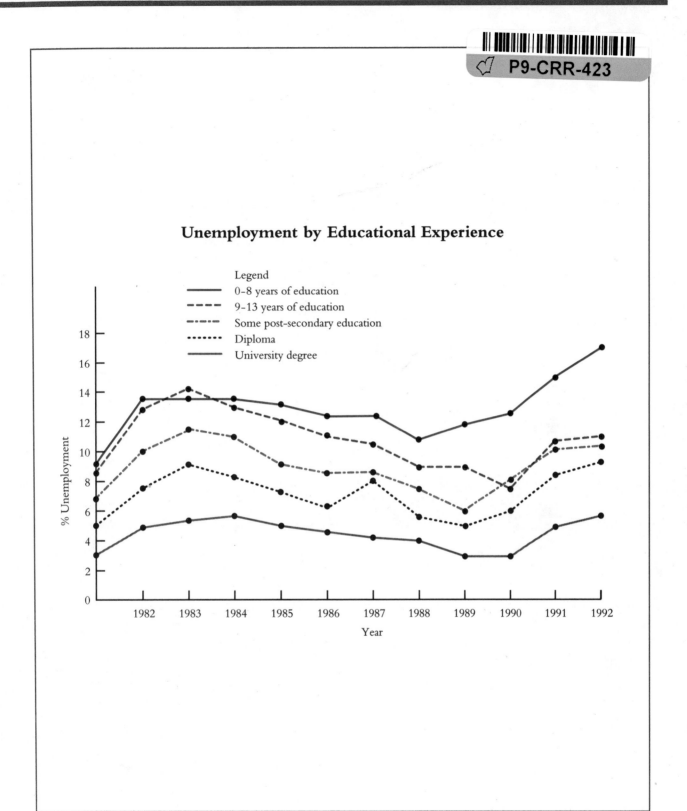

Unemployment by Educational Experience

Legend
— 0–8 years of education
–– 9–13 years of education
–·– Some post-secondary education
···· Diploma
— University degree

ECONOMICS

EIGHT CANADIAN EDITION

Economics

Richard G. Lipsey

Simon Fraser University

Paul N. Courant

The University of Michigan

Douglas D. Purvis

Late, Queen's University

HarperCollins *CollegePublishers*

Executive Editor: John Greenman
Project Coordination and Text Design: Ruttle, Shaw & Wetherill, Inc.
Cover Design: Kay Cannizzaro
Production Manager: Joseph Campanella
Compositor: Interactive Composition Corporation
Printer and Binder: R.R. Donnelley & Sons
Cover Printer: The Lehigh Press, Inc.

ECONOMICS, Eighth Canadian Edition

Library of Congress Cataloging-in-Publication Data

Lipsey, Richard G., 1928-
    Economics / Richard G. Lipsey, Paul N. Courant, Douglas D. Purvis.
    -- 8th Canadian ed.
        p.   cm.
    Includes index.
    ISBN 0-673-46979-4
    1. Economics.   I. Courant, Paul N.   II. Purvis, Douglas D.
    III. Title
    HB171.5.L733   1994
    330--dc20   93-49083
                                                          CIP

To the memory of Douglas Purvis
(1947 – 1993)
Friend, co–author
and
great Canadian

Brief Contents

Preface   xix
Acknowledgments   xxvii
Suggested Outlines for a One-Term Course   xxix
To the Student   xxxi

PART 1

THE NATURE OF ECONOMICS   1

1   ECONOMICS AND SOCIETY   2

2   ECONOMICS AS A SOCIAL
     SCIENCE   23

3   AN OVERVIEW OF THE MARKET
     ECONOMY   42

PART 2

A GENERAL VIEW OF
THE PRICE SYSTEM   57

4   DEMAND, SUPPLY, AND PRICE   58

5   ELASTICITY   82

6   SUPPLY AND DEMAND
     IN ACTION   103

PART 3

CONSUMPTION, PRODUCTION,
AND COST   127

7   HOUSEHOLD CONSUMPTION
     BEHAVIOUR   128

8   USING DEMAND THEORY   159

9   THE ROLE OF THE FIRM   170

10   PRODUCTION AND COST
     IN THE SHORT RUN   183

11   PRODUCTION AND COST IN
     THE LONG RUN AND
     THE VERY LONG RUN   196

PART 4

MARKETS AND PRICING   217

12   COMPETITIVE MARKETS   218

13   MONOPOLY   241

14   PATTERNS OF IMPERFECT
     COMPETITION   258

15   PUBLIC POLICY TOWARD
     MONOPOLY AND
     COMPETITION   284

16   TAKEOVERS, MERGERS,
     AND FOREIGN DIRECT
     INVESTMENT   303

PART 5

THE DISTRIBUTION
OF INCOME   321

17   FACTOR PRICING AND FACTOR
     MOBILITY   322

18   LABOUR MARKETS, UNIONS,
     AND DISCRIMINATION   346

19   NONRENEWABLE NATURAL
     RESOURCES AND CAPITAL   367

PART 6

THE MARKET ECONOMY: PROBLEMS AND POLICIES 383

20 BENEFITS AND COSTS OF GOVERNMENT INTERVENTION 384

21 SOCIAL AND ENVIRONMENTAL REGULATION 406

22 TAXATION AND PUBLIC EXPENDITURE 426

23 CANADIAN SOCIAL POLICY 450

PART 7

INTERNATIONAL TRADE 469

24 THE GAINS FROM TRADE 470

25 THE THEORY AND PRACTISE OF COMMERCIAL POLICY 484

PART 8

NATIONAL INCOME AND FISCAL POLICY 515

26 AN INTRODUCTION TO MACROECONOMICS 516

27 MEASURING MACROECONOMIC VARIABLES 545

28 NATIONAL INCOME AND AGGREGATE EXPENDITURE I: CONSUMPTION AND INVESTMENT 564

29 NATIONAL INCOME AND AGGREGATE EXPENDITURE II: AN OPEN ECONOMY WITH GOVERNMENT 586

30 NATIONAL INCOME AND THE PRICE LEVEL IN THE SHORT RUN 606

31 NATIONAL INCOME AND THE PRICE LEVEL IN THE LONG RUN 628

PART 9

MONEY, BANKING, AND MONETARY POLICY 653

32 THE NATURE OF MONEY AND MONETARY INSTITUTIONS 654

33 THE ROLE OF MONEY IN MACROECONOMICS 682

34 MONETARY POLICY 708

PART 10

MACROECONOMIC PROBLEMS AND POLICIES 731

35 INFLATION 732

36 EMPLOYMENT AND UNEMPLOYMENT 762

37 GOVERNMENT BUDGET DEFICITS 785

38 ECONOMIC GROWTH 806

PART 11

INTERNATIONAL MACROECONOMICS 833

39 EXCHANGE RATES AND THE BALANCE OF PAYMENTS 834

40 MACROECONOMIC POLICY IN AN OPEN ECONOMY 860

Mathematical Notes M-1
Glossary G-1
Index I-1

Detailed Contents

Preface   xix
Acknowledgments   xxvii
Suggested Outlines for a One-Term Course   xxix
To the Student   xxxi

PART 1

THE NATURE OF ECONOMICS   1

1   ECONOMICS AND SOCIETY   2

What is Economics?   3
   Resources and Commodities   3
   Scarcity   3
   Choice   3
   Four Key Economic Problems   6
Alternative Economic Systems   7
   Types of Economic Systems   7
   Command Versus Market Determination   9
Aspects of a Modern Economy   13
   Origins   13
   Living Standards   13
   Ongoing Change   16
   Conclusion   19

   ▨ Box 1-1   The Failure of Central Planning   10

   ▨ Box 1-2   Ends and Means   12

2   ECONOMICS AS A SOCIAL SCIENCE   23

The Distinction Between Positive and Normative   23
The Scientific Approach   25
Is Human Behaviour Predictable?   27
The Importance of Theories   28
The Structure of Theories   28
Testing Theories   30
Can Economics Be Made Value Free?   33

   ▨ Box 2-1   Why Economists Disagree   24

   ▨ Box 2-2   Limits on the Positive-Normative Distinction   26

Appendix to Chapter 2
Graphing Relations Among Variables   36

Representing Theories on Graphs   36
Graphing Observations   38

3   AN OVERVIEW OF THE MARKET ECONOMY   42

Specialization, Surplus, and Trade   42
   The Division of Labour   43
   Markets and Resource Allocation   43
The Decision Makers   44
   Households   45
   Firms   46
   Government   47
Markets and Economies   48
   Markets   48
   Economies   48
   Sectors of an Economy   48
Microeconomics and Macroeconomics   49
   An Overview of Microeconomics   50
   An Overview of Macroeconomics   51

   ▨ Box 3-1   Absolute and Comparative Advantage   44

   ▨ Box 3-2   The Division of Labour   46

PART 2

A GENERAL VIEW OF THE PRICE SYSTEM   57

4   DEMAND, SUPPLY, AND PRICE   58

Demand   58
   Quantity Demanded   58
   What Determines Quantity Demanded?   59
   Demand and Price   59
   The Demand Schedule and the Demand Curve   61
Supply   66
   Quantity Supplied   67
   What Determines Quantity Supplied?   67
   Supply and Price   67
   The Supply Schedule and the Supply Curve   68
Determination of Price by Demand and Supply   70

The Laws of Demand and Supply   72
Prices and Inflation   74

◙ Box 4-1   Stock and Flow Variables   60

◙ Box 4-2   Laws, Predictions, Hypotheses   61

◙ Box 4-3   Demand and Supply: What Really
Happens   74

Appendix to Chapter 4
Foreign Trade   79
The Determination of Imports and
Exports   79
The Law of One Price   79
A Country Facing Given World Prices   79
An Exported Commodity   80

5   ELASTICITY   82

Price Elasticity of Demand   82
The Measurement of Price Elasticity   83
What Determines Elasticity of
Demand?   87
Other Demand Elasticities   90
Income Elasticity of Demand   90
Cross Elasticity of Demand   92
Elasticity of Supply   93
Determinants of Supply Elasticity   94
Long-Run and Short-Run Elasticity
of Supply   95

◙ Box 5-1   Calculating Price Elasticities Using
Averages   86

◙ Box 5-2   Terminology of Elasticity   94

Appendix to Chapter 5
Elasticity: A Formal Analysis   98
Arc Elasticity as an Approximation of Point
Elasticity   98
Point Elasticity According to the Precise
Definition   101

6   SUPPLY AND DEMAND
IN ACTION   103

Who Pays Sales Taxes?   103

Government-Controlled Prices   105
Disequilibrium Prices   105
Price Floors   106
Price Ceilings   107
Rent Controls: A Case Study of Price
Ceilings   109

General Effects of Rent Controls   109
Specific Effects of Rent Controls   109
The Problems of Agriculture   112
Long-Term Trends   113
Short-Term Fluctuations   116
Agricultural Stabilization in Theory   118
Agricultural Policy in Canada   122

◙ Box 6-1   Rent Controls in Toronto   110

◙ Box 6-2   Four General Lessons About Resource
Allocation   114

PART 3

CONSUMPTION, PRODUCTION, AND COST   127

7   HOUSEHOLD CONSUMPTION
BEHAVIOUR   128

The Choices Households Face   128
The Budget Line   128
Shifts in the Budget Line   130
The Choices Households Make   132
Income and Substitution Effects   132
The Role of Tastes   137
Consumers' Surplus   141

◙ Box 7-1   More About the Slope of Demand
Curves   138

◙ Box 7-2   Market and Individual Demand
Curves   140

Appendix A to Chapter 7
Indifference Theory   146
An Indifference Curve   146
The Equilibrium of the Household   148
Derivation of the Demand Curve   150

Appendix B to Chapter 7
Marginal Utility Theory   155
Marginal and Total Utility   155
Maximizing Utility   156
Derivation of the Household's
Demand Curve   158

8   USING DEMAND THEORY   159

Does Demand Theory Require Unrealistic
Rationality?   159
Some Applications of Demand Theory   160

Household Behaviour Under Uncertainty 163
The Market for Insurance 163

■ Box 8-1   Used-Car Prices: The Problem of
"Lemons"   164

9   THE ROLE OF THE FIRM   170

The Organization of Production 170
Forms of Business Organization 170
The Rise of the Modern Corporation 173
Financing of Firms 173
The Firm in Economic Theory 174
Motivation: Profit Maximization 175
Factors of Production 176
The Firm's Costs 176
The Meaning and Significance of Profits 179
Other Definitions of Profits 179
Profits and Resource Allocation 180

■ Box 9-1   Why Are There Firms?   171

■ Box 9-2   Transnational Corporations   174

■ Box 9-3   Opportunity Cost Beyond
Economics   177

10   PRODUCTION AND COST
IN THE SHORT RUN   183

Choices Open to the Firm 183
Time Horizons for Decision Making 183
Connecting the Runs: The Production
Function 184
Short-Run Choices 185
Total, Average, and Marginal Products 185
The Marginal and Average Product
Curves 186
Short-Run Variations in Cost 188
Cost Concepts Defined 189
Short-Run Cost Curves 191
Shifts in Short-Run Cost Curves 192

■ Box 10-1   Diminishing Returns   188

■ Box 10-2   Mario Lemieux's Goal-Scoring
Record   190

11   PRODUCTION AND COST
IN THE LONG RUN AND
THE VERY LONG RUN   196

The Long Run: No Fixed Factors 196
Profit Maximization and Cost
Minimization 198
The Principle of Substitution 199

Cost Curves in the Long Run 200
Shifts in Cost Curves 203
The Very Long Run 203
Innovation, Invention, and Technological
Change 204
The Choices Firms Face 208

■ Box 11-1   Various Concepts
of Efficiency   197

■ Box 11-2   The Significance of Productivity
Growth   205

■ Box 11-3   The Lean Production
Revolution   206

Appendix to Chapter 11
Isoquants: An Alternative Analysis of the Firm's Input
Decisions   212

PART 4
MARKETS AND PRICING   217

12   COMPETITIVE MARKETS   218

Market Structure and Firm Behaviour 218
Market Structure and Behaviour 218
The Significance of Market Structure 219
Elements of the Theory of Perfect
Competition 220
Assumptions of Perfect Competition 220
Demand and Revenue for a Firm in Perfect
Competition 220
Short-Run Equilibrium 223
Rules for All Profit-Maximizing Firms 224
Short-Run Supply Curves 226
Short-Run Equilibrium Price 227
Short-Run Profitability of the Firm 227
Long-Run Equilibrium 228
The Effect of Entry and Exit 228
Conditions for Long-Run
Equilibrium 230
The Long-Run Industry Supply
Curve 232
Changes in Technology 234
Declining Industries 234
The Appeal of Perfect Competition 237

■ Box 12-1   Demand Under Perfect Competition:
Firm and Industry   222

■ Box 12-2   Parable of the Seaside Inn   236

13 MONOPOLY 241

A Single-Price Monopolist 241
  Cost and Revenue in the Short Run 241
  Short-Run Monopoly Equilibrium 244
  Long-Run Monopoly Equilibrium 246
  Entry Barriers 246
Cartels as Monopolies 247
  The Effects of Cartelization 249
  Problems Facing Cartels 249
A Multiprice Monopolist: Price
Discrimination 250
  Why Price Discrimination is Profitable 253
  When Is Price Discrimination
    Possible? 254
  Consequences of Price Discrimination 255
  Normative Aspects of Price
    Discrimination 255

    ◼ Box 13-1   Creative Destruction in Action
    248

    ◼ Box 13-2   The Importance of Entry 252

14 PATTERNS OF IMPERFECT
COMPETITION 258

The Structure of the Canadian Economy 258
  Turnover of Firms 259
  Industrial Concentration 259
Imperfectly Competitive Market Structures 263
  Firms Select Their Products 263
  Firms Choose Their Prices 263
  Other Aspects of the Behaviour
    of Firms 264
Monopolistic Competition 265
  Assumptions of the Theory 265
  Predictions of the Theory 265
  Evaluation of the Theory 266
Oligopoly 268
  Characteristics of Oligopoly 268
  Why Bigness? 268
  The Basic Dilemma of Oligopoly 270
  Cooperation or Competition? 272
  Long-Run Behaviour: The Importance
    of Entry Barriers 275
  Oligopoly and the Functioning of the
    Economy 279

    ◼ Box 14-1   Globalisation of Production
    and Competition 260

    ◼ Box 14-2   Explicit Cooperation
    in OPEC 274

15 PUBLIC POLICY TOWARD
MONOPOLY AND
COMPETITION 284

Economic Efficiency 284
  Efficiency and Inefficiency in Perfect
    Competition and Monopoly 287
  Allocative Efficiency: An Elabouration 288
Canadian Public Policy Toward Monopoly and
  Competition 292
  Direct Control of Natural Monopolies 292
  Direct Control of Oligopolies 295
  Intervention to Keep Firms
    Competing 297

16 TAKEOVERS, MERGERS,
AND FOREIGN DIRECT
INVESTMENT 303

Takeovers, Mergers, and Buyouts 303
  The Effects of Takeovers 304
  Leveraged Buyouts 305
Foreign Investment 307
  Foreign Investment in Developing
    Countries 308
  Foreign Investment in and by Canada:
    Some Facts 310
  Foreign Investment in Canada:
    The Debate 310
The Goals of Firms 313
  The Separation of Ownership from
    Control 314
  Nonmaximizing Theories 315
  The Importance of Nonmaximizing
    Theories 317

PART 5

THE DISTRIBUTION
OF INCOME 321

17 FACTOR PRICING AND FACTOR
MOBILITY 322

Functional Distribution and Size Distribution 322
  Factor Pricing 324
  The Link Between Output and Input
    Decisions 324
The Demand for Factors 325
  The Quantity of a Factor Demanded 325
The Firm's Demand Curve for a Factor 326

Elasticity of Factor Demand   328
The Supply of Factors   330
    The Total Supply of Factors   332
    The Supply of Factors for a Particular
        Use   333
    The Supply of Factors to Individual
        Firms   336
The Operation of Factor Markets   336
    Factor Price Differentials   336
    Policy Issues   338
    Economic Rent   339

    ◾ Box 17-1   More Than One Variable
        Factor   330

    ◾ Box 17-2   The Principles of Derived
        Demand   331

    ◾ Box 17-3   The Supply of Labour   334

    ◾ Box 17-4   Origin of the Term Economic
        Rent   341

18   LABOUR MARKETS, UNIONS,
      AND DISCRIMINATION   346

Labour Markets and Wage Rates   346
    One Wage for Homogeneous Labour   348
    Wage Differentials in Competitive
        Markets   348
    Differentials Arising from Market
        Structures   350
Minimum Wage Laws   355
Modern Labour Unions   357
    Collective Bargaining   357
    Wages Versus Employment   357
Discrimination in Labour Markets   359
    A Model of Labour Market
        Discrimination   359
    Female-Male Differentials   362

    ◾ Box 18-1   Factor Demand When Firms Are
        Not Price Takers   347

    ◾ Box 18-2   Deindustrialisation and the Growth
        of the Service Sector   352

    ◾ Box 18-3   The Historical Development
        of Canadian Unions   358

19   NONRENEWABLE NATURAL
      RESOURCES AND CAPITAL   367

The Economics of Nonrenewable Resources   367
    Determining the Rate of Extraction   367

The Price System as a Conservation
    Mechanism   370
Capital   373
    Two Prices of Capital   373
    Present Value of Future Returns   374
    Equilibrium of the Firm   376
    Equilibrium for the Whole Economy   378

    ◾ Box 19-1   The Rental and Purchase Price
        of Labour   374

    ◾ Box 19-2   The Future Value of a Present
        Sum   377

PART 6

THE MARKET ECONOMY:
PROBLEMS AND POLICIES   383

20   BENEFITS AND COSTS
      OF GOVERNMENT
      INTERVENTION   384

How Markets Coordinate   385
The Case for the Market System   387
The Case for Intervention   389
    Failure to Achieve Efficiency   389
    Other Social Goals   394
Government Intervention   397
    The Tools of Government
        Intervention   397
    The Costs of Government
        Intervention   398
    Government "Imperfection": Social Choice
        Theory   400
    How Much Should Government
        Intervene?   402

    ◾ Box 20-1   A View from the Outside of the
        Inside of Upside Down   386

    ◾ Box 20-2   Distribution Versus Efficiency—
        The Leaky Bucket   395

    ◾ Box 20-3   Arrow's Impossibility
        Theorem   401

21   SOCIAL AND ENVIRONMENTAL
      REGULATION   406

The Economics of Pollution and Pollution
Control   407

The Economic Rationale for Regulating
Pollution   407
Pollution Control in Theory and
Practise   409
Regulation for Health and Safety   415
Health and Safety Information as a Public
Good   415
Health and Safety Regulation in
Practise   420
Benefit-Cost Analysis of Social Regulation   420

■ Box 21-1   Charging for Emissions
at Home   413

■ Box 21-2   Resistance to Market-Based
Environmental Policies   416

22   TAXATION AND PUBLIC
EXPENDITURE   426

Taxation   426
Aspects of the Tax System   426
The Canadian Tax System   428
Evaluating the Tax System   430
Taxes and Equity   431
Efficiency   434
Tax Incidence   435
Public Expenditure   437
Types of Government Expenditures   437
Fiscal Federalism   438
Public Expenditure and the Distribution
of Income   444
Public Expenditure and the Allocation
of Resources   444
Evaluating the Role of Government   445

■ Box 22-1   The Goods and Services
Tax   432

23   CANADIAN SOCIAL POLICY   450

Canada's Social Programs in Perspective   450
The Variety of Social Programs   450
Fiscal, Economic, and Demographic
Setting   451
Issues in Assessing Social Programs   453
Universality   455
An Outline of Selected Programs   456
Human Resource Development
Programs   456
Income Transfer and Security
Programs   457
A Final Word   466

■ Box 23-1 · Poverty in Canada   460

■ Box 23-2   The Rising Cost of Health
Care   464

PART 7

INTERNATIONAL TRADE   469

24   THE GAINS FROM TRADE   470

Sources of the Gains from Trade   470
Interpersonal, Interregional, and International
Trade   470
Gains from Trade with Given Costs   471
Why Opportunity Costs Differ   475
Gains from Specialization with Variable
Costs   477
The Terms of Trade   480

■ Box 24-1   The Gains from Trade Illustrated
Graphically   476

25   THE THEORY AND PRACTISE
OF COMMERCIAL POLICY   484

The Theory of Commercial Policy   484
Methods of Protection   484
The Case for Free Trade   486
The Case for Some Protection   487
Fallacious Trade-Policy Arguments   494
Commercial Policy in the World Today   495
The International Agreements on
Commercial Policy   496
The Crisis in the Multilateral Trading
System   497
Canadian Commercial Policy   498
The Historical Background   499
The Canada-U.S. Free Trade
Agreement   501
The NAFTA   507
The Outlook for Canadian Trade   511

■ Box 25-1   Import Restrictions on Japanese
Cars: Tariffs or Quotas?   488

■ Box 25-2   Gains from Specialization with
Differentiated Products: The Eastman-Stykholt
Analyses   502

■ Box 25-3   Employment Effects of the Canada-
U.S. FTA   505

■ Box 25-4   Hub and Spoke Versus Plurilateral
Regionalism   509

■ Box 25-5   NAFTA and the
Environment   510

PART 8

NATIONAL INCOME AND FISCAL
POLICY   515

26   AN INTRODUCTION TO
MACROECONOMICS   516

What is Macroeconomics?   516
Major Macroeconomic Issues   517
Key Macroeconomic Phenomena   517
Output and Income   518
Employment, Unemployment, and the
Labour Force   524
Inflation and the Price Level   528
The Interest Rate   532
The International Economy   535
Cycles and Trends   538

■ Box 26-1   The Terminology of Business
Cycles   522

■ Box 26-2   How Accurate Are the
Unemployment Figures?   525

■ Box 26-3   Does a Fall in Inflation Hurt
Lenders?   534

■ Box 26-4   The Exchange Rate and the
External Value of the Currency   536

Appendix to Chapter 26
How the CPI is Constructed   542
Measuring the Rate of Inflation   544

27   MEASURING MACROECONOMIC
VARIABLES   545

National Output Concepts   545
Value Added as Output   545
National-Income Accounting: Gross Domestic
Product   546
GDP from the Expenditure Side   548
GDP from the Income Side   551
Income Produced and Income
Received   553
Other Income Concepts   553

Interpreting National Income Measures   554
Real and Nominal Measures   554
Total Values and Per Capita Values and
Productivity   555
What National Income Does Not
Measure   557
Is There a Best Measure of National
Income?   560

■ Box 27-1   Value Added Through Stages
of Production   547

■ Box 27-2   Calculation of Nominal and Real
National Income   556

■ Box 27-3   GDP and Economic
Growth   559

28   NATIONAL INCOME AND
AGGREGATE EXPENDITURE I:
CONSUMPTION AND
INVESTMENT   564

What Determines Desired Expenditure?   564
Some Important Preliminaries   564
Desired Consumption Expenditure   565
Desired Investment Expenditure   570
The Aggregate Expenditure Function   572
Determining Equilibrium National Income   573
Changes in National Income   575
Shifts in the Aggregate Expenditure
Function   576
The Multiplier   577

■ Box 28-1   The Multiplier: A Numerical
Example   580

■ Box 28-2   The Multiplier: An Algebraic
Approach   582

29   NATIONAL INCOME AND
AGGREGATE EXPENDITURE II:
AN OPEN ECONOMY WITH
GOVERNMENT   586

Government: Spending and Taxes   586
Net Exports   588
Equilibrium National Income   592
Shifts in Aggregate Expenditure   595
Net Exports and Equilibrium National
Income   595
Fiscal Policy   596
Lessons and Limitations   599

Appendix A to Chapter 29
Import Content of Autonomous Expenditure   *602*
Appendix B to Chapter 29
The Income-Expenditure Model Treated
   Algebraically   *604*

30   *NATIONAL INCOME AND*
   THE PRICE LEVEL IN THE
   SHORT RUN   *606*

Exogenous Changes in the Price Level   606
   Shifts in the *AE* Curve   606
   Changes in Equilibrium Income   608
   The Aggregate Demand Curve   609
Equilibrium National Income and Price Level   613
   The Aggregate Supply Curve   613
   Macroeconomic Equilibrium   616
Changes in National Income and the
   Price Level   617
   Aggregate Demand Shocks   618
   Aggregate Supply Shocks   622

   ◉ *Box 30-1*   *The Shape of the Aggregate Demand*
   Curve   *611*

   ◉ *Box 30-2*   *The Keynesian* SRAS
   Curve   *619*

   ◉ *Box 30-3*   *More on the Shape of the* SRAS
   Curve   *624*

31   *NATIONAL INCOME AND*
   THE PRICE LEVEL IN THE
   LONG RUN   *628*

Induced Changes in Factor Prices   628

The Long-Run Consequences of Aggregate
   Demand Shocks   631
   Expansionary Shocks   632
   Contractionary Shocks   633
   The Long-Run Aggregate Supply *(LRAS)*
   Curve   634
   Long-Run Equilibrium   636
National Income in the Short and Long Run   637
Fiscal Policy and the Business Cycle   639
   The Basic Theory of Fiscal
   Stabilization   641

   ◉ *Box 31-1*   *Anticipated Demand*
   Shocks   *635*

   ◉ *Box 31-2*   *Demand Shocks and Business*
   Cycles   *640*

   ◉ *Box 31-3*   *Fiscal Policy and the Great*
   Depression   *646*

PART 9
MONEY, BANKING, AND
MONETARY POLICY   *653*

32   *THE NATURE OF MONEY AND*
   MONETARY INSTITUTIONS   *654*

The Nature of Money   656
   What is Money?   656
   The Origins of Money   657
   Modern Money   661
The Banking System   664
   Central Banks   664
   The Canadian Banking System   666
   Reserves   669
Money Creation by the Banking System   672
   The Creation of Deposit Money   673
   Variable Reserve Ratios and Cash
   Drains   675
The Money Supply   676
   Kinds of Deposits   676
   Definitions of the Money Supply   677
   Near Money and Money Substitutes   677
   Conclusion   678

   ◉ *Box 32-1*   *Hyperinflation*   *658*

   ◉ *Box 32-2*   *Terminology of a Modern Financial*
   System   *662*

   ◉ *Box 32-3*   *The Globalisation of Financial*
   Markets   *668*

   ◉ *Box 32-4*   *Deposit Insurance and the Financial*
   System   *671*

33   *THE ROLE OF MONEY IN*
   MACROECONOMICS   *682*

Financial Assets   682

Supply of Money and Demand for Money   686
   The Supply of Money   686
   The Demand for Money   686
Monetary Forces and National Income   689
   Monetary Equilibrium and Aggregate
   Demand   689
   Aggregate Demand, the Price Level, and
   National Income   694

The Strength of Monetary Forces   699
Long-Run Effects on National
   Income   700
Short-Run Effects on National
   Income   700

▣ Box 33-1   *Calculating Present Value*   684

▣ Box 33-2   *The Quantity Theory of
Money*   690

▣ Box 33-3   *The Transmission Mechanism in an
Open Economy*   696

Appendix to Chapter 33
The Slope of the Aggregate Demand Curve   706

34   MONETARY POLICY   708

The Bank of Canada and the Money Supply   708
Open-Market Operations   708
Shifting Government Deposits   711
Monetary Policy With Zero Required
   Reserves   713
Effects of Changes in the Money Supply:
   A Review   713
Instruments and Objectives of Monetary
   Policy   714
Lags and the Controversy over Monetary
   Policy   717
Monetary Policy in Action   719
Monetary Gradualism: 1975–1980   719
Monetary Stringency: 1981–1983   720
Low Inflation and Economic Recovery:
   1983–1987   720
Continued Recovery and Rising Inflation:
   1987–1990   722
The Lessons   723

▣ Box 34-1   *More on Contractionary Monetary
Policy*   710

Appendix to Chapter 34
Securities Markets (Stock Markets)   726

PART 10

MACROECONOMIC PROBLEMS
AND POLICIES   731

35   INFLATION   732

Causes and Consequences of Inflation   732
Why Wages Change   733

From Wages to the *SRAS* Curve   738
Demand Shocks   738
Supply Shocks   740
Inflation as a Monetary Phenomenon   744
Sustained Inflation   745
Accelerating Inflation   745
A Sustained, Constant Rate of
   Inflation   746
Breaking a Sustained Inflation   747
Anti-Inflation Policy in Canada   752
Wage and Price Controls and Monetary
   Gradualism: 1975–1980   753
Stabilizing Inflation: 1981–1988   753
A Policy of Price Stability   756
Conclusion   757

▣ Box 35-1   *The Phillips Curve and the Shifting
SRAS Curve*   736

▣ Box 35-2   *The Phillips Curve and Accelerating
Inflation*   748

▣ Box 35-3   *Constant Inflation*   750

▣ Box 35-4   *Incomes Policies*   754

36   EMPLOYMENT AND
UNEMPLOYMENT   762

Employment and Unemployment in Canada   762
Changes in Total Employment   762
Changes in Unemployment   763
Consequences of Unemployment   763
Kinds of Unemployment   763
Cyclical Unemployment   764
The NAIRU   770
Frictional Unemployment   770
Structural Unemployment   770
Why Does the NAIRU Change?   773
Reducing Unemployment   777
Cyclical Unemployment   777
Frictional Unemployment   777
Structural Unemployment   780
Conclusion   781

▣ Box 36-1   *Real Business Cycle
Theory*   768

▣ Box 36-2   *Industrial Change: An Economist's
Cautionary Tale*   778

37   GOVERNMENT BUDGET
DEFICITS   785

Background to Deficits and Debt   785

Facts About Deficits   786
From Deficits to the National Debt   787
Evaluating the Deficit   789
Why Worry About Deficits?   792
Postponed Tax Liability   793
Ricardo Neutrality   793
Effects of Deficits   793
Proposals to Control the Deficit   798

■ *Box 37-1   Does the National Debt Matter?   796*

■ *Box 37-2   Debt, Deficits, and Sustainability   800*

38   ECONOMIC GROWTH   806

The Nature of Economic Growth   806
Shifts in Aggregate Demand and Aggregate Supply   806
Economic Growth, Efficiency, and Redistribution   808
Saving, Investment, and Growth   809
Benefits and Costs of Growth   810
Benefits of Growth   810
Costs of Growth   810
Theories of Economic Growth   813
The Aggregate Production Function   813
Neoclassical Growth Theory   814
Endogenous Growth   818
Increasing Returns Theories   821
Further Causes of Growth   823
Growth and Competitiveness in Advanced Industrial Economies   823
Are There Limits to Growth?   825
Conclusion   829

■ *Box 38-1   An Open Letter to the Ordinary Citizen from a Supporter of the "Growth Is Good" School   811*

■ *Box 38-2   An Open Letter to the Ordinary Citizen from a Supporter of the "Growth Is Bad" School   812*

■ *Box 38-3   The Brundtland Commission and "Sustainable Development"   826*

PART 11

INTERNATIONAL MACROECONOMICS   833

39   EXCHANGE RATES AND THE BALANCE OF PAYMENTS   834

The Determination of Exchange Rates   834
The Nature of Foreign Exchange Transactions   834
Exchange Rates Changes and Foreign Trade   836
The Exchange of Currencies   838
Changes in Exchange Rates   840
The Behaviour of Exchange Rates   846
The Balance of Payments   849
The Payments Accounts   849
The Meaning of Payments Balances and Imbalances   851

■ *Box 39-1   Managing Fixed Exchange Rates   842*

■ *Box 39-2   Why Total Payments Always Balance: An Illustration   852*

■ *Box 39-3   The Volume of Trade, the Balance of Trade, and the New Mercantilism   855*

40   MACROECONOMIC POLICY IN AN OPEN ECONOMY   860

The Balance of Trade and National Income   860
A Closed Economy   861
An Open Economy with a Fixed Exchange Rate   862
Flexible Exchange Rates   863
International Capital Mobility   867
The Twin Deficits   867
Fiscal and Monetary Policy   869
The Insulation Properties of Flexible Exchange Rates Revisited   871
Canadian Policy   871
1980–1983: Imported Monetary Restraint   871
1984–1987: Recovery and Stable Inflation   872
1987–1991: Anti-Inflation and a Falling Exchange Rate   872
1992–?: Price Stability   872

■ *Box 40-1   Aggregate Supply and the Open-Economy Multiplier   864*

Mathematical Notes   M-1
Glossary   G-1
Index   I-1

Preface

Economics is a living discipline, changing and evolving in response to developments in the world economy and in response to the research of many thousands of economists throughout the world. Through 8 editions, *Economics* has evolved with the discipline. Our purpose in this edition, as in the previous 7, is to provide students with an introduction to the major issues facing the world's economies, to the methods that economists use to study those issues, and to the policy problems that those issues create. Our treatment is everywhere guided by three important principles:

1. Economics is a science, in the sense that it progresses through the systematic confrontation of theory by evidence. Neither theory nor data alone can tell us much about the world, but combined they tell us a great deal.
2. Economics is, and should be seen by students to be, useful. Economic theory and knowledge about the economy have important implications for economic policy. Although we stress these implications, we are also careful to point out cases where too little is known to support strong statements about public policy. Appreciating what is not known is as important as learning what is known.
3. We strive always to be honest with our readers. Although we know that economics is not always easy, we do not approve of glossing over hard bits of analysis without letting readers see what is happening and what has been assumed. We always take whatever space is needed to explain *why* economists draw their conclusions, rather than just asserting the conclusions. We also take pains to avoid simplifying matters so much that students would have to unlearn what they have been taught if they continue their study beyond the introductory course. In short, we have tried to follow Albert Einstein's advise:

Everything should be made as simple as possible, but not simpler.

The Economic Issues of the 1990s

In writing this eighth edition of *Economics*, we have sought to improve the teachability of our presentation of basic economic theory while leaving the overall structure of our presentation largely unchanged. Major changes have been made, however, in the empirical and descriptive material used to illustrate and apply the theory. In doing this, we have tried to reflect the main economic issues of the last decade of the twentieth century.

Globalisation and Growth

The last 20 years have seen enormous worldwide economic changes. Flows of trade and investment between countries have risen so dramatically that it is now common to speak of the "globalisation" of the world economy. Today, it is no longer possible to study any economy without taking into account developments in the rest of the world.

Economic growth and the implications of the globalisation of the world's economy are pressing issues of the day. Forces relating to growth and change in a global context strongly influence the outcomes of many Canadian economic policies, including control of deficits, prevention of environmental degradation and resource depletion, privatizing economic activities, reforming the social safety net, reducing unemployment, and assisting the restructuring of industry. Much of our study of economic principles, and the Canadian economy, has been shaped by such issues.

In the appendix to Chapter 4, foreign trade provides an example of supply and demand in action. Our discussion of agricultural policy in Chapter 7 has a major international dimension. Foreign direct investment and transnational corporations are introduced in the first chapter on the theory of the firm (Chapter 9) and then receive detailed attention in many subsequent chapters, including Chapter 16 on the organization of firms, and Chapter 25 on trade policy. Our treatment of oligopoly in Chapter 14 also allows for global rather than purely national competition. Our discussion of competition policy in Chapter 15 shows the effect of foreign competition on the market power of domestic firms. The newer methods of "lean production" or "flexible manufacturing," first developed in Japan and now displacing the older mass production techniques developed by Henry Ford, are discussed in connection with the firm (Chapters 9, 14, and 16), and with economic growth (Chapter 38). Chapter 25 provides detailed discussions of commercial policies that interfere with the free flow of international trade, and of trade-liberalizing arrangements such as the GATT and the North American Free Trade Agreement (NAFTA).

Our basic framework for macroeconomic theory and policy is also organized around globalisation and growth. In Chapters 26–31 we develop the theory of national income determination in an *open* economy from the outset—rather than starting, as is so often done, with a closed economy which is only opened to international trade and investment many chapters later.

Our analysis of the theory and practise of monetary policy in Chapters 32–34 emphasizes the role of exchange rates. Chapter 37, on deficits, and Chapters 39 and 40, on international monetary economics, all emphasize the relations between domestic and international economic behavior, especially with respect to the twin deficits. In Chapter 38 we study growth to an extent that is unusual in introductory texts.

The Triumph of Market Capitalism

Since the last edition of this book was published, the century-long conflict between capitalism and communism has ended. What a decade ago was the most powerful communist economy in the world, the USSR, has disappeared, both as a nation and as a planned economy. Mixed capitalism, the system of economic organization that has long prevailed in much of the industrialised world, now prevails in virtually all of it. (Although the transformation of formerly planned economies into market economies is proving more difficult than many thought.) Many less developed economies are also moving in this direction. The reasons for the failure of the planned economies of Eastern Europe are discussed in Chapter 1 in contrast to the reasons for the relative success of mixed capitalism.

Declining Growth in Market Economies

At the same time that the formerly communist world of Eastern Europe has moved toward market economies, Canada, the United States, western Europe, and Japan have experienced marked reductions in economic growth.

In Canada, average real wages, having risen steadily from 1900 to 1970, have remained nearly static since the mid 1970s. Steadily rising family incomes have been the exception over the lifetimes of you who are now using this book, rather than the rule that it had been over the lifetimes of readers of most earlier editions. Issues raised by the changing growth performance in most advanced industrial countries are met frequently in both the micro and the macro parts of this book.

Economic Policy

Most chapters of the book contain some discussion of economic policy. We have two main goals in mind in these discussions:

- We aim to give students practise in using economic theory, because applying theory is both a wonderfully effective teaching method and a reliable test of students' grasp of theory.
- We want to introduce students to the major policy issues of today.

Both goals reflect our view that students should see that economics is useful in helping us to understand and deal with the world around us.

Structure and Coverage

Microeconomics

In Part 1, we introduce the issues of scarcity and choice and then briefly discuss comparative economic systems. The problems of converting command economies into market economies will persist for some time, and comparisons with command economies help to establish what a market economy is *by showing what it is not*. In the last part of the chapter, we provide a new survey of a number of national and international trends that introduce students to many of the issues that are studied in more detail later in the book. Chapter 2 makes the important distinction between positive and normative enquiries and goes on to an elementary discussion of the construction and testing of economic theories.

Part 2 deals with demand and supply. After introducing price determination and elasticity in the first two chapters, we apply these tools to a revised and shortened Chapter 6. The case studies are designed to provide practise in applying the tools, rather than to present a full coverage of each case.

The first half of Part 3 deals with the theory of demand. The basic analysis using budget lines and consistent choice is presented in Chapter 7. Both indifference and utility theory are presented in optional appendices. Instructors' tastes differ greatly on how much demand theory is desirable in an introductory course. The structure of Part 3 is designed to let the instructor choose to teach neither, either, or both theories without running into problems later in the book.

The second half of Part 3 begins with Chapter 9, which introduces the firm as an institution and provides a new discussion of multinational corporations. Chapter 10 develops short-run costs. Chapter 11 covers long-run costs and goes on to consider shifts in cost curves due to technological changes that occur in response to economic incentives. This microeconomic application of endogenous growth theory is seldom if ever covered in text books. Yet applied work on competitiveness and firms' responses to changing economic signals shows it to be

extremely important. How firms choose to *innovate* their way out of unprofitable situations is now understood in the applied literature to be a critical part of the microeconomic response to changes in market signals.

The first two chapters of Part 4, Chapters 12 and 13, give the standard theories of perfect competition and monopoly with some discussion of international cartels. Chapter 14 deals with oligopoly, which is the market structure most commonly found in the manufacturing sector. Strategic behaviour plays a central part in the analysis of this chapter.

The first half of Chapter 15 deals with the efficiency of competition and the inefficiency of monopoly. The last half of the chapter is largely concerned with competition policy and public utility regulation.

Chapter 16 deals with the market for corporate control. A discussion of takeovers and mergers leads to a major treatment of foreign direct investment. The belief that existing management is not maximizing profits is an important motive for takeovers. This discussion thus leads naturally to a brief consideration of why firms may and may not maximize their profits in general and to principal-agent problems in particular.

Part 5, on distribution, contains applications to the pricing of labour, renewable resources and capital as well as discrimination.

The first chapter of Part 6 provides a general discussion of market success and market failure, introduces social choice theory, and outlines the arguments for and against government intervention in a market economy. The second chapter deals with environmental and health and safety regulation. The next chapter analyzes taxes and public expenditure while the final one deals with social policy.

The final part of microeconomics focuses primarily on international economics. Chapter 24 gives the basic treatment of international trade, developing both the traditional theory of static comparative advantage and newer theories based on imperfect competition and dynamic comparative advantage. Chapter 25 discusses both the positive and normative aspects of commercial policy, as well as current GATT negotiations and prospects for regional free trade areas, including the NAFTA.

Macroeconomics

Our treatment of macroeconomics is divided into four parts: National Income and Fiscal Policy; Money, Banking, and Monetary Policy; Macroeconomic Problems and Policies; and International Monetary Economics. The themes of internationalization and economic growth are interwoven throughout all four parts.

The first macro chapter, Chapter 26, identifies economic growth and the level of potential national income as the major determinants of a society's material standards of living. In the core macro chapters (28–31), we develop what has now become the standard aggregate-demand–aggregate-supply approach—an approach which we were one of the first elementary textbooks to pioneer. We start with a detailed exposition of the fixed-price (Keynesian cross) model of the determination of equilibrium income in Chapters 28 and 29. In Chapter 28, we consider a simplified economy—one with no international sector or government—to make equilibrium income and the multiplier as teachable as possible. In Chapter 29 we add government and the international sector, thus opening our model economy to international trade at an early point.

From the beginning of our treatment of macro economics, *in contrast to many other introductory texts,* we are careful to distinguish short-run *fluctuations* around equilibrium national income from the long-term *growth* of potential national income. This reflects our desire to emphasize economic growth and to avoid trivializing it by confusing it with the rise in income caused by the removal of a recessionary gap.

In Chapter 30 we develop the aggregate demand curve and the short-run aggregate supply curve. Chapter 31 completes the core model by deriving the vertical long-run aggregate supply curve, which allows us to discuss the different effects of AD shifts in the short and long run. This leads directly to an introduction to fiscal policy and a discussion of business cycles in which both stabilization and growth are treated.

Part 8 focuses on the role of money and financial systems. Chapter 32 discusses the nature of money, including an overview of the evolution from metallic money through to our modern system of fiat currency and deposit money. The chapter concludes with descriptions of the various components of the money supply and the commercial banking system, and of the Bank of Canada. In Chapter 33, we review the determinants of the demand for money and then turn to a detailed discussion of the link between changes in the money supply on the one hand and interest rates, the exchange rate, national income and the price level on the other hand. This chapter builds directly on the material in Chapters 30 and 31, with an emphasis on the distinction between short-run and long-run effects. In Chapter 34, we discuss monetary policy, ending with a review of monetary policy in action over the past 30 years. This provides some important historical context for policy discussions in later parts, as well as an opportunity to draw some general conclusions about the operation of monetary policy.

Part 9, *Macroeconomic Problems and Policies,* deals with some of today's most pressing issues for economic policy. It contains separate chapters on inflation, unemployment, budget deficits, and economic growth, all major concerns of the 1990s. Chapter 35 contains a new discussion of the Bank of Canada's zero inflation policy. Chapter 36 covers modern concerns about unemployment. Chapter 37 deals with deficits, with new stress on the problem of provincial government deficits. Chapter 38 provides a comprehensive summary of what is and is not currently known about the causes of economic growth. Much of the discussion examines current research on endogenous technological innovation, technological diffusion, and the role of transnational corporations. The issue of globalisation is returned to in a long section relating growth to international competitiveness. *Our treatment of economic growth—which we regard as one of the most important macroeconomic issues facing Canada and the world today—goes well beyond the coverage in most other introductory texts.*

The final part deals with international monetary issues. Chapter 39 introduces the basic elements of the balance of payments and international finance. Chapter 40 integrates the international material with the macroeconomic model developed earlier, thus providing an up-to-date discussion of open-economy macroeconomic policy, both monetary and fiscal. In addition to covering open-economy issues, this chapter also reviews and integrates the macroeconomic theory and applications presented earlier, including the key issues of the twin deficits.

★　　★　　★

We hope this menu is attractive and challenging. We hope that students will find our fare stimulating and enlightening. Many of the messages of economics are complex—if economic understanding was only a matter of common sense and simple observation, there would be no need for professional economists and the discipline of economics. To understand economics, one must work hard. Working at this book should help readers gain a better understanding of the world around them and of the policy problems faced by all levels of government. Furthermore, in today's globalised world, the return to education is large. We would like to think that we have contributed in some small part to the understanding that increased investment in human capital by the next generation is necessary to restore their incomes to the rapid growth paths that so benefited our parents and our peers. Perhaps we may even contribute to some income-enhancing accumulation of human capital by some of our readers.

Major Revisions in This Edition

Our revisions have been guided by an extensive series of reviews from users and nonusers of the previous editions of this book. As always, we have strived very hard to improve the "teachability and readability."

Changes in Microeconomics

- Chapter 1 gives a new introduction to the importance of growth as a major long-run determinant of living standards and of the globalisation of markets, thus introducing themes that are carried throughout the whole book.

- In Chapter 3 we have added a new box on comparative advantage that introduces students to the idea of gains from specialization.

- In Chapter 6 a discussion of tax incidence with new figures has been added, and the material on rent controls and agricultural policy has been revised extensively. The coverage of agricultural policy, in particular, has been shortened and recast into an application of supply and demand

rather than a comprehensive treatment of Canadian agricultural policy.

- Chapter 7 now covers all of the minimum necessary material in consumer theory. The treatment of the income and substitution effects has been rewritten, with the teaching table greatly simplified. Consumers' surplus has been brought forward from Chapter 8, which now contains only optional material.

- Two new boxes, one on transnational corporations and one on Coase's theory of the firm, have been added to Chapter 9.

- A new box on what is variously called lean production or flexible manufacturing has been added to Chapter 11. We have focused the last part of the chapter more on the microeconomics of the firm by stressing the endogenous technological changes that are induced by changes in economic signals.

- We have rewritten Chapter 14 to include more material on and examples of, strategic behaviour, contestable markets, game theory, and prisoner's dilemma, as well as two new boxes: "Globalisation of Production and Competition" and "Explicit Cooperation in OPEC."

- The material in Chapter 15 is now organized in terms of economic rather than historical categories.

- Chapter 16 has been reorganized and now includes major coverage of foreign direct investment and the importance of transnational corporations.

- We have completely reorganized the distribution chapters (17, 18 and 19). Chapter 17 now deals with the basic theory of factor markets in three parts: demand for factors, supply of factors, and the working of the market for factors. Chapter 18 covers the important application to labour markets, whereas Chapter 19 deals with exhaustible resources and capital.

- In Chapter 22 we've added a discussion of the Coase theorem and a new box on efficiency and redistribution stressing Okun's "leaky bucket."

- Chapters 22 and 23 give a revised and updated discussion of taxation and social policy.

- Chapter 24 contains an expanded coverage of dynamic comparative advantage, and Chapter

25 now covers the NAFTA as well as the Canada-United States FTA.

Changes in Macroeconomics

- The entire income-expenditure model with fixed prices is covered in two chapters (28–29).

- In Chapter 28, we develop a model of a closed economy without government, which enables students to more easily understand the model. We then add government and foreign trade in Chapter 29.

- The materials from the chapters on business cycles and fiscal policy from the seventh edition have been woven throughout Chapters 26–31, and some of the fiscal policy material is covered in Chapter 37 on budget deficits.

- We have substantially rewritten all three chapters in Part 9, Money, Banking, and Monetary Policy, to make them simpler and shorter. The new, streamlined material is better integrated with earlier material on macro theory and with later material on inflation, in Chapter 35. International issues are also given greater emphasis.

- In Chapter 35 we've added a section on expectations formation, dealing with rational expectations, and a new flow chart to provide a guide to the discussion of demand and supply shocks. We also deal fully with the zero-inflation policy.

- Chapter 36 has been extensively rewritten to give it a more macro cast, which helps to fit it into the rest of the macro chapters.

- Chapter 37 on government deficits has been reworked with added emphasis on the provinces. It also now contains much of the material on fiscal policy that used to occur in an earlier chapter.

- Chapter 38 has been completely rewritten to provide a comprehensive and current summary of the causes of growth. The discussion examines current research on induced technological innovation, diffusion, and the role of transnational corporations.

- Chapter 40 has been reworked to make it more teachable and to provide a full discussion of

Canada's problem of the twin (current account and government) deficits.

Teaching Aids

The use of color. The eighth edition introduces the use of four-color print to the text. Color is used strategically and consistently to enhance the graphs, charts, and tables to further promote student understanding. For example, in graphs, supply curves are always red, and demand curves are always blue. Similarly, aggregate supply curves are red, and aggregate demand curves are blue. Key concepts and results are set apart from the rest of the text in green for emphasis and ease of review.

Tag lines and captions for figures and tables. The boldface tag line below or next to a figure or a table states briefly the central conclusion to be drawn from the illustration; the lightface caption gives information needed to reach that conclusion. Each title, tag line, and caption, along with the figure or table, forms a self-contained unit, useful for reviewing.

Boxes. The boxes contain optional materials of several sorts such as further theoretical material, important developments in the national or global economy, and applications of points already covered in the text. The boxes give flexibility in expanding or contracting the coverage of specific chapters.

End-of-chapter material. Each chapter has a Summary, a list of Topics for Review, and Discussion Questions. The questions are designed for class discussion or for "quiz sections." Answers appear in the *Instructor's Manual.*

Appendixes. All of the appendixes are optional, and contain material that is relevant but not central to a first-year course.

Mathematical notes. Mathematical notes are collected in a separate section at the end of the book. Since mathematical notation and derivation is not necessary to understand the principles of economics but is helpful in more advanced work, this segregation seems to be a sensible arrangement. Students with a mathematical background have often told us that they find the mathematical notes helpful.

Glossary. The glossary covers widely used definitions of the economic terms that are printed in boldface the first time that they are defined in both the micro and the macro parts of the book. It also includes, for ease of reference, some commonly used terms that are not printed in boldface in the text because they are not, strictly speaking, technical terms.

Supplements

Our book is accompanied by a workbook, *Study Guide and Problems,* prepared by Professors Kenneth Grant, William Furlong, and the text authors. This workbook is designed to be used either in the classroom or by students working on their own.

An *Instructor's Manual,* prepared by us, and a *Test Bank,* prepared by Scott Bloom, are available to instructors adopting the book. The test bank is also available in computerized form; contact Harper-Collins Canada Ltd., 1995 Markham Road, Scarborough, Ontario, M1B 5M8.

Two other software programs for students accompany the eighth edition: *Macroview,* a simulation of the Canadian economy, and *Micro Tutorial,* a review of microeconomic concepts.

For this edition, all illustrations in 15 key theory chapters are reproduced as four-color transparency acetates. In addition, the remaining figures in the text are reproduced in the form of transparency masters. All of these are available free to adopters.

Using the Book

Because there are many different kinds of first-year economics courses in colleges and universities, we have included more material than normally would be included in any single course. Although teachers can best design their own courses, it may help if we indicate certain views of our own as to how this book *might* be adapted to different courses.

Sequence

The choice of macro first or micro first is partly a personal one that cannot be decided solely by objective criteria. We believe, however, that there are good reasons for preferring the micro-macro order. The thrust over the past 25 years has been to examine the micro underpinnings of macro functions and to erect macroeconomics on a firmer base of micro behavioural relationships. Virtually every current macro controversy turns on some micro underpinning. For "micro firsters" this poses no problem. For "macro firsters" it is often hard to explain what is at issue.

Changes occur not only in economic theory but also in the topics that excite students. Many of today's problems that students find most challenging—discrimination, social policy, equal-pay legislation, poverty, pollution, and free trade with the United States—are microeconomic in character. The micro-macro order, moreover, reflects the historical evolution of the subject. A century of Classical and neo-Classical development of microeconomics preceded the Keynesian development of macroeconomics.

For those who prefer the macro-micro order, we have attempted to make reversibility easy. The overview chapter that ends Part 1 provides a base on which to build either the microeconomics of Part 2 or the macroeconomics of Part 8. Chapters 4 and 5 should be assigned after Chapter 3, even in macro-first courses. Where further microeconomics concepts are required—as in the macro investment chapter—we have added brief sections to make the treatment self-contained while providing review material for those who have covered the microeconomics section.

One-Term Courses

Thorough coverage of most of the book supposes a two-term course in economics. A number of first courses in economics are only one term (or equivalent) in length. Our book can be easily adapted to such courses and our suggestions for doing so are given on page xxix.

Acknowledgments

The starting point for this book was *Economics,* Tenth Edition, by Richard G. Lipsey, Paul N. Courant, Douglas D. Purvis and Peter O. Steiner. It would be impossible to acknowledge here all the teachers, colleagues, and students who contributed to that book. Hundreds of users have written to us with specific suggested improvements, and much of the credit for the fact that the book does become more and more teachable belongs to them. We can no longer list them individually but we thank them all most sincerely.

Ken Carlaw and Cliff Bekar provided excellent research assistance. A number of individuals provided reviews of the seventh edition that were most helpful in preparing the present edition. These are Torben Andersen, Red Deer College; Keith Baxter, Bishop's University; Torben Drewes, Trent University; Irwin Gillespie, Carleton University; David Gray, University of Ottawa; Michael Hare, University of Toronto; Susan Kamp, University of Alberta; G. Kondort, Lakehead University; Michael Krashinsky, University of Toronto, Scarborough Campus; Wade Locke, Memorial University; Annie Spears, University of Prince Edward Island; Bruce Wilkinson, University of Alberta; and William G. Wolfson, University of Toronto. William Furlong and Kenneth Grant, our two study guide authors, have contributed to this edition as well.

In addition, the following people reviewed the supplements that accompany this book: Beverly Cook, University of New Brunswick; Geoffrey Hainsworth, University of British Columbia; Susan Kamp, University of Alberta; Neil Kaplash, University of Victoria; Keith MacKinnon, York University; Jamshid Shahidi, Kwantlen College; Larry Smith, University of Waterloo; Charles Waddell, University of New Brunswick; Bruce Wilkinson, University of Alberta.

Our special thanks go to Robyn Wills for careful and efficient handling of the manuscript at all stages, and for working cheerfully under stressful conditions that often required efforts over and above the normal call of duty.

This edition is dedicated to the memory of Douglas Purvis whose tragic death in January 1993 not only deprived this book of one of its key coauthors, and the surviving authors of a good friend, but also deprived Canada of one of its finest economists. His name remains on the book as a coauthor in recognition of the substantial work that he did on previous editions and that survives into this one.

Richard G. Lipsey
Paul A. Courant

Suggested Outlines for a One-Term Course

Note: A one-term course can cover no more than about 24 full chapters. The core consists of about 18 chapters. Selections from other chapters, as listed below or according to the instructor's own preferences, can produce courses with various emphases.

Basic core chapters for courses covering both micro and macro:

INTRODUCTION

1. Economics and Society
3. An Overview of the Market Economy

MICROECONOMICS

4. Demand, Supply, and Price
5. Elasticity
9. The Role of the Firm
10. Production and Cost in the Short Run
11. Production and Cost in the Long Run and the Very Long Run
12. Competitive Markets
13. Monopoly
17. Factor Pricing and Factor Mobility
20. Benefits and Costs of Government Intervention

MACROECONOMICS

26. An Introduction to Macroeconomics
27. Measuring Macroeconomic Variables
28. National Income and Aggregate Expenditure I: Consumption and Investment
29. National Income and Aggregate Expenditure II: An Open Economy with Government
30. National Income and the Price Level in the Short Run
31. National Income and the Price Level in the Long Run

32. The Nature of Money and Monetary Institutions
33. The Role of Money in Macroeconomics
38. Economic Growth

Chapters that can be added to give different emphases to different courses:[1]

MICROECONOMICS

*6. Supply and Demand in Action
14. Patterns of Imperfect Competition
15. Public Policy Toward Monopoly and Competition (*Last half)
*16. Takeovers, Mergers, and Foreign Direct Investment
*18. Labour Markets, Unions, and Discrimination
19. Nonrenewable Natural Resources and Capital (*First half)
21. Social and Environmental Regulation
*23. Canadian Social Policy
24. The Gains From Trade
25. The Theory and *Practise of Commercial Policy

MACROECONOMICS

*34. Monetary Policy
35. Inflation
*36. Employment and Unemployment
*37. Government Budget Deficits
39. Exchange Rates and the Balance of Payments
40. Macroeconomic Policy in an Open Economy

---

[1]Chapters marked with an asterisk are particularly appropriate for courses with a heavy policy orientation. Chapters not listed here or in the core seem to us to be lower priority in a one-term course, but they are not necessarily too difficult.

To The Student

A good course in economics will give you insight into how our economy functions and into many currently debated policy issues. Like all rewarding subjects, economics will not be mastered without effort. A book on economics must be worked at. It cannot be read like a novel.

Each of you must develop an individual technique for studying, but the following suggestions may prove helpful. It is usually a good idea to read a chapter quickly in order to get the general run of the argument. At this first reading you may want to skip the "boxes," the figure captions, and any footnotes. Then, after reading the Topics for Review, reread the chapter more slowly, making sure that you understand each step of the argument. With respect to the figures and tables, be sure you understand how the conclusions stated in the brief tag lines with each table or figure have been reached. Working carefully through the analysis in the figure caption is *essential* at this stage. You should be prepared to spend time on difficult sections; occasionally, you may spend an hour on only a few pages. Paper and a pencil are indispensable equipment in your reading. It is best to follow a difficult argument by building your own diagram while the argument unfolds rather than by relying on the finished diagram as it appears in the book. It is often helpful to invent numerical examples to illustrate general propositions. The end-of-chapter questions require you to apply what you have studied. We advise you to outline answers to some of the questions. In short, you should seek to understand economics, not merely to memorize it.

After you have read each part in detail, reread it quickly from beginning to end. It is often difficult to understand why certain things are done when they are viewed as isolated points, but when you reread a whole part, much that did not seem relevant or entirely comprehensible will fall into place in the analysis.

The glossary at the end of the book is there to help. Any time you run into a concept that seems vaguely familiar but is not clear to you, check the glossary. The chances are that the term will be there, and its definition will remind you of what you once understood. If you are still in doubt, check the index entry to find where the concept is discussed more fully. Incidentally, the glossary, along with the captions that accompany figures and tables, the color passages in the text, and the end-of-chapter summaries, will prove helpful when reviewing for examinations.

The bracketed boldfaced numbers in the text itself refer to the mathematical notes that are found starting on page M-1. These will be useful to those of you who like mathematics or prefer mathematical argument to verbal or geometric exposition. Others should ignore them.

We hope that you will find the book rewarding and stimulating. Students who used earlier editions made some of the most helpful suggestions for revision, and we hope you will carry on the tradition. If you are moved to write to us, please do.

ECONOMICS

MICROECONOMICS

MACROECONOMICS

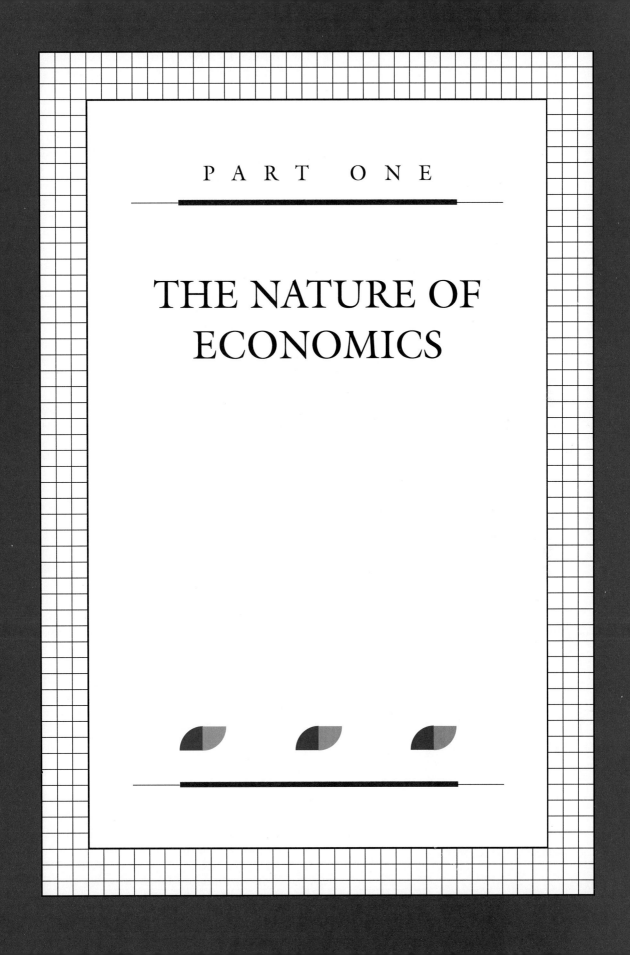

PART ONE

THE NATURE OF ECONOMICS

1

Economics and Society

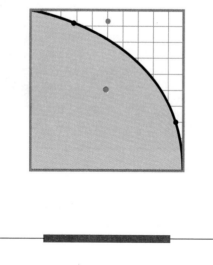

Turn on the TV news, read your local newspaper or the national edition of the *Globe and Mail*, glance at *Macleans* or *The Economist* magazines, and you will see for yourself that many of the world's most pressing problems are economic.

Why did communism fail to deliver acceptable living standards to the citizens of the countries of Eastern Europe and the republics of the former USSR? Why did the developed nations make the adoption of more market-oriented economic policies a precondition of continued foreign aid to the less developed countries of the world? What is the impact of the rise of vast transnational corporations that conduct business over much of the world? Will the population explosion cause the rise of mouths to feed to outrun the growth of food to feed those mouths? Are economists right in urging that environmental protection is often best accomplished using market-price incentives rather than direct government intervention?

Your media survey of press, radio, and TV will also show the importance of economic issues in the problems facing Canada today.

How is it that when the average Canadian enjoys one of the highest living standards the world has ever seen, a standard vastly higher than has been achieved by most of the people who have ever lived on the earth, so many Canadians should feel economically harassed and worry about how to pay the bills? Are Canadians and Americans right to feel threatened by Japanese economic power? Will a North American Free Trade Agreement (NAFTA) be a good or a bad thing for the average Canadian?

Does the size of the massive budget deficits piled up over the last 20 years by both the federal and many provincial governments affect our living standards? Is the Bank of Canada right in believing that a low inflation rate is good for the economy? Why has the distribution of income become more unequal over the past two decades in both Canada and the United States? Will it pay you to go on to higher education? Does it pay the nation to subsidize you to do so?

Of course, not all the world's problems are primarily economic. Political, biological, social, cultural, and philosophical issues often predominate. However, as the following examples suggest, no matter how noneconomic a particular problem may seem, it will almost always have a significant economic dimension.

1. The crises that lead to wars often have economic roots. Nations often fight for oil and rice and land to live on, although the rhetoric of their leaders often evokes God, Glory, and the Fatherland.

2. It took 100,000 years, from the time *Homo sapiens* first appeared on earth until about 1800, for the human population to reach 1 billion. In the next hundred years

a second billion was added. Three billion more came in the next 80 years. The world's population is estimated to be over 10 billion well before the middle of the next century. The economic consequences are steady pressures on the environment everywhere and on local food supplies in poor countries. Unless the human race can find ways to deal with these pressures, increasing millions face starvation and increasing billions face rising levels of environmental degradation.

3. The *greenhouse effect* describes the possibility of a gradual warming of the earth's climate due to a cumulative buildup of carbon dioxide in the atmosphere. *If* the possibility proves a reality, the warming will have significant economic consequences, changing both production possibilities and consumption patterns.

What Is Economics?

So far we have identified a handful of the important current issues on which economics can shed some light. One way to define *economics* is to say that it is the social science that deals with such problems. Another definition, perhaps better known, is Alfred Marshall's: "Economics is a study of mankind in the ordinary business of life." A more penetrating definition might be the following:

Economics is the study of the use of scarce resources to satisfy unlimited human wants.

Scarcity is inevitable and is central to economic problems. What are society's resources? Why is scarcity inevitable? What are the consequences of scarcity?

Resources and Commodities

A society's resources consist of natural endowments such as land, forests, and minerals; human resources, both mental and physical; and manufactured aids to production such as tools, machinery, and buildings.

Economists call such resources **factors of production**[1] because they are used to produce the outputs that people desire. We call these outputs **commodities** and divide them into goods and services. **Goods** are tangible (e.g., cars and shoes), and **services** are intangible (e.g., haircuts and education). Notice the implication of positive value contained in the terms *goods* and *services*. (Compare the terms *bads* and *disservices*.)

People use goods and services to satisfy many of their wants. The act of making them is called **production,** and the act of using them to satisfy wants is called **consumption.** Goods are valued for the services they provide. An automobile, for example, helps to satisfy its owner's desires for transportation, mobility, and possibly status.

Scarcity

For most of the world's 5 1/2 billion human beings, scarcity is real and ever present. In relation to desires (for more and better food, clothing, housing, schooling, entertainment, and so forth), existing resources are woefully inadequate; there are enough to produce only a small fraction of the goods and services that are wanted.

But, one might ask, are not the advanced industrialised nations rich enough that scarcity is nearly banished? After all, they have been characterized as affluent societies. Whatever affluence may mean, it does not mean the end of the problem of scarcity. Most households that earn C$100,000 a year (a princely amount by world standards) have no trouble spending it on things that seem useful to them. Yet it would take nearly twice the present output of the Canadian economy to produce enough to allow all Canadian households to earn that amount.

Choice

Because resources are scarce, all societies face the problem of deciding what to produce and how

---

[1]Definitions of the terms in boldface type can be found in the glossary at the back of the book.

much each person will consume.[2] Societies differ in who makes the choices and how they are made, but the need to choose is common to all. Just as scarcity implies the need for choice, so choice implies the existence of cost. A decision to have more of something requires a decision to have less of something else. The less of something else can be thought of as the cost of having the more of something.

Scarcity implies that choices must be made, and making choices implies the existence of costs.

$$\text{SCARCITY} \rightarrow \text{CHOICE} \rightarrow \text{COSTS}$$

Opportunity Cost

To see how choice implies cost, we look first at a trivial example and then at one that vitally affects all of us; both examples involve precisely the same fundamental principles.

Consider the choice that must be made by a small boy who has 50 cents to spend and who is determined to spend it all on candy. For him there are only two kinds of candy in the world: gumdrops, which sell for 5 cents each, and chocolates, which sell for 10 cents each. The boy would like to buy 10 gumdrops and 10 chocolates, but he knows (or will soon discover) that this is not possible: It is not an *attainable combination* given his scarce resources. However, several combinations are attainable: 8 gumdrops and 1 chocolate, 4 gumdrops and 3 chocolates, 2 gumdrops and 4 chocolates, and so on. Some combinations leave him with money unspent, and he is not interested in them. Only six combinations, as shown in Figure 1-1, are both attainable and use all his money.

After careful thought, the boy has almost decided to buy 6 gumdrops and 2 chocolates, but at the last moment he decides that he simply must have 3 chocolates. What will it cost him to get this

---

[2]There is a partial exception, which is studied later. This occurs when there is a recession in business activity of such severity that there are unemployed amounts of *all* resources. By putting these resources back to work, it is possible for societies to have more of some of the things that they now produce without having less of any other production. Even in such a situation, however, many important choices must be made. For example, those receiving incomes must decide what to buy with these incomes, and the government must decide how much of total national production to allocate to the support of those who are unemployed.

FIGURE 1-1
A Choice Between Gumdrops and Chocolates

A limited amount of money forces a choice among alternatives. Six combinations of gumdrops and chocolates are attainable and use all of the boy's money. The negatively sloped line provides a boundary between attainable and unattainable combinations. The arrows show that the opportunity cost of 1 more chocolate is 2 gumdrops. In this example the opportunity cost is constant, and therefore the boundary is a straight line.

extra chocolate? One answer is 2 gumdrops. As seen in the figure, this is the number of gumdrops he must forgo to get the extra chocolate. Economists describe the 2 gumdrops as the *opportunity cost* of the third chocolate.

Another answer is that the cost of the third chocolate is 10 cents. However, given the boy's budget and his intentions, this answer is less revealing than the first one. Where the real choice is between more of this and more of that, the cost of this is usefully viewed as what you cannot have of that.

The idea of opportunity cost is one of the central insights of economics. The **opportunity cost** of using resources for a certain purpose is the benefit given up by not using them in an alternative way; that is, it is the cost measured in terms of other commodities that could have been obtained instead. If, for example, resources that could have produced 20 miles of road are used instead to produce two small hospitals, the opportunity cost of a hospital is 10 miles of road; looked at the other way round, the opportunity cost of one mile of road is one tenth of a hospital.

Every time a choice must be made, opportunity costs are incurred.

Production Possibilities

Although the choice between gumdrops and chocolates is a minor consumption decision, the essential nature of the decision is the same whatever the choice being made. Consider, for example, the important choice between military and civilian goods and services. If resources are fully employed, it is not possible to have more of both. However, if the government feels able to decrease the size of the military, this will free up the resources needed to produce more for civilian purposes. The opportunity cost of increased civilian output is the forgone military output.

The choice is illustrated in Figure 1-2. Because resources are limited, some combinations—those that would require more than the total available supply of resources for their production—cannot be attained. The negatively sloped curve on the graph divides the combinations that can be attained from those that cannot. Points above and to the right of this curve cannot be attained because there are not enough resources; points below and to the left of the curve can be attained without using all of the available resources; and points on the curve can just be attained if all the available resources are used. The curve is called the **production possibility boundary** or **production possibility curve.** It has a negative slope because, when all resources are being used, having more of one kind of good requires having less of the other kind.

A production possibility boundary illustrates three concepts: scarcity, choice, and opportunity cost. *Scarcity* is indicated by the unattainable combinations above the boundary; *choice,* by the need to choose among the alternative attainable points along the boundary; and *opportunity cost,* by the negative slope of the boundary.

The shape of the production possibility boundary in Figure 1-2 implies that more and more civil-

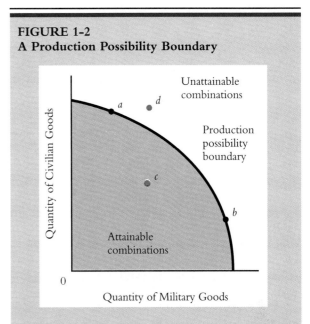

FIGURE 1-2
A Production Possibility Boundary

The **negatively sloped boundary shows the combinations that are just attainable when the society's resources are fully employed.** The quantity of military goods produced is measured along the horizontal axis, the quantity of civilian goods along the vertical axis. Thus any point on the diagram indicates some amount of each kind of good produced. The production possibility boundary separates the attainable combinations of goods, such as *a, b,* and *c,* from unattainable combinations, such as *d.* It is negatively sloped because resources are scarce: When resources are fully employed, more of one kind of good can be produced only if resources are freed by producing less of the other kind of good. Points *a* and *b* represent full and efficient use of society's resources. Point *c* represents either inefficient use of resources or failure to use all the available resources.

ian production must be given up to achieve equal successive increases in military production. This shape, referred to as *concave* to the origin, indicates that the opportunity cost of either good grows larger and larger as we increase the amount of it that is produced. A straight-line boundary, as in Figure 1-1, indicates that the opportunity cost of one good in terms of the other stays constant, no matter how much of it is produced. As we shall see later, the case of rising opportunity cost applies to many important choices.

Four Key Economic Problems

Most problems studied by economists can be grouped under four main headings.

1. What Is Produced and How?

The allocation of scarce resources among alternative uses, called **resource allocation,** determines the quantities of various goods that are produced. Choosing to produce a particular combination of goods means choosing a particular allocation of resources among the industries or regions producing the goods.

Further, because resources are scarce, it is desirable that they be used effectively. Hence it matters which of the available methods of production is used to produce each of the goods.

2. What Is Consumed and by Whom?

What is the relationship between an economy's production of commodities and the consumption enjoyed by its citizens? Economists seek to understand what determines the distribution of a nation's total output among its people. Who gets a lot, who gets a little, and why? What role does international trade play in this?

Questions 1 and 2 fall within **microeconomics,** the study of the allocation of resources and the distribution of income as they are affected by the working of the price system and government policies that seek to influence it.

3. How Much Unemployment and Inflation Exist?

When an economy is in a recession, unemployed workers would like to have jobs, the factories in which they could work are available, the managers and owners would like to be able to operate their factories, raw materials are available in abundance, and the goods that could be produced by these resources are wanted by individuals in the community, but for some reason resources remain unemployed. This means that the economy is operating within its production possibility boundary, at a point such as *c* in Figure 1-2.

The world's economies have often experienced bouts of prolonged and substantial changes in price

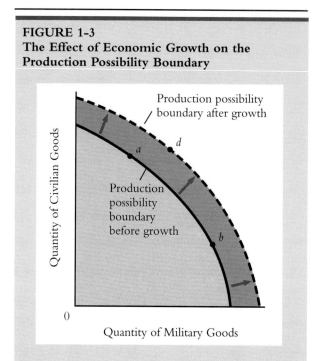

FIGURE 1-3
The Effect of Economic Growth on the Production Possibility Boundary

Economic growth shifts the boundary outward and makes it possible to produce more of all commodities. Before growth in productive capacity, points *a* and *b* were on the production possibility boundary and point *d* was an unattainable combination. After growth, as shown by the dark shaded band, point *d* and many other previously unattainable combinations are attainable.

levels. In recent decades, the course of prices has almost always been upward. The 1970s and early 1980s saw accelerating inflation, not only in Canada but also in most other parts of the world. Then inflation slowed while unemployment soared. Were these two events related? Why do governments worry that reductions in either unemployment or inflation may be at the cost of a temporary increase in the other?

4. Is Productive Capacity Growing?

The capacity to produce commodities to satisfy human wants grows rapidly in some countries, slowly in others, and actually declines in still others. Growth in productive capacity is caused by such things as increases in the number of people working, increases in the amount of capital workers have to work with, and changes in technology that make workers and capital more productive. Over the decades, steady improvements in technology have made labour and capital vastly more productive than they were a century ago. The resulting growth in productive capacity can be represented by an outward shift of the production possibility boundary, as shown in Figure 1-3. If an economy's capacity to produce goods and services is growing, combinations that are unattainable today will become attainable tomorrow. Growth makes it possible to have more of all goods.

Questions 3 and 4 fall within **macroeconomics**, the study of the determination of economic aggregates such as total output, total employment, the price level, and the rate of economic growth.

Alternative Economic Systems

An economic system is a distinctive method of providing answers to the basic economic questions just discussed. All such systems are complex. They include producers of every sort—publicly and privately owned as well as domestically owned and foreign-owned producers. They include consumers of every sort: young and old, rich and poor, working and nonworking. They include laws—such as those relating to property rights—rules, regulations, taxes, subsidies, and everything else that governments use to influence what is produced, how it is produced, and who gets it. They also include customs of every conceivable kind and the entire range of contemporary mores and values.

Types of Economic Systems

Although every economy is in some ways distinct, it is helpful to distinguish three pure types, called *traditional, command,* and *market economies.* These economies differ in the ways in which economic decisions are *coordinated.* All real economies contain some elements of each method.

Traditional Systems

A traditional economic system is one in which behaviour is based primarily on tradition, custom, and habit. Young men follow their fathers' occupations—hunting, fishing, and so on. Women do what their mothers did—typically cooking and field work. There is little change in the pattern of goods produced from year to year, other than those imposed by the vagaries of nature. The techniques of production also follow traditional patterns, except when the effects of an occasional new invention are felt. Finally, production is allocated among the members according to long-established traditions. In short, the answers to the economic questions of what to produce, how to produce, and how to distribute are determined by traditions.

Such a system works best in an unchanging environment. Under static conditions, a system that does not continually require people to make choices can prove effective in meeting economic and social needs.

Traditional systems were common in the nomadic life that preceded the Neolithic agricultural revolution. They have also been found in less distant times. For example, the feudal system, under which most people lived in medieval Europe, was a largely traditional society. Peasants, artisans, and most others living in villages inherited their positions in that society. They also usually inherited their specific jobs, which they handled in traditional ways. For example, blacksmiths made customary charges for dealing with horses brought to them, and it would have been unthinkable for them to decline their services to any villager who requested them.

Today only a few small, isolated, self-sufficient communities still retain mainly traditional systems. Examples can be found in the Canadian Arctic and in Patagonia. Also, in many less developed countries, significant aspects of economic behaviour are still governed by traditional patterns.

Command Systems

In command systems, economic behaviour is determined by some central authority, which makes most of the necessary decisions on what to produce, how to produce it, and who gets it. Such economies are characterized by the *centralization* of decision making. Because centralized decision makers usually lay down elabourate and complex plans for the behaviour that they wish to impose, the terms **command economy** and **centrally planned economy** are usually used synonymously.

The sheer quantity of data required for the central planning of an entire economy is enormous, and the task of analysing it to produce a fully integrated plan can hardly be exaggerated. Moreover, the plan must be a rolling process, continually changing to take account not only of current data but also of future trends in labour supplies, technological developments, and people's tastes for various goods and services. Doing so involves the planners in *forecasting*. This is a notoriously difficult business, not least because of the unavailability of all essential, accurate, and up-to-date information.

A decade ago, over one third of the world's population lived in countries that relied heavily on central planning to deal with the basic economic questions. Today, the number of such countries is small. Even in countries where planning is the proclaimed system, as in China, increasing amounts of market determination are being quietly permitted.

Market Systems

In the third type of economic system, the decisions about resource allocation are made without any central direction. Instead, they result from innumerable independent decisions made by individual producers and consumers; such a system is known as a **free-market economy** or, more simply, a **market economy**. In such an economy, decisions relating to the basic economic issues are decentralized. They are nonetheless coordinated. The main coordinating device is the set of market-determined prices—which is why free-market systems are often called *price systems*. Because much of this book is devoted to studying how market systems work, little more needs to be said about them at this point.

Mixed Systems

Economies that are fully traditional, or fully centrally controlled, or wholly free market are pure types that are useful for studying basic principles. When we look in detail at *any* real economy, however, we discover that its economic behaviour is the result of some mixture of central control and market determination, with a certain amount of traditional behaviour as well. In practise, every economy is a **mixed economy** in the sense that it combines sig-

nificant elements of all three systems—traditional, command, and market—in determining economic behaviour.[3] Furthermore, within any economy, the degree of the mix will vary from sector to sector. For example, in some planned economies, the command principle was used more often to determine behaviour in heavy goods industries, such as steel, than in agriculture. Farmers were often given substantial freedom to produce and sell what they wished in response to varying market prices.

When we speak of a particular economy as being a centrally planned economy, we mean that the degree of the mix is weighted heavily toward the command principle. When we speak of an economy as being a market economy, we mean that the degree of the mix is weighted heavily toward decentralized decision making in response to market signals. It is important to realize that such distinctions are always matters of degree, and that almost every conceivable mix can be found across the spectrum of the world's economies.

Although no country offers an example of either system working alone, some economies, such as those of Canada, France, and South Korea, rely much more heavily on market decisions than others, such as the economies of China, North Korea, and Cuba. Yet even in Canada, the command principle has some sway. Minimum wages, rules and regulations for environmental protection, quotas on some agricultural outputs, and restrictions on the import of items such as textiles, cheap shoes, and poultry are the obvious examples.

Ownership of Resources

We have seen that economies differ as to the principle used for coordinating their economic decisions. They also differ as to who owns their productive resources. Who owns a nation's farms and factories, its coal mines and forests? Who owns its railways, streams, and golf courses? Who owns its houses and hotels?

In a private-ownership economy, the basic raw materials, the productive assets of the society, and the goods produced in the economy are predomi-

---

[3]Although tradition influences behaviour in all societies, we shall have little to say about it in the rest of this book because we are primarily interested in the consequences of making economic decisions through the market and the command principles.

nantly privately owned. By this standard, Canada has primarily a private-ownership economy. However, even in Canada, public ownership extends beyond the usual basic services, such as schools and local transportation systems, to include such other activities as housing projects, forest and range land, and electric power utilities.

In contrast, a public-ownership economy is one in which the productive assets are predominantly publicly owned. This was true of the former USSR, and it is still true to some extent in present-day China. In China, however, legal private ownership exists in many sectors—including the rapidly growing part of the manufacturing sector that is foreign owned—while in practise many peasants now effectively own their land.

The Coordination-Ownership Mix

Leaving aside tradition, because it is not the predominant coordinating method in any modern economy, there are four possible combinations of coordination and ownership principles. Of the two most common combinations, the first is the private-ownership market economy, in which the market principle is the main coordinating mechanism and the majority of productive assets are privately owned. The second most common combination during the twentieth century has been the public-ownership planned economy, in which central planning is the primary means of coordinating economic decisions and property is primarily publicly owned. In 1975, the countries in this class included the USSR, the six other countries of Eastern Europe, China, Cuba, Viet Nam, North Korea, and a number of other countries in Asia and Africa. In 1994, North Korea and Cuba were almost the only countries remaining wholly in this class.

The two other possible combinations are a market economy in which the resources are publicly owned and a command economy in which the resources are privately owned. No modern economy has achieved either of these two hybrid types. Nazi Germany from 1932 to 1945 went some way toward combining private ownership with the command principle. The United Kingdom from 1945 to 1980 went quite a way toward a public-ownership market economy, because many industries and much housing were publicly owned. On balance, however, Germany and the United Kingdom were still best described as private-ownership market economies. (The United Kingdom's privatization program in the 1980s returned most publicly owned assets to private ownership, thus placing that country fully in the ranks of private-ownership market economies.)

Command Versus Market Determination

For over a century, a great debate raged on the relative merits of the command principle versus the market principle for coordinating economic decisions in practise. The USSR, the countries of Eastern Europe, China, and many smaller nations were command economies for much of this century. Canada, the United States, the countries of Western Europe and many others were, and are, primarily market economies. The successes of the USSR and China in the early stages of industrialisation suggested to many observers earlier in this century that the command principle was at least as good for organizing economic behaviour as the market principle, if not better. In the long haul, however, planned economies proved a failure of such disastrous proportions as to seriously depress the living standards of their citizens.

Rarely in human history has such a decisive verdict been delivered on two competing systems. Box 1-1 gives some of the reasons why central planning was a failure in Eastern Europe and the USSR. The discussion is of more than purely historical interest because the reasons for the failure of planned economies give insight into the reasons for the relative success of free-market economies.

The Lessons from the Failure of Command Systems

The failure of planned economies suggests the superiority of decentralized markets over centrally planned ones as coordinating and signaling devices. Put another way, it demonstrates the superiority of mixed economies with substantial elements of market determination over fully planned command economies. However, it does *not* demonstrate, as some have asserted, the superiority of completely free-market economies over mixed economies.

Box 1-1

The Failure of Central Planning

The year 1989 signaled to the world what many economists had long argued: the superiority of a market-oriented price system over central planning as a method of organizing economic activity. The failure of central planning had many causes, but four were particularly significant.

The Failure of Coordination

In centrally planned economies, a body of planners tries to coordinate all the economic decisions about production, investment, trade, and consumption that are likely to be made by the producers and consumers throughout the country. This proved impossible to do with any reasonable degree of efficiency. Bottlenecks in production, shortages of some goods, and gluts of others plagued the Soviet economy for decades. For example, in 1989, much of a bumper harvest rotted on the farm because of shortages of storage and transportation facilities, and for years there was an ample supply of black-and-white television sets and severe shortages of toilet paper and soap.

Failure of Quality Control

Central planners can monitor the number of units produced by any factory and reward those who overfulfill their production targets and punish those who fall short. It is much harder, however, for them to monitor quality. A constant Soviet problem, therefore, was the production of poor-quality products. Factory managers were concerned with meeting their quotas by whatever means were available, and once the goods passed out of their factory, what happened to them was someone else's headache. The quality problem was so serious that very few Eastern European-manufactured products were able to stand up to the newly permitted competition from superior goods produced in the advanced market societies.

In market economies, poor quality is punished by low sales, and retailers soon give a signal to factory managers by shifting their purchases to other suppliers. The incentives that obviously flow from such private-sector purchasing discretion are generally absent from command economies, where purchases and sales are planned centrally.

Misplaced Incentives

In market economies, relative wages and salaries provide incentives for labour to move from place to place, and the possibility of losing one's job provides an incentive to work diligently. This is a harsh mechanism that punishes losers with loss of income (although social programs provide floors to the amount of economic punishment that can be suffered). In planned economies, workers usually have complete job security. Industrial unemployment is rare, and even when it does occur, new jobs are usually found for those who lose theirs. Although

There is no guarantee that free markets will handle, on their own, such urgent matters as controlling pollution and producing sustainable growth. (Indeed, as we shall see in later chapters, much economic theory is devoted to explaining why free markets often fail to do these things.) Mixed economies, with significant degrees of government intervention, are needed to do these jobs.

Furthermore, acceptance of the free market over central planning does not provide an excuse to ignore a country's pressing social issues. Acceptance of the benefits of the free market still leaves plenty of scope to debate the kinds, amounts, and directions of government interventions into the workings of our market-based economy that will help to achieve social goals.

It follows that there is still room for disagreement about the *degree* of the mix of market and the high level of security is attractive to many, it proved impossible to provide sufficient incentives for reasonably hard and efficient work under such conditions. In the words of Oxford historian Timothy Garton Ash, who wrote eyewitness chronicles of the developments in Eastern Europe from 1980 to 1990, the social contract between the workers and the government in the Eastern countries was "We pretend to work, and you pretend to pay us."

Because of the absence of a work-oriented incentive system, income inequalities do not provide the normal free-market incentives. Income inequalities were used instead to provide incentives for party members to tow the line. The major gap in income standards was between party members on the one hand and non-party members on the other. The former had access to such privileges as special stores where imported goods were available, special hospitals providing sanitary and efficient medical care, and special resorts where good vacations were available. In contrast, nonmembers had none of these things.

Environmental Degradation

Fulfilling production plans became the all-embracing incentive in planned economies, to the exclusion of most other considerations, including the environment. As a result, environmental degradation occurred in all the countries of Eastern Europe on a scale unknown in advanced Western nations. A par-ticularly disturbing example occurred in central Asia, where high quotas for cotton output led to indiscriminate use of pesticides and irrigation. Birth defects are now found in nearly one child in three, and the vast Aral Sea has been half drained, causing major environmental effects.

This failure to protect the environment stems from a combination of the pressure to fulfill plans and the lack of a political marketplace where citizens can express their preferences for the environment versus economic gain. Imperfect though the system may be in democratic market economies, their record of environmental protection has been vastly better than that of command economies.

The Price System

In contrast to the failures of command economies, the performance of the free-market price system is impressive. One theme of this book is *market success:* how the price system works to coordinate with relative efficiency the decentralized decisions made by private consumers and producers, providing the right quantities of relatively high-quality outputs and incentives for efficient work. It is important, however, not to conclude that doing things better means doing things perfectly. Another theme of this book is *market failure:* how and why the unaided price system sometimes fails to produce efficient results and fails to take account of social values that cannot be expressed through the marketplace.

government determination in any modern mixed economy—room enough to accommodate such divergent views as could be expressed by conservative, liberal, and modern social democratic parties. People can accept the free market as an efficient way of organizing economic affairs and still disagree about many things. A partial list includes the optimal amount and types of government regulation of, and assistance to, the functioning of the economy; the types of measures needed to protect the environment; whether health care should be provided by the public or the private sector; and the optimal amount and design of social services and other policies intended to redistribute income from more to less fortunate citizens. Some of the issues that arise when we debate the value of alternative economic systems in general, or of specific policies in particular, are discussed in Box 1-2.

Box 1-2

Ends and Means

To understand debates about relative desirability of different systems—as well as countless other debates about economic matters—we need first to distinguish between the goals of our actions and the means that we use to achieve those goals. Our goals are called **ends**; they are the things that we strive for. The things that we use to achieve our ends are our **means**; they are the methods of achieving our goals.

In the economic aspects of life, most people's ends include (1) achieving a satisfactory and, ideally, a rising living standard, (2) maintaining at a reasonable quality the environment in which they live, and (3) as far as possible, protecting themselves and others from the consequences of such serious disasters as the loss of their job, the onset of a major disability, or the bankruptcy of their employer.

All three examples represent a broad group of ends. The first relates to our material living standards. The second relates to the quality of the environment in which we live and work. The third relates to our social welfare system—the system that is intended to shield citizens from the worst consequences of disasters and to provide a living-standard safety net below which no one should be forced to sink for any reason. These are three of our most important economic ends.

Debates over Means

Many political and economic debates relate to the alleged potency of alternative means to achieve agreed ends. Consider some examples.

The two great systems of command and free-market economies were both seen as means to higher living standards and better control over our environment. Starting in 1989, the countries of Eastern Europe made the choice to move toward a free-market system, in part because their citizens thought that it was, among other things, a superior means to the end of higher living standards.

Many Canadians support government intervention into the markets for privately rented accommodations (rent controls) and farm production (price supports and subsidies). This is not because they value intervention for its own sake. Instead, they hope that such intervention will be a means toward higher incomes for producers and/or lower prices to consumers, which in turn means a rise in the living standards of those concerned. Opponents agree that a rise in living standards is desirable but argue that these means are inappropriate to the ends. They say, for example, that the long-term result of government intervention into agricultural markets is that consumers will be worse off and only a few farmers better off than if the market had been left alone.

Debates over Ends

The interests of various groups who are pursuing different ends can also conflict. Everyone may agree, for example, that a particular agricultural policy makes farmers better off but at the expense of consumers who must pay higher prices for their products. In this case, there is a real conflict between groups. The issue then becomes deciding between competing ends—improving the lot of farmers or that of consumers—rather than judging between alternative means to agreed-upon ends.

Conflicts can also emerge over ends because different groups put different values on alternative ends. When environmental groups oppose the establishment of a local pulp mill while potential employees support it, the two groups are applying different values to two competing ends: more local job creation and more environmental protection.

Aspects of a Modern Economy

Throughout this book we study the functioning of a modern, market-based, mixed economy, such as is found in Canada today. By way of introduction, this section gives a few salient aspects that should be kept in mind from the outset.

Origins

The modern market economies that we know today first arose in Europe out of the ashes of the feudal system. As we have already mentioned, the feudal system was a traditional one, in which people did jobs based on heredity (the miller's son became the next generation's miller) and received shares of their village's total output that were based on custom. Peasants were tied to the land. Much land was owned by the crown and granted to the lord of the manor in return for military services. Some of it was made available for the common use of all villagers. Property such as the village mill and blacksmith's shop never belonged to those who worked there and could therefore never be bought and sold by them.

In contrast, modern economies are based on market transactions between people who voluntarily decide whether or not to engage in them. They have the right to buy and sell what they wish, to accept or refuse offered work, and to move to where they want when they want. Key institutions are private property and freedom of contract, both of which must be maintained by active government policies. The government creates laws of ownership and contract and then provides the courts to enforce these laws.

Living Standards

The material living standards of any society depend on how much it can produce. What there is to consume depends on what is produced. If the productive capacity of a society is small, then the living standards of its typical citizen will be low. Only by raising that productive capacity can average living standards be raised. No society can generate increased real consumption merely by voting its citizens higher money incomes.

How much a society can produce depends both on how many of its citizens are at work producing goods and services and on their productivity in their work. How well has the Canadian economy performed in each of these dimensions?

Jobs

In spite of some short-term ups and downs, the trend of total employment has been upward over most of modern Canadian history. For example, in 1952 there were 5.2 million Canadian citizens in civilian employment (excluding the armed forces), whereas in 1992 the figure was 13.9 million. This is a net creation of 8.6 million new jobs over that 40-year period.

These new jobs provided employment for a rising population and for the increasing proportion of that population who wished to work. The percentage of the population over 16 who were in the labour force (i.e., either working or looking for work) rose from 53 percent in 1952 to 66 percent in 1992. This overall increase masked large offsetting movements in male and female participation in the labour force. Over that period, the percentage of women over 16 who were in the labour force rose from 22 to 58 percent, whereas the percentage of men fell from 84 to 74 percent.

Labour Productivity

Labour productivity refers to the amount produced per hour of work. Rising living standards are closely linked to the rising productivity of the typical worker. If each worker produces more, then (other things being equal) there will be more production in total and hence more for each person to consume on average.

In the period from 1750 to 1900, the market economies in Europe and North America became industrial economies. Industry was slower to develop in Canada, but modern mechanized methods of production raised output in agriculture, mines, forests, and other primary industries whose products were required by consumers and producers in more industrialised countries. With mechanization and industrialisation, modern market economies raised ordinary people out of poverty by raising productivity at rates that appeared slow from year to year, but that had dramatic effects on living standards when sustained over long periods of time.

> Over a year, or even over a decade, the economic gains [of the late eighteenth and nineteenth centuries], after allowing for the rise in population, were so little noticeable that it was widely believed that the gains were experienced only by the rich, and not by the poor. Only as the West's compounded growth continued through the twentieth century did its breadth become clear. It became obvious that Western working classes were increasingly well off and that the Western middle classes were prospering and growing as a proportion of the whole population. Not that poverty disappeared. The West's achievement was not the abolition of poverty but the reduction of its incidence from 90 percent of the population to 30 percent, 20 percent, or less, depending on the country and one's definition of poverty.[4]

Figure 1-4 shows the rise in the productivity of Canadian labour from 1946 to 1992. In spite of many short-term variations, the general trend is unmistakably upward. Every hour worked has produced more and more total output during the whole course of this century, including the period from 1947 and 1992 covered by the figure. Over the period shown in the figure, labor productivity doubled and then doubled again. As a result, each person produces four times as much now as he or she did in 1947. The basis of our rising living standards is our ability to produce more and more as time passes. (A helpful device is the *rule of 72:* Divide 72 by the annual growth rate, and the result is approximately the number of years required for income to double.) **[1]**[5]

These are potent sources of increases in living standards. The rising real wages that they generated are shown in Figure 1-5. Over the long period of rising productivity, Canadian citizens (as well as the citizens of most industrial countries) got used to

each generation being substantially better off than each preceding generation. In the middle period from 1938 to 1974, children whose income relative to their contemporaries was the same as their parents' could expect to earn about twice the real income their parents had enjoyed.

Then in the mid-1970s, this productivity growth fell substantially. Currently the typical child 25 years younger than his or her parents can expect to be no more than 30 percent better off than his or her parents. This is a remarkable reduction in the rate that each generation is becoming better off materially. Over long periods of time, however, even 1 percent productivity growth is still a potent force for change, because it doubles real output per worker about every 72 years, or about one human lifetime.

Distribution of Income

What we have just said is not the end of the story. Not only has the rate of increase in aggregate income slowed dramatically in recent years, but the way in which that income is distributed among the various income groups has also altered significantly.

Some of the most dramatic shifts have occurred in the United States. Incomes became progressively more equally distributed up through the 1960s. After that, the trend reversed. Over the 1970s, 1980s, and 1990s the distribution of income has slowly become more unequal. For example, the share of income received by the lowest 20 percent in the income distribution rose from 5.0 percent in 1947 to 5.7 percent in 1968, then fell to 4.6 percent in 1990. That is a 20-percent decrease in the share of total income going to the poorest group over a 25-year period. At the other end of the distribution, the share of income going to the highest 20-percent on the income scale fell from 43.0 percent in 1947 to 40.5 percent in 1968, then rose to 44.3 percent by 1990. That is close to a 10-percent increase in the share of total income going to the richest group in the society.

Interestingly, Canadian data do not show this turnaround. Instead, inequalities have continued to narrow right up to the beginning of the 1990s. For example, the lowest 20 percent of income earners received only 2.8 percent of total income in 1967 and 5.4 percent in 1991. While they are still poor by our standards, they did double their share of an increasing total of the nation's income. In contrast,

---

[4]N. Rosenberg and L. E. Birdzell, Jr., *How the West Grew Rich* (New York: Basic Books, 1986), p. 6.

[5]Notes giving mathematical demonstrations of the concepts presented in the text are designated by boldface reference numbers. These notes can be found at the end of the book beginning on page M-1.

FIGURE 1-4
Output Per Hour Worked in Canada

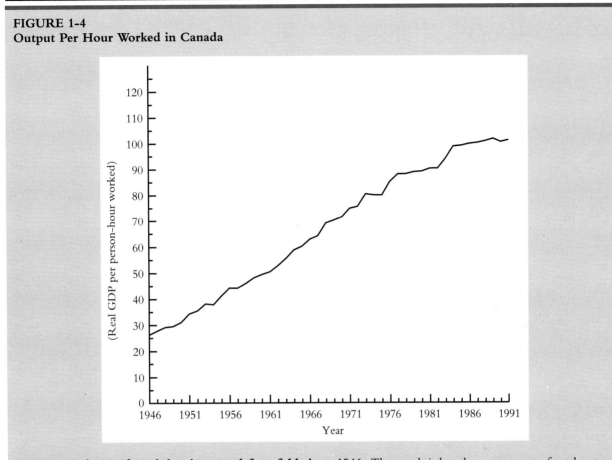

Output per hour of work has increased four fold since 1946. The graph is based on a measure of total output in Canada (the GDP) divided by the total number of hours worked by the Canadian labour force. The data are expressed as a percentage of the value of output per hour worked in 1986 (1986 is therefore shown as 100). The steady improvement, which is the basis for rising living standards, is apparent. So also is the slowdown in growth of output per person hour that began in the mid 1970s. (*Source*: Statistics Canada, 15–204.)

the top 20 percent of income earners received 46.3 percent of the nation's total income in 1967 and 43.7 percent in 1991.

The evidence is that market forces in virtually all advanced countries were pushing in the direction of more income inequality in the 1980s (and in the 1990s as well). The difference between Canada and the United Kingdom on the one hand and the United States and several other countries on the other hand, is that in Canada and the United Kingdom income transfers provided by the social welfare system offset virtually all of the effects of these market forces. For example, two U.S. economists, Maria Hanratty and Rebecca Blank, show that in the 1980s the maximum monthly transfers for low-income people fell by 6.4 percent in the United States but *rose* by 9.6 percent in Canada. The net result of these market forces and differences in welfare support was, according to Boston college professor Peter Gottschalk,[6] that the actual incomes families had to spend, after paying taxes and receiving transfers, became substantially more unequal in the United States, while it hardly changed in Canada between the years 1979 and 1985.

The growing inequality in the distribution of income created by market forces seems to a great

---

[6]As reported in the *American Economic Review*, May 1993, pp. 136-142.

FIGURE 1-5
Average Canadian Wages Over the Decades

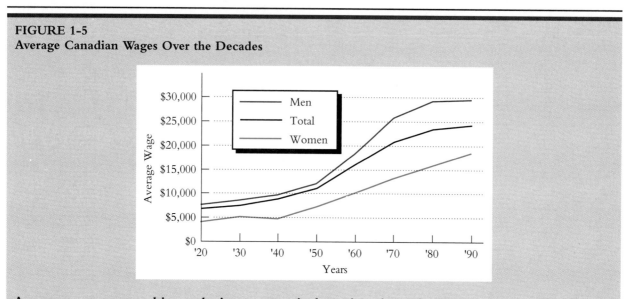

Average wages measured in purchasing-power units have risen dramatically over the decades. From 1920 to 1990 the purchasing power of the average wage earned by Canadians rose by about 250 percent. The purchasing power of women's wages hardly rose from 1920 to 1940 but since then, has risen steadily decade by decade. In contrast, the average wage earned by men rose dramatically through the 1960s, slowed its increase in the 1970s, and did not rise at all in the 1980s.

The data show the average wage for men and for women in each decade from the 1920s to the 1980s. The wages are expressed in 1990 dollars, which means that they show the change in purchasing power of wages over the decades. For example, average wages for women in the decade 1920-1930 were about five thousand 1990 dollars, which means that the wages women earned in that decade would have bought as many goods and services as $5,000 could buy in 1990. The data cover both part-time and full-time work, so part of the discrepancy between male and female wages is accounted for by the larger percentage of women who work part-time compared to men. (*Source*: Statistics Canada, 13–217.)

extent to be due to the increasing need for, and hence higher earnings of, relatively well-educated workers. This in turn is associated with changes in many production processes that demand higher and higher levels of skill. Henry Ford boasted just before 1914 that any job on his assembly line could be taught in 15 minutes to an immigrant worker with an imperfect command of English. Today, many jobs cannot be taught at all unless the workers have many years of education, followed by months of on-the-job training.

Ongoing Change

The growth in incomes over the centuries since market economies first arose has mainly been caused by continual technological change. Our technolo-

gies are our ways of doing things. New ways of doing old things and new things to do are continually being invented and brought into use. These technological changes make labour more productive, and they are constantly changing the nature of our economy. Old jobs are destroyed and new jobs are created as the technological structure slowly evolves.

Job Structure

The most dramatic change in the structure of jobs in the earlier part of this century was in agriculture. In 1900, over 40 percent of the Canadian population were employed on farms. Today, this figure is just over 3 percent!

Figure 1-6 shows the change in occupational structure of the nonagricultural labour force between 1958 and 1993. The most dramatic changes

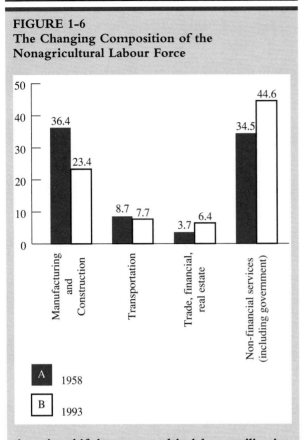

FIGURE 1-6
The Changing Composition of the
Nonagricultural Labour Force

A 1958
B 1993

A major shift has occurred in labour utilization over the last 35 years. The figure shows the percentage of the nonagricultural labour force employed in each of four sectors; for each sector, the first bar shows the percentage in 1958 and the second bar shows the percentage in 1993. The shift has been away from manufacturing and toward the service-oriented (largely white-collar) sectors shown in the last two sets of bars. Although dramatic, these shifts are part of a continuing adjustment that has been going on over the last 200 years. (*Source*: Statistics Canada, 71–201.)

are associated with the decline of jobs in manufacturing and the rise in service industries. The change has been so dramatic that many observers speak of the deindustrialisation of the economy. A better term might be deindustrialisation of employment. Manufacturing employment has declined steadily as more and more output is produced with higher and

higher efficiency using less and less labour. Canadians still produce and consume many manufactured commodities, but a declining proportion of Canadians earn their incomes by working in the manufacturing sector. As explained below, even the shift of employment to services is a complex change whose nature is not fully caught by the phrase "deindustrialisation." If deindustrialisation applies to the Canadian and U.S. economies in any sense of the term, it also applies to the economies of most Western European countries, where similar changes have been observed.

Services in manufacturing. The enormous growth in what are recorded as service jobs overstates the decline in the importance of the manufacturing of goods in our economy. This is because many of the jobs recorded as service jobs in fact are an integral part of the production of manufactured goods.

First, some of the growth has occurred because services that used to be produced within the manufacturing firms have now been decentralized to specialist firms. These often include design, quality control, accounting, legal services, and marketing (e.g., for the first time in its eight editions, the manuscript of this book was handled by an independent firm rather than in-house). Indeed, one of the most significant of the new developments in production is the breakdown of the old hierarchial organization of firms and the development of the production unit as a loosely knit grouping of organizations, each responsible for part of the total activities; some units are owned by the firms, but many are on contract to them.

Second, as a result of the rapid growth of international trade, production and sales have required growing quantities of service inputs for such things as transportation, insurance, banking, and marketing.

Third, as more and more products become high tech, increasing amounts are spent on product design at one end and customer liaison at the other end. These activities, which are all related to the production and sale of goods, are often recorded as service activities.

Services for final consumption. As households' incomes have risen over the decades, households have spent a rising proportion of their incomes on consuming services rather than goods. Today, for example, eating out is common; for your grandparents, it was a luxury. This does not mean, however, that we spend more on food. The extra expenditure goes to pay for the services of those who prepare and serve in restaurants the same ingredients that your grandparents prepared for themselves at home. Young people spend far more on attending live concerts than they used to, and all of us spend vastly more on travel. In 1890, the salesman in a small town was likely to be *the* well-traveled citizen because he had gone 500 miles by train to the provincial capital. Today, such a person would be regarded by many as an untraveled stay-at-home.

New Products

When we talk of each generation having more real income than previous generations, we must not think of just having more and more money to spend on the same set of products that our parents or grandparents consumed. In fact, we consume very few of the products that were the mainstays of expenditure for our great grandparents.

One of the most important aspects of the change that permeates market economies is the continual introduction of new products. It was not until well into this century that electricity was brought to rural areas. Most of the myriad instruments and tools in a modern dentist's office, doctor's office, or hospital did not exist 50 years ago. Penicillin, painkillers, bypass operations, movies, stereos, videocassettes and recorders, pocket calculators, computers, ballpoint pens, compact discs, and fast, safe travel by jet aircraft have all been introduced within living memory. So also have the products that have eliminated much of the drudgery formerly associated with housework. Dishwashers, detergents, disposable diapers, washing machines, vacuum cleaners, refrigerators, deep freezers, and their complement, the supermarket, were not there to help your great grandparents when they first set up house.

Globalisation

Another aspect of the constant change that occurs in evolving market economies is the globalisation that has been occurring at an accelerating rate over the last two decades. At the heart of globalisation lies the rapid reduction in transportation costs and the revolution in information technology. The cost of moving products around the world has fallen greatly in recent decades. More dramatically, our abilities to transmit and to analyse data have been *increasing* dramatically, while the costs of doing so have been *decreasing* equally dramatically.

Many *markets* are globalising; for example, as some tastes become universal to young people, we can see the same designer jeans and leather jackets in virtually all big cities. Many *corporations* are globalising, as they increasingly become what are called *transnationals*. These are massive firms with a physical presence in many countries and an increasingly decentralized management structure. Many *labour markets* are globalising, as the revolutions in communications and transportation allow the various components of any one product to be produced all over the world. A typical compact disc player, TV set, or automobile will contain components made in literally dozens of different countries. We still know where a product is assembled, but it is becoming increasingly difficult to say where it is *made*.

One result of this globalisation of production is that components that can be produced by unskilled labour can now be produced in any low-wage country around the world, where previously they were usually produced in the country that did the assembly. This has proven valuable for developing countries. They have a better chance of becoming competitive in a small range of components than in the integrated production of whole commodities. However, unskilled labour in developed countries is losing (relatively, and possibly absolutely for a while), as their labour becomes less scarce relative to the need for it. In short, the market for unskilled labour is globalising, throwing unskilled labour in advanced countries into direct competition with unskilled labour in poorer countries.

Globalisation has greatly increased the amount of international trade. This has risen roughly twice as fast as total production over the decades since the end of the Second World War in 1945. Canada has always depended greatly on foreign trade. Most of its exports went to the United Kingdom up until 1945. Today, however, the United States is Canada's most important market, in most years taking over 70 percent of all Canadian exports.

Globalisation has also increased U.S. dependence on foreign markets. In 1959, exports only amounted to 4.1 percent of *total U.S. production* (as measured by what is called its GDP). The rest was used domestically. In 1991, the figure was 10.4 percent. The proportion of total U.S. production of *goods* that is exported is much larger than 10 percent. Without the export market, many of the existing sources of U.S. employment and income would not exist.

On the investment side, the most important result of globalisation is that large firms are seeking a physical presence in many major countries. In the 1950s and 1960s, most foreign investment was made by U.S. firms investing abroad to establish a presence in foreign markets. Today, most developed countries see major flows of investment in *both directions,* inward as foreign firms invest in their markets and outward as their own firms invest abroad.

In 1967, 50 percent of all outward-bound foreign investment came from the United States and went to many foreign countries. In 1990, according to United Nations figures, the United States accounted for less than 30 percent of all outward-bound foreign investment. At the same time, the United Kingdom accounted for 16 percent, while Japan and Germany accounted for just under 10 percent each, and Canada 2.1 percent.

On the inward-bound side, the change is more dramatic. In 1967, the United States attracted only 9 percent of all foreign investment made in that year. In 1990, however, the United States attracted 27 percent. Not only do U.S. firms hold massive foreign investments in foreign countries, but foreign firms now hold massive investments in the United States. In 1990, Canada, a much smaller country, received 3.2 percent of all inward-bound foreign investment.

Being a small country with enormous resources beyond the power of domestic capital to develop fully, Canada has always relied heavily on foreign investment for much of its growth. As the Canadian economy matured, however, Canadian firms began to spread abroad making Canada a source of outward bound investment as well as a recipient of inward bound investment. Also, as Canadian firms grew, they took over more and more of the investment in the Canadian market. As a result, foreign ownership of Canadian industry peaked in the early 1970s and has been declining ever since—with a small upsurge around 1990 when Canada's free trade agreement with the United States increased Canada's attractivness to foreign firms seeking to locate in the North American Market.

As a result of these enormous investment flows, many workers in Canada, the United States, the United Kingdom, Germany, France, and most other industrial countries work for foreign-owned firms.[7]

The world is truly globalising in both its trade and investment flows. Today, no country can take an isolationist economic stance and hope to take part in the global economy, where increasing shares of jobs and incomes are created. Not only do a large number of Canadians work for foreign-owned companies operating in Canada, but a growing number of foreigners work for Canadian-owned companies operating abroad.

Conclusion

In this last part of the chapter, we have briefly discussed how people's living standards are affected by the availability of jobs, the productivity of labour in those jobs, and the distribution of the income produced by those jobs. We have seen how the economy is characterized by ongoing change in the structure of jobs, in the production techniques used by the workers, and in the kinds of goods and services produced. We have also seen that these changes exist in the context of a rapidly globalising economy—one in which events occurring in any one country have major consequences in many other countries.

These issues will arise at many places throughout this book. We will study what is happening in more detail and will use economic theory to explain why it is happening. Because most of them are interrelated, it helps to know the basic outlines of all of them before studying any one in more depth.

---

[7]Foreign investment in Canada is discussed in much more detail in Chapter 16.

SUMMARY

1. Most of the world's pressing problems have an economic aspect, and many are primarily economic. A common feature of such problems is that they concern the use of limited resources to satisfy virtually unlimited human wants.

2. Scarcity is a fundamental problem faced by all economies. Not enough resources are available to produce all the goods and services that people would like to consume. Scarcity makes it necessary to choose. All societies must have a mechanism for choosing what commodities will be produced and in what quantities.

3. The concept of opportunity cost emphasizes the problem of scarcity and choice by measuring the cost of obtaining a unit of one commodity in terms of the number of units of other commodities that could have been obtained instead.

4. Answers must be provided for four basic questions in all economies: What commodities are to be produced and how? What commodities are to be consumed and by whom? What will the unemployment and inflation rates be? Will productive capacity change?

5. Different economies resolve these questions in different ways and with varying degrees of efficacy. Economists study how these problems are addressed in various societies and the consequences of using one method rather than another to provide solutions.

6. We can distinguish three pure types of economies: traditional, command, and free market. In practise, all economies are mixed economies in that their economic behaviour responds to mixes of tradition, government command, and price incentives.

7. In the late 1980s, events in Eastern Europe and the USSR led to the general acceptance that the system of fully centrally planned economies had failed to produce minimally acceptable living standards for its citizens. All of these countries are now moving toward greater market determination and less state command in their economies.

8. Market economies are based on private property and freedom of contract. They have generated sustained growth, which, over long periods, has raised material living standards massively.

9. Over the last two centuries, living standards have risen greatly. Recently, however, the rapid growth in labour productivity has slowed and the distribution of income created by market forces has become somewhat more unequal in most advanced industrial countries. In some countries, including Canada and the United Kingdom the effects of these pressures for inequality have been largely offset by the income transfer system that assists low income families.

10. Market economies are characterized by constant change in such things as the structure of jobs, the structure of production, the technologies in use, and the types of products produced.

11. Driven by the revolution in transportation and communications, the world economy is rapidly globalising. National and regional boundaries are becoming less important as transnational corporations locate the production of each component part of a com-

modity in the country that can produce it at the best quality and the least cost.

12. As part of this globalisation, most countries are much more heavily involved in foreign trade than in the past. Most advanced countries have become both host countries for investment by foreign firms and source countries for investment located in foreign countries.

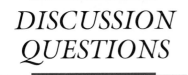

TOPICS FOR REVIEW

Scarcity and the need for choice

Choice and opportunity cost

Production possibility boundary

Resource allocation

Growth in productive capacity

Traditional economies

Command economies

Market economies

Globalisation

DISCUSSION QUESTIONS

1. What does each of the following questions tell you about the policy conflicts perceived by the person making the statement and about how that person has resolved them?

   a. "It is an industry worth several hundred jobs to our province; we cannot afford to forgo it." A provincial premier explaining the decision to organize a killing of wolves in his province so that more game animals could grow up to be shot by hunters.

   b. "The annual seal hunt must be stopped, even if it destroys the livelihood of the seal hunters." An animal rights advocate successfully opposing the former seal hunt in Canada.

   c. "Considering our limited energy resources and the growing demand for electricity, Canada really has no choice but to use all of its possible domestic energy sources, including nuclear energy. Despite possible environmental and safety hazards, nuclear power is a necessity." A provincial hydro authority replying to critics.

   d. "The proposed pulp mills must be opposed because of the pollution they cause, even though they bring new, diversified jobs and even though they are based on the most advanced, pollution-minimizing technologies." An opponent of the proposal to construct new pulp and paper mills in the Peace River District of northern Canada during the 1990s.

   e. "Damn the pollution—we want the jobs." A labour leader in Brazil advocating permission to build new pulp mills in his country.

2. What is the difference between scarcity and poverty? If everyone in the world had enough to eat, could we say that food was no longer scarce?

3. Consider the right to free speech in political campaigns. Suppose that the Flat Earth Society, the Communists, the Conservatives,

the Liberals and the NDP all demand equal time on television in an election campaign. What economic questions are involved? Can there be freedom of speech without free access to the scarce resources needed to make one's speech heard?

4. Evidence accumulates that the use of chemical fertilizers, which increases agricultural production greatly, damages water quality. Show the choice between more food and cleaner water involved in using such fertilizers. Use a production possibility curve with agricultural output on the vertical axis and water quality on the horizontal axis. In what ways does this production possibility curve reflect scarcity, choice, and opportunity cost? How would an improved fertilizer that increased agricultural output without further worsening water quality affect the curve? Suppose that a pollution-free fertilizer were developed; would this mean that there would no longer be any opportunity cost in using it?

5. Identify the coordinating principle and the incentive system suggested by each of the following:
   a. Canada has very high taxes on gasoline, tobacco, and alcohol compared to the United States.
   b. Many U.S. policy makers advocate raising taxes on gas to encourage higher-mileage cars.
   c. Production targets are assigned to a Chinese factory manager by the state planning agency.
   d. British Columbia raises the minimum wages that can legally be paid to anyone in the province.
   e. Many provincial governments direct their agencies to use local suppliers of goods rather than buying from other provinces.
   f. Legislation prohibits the sale and use of cocaine.
   g. The province of Ontario controls the maximum rents at which apartments can be rented and also provides some subsidization of the building of rental accommodations.

6. "The introduction of these new machines must be stopped at all costs; they will destroy our jobs"—a local labour leader. Who gains and who loses if the introduction of new machines is prevented by a strong union? Does the globalisation of the world's economy affect your answer? What would have happened if such sentiments had generally prevailed in the early part of this century?

7. Discuss the following statement by a senior economist: "One of the mysteries of semantics is why the government-managed economies ever came to be called *planned,* and the market economies *unplanned.* It is the former that are in chronic chaos, in which buyers stand in line hoping to buy some toilet paper or soap. It is the latter that are in reasonable equilibrium—where if you want a cake of soap or a steak or a shirt or a car, you can go to the store and find that the item is magically there for you to buy. It is the liberal economies that reflect a highly sophisticated planning system, and the government-managed economies that are primitive and unplanned."

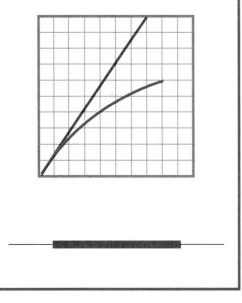

2

Economics as a Social Science

Economics is generally regarded as a social science. What does it mean to be scientific? Can economics hope to be in any way scientific in its study of human behaviour?

The Distinction Between Positive and Normative

The success of modern science rests partly on the ability of scientists to separate their views on what *does* happen from their views on what they *would like* to happen.

Positive statements concern what is, was, or will be. Positive statements, assertions, or theories may be simple or complex, but they are basically about matters of fact. Positive statements assert things about the world. If it is possible for a positive statement to be proved wrong by empirical evidence, we call it a *testable statement*.

Many positive statements are testable, and disagreements over such statements are appropriately handled by an appeal to the facts.

Normative statements concern what one believes ought to be. They state or are based on judgements about what is good and what is bad (called *value judgements*). They are thus bound up with philosophical, cultural, and religious systems.

Normative statements are not testable. Disagreements over such normative statements as "It is wrong to steal" or "It is immoral to have sexual relations out of wedlock" cannot be settled by an appeal to empirical observations.

Different techniques are needed for studying normative and positive questions.

It is therefore useful to separate normative and positive inquiries. We do this not because we think one is less important than the other but merely because they must be handled in different ways.

Some related issues concerning disagreements among economists are discussed in Box 2-1.

The Distinction Illustrated

The statement "It is impossible to break up atoms" is a positive statement that can quite definitely be (and of course has been) refuted by empirical observations. In contrast, the statement "Scientists ought not to break up atoms" is a normative statement that involves ethical judgements. The questions "What government policies will reduce unemployment?" and "What policies will prevent inflation?" are positive ones, whereas the question "Should we be more

Box 2-1

Why Economists Disagree

If you listen to a discussion among economists on "The National," "Sunday Morning," or "As It Happens," or if you read about their debates in the daily press or weekly magazines, you will find that economists frequently disagree with each other. Why do economists disagree, and what should we make of this fact?

In a *Newsweek* column, Charles Wolf, Jr. suggested four reasons: (1) Different economists use different benchmarks (e.g., inflation is down compared with last year but up compared with the 1950s). (2) Economists fail to make it clear to their listeners whether they are talking about short-term or long-term consequences (e.g., tax cuts will stimulate consumption in the short run and investment in the long run). (3) Economists often fail to acknowledge the full extent of their ignorance. (4) Different economists have different values, and these normative views play a large part in most public discussions of policy.

There is surely some truth in each of these assessments, but there is also a fifth reason: the public's *demand for disagreement*. For example, suppose that most economists were in fact agreed on some proposition such as the following: Unions are not a major cause of inflation. This view would be unpalatable to some individuals. Those who are hostile to unions, for instance, would like to blame inflation on them and would be looking for an intellectual champion. Fame and fortune would await the economist who espoused their cause, and a champion would soon be found.

Notice also that any disagreement that does exist will be exaggerated, possibly unintentionally, by the media. When the media cover an issue, they naturally wish to give both sides of it. Normally, the public will hear one or two economists on each side of a debate, regardless of whether the profession is divided right down the middle or is nearly unanimous in its support of one side. Thus the public will not know that in one case a reporter could have chosen from dozens of economists to present each side, whereas in another case the reporter had to spend three days finding someone willing to take a particular side because nearly all the economists contacted thought it was wrong. In their desire to show both sides of all cases, however, the media present the public with the appearance of a profession equally split over all matters.

Thus, anyone seeking to discredit some particular economist's advice by showing that there is disagreement among economists will have no trouble finding evidence of some disagreement. But those who wish to know if there is a majority view or even a strong consensus will find one on a surprisingly large number of issues. For example, a survey published in the *American Economic Review* showed strong agreement among economists on many propositions such as "Rent control leads to a housing shortage" (85 percent yes).

These results illustrate that economists do agree on many issues—where the balance of evidence seems to strongly support certain predictions that follow from economic theories.

concerned about unemployment than about inflation?" is a normative one.

The Importance of the Distinction

As an example of the importance of this distinction, consider the question "Has the payment of gener-

ous unemployment benefits increased the amount of unemployment?" This positive question can be turned into a testable hypothesis, such as "The higher the benefits paid to the unemployed, the higher will be the total amount of unemployment." If we are not careful, however, attitudes and value judgements may get in the way of the study of this hypothesis. Some people are opposed to all welfare measures and believe in an individualistic self-help ethic. They may hope that the hypothesis is correct because its truth could then be used as an argument against welfare measures in general. Others feel that welfare measures are desirable, reducing misery and contributing to human dignity. They may hope that the hypothesis is wrong because they do not want any welfare measures to come under attack. In spite of different value judgements and social attitudes, however, evidence is accumulating on this particular hypothesis. As a result, we have more knowledge than we had 20 years ago of why and by how much unemployment benefits increase unemployment. This evidence could never have been accumulated or accepted if investigators had not been able to distinguish their feelings about how they wanted the answer to turn out from their assessment of evidence on how people actually behaved.[1]

The distinction between positive and normative statements helps us to keep our views on how we would like the world to work separate from our views on how the world actually does work. We may be interested in both. It can only obscure the truth, however, if we let our views on what we would like to be bias our investigations of what actually is. For this reason, the separation of positive from normative statements is one of the foundation stones of science. It is also for this reason that scientific inquiry, as it is normally understood, is usually confined to positive questions. Some important limitations on the distinction between positive and normative are discussed in Box 2-2.

Positive and Normative Statements in Economics

We have seen that normative questions cannot be settled by a mere appeal to facts. In democracies, normative questions relating to government policies are often settled by voting. So on the one hand, we look to observations to shed light on the issue of the extent to which unemployment insurance deters people from working. On the other hand, we use the political process to decide whether or not, when all the pros and cons are considered, we should have such insurance.

Economists need not confine their discussions to positive, testable statements. Economists can usefully hold and discuss value judgements. Indeed, the pursuit of what appears to be a normative statement, such as "unemployment insurance ought to be abolished," will often turn up positive hypotheses that underlie the normative judgement. In this case, there are probably relatively few people who believe that government provision of unemployment insurance is in itself good or bad. Their advocacy or opposition will be based on beliefs that can be stated as positive rather than normative hypotheses; for example, "Unemployment insurance causes people to remain unemployed when they would otherwise take a job" or "Unemployment insurance increases the chance that workers will locate the jobs to which they are best suited by supporting them while they search for the right job."

The Scientific Approach

An important aspect of the scientific approach consists of relating questions to evidence. When presented with a controversial issue, investigators, whether in the natural or the social sciences, will look for relevant evidence.

In some fields, scientists are able to generate observations that provide evidence for use in testing their hypotheses. Experimental sciences such as chemistry and some branches of psychology have an advantage because it is possible for them to produce relevant evidence through controlled laboratory experiments.

Other sciences, such as astronomy, cannot do this. They must wait for natural events to produce observations that can be used as evidence in testing their theories. The evidence that then arises does not come from laboratory conditions under which everything is held constant except the forces being studied. Instead, it arises from situations in which many things are changing at the same time, and great care is therefore needed in drawing conclusions from what is observed.

---

[1]Of course, economists, like all scientists, let what they want to find influence what they do find. For a study of this problem in a different context, see Stephen Jay Gould, *The Mismeasure of Man* (New York: W. W. Norton, 1981). The more likely it is that value judgements will affect our assessments of positive issues, the more important it is that the test of consistency with facts be accepted as an important criterion for the acceptance of theories.

Box 2-2

Limits on the Positive-Normative Distinction

Although the distinction between positive and normative statements is useful, it has a number of limitations.

The Distinction Is Not Unerringly Applied

The fact that the positive-normative distinction aids the advancement of knowledge does not necessarily mean that all scientists automatically and unerringly apply it. Scientists are human beings. Many have strongly held values, and they may let their value judgements get in the way of their assessment of evidence. Nonetheless, the desire to separate what is from what we would like to be is a guiding light, an ideal, of all science. The ability to do so, albeit imperfectly, is attested to by the acceptance, first by scientists and then by the general public, of many ideas that were initially extremely unpalatable—ideas such as the close relationship between humans and other apes.

Not All Positive Statements Are Testable

A positive statement asserts something about some aspect of the universe in which we live. It may be empirically true or false in the sense that what it asserts may or may not be true of the world. If it is true, it adds to our knowledge of what can and cannot happen. Many positive statements are refutable: If they are wrong, this can be ascertained (within a margin for error of observation) by checking them against data. For example, the positive statement that the earth is less than 5,000 years old was once accepted by most people in the West but was tested and refuted by a mass of evidence accumulated in the eighteenth and nineteenth centuries.

The statement "Extraterrestrials exist and frequently visit the earth in visible form" is also a positive statement. It asserts something about the universe, but we could never refute this statement with evidence because, no matter how hard we searched, believers could argue that we did not look in the right places or in the right way, that extraterrestrials do not reveal themselves to nonbelievers, or a host of other reasons. Thus some positive statements are irrefutable.

The Classification Is Not Exhaustive

The classifications *positive* and *normative* do not cover all statements that can be made. For example, there is an important class, called *analytic statements*, whose validity depends only on the rules of logic. Thus the sentence "If all humans are immortal and if you are a human, then you are immortal" is a valid analytic statement. It tells us that *if* two things are true, *then* a third thing must also be true. The validity of this statement is not dependent on whether or not its individual parts are in fact true. Indeed, the sentence "All humans are immortal" is a positive statement that has been decisively refuted. Yet no amount of empirical evidence on the mortality of humans can upset the truth of the *if-then* sentence quoted. Analytic statements—which proceed by logical analysis—play an important role in scientific work and form the basis of much of our ability to theorize.

Not long ago, economics would have been put wholly in the group of nonexperimental sciences. It is still true that the majority of evidence economists use is generated by observing what happens in the economy from day to day. However, a significant and growing amount of evidence is now being generated under controlled laboratory conditions. In the introductory treatment of this book we concentrate on the nonlaboratory aspects of economic evidence, both because this is still the predominant aspect and because the significance of laboratory-generated evidence remains controversial.

Later in this chapter we will consider some of the problems that arise when analysing evidence generated by observing day-to-day behaviour that does not take place under controlled laboratory conditions. For the moment, however, we shall consider some general problems that are more or less common to all sciences and are particularly important in the social sciences.

Is Human Behaviour Predictable?

Social scientists seek to understand and to predict human behaviour. A scientific prediction is based on discovering stable response patterns, but does human behaviour show sufficiently stable responses to factors influencing it to be predictable within some stated margin of error? The question might concern either the behaviour of groups or that of isolated individuals, and it can be settled only by an appeal to evidence and not by armchair speculation.

Group Behaviour Versus Individual Behaviour

There are many situations in which group behaviour can be predicted accurately without certain knowledge of individual behaviour. The warmer the weather, for example, the more people visit the beach and the higher the sales of ice cream. It may be hard to say if or when one individual will buy an ice cream cone, but a stable response pattern can be seen among a large group of individuals. Although social scientists cannot predict which particular individuals will be involved in auto accidents during the next holiday weekend, they can come very close to knowing the total number who will. The more objectively measurable data they have (e.g., the state of the weather on the days in question and the trend in gasoline prices), the more closely they will be able to predict total accidents.

Economists can also predict with fair accuracy what employees as a group will do when their take-home pay rises. Although some individuals may do surprising and unpredictable things, the overall response of workers in spending more when their take-home pay rises is predictable within quite a narrow margin of error. This relatively stable response is the basis of economists' ability to predict successfully the outcome of major changes in income-tax rates that permanently alter people's take-home pay.

Nothing we have said implies that people never change their minds or that future events can be foretold simply by projecting past trends. For example, we cannot safely predict that people will increase their spending next year just because they inased their spending this year. The stability we are discussing relates to a cause-effect response. For example, the next time take-home pay rises significantly (cause), spending by employees will rise (effect).

The "Law" of Large Numbers

Successfully predicting the behaviour of large groups of people is made possible by the statistical "law" of large numbers. Broadly speaking, this law asserts that random movements of many individual items tend to offset one another.

What is implied by this law? Ask any one person to measure the length of a room, and it will be almost impossible to predict in advance what sort of error of measurement will be made. Dozens of things will affect the accuracy of the measurement; furthermore, the person may make one error today and a quite different one tomorrow. But ask 1,000 people to measure the length of the same room, and we can predict within a small margin just how this *group* will make its errors. We can assert with confidence that more people will make small errors than will make large errors; that the larger the error, the fewer will be the number making it; that roughly the same number of people will overstate as will understate the distance; and that the larger the number of people making the measurement, the smaller the average of their errors will tend to be.

If a common cause acts on each member of the group, the average behaviour of the group can be predicted even though any one member may act in a surprising fashion. For example, let each of the 1,000 individuals be given a tape measure that understates actual distances. On the average, the group will now understate the length of the room. It is, of course, quite possible that one member who had in the past been reading her tape measure correctly will now read more than it measures as a result of developing an eye defect. However, something else may have happened to another individual that causes him to underread his tape measure where before he was reading it correctly. Individuals may alter their behaviour for many different reasons, but the group's behaviour, when the inaccurate tape is substituted for the accurate one, is predictable precisely because the odd things that one individual does tend to cancel out the odd things that some other individual does.

Irregularities in individual behaviour tend to cancel each other out, and the regularities tend to show up in repeated observations.

The Importance of Theories

When some regularity between two or more things is observed, curious people ask why. A *theory* provides an explanation, and by doing so, it enables us to predict as-yet unobserved events.

For example, the simple theory of market behaviour that we will study in Part 2 shows how the output of a product affects the price at which it sells and hence affects the incomes of those who produce it. As we will see in Chapter 6, this theory allows us to predict (among other things) that a partial failure of the potato crop will *increase* the income of the average potato farmer!

Theories are used in explaining existing observations. A successful theory enables us to predict things we have not yet seen.

Any explanation whatsoever of how given observations are linked together is a theoretical construction. Theories are used to impose order on our observations, to explain how what we see is linked together. Without theories, there would be only a shapeless mass of observations.

The choice is not between theory and observation but between better or worse theories to explain observations.

The Structure of Theories

A theory consists of (1) a set of definitions that clearly define the *variables* to be used, (2) a set of *assumptions* about the behaviour of the variables, and (3) *predictions* (often called *hypotheses*) that are deduced from the assumptions of the theory and can be tested against actual empirical observations. We shall consider these constituents one by one.

Variables

A **variable** is a magnitude that can take on different possible values. Variables are the basic elements of theories, and each one needs to be carefully defined.

Price is an example of an important economic variable. The price of a commodity is the amount of money that must be given up to purchase one unit of that commodity. To define a price, we must first define the commodity to which it is attached. Such a commodity might be one dozen grade-A large eggs. The price of such eggs sold in, say, supermarkets in Moose Jaw, Saskatchewan, defines a variable. The particular values taken on by that variable might be $1.89 on July 1, 1990, $1.95 on July 8, 1991, and $1.92 on July 15, 1992. There are many distinctions between kinds of variables; we shall discuss only one at this time.

Endogenous and exogenous variables. An **endogenous variable** is a variable that is explained within a theory. An **exogenous variable** influences endogenous variables but is itself determined by factors outside the theory.

Consider the theory that the price of apples in Vancouver, B.C., on a particular day depends on several things, one of which is the weather in the Okangan Valley during the previous apple-growing season. We can safely assume that the state of the weather is not determined by economic conditions. The price of apples in this case is an endogenous variable—something determined within the framework of the theory. The state of the weather in the Okangan Valley is an exogenous variable; changes in it influence prices because the changes affect the output of apples, but the state of the weather is not influenced by apple prices.

Other words are sometimes used for the same distinction. One frequently used pair is *induced* for endogenous and *autonomous* for exogenous; another is *dependent* for endogenous and *independent* for exogenous.

Assumptions

A key element of any theory is a set of assumptions about the behaviour of the variables in which we are interested. Usually, these state how the behaviour of two or more variables relate to each other.

In some cases, these linkages are provided by physical laws. One such case is the relation between the resources each firm uses, which economists call inputs, and that firm's output. In the case of the egg farmer, the output of eggs is related to the inputs of chicken feed, farm labour, and all the other things the farmer uses.

In other cases, these linkages are provided by human behaviour. For example, economists make two basic assumptions about consumers. The first concerns how each consumer's satisfaction, or utility, is related to the quantities of all the goods and services that he or she consumes. The second is that in making their choices on how much to consume, people seek to maximize the satisfaction they gain from that consumption.

Although assumptions are an essential part of all theories, students are often concerned about those that seem unrealistic. An example will illustrate some of the issues involved. Much of the theory that we are going to study in this book uses the assumption that the sole motive of the owners of firms is to make as much money as they possibly can, or, as economists put it, firms are assumed to *maximize their profits.* The assumption of profit maximization allows economists to make predictions about the behaviour of firms. Economists study the effects that the choices open to firms would have on profits. They then predict that the alternative that produces the most profits will be the one selected.

Profit maximization may seem like a rather crude assumption. Surely, for example, the managers of firms sometimes choose to protect the environment rather than pursue certain highly polluting, but profitable, opportunities. Does this not discredit the assumption of profit maximization by showing it to be unrealistic?

The answer is no; to make successful predictions, the theory does not require that managers be solely and unwaveringly motivated by the desire to maximize profits. All that is required is that profits be a sufficiently important consideration that a theory based on the assumption of profit maximization will produce explanations and predictions that are substantially correct.

This illustration shows that it is not always appropriate to criticise a theory because its assumptions seem unrealistic. All theory is an abstraction from reality. If it were not, it would merely duplicate the world in all its complexity and would add nothing to our understanding of it. A good theory abstracts in a useful way; a poor theory does not. If a theory has ignored some genuinely important factors, its predictions will be contradicted by the evidence—at least where an ignored factor exerts an important influence on the outcome.

Predictions

A theory's predictions are the propositions that can be deduced from that theory; they are often called *hypotheses.* An example of a prediction would be a deduction that *if* firms maximize their profits and *if* certain other assumptions of the theory hold true, *then* an increase in the going wage for labour will lower the amount of labour employed.

When the predictions of a theory have been confirmed in a large number of specific cases, they are sometimes referred to as laws.

A scientific prediction is a conditional statement that takes the following form: *If* this occurs, *then* such and such will follow.

For example, *if* a provincial government forces down the rents on residential accommodation (through a policy called *rent control*), *then* a housing shortage will develop.

It is important to realize that this prediction is different from the statement "I prophesy that in two years' time there will be a housing shortage in my city because I believe its provincial government will decide to impose rent controls." The government's decision to introduce rent controls in two years' time will be the outcome of many influences, both economic and political. If the economist's prophecy about a housing shortage turns out to be wrong because in two years' time the government does not impose rent controls, then all that has been learned is that the economist is not a good guesser about the behaviour of the government. However, *if* the government does impose rent controls (in two years' time or at any other time), and *then* a housing shortage does not develop, a conditional (if-then) prediction based on economic theory will have been contradicted.

Expressing Relations Among Variables

Economists deal with many relations among variables. A **function**, also known as a *functional relation*, is a formal expression of a relationship between two or more variables.[2]

The prediction that the quantity of eggs people want to buy is negatively related to the price of eggs is an example of a functional relation in economics. In its most general form, it merely says that as the price of eggs rises, the quantity of desired purchases falls.

In many relations of this kind, economists can be even more specific about the nature of the functional relation. On the basis of detailed factual studies, economists often have a pretty good idea of by how much the quantity demanded will change as a result of specified changes in price; that is, they can predict magnitude as well as direction.

Testing Theories

A theory is tested by confronting its predictions with evidence. It is necessary to discover if certain events are followed by the outcomes predicted by the theory. For example, is the imposition of rent controls followed by a housing shortage? Theories are sometimes tested in conscious attempts to do just that. They are also tested every time an economist uses one to predict the outcome of some spe-

cific event. If economists continued to be mistaken every time they used some theory to make predictions, the theory would soon be called into question.

Theories tend to be abandoned when they are no longer useful, and theories cease to be useful when they cannot predict the outcomes of actions better than the next best alternative. When a theory consistently fails to predict better than the available alternatives, it is either modified or replaced. Figure 2-1 summarizes the discussion of theories and their testing.

Refutation or Confirmation

An important part of a scientific approach to any issue consists of setting up a theory that will explain it and then seeing if that theory can be refuted by evidence.

The alternative to this approach is to set up a theory and then look for confirming evidence. Such an approach is hazardous, because the world is sufficiently complex that some confirming evidence can be found for any theory, no matter how unlikely the theory may be. For example, flying saucers, the Loch Ness monster, fortune telling, and astrology all have their devotees who can quote confirming evidence in spite of the failure of attempts to discover systematic, objective evidence for these things.

An example of the unfruitful approach of seeking confirmation is frequently seen when a leader—be it a Canadian Prime Minister or a foreign leader—is surrounded by followers who provide only evidence that confirms the leader's existing views. This approach is usually a road to disaster, because the leader becomes more and more out of touch with reality.

A wise leader adopts a scientific approach instinctively, constantly checking the realism of accepted views by encouraging subordinates to criticise him or her. This tests how far the leader's existing views correspond to all available evidence and encourages amendment in the light of evidence that conflicts with the current views.

Statistical Analysis

Statistical analysis is used to test the hypothesis that two or more things are related and to estimate the numerical values of the function that describes the relation.

---

[2]When two variables are related in such a way that an increase in one is associated with an increase in the other, they are said to be *positively related*. When two variables are related in such a way that an increase in one is associated with a decrease in the other, they are said to be *negatively related*.

FIGURE 2-1
The Interaction of Deduction and Measurement in Theorizing

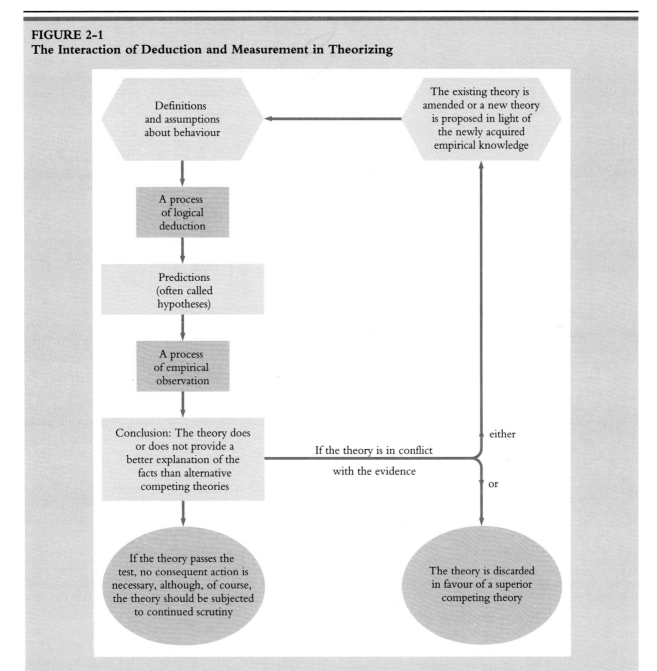

Theory and observation are in continuous interaction. Starting (at the top left) with the assumptions of a theory and the definitions of relevant terms, the theorist deduces by logical analysis everything that is implied by the assumptions. These implications are the predictions of the theory. The theory is then tested by confronting its predictions with evidence. If the theory is in conflict with facts, it will usually be amended to make it consistent with those facts (thereby making it a better theory); in extreme cases it will be discarded to be replaced by a superior alternative. The process then begins again: The new or amended theory is subjected first to logical analysis and then to empirical testing.

In practise, the same data can be used simultaneously to test whether a relationship exists and, if it does exist, to provide a measure of it.

Because economics is primarily a nonlaboratory science, it must utilize the millions of uncontrolled experiments that are going on every day. Households are deciding how to alter their purchases in the face of changing prices and incomes; firms are deciding what to produce and how to produce it; and governments are involved in the economy through their various taxes, subsidies, and controls. Because all these activities can be observed and recorded, a mass of data is continually being produced by the economy.

The variables that interest economists, such as the amount of unemployment, the price of wheat, and the output of automobiles, are generally influenced by many forces that vary simultaneously. If economists are to test their theories about relations among variables in the economy, they must use statistical techniques designed for situations in which other things cannot be held constant.

Fortunately, such techniques exist—although their application is often neither simple nor straightforward. Some of these techniques are studied in elementary statistics courses. More advanced courses in econometrics deal with the array of techniques designed to test economic hypotheses and to measure economic relations in the complex circumstances in which economic evidence is often generated.

The Decision to Reject or Accept

There is no absolute certainty in any knowledge. No doubt some of the things we now think are true will eventually turn out to be false, and some of the things we currently think are false will eventually turn out to be true. Yet even though we can never be certain, we can assess the balance of available evidence. Some hypotheses are so unlikely to be true, given current evidence, that for all practical purposes we may regard them as false. Other hypotheses are so unlikely to be false, given current evidence, that for all practical purposes we may regard them as true. This kind of practical decision must always be regarded as tentative. Every once in a while, we will find that we have to change our mind. Something that looked right will begin to look doubtful, or something that looked wrong will begin to look possible.

Making the decisions just discussed requires accepting some theories (to act as if they were true) and rejecting others (to act as if they were false). Just as a jury can make two kinds of errors (finding an innocent person guilty or letting a guilty person go free), so statistical decision makers can make two kinds of errors. They can reject hypotheses that are true, and they can accept hypotheses that are false. Fortunately, like a jury, they can also make correct decisions—and indeed, they expect to do so most of the time.

Although the possibility of error cannot be eliminated when testing theories against observations, it can be controlled.

The method of control is to decide in advance how large a risk to take in accepting a hypothesis that is in fact false.[3] Conventionally in statistics, this risk is often set at 5 percent or 1 percent. When the 5 percent cutoff point is used, we will accept the hypothesis if the results that appear to establish it could have happened by chance no more than 1 time in 20. Using the 1 percent decision rule gives the hypothesis a more difficult test. A hypothesis is accepted only if the results that appear to establish it could have happened by chance no more than 1 time in 100.

Consider the hypothesis that a certain coin is "loaded," favouring heads over tails. The test consists of flipping the coin 100 times. Say that on a single test, the coin comes up heads 53 times. This result is not strong evidence in favour of the hypothesis, because such an unbalanced result could happen by chance in more than 22 percent of such tests. Thus, the hypothesis of a head-biased coin would not be accepted on the basis of this evidence using either a 1 percent or a 5 percent cutoff. Had the test produced 65 heads and 35 tails, a result that would occur by chance in less than 1 percent of such tests, we would (given either a 1 percent or a 5

---

[3]Return to the jury analogy: Our notion of a person's being innocent unless the jury is persuaded of guilt "beyond a reasonable doubt" rests on our wishing to take only a small risk of accepting the hypothesis of guilt if the person tried is in fact innocent.

percent cutoff) accept the hypothesis of the coin being loaded.[4]

When action must be taken, some rule of thumb is necessary, but it is important to understand first, that no one can ever be certain about being right in rejecting or accepting any hypothesis, and second, that there is nothing magical about arbitrary cutoff points. Some cutoff point must be used whenever decisions have to be made.

Can Economics Be Made Value Free?

We have made two key statements about the positive-normative distinction. First, the ability to distinguish positive from normative questions is a key part of the foundation of science. Second, economists, in common with all scientists, seek to answer positive questions.

Some people who have accepted these points have gone on to argue that there can be a completely value-free inquiry into any branch of science, including economics. After long debate over this issue, the conclusion that most people seem to accept is that a *completely* value-free inquiry is impossible.

Our values become involved at all stages of any enquiry. For example, we must allocate our scarce time. This means that we choose to study some problems rather than other problems. This choice is often influenced by our value judgements about the relative importance of various problems. Also, evidence is never conclusive and so is always open to

more than one interpretation. It is difficult to assess such imperfect evidence without giving some play to one's values. Further, when reporting the results of our studies, we must use words that we know will arouse various emotions in those who read them. So the words we choose and the emphasis we give to the available evidence (and to the uncertainties surrounding it) will influence the impact that the study has on others.

For these and many other reasons, most people who have discussed this issue believe that there can be no totally value-free study of economics.

This does not mean, however, that *everything* is a matter of subjective value judgements. The very real advancements of knowledge in all sciences, natural and social, show that science is not just a matter of opinion or of deciding between competing value judgements.

First, acknowledging the distinction between positive and normative issues helps us to reduce the unconscious influence of our ethical views on our study of positive questions. Second, accepting that the choice among competing theories depends ultimately on their relative abilities to explain the facts does lead to an advance of knowledge over time. Indeed, all genuine sciences have been successful in spite of the fact that individual scientists have not always been totally objective. Individual scientists have sometimes passionately resisted the apparent implications of evidence. The rules of the scientific game—that facts cannot be ignored and must somehow be fitted into the accepted theoretical structure—tend to produce scientific advance in spite of what might be thought of as unscientific, emotional attitudes on the part of many individual scientists.

But if those engaged in scientific debate, in economics or any other science, ever succeed in changing the rules of the game to allow inconvenient facts to be ignored or defined out of existence, a major blow would be dealt to scientific inquiry in economics.

---

[4]The actual statistical testing process is more complex than this example suggests but must be left to a course in statistics.

SUMMARY

1. It is possible, and useful, to distinguish between positive and normative statements. Positive statements concern what is, was, or will be, whereas normative statements concern what ought to be. Disagreements over positive, testable statements are appropriately settled by an appeal to the facts. Disagreements over normative statements cannot be settled in this way.

2. Successful scientific inquiry requires separating positive questions about the way the world works from normative questions about how one would like the world to work, formulating positive questions precisely enough so that they can be settled by an appeal to evidence, and then finding means of gathering the necessary evidence.

3. Social scientists have observed many stable human behaviour patterns. These form the basis for successful predictions of how people will behave under certain conditions.

4. The fact that people sometimes act strangely, even capriciously, does not destroy the possibility of scientific study of group behaviour. The odd and inexplicable things that one person does will tend to cancel out the odd and inexplicable things that another person does.

5. Theories are designed to give meaning and coherence to observed sequences of events. A theory consists of a set of definitions of the variables to be employed and a set of assumptions about how things behave. Any theory has certain logical implications that must be true if the theory is true. These are the theory's predictions.

6. A theory is conditional in the sense that it provides predictions of the type "if one event occurs, then another event will also occur." An important method of testing theories is to confront their predictions with evidence.

7. The progress of any science lies in finding better explanations of events than are now available. Thus, in any developing science, one must expect to discard some present theories and replace them with demonstrably superior alternatives.

8. Theories are tested by checking their predictions against evidence. In some sciences, these tests can be conducted under laboratory conditions in which only one thing changes at a time. In other sciences, testing must be done using the data produced by the world of ordinary events.

9. Although distinguishing positive from normative questions and seeking to answer positive questions are important aspects of science, it does not follow that economic inquiry can be totally value free. Although values intrude at almost all stages of scientific inquiry, the rule that theories should be judged against evidence wherever possible tends to produce advances of positive knowledge over time.

TOPICS FOR REVIEW

Positive and normative statements

Testable statements

The law of large numbers and the predictability of human behaviour

Variables, assumptions, and predictions in theorizing

Functional relations

Conditional prediction versus prophecy

DISCUSSION QUESTIONS

1. What are some of the positive and normative issues that lie behind the disagreements in the following cases?
    a. Economists disagree on whether the Bank of Canada should stimulate the economy this year.
    b. European and U.S. negotiators disagree over the desirability of reducing European farm subsidies.
    c. Economists argue about the merits of a voucher system that allows parents to choose the schools their children will attend.

2. What groups are likely to have a self-interest in a proposal to severely restrict the ability of Japanese-made cars to compete against North American-made cars in the North American market? What are some of the positive issues that might be relevant to deciding on this proposal?

3. A baby doesn't know of the theory of gravity, yet in walking and eating the child soon begins to use the principles of gravity. Distinguish between behaviour and the explanation of behaviour. Do buyers and sellers have to understand economic theory to behave in a pattern consistent with economic theory?

4. "If human behaviour were completely capricious and unpredictable, life insurance could not be a profitable business." Explain. Can you think of any businesses that do not depend on predictable human behaviour?

5. Write five statements about unemployment. Classify each statement as positive or normative. If your list contains only one type of statement, try to add a sixth statement of the other type.

6. Each of the following unrealistic assumptions is sometimes made. See if you can visualize situations in which each of them might be useful.
    a. The earth is flat.
    b. There are no differences between men and women.
    c. People are wholly selfish.

7. What may at first appear to be untestable statements can often be reworded so that they can be tested by an appeal to evidence. How might you do that with respect to each of the following assertions?
    a. Canadian restrictions on the importation of cheap foreign footwear help the poor by protecting jobs for the unskilled in the uncompetitive Canadian footwear industry.
    b. Unemployment insurance is eroding the work ethic and encouraging people to become wards of the state rather than productive workers.
    c. Robotics ought to be outlawed, because it will destroy the future of working people.
    d. Laws requiring equal pay for work of equal value will disadvantage the economic position of women.

8. "The simplest way to see that capital punishment is a strong deterrent to murder is to ask yourself whether you might be more inclined to commit murder if you knew in advance that you ran no risk of ending in the electric chair, in the gas chamber, or on the gallows." Comment on the methodology of social investigation implied by this statement. Suggest an alternative approach.

APPENDIX TO CHAPTER

2

Graphing Relations Among Variables

This appendix is for readers who do not feel fully confident about the use of graphs. Graphs play an important role in economics by representing geometrically both observed data and the relations among variables that are the subject of economic theory.

Because the surface of a piece of paper is two-dimensional, a graph may readily be used to represent pictorially any relation between two variables. Flip through this book and you will see dozens of examples. Figure 2A-1 shows generally how a coordinate graph can be used to represent any two measurable variables.[1]

Representing Theories on Graphs

Figure 2A-2 shows a simple two-variable graph, which will be analysed in detail in Chapter 4. For now it is sufficient to notice that the graph permits us to show the relationship between two variables, the *price* of carrots on the vertical axis and the *quantity* of carrots per month on the horizontal axis.[2] The negatively sloped curve, labeled D for a *demand curve*, shows the relationship between the price of carrots and the quantity of carrots that buyers wish to purchase.

Figure 2A-3 is very much like Figure 2A-2, with one difference. It generalizes from the specific example of carrots to an unspecified commodity and focuses on the slope of the demand curve rather than on specific numerical values. Note that the quantity labeled q_0 is associated with the price p_0, and the quantity q_1 is associated with the price p_1.

Straight Lines and Their Slopes

Figure 2A-4 illustrates a variety of straight lines. They differ according to their slopes. **Slope** is defined as the ratio of the vertical change to the corresponding horizontal change as one moves along a curve.

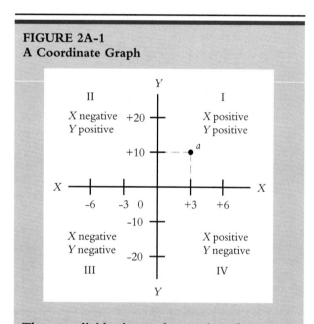

FIGURE 2A-1
A Coordinate Graph

The axes divide the total space into four quadrants according to the signs of the variables. In the upper right-hand quadrant, both X and Y are greater than zero; this is usually called the *positive quadrant*. Point a has *coordinates* $X = 3$ and $Y = 10$ in the coordinate graph. These coordinates *define* point a.

---

[1]Economics is often concerned only with the positive values of variables, and the graph is confined to the upper right-hand (or "positive") quadrant. Whenever a variable has a negative value, one or more of the other quadrants must be included.

[2]The choice of which variable to put on which axis is discussed in the footnote to Figure 5-6 and in math note 4 (regarding math notes, see footnote 5 on p. 14).

FIGURE 2A-2

The Relationship Between the Price of Carrots and the Quantity of Carrots That Purchasers Wish to Buy: A Numerical Illustration

A two-dimensional graph can show how two variables are related. The two variables, the price of carrots and the quantity that people wish to purchase, are shown by the downward-sloping curve labeled *D*. Particular points on the curve are labeled *U* through *Z*. For example, point *Z* shows that at a price of $120, the demand to purchase carrots is 60,000 tons per month.

FIGURE 2A-3

The Relationship Between the Price of a Commodity and the Quantity of the Commodity That Purchasers Wish to Buy

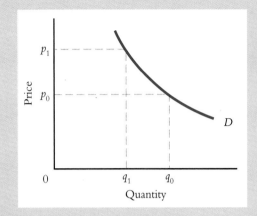

Graphs can illustrate general relationships between variables as well as between specific quantities. Here, in contrast to Figure 2A-2, price and quantity are shown as general variables. The demand curve illustrates a quantitatively unspecified *negative* relationship between price and quantity. For example, at the price p_0 the quantity that purchasers demand is q_0, whereas at the higher price of p_1 purchasers demand the lower quantity of q_1.

The symbol Δ (which is the Greek letter capital delta) is used to indicate a change in any variable. Thus ΔX means "the change in X," and ΔY means "the change in Y." The ratio $\Delta Y/\Delta X$ is the slope of a straight line. When they increase or decrease together, the ratio is positive and the line is positively sloped, as in part (i) of Figure 2A-4. When ΔY and ΔX have opposite signs, that is, when one increases while the other decreases, the ratio is negative and the line is negatively sloped, as in part (ii). When ΔY does not change, the line is horizontal, as in part (iii), and the slope is zero. When ΔX is zero, the line is vertical, as in part (iv), and the slope is often said to be infinite, although the ratio $\Delta Y/\Delta X$ is inderterminate.[2]

Slope is a quantitative measure, not merely a qualitative one. For example, in Figure 2A-5, two upward-sloping straight lines have different slopes.

Line *A* has a slope of 2 ($\Delta Y/\Delta X = 2$); line *B* has a slope of 1/2 ($\Delta Y/\Delta X = 0.5$).

Curved Lines and Their Slopes

Figure 2A-6 shows four curved lines. The line in part (i) is plainly upward sloping; the line in part (ii) is downward sloping. The other two change from one to the other, as the labels indicate. Unlike a straight line, which has the same slope at every point on the line, the slope of a curve changes. The slope of a curve must be measured at a particular point and is defined as *the slope of a straight line that just touches (is tangent to) the straight line at that point.* This is illustrated in Figure 2A-7. The slope at point *A* is measured by the slope of the tangent line *a*. The slope at point *B* is measured by the slope of the tangent line *b*.

FIGURE 2A-4
Four Straight Lines with Different Slopes

The slope of a straight line is constant but can vary from one line to another. The direction of slope of a straight line is characterized by the signs of the ratio $\Delta Y/\Delta X$. In part (i) that ratio is positive because X and Y vary in the same direction; in part (ii) the ratio is negative because X and Y vary in opposite directions; in part (iii) it is zero because Y does not change as X changes; in part (iv) it is infinite.

FIGURE 2A-5
Two Straight Lines with Different Slopes

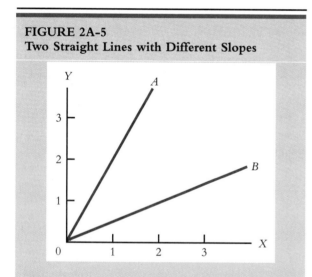

Slope is a quantitative measure. Both lines have positive slopes and thus are similar to Figure 2A-4(i). However, line A is steeper (i.e., has a greater slope) than line B. For each 1-unit increase in X, the value of Y increases by 2 units along line A but only ½ unit along line B. The ratio $\Delta Y/\Delta X$ is 2 for line A and ½ for B.

Graphing Observations

A coordinate graph such as that shown in Figure 2A-1 can be used to show the observed values of two variables as well as the theoretical relationships between them. For example, curve D in Figure 2A-2 might have arisen as a freehand line drawn to generalize actual observations of the points labeled U, V, W, X, Y, and Z.

Although that graph was not constructed from actual observations, many graphs are. To illustrate, we take the very simple hypothesis that the income taxes paid by families increase as their incomes increase.

To test the hypothesis about taxes, we have chosen a random sample of 212 families from data collected by the Survey Research Center of the University of Michigan. We have recorded each family's income and the federal income tax it pays.

One way in which the data may be used to evaluate the hypothesis is to draw what is called a **scatter diagram**, which plots paired values of two variables. Figure 2A-8 is a scatter diagram that re-

---

FIGURE 2A-6
Four Curved Lines

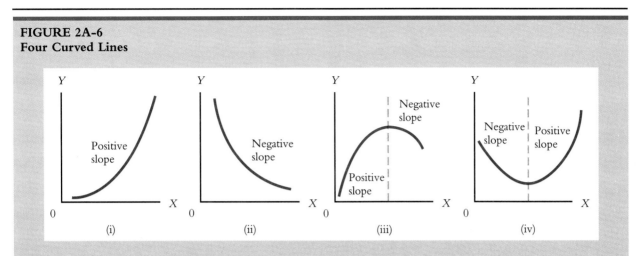

The slope of a curved line is not constant and may change direction. The slopes of the curves in parts (i) and (ii) change in size but not in direction, whereas those in parts (iii) and (iv) change in both size and direction. Unlike that of a straight line, the slope of a curved line cannot be defined by a single number because it changes as the value of X changes.

FIGURE 2A-7
Defining the Slope of a Curve

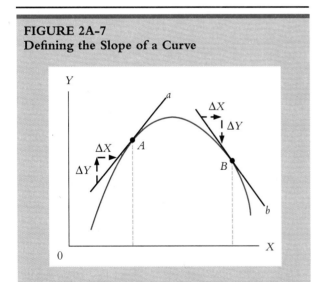

The slope of a curve at any point on the curve is defined by the slope of the straight line that is tangent to the curve at that point. The slope of the curve at point A is defined by the slope of the line a, which is tangent to the curve at point A. The slope of the curve at point B is defined by the slope of the tangent line b.

lates family income to federal income-tax payments. Income is measured on the horizontal axis and taxes paid on the vertical axis. Any point in the diagram represents a particular family's income combined with the tax payment of that family. Thus, each family for which there are observations can be represented on the diagram by a dot, the coordinates of which indicate the family's income and the amount of taxes paid in 1979.

The scatter diagram is useful because if there is a simple relationship between the two variables, it will be apparent to the eye once the data are plotted. For example, Figure 2A-8 makes it apparent that more taxes tend to be paid as income rises. It also makes it apparent that the relationship between taxes and income is approximately linear. A rising straight line fits the data reasonably well between about $10,000 and $40,000 of income. Above $40,000 and below $10,000, the line does not fit the data as well, but because more than two thirds of the families sampled have incomes in the $10,000-to-$40,000 range, we may conclude that the straight line provides a fairly good description of the basic relationship for middle-income families.

The graph also gives some idea of the strength

FIGURE 2A-8
A Scatter Diagram Relating Taxes Paid to Family Income

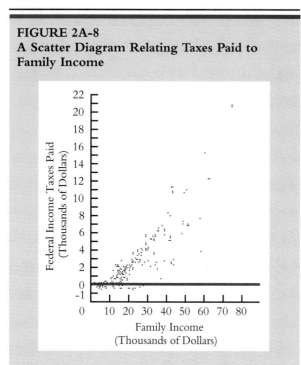

The scatter pattern shows a clear tendency for taxes paid to rise with family income. Family income is measured along the horizontal axis, and federal income taxes paid are measured along the vertical axis. Each dot represents a single family in the sample and is located on the graph according to the family's income and taxes paid. The dots fall mainly within a narrow, rising band, suggesting the existence of a systematic relationship between income and taxes paid, but they do not fall along a single line, which suggests that things other than family income affect taxes paid. The data are for 1979. (Negative amounts of tax liability arise because of such things as capital losses that may be carried forward.)

of the relationship. If income were the only determinant of taxes paid, all the dots would cluster closely around a line or a smooth curve. As it is, the points are somewhat scattered, and several households with the same income show different amounts of taxes paid.

There is some scattering of the dots because the relationship is not perfect; in other words, there is some variation in tax payments that cannot be associated with variations in family income. These variations in tax payments occur mainly for two reasons. First, factors other than income influence tax

payments, and some of these other factors will undoubtedly have varied among the families in the sample. Second, there will inevitably be some errors in measurement. For example, a family might have incorrectly reported its tax payments to the person who collected our data.

TABLE 2A-1 Personal Income and Consumption in Canada, 1965–1991 (1986 dollars)

Year	Disposable personal income per capita	Personal consumption expenditures per capita
1965	$ 6,907	$ 6,450
1966	7,420	6,654
1967	7,369	6,818
1968	7,502	6,987
1969	7,711	7,241
1970	7,854	7,316
1971	7,966	7,619
1972	8,975	8,104
1973	9,778	8,631
1974	10,317	7,008
1975	10,806	9,308
1976	11,244	9,786
1977	11,411	9,965
1978	11,801	10,172
1979	12,137	10,378
1980	12,369	10,472
1981	12,819	10,495
1982	12,757	10,216
1983	12,399	10,481
1984	12,983	10,877
1985	13,294	11,396
1986	13,363	11,758
1987	13,680	12,127
1988	14,106	12,521
1989	14,578	12,777
1990	14,476	12,704
1991	14,009	12,308
1992	13,957	12,157

Source: Statistics Canada 11-210

Real disposable income per capita and real personal consumption expenditures have both grown since 1965. The former has increased from $6,907 to nearly $14,000 over the period, while the latter grew from $6,450 to over $12,000.

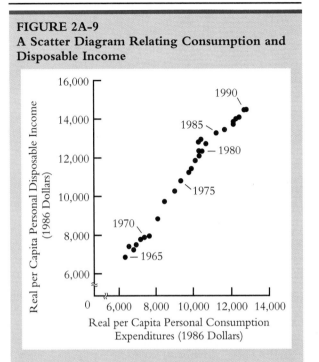

FIGURE 2A-9
A Scatter Diagram Relating Consumption and Disposable Income

This scatter diagram shows paired values of two variables. The data of Table 2A-1 are plotted here. Each dot shows the values of per capita personal consumption expenditures and per capita disposable personal income for a given year. A close, positive, relationship between the two variables is obvious. Note that in this diagram, the axes are shown with a break in them to indicate that not all the values of the variables between $6,000 and zero are given. Since no *observations* occurred in those ranges, it was unnecessary to provide space for them.

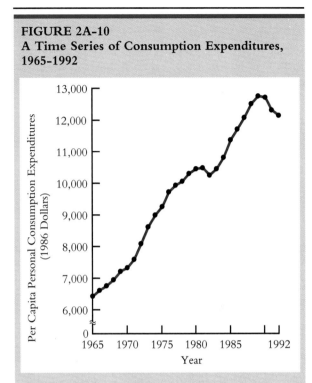

FIGURE 2A-10
A Time Series of Consumption Expenditures, 1965-1992

A time series plot values of a single variable in chronological order. This graph shows that with only minor interruptions, consumptions measured in 1987 dollars rose from 1965 to 1991. The data are given in the last column of Table 2A-1.

Time-Series Data

The data shown in Figure 2A-8 are called *cross-sectional data*. They show incomes and taxes for a single year. Scatter diagrams may also be drawn for observations taken on two variables at successive periods of time. For example, to check for a relation between income and consumption, data could be gathered for several years, as shown in Table 2A-1. These data are plotted on a scatter diagram in Figure 2A-9, and they suggest a systematic relationship.

Observations taken over successive periods of time are called **time-series data**, and plotting them on a scatter diagram involves no new techniques. When cross-sectional data are plotted, each point gives the values of two variables of a particular unit (say a family); when time-series data are plotted, each point tells the values of two variables for a particular period of time.

We could also study the changes in either one of these variables over time. Figure 2A-10 does this for consumption. Time is one variable, and consumption is the other. Such a figure is called a *time-series graph* or a **time series**. The graph makes it easy to see whether or not the variable has changed in a systematic way over time.

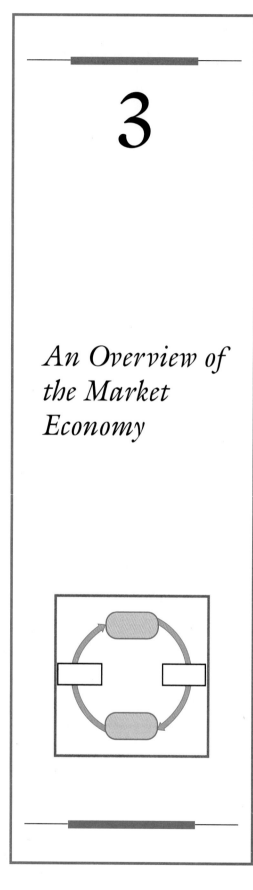

3

An Overview of the Market Economy

Until about 10,000 years ago, all human beings were hunter-gatherers, meeting for their wants and needs with foods that were freely provided in nature. The Neolithic agricultural revolution changed all that. People gradually abandoned their nomadic life of hunting and food gathering and settled down to tend crops and domesticated animals. Since that time, all societies have faced the problem of choice under conditions of scarcity.[1]

Specialization, Surplus, and Trade

Along with permanent settlement, the agricultural revolution brought surplus production. Farmers could produce substantially more than they needed for survival. The agricultural surplus allowed the creation of new occupations. Freed from having to produce their own food, new classes—such as artisans, soldiers, priests, and government officials—turned their talents to performing specialized services and producing goods other than food. They also produced more than they themselves needed and traded the excess to obtain other goods.

The allocation of different jobs to different people is called **specialization of labour.** Specialization has proved to be extraordinarily efficient compared with self-sufficiency, for at least two reasons.

First, individual talents and abilities differ, and specialization allows each person to do the job he or she can do best, while leaving everything else to be done by others. That production is greater with specialization than with self-sufficiency is one of the most fundamental principles in economics. It is called the *principle of comparative advantage.* An example is given in Box 3-1, and a much fuller discussion is found in Chapter 24.

Second, a person who concentrates on one activity becomes better at it than could a jack-of-all-trades. This is called *learning by doing.* It was a factor much stressed by early economists. Modern research into what are called *learning curves* shows that learning by doing is important in many modern industries.

The exchange of goods and services in early societies commonly took place by simple mutual agreement among neighbours. In the course of time, however, trading became centered in particular gathering places called *markets.* Today we use the term *market economy* to refer to a society in which people specialize in productive activities and satisfy most of their material wants through exchanges.

---

[1]Hunter-gatherer societies, which preceded the first fixed settlements and which survive in a few isolated places even today, are traditional societies in which goods are typically held in common and wants can be satisfied with only a few days of work per week and in which, therefore, leisure time is abundant.

Specialization must be accompanied by trade. People who produce only one thing must trade much of their production in order to obtain all the other things they require.

The earliest market economies depended to some considerable extent on **barter**, the trading of goods directly for other goods.[2] However, barter can be a costly process in terms of the time spent searching out satisfactory exchanges. The evolution of money has made trading easier. Money eliminates the inconvenience of barter by allowing the two sides of the barter transaction to be separated. Farmers who have wheat and want hammers do not have to search for individuals who have hammers and want wheat. They take money in exchange for their wheat, then find other people who wish to trade hammers and offer money for the hammers.

By eliminating the need for barter, money greatly facilitates trade and specialization.

The Division of Labour

Market transactions in early economies mainly involved consumption goods and services. Producers specialized in making a commodity and then traded it for the other products they needed. Over the past several hundred years, many technical advances in methods of production have made it efficient to organize agriculture and industry on a large scale. These technical developments have made use of what is called the **division of labour**, which is a further step in the specialization of labour involving specialization within the production process of a particular commodity. The labour involved is divided into a series of repetitive tasks, and each individual performs a single task that may be just one of hundreds of tasks necessary to produce the commodity.

To gain the advantages of the division of labour, it became necessary to organize production in large

---

[2]Not only was barter common in the earliest societies that flourished before the invention of money and in medieval villages, it survived in isolated cases into more recent times. For example, much of the early North American fur trade was barter—trinkets, gems, cloths, and firearms being traded directly for furs.

factories. The typical workers sold their labour services to firms and received money wages in return. With this development, most urban workers became dependent on their ability to sell their labour. Adam Smith, the great eighteenth-century Scottish political economist, was the first to study the division of labour in detail, as discussed in Box 3-2.

Interestingly, recent changes in technology have led to an increased number of self-employed workers who are more like the artisans of old than like factory workers. Even within the factory, a new organizational principle called *lean production* or *flexible manufacturing*, which was pioneered by Japanese auto manufacturers, has led back to a more craft-based form of organization within the factory. In this technique, employees work as a team; each employee is able to do every team member's job rather than one very specialized task at one point on the assembly line. These important developments are further discussed in Chapter 9.

Markets and Resource Allocation

As explained in Chapter 1, *resource allocation* refers to the distribution of the available factors of production among the various uses to which they might be put. There are not enough resources to produce all the goods and services that could be consumed. It is therefore necessary to allocate the available resources among their various possible uses and in so doing to choose what to produce and what not to produce. In a market economy, millions of consumers decide what commodities to buy and in what quantities; a vast number of firms produce these commodities and buy the factor services that are needed to make them; and millions of factor owners decide to whom they will sell these services. These individual decisions collectively determine the economy's allocation of resources.

In a market economy, the allocation of resources is the outcome of countless independent decisions made by consumers and producers, all acting through the medium of markets.

This chapter provides an overview of the market mechanism.

Box 3-1

Absolute and Comparative Advantage

A simple case will illustrate the important principles involved in the gains from specialization.

Absolute Advantage

Suppose that, working full time on his own, Jacob can produce 100 pounds of potatoes *or* 40 sweaters per year, whereas Maria can produce 400 pounds of potatoes *or* 10 sweaters. Maria has an absolute advantage in producing potatoes because she can make more per period than Jacob. However, Jacob has an absolute advantage over Maria in producing sweaters for the same reason. If they both spend *half* their time producing each commodity, the results will be as given in Table-1.

Now let Jacob specialize in sweaters, producing 40 of them, and Maria specialize in potatoes,

producing 400 pounds. Production of both commodities has risen because each person is better than the other person at his or her specialty.

Comparative Advantage

Now make things a little less obvious by giving Maria an absolute advantage over Jacob in both commodities. We do this by making Maria more productive in sweaters so that she can produce 48 of them per year, with all other productivities remaining the same. Table 2 gives the outputs when Jacob and Maria each divide their time equally between the two products. Now compared with Jacob, Maria is four times more efficient at producing potatoes and 20 percent more efficient at producing sweaters.

It is possible to increase their combined production of both commodities by having Maria increase her production of potatoes and Jacob increase his production of sweaters. Table 3 gives an example in which Jacob specializes fully in sweater production and Maria spends 25 percent of her time on sweaters and 75 percent on potatoes. (Her outputs of sweaters and potatoes are thus 25 percent and 75 percent of what she could produce of these commodities if she worked full time on one or the other.) Table 3 shows the results.

In this latter example, Maria is absolutely more efficient than Jacob in both lines of production, but the amount of her advantage is greater in potatoes

TABLE 1   Production of Potatoes and Sweaters with Each Person's Time Divided Equally Between the Two Commodities

Sweaters	Potatoes	
Jacob	50	20
Maria	200	5
Total	250	25

The Decision Makers

Economics is about the behaviour of people, and there are millions of individuals in most economies. To make a systematic study of their behaviour manageable, economists categorize them into three important groups: households, firms, and the government, collectively known as **agents.** Members of

these groups are economic theory's cast of characters; they make the decisions that determine how the nation's resources are allocated.[3]

---

[3]Although we can manage with just three sets of decision makers, it is worth noting that there are others. Probably the most important of those omitted are nonprofit organizations such as private educational establishments, private hospitals, homes for senior citizens, charities, and research organizations such as the Institute for Research on Public Policy (IRPP). These bodies have a significant influence on the allocation of the economy's resources.

TABLE 2	Production of Potatoes and Sweaters with Each Person's Time Divided Equally Between the Two Commodities	
	Potatoes	Sweaters
Jacob	50	20
Maria	200	24
Total	250	44

TABLE 3	Production of Potatoes and Sweaters with Jacob Fully Specialized and Maria Spending 25 Percent of Her Time on Sweaters and 75 Percent on Potatoes	
	Potatoes	Sweaters
Jacob	—	40
Maria	300	12
Total	300	52
Increase over Table 2	50	8

with which she is four times as productive as Jacob than in sweaters with which she is only 20 percent more productive. Economists say that Maria has a **comparative advantage** over Jacob in the line of production in which her margin of advantage is greatest (potatoes, in this case) and that Jacob has a comparative advantage over Maria in the line of production in which his margin of disadvantage is least (sweaters, in this case). This is only an illustration: The principles can be generalized as follows.

Absolute efficiencies are not necessary for there to be gains from specialization.

Gains from specialization occur whenever there are *differences* in the amount of advantage one person enjoys over another in various lines of production.

Total production can always be increased when each person specializes in the production of the commodity in which he or she has a comparative advantage.

A more detailed study of the important concept of comparative advantage and its many applications to international trade and specialization must await the chapter on international trade (which is sometimes studied in courses on microeconomics and sometimes in courses on macroeconomics). In the meantime, it is worth noting that the comparative advantage of individuals and of whole nations may change. Maria may learn new skills and develop a comparative advantage in sweaters that she does not currently have. Similarly, whole nations may develop new abilities and know-how that will change their patterns of comparative advantage.

Households

A **household** is defined as all the people who live under one roof and who make joint financial decisions or are subject to others who make such decisions for them. The members of households are often referred to as *consumers* because they buy and consume most of the consumption goods and services. Economic theory gives households a number of attributes.

First, economists assume that each household makes consistent decisions, as though it were composed of a single individual. Thus, in analysing markets, economists ignore many interesting problems of how each household reaches its decisions, including family conflicts and the moral and legal problems concerning parental control over minors.[4]

[4]Some economists have studied resource allocation within households. This field of study, pioneered by University of Chicago economist and Nobel prize winner, Gary Becker, is often treated in advanced courses in labour economics.

Box 3-2

The Division of Labour

Adam Smith begins his classic *The Wealth of Nations* (1776) with a long study on the division of labour.

> The greatest improvements in the productive powers of labour ... have been the effects of the division of labour.
>
> To take an example ... the trade of the pinmaker; a workman not educated to this business (which the division of labour has rendered a distinct trade), nor acquainted with the use of the machinery employed in it could scarce, perhaps, with his utmost industry, make one pin in a day, and certainly could not make twenty. But in the way in which this business is now carried on ... it is divided into a number of branches .... One man draws out the wire, another straightens it, a third cuts it, a fourth points it, a fifth grinds it at the top for receiving the head; to make the head requires two or three distinct operations; to put it on is a peculiar business, to whiten the pins is another; it is even a trade by itself to put them into the paper; and the important business of making a pin is, in this manner, divided into about eighteen distinct operations, which, in some manufactories, are all performed by distinct hands, though in others the same man will sometimes perform two or three of them.

Smith observes that even in smallish factories, where the division of labour is exploited only in part, output is as high as 4,800 pins per person per day!

Later, Smith discusses the general importance of the division of labour and the forces that limit its application:

> Each animal is still obliged to support and defend itself, separately and independently, and derives no sort of advantage from that variety of talents with which nature has distinguished its fellows. Among men, on the contrary, the most dissimilar geniuses are of use to one another; the different produces of their respective talents, by the general disposition of truck, barter, and exchange, being brought, as it were, into a common stock, where every man may purchase whatever part of the produce of other men's talents he has occasion for.
>
> As it is the power of exchanging that gives occasion to the division of labour, so the extent of this division must always be limited by the extent of that power, or, in other words, by the extent of the market. When the market is very small, no person can have any encouragement to dedicate himself entirely to one employment for want of the power to exchange all that surplus part of the produce of his own labour, which is over and above his own consumption, for such parts of the produce of other men's labour as he has occasion for.

Smith notes that there is no point in specializing to produce a large quantity of pins, or anything else, unless there are enough persons making other commodities to provide a market for all the pins that are produced. Thus the larger the market, the greater is the scope for the division of labour and the higher are the resulting opportunities for efficient production.

Second, economists assume that when buying commodities and selling factor services, households are the principal owners of factors of production. They sell the services of these factors to firms and receive their incomes in return.

Motivation. Economists assume that each household seeks maximum *satisfaction* or *well-being* or *utility,* as the concept is variously called. The household tries to do this within the limits set by its available resources.

Firms

A **firm** is defined as the unit that employs factors of production to produce commodities that it sells to other firms, to households, or to government. For obvious reasons, a firm is often called a producer. Elementary economic theory gives firms several attributes.

First, in elementary economic theory, each firm is assumed to make consistent decisions, as though it were composed of a single individual. This strand of theory ignores the internal problems of how particular decisions are reached by assuming that the firm's internal organization is irrelevant to its decisions. This allows the firm to be treated, at least in elementary theory, as the unit of behaviour on the production or supply side of commodity markets, just as the household is treated as the unit of behaviour on the consumption or demand side.[5]

Second, economists assume that in their role as producers, firms are the principal users of the services of factors of production. In *factor markets* where factor services are bought and sold, the roles of firms and households are thus reversed from what they are in commodity markets: In factor markets, firms do the buying and households do the selling.

Motivation. Economists assume that most firms make their decisions with a single goal in mind: to make as much profit as possible. This goal of *profit maximization* is analogous to the household's goal of utility maximization.

Government

The term **government** is used in economics in a broad sense to include all public officials, agencies, government bodies, and other organizations belonging to or under the direct control of federal, state, and local governments. For example, in Canada, the term *government* includes, among others, the prime minister, the Bank of Canada, city councils, commissions and regulatory bodies, provincial premiers and legislators, mayors, and police forces. It is not important to draw up a comprehensive list, but one should have in mind a general idea of the organizations that have legal and political power to exert control over individual decision makers and over markets.

It is *not* a basic assumption of economics that government always acts in a consistent fashion. Two important reasons for this may be mentioned here.

First, what we call *the government* has many levels and many branches. For example, the mayor of Fredericton, an Alberta MLA, and a federal senator from Quebec represent different constituencies, whereas the Federal Departments of Labour, Finance, and Transport represent different interests, each with its own goals. Therefore, different and conflicting views and objectives are typically found within the government.

Second, decisions on interrelated issues of policy are made by many different bodies. Federal and provincial legislatures pass laws, the courts interpret laws, governments decide which laws to enforce with vigour and which not to enforce, the Department of Finance and the Bank of Canada influence monetary conditions, and a host of other agencies and semiautonomous bodies determine actions in respect to different aspects of policy goals. Because of the multiplicity of decision makers, it would be amazing if fully consistent behaviour resulted.

Motivation. Individual public servants, whether elected or appointed, have personal objectives (such as staying in office, promotion, power, prestige, and personal aggrandizement) as well as public service objectives. Although the balance of importance given to the two kinds of objectives varies among persons and among types of office, both will almost always have some influence. For example, most city councillors would not vote against a measure that slightly reduced the public good if this vote almost guaranteed defeat during the next election. ("After all," the councillor reasons, "if I am defeated, I won't be around to vote against *really* bad measures.")

As this discussion reveals, an important goal of legislators and political officials is the electoral success for themselves and their political party. As a result, measures that impose large political costs and few obvious economic benefits over the short run are unlikely to find favour, even when the long-term economic benefits may be large. In other words, there tends to be a bias toward shortsightedness in an elective system. Although much of this bias reflects a selfish unwillingness to look beyond the present, some of it reflects genuine uncertainty about the future. These issues of government motivation are further discussed in Chapter 20.

---

[5]At the more advanced level, many studies look within the firm to ask questions such as: Does the firm's internal organization affect its behaviour? We briefly consider such questions in Chapter 16.

Markets and Economies

If households, firms, and the government are the main actors, then markets are the stage on which their drama takes place.

Markets

Originally, *markets* were places where goods were bought and sold. The Granville Island market in Vancouver is a modern example of a market in the everyday sense, and many other cities have their own fruit and vegetable markets. Much early economic theory explained price behaviour in just such markets. Why, for example, can you get great bargains at the end of some days, but at the end of other days you buy at prices that appear exorbitant compared to the prices quoted only a few hours earlier?

As theories of market behaviour were developed, they were extended to cover commodities such as wheat. Wheat produced anywhere in the world can be purchased almost anywhere else in the world, and the price of a given grade of wheat tends to be nearly uniform. When we talk about the wheat market, the concept of a market has been extended well beyond the idea of a single place to which the producer, the storekeeper, and the householder go to sell and buy.

Similarly, the *foreign exchange market* has no specific location. Instead, it operates through international telephone and computer networks whereby dealers buy and sell dollars, sterling, francs, yen, and other national currencies. Markets may indeed use all conceivable means of communication, including the press, as in the case of the markets for many secondhand goods such as automobiles. If you have a car to sell or want to buy one, you will discover that the market comprises the local press, specialized magazines, and used-car dealers.

In the modern sense, a **market** refers to any situation in which buyers and sellers can negotiate the exchange of some commodity. In the past, high transportation costs and perishability made many markets quite local. Fresh fruits and vegetables, for example, would only be sold close to their points of production. Today, advances in preservation, the

falling cost of transportation, and the development of worldwide communications networks have led to the globalisation of many markets. A visit to the supermarket will confirm, for example, that food products such as Bulgarian jam, Chilean apples, and Indian rice are no longer confined to markets within their country of origin.

Economies

An **economy** is loosely defined as a set of interrelated production and consumption activities. It may refer to this activity in a region of one country (e.g., the economy of the Maritimes), in a country (the Canadian economy), or in a group of countries (the North American economy). In any economy, the allocation of resources is determined by the production, sales, and purchase decisions made by firms, households, and governments.

In Chapter 1 we learned three important things about economies. First, a *free-market economy* is one in which the decisions of individual households and firms (as distinct from the government) exert the major influence over the allocation of resources. Second, the opposite of a free-market economy is a *command economy,* in which the major decisions about the allocation of resources are made by the government and in which firms produce and households consume only as directed. Third, in practise, all economies are *mixed economies* in that some decisions are made by firms, households, and the government acting through markets, whereas other decisions are made by the government using the command principle.

Sectors of an Economy

Parts of an economy are usually referred to as **sectors** of that economy. For example, the agricultural sector is the part of the economy that produces agricultural commodities.

Market and Nonmarket Sectors

Producers make commodities. Consumers use them. Commodities may pass from one group to the other in two ways. They may be sold by producers and bought by consumers through markets, or they may be given away.

When commodities are bought and sold, producers expect to cover their costs with the revenue they obtain from selling the product. This is called *marketed production,* and this part of the economy's activity belongs to the **market sector.** When the product is given away, the costs of production must be covered from some source other than sales revenue. This is called *nonmarketed production,* and this part of the economy's activity belongs to the **nonmarket sector.** In the case of private charities, the money required to pay for factor services may be raised from the public by voluntary contributions. In the case of production by the government—which accounts for the bulk of nonmarketed production—the money is provided from government revenue, which in turn comes mainly from taxes.

Whenever a government enterprise *sells* its output, its production is in the market sector. Most of the government's output, however, is in the nonmarket sector, often by the very nature of the product provided. For example, one could hardly expect the criminal to pay the judge for providing the service of criminal justice. Other products are in the nonmarket sector because governments have decided that there are advantages to removing them from the market sector. This is the case, for example, with public school education and medical and hospital services in Canada. Public policy places them in the nonmarket sector even though much of their output could be provided by the market sector.

The economic significance of this distinction lies in the *bottom line.* (In accounting, the bottom line refers to profits.) In the market sector, firms face the bottom line test of profitability. If a product cannot be sold for a price that will cover its costs and provide sufficient return to the owners of the firm that makes it, the product will not be made. Production in the nonmarket sector faces no such profitability test. Since the product is provided free and its costs are met by contribution, the decision to produce it depends on the willingness of the government and private bodies to pay its costs and not on its ability to be sold at a cost-covering price.

Private and Public Sectors

An alternative division of an economy's productive activity is between private and public sectors. The **private sector** refers to all production that is in private hands, and the **public sector** refers to all production that is in public hands, that is, owned by

the government. The distinction between the two sectors depends on the legal distinction of ownership. In the private sector, the organization that does the producing is owned by households or other firms; in the public sector, it is owned and controlled by the government. The public sector includes all production of goods and services by the government plus all production of all publicly owned companies and other government-operated industries that is sold to consumers through markets.

The distinction between market and nonmarket sectors is economic; it depends on whether or not producers cover their costs from revenue earned by selling output to users. The distinction between the private and the public sectors is legal; it depends on whether the producing organizations are privately or publicly owned.

Some examples will illustrate these important decisions. The Aluminium Company of Canada (ALCAN) is in the private and market sectors; a Salvation Army soup kitchen is in the private and nonmarket sectors. The provincial hydro authorities are in the public and market sectors. Finally, Canadian health care is in the public and nonmarket sectors.

Microeconomics and Macroeconomics

As we saw in Chapter 1, there are two different but complementary ways of viewing the economy. The first, *microeconomics,* studies the detailed workings of individual markets and interrelationships among markets. The second, *macroeconomics,* suppresses much of the detail and concentrates on the behaviour of broad aggregates.[6]

Microeconomics and macroeconomics differ in the questions each asks and in the level of aggregation each uses. Microeconomics deals with the determination of prices and quantities in individual markets and with the relationships among these markets. Thus, it looks at the details of the market

---

[6]The prefixes *micro* and *macro* derive from the Greek words *mikros* for small and *makros* for large.

economy. It asks, for example, how much labour is employed in the fast-food industry and why the amount is increasing. It asks about the determinants of the output of broccoli, pocket calculators, automobiles, and hamburgers. It asks, too, about the prices of these goods—why some prices go up and others down. For example, economists interested in microeconomics analyse how a new invention, a government subsidy, or a drought will affect the price and output of wheat and the employment of farm workers.

In contrast, macroeconomics focuses on much broader aggregates. It looks at such things as the total number of people employed and unemployed, the average level of all prices, national output, and aggregate consumption. Macroeconomics asks what determines these aggregates and how they respond to changing conditions. Whereas microeconomics looks at demand and supply with regard to particular commodities, macroeconomics looks at aggregate demand and aggregate supply.

An Overview of Microeconomics

Early economists observed the market economy with wonder. They saw that even though commodities were made by many independent producers, the amounts of commodities produced approximately equaled the amounts people wanted to purchase. Natural disasters aside, there were neither vast surpluses nor severe shortages of products. They also saw that in spite of the ever-changing geographical, industrial, and occupational patterns of demand for labour services, most labourers were able to sell their services to employers most of the time. Visitors from the highly regulated economies of Eastern Europe and the former USSR had similar reactions until their command systems were abandoned during the early 1990s. How, they asked, could there be such an abundance of the right things, produced at the right time, and delivered to the right place—something that planned economies conspicuously failed to do?

How does the market produce this order in the absence of conscious coordination? It is one thing to have the same good produced year in and year out when people's wants and incomes do not change; it is quite another thing to have production adjusting continually to changing wants, incomes,

and techniques of production. Yet this adjustment is accomplished relatively smoothly by markets—albeit with occasional, and sometimes serious, interruptions.

Markets work without conscious central control because individual agents make their private decisions in response to publicly known signals such as prices, wages, and profits, and these signals, in turn, respond to the collective actions entailed by the sum of all individual decisions. In short:

The great discovery of eighteenth-century economists was that the price system is a social control mechanism that coordinates decentralized decision making.

In *The Wealth of Nations,* Adam Smith spoke of the price system as "the invisible hand." The system allows decision making to be decentralized under the control of millions of individual producers and consumers but nonetheless to be coordinated. An example may help to illustrate how this coordination occurs.[7]

An Example

Suppose that under prevailing conditions, farmers find it equally profitable to produce either of two crops, carrots or broccoli. As a result, they are willing to produce some of both commodities, thereby satisfying the demands of households to consume both. Now suppose that consumers develop a greatly increased desire for broccoli and a diminished desire for carrots. This change might have occurred because of the discovery of hitherto unsuspected nutritive or curative powers of broccoli.

When consumers buy more broccoli and fewer carrots, a shortage of broccoli and a surplus of carrots develop. To unload their surplus stocks of carrots, merchants reduce the price of carrots, because it is better to sell them at a reduced price than not to sell them at all. Merchants find, however, that they are unable to satisfy all their customers' demands for broccoli. Broccoli has become more scarce, so merchants charge more for it. As the price rises, fewer people are willing and able to purchase broccoli. Thus the rise in its price limits the quantity demanded to the available supply.

---

[7]The example is meant to give some feeling for how the price system works. This intuition is given a more formal expression in the theory laid out in Part 2 of this book.

Farmers see that broccoli production has become more profitable than in the past, because the costs of producing broccoli remain unchanged while its market price has risen. Similarly, they see that carrot production has become less profitable than in the past, because costs are unchanged while the price has fallen. Attracted by high profits in broccoli and deterred by low profits or potential losses in carrots, farmers expand the production of broccoli and curtail the production of carrots. Thus, the change in consumers' tastes, working through the price system, causes a reallocation of resources—land and labour—out of carrot production and into broccoli production.

The reaction of the market to a change in demand leads to a reallocation of resources. Carrot producers reduce their production; they will therefore be laying off workers and generally demanding fewer factors of production. Broccoli producers expand production; they will therefore be hiring workers and generally increasing their demand for factors of production.

Labour can probably switch from carrot to broccoli production without much difficulty. Certain types of land, however, may be better suited for growing one crop than the other. When farmers increase their broccoli production, their demands for the factors especially suited to growing broccoli also increase—and this creates a shortage of these resources and a consequent rise in their prices. Meanwhile, with carrot production falling, the demand for land and other factors of production especially suited to carrot growing is reduced. A surplus results, and the prices of these factors are forced down.

Thus factors particularly suited to broccoli production will earn more and will obtain a higher share of total national income than before. Factors particularly suited to carrot production, however, will earn less and will obtain a smaller share of the total national income than before.

All of the changes illustrated in this example will be studied more fully in subsequent parts of this book. The important thing to notice now is how changes in demand cause both reallocations of resources in the directions required to cater to the new levels of demand and changes in the incomes earned by factors of production.

This example illustrates the point made earlier: *The price system is a mechanism that coordinates individual, decentralized decisions.*

An Overview of Macroeconomics

We can group together all the buyers of the nation's output and call their total desired purchases *aggregate demand.* We can also group together all the producers of the nation's output and call their total desired sales *aggregate supply.*

Major changes in aggregate demand are called *demand shocks,* and major changes in aggregate supply are called *supply shocks.* Shocks cause important changes in the broad averages and aggregates that are the concern of macroeconomics, including total output, total employment, and average levels of prices and wages. Government actions sometimes *cause* demand or supply shocks; at other times, governments are *reacting to* the shocks. In the latter case, the government may attempt to cushion or to change the effects of a demand or a supply shock.

The Circular Flow of Income

One way to gain insight into aggregate demand and aggregate supply is to view the economy as a giant set of flows. We build up a picture of such flows in stages.

In Figure 3-1, all *producers* of goods and services are grouped together in the lower colored area, labeled producers. All *consumers* of goods and services are grouped together in the upper colored area, labeled consumers.[8]

The interactions between producers and consumers take place through two kinds of markets. Goods and services that are produced by firms are sold in markets that are usually referred to as *goods markets.* The services of factors of production (land, labour, and capital) are sold in markets called *factor markets.* The interactions involve flows going in two directions. Flows of goods and services, called *real flows,* are shown flowing counterclockwise in part (i) of the figure. Flows of payments for these goods and services, called *money flows,* are shown flowing clockwise in part (ii) of the figure.

We may now look in a little more detail at the relations just outlined.

Goods markets. The outputs of commodities flow from producers to consumers through what are usu-

[8]Most individuals and firms have a double role. As buyers of goods and services, they play a part in consuming that output; as sellers of factor services and other inputs, they play a part in producing that output.

FIGURE 3-1
Real and Money Flows

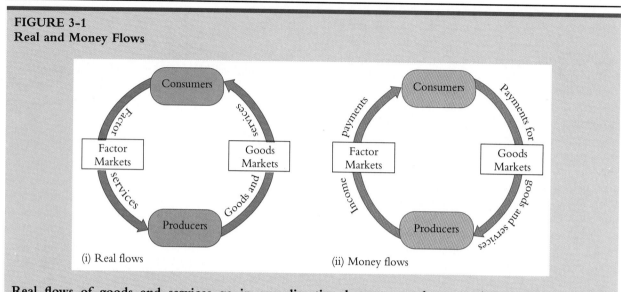

(i) Real flows

(ii) Money flows

Real flows of goods and services go in one direction between producers and consumers, whereas money flows of payments go in the opposite direction. The blue arrows in part (i) show real flows. Goods and services made by producers are sold to those who consume them, and factor services owned by consumers are sold to producers. The red arrows in part (ii) show money flows. Income payments go to consumers in return for the factor services that they sell. Expenditures flow from consumers to producers in return for the goods and services they buy.

ally known as **goods markets**, although that term covers both goods and services. Note that the term is used in the plural form, *goods markets*. Just as firms produce many products, so are there many markets in which products are sold. Households constitute one major group of consumers—indeed the largest, by amount consumed. They buy, for their own use, goods and services such as food, clothing, train journeys, compact discs, and cars. Other consumers include firms that purchase capital goods produced by yet other firms and include foreigners who purchase exports.

Factor markets. Most people earn their incomes by selling factor services to producers. (Exceptions are people receiving payments from such schemes as pension plans and unemployment insurance; they receive an income but not in return for providing their factor services to help in current production.) Most of those who do sell factor services are employees. They sell their labour services to firms in return for wages. Some others own capital and receive interest or profits for providing it. Others own land and derive rents from it. The buying and selling of these factor services takes place in factor markets. The buyers are producers. They use the ser-

vices that they purchase as inputs for the production of goods and services that are sold to consumers.

The circular flow. What we have just described involves two circular *flows*. This concept of a circularity in economic relations is a critical one. It helps us to understand how the separate parts of the economy are related to each other in a system of mutual interaction. For example, the activities of producers affect households, since the wages they pay affect household incomes. The activities of households affect firms, since the goods they buy affect the sales revenues of firms.

The two parts of Figure 3-1 provide alternative ways of looking at the same transactions. Every market transaction is a two-sided exchange in the sense that for every sale, there is a purchase, and for every seller, there is a buyer. The buyer receives goods or services and parts with money; the seller receives money and parts with goods or services.

The blue arrows in part (i) of the figure show the flows of goods and services through markets. They are shown flowing counterclockwise, from consumers to producers and from producers to consumers. The red arrows in part (ii) of the figure show the corresponding flows of money payments.

Flows of payments are going in the opposite direction, that is, clockwise. Payments flow from producers to consumers in order to pay for factor services, and they flow from consumers to producers to pay for goods and services.[9]

To distinguish these two sets of flows, each of which is the counterpart of the other, the blue flows in part (i) are called *real flows* and the red flows in part (ii) are called money, or *nominal,* flows.

Both of these ways of looking at the flows of economic transactions carry an important message. When firms produce goods and services, they create through factor payments the incomes needed to purchase their outputs; when users buy the outputs of firms, their payments create the incomes that firms need to pay for the factors of production that they employ. The main circular flow is shown passing from domestic producers to domestic households and back again. On the way, however, there are several leakages from and additions to this flow around the main circuit.

Other Flows

Figure 3-2 elaborates on the money flows shown in part (ii) of Figure 3-1 (still omitting much of the detail). It does so by allowing for private-sector saving and investment, for government taxing and spending, and for foreign trade. Since we are going to allow for foreign trade, the bottom box is labeled "Domestic Producers" to distinguish them from foreign producers. In addition, since we are going to allow for several classes of consumers of output, the top box is now labeled "Domestic Households" to distinguish that important group from the other purchasers of domestic output: foreigners, the government, and firms that purchase capital goods.

Leakages. As shown in Figure 3-2, payments flow from domestic producers to domestic households by way of payments for factor services. On the way, however, some leaks out of the circular flow because of government taxes, which reduce the flow of income payments that would otherwise go to households.

Payments pass from domestic households to domestic producers when households spend their incomes to buy goods and services made by producers.

Some household income leaks out of the circular flow when households save part of their incomes. The part that is saved is not spent on goods and services. Instead, it is shown flowing into the financial system, which happens, for example, when households deposit their savings in banks, with mortgage companies, or with investment trust companies. Money payments also leak out of the flow because of imports, which are purchases by domestic consumers that create incomes for *foreign* producers.

Injections. The spending of domestic households on domestically produced output creates income for domestic producers. Income is also created by three additional expenditures, often called *injections,* that cause additions to the circular flow. The first is investment expenditure, which goes to purchase the output of other firms. It is expenditure that firms make on capital goods such as machinery or factories that are produced by other firms. This expenditure is shown as a flow coming from the financial system. Such investment expenditures include a firm financing its own investment with funds raised by selling stocks or bonds to households (which is done through intermediary agents) or directly borrowing money from a bank or other financial institution. The second injection is the funds that the government spends on a whole range of goods and services, from national defense through the provision of justice to the building of schools and roads. The third injection comes from the selling of exports in response to the demand from foreign consumers for the output of domestic producers.

Together, the expenditure of domestic households, the investment expenditure of domestic firms, government purchases of goods and services, and exports constitute the aggregate demand for domestic output.[10] When any one of these elements of aggregate demand changes, aggregate output and total income earned by households are likely to change as a result. Thus, studying the determinants of total consumption, investment, government

---

[9]The direction—clockwise or counterclockwise—is of no significance. What is significant is that the real and the money flows are in *opposite directions.* Any real flow is matched by a corresponding money flow going in the other direction.

[10]Figure 3-2 highlights some of the main flows by omitting others. Two of the most important omissions, both of which are added during the study of elementary macroeconomics, are the following: (1) Governments add directly to the incomes of domestic households through what are called *transfer payments,* which include unemployment insurance and social security payments, and (2) some of the money that firms spend on investment comes not from the financial system but from their own profits that they reinvest rather than paying out as dividends.

FIGURE 3-2
The Circular Flow Elabourated

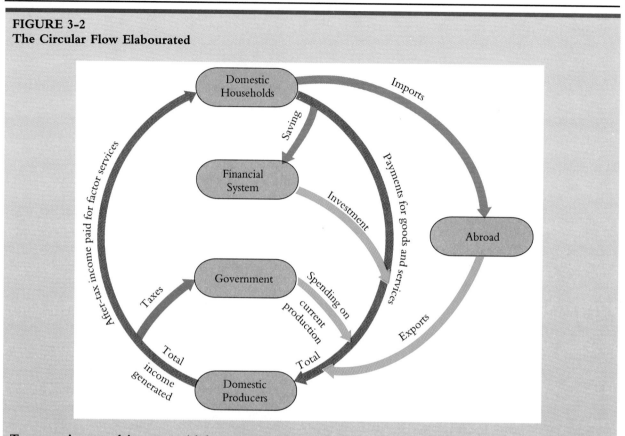

Taxes, savings, and imports withdraw expenditures from the circular flow; government purchases, investment, and exports inject expenditures into the circular flow. From the total income created by domestic producers, some leaks out of the circular flow because of government taxes on incomes. In this simplified version, the rest reaches domestic households as their disposable incomes. Some household income leaks out of the circular flow because of savings and imports; the rest is spent on purchasing the output of domestic firms. To these purchases are also added three injections: investment, government expenditure, and exports. Together these injections, plus household expenditure on domestic output, account for the total purchases of domestic output.

spending, and imports and exports is crucial to understanding the causes of changes both in the nation's total output and in the employment generated by the production of that output.

The Next Step

Soon you will be going on to study microeconomics or macroeconomics. Whichever branch of the subject you first study in detail, it is important to remember that microeconomics and macroeconomics provide complementary, not competing, views of the economy. Both views are needed for a full understanding of the functioning of a modern economy.

SUMMARY

1. Modern market economies are based on the specialization and division of labour, which necessitate the exchange of goods and services. Exchange takes place in markets and is facilitated by the use of money. Much of economics is devoted to the study of how markets work to coordinate millions of individual, decentralized decisions.

2. In economic theory, three groups of agents make the relevant decisions. Households, firms, and governments all interact with each other in markets. Households are assumed to maximize their satisfaction and firms to maximize their profits. Governments may have multiple objectives.

3. A free-market economy is one in which the allocation of resources is determined by production, sales, and purchase decisions made by firms and households acting in response to such market signals as prices and profits.

4. Economies are commonly divided into market and nonmarket sectors and into public and private sectors. These divisions cut across each other; the first is based on the economic distinction of how costs are covered, and the second is based on a legal distinction of ownership.

5. A key difference between microeconomics and macroeconomics is in the level of aggregation. Microeconomics looks at prices and quantities in individual markets and how they respond to various shocks that impinge on those markets. Macroeconomics looks at broader aggregates such as aggregate consumption, employment and unemployment, and the price level.

6. The questions asked in microeconomics and macroeconomics differ, but they are complementary parts of economic theory. They study different aspects of a single economic system, and both are needed for an understanding of the whole.

7. Microeconomics deals with the determination of prices and quantities in individual markets and the relationships among those markets. It shows how the price system provides signals that reflect changes in demand and supply and to which producers and consumers react in an independent but nonetheless coordinated manner.

8. The macroeconomic interactions between households and firms through markets may be illustrated in a circular flow diagram that traces money flows between producers and consumers. These flows are the starting point for studying the circular flow of aggregate income that is the key element of macroeconomics.

9. The circular flow of payments from domestic households to domestic firms and back again is not a closed system for two reasons. First, there are leakages from it in the form of taxes, savings, and imports, all of which cause the spending of domestic households on domestic output to be less than the income that they earn. Second, there are injections in the form of government spending on goods and services, investment spending, and exports, all of which cause the receipts of domestic firms to be greater than the spending of domestic households on domestic output.

TOPICS FOR REVIEW

Specialization and division of labour

Economic decision makers

Markets and market economies

Market and nonmarket sectors of an economy

Private and public sectors of an economy

The price system as a social control mechanism

Microeconomics and macroeconomics

Circular flow of income

DISCUSSION QUESTIONS

1. In recent years, many productive activities have been moved out of the public and nonmarket sectors. Can you give examples of some that have gone to the public and market sector and the private and market sector? What activities currently in the public and nonmarket sector could be moved into the private and market sector? Do you think such a move would be desirable?

2. Can you find examples of production that is allocated to a different sector in Canada and in the United States? (Use the market-nonmarket/public-private classifications.)

3. Suggest some examples of specialization and division of labour among people you know.

4. There is a greater variety of specialists and specialty stores in large cities than in small towns with populations with the same average income. Explain this in economic terms.

5. Define the household of which you are a member. Consider your household's income last year. What proportion of it came from the sale of factor services? Identify other sources of income. Approximately what proportion of the expenditures by your household became income for firms?

6. "It is not from the benevolence of the butcher, the brewer, or the baker that we expect our dinner, but from their regard to their self-interest. We address ourselves, not to their humanity, but to their self-love, and never talk to them of our necessities, but of their advantages." Do you agree with this quotation from The Wealth of Nations? How are our dinner and their self-interest related to the price system? What are assumed to be the motives of firms and of households?

7. Trace the effect of a sharp change in consumer demand away from fatty red meat and toward skinless poultry as a result of continuing reports that too much fatty red meat in a diet is unhealthy.

8. Trace out some significant microeconomic and macroeconomic effects of an aging population, such as is predicted for many industrialised countries in the twenty-first century.

9. Which, if any, of the arrows in Figure 3-2 does each of the following affect initially?
    a. Households increase their consumption expenditures by reducing saving.
    b. The government lowers income-tax rates.
    c. Because of a recession, firms decide to postpone production of some new products.
    d. Consumers like the new model cars and borrow money from the banking system to buy them in record numbers. (Hint: Borrowing may be thought of as negative saving.)

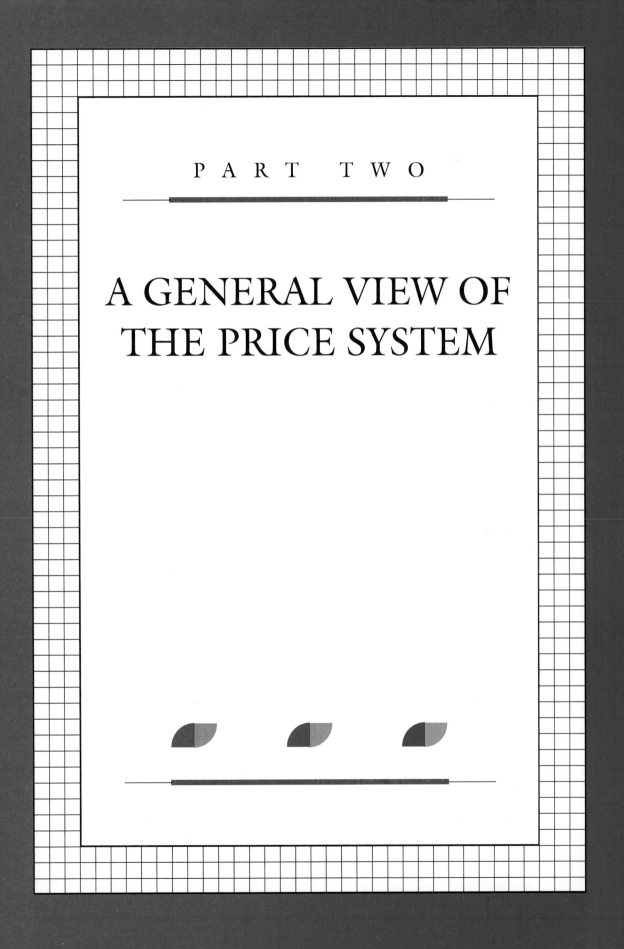

PART TWO

A GENERAL VIEW OF THE PRICE SYSTEM

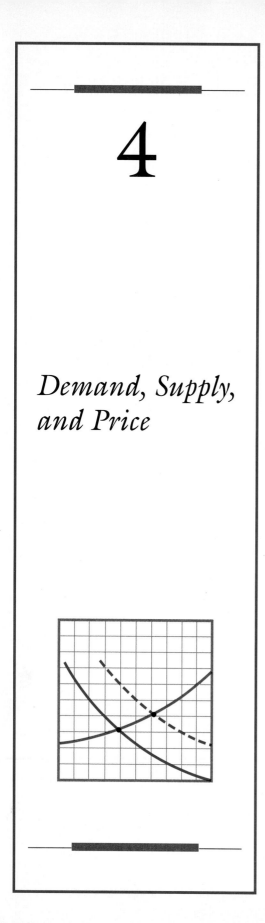

4

Demand, Supply, and Price

Some people believe that economics begins and ends with the laws of supply and demand. However, "economics in one lesson" is, of course, too much to hope for. (An unkind critic of a book with that title remarked that the author needed a second lesson.) Still, the so-called laws of supply and demand are an important part of our understanding of the market system.

As a first step, we need to understand what determines the demand for and the supply of particular goods or services. Then we can see how demand and supply together determine the prices of goods and services and the quantities that are bought and sold. Finally, we examine how the price system allows the economy to respond to the many changes that impinge on it. Demand and supply help us understand the price system's successes and its failures. They also help us understand the consequences of such government intervention as price controls, minimum wage laws, and sales taxes.

Demand

What determines the composition of consumer expenditure in Canada? Why does it change? Why did the fraction of total consumer expenditure for food decline from more than 33 percent in 1910 to less than 13 percent by 1991? Why has the proportion of income spent on services increased from 40 percent to nearly 60 percent in the last 40 years? How have Canadians reacted to the large changes in fuel prices that occurred in the last quarter century?

To see what determines the demand for various goods and services, we consider some typical *commodity.*

Quantity Demanded

The total amount of any particular commodity that all households wish to purchase in some time period is called the **quantity demanded** of that commodity.[1] It is important to notice three things about this concept.

First, quantity demanded is a *desired* quantity. It is the amount households wish to purchase, given the price of the commodity, other prices, their incomes, their tastes, and so

---

[1]In this chapter, we concentrate on the demand of *all* households for commodities. Of course, what all households do is only the sum of what each individual household does. In Chapters 7 and 8, we study the behaviour of individual households in more detail.

on.[2] It may be different from the amount that households actually succeed in purchasing. If sufficient quantities are not available, the amount that households wish to purchase may exceed the amount they actually purchase. To distinguish these two concepts, the term *quantity demanded* is used to refer to desired purchases, and a phrase such as *quantity actually bought* or *quantity exchanged* is used to refer to actual purchases.

Second, *desired* does not refer to idle dreams but to *effective demands*—that is, to the amounts people are willing to buy, given the price they must pay for the commodity.

Third, quantity demanded refers to a continuous *flow* of purchases. It must, therefore, be expressed as so much per period of time, such as 1 million units per day, 7 million per week, or 365 million per year. For example, being told that the quantity of new television sets demanded (at current prices) in Canada is 100,000 means nothing unless you are also told the period of time involved. One hundred thousand television sets demanded per day would be an enormous rate of demand; 100,000 per year would be a much smaller rate. (The important distinction between stocks and flows is discussed in Box 4-1.)

What Determines Quantity Demanded?

The amount of some commodity that all households wish to buy in a given time period is influenced by the following important variables: **[3]**

Commodity's own price

Average household income

Prices of related commodities

Tastes

Distribution of income among households

Population size

It is difficult to determine the separate influence of each of these variables if we consider what happens when everything changes at once. Instead, we consider the influence of the variables one at a time. To do this, we hold all but one of them constant. Then we let the selected variable change and study how these changes affect quantity demanded. We can do the same for each of the other variables in turn, and in this way we can come to understand the importance of each.[3] Once this is done, we can combine the separate influences of the variables to discover what happens when several things change at the same time—as they often do.

Holding all other influencing variables constant is often described by the words "other things being equal," "other things given," or by the equivalent Latin phrase *ceteris paribus.* When economists speak of the influence of the price of wheat on the quantity of wheat demanded, *ceteris paribus,* they refer to what a change in the price of wheat would do to the quantity of wheat demanded if all other forces that influence the demand for wheat remain unchanged.

Demand and Price

We are interested in developing a theory of how prices are determined. To do this, we need to study the relationship between the quantity demanded of each commodity and that commodity's own price. This requires that we hold all other influences constant and ask: How will the quantity of a commodity demanded vary as its own price varies?

A basic economic hypothesis is that the price of a commodity and the quantity that will be demanded are related *negatively*, other things being equal.[4] That is, the lower the price, the

---

[2]When economists say that something is "given," they do not mean that it is provided free! Instead they mean that the quantity is held constant. The expression "given the price of thecommodity" therefore means that the price of the commodity is assumed not to change during the period under discussion.

[3]A relationship in which many variables (in this case, average income, population, tastes, and many prices) influence a single variable (in this case, quantity demanded) is called a *multivariate* relationship. The technique of studying the effect of each of the influencing variables one at a time, while holding the others constant, is common in mathematics, and there is a specific concept, the *partial derivative,* designed to measure such effects.

[4]The famous British economist Alfred Marshall called this fundamental relation the "law of demand." In Box 4-2, we discuss the relationship between laws, predictions, and hypotheses. In Chapters 7 and 8, we derive the law of demand as a prediction that follows from more basic assumptions about consumers' tastes.

Box 4-1

Stock and Flow Variables

One important conceptual issue that arises frequently in economics is the distinction between stock and flow variables. Economic theories use both, and it takes a little practise to keep them straight.

As noted in the text, *a flow variable has a time dimension*; it is so much per unit of time. For example, the quantity of grade A large eggs purchased in Moose Jaw is a flow variable. No useful information is conveyed if we are told that the number purchased was 2,000 dozen eggs unless we are also told the period of time over which these purchases occurred. Two thousand dozen per hour would indicate an active market in eggs, whereas 2,000 dozen per month would indicate a sluggish market.

A stock variable has no time dimension; it is just so much. Thus, the number of eggs in the egg producers' coop warehouse—for example, 20,000 dozen eggs—is a stock variable. All those eggs are there at one time, and they remain there until something happens to change the stock held by the coop. The stock variable is just a number, not a rate of flow of so much per day or per month.

The distinction between stocks and flows can be explained using a bathtub. At any moment, the tub holds so much water. This is the *stock*, and it can be measured in terms of the volume of water, say 25 gallons. There might also be water flowing into the tub from the tap, or out of the tub through the drain; these *flows* are measured as so much water per unit of time, say 200 gallons per hour flowing in and 195 gallons flowing out.

The distinction between stocks and flows is important. Failure to keep it straight is a common source of confusion and even error. In economics, the amount of income earned is a flow; there is so much per year or per month or per hour. The amount of a household's expenditure is also a flow—so much spent per week or per month or per hour. The amount of money in a bank account or a miser's hoard (earned, perhaps, in the past but unspent) is a stock—just so many thousands of dollars. The key test is always whether a time dimension is required to give the variable meaning.

---

higher the quantity demanded, and the higher the price, the lower the quantity demanded.

Why might this be so? Commodities are used to satisfy desires and needs, and there is almost always more than one commodity that will satisfy any desire or need. Hunger may be alleviated by meat or vegetables; a desire for green vegetables can be satisfied by broccoli or spinach. The need to keep warm at night may be satisfied by several woolen blankets, by one electric blanket, or by a sheet and an overworked furnace. The desire for a vacation may be satisfied by a trip to the seashore or to the mountains; the need to get there may be satisfied by different airlines, a bus, a car, or a train. For any general desire or need, there are many different commodities that will satisfy it.

Now consider what happens if income, tastes, population, and the prices of all other commodities remain constant and the price of only one commodity changes. As the price goes up, that commodity becomes an increasingly expensive way to satisfy a want. Some households will stop buying it altogether; others will buy smaller amounts; still others may continue to buy the same quantity. Because many households will switch wholly or partly to other commodities to satisfy the same want, less will be bought of the commodity whose price has risen. As meat becomes more expensive, for example, households may to some extent switch to meat substitutes; they may also forgo meat at some meals and eat less meat at others.

Conversely, as the price goes down, the commodity becomes a cheaper method of satisfying a

Box 4-2

Laws, Predictions, Hypotheses

In what sense can the four propositions developed for supply and demand be called laws? They are not like bills passed by Parliament, interpreted by courts, and enforced by the police; they cannot be repealed if people do not like their effects. Nor are they, like the laws of Moses, revealed to humanity by the voice of God. Are they natural laws similar to Newton's law of gravity? In labeling them *laws,* economists clearly had in mind Newton's laws as analogies.

The term *law* is used in science to describe a theory that has stood up to substantial testing. A law of this kind is not something that has been proved to be true for all times and all circumstances, nor is it regarded as immutable. As observations accumulate, laws may be modified or the range of phenomena to which they apply may be restricted or redefined. Einstein's theory of relativity, as one example, forced such amendments and restrictions on Newton's laws.

The laws of supply and demand have stood up well to many empirical tests, but no one believes that they explain all market behaviour. They are thus laws in the sense that they predict certain kinds of behaviour in certain situations, and the predicted behaviour occurs sufficiently often to lead people to have continued confidence in the predictions of the theory. They are not laws—any more than are the laws of natural science—that are beyond being challenged by present or future observations that may cast doubt on some of their predictions. Nor is it a heresy to question their applicability to any particular situation.

Laws, then, are predictions that account for observed behaviour. It is possible, in economics as in the natural sciences, to be impressed both with the laws we do have and with their limitations: to be impressed, that is, both with the power of what we know and with the magnitude of what we have yet to understand.

---

want. Households will buy more of it. Consequently, they will buy less of similar commodities whose prices have not fallen and which as a result have become expensive *relative to* the commodity in question. When a bumper tomato harvest drives prices down, shoppers switch to tomatoes and cut their purchases of many other vegetables that now look relatively more expensive.

The Demand Schedule and the Demand Curve

A **demand schedule** is one way of showing the relationship between quantity demanded and the price of that commodity, other things being equal. It is a numerical tabulation showing the quantity that is demanded at selected prices.

Table 4-1 is a hypothetical demand schedule for carrots. It lists the quantity of carrots that would be demanded at various prices on the assumption that all other influences on quantity demanded are held constant. We note in particular that average household income is fixed at $30,000, because later we will want to see what happens when income changes. The table gives the quantities demanded for six selected prices, but in fact a separate quantity would be demanded at each possible price from 1 cent to several hundreds of dollars.

A second method of showing the relationship between quantity demanded and price is to draw a graph. The six price-quantity combinations shown in Table 4-1 are plotted on the graph shown in Figure 4-1. Price is plotted on the vertical axis, and quantity is plotted on the horizontal axis. The smooth curve drawn through these points is called a **demand curve.** It shows the quantity that pur-

TABLE 4-1   A Demand Schedule for Carrots

	Price per ton	Quantity demanded when average household income is $30,000 per year (thousands of tons per month)
U	$ 20	110.0
V	40	90.0
W	60	77.5
X	80	67.5
Y	100	62.5
Z	120	60.0

The table shows the quantity of carrots that would be demanded at various prices, *ceteris paribus*. For example, row *W* indicates that if the price of carrots were $60 per ton, consumers would desire to purchase 77,500 tons of carrot per month, given the values of the other variables that affect quantity demanded, including average household income.

chasers would like to buy at each price. The negative slope of the curve indicates that the quantity demanded increases as the price falls.[5]

Each point on the demand curve indicates a single price-quantity combination. The demand curve as a whole shows something more.

The demand curve represents the relationship between quantity demanded and price, other things being equal.

When economists speak of the demand in a particular market as being given or known, they are referring not just to the particular quantity being demanded at the moment (i.e., not just to one point on the demand curve) but instead, to the entire demand curve—to the relationship between desired purchases and all the possible alternative prices of the commodity.

<hr>

[5]Readers trained in other disciplines often wonder why economists plot demand curves with price on the vertical axis. The normal convention is to put the independent variable (the variable that does the explaining) on the X (i.e., horizontal) axis and the dependent variable (the variable that is explained) on the Y axis. This convention calls for price to be plotted on the horizontal axis and quantity on the vertical axis. For reasons explained in the math notes [4], economists reverse this practise in the case of demand curves, while following the normal practise with all other graphs.

FIGURE 4-1
A Demand Curve for Carrots

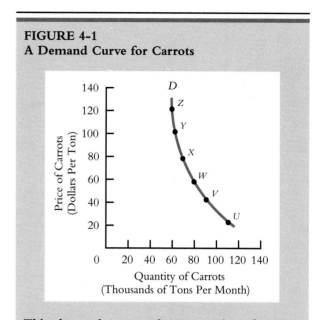

This demand curve relates quantity of carrots demanded to the price of carrots; its negative slope indicates that quantity demanded increases as price falls. The six points correspond to the price-quantity combinations shown in Table 4-1. Each row in the table defines a point on the demand curve. The smooth curve drawn through all of the points and labeled *D* is the demand curve.

Thus the term **demand** refers to the entire relationship between the quantity demanded of a commodity and the price of that commodity (as shown, for example, by the demand schedule in Table 4-1 or the demand curve in Figure 4-1). In contrast, a single point on a demand schedule or curve is the *quantity demanded* at that point. (For example, point *W* in Figure 4-1 corresponds to row *W* in Table 4-1. At *W*, 77,500 tons of carrots a month are demanded at a price of $60 per ton.)

Shifts in the Demand Curve

The demand schedule is constructed and the demand curve is plotted on the assumption of *ceteris paribus*. But what if other things change, as surely they must? For example, what if a household finds itself with more income? If it spends its extra income, it will buy additional quantities of many commodities *even though the prices of those commodities are unchanged*.

If households increase their purchases of any one commodity whose price has not changed, the

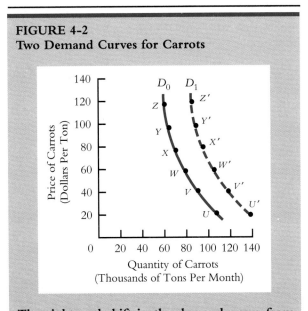

FIGURE 4-2
Two Demand Curves for Carrots

The rightward shift in the demand curve from D_0 to D_1 indicates an increase in the quantity demanded at each price. The lettered points correspond to those in Table 4-2. A rightward shift in the demand curve indicates an increase in demand in the sense that more is demanded at each price and that a higher price would be paid for each quanitity.

purchases cannot be represented by points on the original demand curve. They must be represented on a new demand curve, which is to the right of the old curve. Thus, the rise in household income shifts the demand curve to the right, as shown in Figure 4-2. This illustrates the operation of an important general rule.

A demand curve is drawn on the assumption that everything except the commodity's own price is held constant. A change in any of the variables previously held constant will shift the demand curve to a new position.

A demand curve can shift in many ways; two of them are particularly important. In the first case, more is bought at *each* price, and the demand curve shifts rightward so that each price corresponds to a higher quantity than it did before. In the second case, less is bought at *each* price, and the demand curve shifts leftward so that each price corresponds to a lower quantity than it did before.

The influence of changes in variables other than price may be studied by determining how changes in each variable shift the demand curve. Any change will shift the curve to the right if it increases the amount that households wish to buy, other things remaining equal. It will shift the curve to the left if it decreases the amount that households wish to buy, other things remaining equal. Changes in people's *expectations* about *future* values of variables such as income and prices can also influence current demand. For example, households may increase their purchases this year in response to an announced cut in income tax rates that will increase their after-tax incomes starting next year. For simplicity, however, we consider only the influence of changes in the current values of these variables.

Average household income. If households receive more income on average, they will purchase more of most commodities, even though commodity prices remain the same.[6] In other words, at any given price, a larger quantity will be demanded than was demanded previously. This shift in demand is illustrated in Table 4-2 and Figure 4-2.

A rise in average household income shifts the demand curve for most commodities to the right. This indicates that more will be demanded at each price.

Other prices. We saw that the negative slope of a commodity's demand curve occurs because the lower its price, the cheaper the commodity becomes relative to other commodities that can satisfy the same needs or desires. These other commodities are called **substitutes.** Another way for the same change to come about is for the price of the substitute commodity to rise. For example, carrots can become cheap relative to cabbage either because the price of carrots falls or because the price of cabbage rises. Either change will increase the amount of carrots that households wish to buy.

A rise in the price of a substitute for a commodity shifts the demand curve for the commodity to the right. More will be purchased at each price.

For example, a rise in the price of cabbage could cause the demand curve for carrots to shift to the right, as in Figure 4-2.

[6]Such commodities are called *normal goods.* Commodities for which the amount purchased falls as income rises are called *inferior goods.* These concepts are discussed in Chapter 5.

TABLE 4-2   Two Alternative Demand Schedules for Carrots

Price per ton *p*	Quantity demanded when average household income is $30,000 per year (thousands of tons per month) D_0		Quantity demanded when average household income is $36,000 per year (thousands of tons per month) D_1	
$ 20	110.0	*U*	140.0	*U'*
40	90.0	*V*	116.0	*V'*
60	77.5	*W*	100.8	*W'*
80	67.5	*X*	87.5	*X'*
100	62.5	*Y*	81.3	*Y'*
120	60.0	*Z*	78.0	*Z'*

An increase in average household income increases the quantity demanded at each price. When average income rises from C$30,000 to C$36,000 per year, quantity demanded at a price of C$60 per ton rises from 77,500 tons per month to 100,800 tons per month. A similar rise occurs at every other price. Thus the demand schedule relating columns *p* and D_0 is replaced by one relating columns *p* and D_1. The graphical representations of these two functions are labeled D_0 and D_1 in Figure 4-2.

Complements are commodities that tend to be used jointly. Cars and gasoline are complements; so are golf clubs and golf balls, electric stoves and electricity, and airplane flights to Calgary and lift tickets at Banff. Because complements tend to be consumed together, a fall in the price of either one will increase the demand for both.

A fall in the price of a complementary commodity will shift a commodity's demand curve to the right. More will be purchased at each price.

For example, a fall in the price of hotel rooms at Banff will lead to a rise in the demand for lift tickets at Banff ski slopes, even though the price of those lift tickets is unchanged.

Tastes. Tastes have an effect on people's desired purchases. A change in tastes may be long lasting, such as the shift from fountain pens to ballpoint pens or from typewriters to word processors; or it may be a fad, such as hula hoops or CB radios. In either case, a change in tastes in favour of a commodity shifts the demand curve to the right. More will be bought at each price.

Distribution of income. If a constant total of income is redistributed among the population, demands may change. If, for example, the government increases the deductions that may be taken for children on income tax returns and compensates by raising basic tax rates, income will be transferred from childless persons to households with large families. Demands for commodities more heavily bought by childless persons will decline, while demands for commodities more heavily bought by households with large families will increase.

A change in the distribution of income will cause a rightward shift in the demand curves for commodities bought most by households whose incomes increase and a leftward shift in the demand curves for commodities bought most by households whose incomes decrease.

Population. Population growth does not by itself create new demand. The additional people must have purchasing power before demand is changed. However, extra people of working age who are employed will earn new income. When this happens, the demands for all the commodities purchased by the new income earners will rise. Thus the following statement is usually true:

A general increase in population will shift the demand curves for most commodities to the right, indicating that more will be bought at each price.

The various reasons why demand curves shift are summarized in Figure 4-3.

Movements Along the Demand Curve Versus Shifts of the Whole Curve

Suppose you read in today's newspaper that the soaring price of carrots has been caused by a greatly increased demand for carrots. Then tomorrow you read that the rising price of carrots is greatly reducing the typical household's purchases of carrots, as shoppers switch to potatoes, yams, and peas. The two stories appear to contradict each other. The

FIGURE 4-3
Shifts in the Demand Curve

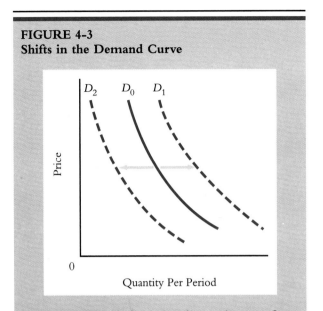

The rightward shift in the demand curve from D_0 to D_1 indicates an increase in demand; a leftward shift from D_0 to D_2 indicates a decrease in demand. An increase in demand means that more is demanded at each price. Such a rightward shift can be caused by a rise in income, a rise in the price of a substitute, a fall in the price of a complement, a change in tastes that favours that commodity, an increase in population, or a redistribution of income toward groups that favour the commodity.

A decrease in demand means that less is demanded at each price. Such a leftward shift can be caused by a fall in income, a fall in the price of a substitute, a rise in the price of a complement, a change in tastes that disfavours the commodity, a decrease in population, or a redistribution of income away from groups that favour the commodity.

first associates a rising price with a rising demand; the second associates a rising price with a declining demand. Can both statements be true? The answer is yes, because they refer to different things. The first describes a shift in the demand curve; the second describes a movement along a demand curve in response to a change in price.

Consider first the statement that the increase in the price of carrots has been caused by an increased demand for carrots. This statement refers to a shift in the demand curve for carrots. In this case the demand curve must have shifted to the right, indicating more carrots demanded at each price. This shift,

as we will see later in this chapter, will increase the price of carrots.

Now consider the statement that fewer carrots are being bought because carrots have become more expensive. This refers to a movement along a given demand curve and reflects a change between two specific quantities being bought—one before the price rose and one afterward.

Possible explanations for the two stories are given in the following:

1. A rise in the population is shifting the demand curve for carrots to the right as more carrots are demanded at each price. This in turn is raising the price of carrots (for reasons we will soon study in detail). This was the first newspaper story.
2. The rising price of carrots is causing each individual household to cut back on its purchase of carrots. This causes an upward movement to the left along any particular demand curve for carrots. This was the second newspaper story.

To prevent the type of confusion caused by our two newspaper stories, economists use a specialized vocabulary to distinguish between shifts of curves and movements along curves.

We have seen that *demand* refers to the *whole* demand curve, whereas *quantity demanded* refers to a specific quantity that is demanded at a specified price, as indicated by a particular point on the demand curve. In Figure 4-1, for example, demand is given by the curve D; at a price of $40, the quantity demanded is 90 tons, as indicated by the point V.

Economists reserve the term **change in demand** to describe a shift in the whole demand curve, that is, a change in the amount that will be bought at *every* price. The term **change in quantity demanded** refers to a change from one point on a demand curve to another point, either on the original demand curve or on a new one.

A change in quantity demanded can result from a change in demand, with the price constant; from a movement along a given demand curve due to a change in the price; or from a combination of the two. [5]

We consider each of these possibilities in turn.

An increase in demand means that the whole demand curve shifts to the right; a decrease in demand means that the whole demand curve shifts to the left. At a given price, an increase in demand causes an increase in quantity demanded, whereas a decrease in demand causes a decrease in quantity demanded.

For example, in Figure 4-2, the shift in the demand curve from D–0 to D–1 represents an increase in demand, and at a price of $40, for example, quantity demanded increases from 90,000 tons to 116,000 tons, as indicated by the move from V to V^1.

A movement down and to the right along a demand curve represents an increase in quantity demanded; a movement up and to the left along a demand curve represents a decrease in quantity demanded.

For example, in Figure 4-2, with demand given by the curve D–1, an increase in price from $40 to $60 causes a movement along D–1 from V^1 to W^1, so that quantity demanded decreases from 116,000 tons to 100,800 tons.

When there is a change in demand *and* a change in the price, the change in quantity demanded is the net effect of the shift in the demand curve and the movement along the new demand curve.

Figure 4-4 shows the combined effect of a rise in demand, shown by a rightward shift in the whole demand curve, and an upward movement to the left along the new demand curve due to an increase in price. The rise in demand causes an increase in quantity demanded at the initial price, whereas the movement along the demand curve causes a decrease in the quantity demanded. Whether quantity demanded rises or falls overall depends on the relative magnitudes of these two changes.

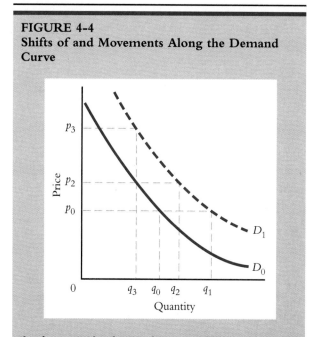

FIGURE 4-4
Shifts of and Movements Along the Demand Curve

An increase in demand means that the demand curve shifts to the right, and hence quantity demanded will be higher at each price. A rise in price causes an upward movement to the left along the demand curve, and hence quantity demanded will fall.

The demand curve is originally D_0 and price is p_0, which means that quantity demanded is q_0. Suppose that demand increases to D_1, which means that at any particular price, there is a larger quantity demanded; for example, at p_0, quantity demanded is now q_1. Now suppose that the price rises above p_0. This causes a movement up and to the left along D_1, and quantity demanded falls below q_1.

The net effect of these two changes can be either an increase or a decrease in the quantity demanded. In this figure, a rise in price to p_2 means that the quantity demanded, q_2, is still in excess of the original quantity demanded, q_0; a rise in price to p_3 means that the final quantity demanded, q_3, is below the original quantity demanded, q_0.

Supply

The Canadian private sector produced goods and services worth about $500 billion in 1992. Econo-mists have as many questions to ask about production and its changing composition as they do about consumption. What determines the amount produced? What determines its composition? Why do the quantities of goods and services produced change? Why has manufacturing output fallen from 31 percent of total private-sector production in

1951 to 27 percent in 1992? Why have agriculture, forestry, and fisheries, as a group, fallen from almost 7 percent in 1955 to just over 2 percent in 1992? Why have services grown from 47 percent to over 55 percent in the same period?

Dramatic changes have occurred within each of these market categories. Why, for example, did the aluminum industry grow much faster than the steel industry? Even within any single industry, some firms prosper and grow while others decline. A large fraction of the firms in a typical industry at the beginning of any decade are no longer present at the end of that decade. Why and how do new jobs, new firms, and new industries come into being while other jobs, firms, and industries shrink or disappear altogether?

All of these questions and many others are aspects of a single question: *What determines the quantities of commodities that will be produced and offered for sale?*

A full discussion of these questions of supply will come later (in Part 4). For now, it suffices to examine the basic relationship between the price of a commodity and the quantity produced and offered for sale and to understand what forces lead to shifts in this relationship.

Quantity Supplied

The amount of a commodity that firms wish to sell in some time period is called the **quantity supplied** of that commodity. Quantity supplied is a flow; it is so much per unit of time. Note also that quantity supplied is the amount that firms are willing to offer for sale; it is not necessarily the amount they succeed in selling, which is expressed by the term *quantity actually sold* or the term *quantity exchanged*. Although households may desire to purchase an amount that differs from what firms desire to sell, they obviously cannot succeed in buying what someone else does not sell. A purchase and a sale are merely two sides of the same transaction. Viewed from the buyer's side, there is a purchase; viewed from the seller's side, there is a sale.

Because desired purchases do not have to equal desired sales, quantity demanded does not have to equal quantity supplied. However, the quantity actually purchased must equal the quantity actually sold because whatever someone buys, someone else must sell.

What Determines Quantity Supplied?

The amount of a commodity that firms will be willing to produce and offer for sale is influenced by the following important variables:[6]

Commodity's own price

Prices of inputs

Goals of firms

State of technology

The situation with supply is the same as with demand: There are several influencing variables, and we will not get far if we try to discover what happens when they all change at the same time. So, again, we use the convenient *ceteris paribus* technique to study the influence of the variables one at a time.

Supply and Price

In order to develop a theory of how commodities get priced, we study the relationship between the quantity supplied of each commodity and that commodity's own price. We start by holding all other influences constant and asking: How do we expect the quantity of a commodity supplied to vary with its own price?

A basic hypothesis of economics is that, for many commodities, the price of the commodity and the quantity that will be supplied are related *positively*, other things being equal.[7] That is to say, the higher the commodity's own price, the more its producers will supply, and the lower the price, the less its producers will supply.

---

[7]In this chapter, we introduce this key relation as an assumption. In later chapters, we will derive it as a prediction from more basic assumptions about the behaviour of firms.

	Price per ton	Quantity supplied (thousands of tons per month)
u	$ 20	5.0
v	40	46.0
w	60	77.5
x	80	100.0
y	100	115.0
z	120	122.5

TABLE 4-3 A Supply Schedule for Carrots

The table shows the quantities that producers wish to sell at various prices, *ceteris paribus*. For example, row *y* indicates that if the price were $100 per ton, producers would wish to sell 115,000 tons of carrots per month.

Why might this be so? It is true because the profits that can be earned from producing a commodity will almost certainly increase if the price of that commodity rises while the costs of inputs used to produce it remain unchanged. This will make firms, which are in business to earn profits, wish to produce more of the commodity whose price has risen.[8]

The Supply Schedule and the Supply Curve

The general relationship just discussed can be illustrated by a supply schedule, which shows the relationship between quantity supplied of a commodity and the price of the commodity, other things being equal. A supply schedule is analogous to a demand schedule; the former shows what producers would be willing to sell, whereas the latter shows what households would be willing to buy, at alternative prices of the commodity. Table 4-3 presents a hypothetical supply schedule for carrots.

---

[8]Notice, however, the qualifying word *many* in the hypothesis printed in green. It is used because, as we shall see in Part 4, there are exceptions to this rule. Although the rule states the usual case, a rise in price (*ceteris paribus*) is not always necessary to produce an increase in quantity supplied.

FIGURE 4-5
A Supply Curve for Carrots

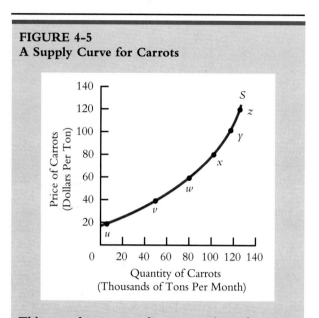

This supply curve relates quantity of carrots supplied to the price of carrots; its positive slope indicates that quantity supplied increases as price increases. The six points correspond to the price-quantity combinations shown in Table 4-3. Each row in the table defines a point on the supply curve. The smooth curve drawn through all of the points and labeled *S* is the supply curve.

A **supply curve**, the graphic representation of the supply schedule, is illustrated in Figure 4-5. Each point on the supply curve represents a specific price-quantity combination; however, the whole curve shows something more.

The supply curve represents the relationship between quantity supplied and price, other things being equal; its positive slope indicates that quantity supplied varies in the same direction as does price.

When economists speak of the conditions of supply as being given or known, they are not referring just to the particular quantity being supplied at the moment, that is, not to just one point on the supply curve. Instead, they are referring to the entire supply curve, to the complete relationship between desired sales and all possible alternative prices of the commodity.

Supply refers to the entire relationship between the quantity supplied of a commodity and the price

TABLE 4-4 Two Alternative Supply Schedules for Carrots

Price per ton p	Quantity supplied before cost-saving innovation (thousands of tons per month) S_0		Quantity supplied after innovation (thousands of tons per month) S_1	
$ 20	5.0	u	28.0	u'
40	46.0	v	76.0	v'
60	77.5	w	102.0	w'
80	100.0	x	120.0	x'
100	115.0	y	132.0	y'
120	122.5	z	140.0	z'

A cost-saving innovation increases the quantity supplied at each price. As a result of a cost-saving innovation, the quantity that is supplied at $100 per ton rises from 115,000 to 132,000 tons per month. A similar rise occurs at every price. Thus, the supply schedule relating p and S_0 is replaced by one relating p and S_1.

FIGURE 4-6
Two Supply Curves for Carrots

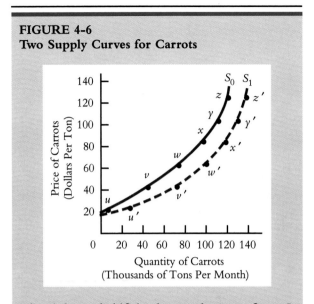

The rightward shift in the supply curve from S_0 to S_1 indicates an increase in the quantity supplied at each price. The lettered points correspond to those in Table 4-4. A rightward shift in the supply curve indicates an increase in supply such that more carrots are supplies at each price.

of that commodity, other things being equal. A single point on the supply curve refers to the *quantity supplied* at that price.

Shifts in the Supply Curve

A shift in the supply curve means that at each price a different quantity will be supplied than previously. An increase in the quantity supplied at each price is shown in Table 4-4 and is graphed in Figure 4-6. This change appears as a rightward shift in the supply curve. In contrast, a decrease in the quantity supplied at each price appears as a leftward shift. A shift in the supply curve must be the result of a change in one of the factors that influence the quantity supplied other than the commodity's own price. The major possible causes of such shifts are summarized in the caption of Figure 4-7 and are considered briefly in the text.

For supply, as for demand, there is an important general rule:

A change in any of the variables (other than the commodity's own price) that affects the amount of a commodity that firms are willing to produce and sell will shift the supply curve for that commodity.

Prices of inputs. All things that a firm uses to produce its outputs, such as materials, labour, and machines, are called the firm's *inputs.* Other things being equal, the higher the price of any input used to make a commodity, the less will be the profit from making that commodity. We expect, therefore, that the higher the price of any input used by a firm, the lower will be the amount that firms will produce and offer for sale at any given price of the commodity.

A rise in the price of inputs shifts the supply curve to the left, indicating that less will be supplied at any given price; a fall in the cost of inputs shifts the supply curve to the right.

Technology. At any time, what is produced and how it is produced depends on what is known. Over time, knowledge changes; so do the quantities of individual commodities supplied. The enormous increase in production per worker that has been going on in industrial societies for about 200 years is largely due to improved methods of production.

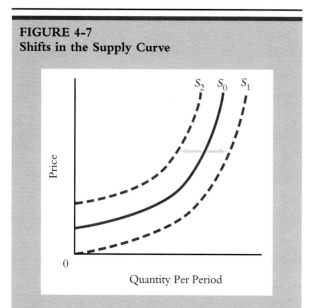

FIGURE 4-7
Shifts in the Supply Curve

A shift in the supply curve from S_0 to S_1 indicates an increase in supply; a shift from S_0 to S_2 indicates a decrese in supply. An increase in supply means that more is supplied at each price. Such a rightward shift can be caused by certain changes in producers' goals, improvements in technology, or decreases in the costs of inputs that are important in producing the commodity.

A decrease in supply means that less is supplied at each price. Such a leftward shift can be caused by certain changes in producers' goals or increases in the costs of inputs that are important in producing the commodity.

The Industrial Revolution is more than a historical event; it is a present reality. Discoveries in chemistry have led to lower costs of production for well-established products, such as paints, and to a large variety of new products made of plastics and synthetic fibers. Such inventions as transistors and silicon chips have radically changed products such as computers, audiovisual equipment, and guidance control systems, and the consequent development of smaller computers is revolutionizing the production of countless other nonelectronic products.

Any technological innovation that decreases production costs will increase the profits that can be earned at any given price of the commodity. Since increased profitability leads to increased production, this change shifts the supply curve to the right, indicating an increased willingness to produce the commodity and offer it for sale at each possible price.

Movements Along the Supply Curve Versus Shifts of the Whole Curve

As with demand, it is important to distinguish movements along supply curves from shifts of the whole curve. Economists reserve the term **change in supply** to describe a shift of the whole supply curve, that is, a change in the quantity that will be supplied at every price. The term **change in quantity supplied** refers to a change from one point on a supply curve to another point, either on the original supply curve or on a new one. That is, an increase in supply means that the whole supply curve has shifted to the right, so that the quantity supplied at any given price has increased; a movement up and to the right along a supply curve indicates an *increase in the quantity supplied* in response to an increase in the price of the commodity.

A change in quantity supplied can result from a change in supply, with the price constant; from a movement along a given supply curve due to a change in the price; or from a combination of the two.

Determination of Price by Demand and Supply

So far, demand and supply have been considered separately. Now we are ready to see how the two forces interact to determine price in a competitive market?[9] Table 4-5 brings together the demand and supply schedules from Tables 4-1 and 4-3. The quantities of carrots demanded and supplied at each price may now be compared.

In this example, there is only one price, $60 per ton, at which the quantity of carrots demanded equals the quantity supplied. At prices less than $60 per ton, there is a shortage of carrots, because the quantity demanded exceeds the quantity supplied. This is often called a situation of **excess demand**. At prices greater than $60 per ton, there is a surplus of carrots, because the quantity supplied exceeds the

---

[9]Roughly, a competitive market is one that has a large number of buyers and sellers, each accounting for a small share of total purchases and sales; this concept, and alternative market structures that occur, are defined more precisely in later chapters.

TABLE 4-5 Demand and Supply Schedules for Carrots and Equilibrium Price

(1) Price per ton p	(2) Quantity demanded (thousands of tons per month) D	(3) Quantity supplied (thousands of tons per month) S	(4) Excess demand (+) or excess supply (−) (thousands of tons per month) D − S
$ 20	110.0	5.0	+105.0
40	90.0	46.0	+44.0
60	77.5	77.5	0.0
80	67.5	100.0	−32.5
100	62.5	115.0	−52.5
120	60.0	122.5	−62.5

Equilibrium occurs where quantity demanded equals quantity supplied—when there is neither excess demand nor excess supply. These schedules are those of Tables 4-1 and 4-3. The equilibrium price is $60. For lower prices, there is excess demand; for higher prices, there is excess supply.

quantity demanded. This is called a situation of **excess supply**.

To discuss the determination of market price, suppose first that the price is $100 per ton. At this price, 115,000 tons are offered for sale, but only 62,500 tons are demanded. There is an excess supply of 52,500 tons per month. We assume that sellers will then cut their prices to get rid of this surplus and that purchasers, observing the stock of unsold carrots, will pay less for what they are prepared to buy.

Excess supply causes downward pressure on price.

Next consider the price of $20 per ton. At this price there is excess demand. The 5,000 tons produced each month are snapped up quickly, and 105,000 tons of desired purchases cannot be made. Rivalry between would-be purchasers may lead them to offer more than the prevailing price in order to outbid other purchasers. Also, perceiving that they could sell their available supplies many times over, sellers may begin to ask a higher price for the quantities that they do have to sell.

Excess demand causes upward pressure on price.

Finally, consider the price of $60. At this price, producers wish to sell 77,500 tons per month, and

purchasers wish to buy that quantity. There is neither a shortage nor a surplus of carrots. There are no unsatisfied buyers to bid the price up, nor are there unsatisfied sellers to force the price down. Once the price of $60 has been reached, therefore, there will be no tendency for it to change.

An equilibrium implies a state of rest, or balance, between opposing forces. The **equilibrium price** is the one toward which the actual market price will tend. It will persist, once established, unless it is disturbed by some change in market conditions.

The price at which the quantity demanded equals the quantity supplied is called the equilibrium price.

The equilibrium price is also called the *market-clearing price*. Any other price is called a **disequilibrium price**: a price at which quantity demanded does not equal quantity supplied. When there is either excess demand or excess supply in a market, that market is said to be in a state of **disequilibrium**, and the market price will be changing.

A condition that must be fulfilled if equilibrium is to be obtained in some market is called an **equilibrium condition**. The equality of quantity demanded and quantity supplied is an equilibrium condition.[7]

This same story is told in graphic terms in Figure 4-8. The quantities demanded and supplied at

FIGURE 4-8
Determination of the Equilibrium Price

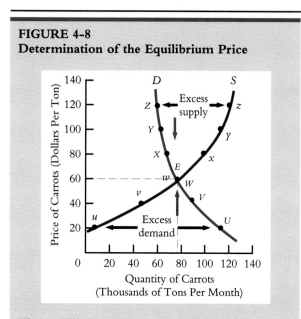

The equilibrium price corresponds to the intersection of the demand and supply curves. Equilibrium is indicated by E, which is point W on the demand curve and point w on the supply curve. At a price of $60, quantity demanded equals quantity supplied. At prices above equilibrium, there is excess supply and downward pressure on price. At prices below equilibrium, there is excess demand and upward pressure on price. The pressures on price are represented by the vertical arrows.

any price can be read off the two curves; the excess supply or excess demand is shown by the horizontal distance between the curves at each price. The figure makes it clear that the equilibrium price occurs where the demand and supply curves intersect. Below that price there is excess demand, and hence upward pressure on the existing price. Above that price there is excess supply, and hence downward pressure on the existing price. These pressures are represented by the vertical arrows in the figure.

The Laws of Demand and Supply

Changes in any of the variables, other than price, that influence quantity demanded or supplied will cause a shift in the supply curve, the demand curve, or both. There are four possible shifts: (1) a rise in demand (a rightward shift in the demand curve), (2)

a fall in demand (a leftward shift in the demand curve), (3) a rise in supply (a rightward shift in the supply curve), and (4) a fall in supply (a leftward shift in the supply curve).

Each of these shifts causes changes that are described by one of the four laws of demand and supply. Each of the laws summarizes what happens when an initial position of equilibrium is upset by some shift in either the demand curve or the supply curve and a new equilibrium position is then established. The sense in which it is correct to call these propositions "laws" is discussed in Box 4-2.

To discover the effects of each of the curve shifts that we wish to study, we use the method known as **comparative statics**, short for *comparative static equilibrium analysis.*[10] In this method, we derive predictions by analysing the effect on the equilibrium position of some change in which we are interested. We start from a position of equilibrium and then introduce the change to be studied. The new equilibrium position is determined and compared with the original one. The difference between the two positions of equilibrium must result from the change that was introduced, because everything else has been held constant.

The four laws of demand and supply are derived in Figure 4-9, which generalizes our specific discussion about carrots. Study the figure carefully. Up to now, we have given the axes specific labels, but from here on we will simplify. Because it is intended to apply to any commodity, the horizontal axis is simply labeled *Quantity.* This should be understood to mean quantity per period in whatever units output is measured. *Price,* the vertical axis, should be understood to mean the price measured as dollars per unit of quantity for the same commodity. The four laws of demand and supply are as follows:

1. A rise in demand causes an increase in both the equilibrium price and the equilibrium quantity exchanged.
2. A fall in demand causes a decrease in both the equilibrium price and the equilibrium quantity exchanged.

---

[10]The term *statics* is used because we are not concerned with the actual path by which the market goes from the first equilibrium position to the second or with the time taken to reach the second equilibrium. Analysis of these movements would be described as dynamic analysis.

FIGURE 4-9
The Four "Laws" of Demand and Supply

(i) The effect of shifts in the demand curve   (ii) The effect of shifts in the supply curve

The effects on equilibrium price and quantity of shifts in either demand or supply are called the laws of demand and supply. *A rise in demand.* In part (i) assume that the original demand and supply curves are D_0 and S, which intersect to produce equilibrium at E_0, with a price of p_0 and an quantity of q_0. An increase in demand shifts the demand curve to D_1, taking the new equilibrium to E_1. Price rises to p_1 and quantity to q_1.

A fall in demand. In part (i) assume that the original demand and supply curves are D_1 and S, which intersect to produce equilibrium at E_1, with a price of p_1 and a quantity of q_1. A decrease in demand shifts the demand curve to D_0, taking the new equilibrium to E_0. Price falls to p_0, and quantity falls to q_0.

A rise in supply. In part (ii) assume that the original demand and supply curves are D and S_0, which intersect to produce equilibrium at E_0, with a price of p_0 and a quantity of q_0. An increase in supply shifts the supply curve to S_1, taking the new equilibrium to E_1. Price falls to p_1, and quantity rises to q_1.

A fall in supply. In part (ii) assume that the original demand and supply curves are D and S_1, which intersect to produce equilibrium at E_1, with a price of p_1 and a quantity of q_1. A decrease in supply shifts the supply curve to S_0, taking the new equilibrium to E_0. Price rises to p_0, and quantity falls to q_0.

3. A rise in supply causes a decrease in the equilibrium price and an increase in the equilibrium quantity exchanged.
4. A fall in supply causes an increase in the equilibrium price and a decrease in theequilibrium quantity exchanged.

Demonstrations of these laws are given in the caption to Figure 4-9. The intuitive reasoning behind each is as follows:

1. A rise in demand creates a shortage, and the unsatisfied buyers bid up the price. This causes a larger quantity to be produced, with the result that at the new equilibrium more is bought and sold at a higher price.
2. A fall in demand creates a surplus, and the unsuccessful sellers bid the price downward. As a result, less of the commodity is produced and offered for sale. At the new equilibrium, both price and quantity bought and sold are lower than they were originally.
3. An increase in supply creates a glut, and the unsuccessful suppliers force the price down. This increases the quantity demanded, and the new equilibrium is at a lower price and a higher quantity bought and sold.
4. A reduction in supply creates a shortage that causes the price to be bid up. This reduces the quantity demanded, and the new equilibrium is at a higher price and a lower quantity bought and sold.

In this chapter, we have studied many forces that can cause demand or supply curves to shift. These shifts were summarized in Figures 4-3 and 4-7. By combining this analysis with the four laws of demand and supply, we can link many real-world

Box 4-3

Demand and Supply: What Really Happens

"The theory of supply and demand is neat enough," said the skeptic, "but tell me what really happens."

"What really happens," said the economist, "is that demand curves have a negative slope; supply curves have a positive slope; prices rise in response to excess demand; and prices fall in response to excess supply."

"But that's theory," insisted the skeptic. "What about reality?"

"That is reality as well," said the economist.

"Show me," said the skeptic.

The economist produced the following passages from the local newspaper.

Recession causes early peak in gas prices. "Nine times out of ten, prices will go up in June. Historically they go up about three cents a litre after May 24th," said one industry spokesman. "This summer the recession has cut into many Canadians' travel plans, and gas sales are down all over the country. In some areas, gas prices have actually fallen."

Increased demand for macadamia nuts causes price to rise above competing nuts. A major producer now plans to double the size of its orchards during the next five years.

OPEC countries once again fail to agree on output quotas for oil. Output soars and prices plummet.

Last summer, Rhode Island officials reopened the northern third of Narragansett Bay, a 9,500-acre fishing ground that had been closed since 1978 because of pollution. Suddenly clam prices dropped, thanks to an underwater population explosion that had transformed the Narragansett area into a clam harvester's dream.

How deep is the art market's recession?... in today's unforgiving economic climate, the sales of contemporary, impressionist, and modern works of art took hits at this week's auctions. Sales totaled just under $100 million compared with $893 million just one year ago. Many paintings on offer went unsold, and those that did sell went for well under their predicted price.

Supply management of the Canadian poultry industry reduces local production, causing Canadian chicken prices to be as much as 30 percent above U.S. prices. This policy could never be sustained if the Federal government did not restrict imports of chicken from the United States.

The skeptic's response is not recorded, but you should be able to tell which clippings illustrate which of the economist's four statements about "what really happens."

---

events that cause demand or supply curves to shift with changes in market prices and quantities. For example, a rise in the price of a commodity's substitute will shift the commodity's demand curve to the right, as in Figure 4-3, thus leading to a rise in both the commodity's price and the quantity that is bought and sold, as in part (i) of Figure 4-9.

The theory of the determination of price by demand and supply is beautiful in its simplicity. Yet, as we shall see, it is powerful in its wide range of applications. The usefulness of this theory in interpreting what we see in the world around us is further discussed in Box 4-3.

Prices and Inflation

The theory we have developed explains how individual prices are determined by the forces of demand and supply. To facilitate matters, we have made *ceteris paribus* assumptions. Specifically, we have assumed the constancy of all prices except the one we are studying (and occasionally one other price, when we wish to see how a change in that price affects the market being studied). Does this mean that our theory is inapplicable to an inflationary world in which all prices are rising at the same time? Fortunately, the answer is no.

The price of a commodity is the amount of money that must be spent to acquire one unit of that commodity. This is called the **absolute price**, or *money price*. A **relative price** is the ratio of two absolute prices; it expresses the price of one good in terms of (i.e., *relative to*) another.

We have mentioned several times that what matters for demand and supply is the price of the commodity in question relative to the prices of other commodities; that is, what matters is the *relative price*.

In an inflationary world, we are often interested in the price of a given commodity as it relates to the average price of all other commodities. If, during a period when the general price level rose by 40 percent, the price of oranges rose by 60 percent, then the price of oranges rose relative to the price level as a whole. Oranges became *relatively* expensive. However, if oranges had risen in price by only 30 percent when the general price level rose by 40 percent, then the relative price of oranges would have fallen. Although the money price of oranges rose substantially, oranges became *relatively* cheap.

In Lewis Carroll's famous story, *Through the Looking-Glass*, Alice finds a country where you have to run in order to stay still. So it is with inflation. A commodity's price must rise as fast as the general level of prices rises just to keep its relative price constant.

It has been convenient in this chapter to analyse changes in particular prices in the context of a constant price level. The analysis is easily extended to an inflationary period by remembering that any force that raises the price of one commodity when other prices remain constant will, given general inflation, raise the price of that commodity more than the price level has risen. For example, a change in tastes in favour of carrots that would raise their price by 20 percent when other prices were constant would raise their price by 32 percent if, at the same time, the general price level rises by 10 percent.[11] In each case, the price of carrots rises 20 percent *relative to the average of all prices*.

In price theory, whenever we talk of a change in the price of one commodity, we mean a change relative to other prices.

If the price level is constant, this change requires only that the money price of the commodity in question rise. If the price level is itself rising, this change requires that the money price of the commodity in question rise more than the price level has risen.

---

[11]Let the price level be 100 in the first case and 110 in the second. Let the price of carrots be 120 in the first case and x in the second. To preserve the same relative price we need x such that $120/100 = x/110$, which makes $x = 132$.

SUMMARY

1. The amount of a commodity that households wish to purchase is called the quantity demanded. It is a flow expressed as so much per period of time. It is determined by tastes, average household income, the commodity's own price, the prices of related commodities, the size of the population, and the distribution of income among households.

2. Quantity demanded is assumed to increase as the price of the commodity falls, other things given. The relationship between quantity demanded and price is represented graphically by a demand curve that shows how much will be demanded at each market price. A movement along a demand curve indicates a change in the quantity demanded in response to a change in the price of the commodity.

3. A shift in a demand curve represents a change in the quantity demanded at each price and is referred to as a change in demand. The demand curve shifts to the right (an increase in demand) if average income rises, if population rises, if the price of a substitute

rises, if the price of a complement falls, or if there is a change in tastes in favour of the product. The opposite changes shift the demand curve to the left (a decrease in demand).

4. The amount of a commodity that firms wish to sell is called the quantity supplied. It is a flow expressed as so much per period of time. It depends on the commodity's own price, the costs of inputs, the goals of the firm, and the state of technology.

5. Quantity supplied is assumed to increase as the price of the commodity increases, ceteris paribus. The relationship between quantity supplied and price is represented graphically by a supply curve that shows how much will be supplied at each market price. A movement along a supply curve indicates a change in the quantity supplied in response to a change in price.

6. A shift in the supply curve indicates a change in the quantity supplied at each price and is referred to as a change in supply. The supply curve shifts to the right (an increase in supply) if the costs of producing the commodity fall or if, for any reason, producers become more willing to produce the commodity. The opposite changes shift the supply curve to the left (a decrease in supply).

7. The equilibrium price is the one at which the quantity demanded equals the quantity supplied. At any price below equilibrium, there will be excess demand; at any price above equilibrium, there will be excess supply. Graphically, equilibrium occurs where the demand and supply curves intersect.

8. Price rises when there is excess demand and falls when there is excess supply. Thus, the actual market price will be pushed toward the equilibrium price, and when it is reached, there will be neither excess demand nor excess supply, and the price will not change until either the supply curve or the demand curve shifts.

9. Using the method of comparative statics, the effects of a shift in either demand or supply can be determined. A rise in demand raises both equilibrium price and equilibrium quantity; a fall in demand lowers both. A rise in supply raises equilibriumquantity but lowers equilibrium price; a fall in supply lowers equilibrium quantity but raises equilibrium price. These are called the laws of demand and supply.

10. Price theory is most simply developed in the context of a constant price level. Price changes discussed in the theory are changes relative to the average level of all prices. The absolute price of a commodity is its price in terms of money; its relative price is its price in relation to other commodities. In an inflationary period, a rise in the relative price of one commodity means that its absolute price rises by more than the price level; a fall in its relative price means that its absolute price rises by less than the price level.

TOPICS FOR REVIEW

Quantity demanded and quantity actually bought

Demand schedule and demand curve

Movement along a curve and shift of a whole curve

Change in quantity demanded and change in demand

Quantity supplied and quantity actually sold

Supply schedule and supply curve

Change in quantity supplied and change in supply

Equilibrium, equilibrium price, and disequilibrium

Comparative statics

Laws of supply and demand

Relative price

DISCUSSION QUESTIONS

1. What shifts in demand or supply curves would produce the following results? (Assume that only one of the two curves has shifted.)
   a. The price of pocket calculators has fallen over the past few years, and the quantity exchanged has risen greatly.
   b. As the average Canadian standard of living rose, both the prices and the consumption of vintage wines rose steadily.
   c. Summer sublets in Kingston, Ontario, are at rents well below the regular rentals.
   d. Changes in styles cause the sale of jeans to decline.
   e. A potato blight causes spud prices to soar.
   f. "Gourmet food market grows as affluent shoppers indulge."
   g. Du Pont increased the price of synthetic fibers, although it acknowledged that demand was weak.
   h. The Edsel was a lemon when it was produced in 1958–1960 but is now a bestseller among cars of its vintage.
   i. Do the same for all the examples given in Box 4-3.

2. Compact disc producers find that they are selling more at the same price than they did two years ago. Is this a shift of the demand curve or a movement along the curve? Suggest at least four reasons why this rise in sales at an unchanged price might occur.

3. What would be the effect on the equilibrium price and quantity of marijuana if its sale were legalized?

4. The relative prices of personal, laptop, and notebook computers dropped continually over time after their initial introduction. Would you explain this falling price in terms of demand or supply changes? What factors are likely to have caused the demand or supply shifts that did occur?

5. Classify the effect of each of the following as (a) a decrease in the demand for fish, (b) a decrease in the quantity of fish demanded, or (c) other. Illustrate each diagrammatically.
   a. The Canadian government closes Grand Banks fishing because of depletion of the stock of cod.
   b. People buy less fish because of a rise in fish prices.
   c. The price of beef falls, and as a result households buy more beef and less fish.
   d. Fears of mercury pollution lead locals to shun fish caught in nearby lakes.
   e. Supermarkets offer bargains in frozen fish.
   f. It is discovered that eating fish is better for one's health than eating meat.
   g. Overfishing greatly reduces the catch of North Atlantic fishing fleets.

6. Predict the effect on the price of at least one commodity of each of the following:
   a. Winter snowfall is at a record high in the Rockies, but drought continues in Eastern ski areas.
   b. A recession decreases employment in Canadian automobile factories.
   c. The French grape harvest is the smallest in 20 years.
   d. Falling trans-Pacific airfares lead to increased Japanese tourism in Canada.

7. Are the following two observations inconsistent? (a) Rising demand for housing causes prices of new homes to soar. (b) Many families refuse to buy homes as prices become prohibitive for them.

8. Some time ago, the U.S. Department of Agriculture predicted that the current excellent weather would result in larger crops of corn and wheat than farmers had expected. But its chief economist warned consumers not to expect prices to decrease because the cost of production was rising and foreign demand for U.S. crops was increasing. "The classic pattern of supply and demand won't work this time," the economist said. Discuss his observation.

APPENDIX TO CHAPTER

4

Foreign Trade

In Chapter 4, we discussed the determination of price in a single domestic market. But what about those goods that are traded internationally? Foreign trade has always been important to Canada. About 25 percent of Canadian national income is currently generated by selling Canadian products in foreign markets—these are Canadian exports. About the same percentage of Canadian national income is spent on purchasing foreign-produced commodities—these are Canadian imports.

The Determination of Imports and Exports

What determines whether a single country, such as Canada, imports or exports some internationally traded commodity? If Canada produces none of the commodity at home—as with coffee and bananas—any domestic consumption must be satisfied by imports. At the other extreme, if Canada is the only (or even the major) world producer, as with nickel, demand in the rest of the world must be met by exports from Canada. What of the many intermediate cases, in which Canada is only one of many producers of an internationally traded commodity, as with beef, oil, and wheat? Will Canada be an exporter or an importer of such commodities, or will it just produce exactly enough to satisfy its domestic demand for the commodity?

The Law Of One Price

Whether Canada imports or exports a commodity for which it is only one of many producers will depend to a great extent on the commodity's price.

The law of one price states that when an easily transported commodity is traded throughout the entire world, it will tend to have a single worldwide price, which economists refer to as the *world price*.

Many basic commodities, such as copper wire, steel pipe, iron ore, and coal, fall within this category. The single price for each good is the price that equates the quantity demanded worldwide with the quantity supplied worldwide.

The single world price of an internationally traded commodity may be influenced greatly, or only slightly, by the demand and supply coming from any one country. The extent of one country's influence will depend on how important its demands and supplies are in relation to the worldwide totals.

A Country Facing Given World Prices

The simplest case for us to study arises when the country, which we will take to be Canada, accounts for only a small part of the total worldwide demand and supply. In this case, Canada does not itself produce enough to influence the world price significantly. Furthermore, Canadian purchasers are too small a proportion of worldwide demand to affect the world price materially. Producers and consumers in Canada thus face a world price that they cannot significantly influence by their own actions.

Notice that in this case the price that rules in the Canadian market must be the world price (adjusted for the exchange rate between the Canadian dollar and the foreign currency). The law of one price says that this must be so. What would happen if the Canadian domestic price diverged from the

FIGURE 4A-1
The Determination of Exports

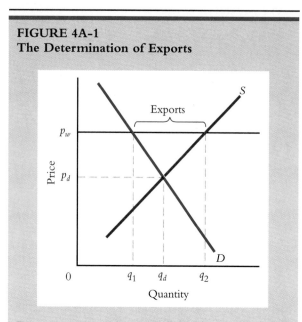

Exports occur whenever there is excess supply domestically at the world price. The domestic demand and supply curves are D and S, respectively. The domestic price in the absence of foreign trade is p_d, with q_d produced *and* consumed domestically. The world price of p_w is higher than p_d. At p_w, q_1 is demanded while q_2 is supplied domestically. The excess of the domestic supply over the domestic demand is exported.

FIGURE 4A-2
The Determination of Imports

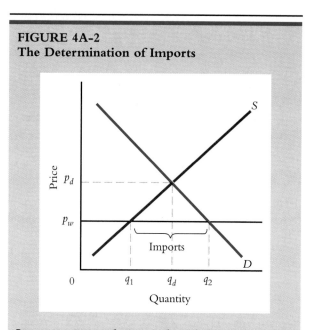

Imports occur whenever there is excess demand domestically at the world price. The domestic demand and supply curves are D and S, respectively. The domestic price in the absence of foreign trade is p_d, with q_d produced *and* consumed domestically. The world price of p_w is less than p_d. At p_w, q_2 is demanded, whereas q_1 is supplied domestically. The excess of domestic demand over domestic supply is satisfied through imports.

world price? If the Canadian domestic price were above the worldwide price, no buyers would buy from a Canadian source, because money could be saved by buying abroad. Conversely, if the Canadian price were below the world price, no supplier would sell in the Canadian market, since more money could be made by selling abroad.

Now let us see what determines the pattern of Canadian foreign trade in such circumstances.

An Exported Commodity

To determine the pattern of Canadian foreign trade, we first show the Canadian domestic demand and supply curves for some commodity, say wheat. The intersection of these two curves tells us what the price and quantity would be *if there were no foreign*

trade. Now compare this no-trade price with the world price of that commodity.[1] If the world price is higher, then the actual price in Canada will exceed the no-trade price. There will be an excess of Canadian supply over Canadian demand, and the surplus production will be exported for sale abroad.

Countries export products whose world price exceeds the price that would rule domestically if there were no foreign trade.

This result is demonstrated in Figure 4A-1.

---

[1] Usually the world price of some commodity is stated in terms of some foreign currency, such as U.S. dollars or Japanese yen. The price must then be converted into Canadian dollars using the current exchange rate between the foreign currency and Canadian dollars.

An Imported Commodity

Now consider some other commodity; for example, oil. Once again, look first at the domestic demand and supply curves, shown this time in Figure 4A-2. The intersection of these curves determines the no-trade price that would rule *if there were no international trade.* The world price of oil is below the Canadian no-trade price, so that, at the price ruling in Canada, domestic demand is larger, and domestic supply is smaller, than if the no-trade price had ruled. The excess of domestic demand over domestic supply is met by imports.

Countries import products whose world price is less than the price that would rule domestically if there were no foreign trade.

This result is demonstrated in Figure 4A-2.

We have now developed the basic theory of how imports and exports are determined in competitive markets. Later in the book, this theory will be used to study the effects on Canadian imports and exports of changes in the world price and of changes in Canadian domestic demand or supply.

5

Elasticity

The laws of demand and supply predict the *direction* of changes in price and quantity in response to various shifts in demand and supply. However, it usually is not enough to know merely whether price and quantity each rise or fall; it is also important to know *how much* each changes.

Measuring and describing the extent of the responsiveness of quantities to changes in prices and other variables is often essential if we are to understand the significance of these changes. This is what the concept of *elasticity* does.

Price Elasticity of Demand

Suppose that there is an increase in a farm crop, that is, a rightward shift in the supply curve. We saw in Figure 4-9 that the equilibrium price will fall and the equilibrium quantity will rise. By how much will each change? The answer depends on a property called the *elasticity of demand*.

This is illustrated in the two parts of Figure 5-1, each of which reproduces the analysis of Figure 4-9 but uses two different demand curves. The two parts of Figure 5-1 have the same initial equilibrium, and that equilibrium is disturbed by the same rightward shift in the supply curve. Because the demand curves are different in the two parts of the figure, the new equilibrium position is different, and hence the magnitude of the effects of the increase in supply on equilibrium price and quantity are different.

A shift in supply will have different quantitative effects, depending on the shape of the demand curve.

The difference may be significant for government policy. Consider what would happen if the rightward shift of the supply curve shown in Figure 5-1 occurs because the government has persuaded farmers to produce more of a certain crop. (It might, for example, have paid a subsidy to farmers for producing that crop.)

Part (i) of Figure 5-1 illustrates a case in which the quantity that consumers demand is relatively responsive to price changes. The rise in production brings down the price, but because the quantity demanded is quite responsive, only a small change in price is necessary to restore equilibrium. The effect of the government's policy, therefore, is to achieve a large increase in the production and sales of this commodity and only a small decrease in price.

Part (ii) of Figure 5-1 shows a case in which the quantity demanded is relatively unresponsive to price changes. As before, the increase in supply at the original price causes a surplus that brings the price down. However, this time the quantity demanded by consumers does not increase much in response to the fall in price. Thus the price continues to

FIGURE 5-1
The Effect of the Shape of the Demand Curve

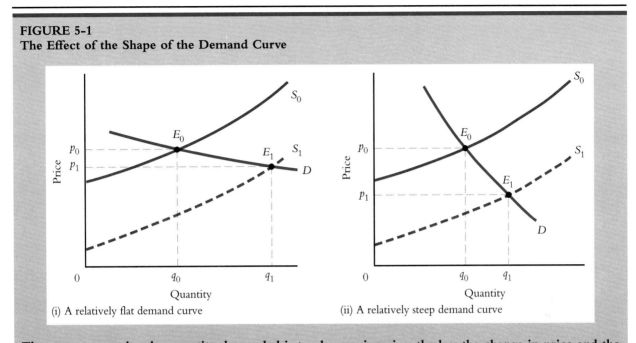

(i) A relatively flat demand curve

(ii) A relatively steep demand curve

The more responsive the quantity demanded is to changes in price, the less the change in price and the greater the change in quantity deriving from any given shift in the supply curve. Both parts of the figure are drawn to the same scale. They show the same initial equilibrium and the same shift in the supply curve. In each part, initial equilibrium is at price p_0 and output q_0 and the new equilibrium is at p_1 and q_1. In part (i) the effect of the shift in supply from S_0 to S_1 is a slight fall in the price and a large increase in quantity. In part (ii) the effect of the identical shift in the supply curve from S_0 to S_1 is a large fall in the price and a relatively small increase in quantity.

drop until, discouraged by lower and lower prices, farmers reduce the quantity supplied nearly to the level that prevailed before they received the subsidy. The effect of the government's policy is to achieve a large decrease in the price of this commodity and only a small increase in the quantity produced and sold.

In both of the cases shown in Figure 5-1, it can be seen that the government's policy has exactly the same effectiveness as far as the farmers' willingness to supply the commodity is concerned—the supply curve shifts are identical. The magnitude of the effects on the *equilibrium* price and quantity, however, are very different because of the different degrees to which the quantity demanded by consumers responds to price changes.

If the purpose of the government's policy is to increase the quantity of this commodity produced and consumed, it will be a great success when the demand curve is similar to the one shown in part (i) of Figure 5-1, but it will be a failure when the demand curve is similar to the one shown in part (ii)

of Figure 5-1. If, however, the purpose of the government's policy is to achieve a large reduction in the price of the commodity, the policy will be a failure when demand is as shown in part (i), but it will be a great success when demand is as shown in part (ii).

The Measurement of Price Elasticity

In Figure 5-1, we were able to say that the curve in part (i) showed a demand that was more responsive to price changes than the curve in part (ii) because two conditions were fulfilled. First, both curves were drawn on the same scale. Second, the initial equilibrium prices and quantities were the same in both parts of the figure. Let us see why these conditions matter.

First, by drawing both figures on the same scale, the curve that looked steeper actually did have the larger absolute slope. (The slope of a demand curve tells us the number of dollars by which price must change to cause a unit change in quantity demanded.) If we had drawn the two curves on different scales, we could have concluded nothing about the relative price changes needed to get a unit change in quantity demanded by comparing their appearances on the graph.[1]

Second, because we started from the same price-quantity equilibrium in both parts of the figure, we did not need to distinguish between percentage changes and absolute changes. If the initial prices and quantities are the same in both cases, the larger absolute change is also the larger percentage change. However, when dealing with different initial price-quantity equilibria, percentage changes are required for comparisons of "more" or "less."

To illustrate, assume we have the data in Table 5-1. They do not tell us much about relative responsiveness because without knowing the original prices and quantities, we do not know if any of the changes shown are large or small. Table 5-2 shows the original *and* new levels of price and quantity. Changes in price and quantity expressed as percentages of the average prices and quantities are shown in the first two columns of Table 5-3. The **price elasticity of demand,** the measure of responsiveness of quantity of a commodity demanded to a change in market price, is symbolized by the Greek letter eta, η. It is defined as

$$\eta = \frac{\text{percentage change in quantity demanded}}{\text{percentage change in price}}$$

This measure is called the **elasticity of demand,** or simply *demand elasticity*. Because the variable causing the change in quantity demanded is the commodity's own price, the term *own price elasticity of demand* is also used. The use of *average* price and quantity is discussed further in Box 5-1. **[8]**

---

[1]It is misleading to infer anything about the responsiveness of quantity to a price change by inspecting the apparent steepness of a graph of a demand curve. By the same token, it can be misleading to infer anything about the relative responsiveness of two different demands by comparing the appearances of their two curves. The reason is that you can make any curve appear as steep or as flat as you wish by changing the scales. For example, a curve that looks steep when the horizontal scale is 1 inch = 100 units will look much flatter when it is drawn on a graph with the same vertical scale but when the horizontal scale is 1 inch = 1 unit.

TABLE 5-1 Price Reductions and Corresponding Increases in Quantity Demanded

Commodity	Reduction in price (cents)	Increases in quantity demanded (per month)
Cheese	20 per pound	7,500 pounds
Men's shirts	20 per shirt	5,000 shirts
Radios	20 per radio	100 radios

The data show, for each of three commodities, the change in quantity demanded in response to the same absolute fall in price. The data are fairly uninformative about the responsiveness of demand to price because they do not tell us either the original price or the original quantity demanded.

Interpreting Numerical Elasticities

Because demand curves have negative slopes, an *increase* in price is associated with a *decrease* in quantity demanded and vice versa. Since the percentage changes in price and quantity have opposite signs, demand elasticity is a negative number. However, we will follow the usual practise of ignoring the negative sign and speak of the measure as a positive number, as we have done in the illustrative calculations in Table 5-3. Thus, the more responsive the quantity demanded (for example, radios relative to cheese), the greater the elasticity of demand and the higher the measure (e.g., 2.0 compared to 0.5).

The numerical value of elasticity can vary from zero to infinity. Elasticity is zero when quantity demanded does not respond at all to a price change. As long as the percentage change in quantity is less than the percentage change in price, the elasticity of demand is less than unity (i.e., less than 1). When the two percentage changes are equal, elasticity is equal to unity. When the percentage change in quantity exceeds the percentage change in price, the elasticity of demand is greater than unity.

When the percentage change in quantity is less than the percentage change in price (elasticity less than 1), demand is said to be **inelastic.** When the percentage change in quantity is greater than the percentage change in price (elasticity greater than 1), demand is said to be an **elastic.** This important terminology is summarized in part A of Box 5-2 on page 94.

TABLE 5-2   Price and Quantity Information Underlying Data of Table 5-1

Commodity	Unit	Original price	New price	Average price	Original quantity	New quantity	Average quantity
Cheese	per pound	$ 1.70	$ 1.50	$ 1.60	116,250	123,750	120,000
Men's shirts	per shirt	8.10	7.90	8.00	197,500	202,500	200,000
Radios	per radio	40.10	39.90	40.00	9,950	10,050	10,000

These data provide the appropriate context for the data given in Table 5-1. The table relates the 20-cent-per-unit price reduction of each commodity to the actual prices and quantities demanded.

A demand curve need not, and usually does not, have the same elasticity over every part of the curve. Figure 5-2 shows that a negatively sloped, straight-line demand curve does not have a constant elasticity. A straight line has constant elasticity only when it is vertical or when it is horizontal. Figure 5-3 illustrates these two cases, plus a third case of a particular *nonlinear* demand curve that also has a constant elasticity.

Price Elasticity and Changes in Total Expenditure

In the absence of sales taxes, the total amount spent by purchasers is also the total revenue received by the sellers, so we can use the terms *total (purchasers') expenditure* and *total (sellers') revenue* interchangeably.[2] How does total expenditure, which is price *times* quantity, react when the price of a product is changed? It turns out that the response of total expenditure depends on the price elasticity of demand.

Because price and quantity move in opposite directions—one falling when the other rises—the change in total expenditure appears to be ambiguous. It is easily shown, however, that the direction of change in total expenditure depends on the relation between percentage changes in the two variables, price and quantity. If the percentage change in price exceeds the percentage change in quantity, then the price change will dominate and total expenditure will change in the same direction as the

price changes; this, of course, is the case of elasticity less than unity. If the percentage change in the price is less than the percentage change in the quantity demanded (elasticity exceeds unity), then the quantity change will dominate and total expenditure will change in the same direction as *quantity* changes (that is, in the opposite direction to the change in price). If the two percentage changes are equal, then total expenditure is unchanged—this is the case of unit elasticity.

The general relationship between elasticity and change in price can be summarized as follows:

1. If demand is elastic, price and total expenditure are negatively related. A fall in price increases total expenditure, and a rise in price reduces it.

TABLE 5-3   Calculation of Demand Elasticities

Commodity	(1) Percentage decrease in price	(2) Percentage increase in quantity	(3) Elasticity of demand (2) ÷ (1)
Cheese	12.5	6.25	0.5
Men's shirts	2.5	2.50	1.0
Radios	0.5	1.00	2.0

Elasticity of demand is the percentage change in quantity divided by the percentage change in price. The percentage changes are based on average prices and quantities shown in Table 5-2. For example, the 20-cent-per-pound decrease in the price of cheese is 12.5 percent of $1.60. A 20-cent change in the price of radios is only 0.5 percent of the average price per radio of $40.

[2]Allowing for sales taxes complicates the analysis substantially and changes the conclusions in small ways but not in broad outline.

Box 5-1

Calculating Price Elasticities Using Averages

The formula in the text stresses that the changes in price and quantity are measured in terms of the *average* values of each. Averages are used in order to avoid the ambiguity caused by the fact that when a price or quantity changes, the change is a different percentage of the original value than it is of the new value. For example, the 20-cent change in the price of cheese shown in Table 5-2 is a different percentage of the original price, $1.70, than it is of the new price, $1.50 (11.8 percent versus 13.3 percent).

Using average values for price and quantity also means that the measured elasticity of demand between any two points A and B is independent of whether the movement is from A to B or from B to A. In the example of cheese in Tables 5-2 and 5-3, the 20-cent change in the price of cheese is unambiguously 12.5 percent of the average price of $1.60, and that percentage applies to a price increase from $1.50 to $1.70, as well as to the decrease discussed in the text.

The implications of using average values for price and quantity for calculating elasticity can be seen as follows. Consider a change from an initial equilibrium with a price of p_0 and an initial quantity of q_0 to a new equilibrium following a shift in

supply with a price of p_1 and a quantity of q_1. The formula for elasticity is then

$$\eta = \frac{(q_1 - q_0)/q}{(p_1 - p_0)/p} \qquad [1]$$

where p and q are the average quantity and average price, respectively. Thus $p = (p_1 + p_0)/2$, and $q = (q_1 + q_0)/2$. These expressions can be substituted for p and q in Equation 1, and canceling the 2s, we get

$$\eta = \frac{(q_1 - q_0)/(q_1 + q_0)}{(p_1 - p_0)/(p_1 + p_0)} \qquad [2]$$

which provides a very convenient formula for calculating elasticity. For example, for the case of cheese in the tables, we have

$$\eta = \frac{7,500/240,000}{0.20/3.20} = \frac{0.03125}{0.0625} = 0.5 \qquad [3]$$

which is as in Table 5-3. Further discussion of the use of averages to calculate elasticity, and of alternative methods, is found in the appendix to this chapter.

2. If demand is inelastic, price and total expenditure are positively related. A fall in price reduces total expenditure, and a rise in price increases it.
3. If elasticity of demand is unity, total expenditure is constant and therefore unrelated to price. A rise or a fall in price leaves total expenditure unaffected.

Table 5-4 and Figure 5-4 illustrate the relationship between elasticity of demand and total expen-

diture; both are based on the straight-line demand curve in Figure 5-2. Total expenditure (equal to the area under the demand curve) at each of a number of points on the demand curve is calculated in Table 5-4, and the general relationship between total expenditure and quantity demanded is shown in Figure 5-4; there we see that expenditure reaches its maximum when elasticity is equal to one. [9]

For example, when a bumper potato crop recently sent prices down 50 percent, quantity sold

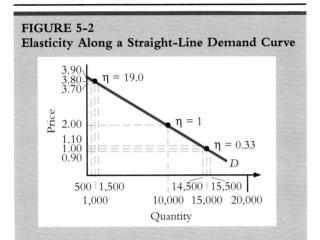

FIGURE 5-2
Elasticity Along a Straight-Line Demand Curve

Moving down a straight-line demand curve, elasticity falls continuously. On this straight-line demand curve, a reduction in price of $0.20 always leads to the same increase (1,000 units) in quantity demanded.[a]

Near the upper end of the curve, where price is $3.80 and quantity demanded is 1,000 units, a reduction in price of $0.20 (from $3.90 to $3.70) is just slightly more than a 5 percent reduction, but the 1,000-unit increase in quantity is a 100 percent increase. Here, elasticity (η) is 19.

Near the lower end, at a price of $1.00 and a quantity of 15,000 units, a price reduction of $0.20 (from $1.10 to $0.90) leads to the same 1,000-unit increase in demand. However, the $0.20 price reduction represents a 20 percent fall, whereas the 1,000-unit increase in quantity demanded represents only a 6.67 percent increase. Here, elasticity is 0.33.

[a]The equation for the demand curve is

$$q^d = 20,000 - 5,000p$$

increased only 15 percent. Demand was clearly inelastic, and the result of the bumper crop was that potato farmers experienced a sharp *fall* in revenues.

Another example can be constructed from Table 5-2. Calculations for what happens to total revenue when the prices of radios, men's shirts, and cheese fall are shown in Table 5-5. In the case of cheese, the demand is inelastic, and a cut in price lowers the sellers' revenue; in the case of radios, the demand is elastic, and a cut in price raises revenue. The borderline case is men's shirts; here, the elastic-

ity is unity, and the cut in price leaves revenue unchanged.

What Determines Elasticity of Demand?

Table 5-6 shows some estimated price elasticities of demand. Evidently, elasticity can vary considerably. The main determinant of elasticity is the availability of substitutes. Some commodities, such as margarine, cabbage, lamb, and Honda Civics, have quite close substitutes—butter, other green vegetables, beef, and the Dodge Colt. A change in the prices of these commodities, *with the prices of their substitutes remaining constant,* will cause much substitution. A fall in price leads consumers to buy more of the commodity and less of the substitutes, and a rise in price leads consumers to buy less of the commodity and more of the substitutes. More broadly defined commodities, such as all foods, all clothing, alcohol, and fuel, have few, if any, satisfactory substitutes. A rise in their prices will cause a smaller fall in quantities demanded than would be the case if close substitutes were available.

A commodity with close substitutes tends to have a more elastic demand than a commodity with no close substitutes.

Closeness of substitutes—and thus measured elasticity—depends on both how the commodity is defined and the time period. This is explored next.

Definition of the Commodity

For food taken as a whole, demand is inelastic over a large price range. It does not follow, however, that any one food, such as white bread or beef, is a necessity in the same sense. Individual foods can have quite elastic demands, and they frequently do.

Clothing provides a similar example. Clothing as a whole is less elastic than individual kinds of clothes. For example, when the price of wool sweaters rises, many households may buy cotton sweaters or down vests instead of buying an additional wool sweater. Thus, although purchases of wool sweaters fall, total purchases of clothing do not.

FIGURE 5-3
Three Demand Curves

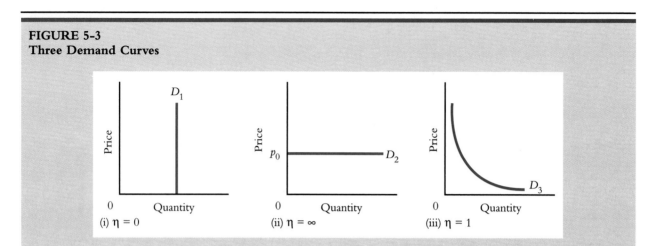

(i) η = 0   (ii) η = ∞   (iii) η = 1

Each of these demand curves has a constant elasticity. D_1 has *zero elasticity:* The quantity demanded does not change at all when price changes. D_2 has *infinite elasticity at the price* p_0: A small price increase from p_0 decreases quantity demanded from an indefinitely large amount to zero. D_3 has *unit elasticity:* A given percentage increase in price brings an equal percentage decrease in quantity demanded at all points on the curve; it is a rectangular hyperbola for which price *times* quantity is a constant.

Any one of a group of related products will have a more elastic demand than the group taken as a whole.

TABLE 5-4   Changes in Total Expenditure for the Demand Curve of Figure 5-2

Price	Quantity	Expenditure
$3.80	1,000	3,800
3.00	5,000	15,000
2.50	7,500	18,750
2.00	10,000	20,000
1.50	12,500	18,750
1.00	15,000	15,000

As price falls along a linear demand curve, total expenditure first rises and then falls.[a] Along the range where price is greater than $2.00, elasticity is greater than one. As a result, the percentage fall in price is smaller than the resulting percentage increase in quantity, and total expenditure rises.

Along the range where price is less than $2.00, elasticity is less than one. As a result, the percentage fall in price is greater than the resulting percentage increase in quantity, and total expenditure falls.

[a]Recall from Figure 5-2 that the equation of the demand curve is

$$q^d = 20,000 - 5,000p$$

FIGURE 5-4
Elasticity of Demand and Total Expenditure

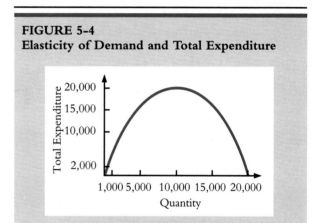

The change in total expenditure on a commodity in response to a change in price depends upon the elasticity of demand. The total expenditure for each possible quantity demanded is plotted for the demand curve in Figure 5-2. For quantities demanded that are less than 10,000, elasticity of demand is greater than one, and hence any increase in quantity demanded will be proportionately larger than the fall in price that caused it. In that range total expenditure is increasing. For quantities greater than 10,000 elasticity of demand is less than one, and hence any increase in quantity demanded will be proportionately smaller than the fall in price that caused it. In that range total expenditures is decreasing. The maximum of total expenditure occurs where the elasticity of demand equals one.

TABLE 5-5   Changes in Total Expenditure (Total Revenue) for the Example of Table 5-2

Commodity	Price X quantity (original prices and quantities)	Price X quantity (new prices and quantities)	Change in revenue (expenditure)	Elasticity of demand from Table 5-3
Cheese	$ 197,625	$ 185,625	−$12,000	0.5
Men's shirts	1,599,750	1,599,750	0	1.0
Radios	398,995	400,995	+ 2,000	2.0

Whether expenditure increases or decreases in response to a price cut depends on whether demand is elastic or inelastic. The $197,625 figure is the product of the original price of cheese ($1.70) and the original quantity (116,250 pounds); $185,625 is the product of the new price ($1.50) and quantity (123,750), and so on.

Long-Run and Short-Run Elasticity of Demand

Because it takes time to develop satisfactory substitutes, a demand that is inelastic in the short run may prove elastic when enough time has passed. For example, at the time when cheap electric power was first brought to rural areas (long after it had come to cities), few farm households were wired for electricity. The initial measurements showed rural demand for electricity to be very inelastic. Some commentators even argued that it was foolish to invest so much money in bringing cheap electricity to farmers because they would not buy it, even at low prices. Gradually, though, farm households became electrified, and as they responded by purchasing electric appliances, measured elasticity steadily increased.

Petroleum provides a more recent example. In the early 1970s, the Organization of Petroleum Exporting Countries (OPEC) cartel shocked the world with a sudden and large increase in the price of oil. At that time, the short-run demand for oil proved to be highly inelastic. Large price increases were met in the short run by very small reductions in quantity demanded. In this case, the short run lasted for several years. Gradually, however, the high price of petroleum products led to such adjustments as the development of smaller, more fuel-efficient cars, economizing on heating oil by installing more efficient insulation, and replacement of fuel oil in many industrial processes with such other power sources as coal and hydroelectricity. The long-run elasticity of demand, relating the change in price to the change in quantity demanded after all adjustments were made, turned out to have an elasticity

of well over 1, although the long-run adjustments took as much as a decade to work out.

The degree of response to a price change, and thus the measured price elasticity of de-

TABLE 5-6   Estimated Price Elasticities of Demand[a] (selected commodities)

Demand significantly inelastic (less than 0.9)	
Potatoes	0.3
Sugar	0.3
Public transportation	0.4
All foods	0.4
Cigarettes	0.5
Gasoline	0.6
All clothing	0.6
Consumer durables	0.8
Demand of close to unit elasticity (between 0.9 and 1.1)	
Beef	
Beer	
Marijuana	
Demand significantly elastic (more than 1.1)	
Furniture	1.2
Electricity	1.3
Lamb and mutton (U.K.)	1.5
Automobiles	2.1
Millinery	3.0

[a]For the United States except where noted.

The wide range of price elasticities is illustrated by these selected measures. These elasticities, from various studies, are representative of literally hundreds of existing estimates. Explanations of some of the differences are discussed in the text.

FIGURE 5-5
Short-Run and Long-Run Demand Curves

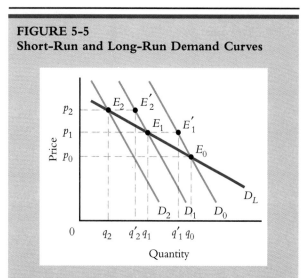

The long-run demand curve is more elastic than the short-run demand curve. D_L is a long-run demand curve. Suppose that consumers are fully adjusted to price p_0. Equilibrium is then at E_0, with quantity demanded q_0. Now suppose that price rises to p_1. In the short run, consumers will react along the short-run demand curve D_0 and adjust consumption to q'_1. Once time has permitted the full range of adjustments to price p_1, however, a new equilibrium E_1 will be reached with quantity q_1. At E_1 there is a new short-run demand curve D_1. A further rise to price p_2 would lead first to a short-run equilibrium at E'_2 but eventually to a new long-run equilibrium at E_2. The long-run demand curve, D_L, is more elastic than any of the short-run curves.

its major effect until the stock of appliances and machines using these commodities has been adjusted. This adjustment may take a long time to occur.

For commodities for which substitutes are developed over a period of time, it is helpful to identify two kinds of demand curves. A *short-run demand curve* shows the response of quantity demanded to a change in price for a given structure of the durable goods that use the commodity and for the existing sets of substitute commodities. A different short-run demand curve will exist for each such structure.

The *long-run demand curve* shows the response of quantity demanded to a change in price after enough time has passed to ensure that all adjustments to the price change have occurred. The relationship between long-run and short-run demand curves is shown in Figure 5-5. The principal conclusion, already suggested in our discussion of elasticity, is this:

The long-run demand curve for a commodity will tend to have a substantially higher elasticity than the short-run demand curves for that commodity.

Other Demand Elasticities

Income Elasticity of Demand

One of the most important determinants of demand is the income of the potential customers. When the Food and Agricultural Organization (FAO) of the United Nations wants to estimate the future demand for some crop, it needs to know by how much world income will grow and how much of that additional income will be spent on that particular foodstuff. As nations get richer, their consumption patterns typically change, with relatively more spent, for example, on meat and relatively less spent on staples such as rice and potatoes.

The responsiveness of demand to changes in income is termed **income elasticity of demand** and is symbolized η_Y.

$$\eta_Y = \frac{\text{percentage change in quantity demanded}}{\text{percentage change in income}}$$

mand, will tend to be greater the longer the time span allowed for quantity to be adjusted to a price change.

Because the elasticity of demand for a commodity changes over time as consumers adjust their habits and substitutes are developed, the demand curve also changes; hence, a distinction can be made between short-run and long-run demand curves. Every demand curve shows the response of consumer demand to a change in price. For such commodities as cornflakes and pillowcases, the full response occurs quickly, and there is little reason to worry about longer-term effects, but other commodities are typically used in connection with highly durable appliances or machines. A change in price of, say, electricity and gasoline may not have

For most goods, increases in income lead to increases in demand—their income elasticity is positive. These are called **normal goods.** Goods for which consumption decreases in response to a rise in income have negative income elasticities and are called **inferior goods.**

The income elasticity of normal goods may be greater than unity (elastic) or less than unity (inelastic), depending on whether the percentage change in the quantity demanded is greater or less than the percentage change in income that brought it about. It is also common to use the terms *income elastic* and *income inelastic* to refer to income elasticities of greater or less than unity. (See Box 5-2 for further discussion of elasticity terminology.)

The reaction of demand to changes in income is extremely important. We know that in most Western countries, economic growth in the first 70 years of this century caused the level of average income to double every 20 to 30 years. This rise in average income has been shared by most citizens. As they found their incomes rising, they increased their demands for most commodities, but the demands for some commodities, such as food and basic clothing, did not increase much, whereas the demands for other commodities increased rapidly. In developing countries, such as Ireland and Mexico, the demand for durable goods is increasing most rapidly as household incomes rise, while in the developed countries of North America and Western Europe, the demand for services has risen most rapidly. The uneven impact of the growth of income on the demands for different commodities has important economic effects, which are studied at several points in this book, beginning with the discussion of agriculture in Chapter 6.

What Determines Income Elasticity?

The variations in income elasticities shown in Table 5-7 suggest that the more basic or staple a commodity, the lower its income elasticity. Food as a whole has an income elasticity of 0.2, consumer durables of 1.8. In Canada, starchy roots such as potatoes are inferior goods; their quantity consumed falls as income rises.

Does the distinction between luxuries and necessities help to explain differences in income elasticities? The table suggests that it does. The case of meals eaten away from home is one example. Such meals are almost always more expensive, calorie for calorie, than meals prepared at home. It would thus be expected that at lower ranges of income, restaurant meals would be regarded as an expensive luxury but that the demand for them would expand substantially as households became richer. This is in fact what happens.

Does this mean that the market demand for the foodstuffs that appear on restaurant menus will also have high income elasticities? Generally, the answer is no. When a household eats out rather than preparing meals at home, the main change is not in what is eaten but in who prepares it. The additional expenditure on food goes mainly to pay cooks and waiters and to yield a return on the restaurateur's capital. Thus, when a household expands its expenditure on restaurant food by 2.4 percent in response to a 1-percent rise in its income, most of the extra expenditure on food goes to workers in service industries; little, if any, finds its way into the pockets of farmers. This is a striking example of the general tendency for households to spend a rising propor-

TABLE 5-7 Estimated Income Elasticities of Demand[a] (selected commodities)

Inferior goods (negative income elasticities)	
Whole milk	−0.5
Pig products	−0.2
Starchy roots	−0.2
Inelastic normal goods (0.0 to 1.0)	
Wine (France)	0.1
All food	0.2
Poultry	0.3
Cheese	0.4
Elastic normal goods (greater than 1.0)	
Gasoline	1.1
Wine	1.4
Cream (U.K.)	1.7
Consumer durables	1.8
Poultry (Sri Lanka)	2.0
Restaurant meals (U.K.)	2.4

[a]For the United States except where noted.

Income elasticities vary widely across commodities and sometimes across countries. The basic source of food estimates by country is the FAO, but many individual studies have been made. Explanations of some of the differences are discussed in the text.

tion of their incomes on services and a lower proportion on foodstuffs as their incomes rise.

The more basic an item is in the consumption pattern of households, the lower is its income elasticity.

So far we have focused on differences in income elasticities among commodities. However, income elasticities for any one commodity also vary with the level of a household's income. When incomes are low, households may eat almost no green vegetables and consume lots of starchy foods, such as bread and potatoes; when incomes are higher, they may eat cheap cuts of meat and more green vegetables along with their bread and potatoes; when incomes are even higher, they are likely to substitute frozen vegetables for canned, and to eat a greater variety of foods.

What is true of individual households is also true of countries. Empirical studies show that for different countries at comparable stages of economic development, income elasticities are similar. However, the countries of the world are at various stages of economic development and so have widely different income elasticities for the same products. Notice in Table 5-7 the different income elasticity of poultry in the United States, where it is a standard item of consumption, and in Sri Lanka, where it is a luxury.

Graphical Representation

Increases in income shift the demand curve to the right for a normal good and to the left for an inferior good. Figure 5-6 shows a different kind of graph, an *income-consumption curve*. The curve resembles an ordinary demand curve in one respect: It shows the relationship of quantity demanded to one other variable, *ceteris paribus*. The other variable is not price, however, but household income. (An increase in the price of the commodity, incomes remaining constant, would shift the curves shown in Figure 5-6 downward.)[3]

The figure shows three different patterns of income elasticity. Goods that consumers regard as ne-

cessities will have high income elasticities at low levels of income but will show low income elasticities beyond some level. The obvious reason is that as incomes rise, it becomes possible for households to devote a smaller proportion of their incomes to meeting basic needs and a larger proportion to buying things they have always wanted but could not afford. Some of the necessities may even become inferior goods. So-called luxury goods will not tend to be purchased at low levels of income but will have high income elasticities once incomes rise enough to permit households to sample the better things of life available to them.

Cross Elasticity of Demand

The responsiveness of demand to changes in the price of another commodity is called the **cross elasticity of demand.** It is often denoted η_{xy} and defined as follows:[4]

$$\eta_{xy} = \frac{\text{percentage change in quantity demanded of one good } (X)}{\text{percentage change in price of another good } (Y)}$$

Cross elasticity can vary from minus infinity to plus infinity. Complementary commodities, such as cars and gasoline, have negative cross elasticities. A large rise in the price of gasoline will lead (as it did in Canada in the 1970s) to a decline in the demand for cars, as some people decide to do without a car and others decide not to buy a second (or third) car. Substitute commodities, such as cars and public transport, have positive cross elasticities. A large rise in the price of cars (relative to public transport) would lead to a rise in the demand for public transport as some people shift from cars to public transport. (See Box 5-2 for a summary of elasticity terminology.)

Measures of cross elasticity sometimes prove helpful in defining whether producers of similar products are in competition. For example, glass bottles and tin cans have a high cross elasticity of demand. The producers of bottles are thus in competi-

---

[3]In Figure 5-6, in contrast to the ordinary demand curve, quantity demanded is on the vertical axis. This follows the usual practise of putting the variable to be explained (called the *dependent variable*) on the vertical axis and the explanatory variable (called the *independent variable*) on the horizontal axis. It is the ordinary demand curve that has the axes "backward."

[4]The change in price of good Y causes the *demand curve* for good X to shift. Holding the price of good X constant means that we can measure the shift in the demand curve in terms of the change in quantity demanded of good X at the given price of good X.

FIGURE 5-6
Income-Consumption Curves of Different Commodities

Different shapes of the curve relating quantity demanded to income correspond to different ranges of income elasticity. Normal goods have rising curves; inferior goods have falling curves. Many different patterns of income elasticity have been observed. The good in part (i) is a typical normal good that is a necessity. It is purchased at all levels of income; even at high levels of income, some fraction of extra income is spent on it, although this fraction steadily decreases. The good in part (ii) is a luxury good that is income-elastic beyond income I_1. The good in part (iii) is a necessity at low incomes but becomes an inferior good for incomes beyond I_2.

tion with the producers of cans. If bottle companies raise their prices, they will lose substantial sales to can producers. Men's shoes and women's shoes have a low cross elasticity. A producer of men's shoes is not in close competition with a producer of women's shoes. If the former raises its price, it will not lose many sales to the latter. Knowledge of cross elasticities can be important in anti-combines investigations in which the issue is whether a firm in one industry is or is not competing with firms in another industry. Whether waxed paper and plastic wrap or aluminum cable and copper cable are or are not substitutes may determine questions of monopoly under the law. The positive or negative sign of cross elasticities tells us whether or not goods are substitutes.

Elasticity of Supply

The concept of elasticity can be applied to supply as well as to demand. **Elasticity of supply** measures the responsiveness of the quantity supplied to a change in the commodity's price. It is denoted η_S and defined as

$$\eta_S = \frac{\text{percentage change in quantity supplied}}{\text{percentage change in price}}$$

This is often called *supply elasticity.* The supply curves considered in this chapter all have positive slopes: An increase in price causes an increase in quantity sold. Such supply curves all have positive elasticities because price and quantity both change in the same direction.

There are important special cases. If the supply curve is vertical—the quantity supplied does not change as price changes—then elasticity of supply is zero. This would be the case, for example, if suppliers produced a given quantity and dumped it on the market for whatever it would bring. A horizontal supply curve has an infinitely high elasticity of supply: A small drop in price would reduce the quantity producers are willing to supply from an indefinitely large amount to zero. Between these two extremes, elasticity of supply varies with the shape of the supply curve.[5]

---

[5]Steepness, which is related to absolute rather than percentage changes, is not always a reliable guide. For example, as is shown in the appendix to this chapter, *any* upward-sloping straight line passing through the origin has an elasticity of +1.0 over its entire range.

Box 5-2

Terminology of Elasticity

Term	Symbol	Numerical measure of elasticity	Verbal description
A. Price elasticity of demand (supply)	η (η_s)		
Perfectly or completely inelastic	Zero		Quantity demanded (supplied) does not change as price changes.
Inelastic		Greater than zero, less than one	Quantity demanded (supplied) changes by a smaller percentage than does price.
Unit elasticity		One	Quantity demanded (supplied) changes by exactly the same percentage as does price.
Perfectly, completely, or infinitely elastic		Infinity	Purchasers (sellers) are prepared to buy (sell) all they can at some price and none at all at an even higher (lower) price
B. Income elasticity of demand	η_Y		
Inferior good		Negative	Quantity demanded decreases as income increases.
Normal good		Positive	Quantity demanded increases as income increases:
Income inelastic		Less than one	Less than in proportion to income increase
Income elastic		Greater than one	More than in proportion to income increase
C. Cross elasticity of demand	η_{xy}		
Substitute		Positive	Price increase of a substitute leads to an increase in quantity demanded of this good (and less of the substitute).
Complement		Negative	Price increase of a complement leads to a decrease in quantity demanded of this good (as well as less of the complement).

Determinants of Supply Elasticity

Supply elasticities are important for many problems in economics. Much of the treatment of demand elasticity carries over to supply elasticity. For example, the ease of substitution can vary in production as well as in consumption. If the price of a commodity rises, how much more can be produced profitably? This depends in part on how easy it is for producers to shift from the production of other commodities to the one whose price has risen. If agricultural land and labour can be readily shifted from one crop to another, the supply of any one crop will be more elastic than if they cannot.

Supply elasticity depends to a great extent on how costs behave as output is varied, an issue that will be treated at length in Part 3. If the costs of producing a unit of output rise rapidly as output rises, then the stimulus to expand production in response to a rise in price will quickly be choked off by increases in costs. In this case, supply will tend to be rather inelastic. If, however, the costs of producing a unit of output rise only slowly as production increases, a rise in price that raises profits will elicit a large increase in quantity supplied before the rise in costs puts a halt to the expansion in output. In this case, supply will tend to be rather elastic.

Long-Run and Short-Run Elasticity of Supply

As with demand, length of time for response is important. It may be difficult to change quantities supplied in response to a price increase in a matter of weeks or months but easy to do so over a period of years. An obvious example is the planting cycle of crops. Also, new oil fields can be discovered, wells drilled, and pipelines built over a period of years, but not in a few months. Thus elasticity of oil supply is much greater over five years than over one year. We explore some of the implications of the distinction between short-run and long-run elasticity in the next chapter.

SUMMARY

1. *Price elasticity of demand,* also called simply *elasticity of demand,* is a measure of the extent to which the quantity demanded of a commodity responds to a change in its price. It is defined as the percentage change in quantity demanded divided by the percentage change in price that brought it about; the percentage changes are usually calculated as the change divided by the *average value.* Elasticity is defined to be a positive number, and it can vary from zero to infinity.

2. When the numerical measure of elasticity is less than unity, demand is *inelastic.* This means that the percentage change in quantity demanded is less than the percentage change in price that brought it about. When the numerical measure exceeds unity, demand is *elastic.* This means that the percentage change in quantity demanded is greater than the percentage change in price that brought it about.

3. Elasticity and total revenue of sellers are related in the following way: If elasticity is less than unity, total revenue is positively associated with price; if elasticity is greater than unity, total revenue is negatively associated with price; and if elasticity is unity, total revenue does not change as price changes.

4. The main determinant of the price elasticity of demand is the availability of substitutes for the commodity. Any one of a group of close substitutes will have a more elastic demand than the group as a whole.

5. Elasticity of demand tends to be greater the longer the time over which adjustment occurs. Items that have few substitutes in the short run may develop many substitutes when consumers and producers have time to adapt.

6. *Income elasticity of demand* is the percentage change in quantity demanded divided by the percentage change in income that brought it about. The income elasticity of demand for a commodity will usually change as income varies. For example, a commodity that has a high income elasticity at a low income (because increases in income bring it within reach of the typical household) may have a low or negative income elasticity at higher incomes (because as incomes rise, it is gradually replaced by a superior substitute).

7. *Cross elasticity of demand* is the percentage change in quantity demanded divided by the percentage change in the price of some other commodity. It is used to define commodities that are substitutes for one another (positive cross elasticity) and commodities that complement one another (negative cross elasticity).

8. *Elasticity of supply* is an important concept in economics. It measures the ratio of the percentage change in the quantity supplied of a commodity to the percentage change in its price. It is the analogue on the supply side to the elasticity of demand. Supply tends to be more elastic in the long run than in the short run.

TOPICS FOR REVIEW

Elasticity of demand

Inelastic and perfectly inelastic demand

Elastic and infinitely elastic demand

Relationship between demand elasticity and total expenditure

Short-run and long-run demand curves

Income elasticity of demand

Income-elastic and income-inelastic demands

Normal goods and inferior goods

Cross elasticity of demand

Substitutes and complements

Elasticity of supply

DISCUSSION QUESTIONS

1. From the following quotations, what, if anything, can you conclude about elasticity of demand?

    a. "Good weather resulted in record corn harvests and sent prices tumbling. For many farmers, the result has been calamitous."

    b. "Ridership always went up when bus fares came down, but the increased patronage never was enough to prevent a decrease in overall revenue."

    c. "As the price of compact disc players fell, producers found their revenues soaring."

    d. "Canadian Airlines International slashes transcontinental fares in an attempt to fill empty seats."

2. Advocates of minimal charges for people using doctors' services in Canada hope that this will greatly reduce the cost to the government while not denying essential medical services to anyone. Opponents argue that even minimal charges will deny critical services to lower-income Canadians. Use elasticity terminology to restate the views of each of these groups.

3. What would you predict about the relative price elasticity of demand of (a) food, (b) vegetables, (c) artichokes, and (d) artichokes sold at the local supermarket? What would you predict about their relative income elasticities?

4. "Avocados have a limited market, not greatly affected by price until the price falls to less than 25 cents a pound. Then they are much demanded by manufacturers of dog food." Interpret this statement in terms of price elasticity.

5. "Laptop and notebook computers were a leader in sales appeal through much of the 1980s. But per capita sales are much lower in Mexico than in Canada and lower in Newfoundland than in British Columbia. Manufacturers are puzzled by the big differences." Can you offer an explanation in terms of elasticity?

6. What elasticity measure or measures would be useful in answering the following questions?
   a. Will cheaper transport into the central city help keep downtown shopping centres profitable? Will it reduce the congestion caused by private cars?
   b. Will raising the bulk postage rate increase or decrease the postal deficit?
   c. Are producers of toothpaste and mouthwash in competition with each other?
   d. What effect will rising gasoline prices have on the sale of cars that run on diesel?

7. Interpret the following statements in terms of the relevant elasticity concept.
   a. "As fuel for tractors has become more expensive, many farmers have shifted from plowing their fields to no-till farming. No-till acreage increased from 30 million acres in 1972 to 95 million acres in 1982."
   b. "Fertilizer makers brace for dismal year as prices soar."
   c. "When farmers are hurting, small towns feel the pain."
   d. "The development of the Hibernia oil field may bring temporary prosperity to Newfoundland merchants."

8. Suggest commodities that you think might have the following patterns of elasticity of demand.
   a. High income elasticity, high price elasticity
   b. High income elasticity, low price elasticity
   c. Low income elasticity, low price elasticity
   d. Low income elasticity, high price elasticity

9. Faced with growing deficits the New York City Opera cut its ticket prices by 20 percent, while the New York Transit Authority raised subway fares. Could both of these approaches to reducing a deficit be right?

APPENDIX TO CHAPTER

5

Elasticity: A Formal Analysis

The verbal definition of elasticity used in the text may be written symbolically in the following form:

$$\eta = \frac{\Delta q}{\text{average } q} \div \frac{\Delta p}{\text{average } p}$$

where the averages are over the range, or arc, of the demand curve being considered.[1] Rearranging terms, we can write

$$\eta = \frac{\Delta q}{\Delta p} \times \frac{\text{average } p}{\text{average } q}$$

This is called **arc elasticity,** and it measures the average responsiveness of quantity to price over an interval of the demand curve.

Most theoretical treatments use a different but related concept called **point elasticity.** This is the measure of responsiveness of quantity to price at a particular point on the demand curve. The precise definition of point elasticity uses the concept of a derivative, which is drawn from differential calculus.

In this appendix we first study arc elasticity, which may be regarded as an approximation of point elasticity. Then we study point elasticity.

Before proceeding, we should notice one further change. In the text of Chapter 5, we reported our price elasticities as positive values and thus implicitly multiplied all our calculations by -1. In theoretical work, it is more convenient to retain the

concept's natural sign. Thus normal demand elasticities will have negative signs, and statements about "more" or "less" elasticity must be understood to refer to the absolute, not the algebraic, value of demand elasticity.

Arc Elasticity as an Approximation of Point Elasticity

Point elasticity measures elasticity at some point *(p, q)*. In the approximate definition, however, the responsiveness is measured over a small range starting from that point. For example, in Figure 5A-1, the elasticity at point 1 can be measured by the responsiveness of quantity demanded to a change in price that takes price and quantity from point 1 to point 2. The algebraic formula for this elasticity concept is

$$\eta = \frac{\Delta q}{\Delta p} \times \frac{p}{q} \qquad [1]$$

This is similar to the definition of arc elasticity, except that, because elasticity is being measured at a point, the p and q corresponding to that point are used (rather than the average p and q over an arc of the curve).

Equation 1 splits elasticity into two parts: $\Delta q/\Delta p$ (the ratio of the change in quantity to the change in price), which is related to the *slope* of the demand curve, and p/q, which is related to the *point* on the curve at which the measurement is made.

Figure 5A-1 shows a straight-line demand curve. To measure the elasticity at point 1, take p and q at that point and then consider a price change, say, to point 2, and measure Δp and Δq as indicated. The slope of the straight line joining

---

[1]The following symbols will be used throughout.

η = elasticity of demand

η_s = elasticity of supply

q = the original quantity

Δq = the change in quantity

p = the original price

Δp = the change in price

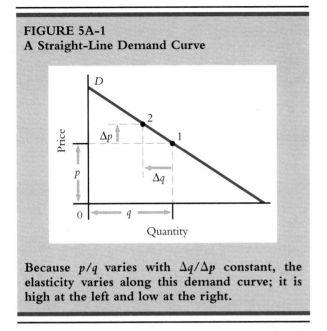

FIGURE 5A-1
A Straight-Line Demand Curve

Because *p/q* varies with Δ*q*/Δ*p* constant, the elasticity varies along this demand curve; it is high at the left and low at the right.

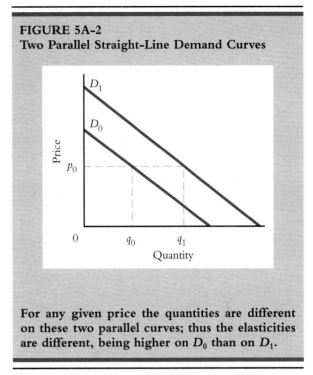

FIGURE 5A-2
Two Parallel Straight-Line Demand Curves

For any given price the quantities are different on these two parallel curves; thus the elasticities are different, being higher on D_0 than on D_1.

points 1 and 2 is Δ*p*/Δ*q*. The term in Equation 1 is Δ*q*/Δ*p*, which is the reciprocal of Δ*p*/Δ*q*. Therefore, the first term in the elasticity formula is the reciprocal of the slope of the straight line joining the two price-quantity positions under consideration.

Although point elasticity of demand refers to a point *(p,q)* on the demand curve, the first term in Equation 1 still refers to changes over an arc of the curve. This is the part of the formula that involves approximation, and, as we shall see, it has some unsatisfactory results. Nonetheless, some interesting theorems can be derived by using this formula as long as we confine ourselves to straight-line demand and supply curves.

1.   *The elasticity of a downward-sloping straight-line demand curve varies from zero at the quantity axis to infinity at the price axis.* First, notice that a straight line has a constant slope, so the ratio Δ*p*/Δ*q* is the same everywhere on the line. Therefore its reciprocal, Δ*q*/Δ*p*, must also be constant. The changes in η can now be inferred by inspecting the ratio *p/q*. Where the line cuts the quantity axis, price is zero, so the ratio *p/q* is zero; thus $\eta = 0$. Moving up the line, *p* rises and *q* falls, so the ratio *p/q* rises; thus elasticity rises. Approaching the top of the line, *q* approaches zero, so the ratio becomes very large. Thus elasticity increases without limit as the price axis is approached.

2.   *Where there are two straight-line demand curves of the same slope, the one farther from the origin is less elastic at each price than the one closer to the origin.* Figure 5A-2 shows two parallel straight-line demand curves. Compare the elasticities of the two curves at any price, say p_0. Because the curves are parallel, the ratio Δ*q*/Δ*p* is the same on both curves. Because elasticities at the same price are being compared on both curves, *p* is the same, and the only factor left to vary is *q*. On the curve farther from the origin, quantity is larger (i.e., $q_1 > q_0$) and hence p_0/q_1 is smaller than p_0/q_0; thus η is smaller.

It follows from theorem 2 that parallel shifts of a straight-line demand curve lower elasticity (at each price) when the line shifts outward and raise elasticity when the line shifts inward.

3.   *The elasticities of two intersecting straight-line demand curves can be compared at the point of intersection merely by comparing slopes, the steeper curve being the less elastic.* In Figure 5A-3 there are two intersecting curves. At the point of intersection, *p* and *q* are common to both curves and hence the ratio *p/q* is the same. Therefore η varies only with Δ*q*/Δ*p*. On the steeper curve, Δ*q*/Δ*p* is smaller than on the flatter curve, so elasticity is lower.

4.   *If the slope of a straight-line demand curve changes while the price intercept remains constant, elastic-*

FIGURE 5A-3
Two Intersecting Straight-Line Demand Curves

Elasticities are different at the point of intersection of these demand curves because the slopes are different, being higher on D_0 than on D_1. Therefore, D_1 is more elastic than D_0 at p_0.

FIGURE 5A-4
Two Straight-Line Demand Curves from the Same Price Intercept

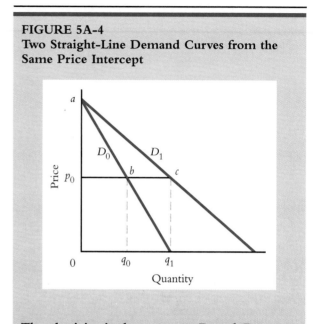

The elasticity is the same on D_0 and D_1 at any price p_0. This situation occurs because the steeper slope of D_0 is exactly offset by the smaller quantity demanded at any price.

ity at any given price is unchanged. This is an interesting case for at least two reasons. First, when more customers having similar tastes to those already in the market enter the market, the demand curve pivots outward in this way. Second, when more firms enter a market that is shared proportionally among all firms, each firm's demand curve shifts inward in this way.

Consider in Figure 5A-4 the elasticities at point b on demand curve D_0 and at point c on the demand curve D_1. We shall focus on the two triangles, abp_0 on D_0 and acp_0 on D_1, formed by the two straight-line demand curves emanating from point a and by the price p_0.

The price p_0 is the line segment $0p_0$. The quantities q_0 and q_1 are the line segments p_0b and p_0c, respectively. The slope of D_0 is $\Delta p/\Delta q = ap_0/p_0b$ and the slope of D_1 is $\Delta p/\Delta q = ap_0/p_0c$. From Equation 1, we can represent the elasticities of D_0 and D_1 at the points b and c, respectively, as

η at point $b = (p_0b/ap_0) \times (0p_0/p_0b) = (0p_0/ap_0)$

η at point $c = (p_0c/ap_0) \times (0p_0/p_0c) = (0p_0/ap_0)$

The two are the same. The reason is that the distance corresponding to the quantity demanded at p_0 appears in both the numerator and the denominator and thus cancels out.

Put differently, if the straight-line demand curve D_0 is twice as steep as D_1, it has half the quantity demanded at p_0. Therefore, in the expression

$$\eta = \frac{\Delta q}{\Delta p} \times \frac{p}{q}$$

the steeper slope (a smaller Δq for the same Δp) is exactly offset by the smaller quantity demanded (a smaller q for the same p).

5. *Any straight-line supply curve through the origin has an elasticity of one.* Such a supply curve is shown in Figure 5A-5. Consider the two triangles with the sides p, q, and the S curve and Δp, Δq, and the S curve. Clearly, these are similar triangles. Therefore, the ratios of their sides are equal: that is,

$$\frac{p}{q} = \frac{\Delta p}{\Delta q} \qquad [2]$$

Elasticity of supply is defined as

$$\eta_s = \frac{\Delta q}{\Delta p} \times \frac{p}{q}$$

FIGURE 5A-5
A Straight-Line Supply Curve Through the Origin

At every point on the curve, p/q equals $\Delta p/\Delta q$; thus elasticity equals unity at every point.

FIGURE 5A-6
Point Elasticity of Demand Measured by the Approximate Formula

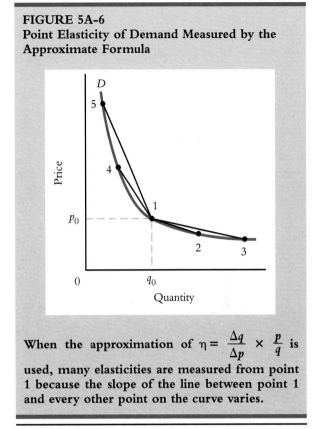

When the approximation of $\eta = \dfrac{\Delta q}{\Delta p} \times \dfrac{p}{q}$ is used, many elasticities are measured from point 1 because the slope of the line between point 1 and every other point on the curve varies.

which, by substitution from Equation 2, gives

$$\eta_s = \frac{q}{p} \times \frac{p}{q} \equiv 1$$

6. *The elasticity measured from any point (p,q), according to Equation 1, is dependent on the direction and magnitude of the change in price and quantity.* Except for a straight line (for which the slope does not change), the ratio $\Delta q/\Delta p$ will not be the same over different ranges of a curve. Figure 5A-6 shows a demand curve that is not a straight line. To measure the elasticity from point 1, the ratio $\Delta q/\Delta p$—and thus η—will vary according to the size and the direction of the price change.

Theorem 6 yields a result that is very inconvenient and is avoided by use of a different definition of point elasticity.

Point Elasticity According to the Precise Definition

To measure the elasticity at a point exactly, it is necessary to know the reaction of quantity to a change in price *at that point,* not over a range of the curve.

The reaction of quantity to price change at a point is called dq/dp, and this is defined to be the reciprocal of the slope of the straight line tangent to the demand curve at the point in question. In Figure 5A-7 the elasticity of demand at a point 1 is the ratio p/q (as it has been in all previous measures), now multiplied by the ratio of $\Delta q/\Delta p$ measured along the straight line T, tangent to the curve at point 1, that is, by dq/dp. Thus the exact definition of point elasticity is

$$\eta = \frac{dq}{dp} \times \frac{p}{q} \qquad [3]$$

The ratio dq/dp, as defined, is in fact the differential calculus concept of the *derivative* of quantity with respect to price.

This definition of point elasticity is the one normally used in economic theory. Equation 1 is mathematically only an approximation of this ex-

FIGURE 5A-7
Point Elasticity of Demand Measured by the Exact Formula

When the exact definition $\eta = \dfrac{dq}{dp} \times \dfrac{p}{q}$ is used, only one elasticity is measured from point 1 because there is only one tangent to the demand curve at that point.

pression. In Figure 5A-7 arc elasticity will come closer to point elasticity the smaller the price change used to calculate the arc elasticity. The $\Delta q/\Delta p$ in Equation 1 is the reciprocal of the slope of the line connecting the two points being compared. As the two points get closer together the slope of the line joining them gets closer to that of the tangent T. (Compare the lines connecting point 1 to b' and b'' in Figure 5A-7.) Thus, the error in using Equation 1 as an approximation of Equation 3 tends to diminish as the size of Δp diminishes.

6

Supply and Demand in Action

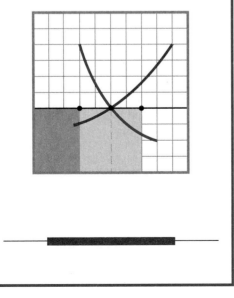

Now that you have mastered the theory of how prices are determined by supply and demand, you have a very powerful tool at your command. However, a full understanding of any theory comes only with practise. This chapter is designed to give you that practise; we start by reviewing some theoretical issues and then turn to some cases drawn from real-world experience. Although we hope that these illustrations are interesting in themselves, the most important reason for studying them is to master the theory so that you can use it to understand other cases.

We start by reviewing and extending our earlier discussion of the method of comparative statics, first encountered on page 72. This method, you will recall, starts from a position of market equilibrium and then introduces the disturbance to be studied. The new equilibrium position is then determined and compared with the original one.

For example, equilibrium in the market for carrots might be disturbed by an increase in supply due to a bumper crop this year; this will in turn lead to a new equilibrium in the market for carrots. A comparison of the price and quantity in the new and the original equilibrium shows the predicted effects of the bumper crop. This comparative statics analysis is illustrated in Figure 5-1 on page 83.

Who Pays Sales Taxes?

One interesting question that supply and demand analysis can shed some light on is: Who pays when provincial governments levy sales taxes on commodities? At the point of sale, sellers typically collect the tax on behalf of the government and then periodically remit the tax collections. When they write the check to the government, these firms feel—with some justification—that they pay. Consumers, however, argue—again, with some justification—that the tax causes the price to go up, and hence they pay.

The question of who bears the burden of a tax is called the question of *tax incidence*.[1] A straightforward application of supply and demand analysis will show that incidence of a sales tax does not depend on whether the government collects it directly from the consumer or from the firm.

The burden of a sales tax is distributed between consumers and sellers in a manner that depends upon the elasticities of supply and demand.

Consider the market for beer, as illustrated in Figure 6-1. Initially, there is no sales tax, and the initial equilibrium is as illustrated by the solid supply and demand curves.

---

[1]Tax incidence is studied further in Chapter 22.

FIGURE 6-1
The Incidence of a Sales Tax

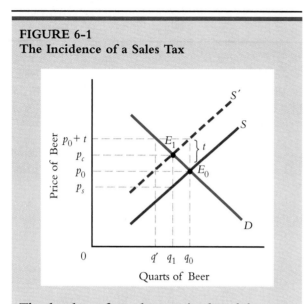

Quarts of Beer

The burden of a sales tax is shared by consumers and producers. The original supply and demand curves for beer are given by the solid lines S and D; equilibrium is at E_0 with price p_0 and quantity q_0.

When a sales tax of t per quart is imposed, the supply curve shifts up to the dashed line S', which lies above the original supply curve by the amount of the tax, t. If the market price were to rise by the amount of the sales tax, to $p_0 + t$, there would now be excess supply. Consumers, facing a price of $p_0 + t$, would reduce their quantity demanded from q_0 to q'. Quantity supplied by firms would remain at q_0 because the rise in the price fully offsets the effect of the tax on their net receipts per unit; that is, when the consumer price rises to $p_0 + t$, the seller price remains at p_0.

The new equilibrium is at E_1. The consumer price rises to p_c (less than $p_0 + t$), the seller price falls to p_s, and the equilibrium quantity falls to q_1.

What happens when a sales tax of t per unit is introduced? A sales tax means that the price paid by the consumer, called the *consumer price,* and the price received by the seller, called the *seller price,* now differ by the amount of the tax, t.

In terms of the figure, the effect of the sales tax can be analysed by considering a new supply curve, S', that is above the original supply curve, S, by the amount of the tax per quart of beer, t. To understand this new curve, consider the situation of sellers at the original equilibrium quantity, q_0. In order to supply that quantity, sellers must receive p_0 per quart

of beer sold. However, for this to occur when there is a sales tax on beer, the consumer must pay a total price of $p_0 + t$. (This is true whether the consumer "pays the tax directly" by giving p_0 to the producers and t to the government, or whether the consumer pays the total $p_0 + t$ to the sellers and the sellers then remit the tax t to the government.) Thus, after the imposition of the sales tax, the supply curve, *which relates quantities supplied to the price consumers pay,* lies above the original supply curve, *which relates quantity supplied to the price received by sellers.*

In terms of the total or tax-inclusive price paid by the consumer, the supply curve shifts up by the amount of the sales tax.

Now consider the situation at the consumer price of $p_0 + t$. Firms will still be willing to sell the original quantity, but households will demand less because the price has risen; there is excess supply and, hence, pressure for the consumer price to fall.

The new equilibrium after the imposition of the sales tax occurs at the intersection of the original demand curve, D, with the tax-shifted supply curve, S'. At this new equilibrium, the quantity demanded at the consumer price is equal to the quantity supplied at the sellers' price. As shown in the figure, compared to the original equilibrium, the quantity exchanged falls. Also, the consumer price rises and the seller price falls, although in each case the change in price is less than the full extent of the sales tax.

After the imposition of a sales tax, the difference between the consumer and seller prices is equal to the tax, and hence the sum of the increase in the consumer price and the decrease in the seller price is equal to the tax. In the new equilibrium, the quantity exchanged is less than that exchanged prior to the imposition of the tax.

The role of elasticities of supply and demand is illustrated in Figure 6-2. In part (i), demand is very inelastic; as a result, the fall in quantity is quite small, whereas the price paid by consumers rises by almost the full extent of the tax. Because neither the price received by sellers nor the quantity sold change very much, sellers bear little of the burden of the tax. In part (ii), the supply curve is quite inelastic; now consumers continue to purchase almost

FIGURE 6-2
Elasticity and Sales Tax Incidence

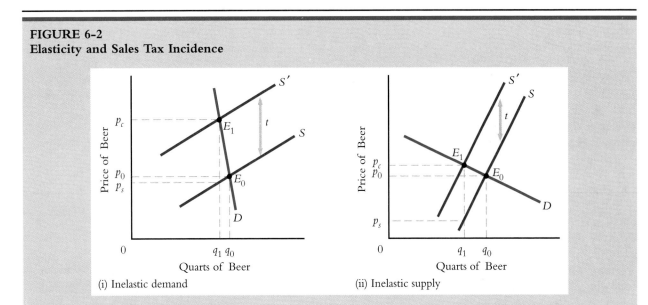

(i) Inelastic demand

(ii) Inelastic supply

The distribution of the burden of a sales tax between consumers and producers depends upon the elasticities of supply and demand. In both parts of the figure, the initial supply and demand curves are given by S and D; the initial equilibrium is at E_0 with equilibrium price p_0 and quantity q_0. A sales tax of t per quart is imposed, causing the supply curve to shift up by the amount of the tax to S'. The new equilibrium is at E_1. The consumer price rises to p_c, the seller price falls to p_s, and the quantity falls to q_1.

In part (i), the demand curve is very inelastic. Because the rise in the consumer price does not induce a very significant fall in quantity demanded, the consumer price rises by almost the full extent of the tax and the seller price falls only a little; as a result, most of the burden of the tax is borne by consumers.

In part (ii), the supply curve is very inelastic. Because the fall in the seller price does not induce a very significant fall in quantity supplied, the seller price falls by almost the full extent of the tax and the consumer price rises only a little; as a result, most of the burden of the tax is borne by producers.

the same quantity with little change in the price, and hence consumers bear little of the burden of the tax.

Government-Controlled Prices

Our next application concerns a number of important cases that arise when the government fixes the price at which a commodity must be sold on the domestic market.

The equilibrium price in a free market occurs at the price at which the quantity demanded equals the quantity supplied. Government **price controls** are policies that attempt to hold the price at some disequilibrium value that could not be maintained in the absence of the government's intervention. Some controls hold the market price below its equilibrium value; this creates a shortage, with quantity demanded exceeding quantity supplied at the controlled price. Other controls hold price above equilibrium; this creates a surplus, with quantity supplied exceeding quantity demanded at the controlled price.

Disequilibrium Prices

Generally, market price changes whenever quantity supplied does not equal quantity demanded. Price then moves toward its equilibrium value, at which point there are neither unsatisfied suppliers nor unsatisfied demanders.

When controls hold price at some disequilibrium value, what determines the quantity actually traded on the market? The key to the answer is the fact that any voluntary market transaction requires both a willing buyer and a willing seller. This means that if quantity demanded is less than quantity supplied, demand will determine the amount actually exchanged, while the rest of the quantity supplied will remain in the hands of the unsuccessful sellers. On the other hand, if quantity demanded exceeds quantity supplied, supply will determine the amount actually exchanged, while the rest of the quantity demanded will represent desired purchases of unsuccessful buyers. This argument is spelled out in more detail in Figure 6-3, which establishes the following general conclusion:

At any disequilibrium price, quantity exchanged is determined by *the lesser* of quantity demanded or quantity supplied.

Price Floors

The government sometimes establishes a **price floor,** which is the minimum permissible price that can be charged for a particular good or a service. A price floor that is set at or below the equilibrium price has no effect, because equilibrium remains attainable. If, however, the price floor is set above the equilibrium, it will raise the price, in which case it is said to be *binding* or *effective.*

Price floors may be established by rules that make it illegal to sell the commodity below the prescribed price, as in the case of the minimum wage (examined in Chapter 17). Further, the government may establish a price floor by announcing that it will guarantee a certain price by buying any excess supply of the product that emerges at that price. Such guarantees are a feature of many agricultural support policies (examined later in this chapter).

The effects of binding price floors are illustrated in Figure 6-4, which establishes the following key result:

Effective price floors lead to excess supply. Either an unsold surplus will exist or some-

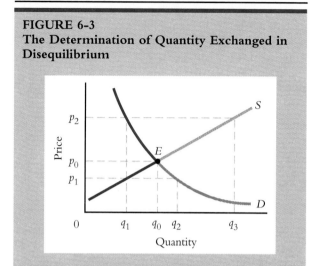

FIGURE 6-3
The Determination of Quantity Exchanged in Disequilibrium

In disequilibrium, quantity exchanged is determined by *whichever is less*, quantity demanded or quantity supplied. At p_0 the market is in equilibrium, with quantity demanded equal to quantity supplied at q_0. For prices below p_0, the quantity exchanged will be determined by the supply curve. For example, the quantity q_1 will be exchanged at the disequilibrium price p_1 in spite of the excess demand of q_1q_2. For prices above p_0, the quantity exchanged will be determined by the demand curve. For example, the quantity q_1 will be exchanged at the disequilibrium price p_2 in spite of the excess supply of q_1q_3. Thus the darker portions of the S and D curves show the actual quantities exchanged at different prices.

one must enter the market and buy the excess supply.

The consequences of excess supply will, of course, differ from commodity to commodity. If the commodity is labour, subject to a minimum wage, excess supply translates into people without jobs. If the commodity is wheat, and more is produced than can be sold, the surplus wheat will accumulate in grain elevators or government warehouses. These consequences may or may not be worth it in terms of the other goals achieved. Whether they are worth it or not, these consequences are inevitable whenever a price floor is set above the market-clearing equilibrium price.

Why might the government wish to incur these consequences? One reason is that those who actu-

FIGURE 6-4
A Price Floor

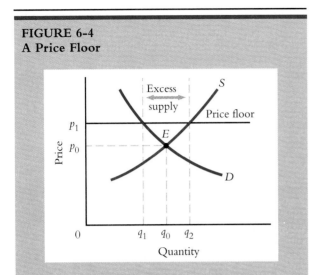

If a price floor is above the equilibrium price, quantity supplied will exceed quantity demanded. The free market equilibrium is at E, with price p_0 and quantity q_0. The government now establishes an effective price floor at p_1. Quantity supplied exceeds quantity demanded by q_1q_2.

If the government does nothing else, this excess supply will either go to waste or accumulate in the sellers' inventories. If the government buys the excess supply, q_2 will be sold—q_1 being bought by ordinary purchasers and q_1q_2 by the government, which will have to store it or find some way of disposing of it.

ally succeed in selling their commodities at the price floor are better off than if they had to accept the lower equilibrium price. Farmers, as well as firms in regulated industries, are among those politically active, organized groups who have gained by persuading the government to establish price floors that enable them to sell their outputs at prices above free-market levels. The losses are spread across the large, diverse set of consumers, each of whom suffers only a small loss (although the *total* loss is considerable).

Price Ceilings

Governments sometimes fix the *maximum prices* at which certain goods and services may be sold. Price controls on oil, natural gas, and rental accommoda-

tion have been frequently imposed by various levels of government—federal, provincial, and local.

Although sometimes referred to as *fixed* or *frozen prices,* most price controls actually specify a **price ceiling,** which is the highest permissible price that producers may legally charge. If the price ceiling is set above the equilibrium price, it has no effect, because the equilibrium remains attainable. If, however, the price ceiling is set below the equilibrium price, the price ceiling lowers the price and is said to be *binding* or *effective*. The effects of price ceilings are shown in Figure 6-5, which establishes the following conclusion:

Effective price ceilings lead to excess demand, with the quantity exchanged being less than its equilibrium amount.

FIGURE 6-5
A Price Ceiling and Black-Market Pricing

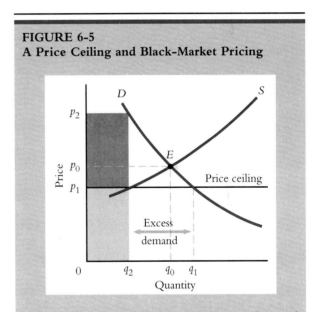

An effective price ceiling causes excess demand and invites a black market. Equilibrium price is at p_0. If a price ceiling is set at p_1, the quantity demanded will rise to q_1 and the quantity supplied will fall to q_2. Quantity actually exchanged will be q_2. Price may not rise legally to restore equilibrium.

If all the available supply of q_2 were sold on a black market, price to consumers would rise to p_2, with black marketeers earning receipts shown by the shaded areas. Because they buy at the ceiling price of p_1 and sell at the black-market price of p_2, their profits are represented by the dark shaded area.

Allocating a Commodity in Short Supply

The free market eliminates excess demand by allowing prices to rise, thereby allocating the available supply among would-be purchasers. Because this does not happen under price ceilings, some other method of allocation must be adopted. Experience suggests what to expect.

First come, first served. If stores sell their available supplies on a first-come, first-served basis, people will rush to those stores that are said to have stocks of the commodity. In some African countries (and until recently, under Communist regimes in many Eastern European countries), prices of essentials are subject to effective price ceilings, and even the rumor that a shop is selling supplies of a scarce commodity can cause a local stampede. Buyers may wait hours to get into the store, only to find that supplies are exhausted before they can be served. This is why standing in lines became a way of life in command economies. Goods are allocated according to the households' willingness and ability to stand in line. For example, a household with a retired grandparent is at an advantage over a household containing two working adults and very young children.

The first-come, first-served principle is also used to allocate scarce quantities in market economies. For example, tickets to rock concerts and sporting events are often priced below the equilibrium level and sold to first-comers.

Sellers' preferences. Instead of selling their supplies on a first-come, first-served basis, storekeepers may decide to keep goods "under the counter" and sell only to customers of their own choosing. For example, in the United States in 1979, the government placed a ceiling on the price of gasoline after supplies had been severely cut by the producing countries. In the face of the resulting shortage, many gas station operators sold only to regular customers. When sellers decide to whom they will (and will not) sell scarce supplies, allocation is by **sellers' preferences.**

Rationing. If the government dislikes these allocation systems, it can ration the commodity. To do so, it prints only enough ration coupons to match the available supply and then distributes the coupons to would-be purchasers, who need both money and coupons to buy the commodity. The coupons may be distributed equally among the population or on the basis of some criterion such as age, family status, or occupation.

Rationing substitutes the government's preferences for the sellers' preferences in allocating a commodity that is in excess demand because of an effective price ceiling.

Rationing was used in Canada and most other belligerent countries during both World War I and World War II.

Black Markets

Price ceilings, with or without rationing, usually give rise to black markets. A **black market** is any market in which goods are sold illegally at prices that violate a legal price control.

Many manufactured products are produced by only a few firms but are sold by many retailers. Thus, although it may be easy to police the few producers, it is often impossible to enforce the price at which the many retailers sell to the general public. If the government is able to control the price received by producers but not by retailers, production remains at a level consistent with the price ceiling because the producers receive only the controlled price. At the retail level, however, the opportunity for a black market arises because purchasers are willing to pay more than the price ceiling for the limited amounts of the commodity that are available.

Effective price ceilings create the potential for a black market, because a profit can be made by buying at the controlled price and selling at the black-market price.

Figure 6-5 illustrates the extreme case in which all the available supply is sold on a black market.[2]

---

[2]This case is extreme because there are law-abiding people in every society and because governments ordinarily have considerable power to enforce their price ceilings. Although *some* of a commodity subject to an effective price ceiling will be sold on the black market, it is unlikely that *all* of that commodity will be.

Does the existence of a black market mean that the goals sought by imposing price ceilings have been thwarted? The answer depends upon what the goals are. For example, a government might be interested mainly in

1. Restricting production (perhaps to release resources for war production)
2. Keeping prices down
3. Satisfying notions of equity in the consumption of a commodity that is temporarily in short supply.

When price ceilings are accompanied by a black market, only the first objective is achieved. Black markets frustrate the second objective. Effective price ceilings on manufacturers plus an extensive black market at the retail level may produce the opposite of the third goal. There will be less to go around than if there were no controls, and the available quantities will tend to go to those with the most money or the least social conscience.

Rent Controls: A Case Study of Price Ceilings

Rent controls have existed in New York, London, Paris, and many other large cities at least since World War II. In Sweden and Britain, where rent controls on unfurnished apartments existed for decades, shortages of rental accommodations were chronic. When British controls were extended to furnished apartments in 1973, the supply of such accommodations dried up, at least until loopholes were found in the law. When rent controls were initiated in Ontario in 1975 and in Rome in 1978, severe housing shortages soon developed in areas where demand was growing.

General Effects of Rent Controls

Rent controls are just a special case of price ceilings.[3] Hence Figure 6-5 can be used to predict some of the effects of *binding* controls:

1. There will be a housing shortage in the sense that quantity demanded will exceed quantity supplied.
2. The available quantity of rental housing will be less than if free-market rents had been charged.
3. The shortage will lead to alternative allocation schemes. Landlords may allocate by sellers' preferences, or the government may intervene, often through security-of-tenure laws, which protect tenants from eviction and thereby give them priority over prospective new tenants.
4. Black markets will appear. For example, landlords may require large "entrance fees" from new tenants, which reflect the difference in value between the free-market and the controlled rents. In the absence of security-of-tenure laws, landlords may force tenants out when their leases expire in order to extract large entrance fees from new tenants.

The province of Ontario instituted rent controls in 1975 and tightened them on at least two subsequent occasions. The controls allow significant increases in rents where these are needed to pass on cost increases. As a result, their restrictive effects have mainly been felt in areas where demand is increasing rapidly. The controls have been severely binding in urban areas that were growing rapidly, and the effects predicted above have all been observed. They are elaborated on in Box 6-1. However, in areas that were not growing, and in most areas during the severe recession of the early 1990s including Toronto, the demand for housing was not rising. As a result, many of the controls did not bind because the free market rents were at or below the controlled ceilings on rents.

Specific Effects of Rent Controls

Further effects of rent control arise because housing is a **durable good,** a good that yields its services gradually over an extended period of time. Once it

[3]Specifics of rent control laws vary greatly; in particular, exemptions for new buildings and allowances for maintenance costs and inflation are often permitted. Some laws have so many exceptions that the controls are rarely binding. For simplicity, we study the case where rent controls are effective in reducing the price of all rental accommodations below the market equilibrium price.

Box 6-1

Rent Controls in Toronto

Throughout the 1980's, Toronto was expanding rapidly. As a result, the demand for rental accommodations grew while the Ontario government's rent controls held rents down. The gap between demand and supply grew, as did the difference between the controlled rental prices and the prices that would have ruled on the free market. This difference created a valuable asset. For example, if you only have to pay $400 per month for an apartment that would rent on the free market for $700 per month, you have $300 of value per month that you do not pay for.

Naturally, people scramble to appropriate such values. *Key money*—the price charged by landlords to gain access to a rent-controlled flat—became prevalent, and the press reported payments running into many thousands of dollars. (Such lump-sum payments are most burdensome on the low-income persons that the rent control policy is supposed to be aiding.) Subletting became common: A tenant pays the landlord the controlled rent and then sublets at the market rent. This is the worst of both worlds as analysed in Figure 6-1. The supplier gets the controlled price and hence supplies only a small quantity, while the ultimate user pays the market price, which, because of the control-induced shortage, is higher than the uncontrolled free-market price would have been. The gain goes to the tenant who is subletting. It serves no allocative purpose since that person is responsible neither for maintaining the existing building nor for erecting new ones.

The growing housing shortage leads to more and more frantic searches for the available space. A feature article in the *Toronto Star* told of searches involving bribing caretakers, hunting through obituary columns, and finding elderly tenants in the hope of being first on the scene when death makes a flat available. Younger people, particularly those in less skilled jobs, told of landlord preferences for middle-aged, middle-class tenants holding white-collar jobs and earning higher incomes—a predictable allocation by sellers' preferences that tended to discriminate against some of the very groups the policy was supposed to help.

None of these events is a surprise to anyone who has studied the effects of rent controls elsewhere in the world. They are the all-too-predictable consequences of the system. City and provincial politicians and many other rent control advocates, however, express surprise at these events—being understandably unwilling to accept the responsibility that they actually bear for them. Efforts continue to be made to avoid the worst effects that have occurred elsewhere, but as long as rents are held below their long-term market equilibrium level—and there would be no point in having controls otherwise—the consequences analysed in this chapter will continue to be felt.

has been built, an apartment can be used for decades and often centuries.

The Supply of Rental Accommodations

The supply of rental accommodations depends on the stock of rental housing available, which in any year is composed mainly of buildings put up in the past. The stock is augmented by conversions of housing from other uses and construction of new buildings; it is diminished by conversions to other uses and by demolition or abandonment.

All of these reactions take time, which suggests that we need to use the distinction between short- and long-run supply that was first introduced in Chapter 5.

Short-run supply. The short-run response of the supply of rental accommodation to changes in rents tends to be quite limited. When rents rise, some conversions from other uses are possible, but it takes years to plan and to build new apartments. When rents fall, some conversions to condominiums and cooperatives may occur, and if rents fall so low that variable cost cannot be covered, buildings will be abandoned, as they were on a large scale in some parts of London, England, and New York City. However:

Quite wide ranges of variations in rents will be met by very small changes in the short-run supply of rental accommodations, making the short-run supply curve quite inelastic.

Long-run supply. If the expected return from investing in new apartments falls significantly below what can be earned on other, comparable investments, funds will go elsewhere. New construction will be halted, and old buildings will be converted to other uses, or, where this is impossible, they will not be replaced when they wear out. If the return rises significantly above the return on comparable investments, there will be a flow of investment funds into the building of new apartments. It takes years to increase the quantity of housing through new construction; reducing the quantity through nonreplacement takes decades.

The long-run supply curve of rental accommodations (which refers to the quantity supplied after enough time has been allowed for all adjustments) is highly elastic under most market conditions.

The Demand for Rental Accommodations

Does the fact that housing is a basic necessity mean that the demand for rental accommodations is highly inelastic? Although some form of shelter is a necessity, rental accommodations have many close substitutes, and empirical estimates show substantial elasticity in the demand *for a square foot* of rental accommodations.

A rise in the price of rental accommodations will lead to the following types of changes: Some people will stop renting and will buy instead; some will move to smaller, lower-grade rental housing; some will move to other areas where rents are lower; some young people will stay longer with their parents; and others will find roommates. For example, in response to a dramatic increase during recent decades in the cost of housing—both purchased and rented—the sharing of apartments among middle-income persons is more common today than it was only a few decades ago; they share in larger numbers per apartment, and they remain sharing for more years of their lives.

The demand for rental accommodation is quite responsive to changes in its (relative) price.

Rent Control and a Growing Housing Shortage

Because the short-run supply of housing is inelastic, rent controls that hold rentals somewhat below their free-market levels cause only a moderate housing shortage in the short run. Indeed, most of the shortage comes from an expansion in quantity demanded rather than from a shrinking in quantity supplied. As time passes, however, fewer new apartments are built, more conversions take place, and older buildings are not replaced as they wear out. As a result, the quantity supplied shrinks steadily. Furthermore, it is not worthwhile for landlords to spend as much on repairs as under free-market conditions, because rent controls lower the return on capital invested in rental accommodations. Concern over the deteriorating quality of housing is a recurring theme when effective rent controls have been in place for some time. This is still true, for example, in the city of Toronto. In other areas of Ontario, however, declining economic activity has led to a declining demand for rental accommodation. In some of these cases, rent controls no longer bind, and the predicted consequences of binding controls do not occur.

Both the long- and the short-run effects of binding rent control are shown in Figure 6-6.

Who Gains and Who Loses

Tenants in rent-controlled accommodations are the principal gainers. As the gap between the controlled and the equilibrium rents grows, those who are lucky enough to be tenants gain more and more.

FIGURE 6-6
Effects of Rent Control in the Short Run and the Long Run

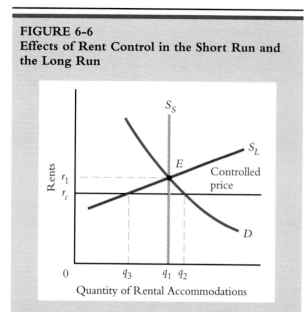

Rent control causes housing shortages that worsen as time passes. The controlled rent of r_c forces rents below their free-market equilibrium value of r_1. The short-run supply of housing is shown by the inelastic curve S_s. Thus quantity supplied remains at q_1 in the short run, and the housing shortage is q_1q_2. Over time, the quantity supplied shrinks, as shown by the long-run supply curve S_L. In long-run equilibrium there are only q_3 units of rental accommodations, fewer than when controls were instituted. The housing shortage of q_3q_2 which occurs after supply has fully adjusted, is larger than the initial shortage of q_1q_2.

The beneficiaries of rent controls are existing tenants; the losers are the present generation of landlords and those would-be tenants of the future who do not succeed in finding rent-controlled accommodations.

Landlords suffer because they do not get the return that they had expected on their investments. Some landlords are large companies, and others are rich individuals. Neither one of these groups attracts great public sympathy—even though the rental companies' stockholders are not all rich. Many other landlords are people of modest means who have put their retirement savings into a small apartment or a few houses. They find that the value of their savings is greatly diminished, and often they find themselves in the ironic position of subsidizing tenants who are far better off than they are.

The other major class of people who suffer from rent controls are potential future tenants. The housing shortage hurts them because the rental housing they would require will not be there in the future. Those who fight to keep rent controls on the apartments that they occupy are behaving in their own best interest. If and when they succeed, they are making life more difficult for future potential tenants—including the next generation of aged couples, welfare families who may wish to move in order to secure better employment opportunities, and young people starting out on new careers—who will encounter a steadily shrinking quantity and quality of available rental housing.

The costs of providing additional housing cannot be voted out of existence; all that can be done is to transfer the costs from one set of persons to another.

Box 6-2 provides some general lessons concerning resource allocation and government attempts to control prices—lessons that apply to all parts of the economy, including the housing market, which we have just studied, and the agricultural sector, to which we now turn.

The Problems of Agriculture

The free operation of the price system in agricultural markets has two common results. The first is a long-run tendency for farm incomes to fall relative to urban incomes in spite of both an extremely rapid rise in agricultural productivity and a long-term shift of labour from the farms. The second is wide year-to-year fluctuations in prices, causing much variability in farm incomes.

To deal with these two problems, governments throughout the Western world have tried a variety of techniques, including price supports, crop insurance, transportation and storage subsidies, and marketing boards. But each of these solutions seems to bring problems of its own, sometimes more serious than the original problems they were meant to solve.

Long-Term Trends

Agriculture's long-term problems arise from both the supply and the demand sides of agricultural markets.

Increasing domestic supply. Since 1900, the output per worker in Canadian agriculture has increased tenfold, roughly twice as fast as manufacturing productivity has increased. In 1900, one farm worker could produce enough food to feed about 2 ½ persons. By 1990, the figure was over 60 persons!

The rapid growth of farm productivity means that the supply curves of Canadian farm products have been shifting rapidly to the right.

Lagging domestic demand. The overall growth of output throughout the entire Canadian economy has resulted in a rising trend for the real income of the average Canadian family during the last 150 years. However, at the levels of income existing in Canada and in other advanced industrial nations, most foodstuffs have low income elasticities of demand because most people are already well fed. Thus, increases in incomes are often spent mostly on consumer durables, entertainment, travel, and dining out.[4]

As Canadian incomes grow, the Canadian demand for agricultural goods also grows, but less rapidly.

Export demand. The contribution of export markets to demand for domestic production has been variable over recent decades. Explosive growth of world population in the past half century has provided an expanding demand for foodstuffs, which, over much of the period, translated into a growing export market for North American produce. This tended to alleviate somewhat the domestic pressures just discussed. Throughout the 1970s, however, many less developed countries succeeded in dramatically increasing their own food production. Furthermore, large European agricultural subsidies

turned the countries of the European Community into exporters of agricultural products rather than importers.

By the beginning of the 1980s, international developments tended to exacerbate the domestic problem of agricultural surpluses instead of alleviating it.

For example, the world price of wheat fell from its peak of $6 per bushel in 1981 to about $2 in 1993. In real terms, this is the lowest price of wheat in Canadian history, including the prices at the depth of the Great Depression of the 1930s.

The importance of exports for Canadian and U.S. agriculture is shown by the increasing concern of the governments of many countries with the agricultural subsidies that are being paid to farmers in Europe, Japan, and several other countries. The non-European governments argue that these subsidies give an unfair foreign-trade advantage to farm products produced in Europe, keeping other countries' farm products out of many potential export markets. In 1993, all eyes were on the negotiations seeking settlement of the so-called Uruguay Round of the General Agreement on Trade and Tariffs (the GATT), in which many of these subsidies were under review; these developments are considered, in more detail, in Chapter 25.

Excess supply. Both the demand and the supply curves in typica.l agricultural markets have been shifting to the right over the whole of this century, with the demand curve shifting more slowly than the supply curve. As a result:

There is a continuing tendency for an excess supply of agricultural produce to develop at existing market prices.

This, in turn, tends to depress market prices. Most agricultural produce tends to have price elasticities of demand significantly less than one; therefore, the fall in price tends to depress agricultural incomes.[5]

---

[4]The enormous increase in the demand for fast foods and other restaurant meals—dining out was a rare luxury a scant 50 years ago—has caused an increase in the demand for the services provided by eating establishments but not for food itself.

[5]Recall from Chapter 5 that the demand elasticity determines the relationship between price fluctuations and total expenditure on a particular commodity or group of commodities; later in this chapter, we review the details in relation to fluctuations in agricultural prices.

Box 6-2

Four General Lessons About Resource Allocation

In this chapter, we examine examples of government intervention in markets that might have been left unregulated. Our discussion suggests four widely applicable lessons.

1. Costs May Be Shifted, But They Cannot Be Avoided

Production, whether in response to free-market signals or to government controls, uses resources; thus it involves costs to members of society. If it takes 5 percent of the nation's resources to provide housing at some stated average standard, those resources will not be available to produce other commodities. If resources are used to produce unwanted wheat, those resources will not be available to produce other commodities. For society, there is no such thing as free housing or free wheat.

The average standard of living depends on the amount of resources available to the economy and the efficiency with which these resources are used. It follows that *costs are real* and are incurred no matter who provides the goods. Rent controls or subsidies to agriculture can change the share of the costs paid by particular individuals or groups, lowering the share for some and raising the share for others, but they cannot make the costs go away.

Different ways of allocating the costs may also affect the total amount of resources used and thus the amount of costs incurred. For example, controls that keep prices and profits of some commodity below free-market levels will lead to increased quantities demanded and decreased quantities supplied. Unless government steps in to provide additional supplies, fewer resources will be allocated to producing the commodity. If government chooses to supply all the demand at the controlled prices, more resources will be allocated to it, which means fewer resources will be devoted to other kinds of goods and services.

2. Free-Market Prices and Profits Encourage Economical Use of Resources

Prices and profits in a market economy provide signals to both demanders and suppliers. Prices that are high and rising (relative to other prices) provide an incentive to purchasers to economize on the commodity. They may choose to satisfy the want in question with substitutes whose prices have not risen so much (because they are less costly to provide) or to satisfy less of that want by shifting expenditure to the satisfaction of other wants.

On the supply side, rising prices tend to produce rising profits. High profits attract further resources into production. Short-term profits that bear no relation to current costs repeatedly occur in market economies. They cause resources to move into those industries with profits until profits fall to levels that can be earned elsewhere in the economy.

Falling prices and falling profits provide the opposite motivations. Purchasers are inclined to buy more; sellers are inclined to produce less and to move resources out of the industry and into more profitable undertakings.

The price system responds to the need for

change in the allocation of resources, say, in response to an external event such as the loss of a source of a raw material or the outbreak of a war. Changing relative prices and profits signal the need for change to which consumers and producers respond.

3. Government Intervention Affects Resource Allocation

Governments intervene in the price system sometimes to satisfy generally agreed-upon social goals and sometimes to help politically influential interest groups. Government intervention changes the allocation of resources that the price system would achieve.

Interventions have allocative consequences because they inhibit the free-market allocative mechanism. Some controls, such as rent controls, prevent prices from rising (in response, say, to an increase in demand with no change in supply). If the price is held down, the signal is not given to consumers to economize on a commodity that is in short supply. On the supply side, when prices and profits are prevented from rising, the profit signals that would attract new resources into the industry are never given. The shortage continues, and the movements of demand and supply that would resolve it are not set in motion.

Other controls, such as agricultural price supports, prevent prices from falling (in response, say, to an increase in supply with no increase in demand). This leads to excess supply, and the signal is not given to producers to produce less or to buyers to increase their purchases. Surpluses continue, and the movements of demand and supply that would eliminate them are not set in motion.

4. Intervention Requires Alternative Allocative Mechanisms

Intervention typically requires alternative allocative mechanisms. During times of shortages, allocation will be by sellers' preferences, on a first-come, first-served basis, or by some system of government rationing. During periods of surplus, there will be unsold supplies unless the government buys and stores the surpluses. Because long-run changes in demand and costs do not induce resource reallocations through private decisions, the government will have to step in. It will have to force resources out of industries in which prices are held too high, as it has tried to do in agriculture, and into industries in which prices are held too low, as it can do, for example, by providing public housing.

Intervention almost always has both benefits and costs. Economics cannot answer the question of whether a particular intervention with free markets is desirable, but it can clarify the issues by identifying benefits and costs and who will enjoy or bear them. In doing so it can identify the competing values involved. This matter will be discussed in detail in Chapters 20 and 21.

Resource Reallocation. Depressed prices, wages, and farm incomes signal the need for resources to move out of agriculture and into other rapidly growing sectors. However necessary they may be, adjustments of this kind prove to be painful to those who live and work on farms, especially when resources move slowly in response to depressed incomes. It is one thing for farmers' sons and daughters to move to the city; it is quite another for existing farmers and their parents to be displaced.

The magnitude of the required supply response has been enormous. In 1900, more than 40 percent of the Canadian labour force worked in agriculture; by 1930 it was down to 29 percent, and by 1992 it had fallen to just over 3 percent.

Notice that analogous problems arise in any industry where growth in demand is low but productivity growth is high. For example, the rapid rise in productivity in automobile production, combined with government subsidies to new auto plants, had created severe excess capacity in the North American auto industry in the 1990s.

Short-Term Fluctuations

The second characteristic agricultural problem is the short-term price volatility typical of many agricultural markets. These short-term fluctuations occur mainly because of forces completely beyond farmers' control. For example, pests, floods, and drought can drastically reduce output, whereas exceptionally favourable weather can cause production to exceed expectations. By now, you should not be surprised to hear that such unplanned fluctuations in output cause fluctuations in farm prices and farm incomes.

Fluctuating Supply with Inelastic Demand

The basic behaviour is illustrated in Figure 6-7. Variations in farm output cause price fluctuations in the direction opposite to crop size. A bumper crop sends prices down; a small crop sends them up. The less elastic is the demand curve, the larger are the price fluctuations.

FIGURE 6-7
The Effect on Price of Unplanned Variations in Output

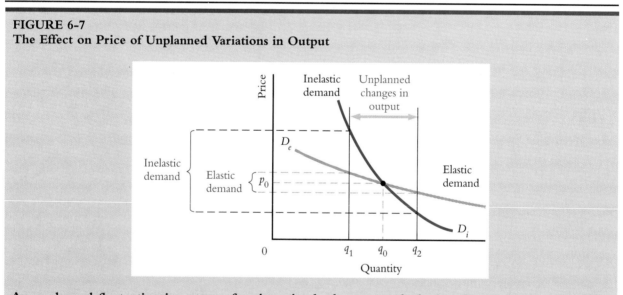

An unplanned fluctuation in output of a given size leads to a much sharper fluctuation in price when the demand curve is inelastic than when it is elastic. Suppose that the expected price is p_0 and the planned output is q_0. The two curves D_i and D_e are *alternative* demand curves. If actual production always equaled planned production, the equilibrium price and quantity would be p_0 and q_0 with either demand curve. Unplanned variation in output, however, causes quantity to fluctuate year by year between q_1 (a bad harvest) and q_2 (a good harvest). When demand is inelastic (shown by the dark blue curve), prices will show large fluctuations. When demand is elastic (shown by the light blue curve), price fluctuations will be much smaller.

What are the effects on the receipts of farmers? In typical cases where demand is inelastic, increases in supply cause decreases in farmers' receipts.

Because farm products typically have inelastic demands, unplanned fluctuations in production tend to cause relatively large fluctuations in price. Therefore, good harvests bring reductions in total farm receipts and bad harvests bring increases in total farm receipts.

Thus, the inelasticity of demand for most farm products explains the apparently paradoxical experience that when nature is bountiful and produces a bumper crop, farmers' receipts dwindle, whereas when nature is moderately unkind and output falls unexpectedly, farmers' receipts rise. The interests of the farmer and the consumer are exactly opposed in such cases.

Fluctuating Demand with Inelastic Supply

As the tide of business activity flows and ebbs, demand curves for all commodities rise and fall. The magnitude of the effects on prices and outputs depend on the elasticity of *supply*.

Industrial products typically have rather elastic short-run supply curves, so shifts in demand cause fairly large changes in outputs but only small changes in prices, as Figure 6-8(i) illustrates. In contrast, agricultural commodities typically have rather inelastic short-run supply curves because land, labour, and machinery devoted to agricultural uses are neither quickly transferred to nonagricultural uses when demand falls nor quickly returned to agriculture when demand rises.

The inelastic short-run supply curves for most agricultural products make farm prices,

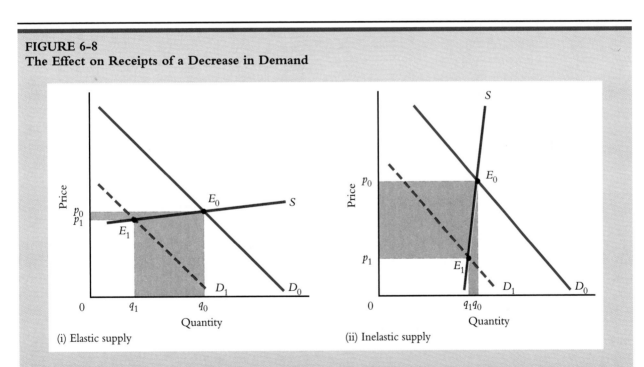

FIGURE 6-8
The Effect on Receipts of a Decrease in Demand

(i) Elastic supply

(ii) Inelastic supply

Both elastic and inelastic supply curves can lead to sharp decreases in receipts, but the effects on prices are very different in the two cases. In each part of the figure, when demand decreases from D_0 to D_1, price and quantity decrease to p_1 and q_1, and total receipts decline by the shaded area. In part (i) the symptom is primarily the sharp decrease in quantity. Employment and total profits earned fall drastically, though wage rates and profit margins on what is produced may remain close to their former level. In part (ii) the symptom is mainly the sharp decrease in price. Output and employment remain high, but the drastic fall in price will reduce profits.

farm receipts, and farm income sensitive to demand shifts.

As Figure 6-8(ii) shows, a sharp drop in demand (a leftward shift of the demand curve) will cause a large reduction in incomes derived from selling farm crops.

Agricultural Stabilization in Theory

Governments throughout the world intervene in agricultural markets in attempts to stabilize agricultural prices and incomes in the face of short-term fluctuations in supply and cyclical fluctuations in demand. We deal with two cases that are relevant to much of Canadian agriculture, first the production of commodities mainly for export and then the production of commodities mainly for domestic consumption. In what follows, we assume that all supply curves refer to planned production per year but that actual production fluctuates around that level for reasons beyond farmers' control.

Exports at World Market Prices

When Canadian production is sold on world markets, the prices are largely independent of the amount sold by Canadian producers because they contribute only a small proportion of total world supply. Thus, domestic producers face a perfectly elastic demand curve, indicating that they can sell all that they wish at the given world price. A government stabilization policy then faces two key problems: first, how to cope with short-term supply fluctuations at home and second, how to react to fluctuations in world prices.

Output fluctuations at given world prices. Figure 6-9 illustrates sales over several years at a given world price when domestic output fluctuates. In years of bumper crops, sales will rise, and price will not be driven down, so incomes will rise. In years of poor crops, sales will fall, but price will not rise, so incomes will fall.

However, the effect of selling on the international market and being only a small part of total world supply is to make the demand curve that domestic producers face perfectly elastic (even though

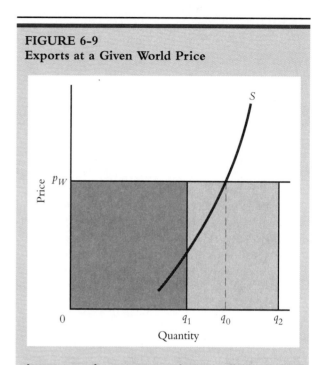

FIGURE 6-9
Exports at a Given World Price

A country that exports only a small portion of the world's supply of some commodity faces a perfectly elastic demand because the world price is not affected by its own sales. The given world price is p_W. The domestic supply curve shows that intended output is q_0 at that price. Unintended fluctuations cause output to vary between q_1 and q_2. When output is at q_1, farm income is given by the dark shaded area. When output is q_2, farm income is given by the total of the light and the dark shaded areas.

the world demand curve is inelastic). Note the contrast with the case where demand is inelastic and farm incomes fluctuate in the direction *opposite* to output: Good harvests depress incomes and bad harvests raise them.

When domestic farmers sell at a given world price that is unaffected by their own volume of sales, their incomes fluctuate in the same direction as their short-term fluctuations in output.

The incomes of farmers who produce nonperishable crops could be stabilized if the government developed a scheme allowing farmers to store their outputs in years of bumper crops and to sell from stocks in years of poor crops. Effectively, sales would always be equal to planned output. Any unplanned excess of production would be stored, and any shortfall would be made up out of sales from stocks. But storage costs money and postpones the receipt of revenue until the sales occur. An alternative would be to sell all the crop each year and then save the extra money received in good years to spend in bad years. This is something that farmers can do on their own without assistance from the government.

Fluctuations in world prices. When world prices fluctuate, it may pay to hold stocks. When the government judges that this year's price is unusually low, it can store some of the output in the hope of selling it later at a better price. When the government judges that this year's price is unusually high, it can sell some of the stocks that it put aside in years when the price was low.

In a world in which future prices were known with certainty, the government would merely calculate the extra revenue that could be obtained by selling at some future price higher than the present one and subtract the costs of storage to see if the crop should be sold now or held. In practise, the future is not known, and the government must use its knowledge of market conditions to guess its best policy. The government will be inclined to store a larger amount this year the more it expects prices to rise in future years and to sell more from stocks if it expects prices to fall in future years. If the government is good at predicting the future state of the market, it will increase farmers' revenues by selling less when prices are low and more when prices are high, as compared with a policy of selling the whole crop each year. If the government's market predictions are wrong, however, the scheme can bring losses.

Sales on the Domestic Market Only

Quite a few Canadian agricultural goods are sold mainly on the domestic market. The difference between this case and the one just considered is that the demand curve facing domestic producers is now negatively sloped and typically inelastic. The analysis of Figure 6-7 now applies, so farm income will fluctuate in the direction opposite to output. Can farm income be stabilized in this case?

Price stabilization. Suppose that the government enters the market, buying and thereby adding to its own stocks when there is a surplus, and selling and thereby reducing its stocks when there is a shortage. If it had enough grain elevators and warehouses, and if its support price were set at a realistic level, the government could stabilize *prices* indefinitely. But this would not stabilize farmers' revenues, which would be high with bumper crops and low with poor crops.

In effect, the government policy imposes a demand curve that is perfectly elastic at the support price. The situation is then analogous to the one analysed in Figure 6-9: The product can be sold at a given world price, and income fluctuates in the same direction as output.

Government price supports at the equilibrium price would not stabilize revenues. They would, however, reverse the pattern of revenue fluctuation.

Revenue stabilization. Obviously, there must be a government buying-and-selling policy that will stabilize farmers' receipts. What are its characteristics? As has been seen, too much price stability causes receipts to vary directly with production, and too little price stability causes receipts to vary inversely with production. It appears that the government should aim at some intermediate degree of price stability. If the government allows prices to vary in inverse proportion to variations in production, receipts will be stabilised. A 10 percent rise in production should be met by a 10 percent fall in price, and a 10 percent fall in production by a 10 percent rise in price.

To stabilize farmers' receipts, the government must make the demand curve unit elastic. It must buy in periods of high output and sell in periods of low output, but only enough to let prices change in inverse proportion to farmers' output.

Prices Above Equilibrium

In practise, stabilization plans, whether they seek to fix prices completely or merely to dampen free market fluctuations, often seek to maintain an average price *above* the average free-market equilibrium

FIGURE 6-10
Price Supports Above the Equilibrium Price

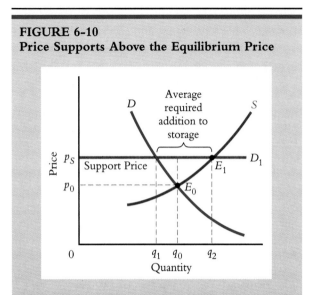

The support price becomes a price floor, and the government must purchase the excess supply at that price. Average annual demand and supply are D and S, respectively. The free-market equilibrium is at E_0. If the government will buy any quantity at p_s, the demand curve becomes the gray curve D_1 and equilibrium shifts to E_1. The average addition to storage is the quantity $q_1 q_2$. The government purchases add to farmers' receipts and to government expenditures.

level. This is because stabilization is not the only goal; governments also desire to give farmers a standard of living comparable with that of city dwellers. This involves *raising* farm incomes in addition to stabilizing them.

The government buys in periods of high output and sells in periods of low output, but as shown in Figure 6-10, it buys much more on average than it sells, with the result that unsold surpluses accumulate. Taxpayers will generally be paying farmers for producing goods that no one is willing to purchase, at least at prices that come near to covering costs.

Subsidies. This is the route taken by the European Community (EC) with its Common Agricultural Policy (CAP). This policy has supported the existing farm population of Europe by guaranteeing stable, high prices. It has also meant that Western Europe has changed from being a net importer of

agricultural products—which it had been for over a century and would still be under free-market determination—into a net exporter. As a result of the CAP, the EC is now faced with mounting stockpiles of many agricultural products.[6] Periodically, it seeks to sell some of the surpluses to outside countries, charging prices well below the costs of production. The net result is that taxpayers in the EC are subsidizing consumers in foreign countries by allowing them to buy goods at prices much below their cost of production. Payments under the CAP now account for well over half of the EC's entire budget, and concern is mounting that the ever-growing payments to farmers may soon outrun the EC's ability to pay.

Quotas. Another way of holding the price above its free-market equilibrium level is to reduce the supply through quotas. Under this system, no one can produce the product without having a government-issued quota. Sufficient quotas are issued to hold production at any desired level below the free-market output. This drives prices above their free-market level. This quota system, which is analysed in Figure 6-11, has the advantage of not causing the accumulation of massive unsold surpluses. It is widely used in Canada.

The quota system, called *supply management* in Canada, affects both the short-term and the long-term behaviour of agricultural markets. Consider short-term fluctuations first. There will still be good crops and poor crops and other natural disturbances, such as outbreaks of disease, that will cause short-term fluctuations in output. A shortfall of output below the quota will drive price upward. Farmers with no crop to sell will lose, but farmers whose outputs fall proportionally less than the price rise will gain. Since most agricultural products have inelastic demands, the typical farmer must gain—the percentage increase in market price will exceed the percentage fall in the aggregate crop.

What about unplanned extra output due to favourable conditions? The farmer is allowed to sell only the amount covered by the quota. The rest must be either destroyed or sold on some secondary

---

[6]Some attempts are made to restrict supply, but these are insufficient to prevent an excess of quantity supplied over quantity demanded at the support price.

FIGURE 6-11
Price Support Through the Use of Quotas

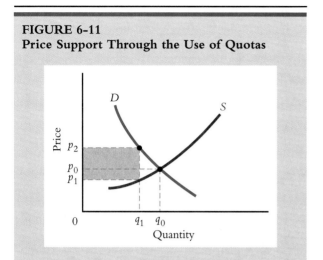

A quota below the equilibrium quantity maintains the price above the equilibrium level without generating surpluses. If a total quota of q_1 is enforced, the price will rise to p_2. Since the supply curve indicates that in a free market producers would be willing to supply q_1 at a lower price p_1, the effect is to provide holders of quotas with additional revenues, represented by the shaded area.

market not covered by the quota system. Farm income is stabilized. The quota output is sold at the market price for that output even when there is surplus output (and the rest goes for what it can get). Given that demand is typically inelastic, without quotas the free-market price would fall by a larger percentage than output would rise, and producers' incomes would shrink drastically.

A quota system guarantees that farmers will get the free-market price of the total quota output when output equals or exceeds the quota and more when output falls short of the quota and demand is inelastic.

Thus, the quota system is superior to the subsidy system in that it really does remove the downside risks caused by unexpected increases in output, and unlike the CAP, it does not lead to accumulating stockpiles of unsold output. The main cost is met by consumers, who on average pay a price that is higher, and consume an output that is lower, than would occur under free-market conditions.

Now consider the long term. We have seen that the quota drives price above its free-market level by restricting output. For purposes of illustration, let us suppose that the quota is for eggs. Those who are producing eggs when the quota system is first instituted must gain. Since production falls, total costs must fall; since demand is inelastic, total revenue must rise. Therefore, egg producers find their profits rising, since they spend less to earn more revenue. No wonder quotas are popular among the original producers!

But do quotas really increase farm income in the long run? Because people leave the industry for such reasons as death and retirement and new people must enter to replace them, existing holders are allowed to transfer their quotas to new would-be egg producers. But the quota is valuable, since it confers the right to produce eggs that earn a large profit as a result of the supply restriction. Therefore, the quota commands a price. The price turns out to be the current value of the extra profits that the quota system has produced.[7]

When the quota system makes production of eggs unusually profitable, more farmers will wish to produce eggs. But this requires a quota. The new demand for egg quotas bids up their price until egg production is no more profitable than other investments with similar risks.

The free-market price of a quota to produce any good will be such that the profitability of that good's production will, after deducting the cost of the quota, be no more than the profitability of other lines of activity carrying similar risks.

---

[7]The reasons why this is so are spelled out in detail in Chapter 12, where we consider entry into a competitive industry. But to show the common sense of the result now, we argue as follows: People have alternative ways of investing their money. For example, someone with money to invest could buy an egg farm, a small factory, a share in a large corporation, or a government bond. When returns are relatively high in one line of activity, people will rush to invest funds in it; when returns are relatively low, people will be reluctant to invest in that activity. This search of investors for the most profitable uses for their funds tends to force equality in the rates of return in alternative investments that are open to investors (making due allowances for differences in risk).

In other words, the whole extra profitability created by the quota system becomes embodied in the price of the quota. The extra profits created by the quota will just provide an acceptable return on the money invested in buying the quota—if it provided more, the price of the quota would be bid up; if it provided less, the price of the quota would fall.

For this reason, new entrants to the industry will earn no more than the return available in other lines of production. Since that would also be the case under market-determined prices and outputs, the quota does not raise the profitability of producing eggs. What it does do is reduce some of the uncertainty due to unexpected short-term fluctuations of output. Farming becomes a somewhat less risky operation than before.

Economics alone cannot tell us whether such a system is good or bad. What it can do is show us who will gain and who will lose and also which alleged sources of gain are effective and which are illusory.

Agricultural Policy in Canada

The main tools of agricultural stabilization in Canada are marketing boards and income supplement programs. Sales through marketing boards account for about half of all farm cash receipts.

Marketing Boards

Basically there are two types of government marketing boards. The first seeks to influence prices by controlling supply. The second accepts prices and acts as a selling agency for producers.

Supply management. The supply management schemes typically are provincially administered systems that restrict output of commodities sold in the Canadian market through quotas issued by provincial marketing boards. They vary from province to province but often cover milk, eggs, cheese, butter, and poultry. The monopoly profits created by these schemes are enormous and can be accurately measured by the prices farmers must pay to purchase quotas. For example, it currently costs $1 million to buy the minimum-size quota needed to operate one family-sized chicken farm in Ontario, and it costs

$3 million to buy the quota needed to operate an average-size dairy farm in the Fraser Valley.

Schemes of this type, analyzed in Figure 6-11, are successful in reducing short-term fluctuations. However, they also greatly increase the cost of becoming a producer, because a quota must be purchased in addition to the physical capital needed for production. The schemes are popular among farmers, because they reduce risk in the short term and because the value of the quotas often rises over the long term. The gains to farmers and food importers are paid for by consumers in the form of higher prices.

Recently, two other important effects of supply management systems have become apparent. First, they harm Canadian manufacturers of food products. Canadian firms producing frozen and canned foods must buy expensive Canadian produce, whereas their foreign competitors can buy their raw foodstuffs at the lower world prices. Second, they reduce competition among users of agricultural products. For example, to allocate scarce supplies of milk, the Fraser Valley Milk Marketing Board channels supplies to selected users of raw milk. These milk processors have no incentive to compete for market share or to introduce new products, because a successful competitor could not get the larger supplies of raw milk needed to increase sales.

The high domestic prices caused by supply management would normally lead to a flood of imports. To prevent this, the federal government used to impose fixed and small quotas on imports of goods subject to supply management. Under the Uruguay Round of the General Agreement on Tariffs and Trade (the GATT), Canada agreed to replace these quotas in 1994-1995 with tariffs which had equivalent effect. In some cases the tariff rates exceeded 300 percent! The slow speed at which these tariff rates are to be reduced under the agreement will allow supply management to persist for many years. Consumers may have to wait until another round of GATT tariff reductions before they get real relief from the high-price effects of marketing boards.

Orderly marketing schemes. The prime example of an orderly marketing scheme is the Canadian Wheat Board, which markets Canadian wheat at prices set on the world wheat market. Each year, the board estimates the average price at which it expects the wheat crop to be sold. Seventy-five percent of that price is then paid to each farmer on delivery of the wheat. After the board sells the wheat, any proceeds in excess of the initial payments are distributed to the producers in proportion to the amount of wheat supplied by each.

The goals of the Wheat Board are not to influence world prices. Instead, by paying farmers 75 percent of the estimated average selling price over the year, the board provides farmers with a secure cash flow early in the selling period. The board also serves to secure farmers' incomes against intrayear fluctuations in wheat prices. It does this by pooling all of its receipts and paying them out to farmers according to the amount of wheat delivered by each farmer but irrespective of the date within the year of that delivery. So the farmer is relieved of worry about what the spot price of wheat may be on the day of delivery.

These functions of the board appear to be in the farmers' interests and not to be disadvantageous to consumers. Most farmers approve of the annual averaging of receipts, most find the information provided by an early estimate of this year's price useful, and most like the early cash flow of 75 percent of the estimated selling price provided on delivery.

Income Supplements

As market conditions for grain deteriorated during the 1980s, the Canadian government provided substantial, and rising, support to maintain farmers' incomes. Federal direct assistance to farmers, mainly those in grain production, rose from $2.8 billion in 1983 to over $6 billion in 1992! (This is about $500 for every Canadian household.)

The result of this assistance is that in spite of deteriorating world market conditions, net farm income rose every year in the 1980s. In 1981, this income was $3.8 billion, of which 94.5 percent came from sales revenue and 5.5 percent from direct government assistance. By 1992, farm income had risen to $5.9 billion, of which just over 19 percent came from government assistance.

In spite of this, many farmers were still experiencing financial difficulties, partly as a result of heavy borrowing and overinvestment in the face of what turned out to be temporary boom conditions in the 1970s. The Economic Council of Canada estimated that in 1988, some 25 percent of all farmers faced financial difficulties, and 10 percent of all farmers were considered nonviable because their incomes (including federal assistance) fell short of their expenses. By 1993 the figure for farmers in difficulties had risen dramatically.

The Future of Agricultural Policy

Is there a better way to make farming an occupation in which people can invest and work without being disadvantaged relative to other citizens and without needing large payments of funds raised from the nation's taxpayers? Most economists believe that a more efficient system would assist farm workers to change occupations and farm producers to change products rather than subsidize them to stay where they are not needed and to produce products that cannot be marketed profitably. Such assistance would require significant outlays—as do the present schemes—but would allow the market to do the job of allocating resources to agriculture.

There is no doubt that a policy of allowing agricultural prices and outputs to be determined on free markets would avoid surplus production, but the human and political costs of this policy have been judged to be unacceptable. The challenge has been to respond to the real hardships of the farm population without intensifying the long-term problems. Canadian farm policy has not always succeeded in doing so; the economic analysis in the previous sections helps us to understand why.

SUMMARY

1. The elementary theory of supply, demand, and price provides powerful tools for analysing and understanding some real-world problems and policies. The chapter illustrates a few of them.

2. The distribution of the burden of a sales tax between consumers who demand the product and producers who supply it is indepen-

dent of who remits the tax to the government. Rather, it depends on the elasticity of the supply of **and demand for the product.**

3. Effective price floors lead to excess supply. Either the potential seller is left with quantities that cannot be sold, or the government must step in and buy the surplus. Effective price ceilings lead to excess demand and provide a strong incentive for black marketeers to buy at the controlled price and sell at the higher free-market price.

4. Rent controls are a persistent and widespread form of price ceiling. The major consequence of effective rent controls is a shortage of rental accommodations that gets worse because of a decline in the quantity of rental housing.

5. The long-term problems of agriculture arise from a high rate of productivity growth on the supply side and a low income elasticity on the demand side. This means that unless many resources are being transferred out of agriculture, quantity supplied increases faster than quantity demanded year after year.

6. Many agricultural prices and incomes are depressed by chronic surpluses in agricultural markets. At various times and places, government policies to protect farm incomes have included buying farmers' output at above free-market prices and limiting production and acreage by quotas. Such policies tend to inhibit the reallocation mechanism and thus to increase farm surpluses above what they would otherwise be and lead to accumulating stocks.

7. Agricultural commodities are subject to wide fluctuations in market prices, which cause fluctuations in producers' incomes. This is because of year-to-year unplanned fluctuations in supplies combined with inelastic demand and because of cyclical fluctuations in demand combined with inelastic supplies. Where demand is inelastic, large crops tend to be associated with low total receipts and small crops with high total receipts.

8. Canadian agricultural stabilization policies operate in two types of markets. In the first, which covers products such as wheat, the bulk of production is exported at prices set in world markets. In this case, there is little that the government can usefully do to stabilise prices or to insulate revenues from fluctuating in response to unplanned fluctuations in output. The government can, however, seek to mitigate fluctuations in revenue that stem from fluctuations in world prices. This is done by storing some of the crop when prices are thought to be unusually low and selling out of stocks when prices are thought to be unusually high.

9. In the second type of market, which includes many products subject to provincial supply management, such as milk, eggs, cheese, and chickens, the product is sold on a domestic market that is protected from foreign competition either by natural factors or by government restrictions on imports. Output is restricted through quotas, causing the actual price to exceed the free-market equilibrium price. Farmers gain by the reduction in short-term price fluctuations and by any increase in the values of their quotas after they have purchased them. Since the quota price reflects the addi-

tional profits brought about by supply restriction, new entrants into the industry do not earn higher returns on their investments than they could earn in other lines bearing similar risks or that they would have earned if the good were produced under free-market conditions.

TOPICS FOR REVIEW

Price floors and price ceilings

The incidence of sales taxes

Allocation by sellers' preferences, rationing, and black markets

Short-run and long-run supply curves

Effects of high productivity growth and low income elasticity

Importance of export demand

Price supports at and above the level of free-market equilibrium

Supply management in domestic markets

DISCUSSION QUESTIONS

1. "When a controlled item is vital to everyone, it is easier to start controlling the price than to stop controlling it. Such controls are popular with consumers, regardless of their harmful consequences." Explain why it may be inefficient to have such controls, why they may be popular, and why, if they are popular, the government might nevertheless choose to decontrol these prices.

2. Discuss the following statements about the housing problem in Vancouver.
   a. "Zoning laws that require that most of Vancouver be restricted to single-family dwellings reflect the exploitation of the poor by the middle class."
   b. "The world is awash with agricultural surpluses while land-starved Vancouver is prevented from spreading into much of the adjacent Fraser Valley by government 'land banks' designed to preserve agricultural land from urbanization."
   c. "More than 40 percent of all rented apartments in Vancouver are illegal and would not be permitted if their owners applied for permission to rent their space legally."

3. It is sometimes asserted that the rising costs of construction are putting housing out of the reach of ordinary citizens. Who bears the heaviest cost when rents are kept down by (a) rent controls, (b) a subsidy to tenants equal to some fraction of their rent payments, and (c) low-cost public housing?

4. From 1991 to 1993, cities such as Toronto experienced decreases in rents in spite of rent controls. This was attributed to declining incomes due to a serious recession. Discuss the implication of removing rent controls under these market conditions.

5. The Kenya Meat Commission (KMC) decided that it was undemocratic to allow meat prices to be out of the reach of the ordinary citizen. It decided to freeze meat prices. Six months later, in

a press interview, the managing commissioner of the KMC made the following statements. Do the facts alleged make sense, given KMC's policy?

a. "The price of almost everything in Kenya has gone up, but we have not increased the price of meat. The price of meat in this country is still the lowest in the world."

b. "Cattle are scarce in the country, but I do not know why."

c. "People are eating too much beef, and unless they diversify their eating habits and eat other foodstuffs, the shortage of beef will continue."

6. Discuss the following statement by University of Saskatchewan professor of agricultural economics Gary Storey: "One of the sad truths of the agricultural policies in Europe and the United States is that they do very little for the future generations of farmers. Most of the subsidies get capitalized into higher land prices, creating windfall gains for current landowners (i.e., gains that they neither expected nor did anything to earn). It creates a situation where the next generation of farmers require, and ask for, increased government support."

7. Compare the following two headlines that appeared within a week of each other.

a. "Bumper potato crop dashes farmers' hopes."

b. "Record high wheat crop leaves farmers smiling."

8. Discuss the following two statements. Do you see a relation between them?

a. "The current financial crisis is so large that it may be beyond the fiscal capability of governments to solve by subsidies and public assistance. Government assistance has not been able to prevent farm financial problems."—George Brinkman, professor of agricultural economics, University of Guelph.

b. "Ironically, the industry is a victim of its own success. Programs [to increase agricultural production in many countries in the 1970s] were so successful that the world is now awash with surplus food. There are mountains of grain, cheese, and beef in storage around the world, and lakes of milk, wine, and olive oil."—Oliver Bertin, journalist.

9. Discuss the following recent headlines in terms of the analysis of this chapter.

a. "Huge grain stockpiles blunt price upturn, economist says."

b. "Farm children plan for careers off the family land."

c. "Subsidies for farmers may be intractable dilemma."

d. "If wheat prices fall, so do land prices."

10. When one Canadian province recently proposed an increase in the provincial sales tax, a critic suggested that this would hurt both producers and consumers. Discuss the sense in which this is true. How would you expect the distribution of the tax burden between the two groups to vary between, say, automobiles and cigarettes? Would you expect the distribution in each market to be different in the short and the long runs?

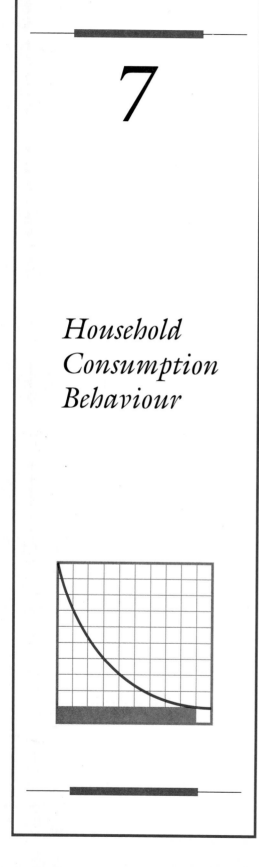

7

Household Consumption Behaviour

In Part 2, we saw that demand is an important part of the explanation of market prices and that the shapes of demand curves influence how markets behave. Why do market demand curves have the shapes they do? To address this question, we need to go behind the demand curve and study the behaviour of individual households, because that behaviour underlies market demand curves.

We start by studying the choices faced by every household that has money to spend and that desires to purchase certain commodities. Later we develop theories of how households make their choices.

The Choices Households Face

To begin, we reduce the problem of choice to its basics by considering a household choosing between just two commodities—food and clothing. Simplifying the problem in this way allows us to see the essential points more easily.

Suppose that the household has a money income of $360 per week and that the prices for food and clothing are $12 per unit for food and $6 per unit for clothing. For the purpose of our example, suppose further that the household does not save; its only choice is how much of its $360 to spend on food ($F$) and how much to spend on clothing (C).

The Budget Line

We can illustrate the household's alternatives using a graph. Look at the solid line *ab* in Figure 7-1. That line, called a **budget line,** shows all the combinations of food and clothing that the household can buy if it spends a fixed amount of money, in this case all its income, at fixed prices of the commodities. (It is also sometimes called an *isocost line,* because all points on it represent bundles of goods with the same total cost.)

The budget line has several important properties:

1. Points on the budget line indicate bundles of commodities that use up the household's entire income. (Try, for example, the point 20 *C,* 20 *F.*)
2. Points between the budget line and the origin indicate bundles of commodities that cost less than the household's income. (Try, for example, the point 20 *C,* 10 *F.*)
3. Points above the budget line indicate combinations of commodities that cost more than the household's income. (Try, for example, the point 30 *C,* 40 *F.*)

The budget line shows all combinations of commodities that are available to the household given the

PART THREE

CONSUMPTION, PRODUCTION, AND COST

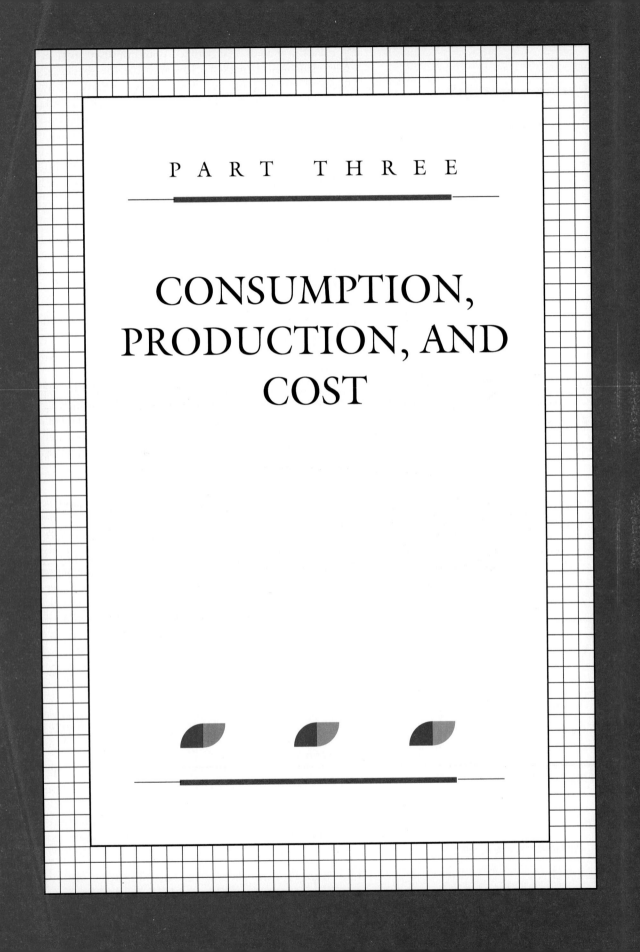

FIGURE 7-1
A Budget Line

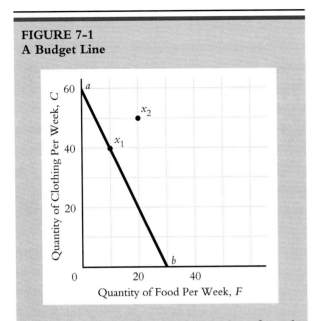

The budget line shows the quantities of goods available to a household given its money income and the prices of goods it buys. Any point in this diagram indicates a combination (or bundle) of so much food and so much clothing. Point x_1, for example, indicates 40 units of clothing and 10 units of food per week.

With an income of $360 a week and prices of $12 per unit for food and $6 per unit for clothing, the household's budget line is *ab*. This line shows all the combinations of F and C available to a household spending this income at these prices. The household could spend all of its money income on clothing and obtain 60 units of clothing and zero food each week. It could likewise go to the other extreme and purchase only food, buying 30 units of F and zero units of C. It could also choose an intermediate position and consume some of both goods; for example, it could spend $120 to buy 10 units of F and $240 to buy 40 units of C (point x_1). Points above the budget line, such as x_2, are not attainable.

represent the quantities of food and clothing chosen, then spending on clothing is equal to P_F times F, and spending on clothing is P_C times C. Thus, the equation for the budget line is

$$E = P_F F + P_C C$$

Now look again at the budget line shown in Figure 7-1. The vertical intercept is 60 units of clothing and the horizontal intercept is 30 units of food. Thus, the slope is equal to -2. The minus sign means that increases in purchases of one of the goods must be accompanied by decreases in purchases of the other. The numerical value of the slope indicates how much of one good must be given up to obtain an additional unit of the other; in our example, the slope of -2 means that it is necessary to forgo the purchase of two units of clothing in order to acquire one extra unit of food.

Recall that in Chapter 4 we contrasted the *absolute*, or *money*, price of a commodity with its *relative* price, which is the ratio of its absolute price to that of some other commodity or group of commodities. One important point is that the relative price determines the slope of the budget line. In terms of our example of food and clothing, the slope of the budget line is determined by the relative price of food in terms of clothing, P_F/P_C; with the price of food (P_F) at $12 per unit and the price of clothing (P_C) at $6 per unit, the slope of the budget line is 2. **[10]**

The significance of the slope of the budget line for food and clothing is that it reflects the *opportunity cost* of food in terms of clothing. In order to increase food consumption while maintaining expenditure constant, the household must move along the budget line and therefore consume less clothing; the slope of the budget line determines how much clothing must be given up to obtain an additional unit of food.

In the example, with fixed income and with the relative price of food in terms of clothing, (P_F/P_C) equal to 2, it is necessary to forgo the purchase of two units of clothing to acquire one extra unit of food. The opportunity cost of a unit of food is thus two units of clothing.

The opportunity cost of food in terms of clothing is measured by the slope of the budget line and also by the relative price ratio, P_F/P_C.

prices of the goods that it purchases and the total income it spends.

We can also show the household's alternatives by using an equation that uses symbols to express the information contained in the budget line. Let E stand for the household's money income, which must be equal to the household's total expenditure on food and clothing. If P_F and P_C represent the money prices of food and clothing, and F and C

Notice that the relative price (in our example $P_F/P_C = 2$) is consistent with an infinite number of absolute prices. If $P_F = \$40$ and $P_C = \$20$, it is still necessary to sacrifice two units of clothing to acquire one unit of food.[1] This shows that relative, not absolute, prices determine opportunity cost.

Shifts in the Budget Line

Changes in the income received by the household or in the prices of the goods it purchases will cause the budget line to shift.

Changes in Money Income

What happens to the budget line when money income changes? If the household's money income is halved from \$360 to \$180 per week, while money prices remain unchanged at \$12 per unit for food and \$6 per unit for clothing, the amount of goods that the household can buy will also be halved. This causes the budget line to shift inward toward the origin, as shown in Figure 7-2. All possible combinations that are now open to the household appear on a budget line that is closer to the origin than the original budget line.

If the household's money income *rises* to \$540, while the money prices of food and clothing remain unchanged, it will be able to increase its purchases of both commodities. The budget line shifts outward, as shown in Figure 7-2.

Variations in the household's money income, with money prices constant, shift the budget line parallel to itself. It shifts inward (toward the origin) when money income falls and outward (away from the origin) when money income rises.

Proportional Changes in All Money Prices

Now return to the initial situation, in which the household has a money income of \$360 and faces prices of \$12 per unit for food and \$6 per unit for clothing. Let the money prices of food and clothing

---

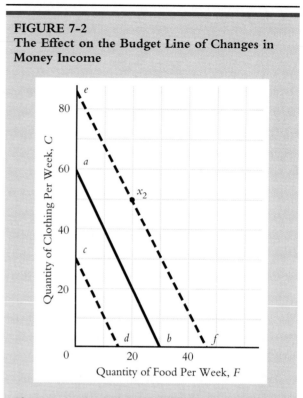

FIGURE 7-2
The Effect on the Budget Line of Changes in Money Income

Changes in the household's money income shift the budget line inward toward the origin when money income falls and outward when money income rises. The original budget line *ab* is reproduced from Figure 7-1. It refers to a money income of \$360 and prices of \$12 per unit for F and \$6 per unit for C. If the household's money income is halved from \$360 to \$180 per week, while prices remain unchanged, the amount of goods the household can buy will also be halved. This causes the budget line to shift inward (toward the origin) to *cd*. If the household spends all its money income on clothing, it can now get 30 units of clothing and zero units of food (point *c* in the figure). If it spends all its money income on food, it can get 15 units of food and zero units of clothing (point *d*).

If the household's money income rises to \$540, while the price of food and clothing remain unchanged, the budget line shifts outward to *ef*. If the household buys only clothing, it can have 90 units of clothing; if it buys only food, it can have 45 units of food. Point x_2, indicating 50 units of C and 20 units of F, is now attainable, as shown by the fact that it lies on the new budget line *ef*.

---

[1] Of course, with a given money income, the household can afford much less of each at these higher money prices, but the opportunity cost of food in terms of clothing remains unchanged.

double to $24 per unit for food and $12 per unit for clothing. This halves the quantities of food and clothing that can be bought and so shifts the budget line inward, parallel to itself. These changes in money prices have exactly the same effect as when prices remain constant at $12 per unit for food and $6 per unit for clothing but money income falls from $360 to $180; they would cause the budget line in Figure 7-2 to shift toward the origin from *ab* to *cd*.

Similarly, a proportional reduction of both money prices causes the budget line to shift outward in exactly the same manner that an increase in money income does. For example, a reduction in the prices of food and clothing to $8 per unit and $4 per unit, respectively, would cause the budget line in Figure 7-2 to shift outward from *ab* to *ef.*

Proportional changes in the money prices of all goods, if money income remains constant, shift the budget line parallel to itself. It shifts outward (away from the origin) when money prices fall and inward (toward the origin) when money prices rise.

Money Income and Real Income

Clearly, there can be offsetting changes in money prices and money incomes that leave the household's real income unchanged. For example, if money income and money prices all rise by 10 percent, the position of the budget line, and hence the choices available to the household, are unchanged.

A proportional change in money income and in all money prices leaves the household neither better nor worse off in terms of its ability to purchase commodities.

The foregoing observations show the importance of the distinction between *money* income and *real* income. A household's **money income** is its income measured in monetary units per period of time—so many dollars per week or per year. A household's **real income** is the *purchasing power* of its money income; it is the quantity of goods and services that can be purchased with that money income.

If money prices remain constant, any change in money income will cause a corresponding change in real income. If the household's money income rises by 10 percent (say, from $10,000 to $11,000), the household is able to buy 10 percent more of all commodities—its purchasing power has risen by 10 percent.

If money prices change, real and money incomes will not change in the same proportion; indeed, they can easily change in *opposite* directions. Consider a situation in which all money prices rise by 10 percent. If money income rises by any amount less than 10 percent, real income falls. If money income also rises by 10 percent, real income will be unchanged. Only if money income rises by more than 10 percent will real income also rise.

A household's ability to purchase goods and services is measured by its real income, not by its money income.

Changes in real income are shown graphically by shifts in the budget line. When the budget line in Figure 7-2 shifts toward the origin, real income falls; when the budget line shifts away from the origin, real income rises.

Changes in Relative Prices

Recall that a *relative price* is the ratio of two absolute prices. The statement "The price of *F* is $12" refers to an absolute price; the statement "The price of *F* is twice the price of *C*" refers to a relative price.

A change in a relative price can occur, and often does, as a result of changes in both of the absolute prices in different proportions. However, the points we wish to make can be established by studying the case in which changes in relative prices occur when one money price remains constant while the other changes.

Let us return to our illustration in which a household with a money income of $360 faces prices of $12 per unit for food and $6 per unit for clothing. Now let the price of food fall to $6 per unit. This lowers the price of food *relative to the price of clothing* and, as shown in Figure 7-3, changes the slope of the budget line. The important conclusion is this:

A change in relative prices alters the slope of the budget line and therefore changes the opportunity cost of food in terms of clothing.

Relative prices and real income. When relative prices change, there is a change in the alternatives

FIGURE 7-3
The Effect on the Budget Line of Changes in the Price of Food

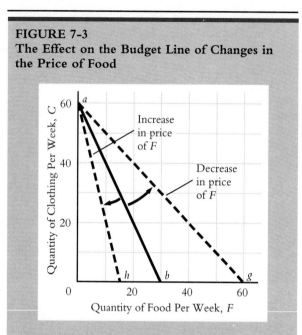

A change in the absolute price of one commodity changes relative prices and thus changes the slope of the budget line. The original budget line *ab* occurred with a money income of $360, with units of C priced at $6 and units of F at $12. A fall in the price of F to $6 doubles the quantity of F obtainable for any given quantity of C purchased and pivots the budget line outward to *ag*. A rise in the price of F to $24 reduces the quantity of F obtainable and pivots the budget line inward to *ah*.

available to the household; that is, there is a change in the amounts of the various commodities that it can afford to purchase. This means that a change in relative prices has an effect on the household's *real income*. As we shall see in the next section, the extent of the effect on real income depends not only on the choices households face but also on the choices they make. For this reason, when relative prices change, the measurement of the effect on real income is more difficult than it is when only money income changes, or when all absolute prices change in proportion so that relative prices remain constant.

The Choices Households Make

The combination of goods and services that a household chooses to purchase will depend on both

what it *can* do and what it *wants* to do. What it can do is shown by its budget line, which we have just studied. What it wants to do is determined by its tastes. Given its budget line and its tastes, what will the household do?

The key assumption about household behaviour is that households maximize what is variously called their *satisfaction,* their *welfare,* their *well-being,* or their *utility.* However it is worded, and whatever the theory used to develop it, the important thing is that households are assumed to try to do as well for themselves as they can.

Facing a choice among alternative consumption bundles, each household is assumed to choose the bundle that it prefers—which is the same as saying that the household makes its choices so as to maximize its satisfactions or its welfare.

Income and Substitution Effects

How does the household react to a change in the price of one good? For purposes of illustration, we consider a fall in price.

A fall in the price of one good affects the consumer in two ways. First, relative prices change, providing an incentive to buy *more* of the good in question because it is cheaper. Second, the household's real income increases, because it can buy more of all commodities (as can be seen, for example, by comparing budget lines *ab* and *ag* in Figure 7-3). This rise in real income provides an incentive to buy different amounts of all goods. (Recall from Chapter 5 that when its real income rises, the household buys more of all normal goods and less of all inferior goods.)

These two effects are illustrated in Figure 7-3. The household initially has a money income of $360 and faces prices of food and clothing of $12 and $6, respectively. The budget line is shown by line *ab* in the figure; given the household's tastes, it will prefer a combination of goods shown by some particular point on this line. The price of food then falls to $6, which shifts the budget line to *ag* in the figure and makes it possible for the household to buy more of both commodities—which is why we say that its real income has risen. The household then chooses its preferred position on the new budget line. The shift in consumption is partly a response to the change in the *slope* of the budget line, reflecting the change in relative prices. It is also partly a response to an *outward* shift in the budget line, reflecting the increase in the household's real income due to the fall in one money price with money income and all other money prices remaining constant.

The *extent* of the rise in real income depends on the share of total expenditures that the household spends on each good. For example, consider the extreme case of a household that spends all of its income on food; it will find that its real income has doubled, because at a price of food of $6, it can now afford to purchase 60 units of food rather than only the 30 units it could afford at the original price of $12. At the other extreme, a household that spends none of its income on food and all of it on clothing finds that its consumption opportunities are unchanged—it can still buy only 60 units of clothing. For intermediate cases, where some of both goods are purchased, there will be some positive effect on real income when the price of food falls, the strength of which will depend on the share of food expenditures in the household's budget.

An Example

To make the example precise, suppose that the household chooses the particular combinations shown in Figure 7-4 and Table 7-1. Suppose that at the initial prices, with budget line *ab*, the household chooses to consume 15 units of food and 30 units of clothing. This combination is indicated by the point E_0 in part (i) of Figure 7-4 and is also described in line 1 of the table. Following the fall in the price of food, with the new budget line of *ag*, we suppose that the household chooses to consume 25 units of food and 35 units of clothing. This combination is indicated by point E_1 in the figure and is described in line 4 of the table.

Substitution effect. To isolate the effect of the change in relative price when the price of food falls, we can consider what would happen if we also reduce the household's money income to restore its original purchasing power. To do this we can reduce money income until the original bundle of food and clothing can just be bought at the new prices. The consumption bundle that the household chooses in this hypothetical situation with the new prices and the reduced money income reflects the effect of the change in relative prices *when the pur-*

chasing power of income is held constant. The resulting change in the household's choice, compared to its initial preferred combination, is called the **substitution effect,** which is the change in quantity demanded as a result of a change in relative prices, with real income held constant.[2]

In our example, the new budget line is *de* in part (ii) of Figure 7-4, and the household chooses the combination indicated by point E' in the figure and described in line 3 of Table 7-1. The substitution effect causes the household to buy more food, the relative price of which has fallen, and less clothing, the relative price of which has risen.

Income effect. Next, we restore the household's money income, which shifts the budget line outward, parallel to itself. Assuming that we are dealing with normal goods, the household will increase its consumption of both food and clothing. The change in the quantity of food demanded as a result of the household's reaction to this shift of its budget line is called the **income effect.** It is shown by the change between lines 3 and 4 in Table 7-1 and points E' and E_1 in part (iii) of Figure 7-4.

Recap. We have now broken down the reaction to a fall in the price of a commodity (food, in our example) into a substitution effect and an income effect. In our numerical example, the substitution effect raises the consumption of food by 6 units, and the income effect raises it by 4 units, making the overall response to the fall in price of food an increase in food consumption of 10 units. Of course, when the price of food falls, the household moves directly from its initial position to its final position, buying 10 more units of food. By breaking this movement into two parts, however, we are able to study the household's total change in quantity demanded as a response to a change in relative prices and a response to a change in real income.

Notice that the size of the income effect depends on the amount of income spent on the good whose price changes and on the amount by which the price changes. In our simple example, where the household was spending one half of its income on food, a 50 percent fall in the food price was equivalent (at the new prices) to a 25 percent in-

---

[2]This measure, which isolates the substitution effect by holding the household's *purchasing power* constant, is known as the *Slutsky effect.* A related but slightly different measure that holds the household's *level of satisfaction* constant is discussed in Chapter 8.

FIGURE 7-4
The Income and Substitution Effects

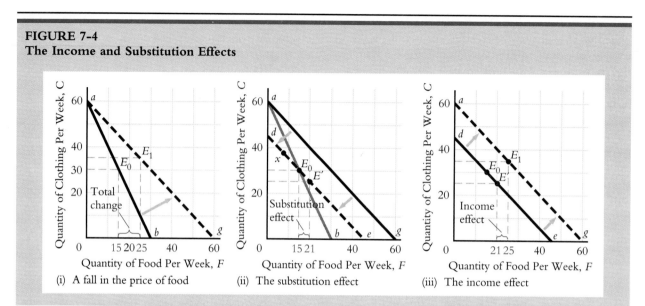

(i) A fall in the price of food (ii) The substitution effect (iii) The income effect

The effect on household choice of a change in price can be broken into (1) a substitution effect measuring the response to a change in relative prices with purchasing power being held constant, and (2) an income effect measuring the response to the change in purchasing power caused by the price change.

(i) The initial budget line is *ab*, and the household's chosen position is E_0, which corresponds to line 1 of Table 7-1. At E_0 food consumption is $15F$ and clothing consumption is $30C$. The price of food then falls, taking the budget line to *ag* and consumption to the bundle indicated by E_1. At E_1 food consumption is $25F$, and hence the total change in the demand for food is $10F$.

(ii) The substitution effect is shown by reducing money income so that the original bundle can just be bought at the new prices. As shown in line 2 of Table 7-1, income must be reduced to $270. Graphically, in part (ii) this shifts the budget line to *de*, where it is parallel to *ag* but passes through E_0. The combined effect of the change in the price and the fall in income is that the budget line rotates through the initial consumption point E_0. The household chooses point E' on *de*, which corresponds to line 3 of Table 7-1. The substitution effect is the movement from E_0 to E'; as shown in part (ii) of the Figure and Table 7-1, the substitution effect on the demand for food is $6F$, as consumption rises from $15F$ to $21F$.

(iii) The income effect is then measured by restoring money income to its original level. Graphically, this shifts the budget line in part (iii) from *de* to *ag*. The household chooses point E_1; this corresponds to line 4 in Table 7-1. The income effect is the change in consumption from E' to E_1. This corresponds to the change from line 3 to line 4 in Table 7-1; the income effect on the demand for food is $4F$ as consumption rises from $21F$ to $25F$. The total increase is therefore the sum of the two effects, or $10F$.

crease in income. Now consider a different case. Assume that the price of petroleum falls by 20 percent. For a household that was spending only 5 percent of its income on gas and oil, this is equivalent (at the new prices) to only a 1 percent increase in purchasing power (20 percent of 5 percent).

Derivation of a Demand Curve

The demand curve relates the quantity of a particular commodity demanded to the commodity's price.

Figure 7-5 shows the derivation of the demand curve for food based on the example in Table 7-1. Part (i) reproduces part (i) of Figure 7-4; it shows the effect of a fall in the price of food on the budget line and on the consumption bundle chosen by the household. Each combination of a price of food and the corresponding quantity of food purchased is then plotted as a point in part (ii) of Figure 7-5. These are each points on the demand curve for food. The line joining them is a negatively sloped demand curve.

TABLE 7-1 The Income and Substitution Effects: A Numerical Example

		Prices		Consumption		Total expenditure
		Food	Clothing	Food	Clothing	
1.	Initial Position Household chooses bundle E_0	$12	$6	15	30	$360
2.	Price of food falls; cost of initial bundle at new prices	$6	$6	15	30	$270
3.	Intermediate Position Household chooses bundle E'	$6	$6	21	24	$270
4.	Final position Household chooses bundle E_1	$6	$6	25	35	$360

The substitution effect measures the response to a change in relative prices when the purchasing power of income is held constant; the income effect measures the response to a change in purchasing power when relative prices are held constant. In the initial position shown in line 1, a consumer with a money income of $360 faces prices of $12 per unit for food and $6 per unit for clothing and chooses to purchase $15F$ and $30C$. This corresponds to point E_0 on budget line ab in part (i) of Figure 7-4.

The money price of food then falls to $6 per unit. As shown in line 2, the household's initial bundle of $15F$ and $30C$ now costs only $270.

Line 3 shows the household's consumption choice at the new prices when its income is reduced to $270. Although the initial bundle of $15F$ and $30C$ could still be bought at the new prices, the household does not choose to do so. Instead, it increases its consumption of (the now cheaper) food and reduces its consumption of clothing; it now purchases $21F$ and $24C$. This corresponds to point E' on budget line de in part (ii) of Figure 7-4.

Line 4 shows what happens when money income is returned to its original level of $360—the consumption of F and C both rise, to $25F$ and $35C$.

The substitution effect is the change in food consumption that results from the change in relative prices, with purchasing power held constant. This is shown by the change in food consumption from $15F$ in line 2 to $21F$ in line 3. The income effect is the change in food consumption that results from the change in purchasing power, with relative prices held constant at their new level. This is shown by the increase in food consumption from $21F$ in line 3 to $25F$ in line 4.

The total change in the demand for food in response to the fall in its price is the sum of the substitution and income effects—in this example, the fall in the price of food from $12 to $6 leads to an increase of 10 units in the quantity of food demanded, from 15 to 25 units per week.

The Slope of the Demand Curve

The negative slope of the demand curve in Figure 7-5 shows that a fall in price leads to an increase in the quantity demanded. Earlier in this book, we merely assumed this slope, but the analysis underlying Figure 7-4 allows us to explain it. As shown in Figure 7-4, the substitution effect leads the household to buy more food, which is the commodity whose price has fallen.

We now ask a fundamental question: Could the substitution effect of a fall in the price of food have led the household to buy less food? Graphically, this would mean that the household would select some bundle that had less food and more clothing than its initial bundle. An example would be the bundle indicated by the point x on budget line de in Figure 7-6, which reproduces part (ii) of Figure 7-4. When the household faced its original budget line, ab, it could have gone to x (by not spending all of its income), but it chose not to do so, going to E_0 instead. So as long as its preferences remain unchanged, the household will not now go to x. This argument leads us to an important conclusion:

FIGURE 7-5
Derivation of the Demand Curve for Food

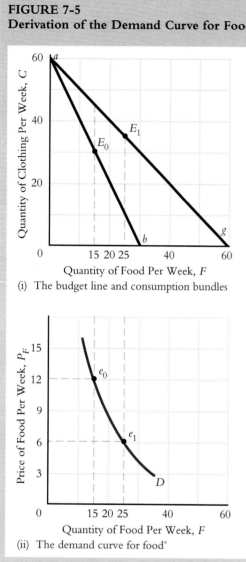

(i) The budget line and consumption bundles

(ii) The demand curve for food°

With a given money income, a change in the price of food causes the budget line to rotate and a new bundle of food and clothing to be purchased. This gives the information needed to derive the demand curve for food. Part (i) reproduces part (i) of Figure 7-4. The household has an income of $360, and prices are initially $12 per unit of food and $6 per unit of clothing. The budget line is ab, and the household consumes at point E_0, purchasing 15 units of food. When the price of food falls to $6 per unit, the budget line shifts to ag. The household consumes at point E_1, purchasing 25 units of food.

Part (ii) plots the quantity of food demanded against the price of food to yield the demand curve for food. Point e_0 corresponds to point E_0 in part (i), where we saw that at a price of $12 per unit, the household purchases 15 units of food. Point e_1 corresponds to point E_1 in part (i); at the lower price of $6 per unit, the household's demand for food rises to 25 units. Considering other prices would give rise to a series of points that when joined would yield the demand curve D.

The substitution effect can *never* lead a household to purchase less of a commodity whose price has fallen.

Now consider the second part of the household's adjustment to the fall in price, the income effect. As we saw in Chapter 5, a rise in income leads the household to buy more of all normal goods. This leads to the second conclusion.

The income effect leads the household to buy more of the commodity whose price has

fallen, provided that it is a normal commodity.

Putting these two effects together gives the following conclusion:

Because of the combined operation of the substitution effect and the income effect, the demand curve for any normal commodity will be negatively sloped, indicating that a fall in price will lead to an increase in quantity demanded.

FIGURE 7-6
The Substitution Effect and Quantity Demanded

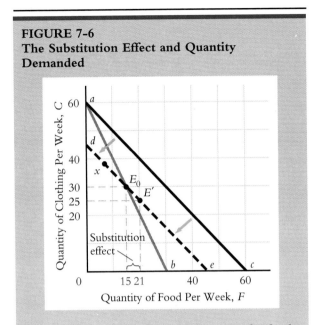

The substitution effect can never lead the household to buy less food when its price falls. The figure reproduces part (ii) of Figure 7-4. At the initial prices and income levels, the budget line is given by *ab*. If the price of food falls and income is reduced so that the household can still choose E_0, the budget line rotates to *de*. Suppose that the household chose a bundle such as *x*, which lies to the left of E_0 on the budget line *de*. However, when the household had budget line *ab*, it could have chosen *x* (by not spending all its income). Instead it rejected *x* in favour of E_0. If the household is consistent, it will not now choose a previously rejected combination. Instead it will choose some position on *de* at, or to the right of, E_0; such points were not available to it when it chose E_0 on budget line *ab*. *Any* point on *de* to the right of E_0 indicates more consumption of food, the good whose price has fallen.

The Role of Tastes

Earlier, we observed that what the household can do depends on its budget line, whereas what it does do depends on its tastes. Yet we appear to have studied the household's reactions to a change in price without saying much about the household's tastes. In fact, we did make use of a simple assump-

tion about tastes. We assumed that households were consistent in the sense that if once they chose bundle of goods *A* over bundle *B*, they would not subsequently choose bundle *B* over bundle *A*. This is what allowed us to say that when the price of food fell and income was adjusted so that the original bundle could just be purchased, the household would never choose a new bundle containing less food because any such bundle could have been chosen in the initial situation. This assumption is laid out in more detail in Box 7-1 for readers who would like to study it further.

Can Demand Curves Ever Have Positive Slopes?

What the great English economist Alfred Marshall called the **law of demand** asserts that, other things being constant, the market price of a product and the quantity demanded in the market are negatively associated; that is, demand curves have negative slopes. Challenges to the law have taken various forms, focusing on Giffen goods, conspicuous consumption goods, and goods whose demands are perfectly inelastic. Let us consider each of these in turn.

Giffen goods. Great interest was attached to the nineteenth-century English economist Sir Robert Giffen's apparent refutation of the law of demand. He is alleged to have observed that when a rise in the price of imported wheat led to an increase in the price of bread, members of the British working class *increased* their consumption of bread. This meant that their demand curve for bread was positively sloped.

  The study of the income and substitution effects (discussed further in Box 7-1) shows that such an exception to the law of demand could occur. There are two requisites: (1) The good must be an inferior good, and (2) the good must take a large proportion of total household expenditure; that is, its income effect must be large. Bread was indeed a dietary staple of the British working classes during the nineteenth century. A rise in the price of bread would cause a large reduction in their real income. This could lead to increased consumption of bread as households cut out their few luxuries in order to be able to consume enough bread to keep alive. Though possible, such cases are all but unknown in the modern world. The reason is that in all but the

Box 7-1

More About the Slope of Demand Curves

This box gives a more precise treatment of the discussion found in the text and then discusses the implications of the negative income effects that arise with inferior goods. The basic assumption about tastes that is used in this approach is called the *consistency assumption*. It states that if the household chose some bundle of goods that we call *A* over some other bundle that we call *B* in one situation, then—so long as the household's tastes do not change—it would never choose *B* over *A* in some subsequent situation in which *A* and *B* are both available to it.

Normally Sloped Demand Curves

Let the initial budget line be *ab* and the chosen position be E_0. This means that the household has chosen the combination indicated by E_0 over all other attainable combinations. The rejected combinations are indicated by the points in the shaded triangle between *ab* and the origin. (Note that when it faces the budget line *ab*, the household can reach any point on *ab* by spending all of its income and can reach any point lying in the shaded area below *ab* by spending less than all its income.) If the household is consistent, it will never choose another bundle within that area when the bundle indicated by E_0 is also available.

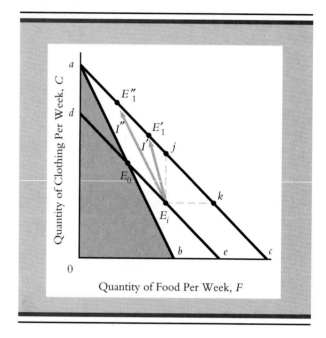

Now let the price of *F* fall, taking the budget line to *ac*. To isolate the substitution effect, we also reduce money income so that the budget line becomes *de*. This new budget line is parallel to *ac*, indicating that the household faces the new relative price. The new budget line also passes through E_0,

poorest societies, typical households do not spend large proportions of their incomes on a single inferior good.

Conspicuous consumption goods. Thorstein Veblen in *The Theory of the Leisure Class* noted that some commodities were consumed not for their intrinsic qualities but because they carried a snob appeal. He suggested that the more expensive such a commodity became, the *greater* might be its ability to confer status on its purchaser.

Consumers might buy diamonds, for example, not because they particularly like diamonds but because they wish to show off their wealth in an ostentatious but socially acceptable way. They are assumed to value diamonds precisely because diamonds are expensive. Thus a fall in price might lead them to stop buying diamonds and to switch to a more satisfactory object of conspicuous consumption. They may behave in the same way with respect to luxury cars, buying them *because* they are expensive. Households that behave in this way will indicating that the household has only its original purchasing power.

Consistency requires that the household cannot choose any point to the left of E_0 on the new budget line *de*, since those points lie within the shaded area that was rejected when E_0 was chosen on the budget line *ab*. The household either stays at E_0 or moves to some point to the right of E_0—say it goes to E_i.

The foregoing argument shows that the substitution effect cannot be positive; when the price of food falls, the household cannot buy less food.

Now consider the income effect. Begin by drawing a vertical and a horizontal line from E_i to cut *ac* at *j* and *k*. Points on *ac* between *j* and *k* indicate an increase in the consumption of both commodities when the budget line goes from *de* to *ac*. This is what must happen if both goods are normal goods. This shows that the income effect of a fall in the price of food must lead to an increase in the demand for food, assuming only that it is a normal (noninferior) good.

So we know that if the price of some product falls, the substitution effect cannot lead to less of it being consumed, and if the good is normal, the income effect leads to more of it being consumed. A fall in the price of any normal good must therefore lead to an increase in its demand; that is, its demand curve has a negative slope.

Positively Sloped Demand Curves

Could the demand curve for F ever be positively sloped? This can happen only if F is an inferior good (a necessary condition). The figure illustrates two cases in which F is inferior. In the first case, the movement of the budget line from *de* to *ac* takes the equilibrium position along the arrow I' to E'_1. In this case, the income effect leads to a fall in the demand for F, but the substitution effect is stronger than the income effect. Hence the overall change in the quantity of F is an increase as the chosen position goes from E_0 to E'_1. In the second case, the negative income effect is stronger, and the equilibrium follows the path I'' from E_i to E''_1. In this case, the income effect of the inferior good outweighs the substitution effect, and the quantity of F demanded falls from that indicated by E_0 to that indicated by E'_1, as a result of a fall in the price of F.

We can now conclude the following:

1. All normal goods have negatively sloped demand curves.
2. All inferior goods for which the substitution effect outweighs the income effect have negatively sloped demand curves.
3. A positively sloped demand curve requires an inferior good for which the income effect outweighs the substitution effect.

have positively sloped *individual demand curves* for diamonds and cars.[3]

Perfectly inelastic demand curves. Even if demand curves never had positive slopes, the substan-

tial insight provided by the law of demand would be diminished if there were important commodities for which changes in price had virtually no effect on quantity demanded.

It is surprising how often the assumption of a vertical demand curve is made implicitly. For example, a common response of urban bus or subway systems to financial difficulties is to propose a percentage increase in fares equal to the percentage increase that they require in their revenues. Even professors are not immune to this type of response. At a

---

[3]Of course, even with conspicuous consumption goods, the quantity demanded may rise when the price of the good goes down as long as its perceived price remains high—as one advertising slogan for a discount department store puts it: "Only you know how little you paid."

Box 7-2

Market and Individual Demand Curves

Market demand curves tell how much is demanded by all purchasers. For example, in Figure 4-1, (page 62) the market demand for carrots is 90,000 tons when the price is $40 per ton. This 90,000 tons is the sum of the quantities demanded by millions of different households. It may be made up of 4 pounds for the Carsons, 7 pounds for the Chows, 1.5 pounds for the Smiths, and so on. The demand curve in Figure 4-1 also tells us that when the price rises to $60, the total quantity demanded falls to 77,500 tons per month. This quantity too can be traced back to individual households. The Carsons might buy only 3 pounds, the Chows 6.5 pounds, and the Smiths none at all. Notice that we have now described two points not only on the market demand curve but also on the demand curves of each of these households.

The market demand curve is the horizontal sum of the demand curves of individual households.

It is the horizontal sum because we wish to add quantities demanded at a given price, and quantities are measured in the horizontal direction on a conventional demand curve.

The figure illustrates aggregation over two households. At a price of $3, household A purchases 2 units and household B purchases 4 units; thus together they purchase 6 units, yielding one point on the market demand curve. No matter how many households are involved, the process is the same: Add the quantities demanded by all households at each price, and the result is the market demand curve.

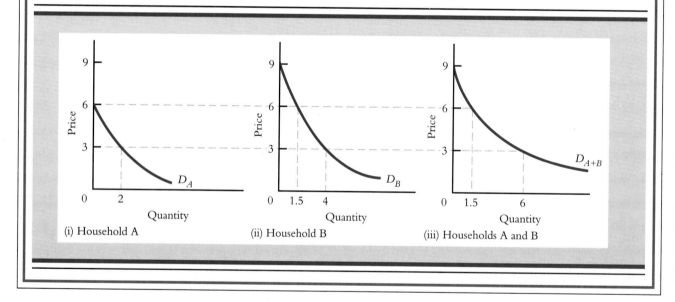

(i) Household A   (ii) Household B   (iii) Households A and B

meeting of an association of university professors, a motion was introduced "to raise annual dues by 20 percent in order to raise revenues by 20 percent," in spite of the empirical evidence showing that a previous increase in dues had led (as our theory would predict) to a drop in membership.

It was once widely argued that the demand for gasoline was almost perfectly inelastic, on the grounds that people who had paid thousands of dollars for cars would not balk at paying a few cents extra for gasoline. The events of the past two decades have proved how wrong this argument is:

Higher gasoline prices in the early 1980s led to production of smaller cars, to more car pools, to more economical driving speeds, and to less pleasure driving. Falling gasoline prices in the mid-1980s led to a reversal of these trends.

Market demand curves. Even if some individual households were to exhibit one or more of the exceptions to the law of demand discussed above, their actions would normally be swamped by those of households whose behaviour conformed to the law of demand. For example, even if a few wealthy customers reduced their purchases of diamonds when their price fell, this behaviour would be swamped by the normal behaviour of households with somewhat lower incomes who would now be able to afford diamonds. Thus the *market* demand curve would still be negatively sloped. Box 7-2 shows the link between the household demand curves studied in this chapter and the market demand curves encountered in earlier chapters.

In summary, a mass of accumulated evidence confirms that most demand curves do in fact have a negative slope.

The hypothesis that demand curves are negatively sloped is strongly supported by the evidence.

Consumers' Surplus

Imagine yourself facing an either-or choice concerning some particular commodity: You can have the amount you are now consuming, or you can have none of it. Assume that you would be willing to pay as much as $100 per month for that amount rather than do without it. Further assume that you actually buy that amount of the commodity for $60 instead of $100. What a bargain! You have paid $40 less than the top figure you were willing to pay. Yet this sort of bargain occurs every day in any economy in which prices do the rationing. Indeed, it is so common that the $40 "saved" in this example has been given a name: *consumers' surplus.* We will define the term later; first, let us look at how this surplus arises.

Consumers' surplus is a direct consequence of negatively sloped demand curves. To illustrate this

TABLE 7-2   Consumers' Surplus on Milk Consumption by One Consumer

(1) Glasses of milk consumed per week	(2) Amount the consumer would pay to get this glass	(3) Consumer's surplus on each glass if milk costs 30 cents per glass
First	$3.00	$2.70
Second	1.50	1.20
Third	1.00	.70
Fourth	.80	.50
Fifth	.60	.30
Sixth	.50	.20
Seventh	.40	.10
Eighth	.30	.00
Ninth	.25	—
Tenth	.20	—

Consumers' surplus on each unit consumed is the difference between the market price and the maximum price the consumer would pay to obtain that unit. The table shows the value that one consumer, Mrs. Swartz, puts on successive glasses of milk consumed each week. Her negatively sloped demand curve shows that she would be willing to pay progressively smaller amounts for each additional unit consumed. As long as she would be willing to pay more than the market price for any unit, she obtains a consumers' surplus on it when she buys it. The marginal unit is the one valued just at the market price and on which no consumers' surplus is earned.

connection, suppose that we have collected the information in Table 7-2 on the basis of an interview with Mrs. Swartz. Our first question to Mrs. Swartz is, "If you were getting no milk at all, how much would you be willing to pay for one glass per week?" With no hesitation, she replies $3.00. We then ask, "If you had already consumed that one glass, how much would you pay for a second glass per week?" After a bit of thought she answers $1.50. Adding one glass per week with each question, we discover that she would be willing to pay $1.00 to get a third glass per week and 80, 60, 50, 40, 30, 25, and 20 cents for successive glasses from the fourth to the tenth glass per week.

The sum of the values that she places on each glass of milk gives us the *total value* that she places on all 10 glasses. In this case, Mrs. Swartz values 10 glasses of milk per week at $8.55. This is the amount she would be willing to pay if faced with the either-or choice of 10 glasses or none. This is also the amount she would be willing to pay if she were offered the milk one glass at a time and charged the maximum she was willing to pay for each.

However, Mrs. Swartz does not have to pay a different price for each glass of milk she consumes each week; she can buy all she wants at the prevailing market price. Suppose the price is 30 cents per glass. She will buy eight glasses per week (one each weekday and two on Sunday) because she values the eighth glass just at the market price but all earlier glasses at higher amounts. She does not buy a ninth glass because she values it at less than the market price.

Because she values the first glass at $3.00 but gets it for 30 cents, she makes a "profit" of $2.70 on that glass. Between her $1.50 valuation of the second glass and what she has to pay for it, she clears a "profit" of $1.20. She clears a "profit" of 70 cents on the third glass, and so on. These "profits," which are shown in column 3 of Table 7-2, are called her consumers' surplus on each glass.

Her total consumers' surplus of $5.70 per week can be calculated by summing her surplus on each glass; the same total can be calculated by first summing what she would pay for all eight glasses, which is $8.10, and then by subtracting the $2.40 that she does pay.

The value placed by each household on its total consumption of some commodity can be estimated in at least two ways: The valuation that the household places on each successive unit may be summed, or the household may be asked how much it would pay to consume the amount in question if the alternative were to have none of that commodity.[4]

Although other households would put different numerical values into Table 7-2, the negative slope

[4]This is only an approximation, but it is good enough for our purposes. More advanced theory shows that the calculations presented here overestimate consumers' surplus because they ignore the income effect. Although it is sometimes necessary to correct for this bias, no amount of refinement upsets the general result that we establish here: When consumers can buy all units they require at a single market price, they pay much less than they would be willing to pay if facing a choice between having the quantity they consume and having none.

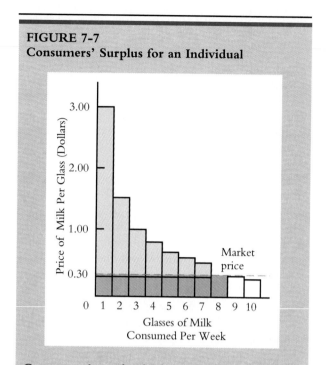

FIGURE 7-7
Consumers' Surplus for an Individual

Consumers' surplus is the sum of the extra valuations placed on each unit above the market price paid for each. This figure is based on the data in Table 7-2. Mrs. Swartz pays the amounts shown in the dark shaded area for the eight glasses of milk she will consume per week when the market price is 30 cents per glass. The total value she places on these eight glasses is the entire shaded area. Hence her consumers' surplus is the light shaded area.

of the demand curve implies that the figures in column 2 would be declining for each household. Because a household will go on buying additional units until the value placed on the last unit equals the market price, it follows that there will be a consumers' surplus on every unit consumed except the last one.

In general, **consumers' surplus** is the difference between the total value that consumers place on all the units consumed of some commodity and the payment they must make to purchase that amount of the commodity.

The data in columns 1 and 2 of Table 7-2 give Mrs. Swartz's demand curve for milk. It is her demand curve because she will go on buying glasses of milk as long as she values each glass at least as much as the market price she must pay for it. When the market price is $3.00 per glass, she will buy only one glass; when it is $1.50, she will buy two glasses; and so on. The total valuation she places on her milk consumption is the area below her demand curve, and her consumers' surplus is the part of the area that lies above the price line. This is shown in Figure 7-7.

Figure 7-8 shows that the same relationship holds for the smooth market demand curve that indicates the total amount all consumers would buy at each price.[5]

A Preview

In this chapter, we have presented the minimum amount of demand theory that is needed for the rest of this book. In the next chapter we shall present a number of applications. The two appendixes to this chapter present more formal theories of household tastes that lead to the prediction of negatively sloped demand curves. Some of you will skip both of these appendixes; others will read one or both. Whatever you do, remember that although abstract in its current presentation, modern demand theory grew up to handle a number of real and interesting problems. We shall see how the theory can be applied to real issues both in the next chapter and later in this book.

---

[5]Figure 7-7 is a bar chart because we only allowed Mrs. Swartz to vary her consumption in discrete units of one glass at a time. Had we allowed her to vary her consumption of milk one drop at a time, we could have traced out a continuous curve similar to the one shown in Figure 7-8.

FIGURE 7-8
Consumers' Surplus for the Market

Total consumers' surplus is the area under the demand curve and above the price line. The demand curve shows the amount consumers would pay for each unit of the commodity if they had to buy their units one at a time. The area under the demand curve shows the total valuation that consumers place on all units consumed. For example, the total value that consumers place on q_0 units is the entire shaded area under the demand curve up to q_0. At a market price of p_0, the amount paid for q_0 units is the dark shaded area. Hence consumers' surplus is the light shaded area.

SUMMARY

1. The budget line shows all combinations of commodities that are available to the household, given its money income and the prices of the goods it purchases.
2. The budget line is shifted parallel to itself by either a change in money income, with all money prices being held constant, or a proportionate change in all money prices, with money income being held constant.
3. Changes in relative prices change the slope of the budget line.
4. The budget line describes what the household *can* purchase; what it *does* purchase depends also on its tastes.
5. A change in one money price has an income effect and a substitution effect. The substitution effect is the reaction of the household to the change in relative prices, with real income held constant. It can be measured by allowing price to change and then by altering money income until the original bundle can just be purchased. In this situation, a consistent household would never reduce its purchases of the commodity whose relative price has fallen. The in-

come effect is then measured by a parallel shift of the budget line to restore its initial money income. The income effect of a fall in one money price will lead to an increase in the purchases of all normal commodities.

6. The combined effect of the income and the substitution effects ensures that the quantity demanded of any normal good will increase when its money price falls, other things being equal. This means that normal goods have negatively sloped demand curves.

7. Three conceivable exceptions to the law of negatively sloped demand curves are a Giffen good, which can only arise in the case of an inferior good on which a household spends much of its income; conspicuous consumption goods, which are goods consumed *because* they are expensive; and goods with perfectly inelastic demands. Such exceptions rarely, if ever, cause actual market demand curves to have a positive slope.

8. Consumers' surplus arises because a household can purchase every unit of a commodity at a price equal to the value it places on the last unit purchased. The negative slope of demand curves implies that the value households place on all other units purchased exceeds the value of the last unit purchased, and hence that all but the last unit purchased yield a consumers' surplus.

9. The total value that consumers place on some quantity of a commodity consumed is given by the area under the demand curve up to that quantity. The amount that is paid to purchase the commodity is given by an area below the market price up to that quantity. Consumers' surplus is the difference between the two.

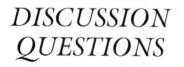

TOPICS FOR REVIEW

Causes of shifts in the budget line

Real income and money income

Absolute (or money) prices and relative prices

Relative prices and real income

Income effect and substitution effect

The law of demand and its possible exceptions

Consumers' surplus

DISCUSSION QUESTIONS

1. When the prices of fuel oil and gasoline rose drastically in the early 1980s, many Canadians reported that they felt worse off. To what extent do you think this reduction in real income was due to the income effect, and to what extent due to the substitution effect?

2. Explain the transactions described in the following quotations in terms of the value of the commodity. Interpret "worthless" and "priceless" as used here.

   a. "Bob Koppang has made a business of selling jars of shredded currency. The money is worthless, and yet he's sold 53,000 jars already and has orders for 40,000 more—at $5 a jar. Each jar contains about $10,000 in shredded bills."

   b. "In February 1987, Vincent Van Gogh's priceless painting "Sunflowers" sold at auction for $39 million."

3. In an effort to promote responsible drinking and to encourage the use of designated drivers, many campus bars in the country have started offering soft drinks at very low prices, sometimes even free. Describe the results you would expect in terms of the income and substitution effects.

4. Between 1980 and 1993, the cost of purchasing a representative bundle of consumers' goods rose by about 100 percent, as measured by the Consumer Price Index. What else would you need to know to find out what had happened to the average Canadian citizen's real income?

5. Mary is willing to pay $10 for the first widget that she purchases each year, $9 for the second, $8 for the third, and so on down to $1 for the tenth and nothing for the eleventh. How many widgets will she buy, and what will be her consumers' surplus, if widgets cost $3 each? What will happen if the price of widgets rises to $5? Can you state a generalization about the relationship between consumers' surplus obtained and the price of a commodity?

6. Professors Jeff Biddle and Daniel Hamermesch of Michigan State University have recently estimated that a 25 percent increase in wages will cause the average individual to reduce the time that he or she spends sleeping by about 1 percent. Interpret this in terms of the substitution effect. Would you expect to find an income effect on the amount of time that a person spends sleeping?

7. A middle-aged business executive reports that she now drinks a lot more French wine than she used to when she first started working for the company, even though imported wine is now much more expensive than it used to be. Do you think she has a positively sloped demand curve for French wine?

APPENDIX A TO CHAPTER

7

Indifference Theory

The history of demand theory has seen two major breakthroughs. The first was marginal utility theory, which assumed that the utility that people received from consuming commodities could be measured objectively. By distinguishing total and marginal values, this theory, which is discussed in Appendix 7B, helped explain the so-called paradox of value that is discussed in Chapter 8.

The second breakthrough came with indifference theory, which showed that demand theory could dispense with the dubious assumption of measurable utility on which marginal utility theory was based. All that is needed in this theory is the assumption that households could say which of two consumption bundles they preferred without having to say *by how much* they preferred it.

Appendix A develops the modern indifference theory; Appendix B deals with marginal utility theory.

An Indifference Curve

Indifference theory, which is sometimes called the modern theory of demand, is based on *indifference curves.* To understand these curves, we start with an imaginary household that currently has available to it some specific bundle of goods, say 18 units of clothing and 10 units of food. Now offer the household an alternative bundle of 13 units of clothing and 15 units of food. This alternative combination of goods has 5 fewer units of clothing and 5 more units of food than the first one. Whether the household prefers this bundle depends on the relative valuation that it places on 5 more units of food and 5 fewer units of clothing. If it values the extra food more than the forgone clothing, it will prefer the new bundle to the original one. If it values the food

TABLE 7A-1   Alternative Bundles Giving a Household Equal Satisfaction

Bundle	Clothing	Food
a	30	5
b	18	10
c	13	15
d	10	20
e	8	25
f	7	30

These bundles all lie on a single indifference curve. Since all of these bundles of food and clothing give equal satisfaction, the household is indifferent among them.

less than the clothing, it will prefer the original bundle. If the household values the extra food the same as it values the forgone clothing, it is said to be *indifferent between* the two bundles.

Assume that after much trial and error, we have identified several bundles among which the household is indifferent. In other words, each bundle gives the household equal satisfaction. They are shown in Table 7A-1.

There will, of course, be combinations of the two commodities other than those enumerated in Table 7A-1 that will give the same level of satisfaction to the household. All of these combinations are shown in Figure 7A-1 by the smooth curve that passes through the points plotted from the table. This curve, called an **indifference curve,** shows all combinations of commodities that yield the same satisfaction to the household; the household is indifferent between the combinations indicated by any two points on one indifference curve.

Next we wish to compare bundles of goods that are on the curve with points off the curve, which means they are either above the curve or below it. To do this, we assume that the household *always prefers more to less.* To be more specific, if bundle A contains more of both goods than bundle B, the household will always choose A when given a free choice between A and B. We can now show that any points above the curve show combinations of food and clothing that the household would prefer to combinations indicated by points on the curve. Consider, for example, the combination of 20 units of food and 18 units of clothing, represented by point *g* in Figure 7A-1. Although it may not be obvious that this bundle must be preferred to bundle *a* (which has more clothing but less food), it is obvious that it will be preferred to bundle *c,* because there is both less clothing and less food represented at *c* than at *g.* Inspection of the graph shows that *any* point above the curve will be obviously superior to *some* points on the curve in the sense that it will contain both more food and more clothing than those points on the curve. However, since all points on the curve are equal in the household's eyes, any point above the curve must be superior to *all* points on the curve. By a similar argument, all points below and to the left of the curve represent bundles that are inferior to bundles represented by points on the curve.

The Hypothesis of Diminishing Marginal Rate of Substitution

When the household moves downward to the right along the indifference curve in Figure 7A-1, it is reducing its consumption of clothing and increasing its consumption of food. What is the maximum amount of clothing that the household would be prepared to give up to get one more unit of food? The answer to this question measures what is called the marginal rate of substitution of clothing for food. The **marginal rate of substitution (MRS)** is the maximum amount of one commodity that a consumer would be prepared to give up in order to get one more unit of another commodity.

The first basic assumption of indifference theory is that the algebraic value of the *MRS* is always negative.

A negative *MRS* means that, in order to increase its consumption of one commodity, the household is prepared to decrease its consumption

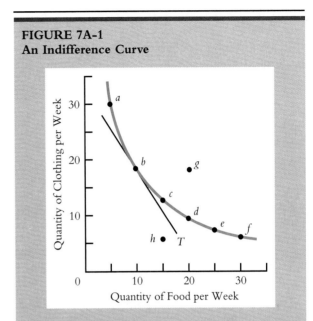

FIGURE 7A-1
An Indifference Curve

This indifference curve shows combination of food and clothing that yield equal satisfaction and among which the household is indifferent. Points *a* through *f* are plotted from Table 7-1. The smooth curve through them is an indifference curve; each combination on it gives equal satisfaction to the household. Point *g* above the line is a preferred combination to any point on the line; point *h* below the line is an inferior combination to any point on the line. The slope of the line *T* gives the marginal rate of substitution at point *b.* Moving down the curve from *b* to *f,* the slope flattens, showing that the more food and the less clothing the household has, the less willing it will be to sacrifice further clothing to get more food.

of a second. The negative value of the marginal rate of substitution is indicated graphically by the negative slope of all indifference curves. (See, for example, the curve in Figure 7A-1.)

The second basic assumption of indifference theory is that the marginal rate of substitution between any two commodities depends on the amounts of the commodities currently being consumed by the household.

Consider a case in which the household has a lot of clothing and only a little food. Common sense suggests that the household might be willing to give up quite a bit of its plentiful clothing in order to get one unit more of scarce food. It suggests as well that a household with a little clothing and a lot of food would be willing to give up only a little of its scarce clothing in order to get one more unit of already plentiful food.

This example illustrates the hypothesis of diminishing marginal rate of substitution. The less of one commodity, A, and the more of a second commodity, B, that the household has already, the smaller will be the amount of A that it will be willing to give up in order to get one additional unit of B. The hypothesis says that the marginal rate of substitution changes when the amounts of two commodities consumed change. The graphical expression of this is that the slope of any indifference curve becomes flatter as the household moves downward and to the right along the curve. In Figure 7A-1, a movement downward and to the right means that less clothing and more food is being consumed. The decreasing steepness of the curve means that the household is willing to sacrifice less and less clothing to get each additional unit of food. **[11]**

The hypothesis is illustrated in Table 7A-2, which is based on the example of food and clothing in Table 7A-1. The last column of the table shows the rate at which the household is prepared to sacrifice units of clothing per unit of food obtained. At first, the household will sacrifice 2.4 units of clothing to get 1 unit more of food, but as its consumption of clothing diminishes and its consumption of food increases, the household becomes less and less willing to sacrifice further clothing for more food.[1]

The Indifference Map

So far, we have constructed only a single indifference curve. However, starting at any other point of Figure 7A-1, such as g, there will be other combinations that will yield equal satisfaction to the household. If the points indicating all of these combinations are connected, they will form another indifference curve. This exercise can be repeated as

---

[1]In the text, we have discussed movements between distinctly separated points on the indifference curve. The rate at which the household will give up clothing to get food at any point on the curve is shown by the slope of the tangent to the curve at that point. The slope of the line T, which is a tangent to the curve at point b in Figure 7A-1, is the slope of the curve at that precise point. It tells us the rate at which the household will sacrifice clothing per unit of food obtained when it is currently consuming 18 units of clothing and 10 units of food (the coordinates of point b).

TABLE 7A-2   The Marginal Rate of Substitution Between Clothing and Food

Movement	(1) Change in clothing	(2) Change in food	(3) Marginal rate of substitution (1) ÷ (2)
From a to b	−12	5	−2.4
From b to c	− 5	5	−1.0
From c to d	− 3	5	−0.6
From d to e	− 2	5	−0.4
From e to f	− 1	5	−0.2

The marginal rate of substitution of clothing for food declines as the quantity of food increases. This table is based on Table 7A-1. When the household moves from a to b, it gives up 12 units of clothing and gains 5 units of food; it remains at the same level of overall satisfaction. The household at point a is prepared to sacrifice 12 units of clothing for 5 units of food (i.e., $12/5 = 2.4$ units of clothing per unit of food obtained). When the household moves from b to c, it sacrifices 5 units of clothing for 5 units of food (a rate of substitution of 1 unit of clothing for each unit of food).

many times as we wish, and we can generate as many indifferene curves as we wish. The farther any indifference curve is from the origin, the higher will be the level of satisfaction given by any of the combinations of goods indicated by points on the curve.

A set of indifference curves is called an **indifference map,** an example of which is shown in Figure 7A-2. It specifies the household's tastes by showing its rate of substitution between the two commodities for every possible level of current consumption of these commodities. When economists say that a household's tastes are *given,* they do not mean that the household's current consumption pattern is given; rather, they mean that the household's entire indifference map is given.

The Equilibrium of the Household

An indifference map describes the preferences of a household. As we saw in Chapter 7, a budget line describes the possibilities open to a household. To

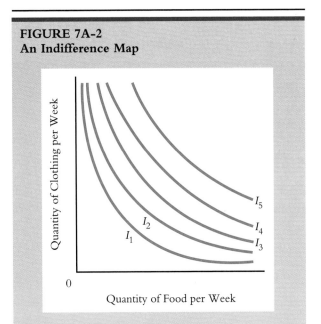

FIGURE 7A-2
An Indifference Map

An indifference map consists of a set of indifference curves. All points on a particular curve indicate alternative combinations of food and clothing that give the household equal satisfaction. The farther the curve is from the origin, the higher is the level of satisfaction it represents. For example, I_5 is a higher indifference curve than I_4, which means that all the points on I_5 yield a higher level of satisfaction than do the points on I_4.

predict what a household will actually do, both sets of information must be combined. This is done in Figure 7A-3. The household's budget line is shown by the straight line, and the curves from the indifference map are also shown. Any point on the budget line is attainable, but which point will actually be chosen by the household?

Because the household wishes to maximize its satisfaction, it wishes to reach its highest attainable indifference curve. Inspection of Figure 7A-3 shows that, if the household purchases any bundle on its budget line at a point cut by an indifference curve, a higher indifference curve can be reached. Only when the bundle purchased is such that the indifference curve is tangent to the budget line is it impossible for the household to alter its purchases and reach a higher curve.

The household's satisfaction is maximized at the point where an indifference curve is tangent to the budget line.

At such a tangency position, the slope of the indifference curve (the household's marginal rate of substitution for the two goods) is the same as the slope of the budget line (the relative prices of the two goods in the market).

The intuitive explanation for this result is that if the household values goods differently than the market does, there is room for profitable exchange. The household can give up some of the goods it values relatively less than the market does and take in return some of the goods it values relatively more than the market does. When the household is prepared to exchange goods at the same rate as they can be traded on the market, there is no further opportunity for it to raise its satisfaction by substituting one commodity for the other.

The theory thus proceeds by supposing that the household is presented with market prices it cannot change and then analysing how the household adjusts to these prices by choosing a bundle of goods such that, at the margin, its own subjective evaluation of the goods coincides with the valuations given by market prices.

We now use this theory to predict the typical household's response to a change in its income and in prices.

The Household's Reaction to a Change in Income

We have seen that changes in income lead to parallel shifts of the budget line—toward the origin when income falls and away from the origin when income rises. For each level of income, there will be an equilibrium position at which an indifference curve is tangent to the relevant budget line. Each such equilibrium position means that the household is doing as well as it possibly can at that level of income. If we move the budget line through all possible levels of income, and if we join up all the points of equilibrium, we will trace out what is called an **income-consumption line,** an example of which is shown in Figure 7A-4. This line shows how the consumption bundle changes as income changes, with relative prices being held constant.

The Household's Reaction to a Change in Price

We already know that a change in the relative price of the two goods changes the slope of the budget line. Given a price of clothing, for each possible

FIGURE 7A-3
The Equilibrium of a Household

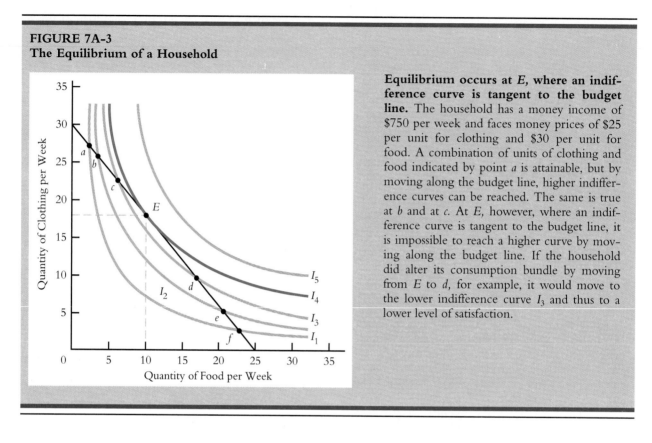

Equilibrium occurs at E, where an indifference curve is tangent to the budget line. The household has a money income of $750 per week and faces money prices of $25 per unit for clothing and $30 per unit for food. A combination of units of clothing and food indicated by point *a* is attainable, but by moving along the budget line, higher indifference curves can be reached. The same is true at *b* and at *c*. At *E*, however, where an indifference curve is tangent to the budget line, it is impossible to reach a higher curve by moving along the budget line. If the household did alter its consumption bundle by moving from *E* to *d*, for example, it would move to the lower indifference curve I_3 and thus to a lower level of satisfaction.

price of food there is an equilibrium consumption position for the household. If we connect these positions, we will trace out a **price-consumption line,** as is shown in Figure 7A-5. Notice that in this example, as the relative prices of food and clothing change, the relative quantities of food and clothing purchased also change. In particular, as the price of food falls, the household buys more food and less clothing.

Derivation of the Demand Curve

If food and clothing were the only two commodities purchased by households, we could derive a demand curve for food from the price-consumption line in Figure 7A-5, much as we did in Chapter 7. (See pages 136–137.) Now, however, we can be more precise. The price-consumption line shows how the quantity of food demanded varies as the price of food changes, with the price of clothing remaining unchanged. To use indifference theory to derive the type of demand curve introduced in

Chapter 4, it is necessary to depart from our simplified world of only two commodities.

What happens to the household's demand for some commodity, say gasoline, as the price of that commodity changes, *all other prices being held constant?* In part (i) of Figure 7A-6, a new type of indifference map is plotted, in which gallons of gasoline per month are measured on the horizontal axis and the value of all other goods consumed per month is plotted on the vertical axis. We have in effect used *everything but gasoline* as the second commodity. The indifference curves give the rate at which the household is prepared to substitute gasoline for money (which allows it to buy all other goods) at each level of consumption of gasoline and of all other goods.

To illustrate the derivation of demand curves, we use the numerical example shown in Figure 7A-6. The household is assumed to have an after-tax money income of $2,000 per month. This money income is plotted on the vertical axis, showing that if the household consumes no gasoline, it can consume $2,000 worth of other goods each month. When gasoline costs 0.75 per litre, the household

FIGURE 7A-4
The Income-Consumption Line

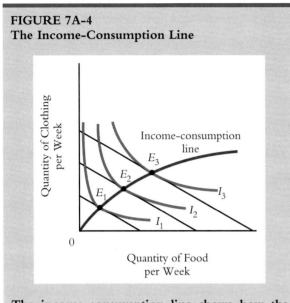

The income-consumption line shows how the household's purchases react to a change in money income with relative prices being held constant. Increases in money income shift the budget line outward parallel to itself, moving the equilibrium from E_1 to E_2 to E_3. By joining all the points of equilibrium, an income-consumption line is traced out.

FIGURE 7A-5
The Price-Consumption Line

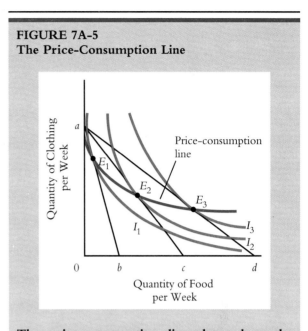

The price-consumption line shows how the household's purchases react to a change in one price with money income and other prices being held constant. Decreases in the price of food (with money income and the price of clothing being held constant) pivot the budget line from ab to ac to ad. The equilibrium position moves from E_1 to E_2 to E_3. By joining all the points of equilibrium, a price-consumption line is traced out, showing more food and less clothing bought as the price of food falls.

could buy a maximum of 2,667 litres per month. This gives rise to the innermost budget line. Given its tastes, the household reaches equilibrium at point E_0, consuming 600 litres of gasoline and $1,550 worth of other commodities.[2] Next, let the price of gasoline fall to 0.50 per litre. Now the maximum possible consumption of gasoline is 4,000 litres per month, giving rise to the middle budget line in the figure. The household's equilibrium is, as always, at the point where the new budget line is tangent to an indifference curve. At this point, E_1, the household is consuming 1,200 litres of gasoline per month and spending $1,400 on all other goods. Finally, let the price fall to $0.25 per litre. The household can now buy a maximum of 8,000 litres per month, giving rise to the outermost of the three budget lines. The household reaches equilibrium by

consuming 2,200 litres of gasoline per month and by spending $1,450 on other commodities.

If we let the price vary over all possible amounts, we will trace out a complete price-consumption line, as shown in the figure. The points derived in the preceding paragraph are merely three points on this line.

We have now derived all that we need to plot the household's demand curve for gasoline, since we know how much the household will purchase at each price. To draw the curve, we merely replot the data from part (i) of Figure 7A-6 onto a demand graph, as shown in part (ii) of Figure 7A-6.

Like part (i), part (ii) has quantity of gasoline on the horizontal axis. By placing one graph under the other, we can directly transcribe the quantity determined on the upper graph to the lower one. We first do this for the 600 litres consumed on the innermost budget line. We now note that the price of

[2]This household must do a lot of traveling! If we chose more realistic figures for its consumption of gasoline, however, the various equilibrium positions would all be so close to the horizontal axis that the graph would be difficult to read.

FIGURE 7A-6
Derivation of a Household's Demand Curve

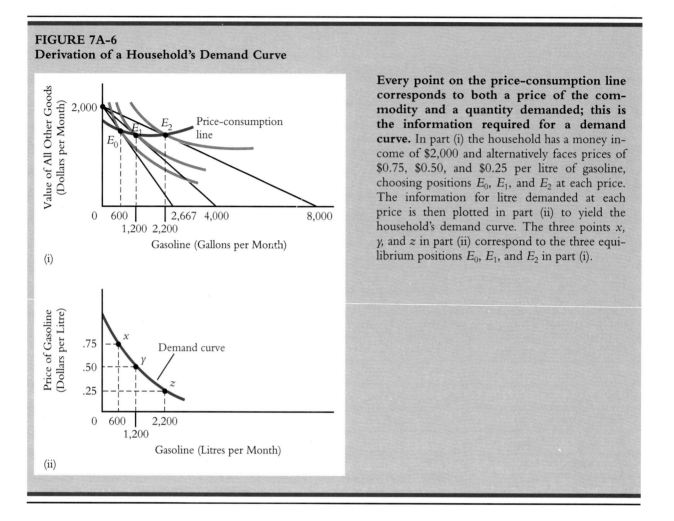

Every point on the price-consumption line corresponds to both a price of the commodity and a quantity demanded; this is the information required for a demand curve. In part (i) the household has a money income of $2,000 and alternatively faces prices of $0.75, $0.50, and $0.25 per litre of gasoline, choosing positions E_0, E_1, and E_2 at each price. The information for litre demanded at each price is then plotted in part (ii) to yield the household's demand curve. The three points x, y, and z in part (ii) correspond to the three equilibrium positions E_0, E_1, and E_2 in part (i).

gasoline that gives rise to that budget line is $0.75 per litre. Plotting 600 litres against $0.75 in part (ii) produces the point x, derived from point E_0 in part (i). This is one point on the household's demand curve. Next we consider the middle budget line, which occurs when the price of gasoline is $0.50 per litre. We take the figure of 1,200 litres from point E_1 in part (i) and transfer it to part (ii). We then plot this quantity against the price of $1.00 to get the point y on the demand curve. Doing the same thing for point E_2 yields the point z in part (ii): price $0.25, quantity 2,200 litres.

Repeating the operation for all prices yields the demand curve in part (ii). Note that the two parts of Figure 7A-6 describe the same behaviour. Both parts measure the quantity of gasoline on the horizontal axes; the only difference is that in part (i) the price of gasoline determines the slope of the budget line, whereas in part (ii) the price of gasoline is plotted explicitly on the vertical axis.

The Slope of the Demand Curve

The price-consumption line in part (i) of Figure 7A-6 indicates that as price decreases, the quantity of gasoline demanded increases, thus giving rise to the negatively sloped demand curve in part (ii). As we saw in Chapter 7, the key to understanding the negative slope of the demand curve is to distinguish between the income effect and the substitution effect of a change in price. Let us see how this distinction is made using indifference curves.

Income and Substitution Effects

In Chapter 7, we eliminated the income effect by changing money income *until the original bundle of*

FIGURE 7A-7
The Income Effect and the Substitution Effect in Indifference Theory

The substitution effect is defined by sliding the budget line around a fixed indifference curve; the income effect is defined by a parallel shift of the budget line. The original budget line is at ab, and a fall in the price of gasoline takes it to aj. The original equilibrium is at E_0 with q_0 of gasoline being consumed, and the final equilibrium is at E_2 with q_2 of gasoline being consumed. To remove the income effect, imagine reducing the household's money income until it is just able to attain its original indifference curve. We do this by shifting the line aj to a parallel line nearer the origin $a_1 j_1$ that just touches the indifference curve that passes through E_0. The intermediate point E_1 divides the quantity change into a substitution effect $q_0 q_1$ and an income effect $q_1 q_2$.

goods could just be consumed. In indifference theory, however, the income effect is removed by changing money income until the original level of *satisfaction*—the original indifference curve—can just be achieved. This results in a slightly different measure of the income effect, but the principle involved in separating the total change into an income effect and a substitution effect is exactly the same as in Chapter 7.[3]

The separation of the two effects according to indifference theory is shown in Figure 7A-7. The figure shows in greater detail part of the price-consumption line first drawn in Figure 7A-6. Points E_0 and E_2 are on the price-consumption line for gasoline. We can think of the separation occurring in the following way. After the price of the good has fallen, we reduce money income *until the original indifference curve can just be obtained.* This leads the household to move from point E_0 to an intermediate point E_1, and this response is defined as the substitution effect. Then, to measure the income effect, we restore money income. The household moves from the point E_1 to the final point E_2, and this response is defined as the income effect.

Now compare this indifference theory definition with the Slutsky definition used in Chapter 7. In Chapter 7, we measured the substitution effect of any price change by altering money income until the original bundle of goods can just be purchased. Here, we measure the substitution effect by altering money income until the original level of satisfaction—the original indifference curve—can just be attained.

The advantage of the Slutsky definition is that it is operational; the change in money income required to allow the original bundle to be purchased

---

[3] The approach used in Chapter 7 (see pages 132–134) defines constant real income as constant purchasing power. The introduction of indifference curves allows a slightly more sophisticated concept of constant real income—constant satisfaction as expressed by the original indifference curve. However, the two are very similar in practise, and indeed, in most empirical applications, the approach taken in Chapter 7 (the Slutsky equation) is used.

at the new prices can be simply calculated. The disadvantage is that this change does not leave unchanged the household's real income, defined as its level of satisfaction. The advantage of the indifference curve approach is that the change does leave the household's level of satisfaction unchanged and hence defines the substitution effect as the response to changes in relative prices with real satisfaction unchanged. The disadvantage is that the measurement is not easily made operational; we have to know each household's tastes to be able to make the required change in money income.

SUMMARY

1. The budget line describes what the household *can* purchase; indifference curves describe the household's tastes and, therefore, refer to what it *would like* to purchase. A single indifference curve joins combinations of commodities that give the household equal satisfaction and among which it is therefore indifferent. An indifference map is a set of indifference curves.

2. The basic hypothesis about tastes is that of a diminishing marginal rate of substitution. This hypothesis states that the less of one good and the more of another the household has, the less willing it will be to give up some of the first good to get an additional unit of the second. This means that indifference curves are downward sloping and convex to the origin.

3. The household achieves an equilibrium that maximizes its satisfactions, given its budget line, at the point at which an indifference curve is tangent to its budget line.

4. The income-consumption curve shows how quantity consumed changes as income changes when relative prices are held constant.

5. The price-consumption curve shows how quantity consumed changes as relative prices change. When prices change, the household will consume more of the commodity whose relative price falls.

6. The price-consumption curve relating the purchases of one particular commodity to all other commodities contains the same information as a conventional demand curve. The horizontal axis measures quantity, and the slope of the budget line measures price. Transferring this price-quantity information to a diagram whose axes represent price and quantity yields a demand curve.

7. The effect of a change in price of one commodity, all other prices and money income being held constant, changes not only relative prices but also real incomes. A change in price affects consumption through both the substitution effect and the income effect.

APPENDIX B TO CHAPTER

7

Marginal Utility Theory

In this second appendix to Chapter 7, we study the marginal utility theory of household demand.

Marginal and Total Utility

We confine our attention for the moment to the consumption of a single commodity. The satisfaction that a consumer receives from consuming that commodity is called its **utility. Total utility** refers to the total satisfaction resulting from the consumption of that commodity by a consumer. **Marginal utility** refers to the change in satisfaction resulting from consuming a little more or a little less of that commodity. For example, the total utility of consuming 14 eggs per week is the total satisfaction that those 14 eggs provide. The marginal utility of the fourteenth egg consumed is the additional satisfaction provided by the consumption of that egg. Thus marginal utility is the difference in total utility gained by consuming 13 eggs and by consuming 14.[1]

The Hypothesis of Diminishing Marginal Utility

The basic hypothesis of utility theory, sometimes called the *law of diminishing marginal utility,* is as follows:

The utility that any household derives from successive units of a particular commodity diminishes as total consumption of the commodity increases while the consumption of all other commodities remains constant.

Consider water. Some minimum quantity is essential to sustain life, and a person would, if necessary, give up all of his or her income to obtain that quantity of water. Thus the marginal utility of that much water is extremely high. More than this bare minimum will be drunk, but the marginal utility of successive glasses of water drunk over a period of time will decline steadily.

Evidence for this hypothesis will be considered later, but you can convince yourself that it is at least reasonable by asking a few questions. How much money would induce you to cut your consumption of water by one glass per week? The answer is very little. How much would induce you to cut it by a second glass? By a third glass? To only one glass consumed per week? The answer to the last question is quite a bit. The fewer glasses you are consuming already, the higher the marginal utility of one more or one less glass of water.

Water has many uses other than for drinking. A fairly high marginal utility will be attached to some minimum quantity for bathing, but much more than this minimum will be used only for more frequent baths or having a water level in the bathtub higher than is absolutely necessary. The last weekly litre used for bathing is likely to have a low marginal utility. Again, some small quantity of water is necessary for brushing teeth, but many people leave the water running while they brush. The water going down the drain between wetting and rinsing the brush surely has a low utility. When all the extravagant uses of water by the modern consumer are considered, the marginal utility of the last, say, 30 percent of all units consumed is probably very low, even though the total utility of *all* the units consumed is extremely high.

---

[1]Here and elsewhere in elementary economics, it is common to use interchangeably two concepts that mathematicians distinguish. Technically, *incremental* utility is measured over a discrete interval, such as from 9 to 10, whereas *marginal* utility is a rate of change measured over an infinitesimal interval. However, common usage applies the word *marginal* when the last unit is involved, even if a one-unit change is not infinitesimal. [12]

Utility Schedules and Graphs

The schedule in Table 7B-1 is hypothetical. It is constructed to illustrate the assumptions that have been made about utility, using movie attendance as an example. The table shows that total utility rises as the number of movies attended each month rises. Everything else being equal, the more movies the household attends each month, the more satisfaction it gets—at least over the range shown in the table. However, the marginal utility of each additional movie per month is less than that of the previous one, even though each movie adds something to the household's satisfaction. The schedule in Table 7B-1 shows that marginal utility declines as quantity consumed rises. **[13]**

Maximizing Utility

A basic assumption of the economic theory of household behaviour is that households try to make themselves as well off as they possibly can in the circumstances in which they find themselves. In other words, the members of a household seek to maximize their total utility.

The Equilibrium of a Household

How can a household adjust its expenditure so as to maximize its total utility? Should it go to the point at which the marginal utility of each commodity is the same, that is, the point at which it would value equally the last unit of each commodity consumed? This would make sense only if each commodity had the same price per unit. However, if a household must spend $3 to buy an additional unit of one commodity and only $1 to buy one unit of another, the first commodity would represent a poor use of its money if the marginal utility of each were equal. The household would be spending $3 to get satisfaction equal to what it would have acquired for only $1.

The household that is maximizing its utility will allocate its expenditures among commodities so that the utility of the last dollar spent on each is equal.

Imagine that the household is in a position in which the utility of the last dollar spent on carrots

TABLE 7B-1 Total and Marginal Utility Schedules

Number of movies attended per month	Total utility	Marginal utility
0	0	
1	30	30
2	50	20
3	65	15
4	75	10
5	83	8
6	89	6
7	93	4
8	96	3
9	98	2
10	99	1

Total utility rises, but marginal utility declines as this household's consumption increases. The marginal utility of 20, shown as the second entry in the third column, arises because total utility increases from 30 to 50—a difference of 20—with attendance at the second movie. To indicate that the marginal utility is associated with the change from one rate of movie attendance to another, the figures in the third column are recorded between the rows of the figures in the second column. When plotting marginal utility on a graph, it is plotted at the midpoint of the interval over which it is computed.

yields three times the utility of the last dollar spent on Brussels sprouts. In this case, total utility can be increased by switching a dollar of expenditure from Brussels sprouts to carrots and by gaining the difference between the utilities of a dollar spent on each.

The utility-maximizing household will continue to switch its expenditure from Brussels sprouts to carrots as long as a dollar spent on carrots yields more utility than a dollar spent on Brussels sprouts. This switching, however, reduces the quantity of Brussels sprouts consumed and, given the law of diminishing marginal utility, raises the marginal utility of Brussels sprouts. At the same time, switching increases the quantity of carrots consumed and thereby lowers the marginal utility of carrots.

Eventually, the marginal utilities will have changed enough so that the utility of a dollar spent on carrots is just equal to the utility of a dollar spent on Brussels sprouts. At this point, there is nothing to be gained by a further switch of expenditure from Brussels sprouts to carrots. If the household persists in reallocating its expenditure, it will further reduce the marginal utility of carrots (by consuming more of them) and raise the marginal utility of Brussels sprouts (by consuming less of them). Total utility will no longer be at its maximum, because the utility of a dollar spent on Brussels sprouts will exceed the utility of a dollar spent on carrots.

Let us now consider the conditions for maximizing utility in a more general way. Denote the marginal utility of the last unit of commodity X by MU_x and its price by p_x. Let MU_y and p_y refer, respectively, to the marginal utility of a second commodity Y and its price. The marginal utility per dollar of X will be MU_x/p_x. For example, if the last unit adds 30 units to utility and costs \$2, its marginal utility per dollar is $30/2 = 15$.

The condition required for a household to maximize its utility is, for any pair of commodities,

$$\frac{MU_x}{p_x} = \frac{MU_y}{p_y} \qquad [1]$$

This says that the household will allocate its expenditure so that the utility gained from the last dollar spent on each commodity is equal.

This is the fundamental equation of the utility theory of demand. Each household demands each good (for example, movie attendance) up to the point at which the marginal utility per dollar spent on it is the same as the marginal utility of a dollar spent on another good (for example, water). When this condition is met, the household cannot shift a dollar of expenditure from one commodity to another and increase its utility.

An Alternative Interpretation of Household Equilibrium

If we rearrange the terms in Equation 1, we can gain additional insight into household behaviour.

$$\frac{MU_x}{MU_y} = \frac{p_x}{p_y} \qquad [2]$$

The right side of this equation states the *relative* price of the two goods. It is determined by the

market and is outside the control of the individual household; the household reacts to these market prices but is powerless to change them. The left side states the relative ability of the goods to add to the household's satisfaction and is within the control of the household. In determining the quantities of different goods it buys, the household also determines their marginal utilities.

If the two sides of Equation 2 are not equal, the household can increase its total satisfaction by rearranging its purchases. Assume, for example, that the price of a unit of X is twice the price of a unit of Y ($p_x/p_y = 2$), while the marginal utility of a unit of X is three times that of a unit of Y ($MU_x/MU_y = 3$). Under these conditions, it is worthwhile for the household to buy more of X and less of Y. For example, if the household reduces its purchases of Y by 2 units, enough purchasing power is freed to buy a unit of X. Since one extra unit of X bought yields 1.5 times the satisfaction of 2 units of Y forgone, the switch is worth making. What about a further switch of X for Y? As the household buys more of X and less of Y, the marginal utility of X falls and the marginal utility of Y rises. The household will go on rearranging its purchases—reducing Y consumption and increasing X consumption—until, in this example, the marginal utility of X is only twice that of Y. At this point, total satisfaction cannot be further increased by rearranging purchases between the two commodities.

Now consider what the household is doing. It faces a set of prices that it cannot change. The household responds to these prices and maximizes its satisfaction by adjusting the things it can change—the quantities of the various goods it purchases—until Equation 2 is satisfied for all pairs of commodities.

This sort of equation—one side representing the choices that the outside world gives decision makers and the other side representing the effect of those choices on their welfare—recurs in economics. It reflects the equilibrium position reached when decision makers have made the best adjustment that they can to the external forces that limit their choices.

When it enters the market, every household faces the same set of market prices. When all households are fully adjusted to these prices, each will have identical ratios of its marginal utilities for each pair of goods. Of course, a rich household may consume more of each commodity than a poor household. However, the rich and the poor households (and every other household) will adjust their *relative* purchases of each commodity so that the relative marginal utilities are the same for all. Thus if the price of X is twice the price of Y, each household will purchase X and Y to the point at which the household's marginal utility of X is twice its marginal utility of Y. Households with different tastes will, however, have different marginal utility schedules and so may consume differing relative quantities of commodities, even though the ratios of their marginal utilities are the same for all households.

Derivation of the Household's Demand Curve

To derive the household's demand curve for a commodity, it is only necessary to ask what happens when there is a change in the price of that commodity. As an example, let us do this for candy. Take Equation 2 and let X stand for candy and Y for all other commodities. What will happen if, with all other prices remaining constant, the price of candy rises? The household that started from a position of equilibrium will now find itself in a position in which

$$\frac{MU \text{ of candy}}{MU \text{ of } Y} < \frac{\text{price of candy}}{\text{price of } Y} \qquad [3]$$

To restore equilibrium, it must buy less candy, thereby raising its marginal utility until once again Equation 2 (where X is candy) is satisfied. The hypothesis of diminishing marginal utility tells us that the marginal utility of candy *per dollar* falls when its price rises. The household began with the utility of the last dollar spent on candy equal to the utility of the last dollar spent on all other goods, but the rise in candy prices changes this. The household buys less candy (and more of other goods) until the marginal utility of candy rises enough to make the utility of a dollar spent on candy the same as it was originally.

This analysis leads to the basic prediction of demand theory:

A rise in the price of a commodity (with income and the prices of all other commodities being held constant) will lead to a decrease in the quantity of the commodity demanded by each household.

If this is what each household does, it is also what all households taken together do. Thus the theory predicts a downward-sloping market demand curve.

SUMMARY

1. Marginal utility theory distinguishes between the total utility gained from the consumption of all units of some commodity and the marginal utility resulting from the consumption of one more unit of the commodity.

2. The basic assumption made in utility theory is that the utility the household derives from the consumption of successive units of a commodity per period of time diminishes as the consumption of that commodity increases.

3. Households are assumed to maximize utility and thus reach equilibrium when the utility derived from the last dollar spent on each commodity is equal. Another way of putting this is that the marginal utilities derived from the last unit of each commodity consumed will be proportional to their prices.

4. Demand curves have negative slopes because when the price of one commodity, X, falls, each household restores equilibrium by increasing its purchases of X sufficiently to restore the ratio of X's marginal utility to its now lower price (MU_x/p_x) to the same level as it has achieved for all other commodities.

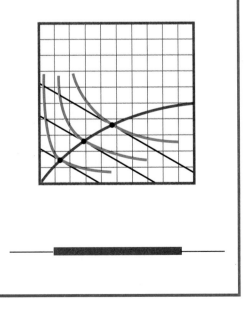

8

Using Demand Theory

In Chapter 7, we covered some basic material concerning the theory of demand. In this chapter, we go further and develop some applications of this theory. We start by asking the important question of whether demand theory assumes an unreasonable amount of rational behaviour on the part of consumers. We then go on to some applications. Finally, we consider the important case of choices when outcomes are less than certain.

Does Demand Theory Require Unrealistic Rationality?

The theory of household behaviour uses the key assumption that households always act rationally in their pursuit of satisfaction. This assumption of rationality appears in slightly different form in various theories, but it always amounts to assuming that, facing alternatives, each household consistently chooses the one it prefers.

It is tempting to dismiss demand theory with the objection that consumer rationality is an unrealistic assumption. After all, there are people who sometimes spend a week's pay on a binge or a frivolous purchase that they afterward regret.

To assess the significance of such observed "irrationalities," it is helpful to distinguish three possible uses of demand theory. The first is to study the aggregate behaviour of all households—as illustrated, for example, by the market demand curve for gasoline or carrots. The second use is to make statements about a particular household's probable actions. The third is to make statements about what each household will certainly do.

The criticism that the assumption of rationality is not realistic applies primarily to the third use of demand theory. Observations of unusual or irrational behaviour refute only the prediction that *all* households *always* behave as assumed by the theory. To predict the existence of a relatively stable negatively sloped market demand curve (the first use) or to predict what an individual household will probably do (the second use), we do *not* require that *all* households behave as assumed by the theory all of the time. Consider two illustrations.

First, some households may always behave in a manner inconsistent with the theory. Households whose members have serious emotional disturbances are one obvious example. The erratic behaviour of such households will not cause market demand curves to depart from their downward slope, as long as these households account for a minority of total purchasers of any product. Their erratic behaviour will be swamped by the normal behaviour of the majority of households.

Second, occasional impulse buying or downright irrationality on the part of any household will not upset the downward slope of the market demand curve as long as these isolated inconsistencies do not occur at the same time and in the same way in all households. As long as such inconsistencies are unrelated across households, occurring now in one and now in another, their effects will tend to offset each other; thus their total effect will be small and will be offset by the normal behaviour of the majority of households.

The negative slope of the demand curve requires only that at any moment in time *most* households are behaving as predicted by the theory. This is compatible with inconsistent behaviour on the part of some households all of the time and on the part of all households some of the time.

Some Applications of Demand Theory

Consumers' surplus, which we studied in Chapter 7, is an important and useful concept. Understanding it is the key to understanding the theory of demand. We shall now see how it helps us to explain some real-world events that on the surface seem paradoxical. In later chapters, consumers' surplus will play a key role in our analysis of certain aspects of the performance of the market system.

The Paradox of Value

Early economists, struggling with the problem of what determines the relative prices of commodities, encountered what they called the *paradox of value*: Many necessary commodities, such as water, have prices that are low compared with the prices of luxury commodities, such as diamonds. Water is necessary to our existence, whereas diamonds are used mostly for frivolous purposes and could disappear from the face of the earth tomorrow without causing any real hardship. Does it not seem odd, then, these economists asked, that water is so cheap and diamonds are so expensive? It took a long time to resolve this apparent paradox, so it is not surprising that even today analogous confusions cloud many policy discussions.

The key to resolving this "paradox" lies in the important distinction between what one would pay to avoid having one's consumption of a commodity reduced to zero and what one would pay to gain the use of one more unit of that commodity. This point involves a distinction between total and mar-

ginal values that is frequently encountered in many branches of economics.

We have seen already that the area under the demand curve shows what the household would pay for the commodity if it had to purchase it unit by unit. It is thus a measure of the total value that the household places on *all* of the units it consumes. In Figure 7-8, the *total* value of q_0 units is the entire shaded area (light and dark) under the demand curve.

What about the *marginal value* that the household places on one more or one less than the q_0 units it is currently consuming? This is given by the commodity's market price, which is p_0 in this case. Facing a market price of p_0, the household buys all the units that it values at p_0 or greater but does not purchase any units that it values at less than p_0. It follows that the household places on the last unit consumed of any commodity a value that is measured by the commodity's price.

Now look at the total market value of the commodity. This is the amount that everyone spends to purchase it. It is price multiplied by quantity. In Figure 7-8, on page 143, this is the dark shaded rectangle with sides $0p_0$ and $0q_0$.

We have seen that the total value that consumers place on a given amount of a commodity, as measured by the relevant area under the demand curve, is different from the total market value of a commodity, as given by the commodity's price multiplied by the quantity consumed. Being different, the two values do not have to be related. Figure 8-1 illustrates a case in which a good with a total high value has a low market value, and vice versa.

The resolution of the paradox of value is that a good that is very plentiful, such as water, will have a low price and will thus be consumed to the point where all households place a low value on the last unit consumed, whether or not they place a high value on their total consumption of the commodity. By contrast, a commodity that is relatively scarce will have a high market price, and consumption will therefore stop at a point where consumers place a high value on the last unit consumed, regardless of the value that they place on their total consumption of the good.

We have now reached an important conclusion:

Because the market price of a commodity depends not only on demand but also on supply, there is nothing paradoxical in there

FIGURE 8-1
Total Value Versus Market Value

(i) Water

(ii) Diamonds

The market value of the amount of some commodity bears no necessary relationship to the total value that consumers place on that amount. The graph presents hypothetical demand curves for water and diamonds, that are meant to be stylized versions of the real curves. The total value that households place on water, as shown by the area under the demand curve, is great—indeed, we do not even show the curve for very small quantities because people would pay all they had rather than be deprived completely of water. The total valuation that households place on diamonds is shown by the area under the demand curve for diamonds. This is clearly less than the total value placed on water.

The low supply of diamonds makes diamonds scarce and keeps diamonds high in price, as shown by p_d in part (ii) of the figure. The total market value of diamonds sold, indicated by the light shaded area of $p_d q_d$, is high.

The large supply of water makes water plentiful and makes water low in price, as shown by p_w in part (i) of the figure. Thus the total market value of water consumed, indicated by the dark shaded area of $p_w q_w$, is low.

being a commodity on which consumers place a high total value selling for a low price and hence having only a small amount spent on it.

Necessities, Luxuries, and Elasticity

People often distinguish between *necessities*—commodities that are difficult to do without—and *luxuries*—commodities that could be fairly easily dispensed with. The distinction is somewhat arbitrary; for example, are eggs a necessity or a luxury? Nonetheless, some sense can be made of the distinction by comparing the *total* values that households place on their consumption of different commodities. In Chapter 7, we learned to measure these total values by the areas under demand curves.

Using this terminology, we would say that a necessity has a very large area under its demand curve; a luxury has a smaller area under its demand curve.

A frequent error occurs when people try to use knowledge of total values to predict demand elasticities. It is sometimes argued that because luxuries can be given up, they have highly elastic demands; when their prices rise, households can stop purchasing them. It is likewise argued that necessities have highly inelastic demands because when prices rise, households have no choice but to continue to buy them.

However, elasticity of demand depends on how consumers value commodities at the margin, not on how much they value the total consumption of the commodity. The relevant question for the determination of elasticity is, "How much do households value a bit more of some commodity?" and not, "How much do they value *all* of the commodity that they are now consuming?"

Demand theory leads to the prediction that when the price of a commodity rises, each household will reduce its purchases of that commodity until it values the last unit consumed of the commodity at the price that it must pay for that unit. Will the reduction in quantity required to raise the valuation be a little or a lot? This depends on the shape of the demand curve in the relevant range. If a large change in quantity is required, demand will be elastic. If a small change will suffice, demand will be inelastic. Figure 8-2 presents two possible responses to an increase in price. It leads to this important conclusion:

The size of the response of quantity demanded to a change in price depends on the value that households place on having a bit more or a bit less of the commodity and has no necessary relationship to the value that they place on their total consumption of the quantity in question.

Free, Scarce, and Freely Provided Goods

A **free good** is one for which the quantity supplied exceeds the quantity demanded at a price of zero. Such goods will not command positive prices in a market economy. A household can become better off by increasing its consumption of free goods as long as it places a positive value on the extra units consumed. It follows that free goods will be consumed up to the point at which the value that households place on another unit consumed is zero. At some times in some places, air, water, salt, sand, and wild fruit have been free goods. Note that a good may be free at one time or place but not at another.

A **scarce good** is one for which the quantity demanded exceeds the quantity supplied at a price of zero. If all such goods had zero prices, the total amount that people would want to consume would greatly exceed the amount that could be produced. Such goods therefore will command positive prices in a market economy. Most goods are scarce goods.

Many people have strong views about the prices that are charged for certain commodities. These views are often an emotional reaction to the total

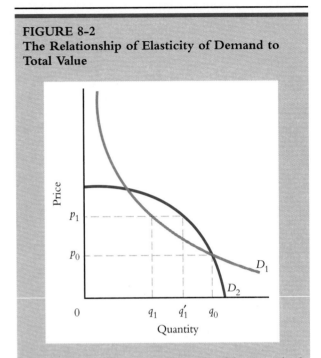

FIGURE 8-2
The Relationship of Elasticity of Demand to Total Value

Elasticity of demand is determined by marginal valuation in the relevant range, not total value. Consider two alternative demand curves for a commodity, D_1 and D_2. Suppose the price is p_0. Given either demand curve, the household consumes the quantity q_0, where the last unit consumed is valued at p_0. When the price rises to p_1, households cut their consumption.

If dark blue line D_2 is the demand curve, consumption falls to only q_1', and the demand for the product is quite inelastic. If, however, the light blue line D_1 is the demand curve, consumption falls to q_1, and the demand for the product is more elastic.

Total value depends on the whole area under the curve. Depending on the shape of the curve up to q_0, either curve can show more or less total value than the other. Thus total value has no influence on market behaviour in response to a change in price from p_0 to p_1.

values of the goods rather than to their marginal values. Here is an example: "Because water is such a complete necessity of life to rich and to poor, it is wrong to make people pay for water. Instead, the government should provide free water for everyone."

When deciding between a zero price and a modest price for water, the relevant question for the consumer is not, "Is water so necessary that we want everyone to be provided with some of it?" but rather "Are the marginal uses of water so important that we are willing to use scarce resources to provide the necessary quantities?" The distinction is important because the two questions have different answers.

The evidence that we have about the consumption of water at various prices suggests that the demand curve for water has a shape similar to the curve shown in part (i) of Figure 8-1. If so, the difference in consumption that results from providing water free or charging a modest price for it will be large. The additional water consumed, however, is costly to provide, and its provision requires scarce resources that could have been used to produce other commodities. If the value that households place on the commodities forgone is higher than the value that they place on the extra water consumed, households are worse off as a result of receiving water free. A charge for water would release resources from water production to produce commodities that households value more highly at the margin. Of course, some minimum quantity of water could be provided free to every household, but the effects of this would be quite different from the effects of making all water free.

It follows that neither the gain to consumers of encouraging a little more consumption of some commodity nor the loss from inducing a little less can be inferred from a knowledge of the total value placed on all of the consumption of that commodity.

Similar considerations apply to food, medical services, and a host of other commodities that are necessities of life but that also have numerous low-value uses that will be encouraged if a scarce commodity is provided at a zero price.

Household Behaviour Under Uncertainty

So far we have studied how households choose between alternatives that are *certain*. As we have just seen, the theory of demand that results from this approach is very powerful in explaining many observable real-world events. However, many, if not all, of the choices that households make involve *uncertainty*. Of course, for many problems, the role of uncertainty is incidental and the standard analysis assuming certainty is perfectly adequate. However, there are some situations in which uncertainty is central to the issue.

Uncertainty arises whenever decisions are made with imperfect information about the alternatives. It is present in virtually all aspects of economic life. Whenever some of the effects of an action will be felt in the future, that action will have some uncertainty attached to it. This is obviously true of speculative purchases of gold, real estate, and stocks. This is also true when you buy a consumer durable; for example, because you cannot be sure about the reliability and durability of an automobile, you are uncertain about the value of the services that the car will deliver should you purchase it. Box 8-1 takes up the interesting problems that this poses for the used-car market.

How does uncertainty influence household decisions? How do markets cope with uncertainty? We can explore these questions by considering the market for insurance. As we shall see, the *expected value* of the possibilities that might arise proves very useful in this exercise. The *expected value* of an uncertain event is the weighted average calculated by adding up the values of the various possible outcomes, each weighted by the probability of its occurrence. (The numerical example in footnote 1 on page 165 could be studied now if you are unfamiliar with this concept.)

The Market for Insurance

We shall first study household demand for insurance, and then we shall look briefly at the behaviour of insurance firms.

The Demand for Insurance

Suppose that there is 1 chance in 100 that some unfavourable outcome will happen in which you will lose some asset (possibly your house) that you value at $100,000, and suppose that there are 99 chances in 100 that nothing at all will happen to this asset. The most likely outcome is that nothing will happen, but there is a small chance that you will incur a very big loss.

Box 8-1

Used-Car Prices: The Problem of "Lemons"

It is common for people to regard the large loss of value of a new car in the first year of its life as a sign that consumers are overly style conscious and will always pay a big premium for the latest in anything. Professor George Akerlof of the University of California at Berkeley suggests a different explanation, based on the proposition that the flow of services expected from a one-year-old car that is *purchased on the used-car market* will be lower than those expected from an *average* one-year-old car on the road. Consider his theory.

Any particular model year of automobiles will include a certain proportion of "lemons"—cars that have one or more serious defects. Purchasers of new cars of a certain year and model take a chance on their car's turning out to be a lemon. Those who are unlucky and get a lemon are more likely to resell their car than those who are lucky and get a quality car. Hence, the used-car market will contain a disproportionately large number of lemons for sale.

Thus, buyers of used cars are right to be on the lookout for low-quality cars, while salespeople are quick to invent reasons for the high quality of the cars they are selling ("It was owned by a little old lady who drove it only on Sundays"). Because it is difficult to identify a lemon or a badly treated used car before buying it, the purchaser is prepared to buy a used car only at a price that is low enough to offset the probability that it is of poor quality.

This is a rational consumer response to uncertainty and helps to explain why 1-year-old cars typically sell for a discount that is much larger than can be explained by the physical depreciation that occurs in one year in the *average* car of that model. The large discount reflects the lower services that the purchaser can expect from a used car because of the higher probability that it will be a lemon.

Suppose that someone now offers you an insurance policy that costs $1,000. If nothing else happens, you simply lose the $1,000. However, if the disaster occurs and you suffer the loss of $100,000, you will be fully compensated.

If you buy the policy, you give up $1,000 for certain, but you are no longer at risk. If you do not buy the policy, you are taking a risk. The possible outcomes from having no insurance are 1 chance in 100 of losing $100,000 and 99 chances in 100 of losing nothing. This gives an expected value of $-\$100,000 \ (1/100) + \$0 \ (99/100) = -\$1,000$. The insurance policy represents what might be called a *fair game* because the expected values of both courses of action are the same—a loss of $1,000.

Although the expected values of the two choices are the same, the choices are obviously not identical. Not buying the insurance is a much riskier choice than buying it. If you do not buy the insurance and are lucky, you save the $1,000 insurance premium; however, if you are unlucky, you lose $100,000. If you buy the insurance, you lose $1,000 for certain.

Someone who is risk averse would buy the policy because it reduces risk without reducing expected income; for the same reasons, someone who is a risk lover (a gambler?) would not. Because both courses have the same expected value, a person who feels neutral towards risk would be indifferent to either buying the insurance policy or not buying it—if there were no other considerations.

This discussion assumes that the insurance policy offers a fair bet, but insurance companies must themselves make money, so they do not offer their policyholders mathematically fair policies. In the case in which the risk was 1 chance in 100 of losing $100,000, the policy would actually cost more than $1,000—say, $1,200. Now the expected return from buying the policy remains at $1,000, but the cost of the policy is $1,200; thus the expected value of buying the policy is negative. This makes insurance less attractive, and fewer people would buy it; in particular, people who are risk neutral would no longer buy it, although people who are sufficiently risk averse would.

The Supply of Insurance

When households buy insurance, they are essentially trading risk with those who sell them the insurance. Why are firms willing to supply insurance to households who demand it?

An insurance firm takes your money and agrees to pay out a certain sum should the unlucky event strike you. It expects to make profits on the difference between the premiums it charges and the amount of claims it expects to pay to its customers. These profits, however, are not guaranteed. Conceivably, the insurance firm itself could have a run of bad luck in which many of the people it insures suffer losses at the same time. Indeed, conceivably, it could even incur losses sufficiently large to cause it to go bankrupt.

How can insurance companies afford to absorb their customers' risks? The main explanation of insurance company behaviour relies on their ability to engage in *risk pooling* and *risk sharing* in order to reduce the total amount of risk that has to be borne by them and their customers.

Risk pooling. To see what is involved in the pooling of risks, consider two individuals who receive an income that varies according to the toss of a coin. (The coin toss is simply an example used to illustrate the principles that apply for any source of uncertainty.) Each individual tosses a coin each month. If the coin comes up heads, John receives $500; if it comes up tails, he receives nothing. The same applies to June: She receives $500 if she tosses heads and nothing if she tosses tails. The expected value of each person's income is $500 (0.5) = $250 per month. Over a long period of time, each person's monthly income will indeed average close to $250, but John and June may not like the possibility

of going from $500 to nothing on the toss of a coin each month.

Suppose that they decide to pool their incomes each month and each take one half of the resulting amount. The expected value of each person's income is still $250 per month, but now the variation from month to month will be diminished.[1] The result is shown in Table 8-1. When they were operating on their own, each person's income deviated from its expected value by $250 each month; in good months it was $250 above the expected value, and in bad months it was $250 below the expected value. When the two incomes are pooled, the expected value is reached whenever one person is lucky and the other is unlucky, which will be about half the time. Only in one quarter of the outcomes will income be above $250, and only in one quarter of the outcomes will it be below $250. These results each require that they both be lucky or unlucky at the same time.

The key to this result is that the events must be independent. The result of John's coin toss was independent of the result of June's. In the case in which their incomes were not pooled, for either of them the zero-income result occurs whenever they themselves are unlucky. The probability of the zero-income result is less likely when they pool their incomes, because it requires that they both be unlucky at the same time.

If three people pool their incomes, each receives zero only when all three are unlucky at the same time. This case occurs with a probability of 1 chance in 8. If four people pool their incomes, the extreme case of each receiving $0 income will occur only with a probability of 1/16. By the time 10 people are involved, the extreme case will occur only 1 time in 2 raised to the tenth power—a very small fraction indeed.

The larger the number of independent events that are pooled, the less and less likely it is that extreme results will occur.

The same reasoning applies to all kinds of chance events, as long as they are independent of

---

[1]This can be seen by evaluating the four possible outcomes: There is a 25 percent chance of each individual's share of the pool being $500, a 50 percent chance of it being $250, and a 25 percent chance of it being $0. This sums to $500 (0.25) + $250 (0.5) + $0 (0.25) = $125 + $125 + $0 = $250.

TABLE 8-1 Incomes When Risks Are and Are Not Pooled

	Risks not pooled		Risks pooled
	John	June	Each
Tails–tails	$ 0	$ 0	$ 0
Tails–heads	0	500	250
Heads–tails	500	0	250
Heads–heads	500	500	500

Pooling of independent risks reduces risk. Each person gets an income of $500 if he or she tosses heads and nothing if he or she tosses tails. There are four possible results. In two of them, one head and one tail occurs. In the other two, either two tails or two heads occurs. When each accepts his or her own risks, each expects an income of $500 half the time and zero the other half. When the incomes are pooled and then split, only one combination in four gives them zero income, while half of the time they will get $250. The deviations of their monthly incomes from the expected value of $250 is decreased by pooling, but the expected value itself is unchanged.

one another. Suppose that there is 1 chance in 1,000 that any given house in the country will burn down in any given year, and suppose that an insurance company collects a premium from the owners of these houses and offers them full compensation if their house burns down.

If the company is so small that it can only insure 10 houses, it may be unlucky in having 10 owners who just happen to be careless at the same time and have their houses burn down accidentally. This is unlikely but not impossible. A bad bit of luck that destroys all 10 insured houses would ruin the company; it could not meet all of its insured risks at the same time. Suppose, however, that the company is large enough to insure 100,000 houses. Now it is pooling its risks over a large number, and the chances are high that something very close to 1 house in 1,000 insured will burn down. With 100,000 houses insured, the most likely outcome is that 100 houses will burn down. The company might be unlucky and have 110 burn down or lucky and have only 90 burn down, but to have even 150 burn down is very unlikely indeed, as long

as the chance of a fire burning down one house is independent of the chance of a fire burning down another. (Insurance companies are careful to spread the houses that they insure over a wide geographic area!)

This requirement of independence is why insurance policies normally exclude wars and other situations in which some common cause acts on all the insured units. A war may lead to a vast number of houses being destroyed. Because the cause of the loss of one house is not independent of the cause of the loss of another, if the insurance company suffers losses on any house because of war, there is a high probability that it will suffer losses on a large proportion of its insured properties, and this could ruin the insurance company.

The basic feature in insurance is the pooling of independent events, which is what makes extreme outcomes unlikely. A common cause that has a similar effect on all insured items defeats the principle on which insurance is based.

Risk sharing. Let us say that a famous concert pianist wants to insure her hands against any event that would end her career as a performer. The amount insured would be colossal, amounting to all the income that she would have earned over her life if her hands had not been harmed. The company can calculate the chances that any randomly chosen person in the population will suffer such a loss. It is not insuring an entire population, however; only one person is involved. If there is no catastrophe, the company will gain its premium; if there is a catastrophe, the company will suffer a large loss.

The trick in being able to insure the pianist, or any unique person or thing posing the risk of a large loss, lies in what is called *risk sharing*. One company writes a policy for the pianist and then breaks the policy up into a large number of subpolicies. Each subpolicy carries a fraction of the payout and earns a fraction of the premium. The company then sells each subpolicy to a different firm.

Assume, for the purposes of illustration, that 100 firms each write one such primary policy, for example, one on a pianist's hands, one on a football player's legs, one on a rare painting being flown to Japan for an exhibit, and so on. Each then breaks its primary policy up into 100 subpolicies and sells each subpolicy to the other 99 firms. Each firm ends up holding risks that are independent of each other, no one of which is large enough to threaten the firm should it give rise to a claim.

Moral Hazard and Adverse Selection

Insurance markets work quite well at reducing the risk that individuals must contend with *and* at reducing the overall risk in the economy. However, there are problems that reduce the ability of insurance companies to exploit the principles of risk pooling and risk sharing to insure households against some risks. Two of the most interesting are *moral hazard* and *adverse selection.*

When having insurance leads people to behave less carefully, thus raising the insurance company's expected costs, the situation is described as displaying **moral hazard.** For example, car owners might be much more willing to park their cars in an unsavoury part of town where the risk of theft is high and might be less diligent about locking them regularly if their cars are insured against theft. If this effect is strong enough, insurance companies will not find it profitable to offer insurance against the particular event, and hence car owners will have to bear the risk themselves. Often the problem is sufficient to make it impossible for the car owners to obtain complete insurance; the insurance company offers only *partial coverage* by requiring that the car owner pay the first, say, $250 dollars in the event of a claim.

Another problem is that not everyone buys insurance, so the full benefits of risk pooling are not available to the insurance company. In particular, for any policy that is offered, *those most likely to make a claim are also most likely to purchase the policy.* This is referred to as **adverse selection,** because from the insurer's viewpoint the wrong people have chosen to buy the policy. (The lemons problem discussed in Box 8-1 is an example of adverse selection.)

If insurance companies can distinguish among different potential customers, they can customize policies to suit each group's characteristics. For example, life insurance companies usually require that applicants have a medical examination, and they charge higher premiums to those who are thus demonstrated to be higher risks.

When insurance companies cannot distinguish among different potential customers and thus have to make any policy available on the same terms to all potential customers, they will have to charge a high enough premium to allow for the increased risks created by adverse selection. This may mean that potential customers who know themselves to be low-risk individuals will choose not to buy the policy. If these people could convince the insurance company that they are low risks, there is a price at which the insurance company would be able to sell them insurance and still make a profit, but, of course, everybody would like to convince the insurance company that they are low-risk individuals and hence benefit from the lower premiums.

Thus, adverse selection can create a situation in which some individuals cannot purchase insurance. One way in which insurance companies deal with this problem is to identify characteristics (often age, sex, or occupation) that are related to risk and then to offer different policies to individuals with different characteristics; however, in many places legislation has been introduced that makes such discrimination illegal.

SUMMARY

1. It is important to distinguish between total and marginal values, because choices concerning a bit more and a bit less cannot be predicted from a knowledge of total values. The paradox of value involves a confusion between total value and marginal value.

2. Elasticity of demand is related to the marginal value that households place on having a bit more or a bit less of some commodity; it bears no necessary relationship to the total value that households place on all of the units consumed of that commodity.

3. Households will consume any good that has a zero price up to the point where the marginal value that they place on further consumption is zero.

4. People who are risk averse would choose to buy insurance as long as the premium does not exceed the expected value of the risky alternative by more than their aversion to risk.

5. Insurance companies can absorb risk from such people and then reduce the risk that they themselves bear by exploiting the principles of risk pooling and risk sharing. These principles operate when the risky events being insured are independent of one another.

6. Insurance markets may fail to operate effectively if there are serious problems of moral hazard or adverse selection. Moral hazard arises when having insurance causes people to behave in a manner that increases the chance of losses, thus reducing the expected profits of the insurance company. Adverse selection arises when potential customers have different risk characteristics and insurance companies cannot easily distinguish the various groups.

TOPICS FOR REVIEW

The paradox of value

Necessities and luxuries

Free goods and scarce goods

The market for insurance

Risk pooling and risk sharing

Moral hazard and adverse selection

DISCUSSION QUESTIONS

1. The measured elasticity of demand for salt is quite low. Why do you think this is so? Does this low elasticity imply that if one firm were to monopolise the sales of salt in the whole country, it could go on raising its revenues indefinitely by continually increasing the price of salt?

2. Consider a household that, on average, uses 1,500 kilowatt-hours (kwh) of electricity per month at a price of 5 cents per kwh. Suppose that the local utility company, the only supplier of electricity, adopts a new policy whereby its customers will be billed $100 per month plus 5 cents for each kwh in excess of 2,000 that a household uses in any month. How will this affect the household's demand for electricity? How will this affect the consumers' surplus that it derives from the consumption of electricity?

3. Some jurisdictions prohibit insurance companies from requiring tests for the HIV virus as a condition for purchasing life insurance.
   a. What effects will this have on the market for life insurance in those areas?
   b. Suppose that the rule also extended to all other types of insurance. What effects would this have?

4. What do you think about someone who buys two lottery tickets instead of one and tells you that he or she does this in order "to increase my chances of coming out a winner"?

5. How might people's behaviour differ in serving themselves at a fixed-price buffet and at a restaurant where orders are taken from an à la carte menu? Discuss the marginal and average values of food consumed in each case.

6. Describe the difference in behaviour at a campus party at which drinks are free between someone who imbibes up to the point where the *marginal* value of more alcohol consumed is zero and someone who imbibes up to the point where the *average* value of alcohol consumed is zero.

7. Which of these implied choices involve a consideration of marginal values, and which involve a consideration of total values?

   a. Parliament debates whether 17-year-olds should be given the vote.

   b. A diet calls for precisely 1,200 calories per day.

   c. My doctor says that I must give up smoking and drinking or else accept an increased chance of heart attack.

   d. When Armand Hammer decided to buy the Rembrandt painting "Juno" for $3.25 million, he called it the "crown jewel of my collection."

   e. I enjoyed my golf game today, but I was so tired that I decided to stop at the seventeenth hole.

9

The Role of the Firm

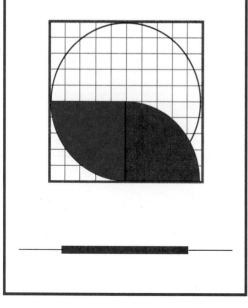

Ask almost anyone you know to name 10 Canadian firms. The odds are overwhelming that the list will include several of these firms: Northern Telecom, Alcan, Air Canada, Canadian Airlines International, Brascan, Macmillan Blodel, McCains Foods, Canadian Pacific, the Toronto Dominion Bank, and Canadian Tire. Drive around Gananoque, Ontario, and note at random 10 firms that come into view. They will likely include a Loblaw's supermarket, a Harding's Drugstore, a PetroCan service station, a Donevan's Hardware, the Modern Café, and the Bank of Montreal. Drive through Saskatchewan or Manitoba and look around you: Every farm is a business, or firm, as well as a home.

Firms develop and survive because they are efficient institutions for organizing resources to produce goods and services and for organizing their sales and distribution. An interesting insight into the nature of the firm is presented in Box 9-1.

It is not difficult to count ways in which Alcan, Haabs, and the Manitoba farm are different. However, we can gain insight by treating them all under a single heading, that is, by seeing what they have in common. This is what much of economic theory does. Economists usually assume that the firm's behaviour can be understood in terms of a common motivation. In predicting what decisions are made, it is irrelevant whether the firm is Ma and Pa's Bar and Grill or the Northern Telecom or whether a particular decision is made by the board of directors, the third vice-president in charge of advertising, or the owner-manager. Criticisms that economic theory neglects differences among firms will be considered in Chapter 16.

Before studying how the firm is treated in economic theory, we shall examine more closely the firm in Canada today.

The Organization of Production

Forms of Business Organization

There are three major forms of business organization in the private sector: the single proprietorship, the partnership, and the corporation. In the **single proprietorship,** one owner makes all the decisions and is personally responsible for all of the firm's actions and debts. In the **partnership,** there are two or more joint owners, each of whom may make binding decisions and may be personally responsible for all of the firm's actions and debts. In the **corporation,** the firm has a legal existence separate from that of the owners. The owners are the firm's shareholders, and they

Box 9-1

Why Are There Firms?

In previous chapters (and in many that follow) we study the role of markets in allocating resources. As we have seen, markets work through the forces of supply and demand; people with a particular good or service to sell and people who wish to purchase that good or service satisfy their mutual desires by exchanging with each other.

However, not all mutually advantageous trade occurs through markets; often it occurs within institutions, and in particular, within firms. As we will see in this chapter, there are many kinds and sizes of firms. Most economists, like most other people, are inclined to simply take the existence of firms for granted. But in a famous article published in 1937, Professor Ronald Coase of the University of Chicago, the recipient of the 1991 Nobel Prize in Economic Science, took up the question posed in the title of this box.[1]

The key to understanding Coase's argument is to recognise that there are costs associated with transactions. When a firm purchases something, it must identify the market and then find what different quantities and qualities are available at what prices. This takes time and money; it usually involves some uncertainty. When the firm decides instead to produce the thing itself, it uses the command principle and orders the commodity to be made to its desired specifications. The transactions costs may be lower, but the advantages of buying in a competitive market are lost. Furthermore, as the firm gets larger, the inefficiencies of the command system tend to become large compared with the efficiencies involved in decentralizing through the market system.

The firm must choose when to transact internally and when to transact through the market. For example, a car manufacturer must decide whether to purchase a certain component by contracting with a parts manufacturer to supply it, or to supply the component to itself by producing it. Coase viewed the firm as an institution that economizes on transactions costs, and thus he argued that the market works best when transactions costs are low, but when transactions costs are high there is an incentive for the firm to use internal mechanisms in place of market transactions.

Coase's insights have stimulated a great deal of further research by economists such as Professor Oliver Williamson of the University of California at Berkeley. This research has contributed to the understanding of the interaction of institutions and markets. Organization theorists have stressed that firms sometimes require less information than markets do for certain types of transactions; for example, transactions within firms do not require the decision makers to always know what market prices are. Some research even shows that transactions within firms sometimes *generate* information that is useful to the firm; for example, a close relationship between the producer of a particular component and the user might lead to improvements in its design. Another aspect is that when firms internalize a production process, they use one type of contract (say, with their employees) to replace a set of often more complicated contracts with external suppliers.

Coase's analysis has proven remarkably robust over the years, and its influence has spread throughout economics. As economic historian Douglas North recently put it, "Whenever transactions costs are high, institutions become important."

---

[1] "The Nature of the Firm," *Economica* 4 (1937), pp. 386–405.

risk only the amount that they put up to purchase their shares. The owners elect a board of directors, which hires managers to run the firm under the board's supervision.

Corporations account for more than two thirds of the nation's privately produced income.

In manufacturing, transportation, public utilities, and finance, corporations do almost all of the nation's business. In trade and construction they do about one half of the total business. In services, which are now the economy's dominant employer, partnerships and individual proprietorships outnumber corporations.

The Single Proprietorship and the Partnership

The major advantage of the single proprietorship is that the owner is the boss who maintains full control over the firm. The disadvantages are, first, that the size of the firm is limited by the amount of capital that the owner can personally raise and second, that the owner is personally responsible by law for all debts of the firm; this is called *unlimited liability.*

The ordinary partnership overcomes to some extent the first disadvantage of the single proprietorship but not the second. Ten partners may be able to finance a much bigger enterprise than one owner could, but they are still subject to unlimited liability. Each partner is fully liable for all of the debts of the firm. Partnerships are traditional in many professions, including law, medicine, and (until recently) brokerage. Partnerships survive in these professions partly because they depend heavily on a relationship of trust between owners and clients, and the partners' unlimited liability for one another's actions is thought to enhance public confidence in the firm.

The **limited partnership,** which has two classes of partners (general and limited), provides protection against some of the risks of the general partnership. The firm's *general partners,* who are responsible for the operation of the firm, have unlimited liability; the firm's *limited partners* are liable only for the amount that they have invested; this is called **limited liability.** Limited partners can neither participate in the running of the firm nor make agreements on its behalf.

The Corporation

The corporation is regarded by law as an entity separate from the individuals who own it. It can enter into contracts, sue and be sued, own property, contract debts, and generally incur obligations that are the legal obligations of the corporation but not of its *owners.* The corporation's right to be sued may not seem to be an advantage, but it is, because it allows others to enter into enforceable contracts with the corporation.

Although some corporations are owned by just a few persons, who also manage the business, the most important type of corporation is one that sells shares to the general public. Those who invest their money by buying its stock, called its **stockholders** or **shareholders,** are the corporation's owners. All profits belong to the stockholders. Profits that are paid out to them are called **dividends;** profits that are retained to be reinvested in the firm's operations are called **undistributed profits.**

Stockholders, who are entitled to one vote for each share that they own, elect a board of directors. This board of directors defines general policy and hires senior managers whose job it is to translate this general policy into detailed decisions. This chain of command, from owner to director to manager, gives rise to what is called a *principal-agent* problem: how can the managers (the agents) be induced to act in the interests of the shareholders (the principals)?

Should the corporation fail, the personal liability of any one stockholder is limited to whatever money that stockholder has actually invested in the firm.

From a stockholder's viewpoint, one of the most important aspects of the corporation is its limited liability.

One advantage to the corporation is that it can raise capital from a large number of individuals. Each individual who invests money in the firm shares in the firm's profits but has no personal liability beyond risking the loss of the amount invested. Thus, investors know how much they have at risk. Because shares are easily transferred from one person to another, a corporation has a continuity of life that is unaffected by frequent changes in investors.

Fifty years ago, most corporations had a physical presence in only one country. Many corporations exported some or even all of their production, and some corporations imported some of their inputs, but they did not produce outside of the country in which they were incorporated. Today, a great deal of production takes place in **transnational corporations,** which have a physical presence in more than one country. This development, which has many important implications for the functioning of the economy, is discussed further in Box 9-2.

The Rise of the Modern Corporation

The direct predecessors of the modern corporation were the English chartered companies of the sixteenth century. The Muscovy Company, chartered in 1555; the East India Company, chartered in 1600; and the Hudson's Bay Company, chartered in 1609 and still operating nearly 400 years later, are famous examples of early joint-stock ventures with limited liability. Their need for many investors to finance a ship that would not return with its cargo for years—if it returned at all—made this form of organization desirable.

In the next three centuries, the need to commit large amounts of capital for long periods of time and to diversify risks was felt in other fields, and charters were granted for insurance, turnpikes and canals, and banks, as well as for foreign trade. Exploiting the new techniques of the Industrial Revolution required the growth of large firms in many branches of manufacturing. The increasing need for large firms led to the passage of laws permitting incorporation with limited liability *as a matter of right rather than as a special grant of privilege.* Such laws became common in England and in North America during the late nineteenth century.

In their important book, *How the West Grew Rich,* economic historians Nate Rosenberg and L. E. Birdzell argue that it is important for countries to be able to evolve institutions that are appropriate to changing economic circumstances. Those countries that develop new institutions suited to the changing world environment are likely to prosper most. In the 1990s, adaptation is needed to the rapid developments in information and communication technology. Some commentators argue that new management techniques and new types of industrial structures explain much of Japan's rapid growth in the past quarter century.

Financing of Firms

The money that a firm raises for carrying on its business is sometimes called its **financial** (or *money*) **capital.** This is distinct from its **real** (or *physical*) **capital,** the physical assets of the firm that constitute plant, equipment, and inventories. Money capital may be broken down into **equity capital,** which refers to funds provided by the owners of the firm, and **debt,** which refers to the funds that have been borrowed from persons or institutions who are not owners of the firm.

The use of the term *capital* to refer to both an amount of money and a quantity of goods can be confusing, but it is usually clear from the context which is being referred to. The two uses are not independent, for much of the money capital raised by a firm will be used to purchase the capital goods that the firm requires for production.

Equity Financing

The firm can raise equity capital in two ways. One is to sell newly issued shares. The other is to reinvest, or plow back, some of its own profits. Although shareholders do not receive reinvested profits directly as their dividend income, they benefit from the rise in value of their shares (called *capital gains*) that occurs if the funds are reinvested profitably. Reinvestment has become an important source of funds in modern times.

Debt Financing

Firms can also raise money by issuing debt, either by selling bonds or by borrowing from financial institutions. A **bond** is a promise to pay interest each year and to repay the amount borrowed, called the *principal,* at a stated time in the future (say, 20 years hence). Bank loans are often short term; sometimes the firm even commits to repaying the principal on demand. Debt holders are *creditors,* not owners, of the firm: They have loaned money to the firm in return for the firm's promise to pay interest on the loan and, of course, to repay the principal. The commitment to make interest payments is a legal obligation that must be met whether or not profits have been made. Many a firm that would have survived a temporary crisis had all its capital been equity financed has been forced into bankruptcy because it could not

Box 9-2

Transnational Corporations

Over the past half century, the concept of a *national* economy has become less precise as a growing portion of production has been undertaken by firms with production facilities in more than one country.[1] Such firms are sometimes called *multinational corporations,* but are officially designated by the United Nations as *transnational corporations* (TNCs). TNCs encourage global competition as well as the transfer of technological know-how among countries.

In 1985, some 600 TNCs had sales of more than US$1 billion each. A dominant group of 74 of these accounted for half of the group's total sales. More than 75 percent of the total sales of all 600 TNCs occurred in the petroleum, chemicals, machinery and equipment, and motor vehicle industries. Fully 45 percent of the 600 firms in the "billion-dollar club" are based in the United States, and just over 45 percent are in eight other developed nations—Switzerland, the Netherlands, Canada, the United Kingdom, Sweden, France, Japan, and Germany.

The 1980s saw many changes in the behaviour of TNCs. The United States changed from being the leading provider of foreign investment through its TNCs to being the world's leading recipient of investment from foreign TNCs. Japan has become a leading foreign investor through TNCs. The Japanese transnationals have demonstrated a superior ability to innovate in high-tech activities such as the application of microelectronics-based technologies to manufacturing systems and to the handling of information in the service sector. Finally, the less developed countries (LDCs) have suffered large reductions in the amount of foreign capital that they import through foreign TNCs. (As a result, most of the LDCs have ended their anti-foreign-capital rhetoric and instead have adopted policies designed to attract such investment.)

The world is still in the phase of what the United Nations calls the "continuing transnationalization of world economic activity." Rapid expansion of TNCs from Japan, Western Europe, Australia, Canada, and Korea suggests, however, that although the location of expanding TNCs may have

[1] The material in this box draws on *Transnational Corporations in World Development: Trends and Prospects* (New York: United Nations, 1988).

---

meet its contractual obligations to pay interest to its debt holders. Debt holders, and all other creditors, have the first claims on the firm's funds. Only when they have been repaid in full can the stockholders attempt to recover anything for themselves.

The Firm in Economic Theory

Obviously, IBM and the Main Street Deli make decisions differently. Within a single large corporation, not all decisions are made by the same people or in the same way. For example, someone at IBM decided to introduce a small computer in 1981. Someone else decided to call it the IBM Personal Computer and market it for home use. Someone else decided how and where to produce it. Someone else decided its price. Someone else decided how best to promote its sales. The common aspect of these decisions is that all were in pursuit of the same goal—to earn profits for IBM. Basic economic theory assumes that the same principles underlie each decision made within a firm regardless of who makes it.

changed, the overall expansion continues.

The TNCs' primary instrument for developing foreign operations up until 1980 was foreign direct investment (FDI)—acquiring the controlling interest in foreign production facilities either by purchasing existing facilities or by building new ones. During the 1980s, however, FDI fell dramatically, and other instruments became more common. The most important of these are joint ventures with domestic firms located in countries where the TNCs wish to develop an interest, and licensing arrangements whereby a domestic firm produces a TNC's product locally.

There are many reasons for a company to transfer some of its production beyond its home base (thus becoming a TNC) rather than producing everything at home and then exporting the output. First, local conditions matter. As products become more sophisticated and differentiated, locating production in large local markets allows more flexible responses to local needs than can be achieved through centralized production back home. Second, nontariff barriers to trade make location in large foreign markets, such as the United States and the European Community, less risky than sending exports from the home base. Third, many of the TNCs are now in rapidly developing service industries such as advertising, marketing, public management, accounting, law, and financial services where a physical presence is needed in the country in which the service is sold. Fourth, the computer and communications revolutions have allowed production to be disintegrated on a global basis. Components of any one product are often manufactured in many countries, each component being made where its production is cheapest.

As a result of transnationalization, TNCs account for a large proportion of the foreign trade of many developed countries. This has long been so for the United States and is now becoming true for several other countries, particularly Japan. Although all types of TNCs have grown, much of the growth in recent years has been concentrated in small and medium-size TNCs, including some based in less developed countries. As the United Nations puts it, "This dynamic aspect of the growth of TNCs is one of the major channels by which economic change is spread throughout the world."

Motivation: Profit Maximization

In building a theory of how firms behave, economists usually assume that firms try to make their profits as large as possible. In other words, firms are assumed to *maximize their profits,* which are the difference between the value of sales and the costs to the firm of producing what is sold.

Why is this assumption made? First, it is necessary to make *some* assumption about what motivates decision makers if the theory is to predict how they will act. Second, a great many of the predictions of theories based on this assumption have been confirmed by observation. Third, no single alternative assumption has yet been shown to yield more accurate predictions. However, the assumption has been criticised, and alternatives have been suggested (see Chapter 16).

The assumption of profit maximization provides a principle by which firms' actions can often be successfully predicted.

Economists predict the behaviour of firms by studying the effect that making each choice available to the firm would have on profits. They then predict that firms will select the alternative that yields the largest profits. This theory does not say that profit is the *only* factor that influences the firm's behaviour; rather, it says that profits are important enough that assuming profits to be the firm's sole objective will produce predictions that are substantially correct.

Factors of Production

Firms seek profits by producing and selling commodities. The materials and services of factors of production, called **factor services,** that the firm uses in its production process are called **inputs,** and the goods and services that are produced are called **outputs.** One way of looking at production is to regard the inputs as being used up, or sacrificed, to gain the outputs.

Hundreds of inputs enter into the output of most goods and services. Among the inputs entering into the output of automobiles are sheet steel, rubber, spark plugs, electricity, machinists, cost accountants, forklift operators, managers, and painters. These inputs can be grouped into four broad classes: (1) those that are inputs to the automobile manufacturer but outputs to some other manufacturer, such as spark plugs, electricity, and sheet steel; (2) those that are provided directly by nature, such as the land used by the automobile plant; (3) those that are provided directly by households, such as the services of workers; and (4) those that are provided by machines, such as drill presses and robots.

Inputs in the first group just mentioned are called **intermediate products.** They are goods that are produced by other firms. They appear as inputs only because the stages of production are divided among different firms so that at any one stage, a firm is using as inputs goods produced by other firms. If these products are traced back to their sources, all production can be accounted for by the services of only three kinds of inputs, which are called *factors of production:* Economists call all gifts of nature, such as land and raw materials, **land;**[1] all

physical and mental contributions that are provided by people, **labour**; and all manufactured aids to further production, such as machines, **capital.**

Extensive use of capital is one distinguishing feature of modern production. Instead of making consumer goods with only the aid of simple natural tools, productive effort goes into the manufacture of tools, machines, and other goods that are desired not in themselves but as aids to making other goods.

The Firm's Costs

Profits are the difference between the value of the goods that a firm sells and the cost of producing these goods. In later chapters, we will look at the firm's sales revenues. Here, we are concerned with cost. **Cost,** to the producing firm, is the value of inputs used to produce its output.

Notice the use of the word *value* in the definition. A given output produced by a given technique, say, 6,000 cars produced each week by General Motors with its present production methods, has a given set of inputs associated with it—so many working hours of various types of labourers, supervisors, managers, and technicians; so many tons of steel, glass, and aluminum; so many kilowatt-hours of electricity; and so many hours of the time of various machines. The cost of each can be calculated, and the sum of these separate costs is the total cost to General Motors of producing 6,000 cars per week.

Opportunity Cost

Although the details of economic costing vary, they are governed by a common principle called *opportunity cost,* a concept introduced in Chapter 1.

The opportunity cost of using something in a particular venture is the benefit forgone by not using it in its best alternative use.

Box 9-3 considers some general applications of the principle of opportunity cost.

To measure opportunity cost, the firm must assign to each input that it uses a monetary value equal to what it has sacrificed to use the input. Applying this principle to specific cases is not quite as easy as it may seem at first.

---

[1]Recently, economists have begun to distinguish between land and the natural resources that are on or below the land. In Chapter 18, we discuss the pricing and use of natural resources as inputs in production.

Box 9-3

Opportunity Cost Beyond Economics

Opportunity cost is one of the great insights of economics. It plays a vital role in economic analysis, but it is also a fundamental principle that applies to a wide range of situations. Consider some examples:

George Bernard Shaw, on reaching his ninetieth birthday, was asked how he liked being 90. He is reputed to have said, "It's fine, when you consider the alternative."

Llewelyn Formed likes to watch both Lloyd Robertson and Peter Mansfield. If he finally decides to watch Peter Mansfield, what is the opportunity cost of this decision?

Lisa Hearthrob, 31 years old and single, is thinking about marrying. Although she thinks Ray Gular is a great guy, she realizes that if she marries him, she will give up the chance of wedded bliss with another guy she may meet next year, so she decides to wait a while. What other information do you need to determine the opportunity cost of this decision?

Serge Ginn, M.D., complains that now that he is earning large fees, he can no longer afford to take the time for a vacation trip to Europe. In what way does it make sense to say that the opportunity cost of his vacation depends on his fees?

Retired General Robert Russ has decided to contribute $5,000 to a local charity. His lawyer points out to him that, because such contributions can be deducted from taxable income, the real cost of his contribution is the same as if he were giving an extra $3,450 to his spendthrift stepson (who refers to him as Gen. R. Russ). Is the opportunity cost of the contribution to the zoo $5,000 or $3,450?

Purchased and Hired Factors

Assigning costs is a straightforward process when inputs purchased in one period are used up in the same period and when the price that the firm pays is determined by forces beyond its control. Inputs of intermediate products purchased from other firms fall into this category. If a firm pays $110 per ton for steel, it has sacrificed its claims to something else the $110 can buy, and thus the purchase price is a reasonable measure of the firm's opportunity cost of using one ton of steel.

Inputs of hired factors of production are also in this category. Firms hire labour, and the opportunity cost is the price that must be paid for these labour services. This includes the wage rate and all related expenses, such as contributions to pension funds, unemployment and disability insurance, and other fringe benefits. Firms also use borrowed money. Interest payments measure the opportunity cost of borrowed funds, because the money paid out as interest could have been used to buy something else of equivalent monetary value.

Imputed Costs

Some of the inputs that the firm uses are neither purchased nor hired for current use. Their use requires no payment to anyone outside the firm, so the costs of using them are not obvious. Nonetheless, their use does entail a cost. The opportunity cost of these inputs is the amount that the firm would earn if it were to shift the inputs to their next best use. When these costs are calculated, they are called **imputed costs,** costs that must be inferred because they are not made as money payments. The following examples all involve imputed costs.

Using the firm's own money. Consider a firm that uses $100,000 of its own money, which instead it could have loaned out at 10 percent per year, yielding $10,000 per year. This amount should be deducted from the firm's revenue as the cost of funds used in production. If the firm earns only $6,000 over all other costs, one should not say that the firm made a profit of $6,000 but that it lost $4,000. If it had closed down completely and merely loaned out its money to someone else, it could have earned $10,000.

Costs of durable assets. The costs of using assets owned by the firm, such as buildings, equipment, and machinery, include a charge, called **depreciation,** for the loss in value of an asset over a period of time because of its use in production, due to physical wear and tear and to obsolescence. The economic cost of owning an asset for a year is the loss in value of the asset during the year. Accountants use several conventional methods to show depreciation based on the price originally paid for the asset, which is called its *historical cost.* One of the most common is *straight-line depreciation,* in which the same amount of historical cost is deducted in every year of useful life of the asset. Although historical cost is often a useful approximation, in some cases it may differ substantially from the depreciation required by the opportunity-cost principle. Consider two examples.

Assets that may be resold. A woman buys a new automobile for $15,000. She intends to use it for 6 years and then sell it for $6,000. She may think that, using straight-line depreciation, this will cost her $1,500 per year. If after 1 year, however, the value of her car on the used-car market is $12,000, it has cost her $3,000 to use the car during the first year. Why should she charge herself $3,000 depreciation during the first year? After all, she does not intend to sell the car for 6 years. The answer is that one of the purchaser's alternatives is to buy a 1 year old car and operate it for 5 years. Indeed, that is the position she is in after the first year. Whether she likes it or not, she has paid $3,000 for the use of the car during the first year of its life. If the market had valued her car at $14,000 after one year (instead of $12,000), the correct depreciation would have been only $1,000.

Sunk costs. In the example just given, an active used-asset market was available. At the other extreme, consider an asset that has no alternative use. This is sometimes called a *sunk cost.* Suppose, for example, that a firm has a set of machines that it purchased a few years ago for $100,000. These machines were expected to last 10 years, and the firm's accountant calculates the depreciation costs of these machines by the straight-line method at $10,000 per year. Assume also that the machines can be used to make one product and nothing else. Suppose, too, that they are installed in the firm's plant, they cannot be leased to any other firm, and their scrap value is negligible. In other words, the machines have no value except to this firm in its current operation. Suppose that the machines are used to produce the product, the cost of all other factors used will amount to $25,000, and the goods produced can be sold for $29,000.

Now, if the accountant's depreciation "costs" of running the machines are added in, the total cost of operation comes to $35,000; with revenues at $29,000, this yields an annual loss of $6,000 per year. It appears that the goods should not be made!

The fallacy in this argument lies in adding a charge based on the sunk cost of the machines as one of the costs of current operations. The machines have no alternative uses whatsoever. Clearly, their *opportunity cost is zero.* The total cost of producing this line of goods is thus only $25,000 per year (assuming that all other costs have been correctly assessed), and the line of production shows an annual return over all relevant costs of $4,000, not a loss of $6,000.

To see why the second calculation leads to the correct decision, we notice that if the firm abandons this line of production as unprofitable, it will have no money to pay out and no revenue received on this account. If the firm takes the economist's advice and pursues the line of production, it will pay out $25,000 and receive $29,000, thus making it $4,000 per year better off than if it had not done so. Clearly, the production is worth undertaking. The amount that the firm happens to have paid out for the machines in the past has no bearing whatever on deciding on the correct use of the machines once they are installed on the premises.

Because they involve neither current nor future costs, sunk costs should have no influence on deciding what is currently the most profitable thing to do.

The principle of "let bygones be bygones" extends well beyond economics and is often ignored in poker, in war, and in love. Because you have invested heavily in a poker hand, a war, or a courtship does not mean that you should stick with it if the prospects of winning become very small. At every moment of decision making, maximizing behaviour is based on how benefits from this time forward compare with current and future costs.

Risk taking. One difficulty in imputing costs has to do with risk taking. Business enterprise is often a risky affair. Uninsured risks are borne by the owners of the firm, who, if the enterprise fails, may lose the money that they have invested in the firm.

Risk must be borne by someone. If a firm does not obtain a return that is sufficient to compensate for the risks involved, it will not be able to persuade people to invest in it. Those who buy the firm's shares expect a return that exceeds what they could have obtained if they had invested their money in a virtually riskless manner, say, by buying a government bond.

Suppose that a businesswoman invests $100,000 in a class of risky ventures and expects that most of the ventures will be successful but that some will fail. In fact, she expects that about $5,000 will be a total loss. (She does not know which specific ventures will be the losers; if she did, she would not invest in them.) Suppose further that she could earn a 10 percent return on an otherwise equivalent but riskless use of her funds. To earn a net revenue of $10,000 while recovering the $5,000 of expected losses, she needs to earn $15,000 from the $95,000 of successful investments. This is a rate of return of 15.8 percent. She charges 10 percent for the use of her capital and 5.8 percent for bearing the risk inherent in this type of venture.

Patents, trademarks, and other special advantages. Suppose that a firm owns a valuable patent or a highly desirable location or produces a popular brand-name product such as Coca-Cola or Miller Lite. Each of these involves an opportunity cost to the firm in production (even if it was acquired free) because if the firm does not choose to use the special advantage itself, it could sell or lease it to others.

The Meaning and Significance of Profits

Economic profits, sometimes also called *pure profits* or just *profits,* are the difference between the revenues received by the firm from the sale of output and the opportunity cost of all the inputs used to make the output. If costs are greater than revenues, such "negative profits" are called *losses.*

This definition *includes* in costs (and thus *excludes* from profits) the imputed returns to capital and to risk taking. By doing so, it gives a special meaning to the words *profits* and *losses*—a meaning that differs somewhat from everyday usage. Table 9-1 illustrates how the terms *cost* and *profit* are used by economists.

Other Definitions of Profits

Firms define *profits* as the excess of revenues over costs as measured by the conventions of accounting. Accountants charge neither for risk taking nor for the use of the owner's own capital, and thus these items are recorded by the firm as part of its profits. When a firm says it needs a certain amount of profit to stay in business, it is making sense within its definition, for its "profits" must be large enough to pay the costs of those inputs that accounting conventions do not include as costs.

Economists would express the same notion by saying that the firm needs to cover *all* of its costs, including those that are not used in accounting. If the firm is covering all of its opportunity costs, it could not do better by using its resources in any other line of activity than the one currently being followed.

A situation in which revenues equal costs, including opportunity costs, is one in which economic profits are zero; such a situation is consistent with the firm remaining in business because all factors, hidden as well as visible, are being rewarded at least as well as they would be in their *best* alternative uses.[2]

Profits and Resource Allocation

When resources are valued by the opportunity cost principle, their costs show how much these resources would earn if they were used in their best alternative uses. If there is an industry in which revenues exceed opportunity costs, the firms in that industry will be earning profits. Thus, the owners of factors of production will want to move resources into that industry because they could earn more there than in their present uses. Conversely, if in some other industry, firms are incurring losses, resources in that industry could earn more revenues in other uses, and their owners will want to move them to those other uses. Only when economic profits are zero is there no incentive for resources to move into or out of an industry.

Profits and losses play a crucial signaling role in the workings of a free-market system.

---

[2]In an alternative usage, the term *normal profits* is sometimes used to describe the firm's return on capital and its risk premium, whereas the term *super normal profits* is used for what we call *economic profits*. This alternative defines profits in the business sense and then divides them between the return on capital and risk called "normal," and profits above all economic costs, called "super normal." In this usage, "super normal profits" are what we call "economic profits."

TABLE 9-1   The Calculation of Economic Profits: An Example

Gross revenue from sales	$1,000
Less: direct cost of production (materials, labour, electricity, etc.)	−650
"Gross profits" (or "contributions to overhead")	350
Less: indirect costs (depreciation, overhead, management salaries, interest on debt, etc.)	−140
"Net profits"	210
Income taxes payable	−74
After-tax "net profits"	136
Less: imputed charges for own capital used and for risk taking (normal profits)	−130
Economic profits	$ 6

Economic profits are less than profits as defined by accountants. The main difference between economic profits and what a firm calls its net profits is in the subtraction of the imputed charges for use of capital owned by the firm and for risk taking. Income tax is levied on whatever definition of profits the taxing authorities choose, usually closely related to net profits. Although economic profits are necessarily less than net profits, they can be greater or less than normal profits, which include only the imputed charges for capital and risk. (In this example they are much less.)

SUMMARY

1. The firm is the economic unit that produces and sells commodities. The definition of the firm used in economics abstracts from real-life differences in the size and form of the organization of firms.

2. The single proprietorship, the partnership, and the corporation are the major forms of business organization in Canada today. The corporation is by far the most common wherever large-scale production is required. The corporation is recognised as a legal entity; the liability of its owners, or shareholders, is limited to the amount of money that they have invested in the organization. Corporate ownership is readily transferred by the sale of shares of the company's stock in securities markets.

3. Firms can raise money through equity financing or debt financing. A firm's owners provide equity capital both when they purchase newly issued shares and when the firm reinvests its profits. The firm obtains debt financing from creditors either by borrowing from financial institutions or by selling bonds to the public.

4. Economic theory assumes that the same principles underlie each decision made within the firm and that the actual decision is uninfluenced by who makes it. The key behavioural assumption is that the firm seeks to maximize its profit.

5. Production consists of transforming inputs (the services of factors of production) into outputs (goods and services). It is often convenient to divide factors of production into categories. One common classification is land, labour, and capital. Land includes land and natural resources, labour means all human services, and capital denotes all manufactured aids to further production. An outstanding feature of modern production is the use of capital goods.

6. The opportunity cost of using a resource is the value of that resource in its best alternative use. If the opportunity cost of using a resource in one way is less than or equal to the gain from using the resource in this way, there is no better way of using it.

7. Measuring opportunity cost to the firm requires imputing the cost of resources not purchased or hired for current use. Among these imputed costs are those for the use of the owners' money, depreciation, risk taking, and any special advantages, such as trademarks, that the firm possesses.

8. A firm that is maximizing profits, defined as the difference between revenue and the opportunity cost of all the resources that it uses, is making the best allocation of the resources under its control, according to the firm's evaluation of its alternatives.

9. When a firm is earning zero *economic profits,* its revenue is covering all of its opportunity costs. This means that it could do better by using its resources in other ways.

10. Economic profits and losses provide important signals concerning the reallocation of resources. Profits earned in an industry provide a signal that more resources can profitably move into the industry. Losses show that resources have more profitable uses elsewhere and serve as a signal that some of these resources should be transferred out of that industry.

TOPICS FOR REVIEW

Role of profit maximization

Single proprietorship, partnership, and corporation

Debt and equity financing

Inputs and factors of production

Opportunity costs and imputed costs

Alternative definitions of profits

Profits and resource allocation

1. Can the economic theory of the firm be of any help in analysing the decisions of such nonprofit organizations as governments, churches, and colleges? What role, if any, does the notion of opportunity cost play for them?

2. "There is no such thing as a free lunch." Can anything be free? In earlier decades, gasoline stations routinely provided many free services, including windshield cleaning, tire inflation, and road maps. Now many sell road maps and have discontinued free services. Indeed, self-service stations have become increasingly popular with motorists who like the lower gasoline prices at these stations. Under what conditions will profit-maximizing behaviour lead to the coexistence of full-service and self-service gasoline stations? What would determine the proportions in which each occurs?

3. What is the opportunity cost of the following?
   a. Fining a politician $10,000 and imprisoning her for a year.
   b. Lending $500 to a friend.
   c. Towing icebergs to Saudi Arabia to provide drinking water at the cost of 50 cents per cubic meter.

4. According to *Forbes* magazine (June 13, 1988), "Unredeemed frequent-flyer coupons, the bright promotional idea dreamed up first by American Airlines in 1981 and subsequently copied by just about everyone else" mean that "the industry owes passengers about 25 billion miles of free travel . . . [and] if all the miles earned were cashed in, it would cost the airlines $1.7 billion." How would you go about estimating the cost to the airlines of the 25 billion frequent-flyer miles that are now outstanding?

5. Having bought a used car from Smiling Sam for $2,000, you drive it for two days, and it stops. You now find that it requires an extra $1,500 before it will run. Assuming that the car is not worth $3,500 fixed, should you make the repairs?

6. "To meet the legislated standard of 3.4 grams of carbon monoxide per mile driven, General Motors has calculated that it will cost $100 million and prolong 200 lives by one year each, thus costing $500,000 per year of extra life. Human lives are precious, which is why it is so sad to note another use of that money. It has been estimated that the installation of special cardiac-care units in ambulances could prevent premature deaths each year at an average cost of only $200 for each year of extra life."

   Assume that the facts in this quotation are correct. If the money spent on carbon monoxide control would have been spent on cardiac-care units instead, what is the opportunity cost of the carbon monoxide requirement? If the money would not have been so spent but simply reduced automobile companies' costs, what is the opportunity cost?

7. Which concept of profits is implied in the following quotations?
   a. "Profits are necessary if firms are to stay in business."
   b. "Profits signal firms to expand production and investment."
   c. "Accelerated depreciation allowances lower profits and thus benefit the company's owners."

10

Production and Cost in the Short Run

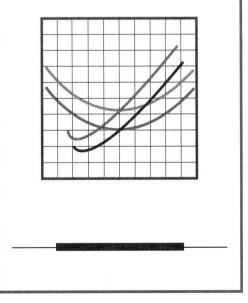

Every firm knows that its total costs of production are positively related to its output. If it produces more, it must pay more to hire additional workers and to buy more of other inputs. Perhaps more interestingly, many firms also find that their costs *per unit of output* are systematically related to their outputs. Both very low and very high levels of output are usually associated with high unit costs, whereas intermediate levels that are near the plant's normal output capacity are typically associated with lower unit costs of production. In Chapter 9, we defined costs of production. In this chapter, we see how and why costs vary with the rate of production and with changes in factor prices.

Choices Open to the Firm

Consider a firm that is producing a single product in a number of plants. Suppose its sales have increased, and it decides that production should be increased correspondingly. Should a single plant be operated for longer hours, using overtime shifts, or should several plants each be operated for a slightly longer period of time? Such decisions concern how best to use *existing* plants and equipment. They involve time periods that are too short in which to build new plants or to install more equipment.

Rather different decisions must be made when managers make their long-range plans. Should the firm adopt a highly automated process that will greatly reduce its wage bill? Or should it continue to build new plants that use current techniques? These matters concern what a firm should do when it is changing or replacing its plant and equipment. Such decisions may take a long time to put into effect.

In the examples just given, managers make decisions from known possibilities. Many firms also have research and development (R&D) staffs whose job it is to discover new products and new methods of production. Such firms must decide how much money to devote to R&D and in what areas the payoff for new development will be largest. If, for example, a shortage of a particular labour skill or raw material is anticipated, the research staff can be told to try to find ways to economize on that input or even to eliminate it from the production process.

Time Horizons for Decision Making

Economists organize the decisions that firms make into three classes: (1) how best to employ existing plant and equipment—the *short run;* (2) what new plant and equipment and production processes to select, given known technical possibilities—the *long run;* and (3) how to encourage, or adapt to, the development of new techniques—the *very long run.*

The Short Run

The **short run** is a time period in which the quantity of some inputs, called **fixed factors,** cannot be increased.[1] A fixed factor is usually an element of capital (such as plant and equipment), but it might be land, the services of management, or even the supply of skilled labour. Inputs that can be varied in the short run are called **variable factors.**

The short run does not correspond to a specific number of months or years. In some industries, it may extend over many years; in others, it may be a matter of months or even weeks.

In the electric power industry, for example, it takes 3 or more years to acquire and install a steam-turbine generator. An unforeseen increase in demand will involve a long period during which the extra demand must be met with the existing capital equipment. In contrast, a machine shop can acquire new equipment or sell existing equipment in a few weeks. An increase in demand will have to be met with the existing stock of capital for only a brief time, after which it can be adjusted to the level made desirable by the higher demand.

The Long Run

The **long run** is a time period in which all inputs may be varied but in which the basic technology of production cannot be changed. Like the short run, the long run does not correspond to a specific length of time.

The long run corresponds to the situation faced by the firm when it is planning to go into business,

to expand the scale of its operations, to branch out into new products or new areas, or to change its method of production. The firm's *planning decisions* are long-run decisions because they are made from given technological possibilities but with freedom to choose from a variety of production processes that will use factor inputs in different proportions.

The Very Long Run

Unlike the short run and the long run, the **very long run** is a period of time in which the technological possibilities available to a firm will change. Modern industrial societies are characterized by continuously changing technologies that lead to new and improved products and production methods.

Some of these technological advances are made by the firm's own research and development efforts. For example, much of the innovation in cameras and films has been made by Kodak and Polaroid. Some firms adopt technological changes developed by others. For example, the transistor and the electronic chip have revolutionized dozens of industries that had nothing to do with developing them. Firms must regularly decide how much to spend in efforts to change technology either by developing new techniques or by adapting techniques that have been developed by others.

Connecting the Runs: The Production Function

The **production function** describes the precise physical relationship between factor inputs and output.

The various runs are simply different aspects of the same basic problem: getting output from inputs efficiently. They differ in terms of what the firm is able to change.

A simplified production function in which there are only two factors of production, labour and capital, will be considered here, but the conclusions apply equally when there are many factors. (Capital is taken to be the fixed factor, and labour is taken to

---

[1]Sometimes, it is physically impossible to increase the quantity of a fixed factor in a short time. For instance, there is no way to build a hydroelectric dam or a nuclear power plant in a few months. In other cases, it might be physically possible but prohibitively expensive to increase the quantity of a fixed factor in a short time. For example, a suit-manufacturing firm could conceivably rent a building, buy and install new sewing machines, and hire a trained labour force in a few days if money were no consideration. Prohibitive costs, along with physical impossibility, are both sources of fixed factors.

be the variable one.) This chapter deals with the short-run situations in which output and cost change as different amounts of the variable input, labour, are used. Long-run situations in which both factors can be varied, and very-long-run situations in which the production function changes, are both covered in Chapter 11.

Short-Run Choices

Total, Average, and Marginal Products

Suppose that a firm starts with a fixed amount of capital (say, four units) and contemplates applying various amounts of labour to it. Table 10-1 shows three different ways of looking at how output varies with the quantity of the variable factor.

Total product (TP) is the total amount that is produced during a given period of time. If the inputs of all but one factor are held constant, total product will change as more or less of the variable factor is used. This variation is shown in columns 1 and 2 of Table 10-1, which gives a total product schedule. Figure 10-1(i) shows such a schedule graphically. (The shape of the curve will be discussed shortly.)

Average product (AP) is the total product divided by the number of units of the variable factor used to produce it. If we let the number of units of labour be denoted by L, the average product can be written as

$$AP = \frac{TP}{L}$$

Notice in column 3 of Table 10-1 that as more of the variable factor is used, average product first rises and then falls. The level of output at which average product reaches a maximum (34 units in the example) is called the *point of diminishing average productivity.* Up to that point, average productivity is increasing; beyond that point, average productivity is decreasing.

Marginal product (MP), sometimes called *incremental product* or **marginal physical product**

TABLE 10-1 Variation of Output with Capital Fixed and Labour Variable

(1) Quantity of labour (L)	(2) Total product (TP)	(3) Average product (AP)	(4) Marginal product (MP)
0	0	0	
			15
1	15	15.0	
			19
2	34	17.0	
			14
3	48	16.0	
			12
4	60	15.0	
			2
5	62	12.4	

The relationship between changes in output and changes in the quantity of labour can be looked at in three ways. Capital is assumed to be fixed at four units. As the quantity of labor increases, the level of output (the total product) increases. Average product increases at first and then declines. The same is true of marginal product.

Marginal product is shown between the lines because it refers to the *change* in output from one level of labour input to another. When the schedule is graphed, marginal products are plotted at the midpoint of the interval. For example, the marginal product of 12 would be plotted to correspond to a quantity of labour of 3.5.

(MPP), is the change in total product resulting from the use of one unit more of the variable factor:[2] **[14]**

$$MP = \frac{\Delta TP}{\Delta L}$$

Computed values of marginal product are shown in column 4 of Table 10-1. The figures in this column are placed between the other lines of the table to stress that the concept refers to the *change* in output caused by the *change* in quantity of the variable factor. For example, the increase in labour from 3 to 4 units ($\Delta L = 1$) raises output by 12 from 48 to 60 ($\Delta TP = 12$). Thus the MP equals 12, and it is recorded between 3 and 4 units of labour. Note that the MP in the example first rises and then falls as

---

[2]Δ is read "change in." For example, ΔL is read "change in quantity of labour."

FIGURE 10-1
Total Product, Average Product, and Marginal Product Curves

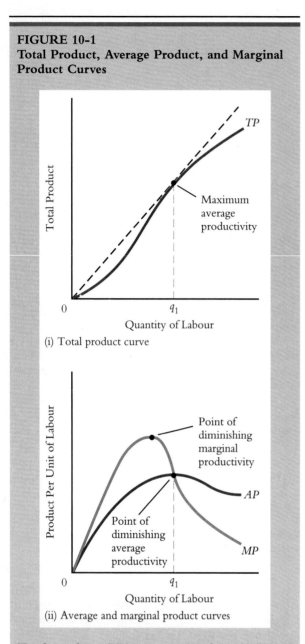

(i) Total product curve

(ii) Average and marginal product curves

Total product *(TP)*, average product *(AP)*, and marginal product *(MP)* curves often have the shapes shown here. The total product curve in part (i) shows the total product steadily rising, first at an increasing rate and then at a decreasing rate. This causes both the average and the marginal product curves in part (ii) to rise at first and then to decline. The point of diminishing average productivity (also called the point of maximum average productivity) is q_1. At this point $MP = AP$.

output increases. The level of output at which marginal product reaches a maximum is called the **point of diminishing marginal productivity.**

Figure 10-1(ii) plots average product and marginal product curves. Although three different schedules are shown in Table 10-1 and three different curves are shown in Figure 10-1, they are all aspects of the same single relationship described by the production function. As we vary the quantity of labour, with capital being fixed, output changes. Sometimes it is interesting to look at total output, sometimes at average output, and sometimes at the marginal change in output.

Finally, bear in mind that the schedules in Table 10-1 and the curves in Figure 10-1 all assume a specified quantity of the fixed factor. If the quantity of capital were, say, 10 units instead of the 4 that were assumed, there would be a different set of total product, average product, and marginal product curves. The reason is that if for any specified amount of labour there is more capital to work with, labour can produce more output; that is, the total product will be greater.

The Marginal and Average Product Curves

The Law of Diminishing Returns

The variations in output that result from applying more or less of a variable factor to a given quantity of a fixed factor are the subject of a famous economic relation. Usually it is called the **law of diminishing returns.** (Sometimes it is also called the *law of variable proportions.*)

The law of diminishing returns states that if increasing amounts of a variable factor are applied to a given quantity of a fixed factor, eventually a situation will be reached in which each additional unit of the variable factor adds less to total product than did the previous unit; that is, the marginal product of the variable factor will decline.

The common-sense explanation of the law of diminishing returns is that as output is increased in the short run, more and more of the variable factor is combined with a given amount of the fixed factor. As a result, each unit of the variable factor has less and less of the fixed factor to work with. When the fixed factor is capital and the variable factor is labour, each unit of labour gets a declining amount of capital to assist it as the total output grows. It is not surprising, therefore, that sooner or later equal increases in labour eventually begin to add diminishing amounts to total output.

It is possible that marginal product might diminish from the outset, so that the first unit of labour contributes most to total production and each successive unit contributes less than the previous unit. It is also possible for the marginal product to rise at first and to decline only at some higher level of output. In this case, the law might more accurately be described as the law of *eventually diminishing marginal returns.*

To illustrate this second case, let us consider the use of workers in a manufacturing operation. If there is only one worker, that worker must do all the tasks, shifting from one to another and becoming competent in each. As a second, third, and subsequent workers are added, each can specialize in one task, becoming expert at it. This process, as we noted in Chapter 1, is called the *division of labour.* If additional workers allow more efficient divisions of labour, marginal product will rise: Each newly hired worker will add more to total output than did each previous worker. However, according to the law of diminishing returns, the scope for such economies must eventually disappear, and sooner or later the marginal products of additional workers must decline. When this happens, each additional worker who is hired will increase total output by less than did the previous worker. This case, in which marginal product rises at first and then declines, is illustrated in Figure 10-1.

Eventually, as more and more of the variable factor is employed, marginal product may reach zero and then become negative. It is not hard to see why if you consider the extreme case, in which there would be so many workers in a limited space that additional workers would simply get in the way.

So far we have spoken of diminishing marginal returns, but average returns also are expected to diminish. The *law of diminishing average returns* states that if increasing quantities of a variable factor are applied to a given quantity of fixed factors, the average product of the variable factor will eventually decrease. Both diminishing marginal and average products are illustrated in Table 10-1. **[15]**

The significance of diminishing returns. Empirical illustrations of both diminishing marginal and diminishing average returns occur frequently. Some examples are illustrated in Box 10-1. One might wish that it were not so. There would then be no reason to fear a food crisis caused by the population explosion in less developed countries. If the marginal product of additional workers applied to a fixed quantity of land were constant, food production could be expanded in proportion to population growth merely by keeping a constant fraction of the population on farms. With fixed techniques, however, diminishing returns dictate an inexorable decline in the marginal product of each additional labourer because an expanding population must work with a fixed supply of agricultural land.

Thus, unless there is a steady improvement in the techniques of production used in countries with widespread subsistence agriculture, continuous population growth will bring with it, according to the law of diminishing returns, declining average living standards and eventually widespread famine.[3] This gloomy prediction of the nineteenth-century English economist Thomas Malthus is discussed further in Box 11-2.

The Relationship Between Marginal and Average Curves

Notice that in part (ii) of Figure 10-1, the MP curve cuts the AP curve at the AP's maximum point. It is important to understand how these curves are related. **[16]**

The average product curve is positively sloped as long as the marginal product curve is *above* it; whether the marginal product curve is itself positively or negatively sloped is irrelevant. If an additional worker is to raise the average product of all workers, that additional worker's output must be greater than the average output of the other workers. It is immaterial whether the new worker's contribution to output is greater or less than the contribution of the worker hired immediately before; all that matters is that the new worker's contribution to output exceeds the average output of *all workers hired previously.* (The relationship between marginal and average measures is illustrated further in Box 10-2 on page 190.)

---

[3]In many poor countries, people subsist mainly on what they and their neighbours can grow locally.

Box 10-1

Diminishing Returns

The law of diminishing returns operates in a wide range of circumstances.

British Columbia's Campbell River, a noted sport fishing area, has become the centre of a thriving, well-promoted tourist trade. As fishing has increased, the total number of fish caught has steadily increased, but the number of fish per person fishing has decreased and the average hours fished for each fish caught has increased.

When Southern California Edison was required to modify its Mojave power plant to reduce the amount of fly ash emitted into the atmosphere, it discovered that a series of filters applied to the smokestacks could do the job. A single filter eliminated one half of the discharge. Five filters in series reduced the fly ash discharge to the 3 percent allowed by law. When a state senator proposed a new standard that would permit no more than 1 percent fly ash emission, the company brought in experts who testified that this would require at least 15 filters per stack and would triple the cost.

Public opinion pollsters, as well as all students of statistics, know that you can use a sample to estimate characteristics of a very large population. Even a relatively small sample can provide a useful estimate—at a tiny fraction of the cost of a complete enumeration of the population. However, sample estimates are subject to sampling error. If, for example, 38 percent of a sample approves of a certain policy, the percentage of the population that approves of it is likely to be close to 38 percent, but it might well be anywhere from 36 to 40 percent. The theory of statistics shows that the size of the expected sampling error can be reduced by increasing the sample size. However, the theory also shows that successive reductions in the sampling error require larger and larger increases in the sample size. Suppose that the original sample was 400; if quadrupling the sample to 1,600 would halve the chance of an error of any given size from occurring, then in order to halve it again, the new sample would have to be quadrupled again—to 6,400. In other words, increasing the sample size leads to diminishing marginal returns in terms of accuracy.

During the early days of World War II, so few naval ships were available that each North Atlantic convoy had only a few escort vessels to protect it from German submarines. The escorts dashed about from one side of the convoy to the other and ended up sinking very few submarines. As the construction program made more ships available, the escorts could stay in one position in the convoy: Some could close in on the various flanks; others could hunt farther afield. Not only did the total number of submarines sunk per convoy crossing rise, but also the number of submarines sunk per escort vessel rose. Still later in the war, as each successive convoy was provided with more and more escort vessels, the number of submarines sunk per convoy crossing continued to rise, but the number of submarines sunk per escort vessel began to fall sharply.

Short-Run Variations in Cost

We now shift our attention from the firm's production function to its costs. The majority of firms cannot influence the prices of the inputs that they employ; instead they must pay the going market price for their inputs. For example, a shoe factory in Montreal, a metal manufacturer in Sarnia, a rancher in Red Deer, and a boat builder in Prince Rupert are each too small a part of the total demand for the factors that they use to be able to influence their prices significantly. The firms must pay the going rent for the land that they need, the going wage rate for the labour that they employ, and the going interest rate that banks charge for loans; so it

TABLE 10-2 Variation of Costs with Capital Fixed and Labour Variable

(1) Labour (L)	(2) Output (q)	(3) Fixed (TFC)	(4) Variable (TVC)	(5) Total (TC)	(6) (MC)	(7) Fixed (AFC)	(8) Variable (AVC)	(9) Total (ATC)
			Total cost ($)		Marginal cost ($ per unit)		Average cost ($ per unit)	
0	0	100	0	100		—	—	—
					0.67			
1	15	100	10	110		6.67	0.67	7.33
					0.53			
2	34	100	20	120		2.94	0.59	3.53
					0.71			
3	48	100	30	130		2.08	0.62	2.71
					0.83			
4	60	100	40	140		1.67	0.67	2.33
					5.00			
5	62	100	50	150		1.61	0.81	2.42

The relationship of cost to level of output can be looked at in several ways. These cost schedules are computed from the product schedule of Table 10-1, given the price of capital of $25 per unit and the price of labour of $10 per unit. Marginal cost (in column 6) is shown between the lines of total cost because it refers to the *change* in cost divided by the *change* in ouput that brought it about. For example, the *MC* of $0.71 is the $10 increase in total cost (from $120 to $130) divided by the 14-unit increase in output (from 34 to 48). In constructing a graph, marginal costs should be plotted midway in the interval over which they are computed. For example, the *MC* of $0.71 would be plotted at an output of 41.

is with most other firms.[4] Given these prices and the physical returns summarized by the product curves, the costs of different levels of output can be calculated.

Cost Concepts Defined

The following definitions of several cost concepts are closely related to the product concepts just introduced.

Total cost *(TC)* is the total cost of producing any given level of output. Total cost is divided into two parts, total fixed cost and total variable cost. **Total fixed cost *(TFC)*** does not vary with the level of output; it is the same whether output is 1

unit or 1 million units. This cost is also referred to as *sunk cost, overhead cost,* or *unavoidable cost.* A cost that varies directly with output, rising as more output is produced and falling as less output is produced, is called a **total variable cost *(TVC)*** (also a *direct* or *avoidable cost).* In the example in Table 10-1, labour is the variable factor of production, and wages are therefore a variable cost.

Average total cost *(ATC)*, also called **average cost *(AC)*,** is the total cost of producing any given number of units of output divided by that number. Average total cost can be separated into **average fixed costs *(AFC)*,** fixed cost divided by quantity of output, and **average variable costs *(AVC)*,** variable cost divided by quantity of output.

Although average *variable costs* may rise or fall as production is increased (depending on whether output rises more rapidly or more slowly than total variable costs), it is clear that average *fixed costs* decline continuously as output increases. A doubling of output always leads to a halving of fixed costs per unit of output. This is a process popularly known as *spreading one's overhead.*

Marginal cost *(MC)*, sometimes called *incremental cost,* is the increase in total cost resulting from raising the rate of production by one unit. Because fixed costs do not vary with output, marginal fixed

---

[4]The firm that is a large enough employer of labour or user of land or capital to affect the prices of its factor services is the exception rather than the rule. The exceptions are very large firms, such as General Motors, and firms in one-company towns. (Even such firms cannot set just any wage they wish because their workers always have the option of moving to another town.) The important problems that arise when a firm can influence the wage rate that it pays to its employees are considered in Chapter 18.

Box 10-2

Mario Lemieux's Goal-Scoring Record

The relationship between the concepts of marginal and average measures is very general. An interesting example comes from Mario Lemieux's goals-per-season record for the first nine years after he joined the NHL's Pittsburgh Penguins for the 1984–1985 season, as shown in the table.

Mario Lemieux's Goals Per Season

Season	(1) Career total at start of season	Old average (2) Career average at start of season	Marginal (3) Goals scored during season	New average (4) Career average at end of season
1984–1985	—	—	43	43.00
1985–1986	43	43.00	48	45.50
1986–1987	91	45.50	54	48.33
1987–1988	145	48.33	70	53.75
1988–1989	215	53.75	85	60.00
1989–1990	300	60.00	45	57.50
1990–1991	345	57.50	19	52.00
1991–1992	364	52.00	44	51.00
1992–1993	408	51.00	69	53.00

For each season, the first column shows the total number of NHL goals that Lemieux had scored as of the start of the season. In the second column, that total is divided by the number of seasons he had played to calculate his career *average* goals per season. The third column gives the number of goals he scored that season—that is, his *marginal* goals-per-season production. The fourth column then gives his new *average* goals per season as of the end of the season. It is calculated as his new career total goals scored, the sum of columns 1 and 3, divided by his total number of seasons.

Note that in each of his first five seasons, Lemieux's marginal production exceeded his start-of-season average, and as a result his average rose. *Whenever his marginal performance during a season is better than his career average at the start of the season, his career average rises.* For example, Lemieux entered the 1987–1988 season having averaged 48.33 goals per season in his first three years. That year, he scored 70 goals, so his *marginal* production exceeded his average. Thus the average that he carried forward from the 1987–1988 season rose to 53.75.

In 1989–1990, Lemieux missed a lot of the season due to injury, and as a result he had a below-average year. He entered the season with a career average of 60 goals per season, but his production that year was only 45 goals, so at the end of the season his career average had fallen to 57.5. This experience was repeated in 1990–1991 and 1991–1992. *Whenever his performance during a season is worse than his career average at the start of the season, his career average falls.* In 1992–1993 he was back in form; his season's goals exceeded his lifetime average, and that average rose.

This illustrates the important relationship between marginal (in this case, current-season) and average (in this case, career) measures:

If the average is to rise, all that matters is that the marginal be above the average; if the average is to fall, all that matters is that the marginal be below the average.

Notice that what matters is whether his year's goals (his marginal production) exceed or fall short of his existing average. It does not matter if the marginal production increases or decreases between any two years. For example, in the years 1990–1992 his marginal production fell from 45 to 19, then rose to 44. Because each of these figures was below his current average, that average fell.

FIGURE 10-2
Total Cost, Average Cost, and Marginal Cost Curves

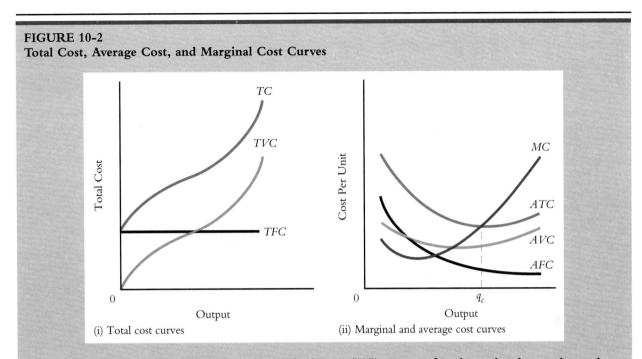

(i) Total cost curves

(ii) Marginal and average cost curves

Total cost (TC), average cost (AC), and marginal cost (MC) curves often have the shapes shown here.
Total fixed cost does not vary with output. Total variable cost and the total of all costs $(TC = TVC + TFC)$ rise with output, first at a decreasing rate and then at an increasing rate. The total cost curves in part (i) give rise to the average and marginal curves in part (ii). Average fixed cost (AFC) declines as output increases. Average variable cost (AVC) and average total cost (ATC) fall and then rise as output increases. Marginal cost (MC) does the same, intersecting ATC and AVC at their minimum points. Capacity output is q_c, the minimum point on the ATC curve.

costs are always zero. Therefore, marginal costs are necessarily marginal variable costs, and a change in fixed costs will leave marginal costs unaffected. For example, the marginal cost of producing a few more potatoes by farming a given amount of land more intensively is not affected by the rent paid for the land. **[17]**

Short-Run Cost Curves

Using the production relationships found in Table 10-1, assume that the price of labour is $10 per unit and that the price of capital is $25 per unit. The cost schedules that result from these values are shown in Table 10-2 on page 189.

Figure 10-2 shows cost curves that are similar in shape to those arising from the data in Table 10-2. Notice that the marginal cost curve cuts the average total cost curve and the average variable cost curve

at their lowest points. This is another example of the relationship between a marginal and an average curve. The ATC curve, for example, has a negative slope as long as the MC curve is below it; it makes no difference whether the MC curve is itself negatively or positively sloped.

To see this, consider an example in which 10 units are produced each week at an average cost of $5 per unit (total cost equals $50). The average cost of producing 11 units will exceed $5 if the eleventh unit adds more than $5 to the cost (MC exceeds AC) and will be less than $5 if the eleventh unit adds less than $5 to the cost (MC is less than AC). The marginal cost of the tenth unit does not matter for this calculation. (It could be above, below, or equal to the eleventh unit's marginal cost.)

Short-run average variable cost. In Figure 10-2 the average variable cost curve reaches a minimum and then rises. With fixed factor prices, when average product per worker is at a maximum, average variable cost is at a minimum. [18] Common sense tells us that since each additional worker adds the same amount to cost but a different amount to output, when output per worker rises, the cost per unit of output must fall, and vice versa.

Eventually diminishing average productivity implies eventually increasing average variable costs.

Short-run average total cost curve. Short-run ATC curves are often U-shaped. This reflects the assumptions that (1) average productivity increases when output is low, but that (2) at some level of output, average productivity begins to fall fast enough to cause average variable costs to increase faster than average fixed costs are falling. When this happens, ATC increases.

Marginal cost curves. In part (ii) of Figure 10-2, the marginal cost curve is shown as a negatively sloped curve that reaches a minimum and then rises. This is the reverse of the shape of the marginal product curve in part (ii) of Figure 10-1. The reason for the reversal is as follows: If extra units of a variable factor that is bought at a fixed price per unit result in increasing quantities of output (marginal *product rising)*, the cost per unit of extra output must be falling (marginal *cost falling)*. However, if marginal product is falling, marginal cost will be rising. Thus, the law of eventually diminishing marginal product implies eventually increasing marginal cost. [9]

Total variable cost. In part (i) of Figure 10-2, total variable cost is shown as an upward-sloping curve, indicating that total variable cost rises with the level of output. This is true as long as marginal cost is positive, because the total variable cost of producing any given level of output is just the sum of the marginal costs of producing each unit of output up to the given level of output. [20]

Definition of Capacity

The level of output that corresponds to the minimum short-run average total cost is often called the **capacity** of the firm. In this sense, capacity is the largest output that can be produced without encountering rising average costs per unit. In part (ii) of Figure 10-2, capacity output is q_c units, but higher outputs can be achieved, provided that the

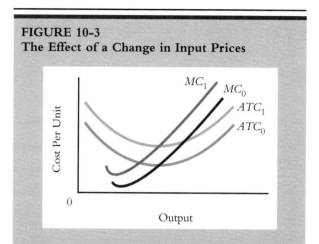

FIGURE 10-3
The Effect of a Change in Input Prices

A change in any input price shifts the average total cost curve and the marginal cost curve. The original average total cost and marginal cost curves are shown by ATC_0 and MC_0. A rise in the price of a variable input—for example, the wage rate—rises the cost of producing each level of output. As a result, the average total cost curve and the marginal cost curve shift upward to ATC_1 and MC_1.

Conversely, a fall in the price of a variable input used by the firm shifts the average total cost curve and the marginal cost curve downward; if the original curves are ATC_1 and MC_1, after the fall in the price of the variable input the curves will be ATC_0 and MC_0.

firm is willing to accept the higher per unit costs that accompany any level of output that is "above capacity." A firm that is producing at an output less than the point of minimum average total cost has **excess capacity.**

The technical definition gives the word *capacity* a meaning that is different from the one used in everyday speech, in which it often means an upper limit that cannot be exceeded. The technical definition is, however, a useful concept in economic and business discussions.

Shifts in Short-Run Cost Curves

So far we have seen how costs vary as output varies, with input prices being held constant. Figure 10-3 shows the effect on a firm's cost curves of a change in the price of any variable input. A rise in the price of any input used by the firm must raise the price of producing any given quantity of output. A fall in the price of any input has the opposite effect.

This is a very simple relationship, but it is important nonetheless.

A change in the price of any variable input used by the firm will shift its variable and total cost curves—upward for a price increase and downward for a price decrease.

There is thus a set of average and marginal costs curves that correspond to each price of the variable factor.

A Family of Short-Run Cost Curves

A short-run cost curve shows how costs vary with output for a given quantity of the fixed factor, say, a given size of plant.

There is a different short-run cost curve for each given quantity of the fixed factor.

A small plant that manufactures nuts and bolts will have its own short-run cost curve. A medium-size plant and a large plant will each have its own short-run cost curve. If a firm expands and replaces its small plant with a medium-size plant, it will move from one short-run cost curve to another. This change from one plant size to another is a long-run change. We shall discuss how short-run cost curves for plants of different sizes are related to each other in Chapter 11.

SUMMARY

1. A firm's production decisions can be classified into three groups: (a) how best to employ existing plants and equipment—the short run; (b) what new plant and equipment and production processes to select, given known technical possibilities—the long run; and (c) how to encourage or to adapt to technological changes—the very long run.

2. The short run involves decisions in which one or more factors of production are fixed. The long run involves decisions in which all factors are variable but technology is given. The very long run involves decisions in which technology can change.

3. The production function shows the output that results from each possible combination of inputs. Short-run and long-run situations can be interpreted as implying different kinds of constraints on the production function. In the short run, the firm is constrained to use no more than a *given* quantity of some fixed factor; in the long run, it is constrained only by the available techniques of production.

4. The theory of short-run costs is concerned with how output varies as different amounts of the variable factor are combined with given amounts of the fixed factors. The concepts of total, average, and marginal product represent alternative relationships between output and the quantity of the variable factor of production.

5. The law of diminishing returns asserts that if increasing quantities of a variable factor are combined with given quantities of fixed factors, the marginal and the average products of the variable factor will eventually decrease. If factor prices are fixed, this hypothesis implies that marginal and average costs will eventually rise as output is increased.

6. Given physical productivity schedules and the prices of inputs, it is a matter of simple arithmetic to develop the whole family of short-run cost curves, one for each quantity of the fixed factor.

7. Short-run average total cost curves are often U-shaped. Average productivity increases at low levels of outputs but eventually declines rapidly enough to offset advantages of spreading overheads. The output corresponding to the minimum point of a short-run average total cost curve is called the plant's capacity.

8. Changes in factor prices shift the short-run cost curves—upward when prices rise and downward when prices fall. Thus there is a whole family of short-run curves, one for each set of factor prices.

TOPICS FOR REVIEW

Short run, long run, and very long run

Total product, average product, and marginal product

The law of diminishing returns

Marginal product curves and average product curves

Relationship between productivity and cost

Total cost, marginal cost, and average cost

Short-run cost curves

Capacity and excess capacity

DISCUSSION QUESTIONS

1. Does the short run consist of the same number of months for increasing output as for decreasing it? Must the short run in an industry be the same length for all firms in the industry? Under what circumstances might the long run actually involve a longer time span than the very long run for one particular firm?

2. Use the distinction between long run and short run to discuss each of the following.
   a. A guaranteed annual employment contract of at least forty-eight 40-hour weeks of work for all employees.
   b. A major economic recession during which there is substantial unemployment of labour and in which equipment is being used at well below capacity levels of production.
   c. A speeding up of delivery dates for new easy-to-install equipment.

3. Indicate whether each of the following conforms to the hypothesis of diminishing returns and if so, whether it refers to marginal returns, average returns, or both.
   a. "The bigger they are, the harder they fall."
   b. "As more and more of the population receives smallpox vaccinations, the reduction in the smallpox disease rate for each additional 100,000 vaccinations becomes smaller."
   c. "Five workers produce twice as much today as 10 workers did 40 years ago."
   d. "Diminishing returns set in last year when the rising rural population actually caused agricultural output to fall."

4. Consider the education of a human being as a process of production. Regard years of schooling as one variable factor of production. What are the other factors? What factors are fixed? At what point would you expect diminishing returns to set in?

5. Discuss each of the following news items in terms of its effects on cost. (You will have to decide which concept of cost is most likely to be affected.)

   a. An educational research institute reports that the increasing level of education of youth has led both to higher productivity and to increases in the general level of wages.

   b. During one recent winter, many factories were forced by fuel shortages to reduce production and to operate at levels of production far below capacity.

   c. NASA, the U.S. space agency, reports that the space program has led to the development of electronic devices that have brought innovations to many industries.

6. "Because overhead costs are fixed, increasing production lowers costs. Thus small businesses are sure to be inefficient. This is a dilemma of modern society, which values both smallness *and* efficiency." Discuss.

7. Look again at the examples of diminishing returns given in Box 10-1. Indicate for each whether it refers to marginal returns, average returns, or both, and identify what is being held constant and what is varying.

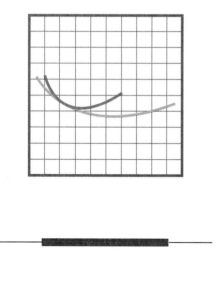

11

Production and Cost in the Long Run and the Very Long Run

In the first part of this chapter, we look at *long-run* behaviour, in which firms are free to vary all factors of production. Should firms use a great deal of capital and only a small amount of labour? Should they use less capital and more labour? What effects do these decisions have on firms' costs?

In the second part of the chapter, we examine the *very long run*. The discussion concerns the improvements in technology and productivity that have dramatically increased output and incomes in all industrial countries during the past 100 years. Evidence shows that such improvements are an important part of the response of firms to signals such as changes in factor prices.

The Long Run: No Fixed Factors

In the short run, in which only one factor can be varied, the only way to produce a given output is to adjust the input of the variable factor. Thus, once the firm has decided on a rate of output, there is only one possible way of achieving it. In the long run, all factors can be varied, so there are numerous technically possible ways to produce any given output. The firm must decide both on a level of output *and* on how to produce that output. Specifically, this means that firms in the long run must choose the nature and amount of plant and equipment, as well as the size of their labour force.

In making this choice, the firm will wish to avoid being technically inefficient, which means using more of *all* inputs than are necessary. Being technically efficient is not enough, however. To be economically efficient, the firm must choose from among the many technically efficient options the one that produces a given level of output at the lowest possible cost. (The distinction between various types of efficiency sometimes causes confusion, particularly when engineers and economists are involved in the same decision-making process. Box 11-1 elabourates on this distinction.)

Long-run planning decisions are important. A firm that decides to build a new steel mill and to invest in machinery that will go into it will choose among many alternatives. Once installed, that equipment is fixed for a long time. If the firm makes a wrong choice, its survival may be threatened; if it estimates shrewdly, it may be rewarded with large earnings.

Long-run decisions are risky because the firm must anticipate what methods of production will be efficient, not only today but also for many years in the future, when the costs of labour and raw materials will no doubt have changed. The decisions are also risky because the firm must estimate how much output it will want to produce. Is the

Box 11-1

Various Concepts of Efficiency

In popular discussion, in business decision making, and in government policies, three different types of efficiency concepts are encountered. These are engineering, technical, and economic efficiency. Each is a valid concept, and each conveys useful information. However, the use of one concept in a situation in which another is appropriate is a potential source of error and waste.

Engineering efficiency refers to the *physical* amount of some *single key input* that is used in production. It is measured by the ratio of that input to output. For example, the engineering efficiency of an engine refers to the ratio of the amount of energy in the fuel burned by the engine to the amount of usable energy produced by the engine. The difference goes in friction, heat loss, and other unavoidable sources of waste. Saying that a steam engine is 40 percent efficient means that 40 percent of the energy in the fuel that is burned in the boiler is converted into work that is done by the engine, while the other 60 percent is lost.

Technical efficiency (or technological efficiency) is related to the *physical* amount of *all factors* used in the process of producing some commodity. A particular method of producing a given output is technically inefficient if there exist other ways of producing the output that will use less of at least one input while not using more of any others. (Economists often call technical inefficiency *X-inefficiency*.)

Economic efficiency is related to the *value* of all inputs used in producing a given output. The production of a given output is economically efficient if there is no other way of producing the output that will use a smaller total value of inputs.

What is the relationship between economic efficiency and these other two concepts?

We have seen that engineering efficiency measures the efficiency with which a single input is used. Although knowing the efficiency of any given gasoline, electric, or diesel engine is interesting, increasing this efficiency is not necessarily economically efficient, because doing so usually requires the use of other valuable resources. For example, the engineering efficiency of a gas turbine engine can be increased by using more and stronger steel in its construction. Raising the engineering efficiency of an engine saves on fuel, but at the cost of using more of other inputs. To know whether this is worth doing, the firm must compare the value of the fuel saved with the value of the other inputs used. The optimal level of engineering efficiency is achieved by increasing efficiency to the point where the value of the input saved exceeds the value of the extra resources used, but not into the range where the costs exceed the value of the input saved.

Technical efficiency is desirable as long as inputs are costly to the firm in any way. If a technically inefficient process is replaced by a technically efficient process, there is a saving. We do not need to put a precise value on the cost of inputs to make this judgement. All we need to know is that inputs have a positive cost to the firm, so that saving on these costs is desirable.

Usually, however, any given output may be produced in any one of many alternative, technically efficient ways in the long run. Avoiding technical inefficiency is clearly a necessary condition for producing any output at the least cost. The existence of technical inefficiency means that costs can be reduced by reducing some inputs and not increasing any others. Avoiding technical efficiency is not, however, a sufficient condition for producing at lowest possible cost. The firm must still ask which of the many technically efficient methods it should use. This is where the concept of economic efficiency comes in. The appropriate method is the one that uses the smallest value of inputs. This ensures that the firm spends as little as possible on its given output; in terms of opportunity cost, the firm sacrifices the least possible value with respect to other things that it might do with those inputs.

industry to which it belongs growing or declining? Will new products emerge to render its existing products less useful than an extrapolation of past sales suggests?

Profit Maximization and Cost Minimization

Any firm that is trying to maximize its profits in the long run should select the economically efficient method, which is the method that produces its output at the lowest possible cost. This implication of the hypothesis of profit maximization is called **cost minimization:** From the alternatives open to it, the profit-maximizing firm will choose the least costly way of producing whatever specific output it chooses.

Choice of Factor Mix

If it is possible to substitute one factor for another to keep output constant while reducing total cost, the firm is not using the least costly combination of factors. In such a situation, the firm should substitute one factor for another factor, as long as the marginal product of the one factor *per dollar* expended on it is greater than the marginal product of the other factor *per dollar* expended on it. The firm is not minimizing its costs as long as these two magnitudes are unequal. For example, if an extra dollar spent on labour produces more output than an extra dollar spent on capital, the firm can reduce costs by spending less on capital and more on labour.

If we use K to represent capital, L to represent labour, and p to represent the price of a unit of the factor, the necessary condition for cost minimization is as follows:

$$\frac{MP_K}{p_K} = \frac{MP_L}{p_L} \qquad [1]$$

Whenever the two sides of Equation 1 are not equal, there are possibilities for factor substitutions that will reduce costs.

To see why this equation must be satisfied if costs of production are to be minimized, consider a situation where the equation is not satisfied. Sup-

pose, for example, that the marginal product of capital is 20 and its price is $2, making the left side of Equation 1 equal to 10. Suppose that the marginal product of labour is 32 and its price is $8, making the right side of Equation 1 equal to 4. Thus, the last dollar spent on capital adds 10 units to output, whereas the last dollar spent on labour adds only 4 units to output. In such a case, the firm could maintain its output level and reduce costs by using $2.50 less of labour and spending $1.00 more on capital. Making such a substitution of capital for labour would leave output unchanged and reduce costs by $1.50. Thus, the original position was not cost minimizing.[1]

By rearranging the terms in Equation 1, we can look at the cost-minimizing condition a bit differently.[2]

$$\frac{MP_K}{MP_L} = \frac{p_K}{p_L} \qquad [2]$$

The ratio of the marginal products on the left side of the equation compares the contribution to output of the last unit of capital and the last unit of labour. If the ratio is 4, this means that 1 unit more of capital will add 4 times as much to output as 1 unit more of labour. The right side of the equation shows how the cost of 1 unit more of capital compares to the cost of 1 unit more of labour. If the ratio is also 4, the firm cannot reduce costs by substituting capital for labour or vice versa. Now suppose that the ratio on the right side of the equation is 2. Capital, though twice as expensive, is four times as productive. It will pay the firm to switch to a method of production that uses more capital and less labour. If, however, the ratio on the right side is 6 (or *any* number more than 4), it will pay to switch to a method of production that uses more labour and less capital.

We have seen that when the ratio $MP_K\backslash MP_L$ is 4, while the ratio $p_K\backslash p_L$ is 2, the firm will substitute capital for labour. This substitution is measured by changes in the **capital-labour ratio**—the amount of capital per worker used by the firm.

---

[1] The argument in this paragraph assumes that the marginal products do not change when expenditure changes by a small amount.

[2] The appendix to this chapter provides a graphical analysis of this condition, which is similar to the analysis of household behaviour in Chapter 7A.

How far does the firm go in making this substitution? There is a limit, because the law of diminishing returns dictates that as the firm uses more capital, the marginal product of capital falls, and as it uses less labour, the marginal product of labour rises. Thus the ratio $MP_K \backslash MP_L$ falls. When it reaches 2 in the present example, the firm need substitute no further. The ratio of the marginal products is equal to the ratio of the prices.

Equation 2 shows how the firm can adjust the elements over which it has control (the quantities of factors used, and thus the marginal products of the factors) to the prices of the factors given by the market.

Long-Run Equilibrium of the Firm

The firm will have achieved its equilibrium capital-labour ratio when there is no opportunity for cost-reducing substitutions. This occurs when the marginal product per dollar spent on each factor is the same (Equation 1) or, equivalently, when the ratio of the marginal products of factors is equal to the ratio of their prices (Equation 2).

The Principle of Substitution

Suppose that a firm is meeting the cost-minimizing conditions shown in Equations 1 and 2 and that the cost of labour increases while the cost of capital remains unchanged. The least-cost method of producing any output will now use less labour and more capital than was required to produce the same output before the factor prices changed.

Methods of production will change if the relative prices of factors change. Relatively more of the cheaper factor and relatively less of the more expensive factor will be used.

This is called the **principle of substitution,** and it follows from the assumption that firms minimize their costs.

The principle of substitution plays a central role in resource allocation, because it relates to the way in which individual firms respond to changes in relative factor prices that are caused by the changing relative scarcities of factors in the economy as a whole. Individual firms are motivated to use less of factors that become scarcer to the economy and more of factors that become more plentiful. Here are two examples of the principle of substitution in action.

In recent decades, construction workers' wages have risen sharply relative to the wages of factory labour and the cost of machinery. In response, many home builders have shifted from on-site construction to panelization, a method of building that uses standardized modules. The wiring, plumbing, insulation, and painting of these standardized modules are all done at the factory. The bulk of the factory work is performed by machinery and by assembly line workers whose wages are only half those of on-site construction workers.

Some countries have plentiful land and small populations. Their land prices are low, and because their labour is in short supply, their wage rates are high. In response, their farmers make lavish use of the cheap land while economizing on expensive labour; thus their production processes use low ratios of labour to land. Other countries are small in area but have large populations. The demand for land is high relative to its supply, and land is relatively expensive, whereas labour is relatively cheap. In response, farmers economize on land by using much labour per unit of land; thus their production processes use high ratios of labour to land.

Once again, we see the price system functioning as an automatic control system. No single firm needs to be aware of national factor surpluses and scarcities. These are reflected by market prices, so individual firms that never look beyond their own profits are led to economize on factors that are scarce to the nation as a whole.

This discussion suggests why methods of producing the same commodity differ among countries. In the United States, where labour is highly skilled and expensive, a farmer with a large farm may use elaborate machinery to economize on labour. In China, where labour is abundant and capital is scarce, a much less mechanized method of production is appropriate. The Western engineer who believes that the Chinese are inefficient because they are using methods long ago discarded in the West is missing the truth about efficiency in the use of resources; where factor scarcities differ across nations, so will the most efficient methods of production.

Cost Curves in the Long Run

When all factors can be varied, there is a least-cost method of producing each possible level of output. Thus, with given factor prices, there is a minimum achievable cost for each level of output; if this cost is expressed as a quantity per unit of output, we obtain the long-run average cost of producing each level of output. When this least-cost method of producing each output is plotted on a graph, the result is called a **long-run average cost (*LRAC*) curve.** Figure 11-1 shows one such curve.

This cost curve is determined by the technology of the industry (which is assumed to be fixed) and by the prices of the factors of production. It is a boundary in the sense that points below it are unattainable; points on the curve, however, are attainable if sufficient time elapses for all inputs to be adjusted. To move from one point on the *LRAC* curve to another requires an adjustment in all inputs, which may, for example, require building a larger, more elabourate factory.

The *LRAC* curve is the boundary between cost levels that are attainable, with known technology and given factor prices, and those that are unattainable.

Just as the short-run cost curves discussed in Chapter 10 relate to the *production function* describing the physical relationship between factor inputs and output, so does the *LRAC* curve. The difference is that in deriving the *LRAC* curve, there are no fixed factors, so all factors are treated as variable. Because all costs are variable in the long run, we do not need to distinguish among *AVC, AFC,* and *ATC,* as we did in the short run; in the long run there is only one *LRAC* for any given set of input prices.

The Shape of the Long-Run Average Cost Curve

The *LRAC* curve shown in Figure 11-1 first falls and then rises. This curve is often described as U-shaped, although saucer-shaped might be a more accurate description of the evidence from many empirical studies.

Decreasing costs. Over the range of output from zero to q_m, the firm has falling long-run average costs: An expansion of output permits a reduction of costs per unit of output. Technologies with this property are referred to as exhibiting **economies of scale.** (Of course, when output is increased, such economies of scale will be realized only after enough time has elapsed to allow changes in all factor inputs.) The prices of factors are assumed to be constant, and thus the decline in long-run average cost occurs because output is increasing *more than* in proportion to inputs as the scale of the firm's production expands. Over this range of output, the decreasing-cost firm is often said to enjoy long-run **increasing returns.**[3]

Increasing returns may occur as a result of increased opportunities for specialization of tasks made possible by the division of labour. Adam Smith's classic discussion of this important point is given in Box 3-2. Even the most casual observation of the differences in production techniques used in large and small plants will show that larger plants use greater specialization.

These differences arise because large, specialized equipment is useful only when the volume of output that the firm can sell justifies employment of that equipment. For example, assembly line techniques, body-stamping machinery, and multiple-boring engine-block machines in automobile production are economically efficient only when individual operations are repeated thousands of times. Use of elabourate harvesting equipment (which combines many individual tasks that would otherwise be done by hand and by tractor) provides the least-cost method of production on a big farm but not on a few acres.

Typically, as the level of planned output increases, capital is substituted for labour and complex machines are substituted for simpler machines. Robotics is a contemporary example. Electronic de-

---

[3]Economists often shift back and forth between speaking in physical terms (i.e., *increasing returns to scale*) and cost terms (i.e., *decreasing costs of production*). Under constant input prices as assumed in the text, the same relationship can be expressed in either way.

FIGURE 11-1
A Long-Run Average Cost Curve

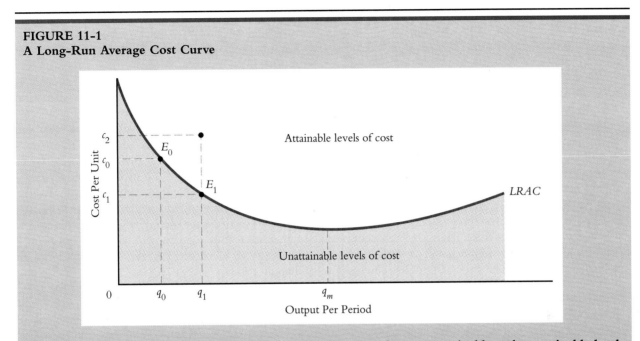

The long-run average cost *(LRAC)* curve provides a boundary between attainable and unattainable levels of costs. If the firm wishes to produce output q_0, the lowest attainable cost level is c_0 per unit. Thus, point E_0 is on the *LRAC* curve. E_1 represents the least-cost method of producing q_1. Suppose that a firm is producing at E_0 and desires to increase output to q_1. In the long run a plant optimal for output q_1 can be built, and the cost of c_1 per unit can be attained. However, in the short run it will not be able to vary all factors, and thus costs per unit will be above c_1, say c_2. At output q_m, the firm attains its lowest possible per unit cost of production for the given technology and factor prices.

vices can handle huge numbers of operations quickly, but unless the level of production requires such a large volume of operations, robotics or other forms of automation will not provide the least-cost method of production.

The foregoing discussion refers to the technology of production, which is one major source of increasing returns to scale. A second source lies in the geometry that is intrinsic to the three-dimensional world in which we live. To illustrate how geometry matters, consider a firm that wishes to store a gas or a liquid. The firm is interested in the *volume* of storage space. However, the materials cost of a storage container is related to the *area* of its surface. When the size of a container is increased, the storage capacity, which is determined by its volume, increases

faster than its surface area.[4] This is a genuine case of increasing returns—the output, in terms of storage capacity, increases more proportionately than the increase in the costs of the required construction materials.

---

[4]For example, consider a cubic container with metal sides, bottom, and lid, all of which measure 1 metre by 1 metre. To build this container, 6 square metres of metal is required (6 sides, each 1 square metre), and it will hold 1 cubic metre of gas or liquid. Now increase all of the lengths of each of the container's sides to 2 metres. Now 24 square metres of metal is required (6 sides, each 4 square metres), and the container will hold 8 cubic metres of gas or liquid (2 metres x 2 metres x 2 metres). So increasing the amount of metal in the container's walls fourfold has the effect of increasing its capacity eightfold.

A third source of increasing returns consists of inputs that do not have to be increased as the output of a product is increased, even in the long run. For example, there are often large fixed costs in developing new products, such as a new generation of airplanes or a more powerful computer. These R&D costs have to be incurred only once for each product and hence are independent of the scale at which the product is subsequently produced. Even if the product's *production costs* increase in proportion to output in the long run, average total costs, including *product development costs,* will fall as the scale of output rises. The influence of such once-and-for-all costs is that, other things being equal, they cause average total costs to be falling over the entire range of output. (The significance of such once-and-for-all costs is further discussed in Chapter 14.)[5]

Increasing costs. Over the range of outputs greater than q_m, the firm encounters rising long-run costs. An expansion in production, even after sufficient time has elapsed for all adjustments to be made, will be accompanied by a rise in average costs per unit of output. If costs per unit of input are constant, the firm's output must be increasing *less than* in proportion to the increase in inputs. When this happens, the increasing-cost firm is said to encounter long-run **decreasing returns.**[6] Decreasing returns imply that the firm suffers some diseconomy of scale. As its scale of operations increases, diseconomies are encountered that increase its per unit cost of production.

These diseconomies may be associated with the difficulties of managing and controlling an enterprise as its size increases. For example, planning problems do not necessarily vary in direct propor-

tion to size. At first, there may be scale economies as the firm grows, but sooner or later planning and coordination problems may multiply more than in proportion to the growth in size. If so, management costs per unit of output will rise. Other sources of scale diseconomies concern the possible alienation of the labour force as size increases and the difficulties of providing appropriate supervision as more and more tiers of supervisors and middle managers come between the person at the top and the workers on the shop floor. Control of middle-range managers may also become more difficult. As the firm becomes larger, managers may begin to pursue their own goals rather than devote all of their efforts to making profits for the firm. (This is the principal-agent problem that is discussed in detail in Chapter 16.)

Constant costs. In Figure 11-1, the firm's long-run average costs fall until output reaches q_m and rises thereafter. Another possibility should be noted. The firm's *LRAC* curve might have a flat portion over a range of output around q_m. With such a flat portion, the firm would be encountering constant costs over the relevant range of output. This means that the firm's long-run average costs per unit of output do not change as its output changes. Because factor prices are assumed to be fixed, the firm's output must be increasing *exactly in proportion* to the increase in inputs. A firm in this situation is said to be encountering **constant returns to scale.**

Relationship Between Long-Run and Short-Run Costs

The short-run cost curves mentioned at the conclusion of Chapter 10 and the long-run curve studied in this chapter are all derived from the same production function. Each curve assumes given prices for all factor inputs. In the long run, all factors can be varied; in the short run, some must remain fixed. The long-run average cost (*LRAC*) curve shows the lowest cost of producing any output when all factors are variable. Each short-run average total cost (*SRATC*) curve shows the lowest cost of producing any output when one or more factors are held constant at some specific level.

No short-run cost curve can fall below the long-run curve, because the *LRAC* curve represents the lowest attainable cost for each possible output.

---

[5]This phenomenon is similar to what happens in the short run when averaged fixed costs fall with output. The difference is that fixed short-run production costs are variable long-run production costs. If the firm increases its scale of output for some product, it will incur more capital costs in the long run as a larger plant is built. However, its costs of developing that product are not affected.

[6]Long-run decreasing returns differ from short-run diminishing returns. In the short run, at least one factor is fixed, and the law of diminishing returns ensures that returns to the variable factor will eventually diminish. In the long run, all factors are variable, and it is possible that physically diminishing returns would never be encountered—at least as long as it was genuinely possible to increase inputs of all factors.

FIGURE 11-2
Long-Run Average Cost and Short-Run Average Cost Curves

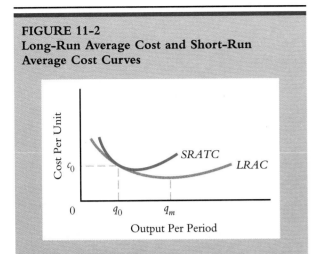

The short-run average total cost (*SRATC*) curve is tangent to the long-run average cost (*LRAC*) curve at the output for which the quantity of the fixed factors is optimal. If output is varied around q_0 units with plant and equipment fixed at the optimal level for producing q_0, costs will follow the short-run cost curve. Whereas *SRATC* and *LRAC* are at the same level for output q_0, where the fixed plant is optimal for that level, for all other outputs there is too little or too much plant and equipment, and *SRATC* lies above *LRAC*. If some output other than q_0 is to be sustained, costs can be reduced to the level of the long-run average cost curve when sufficient time has elapsed to adjust the plant and equipment.

As the level of output is changed, a different-size plant is normally required to achieve the lowest attainable cost. This is shown in Figure 11-2, where the *SRATC* curve lies above the *LRAC* curve at all outputs except q_0.

As we observed at the end of Chapter 10, an *SRATC* curve, such as the one shown in Figure 11-2, is one of many such curves. Each curve shows how costs vary as output is varied from a base output, holding the fixed factor at the quantity most appropriate to that output. Figure 11-3 shows a family of short-run average total cost curves, along with a single long-run average cost curve. The long-run average cost curve sometimes is called an **envelope,** because it encloses a series of short-run average total cost curves by being tangent to them. Each *SRATC* curve is tangent to (touches) the long-run average cost curve at the level of output

for which the quantity of the fixed factor is optimal and lies above it for all other levels of output.

Shifts in Cost Curves

The cost curves derived so far show how cost varies with output, given constant factor prices and fixed technology. Changes in either technological knowledge or factor prices will cause the entire family of short-run and long-run average cost curves to shift. Loss of existing technological knowledge is rare, so technological change normally causes change in only one direction, shifting cost curves downward. Improved ways of producing existing commodities make lower-cost methods of production available. (Technological change will be discussed in more detail later in this chapter.)

Changes in factor prices can exert an influence in either direction. If a firm has to pay more for any factor that it uses, the cost of producing each level of output will rise; if the firm has to pay less for any factor that it uses, the cost of producing each level of output will fall.

A rise in factor prices shifts the family of short-run and long-run average cost curves upward. A fall in factor prices, or a technological advance, shifts the entire family of average cost curves downward.

Although factor prices usually change gradually, sometimes they change suddenly and drastically. For example, in the mid-1980s, oil prices fell dramatically; the effect was to shift downward the cost curves of all users of oil and oil-related products.

The Very Long Run

In the long run, profit-maximizing firms do the best they can to produce known products with the techniques and the resources currently available. This means being *on,* rather than above, their long-run cost curves. In the very long run, the tech-

FIGURE 11-3
The Envelope Relationship Between the Long-Run Average Cost Curve and All of the Short-Run Average Cost Curves

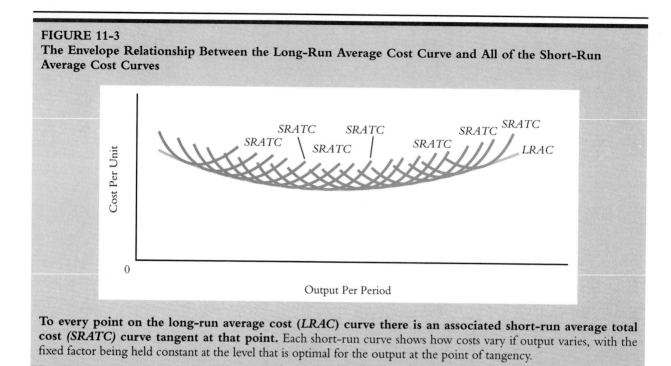

To every point on the long-run average cost (*LRAC*) curve there is an associated short-run average total cost (*SRATC*) curve tangent at that point. Each short-run curve shows how costs vary if output varies, with the fixed factor being held constant at the level that is optimal for the output at the point of tangency.

niques and resources that are available change. Such changes cause *shifts* in long-run cost curves.

The decrease in costs that can be achieved by choosing from among available factors of production, known techniques, and alternative levels of output is necessarily limited. Improvements by invention and innovation are potentially limitless, however, and hence sustained growth in living standards is critically linked to *technological change.*

Technological change refers to all changes in the available techniques of production. To measure its extent, economists use the notion of **productivity,** defined as a measure of output produced per unit of resource input. The rate of increase in productivity provides a measure of the progress caused by technological change. The significance of such growth is explored further in Box 11-2.[7]

Innovation, Invention, and Technological Change

Technological change was once thought to be mainly a random process, brought about by inventions made by crackpots and eccentric scientists working in garages and scientific laboratories. As a result of recent research by economists such as Nathan Rosenberg of Stanford University and Eric von Hipple of MIT, we now know better.

Changes in technology are often *endogenous responses* to changing economic signals; that is, they result from responses by firms to the same things that induce the substitution of one factor for another within the confines of a given technology.

In our discussion of long-run demand curves in Chapter 5, we looked at just such technological changes in response to rising relative prices when we spoke of the development of smaller, more fuel-

[7]One widely used measure of productivity is output *per hour* of labour. Other possible measures include output *per worker,* output *per person,* and output *per unit* of inputs, measured by an index number.

Box 11-2

The Significance of Productivity Growth

Economics used to be known as the dismal science because some of its predictions were dismal. Malthus and other classical economists predicted that the pressure of more and more people on the world's limited resources would cause a decline in output per person due to the operation of the law of diminishing returns. Human history would see more and more people living less and less well and the surplus population, which could not be supported, dying off from hunger and disease.

This prediction has proved wrong for the developed countries for two main reasons. First, their populations have not expanded as rapidly as predicted by early economists, who were writing before birth control techniques were widely used. Second, pure knowledge and its applied techniques have expanded so rapidly during the past 150 years that the ability to squeeze more out of limited resources has expanded faster than the population. We have experienced sustained growth in productivity that has permitted increases in output per person.

Growth in productivity permits increases in output per person and thus contributes to rising standards of living.

Productivity increases are a powerful force for increasing living standards. An apparently modest rate of increase in productivity of 2 percent per year leads to a doubling of output per hour of labour every 35 years. Productivity in Canada has increased at a rate somewhat greater than this throughout most of the twentieth century.

The growth rates of other countries have been even higher. Between 1945 and 1980, German productivity increased at 5 percent per year, doubling its output every 14 years. In Japan, it increased at more than 9 percent per year, a rate that doubles output per hour of labour approximately every 8 years! In many countries, a stable rate of productivity growth came to be taken for granted as an automatic source of ever-increasing living standards.

During the 1970s, the rate of productivity growth in most industrialised countries dropped sharply below its historical trend, and the slowdown was particularly acute in Canada and the United States. Since 1982, however, productivity growth has resumed at almost 2 percent per year. It remains to be seen whether the slowdown was a one-time occurrence or whether the accustomed doubling of productivity in every generation is a thing of the past.

A permanent slowdown in productivity growth would have severe consequences. Declining productivity growth means that living standards rise more slowly.

efficient cars in the wake of rising gasoline prices. Similarly, much of the move to substitute capital for labour in manufacturing, transportation, communications, mining, and agriculture in response to rising wage rates has taken the form of inventing new labour-saving methods of production.

Invention and Innovation

Invention is the discovery of something new, such as a production technique or a product. **Innovation** is the introduction of an invention into methods of production. Invention is thus a precondition to innovation.

Innovation is a costly and very risky activity engaged in by firms in the hope of gaining profits; it results from responses to signals of current and expected prices and costs, that is, responses to profit incentives. Profit incentives are in turn affected by many aspects of the economic climate, among them the rate of growth of the economy, the cost and availability of money for investment, and all sorts of government policies, from taxes to regulations.

Box 11-3

The Lean Production Revolution

Production techniques are currently being revolutionized by the introduction, in many industries and in many countries, of *lean production techniques,* or as they are sometimes called, *flexible manufacturing.*[1] This is the most fundamental change to occur since the introduction of mass production—a technique brought to full development by Henry Ford early in the twentieth century. To understand the lean production revolution pioneered by the Japanese, one must distinguish the three types of production methods used today.

Craft methods employ highly skilled workers to make nonstandardized products that are often tailor-made for individual purchasers. The result is usually an expensive product of high quality, made by artisans who get considerable job satisfaction.

Mass-production methods are based on specialization and division of labour, as first analysed by Adam Smith in the eighteenth century (see Box 3-2). They use skilled personnel to design products and production methods. They then employ relatively unskilled labour to produce standardized parts and to assemble them using highly specialized, single-purpose machines. The parts are usually manufactured in separate locations, often by distinct companies, and then assembled on a central production facility, often called an *assembly line.* The design of the product is centralized, and manufacturers bid competitively to produce parts to the stated specifications. The cost of changing the specialized equipment from the production of one product variant to another is high, and thus specific product types are produced for as long as possible. The result is a standardized product, made in a fairly small number of variants and produced at low cost with moderate quality. The work is repetitive, and workers are regarded as variable costs to be laid off or taken on as the desired rate of production varies.

Lean production methods combine the flexibility and high quality standards of craft production with the low cost of mass-production techniques. They are lean because they use less of all inputs, including time, labour, capital, and inventories, compared with either of the other techniques. They are flexible because the costs of switching from one product line to another are minimized.

In lean production, workers are organized as teams; each worker is encouraged to do all of the tasks assigned to the team, using equipment that is less highly specialized than what is used in mass-production techniques. This emphasizes individuality and initiative rather than a mind-numbing repetition of one unskilled operation. It also helps workers to identify places where improvements can be made and encourages them to follow up on these. Finally, it reduces the costs of switching equipment from production of one product variant to another.

In mass-production plants, stopping an assembly line to correct a problem at one point stops work at all points. So stopping the line is regarded as a serious matter, and keeping the assembly line running is the sole responsibility of a senior line manager. To reduce stoppages, large stocks of each part are held, and defective parts are discarded. Faults in assembly, which are treated as random events, are left to be corrected after the product has been assembled—often an expensive procedure. Stops are nonetheless frequent to correct materials-supply and coordination problems. In lean production, every worker has the ability to stop production whenever a fault is

---

[1]The material in this box is adapted from J. P. Womack, D. T. Jones, and D. Roos, *The Machine That Changed the World* (New York: Maxwell Macmillan, 1990).

discovered. Parts are delivered by the suppliers to the work stations "just in time." Defective parts are put aside so that their source can be identified, and any defects are treated as events with patterns of causes that need to be understood. When lean methods are first introduced, stoppages are frequent as problems are identified and investigated. As the sources are found and removed, work stoppages diminish, and the typical mature lean production line—wherein any worker can stop the line—stops much less frequently than the typical mass-production assembly line, where only the line foreman can press the stop button.

The result for labour is much more worker identification with the job and much more worker satisfaction than under mass-production techniques. Employers find that their labour force develops substantial skills, and they try to hold on to workers rather than treating them as strictly variable factors. (Some union leaders feel that workers lose when they and management form a cooperative rather than an adversarial relation and consequently oppose the introduction of lean production methods.)

Product design is expensive. Mass-production firms try to reduce the costs by using specialist designers. For example, one person may spend his or her life trying to improve window-opening mechanisms. The specialization creates problems both in coordinating the work of various designers and in getting good feedback from parts producers and assembly line workers to designers. The best theoretical design is of little use if it poses costly production problems. Lean producers use design teams that are nonspecialized and work closely with production engineers and parts producers. This creates more flexibility and better feedback, from the practical problems that arise in production to the basic design of products. It also allows parts producers to be presented with broad specifications of the required parts while they do their own R&D to develop the detailed specifications.

The use of design teams also cuts product development time dramatically. In the specialized design techniques, the designing must be done in a linear manner: The product design must be worked out in detail before the machine makers begin to design the specialized equipment needed to do the work. In the lean design team, everyone is working together. As the new product begins to take shape, the tool designers can begin to work on their outline plans; as the product design becomes better specified, the design of the tools can likewise be more fully developed.

Although lean production methods still have scale economies—unit costs fall as the volume of output increases—their main effect is to shift the whole long-run cost curve dramatically downward. Lean methods are also effective in the very long run, especially in developing successful new products that can be produced efficiently and cheaply.

Japanese automobile firms using these methods have been able to achieve unit costs of production below those of mass-production-based North American car factories that have twice their volume of output. They have also been able to lead in international competition to design new products efficiently and rapidly. Lean production methods are a major source of the Japanese competitive advantage, both in automobiles and in a range of other manufactured goods. The ability of firms in other countries to compete successfully with these Japanese firms may depend on the speed with which they can institute lean methods in their own production processes.

Invention is cumulative in effect. A useful invention is adopted; a useless one is discarded. The cumulative impact of many small, useful devices and techniques may be as great as the impact of one occasional dramatic mechanism such as the steam engine, the cotton gin, or the sewing machine. Indeed, few famous inventions have sprung from a single act of creative inspiration; usually each builds on the contributions of prior inventors. The backlog of past inventions constitutes society's technical knowledge, and that backlog in turn feeds innovation.

Kinds of Technological Change

Consider three kinds of change that influence production and cost in the very long run.

New techniques. Throughout the nineteenth and twentieth centuries, changes in the techniques available for producing existing products have been dramatic; this is called *process innovation*. About the same amount of coal is produced in North America today as was produced 50 years ago, but the number of coal miners is less than one tenth what it was then. Eighty years ago, roads and railways were built by gangs of workers who used buckets, spades, and draft horses. Today bulldozers, giant trucks, and other specialized equipment have banished the workhorse completely from construction sites and to a great extent have displaced the pick-and-shovel worker.

An important new production technique called *lean production* (also often called *flexible manufacturing*) is rapidly replacing the long-established *mass-production, assembly-line* techniques in many industries. Lean production, which was pioneered by the Japanese automobile industry and is spreading throughout Western industrialised countries, is a more flexible, lower-cost method of production that produces higher-quality products and reduces the cost of developing new products. Lean production typically has a lower long-run cost curve than conventional mass production and a more rapidly downward-shifting cost curve in the very long run. Lean production is discussed further in Box 11-3.

New products. New goods and services are constantly being invented and marketed; this is called *product innovation*. Color television, polio vaccine, personal computers, and many other current consumer products did not exist a mere generation or

two ago. Other products have changed so dramatically that the only connection they have with the "same" commodity that was produced in the past is the name. A 1993 Ford is very different from a 1923 Ford, and it is even different from a 1963 Ford in size, safety, and gasoline consumption. Modern jets are revolutionary compared with the DC-3—the workhorse of the airlines during the 1930s and 1940s. The DC-3 itself bore little resemblance—beyond having wings and an engine—to the Wright brothers' original flying machine.

Improved inputs. Improvements in such intangibles as health and education raise the quality of labour services. Today's workers and managers are healthier and better educated than their grandparents. Many of today's unskilled workers are literate and competent in arithmetic, and their managers are apt to be trained in modern scientific methods of business management and computer science.

Similarly, improvements in material inputs occur. For example, the type and quality of metals have changed. Steel has replaced iron, and aluminum substitutes for steel in a process of change that makes a statistical category such as "primary metals" seem unsatisfactory. Even for a given category, say, steel, today's product is lighter, stronger, and more flexible than the "same" product manufactured only 20 years ago.

The Choices Firms Face

When firms receive signals that the economic environment they face, and can expect to face in the future, is changing, they can respond in a number of ways.

Suppose that the price of a key input rises and that this increase is expected to persist into the future. One option for the firm is to make what we have called a long-run response by substituting away from the use of the input by changing its production techniques within the confines of existing technology. Another option is to invest in research in order to develop new production techniques that innovate away from the input. Often, both responses are adopted, but because both involve the use of costly resources, the responses are often substitutes in the sense that a particular firm may have to choose to emphasize one or the other.

It is important to recognise that the two options can involve quite different actions and can ultimately have quite different implications for productivity. For example, consider three possible responses to a trend increase in labour costs.

- One firm might reallocate a lot of its production activities to Mexico or Southeast Asia, where labour costs are relatively low and hence labour-intensive production techniques remain quite profitable.

- A second might elect to replace existing equipment with alternative machines that are more expensive than the ones now in use but that use less labour and hence become more attractive in the face of increased labour costs.

- A third might elect to devote resources to developing new production techniques that use much less labour than existing techniques—in effect this response innovates the increased labour costs away.

All three are possible reactions to the changed circumstances. All three are observed to occur. The first two are largely predictable in advance and will lead to improved efficiency relative to continued reliance on the original production methods. The third response, depending upon the often unpredictable results of the innovation, may reduce costs sufficiently to warrant the investment in research and development, and it may even lead to substantially more effective production techniques that allow the firm to maintain an advantage over its competitors for a number of years.

In predicting any industry's response to changes in its operating environment, it is important to consider the effects of endogenous innovations in technology as well as substitution based on changes in the use of existing technologies.

SUMMARY

1. There are no fixed factors in the long run. Profit-maximizing firms choose from the alternatives open to them the least-cost method of achieving any specific output. A long-run cost curve represents the boundary between attainable and unattainable levels of cost for the given technology.

2. The principle of substitution says that efficient production will use cheaper factors lavishly and more expensive ones economically. If the relative prices of factors change, relatively more of cheaper factors and relatively less of more expensive ones will be used.

3. The shape of the long-run cost curve depends on the relationship of inputs to outputs as the whole scale of a firm's operations changes. Increasing, constant, and decreasing returns lead, respectively, to decreasing, constant, and increasing long-run average costs.

4. The long-run and short-run cost curves are related. Every long-run cost corresponds to *some* quantity of each factor and is thus on some short-run cost curve. The short-run cost curve shows how costs vary when that particular quantity of a fixed factor is used to produce outputs greater than or less than the output for which it is optimal.

5. Cost curves shift upward or downward in response to changes in the prices of factors or changed technology. Increases in factor prices shift cost curves upward. Decreases in factor prices and technological advances shift cost curves downward.

6. Over the very long run, the most important influence on costs of production and on standards of living has been the increases in output made possible by technological change. This refers to all

changes in available techniques of production that lead to an increase in measured productivity.

7. Changes in technology are often *endogenous responses* to changing economic signals; that is, they result from responses by firms to the same things that induce the substitution of one factor for another in a given technology.

8. Innovation is the key to productivity growth. It requires invention but also profitable opportunities for the introduction of available knowledge. The state of the economy, the institutional climate, and differences in technological possibilities in sectors where demand is growing and declining all affect the opportunities for innovation. Innovation can lead to technological change due to the introduction of new techniques, new products, and improved inputs.

9. In trying to understand any industry's response to changes in its operating environment, it is important to consider the effects of endogenous innovations in technology as well as substitution based on changes in the use of existing technologies.

TOPICS FOR REVIEW

Implication of cost minimization

Interpretation of $MP_K/MP_L = p_K/p_L$ and $MP_K/p_K = MP_L/p_L$

The principle of substitution

Increasing, decreasing, and constant returns

Economies of scale

Envelope curve

Technological change and productivity growth

Invention and innovation

Determinants of innovation

DISCUSSION QUESTIONS

1. Faced with high relative labour costs, . . . American consumer electronics firms moved to locate labour-intensive activities in . . . Asian countries, leaving the product and production process essentially the same. . . . Japanese rivals . . . set out instead to eliminate labour through automation. Doing so involved reducing the number of components *which further lowered cost and improved quality.* Japanese firms were soon building assembly plants in the United States, the place American firms had sought to avoid.

   —M. Porter, *The Competitive Advantage of Nations,* p. 85.

   Discuss these reactions in terms of long-run and very-long-run changes.

2. Discuss the following quotation in terms of the incentives that lead to the establishment of a major field of pure research.

   > Solid-state physics...attracted only a few physicists before the advent of the transistor. In fact, the subject was not even taught at most universities. This situation was transformed...by the invention of the

transistor in 1948. The transistor demonstrated the potentially high payoff of solid-state research and led to a huge concentration of [pure research]resources in that field. Shockley [the inventor of the transistor] even ran a six-day course at Bell Labs in June 1952 for professors from some thirty universities as part of an attempt to encourage the establishment of courses in transistor physics. Clearly, the main flow of scientific knowledge during this period was from industry to the university.

—N. Rosenberg, *Inside the Black Box,* p. 155

3. Why does the profit-maximizing firm choose the least-cost method of producing any given output? Might a non-profit-maximizing organization such as a university, church, or government intentionally choose a method of production other than the least-cost one?

4. The chairman of a multinational oil company recently said, "Our government has adopted a gratuitously hostile attitude. Industry has been compelled to spend more and more of its research dollars to comply with environmental, health, and safety regulations—and to move away from longer-term efforts aimed at major scientific advance." If this is true, is it necessarily a sign that government policies are misguided?

5. Use the principle of substitution to predict the effect of each of the following.

    a. During the 1960s, salaries of professors rose much more rapidly than those of teaching assistants. During the 1970s, salaries of teaching assistants rose more than those of professors. During the 1980s, the relative salaries of these two groups did not change greatly.

    b. The cost of land in big cities increases more than the cost of high-rise construction.

    c. Gold leaf is produced by pounding gold with a hammer. The thinner it is, the more valuable it is. The price of gold is set on the world market, but the price of labour varies among countries.

    d. Wages of textile workers rise more in Canada than in the Southern United States.

6. Israel, a small country, imports the "insides" of its automobiles, but it manufactures the bodies. If this makes economic sense, what does it tell us about cost conditions of automobile manufacturers?

7. Name five important modern products that were not available when your parents were your age.

8. Each of the following is a means of increasing productivity. Discuss which groups within a society might oppose each one.

    a. A labour-saving invention that permits all goods to be manufactured with less labour than before.

    b. Rapidly increasing growth of population in the economy.

    c. Removal of all government production safety rules.

    d. Reduction in corporate income taxes.

    e. Reduction in production of services and increase in agricultural production.

APPENDIX TO CHAPTER

11

Isoquants: An Alternative Analysis of the Firm's Input Decisions

The production function gives the relationship between the factor inputs that the firm uses and the output that it obtains. In the long run, the firm can choose among many different combinations of inputs that will yield the same output. The production function and the long-run choices open to the firm can be represented graphically using what are called *isoquants*.

A Single Isoquant

Table 11A-1 illustrates a hypothetical example in which several combinations of two inputs (labour and capital) can produce a given quantity of output. The data from Table 11A-1 are plotted graphically in Figure 11A-1. A smooth curve is drawn through the points to indicate that there are additional ways, which are not listed in the table, of producing 6 units.

This curve is called an **isoquant.** It shows the whole set of technologically efficient factor combinations for producing a given level of output—6 units in this case. This is an example of graphing a relationship among three variables in two dimensions. It is analogous to the contour line on a map, which shows all points of equal altitude, and to an indifference curve (discussed in Chapter 7A), which shows all combinations of commodities that yield an equal utility.

As we move from one point on an isoquant to another, we are *substituting one factor for another* while holding output constant. If we move from point *b* to point *c*, we are substituting 1 unit of labour for 3 units of capital. The marginal rate of substitution measures the rate at which one factor is substituted

TABLE 11A-1 Alternative Methods of Producing 6 Units of Output: Points on an Isoquant

Method	K	L	ΔK	ΔL	Rate of substitution $\Delta K / \Delta L$
a	18	2	−6	1	−6.00
b	12	3	−3	1	−3.00
c	9	4	−3	2	−1.50
d	6	6	−2	3	−0.67
e	4	9	−1	3	−0.33
f	3	12	−1	6	−0.17
g	2	18			

An isoquant describes the firm's alternative methods for producing a given output. The table lists some of the methods indicated by a production function as being available to produce 6 units of output. The first combination uses a great deal of capital (K) and very little labour (L). As we move down the table, labour is substituted for capital in such a way as to keep output constant. Finally, at the bottom, most of the capital has been replaced by labour. The rate of substitution between the two factors is calculated in the last three columns of the table. Note that as we move down the table, the absolute value of the rate of substitution declines.

for another with output being held constant. Graphically, the marginal rate of substitution is measured by the slope of the isoquant at a particular point.[1] Table 11A-1 shows the calculation of some

---

[1]Sometimes the term *marginal rate of technical substitution* is used to distinguish this concept from the analogous one that arises in consumer theory; see Chapter 7A. Henceforth we adopt the standard convention of defining the marginal rate of substitution as the negative of the slope of the isoquant, so that it is a positive number.

FIGURE 11A-1
An Isoquant for Output of 6 Units

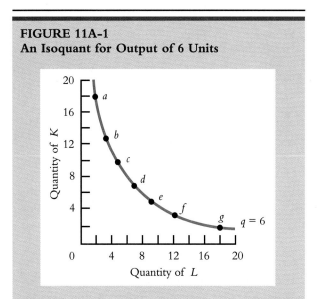

Isoquants are negatively sloped and convex. The negative slope reflects the requirement of technical efficiency. A method that uses more of one factor must use less of the other factor if it is to be technically efficient. The convex shape of the isoquant reflects a diminishing marginal rate of substitution. The lettered points on the graph are plotted from the data in Table 11A-1. Starting from point *a*, which uses relatively little labour and much capital, and moving to point *b*, 1 additional unit of labour can substitute for 6 units of capital (while holding production constant). However, from *b* to *c*, 1 unit of labour substitutes for only 3 units of capital. This diminishing rate is expressed geometrically by the flattening of the slope of the isoquant.

The **marginal rate of substitution between two factors of production is equal to the ratio of their marginal products.**

Isoquants satisfy two important conditions: They are negatively sloped, and they are convex, viewed from the origin. What is the economic meaning of these conditions?

The negative slope indicates that each factor input has a positive marginal product. If the input of one factor is reduced and that of the other is held constant, output will be reduced. Thus, if one input is decreased, production can be held constant only if the other factor input is increased. The marginal rate of substitution has a negative value. Decreases in one factor must be balanced by increases in the other factor if output is to be held constant.

To understand convexity, consider what happens as the firm moves along the isoquant of Figure 11A-1 downward and to the right. Labour is being added and capital reduced to keep output constant. If labour is added in increments of exactly 1 unit, how much capital may be dispensed with each time? The key to the answer is that both factors are assumed to be subject to the law of diminishing returns. Thus, the gain in output associated with each additional unit of labour added is *diminishing,* whereas the loss of output associated with each additional unit of capital forgone is *increasing.* It therefore takes ever-smaller reductions in capital to compensate for equal increases in labour. This implies that the isoquant is convex viewed from the origin.

An Isoquant Map

The isoquant of Figure 11A-1 is for 6 units of output. There is another isoquant for 7 units, another for 7,000 units, and a different one for every other rate of output. Each isoquant refers to a specific output and connects combinations of factors that are technologically efficient methods of achieving that output. If we plot a representative set of these isoquants from the same production function on a single graph, we get an **isoquant map** like that in Figure 11A-2. The higher the level of output along a particular isoquant, the farther the isoquant is from the origin.

rates of substitution between various points of the isoquant. **[21]**

The marginal rate of substitution is related to the marginal products of the factors of production. To see how, consider an example. Assume that at the present level of inputs of labour and capital, the marginal product of labour is 2 units of output, while the marginal product of capital is 1 unit of output. If the firm reduces its use of capital and increases its use of labour to keep output constant, it needs to add only 1\2 unit of labour for 1 unit of capital given up. If, at another point on the isoquant with more labour and less capital, the marginal products are 2 for capital and 1 for labour, then the firm will have to add 2 units of labour for every unit of capital it gives up. The general proposition is this:

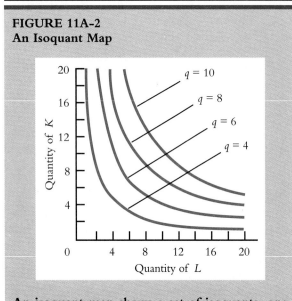

FIGURE 11A-2
An Isoquant Map

An isoquant map shows a set of isoquants, one for each level of output. The figure shows four isoquants drawn from the production function and corresponding to 4, 6, 8, and 10 units of production.

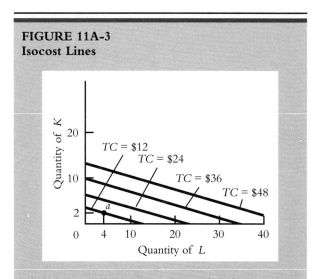

FIGURE 11A-3
Isocost Lines

Each isocost line shows alternative factor combinations that can be purchased for a given outlay. The graph shows the four isocost lines that result when labour costs $1 per unit and capital $4 per unit, and when expenditure is held constant at $12, $24, $36, and $48, respectively. The line labeled $TC = 12 represents all combinations of the two factors that the firm could buy for $12. Point *a* represents 2 units of K and 4 units of L.

Conditions for Cost Minimization

Finding the efficient way of producing any output requires finding the least-cost factor combination. To do this requires that when both factors are variable, factor prices be known. Suppose, to continue the example, that capital is priced at $4 per unit and labour at $1 per unit. In Chapter 7, a budget line was used to show the alternative combinations of goods that a household could buy; here an *isocost line* is used to show alternative combinations of factors that a firm can buy for a given outlay. Four different isocost lines appear in Figure 11A-3. The slope of each reflects *relative* factor prices, just as the slope of the budget line in Chapter 7 represented relative product prices. For given factor prices, a series of parallel isocost lines will reflect the alternative levels of expenditure on factor purchases that are open to the firm. The higher the level of expenditure, the farther the isocost line is from the origin.

In Figure 11A-4, the isoquant and isocost maps are brought together. The economically most efficient method of production must be a point on an isoquant that just touches (i.e., is tangent to) an isocost line. If the isoquant cuts the isocost line, it is possible to move along the isoquant and reach a lower level of cost. Only at a point of tangency is a movement in either direction along the isoquant a movement to a higher cost level. The lowest attainable cost of producing 6 units is $24. This cost level can be achieved only by operating at A, the point where the $24 isocost line is tangent to the 6-unit isoquant. The lowest average cost of producing 6 units is thus $24/6 = $4 per unit of output.

The least-cost position is given graphically by the tangency point between the isoquant and the isocost lines.

Notice that point A in Figure 11A-4 indicates not only the lowest level of cost for 6 units of output but also the highest level of output for $24 of cost. Thus we find the same solution if we set out *either* to minimize the cost of producing 6 units of output *or* to maximize the output that can be obtained for

FIGURE 11A-4
The Determination of the Least-Cost Method of Output

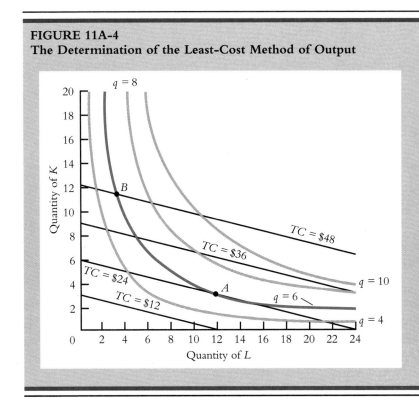

Least-cost methods are represented by points of tangency between isoquant and isocost lines. The isoquant map of Figure 11A-2 and the isocost lines of Figure 11A-3 are brought together. Consider point A. It is on the 6-unit isoquant and the $24 isocost line. Thus it is possible to achieve the output q = 6 for a total cost of $24. There are other ways to achieve this output, for example, at point B, where TC = $48. Moving along the isoquant from point A in either direction increases cost. Similarly, moving along the isocost line from point A in either direction lowers output. Thus either move would raise cost per unit.

$24. One problem is said to be the *dual* of the other.

The slope of the isocost line is given by the ratio of the prices of the two factors of production. The slope of the isoquant is given by the ratio of their marginal products. When the firm reaches its least-cost position, it has equated the price ratio (which is given to it by the market prices) with the ratio of the marginal products (which it can adjust by varying the proportions in which it hires the factors). In symbols,

$$\frac{MP_K}{MPL} = \frac{p_K}{pL}$$

This is equivalent to Equation 2 on page 198. We have now derived this result by use of the isoquant analysis of the firm's decisions. [22]

The Principle of Substitution

Suppose that with technology unchanged, that is, with the isoquant map being held fixed, the price of one factor changes. Suppose that with the price of capital unchanged at $4 per unit, the price of labour rises from $1 to $4 per unit. Originally, the efficient factor combination for producing 6 units was 12 units of labour and 3 units of capital. It cost $24. To produce that same output in the same way would now cost $60 at the new factor prices. Figure 11A-5 shows why this is not efficient. The slope of the isocost line has changed, which makes it efficient to substitute the now relatively cheaper capital for the relatively more expensive labour.

This illustrates the principle of substitution.

Changes in relative factor prices will cause a partial replacement of factors that have become relatively more expensive by factors that have become relatively cheaper.

Of course, substitution of capital for labour cannot fully offset the effects of a rise in cost of labour, as Figure 11A-5(i) shows. Consider the output attainable for $24. In the figure, there are two isocost lines representing $24 of outlay—at the old and new prices of labour. The new isocost line for $24 lies inside the old one (except where no labour is used).

FIGURE 11A-5
The Effects of a Change in Factor Prices on Costs and Factor Proportions

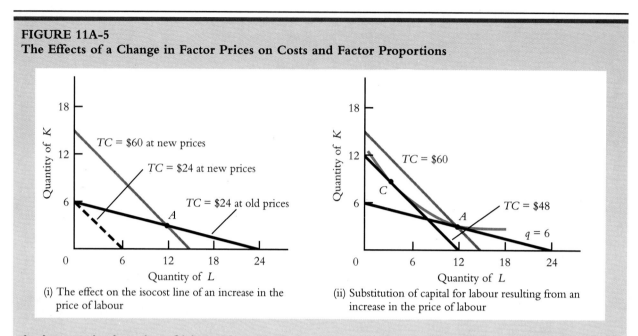

(i) The effect on the isocost line of an increase in the price of labour

(ii) Substitution of capital for labour resulting from an increase in the price of labour

An increase in the price of labour pivots the isocost line inward and thus increases the cost of producing any output. It also changes the slope of the isocost line and thus changes the least-cost method of producing. In part (i) the rise in the price of L from $1 to $4 per unit (with the price of K being held constant at $4) pivots the $24 isocost line inward to the dashed line. Any output previously produced for $24 will cost more at the new prices if it uses any labour. The new cost of producing at A rises from $24 to $60. In part (ii) the steeper isocost line is tangent to the isoquant at C, not A, so that more capital and less labour is used. Costs at C are $48, which is higher than they were before the price increase, but not as high as they would be if no factor substitution had occurred.

The isocost line must therefore be tangent to a lower isoquant. This means that if production is to be held constant, higher costs must be accepted. However, because of substitution, it is not necessary to accept costs as high as those that would accompany an unchanged factor proportion. In the example, 6 units can be produced for $48 rather than the $60 that would be required if no change in factor proportions were made.

This leads to the following predictions:

A rise in the price of one factor with all other factor prices being held constant will (1) shift upward the cost curves of commodities that use that factor and (2) lead to a substitution of factors that are now relatively cheaper for the factor whose price has risen.

Both of these predictions were stated in Chapter 11; now they have been derived formally by using isoquants.

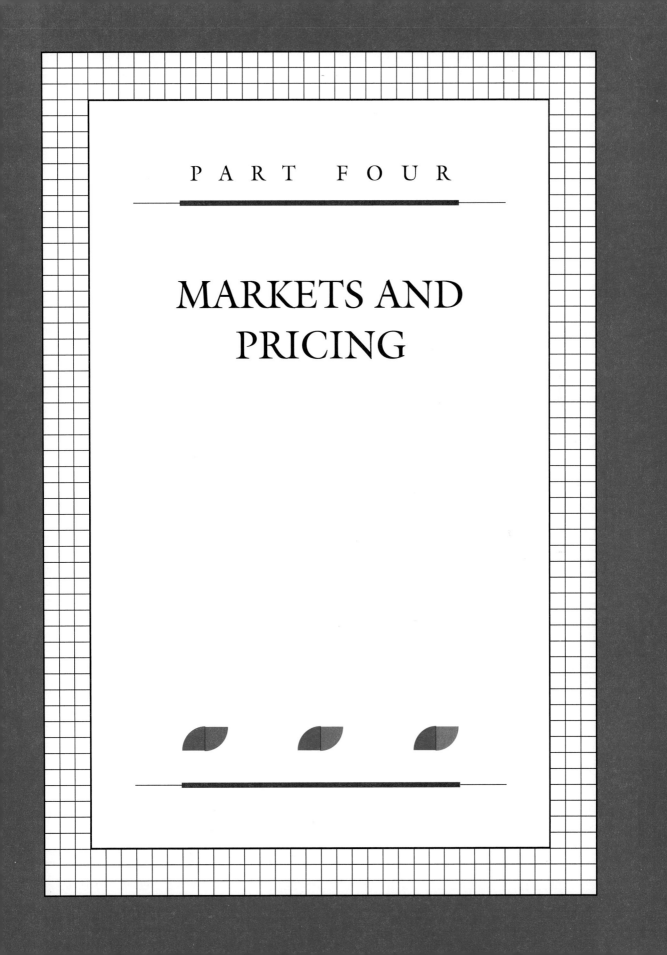

PART FOUR

MARKETS AND PRICING

12

Competitive Markets

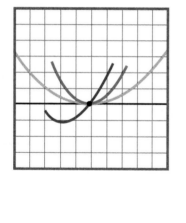

Does PetroCan compete with Imperial Oil in the sale of gasoline? Does Visa compete with American Express? Does a wheat farmer from Biggar, Saskatchewan, compete with a wheat farmer from Brandon, Manitoba? If we use the ordinary meaning of the word *compete,* the answer to the first two questions is plainly yes, and the answer to the third is probably no.

PetroCan and Imperial Oil both advertise extensively to persuade car drivers to buy *their* products. Everything from new mileage-stretching additives to free dishes is used to tempt drivers to buy one brand of gasoline rather than another. A host of world travelers in various tight spots attest on television to the virtues of Visa, while discreet ads in many magazines tell us that the American Express card is *the* prestigious credit card to carry.

When we shift our attention to firms producing wheat, however, we see that there is nothing that the Saskatchewan farm family can do to affect either the sales or the profits of the Manitoba farm family. There would be no point in doing so even if they could, since the sales and profits of the Manitoba farm have no effect on those of the Saskatchewan farm.

To sort out the questions of who is competing with whom and in what sense, it is useful to distinguish between the behaviour of individual firms and the *type of market* in which they operate. In everyday use, the word *competition* usually refers to competitive behaviour. Economists, however, are interested both in the competitive behaviour of individual firms and in a quite distinct concept, competitive market structure.

Market Structure and Behaviour

The term **market structure** refers to all the features that may affect the behaviour and performance of the firms in a market (for example, the number of firms in the market, or the type of product that they sell).

Competitive Market Structure. The competitiveness of the market refers to the extent to which individual firms have power to influence market prices or the other terms on which their product is sold. *The less power an individual firm has to influence the market in which it sells its product, the more competitive that market is.*

The extreme form of competitiveness occurs when each firm has zero market power. In such a case, there are so many firms in the market that each must accept the price set by the forces of market demand and market supply. The firms perceive themselves as being able to sell as much as they choose at the prevailing market price and as having no power to influence that price. If the firm charged a higher price, it would obtain no sales; so many other firms would be selling at the market price that buyers would take their business elsewhere.

This extreme is called a *perfectly competitive market structure.* (Usually the term "structure" is dropped and economists speak of a *perfectly competitive market.*) In it, there is no need for individual firms to compete actively with one another, since none has any power over the market. One firm's ability to sell its product does not depend on the behaviour of any other firm. For example, the Saskatchewan and Manitoba wheat farmers operate in a perfectly competitive market over which they have no power. Neither can change the market price for its wheat by altering its own behaviour.

Competitive behaviour. In everyday language, the term *competitive behaviour* refers to the degree to which individual firms actively compete with one another. For example, PetroCan and Imperial Oil certainly engage in competitive behaviour. It is also true, however, that both companies have some real power over their market. Either firm could raise its prices and still continue to attract customers. Each has the power to decide, within limits set by buyers' tastes and the prices of competing products, the price that people will pay for their gasoline and oil. So even though they actively compete with each other, they do so in a market that does not have a perfectly competitive structure.

In contrast, the Saskatchewan and Manitoba wheat farmers do not engage in *competitive behaviour,* because the only way they can affect their profits is by changing their outputs of (or their costs of producing) wheat.

Behaviour versus structure. The distinction that we have just made explains why firms in perfectly competitive markets (e.g., the Saskatchewan and the Manitoba wheat producers) do not compete actively with each other, whereas firms that do compete actively with each other (e.g., PetroCan and Imperial Oil) do not operate in *perfectly* competitive markets.

The Significance of Market Structure

PetroCan and Imperial Oil are two of several large firms in the oil *industry.* They produce petroleum products and sell them in various *markets.* The terms *industry* and *market* are familiar from everyday use. However, economists give them precise definitions that we need to understand.

We noted earlier that a *market* consists of an area over which buyers and sellers can negotiate the exchange of some commodity. The firms that produce a well-defined product or a closely related set of products constitute an **industry.** In earlier chapters, we developed and used market demand curves; here we note that the market demand curve for any particular product is the demand curve facing the *industry* that produces the product.

When the managers of a firm make their production and sales decisions, they need to know what quantity of a product their firm can sell at various prices. Their concern is, therefore, not with the *market* demand curve for their industry's product, but rather with the demand curve for their firm's own output of that product. If they know the demand curve that their own firm faces, they know the sales that their firm can make at each price it might charge, and thus they know its potential revenues. If they also know their firm's costs for producing the product, they can calculate the profits that would be associated with each rate of output. They can with this information choose the output that maximizes profits.

Recall that economists define market structure as the characteristics that affect the behaviour and performance of firms that sell in that market. These characteristics determine, among other things, the relationship between the market demand curve for the industry's product and the demand curve facing each firm in that industry.

To reduce the analysis of market structure to manageable proportions, economists focus on four theoretical market structures that cover most actual cases. These are called *perfect competition, monopoly, monopolistic competition,* and *oligopoly.* Perfect competition will be dealt with in the rest of this chapter;

the others will be dealt with in the chapters that follow.

Elements of the Theory of Perfect Competition

The perfectly competitive market structure—usually referred to simply as *perfect competition*—applies directly to a number of real-world markets. It also provides an important benchmark for comparison with other market structures.

Assumptions of Perfect Competition

The theory of **perfect competition** is built on a number of key assumptions relating to the firm and to the industry.

Assumption 1: All the firms in the industry sell an identical product. Economists describe this by saying that the firms sell a **homogeneous product.**

Assumption 2: Customers know the nature of the product being sold and the prices charged by each firm.

Assumption 3: The level of a firm's output at which its long-run average total cost reaches a minimum is small relative to the industry's total output (when price is such that firms are covering all costs).

Assumption 4: The *firm* is a **price taker.** This means that the firm can alter its rate of production and sales without significantly affecting the market price of its product. This is why a firm operating in a perfectly competitive market has no power to influence that market through its own individual actions. It must passively accept whatever happens to be the ruling price, but it can sell as much as it wants at that price.[1]

Assumption 5: The *industry* is assumed to be characterized by *freedom of entry and exit;* that is, any new firm is free to enter the industry and start producing if it so wishes, and any existing firm is free to cease production and leave the industry. Existing firms cannot bar the entry of new firms, and there are no legal prohibitions or other artificial barriers to entering or exiting the industry.

An illustration. The Saskatchewan and the Manitoba wheat farmers whom we considered earlier provide us with good illustrations of firms that are operating in a perfectly competitive market.

Because each individual wheat farmer is just one of a very large number of producers who are all growing the same product, one firm's contribution to the industry's total production is only a tiny drop in an extremely large bucket. Each firm will correctly assume that variations in its output have no significant effect on the world price of wheat. Thus, each firm, knowing that it can sell as much or as little as it chooses at that price, adapts its behaviour to a given market price of wheat. Furthermore, anyone who has enough money to buy or rent the necessary land, labour, and equipment can become a wheat farmer.

There is nothing that existing farmers can do to stop another farmer from growing wheat, and there are no legal deterrents to becoming a wheat farmer.

The difference between the wheat farmers and PetroCan is in *degree of market power.* Each firm that is producing wheat is an insignificant part of the whole market and thus has no power to influence the price of wheat. The oil company does have power to influence the price of gasoline, because its own sales represent a significant part of the total sales of gasoline.

Box 12-1 explores further the reasons why each firm that is producing wheat finds the world price of wheat to be beyond its influence.

Demand and Revenue for a Firm in Perfect Competition

A major distinction between firms operating in perfectly competitive markets and firms operating in

---

[1]To emphasize its importance, we identify price taking as a separate assumption, although, strictly speaking, it is implied by the first three assumptions.

FIGURE 12-1
The Demand Curve for a Competitive Industry and for One Firm in the Industry

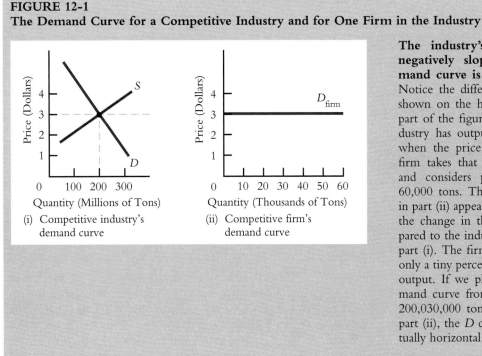

(i) Competitive industry's demand curve

(ii) Competitive firm's demand curve

The industry's demand curve is negatively sloped; the firm's demand curve is virtually horizontal. Notice the difference in the quantities shown on the horizontal scale in each part of the figure. The competitive industry has output of 200 million tons when the price is $3. The individual firm takes that market price as given and considers producing up to, say, 60,000 tons. The firm's demand curve in part (ii) appears horizontal because of the change in the quantity scale compared to the industry's demand curve in part (i). The firm's output variation has only a tiny percentage effect on industry output. If we plotted the industry demand curve from 199,970,000 tons to 200,030,000 tons on the scale used in part (ii), the D curve would appear virtually horizontal.

any other type of market is in the shape of the firm's own demand curve.

The demand curve facing each firm in perfect competition is horizontal, because variations in the firm's output over the range that it needs to consider have no noticeable effect on price.

The horizontal (perfectly elastic) demand curve does not mean that the firm could actually sell an infinite amount at the going price. It means, rather, that the variations in production *that it will normally be possible for the firm to make* will leave price virtually unchanged, because their effect on total industry output will be negligible.

Figure 12-1 contrasts the demand curve for the product of a competitive industry with the demand curve facing a single firm in that industry.

Total, average, and marginal revenue. To study the revenues that firms receive from the sales of their products, economists define three concepts called total, average, and marginal revenue. These are the revenue counterparts of the concepts of total, average, and marginal cost that we considered in Chapter 10.

Total revenue (TR) *is the total amount received by the seller from the sale of a product.* If q units are sold at p dollars each,[2] $TR = p \cdot q$.

Average revenue (AR) *is the amount of revenue per unit sold.* This is equal to the price at which the product is sold.

Marginal revenue (MR), *sometimes called incremental revenue,* is the change in a firm's total revenue resulting from a change in its rate of sales by one unit. Whenever output changes by more than one unit, the change in revenue must be divided by the change in output to calculate marginal revenue. For example, if an increase in output of 3 units per month is accompanied by an increase in revenue of

---

[2]Four common ways of indicating that any two variables such as p and q are to be multiplied are $p \cdot q$, $p \times q$, $(p)(q)$, and pq.

Box 12-1

Demand Under Perfect Competition: Firm and Industry

Because all products have negatively sloped market demand curves, *any* increase in the industry's output will cause *some* fall in the market price. However, any conceivable increase that one wheat farm could make in its output has such a negligible effect on the industry's price that the farmer correctly ignores it. (For our purposes, the farm is a firm producing wheat.)

The calculations given below arrive at the elasticity of demand facing one wheat farmer in two steps. Step 1 shows that a 200 percent variation in the farm's output leads to only a very small percentage variation in the world price. Thus, as step 2 shows, the elasticity of demand for the farm's product is very high: 71,428!

Although the arithmetic used in reaching these measures is unimportant, understanding why the wheat farmer is a price taker in these circumstances is vital.

Here is the argument that the calculations summarize. The market elasticity of demand for wheat is approximately 0.25. This means that if the quantity of wheat supplied in the world increased by 1 percent, the price would have to fall by 4 percent to induce the world's wheat buyers to purchase the extra wheat.

Even huge farms produce a very small fraction of the total world crop. In a recent year, one large farm produced 1,750 metric tons of wheat. This was only 0.0035 percent of the world production of 500 million metric tons. Suppose that the farmer decided in one year to produce nothing and in another year managed to produce twice the farms' normal output of 1,750 metric tons. This is an extremely large variation in one farm's output.

The increase in output from zero to 3,500 metric tons represents a 200 percent variation measured around the farm's average output of 1,750 metric tons. Yet the percentage increase in world output is only (3,500/500 million)100 = 0.0007 percent. The table shows that this increase would lead to a decrease in the world price of 0.0028 percent (2.8 cents in $1,000) and give the farm's own demand curve an elasticity of over 71,000! This is an enor-

$1,500, the marginal revenue resulting from the sale of *one extra unit* per month is $1,500/3, or $500. At any existing level of sales, marginal revenue shows what revenue the firm would gain by selling one unit more and what revenue it would lose by selling one unit less. [23]

To illustrate each of these revenue concepts, consider a firm that is selling an agricultural commodity in a perfectly competitive market at a price of $3 per ton. Total revenue rises by $3 for every ton sold. Because every ton brings in $3, the average revenue per ton sold is clearly $3. Furthermore, because each *additional* ton sold brings in $3, the marginal revenue of an extra ton sold is also $3. Table 12-1 shows calculations of these revenue con-

cepts for a range of outputs between 10 and 13 tons.

The important point illustrated in Table 12-1 is that as long as the firm's output does not significantly affect the price of the product it sells, marginal revenue is, for all intents and purposes, equal to average revenue (which is *always* equal to price). Graphically, as shown in part (i) of Figure 12-2, average revenue and marginal revenue are the same horizontal line drawn at the level of market price. Because the firm can sell any quantity it chooses at this price, the horizontal line is also the *firm's demand curve;* it shows that any quantity the firm chooses to sell will be associated with this same market price.

mous elasticity of demand. The farm would have to increase its output by over 71,000 percent to bring about a 1 percent decrease in the price of wheat! Because the farm's output cannot be varied this much, it is not surprising that the farmer regards the price of wheat as unaffected by any change in output that this one farm could conceivably make. For all intents and purposes, the wheat-producing firm faces a perfectly elastic demand curve for its product; *it is a price taker.*

Calculation of the Firm's Elasticity of Demand (η_F) from Market Elasticity of Demand (η_M)

Given:

World elasticity of demand (η_F) = 0.25
World output = 500,000,000 metric tons

A large farm with an average output of 1,750 metric tons varies its output between 0 and 3,500 tons. The variation of 3,500 tons represents 200 percent of the farm's average output of 1,750 metric tons. This causes world output to vary by only $(3,500/500,000,000)100 = 0.0007$ percent.

Step 1: Find the percentage change in world price. We know that the market elasticity is 0.25. This means that the percentage change in quantity must be one quarter as big as the percentage change in price. Put the other way round, the percentage change in price must be four times as big as the percentage change in quantity. We have just seen that world quantity changes by 0.0007 percent, so world price must change by $(0.0007)(4) = 0.0028$ percent.

Step 2: Find the firm's elasticity of demand. This is the percentage change in its *own output* divided by the resulting percentage change in the world price. This is 200 percent divided by 0.0028 percent. Clearly the percentage change in quantity vastly exceeds the percentage change in price, making elasticity very high. Its precise value is 200/0.0028, or 2,000,000/28, which is 71,429.

If the market price is unaffected by variations in the firm's output, then the firm's demand curve, its average revenue curve, and its marginal revenue curve all coincide in the same horizontal line.

This result can be stated in a slightly different way that turns out to be important for our later study:

For a firm in perfect competition, price equals marginal revenue.

This means, of course, that total revenue rises in direct proportion to output, as shown in part (ii) of Figure 12-2.

Short-Run Equilibrium

We learned in Chapter 11 how each firm's costs vary with its output. In the short-run, the firm has one or more fixed factors, and the only way in which it can change its output is by using more or less of the factor inputs that it can vary. Thus the firm's short-run cost curves are relevant to its decision regarding output.

We have just learned how the revenues of each price-taking firm vary with its output. The next step is to combine information about the firm's

TABLE 12-1 Revenue Concepts for a Price-Taking Firm

Price p	Quantity q	$TR =$ $p \cdot q$	$AR =$ TR/q	$MR =$ $\Delta TR/\Delta q$
$3	10	$30	$3	
3	11	33	3	$3
3	12	36	3	3
3	13	39	3	3

When the firm is a price taker, $AR = MR = p$. Marginal revenue is shown between the lines because it represents the change in total revenue (e.g., from $33 to $36) in response to a change in quantity (from 11 to 12 units): $MR = (36 - 33)/(12 - 11) = \$3$ per unit.

costs and revenues to determine the level of output that will maximize its profits. We start by stating two rules that apply to *all* profit-maximizing firms, whether or not they operate in perfectly competitive markets. The first determines whether or not the firm should produce at all, and the second determines how much it should produce.

Rules for All Profit-Maximizing Firms

Should the Firm Produce at All?

The firm always has the option of producing nothing. If it exercises this option, it will have an operating loss that is equal to its fixed costs. If it decides to produce, it will add the variable cost of production to its costs and the receipts from the sale of its product to its revenue. Therefore, it will be worthwhile for the firm to produce as long as it can find some level of output for which revenue exceeds variable cost. However, if its revenue is less than its variable cost at *every* level of output, the firm will actually lose more by producing than by not producing.

Rule 1: **A firm should not produce at all if for *all* levels of output the total variable cost of producing that output exceeds the total revenue derived from selling it or, equivalently, if the average variable cost of producing the output exceeds the price at which it can be sold. [24]**

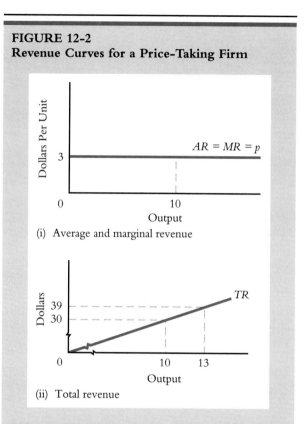

FIGURE 12-2
Revenue Curves for a Price-Taking Firm

(i) Average and marginal revenue

(ii) Total revenue

This is a graphical representation of the revenue concepts in Table 12-1. Because price does not change, neither marginal revenue nor average revenue varies with output. When price is constant, total revenue (which is price times quantity) is an upward-sloping straight line starting from the origin.

The shut-down price. The **shut-down price** is the price at which the firm can just cover its average variable cost. This price leaves it indifferent between producing and not producing. At any lower price, the firm will shut down. For example, in part (i) of Figure 12-5 on page 227, the shut-down price is $2. The firm can just cover its average variable cost by producing q_0 units, while any other output would not produce enough revenue to cover variable costs. For any price below $2, there is no output at which variable costs can be covered.

How Much Should the Firm Produce?

If a firm decides that (according to Rule 1) production is worth undertaking, it must decide how much to produce. Common sense dictates that on a unit-by-unit basis, if any unit of production adds more to revenue than it does to cost, producing and selling that unit will increase profits. However, if any unit adds more to cost than it does to revenue, producing and selling that unit will decrease profits. Using the terminology introduced earlier, a unit of production raises profits if the marginal revenue obtained from selling it exceeds the marginal cost of producing it; it lowers profits if the marginal revenue obtained from selling it is less than the marginal cost of producing it.

Now let a firm with some existing rate of output consider increasing or decreasing that output. If a further unit of production will increase the firm's profits, the firm should expand its output. However, if the last unit produced reduced profits, the firm should contract its output. From this it follows that the only time the firm should leave its output unaltered is when the last unit produced adds the same amount to costs as it does to revenue.

The results in these two paragraphs can be combined in the following rule:

Rule 2: **Whenever it is worthwhile for the firm to produce at all, it should produce the output at which marginal revenue equals marginal cost. [25]**

The two rules that we have stated refer to each firm's own costs and revenues, and they apply to all profit-maximizing firms, whatever the market structure in which they operate.[3]

Rule 2 Applied to Price-Taking Firms

Rule 2 tells us that any profit-maximizing firm that produces at all will produce at the point where marginal cost equals marginal revenue. However, we have already seen that for price-taking firms, marginal revenue is the market price. Combining these two results gives us an important conclusion:

A firm that is operating in a perfectly competitive market will produce the output that

FIGURE 12-3
The Short-Run Equilibrium of a Competitive Firm

The firm chooses the output for which $p = MC$ above the level of AVC. When $p = MC$, as at q_E, the firm would decrease its profits if it changed its output. At any point to the left of q_E, say, q_0, price is greater than the marginal cost, and it is worthwhile for the firm to increase output (as indicated by the arrow on the left). At any point to the right of q_E, say, q_1, price is less than the marginal cost, and it is worthwhile for the firm to reduce output (as indicated by the arrow on the right). The short-run equilibrium output for the firm is q_E.

equates its marginal cost of production with the market price of its product (as long as price exceeds average variable cost).

In a perfectly competitive industry, the market determines the price at which the firm sells its product. The firm then picks the quantity of output that maximizes its profits. We have seen that this is the output for which price equals marginal cost.

When the firm has reached a position where its profits are maximized, it has no incentive to change its output. Therefore, unless prices or costs change, the firm will continue to produce this output because it is doing as well as it can do, given the market situation. The firm is in *short-run equilibrium,* as illustrated in Figure 12-3.

In a perfectly competitive market, each firm is a quantity adjuster. It pursues its goal of profit maximization by increasing or decreasing quantity until it equates its short-run

---

[3]A third rule is needed to distinguish between profit-*maximizing* and profit-*minimizing* positions: The marginal cost curve must cut the marginal revenue curve from below. This rule is not, however, needed for the discussion that follows, so we say nothing further about it. We only consider situations in which it is met.

FIGURE 12-4
The Short-Run Equilibrium of a Firm Using Total Cost and Revenue Curves

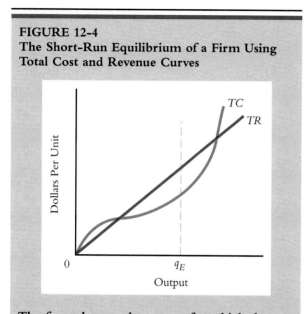

The firm chooses the output for which the gap between the total revenue and the total cost curves is the largest. At each output, the vertical distance between the *TR* and the *TC* curves shows by how much total revenue exceeds total cost. In the figure, the gap is largest at output q_E, which is thus the profit-maximizing output.

marginal cost with the price of its product that is given to it by the market.

Figure 12-3 shows the equilibrium of the firm using average cost and revenue curves. We can, if we wish, show the same equilibrium using total cost and revenue curves. Figure 12-4 combines the total cost curve first drawn in Figure 10-2 with the total revenue curve first shown in Figure 12-2. It shows the profit-maximizing output as the output with the largest positive difference between total revenue and total cost. This must, of course, be the same output as we located in Figure 12-3 by equating marginal cost and marginal revenue.

Short-Run Supply Curves

We have seen that in a perfectly competitive market, the firm responds to a price that is set by the forces of demand and supply. By adjusting the quantity it

produces in response to the current market price, the firm helps to determine the market supply. The link between the behaviour of the firm and the behaviour of the competitive market is provided by the *market supply curve.*

The supply curve for one firm.   The firm's supply curve is derived in part (i) of Figure 12-5, which shows a firm's marginal cost curve and four alternative prices. The horizontal line at each price is the firm's demand curve when the market price is at that level. The firm's marginal cost curve gives the marginal cost corresponding to each level of output. We require a supply curve that shows the quantity that the firm will supply at each price. For prices below average variable cost, the firm will supply zero units (Rule 1). For prices above average variable cost, the firm will equate price and marginal cost (Rule 2, modified by the proposition that *MR* $=p$ in perfect competition). This leads to the following conclusion:

In perfect competition, the firm's supply curve is its marginal cost curve for those levels of output for which marginal cost is above average variable cost.

The supply curve of an industry.   To illustrate what is involved, Figure 12-6 shows the derivation of an industry supply curve for an industry containing only two firms. The general result is as follows:

In perfect competition, the industry supply curve is the horizontal sum of the marginal cost curves (above the level of average variable cost) of all firms in the industry.

The reason for this is that each firm's marginal cost curve shows how much that firm will supply at each given market price, and the industry supply curve is the sum of what each firm will supply.

This supply curve, based on the short-run marginal cost curves of all the firms in the industry, is the industry's supply curve that was first encountered in Chapter 4. We have now established the profit-maximizing behaviour of individual firms that lies behind that curve. It is sometimes called a **short-run supply curve,** because it is based on the short-run, profit-maximizing behaviour of all the firms in the industry. This distinguishes it from a *long-run supply curve,* which relates quantity supplied

FIGURE 12-5
Derivation of the Supply Curve for a Price-Taking Firm

(i) Marginal cost and average variable cost curves

(ii) Supply curve

The supply curve of the price-taking firm, shown in part (ii), is the same as its MC curve, shown in part (i). For prices below $2, output is zero, because there is no output at which AVC can be covered. Thus the point E_0, where the price of $2 is just equal to AVC, is the point at which the firm will shut down, and $2 is the shut-down price. As price rises to $3, $4, and $5, equilibrium shifts to E_1, E_2, and E_3, taking output to q_1, q_2, and q_3. At any of these prices, the firm's revenue exceeds its variable costs of production. An example of the excess is shown in part (i) of the figure by the shaded area associated with price p_1 (= $3) and output q_1. This amount is available to help cover fixed costs and, once these are covered, to provide a profit.

to the price that rules in long-run equilibrium (which we will study later in this chapter).

Short-Run Equilibrium Price

The price of a product sold in a perfectly competitive market is determined by the interaction of the industry's short-run supply curve and the market demand curve. Although no one firm can influence the market price significantly, the collective actions of all firms in the industry (as shown by the industry supply curve) and the collective actions of households (as shown by the market demand curve) together determine the equilibrium price. This occurs at the point where the market demand curve and the industry supply curve intersect.

At the equilibrium price, each firm is producing and selling a quantity for which its marginal cost equals price. No firm is motivated to change its output in the short run. Because total quantity demanded equals total quantity supplied, there is no reason for market price to change in the short run; the market and all the firms in the industry are in short-run equilibrium.

Short-Run Profitability of the Firm

We know that when an industry is in short-run equilibrium, each firm is maximizing its profits. However, we do not know *how large* these profits are. It is one thing to know that a firm is doing as well as it can, given its particular circumstances; it is another thing to know how well it is doing.

Figure 12-7 shows three possible positions for a firm in short-run equilibrium. In all cases, the firm is maximizing its profits by producing where price

FIGURE 12-6
Derivation of the Supply Curve for a Competitive Industry

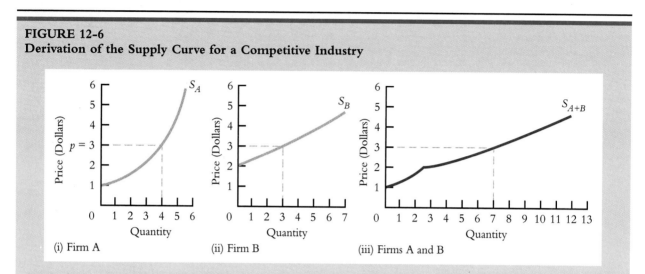

(i) Firm A   (ii) Firm B   (iii) Firms A and B

The industry's supply curve is the horizontal sum of the supply curves of each of the firms in the industry. At a price of $3, Firm A would supply 4 units and Firm B would supply 3 units. Together, as shown in part (iii), they would supply 7 units. If there are hundreds of firms, the process is the same. Each firm's supply curve (derived as in Figure 12-5) shows what the firm will produce at any given price p. The industry supply curve relates the price to the sum of the quantities produced by each firm. In this example, because Firm B does not enter the market at prices below $2, the supply curve S_{A+B} is identical to S_A up to the price $2 and is the sum of $S_A + S_B$ above $2.

equals marginal cost, but in part (i) the firm is suffering losses, in part (ii) it is just covering all of its costs (breaking even), and in part (iii) it is making profits, because average revenue exceeds average total cost. In part (i), we could say that the firm is minimizing its losses rather than maximizing its profits, but both statements mean the same thing. In all three cases, the firm is doing as well as it can, given its costs and the market price.

Long-Run Equilibrium

Although Figure 12-7 shows three possible short-run equilibrium positions for the firm in perfect competition, not all of them are possible long-run equilibrium positions.

The Effect of Entry and Exit

The key to long-run equilibrium under perfect competition is entry and exit. We have seen that when firms are in *short-run equilibrium,* they may be making profits, suffering losses, or just breaking even. Because costs include the opportunity cost of capital, firms that are just breaking even are doing as well as they could do by investing their capital elsewhere. Thus, there will be no incentive for such firms to leave the industry. Similarly, if new entrants expect to just break even, there will be no incentive for firms to enter the industry, because capital can earn the same return elsewhere in the economy. If, however, existing firms are earning revenues in excess of all costs, including the opportunity cost of capital, new capital will enter the industry to share in these profits. If existing firms are suffering losses, capital will leave the industry, because a better return can be obtained elsewhere in the economy. Let us now consider this process in a little more detail.

An entry-attracting price.   First, let all firms in the competitive industry be in the position of the firm shown in part (iii) of Figure 12-7. New firms, attracted by the profitability of existing firms, will enter the industry. Suppose that in response to the high profits that the 100 existing firms are making, 20 new firms enter. The market supply curve that formerly added up the outputs of 100 firms must

FIGURE 12-7
Average Short-Run Equilibrium Positions of a Competitive Firm

(i) Losses   (ii) Zero profit   (iii) Positive profit

When it is in short-run equilibrium, a competitive firm may be suffering losses, breaking even, or making profits. The diagrams show a firm with given costs facing alternative prices p_1, p_2, and p_3. In each part, equilibrium occurs at the point where $MC = MR$ = price. Because in all three cases price exceeds AVC (which is only shown in part i), the firm is in short-run equilibrium at E_1 in part (i), E_2 in part (ii), and E_3 in part (iii).

In part (i) price is p_1, and the firm is suffering losses, shown by the shaded area, because price is below average total cost. Because price exceeds average variable cost, it is worthwhile for the firm to keep producing, but it is *not* worthwhile for it to replace its capital equipment as the capital wears out.

In part (ii) price is p_2, and the firm is just covering its total costs. It is worthwhile for the firm to replace its capital as it wears out, since it is covering the full opportunity cost of its capital.

In part (iii) price is p_3, and the firm is earning profits, shown by the shaded area.

now add up the outputs of 120 firms. At any price, more will be supplied because there are more producers.

With an unchanged market demand curve, this shift in the short-run industry supply curve means that the previous equilibrium price will no longer prevail. The shift in supply will lower the equilibrium price, and both new and old firms will have to adjust their output to this new price. This is illustrated in Figure 12-8. New firms will continue to enter, and the equilibrium price will continue to fall, until all firms in the industry are just covering their total costs. Firms will then be in the position of the firm shown in part (ii) of Figure 12-7, which is called a *zero-profit equilibrium*.

Profits in a competitive industry are a signal for the entry of new firms; the industry will expand, pushing price down until the profits fall to zero.

An exit-inducing price. Now let the firms in the industry be in the position of the firm shown in part (i) of Figure 12-7. Although the firms are covering their variable costs, the return on their capital is less than the opportunity cost of capital. They are not covering their total costs. This is a signal for the exit of firms. Old plants and equipment will not be replaced as they wear out. As a result, the industry's short-run supply curve shifts leftward, and the market price rises. Firms will continue to exit, and the market price will continue to rise, until the remaining firms can cover their total costs, that is, until they are all in the zero-profit equilibrium illustrated in part (ii) of Figure 12-7. The exit of firms then ceases.

Losses in a competitive industry are a signal for the exit of firms; the industry will contract, driving the market price up until the remaining firms are covering their total costs.

FIGURE 12-8
The Effect of New Entrants

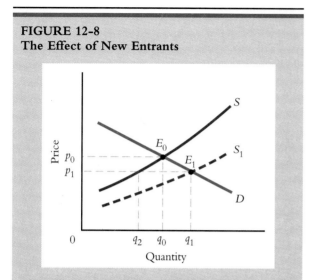

New entrants shift the supply curve to the right and lower the equilibrium price. Initial equilibrium is at E_0. The entry of new firms shift the supply curve to S_1. Equilibrium price falls to p_1, while output rises to q_1. Before the entry of new firms, only q_2 would have been produced had the price been p_1. The extra output is supplied by the new productive capacity.

The break-even price. Because firms exit when they are motivated by their losses and enter when they are motivated by their profits, this conclusion follows:

The long-run equilibrium of a competitive industry occurs when firms are earning zero profits.

The firm in part (ii) of Figure 12-7 is in a zero-profit, long-run equilibrium. For that firm, the price p_0 is sometimes called the **break-even price.** It is the price at which all costs, including the opportunity cost of capital, are being covered. The firm is just willing to stay in the industry. It has no incentive to leave, nor do other firms have an incentive to enter.

In the preceding analysis, we see profits serving the function of providing signals that guide the allocation of scarce resources among the economy's industries. It is also worth noting that freedom of entry will tend to push profits towards zero in any industry whether or not it is perfectly competitive.

Conditions for Long-Run Equilibrium

There are four conditions for a competitive industry to be in long-run equilibrium.

1. Existing firms must be doing as well as they can, given their existing capital. This means that short-run marginal costs of production must be equal to market price.
2. Existing firms must not be suffering losses. If they are suffering losses, they will not replace their capital. In this case, the size of the industry will shrink over time.
3. There must be no incentive for new firms to enter the industry. The absence of an incentive for entry requires that existing firms are not earning profits on their existing plants; if they were, new entrants could duplicate these facilities and earn profits themselves.
4. Existing firms must not be able to increase their profits by changing the size of their production facilities. This implies that each existing firm must be at the minimum point of its long-run cost curve.

This last condition is new to our discussion. Figure 12-9 shows that if the condition does not hold, a firm can increase its profits. Although the firm is in short-run equilibrium, in which it is just covering all of its costs when operating its existing plant, there are unexploited economies of scale. By building a new plant with a larger capacity than its existing plant, the firm can reduce its average cost. Because in its present position average cost is just equal to price, any reduction in average cost must yield profits.

For a price-taking firm to be in long-run equilibrium, it must be producing at the minimum point on its *LRAC* curve.

The level of output at which *LRAC* reaches a minimum is known as the firm's **minimum efficient scale (MES).**[4]

---

[4]With a U-shaped cost curve, as in Figure 12-9, there is only one point of efficient scale, so the qualification "minimum" is redundant. Empirical evidence shows, however, that many manufacturing plants have cost curves that are flat over a range of minimum average cost. The qualification minimum is then needed to indicate the *smallest* output at which average costs are minimized.

FIGURE 12-9
Short-Run Versus Long-Run Equilibrium of a Competitive Firm

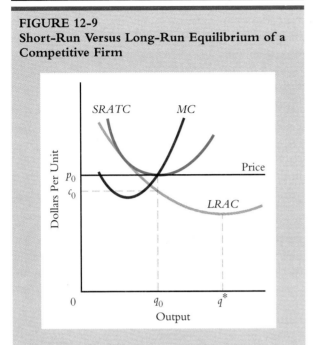

A competitive firm that is not at the minimum point on its *LRAC* curve cannot be in long-run equilibrium. A competitive firm with short-run cost curves *SRATC* and *MC* faces a market price of p_0. The firm produces q_0, where *MC* equals price and total costs are just being covered. However, the firm's long-run cost curve lies below its short-run curve at output q_0. The firm could produce output q_0 at cost c_0 by building a larger plant so as to take advantage of economies of scale. Profits would rise, because average total costs of c_0 would then be less than price p_0. The firm cannot be in long-run equilibrium at any output below q^* because, with any such output, average total costs can be reduced by building a larger plant. The output q^* is the *minimum efficient scale* of the firm.

FIGURE 12-10
The Equilibrium of a Firm When the Industry Is in Long-Run Equilibrium

In long-run competitive equilibrium the firm is operating at the minimum point on its *LRAC* curve. In long-run equilibrium each firm must be (1) maximizing short-run profits, $MC = p$; (2) earning profits of zero on its existing plant, $SRATC = p$; and (3) unable to increase its profits by altering the scale of its operations. These three conditions can be met only when the firm is at E, the minimum point on its *LRAC* curve, with price p^* and output q^*.

When each firm in the industry is producing at the minimum point of its long-run average cost curve and just covering its costs (i.e., each is in the position shown in Figure 12-10), the whole industry is in equilibrium. Because marginal cost equals price, no firm can improve its profits by varying its output in the short run. Because *LRAC* is above price at all possible outputs except the current one, where it is equal to the price, there is no incentive for any existing firm to move along its long-run cost curve by altering the scale of its operations. Because there are neither profits nor losses, there is no incentive for entry into or exit from the industry.

In long-run competitive equilibrium, the firm's average cost of production is the lowest attainable cost, given the limits of known technology and factor prices.

To summarize, the conditions for long-run equilibrium for a competitive industry are as follows: (1) Existing firms produce at the point where marginal cost equals price; (2) existing firms have no incentive to exit (existing firms are not making losses); (3) potential new firms have no incentive to enter (existing firms are not making profits); and (4) existing firms produce at the minimum point on their long-run average cost curve.[5] This is the position shown in Figure 12-10. (Note that conditions 2 and 3 can be combined into a single condition that the total revenues of existing firms should exactly equal their total costs.)

---

[5]Because all costs are variable in the long run, there is no need to distinguish long-run average variable cost from long-run average total cost. They are identical, and we refer to them, as we learned to do in Chapter 11, merely as long-run average costs (*LRAC*).

The Long-Run Industry Supply Curve

Consider a competitive industry that is in the type of long-run equilibrium that we have just studied. The market demand for the industry's product then increases. The reactions to this demand shift are a familiar story by now. First, price will rise, and, in response, existing firms will increase their outputs and earn profits. New firms, attracted by the profits, will enter the industry. As the industry's capacity expands, price will fall, and this process will continue until profits have been eliminated. At that time, existing firms will once again be just covering their full costs.

This is familiar ground, but there is one further question that we could ask. When all the dust has settled, will the new long-run equilibrium price be higher than, lower than, or the same as the original price? A similar analysis could be made for a fall in demand, and the same question could be asked.

The adjustment of a competitive industry to the types of changes that we have just discussed is shown by what is sometimes called the **long-run industry supply (LRS) curve.** This curve shows the relationship between the market price and the quantity produced in a competitive industry when it is in long-run equilibrium. Note, however, that the curve does not take *very*-long-run reactions into account and so is drawn on the assumption that technological knowledge is constant. (Very-long-run changes in technology will *shift* the *LRS* curve.) Figure 12-11 shows the derivation of this curve and its various possible shapes.

In part (i) of the figure, the *LRS* curve is horizontal. This indicates that the industry will adjust its size to provide whatever quantity is demanded at a constant price. An industry with a horizontal *LRS* curve is said to be a *constant-cost industry*. This situation occurs when the long-run expansion of the industry, due to the entry of new firms, leaves the long-run cost curves of existing firms unchanged. Because new firms have access to the same technology and face the same factor prices as existing firms, their cost curves will be the same as those of existing firms. It follows that the cost curves of all firms, new or old, will be unaffected by expansion (or contraction) of the industry. Thus, long-run, zero-profit equilibrium can be reestablished only when price is returned to its original level—which was,

and still is, equal to each firm's unchanged minimum long-run average total cost. In other words, because cost curves are unaffected by the expansion or contraction of the industry, each firm must start from, and return to, the long-run equilibrium position shown in Figure 12-10—*which means that market price must also do the same.*

Changing factor prices and a positively sloped long-run supply curve. When an industry expands its output, it needs more inputs. The increase in demand for these inputs may bid up their prices.[6]

If costs rise with increasing levels of industry output, so too must the price at which the producers are able to cover their costs. As the industry expands, the short-run supply curve shifts outward, but the firms' *SRATC* curves shift upward because of rising factor prices. The expansion of the industry comes to a halt when price is equal to firms' minimum *LRAC*. Because costs have risen, this must occur at a higher price than ruled before the expansion began, as illustrated in part (ii) of Figure 12-11. A competitive industry with rising long-run supply prices is often called a *rising-cost industry.*

Can the long-run supply curve be negatively sloped? So far we have suggested that the long-run supply curve may be constant or rising.[7] Could it ever decline, thereby indicating that higher outputs were associated with lower prices in long-run equilibrium?

It is tempting to answer yes, because of the opportunities of more efficient scales of operation using greater mechanization and more effective specialization of labour. However, this answer would not be correct for perfectly competitive industries, because each firm in long-run equilibrium must already be at the lowest point on its *LRAC* curve. If a firm could lower its costs by building a larger, more mechanized plant, it would be profitable to do so without waiting for an increase in market demand. Because any single firm perceives that it can sell all it wishes at the going market price, it will be profitable for the firm to expand the scale of its operations as long as its *LRAC* is falling.

---

[6]In a fully employed economy, the expansion of one industry implies the contraction of some other industry. What happens to factor prices depends on the proportions in which the expanding and the contracting industries use the factors.

[7]The discussion of returns to scale on pages – of Chapter 11 is relevant here.

FIGURE 12-11
Long-Run Industry Supply Curves

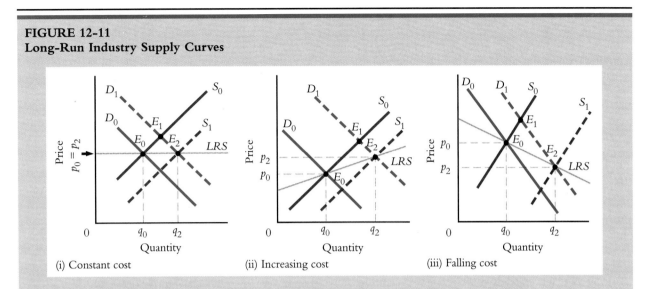

(i) Constant cost (ii) Increasing cost (iii) Falling cost

The long-run industry supply curve may be horizontal, positively sloped, or negatively sloped. In all three parts, the initial curves are at D_0 and S_0, yielding equilibrium at E_0, with price p_0 and output q_0. A rise in demand shifts the demand curve to D_1, taking the short-run equilibrium to E_1. New firms now enter the industry, shifting the supply curve outward, pushing down price until pure profits are no longer being earned. At this point the supply curve is S_1 and the new equilibrium is E_2, with price at p_2 and output q_2.

In part (i), price returns to its original level, making the long-run supply curve horizontal. In part (ii), profits are eliminated before price falls to its original level, giving the LRS curves a positive slope. In part (iii), the price falls below its original level before profits are eliminated, giving the LRS curve a negative slope.

The scale economies that we have just considered are within the control of the firm; they are said to be *internal economies of scale*. A perfectly competitive industry might, however, have falling long-run costs if industries that supply its inputs have increasing returns to scale. Such effects are outside the control of the perfectly competitive firm and are called *external economies of scale*. Whenever expansion of an industry leads to a fall in the prices of some of its inputs, the firms will find their cost curves shifting downward as they expand their outputs.

As an illustration of how the expansion of one industry could cause the prices of some of its inputs to fall, consider the early stages of the growth of the automobile industry. As the output of automobiles increased, the industry's demand for tires grew greatly. This, as was suggested earlier, increased the demand for rubber and tended to raise its price, but it also provided the opportunity for tire manufacturers to build larger plants that exploited the scale economies available in tire production. These economies were large enough to offset any factor

price increases, and tire prices charged to automobile manufacturers fell. Thus automobile costs fell because of lower prices of an important input. This case is illustrated in part (iii) of Figure 12-11. An industry that has a declining long-run supply curve is often called a *declining-cost industry*.

Notice that although the economies were external to the automobile industry, they were internal to the tire industry. This in turn requires that the supplying industry not be perfectly competitive. If it were, all its scale economies would already have been exploited, so this case refers to a perfectly competitive industry that uses an input produced by a non-perfectly-competitive industry whose own scale economies have not yet been fully exploited because demand is insufficient.

Another example is provided by perfectly competitive agricultural industries that buy their farm machinery from the agricultural implements industry, which is dominated by a few large firms.

We can now use our long-run theory to understand two commonly encountered but often misunderstood real-world situations.

Changes in Technology

Consider a competitive industry in long-run equilibrium. Because the industry is in equilibrium, each firm must be in zero-profit equilibrium. Now assume that technological development lowers the cost curves of newly built plants. Because price is just equal to the average total cost for the existing plants, new plants will be able to earn profits, and some of them will now be built. The resulting expansion in capacity shifts the short-run supply curve to the right and drives price down.

The expansion in capacity and the fall in price will continue until price is equal to the short-run average total cost of the *new* plants. At this price, old plants will not be covering their long-run costs. As long as price exceeds their average variable cost, however, such plants will continue in production. As the outmoded plants wear out, they will gradually be closed. Eventually, a new long-run equilibrium will be established in which all plants will use the new technology.

What happens in a competitive industry in which technological change does not occur as a single isolated event but more or less continuously? Plants built in any one year will tend to have lower costs than plants built in any previous year. This common occurrence is illustrated in Figure 12-12.

Industries that are subject to continuous technological change have a number of common characteristics. One of them is that plants of different ages and at different levels of efficiency exist side by side. This characteristic is dramatically illustrated by the many different vintages of farm equipment found in any long-established farm. This is also true of particular pieces of high-tech equipment, as a survey of the firms in any computerized industry, or of your friends' PCs, will show. In all these and many more cases, different vintages with different efficiencies exist side by side, and older models are not discarded as soon as a better model comes on the market.

Critics who observe the continued use of older, less efficient plants and equipment often urge that something be done "to eliminate these wasteful practises." These critics miss the point of economic efficiency. If the plant or piece of equipment is already there, the plant or equipment can be profitably operated as long as its revenues more than cover its *variable* costs. As long as a plant or equipment can produce goods that are valued by consumers at an amount above the value of the resources currently used up for their production (variable costs), the value of society's total output is increased by utilizing it.

A second characteristic of a competitive industry that is subject to continuous technological change is that price is governed by the *minimum ATC* of the most efficient plants.[8] Entry will continue until plants of the latest vintage are just expected to earn normal profits over their lifetimes. The benefits of the new technology are passed on to consumers because all of the units of the commodity, whether produced by new or old plants, are sold at a price that is related solely to the *ATCs* of the new plants. Owners of older plants find that their returns over variable costs fall steadily as more and more efficient plants drive the price of the product down.

A third characteristic is that old plants are discarded (or "mothballed") when the price falls below their *AVCs*. This may occur well before the plants are physically worn out. In industries with continuous technological progress, capital is usually discarded because it is *economically obsolete,* not because it is physically worn out. Old capital is obsolete when the market price of output does not even cover its average variable cost of production.

Declining Industries

What happens when a competitive industry in long-run equilibrium begins to suffer losses due to a permanent and continuing decrease in the demand for its products? As market demand declines, market price falls, and firms that were previously covering average total costs are no longer able to do so. They find themselves in the position shown in part (i) of Figure 12-7. Firms suffer losses instead of breaking even; the signal for the exit of capital is given, but exit takes time.

---

[8]Price will not necessarily equal minimum *ATC*. If firms anticipate the future changes, they will install new capital only when they expect to cover costs over the lifetime of the capital. This means that there must be sufficient profits in early years to match the losses in later years. Thus, price will exceed average costs in the newest, most efficient plants.

FIGURE 12-12
Plants of Different Vintages in an Industry with Continuous Technological Progress

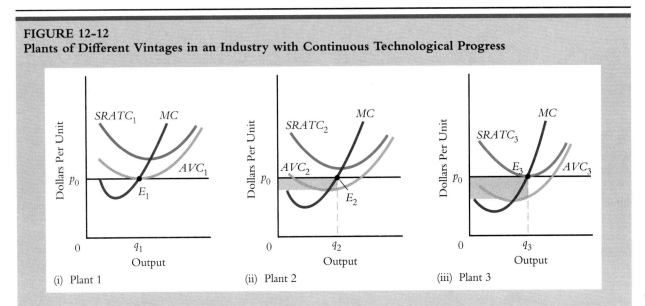

(i) Plant 1   (ii) Plant 2   (iii) Plant 3

Entry of progressively lower-cost firms forces price down, but older plants with higher costs remain in the industry as long as price covers average variable cost. Plant 3 is the newest plant with the lowest costs. Long-run equilibrium price will be determined by the average total costs of plants of this type, because entry will continue as long as the owners of the newest plants expect to earn profits from them. Plant 1 is the oldest plant in operation. It is just covering its AVC, and if the price falls any further, it will be closed down. Plant 2 is a plant of intermediate age. It is covering its variable costs and earning some contributions toward its fixed costs. In parts (ii) and (iii), the excess of revenues over variable costs is indicated by the shaded area.

The Response of Firms

The economically efficient response to a steadily declining demand is to continue to operate with existing equipment as long as its variable costs of production can be covered. As equipment becomes obsolete because it cannot cover even its variable cost, it will not be replaced unless the new equipment can cover its total cost. As a result, the capacity of the industry will shrink. If demand keeps declining, capacity must keep shrinking.

Declining industries typically present a sorry sight to the observer. Revenues are below long-run total costs, and as a result, new equipment is not brought in to replace old equipment as it wears out. The average age of equipment in use thus rises steadily. The untrained observer, seeing the industry's plight, is likely to blame it on the old equipment.

The antiquated equipment in a declining industry is often the effect rather than the cause of the industry's decline.

An interesting illustration of the importance of the distinction between fixed and variable costs—one that is familiar to many hotel users—is given in Box 12-2.

The Response of Governments

Governments are often tempted to support declining industries because they are worried about the resulting job losses. Experience suggests, however, that propping up genuinely declining industries only delays their demise—at significant national cost. When the government finally withdraws its support, the decline is usually more abrupt and hence more difficult to adjust to than it would have been had the industry been allowed to decline gradually under the market force of steadily declining demand.

Once governments recognise the decay of certain industries and the collapse of certain firms as an unavoidable consequence of economic growth, a more effective response is to provide welfare and re-

Box 12-2

Parable of the Seaside Inn

Why do some resort hotels stay open during the off-season, even though to do so they must offer bargain rates that do not even cover their "full costs"? Why do the managers of other hotels allow them to fall into disrepair even though they are able to attract enough customers to stay in business? Are the former being overly generous, and are the latter being irrational penny pinchers?

To illustrate what is involved, consider an imaginary resort hotel called the Seaside Inn. Its revenues and costs of operating during the four months of the season and during the eight months of the off-season are shown in the table. When the profit-maximizing price for its rooms is charged, the hotel earns a return over its total variable costs of $22,000 during the season, as shown in the table. This surplus goes toward meeting the hotel's fixed costs of $24,000.

If it were to charge the same rates during the off-season, it could not attract enough customers even to cover its costs of maids, bellhops, and managers. The hotel discovers, however, that by charging lower rates during the off-season, it can rent some of its rooms and earn revenues of $20,000. Its costs of staying open are $18,000, and if it allocates the same portion of its fixed costs of $24,000 to each month that it stays open, it will not be covering its total costs (fixed plus variable costs) in the off-season, but it will be earning a surplus of $2,000 over variable costs. This surplus, though relatively small, can go toward covering some part of the fixed costs. Therefore, the hotel stays open during the whole year by offering off-season bargain rates to grateful guests. (Indeed, if it were to close during the winter months, it would not be able to cover its total fixed and variable costs solely through its in-season operations.)

Now assume that the off-season revenues fall to $19,000 (everything else remaining the same). The short-run condition for staying open, $TR > TVC$, is met both for the season and for the off-season. However, the long-run condition is not met, since the TR over the whole year of $77,000 is less than the total costs of $78,000, all of which are variable in the long run. The hotel will remain open as long as it can do so with its present capital—it will produce in the short run. However, it will not be worthwhile for the owners to replace the capital as it wears out.

It will become one of those run-down hotels about which guests ask, "Why don't they do something about this place?"—but the owners are behaving rationally. They are operating the hotel as long as it covers its variable costs, but they are not putting any more investment into it, since it cannot cover its fixed costs. Sooner or later, the fixed capital will become too old to be run, or at least to attract customers, and the hotel will be closed.

The Seaside Inn (*total costs and revenues*)

Season	Total revenue TR	Total variable cost TVC	Contribution to fixed costs TR-TVC	Total fixed costs
Season	$58,000	$36,000	$22,000	
Off-season	$20,000	$18,000	$ 2,000	
Total	$78,000	$54,000	$24,000	$24,000

training schemes that cushion the impacts of change. These can moderate the effects on the incomes of workers who lose their jobs and make it easier for them to transfer to expanding industries. Intervention that is intended to increase mobility while reducing the social and personal costs of mobility is a viable long-run policy; trying to freeze the existing industrial structure by shoring up an inevitably declining industry is not.

The Appeal of Perfect Competition

Consider an economy in which all markets are perfectly competitive. In this economy, there are many firms and many households. Each is a price taker, responding as it sees fit to signals that are sent to it by the market. No single firm or consumer has any power over the market; instead, each is a passive quantity adjuster responding to market signals. Yet, the impersonal force of the market produces an appropriate response to all changes. If tastes change, for example, prices will change, and the allocation of resources will change in the appropriate direction. Throughout the entire process, no one firm has any power over any other firm. Dozens of firms react to the same price changes, and if one firm refuses to react, countless other profit-maximizing firms will be eager to make the appropriate changes.

Market reactions, not public policies, eliminate shortages or surpluses. There is need neither for regulatory agencies nor for bureaucrats to make arbitrary decisions about who may produce what, how to produce it, or how much it is permissible to charge for the product. If there are no government officials to make such decisions, no bribes will be necessary to influence their decisions.

In the impersonal decision-making world of perfect competition, neither private firms nor public officials wield economic power. The market mechanism, like an invisible hand, determines the allocation of resources among competing uses.

The theory of perfect competition is an intellectual triumph in showing how a price system can work to coordinate decentralized decision making by allowing all necessary adjustments to occur, in spite of the fact that no one foresees them or provides any overall plan for them. Moreover, as we shall see in Chapter 15, a perfectly competitive economy will generally be economically efficient.

The British historian Lord Acton once observed, "Power tends to corrupt; absolute power corrupts absolutely." To someone who fears power, either in the hands of the government or in such private organizations as large firms, the perfectly competitive model has a strong appeal. It describes an economy that functions effectively without any private or public group exercising any significant market power.

Although the price system often allocates resources in ways that are quite similar to the perfectly competitive economy, and although some markets are indeed perfectly competitive, in our world many groups have power over many markets. Large firms often set prices, determine what will be produced, and decide what research will take place. Labour unions often influence wages by offering or withdrawing their labour services. Governments influence many markets by being the dominant purchaser, as well as by regulating many others. Economic and social policy would be much simpler than it is if the entire economy were perfectly competitive. As it is, however, those who fear the concentration of market power can only regret that the perfectly competitive model does not describe the world in which we live; so many problems would disappear if only it did.

SUMMARY

1. Market behaviour is concerned with the degree to which individual firms compete against one another; market structure is concerned with the type of market in which firms operate. Market structure affects the degree of power that individual firms have to influence the price of the product.

2. Five key assumptions of the theory of perfect competition are as follows: (1) All firms produce a homogeneous product; (2) purchasers know the nature of the product and the price charged for it; (3) each firm's minimum efficient scale occurs at a level of output that is small relative to the industry's total output; (4) firms are price takers; and (5) the industry displays freedom of entry and exit. A firm that is a price taker will adjust to varying market conditions by altering its output.

3. A profit-maximizing firm will produce at a level of output at which (a) price is at least as great as average variable cost and (b) marginal cost equals marginal revenue. In perfect competition, firms are price takers, so marginal revenue is equal to price. Thus, a profit-maximizing firm operating in a perfectly competitive market equates marginal cost to price.

4. Under perfect competition, each firm's short-run supply curve is identical with its marginal cost curve above average variable cost. The perfectly competitive industry's short-run supply curve is the horizontal sum of the supply curves of the individual firms (i.e., the horizontal sum of the firms' marginal cost curves).

5. If a profit-maximizing firm is to produce at all, it must be able to cover its variable cost. However, such a firm may be suffering losses (price is less than average total cost), making profits (price is greater than average total cost), or just breaking even (price is equal to average total cost).

6. In the long run, profits or losses will lead to the entry or the exit of capital into or out of the industry. This pushes any competitive industry to a long-run, zero-profit equilibrium and moves production to the level that minimizes average cost.

7. The long-run response of an industry to steadily changing technology is the gradual replacement of less efficient plants by more efficient ones. Older plants will be discarded and replaced by more modern ones only when price falls below average variable cost.

8. The long-run response of a declining industry will be to continue to satisfy demand by employing its existing plants as long as price exceeds short-run average variable cost. Despite the antiquated appearance that results, this response is the correct one.

9. The great appeal of perfect competition as a means of organizing production lies in the decentralized decision making of myriad firms and households. No individual firm or household exercises power over the market. At the same time, it is not necessary for the government to intervene to determine resource allocation and prices.

TOPICS FOR REVIEW

Competitive behaviour and competitive market structure

Rules for maximizing profits

Perfect competition

Price taking and a horizontal demand curve

Relationship of supply curves to marginal cost curves

Short-run and long-run equilibrium of firms and industries

Entry and exit in achieving long-run equilibrium

DISCUSSION QUESTIONS

1. A number of agricultural products, such as milk, eggs, and chickens, are produced under conditions that come close to perfect competition whenever governments do not regulate these markets. What are the main features of these industries that make them perfectly competitive? Use the theory you have learned in this chapter to predict the consequences of the introduction of government supply management schemes that attempt to raise farmers' incomes by restricting total output through quotas.

2. In the 1970s, prices obtained for Canadian wheat rose substantially relative to other agricultural products. Explain how each of the following may have contributed to this result.
   a. Crop failures caused by unusually bad weather around the world occurred in several years.
   b. There was a rising demand for beef and chickens because of rising population and rising per capita income.
   c. Great scarcities in fishmeal, a substitute for grain in animal diets, occurred because of a mysterious decline in the anchovy harvest off Peru.
   d. Increased Soviet purchases of grain on the world market.

3. In the late 1980s and continuing into the 1990s, the prices obtained for Canadian wheat fell dramatically relative to other agricultural products. Explain how each of the following may have contributed to the result.
   a. The green revolution has made more and more countries self-sufficient in food.
   b. Reforms in Russian agricultural production led to bumper harvests in the late 1980s.
   c. Subsidies have turned the European Community from a net importer to a net exporter of agricultural produce.

4. Discuss the common allegation that when all firms in an industry are charging the same price, this indicates the absence of competition and the presence of some form of price-setting agreement.

5. Which of the assumptions listed on page 220 does the following newspaper story relate to? "Recently Ken Chapman booked a $932 round-trip ticket at noon. While he slept that night, a new computer program searched for a better deal. Sixteen hours later a new fare became available and Mr. Chapman is now ticketed to travel for $578." Will this new procedure make the airline industry more or less competitive? Will it make it perfectly competitive?

6. Which of the following observed facts about an industry are inconsistent with its being a perfectly competitive industry?
   a. Different firms use different methods of production.
   b. The industry's product is extensively advertised by a trade association.
   c. Individual firms devote a large fraction of their sales receipts to advertising their own product brands.
   d. There are 24 firms in the industry.
   e. All firms made large profits in 1992.

7. In which of the following sectors of the Canadian economy might you expect to find competitive *behaviour?* In which might

you expect to find industries that are classified as operating under perfectly competitive *market structures?*

   a. Manufacturing

   b. Agriculture

   c. Transportation and public utilities

   d. Wholesale and retail trade

   e. Illegal drugs

8. The typical office in 1993 uses personal computers of various vintages, with the newest machines having the largest output per unit of cost. There are also old machines which, although still able to function, are not in use at all.

   a. What determines the second-hand price of the older machines?

   b. What is the economic value of the machines that are retained but no longer used?

9. Suppose entry into an industry is not artificially restricted but takes time because of the need to build plants, to acquire technical know-how, and to establish a marketing organization. Can such an industry be characterized as perfectly competitive? Does ease of entry imply ease of exit, and vice versa?

10. What, if anything, does each one of the following tell you about ease of entry into or exit from an industry?

   a. Profits have been very high for two decades.

   b. No new firms have entered the industry for 20 years.

   c. The average age of the firms in the 40-year-old industry is less than 7 years.

   d. Most existing firms are using obsolete equipment alongside newer, more modern equipment.

   e. Profits are low or negative; many firms are still producing, but from steadily aging equipment.

13

Monopoly

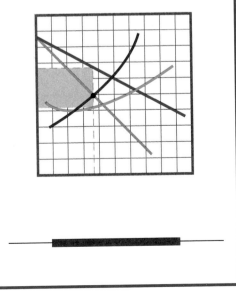

Is Quebec Hydro a monopoly? Are Bombadier, Algomo Steel, provincial liquor boards, the post office, the National Hockey League, or the Coca-Cola Company monopolies? The word *monopoly* comes from the Greek words *monos polein*, which mean "alone to sell." Economists say that a **monopoly** occurs when the output of an entire industry is produced and sold by a single firm, called a **monopolist** or a *monopoly firm*.

A Single-Price Monopolist

The first part of this chapter deals with a monopoly firm that charges a single price for its product. The firm's profits, like those of all firms, will depend on the relationship between its production costs and its sales revenues.

Cost and Revenue in the Short Run

We saw in Chapter 10 that U-shaped short-run cost curves are a consequence of the law of diminishing returns. Because this law applies to the conditions under which goods are produced rather than to the market structure in which they are sold, monopoly firms have U-shaped short-run cost curves just as perfectly competitive firms do.

Because a monopoly firm is the sole producer of the product that it sells, its demand curve is identical with the market demand curve for that product. The market demand curve, which shows the total quantity that buyers will purchase at each price, also shows the quantity that the monopolist will be able to sell at each price. Thus, the monopoly firm, unlike the perfectly competitive firm, faces a negatively sloped demand curve. This means that it faces a trade-off between the price it charges and the quantity it sells. Sales can be increased only if price is reduced, and price can be increased only if sales are reduced.

Average and Marginal Revenue

Starting with the market demand curve, the monopoly firm's average and marginal revenue curves can be readily derived. When the monopoly firm charges the same price for all units sold, average revenue per unit is identical with price. Thus the market demand curve is also the firm's *average revenue curve*.

Now consider the monopoly firm's *marginal revenue* resulting from the sale of an additional (or marginal) unit of production. Because its demand curve is negatively sloped, the monopoly firm must lower the price that it charges on *all* units in order to sell an *extra* unit.

It follows that the addition to its revenue resulting from the sale of an extra unit is less than the price that it receives for that unit (less by the amount that it loses as a result of cutting the price on all the units that it was selling already).

The monopoly firm's marginal revenue is less than the price at which it sells its output. [26]

This proposition is explored in Table 13-1 and Figure 13-1. Consider Table 13-1 first.

Notice that the change in total revenue associated with a change of $1 in price and the change in total revenue associated with a change of one unit of output are both plotted between the rows that refer to specific prices. This is done because the figures refer to what happens when the price is changed between the amounts shown in two adjacent rows.

Notice also that when price is reduced starting from $10, total revenue rises at first and then falls. The maximum total revenue is reached in this example at a price of $5. Because marginal revenue gives the change in total revenue resulting from the sale of one more unit of output, marginal revenue is positive whenever total revenue is increased by selling more, but it is negative when total revenue is reduced by selling more.

The method of calculating marginal revenue shown in the table involves subtracting the total revenue associated with one price from the total revenue associated with another price and then apportioning the change among the number of extra units sold.

Now look at Figure 13-1. It plots the entire demand curve that gave rise to the individual figures for price and quantity shown in Table 13-1. It also plots the entire marginal revenue curve and locates the specific points on it that were calculated in the table. For purposes of illustration, a straight-line demand curve has been chosen.[1]

Notice that marginal revenue is positive up to 50 units of sales, indicating that reductions in price between $10 and $5 increase total revenue. Notice also that marginal revenue is negative for sales

---

[1] It is helpful when you are drawing these curves to remember that if the demand curve is a negatively sloped straight line, the *MR* curve also has a negative slope but is twice as steep. Its price intercept (where $q = 0$) is the same as that of the demand curve, and its quantity intercept (where $p = 0$) is one half that of the demand curve. [27]

TABLE 13-1 A Numerical Example of a Monopoly Firm's Average, Marginal, and Total Revenues

(i) Price (average revenue)	(ii) Quantity sold	(iii) Total revenue (p)(q)	(iv) Change in total revenue ΔTR	(v) Marginal revenue $\Delta TR/\Delta q$
10	0	0		
9	10	90	90	9
8	20	160	70	7
7	30	210	50	5
6	40	240	30	3
5	50	250	10	1
4	60	240	−10	−1
3	70	210	−30	−3
2	80	160	−50	−5
1	90	90	−70	−7
0	100	0	−90	−9

Marginal revenue is less than price because price must be lowered to sell an extra unit. Columns (i) and (ii) of the table give specific points on the demand curve shown in Figure 13-1. The data show that every time the firm alters its price by $1, its sales change by 10 units. Column (iii) gives the total revenue associated with each price, which is that price multiplied by the quantity sold. Column (iv) gives the change in total revenue as the price is altered by $1. However, every time the price changes by $1, the quantity sold changes by 10 units. To calculate the change in revenue associated with a unit change in quantity, the change in column (iv) must be divided by 10 to get the change in revenue per unit change in quantity. The result is recorded in column (v), which is the marginal revenue.

For example, the fifth row of the table shows that when the price is $6, sales are 40 units, making a total revenue of $240, whereas the sixth row shows that when the price is $5, sales are 50 units, making a total revenue of $250. Reading across the table, the next entry is written between the two rows for prices $6 and $5. It records that when price is altered between these two amounts, the change in total revenue is $10 (i.e., $250 − $240). However, this change is associated with a change in sales of 10 units. The entry of $1 shown in the last column is obtained by dividing the change in total revenue of $10 by the change in output of 10 units. This gives the change in total revenue *per unit of sales* when price alters between $6 and $5.

greater than 50 units, indicating that reductions in price below $5 cause total revenue to fall.

The figure also illustrates the two opposing forces that are set up when price is cut. First, the

FIGURE 13-1
Average and Marginal Revenue Curves for a Monopoly Firm

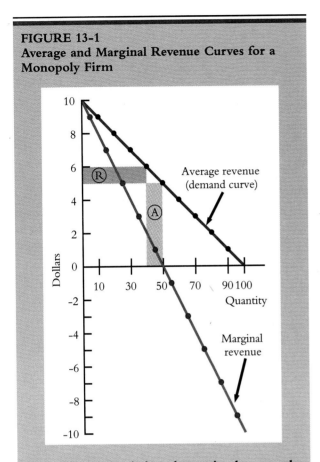

Marginal revenue is less than price because the price at which existing units are sold must be reduced in order to sell more units. The figure shows an example of a demand curve facing a monopoly firm and the resulting marginal revenue curve. The specific points shown by the black dots on the AR curve, and by the blue dots on the MR curve, are recorded in Table 13-1.

The shaded areas on the graph give another way of looking at the example given in the second paragraph of Table 13-1. The blue shaded area, labeled R, shows the reduction in revenue on the existing sales of 40 units when price is cut from $6 to $5. This is a $1 reduction on 40 units, making a total reduction of $40. However, the price cut causes sales to rise by 10, from 40 to 50 units. These are sold at the new price of $5, making an addition to revenue of $50, as shown by the red shaded area, which is marked A. The difference between the addition to revenue of $50 and the reduction of $40 is $10. But this is the result of 10 extra units being sold, which makes $1 *per extra unit* sold. This is the marginal revenue of $1 plotted in the figure between the quantities of 40 and 50 units.

units already sold bring in less money at the new lower price than at the original higher price. The loss is the amount of the price cut multiplied by the number of units already being sold. Second, new units are sold, which brings in more revenue. The extra revenue is the new units sold multiplied by the price at which they are sold. The *net change* in total revenue is the difference between these two amounts. In the example shown in the figure in which price is cut from $6 to $5, the increase resulting from the sale of new units exceeds the decrease resulting from existing sales now being made at a lower price. Marginal revenue is thus positive.

The proposition that marginal revenue is always *less than* average revenue, which has been illustrated numerically in Table 13-1 and graphically in Figure 13-1, provides an important contrast with perfect competition. You will recall that in perfect competition, the firm's marginal revenue from selling an extra unit of output is *equal to* the price at which that unit is sold. The reason for the difference is not difficult to understand. The perfectly competitive firm is a price taker; it can sell all it wants at the given market price. The monopoly firm faces a negatively sloped demand curve; it must reduce the market price in order to increase its sales.

Marginal Revenue and Elasticity

Now look at Figure 13-2. This duplicates the demand and marginal revenue curves shown in Figure 13-1.[2] In Chapter 5 we discussed the relationship between the elasticity of the market demand curve and the total revenue derived from selling the product. Figure 13-2 summarizes this earlier discussion and extends it to cover marginal revenue.

Over the range in which the demand curve is elastic, total revenue rises as more units are sold; marginal revenue must therefore be positive. Over the range in which the demand curve is inelastic, total revenue falls as more units are sold; marginal revenue must therefore be negative.

---

[2]To fit the figure onto the page, the scale on the vertical price axis has been shrunk somewhat. This makes the curve look flatter than the curve in Figure 13-1, *although they each show exactly the same data*. This illustrates the point made in Chapter 5 that the apparent steepness of one curve is not a good guide to its elasticity, because that steepness can be altered merely by changing the scale on the axes.

FIGURE 13-2
Relationship Between Total, Average, and Marginal Revenue and Elasticity of Demand

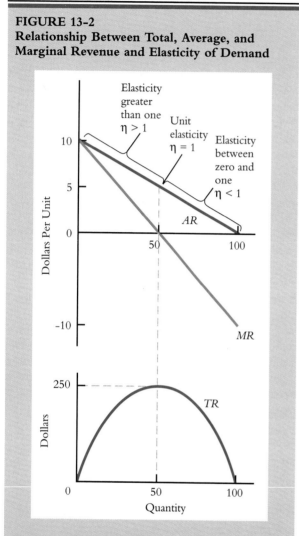

For a monopolist, MR is always less than price; when TR is rising, MR is greater than zero and elasticity is greater than one. The monopoly firm's demand curve is its *AR* curve; the *MR* curve is below the *AR* curve because the demand curve has a negative slope.

In the example shown, for outputs from 0 to 50, marginal revenue is positive, elasticity is greater than one, and total revenue is rising. For outputs from 50 to 100, marginal revenue is negative, elasticity is less than one, and total revenue is falling.

Short-Run Monopoly Equilibrium

To show the profit-maximizing position of a monopoly firm, we bring together information about its revenues and its costs and then apply the two rules developed in Chapter 12. Recall that these two rules are (1) the firm should not produce at all unless there is some level of output for which price is at least equal to total variable cost, and (2) if the firm does produce, its output should be set at the point where marginal cost equals marginal revenue.

When the monopoly firm equates marginal cost with marginal revenue, it reaches the equilibrium shown in Figure 13-3. The output is found as the quantity for which marginal cost equals marginal revenue. The price is read off the demand curve, which shows the price corresponding to that output.

Notice that because marginal revenue is always less than price for the monopoly firm, when marginal revenue is equated with marginal cost, both are less than price.

When a monopoly firm is in equilibrium, its marginal cost is always less than the price it charges for its output.

Competition and monopoly compared. The comparison with firms in perfect competition is important. In perfect competition, firms face perfectly elastic curves, so that price and marginal revenue are the same. Thus, when they equate marginal cost to marginal revenue, they ensure that marginal cost also equals price. In contrast, a monopoly firm faces a negatively sloped demand curve for which marginal revenue is less than price. Thus, when it equates marginal cost to marginal revenue, it ensures that marginal cost will be less than price.

The relationship between elasticity and revenue discussed above has an interesting implication for the monopoly firm's equilibrium. Because marginal cost is always greater than zero, a profit-maximizing monopoly (which produces where $MR = MC$) will always produce where marginal revenue is positive, that is, where demand is elastic. If the firm were producing where demand was inelastic, it could reduce its output, thereby increasing its total revenue and reducing its total costs. No such restriction applies to firms in perfect competition. Each adjusts to its own perfectly elastic demand curve, not to the market demand curve. Thus the equilibrium can occur where the market demand curve is either elastic or inelastic.

A profit-maximizing monopoly will never sell in the range where the demand curve is inelastic.

FIGURE 13-3
Short-Run Profit-Maximizing Position of a Monopolist

(i) Positive profits

(ii) Zero profits

Profit-maximizing output is q_0, where $MR = MC$; price is p_0, which is above MC at that output. The rules for profit maximization require $MR = MC$ and $p > AVC$. (AVC is not shown in the graph, but it must be below ATC.) Whether or not there are profits depends on the position of the ATC curve. In part (i), where average total cost is ATC_1, there are profits, as shown by the shaded area. In part (ii), where average total cost is ATC_2, profits are zero. If average total costs were ATC_3, the monopolist would suffer the losses shown by the gray shaded area.

Monopoly profits. The fact that a monopoly firm produces the output that maximizes its profits tells us nothing about how large these profits will be or even whether there will be any profits at all. Profits may be positive, as shown in part (i) of Figure 13-3. As part (ii) of Figure 13-3 shows, however, the profit-maximizing monopolist may break even or suffer losses. Nothing guarantees that a monopoly firm will make profits in the short run, but if it suffers persistent losses, it will eventually go out of business.

No supply curve for a monopoly. In describing the monopolist's profit-maximizing behaviour, we did not introduce the concept of a supply curve, as we did in the discussion of perfect competition. In perfect competition, the industry short-run supply curve depends only on the marginal cost curves of the individual firms. This is true because, under perfect competition, profit-maximizing firms equate marginal cost with price. Given marginal costs, it is possible to know how much will be produced at each price. This is not the case, however, with a monopoly.

For a monopoly firm, there is no unique relationship between market price and quantity supplied.[3]

Firm and industry. Because the monopolist is the only producer in an industry, there is no need for separate theories about the firm and the industry, as is necessary with perfect competition. The monopolist *is* the industry. Thus the short-run, profit-maximizing position of the firm, as shown in Figure 13-3, is also the short-run equilibrium of the industry.

---

[3]This can be proved by drawing a monopoly firm's marginal cost curve and any marginal revenue curve to intersect the MC curve at some output that we call q^*. Now draw as many other different MR curves as you like, all of which intersect MC at q^*. All of these curves give rise to an equilibrium output of q^*, but because each MR curve is different, each must be associated with a different demand curve *and hence a different price at which* q^* is sold. This shows that a given quantity may be associated with many different prices, depending on the slope of the demand curve that faces the monopoly firm.

Long-Run Monopoly Equilibrium

In a monopolised industry, as in a perfectly competitive one, losses and profits provide incentives for exit and entry.

If the monopoly firm is suffering losses in the short run, it will continue to operate as long as it can cover its variable costs. In the long run, however, it will leave the industry unless it can find a scale of operations at which its full opportunity costs can be covered.

If the monopoly firm is making profits, other firms will wish to enter the industry in order to earn more than the opportunity cost of their capital. If such entry occurs, the equilibrium position shown in part (i) of Figure 13-3 will change, and the firm will cease to be a monopolist.

Entry Barriers

Impediments that prevent entry are called **entry barriers;** they may be either natural or created.

If a monopoly firm's profits are to persist in the long run, the entry of new firms into the industry must be prevented by effective entry barriers.

Natural Barriers

Natural barriers most commonly arise as a result of economies of scale. When the long-run average cost curve is negatively sloped over a large range of output, big firms have significantly lower average total costs than small firms.

You will recall from Chapter 11 that the *minimum efficient scale (MES)* is the smallest-sized firm that can reap all of the economies of large-scale production. It occurs at the level of output where the firm's long-run average total cost curve reaches a minimum.

Now suppose that the technology of an industry is such that one firm's *MES* would be 10,000 units per week at an average total cost of $10 per unit. Further assume that at a price of $10, the total quantity demanded is 11,000 units per week. Under these circumstances, only one firm can operate at or near its *MES*.

A **natural monopoly** occurs when the industry's demand conditions allow only one firm, at most, to cover its costs while producing at its *MES*. In a natural monopoly, there is no price at which two firms can both sell enough to cover their total costs.

Another type of natural barrier is *set-up cost*. If a firm could be catapulted fully grown into the market, it might be able to compete effectively with the existing monopolist. However, the cost to the new firm of entering the market, developing its products, and establishing such things as its brand image and its dealer network may be so large that entry would be unprofitable.

Created Barriers

Many entry barriers are created by conscious government action and are therefore condoned by it. Patent laws, for instance, may prevent entry by conferring on the patent holder the sole legal right to produce a particular commodity for a specific period of time.

Patent protection has led to a major and prolonged battle among nations fought out in international organizations that seek to enforce conditions for fair trade and investment. The major developed countries, where much of the research and development is done, have sought to extend patent rights to other countries. They argue that without the temporary monopoly profits that a patent creates, the incentive to develop new products will be weakened. The less developed countries have sought to maintain weak or nonexistent patent laws. This allows them to produce new products under more competitive conditions and to avoid paying monopoly profits to the original patent holders in developed countries.

A firm may also be granted a charter or a franchise that prohibits competition by law. Regulation and licensing of firms, often in service industries, can restrict entry severely.

Other barriers can be created by the firm or firms already in the market. In extreme cases, the threat of force or sabotage can deter entry. The most obvious entry barriers of this type are encountered in organized crime, where operation outside of the law makes available an array of illegal but potent barriers to new entrants. Legitimate firms must use legal tactics—ranging from the threat of price cutting, designed to impose unsustainable losses on a new entrant, to heavy brand-name advertising—

intended to increase a new entrant's set-up costs. (These and other created entry barriers will be discussed in much more detail in Chapter 14.)

The Significance of Entry Barriers

Because there are no entry barriers in perfect competition, profits cannot persist in the long run.

Profits attract entry, and entry erodes profits.

In monopoly, however, profits can persist in the long run whenever there are effective barriers to entry.

Entry barriers frustrate the adjustment mechanism that would otherwise push profits to zero in the long run.

"Creative Destruction"

In the very long run, technology changes. New ways of producing old products are invented, and new products are created to satisfy both familiar and new wants. What has this to do with entry barriers? The answer is that a monopoly that succeeds in preventing the entry of new firms capable of producing its commodity will sooner or later find its barriers circumvented by innovations. One firm may be able to use new processes that avoid some patent or other barrier that the monopolist relies on to bar entry of competing firms. Another firm may compete by producing a new product that, although somewhat different, still satisfies the same need as the monopoly firm's product. Yet another firm might get around a natural monopoly by inventing a technology that produces at a low *MES* and ultimately allows several firms to enter the market and still cover costs.

A distinguished economist, the late Joseph Schumpeter, took the view that entry barriers were not a serious problem in the very long run. He argued that monopoly profits provide one of the major incentives for people who risk their money by financing inventions and innovations. In his view, the large, short-run profits of a monopoly provide a strong incentive for others to try to usurp some of these profits for themselves. If a frontal attack on the monopolist's barriers to entry is not possible, the barriers will be circumvented by such means as the development of similar products against which the monopolist will not have entry protection.

Schumpeter called the replacing of one monopoly by another through the invention of new products or new production techniques the *process of creative destruction*. He argued that this process precludes the very-long-run persistence of barriers to entry into industries that earn large profits.

He pushed this argument further and argued that because creative destruction depends on innovation, the existence of monopoly profits is a major incentive to economic growth. A key part of his argument can be found in the following words:

> What we have got to accept is that it [monopoly] has come to be the most powerful engine of progress and in particular of the long-run expansion of total output not only in spite of, but to a considerable extent through, this strategy [i.e., creating monopolies], which looks so restrictive when viewed in the individual case and from the individual point of time.
>
> In this respect, perfect competition is not only impossible but inferior, and has no title to being set up as a model. It is hence a mistake to base the theory of government regulation of industry on the principle that big business should be made to work as the respective industry would work in perfect competition.[4]

Schumpeter was writing at a time when the two dominant market structures studied by economists were perfect competition and monopoly. His argument easily extends, however, to any market structure that allows profits to exist in the long run. Today, there are few examples of pure monopolies, but there are many industries in which profits can be earned for long periods of time. Such industries, which are called *oligopolies*, are candidates for the operation of the process of creative destruction. We study these industries in detail in Chapter 14. In the meantime, Box 13-1 provides a few examples.

Cartels as Monopolies

Until now, a monopoly has meant that there is only one firm in an industry. A second way in which a monopoly can arise is for many firms in an industry

---

[4]Joseph Schumpeter, *Capitalism, Socialism, and Democracy*, 3d ed. (New York: Harper & Row, 1950), p. 106.

Box 13-1

Creative Destruction in Action

Creative destruction, the elimination of one product by a superior product and one production process by a superior process, is a major characteristic of all advanced countries. It eliminates the strong market position of the firms and workers who make the threatened product or operate the threatened process.

The steel nibbed pen eliminated the quill pen with its sharpened bird's feather nib. The fountain pen eliminated the steel pen and its accompanying ink well. The ball point pen virtually eliminated the fountain pen. Who knows what will come next in writing implements.

The hand cranked adding machine replaced the Dickensian clerk adding up long columns of figures in his head. (This was an all male occupation.) The electrically driven, mechanical desk calculator eliminated the hand cranked version. The electronic desk calculators eliminated the mechanical calculator. And the pocket calculator eliminated the slide rule (which was a device for doing calculations based on logarithms). The personal computer largely replaced the electronic calculator (except for pocket use). Each step vastly increased the speed and accuracy with which calculations could be completed. A modern PC will do in a fraction of a second what the Dickensian clerk did in a week and what a desk calculator could do in half a day.

The silent films eliminated vaudeville. The talkies eliminated the silent film and colour eliminated black and white. The TV seriously reduced the demand for films (and radio) while not eliminating either of them. Cable greatly reduced the demand for direct TV reception by offering better pictures and a more varied selection. The satellite is threatening to eliminate cable by offering much more selection. Predictably, the cable operators appealed to the Canadian regulators to protect their market by disallowing satellite TV.

In the 1920s and 1930s, the supermarket threatened the small grocery store as the main shopping media for the typical family. The small store fought back with assistance from the courts and the regulators and were able to slow the advance of the super-

markets. But in the end, the big stores were seen to offer a superior product and they pushed the small operations into the niche of the convenience store.

For long distance passenger travel by sea, the steamship eliminated the sailing vessel around the turn of the twentieth century. The airplane eliminated the ocean liner in the 1950s and 1960s. For passenger travel on land, the train eliminated the stage coach while the bus competed with the train without eliminating it. The airplane wiped out the passenger train in most of North America while leaving the bus still in a low cost niche used mainly for short and medium distances.

The above are all product innovations. Production process also undergoes the same type of creative destruction. The laborious hand setting of metal type for printing was replaced by the linotype that allowed the type to be set by a keyboard operator but which still involved a costly procedure for making corrections. The linotype was swept away by computer typesetting and much of the established printing shop operations have recently been replaced by desk top publishing.

Masses of assembly line workers, operating highly specialized and inflexible machines replaced the craftsman when Henry Ford invented the techniques of mass production. A smaller number of less specialized flexible manufacturing workers, operating sophisticated and less specialized machinery, have replaced the assembly line workers who operated the traditional factory.

The cases can be extended almost indefinitely and they all illustrate the same general message. Technological change transforms the products we consume, how we make those products, and how we work. It continually sweeps away positions of high income and economic power established by firms that were in the previous wave of technological change and by those who work for them. It is an agent of dynamism in our economy, an agent of change and economic growth, but it is not without its dark side in terms of the periodic loss of privileged positions on the part of the replaced firms and their workers.

to agree to cooperate with one another, to behave as if they were a single seller, in order to maximize joint profits, eliminating competition among themselves. Such a group of firms is called a **cartel**. A cartel that includes *all* firms in the industry can behave in the same way as a single-firm monopoly that owned all of these firms. The firms can agree among themselves to restrict their total output to the level that maximizes their joint profits.[5]

The Effects of Cartelization

Because perfectly competitive firms are price takers, they accept the market price as given and increase their output until their marginal cost equals price. In contrast, a monopoly firm knows that increasing its output will depress the market price. Taking account of this, the monopolist increases its output only until marginal revenue is equal to marginal cost. If all the firms in a perfectly competitive industry form a cartel, they too will be able to take account of the effect of their *joint output* on price. They can agree to restrict industry output to the level that maximizes their joint profits (where the industry's marginal cost is equal to the industry's marginal revenue). The incentive for firms to form a cartel lies in the cartel's ability to restrict output, thereby creating profits.

When a perfectly competitive industry is cartelized, the firms can agree to restrict their joint output to the profit-maximizing level. One way to do this is to establish a quota for each firm's output. Say that the profit-maximizing output is two thirds of the perfectly competitive output. When the cartel is formed, each firm could be given a quota equal to two thirds of its competitive output.

The effect of cartelizing a perfectly competitive industry and of reducing its output through production quotas is shown in more detail in Figure 13-4.

FIGURE 13-4
Effect of Cartelizing an Industry in Perfectly Competitive Equilibrium

Cartelization of a perfectly competitive industry can always increase that industry's profits. Equilibrium for a perfectly competitive industry occurs at E_0, where the supply and the demand curves intersect. Equilibrium price and output are p_c and q_c. Because the industry demand curve is negatively sloped, marginal revenue is less than price. In the graph, marginal revenue is m_c at the competitive equilibrium output of q_c.

If the industry is cartelized, profits can be increased by reducing output. All units between q_m and q_c add less to revenue than to cost—the marginal revenue curve lies below the marginal cost curve. (Recall from Figure 12-6 that the industry's supply curve is the sum of the supply curves, and hence of the marginal cost curves, of each of the firms in the industry.) If the units between q_m and q_c are not produced, output is reduced to q_m and price rises to p_m. This price-output combination maximizes the industry's profits because it is where industry marginal revenue equals industry marginal cost.

---

[5]In this chapter, we deal with the simple case in which *all* of the firms in a perfectly competitive industry form a cartel in order to act as if they were a monopoly. Cartels are sometimes formed by a group of firms that account for a significant part, but not all, of the total supply of some commodity. The effect is to create what is called an *oligopoly*. The most famous example of this type is the Organization of Petroleum Exporting Countries, best known as OPEC. We shall return to this type of cartel in Chapter 14.

Problems Facing Cartels

Cartels encounter two characteristic problems. The first is ensuring that members follow the behaviour that will maximize the industry's *joint* profits, and the second is preventing these profits from being eroded by the entry of new firms.

Enforcement of output restrictions. The managers of any cartel want the industry to produce its profit-maximizing output. Their job is made more difficult if individual firms either stay out of the cartel or enter and then cheat on their output quotas. Any one firm, however, has an incentive to do just this: to be either the one that stays out of the organization or the one that enters and then cheats on its output quota. For the sake of simplicity, assume that all firms enter the cartel, so enforcement problems are concerned strictly with cheating by its members.

If Firm X is the only firm to cheat, it is in the best of all possible situations. All other firms restrict output and hold the industry price near its monopoly level. They earn profits but only by restricting output. Firm X can then reap the full benefit of the other firms' output restraint and sell some additional output at the high price that has been set by the cartel's actions. However, if all of the firms cheat, the price will be pushed back to the competitive level, and all of the firms will return to their zero-profit position.

This conflict between the interests of the group and the interests of the individual firm is the cartel's dilemma. Provided that enough firms cooperate in restricting output, all firms are better off than they would be if the industry remained perfectly competitive. Any one firm, however, is even better off if it remains outside or enters and cheats. However, if all firms act on this incentive, all will be worse off than if they had joined the cartel and restricted output.

Cartels tend to be unstable because of the incentives for individual firms to violate the output quotas needed to enforce the monopoly price.

The conflict between the motives for cooperation and the motives for independent action is analysed in more detail in Figure 13-5.

Cartels and similar output-restricting arrangements have a long history. For example, schemes to raise farm incomes by limiting crops bear ample testimony to the accuracy of the prediction that cartels will be unstable. Industry agreements concerning crop restriction often break down, and prices fall as

individual farmers exceed their quotas. This is why most crop restriction plans are now operated by governments rather than by private cartels. Government marketing boards of the type discussed in Chapter 6, backed by the full coercive power of the state, can force monopoly behaviour on existing producers and can effectively bar the entry of new ones.

Restricting entry. A cartel must not only police the behaviour of its members but also must be able to prevent the entry of new producers. An industry that can support a number of individual firms must have no overriding natural entry barriers. Thus, if it is to maintain its profits in the long run, a cartel of many separate firms must create barriers that prevent the entry of new firms that are attracted by the cartel's profits. Successful cartels are often able to license the firms in the industry and to control entry by restricting the number of licenses. At other times, the government has operated a quota system and has given it the force of law. If no one can produce without a quota and the quotas are allocated among existing producers, entry is precluded. Box 13-2 provides an example of the typical fate of a cartel that cannot control entry.

A Multiprice Monopolist: Price Discrimination

So far in this chapter, we have assumed that the monopoly firm charges the same price for every unit of its product, no matter where or to whom it sells that product.[6] A monopoly firm will also, as we shall soon see, find it profitable to sell different units of the same product at different prices whenever it gets the opportunity.[7] Because it is also prevalent in oligopolistic markets, the range of examples quoted covers both types of market structure.

---

[6]The rest of this chapter may be omitted without any loss of continuity.

[7]Although multiple price systems are found among many monopolists, such as electricity and water supply firms, they are also found in industries that contain several large firms. Thus, we could discuss such practises under monopoly in this chapter or under oligopoly in Chapter 14. We deal with it here because it naturally arises whenever monopoly is discussed.

FIGURE 13-5
Conflicting Forces Affecting Cartels

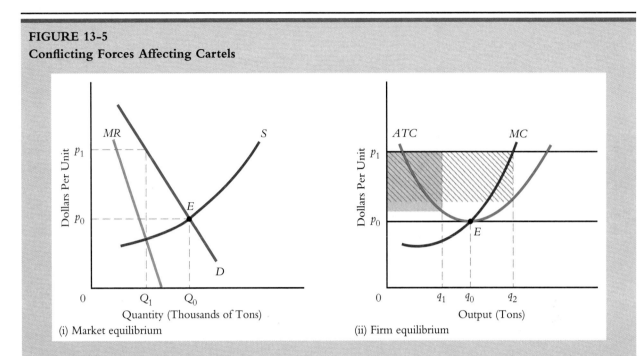

(i) Market equilibrium   (ii) Firm equilibrium

Cooperation leads to the monopoly price, but individual self-interest leads to production in excess of the monopoly output. Market conditions are shown in part (i), and the situation of a typical firm is shown in part (ii). (Note the change of scale between the two graphs.) Initially, the market is in competitive equilibrium with price p_0 and quantity Q_0. The individual firm is producing output q_0 and is just covering its total costs.

The cartel is formed and then enforces quotas on individual firms that are sufficient to reduce the industry's output to Q_1, the output where the supply curve cuts the marginal revenue curve. Q_1 is thus the output that maximizes the joint profits of the cartel members. Price rises to p_1 as a result. The typical firm's quota is q_1. The firm's profits rise from zero to the amount shown by the gray-shaded area in part (ii). Once price is raised to p_1, however, the individual firm would like to increase output to q_2, where marginal cost is equal to the price set by the cartel. This would allow the firm to earn profits, shown by the diagonally striped area. However, if all firms increase their outputs above their quotas, industry output will increase beyond Q_1, and the profits earned by all firms will fall.

Raw milk is often sold at one price when it is to be used as fluid milk but at a lower price when it is to be used to make ice cream or cheese. Doctors in private practise often charge for their services according to the incomes of their patients. Movie theaters often have lower admission prices for children than for adults. Railroads charge different rates per ton per mile for different products. Electric companies sell electricity at one rate to homes and at a lower rate to firms. Airlines often charge less to people who stay over a Saturday night than to those who come and go within the week.

Price discrimination occurs when a producer charges different prices for different units of the same commodity for reasons not associated with differences in cost. Not all price differences represent price *discrimination*. Quantity discounts, differences between wholesale and retail prices, and prices that vary with the time of day or the season of the year may not represent price discrimination, because the same product sold at a different time, in a different place, or in different quantities may have different costs. If an electric power company has unused capacity at certain times of the day, it may be cheaper for the company to provide service at those hours than at peak demand hours. If price differences reflect cost differences, they are not discriminatory.

When a price difference is based on different buyers' valuations of the same product, it is discriminatory. It does not cost a movie theater operator less to fill seats with children than with adults,

Box 13-2

The Importance of Entry

In most cities, there are many barber shops, and anyone who qualifies can set up as a barber. Suppose that in some town the going price for haircuts is $20 and that at this price all barbers believe their incomes are too low. The barbers hold a meeting and decide to form a *cartel* (which they call a "trade association"). They agree on the following points: First, all barbers in the city must join the association and abide by its rules; second, new barbers who meet certain professional qualifications will be required to join the association before practising their trade; third, the association will recommend a price for haircuts that no barber shall undercut. Their trade association has created a monopoly where previously there were many barbers who were free to compete with each other in any dimension, including price.

The barbers intend to raise the price of haircuts in order to raise their incomes. You are called in as a consulting economist to advise them of the probable success of their plan. Suppose you are persuaded that the organization does have the requisite strength to enforce a price rise to, say, $24. What are your predictions about the consequences?

You now need to distinguish between the short-run and the long-run effects of an increase in the price of haircuts. In the short run, the number of barbers is fixed. Thus, in the short run, the answer depends only on the elasticity of the demand for haircuts.

If the demand elasticity is less than 1, total expenditure on haircuts will rise and so will the incomes of barbers; if demand elasticity exceeds 1, the barbers' revenues will fall. Thus, you need some empirical knowledge about the elasticity of demand for haircuts.

Suppose that on the basis of the best available evidence you estimate the elasticity of demand over the relevant price range to be 0.50. You then predict that barbers will be successful in raising their incomes in the short run. A 20 percent rise in price will be met by a 10 percent fall in business, so the total revenue of the typical barber will rise by about 8 percent.*

Now what about the long run? If barbers were just covering their total costs before the price change, they will now be earning profits. Barbering will become an attractive trade relative to others requiring equal skill and training, and there will be a flow of barbers into the industry. As the number of barbers rises, the same amount of business must be shared among more and more barbers, so the typical barber will find business—and thus profits—decreasing. Profits may also be squeezed from another direction. With fewer customers coming their way, barbers may compete for the limited number of customers. The association does not allow them to compete through price cuts, but they can compete in service. They may spruce up their shops, offer their customers expensive magazines to read, and so forth. This kind of competition will raise operating costs.

Such changes will continue until barbers are just covering their opportunity costs, at which time there will be no further attraction for new entrants. The industry will settle down in a new long-run equilibrium in which individual barbers make incomes only as large as they did before the price rise. There will be more barbers than there were in the original situation, but each barber will be working for a smaller fraction of the day and will be idle for a larger fraction (the industry will have excess capacity). Barbers may prefer this situation; they will have more leisure. Customers may or may not prefer it. They will have shorter waits even at peak periods, and they will be able to read a wide range of magazines, but they will pay more for haircuts.

You were hired, however, to report to the barbers with respect to the effect on their incomes, not the effect on their leisure. The report that you finally present will thus say, "You will succeed in the short run (because your monopoly will face a demand curve that is inelastic), but your plan is bound to be self-defeating in the long run unless you are able to prevent the entry of new barbers."

---

*Let p and q be the price and quantity before the price increase. Total revenue after the increase is then given by TR = $(1.2p)(0.9q) = 1.08pq$.

but it may be worthwhile for the movie theater to let the children in at a discriminatory low price if few of them would attend at the full adult fare and if they take up seats that otherwise would be empty.

Why Price Discrimination Is Profitable

Why should a firm want to sell some units of its output at a price that is well below the price that it receives for other units of its output? The simple answer is because it is profitable to do so. Why should it be profitable?

Persistent price discrimination is profitable either because different buyers are willing to pay different amounts for the same commodity or because one buyer is willing to pay different amounts for different units of the same commodity. The basic point about price discrimination is that in either of these circumstances, sellers may be able to capture some of the consumers' surplus that would otherwise go to buyers.

Discrimination among units of output. Look back to Table 7-2 on page 141, which shows the consumers' surplus received by one consumer when she bought eight glasses of milk at a single price. If the firm could sell her each glass separately, it could capture this consumers' surplus. It would sell the first unit for $3.00, the second unit for $1.50, the third unit for $1.00, and so on until the eighth unit was sold for 30 cents. The firm would get total revenues of $8.10 rather than the $2.40 obtained from selling eight units at the single price of 30 cents each. In this example, the firm is able to discriminate perfectly and to extract the entire consumers' surplus.

Perfect price discrimination occurs when the entire consumers' surplus is obtained by the firm. This usually requires that each unit be sold at a separate price. In practise, perfect discrimination is seldom possible. Suppose, however, that the firm could charge two different prices, one for the first four units sold and one for the next four units sold. If it sold the first four units for 80 cents and the next four units for 30 cents, it would receive $4.40—less than it would receive if it could discriminate perfectly but more than it would receive if it sold all units at 30 cents.

Discrimination among buyers. Think of the demand curve in a market that is made up of individual buyers, each of whom has indicated the maximum price that he or she is prepared to pay for a single unit. Suppose, for the sake of simplicity, that there are only four buyers, the first of whom is prepared to pay any price up to $4, the second of whom is prepared to pay $3, the third, $2, and the fourth, $1. Suppose that the product has a marginal cost of production of $1 per unit for all units. If the selling firm is limited to a single price, it will maximize its profits by charging $3, selling two units, and earning profits of $4. If the seller can discriminate among each of the buyers, it could charge the first buyer $4 and the second $3, thus increasing its profits from the first two units to $5. Moreover, it could also sell the third unit for $2, thus increasing its profits to $6. It would be indifferent about selling a fourth unit because the price would just cover marginal cost.

Discrimination among markets. Let the monopoly firm sell in two different markets. For example, it might be the only seller in a tariff-protected home market, while in foreign markets it sells in competition with so many other firms that it is a price taker. In this case, the firm would equate its marginal cost to the price in the foreign market but to marginal revenue in the domestic market. As a result, it would charge a higher price on sales in the home market than on sales abroad.

Price discrimination more generally. Demand curves have a negative slope because different units are valued differently, either by one individual or by different individuals. This fact, combined with a single price for a product, gives rise to consumers' surplus.

The ability to charge multiple prices gives a seller the opportunity to capture some (or, in the extreme case, all) of the consumers' surplus.

In general, the larger the number of different prices that can be charged, the greater is the firm's ability to increase its revenue at the expense of consumers. This is illustrated in Figure 13-6.

It follows that if a selling firm is able to discriminate through price, it can increase revenues received (and thus also profits) from the sale of any

FIGURE 13-6
Price Discrimination

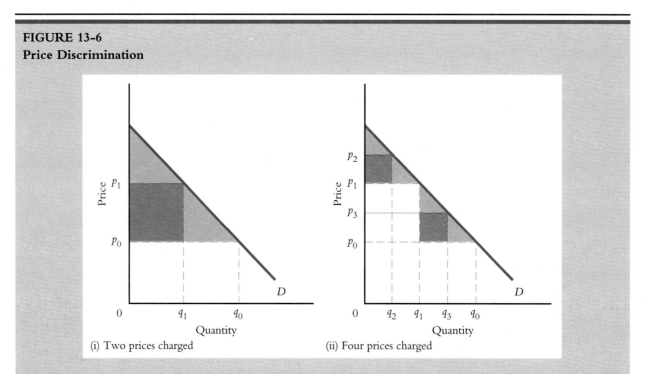

(i) Two prices charged   (ii) Four prices charged

Multiple prices permit a seller to capture consumers' surplus. Suppose in either graph that if a single price were charged, it would be the price p_0. Quantity q_0 would be sold, and consumers' surplus would be the entire area above p_0 and below the demand curve. Part (i) assumes that the market can be segregated in such a way that two prices are charged: p_1 for the first q_1 units and p_0 for the remaining $q_1 q_0$ units. Consumers' surplus is reduced to the two light blue triangles, and the seller's revenue is increased by the dark blue rectangle. Part (ii) assumes that the market can be segregated in such a way that four prices are charged: p_2 for the first q_2 units, p_1 for the units between q_2 and q_1, and so on. Consumers' surplus is further reduced to the light blue triangles, and the seller's revenue is further increased by the two dark blue rectangles. At the extreme, if a different price could be charged for each unit, producers could extract every bit of the consumers' surplus, and the price discrimination would be perfect.

given quantity. [28] However, price discrimination is not always possible, even if there are no legal barriers to its use.

When Is Price Discrimination Possible?

Discrimination among units of output sold to the same buyer requires that the seller be able to keep track of the units that a buyer consumes in each period. Thus, the tenth unit purchased by a given buyer in a given month can be sold at a price that is different from the fifth unit *only* if the seller can keep track of who buys what. This can be done by an electric company through its meter readings or by a magazine publisher by distinguishing between re-

newals and new subscriptions. It can also be done by distributing certificates or coupons that allow, for example, a car wash at a reduced price on a return visit.

Discrimination among buyers is not possible if the buyers who face the low price can easily resell the goods to the buyers who face the high price. For example, even though the local butcher might like to charge the banker twice as much for buying his steak as he charges the taxi driver, he cannot succeed in doing so. The banker can always shop for meat in the supermarket, where her occupation is not known. Even if the butcher and the supermarket agreed to charge her twice as much, she could hire the taxi driver to shop for her. However, the surgeon in private practise may succeed in discriminating (especially if other reputable surgeons do the same), because it will not do the banker much good to hire the taxi driver to have her operation for her.

Price discrimination is possible if the seller can either distinguish individual units bought by a single buyer or separate buyers so that resale among them is impossible.

The ability to prevent resale tends to be associated with the character of the product or the ability to classify buyers into readily identifiable groups. Services are less easily resold than goods; goods that require installation by the manufacturer (e.g., heavy equipment) are less easily resold than movable goods such as household appliances.

An interesting example of nonresalability occurs in the case of plate glass. Small pieces of plate glass are much cheaper to buy per square metre than bigger pieces, but the person who needs glass for a picture window that is 6 by 10 metres cannot use four pieces of glass that are 3 by 5 metres. Transportation costs, tariff barriers, and import quotas separate classes of buyers geographically and may make discrimination possible.

Of course, it is not enough to be able to separate different buyers or different units into separate classes. The seller must also be able to control the supply going to each group. There is no point, for example, in asking more than the competitive price from some buyers if they can simply go to other firms who sell the good at the competitive price.

Consequences of Price Discrimination

The consequences of price discrimination are summarized in the following two propositions.

Proposition 1: For any given level of output, the most profitable system of discriminatory prices will provide higher total revenue to the firm than the profit-maximizing single price.

This proposition, which was illustrated in Figure 13-6, requires only that the demand curve have a negative slope. To see that the proposition is plausible, remember that a monopolist with the power to discriminate could produce exactly the same quantity as a single-price monopolist and charge everyone the same price. Therefore, it need never receive *less* revenue, and it can do better if it can raise the price on even one unit sold, as long as the price need not be lowered on any other.

Proposition 2: Output under price discrimination will generally be larger than under a single-price monopoly.

Remember that a monopoly firm that must charge a single price for a product will produce less than would all the firms in a perfectly competitive industry, because it knows that selling more depresses its price. Price discrimination allows it to avoid this disincentive. To the extent that the firm can sell its output in separate blocks, it can sell another block without spoiling the market for the block that is already being sold. In the case of perfect price discrimination, in which every unit of output is sold at a different price, the profit-maximizing monopolist will produce every unit for which the price charged is greater than or equal to its marginal cost. It will therefore produce the same quantity as does the firm in perfect competition.

Normative Aspects of Price Discrimination

The predicted combination of higher average revenue and higher output does not in itself have any *normative* significance—it does not tell us if the result is good or bad, desirable or undesirable. The ability of the discriminating monopolist to capture some of the consumers' surplus will seem undesirable to consumers but not to the monopolist. How outsiders view the transfer may depend on who gains and who loses.

For instance, when railroads discriminated against farmers, the results aroused public anger. It seems acceptable to many, however, that doctors should practise price discrimination in countries where medical services are provided through the market, charging lower prices to poor patients than to wealthy ones. Nor does everyone disapprove when airlines discriminate by giving senior citizens and vacationers lower fares than business travelers.

Discrimination usually results in a higher output than would occur if a single price were charged. However, it also transfers income from buyers to sellers. When buyers are poor and sellers are rich, this may seem undesirable. Sometimes, however, it allows lower-income people to buy a product that they would be unable to afford if it were sold at the single profit-maximizing price.

SUMMARY

1. Monopoly is a market structure in which an entire industry is supplied by a single firm. The monopoly firm's own demand curve is identical with the market demand curve for the product. The market demand curve is the monopoly firm's average revenue curve, and its marginal revenue curve always lies below its demand curve.

2. When a single-price monopoly is maximizing its profits, marginal revenue is positive and thus elasticity of demand is greater than unity. The amount of profits that a monopoly earns may be large, small, zero, or negative in the short run, depending on the relationship between demand and cost. For monopoly profits to persist in the long run, there must be effective barriers to the entry of other firms. Entry barriers can be natural or created.

3. Monopoly power is limited by the presence of substitute products, the development of new products, and the entry of new firms. In the very long run, it is difficult to maintain entry barriers in the face of the process of creative destruction—the invention of new processes and new products to attack the entrenched position of existing monopolists.

4. A group of firms may form a cartel by agreeing to restrict their joint output to the monopoly level. Cartels tend to be unstable because of the strong incentives for each individual firm to cheat by producing more than its quota allows.

5. A price-discriminating monopolist can capture some of the consumers' surplus that exists when all of the units of a product are sold at a single price. Successful price discrimination requires that the firm be able to control the supply of the product offered to particular buyers and to prevent the resale of the product.

6. For any given level of output, a profit-maximizing monopolist who can enforce discriminatory prices will earn larger profits and produce higher output than will a single-price monopoly.

TOPICS FOR REVIEW

Relationship between price and marginal revenue for a monopolist

Relationships among marginal revenue, total revenue, and elasticity for a monopolist

Potential monopoly profits in perfectly competitive equilibrium

Natural and created entry barriers

Cartels as monopolies

Causes and consequences of price discrimination

DISCUSSION QUESTIONS

1. If you walk through the cabin of any commercial airliner traveling across Canada, you will find people who paid many different prices for the same trip: full-fare business class, round-the-world business class, full economy, various discount tickets, advanced seat sale and package tours (with even lower airfares). Does all of this represent price discrimination? Discuss the possible social value (positive or negative) of these differences.

2. Most provincial hydro authorities are state-owned monopolies. Should they be allowed to prohibit private manufacturers from

generating electricity for their own use if they can do so more cheaply than the hydro's price? What if the private firms want to sell their electricity to the local municipality for domestic use?

3. Three of the four U.S. companies that manufacture matzos—the unleavened bread eaten during the Jewish Passover celebration—recently combined to control 90 percent of the total market. When the owner of the new firm was approached by a marketing specialist about doing special promotions, the *New York Times* reported his reply to be "Why? We already own the market."

   What does this tell you about the new firm's attitude with respect to competitive behaviour? In analysing the firm's price output decisions, would it be reasonable to use monopoly theory? What does the quotation tell you about the firm's belief about the sensitivity of market demand to promotion schemes?

4. Imagine a monopoly firm that has fixed costs but no variable or marginal costs, for example, a firm that owns a spring of water that can produce indefinitely once certain pipes are installed in an area where no other source of water is available. What would be the firm's profit-maximizing price? What elasticity of demand would you expect at that price? Would this seem to be an appropriate pricing policy if the water monopoly were municipally owned?

5. Liquor retailing is a competitive industry in most U.S. states but a government monopoly in most Canadian provinces. In what ways would you expect the industry in the two countries to differ?

6. Airline rates to Europe are higher in summer than in winter. Railroads charge lower fares during the week than on weekends on some routes. Electric companies charge consumers lower rates the more electricity they use. Are these all examples of price discrimination? What additional information would you like to have before answering this question?

7. Discuss whether each of the following represents price discrimination. In your view, which are the most socially harmful?
   a. Weekend airline fares that are less than full fare.
   b. First-class fares that are 50 percent greater than tourist fares, recognising that two first-class seats use the space of three tourist seats.
   c. Discounts on car sales negotiated from list price, for which sales personnel are authorized to bargain and to get as much in each transaction as the traffic will bear.
   d. Higher tuition for out-of-province students at provincial colleges and universities.
   e. Higher tuition for medical students than for arts students.

14

Patterns of Imperfect Competition

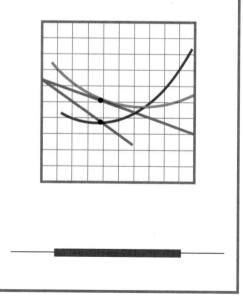

The two market structures that we have studied so far are important "polar" cases. They define the extremes of market power over an industry, just as the North and the South Poles define the limits of traveling north and traveling south. Under perfect competition, firms are price takers; price is driven to the level of marginal cost; and economic profits are zero, which means that firms are just covering the opportunity cost of their capital. Under monopoly, the firm is a price setter; it sets price above marginal cost, and it may earn more than the opportunity cost of its capital.

Although they provide important insights, these two polar theories are insufficient for an understanding of the behaviour of all Canadian firms.

The Structure of the Canadian Economy

Canada is a large, resource-rich country with a small population.[1] In area, it is the second largest in the world; in population, it is one of the smallest of the developed industrial nations. Much of Canadian industry is devoted directly to exploiting its rich resources, among them lumber, minerals, and power, and to producing products that depend on these resources, such as plywood, steel, and aluminum (an enormous user of power).

Because of the Canadian market's small size, many Canadian firms cannot grow to efficient size unless they can export a substantial part of their production. In the past, many inefficient small firms have survived only because of tariffs on imported goods. For this reason, Canadian industry has always had three main market sectors. The exporting sector is efficient enough to compete in foreign markets and thus achieve the scale of output needed to reap available economies of scale. The import-competing sector produces mainly for the local market, sometimes behind tariff protection and always in competition with foreign producers. The nontraded sector serves a local market that is protected from foreign competition by natural barriers of transport costs and perishability. (In this context, *traded* and *nontraded* refer to *foreign trade*.)

Over the whole of the twentieth century, reductions in transport costs, plus technological developments to reduce perishability, have steadily shrunk the nontraded goods sector until today there are few goods (and a shrinking number

---

[1]This section relies heavily on the excellent discussion of these topics in Christopher Green's *Canadian Industrial Organization and Policy* (Toronto: McGraw-Hill's Ryerson, 1990).

of services) that are not open to potential competition from imports.

Over the last half of the twentieth century, Canadian tariffs have been steadily reduced. As a result, industries that could not survive foreign competition have shrunk in size, while those that could compete have grown. Canadian industry is now able to compete in world markets in a wide range of goods. This expansion of sales through exports has caused falling costs, rising per capita outputs, and rising real wages for the typical employee.

The nontraded sector has often been characterized by large numbers of small competing firms. The industries in the (now shrinking) protected part of the economy have usually each been restricted to a few large, often foreign-owned firms that came to Canada to serve the tariff-protected home market. Many of the exporting industries contain only a few large firms, but these are often in active competition with firms in other countries. These large firms are often the major firms in older industries, usually producing established products but sometimes developing new ones. In other cases, exporters are small or medium-size firms.

Box 14-1 elaborates further on the globalisation of both production and competition that has affected all trading actions in the last two decades.

Turnover of Firms

One characteristic of market economies is constant change. As a result, new firms are continually coming into existence to produce new products. Typically, an entrepreneur will have a bright idea for a new product and raise money to finance the necessary research and development (R&D). This will be a "start-up" firm. *If* the entrepreneur succeeds (most fail), the firm will grow. Hence, at any one time in the manufacturing sector, small and middle-size firms coexist with large ones. Some of them are new and growing, while some of them are stable, having reached the size that can be supported by the market for the products that they produce.

Turnover of firms is high in market economies. Even in stable industries—at least those that have many firms—existing firms grow, prosper, and decay only to be replaced by other younger, more dynamic firms. The great English economist and observer of industry Alfred Marshall likened this

process to the life cycle of *trees* (firms) through birth, growth, and decay while the *forest* (the industry) remained stable in size. In growing industries, however, the process of firm turnover will result in a net addition to the size of the industry and possibly also to the number of firms. In declining industries, the reverse holds true. The important point to notice is the continual turnover of firms and jobs. In the Canadian economy, as in all market economies, firms are constantly being born and constantly dying. This means that jobs are constantly being created and constantly being destroyed.

Industrial Concentration

An industry that is highly concentrated contains few firms, whereas an industry that has a low degree of concentration contains many firms. You will recall that monopoly and perfect competition lie at the two extremes of concentration. A monopoly is an industry with only one firm, and perfect competition is an industry with so many firms that no one of them has any influence on market price. Most industries lie between these two extremes of concentration.

Concentration Ratios

When measuring whether an industry has power concentrated in the hands of only a few firms or dispersed over many, it is not sufficient to count the number of firms. For example, an industry with one enormous firm and 29 small ones is more concentrated in any meaningful sense than an industry with only five firms, all of which are of equal size. One way to get around the problem that number of firms is not a good criterion is to calculate what is called a **concentration ratio**, which shows the fraction of total market sales controlled by the largest group of sellers. Common types of concentration ratios cite the share of total market sales made by the largest four or eight firms.

A problem in using concentration ratios is to define the market with reasonable accuracy. On the one hand, the market may be much smaller than the whole country. For example, concentration ratios in national cement sales are low, but they understate the market power of cement companies because high transportation costs divide the cement *industry* into a series of regional *markets,* in each of which

Box 14-1

Globalisation of Production and Competition

Up until the last half of the nineteenth century, people and news traveled by sailing ship, so that it took months to communicate across various parts of the world. Advances since then have sped up both communications and travel, and people come to take them for granted. In the past three decades, the pace of change in communication technology has accelerated. The world has witnessed a communication revolution that has dramatically changed the way business decisions are made and implemented.

Three decades ago, telephone links were laboriously and unreliably connected by operators, satellites were newfangled and not especially useful toys for rocket scientists, photocopying and telecopying were completely unknown, mail services to overseas destinations took weeks, computers were in their infancy, and jets were just beginning to replace the much slower and less reliable propeller aircraft. Today, direct dialing is available to most parts of the world, at a fraction of what long distance calls cost 30 years ago, while faxes, satellite links, fast jet travel, computer networks, cheap courier services, and a host of other developments have made communication that is reliable, and often instantaneous, available throughout the world.

The communication revolution has been a major contributor to the development of what has become known as the "global village," a term first used by Canadian author Marshall McLuhan in his writing about the social implications of changes in communication technology.

Three important characteristics of the global village are the internationalization of production, an increase in competition, and a decline in the power of the nation-state.

Production

The communication revolution has allowed many large international companies, known as transnational corporations (TNCs), to decentralize their production processes. They are now able to locate their research and development (R&D) where the best scientists are available. They can produce various components in dozens of places, locating each activity in a country where costs are cheapest for that type of production. They can then ship all the parts, as they are needed, to an assembly factory where the product is "made."

The globalisation of production has brought employment and rising real wages to people in many less developed countries. At the same time, it has put less skilled labour in the developed countries under strong competitive pressures.

Competition

The communication revolution has also caused an internationalization of competition in almost all in-

there are relatively few firms. On the other hand, the market may be larger than one country. This is a particularly important consideration in a small trading country such as Canada. For example, a single Canadian firm in one industry does not have a monopoly if it is in competition with five U.S. firms that can easily sell in the Canadian market. When appropriately used, however, concentration ratios tell us how much production for a given market is concentrated in the hands of a few firms.

Concentration in Canada

According to McGill University professor Christopher Green, the concentration ratios that are typical dustries. National markets are no longer protected for local producers by high costs of transportation and communication or by the ignorance of foreign firms. Walk into a local supermarket or department store today, and you will have no trouble in finding products representing most of the countries in the United Nations.

Consumers gain by being able to choose from an enormous range of well-made, low-priced goods and services. Firms that are successful gain world-wide sales. Firms that fall behind even momentarily may, however, be wiped out by competition coming from many quarters. Global competition is fierce competition, and firms need to be fast on the uptake—either of other people's new ideas or of their own—if they are to survive.

A few short decades ago, many Canadian industries contained a few large firms that had little to worry about if they could restrain their urges to compete with each other. Today, there are few such industries. If Canadian producers slack off, they are likely to lose market shares to a host of foreign imports.

Economic Policy

The international character of TNCs means that national economic policies have been seriously constrained. Much international trade takes place between segments of single TNCs. This gives them the chance, through their accounting practises, to localize their profits in countries where corporate taxes are lowest and their costs in countries where cost writeoffs are highest.

The internalization of production also allows TNCs to shift production around the world. So tough national policies that reduce profitability may be self-defeating as firms move production elsewhere. Generous policies that seek to attract production may only succeed in attracting small and specialized parts of it. Sweden has given generous tax treatment to R&D expenditures, seeking to attract firms to do their high-tech, high-wage production in that country. Instead, however, many firms have come to Sweden to do their R&D and then have transferred the knowledge to countries where production costs are lower. The net result is that Swedish taxpayers are subsidizing world consumers by paying for R&D that is generating production in other countries.

The examples given here illustrate an important development: Globalisation of production, and consequently of competition, means a great reduction in the scope for relatively small countries, such as Canada, to implement distinctive economic policies.

of various sections of the Canadian economy differ greatly from one another. In agriculture, concentration ratios are very low. The market structure is close to perfect competition, except where government supply management has created cartels. In forestry, four firms account for 18 percent of the total sales, but the remainder is accounted for by numerous small firms. Most of these firms, large and small, sell in highly competitive international markets. In manufacturing, the degree of concentration ranges from very high to very low. In approximately half of all Canadian manufacturing industries, the top four firms control over 50 percent of the sales. In transportation, communication, and energy utilities, the degree of concentration is even higher. There are two firms in rail transportation and two main firms (with some fringe competitors) in air transport and in television networks. There is either monopoly or publicly owned firms in telecommunication, electric energy, and water and natural gas pipelines. Various parts of the wholesale trade have low to medium degrees of concentration, while in the retail trades, the ratios range from low to high. In community, business, and personal services, concentration tends to be quite low (except in small towns, where there are many natural monopolies). Finally, in insurance and real estate, concentration is quite low, while in the financial industries concentration is often high.

This is quite a varied story, and we can gain further insight into this experience of concentration by examining the manufacturing sector in greater detail.

Concentration in Canadian Manufacturing

Although similarities in standard of living, consumption patterns, and education in Canada and the United States have led to many similarities in industrial structure, the Canadian manufacturing sector is substantially more concentrated than the American. This is partly because the small size of the Canadian economy leaves room for fewer firms operating at minimum efficient scale than does the larger American economy. But the Canadian economy is a very open economy, and for many industries the relevant market is the combined Canadian-American market.

Three economists, John Baldwin and John McVey of Statistics Canada and Paul Gorecki now with the Northern Ireland Development Council, have corrected the published data to allow for foreign as well as domestic competition. They estimate market size on the basis of what is sold, whether or not it is produced in Canada, and the importance of one firm in that market is estimated on the basis of what it sells in that market no matter where these goods were produced.

Table 14-1 gives the results based on the published four-firm concentration ratios for Canada and the corrected figures derived by the three economists. It shows that when the corrections are made, the number of Canadian industries that have low concentration ratios rises and the number that

TABLE 14-1   Distribution of Concentration Ratios for 140 Canadian Manufacturing Industries

Concentration ratio categories	Industry count	
	Unadjusted ratio	Adjusted ratio
0–24.9	17	41
25–49.9	50	58
50–74.9	45	34
75–100	28	7
All industries	140	140

Source: John Baldwin, Paul Gorecki, and John McVey, Economic Council of Canada, manuscript.

The standard concentration ratios overstate the degree of concentration in Canadian industries. The first column shows the four-firm concentration ratio. For example, 0–24.9 indicates a low degree of concentration, since the four largest firms account for less than 25 percent of the sales, whereas 75–100 indicates a high level of concentration, with the four largest firms accounting for more than 75 percent of all sales. The second column gives the number of industries in each concentration ratio class according to the standard figures. The last column gives the distribution of the same industries when corrections are made for plants with multi-industry outputs and for the importance of imports in the Canadian market. When the corrected figures are substituted for the usual ones, the fall in measured concentration of the typical Canadian industry is striking.

have high ratios falls.[2]

The table shows that even with the corrected data, in about 70 percent of Canadian manufacturing industries, the four largest firms control over 25 percent of the value of sales. Such industries are not monopolies, because there are several firms in the industry, and these firms engage in rivalrous behaviour. But neither do these firms operate in perfectly competitive markets. Often there are only a few

---

[2]Although more recent estimates are not available, the main point of the table still holds: When the relevant international market is used, Canadian firms have much less market power than appears from an inspection solely of the Canadian section of the market.

major rival firms in an industry, but even when there are many, *they are not price takers.* Virtually all consumer goods are differentiated products, and any one firm will typically have several lines of a product that differ more or less from one another and from competing lines produced by other firms. To explain and predict behaviour in these markets, we need theories of market structures other than the two polar cases studied so far.

Imperfectly Competitive Market Structures

The market structures that we are now going to study are called *imperfectly competitive.* The word *competitive* emphasizes that we are not dealing with monopoly, and the word *imperfect* emphasizes that we are not dealing with perfect competition (in which firms do not compete actively against each other). What is referred to, then, is rivalrous competitive behaviour among firms that have a significant degree of market power.

We first note patterns of firm behaviour that are typical of imperfectly competitive market structures.

Firms Select Their Products

If a new farmer enters the wheat industry, the full range of products that can be produced is already in existence. In contrast, if a new firm enters the cigarette industry, that firm must decide on the characteristics of the new cigarettes that it is to produce. It will not produce cigarettes that are identical to those already in production. Rather, it will develop, possibly at substantial cost, one or more new cigarettes, each of which will have its own distinctive characteristics. As a result, firms in the cigarette industry sell an array of differentiated products, no two of which are identical.

The term **differentiated product** refers to a group of commodities that are similar enough to be called the same product but dissimilar enough that they can be sold at different prices. For example, although one brand of face soap is similar to most others, soaps differ from each other in their chemical composition, colour, smell, softness, brand name, reputation, and a host of other characteristics that matter to customers. So all face soaps taken together are one differentiated product.

Most (but not all) firms in imperfectly competitive market structures sell differentiated products. In such industries, the firm itself must decide on what characteristics to give the products that it will sell. Having done so, it must then develop such a product and market it.

Firms Choose Their Prices

Because firms in perfect competition sell a homogeneous product, they face a market price that they are quite unable to influence. So they adjust their quantities to this price (firms are price takers and quantity adjusters).

In all other market structures, firms have negatively sloped demand curves and thus face a tradeoff between the price that they charge and the quantity that they sell. Whenever different firms' products are not perfect substitutes, the firms must decide on a price to quote. For example, no market sets a single price for razor blades or television sets by equating overall demand with overall supply. What is true for razor blades and for television sets is true for virtually all consumer goods and many capital goods. Any one manufacturer will typically have several product lines that differ more or less from each other and from the competing product lines of other firms. Each product has a price that must be set by its maker. Of course, a certain amount of haggling is possible, particularly at the retail level, but this is usually within well-defined limits set by the price charged by the manufacturer.

In such circumstances, economists say that firms *administer* their price. An **administered price** is a price set by the conscious decision of an individual firm rather than by impersonal market forces. Firms that administer their prices are said to be **price makers.**

Each firm has expectations about the quantity it can sell at each price that it might set. *Unexpected* market fluctuations then cause unexpected variations in the quantities that are sold at the administered prices.

In market structures other than perfect competition, firms set their prices and then let demand determine sales. Changes in market conditions are signaled to the firm by changes in the quantity that the firm sells at its current administered price.

The changed conditions may or may not then lead firms to change their prices.

Short-run price stability. One striking contrast between perfectly competitive markets, on the one hand, and markets for differentiated products, on the other hand, concerns the behaviour of prices. In perfect competition, prices change continually in response to changes in demand and supply. In markets where differentiated manufactured products are sold, prices change less frequently. Manufacturers' prices for automobiles, radios, television sets, and men's suits do not change with anything like the frequency that prices change in markets for basic materials or stocks and bonds. (Retail markups are, however, more often varied in response to short-term fluctuations in market conditions.)

Modern firms that sell differentiated products typically have hundreds, and sometimes even thousands, of distinct products on their price lists. Changing such a long list of administered prices at the same frequency that competitive market prices change would be physically impossible. Changing them at all involves costs. These include the costs of printing new list prices and notifying all customers, the difficulty of keeping track of frequently changing prices for purposes of accounting and billing, and the loss of customer and retailer goodwill due to the uncertainty caused by frequent changes in prices. These costs are often a significant consideration to multiproduct manufacturing firms.

Because producers of differentiated products must administer their own prices, firms must decide on the *frequency* with which they change these prices. In making this decision, the firm will balance the cost of making price changes against the revenue lost by not making price changes. Clearly, the likelihood that the firm will make costly price changes rises with the size of the disturbance to which it is adjusting and the probability that the disturbance will not be reversed.

Thus, transitory fluctuations in demand may be met by changing output with prices constant, while increases in costs that accompany inflation and reductions that accompany major technological changes tend to be passed on fairly rapidly through price changes. Because few firms expect inflationary price increases to be reversed, they know that they must raise their prices to cover them. Even in these cases, however, they do so periodically, rather than continuously, because of the costs incurred in making such changes. Intense rivalry among competing firms tends to drive prices down when technological developments reduce costs.

Other Aspects of the Behaviour of Firms

Several other important aspects of the observed behaviour of firms in imperfect competition could not occur under either perfect competition or monopoly.

Nonprice competition. Many firms spend large sums of money on advertising. They do so in an attempt both to shift the demand curves for the industry's products and to attract customers from competing firms. Many firms engage in a variety of other forms of nonprice competition, such as offering competing standards of quality and product guarantees. Any kind of sales-promotion activity undertaken by a single firm would not happen under perfect competition; any such scheme directed at competing firms in the same industry is, by definition, inconsistent with monopoly.

Unexploited scale economies. Many firms in industries that contain more than one firm appear to be operating on the downward-sloping portions of the long-run average cost curves for many of the individual product lines that they produce. Although this is possible under monopoly, firms in perfect competition must, in the long run, be at the minimum point of their long-run average cost curves. (See Figure 12-10 on page 231.)

One set of reasons is found in high development costs and short product lives. Many modern products involve large development costs. For example, it will cost roughly $1 billion just to design the wing of the new McDonnell Douglas airliner! Today, many products are only sold for a few years before being replaced by a new, superior product. For example, the CEO of a large telecommunication firm recently stated that 80 percent of the products his firm sells today did not exist five years ago! In such cases, firms face steeply falling long-run average total cost curves. The more units that are sold, the less are the fixed development costs per unit. Given perfect competition, these firms would go on increasing outputs and sales until rising marginal costs of production balanced the falling fixed unit costs. As it is, they cannot sell all they would like to at the going price, and they often produce on the falling portion of their average total cost curves all through the product's life cycle.

Entry prevention. Firms in many industries engage in activities that are designed to hinder the entry of new firms, thereby preventing existing pure profits from being eroded by entry. We will consider these activities in much more detail later in the chapter.

Monopolistic Competition

The theory of **monopolistic competition** was originally developed to deal with the phenomenon of product differentiation.[3] This market structure is similar to perfect competition in that the industry contains many firms and exhibits freedom of entry and exit. It differs, however, in one important respect. Whereas firms in perfect competition sell a *homogeneous product* and are price takers, firms in monopolistic competition sell a differentiated product and have some power over the price of their own product.

Product differentiation leads to, and is enhanced by, the establishment of brand names and advertising, and it gives each firm a degree of monopoly power over its own product. Each firm can raise its price, even if its competitors do not, without losing all its sales. This is the monopolistic part of the theory. However, each firm's monopoly power is se-

verely restricted in both the short run and the long run. The short-run restriction comes from the presence of similar products sold by many competing firms; this causes each firm's demand curve to be much more elastic than the industry's demand curve. The long-run restriction comes from free entry into the industry. These restrictions comprise the competition part of the theory.

Assumptions of the Theory

The theory of monopolistic competition is based on three key assumptions.

1. *Each firm produces one specific variety, or brand, of the industry's differentiated product.* Each firm thus faces a demand curve that, although it is negatively sloped, is highly elastic, because other varieties of the same product that are sold by other firms provide many close substitutes.
2. *The industry contains so many firms that each one ignores the possible reactions of its many competitors when it makes its own price and output decisions.* There are too many firms for it to be possible for any one firm to try to take the other firms' separate reactions into account. In this way, firms in monopolistic competition are similar to firms in perfect competition. They make decisions based on their own demand and cost conditions and do not consider interdependence between their own decisions and those of the other firms in the industry. This is the key aspect that distinguishes the market structure of monopolistic competition from the market structure of oligopoly, which we discuss later in the chapter.
3. *There is freedom of entry and exit in the industry.* If profits are being earned by existing firms, new firms have an incentive to enter. When they do, the demand for the industry's product must be shared among more brands, and this is assumed to take demand equally from all existing firms.

Predictions of the Theory

Product differentiation, which is the only thing that makes monopolistic competition different from per-

---

[3]This theory was first developed by the U.S. economist Edward Chamberlin in his pioneering book, *The Theory of Monopolistic Competition* (Cambridge, MA: Harvard University Press, 1933).

fect competition, has important consequences for behaviour in both the short and the long run.

The Short-Run Equilibrium of the Firm

In the short run, a firm that is operating in a monopolistically competitive market structure is similar to a monopoly. It faces a negatively sloped demand curve and maximizes its profits by equating marginal cost with marginal revenue. If the demand curve cuts the average total cost curve, as is shown in part (i) of Figure 14-1, the firm can make profits over and above the opportunity cost of its capital.

The Long-Run Equilibrium of the Industry

Profits, as shown in part (i) of Figure 14-1, provide an incentive for new firms to enter the industry. As they do so, the total demand for the industry's product must be shared among this larger number of firms, so each gets a smaller share of the total market. This shifts the demand curve for each existing firm's product to the left. Entry, and the consequent leftward shifting of the existing firms' demand curves, continues until profits are eliminated. When this has occurred, each firm is in the position shown in part (ii) of Figure 14-1. Its demand curve has shifted to the left until the curve is *tangent* to the average total cost curve. At this output, the firm is just covering all of its costs. At any other output, it would be suffering losses, because average total costs would exceed average revenue.

To see why this "tangency solution" provides the only possible equilibrium, consider the two possible alternatives. First, suppose that the demand curve *nowhere touched* the average total cost curve. There would then be no output at which costs could be covered, and exit would occur. Second, suppose that the demand curve *cut* the average total cost curve. There would then be a range of output over which profits could be earned, and entry would occur.

The excess capacity theorem. Part (ii) of Figure 14-1 makes it clear that monopolistic competition results in a long-run equilibrium of zero profits, even though each individual firm faces a negatively sloped demand curve. It does this by forcing each firm into a position in which it has excess capacity; that is, each firm is producing an output less than that corresponding to the lowest point on its average total cost curve. If the firm were to increase its output, it would reduce its cost per unit, but it does

not do so, because selling more would reduce revenue by more than it would reduce cost. This result is often called the **excess capacity theorem.**

In monopolistic competition, commodities are produced at a point where average total costs are falling, in contrast to perfect competition, where they are produced at their lowest possible cost.

Evaluation of the Theory

Alleged Inefficiency

The excess capacity theorem once aroused passionate debate among economists because it seemed to show that all industries that sell differentiated products would produce them inefficiently at a higher cost than was necessary. Because product differentiation is a characteristic of virtually all modern consumer goods industries, this suggested that modern market economies were systematically inefficient. A few decades ago, many critics of market economies called for state intervention to eliminate unnecessary product differentiation, thus ensuring efficient (i.e., cost-minimizing) levels of production in consumer goods industries.

Subsequent analysis by economists such as William Baumol, Kelvin Lancaster, and Joseph Stiglitz has shown that the charge of inefficiency has not been proved. The "excess capacity" of monopolistic competition does not necessarily indicate inefficiency (and hence waste of resources), because when firms can choose the characteristics of their own products, minimizing the costs of producing a *given set of products* is not necessarily the most efficient thing to do. Differentiated products provide consumers with a choice among a variety of products, and it is clear that consumers have different tastes and needs with respect to differentiated products.

From society's point of view, there is a trade-off between producing more brands to satisfy diverse tastes and producing fewer brands at a lower cost per unit.

Monopolistic competition produces a wider range of products but at a somewhat higher cost per unit than perfect competition. Consumers clearly

FIGURE 14-1
Equilibrium of a Firm in Monopolistic Competition

(i) Short-run equilibrium

(ii) Long-run equilibrium

Short-run equilibrium for a monopolistically competitive firm is the same as for a monopolist. In the long run, a monopolistically competitive industry has zero profits and excess capacity. Short-run equilibrium occurs in part (i) at E_S, the output for which $MR = MC$. Price is p_S and quantity is q_S. Profits may exist; in this example they are shown by the shaded area. Starting from the short-run equilibrium shown in part (i), entry of new firms shifts the firm's demand curve to the left and eliminates profits. In part (ii), point E_L, where demand is tangent to ATC, is the long-run equilibrium. Price is p_L and quantity is q_L. Price is greater and quantity is less than the perfectly competitive equilibrium price and quantity (p_C and q_C). At equilibrium, the monopolistically competitive firm has excess capacity of $q_L q_C$.

value variety, so the benefits of variety must be matched against the extra cost that variety imposes in order to find the socially *optimal* amount of product differentiation. Product differentiation is wasteful only if the costs of providing variety exceed the benefits conferred by providing that variety.

The optimal number of varieties of a differentiated product is attained when the gain to consumers from adding one more variety equals the loss from having to produce each existing variety at a higher cost because less of each is produced.

Depending on consumers' tastes and firms' costs, monopolistic competition may result in too much, too little, or the optimal amount of product variety.

Empirical Relevance

Controversy raged for decades as to the empirical relevance of monopolistic competition. Of course, product differentiation is an almost universal phenomenon in consumer goods and in many other

industries. Nonetheless, many economists maintain that this market structure is seldom found in practise.

To see why they argue in this way, we need to distinguish between products and firms. In many manufacturing industries, numerous differentiated products are produced by only a few firms. In breakfast foods, for example, a vast variety of products is produced by three major firms (Kellogg's, Nabisco, and General Foods). Similar circumstances exist in soap, chemicals, cigarettes, consumer electronics, and numerous other industries in which *many* similar products are produced by *a few* very large firms. Clearly, these industries are neither perfectly competitive nor monopolies. Are they monopolistically competitive? The answer is no, because they contain only a few firms that often take account of one another's reactions when they are determining their own behaviour (thus violating the second assumption listed above). Furthermore, they often earn large profits without attracting new entrants (thus violating the third assumption listed above). In fact, these firms operate under a market structure that is called *oligopoly*, which we shall consider in the next section.

While accepting that many differentiated products are produced by industries that are not monopolistically competitive, some economists find that the theory of monopolistic competition is useful for analysing industries where concentration ratios are low and the product is differentiated, such as restaurants and gas stations.

Oligopoly

Many Canadian industries are characterized by a small number of firms, each of which accounts for a significant fraction of Canadian production. The market structure that embraces such industries is called *oligopoly*, from the Greek words *oligos polein*, meaning "few to sell." An **oligopoly** is an industry that contains two or more firms, at least one of which produces a significant portion of the industry's total output. Whenever there is a high concentration ratio for the firms that are serving one particular market, that market is oligopolistic.

Characteristics of Oligopoly

The market structures of oligopoly, monopoly, and monopolistic competition are similar in that firms in all of these markets face negatively sloped demand curves.

In contrast to a monopoly (which has no competitors) and to a monopolistically competitive firm (which has many competitors), an oligopolistic firm faces a few competitors. The number of competitors is small enough for each firm to realize that its competitors may respond to anything it does and that it should take such possible responses into account. In other words, oligopolists are aware of the interdependence among the decisions made by the various firms in the industry, and they engage in the type of rivalrous behaviour discussed on page 227.

This is the key difference between oligopolists on the one hand and perfect or monopolistic competitors, and monopolies, on the other hand. Oligopolists are aware of their impact on competing firms and they may take their competitors' expected reactions into account when deciding on any course

of action. We say that they engage in **strategic behaviour,** which means that they take explicit account of the impact of their decisions on competing firms and of the reactions they expect competing firms to make. In contrast, firms in perfect competition engage in **nonstrategic behaviour,** which means they make decisions based on their own costs and their own demand curves without considering any possible reactions from their large number of competitors. Monopolists also do not engage in strategic behaviour; this, however, is because they have no competitors rather than too many.

Oligopolistic industries are of many types. In some industries, there are only a few firms (three, in the case of cigarettes). In others, there are many firms, but only a few dominate the market. For example, there are 38 manufacturers of mixed fertilizers, of which the largest four account for 70 percent of total sales. In still other cases, there are many firms and although the largest have significant shares, they do not dominate the market. For example, there are 36 manufacturers of refined petroleum products, but the four largest firms together account for only about one third of the aggregate value of output. Oligopoly is consistent with a large number of small sellers, called a "competitive fringe," as long as a "big few" dominate the industry's production.

In oligopolistic industries, prices are typically administered. Products are usually differentiated. The intensity and the nature of rivalrous behaviour vary greatly from industry to industry and from one period of time to another. This variety has invited extensive theorizing and empirical study.

Why Bigness?

Several factors contribute to explaining why so many industries are dominated by a few large firms. Some are "natural," and some are created by the firms themselves.

Natural Causes of Bigness

Economies of scale.   Much factory production uses the principle of the division of labour that we first studied in Chapter 3. The production of a commodity is broken up into hundreds of simple, repetitive tasks. This type of division of labour is the basis of the assembly line, which revolutionized the production of many goods in the early twentieth century, and it still underlies economies of large-scale production in many industries. Such division of labour is, as Adam Smith observed long ago, dependent on the size of the market (see Box 3-2 on page 46). If only a few units of a product can be sold each day, there is no point in dividing its production into a number of tasks, each of which can be done in a few minutes. So big firms with large sales have an advantage over small firms with small sales whenever there is great scope for economies based on an extensive division of labour.

Economies of scope. Modern industries produce many differentiated products that give rise to a different type of large-scale advantage. To develop a new product is costly, and it may be only a matter of a few years before it is replaced by some superior version of the same basic product. These fixed costs of product development must be recovered in the revenues from sales of the product. The larger the firm's sales, the less the cost that has to be recovered from each unit sold. Consider a product that costs $1 million to develop and to market. If 1 million units are to be sold, $1 of the selling price of each unit must go toward recovering the development costs. If, however, the firm expects to sell 10 million units, each unit need only contribute 10 cents to these costs, and the market price can be lowered accordingly. With the enormous development costs of some of today's high-tech products, firms that can sell a large volume have a distinct pricing advantage over firms that sell a smaller volume.

Other scope economies are related to financing and to marketing. It is costly to enter a market, to establish a sales force, and to make consumers aware of a product. These costs are often nearly as high when a small volume is being marketed as when a large volume is being marketed. Thus the smaller the volume of the firm's sales, the higher the price must be if the firm is to cover all of these costs. Notice that these economies, which are related to the size of the firm, are related neither to the amount the firm produces of any one of its differentiated products, nor to the size of any one of its plants. Economies that depend on the overall size of the *firm* rather than on the size of its *plants* or the volume of production of any one commodity are called the **economies of scope.**

Where size confers a cost advantage either through economies of scale or of scope, there may be room for only a few firms, even when the total market is quite large. This cost advantage of size will dictate that the industry be an oligopoly, unless government regulation prevents the firms from growing to their efficient size.

Firm-Created Causes of Bigness

The number of firms in an industry may be decreased while the average size of the survivors rises due to *strategic behaviour* of the firms themselves. Firms may grow by buying out rivals (acquisitions), or merging with them (mergers), or by driving rivals into bankruptcy through predatory practises. This process increases the size and market shares of the survivors and may, by reducing competitive behaviour, allow them to earn larger profit margins.

The surviving firms must then be able to create and sustain barriers to entry where natural ones do not exist. The industry will then be dominated by a few large firms only because they are successful in preventing the entry of new firms that would lower the industry's concentration ratio.

Is Bigness Natural or Firm Created?

Most observers would agree that the general answer to the question posed in the heading to this section is "some of both." Some industries have high concentration ratios because the efficient size of the firm is large relative to the overall size of the industry's market. Other industries may have higher concentration ratios than efficiency considerations would dictate because the firms are seeking enhanced market power through size and entry restriction. The issue that is debated is the relative importance of these two forces, one coming from the efficiencies of large scale and scope and the other coming from the desire of firms to create market power by growing large.

Harvard economist Alfred D. Chandler, Jr., is a champion of the view that the major reason for the persistence of oligopolies in the manufacturing sector is the efficiency of large-scale production. His monumental work *Scale and Scope: The Dynamics of Industrial Capitalism*[4] argues this case in great detail for the United States, the United Kingdom, and Germany.

---

[4]A. D. Chandler, Jr., *Scale and Scope: The Dynamics of Industrial Capitalism* (Cambridge, MA: Harvard University Press, 1990).

U.S. antitrust law is based on the presumption that large size is undesirable and not justified by the benefits of scale and scope economies. If Chandler is right, however, size efficiency is the most important reason for high concentration ratios and, although strategic reasons are probably important in some cases, they are of secondary importance as an overall explanation. Canadian anticombines policy is more in line with Chandler's views, since the policy condemns neither size nor high market shares per se.

The Basic Dilemma of Oligopoly

Oligopoly behaviour is necessarily *strategic behaviour.* In deciding on strategies, oligopolists face a basic dilemma between competing and cooperating.

The firms in an oligopolistic industry will make more profits as a group if they cooperate; any one firm, however, may make more profits for itself if it defects while the others cooperate.

This result is similar to the one established in Chapter 13 for the cartelization of a perfectly competitive industry.[5] In a perfectly competitive industry, however, there are so many firms that they cannot reach the cooperative solution unless some central governing body is formed, by either themselves or the government, to force the necessary behaviour on all firms. In contrast, the few firms in an oligopolistic industry will themselves recognise the possibility of cooperating to avoid the loss of profits that will result from competitive behaviour.

The cooperative solution. If the firms in an oligopolistic industry cooperate, either overtly or tacitly, to produce among themselves the monopoly output, they can maximize their joint profits. If they do this, they will reach what is called a **coop-**

erative solution, which is the position that a single monopoly firm would reach if it owned all the firms in the industry.

The noncooperative equilibrium. We have seen that if all the firms in an oligopolistic industry are at the cooperative solution, it will usually be worthwhile for any one of them to cut its price or to raise its output, as long as the others do not do so. However, if everyone does the same thing, they will be worse off as a group and may all be worse off individually. An equilibrium that is reached by firms when they proceed by calculating only their own gains, without considering the reactions of others, is called a **noncooperative equilibrium.**

An Example from Game Theory

The **theory of games** is a study of rational decision making in situations in which a number of players compete, knowing that other players will react to their moves, and taking account of their expected reactions when making moves. For example, firm A asks: "Shall I raise or lower my price or leave it unchanged?" Before arriving at an answer it asks: "What will the other firms do in each of these cases, and how will their actions affect the profitability of whatever decision I make?"

When game theory is applied to oligopoly, the players are firms, their game is played in the market, their strategies are their price or output decisions, and the payoffs are their profits.

A game-theory illustration of the basic dilemma of oligopolists, to cooperate or to compete, is shown in Figure 14-2 for the case of a two-firm oligopoly, called a **duopoly.** The simplified game, adopted for the purposes of illustration, allows only two strategies for *each firm:* Produce an output equal to one half of the monopoly output or two thirds of the monopoly output. Even this simple game, however, is sufficient to illustrate several key ideas in the modern theory of oligopoly.

Figure 14-2 presents what is called a *payoff matrix.* The data in the matrix show that if both sides cooperate, *each producing* one half of the monopoly output, they achieve the cooperative solution and jointly earn the monopoly profits by *jointly producing*

---

[5]The basic reason is that when only one firm increases its output by 1 percent, the price falls by less than when all firms do the same. Thus, when the point is reached at which profits will be *reduced* if all firms expand output together, it will still pay one firm to expand output *if* the others do not do the same.

FIGURE 14-2
The Oligopolist's Dilemma: To Cooperate or to Compete

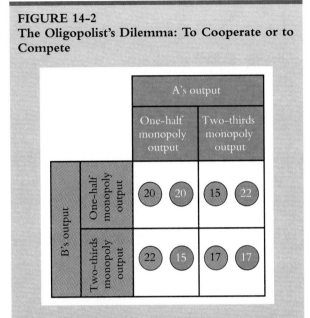

Cooperation to determine the overall level of output can maximize joint profits, but it leaves each firm with an incentive to alter its production. The figure gives what is called a payoff matrix for a two-firm duopoly game. Only two levels of production are considered in order to illustrate the basic problem. A's production is indicated across the top, and its profits (measured in millions of dollars) are shown in the blue circles within each square. B's production is indicated down the left side, and its profits (in millions of dollars) are shown in the red circles within each square. For example, the top right square tells us that if B produces one-half, while A produces two thirds, of the output that a monopolist would produce, A's profits will be $22 million, while B's will be $15 million.

If A and B cooperate, each produces one half the monopoly output and earns profits of $20 million, as shown in the upper left box. However, at that position, known as the cooperative solution, each firm can raise its profits by producing two thirds of the monopoly output, provided that the other firm does not do the same.

Now assume that A and B make their decisions noncooperatively. A reasons that whether B produces either one half or two thirds of the monopoly output, A's best output is two-thirds. B reasons similarly. In this case they reach the noncooperative equilibrium, where each produces two thirds of the monopoly output, and each makes less than it would if the two firms cooperated.

the output that a monopolist would produce. As a group, they can do no better.

Once the cooperative position is attained, the data in the figure show that if A cheats and produces more, its profits will increase. However, B's profits will be reduced: A's behaviour drives the industry's prices down, so B earns less from its unchanged output. Because A's cheating takes the firms away from the joint profit-maximizing monopoly output, their joint profits must fall. This means that B's profits fall by more than A's rise.

Figure 14-2 shows that similar considerations also apply to B. It is worthwhile for B to depart from the joint maximizing output, as long as A does not do so. So both A and B have an incentive to depart from the joint profit-maximizing level of output.

Finally, Figure 14-2 shows that when either firm does depart from the joint-maximizing output, the other has an incentive to do so as well. When each follows this selfish strategy, they reach a noncooperative equilibrium at which they jointly produce one and a third times as much as the monopolist would. Each then has profits that are lower than at the cooperative solution.

Nash equilibrium. The noncooperative equilibrium shown in Figure 14-2 is called a *Nash equilibrium*, after the U.S. mathematician John Nash, who developed the concept in the 1950s. A **Nash equilibrium** is one in which each firm's best strategy is to maintain its present behaviour *given the present behaviour of the other firms.*

It is easy to see that there is one Nash equilibrium in Figure 14-2. In the bottom-right cell, the best decision for each firm, given that the other firm is producing two thirds of the monopoly output, is to produce two thirds of the monopoly output itself. Between them, they produce a joint output of one and a third times the monopoly output. Neither firm has an incentive to depart from this position, except through cooperation with the other. In any other cell, each firm has an incentive to alter its output *given the output of the other firm.*[6]

---

[6]The cooperative position or solution is not an equilibrium, only what results if everyone does cooperate. In contrast, the Nash equilibrium is a genuine equilibrium because each individual firm following its own self interest has no incentive to move away from it once it is established.

The basis of a Nash equilibrium is rational decision making in the absence of cooperation. Its particular importance in oligopoly theory is that it is the only type of self-policing equilibrium. It is self-policing in the sense that there is no need for group behaviour to enforce it. Each firm has a self-interest to maintain it, because no move will improve its profits, given what other firms are currently doing.

If a Nash equilibrium is established—by any means whatsoever—no firm has an incentive to depart from it by altering its own behaviour.

Strategic behaviour. We have seen how the Nash equilibrium in Figure 14-2 can be arrived at when firms cheat on an agreement to reach the cooperative solution. The same equilibrium will be attained if each firm behaves strategically by choosing its optimal strategy, taking into account what the other firm may do. Let us see how this works.

Suppose that firm A reasons as follows: "B can do one of two things; what is the best thing for me to do in each case? First, what if B produces one half of the monopoly output? If I do the same, I receive a profit of 20, but if I produce two thirds of the monopoly output, I receive 22. Second, what if B produces two thirds of the monopoly output? If I produce one half of the monopoly output, I receive a profit of 15, whereas if I produce two thirds, I receive 17. Clearly, my best strategy is to produce two thirds of the monopoly output in either case."

B will reason in the same way.

As a result, they end up producing one and a third times the monopoly output between themselves, and each earns a profit of 17.

Cooperation or Competition?

We have seen that although oligopolists have an incentive to cooperate, they may be driven, through their own individual decisions, to produce more and earn less than they would if they cooperated. Our next step is to look in more detail at the types of cooperative and competitive behaviour that oligopolists may adopt. We can then go on to study the forces that influence the balance between cooperation and competition in actual situations.

Types of Cooperative Behaviour

When firms agree to cooperate in order to restrict output and to raise prices, their behaviour is called **collusion.** Collusive behaviour may occur with or without an actual agreement to collude. Where explicit agreement occurs, economists speak of *overt* or *covert collusion,* depending on whether the agreement is open or secret. Where no explicit agreement actually occurs, economists speak of **tacit collusion.** In this case, all firms behave cooperatively without an explicit agreement to do so. They merely understand that it is in their mutual interest to restrict output and to raise prices.

In terms of Figure 14-2, Firm A decides to produce one half of the monopoly output, hoping that Firm B will do the same. Firm B does what A expects, and they achieve the cooperative equilibrium without ever explicitly cooperating.

Explicit cooperation. The easiest way for firms to ensure that they will all maintain their joint profit-maximizing output is to make an explicit agreement to do so. Such collusive agreements have occurred in the past, although they have been illegal among privately owned firms in Canada for a long time. When they are discovered today, they are rigorously prosecuted. We shall see, however, that such agreements are not illegal everywhere in the world, particularly when they are supported by national governments.

We saw in Chapter 13 that when a group of firms gets together to act in this way, it is called a *cartel.* Cartels show in stark form the basic conflict between cooperation and competition that we just discussed. Full cooperation always allows the industry to achieve the result of monopoly. It also always presents individual firms with the incentive to cheat. The larger the number of firms, the greater the temptation for any one of them to cheat. After all, the cheating of one small firm may not be noticed, because it will have a negligible effect on price. The problems all cartels face are seen most vividly, therefore, in the case that we studied in Chapter 13, in which the number of firms is so large that most of them are price takers. This is why cartels that involve firms in industries that would otherwise be perfectly competitive tend to be unstable.

Cartels may also be formed by a group of firms that would otherwise be in an oligopolistic market.

The smaller the group of firms that forms a cartel, the more likely that the firms will let their joint interest in cooperating guide their behaviour. Although cheating may still occur, the few firms in the industry can easily foresee the outcome of an outbreak of rivalrous behaviour among themselves.

The most famous modern example of a cartel that encourages explicit cooperative behaviour among oligopolists is the Organization of Petroleum Exporting Countries (OPEC). This cartel is discussed in more detail in Box 14-2.

Tacit cooperation. While collusive behaviour that affects prices is illegal, a small group of firms that recognise the influence that each has on the others may act without any explicit agreement to achieve the cooperative equilibrium. In such *tacit* agreements, the two forces that push toward cooperation and competition are still evident.

First, firms have a common interest in cooperating to maximize their joint profits at the cooperative solution. Second, each firm is interested in its own profits, and any one of them can usually increase its profits by behaving competitively.

Types of Competitive Behaviour

Although the most obvious way for a firm to violate the cooperative solution is to produce more than its share of the joint profit-maximizing output, there are other ways in which rivalrous behaviour can break out.

Competition for market shares. Even if *joint* profits are maximized, there is the problem of market shares. How is the profit-maximizing level of sales to be divided among the competing firms? Competition for market shares may upset the tacit agreement to hold to joint-maximizing behaviour. Firms often compete for market shares through various forms of nonprice competition, such as advertising and variations in the quality of their product. Such costly competition may reduce industry profits.

Covert cheating. In an industry that has many differentiated products and in which sales are often by contract between buyers and sellers, covert rather than overt cheating may seem attractive. Secret discounts and rebates can allow a firm to increase its sales at the expense of its competitors while appearing to hold to the tacitly agreed monopoly price.

Very-long-run competition. As we first discussed in Chapter 11, very-long-run considerations may also be important. When technology and product characteristics change constantly, there may be advantages to behaving competitively. A firm that behaves competitively may be able to maintain a larger market share and earn larger profits than it would if it cooperated with the other firms in the industry, even though all the firms' joint profits are lower. In our world of constant change, a firm that thinks it can *keep* ahead of its rivals through innovation has an incentive to compete even if that competition lowers the joint profits of the whole industry. Such competitive behaviour contributes to the long-run growth of living standards and may provide social benefits over time that outweigh any losses due to the restriction of output at any point in time.

For these and for other reasons, there are often strong incentives for oligopolistic firms to compete rather than to maintain the cooperative solution, even when they understand the inherent risks to their joint profits.

Cooperative or Noncooperative Outcomes?

Empirical research by such economists as Joe Bain and Nobel laureate Herbert Simon suggests that the relative strengths of the incentives to cooperate and to compete vary from industry to industry in a systematic way, depending on observable characteristics of firms, markets, and products. What are some of the characteristics that will affect the strength of the two incentives?

1. *The tendency toward joint maximization of profits is greater for smaller numbers of sellers than for larger numbers of sellers.* This involves both motivation and ability. When there are few firms, they will know that one of them cannot gain sales without inducing retaliation by its rivals. Also, a few firms can tacitly coordinate their policies with less difficulty than can many firms.

2. *The tendency toward joint maximization of profits is greater for producers of similar products than for producers of sharply differentiated products.* The more nearly identical the products of sellers, the closer the direct rivalry for customers and the less able one firm is to gain a lasting advantage over its rivals. Such sellers will tend to prefer joint efforts to achieve a larger pie over individual attempts to increase their own shares.

Box 14-2

Explicit Cooperation in OPEC

The experience of the Organization of Petroleum Exporting Countries (OPEC) in the 1970s and 1980s illustrates the power of cooperative behaviour to create short-run profits, as well as the problems of trying to exercise long-run market power in an industry without substantial entry barriers.

OPEC did not attract worldwide attention until 1973, when its members voluntarily restricted their output by negotiating quotas among themselves. In that year, OPEC countries accounted for about 70 percent of the world's supply of crude oil and 87 percent of the world's oil exports. So, although it was not a complete monopoly, the cartel came close to being one. By reducing output, the OPEC countries were able to drive up the world price of oil and to earn massive profits both for themselves and for non-OPEC producers, who obtained the high prices without having to limit their output. After several years of success, however, OPEC began to experience the typical problems of cartels.

New Entry

New entry became a problem. The high price of oil encouraged the development of new supplies, and within a few years new productive capacity was coming into use at a rapid rate in non-OPEC countries.

Long-Run Adjustment of Demand

The short-run demand for oil proved to be highly inelastic. Over time, however, adaptations to reduce the demand for oil were made within the confines of existing technology. Homes and offices were insulated more efficiently, and smaller, more fuel-efficient cars became popular. This is an example of the distinction between the short-run and long-run demand for a commodity, first introduced in Chapter 5.

Innovation in the Very Long Run

Innovation further reduced the demand for oil in the very long run. Over time, technologies that were more efficient in their use of oil, as well as alternative energy sources, were developed. Had the oil prices stayed up longer than they did, major breakthroughs in solar and geothermal energy would surely have occurred.

This experience in both the long run and the very long run shows the price system at work, signaling the need for adaptation and providing the in-

---

3. *The tendency toward joint maximization of profits is greater in a growing market than in a contracting market.* When demand is growing, firms can produce at full capacity without any need to steal customers from their rivals. When firms have excess capacity, they are tempted to give price concessions to attract customers. When their rivals retaliate, price cuts become general.

4. *The tendency toward joint maximization of profits is greater when the industry contains a dominant firm rather than a group of more or less equal competitors.* A dominant firm may become a *price leader,* a firm that sets the industry's price while all other firms fall into line. Even if a dominant firm is not automatically a price leader, other firms may look to it for judgement about market conditions, and its decisions may become a tentative focus for tacit agreement.

5. *The tendency toward joint maximization of profits is greater when nonprice rivalry is absent or limited.* When firms seek to suppress their basic rivalry by avoiding price competition, rivalry will tend to break out in other forms unless it is expressly curtailed. Firms may seek to increase their mar-

centives for that adaptation. It also provides an illustration of Schumpeter's concept of creative destruction, which we first discussed in Chapter 13. In order to share in the profits generated by high energy prices, new technologies and new substitute products were developed, and these destroyed much of the market power of the original cartel.

Cheating

At first, there was little incentive for OPEC countries to violate quotas. Members enjoyed such undreamed-of increases in their incomes that they found it difficult to use all of their money productively. As the output of non-OPEC oil grew, however, OPEC's output had to be reduced to hold prices high. Incomes in OPEC countries declined sharply as a result.

Many OPEC countries had become used to their enormous incomes, and their attempts to maintain them in the face of falling output quotas brought to the surface the instabilities inherent in all cartels. In 1981, the cartel price reached its peak of US$35 per barrel (oil prices are traditionally quoted in U.S. dollars). In real terms, this was about five times as high as the 1972 price, but production quotas were less than one half of OPEC's capacity. Eager to increase their oil revenues, many individual OPEC members gave in to the pressure to cheat and produced in excess of their production quotas. In 1984, Saudi Arabia indicated that it would not tolerate further cheating by its partners and demanded that others share equally in reducing their quotas yet further. However, agreement proved to be impossible. In December 1985, OPEC decided to eliminate production quotas and let each member make its own decisions about output.

After the Collapse

OPEC's collapse as an output-restricting cartel led to a major reduction in world oil prices. Early in 1986, the downward slide took the price to $20 per barrel, and it fell to $11 per barrel later in the year. Allowing for inflation, this was around the price that had prevailed just before OPEC introduced its output restrictions in 1973. Prices have been volatile since then, oscillating between about $12 per barrel, which is close to the perfectly competitive price, and $20 per barrel, which seems to be all that can be sustained under the modest output restrictions that can currently be obtained.

ket shares through extra advertising, changes in the quality of the product, the establishment of new products, giveaways, and a host of similar schemes that leave their prices unchanged but increase their costs and so reduce their joint profits.

6. *The tendency toward joint maximization of profits is greater when the barriers to entry of new firms are greater.* The high profits of existing firms attract new entrants, who will drive down price and reduce profits. The greater the barriers to entry, the less this will occur. Thus, the greater the entry barriers, the closer the profits of existing firms can be to their joint- maximizing level without being reduced by new entrants.

Long-Run Behaviour: The Importance of Entry Barriers

Suppose that firms in an oligopolistic industry succeed in raising prices above long-run average total costs and earn substantial profits that are not completely eliminated by nonprice competition. In the absence of significant barriers to entry, new firms will enter the industry and erode the profits of existing firms, as they do in monopolistic competition. Natural barriers to entry were discussed in Chapter 13. They are an important part of the explanation of the persistence of profits in many oligopolistic industries.

Where such natural barriers do not exist, however, oligopolistic firms can earn profits in the long run only if they can create entry barriers. To the extent to which this is done, existing firms can move toward joint profit-maximization without fear that new firms, attracted by the high profits, will enter the industry. We discuss next some types of created barriers.

Brand Proliferation

By altering the characteristics of a differentiated product, it is possible to produce a vast array of variations on the general theme of that product. Think, for example, of automobiles with a little more or a little less acceleration, braking power, top speed, cornering ability, gas mileage, and so on, compared with existing models.

Although the multiplicity of existing brands is no doubt partly a response to consumers' tastes, it can have the effect of discouraging the entry of new firms. To see why, suppose that the product is the type for which there is a substantial amount of brand switching by consumers. In this case, the larger the number of brands sold by existing firms, the smaller the expected sales of a new entrant.

Say, for example, that an industry contains three large firms, each selling one brand of cigarettes, and say that 30 percent of all smokers change brands in a random fashion each year. If a new firm enters the industry, it can expect to pick up 25 percent of the smokers who change brands (the smoker has available one out of the new total of four brands). This would give the new firm 7.5 percent (25 percent of 30 percent) of the total market the first year merely as a result of picking up its share of the random switchers, and it would keep increasing its share for some time thereafter. If, however, the existing 3 firms have 5 brands each, there would be 15 brands already available, and a new firm selling 1 new brand could expect to pick up only one sixteenth of the brand switchers, giving it less than 2 percent of

the total market the first year, with smaller gains also in subsequent years. This is an extreme case, but it illustrates a general result.

The larger the number of differentiated products that are sold by existing oligopolists, the smaller the market share available to a new firm that is entering with a single new product.

Set-Up Costs

Existing firms can create entry barriers by imposing significant fixed costs on new firms that enter their market. This is particularly important if the industry has only weak natural barriers to entry, because the minimum efficient scale occurs at an output that is low relative to the total output of the industry.

Advertising is one means by which existing firms can impose heavy set-up costs on new entrants. Advertising, of course, serves purposes other than that of creating barriers to entry. Among them, it performs the useful function of informing buyers about their alternatives, thereby making markets work more smoothly. Indeed, a new firm may find that advertising is essential, even when existing firms do not advertise at all, simply to call attention to its entry into an industry in which it is unknown.

Nonetheless, advertising can also operate as a potent entry barrier by increasing the set-up costs of new entrants. Where heavy advertising has established strong brand images for existing products, a new firm may have to spend heavily on advertising to create its own brand images in consumers' minds. If the firm's sales are small, advertising costs *per unit sold* will be large, and price will have to be correspondingly high to cover those costs.

Figure 14-3 illustrates how heavy advertising can shift the cost curves of a firm with a low minimum efficient scale (*MES*) to make it one with a high *MES*. In essence, what happens is that a high *MES* of advertising is added to a low *MES* of production, with the result that the overall *MES* is raised.

A new entrant with small sales but large set-up costs finds itself at a substantial cost disadvantage relative to its established rivals.

Any once-and-for-all cost of entering a market has the same effect as a large initial advertising ex-

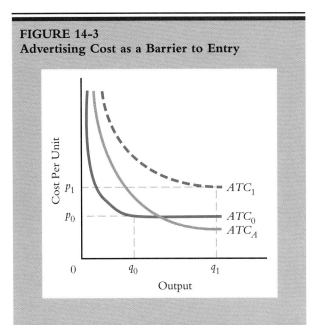

FIGURE 14-3
Advertising Cost as a Barrier to Entry

Large advertising costs can increase the minimum efficient scale (*MES*) of production and
thereby increase entry barriers. The ATC_0 curve
shows that the *MES* without advertising is at q_0. The
curve ATC_A shows that advertising cost per unit falls
as output rises. Advertising increases total cost to
ATC_1, which is downward sloping over its entire
range. Advertising has given a scale advantage to large
sellers and has thus created a barrier to entry.

penditure. For example, with many consumer
goods, the cost of developing a new product that is
similar, but not identical, to existing products may
be quite substantial. Even if there are few
economies of scale in the *production* of the product,
its large fixed *development* cost can lead to a falling
long-run average total cost curve over a wide range
of output.

An Application

The combined use of brand proliferation and advertising as an entry barrier helps to explain one apparent paradox of everyday life—that one firm often
sells multiple brands of the same product, which
compete actively against one another as well as
against the products of other firms.

The soap and cigarette industries provide classic
examples of this behaviour. Because all available

scale economies can be realized by quite small
plants, both industries have few natural barriers to
entry. Both contain a few large firms, each of which
produces an array of heavily advertised products.
The numerous existing products make it harder for
a new entrant to obtain a large market niche with a
single new product. The heavy advertising, although it is directed against existing products, creates an entry barrier by increasing the set-up costs
of a new product that seeks to gain the attention of
consumers and to establish its own brand image.

Predatory Pricing

A firm will not enter a market if it expects continued losses after entry. One way in which an existing
firm can create such an expectation is to cut prices
below costs whenever entry occurs and to keep
them there until the entrant goes bankrupt. The existing firm sacrifices profits while doing this, but it
sends a discouraging message to potential future rivals, as well as to present ones. Even if this strategy
is costly in terms of lost profits in the short run, it
may pay for itself in the long run by creating *reputation effects* that deter the entry of new firms at other
times or in other markets that the firm controls.

Predatory pricing is controversial. Some economists argue that pricing policies that appear to be
predatory can be explained by other motives and
that existing firms only hurt themselves when they
engage in such practises instead of accommodating
new entrants. Others argue that predatory pricing
has been observed and that it is in the long-run interests of existing firms to punish the occasional
new entrant even when it is costly to do so in the
short run.

The courts have taken the position that predatory pricing does occur. A number of firms have
been convicted of using it as a method of restricting
entry.

Contestable Markets and Potential Entry

The theory of contestable markets, developed by
Professors William Baumol, John Panzar, and
Robert Willig, holds that markets do not have to
contain many firms or to experience actual entry
for profits to be held near the competitive level.
Potential entry can do the job just as well as actual entry, as long as (1) entry can be easily accomplished, and (2) existing firms take potential

entry into account when making price and output decisions.

The theory. Entry is usually costly to the entering firm. It may have to build a plant, it may have to develop new versions of the industry's differentiated product, or it may have to advertise heavily in order to call attention to its product. These and many other initial expenses are often called *sunk costs of entry.* A sunk cost of entry is a cost that a firm must incur to enter the market and that cannot be recovered if the firm subsequently exits. For example, if an entering firm builds a product-specific factory that has no resale value, this is a sunk cost of entry. However, the cost of a factory that is not product-specific and that can be resold for an amount that is close to its original cost is not a sunk cost of entry.

A market in which new firms can enter and leave without incurring any sunk costs of entry is called a perfectly **contestable market.** A market can be perfectly contestable even if the firm must pay some costs of entry, as long as these can be recovered when the firm exits. Because all markets require at least some sunk costs of entry, contestability must be understood as a variable. The lower the sunk costs of entry, the more contestable the market.

In a contestable market, the existence of profits, even if they are due to transitory causes, will attract entry. Firms will enter to gain a share of these profits and will exit when the transitory situation has changed.

Consider, for example, the market for air travel on the lucrative Toronto-Ottawa-Montreal triangle. This market would be quite contestable *if* counter and loading space were available to new entrants at the three cities' airline terminals whatever their nationality. An airline that was not currently serving the cities in question could shift some of its existing planes to the market with small sunk costs of entry. Some training of personnel would be needed for them to become familiar with the route and the airport. This is a sunk cost of entry that cannot be recovered if the cities in question are no longer to be served. However, most of the airline's costs would not be sunk costs of entry. If it subsequently decides to leave the area, the rental of terminal space will stop, and the airplanes and the ground equipment can be shifted to another location. Alfred Kahn, for-

mer head of the U.S. Civil Aeronautics Board and architect of airline deregulation, captured this point by referring to commercial aircraft as "marginal cost with wings."

Sunk costs of entry constitute a barrier to entry, and the larger these are, the larger the profits of existing firms can be without attracting new entrants. The flip side of this coin is that firms operating in markets without large sunk costs of entry will not earn large profits. Strategic considerations will lead them to keep prices near the level that would just cover their total costs. They know that if they charge higher prices, firms will enter to capture the profits while they last and then exit.

Contestability, where it is possible, is a force that can limit the profits of existing oligopolists. Even if entry does not occur, the ease with which it can be accomplished may keep existing oligopolists from charging prices that would maximize their joint profits.

Contestability is just another example, in somewhat more refined form, of the key point that the possibility of entry is the major force preventing the exploitation of market power to restrict output and to raise prices.

Empirical relevance. Most economists take the view that, although contestable markets are an elegant extension of competitive markets in theory, there are at least *some* barriers to entry in almost all real markets—and very large barriers in many markets. Setting up an effective organization to produce or to sell almost anything incurs fixed costs. In the case of airlines, for instance, the new company at a given airport must hire and train staff, advertise extensively to let customers know that it is in the market, set up baggage-handling facilities, and overcome whatever loyalties customers have to the preexisting firms. Also, limited space, both in terminals and in take-off and landing slots, greatly restricts the opportunities for quick and easy entry. New firms in almost all industries face entry costs that are analogous to these. Entering a manufacturing industry usually requires a large investment in industry-specific, and sometimes product-specific, plants and equipment as well as product design.

These considerations suggest that contestability, in practise, is something to be measured, rather than simply asserted. The higher the costs of entry, the less contestable is the market, and the higher the profits that existing firms can earn without inducing entry. Current evidence suggests that in practise a high degree of contestability is quite rare.

Oligopoly and the Functioning of the Economy

Oligopoly is found in many industries and in all advanced economies. It typically occurs in industries where both perfect and monopolistic competition are made impossible by the existence of major economies of scale or of scope (or both). In such industries, there is simply not enough room for a large number of firms all operating at or near their minimum efficient scales.

Three questions are important for the evaluation of the performance of the oligopolistic market structure. First, do oligopolistic markets allocate resources very differently than perfectly competitive markets? Second, in their short-run and long-run price-output behaviour, where do oligopolistic firms typically settle between the extreme outcomes of earning zero profits and earning the profits that would be available to a single monopolist? Third, how much do oligopolists contribute to economic growth by encouraging innovative activity in the very long run? We consider each of these questions in turn.

The Market Mechanism Under Oligopoly

We have seen that under perfect competition, prices are set by the impersonal forces of demand and supply, whereas firms in oligopolistic markets administer their prices. The market signaling system works slightly differently when prices are administered rather than being determined by the market. Changes in the market conditions for both inputs and outputs are signaled to the perfectly competitive firm by changes in the prices of its inputs and its outputs. Changes in the market conditions for inputs are signaled to oligopolistic firms by changes in the prices of their inputs. Changes in the market conditions for the oligopolist's output are typically signaled, however, by changes in the volume of sales at administered prices.

Increases in costs of inputs will shift cost curves upward, and oligopolistic firms will be led to raise prices and lower outputs. Increases in demand will cause the sales of oligopolistic firms to rise. Firms will then respond by increasing output, thereby increasing the quantities of society's resources that are allocated to producing that output. They will then decide whether or not to alter their administered prices.

The market system reallocates resources in response to changes in demands and costs in roughly the same way under oligopoly as it does under perfect competition.

Profits Under Oligopoly

Some firms in some oligopolistic industries succeed in coming close to joint-profit maximization in the short run. In other oligopolistic industries, firms compete so intensely among themselves that they come close to achieving competitive prices and outputs.

In the long run, those profits that do survive competitive behaviour among existing firms will tend to attract entry. These profits will persist only insofar as entry is restricted either by natural barriers, such as large minimum efficiency scales for potential entrants, or by barriers created and successfully defended by the existing firms.

Very-Long-Run Competition

Once we allow for the effects of technological change, we need to ask which market structure is most conducive to the sorts of very-long-run changes that we discussed in Chapter 11. These are the driving force of the economic growth that has so greatly raised living standards over the last two centuries. They are intimately related to Schumpeter's concept of creative destruction, which we first encountered in our discussion of entry barriers in Chapter 13 (on pages 246–247).

To the many examples of creative destruction given in Box 13-1, we add just a few more arising from the modern revolutions in the transmission and analysis of information. In recent years, the development of facsimile transmission and electronic mail eliminated the monopoly of the post office in delivering hard-copy (as opposed to oral) communications. In their myriad uses, microcomputers for the home and the office swept away the markets of many once-thriving products and services. For instance, in-store computers answer customer questions, decreasing the need for salespeople. Aided by computers, just-in-time inventory systems greatly reduce the investment in inventories required of existing firms and new entrants alike. Computer-based flexible manufacturing systems allow firms to switch production easily and inexpensively from one product line to another, thereby reducing the minimum scale at which each can be produced profitably. One day, computers may even displace the college textbook.

An important defense of oligopoly relates to this process of creative destruction. Some economists have adopted Schumpeter's concept of creative destruction to develop theories that intermediate market structures, such as oligopoly, lead to more innovation than would occur in either perfect competition or monopoly. They argue that the oligopolist faces strong competition from existing rivals and cannot afford the more relaxed life of the monopolist. At the same time, however, oligopolistic firms expect to keep a good share of the profits that they earn from their innovative activity.

The empirical evidence is broadly consistent with this view. Professor Jesse Markham of Harvard University concluded a survey of empirical findings thusly:

If technological change and innovational activity are, as we generally assume, in some important way a product of organized R&D activities financed and executed by business companies, it is clear that the . . . payoffs that flow from them can to some measurable extent be traced to the doorsteps of large firms operating in oligopolistic markets.

Everyday observation provides some confirmation of this finding. Leading North American firms that operate in highly concentrated industries, such as Bombardier, Alcan, Du Pont, Xerox, Northern Telecom, and 3M, have been highly innovative over many years.

A Final Word

Oligopoly is an important market structure in modern economies because there are many industries in which the minimum efficient scale is simply too large to support many competing firms. The challenge to public policy is to keep oligopolists competing, rather than colluding, and using their competitive energies to improve products and to lower costs, rather than merely to erect entry barriers.

SUMMARY

1. Some Canadian industries fit the perfectly competitive model, but almost none are pure monopolies. Most have intermediate market structures that are called imperfectly competitive.

2. Most of the firms operating in these intermediate market structures sell differentiated products whose characteristics they chose themselves. They also administer their prices, do not change their prices as often as prices change in perfectly competitive markets, engage in nonprice competition, sometimes have unexploited economies of scale, and sometimes take actions designed to prevent the entry of new firms.

3. Monopolistic competition is a market structure that has the same characteristics as perfect competition, except that the many firms each sell one variety of a differentiated product rather than all selling a single homogeneous product. Firms face negatively sloped demand curves and may earn monopoly profits in the short run. In the long run, new firms enter the industry whenever profits can be made and the equilibrium requires that each firm earns zero profits. Each firm's demand curve is tangent to its average total cost curve, which means that each firm is producing less than its minimum-cost level of output.

4. Monopolistic competition does not necessarily result in inefficiency. Even though each firm produces at a cost that is higher

than the minimum attainable cost, the resulting product choice is valued by consumers and so may be worth the extra cost.

5. Oligopolies are dominated by a few large firms that usually sell differentiated products and have significant market power. They can maximize their joint profits if they cooperate to produce the monopoly output. By acting individually, each firm has an incentive to depart from this cooperative solution, but rivalrous behaviour reduces profits and may lead to a noncooperative Nash equilibrium from which no one firm has an incentive to depart.

6. Strategic behaviour, in which each firm chooses its best strategy in the light of other firms' possible decisions, may also lead to a Nash equilibrium.

7. Tacit cooperation is possible but often tends to break down as firms struggle for market share, indulge in nonprice competition, and seek advantages through the introduction of new technology.

8. Oligopolistic industries are likely to come closer to the joint profit-maximizing, cooperative position (a) the smaller the number of firms in the industry, (b) the less differentiated their products, (c) when the industry's demand is growing rather than shrinking, (d) when the industry contains a dominant firm, (e) the less the opportunity for nonprice competition, and (f) the smaller the barriers to entry.

9. Oligopolistic industries will exhibit profits in the long run only if there are significant barriers to entry. Natural barriers relate to scale and scope of economies in production marketing and to large entry costs. Firm-created barriers can be created by proliferation of competing brands, heavy brand-image advertising, and the threat of predatory pricing when new entry occurs. Contestable market theory holds that *potential* entry may be sufficient to hold profits down and emphasizes the importance of sunk costs as an entry barrier.

10. In the presence of major scale economies, oligopoly may be the best of the feasible alternative market structures. Evaluation of oligopoly depends on how much interfirm competition (a) drives the firms away from the cooperative, profit-maximizing solution and (b) leads to innovations in the very long run.

TOPICS FOR REVIEW

Concentration ratios

Reasons for the persistence of large firms

Administered prices

Product differentiation

Monopolistic competition

The excess capacity theorem

The cooperative, joint profit-maximizing solution

The noncooperative equilibrium

Strategic behaviour

Types of collusion

OPEC as a cartel

Firm-created entry barriers

Contestable markets

DISCUSSION QUESTIONS

1. Most Canadian provinces have laws requiring a company to produce beer in the province if it wishes to sell there. What do you think this does to the price of beer? What would be the consequences of repealing these laws? Why can small, high-cost local beers exist in open competition with large, low-cost, nationally sold beers?

2. It is sometimes said that there are more drugstores and gasoline stations than are needed. In what sense might that be correct? Does the consumer gain anything from this plethora of retail outlets?

3. Do you think any of the following industries might be monopolistically competitive? Why or why not?
   a. Textbook publishing. (Fact: Over 50 elementary economics textbooks are in use somewhere in North America this year.)
   b. Postsecondary education.
   c. Cigarette manufacturing.
   d. Restaurant operation.
   e. Automobile retailing.

4. What bearing did each of the following have on the eventual inability of OPEC to maintain a monopoly price for oil?
   a. Between 1979 and 1985, OPEC's share of the world oil supply decreased by half.
   b. "Saudi Arabia's interest lies in extending the life span of oil to the longest possible period," said Sheik Yamani.
   c. During the 1970s, government policies in many oil-importing countries protected consumers from oil price shocks by holding domestic prices well below OPEC levels.
   d. The former Soviet Union, in order to earn Western currency to pay for grain, increased its oil exports to the West during the 1980s, becoming the world's second largest oil exporter. In the 1990s, Russian oil exports dwindled as its industry fell into disrepair.
   e. In the late 1980s, Iran became increasingly concerned with maximizing its own oil revenues in order to pay for its war with Iraq.
   f. Iraq in 1990 occupied Kuwait, and many wells there were set on fire before Iraq was driven out in 1991 by Operation Desert Storm.
   g. Other OPEC countries are able to make up for the lost Kuwait production by raising their outputs at a marginal cost far below the current world price.

5. "The periods following each of the major OPEC price shocks proved to the world that there were many available substitutes for gasoline, among them bicycles, car pools, moving closer to work, cable TV, and Japanese cars." Discuss how each of these may be a substitute for gasoline.

6. The game shown in Figure 14-2 is often known as a prisoner's dilemma game. This is the story that lies behind the name:

> Two men are arrested for jointly committing a crime and are interrogated separately. They know that if they both plead innocent they will get only a moderate sentence. Each is told, however, that if either protests innocence while the other admits guilt, the one who claims innocence will get a severe sentence while the other will get off completely free. If both plead guilty, however, each will get a medium sentence that is worse than the moderate one but better than the severe one.

Draw up a payoff matrix to summarize this game. How does it compare with Figure 14-2? What is the outcome if each prisoner tries to minimize his sentence under each possible choice by the other prisoner? What would they do if they could communicate?

7. Another example of a prisoner's dilemma can arise when two firms are making sealed bids on a contract. For simplicity, assume that only two bids are permitted, either a high or a low price. The high price yields a profit of $10m, whereas the low price yields a profit of $7m. If they put in the same price, they share the job and each earns half the profits. If they give different bids, the lower one gets the job and all the profits. Draw up the payoff matrix and determine the outcomes under strategic and cooperative behaviour.

8. Can you think of other examples of competition among a few firms that might be of the prisoner's dilemma type?

9. The Canadian airline industry is an oligopoly. Do the firms price discriminate? Why or why not? What features of the market facilitate price discrimination and what make it difficult or impossible? Does the behaviour of the firms seem likely to get them close to or far away from the cooperative solution? Until recently, European airlines operated under a price-setting arrangement. How would you expect prices to differ between Canada and Europe?

10. Compare the effects on the automobile and the wheat industries of each of the following. In light of your answers, discuss general ways in which oligopolistic industries fulfil the same general functions as perfectly competitive industries.
    a. Large rise in demand.
    b. Large rise in costs of production.
    c. Temporary cut in supplies coming to market due to a 3-month rail strike.
    d. Rush of cheap foreign imports.

11. Evidence suggests that the profits earned by all the firms in many oligopolistic industries are less than the profits that would be earned if the industry were monopolised. What are some reasons why this might be so?

15

Public Policy Toward Monopoly and Competition

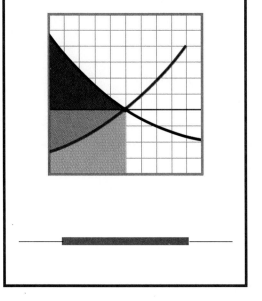

Monopoly has long been regarded with suspicion. In *The Wealth of Nations* (1776), Adam Smith developed a stinging attack on monopolists. Since then, most economists have criticised monopoly and advocated competition.

In this chapter, we first consider what economic theory has to say about the relevant advantages of the two polar market structures of monopoly and competition. Next, we examine intermediate market forms and then go on to study public policies that are directed at encouraging competition and discouraging monopoly.

Part of the appeal of competition and the distrust of monopoly is noneconomic, being based on a fear of concentration of power. This was discussed in Chapter 12. Much of the attraction of competition and the dislike of monopoly, however, has to do with the understanding that competition is efficient in ways that monopoly is not. To understand the issue, we must first define *efficiency*.

Economic Efficiency

Economic efficiency requires avoiding the waste of resources. When labour is unemployed and factories lie idle (as occurs in serious recessions), their potential output is lost. If these resources were employed, total output would be increased and hence everyone could be made better off. However, full employment of resources by itself is not enough to prevent the waste of resources. Even when resources are being fully used, they may be used inefficiently. Let us look at three examples of inefficiency in the use of fully employed resources.

1. If firms do not use the least costly method of producing their chosen outputs, they waste resources. For example, a firm that produces 30,000 pairs of shoes at a resource cost of $400,000 when it could have been done at a cost of only $350,000 is using resources inefficiently. The lower-cost method would allow $50,000 worth of resources to be transferred to other productive uses.
2. If within an industry, the cost of producing its last unit of output is higher for some firms than for others, the industry's overall cost of producing its output is higher than necessary.
3. If too much of one product and too little of another product are produced, resources are being used inefficiently. To take an extreme example, suppose that so many shoes are produced that every consumer has all the shoes he or she could possibly want and so places a zero value on obtaining an additional pair of shoes. Fur-

ther assume that fewer coats are produced relative to demand, so that each consumer places a positive value on obtaining an additional coat. In these circumstances, each consumer can be made better off if resources are reallocated from shoe production, where the last shoe produced has a low value in the eyes of each consumer, to coat production, where one more coat produced would have a higher value to each consumer.

These examples suggest that we must refine our ideas of the waste of resources beyond the simple notion of ensuring that all resources are employed. The sources of inefficiency just outlined suggest important conditions that must be fulfilled if economic efficiency is to be attained. These conditions are conveniently collected into two categories, called *productive efficiency* and *allocative efficiency*, which were studied long ago by the Italian economist Vilfredo Pareto (1848–1923). Indeed, efficiency in the use of resources is often called Pareto optimality or Pareto efficiency in his honour.

Productive Efficiency

Productive efficiency has two aspects, one concerning production within each firm and one concerning the allocation of production among the firms in an industry.

The first condition for **productive efficiency** is that each firm should produce any given output at the lowest possible cost. In the short run, with only one variable factor, the firm has no problem of choice of technique. It merely uses enough of the variable factor to produce the desired level of output. In the long run, however, more than one method of production is available. Productive efficiency requires that the firm use the least costly of the available methods of producing any given output. This means that firms will be located on, rather than above, their long-run average cost curves.

In Chapter 11 we studied the condition for productive efficiency within the firm (see page 198):

Productive efficiency requires that each firm produce its given output by combining factors of production in such a way that the ratio of the marginal products of each pair of factors is made equal to the ratio of their prices.

This is the same thing as saying that $1 spent on every factor should yield the same output. If this is not so, the firm can reduce the resource costs of producing its given output by altering the inputs it uses. It should substitute the input for which $1 of expenditure yields the higher output for the input for which $1 of expenditure yields the lower output.[1]

Any firm that is not being productively efficient is producing at a higher cost than is necessary. This must reduce its profits. It follows that any profit-maximizing firm will seek to be productively efficient no matter which market structure—perfect competition, monopoly, oligopoly, or monopolistic competition—it operates within.

There is a second condition for productive efficiency. This ensures that the total output of each industry is allocated among its individual firms in such a way that the total cost of producing the industry's output is minimized.

Productive efficiency requires that the marginal cost of producing its last unit of output must be the same for each firm in any industry.

If an industry is productively inefficient, it is possible to reduce the industry's total cost of producing any given total output by reallocating production among the industry's individual firms. To illustrate, suppose that the Jones Brothers shoe manufacturing firm has a marginal cost of $70 for the last shoe of some standard type that it produces, while Gonzales, Inc., has a marginal cost of only $65 for the same type of shoe. If the Jones plant produces one less pair of shoes while the Gonzales plant produces one more, total shoe output is unchanged, but total industry costs are reduced by $5. Thus, $5 worth of resources will be freed to increase the production of other commodities.

Clearly, this cost saving can go on as long as the two firms have different marginal costs. However, as the Gonzales firm produces more shoes, its marginal cost rises, and as the Jones firm produces fewer

---

[1]As we saw in Box 11-1, producing at least cost within the firm also involves a more obvious type of efficiency, called *technical efficiency*. Technical efficiency requires that the firm not adopt a method of production if there exists another method that uses *less of all inputs*. Productive (economic) efficiency then ensures that the firm chooses the method that uses the lowest *value* of resources from among the technically efficient methods.

shoes, its marginal cost falls. (By producing more, the Gonzales firm is moving upward to the right along its given *MC* curve, whereas by producing less, the Jones firm is moving downward to the left along its given *MC* curve.) Say, for example, that after Gonzales, Inc., increases its production by 1,000 shoes per month, its marginal cost *rises* to $67, whereas when Jones Brothers reduces its output by the same amount, its marginal cost *falls* to $67. Now there are no further cost savings to be obtained by reallocating production between the two firms.

Figure 15-1 shows a production possibility curve of the sort that was first introduced in Figure 1-2. Productive *inefficiency* implies that the economy is at some point inside the curve. In such a situation, it is possible to produce more of some goods without producing less of others.

Productive efficiency implies being on, rather than inside, the economy's production possibility curve.

Allocative Efficiency

Allocative efficiency concerns the relative quantities of the commodities to be produced. It concerns the choice between alternative points on the production possibility curve, such as points *b*, *c*, and *d* in Figure 15-1.

Allocative efficiency is defined as a situation in which it is impossible to change the allocation of resources in such a way as to make someone better off without making someone else worse off. Changing the allocation of resources implies producing more of some goods and less of others, which in turn means moving from one point on the production possibility curve to another. This is called changing the *mix* of production.

From an allocative point of view, resources are said to be used *inefficiently* when using them to produce a different bundle of goods makes it *possible* for at least one person to be better off while making no other person worse off. Conversely, resources are said to be used *efficiently* when it is *impossible*, by using them to produce a different bundle of goods, to make any one person better off without making at least one other person worse off.

This tells us what is meant by allocative efficiency, but how do we find the efficient point on

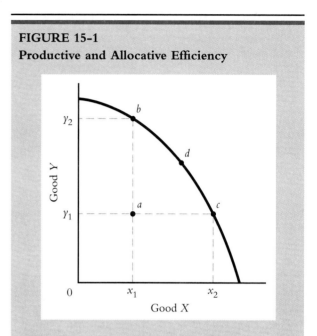

FIGURE 15-1
Productive and Allocative Efficiency

Any point on the production possibility curve is productively efficient; not all points on this curve are allocatively efficient. The curve shows all combinations of two goods *X* and *Y* that can be produced when the economy's resources are fully employed and being used with productive efficiency.

Any point inside the curve, such as *a*, is productively inefficient. If the inefficiency exists in industry *X*, production could be reallocated among firms in that industry in such a way as to raise production of *X* from x_1 to x_2. This would take the economy from point *a* to point *c*, raising production of *X* without any reduction in production of *Y*. Similarly, if the inefficiency exists in industry *Y*, production of *Y* could be increased from y_1 to y_2, which would take the economy from point *a* to point *b*. If both industries are allocatively inefficient, production can be increased to take the economy to some point on the curve *between b* and *c*, thus increasing the production of *both* commodities.

Allocative efficiency concerns being at the most efficient point on the production possibility curve. Assessing allocative efficiency means judging among points on the curve, such as *b*, *c*, and *d*. Usually only one such point will be allocatively efficient, while all others will be inefficient.

the production possibility curve? For example, how many shoes, dresses, and hats should be produced to achieve allocative efficiency? The answer is as follows:

The economy's allocation of resources is efficient when, for each good produced, its marginal cost of production is equal to its price.

To understand the reasoning behind this answer, we need to recall a point that was established in our discussion of consumers' surplus in Chapter 7. The price of any commodity indicates the value that each consumer places on the last unit consumed of that commodity. Faced with the market price of some commodity, the consumer goes on buying units until the last one is valued exactly at its price. Consumers' surplus arises because the consumer would be willing to pay more than the market price for all but the last unit that is bought. On the last unit bought (i.e., the marginal unit), however, the consumer only breaks even, because the valuation placed on it is just equal to its price.

Now assume that some commodity, say, shoes, sells for $60 per pair but has a marginal cost of $70. If one less pair of shoes were produced, the value that all households would place on the pair of shoes not produced would be $60. Using the concept of opportunity cost, however, we see that the resources that would have been used to produce that last pair of shoes could instead produce another good (say, a coat) valued at $70. If society can give up something that its members value at $60 and get in return something that its members value at $70, the original allocation of resources is inefficient. By reallocating resources, someone can be made better off, and no one need be worse off.

This is easy to see when the same household gives up the shoes and gets the coat, but it follows even when different households are involved. In this case, the market value of the gain to the household that gets the coat exceeds the market value of the loss to the household that gives up the shoes. The gaining household *could* afford to compensate the losing household and still come out ahead.

Assume next that shoe production is cut back until the price of a pair of shoes rises from $60 to $65, while its marginal cost falls from $70 to $65. Efficiency is achieved in shoe production because $p = MC = \$65$. Now if one less pair of shoes were produced, $65 worth of shoes would be sacrificed, while, at most, $65 worth of other commodities could be produced with the freed resources.

In this situation, the allocation of resources to shoe production is efficient, because it is not possible to change it to make someone better off without making someone else worse off. If one household were to sacrifice the pair of shoes, it would give up goods worth $65 and would then have to obtain for itself all of the new production of the alternative commodity produced just to break even. It cannot gain without making another household worse off. The same argument can be repeated for every commodity, and it leads to the conclusion that we have stated already: The allocation of resources is efficient when each commodity's price equals its marginal cost of production.

Efficiency and Inefficiency in Perfect Competition and Monopoly

We now know that for productive efficiency, marginal cost should be the same for all firms in any one industry and that for allocative efficiency, marginal cost should be equal to price in each industry. Do the market structures of perfect competition and monopoly lead to productive and allocative efficiency?

Perfect Competition

Productive efficiency. We saw in Figure 12-9 that in the long run under perfect competition, each firm produces at the lowest point on its long-run average cost curve. Therefore, no one firm could lower its costs by altering its own production.

We also know that in perfect competition, all firms in an industry face the same price of their product and that they equate marginal cost to that price. It follows immediately that marginal cost will be the same for all firms. Because all firms in the industry have the same cost of producing their last unit of production, no reallocation of production among the firms could reduce the total industry cost of producing a given output.

Productive efficiency is achieved under perfect competition because all firms in an industry have identical marginal costs and identical minimum costs in long-run equilibrium.

Allocative efficiency. We have seen already that perfectly competitive firms maximize their profits by equating marginal cost to price. Thus, when perfect competition is the market structure for the whole economy, price is equal to marginal cost in each line of production.

Allocative efficiency is achieved when perfect competition prevails throughout the economy, because price will be equal to marginal cost for all commodities.

Monopoly

Productive efficiency. Monopolists have an incentive to be productively efficient, because their profits will be maximized when they adopt the lowest-cost method that can be used to produce whatever level of output they choose. Thus, profit-maximizing monopolists will operate on their LRAC curves. Furthermore, when they have more than one plant producing the same product, they will allocate production among those plants so that the cost of producing the last unit of output is the same in all plants.

Allocative efficiency. Although a monopoly firm will be productively efficient, it will choose a level of output that is too low to achieve allocative efficiency. This follows from what we saw in Chapter 13 (page 244) that the monopolist chooses an output at which the price charged is *greater than* marginal cost. This violates the conditions for allocative efficiency, because the amount that consumers pay for the last unit of output exceeds the opportunity cost of producing it.

Consumers would be prepared to buy additional units for an amount that is greater than the cost of producing these units. Some consumers could be made better off, and none need be made worse off, by shifting extra resources into production of the monopolised commodity, thus increasing the production of the product. From this follows the classic efficiency-based preference for competition over monopoly:

Monopoly is allocatively inefficient, because the monopolist's price always exceeds its marginal cost.

This result has important policy implications for economists and for policy makers, as we shall see later in this chapter.

Efficiency in Other Market Structures

Note that the result just stated extends beyond the case of a simple monopoly. Whenever a firm has any power over the market, in the sense that it faces a negatively sloped demand curve rather than one that is horizontal, its marginal revenue will be less than its price. Thus, when it equates marginal cost to marginal revenue, as do all profit-maximizing firms, marginal cost will also be less than price, which is inefficient. Thus, strictly speaking, both oligopoly and monopolistic competition are also allocatively inefficient.

Oligopoly is an important market structure in today's economy, because in many industries the minimum efficient scale is simply too high to support a large enough number of competing firms to make each a price taker. Although oligopoly does not achieve the conditions for allocative efficiency, it nevertheless may produce more satisfactory results than monopoly. We observed one reason why this might be so in Chapter 14: Competition among oligopolists may encourage very-long-run innovations that result in both new products and cost-reducing methods of producing old ones.

An important defense of oligopoly as an acceptable market structure is that it may be the best of the available alternatives when minimum efficient scale is large. As we observed at the end of Chapter 14, the challenge to public policy is to keep oligopolists competing and using their competitive energies to improve products and to lower costs rather than to restrict interfirm competition and to erect entry barriers. As we shall see later in this chapter, much public policy has just this purpose. What economic policy makers call *monopolistic practises* include not only output restrictions operated by firms with complete monopoly power, but also anticompetitive behaviour among firms that are operating in oligopolistic market structures.

Allocative Efficiency: An Elabouration

We have already established the basic points of productive and allocative efficiency.[2] However, fuller

---

[2]The section from here to page 292 can be skipped without loss of continuity.

interpretation of the normative significance of allocative efficiency can be given by using the concepts of consumers' and producers' surplus.

Consumers' and Producers' Surplus

We saw in Chapter 7 that consumers' surplus is the difference between the total value that consumers place on all the units consumed of some commodity and the payment that they actually make for the purchase of that commodity. Consumers' surplus is shown once again in Figure 15-2.

Producers' surplus is analogous to consumers' surplus. It occurs because all units of each firm's output are sold at the same market price, while, given a rising supply curve, each unit except the last is produced at a marginal cost that is less than the market price.

Producers' surplus is defined as the amount that producers are paid for a commodity less the total variable cost of producing the commodity. The total variable cost of producing any output is shown by the area under the supply curve up to that output.[3] Thus, producers' surplus is the area above the supply curve and below the line giving market price. Producers' surplus is also shown in Figure 15-2.

The Allocative Efficiency of Perfect Competition Revisited

If the total of consumers' and producers' surplus is not maximized, the industry's output could be altered to increase that total. The additional surplus could then be used to make some households better off without making any others worse off.

---

[3]The marginal cost shows the addition to total cost caused by producing one more unit of output. Summing these additions over each unit of output, starting with the first, yields the total variable cost of output. For example, the sum of the marginal costs of producing the first 10 units of output is the total variable cost associated with 10 units of output. Graphically, this process of summation is shown by the whole area under the marginal cost curve. Because, as we have already seen, the industry supply curve under perfect competition is merely the sum of the marginal cost curves of all the firms in the industry, the area under that supply curve up to some given output is the total of all the firms' variable costs of producing that output. Similarly, the area under a monopolist's marginal cost curve up to some given output is the total of the monopolist's variable costs of producing that output.

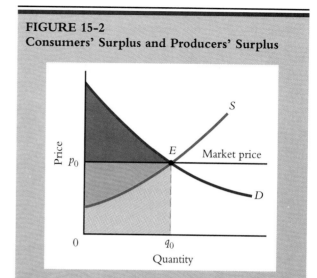

FIGURE 15-2
Consumers' Surplus and Producers' Surplus

Consumers' surplus is the area under the demand curve and above the market price line. Producers' surplus is the area above the supply curve and below the market price line. The equilibrium price and quantity in this competitive market are p_0 and q_0, respectively. The total value that consumers place on q_0 of the commodity is given by the sum of the three shaded areas. The amount that they pay is p_0q_0, the rectangle that consists of the two lighter shaded areas. The remainder, shown as the dark blue shaded area, is *consumers' surplus.*

The receipts to producers from the sale of q_0 units are also p_0q_0. The area under the supply curve, the red shaded area, is total variable cost, the minimum amount that producers require to supply the output. The difference, shown as the light blue shaded area, is *producers' surplus.*

Allocative efficiency occurs where the sum of consumers' and producers' surplus is maximized.

The allocatively efficient output occurs under perfect competition where the demand curve intersects the supply curve, that is, the point of equilibrium in a competitive market. This is shown graphically in Figure 15-3. For any output that is less than the competitive output, the demand curve lies above the supply curve, which means that the value consumers put on the last unit of production exceeds its marginal cost of production. Suppose, for example, that the current output of shoes is such that consumers value at $70 an additional pair of

FIGURE 15-3
The Allocative Efficiency of Perfect Competition

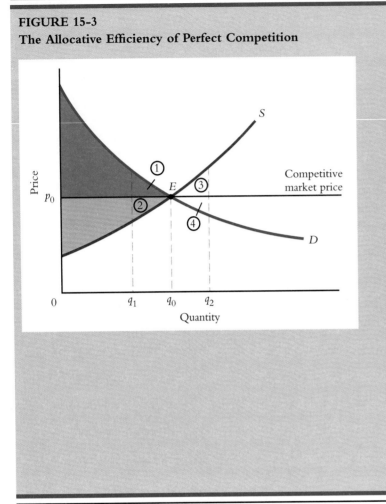

Competitive equilibrium is allocatively efficient because it maximizes the sum of consumers' and producers' surplus. The competitive equilibrium occurs at the price-output combination $p_0 q_0$. At this equilibrium, consumers' surplus is the dark shaded area above the competitive market price line, while producers' surplus is the light shaded area below the competitive market price line.

For any output that is less than q_0, the sum of the two surpluses is less than at q_0. For example, reducing the output to q_1 but keeping price at p_0 lowers consumers' surplus by area 1 and lowers producers' surplus by area 2.

For any output that is greater than q_0, the sum of the surpluses is also less than at q_0. For example, if producers are forced to produce output q_2 and to sell it to consumers, who are in turn forced to buy it at price p_0, producers' surplus is reduced by area 3 (the amount by which variable costs exceed revenue on those units), while the amount of consumers' surplus is reduced by area 4 (the amount by which expenditure exceeds consumers' satisfactions on those units).

Only at competitive output, q_0, is the sum of the two surpluses maximized.

shoes that adds $60 to costs. If it is sold at any price between $60 and $70, both producers and consumers gain; there is $10 of potential surplus to be divided between the two groups. In contrast, the last unit produced and sold at competitive equilibrium adds nothing to either consumers' or producers' surplus, because consumers value it at exactly its market price, and it adds the full amount of the market price to producers' costs.

If production were pushed beyond the competitive equilibrium, the sum of the two surpluses would fall. Assume, for example, that firms were forced to produce and sell further units of output at the competitive market price and that consumers were forced to buy these extra units at that price. (Note that neither group would do so voluntarily.) Firms would lose producers' surplus on those extra units, because their marginal costs of producing the

extra output would be above the price that they received for it. Purchasers would lose consumers' surplus because the valuation that they placed on these extra units, as shown by the demand curve, would be less than the price that they would have to pay.

The sum of producers' and consumers' surplus is maximized *only at the perfectly competitive output*, which is thus the only level of output that is allocatively efficient.

The Allocative Inefficiency of Monopoly Revisited

We have just seen in Figure 15-3 that the output in perfectly competitive equilibrium maximizes the sum of consumers' and producers' surplus. It fol-

FIGURE 15-4
The Allocative Inefficiency of Monopoly

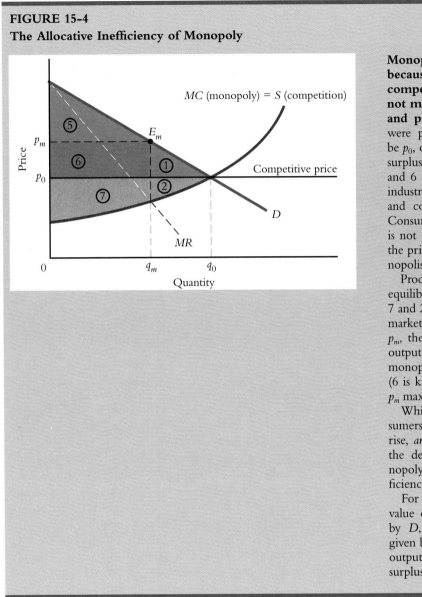

Monopoly is allocatively inefficient because it produces less than the competitive output and thus does not maximize the sum of consumers' and producers' surplus. If this market were perfectly competitive, price would be p_0, output would be q_0, and consumers' surplus would be the sum of areas 1, 5, and 6 (the blue shaded areas). When the industry is monopolized, price rises to p_m, and consumers' surplus falls to area 5. Consumers lose area 1 because that output is not produced; they lose area 6 because the price rise has transferred it to the monopolist.

Producers' surplus in a competitive equilibrium would be the sum of areas of 7 and 2 (the gray shaded areas). When the market is monopolized and price rises to p_m, the surplus area 2 is lost because the output is not produced. However, the monopolist gains area 6 from consumers (6 is known to be greater than 2 because p_m maximizes profits).

While area 6 is transferred from consumers' to producers' surplus by the price rise, *areas 1 and 2 are lost*. They represent the deadweight loss resulting from monopoly and account for its allocative inefficiency.

For all output between q_m and q_0, the value of the output to consumers, given by D, exceeds the cost of production, given by MC. Thus failure to produce this output reduces consumers' plus producers' surplus.

lows that the lower monopoly output must result in a smaller total of consumers' and producers' surplus.

The monopoly equilibrium is not the outcome of a voluntary agreement between the one producer and the many consumers. Instead, it is imposed by the monopoly firm by virtue of the power it has over the market. When the monopoly chooses an output below the competitive level, market price is higher than it would be under perfect competition. As a result, consumers' surplus is diminished, and producers' surplus is increased. In this way the mo-

nopoly firm gains at the expense of consumers. This is not the whole story, however.

When output is below the competitive level, there is always a *net* loss of surplus. More is given up by consumers than is gained by the monopolist. Some surplus is lost by society, because output between the monopolistic and the competitive levels is not produced. This loss of surplus is called the *deadweight loss of monopoly*. It is illustrated in Figure 15-4.

It follows that there is a conflict between the private interest of the monopoly producer and the public interest of all the nation's consumers. This creates a rational case for government intervention to prevent the formation of monopolies if possible and if not, then to control their behaviour.

Canadian Public Policy Toward Monopoly and Competition

Monopolies, cartels, and price-fixing agreements among oligopolists, whether explicit or tacit, have met with public suspicion and official hostility for over a century. These and other noncompetitive practises are collectively referred to as *monopoly practises*. Note that such practises are *not* just what monopolists do; they include noncompetitive behaviour of firms that are operating in other market structures. The laws and other instruments that are used to encourage competition and discourage monopoly practises make up **competition policy** and are used to influence both the market structure and the behaviour of individual firms. By and large, Canadian competition policy has sought to create more competitive market structures where possible, and to discourage monopolistic practises where competitive market structures could not be established. In addition, federal, provincial, and local governments all employ *economic regulations,* which prescribe the rules under which firms can do business, and in some cases determine the prices that businesses can charge for their output.

The goal of economic efficiency provides rationales both for competition policy and for economic regulation. Competition policy is used to promote efficiency by increasing competitive behaviour among firms. Where effective competition is not possible (as in the case of a natural monopoly, such as an electric power company), economic regulation of privately owned firms or public ownership is often used as a substitute for competition. The purpose is to protect consumers from the high prices and reduced output that result from the use of monopoly power.[4]

---

[4]A second kind of regulation, *social regulation,* involves a government's rules that require firms to consider the health, safety, environmental, and other social consequences of their behaviour. Social regulation is discussed in Chapter 21.

Public policies are indeed used in these ways, but they are also often used in ways that reduce economic efficiency. One reason is that efficiency is not the only thing that policy makers have been concerned with in the design and implementation of competition policy. Most public policies have the potential to redistribute income, and people often use them for private gain, regardless of their original public purpose. This is studied more generally in Chapter 20.

We shall study three aspects of Canadian competition policy: first, the direct control of natural monopolies; second, the direct control of oligopolies; and, third, the creation of competitive conditions. The first is a necessary part of any competition policy, the second has been important in the past but is less so now, and the third constitutes the main current thrust of Canadian competition policy.

Direct Control of Natural Monopolies

The clearest case for public intervention arises with a natural monopoly, an industry in which scale effects are so dominant that there is room for only one firm to operate at the minimum efficient scale. Canadian policy makers have not wanted to compel the existence of several smaller, less efficient producers whenever a single firm would be much more efficient; neither have they wanted to give a natural monopolist the opportunity to restrict output, raise prices, and reap monopoly profits.

One response to natural monopoly is for government to assume *ownership* of the single firm, setting it up as a crown corporation. (In Canada, any government-owned firm is called a **crown corporation**.) The government appoints a board of directors who are supposed to set policies guided by their understanding of the national interest. Another response has been to allow private ownership but to *regulate* the monopoly firm's behaviour.

Short-Run Price and Output

Whether the state nationalizes or merely regulates privately owned natural monopolies, the industry's pricing policy is determined by the government. Usually, the industry is asked to follow some policy other than profit maximization.

Marginal cost pricing. Sometimes the government dictates that the natural monopoly should try to set price equal to short-run marginal cost in an effort to maximize consumers' plus producers' surpluses in that industry. Setting price equal to marginal cost means adopting some combination of output and price that lies on the marginal cost curve. Furthermore, a price that clears the market for any given quantity produced must lie on the demand curve. So marginal cost pricing with neither shortages nor surpluses, implies producing the quantity at which the marginal cost curve cuts the demand curve. According to economic theory, this policy, which is called **marginal cost pricing,** provides the efficient solution.

Marginal cost pricing does, however, create some problems. The natural monopoly may still have unexploited economies of scale and may hence be operating on the falling portion of its average total cost curve. In this case, marginal cost will be less than average total cost, and pricing at marginal cost will lead to losses. This is shown in part (i) of Figure 15-5.

A falling-cost natural monopoly that sets price equal to marginal cost will suffer losses.

Demand, however, may be sufficient to allow the firm to produce on the rising portion of its average total cost curve, that is, where output exceeds what is needed to achieve the minimum efficient scale. At any such output, marginal cost exceeds average total cost. If the firm is directed to equate marginal cost to price, it will earn profits. This is shown in part (ii) of the figure.[5]

When a rising-cost natural monopoly sets price equal to marginal cost, it will earn profits.

Average cost pricing. Sometimes, natural monopolies are directed to produce the output that will just cover total costs, thus earning neither profits nor losses. This means that the firm produces to the point where average revenue equals average total cost, which is where the demand curve cuts the average total cost curve. Part (i) of Figure 15-5 shows that for a falling-cost firm, this pricing policy requires producing at less than the allocatively efficient output. The losses that would occur under marginal cost pricing are avoided by producing less than the efficient output.[6] Part (ii) shows that for a rising-cost firm, the policy requires producing at more than the economically efficient output. The profits that would occur under marginal cost pricing are dissipated by producing more than the efficient output.

Generally, average cost pricing will not result in allocative efficiency.

Long-Run Investment Policies

The optimal pricing policy makes price equal to short-run marginal cost. The position of the short-run marginal cost curve (as well as the short-run average cost curve) depends, however, on the amount of fixed capital that is currently available to be combined with the variable factor. What should determine the long-run investment decision to accumulate fixed capital?

The efficient answer, if marginal cost pricing is being followed, is to compare the current market price with the long-run marginal cost. The former expresses the value consumers place on one additional unit of output. The latter expresses the full resource cost of providing an extra unit of output, including capital costs.[7] If price exceeds long-run marginal cost, capacity should be expanded. If it is less, capacity should be allowed to decline as capital wears out.

---

[5]Sometimes, a natural monopoly is defined as one where long-run costs are falling when price equals marginal cost. This, however, is only *sufficient* for a natural monopoly; it is not *necessary*. Demand may be such that one firm is producing, with price equals marginal cost, on the rising portion of its long-run cost curve, while there is no price at which two firms could both cover their costs. For example, if a firm's minimum efficient scale is 1 million units of output and demand is sufficient to allow the firm to cover costs at 1.2 million units, there may be no price at which two firms, with their combined *MES* of 2 million units, can cover their full costs.

[6]Note that the losses are financial losses, not social welfare losses. Every unit produced between the points where *AC* equals price and where *MC* equals price adds to consumers' surplus but brings private financial loss to the producer.

[7]To make the correct comparison, the cost of capital must be expressed at its current rental price so that it can be added to such other costs as wages and fuel.

FIGURE 15-5
Pricing Policies for Natural Monopolies

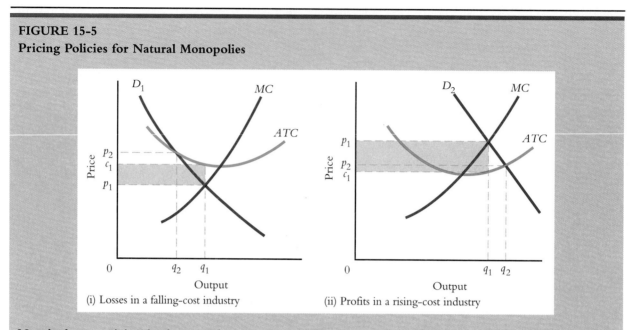

(i) Losses in a falling-cost industry   (ii) Profits in a rising-cost industry

Marginal cost pricing leads to profit or losses, whereas average cost pricing violates the efficiency condition. In each part, the output at which marginal cost equals price is q_1 and price is p_1.

In part (i), average costs are falling at output q_1, so marginal costs are less than the average cost of c_1. There is a loss of $c_1 - p_1$ on each unit, making a total loss equal to the shaded area.

In part (ii), average cost of c_1 is less than price at output q_1. There is a profit of $p_1 - c_1$ on each unit sold, making a total profit equal to the shaded area.

In each part of the diagram, the output at which average cost equals price is q_2 and the associated price is p_2. In part (i), marginal cost is less than price at q_2, so output is below its optimal level. In part (ii), marginal cost exceeds price at q_2, so output is greater than its optimal level.

The efficient pricing system rations the output of existing capacity by setting price equal to the short-run resource cost of producing another unit. It also adjusts capacity in the long run until the full marginal cost of producing another unit of output is equal to the price.

Provincial Hydro Authorities: An Example

The use of average cost pricing tends to distort investment decisions. Assume, for example, that there are three methods of generating electricity: cheap hydroelectric plants, medium-cost plants using fossil fuels, and expensive nuclear power stations. All of the hydroelectric sites have been used, and further fossil fuel plants are considered undesirable on environmental grounds, so new capacity must come

from nuclear energy plants. The provincial hydro authority uses average cost pricing, so users pay more than the cost of the cheap hydroelectricity and less than the costs of expensive nuclear power. The hydro authority finds that there is excess demand for electricity at its current market price and proposes to install new capacity. Should it do so?

The relevant test is not the existence of excess demand at the current price, because the long-run cost of providing more electricity exceeds that price. The cost is, in fact, the full long-run marginal cost of providing electricity from nuclear plants. On efficiency grounds, another plant should be built only if there is excess demand at a price that equals that full long-run cost.

This case illustrates the inefficient policies often adopted by nationalized and regulated industries adopted by nationalized and regulated industries that face rising long-run costs. If they priced at marginal cost, they would make profits, so they price at average cost. As a result, market price does not then provide the correct signal about the social value of further investment.

If a rising-cost firm installs enough capacity to meet all the demand when price is set equal to average cost, it will create more capacity than is socially optimal.

Such socially wasteful policies have been adopted by several provincial hydro authorities, including Ontario Hydro. On the one hand, such authorities have resisted recommendations that they price at marginal cost, because that would mean "making profits at consumers' expense." On the other hand, they have increased capacity whenever demand exceeded supply at a price equal to average cost; they thus require that consumers pay enough in electricity costs to cover the building of new plants whose output consumers would be unwilling to buy if asked to pay its full costs of production. As recently as 1993, Ontario Hydro accepted many of these criticisms. It has abandoned massive schemes for continued expansion and is greatly reducing its staff. It also raised prices closer to marginal cost—amidst great public outcry.

The Very Long Run

Natural monopoly is a long-run concept, meaning that *given existing technology,* there is room for only one firm to operate profitably. In the very long run, however, technology changes. Not only does today's competitive industry sometimes become tomorrow's natural monopoly, but today's natural monopoly sometimes becomes tomorrow's competitive industry.

A striking example is the telecommunication industry. Fifteen years ago, message transmission was a natural monopoly. Now, technological developments such as satellite transmission, electronic mail, and fax machines have made this activity highly competitive. In many countries, an odd circumstance then arose: Nationalized industries sought to maintain their profitability by prohibiting entry into what would otherwise become a fluid and competitive industry. Since it has the full force of the legal system behind it, the public firm may be more suc-

cessful than the privately owned firm in preserving its monopoly long after technological changes have destroyed its naturalness.

Market economies change continually under the impacts of innovation and growth; to be successful, government policy must also be adopted continually to keep it relevant to the ever-changing existing situation.

Direct Control of Oligopolies

Governments have from time to time intervened in industries that were oligopolies, rather than natural monopolies, seeking to enforce the type of price and entry behaviour that was thought to be in the public interest. Such intervention has typically taken two distinct forms. In the United Kingdom, it was primarily nationalization of whole oligopolistic industries, such as railways, steel, and coal mining, which were then to be run by government-appointed boards. In the United States, firms in such oligopolistic industries as airlines, railways, and electric power companies were left in private hands, but their decisions were regulated by government-appointed bodies that set prices and regulated entry. As so often happens, Canada followed a mixture of the British and the American practises. Many Canadian crown corporations, which are in effect nationalized firms, were set up, and many firms that were left in private hands were regulated. For example, in the regulated railway industry, the CPR was privately owned, while the CNR was a crown corporation.

Skepticism About Direct Control

In recent times, policy makers have become increasingly skeptical of their ability to improve the behaviour of oligopolistic industries by having the state control the details of their behaviour through either ownership or regulation. Several experiences have been important in determining this skepticism.

First, oligopolistic market structures have provided much of the economic growth in this century. New products, and new ways of producing old products, have followed each other in rapid succession, all leading to higher living standards and higher productivity. Many of these innovations have such as automobiles, agricultural implements, steel, petroleum refining, chemicals, and telecommunication. As long as governments can keep oligopolists competing with each other, rather than cooperating to produce monopoly profits, most economists see no need to regulate such things as the prices at which oligopolists sell their products and the conditions of entry into oligopolistic industries.

Second, many regulatory bodies have imposed policies that were not related to the cost of each of the services being priced. These prices involved what is called *cross subsidization,* whereby profits that are earned in the provision of one service are used to subsidize the provision of another at a price below cost. Typically, regulators have required that long-distance telephone calls subsidize local calls, first-class mail subsidize third-class mail, and long-haul airline rates subsidize short-haul rates. These pricing policies have forced users of the profitable service to subsidize users of the unprofitable service. When these users are firms that compete with unregulated firms in other countries, international competitiveness can be reduced. For example, until very recently, Canadian firms using long-distance telephones were placed at a disadvantage with respect to firms using similar services in the United States, where competition holds long-distance rates close to the cost of providing the service.

Third, the record of postwar government intervention into regulated industries seemed poorer in practise than its supporters had predicted. When industries were *nationalized,* antagonism often persisted between management, concerned with financial viability, and workers, concerned with take-home pay. As a result, it was not long before the unexpected became commonplace: strikes against the industries that the people themselves owned. When industries were *regulated,* the results were often less beneficial to consumers than had been expected. Research by economists slowly established that in many industries, regulatory bodies were captured by the very firms that they were supposed to be regulating. As a result, the regulatory bodies that were meant to ensure competition often acted to enforce monopoly practises that would have been illegal if instituted by the firms themselves.

This last point, which entails the use of regulatory policy to protect firms from too much competition rather than to protect consumers from too little, is discussed in more detail below.

Protection *Against* Competition

Regulatory bodies have frequently protected firms rather than consumers. For example, Canadian and American railroad rates were originally regulated in order to keep profits down by establishing schedules of *maximum* rates. By the 1930s, however, concern had grown over the depressed economic condition of the railroads and the emerging vigorous competition from trucks and barges. The regulators then became the protectors of the railroads, permitting them to establish *minimum* rates for freight of different classes, allowing price discrimination, and encouraging other noncompetitive practises. Moreover, the regulators became leading advocates of including trucking under the regulatory umbrella. Restricting entry into trucking and setting minimum rates for trucks was unmistakably protectionist. The only reason for regulating the large carriers was to control their competition with the railroads. The big road carriers were limited in where they could go and how low a price they could quote. As a result, they became targets for small, unregulated truckers, who could cut rates and thus draw away customers without fear of retaliation. To eliminate the rate competition, regulation was extended to small truckers.

Airline regulation in Canada and the United States provides another example. When airline routes and fares were first regulated, there was arguably so little demand that competition could not have been effective. By the mid-1960s, however, the regulation was plainly protectionist and designed to shield the major carriers from competition in both countries. Supporters of regulation argued that unrestricted competition would be so intense that it might ruin the industry and even invite cost-cutting practises that endangered public safety. Critics argued that competition might destroy some existing airlines but would prepare the ground for an efficient industry, while regulation could still be used to enforce such things as minimum safety standards on private airline firms.

For decades, Canadian regulation of airline prices consistently blocked price competition. Foreign airlines wishing to cut fares between Canada and Europe have been barred from doing so. Until recently, airlines other than Air Canada and CAI were prevented from introducing cheap transcontinental fares. In the circumstances, it was hard to see Canadian airline regulation as protecting the interests of passengers against the predatory behaviour of the carriers.

Why did regulatory bodies shift from protecting consumers to protecting firms? One thesis championed by the American professor George Stigler is that the regulatory commissions were gradually captured by the firms they were supposed to regulate. In part, this capture was natural enough. When regulatory bodies were hiring staff, they needed people who were knowledgeable in the industries they were regulating. Where better to go than to people who had worked in these industries? Naturally, these people tended to be sympathetic to firms in their own industries. Also, since many of them aspired to go back to those industries once they had gained experience within the regulatory bodies, they were not inclined to arouse the wrath of industry officials by imposing policies that were against the firms' interests.

Deregulation and Privatization

The 1980s witnessed a movement in virtually all advanced industrial nations and the vast majority of less developed nations to reduce the level of government control over industry. A number of forces had been pushing in this direction: (1) the experience that regulatory bodies often sought to reduce, rather than increase, competition; (2) the dashing of the unreasonable hopes that nationalized industries would work better than private firms in the areas of efficiency, productivity growth, and industrial relations; (3) the realization that replacing a private monopoly with a publicly owned one would not greatly change the industry's performance and that replacing privately owned oligopolists by a publicly owned monopoly might actually worsen the industry's performance; (4) the awareness that falling transportation costs and revolutions in data processing and communication exposed local industries to much more widespread international competition than they had previously experienced domestically; and (5) concern over the cross subsidization often required by regulatory bodies.

The natural outcomes of these revised views were the privatization of crown corporations, and deregulation. Both were intended, among other things, to leave prices and entry free to be determined by private decisions.

Privatization went a long way in the United Kingdom in the 1980s. Most of the nationalized industries, both those containing a few large firms and those containing many smaller firms, were returned to private ownership. In Canada, hundreds of crown corporations that the government had acquired for a variety of reasons but were neither natural monopolies nor operating in highly concentrated oligopolistic industries were sold off.[8] Also, many crown corporations operating in oligopolistic industries such as Air Canada and PetroCan were privatized. Many industries, such as airlines and gas and oil, were deregulated. Prices were freed, to be set by the firms in the industry, and entry was no longer restricted by government policy.

Intervention to Keep Firms Competing

The least stringent form of government intervention is designed neither to force firms to sell at particular prices nor to regulate the conditions of entry and exit; it is designed, instead, to encourage competitive behaviour by preventing firms from merging unnecessarily or from engaging in certain anticompetitive practises such as colluding to set monopoly prices. Here, the policy seeks to create the most competitive market structure possible and then to prevent firms from reducing competition by engaging in certain forms of cooperative behaviour.

The Thrust of Canadian Policy

Laws designed for these purposes are called **combine laws** in Canada. They have provided the main thrust of Canadian competition policy since its inception in the nineteenth century. They prohibit monopolies, attempts to monopolise, and conspiracies in restraint of trade. Throughout the history of Canadian competition policy, legislation has been directed chiefly at the misuse of market power by single firms or groups of firms and only rarely at mergers *per se*.

---

[8]It has always been difficult to estimate the number of government-owned corporations in Canada, since these are underrepresented on many official lists. Marsha Gordon, in *Government in Business* (Montreal: C. D. Howe Institute, 1981, p. 3), gives the number as 464 federal corporations in 1981; numerous others were either wholly or partly owned by provincial governments. Since that time, the number has been reduced significantly through the government's privatization policy.

This acceptance of the need for relatively large firms in the business sector was partly a function of the small size of the Canadian economy in the days when most production was solely for the domestic market. Firms that were large enough to exploit the available economies of scale were likely to be large in relation to the total market. This meant that there would be fewer firms in Canadian industries dominated by scale effects than would be found in similar industries in such relatively large economies as the United States.

The Development of Canadian Policy

The first Canadian combine laws were adopted in 1889 and 1890, when legislation made it an offense to combine, to agree to lessen competition unduly, or to restrain trade. Because the proscribed behaviour was illegal, an offense was a criminal act to be handled by the criminal justice system. The laws have been changed frequently since that time, but their basic procompetition stance still prevails in current legislation.

By the 1950s, Canadian anticombine laws had evolved to make illegal three broad classes of activity: (1) combinations, such as price-fixing agreements that unduly lessen competition; (2) mergers or monopolies that may operate to the detriment of the public interest; and (3) unfair trade practises.

Many cases of unfair trade practises were successfully pursued under these laws, but compared to the United States, few cases were brought against mergers, and none of those that were brought were successful. The reason most often cited for this lack of success was the inability of criminal legislation to cope with complex economic issues. Under criminal law, the government must prove beyond a reasonable doubt that the accused has committed the offense. As an added complication, Canadian courts have been much less willing than American courts to assess economic evidence.

Current Canadian Policy

A major review of Canadian legislation was undertaken in the late 1960s by the Economic Council of Canada. Its recommendations, published in a report in 1969, together with those of a committee of experts appointed by the Department of Consumer and Corporate Affairs, formed the basis of the amendments to the Combines Investigation Act that

are still in force. Of the recommendations that were accepted, some were put into practise in 1976 and the remainder in 1986.

Amendments of 1976. The first set of amendments, proclaimed in 1976, included several provisions: (1) extending the Combines Investigation Act to service industries, (2) allowing *civil* (rather than criminal) actions to be brought for damages resulting from contravention of the act, and (3) strengthening legislation against misleading advertising. Claims about product quality must now be based on adequate tests. Advertising a product at a bargain price when the supplier does not, or cannot, supply the product in reasonable quantities and supplying a product at a price higher than the advertised price are prohibited. In 1992, the court levied a record fine against one individual of $500,000 for seriously misleading advertising. Also, the Restrictive Trade Practices Commission was given the power to protect customers by prohibiting suppliers from (1) refusing to supply without good reason, (2) requiring exclusive dealerships, (3) restricting the way a good is sold, or (4) requiring tied sales. As a result, retailing practises for many goods have changed considerably.

Amendments of 1986. In 1986, after four previous attempts had failed, the final set of amendments to the act were passed. The resulting act has three central themes: economic efficiency, adaptability, and international trade. The new act created a specialized Competition Tribunal to deal with civil matters now that competition policy has been taken out of the sphere of the criminal law. This tribunal is empowered to hear applications and issue orders in respect of reviewable practises contained in the Act.

The tribunal can also accept consent orders from the director of investigations on terms agreed on by the parties involved without hearing further evidence. When this happens, Canadian procedures, which used to be very public ones (what economists call *transparent*), now go on very much behind the scenes in private negotiations between the firms involved and the director of investigations. Furthermore, in the important case of the takeover of Texaco Oil Company by Imperial Oil, a carefully worked out agreement among the parties and the director of investigations was seriously amended by the tribunal. This showed that the tribunal was un-willing merely to rubber-stamp agreements worked out behind the scenes under the auspices of the di-rector.

Under the new act, mergers are also placed under civil law, the statutory test being whether or not the merger "substantially lessens competition." For the first time in Canada, economic considera-tions are stated to be directly relevant in judging the acceptability of a merger. When reviewing a merger, the director is to consider such things as ef-fective competition after the merger, the degree of foreign competition, barriers to entry, the availabil-ity of substitutes, and the financial state of the merging entities. Furthermore, an allowable defense of a merger is that the gains in efficiency more than offset any reductions in competition.

This new merger legislation has had some sub-stantial effects on business mergers for the first time in the history of Canadian competition policy. Many firms have consulted with the director before concluding a merger. As a result, some proposed mergers have been amended, and a few have been abandoned. Many mergers that have gone forward have been investigated, and the terms of some have been substantially modified.

Several provisions of the Act were challenged in the courts in cases that several times reached the Supreme Court of Canada. A summary of the key issues decided by the courts was recently given by the Director of Investigation and Research of the Bureau of Competition Policy in the following words[9]:

■ The constitutionality of the price-fixing provi-sions of the Act has been unequivocally upheld by a unanimous judgement of the Supreme Court of Canada. In this decision, the Supreme Court, for the first time, provided a comprehen-sive analytical framework for the interpretation of Canada's price-fixing laws;

■ The Supreme Court upheld the power of the Competition Tribunal to enforce its decisions through contempt orders;

■ The Supreme Court upheld the constitutionality of the misleading advertising provisions of the Act;

■ The Supreme Court denied leave to appeal from a unanimous appellate court decision affirming the constitutionality of the merger provisions of the Act as well as that of the Competition Tri-bunal;

■ The Competition Tribunal recently issued deci-sions in the first two fully contested merger cases under the 1986 *Competition Act* as well as its sec-ond abuse of dominance decision; and

■ The courts imposed record fines against both in-dividuals and firms in price-fixing cases, as well as record individual fines under the Act in a mis-leading representation case.

In summarizing the effects of these legal deci-sions the Director had this to say:

> The recent case law, together with the release of en-forcement guidelines concerning mergers (April 1991), price discrimination (September 1992), predatory pricing (May 1992) and misleading adver-tising (September 1991), have considerably advanced the important objectives of providing guidance to the business and legal communities with respect to the enforcement of Canada's competition law. En-forcement guidelines, in particular, have become an important tool in the Bureau of Competition Pol-icy's efforts towards articulating and clarifying en-forcement policies and practises.

Conclusion

The new act will not be the end of the evolution of Canadian combine legislation, but it appears to have marked the end of a major chapter. Canadian legis-lation has for a long time provided substantial pro-tection to consumers against the misuse of market power by large firms. For the first time, it now also seems to provide some substantial protection against the creation, through mergers, of market power that is not justified by gains to efficiency or international competitiveness. Many observers are optimistic that these laws, no doubt to be further refined in the fu-ture, will provide more protection to consumers than direct government intervention did—either through government ownership of particular firms or through government control of prices and condi-tions of entry.

---

[9]Public Lecture, Fordam Corporate Law Institute, New York, Oct. 22, 1992.

SUMMARY

1. Resources are said to be used efficiently when it is impossible, by using them differently, to make any one household better off without making at least one other household worse off. Economists distinguish two main kinds of efficiency: productive and allocative.

2. Productive efficiency exists for given technology when output is being produced at the lowest attainable cost for that level of output. This requires first, that firms be on, rather than above, their relevant cost curves and second, that all firms in an industry have the same marginal cost.

3. Allocative efficiency is achieved when it is impossible to change the mix of production in such a way as to make someone better off without making someone else worse off. The allocation of resources will be efficient when each commodity's price equals its marginal cost.

4. Perfect competition achieves both productive and allocative efficiency. Productive efficiency is achieved because the same forces that lead to long-run equilibrium lead to production at the lowest attainable cost. Allocative efficiency is achieved because in competitive equilibrium, price equals marginal cost for every product. The economic case against monopoly rests on its allocative inefficiency, which arises because price exceeds marginal cost in equilibrium.

5. Very-long-run considerations, such as the effect of market structure on innovation and the incentive effects of monopoly profits, are important in evaluating market structures. Joseph Schumpeter advocated the view that the incentive to innovate is so much greater under monopoly that monopoly is to be preferred to perfect competition, despite its allocative inefficiency. Though few modern economists go that far, the empirical evidence suggests that technological change and innovation can to a measurable extent be traced to the efforts of large firms operating in oligopolistic industries.

6. Efficiency of natural monopolies requires that price be set equal to short-run marginal cost and that investment be undertaken whenever that price exceeds the full long-run marginal cost of providing another unit of output. Average cost pricing results in too much output in the short run and too much investment in the long run in rising-cost industries and too little output and too little investment in falling-cost industries.

7. Direct control of pricing and entry conditions of some key oligopolistic industries has been common in the past, but deregulation is reducing such control. The move to deregulation was largely the result of the experiences that oligopolistic industries are a major engine of growth, as long as their firms are kept competing; that direct control of such industries has produced disappointing results in the past; and that forced cross subsidization can have serious consequences for some users.

8. Canadian combine laws have always recognised the need for firms that are large in relation to the domestic market if size efficiencies are to be exploited. Such laws seek to restrict growth in size through mergers where the size is not justified by efficiencies and

seek to prevent the unwarranted exploitation of market power where such power is necessary. Recently, such laws have been removed from the criminal code, where enforcement proved difficult, and placed in the civil code, where enforcement appears to be easier.

TOPICS FOR REVIEW

Productive and allocative efficiency

Consumers' and producers' surplus

Pareto optimality

Economies of scale and of scope

Effect of costs on market structure

Effect of market structure on costs

Marginal and average cost pricing

Deregulation

Privatization

Canadian competition policy

DISCUSSION QUESTIONS

1. "Suppose that allocative inefficiency of some economy amounts to 5 percent of the value of production." What does this statement mean? If it is true, would consumers be better off if policy measures succeeded in eliminating the allocative inefficiency? Why or why not?

2. If the many plants producing a given product were built at different times, have different levels of capacity, and have different cost curves, is it possible that producing the industry's output using all of them is productively efficient? Show why or why not.

3. Consider an innovation that lowers the marginal cost of production by the same amount in two industries, one of which is perfectly competitive and the other a single-firm monopoly. Show that prices will fall as a response to a change in marginal costs in each industry but that prices and quantities will change less in monopoly than in competition.

4. "Canadian air travellers opting for U.S. carriers were [partly] responsible for Canadian airlines deregulation"—C. D. Howe Institute

"Canadian consumers crossing the border to buy cheap U.S. groceries may be responsible for the end of supply management in Canada."—Canadian business economist

What market forces are behind these quotations? What difficulties do they reveal for the regulation of particular industries?

5. Would competition laws be necessary in an economy of perfect competition? Would they be beneficial in an economy of natural monopoly?

6. What points in Part 4 of this book are illustrated by the following quotations from the speech by the Bureau of Competition Policy's

Director of Investigation and Research that is referenced in the text of this chapter?

a. "The assessment of unilateral monopolistic practises is a complex and challenging task. Practises which are harmful to competition in a particular context can be pro-competitive or competitively neutral in other market circumstances."

b. "The difference of opinion [between the Bureau and the Competition Tribunal] was in regard to the supply elasticity of the fringe; in this case, the competitors and potential competitors to the [merged] parties post-merger. Interestingly, these fringe competitors were located in bordering U.S. states."

c. "The grounds of appeal address the following concerns . . . the approach to market definition, particularly where product differentiation and dynamic market considerations are an issue."

d. "These issues require careful consideration, to ensure that competition policy deals effectively with anticompetitive practises without interfering with arrangements that facilitate beneficial innovation or otherwise enhance the efficiency of marketplace transactions."

7. Price-fixing agreements are (with some specific exemptions) violations of federal laws. Consider the effects of the following. In what way, if at all, should they be viewed as being similar to price-fixing agreements?

a. A manufacturer "recommends" minimum prices to its dealers.

b. A manufacturer publishes a product price list that is changed only every three months.

c. A trade association publishes "average industry total costs of production" every month.

8. "In a competitive market, the least-cost production techniques are revealed by entry and exit, whereas in public utility regulation, they are revealed by commission rate hearings. It is easier to fool the commission than the market. Therefore, wherever possible, competition should be permitted." Discuss.

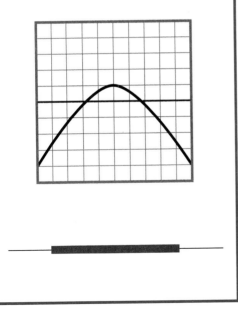

16

Takeovers, Mergers, and Foreign Direct Investment

Takeovers, mergers, and buyouts seem to come in waves. Some are driven by technological changes that increase the minimum efficient scale of firms in many industries. They tend to have long-lasting effects. Such was the merger wave at the beginning of this century and the wave of international takeovers in the 1980s and 1990s. Some are based on experiments that prove to be either outright failures or far less valuable than originally thought. Such was the wave of conglomerate mergers in the 1970s that often involved firms selling widely different products in widely different markets. Although some of the conglomerates formed in that period survived, many were dismantled in the wave of buyouts that occurred in the 1980s.

How should we judge such takeovers, mergers, and buyouts? Do takeovers of some domestic firms by other domestic firms significantly reduce competition and efficiency in domestic markets? Do takeovers of domestic firms by foreign firms threaten the well-being of the Canadian economy? If a firm is maximizing its profits, why would anyone pay a premium to take it over?

In this chapter, we examine what has come to be known as the *market for corporate control,* where takeovers, mergers, and buyouts take place. We also examine the standard assumption that firms always maximize profits and briefly consider a number of alternative theories of the motivation of firms. These two sets of issues are related, because if firms always succeed in maximizing their profits, one major reason for acquiring existing firms on the market for corporate control would be eliminated.

Later in this chapter, we will study nonmaximizing behaviour. In the meantime, we merely observe that there are many reasons why managers may not maximize their firms' profits. For example, they may be incompetent, or they may look after their own interests rather than the interests of their firm's shareholders.

Takeovers, Mergers, and Buyouts

A **takeover** occurs when Company A buys Company B (which then becomes a part of A). A **merger** occurs when Companies A and B join together, often combining even their names. A **buyout** occurs when a group of investors, rather than an existing firm, buys up a firm.

Three types of takeovers and mergers are commonly distinguished: horizontal, vertical, and conglomerate. When takeovers or mergers are among companies producing the same product, they are termed *horizontal.* An example was the merger of Texaco and Imperial Oil, both producers of oil products. Takeovers or mergers among businesses producing in different stages of the production process are termed *vertical,* which may be forward or backward. A forward takeover or merger involves moving toward the market in which the product is sold—for example, the acquisition of retail gas stations by the oil-refining companies. A backward takeover or merger involves one firm's acquisition of other firms that supply its inputs—for example, the purchase of a printing company by a publishing company. A *conglomerate takeover or merger* takes place between firms without obvious common interests in production. Insofar as lower costs result from conglomerate mergers, they are usually associated with managerial, marketing, or financial economies or with risk reduction through diversification.

Buyouts, mergers, and takeovers are transactions in the **market for corporate control.** This market, like any other, has both buyers (those who would acquire the rights to control a firm) and sellers (the current owners of the firm). As in other markets, the expected outcome is that the assets being bought and sold will wind up in the hands of those who value them most. These will tend to be those who can come closest to maximizing the firm's profits.

The wave of buyouts and takeovers that began in the 1970s and extended into the early 1980s has been interpreted in just this light—as an efficiency-enhancing response to unrealized profit opportunities that improves the overall quality of management and the productivity of the target firms. An alternative interpretation is that it was a speculative binge of no intrinsic value that posed a number of longer-term threats to the health of the economy. Furthermore, as we will see, when takeovers involve foreign firms, as many did in the 1980s and 1990s, they are often also assumed to pose a threat because of loss of control over the domestic economy.

A *takeover* begins when the management of the acquiring firm makes a **tender offer** to the stockholders of the target firm. Tender offers are promises to purchase stock at a specified price for a limited period of time, during which the acquiring firm hopes to gain control of the target company. Typically, the prices offered are considerably higher than the prevailing stock market price. The takeover is called a *hostile takeover* when the current management of the target firm opposes it.

The Effects of Takeovers

Do takeovers improve economic efficiency? The main argument in favour is that after a takeover, the new management can make more efficient use of the target firm's assets. The acquiring firm should be able to exploit profit opportunities that the target management is not exploiting. This can be done by such means as operating the target firm more efficiently, providing funds that the target firm could not obtain, or providing access to markets that would be too expensive for the target firm to open up on its own. If this is true, the value of the target firm will rise in response to a takeover, reflecting the expectation of increased future profits.[1] Further, if the *acquiring* firm's managers are acting in the best interest of *their* stockholders, the value of the acquiring firm should also rise when it is successful in a takeover bid.

Returns to Shareholders of Target Companies

Evidence on the effects of takeovers strongly supports the proposition that they benefit the stockholders of target firms. Estimates of the magnitude of the gains vary, but even the low estimates exceeded 20 percent of pretakeover stock value during the period from 1962 through 1985. Estimates of the average gains in successful tender offers during the 1980s range from about 30 percent to more than 50 percent.

Returns to Stockholders of Acquiring Companies

The benefits to stockholders in the acquiring firms vary greatly from takeover to takeover. Sometimes the benefit is large; at other times it is negative (the takeover *lowers* the acquiring firm's profits). Indeed, the best evidence is that the *average benefit* in the 1980s was slightly negative. How could this be?

One answer is that this is what we would expect if the market for corporate control is highly competitive. A typical takeover starts when an exist-

---

[1]Any takeover bid is likely to raise the value of a firm on the stock market. A profitable takeover raises these values permanently; a misjudged takeover does so only temporarily.

ing firm is perceived to be operating at well below its potential profitability. Other firms will want to take the firm over and will bid up the value of its shares to reflect the potential they see to raise the firm's profits once they own it. The result is a large rise in the price of the target firm's shares to the benefit of the owners, whereas the firm that finally makes the successful takeover pays about the price that makes its investment yield normal profits (plus a risk premium to cover the possibility that it may have guessed wrong about the potential of the target firm). Indeed, expectations about the potential of the target firm are subject to a wide margin of error. As a result, some takeovers will turn out to be more valuable than the market thought, and the takeover firm will gain. Others will turn out to be less valuable than expected, and the takeover firm will lose. If, however, the market judges correctly on average, takeovers will only prove normally profitable on average for the firm making the takeover.

Benefits to the Economy

Most economists believe that takeovers provide a useful discipline that helps to restrain managers from acting in nonmaximizing ways. Many also feel that each particular bout of takeovers and mergers is helping to chart new waters. As technology changes, there are changes in the advantages of scale and scope in market demand and market size. To meet the new circumstances, new forms of organization are often necessary and are sometimes effected through mergers, takeovers, and buyouts (and sometimes through the downsizing of firms). When firms react to rapidly changing circumstances, they must learn by experience. It is not surprising that, even though people generally move in the right direction, some make mistakes. In particular, a merger movement may go too far so that, among the profit-increasing mergers, takeovers, or buyouts, there are also some profit-reducing ones. Over time, the successful ones will be solidified and unsuccessful ones abandoned.

This is what we would expect in a world of rapid change, where people must learn appropriate responses through experience. It makes assessment of any current wave of mergers, buyouts, or takeovers difficult until the whole process is completed. Before then, it is hard to distinguish between some spectacular, attention-getting failures that are an inevitable part of the learning process

and a more general failure of the concept behind the wave.

In the absence of evidence to show that a particular wave of takeovers was efficiency decreasing, most economists would probably favour leaving the market for corporate control free from major government intervention.

Leveraged Buyouts

A **leveraged buyout (LBO)** refers to the buying of a firm by new owners where the required funds are raised by bonds sold to the public. (*Leverage* is nothing more than a financial term for *debt,* so a "highly leveraged firm" is one that has much debt relative to equity.) The group wishing to take over the firm borrows most of the money needed to buy up the existing shares. When the deal is completed, a public company, owned by many shareholders, has been turned into a private one, owned by a few buyers who financed their purchase by issuing debt.

Junk bonds are bonds sold to finance leveraged buyouts. They involve a relatively high risk, since the new management must make profits sufficient to meet the large interest payments on these bonds in bad times as well as in good times. In contrast, when finance is by equities, a year of low profits can be a year of low dividend payments without threatening the financial solvency of the firm. Junk bonds carry high interest rates, and the amounts by which these exceed the interest on a safe government bond reflect the market's assessment of the risks involved in the newly financed enterprises.

Leveraged buyouts occur for many reasons, but two of the most important in recent years have been to dismantle unprofitable conglomerates formed in an earlier wave of mergers and to provide a defense of existing management against hostile takeover bids.

Dismantling Conglomerates

The 1970s saw a wave of what were called **conglomerate mergers.** These were the merging into a single conglomerate firm of several firms producing quite different products and operating in quite different industries. One important idea behind these mergers was risk sharing. Typically, as economic growth proceeds, some industries decline while others grow. If a firm is in an industry that is declining, there may be little it can do to stem its own decline no matter how progressive its management. But if a firm straddles many industries, so went the argument, it may spread its risks among them. Since it is unlikely that all of the industries in which it is involved will be declining at the same time, the conglomerate firm may "win with the swings while losing with the roundabouts." Other reasons associated with these takeovers were to gain economies of scope. For example, a large conglomerate might find it easier to raise cash from outside lenders or to move cash from one enterprise to another within its structure, or it might be able to share its marketing expertise across its firms.

In practise, many conglomerate mergers proved ill-founded. In an impressive demonstration of the virtues of the division of labour, management based in one industry proved to be ill-equipped to assist in the management of firms based in other industries. Neither did the expected economies of scope emerge in any large way. Much marketing and financial expertise proved to be industry-specific, and any economies that could be realized often turned out to be smaller than the inefficiencies of trying to unite firms across industries. (To the extent that the separate units of the conglomerate were left to behave completely independently, there was no advantage in having the conglomerate in the first place.)

Investors also found problems with conglomerates. By buying the stock of a conglomerate, they were forced to take a stake in *all* of its enterprises. They could not sell off their ownership in one of the conglomerate's parts whose performance they disliked while holding on to a share of another part whose performance they did like.

For these and other reasons, many of the conglomerates formed in the 1970s were judged to be failures by the mid-1980s. The result of this failure was that the current value of the whole firm was less than the potential value of the sum of its individual parts, if they could be allowed to operate independently. Smart operators perceived this. They decided to buy up the conglomerates, break them up into their constituent parts, allow them to operate long enough so that their profits would be seen to rise, and then sell the parts for more in total than they had paid for the whole firm.

When buyers make the correct assessment, they pay off the junk bonds out of the proceeds of the sales and pocket the balance as a return for perceiv-

ing that efficiency could be increased by breaking up the conglomerates. The new purchasers finance much of their acquisition by issuing equities so that the firm is no longer fully debt-financed.

When buyers guess wrong, either because there is no advantage in breaking up the conglomerate or, more usually, because establishing the advantage takes longer than expected, they have to default on their junk bond payments, and the investors lose their money.

In spite of the great publicity attached to the failure of some leveraged buyouts and the consequent default of their junk bonds, many such buyouts have been successful. The conglomerates have been broken up, the individual parts sold at a profit, and the junk bondholders paid off. The failures show, as the high interest rate on junk bonds attests, that leveraged buyouts are risky. If there had been no failure, the market would have been wrong in demanding a junk bond risk premium in the first place.

Leveraged buyouts and junk bonds got a bad public image. This was partly due to the excesses of a number of shady characters who exploited the mania for takeovers for their own personal benefit. Sometimes they operated just within the law and other times well outside of it. They raised money through junk bonds, paid themselves massive salaries, engaged in insider trading[2] and otherwise manipulated the market. Some ended up in jail after highly publicized criminal trials.

In spite of these excesses, leveraged buyouts did serve a valuable purpose in allowing the market for corporate control to do what it is supposed to do.

Someone who perceives that a firm's current management practises, or its internal organization, are inefficient can make a gain by buying the firm at its current value and then selling at an increased value after the firm's efficiency has been increased.

Defense Against Takeovers

Leveraged buyouts have also been used by the current management of a firm as a defense against hos-

---

[2]Insider trading means making money on the market by utilizing information about forthcoming events gained while pursuing one's job such as helping to manage a company.

tile takeover bids. If the current managers feel that they can run the firm as well as a prospective new management that is making a hostile takeover bid, they can raise money on the junk bond market and make the buyout themselves. If they succeed, and if they are right in assuming that they can operate the firm well enough to justify the amounts paid for its purchase, they will be able to show a profit above the price that they pay for the firm.

Notice, however, that the current management cannot have been maximizing profits in the first place, or there would have been no incentive for a takeover. To buy the firm themselves in order to prevent the takeover, they must know how to maximize profits in the future.

The 1980s saw the development of a number of tactics designed to protect target firms from hostile takeovers and buyouts. These tactics are known collectively as *poison pills.* For example, the target firm can acquire a firm that competes with the potential buyer, thus increasing the possibility of running afoul of the competition laws. Also, the target firm may make a highly leveraged acquisition of another firm, thus leaving it with few liquid funds and much debt—a financial position that is likely to deter potential leveraged buyers. These are both market tactics. A political tactic is to attempt to get the laws changed to make takeovers more difficult. Popular hostility to takeovers and junk bonds has made this political route attractive to firms, and a number of U.S. states have adopted legislation that strongly deters all hostile takeovers and buyouts. Such legislation has the effect of shielding inefficient management from market disciplines. Major investors, such as pension fund managers, complain that this prevents them from maximizing the returns from their investment, and many economists fear that it will make it harder for the market to correct major inefficiencies in the operations of firms. By and large, Canadian provinces have not followed this U.S. lead.

Foreign Investment

When takeovers, buyouts, and mergers involve a domestic firm being taken over by a foreign firm, a further consideration is added: How much should we worry about the nationality of the owners of firms that operate in our country? This question arises most dramatically when a foreign takeover occurs. It pertains more generally to all **foreign direct investment (FDI)**, that is investment which gives foreign owners control over the behaviour of firms in which the investment is made. In Canada's case, FDI gives foreign owners control over the decisions of producers located in Canada (just as FDI made abroad gives Canadians control over the decisions of producers located in foreign countries). In contrast, the other major category of foreign investment, called **portfolio investment**, involves no control. Major components of portfolio investment are foreign holdings of government and private sector debt, usually in the form of bonds and treasury bills. (A treasury bill is short term government debt repayable in a matter of months.) Portfolio investment does not usually arouse the popular concerns that occur over FDI. The latter often causes great interest and concern whether it is the formation of a new foreign-owned firm in Canada, new investment by an existing foreign-owned firm such as building a factory (called "greenfield" investment), or a takeover of a Canadian-owned firm by a foreign-owned firm (called a "brownfield investment").

In the past, the major form of foreign investment was greenfield investment, and it is still important, for instance, in the establishment of Japanese transplant automobile factories in North America. In the last decade or so, more and more FDI has taken the form of mergers or acquisitions of domestically owned firms by foreign-owned firms. Large companies have deemed it necessary to have a physical presence in each of what are called the *triad* set of countries. These are (1) Canada and the United States, (2) Japan and Southeast Asia, and (3) the countries of Western Europe. Developing that presence was usually done through takeovers and mergers rather than by greenfield investment. More and more stand-alone companies found it hard to compete in the globalising marketplace, so they welcomed mergers with firms operating throughout the TRIAD.

For example, in 1991, 22 percent of the mergers in the United States involved one or more foreign-owned company, while the comparable figure in Canada was 73 percent. These are historically high figures for both countries. The much smaller size of the Canadian economy explains why in a globalising world, a higher proportion of Canadian than American mergers will involve foreign firms. Both figures illustrate the key development of the 1980s and early 1990s that much FDI took the form of international mergers as transnational corporations sought to position themselves in the markets of the world's major economies.

Foreign Investment in Developing Countries

Foreign investment has long been a major factor in world development. The residents of newly settled areas, such as North and South America in the seventeenth, eighteenth, and nineteenth centuries, could not hope to generate enough savings to finance the rapid development of their vast potential. Investment funds were required in large amounts to build *infrastructure* (such as roads, dams, city halls, post offices, and bridges), *private productive facilities* (such as factories, machines, and offices), and *housing* both for rental and for ownership. In the first instance, the economic growth of all such countries was financed by foreign investment.

As these economies grew, they produced larger and larger flows of their own domestic savings. These savings financed an increasing proportion of domestic investment, they helped buy back much of the foreign ownership in their country, and they provided a flow of foreign investment going to other, newer countries. This was the pattern in the United States, which was a net importer of capital from abroad until the early part of the twentieth century but became, as the century advanced, a net exporter of capital.[3]

The same pattern has been observed in Canada, but it has not yet gone as far as in the United States. This is due mainly to Canada's smaller size in relation to the investment needed to exploit its huge resources. Canada has always been a recipient of a great deal of foreign investment. As the Canadian economy grew, however, the flow of domestic savings increased. This had several effects. First, a larger and larger proportion of new investment in Canada

has been financed by domestic rather than by imported capital. Second, the share of total capital investment located in Canada that is foreign owned rose more and more slowly, until it peaked at about 40 percent in 1972, after which it fell until the late 1980s.[4] Third, Canada became a rising source of foreign investment in other countries as successful Canadian firms expanded into foreign markets and private Canadian investors added foreign investments to their portfolios of assets.

World Attitudes to Transnationals

World attitudes toward foreign investment were fairly tolerant throughout most of the period since the Industrial Revolution. Most people saw such investment as a benign force leading to more rapid growth in both total population and output per person than could be financed through domestic savings alone. Then, in the late 1950s and the 1960s, attitudes in many countries became more hostile to foreign investment. This change was partly the result of the growth of what was then called the *multinational enterprise,* now called the *transnational corporation (TNC).* (See Box 9-2 on page 174.) These are firms that are present in many countries: A domestic firm may engage in international trade by selling its goods in many countries; a transnational corporation produces its goods in many countries.

TNCs may be highly centralized, with head offices, research and development, and all major policy determination located in the home country. They may also be quite decentralized, with research, product development, and policy determination being done in many different countries.

TNCs have become increasingly important over the years and now account for the majority of international trade and foreign investment. Indeed, much international trade is between different units of the same TNC (intra-TNC trade). Also, the typical organization of a TNC has undergone changes. Although all types have always existed, the typical form in earlier times was a highly centralized firm. Today, with the demands for specialized products carefully tailored to the specific needs of each country and with the ability to produce small runs of each product variation efficiently thanks to computer-assisted production, decentralized organizations are becoming increasingly common.

---

[3]In the 1980s, this pattern was reversed, with the United States once again becoming a net importer of capital, until by 1990 it was home to more foreign capital than any other country in the world.

[4]More recently, the share has risen, for reasons that will be discussed shortly.

In the 1950s and 1960s, the rise of the TNC was seen as an ominous development. People correctly perceived that TNCs would make it more difficult for individual countries to maintain economic policies that differed from those of their trading partners. For example, TNCs have the ability, through internal accounting, to shift costs to areas where local tax laws permit the greatest cost write-offs and to shift profits to areas where profit taxes are lowest. They can also shift R&D to where tax advantages or subsidies are largest and then make the results of this R&D available throughout their entire organization—which often means throughout the entire world.

TNCs are able to exploit country-specific economic policies by locating each activity in the country whose policies are most favourable to that activity.

This ability represented an inevitable weakening of the power of the governments of individual countries.

Throughout the 1960s and 1970s, the rise of TNCs aroused worldwide concerns. Since many of the most successful early TNCs were American, many observers in other countries feared the spread of American economic dominance and cultural influence. Influential books in Europe decried the growth of U.S. economic and cultural imperialism and urged that TNCs be kept out as a defense. Today, with North American firms all too often on the defensive against Japanese and European firms, the fear of U.S. dominance seems but a quaint reminder to Europeans of the human tendency to think that whatever is now happening will always happen.

By the 1980s, attitudes toward TNCs had softened again. Several developments were responsible. First, it was clear to industrial nations that TNCs were here to stay. As world trade became more and more globalised under the impact of the communication and computer revolutions, TNCs became increasingly important, until it became apparent that no advanced country could do without them. Second, less developed countries came to the same realization and put out a welcome mat. As the executive director of the United Nations Center on TNCs recently said:

> The 1980s have witnessed major changes in the world production system, with TNCs being the

principal forces shaping the future of technological innovation. At the same time, a more pragmatic and businesslike relationship between host governments and TNCs has emerged within the past decade. Many developing countries, burdened by debt and economic stagnation, have liberalised their policies towards TNCs while these corporations have displayed greater sensitivity to the development and economic goals of host countries. The era of confrontation has receded and been replaced by a practical search for a meaningful and mutually beneficial accommodation of interests.[5]

Canadian Attitudes to Transnationals

Official Canadian views have matched these swings in world views. Until the 1960s, Canada welcomed foreign investment as a means to achieving economic growth that would have been impossible if it had to be financed by domestic savings alone. Then, in the 1960s, suspicion of foreign (particularly American) investment grew. This resulted in the formation of the Foreign Investment Review Agency (FIRA) in the 1970s. This agency had the right to screen all new foreign direct investment coming into Canada. It turned down about 5 percent of the applications that it reviewed—quite a high rejection rate by international standards. It imposed requirements with respect to domestic production and exports on many of the investments that it did accept. Its presence also discouraged some unknown number of other firms from applying in the first place, making its overall effect in limiting foreign investment in the country hard to discern.

In line with the change in world opinion about TNCs, in 1984, the new Conservative government replaced FIRA with an organization called Investment Canada. Canadian officials announced that Canada once again welcomed foreign investment. Although Investment Canada still has the power to review foreign takeovers of Canadian firms, it has turned down no applications since it came into existence. It has, however, insisted on some conditions before approving some deals. For example, when the Canadian laser company Lumonics was taken over by the Japanese conglomerate Sumatoma (because Lumonics could not raise sufficient capital in Canada), Investment Canada insisted on a number

---

[5]United Nations Center on Transnational Corporations, *Transnational Corporations in World Development: Trends and Prospects* (New York: United Nations, 1988), p. iii.

of assurances designed to keep the creative activities of Lumonics located in Canada.

In the Canada-U.S. Free Trade Agreement (FTA), Canada agreed to raise the threshold of review of U.S. takeovers of Canadian firms from a firm size of $5 million to $150 million. Critics decried this reduction in ability to screen foreign takeovers of Canadian firms. Supporters pointed out, first, that fully 80 percent of nonfinancial capital in Canada was located in firms larger than $150 million and so was still subject to review and, second, that in return for this Canadian concession, the United States had in effect exempted Canadian firms wishing to operate in that country from any review that the United States might subsequently initiate.[6]

Foreign Investment in and by Canada: Some Facts

Canada is heavily reliant on foreign investment: About 20 percent of its total economy was foreign owned in 1991. The percentages vary greatly among industries, being about 45 percent in manufacturing and over 85 percent in the car and rubber industries.

Canada is the largest single host country for U.S. foreign investment—just over $100 billion in 1991. The United States once accounted for over 75 percent of the stock of all foreign direct investment in Canada, but this share has been gradually declining for many years. It stood at about 65 percent in 1991.

Canadian foreign direct investment in the United States totaled nearly $55 billion in 1991. The gap between the two countries' investment positions has been steadily narrowing since 1975. In recent years, Canadian TNCs have been far more aggressive investors in the United States than vice

versa. As a result, Canadian direct investment in the United States grew by 800 percent in the period 1977-1991, while U.S. direct investment in Canada grew by only 230 percent over the same period. If present trends continue, Canadian investors will own as much of the U.S. capital stock as U.S. investors own of the Canadian capital stock shortly after the start of the twenty-first century.

Foreign Investment in Canada: The Debate

By and large, but with some notable exceptions, economists have been skeptical of the view that Canada loses by foreign investment. Among the benefits attributed to foreign investment are (1) more total investment than could be possible if all investment had to be financed by domestic savings, hence a larger population than could otherwise be supported by the full infrastructure; (2) a higher rate of growth due to a more rapid rise in the capital available for each worker; and (3) participation in the world's division of labour as brought about by TNCs. Among the alleged costs are (1) profits earned by foreigners rather than domestic capitalists, (2) loss of control over resource development, (3) loss of control over one's own economy, and (4) loss of good managerial and research jobs to foreign locations favoured by TNCs.

Potential Benefits

The first two advantages listed have already been discussed in our treatment of economic growth of countries that have not yet generated domestic savings large enough to finance their own domestic economic growth. The third point is key in today's globalised world. The growth of global production and globalised competition, with its attendant growth of the TNCs, means that many individual firms are developing a presence over the entire trading world. If ownership of TNCs is spread evenly over the whole advanced world, no single country can expect to own the majority of the capital in a TNC that is operating within its borders. This important point can be illustrated by a numerical example.

Assume that 60 percent of the production of goods and services in each country is done by local firms serving the domestic market, while 40 percent

---

[6]When the FTA was signed in 1988, the United States had no review mechanism for foreign investment, but the growing concern over such investment makes such a review possible in the future. By conferring national treatment on Canadian investors in the United States, the agreement effectively exempts Canada from any new U.S. practises that discriminate between foreign and domestic investors. (See Chapter 25 for a full discussion of national treatment, which in effect means that whatever laws, rules, and regulations—no more and no less—apply to domestic units also apply to foreign units to which national treatment is extended.)

is done by TNCs serving the world market. This means that a typical country can expect to own the 60 percent of its capital that is devoted to domestic production alone, plus *its share* of the 40 percent that is owned by TNCs. If the country in question is similar to Canada, domestic output will account for about 4 percent of the world production of internationally traded commodities. If it owns its share of the TNC capital involved in this production, it will own 4 percent of the 40 percent of the capital in its country that is owned by TNCs. (It will also own 4 percent of the TNC capital that is producing in other countries.) This means that the country will own 61.6 percent of the total capital producing within its borders (the 60 percent that is local capital, plus 4 percent of the 40 percent that is owned by TNCs, which is 1.6 percent of the country's total capital). The percentage owned by foreigners will be 38.4.

In such a world, to insist that the majority of the TNC production facilities located in Canada should be owned in Canada is to insist that Canada own the majority of the world's TNCs (which would require an amount vastly in excess of all Canadian wealth). The only other alternative would be to insist that production in Canada should be by domestically owned companies serving the domestic market alone and not by TNCs, which would condemn Canada to inefficient local production of most of its internationally traded goods.[7] The point is that when production is in the hands of TNCs, no one country can hope to own the bulk of TNC capital located within its borders; instead, if TNC ownership is spread more or less evenly throughout the developed world, each country will own a small proportion of the capital within its own borders—and a small proportion of the capital located in each of the other countries.

Another aspect of this point concerns the growth of firms that develop new products. Many new products are developed by TNCs. Others, however, are invented and developed by entrepreneurs starting out in their own firms—firms that grow as their new products catch on. There comes a critical point in the development of such firms when they must decide how to market their products internationally, which today effectively means over much of the world. A few manage to handle this themselves and grow to become new TNCs. More often, however, the costs and risks of creating world market links and developing the international know-how that goes with being a large TNC are just too great to be acceptable to the still small firm.

So the entrepreneur sells the firm to an existing TNC that can develop its potential. No one has been exploited. The successful entrepreneur sells out for a handsome profit, and the TNC gets a new product that its world network allows it to market efficiently. Typically, however, the TNC will be foreign owned, since, as we just determined, most TNCs operating within any one country will be foreign owned. Public policy critics are likely to perceive a national loss when the home entrepreneur is "forced" to sell out (no matter how willingly the sale was made). The point is, however, that it may be both profitable and efficient for the small entrepreneur to sell his or her company to a TNC that already has the needed world marketing capacity rather than to develop it over again, at great cost and risk. Furthermore, if public policy prevents selling out to a TNC, future entrepreneurs may be less willing to develop new products because they cannot be sold to firms capable of marketing on a world scale.

Alleged Costs

Loss of profits to foreigners. Insofar as the industries are competitive, profits are merely normal returns on capital. If foreigners provide capital that Canadians cannot provide, they get only the normal return. Employment, wages, and many other benefits stay in Canada.

More recently, however, economists have been interested in the economic profits that accompany innovations in oligopolistic industries. In oligopolies, profits can persist well into the long run, and the owners of the firm may make more than the normal return on capital. If so, ownership matters. The owners are gaining more than is being made by investors in other industries who earn just the normal return on capital. How large such profits are, and whether or not they provide a reason for public intervention to hold the profits at home, is a subject of current debate.

Loss of control over industry. All industries in Canada are subject to Canadian law. Canada can, for

---

[7]Canada could do this by imposing high tariff barriers, but not only would this be forbidden under our commitments to such international organizations as the GATT, but it would also be extremely harmful to our living standards, as shown in Chapters 24 and 25.

example, regulate the rate of resource extraction in oil and gas and impose that regulation equally on Canadian and foreign- owned firms operating in Canada. It can also have tough environmental and other laws that impose requirements on all firms in Canada.

TNCs, however, do pose a serious problem called *extraterritoriality,* which is the extension of the laws of the country where the TNC is owned to activities of that firm in other countries. The usual international principle is *national treatment,* under which foreign-owned TNCs operating in a host country are governed by the host country's laws. The United States, however, has championed the principle of extraterritoriality by sometimes trying to make U.S. multinationals that operate in other countries follow U.S. rather than host-country laws. Thus, for example, if the United States has prohibitions against trading with Cuba or China, it tries to apply these laws not only to foreign TNCs operating within the United States but also to U.S. TNCs operating in Canada and other foreign countries. Host countries have resisted these attempts to extend U.S. legal jurisdiction beyond American borders, and the issue remains unresolved. The solution lies in attempts to limit the operation of extraterritoriality; solving the problem by banning TNCs would be like cutting off one's leg to cure a boil on it, since TNCs are a key part of the international trading scene.

Many people worried that the Canada-U.S. Free Trade Agreement eroded Canadian sovereignty with respect to control over TNCs. Defenders of the agreement argued that such concerns were based on a misunderstanding of the principle of national treatment, which allows Canada and the United States each to impose its own requirements on firms operating within its borders. These requirements may differ between the two countries; all that is required by national treatment is that foreign and domestic firms be treated equally in any one country. The only thing neither country can do is use its laws to discriminate by applying tougher laws to foreign owned than to domestically owned firms. So the FTA would appear to have introduced no new reason why foreign investment should limit Canada's ability to control its economy and its environment as it wishes.

Loss of key activities.   Some industries are firmly rooted in a country by virtue of natural advantages. For example, Canadian oil must be extracted in Canada, and Canadian lumber must be cut in Canada. Thus, the oil and lumber industries are firmly rooted in Canada as long as supplies of the important natural resources exist. Other industries—high-tech ones are important examples—are much more footloose. They can be moved among countries to wherever the economic climate and economic policies are most favourable to them. The key characteristic of these industries is that they are knowledge intensive. When head offices determine the location of R&D and other knowledge-intensive activities, they make decisions that influence the course of a country's economic development. They could conceivably direct the types of production with the highest values to their home countries and keep lower-value production, which produces lower wages, in host countries.

A similar issue relates to what are called *key industries.* Some observers believe that certain key industries have important *spillovers* to the rest of the economy. Keeping these key industries at home will favourably affect the value of economic activity elsewhere in the economy. If a TNC takes over one of these key industries, it may relocate the industry to its home country, thereby harming the economies of the other country. Shipbuilding and steel production were thought to be key industries in the 1960s, and many people believe that aircraft and high-tech industries such as chips and computers are key industries today.

These are important and unresolved issues. No one is sure how important these possibilities are. Furthermore, it is not easy to see what practical policy measures should be recommended if these possibilities are shown to be important. This later issue is discussed next.

What Could Be Done?

Say that foreign investment was thought to have some harmful effects. What could be done?

It would be impractical to prohibit all, or even most, foreign investment. First, this would greatly reduce the amount of capital available in Canada, with adverse effects on Canadian economic growth. Second, this would deny Canada's participation in the large segment of international trade that is dominated by TNCs, most of which cannot be owned by Canadians. For a small trading nation such as Canada, with around 25 percent of its GDP generated by exports, that would be a serious matter.

Given the volume of Canadian savings, the most

that could be done would be to redirect foreign investment from some industries into others. This would be done by discouraging foreign investment in some key industries, hoping both that Canadian investment would flow into these industries and that foreign investment would fill in the gaps where the Canadian investment would otherwise have gone. For such a policy to be successful, bureaucrats must be able to discern the areas where it is advantageous to prevent foreign investment, Canadian capital must flow into these areas, and foreign capital must fill the gaps created by the reallocation of Canadian investment. Such a policy is full of risks, of which the following are merely illustrative.

First, because Canadian investment did not flow into the designated activities in the first place, there is a risk that it may not do so after the restrictions are imposed. Second, there is a risk that the activities will be transferred abroad if foreign TNCs are prevented from engaging in them in Canada. This is particularly likely where a foreign takeover of a Canadian firm is designed to make it a part of a large international organization with the linkages necessary for the firm's success. In this case, the substitution is not of Canadian-owned for foreign-owned activity in Canada but of foreign-located for Canadian-located activity. Third, politicians and administrators must be able to identify and promote those activities that are best held in Canadian ownership. Large firms, such as the CPR, CIL, CAI, and Noranda, are the ones that would cause the most political problems if they were taken over by foreigners. Unfortunately, these most visible and best-known companies are not necessarily the ones with the greatest potential payoff from restricting foreign ownership, since they are likely to be only normally profitable. If there is a case to hold ownership at home, it is likely to be stronger for small and midsize industries that are not household names but are at the forefront of industrial development. Yet it is not clear that these are the industries that the political process would hold at home if foreign investment were once again to be seriously controlled.

Conclusion

The worldwide debate about the value of foreign investment is not as heated as it was a decade or two ago. Most countries are aware of the value of foreign investment in economic growth and of the need in today's globalised world for TNCs, most of which cannot be owned by any one small country.

There is debate about the value of encouraging domestic ownership of certain key industries and about the value of controlling the activities of TNCs within one country by such means as requiring local R&D expenditure. There is also an awareness of how easy it is to kill the goose that lays the golden egg by passing laws that drive TNCs to relocate abroad.

The prevailing view in the Canadian government since the mid 1980s has been that foreign investment is beneficial on balance and that it should be subject to only a minimum of controls. According to this view, TNCs are profit maximizers who will locate activities where it is most profitable to do so rather than hold them in their home country as a matter of course. In that case, the market activities of TNCs will produce the most efficient international allocation of resources and the highest possible living standards in both home and host countries. Furthermore, according to this view, the international economy with globalised competition is so complex and sophisticated that investment-regulating intervention is all too likely to do more harm than good. Critics are not so sure. They advocate controls to hold certain key industries under domestic ownership and certain key activities, such as R&D, in home locations.

The Goals of Firms

We have seen two major reasons why one firm may take over another. First, a stand-alone firm in one country may do better when restructured as a part of a large TNC. In this case, the firm's managers may have been maximizing the firm's profits as a stand-alone firm. Second, the firm's managers may not be maximizing its profits. In this case, a takeover firm can raise the original firm's profits without changing its organizational structure. The new management, whether another domestic or a foreign firm, can then, after the takeover, exploit profitable opportunities that are being ignored by the present management.

The view that many firms may systematically maximize something other than profits is made plausible by the nature of the modern corporation. One hundred years ago, the single-proprietor firm, whose manager was its owner, was common in many branches of industry. In such firms, the singleminded pursuit of profits would be expected. Today, however, ownership is commonly diversified among thousands of stockholders, and the firm's managers are rarely its owners. Arranging matters so that managers always act in the best interests of stockholders is, as we shall see, anything but straightforward. Thus there is potential for managers to maximize something other than profits.

The Separation of Ownership from Control

In corporations, the stockholders elect directors, who appoint managers. Directors are supposed to represent stockholders' interests and to determine broad policies that the managers will carry out. In order to conduct the complicated business of running a large firm, a full-time professional management group must be given broad powers of decision. Although managerial decisions can be reviewed from time to time, they cannot be supervised in detail. The links between the directors and the managers are typically weak enough so that top management often truly controls the corporation over long periods of time.

As long as directors have confidence in the managerial group, they accept and ratify their proposals. Stockholders in turn elect and reelect directors who are proposed to them. If the managerial group does not satisfy the directors' expectations, it may be replaced, but this is a disruptive and drastic action that is seldom employed.

Within wide limits, then, effective control of the corporation's activities resides with the managers. Although the managers are legally employed by the stockholders, they remain largely independent of them. Indeed, the management group typically asks for, and gets, the *proxies* of enough stockholders to elect directors who will reappoint it, and thus it perpetuates itself in office. (A **proxy** authorizes a person who is attending a stockholders' meeting to cast a stockholder's vote.) In the vast majority of cases, nearly all votes cast are in the form of proxies.

None of this matters unless the managers pursue interests different from those of the stockholders. Do the interests of the two groups diverge? To study this question, we need to look at what is called principal-agent theory.

Principal-Agent Theory

If you (the *principal*) hire the boy down the block (your *agent*) to mow your lawn while you are away, all you can observe is how the lawn looks when you come back. He *could* have mowed it every 10 days, as you agreed, or he could have waited until two days before you were due home and mowed it only once. By prevailing on a friend or a neighbor to *monitor* your employee's behaviour, you could find out what he actually did, but only at some cost.

When you direct a physician to diagnose and to treat your lower back pain, it is almost impossible for you to monitor the physician's effort and diligence on your behalf. You have not been to medical school, and much of what the physician does will be a mystery to you.

This latter situation is close to the relationship that exists between stockholders and managers. The managers have information and expertise that the stockholders do not have—indeed, that is *why* they are the managers. The stockholders can observe profits, but they cannot directly observe the managers' efforts. To complicate matters further, even when the managers' behaviour can be observed, the stockholders do not generally have the expertise to evaluate whether that behaviour was the best available. Everyone can see how the firm does do, but it takes very detailed knowledge of the firm and the industry to know how well it *could* have done. Boards of directors, who represent the firm's stockholders, can acquire some of the relevant expertise and monitor managerial behaviour, but, again, this is costly.

These examples illustrate the **principal-agent problem:** the problem of designing mechanisms that will induce *agents* to act in their *principals'* interests. In general, unless there is costly monitoring of the agent's behaviour, the problem cannot be completely solved. Hired managers (like hired gardeners) will generally wish to pursue their own goals. They cannot ignore profits, because if they perform badly enough, they will lose their jobs. Just how much latitude they have to pursue their own goals at the expense of profits will depend on many things, including the degree of competition in the industry and the possibility of takeover by more profit-oriented management.

Principal-agent analysis shows that when ownership and control are separated, the self-interest of agents will tend to make profits

lower than in a perfectly frictionless world in which principals act as their own agents.

We know that in the case of firms, the principals, the stockholders, are interested in maximizing profits. What different motives might their agents, the managers, have?

Sales Maximization

If agents do not maximize profits on behalf of the principals, what do they do? One alternative is that they seek to maximize sales. Suppose that the managers need to make some minimum level of profits to keep the stockholders satisfied. Beyond this they are free to maximize their firm's sales revenue. This is a sensible policy on the part of management, the argument runs, because salary, power, and prestige all depend more on the size of a firm than on its rate of profits. Generally, the manager of a large, normally profitable corporation will earn a salary that is considerably higher than the salary earned by the manager of a small but highly profitable corporation.

The sales-maximization hypothesis says that managers of firms seek to maximize their firms' sales revenue, subject to a profit constraint.

Sales maximization subject to a profit constraint leads to the prediction that a firm's managers will sacrifice some profits by setting price below and output above their profit-maximizing levels. (See Figure 16-1.)

Failure to Minimize Costs

The sales-maximization hypothesis implies that the firm's managers will choose to produce more than the profit-maximizing level of output. It is also possible that firms will produce their chosen output at greater than minimum cost. Why would a firm's managers fail to minimize costs?

There are many possible answers, but the most straightforward one is that minimizing costs can demand a great deal of detailed managerial attention, and if management can avoid doing so, it would prefer not to make the necessary effort. Moreover, it is usually costly for a firm to change its routine behaviour. If this is so, one firm may operate at a higher cost than another, but it will still not be worthwhile for the first firm to copy the behaviour

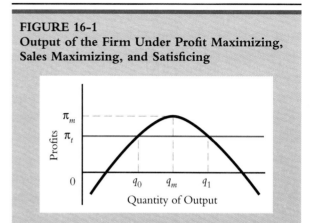

FIGURE 16-1
Output of the Firm Under Profit Maximizing, Sales Maximizing, and Satisficing

The "best" level of output depends on the motivation of the firm. The curve shows the level of profits associated with each level of output. A profit-maximizing firm produces output q_m and earns profit π_m. A sales-maximizing firm, with a minimum profit constraint of π_t, produces the output q_1.

A satisficing firm with a target level of profits of π_t is willing to produce any output between q_0 and q_1. Thus satisficing allows a range of outputs on either side of the profit-maximizing level, whereas sales maximization results in a higher output than profit maximization.

of the second firm. The *transactions costs* of making the change could outweigh the benefits. As with sales maximization, pressure from stockholders, competition from other firms, and threat of takeover will limit the extent to which economic or technological inefficiency can survive, but they may not eliminate inefficiency.

Nonmaximizing Theories

Many students of corporate behaviour, particularly economists based in business schools, criticise the profit-maximization assumption from a perspective different from that given by principal-agent theory. They argue that there are other reasons for doubting that modern corporations are "simple profit-maximizing computers." They believe that corporations are *profit oriented* in the sense that, other things being equal, more profits are preferred to less profits. They do not believe, however, that corporations are profit maximizers.

Full-Cost Pricing

Most manufacturing firms sell differentiated products and are price setters. As we saw in Chapter 14, they must quote a price for each of their products rather than accept a price that has been set in some impersonal competitive market. Simple profit-maximizing theory predicts that these firms will change their prices in response to every change in demand and cost that they experience. Yet students of large firms have long observed that except during periods of rapid inflation, such price flexibility rarely is observed. In the short run, prices of manufactured goods do not appear to vary in response to every shift in demand.

This short-run behaviour is consistent with the hypothesis of **full-cost pricing,** originally advanced in the 1930s by Robert Hall, a British economist, and Charles Hitch, an American economist, following a series of detailed case studies of actual pricing decisions. Case studies in the intervening decades have continued to reveal the widespread use of full-cost pricing procedures.

The full-cost pricer, instead of equating marginal revenue with marginal cost, sets price equal to average cost at normal-capacity output plus a fixed markup.

The full-cost pricing firm changes its prices when its average costs change substantially (as a result of such events as a new union contract or a sharp change in the prices of key raw materials), and it may occasionally change its markup. However, its short-run pricing behaviour is rather unresponsive to changes in demand.

A nonmaximizing interpretation of full-cost pricing. Some modern critics of profit-maximizing theory hold that the prevalence of conventional full-cost practises shows that prices are typically not at their profit-maximizing level. They also hold that full-cost pricing shows that firms are creatures of custom that make only occasional profit-oriented changes at fairly infrequent intervals.

A profit-maximizing interpretation of full-cost pricing. The short-term stickiness of oligopolistic prices can be accounted for under profit-maximizing theory by the costs for a multi-product firm to change its list prices. The possible conflict between full-cost and profit-maximizing theory then concerns only the setting of the markup that relates prices to costs. If markups are arbitrary and only rarely revised, there is conflict. If, however, the markup is the profit-maximizing one for normal-capacity output, full-cost pricing can be consistent with profit maximization.

Satisficing Theory

A major group of critics of profit maximization develop their argument as follows: Firms operate in highly uncertain environments. Their long-term success or failure is determined largely by their ability to administer innovation and change. But the risks of innovation are large, and the outcomes are highly uncertain. Rational firms tend, therefore, to be quite risk averse. They develop routines of behaviour that they follow as long as they are successful. Only when profits fall low enough to threaten their survival do they adopt risky courses of action.

Michael Porter of Harvard University holds this view and argues on the basis of considerable evidence that firms react to the stick of threatened losses of existing profit more than to the carrot of possible increases in profit. Other supporters of this view, such as Richard Nelson and Sidney Winter, argue that firms simply cannot handle the task of scrutinizing all possibilities, calculating the probable outcomes, and then choosing among these so as to maximize their expected profits. Instead, in their view, firms carry on with existing routines as long as these produce *satisfactory* profits, and only when profits fall to unacceptably low levels do the firms search for new ways of doing old things or new lines of activity.

One way of formalizing these views is the theory of **satisficing.** It was first put forward by Professor Herbert Simon of Carnegie-Mellon University, who in 1978 was awarded the Nobel Prize in economics for his work on the behaviour of firms. He wrote, "We must expect the firm's goals to be not maximizing profits but attaining a certain level or rate of profit, holding a certain share of the market or a certain level of sales." In general, a firm is said to be satisficing if the goal of its behaviour is to provide a *satisfactory* (rather than optimal) level of performance.

According to the satisficing hypothesis, firms could produce any one of a range of outputs that produce profits at least equal to the target level. This contrasts with the unique output that is predicted by profit-maximizing theory. Figure 16-1 compares satisficing behaviour with sales- and profit-maximizing behaviour.

The theory of satisficing predicts not a unique equilibrium output but a range of possible outputs that includes the profit-maximizing output.

The Importance of Nonmaximizing Theories

An impressive array of empirical and theoretical evidence can be gathered in support of nonmaximizing theories. What would be the implications if they were accepted as being better theories of the behaviour of the economy than the "standard model," which is based on the assumption of profit maximization?

To the extent that existing non-profit-maximizing theories are correct, the economic system does not perform with the delicate precision that follows from profit maximization. Firms will not always respond quickly and precisely to small changes in market signals from either the private sector or government policy. Nor are they certain to make radical changes in their behaviour even when the profit incentives to do so are large.

The nonmaximizing theories imply that in many cases, firms' responses to small changes in market signals will be of uncertain speed and direction.

According to all existing theories, maximizing and nonmaximizing, firms will tend to sell more when demand increases and less when it decreases. They will also tend to alter their prices and their input mixes when they face *sufficiently large* changes in input prices. Moreover, there are limits to the extent to which the nonmaximizing behaviour can survive in the marketplace. Failure to respond to profit opportunities can lead to takeover by a more profit-oriented management—which is what we discussed earlier in the chapter. Although the threat of takeover does not force managers to maximize

profits at all times, it does put real limits on the extent to which they can ignore profits.

Profits are a potent force in the life and death of firms. The resilience of profit-maximizing theory and its ability to predict the economy's reactions to many major changes (such as the dramatic variations in energy prices that have occurred over the past two decades) suggest that firms are at least strongly motivated by the pursuit of profits.

Three key points are at issue here.

1. The extent to which firms respond predictably to changes in such economic signals as output and input prices, taxes and subsidies.
2. The extent to which nonmaximizing behaviour provides scope for profit-oriented takeovers, mergers, and buyouts.
3. The way in which firms manage very-long-run change. One of the most important lessons learned by economists in the last decade is that much oligopolistic competition takes place over very-long-run matters. How the firm performs relative to its domestic or foreign competitors with respect to product and process innovation will be the major determinant of its competitive performance over a decade or so. These matters require making decisions on highly uncertain issues. Many investigators believe that the performance of firms in these matters is best understood by theories that take account of the firm's organizational structure and the routines that it uses to guide its decision making.

In the past decade or so, the question of how firms behave has received renewed attention from both economists and organization theorists. Almost everyone in the field agrees that firms do not exactly maximize profits at all times and in all places. At the same time, almost everyone agrees that firms cannot stray too far from the goal of profit maximization. Just how far is too far depends on the circumstances in which firms operate and the mechanisms that firms' owners can use to influence managers. Just how much firms' nonmaximizing behaviour influences how they manage change is another important unsettled issue. These areas are at the frontier of current economic research.

SUMMARY

1. In the market for corporate control, would-be buyers of firms deal with would-be sellers (in friendly takeovers, mergers, and buyouts) as well as with reluctant sellers (in hostile takeovers). Buyers who believe that they can operate a firm more profitably than its present management or than its present organization allows can afford to pay more than the present market value of the firm's equities to acquire it. The possibility of such purchases provides an incentive for current managers to come close to maximizing the firm's profits and encourages their replacement by new buyers when they do not.

2. Another major reason for a takeover of a domestic firm by a foreign TNC is to integrate the local firm into the large multinational organization.

3. Leveraged buyouts, financed by junk bonds, have been a means of buying out firms whose organization is too large and cumbersome—often as a result of conglomerate mergers of earlier decades. If the deal is successful, the firm is broken up into its constituent parts, which are sold for a total exceeding the purchase price of the whole. The junk bonds are then retired, with a profit left over for the purchasers. This is the market system working to undo an earlier experiment (conglomerate mergers) that proved to be a failure.

4. Foreign direct investment has played a large part in opening up less developed countries over the past few centuries. In their time, Canada and the United States were less developed than the United Kingdom and some other European countries and were the recipients of foreign investment that flowed from Europe to the New World.

5. As the countries of the New World grew, they were able to generate a rising flow of domestic savings, which reduced their need for new investment, repatriated some old foreign investment, and provided a flow of investment to newer, less developed countries. The United States has experienced this entire cycle. Canada, having a smaller population in a larger geographical area, still needs foreign investment. However, the flow is a much smaller proportion of total investment than it has been in the past, and since 1975, Canada has been a net exporter of foreign direct investment, sending more abroad to buy foreign assets than it takes in from foreigners who buy Canadian assets.

6. The growth of transnational corporations means that no country can hope to own a majority of the capital that is devoted to the production within its borders of internationally traded commodities. The TNCs also have the power to arbitrate national policies, thereby reducing the effectiveness of many policies designed to give advantages to the initiating country.

7. There is debate in Canada about the benefits and costs of foreign investment, but such investment could not be dispensed with, since the wealth involved vastly exceeds Canadians' ability to buy it. The most that can be expected from an active policy to influence foreign investment is to redirect such investment out of some industries and into others. Economists and others do not agree,

however, on which sectors should be targeted for reducing the degree of foreign ownership (and which should increase as a result of redirecting that investment).

8. Principal-agent theory gives support to the idea that corporate managers will not always operate in the best interests of the stockholders; that is, the managers may pursue their own interests rather than simply maximizing profits. Sales maximization is an example of such a pursuit.

9. Even if individual firms do not always maximize profits, it is possible that the industry will be characterized by behaviour that is approximately profit maximizing. The reason is that those firms that come closest to maximizing profits will prosper and grow while those further away from profit maximization will shrink or fail altogether.

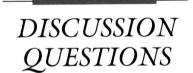

TOPICS FOR REVIEW

Mergers, takeovers, and buyouts

Leveraged buyouts

Junk bonds

Transnational corporations

Foreign direct investment

Portfolio investment

Sales maximization

Satisficing

DISCUSSION QUESTIONS

1. In light of principal-agent theory, why might dentists and lawyers be required to subscribe to professional codes of ethics that prevent (or at least limit) their ability to sell unneeded services to their clients? Why do we not see similar codes of ethics for automobile mechanics?

2. In his now-famous article "Who Is Us?" Robert Reich criticises U.S. policy for giving assistance to domestically *owned* rather than domestically *located* TNCs. Why, he asks, should a U.S.- (or Canadian-) owned firm get R&D assistance for research done in Taiwan to produce goods in Singapore that is denied to a Japanese-owned firm doing research in California (or Toronto) to develop new products to be produced in Kentucky (or Winnipeg)? Who gains the benefits from subsidies provided by governments (and paid for by taxpayers) to each of these types of firms?

3. *The London Economist* ran the following story in 1988, under the headline "Someone's Wrong":

> Notice the curious paradox involved in the biggest and third biggest takeover deals in history? Kohlberg Kravis Roberts is offering $20.3 billion so RJR Nabisco can split its tobacco companies away from the food-making parts of its empire by taking Winston, Camel and Salem private, while selling off Nabisco and Del Monte. [*Note:* Kohlberg's eventual winning bid was billions higher.] Over at Philip Morris, the exact opposite is going on: The company is willing to

pay $11.5 billion to add another food company, Kraft, to its existing tobacco and food business (Marlboro, Benson and Hedges, General Foods). More than $30 billion is therefore riding on two flatly contradictory views of the best future for the food and tobacco business. LBOs may be fashionable, but no one can accuse the American investors of herd instinct.

    a. Why does The Economist find these behaviours so puzzling?

    b. Think of some explanations for the puzzle and discuss them.

4. Comment on these lead lines to recent newspaper stories.

    a. "Critic calls takeovers and mergers *fiscal roulette* that does nothing to contribute to Canadian national income."

    b. "The candidate called on Canadians to take back their country by ending all foreign ownership."

    c. "Union leaders worry that concern over Quebec separation may cause exodus of foreign investment from Canada."

5. Assume that each of the following assertions is factually correct. Taken together, what would they tell you about the prediction that big business is increasing its control of the North American economy?

    a. The share of total manufacturing assets owned by the 100 largest corporations has been rising over the past 25 years.

    b. The number of new firms begun each year has increased over the past 25 years.

    c. The share of manufacturing in total production has been decreasing for 40 years.

    d. Profits as a percentage of national income are no higher now than half a century ago.

6.   We have become accustomed to a quality of life that can survive only through profits. For profits not only create jobs and goods, they furnish essential tax revenues. Federal, state, and local taxes finance the countless programs that our citizens demand—from paving the roads on which we drive to building our country's defense forces . . . to helping millions of Americans who need some form of assistance.

Comment on this excerpt from an Allied Chemical Corporation advertisement.

7. "Our list prices are really set by our accounting department: They add a fixed markup to their best estimates of fully accounted cost and send these to the operating divisions. Managers of these divisions may not change those prices without permission of the board of directors, which is seldom given. Operating divisions may, however, provide special discounts if necessary to stay competitive." Does this testimony by the president of a leading manufacturing company suggest that his firm is a profit maximizer?

8. The leading automobile tire manufacturers sell original equipment (OE) tires to automobile manufacturers at a price below the average total cost of all the tires they make and sell. This happens year after year. Is this consistent with profit-maximizing behaviour in the short run? In the long run? If it is not consistent, what does it show? Do OE tires compete with replacement tires?

PART FIVE

THE DISTRIBUTION OF INCOME

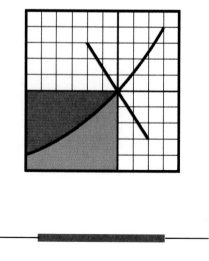

17

Factor Pricing and Factor Mobility

Why, during the first seven decades of the twentieth century, did the proportion of total earned income going to the poorest 20 percent of Canadian citizens rise while the proportion going to the top 20 percent fell? Why was this trend reversed in the early 1970s, with the share of earned income going to the poorest 20 percent falling and the share going to the top 20 percent rising?[1] Are these changes in income shares due to the changing structure of the economy? Are they influenced by government policy and by social changes, such as increased gender equality, affirmative action, and the decline of unions? These and many other related questions take us into the determination of the distribution of income, which is the subject of Part 5.

Functional Distribution and Size Distribution

The founders of classical economics, Adam Smith and David Ricardo, were concerned with the distribution of income among what were then the three great social classes: workers, capitalists, and landowners. They defined three factors of production as labour, capital, and land. The return to each factor was treated as the income of the respective social class.

Smith and Ricardo were interested in what determined the income of each class relative to the total national income. Their theories predicted that, as society progressed, landlords would become relatively better off and capitalists would become relatively worse off. Karl Marx had a different theory. His theory predicted that as growth occurred, capitalists would become relatively better off and workers would become relatively worse off (at least until the whole capitalist system collapsed).

These nineteenth-century debates focused on what is now called the **functional distribution of income,** defined as the distribution of total income among the major factors of production. Table 17-1 shows data for the functional distribution of income in Canada in 1992.

Although functional distribution categories (wages, rent, profits) pervade current statistics, modern economists have shifted their emphasis to another way of looking at differ-

---

[1]We need to say earned income because this is the income produced by market forces. Because of the operation of the Canadian tax and income support systems, the rise in inequalities of income that the unaided market would have produced (and that actually did occur in the United States even after taxes and income transfers) did not occur in Canada.

TABLE 17-1 Functional Distribution of National Income in Canada, 1992

Type of income	Billions of dollars	Percentage of total
Employee compensation	389.2	76.1
Corporate profits	31.9	6.2
Proprietor's income, including rent	37.1	7.2
Interest	53.5	10.5
Total	511.7	100.0

Source: Statistics Canada, 13–207.

Total income is classified here according to the nature of the factor service that earned the income. Although these data show that employee compensation accounts for over 75 percent of national income, this does not mean that workers and their families receive only that proportion of national income. Many households will have income in more than one category listed in the table.

TABLE 17-2 Incomes of Canadian Families, 1991

Income class	Percentage of families
Less than $9,999	2.5
$10,000–$19,999	11.6
$20,000–$29,999	18.9
$30,000–$39,999	19.9
$40,000–$49,999	16.7
$50,000–$59,999	12.3
$60,000 and over	18.1

Source: Statistics Canada, 13–210.

Although median family income in 1991 was about $38,500, many families received much less than this, and some received a great deal more. While 18 percent of Canadian families had very comfortable incomes of more than $60,000, over 13 percent had to subsist on incomes below $20,000. The figures are after taxes have been paid and transfers received.

ences in incomes, called the **size distribution of income.** This term refers to the distribution of income among different households without reference to the source of the income or the social class of the household. Tables 17-2 and 17-3 show that in Canada in 1991 there was substantial inequality in the size distribution of income, but that Canadian taxes and income transfers substantially reduced that income inequality.

Inequality in the distribution of income is shown graphically in Figure 17-1. This curve of income distribution, called a **Lorenz curve,** shows how much of total income is accounted for by given proportions of the nation's households. (The farther the curve bends away from the diagonal, the more unequal is the distribution of income.)

Today, most economists devote more attention to the size distribution of income than to the functional distribution. After all, some capitalists (such as the owners of small retail stores) are in the lower part of the income scale, and some wage earners (such as professional athletes) are at the upper end of the income scale. Moreover, if someone is poor, it matters little whether that person is a landowner or a worker.

To understand the size distribution of income, we must first study how individual incomes are de-

termined. Superficial explanations of differences in income, such as "People earn according to their ability," are clearly inadequate. Incomes are distributed much more unequally than any *measured* index of ability, be it IQ, physical strength, or typing skill. In what sense was Wayne Gretsky four times as able

TABLE 17-3 Inequality in Family Income Distribution, 1991

Family income rank	Percentage share of aggregate income	
	Before taxes and transfers	After taxes and transfers
Lowest fifth	2.4	7.7
Second fifth	10.4	13.3
Middle fifth	17.7	18.1
Fourth fifth	25.4	23.6
Highest fifth	44.1	37.3

Source: Statistics Canada, 13–210.

The distribution of income is unequal before and after taxes. The first column shows the inequality of income produced by market forces. The second column shows that the Canadian tax and income transfer system, which is discussed in detail in Part 6, substantially reduced income inequalities.

FIGURE 17-1
A Lorenz Curve of Family Income in Canada

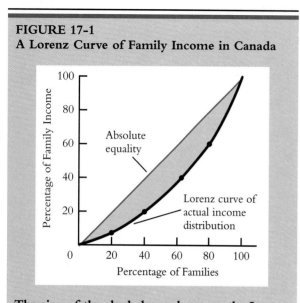

The size of the shaded area between the Lorenz curve and the diagonal is a measure of the inequality of income distribution. If there were complete income equality, the bottom 20 percent of income receivers would receive 20 percent of the income, and so forth, and the Lorenz curve would coincide with the diagonal line. Because the lowest 20 percent receive only 6 percent of the income, the Lorenz curve lies below the diagonal line. The extent to which it bends away from the straight line indicates the amount of inequality in the distribution of income.

a hockey player as Trevor Linden? He averages only about 40 more goals per season, yet he earns four times as much. However, if answers that are couched in terms of worth and ability are easily refuted, so are answers such as "It's all a matter of luck" or "It's just the system." In this chapter, we investigate answers that run deeper than superficial explanations.

Factor Pricing

In this chapter we confine ourselves to goods and factor markets that are perfectly competitive. This means that individual firms are price takers in both markets. On the one hand, they face a given price for the product they produce, and that price is both their average and marginal revenue. On the other hand, they face a given price of each factor that they buy, and that price is both the average and marginal cost of the factor.

Dealing first with firms that are price takers in product and factor markets allows us to study the principles of factor price determination in the simplest context. Once these are understood, it is relatively easy to allow for monopolistic elements in either or both types of markets. This is done in Chapter 18.

The income that a factor earns depends on the price charged for its services and on the quantity that is employed. To determine factor incomes, therefore, we need to ask how markets determine these prices and quantities. To anticipate, the answer is that factor prices and quantities are determined in just the same way as are the prices and quantities of goods—by demand and supply. What is new about factor pricing arises from the *determinants* of factor demands and factor supplies.

The Link Between Output and Input Decisions

In Chapters 10 and 11, we saw how firms' costs varied with their outputs and how they could achieve cost minimization by finding the least costly combination of factors to produce any given output. In Chapter 12, we saw that firms in perfect competition decided how much to produce by equating their marginal costs to given market prices. We also saw how the market supply curve interacted in each goods market with the market demand curve of consumers. This interaction determines the market price as well as the quantity that is produced and consumed.

These events in goods markets have implications for factor markets. The decisions of firms on how much to produce, and how to produce it, imply specific demands for various quantities of the factors of production. These demands, together with the supplies of the factors of production (which are determined by the owners of the factors), come together in factor markets. Together, they determine the quantities of the various factors of production that are employed, their prices, and the incomes earned by their owners.

The above discussion shows that there is a close relationship between the production and pricing of the goods and services produced by firms on the one hand and the pricing, employment, and incomes earned by the factors of production they hire on the other hand. They are two aspects of a single set of economic activities relating to the production of goods and services and the allocation of the nation's resources among their various possible uses. This discussion provides a brief introduction to one of the great insights of economics:

When demand and supply interact to determine the allocation of resources among various lines of production, they also determine the incomes of the factors of production that are used in making the outputs.

The rest of this chapter is an elaboration of this important theme. We first study the demand for factors, then their supply, and finally how they come together to determine factor prices and quantities.

The Demand for Factors

Firms require the services of land, labour, capital, and natural resources[2] to be used as inputs. Firms also use the products of other firms as their inputs, such as steel, plastics, and electricity.

If we investigate the production of these produced inputs, we will find that they, too, are made by using land, labour, capital, natural resources, and other produced inputs. If we continue following through the chain of outputs used as inputs, we can account for all of the economy's output in terms of inputs of the basic factors of production—land, labour, and capital, and natural resources. The theory of factor pricing applies to *all* inputs used by a firm. The theory of distribution explains the division of total national income among the owners of the basic factors: land, labour, capital, and natural resources.

---

[2] Although natural resources are often included with land as a single factor of production, they have so many important special characteristics that it is sometimes worthwhile to treat them as a separate factor. Some of the issues involved with pricing natural resources are discussed in the final section of Chapter 18.

Firms require inputs not for their own sake but as a means to produce goods and services. For example, the demand for computer programmers and technicians is growing as more and more computers are used. The demand for carpenters and building materials rises and falls as the amount of housing construction rises and falls. Thus, demand for any input is derived from the demand for the goods and services that it helps to produce; for this reason, the demand for a factor of production is called a **derived demand.**

Derived demand provides a link between the markets for output and the markets for inputs.

The Quantity of a Factor Demanded

We start by deriving a famous relation that holds in equilibrium for every factor employed by a wide class of firms. In Chapter 12, we established the rules for the maximization of a firm's profits in the short run. When one factor is fixed and another is variable, the profit-maximizing firm increases its output until the last unit produced adds just as much to cost as to revenue, that is, until marginal cost equals marginal revenue. Another way of stating that the firm maximizes profits is to say that *the firm will increase production up to the point at which the last unit of the variable factor employed adds just as much to revenue as it does to cost.*

The addition to total cost resulting from employing one more unit of a factor is its price. (Recall that the firm is assumed to buy its factors in competitive markets.) So if one more worker is hired at a wage of $15 per hour, the addition to the firm's costs is $15.

The amount that a unit of a variable factor adds to revenue is the amount that the unit adds to total output multiplied by the change in revenue caused by selling an extra unit of output.

In Chapter 10, we called the variable factor's addition to total output its *marginal product*. When dealing with factor markets, economists use the term **marginal *physical* product** (MPP) to avoid confusion with the revenue concepts that they also need to use.

The change in revenue caused by selling one extra unit of output is just the price of the output,

P (since the firm is a price taker in the market for its output).

The resulting amount, which is *MPP* × *P*, is called the factor's **marginal revenue product** and given the symbol *MRP*. **[29]**

For example, if the variable factor's marginal physical product is two units per hour and the price of a unit of output is $7.50, then the factor's marginal revenue product is $15 ($7.50 × 2).

We can now restate the condition for a firm to be maximizing its profits in two ways. First:

The addition to total costs caused by hiring another unit of the variable factor =
The factor's marginal revenue product (*MRP*)   [1]

Because the firm is a price taker in both its input and output markets, we can restate Equation 1 by noting that the term before the equal sign is just the price of a unit of the variable factor, which we call *w*, while the term after the equal sign is the factor's marginal physical product, *MPP*, multiplied by the price at which the output is sold, which we call *P*. In words, this gives us:

Price of a unit of the variable factor =
The factor's marginal physical product multiplied by its market price   [2a]

and in symbols:

$$w = MPP \times P \qquad [2b]$$

To check your understanding of Equation 2, consider an example. Suppose that the variable factor is available to the firm at a cost of $10 a unit (*w* =$10). Suppose also that employing another unit of the factor adds three units to output (*MPP* = 3). Suppose further that output is sold for $5 a unit (*P* = $5). Thus the additional unit of the variable factor adds $15 to the firm's revenue and $10 to its costs. Hiring one more unit of the factor brings in $5 more than it costs. *The firm will take on more of the variable factor whenever its marginal revenue product exceeds its price.* Now alter the example so that the last unit of the variable factor taken on by the firm has a marginal physical product of one unit of output—it adds only one extra unit to output—and so adds only $5 to revenue. Clearly, the firm can increase

profits by cutting back on its use of the factor, since laying off one unit reduces revenues by $5 while reducing costs by $10. *The firm will lay off units of the variable factor whenever its marginal revenue product is less than its price.* Finally, assume that another unit of the factor taken on, or laid off, has an *MPP* of two units, so that it increases revenue by $10. Now the firm cannot increase its profits by altering its employment of the variable factor in either direction. *The firm cannot increase its profits by altering employment of the variable factor whenever the factor's marginal revenue product equals its price.*

This example illustrates what was said earlier: We are doing nothing that is essentially new; instead, we are merely looking at the firm's profit-maximizing behaviour from the point of view of its inputs rather than its output. In Chapters 12 and 13, we saw the firm varying its output until the marginal cost of producing another unit was equal to the marginal revenue derived from selling that unit. Now we see the same profit-maximizing behaviour in terms of the firm varying its inputs until the marginal cost of another unit of input is just equal to the revenue derived from selling the unit's marginal product.

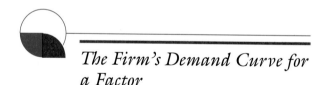

The Firm's Demand Curve for a Factor

We now know what determines the quantity of a variable factor a firm will buy when faced with some specific price of the factor and some specific price of its output. Next we wish to derive the firm's whole demand curve, which tells us how much the firm will buy at *each* price of the variable factor.

To derive a firm's demand curve for a factor, we start by considering the right-hand side of Equation 2b, which tells us that the factor's marginal revenue product is made up of a physical component and a value component.

The physical component of MRP.   As the quantity of the variable factor varies, output will vary. The hypothesis of diminishing returns, first discussed in Chapter 10, predicts what will happen: As the firm

FIGURE 17-2
From Marginal Physical Product to Demand Curve

(i) The *MPP* curve   (ii) The *MRP* curve and the demand curve

Each additional unit of the factor employed adds a certain amount to total product [part (i)] and hence a certain amount to total revenue [part (ii)], and this determines the amount of the factor firms will demand at each price. Part (i) assumes data that are consistent with marginal productivity theory; it shows the addition to the firm's *output* produced by additional units of labour hired. The curve is negatively sloped because of the law of diminishing returns.

Part (ii) shows the addition to the firm's *revenue* caused by the employment of each additional unit of labour. It is the marginal physical product from part (i) multiplied by the price at which that product is sold. In this case the price is assumed to be $5. (The multiplication is by market price because the firm is assumed to be a price taker in the market for its output.)

Since the firm equates the price of the variable factor, which is labour in this case, to the factor's marginal revenue product, it follows that the *MRP* curve, in part (ii), is also the demand curve for labour, showing how much will be employed at each price.

adds further units of the variable factor to a given quantity of the fixed factor, the additions to output will eventually get smaller and smaller. In other words, the factor's marginal physical product declines. This is illustrated in part (i) of Figure 17-2, which uses hypothetical data that have the same general characteristics as the data in Table 10-1 on p. 185. The negative slope of the *MPP* curve reflects the operation of the law of diminishing returns: Each unit of labour adds less to total output than the previous unit.

The value component of MRP. To convert the marginal physical product curve of Figure 17-2(i) into a curve showing the marginal revenue product of the variable factor, we need to know the value of the extra physical product. As long as the firm sells its output in a competitive market, this value is sim-

ply the marginal physical product multiplied by the market price at which the firm sells its product.[3]

This operation is illustrated in part (ii) of Figure 17-2, which shows a marginal revenue product

_____

[3]The basic principle is that firms should equate the addition to cost of buying another unit of a variable factor with the addition to revenue caused by selling the output of that unit, which we call the factor's marginal revenue product, *MRP.* The *MRP* is always composed of a physical component, which is the factor's *MPP*, and a value component, which is the marginal revenue of selling those extra physical units of output. Because in this chapter, our firms are price takers in their output markets, the marginal revenue is just the price they face in that market. If the firm faces a negatively sloped demand curve, we know from Chapter 13 that the addition to the revenue from selling further units is not the market price, because marginal revenue is less than price. In Chapter 18 we will derive the demand for a factor on the part of a firm that faces a negatively sloped demand curve for its output.

curve for labour on the assumption that the firm sells its product in a competitive market at a price of $5 a unit. This curve shows how much would be added to revenue by employing one more unit of the factor *at each level of total employment of the factor.*

From MRP to the demand curve.   Equation 2b states that the profit-maximizing firm will employ additional units of the factor up to the point at which the *MRP* equals the price of the factor. If, for example, the price of the variable factor were $2,000 per month in the example shown in Figure 17-2, then it would be most profitable to employ 60 workers. (There is no point in employing a sixty-first, since that would add just less than $2,000 to revenue but a full $2,000 to costs.) So the profit-maximizing firm hires the quantity of the variable factor that equates the marginal revenue product with the price of the variable factor. Thus, the curve that relates the quantity of the variable factor employed to its *MRP* is also the curve that relates the quantity of the variable factor the firm wishes to employ to its price.

The *MRP* curve of the variable factor is the same as the demand curve for that variable factor.

The Slope of an Industry's Demand Curve for the Factor

So far, we have seen how a single firm that takes its market price as given will vary its quantity demanded for a factor as that factor's price changes. But when a factor's price changes and *all firms* in a competitive industry vary the amount of the factor that they demand in order to vary their output, the price of the industry's product changes. That change will have repercussions on desired output and the quantity of the factor demanded.

For example, a fall in carpenters' wages will reduce the cost of producing houses, thus shifting the supply curve of houses to the right. Price-taking construction firms would plan to increase construction, and hence increase the quantity of carpenters demanded, by some specific amount if the price of houses does not change. Because the demand curve for houses is negatively sloped, however, the increase in output leads to a fall in the market price of houses. As a result, each individual firm will in-

crease its desired output *by less* than it had planned to do before the market price changed.

An increase in carpenters' wages has the opposite effect. The cost of producing houses rises; the supply curve shifts to the left; and the price of houses rises. As a result, the individual firm will cut its planned output and employment of factors of production by less than it would have done if market price had not changed.

The industry's demand curve for a factor, relating the quantity demanded to the factor's price, is steeper when the reaction of market price is allowed for than it would be if firms faced an unchanged product price.

It may be useful to summarize the reasoning used so far.

1. The derived demand curve for a factor of production on the part of a *price-taking* firm will have a negative slope because of the law of diminishing returns. As more of the factor is employed in response to a fall in its price, its marginal product falls, and no further units will be added once its marginal value product falls to the factor's new price.
2. An industry's demand curve for a factor is less elastic than suggested by point 1. As the industry expands output in response to a fall in a factor's price, the price of the firm's output will fall, causing the final increase in each firm's output, and hence employment of factors, to be less than would occur if the output price remained unchanged.

Elasticity of Factor Demand

The elasticity of demand for a factor measures the *degree* of the response of the quantity demanded to a change in its price. The influences that were discussed in the preceding sections explain the *direction* of the response; that is, the quantity demanded is negatively related to price. You should not be surprised, therefore, to hear that the amount of the response depends on the strength with which these influences operate. This section gives the four principles of derived demand that come from the work of the English economist Alfred Marshall (1842–1924).

Diminishing Returns

The first influence on the slope of the demand curve is the diminishing marginal productivity of a factor. If marginal productivity declines rapidly as more of a variable factor is employed, a fall in the factor's price will not induce many more units to be employed. Conversely, if marginal productivity falls only slowly as more of a variable factor is employed, there will be a large increase in quantity demanded as price falls.

The faster the marginal productivity of a factor declines, the lower is the elasticity of each firm's demand curve for the factor.

For example, both labour and fertilizers are used by truck farmers who produce vegetables for sale in nearby cities. For many crops, additional doses of fertilizer add significant amounts to yields over quite a wide range of fertilizer use. Although the marginal product of fertilizer does decline, it does so rather slowly as more and more fertilizer is used. In contrast, although certain amounts of labour are needed for planting, weeding, and harvesting, there is only a small range over which additional labour can be used productively. The marginal product of labour, although high for the first units, declines rapidly as more and more labour is used.

Under these circumstances, truck farming firms will have an elastic demand for fertilizer and an inelastic demand for labour.

Substitution

In the long run, all factors are variable. If one factor's price rises, firms will try to substitute relatively cheaper factors for it. For this reason, the slope of the demand curve for a factor is influenced by the ease with which other factors can be substituted for the factor whose price has changed.

The greater the ease of substitution, the greater is the elasticity of demand for the factor.

The ease of substitution depends on the substitutes

that are available and on the technical conditions of production. It is often possible to vary factor proportions in surprising ways. For example, in automobile manufacturing and in building construction, glass and steel can be substituted for each other simply by varying the dimensions of the windows. Another example is that construction materials can be substituted for maintenance labour in the case of most durable consumer goods. This is done by making the product more or less durable and more or less subject to breakdowns by using more or less expensive materials in its construction.

Such substitutions are not the end of the story. Plant and equipment are being replaced continually, which allows more or less capital-intensive methods to be built into new plants in response to changes in factor prices. Similarly, engines that use less gasoline per kilometre tend to be developed when the price of gasoline rises severely.

Box 17-1 provides an optional formal treatment of the argument just given.

Importance of the Factor

Other things being equal, the larger the fraction of the total costs of producing some commodity that are made up of payments to a particular factor, the greater is the elasticity of demand for that factor.

To see this, suppose that wages account for 50 per-cent of the costs of producing a good and raw materials account for 15 percent. A 10 percent rise in the price of labour raises the cost of producing the commodity by 5 percent (10 percent of 50 percent), but a 10 percent rise in the price of raw materials raises the cost of the com-modity by only 1.5 percent (10 percent of 15 percent). The larger is the increase in the cost of production, the larger is the shift in the commodity's supply curve and hence the larger the decreases in quantities demanded both of the commodity and the factors used to produce it.

Elasticity of Demand for the Output

Other things being equal, the more elastic the demand for the commodity the factor helps to make, the more elastic is the demand for the factor.

Box 17-1

More Than One Variable Factor

When a firm can vary the amounts of several factors that it uses, profit maximization requires that the last dollar it spends on each factor brings in the same amount of revenue.

To see how this works out for two factors, call their prices p_A and p_B and their marginal revenue products MRP_A and MRP_B. The amount of extra revenue per dollar spent on factor A is MRP_A/p_A and per dollar spent on factor B is MRP_B/p_B. For example, if one more unit of A costs \$3 and adds \$6 to revenue, it yields \$2 of revenue per dollar spent on it. If one more unit of B cost \$5 and adds \$10 to revenue, it also yields \$2 of revenue per dollar spent on it. If the firm wants to equate these *MRPs* per dollar spent on the factor, it must set

$$\frac{MRP_A}{p_A} = \frac{MRP_B}{p_B} \qquad [1]$$

We know that the marginal revenue product is $MRP \times P$ for firms that are price takers in their output markets where they face the price P. So we can rewrite Equation 1 as

$$\frac{MPP_A \times P}{p_A} = \frac{MPP_B \times P}{p_B} \qquad [2]$$

If we eliminate the common P term, we have

$$\frac{MPP_A}{p_A} = \frac{MPP_B}{p_B} \qquad [3]$$

This is Equation 1 on page 198, except that we are now calling the factor's marginal product *MPP* (to distinguish it from *MRP*), whereas we called it *MP* in the earlier treatment, because there was no possibility of confusion there.

Equation 1 can be rewritten as follows:

$$\frac{MRP_A}{MRP_B} = \frac{p_A}{p_B} \qquad [4]$$

Those who have studied Appendix B to Chapter 7 can compare Equation 4 with equation [2] on page 157. In Equation 4, the firm is given prices of the two factors, and it adjusts to these by altering the quantities of the two inputs until it has the profit-maximizing amount of each. This behaviour is similar to that of the household shown on page 157. The household is given the prices of two commodities and it adjusts its consumption until its utility is maximized (which it does by making the ratios of the marginal utilities equal the ratio of their prices).

Those who have studied the Appendix to Chapter 11 have seen the analysis of this box done with indifference curves.

If an increase in the price of the commodity causes a large decrease in the quantity demanded—that is, if the demand for the commodity is elastic—there will be a large decrease in the quantity of a factor needed to produce it in response to a rise in the factor's price. However, if an increase in the price of a commodity causes only a small decrease in the quantity demanded—that is, if the demand for the commodity is inelastic—there will be only a small decrease in the quantity of the factor required in response to a rise in its price.

In Box 17-2, the last two forces affecting the elasticity of the derived demand curves that have just been discussed are related more specifically to the market for the industry's output.

The Supply of Factors

When we consider the supply of any factor of production, we must consider the amount supplied to

Box 17-2

The Principles of Derived Demand

The great English economist Alfred Marshall referred to the two propositions derived below as two of the principles of derived demand.

1. The larger the proportion of total costs accounted for by a factor, the more elastic is the demand for it.

Consider the left-hand figure shown. The demand curve for the *industry's product* is D and, given the factor's original price, the *industry supply curve* is S_0. Equilibrium is at E_0 with output at q_0.

Suppose that the factor's price then falls. If the factor accounts for a small part of the industry's total costs, each firm's marginal cost curve shifts downward by only a small amount. So also does the industry supply curve, as illustrated by the supply curve S_1. Output only expands a small amount to q_1, which implies only a small increase in the quantity of the variable factor demanded.

If the factor accounts for a large part of the industry's total costs, each firm's marginal cost curve shifts downward a great deal. So also does the industry supply curve, as illustrated by the curve S_2.

Output expands greatly to q_2, which implies a large increase in the quantity of variable factor demanded.

2. The more elastic the demand curve for the product made by a factor, the more elastic is the demand for the factor.

Consider the right-hand figure. The original demand and supply curves for the industry's product intersect at E_0 to produce an industry output of q_0. A fall in the price of a factor causes the industry's supply curve to shift downward to S_1.

When the demand curve is relatively inelastic, as shown by the curve D_i, the industry's output only increases by a small amount, to q_1. The quantity of the variable factor demanded will only increase by a correspondingly small amount.

When the demand curve is relatively elastic, as shown by the curve D_e, the industry's output increases by a large amount, to q_2. The quantity of the variable factor demanded will then increase by a correspondingly large amount.

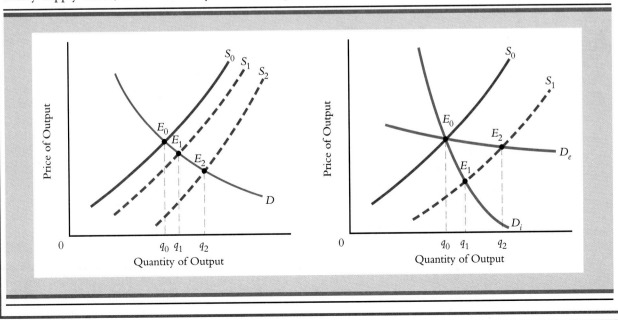

the economy as a whole, to each industry and occupation, and to each firm. The elasticity of supply of a factor will normally be different at each of these levels of aggregation. We start with the highest level of aggregation, the total supply of each factor to the economy as a whole.

The Total Supply of Factors

At any one time, the total quantity of each factor of production is given. For example, in each country the labour force is of a certain size, there is so much arable land available, and there is a given supply of discovered petroleum. However, these quantities can and do change in response to both economic and noneconomic forces. Sometimes the change is very gradual, as when a climatic change slowly turns arable land into desert or when a medical discovery lowers the rate of infant mortality and hence increases the rate of population growth, thereby eventually increasing the potential supply of adult labour. Sometimes the changes can be quite rapid, as when a boom in business activity brings retired persons back into the labour force or a rise in the price of agricultural produce encourages the draining of marshes to add to the quantity of arable land supplied.

Total Supply of Capital

The supply of capital in a country consists of the stock of existing machines, plants, equipment, and so on. Capital is a manufactured factor of production, and its total quantity is in no sense fixed, although it changes only slowly. Each year, the stock of capital goods is diminished by the amount that becomes physically or economically obsolete and is increased by the amount that is newly produced. The difference between these is the net addition to, or net subtraction from, the capital stock. On balance, the trend has been for the capital stock to grow from decade to decade over the past few centuries. In Chapter 18, we shall consider in some detail the determinants of investment in capital.

Total Supply of Land

The total area of dry land in a country is almost completely fixed, but the supply of *fertile* land is not fixed. Considerable care and effort are required to

sustain the productive power of land. If farmers earn low incomes, they may not provide the necessary care and the land's fertility may be destroyed within a short time. In contrast, high earnings from farming may provide the incentive to increase the supply of arable land by irrigation and other forms of reclamation.

Total Supply of Labour

The number of people willing to work is called the *labour force;* the total number of hours they are willing to work is called the **supply of effort** or, more simply, the **supply of labour.** The supply of effort depends on three influences: the size of the population, the proportion of the population willing to work, and the number of hours worked by each individual. Each of these is partly influenced by economic forces.

Population. Populations vary in size, and these variations are influenced to some extent by economic forces. There is some evidence, for example, that the birth rate and the net immigration rate (immigration minus emigration) is higher in good times than in bad. Much of the variation in population is, however, explained by factors outside economics.

The labour force. The proportion of the total population or of some subgroup such as men, women, or teenagers that is willing to work is called that group's **labour force participation rate.** This rate varies in response to many influences, for example, changes in attitudes and tastes. The enormous rise in female participation rates in the last three decades is a case in point. A force that is endogenous to the economic system is the demand for labour. Generally, a rise in the demand for labour, and an accompanying rise in earnings, will lead to an increase in the proportion of the population willing to work. More married women and elderly people enter the labour force when the demand for labour is high. For the same reasons, the labour force tends to decline when earnings and employment opportunities decline.

Hours worked. Not only does the wage rate influence the number of people in the labour force (as we observed earlier), it is also a major determinant of hours worked. Workers trade their leisure for incomes. By giving up leisure (in order to work), they obtain income with which to buy goods. They can, therefore, be thought of as trading leisure for goods.

A rise in the wage rate implies a change in the relative price of goods and leisure. Goods become cheaper relative to leisure, since each hour worked buys more goods than before. The other side of the same change is that leisure becomes more expensive, since each hour of leisure consumed is at the cost of more goods forgone.

This change in relative prices has both the income and the substitution effects that we studied on pages 132–135. The substitution effect leads the individual to consume more of the relatively cheaper goods and *less* of the relatively more expensive leisure—that is, to trade more leisure for goods. The income effect, however, leads the individual to consume more goods and *more* leisure. The rise in the wage rate makes it possible for the individual to have more goods and more leisure. For example, if the wage rate rises by 10 percent and the individual works 5 percent fewer hours, more leisure and more goods will be consumed.

Because the income and the substitution effects work in the same direction for the consumption of goods, we can be sure that a rise in the wage rate will lead to a rise in goods consumed. Because, however, the two effects work in the opposite direction for leisure:

A rise in the wage rate leads to less leisure being consumed (more hours worked) when the substitution effect is the dominant force and to more leisure consumed (fewer hours worked) when the income effect is the dominant force.

Box 17-3 provides an optional analysis of these two cases using indifference curves.

Much of the long-run evidence tends to show that as real hourly wage rates rise for the economy as a whole, people wish to reduce the number of hours they work.

The Supply of Factors for a Particular Use

Most factors have many uses. A given piece of land can be used to grow any one of several crops, or it can be subdivided for a housing development. A computer programmer in Montreal can work for one of several firms, for the government, or for McGill University. A lathe can be used to make many different products, and it requires no adaptation when it is turned for one use or another. Plainly, it is easier for any one user to acquire more of a scarce factor of production than it is for all users to do so simultaneously.

One user of a factor can bid resources away from another user, even though the total supply of that factor may be fixed.

Factor Mobility

When we are considering the supply of a factor for a particular use, the most important concept is *factor mobility.* A factor that shifts easily between uses in response to small changes in incentives is said to be *mobile.* Its supply to any one of its uses will be elastic, because a small increase in the price offered will attract many units of the factor from other uses. A factor that does not shift easily from one use to another, even in response to large changes in remuneration, is said to be *immobile.* It will be in inelastic supply in any one of its uses, because even a large increase in the price offered will attract only a small inflow from other uses. Often a factor may be immobile in the short run but mobile in the long run.

An important key to factor mobility is time. The longer the time interval, the easier it is for a factor to convert from one use to another.

Consider the factor mobility among particular uses of each of the three key factors of production.

Capital. Some kinds of capital equipment— lathes, trucks, and computers, for example—can be shifted readily among uses; many others are comparatively unshiftable. A great deal of machinery is quite specific: Once built, it must be used for the purpose for which it was designed, or it cannot be used at all. (It is the immobility of much fixed capital equipment that makes the exit of firms from declining industries the slow and difficult process described in Chapter 12.)

In the long run, however, capital is highly mobile. When capital goods wear out, a firm may simply replace them with identical goods, or it

Box 17-3

The Supply of Labour

The discussion in the text can be formalized for those who have studied indifference curves in Chapter 8. The key proposition is the following:

Because a change in the wage rate has an income effect and a substitution effect that pull in opposite directions, the supply curve of labour may have a positive or a negative slope.

Part (i) of the figure plots leisure on the horizontal axis and the consumption of goods (measured in dollars) on the vertical axis. The budget line always starts at 24, indicating that everyone is endowed with 24 hours a day that he or she may either consume as leisure or trade for goods by working.

At the original wage rate, the individual could obtain q_a of goods by working 24 hours (i.e., the hourly wage rate is $q_a/24$). Equilibrium is at E_0, where the individual consumes l_0 of leisure and works $24 - l_0$ hours in return for q_0 of goods.

The wage rate now rises so that q_b becomes available if 24 hours are worked (i.e., the hourly wage rate is $q_b/24$). Equilibrium shifts to E_1. Consumption of leisure falls to l_1, and the individual works $24 - l_1$ hours in return for a consumption of q_1 goods. The rise in wages increases hours worked.

The hourly wage rate now rises further to $q_c/24$, and equilibrium shifts to E_2. Consumption of leisure rises to l_2, whereas $24 - l_2$ hours are worked in return for an increased consumption of q_2 goods. This time, therefore, the rise in the wage rate lowers hours worked.

Part (ii) of the figure shows the same behaviour as in part (i), using a supply curve. It plots the number of hours worked against the wage rate. At wage rates of up to w_1, the individual is not in the labour force, since no work is offered. As the wage rate rises from w_1 to w_2, more and more hours are worked, so the supply curve of effort has the normal positive slope. The wage rates that result in E_0 and E_1 in part (i) of the figure lie in this range. Above w_2 and q_2, the quantity of effort falls as wages rise, so that the supply curve has a negative slope. This latter case is often referred to as a *backward-bending supply curve of labour*. The wage that gives rise to equilibrium E_2 in part (i) lies in this range.

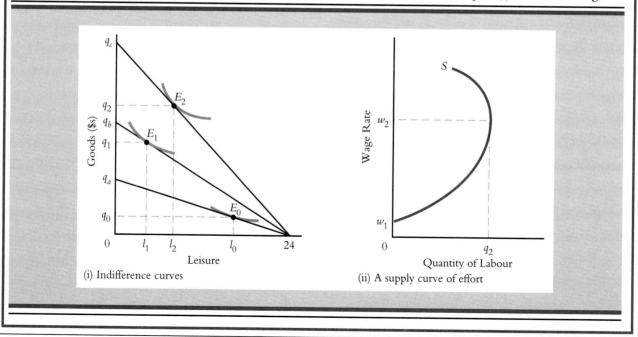

(i) Indifference curves

(ii) A supply curve of effort

may exercise other options. It may buy a newly designed machine to produce the same goods, or it may buy machines to produce totally different goods. Such decisions lead to changes in the long-run allocation of a country's stock of capital among various uses.

Land. Land, which is physically the least mobile of factors, is one of the most mobile in an economic sense. Consider agricultural land. Within one year, one crop can be harvested and a totally different crop can be planted. A farm on the outskirts of a growing city can be sold for subdivision and development on short notice. Once land is built on, its mobility is much reduced. A site on which a hotel has been built can be converted into a warehouse site, but it takes a large differential in the value of land use to make that transfer worthwhile, because the hotel must be torn down.

Although land is highly mobile among alternative uses, it is completely immobile as far as location is concerned. There is only so much land within a given distance of the centre of any city, and no increase in the price paid can induce further land to be located within that distance. This locational immobility has important consequences, including high prices for desirable locations and the tendency to build tall buildings to economize on the use of scarce land, as in the centre of large cities.

Labour. Labour is unique as a factor of production in that the supply of the service often requires the physical presence of the person who supplies it.[4]

Absentee landlords, while continuing to live in the place of their choice, can obtain income from land that is located in remote parts of the world. Investment can be shifted from iron mines in South Africa to mines in Labrador, while the owners commute between Toronto and Hawaii. However, when a worker who is employed by a firm producing men's ties in Montreal decides to supply labour service to a firm producing women's shoes in Mississauga, the worker must physically travel to Mississauga. This has an important consequence.

Because of the frequent need for labour's physical presence when its services are provided for the production of commodities, nonmonetary considerations are much more important for the supply of labour than for other factors of production.

People may be satisfied with or frustrated by the kind of work they do, where they do it, the people with whom they do it, and the social status of their occupations. Since these considerations influence their decisions about what they will do with their labour services, they will not always move just because they could earn a higher wage.

Nevertheless, labour does move among industries, occupations, and areas in response to changes in the signals provided by wages and opportunities for employment. The ease with which movement occurs depends on many forces. For example, it is not difficult for a secretary to shift from one company to another in order to take a job in Calgary, Alberta, instead of in Weyburn, Saskatchewan, but it can be difficult for a secretary to become an editor, a model, a machinist, or a doctor within a short period of time. Workers who lack ability, training, or inclination find certain kinds of mobility to be difficult or impossible.

Some barriers to movement may be virtually insurmountable once a person's training has been completed. It may be impossible for a farmer to become a surgeon or for a truck driver to become a professional athlete, even if the relative wage rates change greatly. However, the children of farmers, doctors, truck drivers, and athletes, when they are deciding how much education or training to obtain, are not nearly as limited in their choices as their parents, who have already completed their education and are settled in their occupations.

In any year, some people enter the labour force directly from school, and others leave it through retirement or death. The turnover in the labour force owing to these causes is 3 or 4 percent per year. Over a period of 10 years, the allocation of labour can change dramatically merely by directing new entrants to jobs other than the ones that were left vacant by workers who left the labour force.

The role of education in helping new entrants adapt to available jobs is important. In a society in which education is provided to all, it is possible to achieve large increases in the supply of any needed labour skill within a decade or so. These issues are

---

[4]Labour must be physically present if it is helping in the direct production of most goods, such as automobiles, and of some services, such as haircuts. In other cases, however, labour services, such as consulting, design of a product, or writing advertising copy, can be supplied at a distance and its product communicated to the purchaser by such means as phone, fax, or mail.

discussed at more length in the first part of Chapter 18.

The labour force as a whole is mobile, even though many individual members in it are not.

The Supply of Factors to Individual Firms

Most firms usually employ a small proportion of the total supply of each factor that they use. As a result, they can usually obtain their factors at the going market price. For example, a firm of management consultants can usually augment its clerical staff by placing an ad in the local paper and paying the going rate for clerks. In doing so, the firm will not affect the rate of pay earned by clerks in its area.

Most individual firms are price takers in factor markets.

The Operation of Factor Markets

The determination of the price, quantity, and income of a factor in a single market poses no new problem. Figure 17-3 shows a competitive market for a factor in which the intersection of the demand and the supply curve determines the factor's price and the quantity of it that is employed. The price times quantity is the factor's total income, and that amount, divided by the total income earned by all factors in the economy (so-called national income), represents that factor's share of the nation's total income.

Factor Price Differentials

First consider labour. If every labourer were the same, if all benefits were monetary, and if workers

FIGURE 17-3
The Determination of Factor Price and Income in a Competitive Market

In competitive factor markets, demand and supply determine factor prices, quantities of factors used and factor incomes. With demand and supply curves D_0 and S, the price of the factor will be p_0 and the quantity employed will be q_0. The total income earned by the factor is the light gray shaded area. A shift in demand from D_0 to D_1 raises equilibrium price and quantity to p_1 and q_1, respectively. The income earned by the factor rises by an amount equal to the dark gray shaded area.

moved freely among markets, then the price of labour would tend to be the same in all uses. Workers would move from low-priced jobs to high-priced ones. The quantity of labour supplied would diminish in occupations in which wages were low, and the resulting labour shortage would tend to force those wages up; the quantity of labour supplied would increase in occupations in which wages were high, and the resulting surplus would force wages down. The movement would continue until there were no further incentives to change occupations, that is, until wages were equalized in all uses.

In fact, however, wage differentials commonly occur. These differentials may be divided into two distinct types: those that exist only in disequilibrium situations and those that persist in equilibrium.

As it is with labour, so it is with other factors of production. If all units of any factor of production were identical and moved freely among markets, all units would receive the same remuneration in equilibrium. In fact, however, different units of any one factor receive different remunerations.

Disequilibrium Differentials

Some factor-price differentials reflect a temporary state of disequilibrium. They are brought about by circumstances such as the growth of one industry and the decline of another. The differentials themselves lead to reallocation of factors, and such reallocations in turn act to eliminate the differentials.

Consider the effect on factor prices of a rise in the demand for air transport and a decline in the demand for rail transport. The airline industry's demand for factors increases while the railroad industry's demand for factors decreases. Relative factor prices will go up in airlines and down in railroads. The differential in factor prices causes a net movement of factors from the railroad industry to the airline industry, and this movement causes the differentials to lessen and eventually to disappear. How long this process takes will depend on how easily factors can be reallocated from one industry to the other, that is, on the degree of factor mobility.

Equilibrium Differentials

Some factor price differentials persist in equilibrium, without generating any forces that will eliminate them. These **equilibrium differentials** can be explained by intrinsic differences in the factors themselves and, for labour, by differences in the cost of acquiring skills and by different nonmonetary advantages of different occupations.

Intrinsic differences. If various units of a factor have different characteristics, the price that is paid may differ among these units. If intelligence and dexterity are required to accomplish a task, intelligent and manually dexterous workers will earn more than less intelligent and less dexterous workers. If land is to be used for agricultural purposes, highly fertile land will earn more than poor land. These differences will persist even in long-run equilibrium.

Acquired differences. If the fertility of land can be increased by costly methods, then more fertile land must command a higher price than less fertile land. If it did not, landlords would not incur the costs of improving fertility. The same holds true for labour. It is costly to acquire most skills. For example, a mechanic must train for some time, and unless the earnings of mechanics remain sufficiently above

what can be earned in less skilled occupations, people will not incur the cost of training.

Nonmonetary advantages. Whenever working conditions differ among various uses for a single factor, that factor will earn different equilibrium amounts in its various uses. The difference between a test pilot's wage and a chauffeur's wage is only partly a matter of skill; the rest is compensation to the worker for facing the higher risk of testing new planes as compared to driving a car. If both were paid the same, there would be an excess supply of chauffeurs and a shortage of test pilots.

Academic researchers commonly earn less than they could earn in the world of commerce and industry because of the substantial nonmonetary advantages of academic employment. If chemists were paid the same in both sectors, many chemists would prefer academic to industrial jobs. Excess demand for industrial chemists and excess supply of academic chemists would then force chemists' wages up in industry and down in academia until the two types of jobs seemed equally attractive on balance.

The same forces account for equilibrium differences in regional earnings of otherwise identical factors. People who work in remote logging or mining areas are paid more than people who do jobs requiring similar skills in large cities. Without higher pay, not enough people would be willing to work at sometimes dangerous jobs in unattractive or remote locations. Similarly, because many people prefer living in the Maritimes to living in the Yukon, equilibrium wages in comparable occupations are lower in the Maritimes than in the Yukon.

Differentials and Factor Mobility

The distinction between equilibrium and disequilibrium differentials is closely linked to factor mobility.

Disequilibrium differentials lead to, and are eroded by, factor movements; equilibrium differentials are not eliminated by factor mobility.

Equalizing net advantage. The behaviour that causes the erosion of disequilibrium differentials is summarized in the assumption of the *maximization of net advantage:* The owners of factors of production will allocate them to uses that maximize the net advantages to themselves, taking both monetary and nonmonetary rewards into consideration. If net advantages were higher in occupation A than in occupation B, factors would move from B to A. The increased supply in A and the lower supply in B would drive factor earnings down in A and up in B until net advantages would be equalized, after which no further movement would occur. This analysis gives rise to the prediction of *equal net advantage:* In equilibrium, units of each kind of factor of production will be allocated among alternative possible uses in such a way that the net advantages in all uses are equalized.

Although nonmonetary advantages are important in explaining differences in levels of pay for labour in different occupations, they tend to be quite stable over time. As a result, monetary advantages, which vary with market conditions, lead to changes in *net advantage.*

A change in the relative price of a factor between two uses will change the net advantages of the uses. It will lead to a shift of some units of that factor to the use whose relative price has increased.

This implies a positively sloped supply curve for a factor in any particular use. When the price of a factor rises in that use, more will be supplied to that use. This factor supply curve (like all supply curves) can also *shift* in response to changes in other variables. For example, an improvement in the safety record in a particular occupation will shift the labour supply curve to that occupation.

Policy Issues

The distinction between equilibrium and disequilibrium factor price differentials raises an important consideration for policy. Trade unions, governments, and other bodies often have explicit policies about earnings differentials, sometimes seeking to eliminate them in the name of equity. The success of such policies depends to a great extent on the kind of differential that is being attacked. Policies that attempt to eliminate equilibrium differentials will encounter severe difficulties.

Pay Equity

Much recent government legislation seeks to establish *equal pay for work of equal value,* or *pay equity.* These laws can work as intended whenever they remove pay differentials that are due to prejudice. They run into trouble, however, whenever they require equal pay for jobs that have different nonmonetary advantages.

To illustrate the problem, say that two jobs demand equal skills, training, and everything else that is taken into account when deciding what is work of equal value but that, in a city with an extreme climate, one is an outside job and the other is an inside job. If some pay commission requires equal pay for both jobs, there will be a shortage of people who are willing to work outside and an excess of people who want to work inside. Employers will seek ways to attract outside workers. Higher pensions, shorter hours, longer holidays, overtime paid for but not worked, and better working conditions may be offered. If these are allowed, they will achieve the desired result but will defeat the original purpose of equalizing the monetary benefits of the inside and outside jobs; they will also cut down on the number of outside workers that employers will hire, since the total cost of an outside worker to an employer will have risen. If the authorities prevent such cheating, the shortage of workers for outside jobs will remain.

In Chapter 18, we discuss the effects of discrimination on wage differentials. Although discrimination is often important, it remains true that many factor price differentials are a natural market consequence of supply and demand conditions that have nothing to do with inequitable treatment of different groups in the society. Generally, mobility of factors tends to establish equilibrium levels of factor prices at which disequilibrium differentials are eliminated and equilibrium differentials are stabilized.

Policies that seek to eliminate factor price differentials without consideration of what caused them or how they affect the supply of the factor are likely to have perverse results.

Regional Income Equalization

Many Canadian policies are designed to reduce regional differences in per capita incomes. The problems that these policies encounter are most easily seen by asking if it would be possible to equalize per capita incomes and unemployment rates across the provinces. The answer to this question is almost certainly no—at least when we consider the kinds of policy tools likely to be available to any foreseeable Canadian government.

As long as provinces differ in their nonmonetary attractiveness, there will be equilibrium differences in their per capita incomes and/or unemployment rates.

Suppose that Province A—despite strong physical, climatic, and social attractions—has a set of natural endowments that will not produce as high an income per person employed as Province B. Deficiencies in economic opportunities in a particular province might arise for many reasons: An inadequate resource base, technological backwardness, slow growth in demand for one region's products, and rapid natural growth of the labour force are just a few.

Suppose that because of migration costs, cultural and language differences, climatic advantages, or other local amenities, many people choose to live in Province A even though they earn lower incomes there. Markets can adjust to such regional differences in two basic ways.

If wages and prices are flexible, real wages and incomes will fall in Province A for the kinds of workers who are in excess supply. The falling real wages will give the province an advantage in new lines of production. Real wages will continue to fall until everyone who is willing to stay at the lower wage has a job and those who are not have migrated. In long-run equilibrium, Province A is a low-wage, low-income province, but it has no special unemployment problem. Those who do not value its amenities as much as they value the higher incomes to be earned in Province B, or who are subject to lower migration costs, will have left. What the price system does is equalize total advantages. It does not equalize economic advantage, because the noneconomic advantages of living in Province A exceed those of living in Province B.

The second possibility arises because wages are not totally flexible. Minimum wage laws, national unions, and nationwide pay scales for the federal civil service put substantial restraints on possible interprovincial wage differentials. People who prefer Province A remain there, yet wages do not fall to create a wage incentive to employ more people in A

and to move to B. Instead, unemployment rates in A rise until (1) the extra uncertainty of finding a job and (2) the lower lifetime income expectations because of bouts of unemployment just balance both the nonpecuniary advantages that A enjoys over B and the costs of moving from A to B. In the long run, those who are willing to stay in spite of the higher unemployment remain, and the others leave.

In these circumstances, increasing local demand, even where that is possible, will lower the rate of emigration but *not* the unemployment rate. This is because in the long run, A's unemployment rate must remain sufficiently high relative to B's to balance the relative amenity and migration-cost advantages that Province A enjoys over B.

In these circumstances, market restrictions, such as laws that require the employment of local labour only and labour market policies such as employment subsidies, will not reduce unemployment, although they will increase employment. As new jobs are created, the rate of emigration slows so that the rate of unemployment is unchanged. Unless the province's policies are sufficient to create jobs for everyone entering its labour force, all that will happen when more jobs are created is that fewer people will migrate. The local supply rises as fast as the local demand for labour, and the unemployment rate is left unchanged.

The foregoing argument does not imply that we should ignore regions that have lower incomes or higher unemployment rates. However, it is important to realize that if the differential is an equilibrium phenomenon, no amount of policy intervention will remove it. If the policies continue to be strengthened as long as these differentials in unemployment persist, expenditures will rise and rise and rise, and the ultimate goal of equalization will continue to prove elusive.

Economic Rent

One of the most important concepts in economics is that of *economic rent*.

A factor must earn a certain amount in its present use to prevent it from moving to another use.[5] If

---

[5] Alfred Marshall called this amount the factor's *transfer earnings*.

there were no nonmonetary advantages in alternative uses, the factor would have to earn its opportunity cost (what it could earn elsewhere) to prevent it from moving elsewhere. This is usually true for capital and land. Labour, however, gains important nonmonetary advantages in various jobs, and it must earn in one use enough to equate the two jobs' total advantages—monetary and nonmonetary.

Any excess that any factor earns over the minimum amount needed to keep it at its present use is called its **economic rent.** Economic rent is analogous to economic profit as a surplus over the opportunity cost of capital. The concept of economic rent is crucial in predicting the effects that changes in earnings have on the movement of factors among alternative uses. However, the terminology of rent is confusing, because economic rent is often called simply *rent,* which can of course also mean the full price paid to hire something, such as a machine or a piece of land. How the same term came to be used for these two different concepts is explained in Box 17-4.

The Division of Factor Earnings

In most cases, economic rent makes up part of the actual earnings of a factor of production. The distinction is most easily seen, however, by examining two extreme cases. In one, everything a factor earns is rent; in the other, none is rent.

The possibilities are illustrated in Figure 17-4. When the supply curve is perfectly inelastic (vertical), the same quantity is supplied, whatever the price. Evidently, there is no minimum that the factor needs to be paid to keep it in its present use, since the quantity supplied does not decrease, no matter how low the price goes. In this case, the whole of the payment is economic rent. The price actually paid allocates the fixed supply to those who are most willing to pay for it.

When the supply curve is perfectly elastic (horizontal), none of the price paid is economic rent. If any lower price is offered, nothing whatsoever will be supplied. All units of the factor will transfer to some other use.

The more usual situation is that of a gradually rising supply curve. A rise in the factor's price serves the allocative function of attracting more units of the factor into the market in question, but the same rise provides additional economic rent to all units of the factor that are already employed. We know that

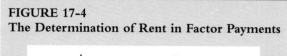

FIGURE 17-4
The Determination of Rent in Factor Payments

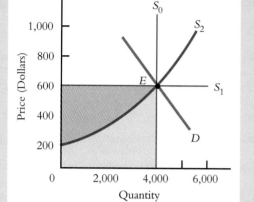

The amount of rent in factor payments depends on the shape of the supply curve. A single demand curve is shown with three different supply curves. In each case the competitive equilibrium price is $600, and 4,000 units of the factor are hired. The total payment ($2.4 million) is represented by the entire shaded area.

When the supply curve is vertical (S_0), the whole payment is economic rent, because a decrease in price would not lead any units of the factor to move elsewhere.

When the supply curve is horizontal (S_1), none of the payment is rent, because even a small decrease in price offered would lead all units of the factor to move elsewhere.

When the supply curve is positively sloped (S_2) part of the payment is rent. As shown by the height of the supply curve, at a price of $600 the 4,000th unit of the factor is receiving just enough to persuade it to offer its services in this market, but the 2,000th unit, for example, is earning well above what it requires to stay in this market. The aggregate of economic rents is shown by the dark red shaded area, and the aggregate of what must be paid to keep 4,000 units in this market is shown by the light red shaded area.

the extra pay that is going to the units already employed is economic rent, because the owners of these units were willing to supply them at the lower price. The general result for a positively sloped supply curve is stated as follows.

If the demand for a factor in any of its uses rises relative to the supply available to that

Box 17-4

Origin of the Term Economic Rent

In the early nineteenth century, there was a public debate about the high price of wheat in England. The price was causing great hardship, because bread was a primary source of food for the working class. Some people argued that wheat had a high price because landlords were charging high rents to tenant farmers. In short, it was argued that the price of wheat was high because the rents of agricultural land were high. Some of those who held this view advocated restricting the rents that landlords could charge.

David Ricardo, a great British economist who was one of the originators of classical economics, argued that the situation was exactly the reverse. The price of wheat was high, he said, because there was a shortage, which was caused by the Napoleonic Wars. Because wheat was profitable to produce, there was keen competition among farmers to obtain land on which to grow wheat. This competition in turn forced up the rent of wheat land. Ricardo advocated removing the tariff so that imported wheat could come into the country, thereby increasing its supply and lowering both the price of wheat and the rent that could be charged for the land on which it was grown.

The essentials of Ricardo's argument were these: The supply of land was fixed. Land was regarded as having only one use, the growing of wheat. Nothing had to be paid to prevent land from transferring to a use other than growing wheat, be-

cause it had no other use. No landowner would leave land idle as long as some return could be obtained by renting it out. Therefore, all the payment to land, that is, rent in the ordinary sense of the word, was a surplus over and above what was necessary to keep it in its present use.

Given a fixed supply of land, the price of land depended on the demand for land, which depended on the demand for wheat. *Rent,* the term for the payment for the use of land, thus became the term for a surplus payment to a factor over and above what was necessary to keep it in its present use.

Later, two facts were realized. First, land often had alternative uses, and from the point of view of any one use, part of the payment made to land would necessarily have to be paid to keep it in that use. Second, factors of production other than land also often earned a surplus over and above what was necessary to keep them in their present use. Television stars and great athletes, for example, are in short and fairly fixed supply, and their potential earnings in other occupations often are quite moderate. However, because there is a huge demand for their services as television stars or athletes, they may receive payments greatly in excess of what is needed to keep them from transferring to other occupations. This surplus is now called *economic rent,* whether the factor is land, labour, or a piece of capital equipment.

---

use, its price will rise in that use. This will serve the allocative function of attracting additional units into that use. It will also increase the economic rent to all units of the factor already in that use.

Determinants of the Division

The proportion of a given payment to a factor that is economic rent varies from situation to situation. We

cannot point to a factor of production and assert that some fixed fraction of its income is always its economic rent. The proportion of its earnings that is rent depends on the alternatives that are open to it.

Focus first on a narrowly defined use of a given factor, say, its use by a particular firm. From that firm's point of view, the factor will be highly mobile, since it could readily move to another firm in the same industry. The firm must pay the going wage or risk losing that factor. Thus, from the perspective of the single firm, a large proportion of the payment made to a factor is needed to prevent it from transferring to another use.

Focus now on a more broadly defined use, for example, the factor's use in an entire industry. From the industry's point of view, the factor is less mobile, because it would be more difficult for it to gain employment quickly outside the industry. From the perspective of the particular *industry* (rather than the specific *firm* within the industry), a larger proportion of the payment to a factor is economic rent.

From the even more general perspective of a particular *occupation,* mobility is likely to be less, and the proportion of the factor payment that is economic rent is likely to be more. It may be easier, for example, for a carpenter to move from the construction industry to the furniture industry than to retrain as a computer operator.

As the perspective moves from a narrowly defined use of a factor to a broadly defined use of a factor, the mobility of the factor decreases; as mobility decreases, the share of the factor payment that is economic rent increases.

Consider how this applies to the often controversial large salaries that are received by some highly specialized types of labourers, such as superstar singers and professional athletes. These performers have a style and a talent that cannot be duplicated, whatever the training. The earnings that they receive are mostly economic rent from the viewpoint of the occupation: These performers enjoy their occupations and would pursue them for much less than the high remuneration that they actually receive. For example, John Olerud would choose baseball over other alternatives even at a much lower salary. However, because of Olerud's amazing skills as a batter, most teams would pay handsomely to have him on their rosters, and he is able to command a high salary from the team he does play for. From the perspective of the firm, the Toronto Bluejays, most of Olerud's salary is required to keep him from switching to another team and hence is not economic rent. From the point of view of the baseball industry, however, much of his salary is economic rent.

SUMMARY

1. The functional distribution of income refers to the shares of total national income going to each of the major factors of production; it focuses on sources of income. The size distribution of income refers to the shares of total national income going to various groups of households; it focuses only on the size of income, not its source.

2. The income of a factor of production is composed of two elements: the price paid per unit of the factor and the quantity of the factor used. The determination of factor prices and quantities is an application of the same price theory that is used to determine product prices and quantities.

3. The firm's decisions on how much to produce and how to produce it imply demands for factors of production, which are said to be *derived* from the demand for goods that they help to produce.

4. A profit-maximizing firm will hire units of a variable factor until the last unit adds as much to cost as it does to revenue. This means that the marginal cost of the factor would be equated with its marginal revenue product, which is its marginal physical product multiplied by the marginal revenue associated with the sale of another unit of output. When the firm is a price taker in input markets, the marginal cost of the factor is its price per unit. When the firm sells its output in a competitive market, the mar-

ginal revenue product is the factor's marginal physical product multiplied by the market price of the output.

5. A price-taking firm's demand for a factor is negatively sloped, because the law of diminishing returns implies that the marginal physical product of a factor declines as more of that factor is employed (with other inputs held constant). The industry's demand is negatively sloped, because of diminishing returns and because the price of the product falls as more is produced under the influence of a fall in a factor's price.

6. The industry's demand for a factor will be more elastic: (a) the faster the marginal physical product of the factor declines as more of the factor is used, (b) the easier it is to substitute one factor for another, (c) the larger is the proportion of total variable costs accounted for by the cost of the factor in question, and (d) the more elastic is the demand for the good that the factor helps to make.

7. The total supply of each factor is fixed at any moment but varies over time. The supply of labour depends on the size of the population, the participation rate, and hours worked. A rise in the wage rate has a substitution effect, which tends to induce more work, and an income effect, which tends to induce less work (more leisure consumed).

8. The supply of a factor to a particular use is more elastic than its supply to the whole economy, because one user can bid units away from other users. The elasticity of supply to a particular use depends on factor mobility, which tends to be greater the longer the time allowed for a reaction to take place.

9. The income of a factor of production is composed of two elements: the price paid per unit of the factor and the quantity of the factor used. Factor prices and quantities are determined by the interactions of demand and supply in factor markets.

10. Factor price differentials often occur in competitive markets. Disequilibrium differentials in the earnings of different units of factors of production induce factor movements that eventually remove the differentials. Equilibrium differentials reflect differences among units of factors as well as nonmonetary benefits of different jobs; they can persist indefinitely.

11. Equal net advantage is a theory of the allocation of the total supply of factors to particular uses. Owners of factors will choose the use that produces the greatest net advantage, allowing for monetary and nonmonetary advantages of a particular employment. In so doing, they will cause disequilibrium factor price differentials to be eliminated.

12. Some amount *must* be paid to a factor in order to prevent it from transferring to another use. Economic rent is the difference between that amount and a factor's actual earnings. Whenever the supply curve is positively sloped, part of the total pay going to a factor is needed to prevent it from transferring to another use, and part of it is rent. The proportion of each depends on the mobility of the factor. The more narrowly defined the use, the larger the fraction that is transfer earnings and the smaller the fraction that is economic rent.

TOPICS FOR REVIEW

Functional distribution and size distribution of income

Derived demand

Marginal physical product

Marginal revenue product

Factor mobility

Disequilibrium and equilibrium differentials

Equal net advantage

Economic rent

DISCUSSION QUESTIONS

1. Other things being equal, how would you expect each of the following to affect the size distribution of after-tax income? Do any of them lead to clear predictions about the functional distribution of income?
   a. An increase in unemployment.
   b. Rapid population growth in an already crowded city.
   c. An increase in food prices relative to other prices.
   d. An increase in social insurance benefits and taxes.
   e. Elimination of the exemption from capital gains taxes of a family's principal residence.

2. Consider the effects on the overall level of income inequality of each of the following.
   a. Increasing participation of women in the labour force as many women shift from work in the home to full-time jobs in the workplace.
   b. Increasing use by fruit growers of migrant workers who are in the country on temporary visas.
   c. Increasing numbers of minority group members studying law and medicine.
   d. Cuts in the rates of income tax, together with the elimination of some personal income tax deductions.

3. How much of the following payments for factor services is likely to be economic rent?
   a. The $750 per month that a landlord receives for an apartment leased to students.
   b. The salary of the prime minister of Canada.
   c. The large annual income earned by the singer Bryan Adams.
   d. The salary of a window cleaner who says, "It's dangerous, dirty work, but it beats driving a truck."

4. Which of the following are disequilibrium differentials and which are equilibrium differentials in factor prices?
   a. Differences in earnings of football coaches and wrestling coaches.
   b. A bonus for signing on offered by a construction company seeking carpenters in a tight labour market.
   c. Differences in monthly rent charged for three-bedroom houses in different parts of the same metropolitan area.
   d. Higher prices per square foot of condominium space in Vancouver compared with Halifax.

5. Equal pay for work of equal value is a commonly held goal, but "equal value" is hard to define. What would be the consequences of legislation that enforces equal pay for what turns out to be work of unequal value?

6. Rent controls often succeed in reducing rents paid by tenants in the short run but at the cost of a growing housing shortage in the long run. What does this tell us about the nature of the earnings of landlords in the short and the long run?

7. The demands listed here have been increasing rapidly in recent years. What derived demands would you predict have risen sharply? Where will the extra factors of production that are demanded be drawn from?
   a. Demand for gasoline.
   b. Demand for medical services.
   c. Demand for international and interregional travel.

8. Can the following factor prices be explained by the theory that factors are paid their marginal revenue products?
   a. The actor James Garner is paid $25,000 for appearing in a 10-second commercial. The model who appears in the commercial with him is paid $500.
   b. The same jockey who is riding the same horse is paid 50 percent more money for winning a 3/4-mile race with a $150,000 first prize than a 1 1/2-mile race with a $100,000 first prize.
   c. The manager of the New York Yankees is paid not to manage during the third year of a three-year contract.
   d. Some years ago the Los Angeles Kings lured hockey superstar Wayne Gretzky away from the Edmonton Oilers, which he has led to several Stanley Cup titles, by an offer that the Oilers—one of the richest clubs in the National Hockey League—were unwilling to match.

9. Consider the large-scale substitution of jumbo jets, each of which has a seating capacity of about 400, for jets with a seating capacity of about 125. What kinds of labour service would you predict will experience an increase in demand and what kinds will experience a decrease? Under what conditions would airplane pilots (as a group) be made better off economically by virtue of this substitution?

10. From the point of view of the Toronto Bluejays, what proportion of Jo Carter's $5 million salary was a rent; from the point of view of the baseball industry as a whole how much was a rent?

18

Labour Markets, Unions, and Discrimination

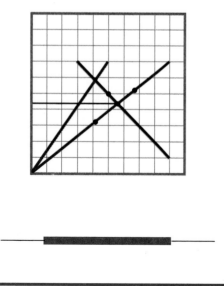

The competitive theory of factor price determination that we developed in Chapter 17 tells us a great deal about factor prices, factor movements, and the distribution of income. In this chapter, we apply that theory to the labour market. In the process, we extend the theory to cover situations in which suppliers and/or demanders are not price takers in factor markets. In Chapter 19, we apply it to the markets for nonrenewable resources and to capital.[1]

In Chapter 17, we assumed the firm sold its output in a competitive market. Box 18-1 describes how the demand for a factor is derived when the firm faces a negatively sloped demand curve for its product—that is, it can set its product price. All that matters for the text is that in all cases we can derive a demand curve showing how much of the factor the firm would wish to employ at alternative, given prices of the factor and that this curve depends on how much an additional unit of the factor would add to the firm's revenue.

Labour Markets and Wage Rates

We observed in Chapter 17 that the need for many workers to be physically present when their labour services are used differentiates much of labour from all other factors of production. As a result, nonmonetary factors, such as location of employment and other working conditions, are more important in the labour market than in markets for other factors of production.

Considerations other than material advantage also enter the relationship between employer and employee, for it is a relationship that involves loyalty, fairness, appreciation, and justice along with paychecks and productivity. It is also a relationship that may involve both actual and perceived discrimination on the basis of such things as gender, race, and age. The performance of labour markets will be affected by all of these noneconomic considerations and more.

Labour unions, employers' associations, collective bargaining, and government intervention in market-wage determination are important features of labour markets. They influence wages and working conditions and affect the levels of employment and unemployment in many industries. This means that the basic theory of factor price determination must be augmented before it can be applied to the full range of problems concerning the determination of wages.

---

[1]There is no need to say more about land for urban and agricultural uses beyond what has already been said in Chapter 17, because such land is usually sold on competitive markets where there are many potential purchasers. Nonrenewable resources, however, pose some special problems that require a treatment of their own.

Box 18-1

Factor Demand When Firms Are Not Price Takers

So far we have assumed that firms are price takers in the markets in which they sell their outputs. What if they face negatively sloped demand curves in these markets? The short answer is as follows.

In going from marginal physical product to marginal revenue product we multiply by price for a price-taking firm and by marginal revenue for a price-setting firm.

We need, however, to explain this in more detail.

We start, as in Chapter 17, with the factor's marginal physical product MPP. The value of that product to the firm is the amount that it adds to its revenue. For a firm in perfect competition, this is the price at which that product is sold. However, any firm that faces a negatively sloped demand curve—whether it is in monopolistic competition, oligopoly or monopoly—only gains the marginal revenue associated with the sale of the extra output. This is less than the price at which the output is sold because selling it drives down the price of all the units that the firm is already selling.

We can now state the general rule and its two specific applications which depend on the market in which the firms sells its output.

General rule

MRP = marginal physical product multiplied by the increase in revenue resulting from the sale of the extra output.   [1]

A price-taking firm

MRP = marginal physical product multiplied by the market price of the product.   [2]

A price-setting firm

MRP = marginal physical product multiplied by the marginal revenue at the existing level of output.   [3]

To illustrate, assume that production rises from 1,200 units per day to 1,250 units when the number of workers employed rises from 99 to 100. The MPP of the 100th worker is 50 units a day. Now assume that selling the extra 50 units of output drives the price down from $10 to $9.80 per unit. Total revenue rises from $12,000 (1,200 × $10) to $12,225 (1,250 × $9.80) when employment rises from 99 to 100. The 100th worker's MRP is $225 per day even though the 50 units he adds to output sell for $490.

The MRP of $225 may be thought of as the worker's MPP of 50 units multiplied by the MR per unit, which is $4.5. (The marginal revenue per unit, when sales rise from 1,200 to 1,250 is the $225 increase in revenue divided by the 50 unit increase in price which is $4.5 per unit of output.)[1]

---

[1] We have avoided unnecessary terminology by referring to both [2] and [3] as *marginal revenue product*. Sometimes, however, when it is desirable to distinguish between then, [2] is called *the value of the marginal product*, while the terms *marginal revenue product,* or *marginal value product,* are reserved for [3].

One Wage for Homogeneous Labour

If all workers were identical and labour markets were perfectly competitive, everyone would earn the same wage in equilibrium, and that wage would be equal to the marginal revenue product of labour.[2] We know that in the real world this is not the case. Some people work full time and are in poverty; others are able to live very well on what they earn from working. Generally, the more education and experience a worker has, the higher his or her wages will be. Given equal education and experience, women currently earn less than men (on average). Workers in highly unionized industries tend to get paid more than workers with similar skills and experience in nonunionized industries. These differentials arise both because all workers are not identical and because many important noncompetitive forces operate in labour markets. We now look more systematically at the reasons why different labour groups earn different incomes.

Wage Differentials in Competitive Markets

Where there are many employers (buyers) and many nonunion workers (sellers), there is a competitive factor market of the kind discussed in Chapter 17. Under competitive conditions, the wage rate and level of employment are set by supply and demand. No worker or group of workers, and no firm or group of firms, would be able to affect the market wage. Indeed, if all workers and all jobs were identical, there would be only one market wage.

In practise, there are many kinds of workers and many kinds of jobs. When considering these, we can think of a series of related labour markets rather than a single national market. In competitive equilibrium, we can distinguish several major sources of differences in pay.

Differentials Arising from Luck

Large incomes will be earned by those who have scarce skills that cannot be taught and that are highly valued—for example, the physical ability to be a professional baseball star. In this case, there is a small and inelastic supply of the relevant kind of labour and a large enough demand, so that the market-clearing wage is high. There are also less extreme cases. Some people are endowed with the ability to make others feel good—they make superior salespersons and therapists. Some people enjoy working hard more than others; they are thus more valuable on the job and often get paid more. All of these are equilibrium differentials in the sense defined in Chapter 17.

Genetic inheritance and early environment, both of which are beyond the individual's control, can have important effects on the ability to earn income as an adult.

Differentials Arising from Working Conditions

Given identical skills, workers will be rewarded for working under relatively onerous or risky conditions. Thus, construction workers who work the high iron, assembling the frames for skyscrapers, are paid more than workers who do similar work at ground level. Other things being equal, risk and unpleasantness will reduce the supply of labour, raising the wage above what it would otherwise be.

In competitive labour markets, supply and demand set the equilibrium wage, but the wage will differ according to the nonmonetary advantages of the job.

Differentials Arising from Human Capital

A machine is physical capital. It requires an investment of time and money to create it, and once created, it yields valuable services over a long time. In the same way, labour skills require an investment of time and money to acquire, and once acquired, they yield an increased income to their owner over a long time. Since investment in labour skills is similar to investment in physical capital, acquired skills are called **human capital.** The supply of some particular skill increases when more people find it worthwhile to acquire the necessary human capital and decreases when fewer do so. The more costly it is to acquire the skill required for a particular job, the higher its pay must be to attract people to train for it.

---

[2]Remember that unless otherwise specified, we are dealing with wages relative to the price level, and the wage is the price of labour. For a review of relative prices, see Chapter 4, pages 74–75.

The stock of skills acquired by individual workers is called human capital; investment in this capital is usually costly, and the return is usually in terms of higher labour productivity and hence higher earning power.

The two main ways in which human capital is acquired are through formal education and on-the-job training.

Formal education. Compulsory education is an attempt to provide some minimum human capital for all citizens. Some people, either through luck in the school they attend, or through their own efforts, profit more from their early education than do others. They acquire more human capital than their less fortunate contemporaries. Subsequent income differentials reflect these differences in human capital acquired in the early stages of education.

Those who decide to stay in school beyond the years of compulsory education are deciding to invest voluntarily in acquiring further human capital. The cost is measured by the income that could have been earned if the person had entered the labour force immediately, plus any out-of-pocket costs for such items as fees and equipment. The return is measured by the higher income earned when a better job is obtained. (There is also a consumption return whenever higher education is preferred to employment.)

If the demand for labour with more human capital rises, the earnings of such labour will rise. This will raise the expected return to those currently deciding whether to make the investment themselves. If the demand for labour with low amounts of human capital falls off, the earnings of such persons will fall. This will lower the costs of staying on in school and acquiring more capital, since the earnings forgone by not going to work are reduced. A rise in unemployment will also lower the costs, because the probability of earning a steady income will be reduced, and this will reduce the expected loss from not entering the labour force early.

Market forces adjust the overall costs and benefits of acquiring human capital, and individuals respond according to their varying personal assessments of costs and benefits.

The evidence suggests that in most advanced industrial countries the demand for people with university education has been rising relative to the demand for those with high school graduation or less.

The return to human capital resulting from investment in higher education seems to have been increasing substantially over the 1980s and 1990s.

The evidence also suggests that more people stay on in further education when times are bad than when times are good. The reason is that the opportunity cost of education, measured in terms of expected earnings forgone, is lower when unemployment rates are high and earnings are depressed than when unemployment rates are low and earnings are buoyant.

In the long run, decisions to acquire human capital help to erode differentials in income. Market signals change the costs and benefits of acquiring human capital in such specific forms as skill in electronics, accountancy, law, or medicine. By reacting to these signals, young people help to increase the supplies of high-income workers and reduce the supplies of low-income workers, thus eroding the differentials that exist at a given time.

Of course, people's ability to acquire human capital is limited by their genetic inheritance and their past experiences. Those with below-average IQs are unlikely to become computer programmers. Those handicapped by inadequate elementary and high school education will find it difficult to become highly skilled technicians in their thirties. (A few dedicated and highly intelligent ones may manage to do so later in life, but for most, the handicaps of bad early training are too great to overcome.)

On-the-job education. Differentials according to age are readily observable in most firms and occupations. To a significant extent, these differentials are a response to human capital acquired on the job.

Acquiring this type of human capital is important in creating rising wages for employees and for making firms competitive. Evidence suggests that people who miss on-the-job training early in life are handicapped relative to others throughout much of their later working career. This makes prolonged unemployment early in one's potential working career more serious than just the wages lost at the time. It also appears that different countries' firms have different practises with respect to investing in their employees' human capital. For example, Japanese auto companies operating in North America spend substantially more on employee training than do North American auto companies. To some extent, this is because the Japanese methods of flexible manufacturing (discussed in Box 11-3 on page 206) require more worker flexibility and training than do North American mass production methods.

Another possible source of differentials is a shift in the pattern of demand from manufacturing jobs that require more human capital to service jobs that require less. Box 18-2 discusses this shift, arguing among other things that although some service jobs do require little human capital, others require a great deal.

Differentials Arising from Gender

Crude statistics show that incomes vary by gender. More detailed studies suggest that a significant part of these differences can be explained by such factors as the amount of human capital acquired through both formal education and on-the-job experience. When all such explanations are allowed for, however, there remains a core of difference consistent with significant discrimination based on sex.

Some forms of discrimination make it difficult, or impossible, for certain groups to take certain jobs, even if they are equipped by skill and education for these jobs. Until very recently, nonwhites and women found many occupations closed to them. Even today, when overt discrimination in hiring is illegal, the evidence suggests that more subtle forms of discrimination sometimes exist.

To the extent that such discrimination occurs, it reduces the supply of labour in the exclusive jobs. It also increases the supply in jobs that are relatively open to the groups subject to discrimination. This raises the wages in the jobs for which entry is made difficult through discrimination and lowers them in the jobs that are open to all comers. These matters are discussed in more detail later in this chapter.

Differentials Arising from Market Structures

One major reason for wage differences is found in the different structures of markets in which various groups of labour sell their services. In Part 4, we distinguished different structures for the markets in which firms sell their outputs. The inputs that firms use are also bought in markets that can have different structures. Although some markets are perfectly competitive, many show monopolistic elements on either the demand or the supply side.

To study the influence of different labour market structures (as well as to keep the analysis simple), we consider the case of an industry that employs only one kind of worker for one kind of job. Furthermore, we assume that all of the workers involved have the same level of skill.

Monopoly: A Union in a Competitive Market

For the purposes of our discussion of labour markets, a **union** (or *trade union*, or *labour union*) is an association that is authorized to represent workers in negotiations with their employers. Box 18-3 on page 358 discusses some details of unions in Canada but should not be read until this section on the influence of market structures is completed.

Suppose that a union enters a competitive labour market to represent all of the workers. As the single seller of labour for many buyers, the union is a monopoly. If it uses its power, it will negotiate a wage above the competitive level. By doing so, it is establishing a minimum wage below which no one will work. This changes the supply curve of labour. The industry can hire as many units of labour as are prepared to work at the union wage but no one at a lower wage. Thus the industry (and each firm) faces a supply curve that is horizontal at the level of the union wage up to the maximum quantity of labour that is willing to work at that wage.

This situation is shown in Figure 18-1, in which the intersection of this horizontal supply curve and the demand curve establishes a higher wage rate and a lower level of employment than the competitive equilibrium.

There will be some workers who would like to obtain work in the industry or occupation but cannot. A conflict of interest has been created between serving the interests of the union's employed and its unemployed members.

An alternative way to achieve the higher wage level is to shift the supply curve to the left. The union may do this by restricting entry into the occupation by methods such as lengthening the required period of apprenticeship and reducing openings for trainees. Alternatively, the union may

FIGURE 18-1
Effect on Wages of Union Entry in a Competitive Labour Market

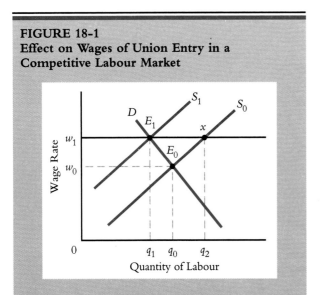

A union can raise the wages of those who continue to be employed in a competitive labour market at the expense of the level of employment. The competitive equilibrium is at E_0, the wage is w_0, and the employment is q_0. If a union enters this market and sets a wage of w_1, a new equilibrium will be established at E_1. The supply curve has become $w_1 x S_0$. At the new wage, w_1, employment will be q_1, and there will be $q_1 q_2$ workers who would like to work but whom the industry will not hire. The decrease in employment due to the wage increase is $q_1 q_0$.

The wage w_1 can be achieved without generating a pool of persons who are seeking but unable to find work in the occupation. To do so, the union must restrict entry into the occupation and shift the supply curve to the left to S_1. Employment will again be q_1.

This figure can also be used to illustrate the effect of government's imposing a minimum wage of w_1 on the market where the competitive equilibrium is at E_0. The q_1 workers who remain employed benefit by the wage increase. The $q_1 q_0$ workers who lose their jobs in this industry suffer to the extent that they fail to find new jobs at a wage of w_0 or more.

shift the supply curve by persuading the government to impose restrictive licensing or certification requirements on those who would work.

Raising earnings by restricting entry is not limited to unions. It occurs in many professions. Because high standards are regarded as necessary to protect the public from incompetent practitioners, many professions have found it publicly acceptable to control supply by limiting entry. One method is to make the training period longer and more costly than is necessary. This and other measures restrict supply and raise earnings without the embarrassing consequences of a pool of unemployed, or under-employed, members of the profession.

Monopsony: A Single Buyer in the Market

A **monopsony** is a market in which there is only one buyer; it is to the buying side of the market what monopoly is to the selling side. Although monopsony is not the most common case, it does sometimes arise. For example, many small towns contain only one industry and often only one large plant or mine. Although the town provides alternative sources of employment in retailing and service establishments, the one industrial employer has substantial monopsony power over the town's labour market. In other cases, local labour markets may contain only a few large industrial employers. Individually, each has substantial market power, and if they all act together, either explicitly or tacitly, they can behave as if they were a single monopsonist. Our analysis applies whenever employers have substantial monopsony power, but, for concreteness, we consider a case in which the few firms operating in one labour market form an employers' hiring association in order to act as a single buying unit.

Monopsonistic labour markets in the absence of unions. Suppose that there are many workers and that they are not members of a union. The employers' association can offer any wage rate it chooses, and the workers must either accept employment at that rate or find a different job.

Suppose that the monopsonist decides to hire some specific quantity of labour. The labour supply curve shows the wage that it must offer. To the monopsonist, this wage is the *average cost curve* of labour. In deciding how much labour to hire, however, the monopsonist is interested in the marginal cost of hiring additional workers. The monopsonist wants to know how much its costs will rise if it takes on more labour.

Whenever the supply curve of labour is positively sloped, the marginal cost of employing extra units will exceed the average cost. It exceeds the wage paid (the average cost) because the increased wage rate necessary to attract an extra worker must also be paid to *everyone already employed.* [30]

Box 18-2

Deindustrialisation and the Growth of the Service Sector

The growth of employment in services and the retail trade over the past decades has been dramatic in all industrialised nations. The growth has been concentrated in several areas: transportation and communication, eating and drinking, health care, education, retail services such as hotels and entertainment, and a host of business services. In Canada in 1990, *total* employment in the manufacturing of durable goods was equal to the *increase* in employment in services over the previous two decades.

In one sense this is good news, for without these new job opportunities, overall unemployment would have been high. But many people worry about the effects of deindustrialisation on the economy.

Some fear that productivity is lower and the opportunities for growth are much more limited in service industries than in goods-producing industries. They argue that the possibilities for using more capital per unit of labour employed, which raises labour productivity, are less in selling hamburgers than in manufacturing. Another concern, stressed by the Economic Council of Canada in *Good Jobs, Bad Jobs,* is that many of the new jobs in the service sector are "bad jobs" characterized by low pay and little security.

However, there are reasons to be cautious about accepting some of the pessimism concerning the growth of services. First, we need to keep a sense of perspective about the emergence of low-paying service jobs. As noted in the text, the trend toward services has been going on for over a century. Yet disposable income per employed person has been rising throughout this period; as a nation, we are getting wealthier, not poorer. Further, the size distribution of income has not changed dramatically over this period, so the increased wealth has been experienced by individuals in all income classes.

Second, to a considerable extent, the decrease in the share of manufacturing in total employment is a result of that sector's dynamism. More and more manufactured goods have been produced by fewer and fewer workers, leaving more workers to produce services. This movement is analogous to the one out of agriculture earlier in the century. At the turn of the century, nearly 50 percent of the Canadian labour force worked on farms. Today less than 5 percent of the employed work in farming, yet they produce more total output than did the 50 percent in 1900. (A similar shift also occurred in the United States.) This deagriculturalization freed workers to move into manufacturing, raising our living standards and transforming our way of life. In like manner, deindustrialisation is freeing workers to move into services, and by replacing the grimy blue-collar jobs of pollution-creating smokestack industries with white-collar jobs in the relatively clean service industries, it will once again transform our way of life.

Third, to a considerable extent, the decrease in the share of manufacturing in total employment also follows from consumers' tastes. Just as consumers in the first half of the century did not want to go on consuming more and more food products as their incomes rose, today's consumers do not wish to spend all of their additional income on manufacturing products. Households have chosen to spend a high proportion of their increased incomes on services, thus creating employment opportunities in that sector.

Fourth, although some service industries—particularly personal services and fast foods—do generate low-paying jobs, so do many manufacturing industries. Two decades ago, pessimists worried that the new industrial revolution of automation and computerization was going to destroy most of the jobs for the unskilled. But the growth in the service sector fully compensated for the lost low-skilled jobs in manufacturing.

Finally, it is easy to underestimate the scope for quality, quantity, and productivity increases in services. As one example of productivity increases, compare your local bank with what you see in a movie filmed in a bank no more than 30 years ago. As another, note that since 1950, output per full-time worker has grown about twice as fast in the communication industry as it has in manufacturing. In its study, the Economic Council of Canada stresses that the services sector is changing quickly. There has been some trend toward the mass production techniques that provided much of the basis for productivity growth in the goods sector earlier in this century. Services are also becoming globalised, so international trade will provide more opportunity for specialization and, hence, increased productivity. Also, much of the recent growth in demand for services comes as an input into goods-producing industries—either indirectly in the form of bundling sales with, say, maintenance contracts, or directly through productivity-enhancing management skills, inventory control methods, and the like. These contribute to the value added of the goods sector and hence to real national income.

It is also the case that many quality improvements in services go unrecorded. Today's hotel room is vastly more luxurious than a hotel room of 40 years ago, yet this is unlikely to show up in our national income statistics as a quality improvement. All that the statistics are likely to reflect is that the price of a hotel room has risen.

Measuring such technological improvements is even more difficult when they take the form of entirely new products. Airline transportation, telecommunication, fast-food chains, and financial services are prominent examples. The resulting increase in output is not always properly captured in our existing statistics.

It is easy to become concerned when looking at the official statistics, which show slow growth rates and low wages earned in some service jobs. Indeed, the council's report confirms that the shift in employment toward services is, like most changes that hit the economy, a mixed blessing. It entails a significant increase in the number of "bad" service-sector jobs with low pay, low job security, and sometimes poor working conditions. However, if we look at the growth in real standards of living, there is little reason to think that the shift in employment from industries to services in the second half of the twentieth century—which, after all, is driven by our rising real incomes—will be any less beneficial to industrialised nations than the shift from agriculture to manufacturing in the first half of the century.

For example, assume that 100 workers are employed at $8 per hour and that in order to attract an extra worker, the wage must be raised to $8.01 per hour. The marginal cost of the 101st worker is not the $8.01 per hour paid to the worker, but $9.01 per hour—made up of the extra 1 cent per hour paid to the 100 existing workers and $8.01 paid to the new worker. Thus, the marginal cost is $9.01; the average cost, $8.01.[3]

The profit-maximizing monopsonist will hire labour up to the point at which the marginal cost just equals the amount that the firm is willing to pay for an additional unit of labour. That amount is determined by labour's marginal revenue product and is shown by the demand curve illustrated in Figure 18-2.

Monopsonistic conditions in a labour market will result in a lower level of employment and a lower wage rate than would rule when labour is purchased under competitive conditions.

The common sense of this result is that the monopsonistic employer is aware that by hiring more workers, it drives up the wage paid to all workers. It will therefore stop short of the point that is reached when the wages are negotiated by many separate firms, no one of which can exert an influence on the wage rate.

Monopoly versus monopsony: A union in a monopsonistic market. Suppose that the workers in this industry organize themselves under a single union. The monopsonistic employer's organization now faces a monopoly union, and the two sides will settle the wage through *collective bargaining*, a process which is discussed in a later section. The outcome of this bargaining process will depend on the objective that each side sets and on the skill each has in bargaining for its objective. We have seen that, left to itself, the employer's organization will set the monopsonistic wage shown in Figure 18-2. To understand the range over which the wage may be set

[3]This marginal cost of hiring an extra worker must not be confused with the marginal cost of producing an extra unit of output. Assume that the extra worker in the example increased total output by three units. Since the worker adds $9.01 to cost and three units to output, the marginal cost of producing one extra unit of output is 9.01/3, which is $3 (to the nearest cent).

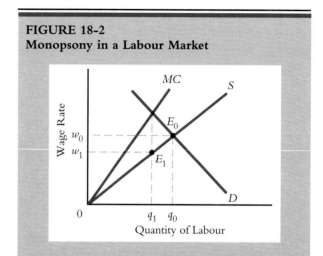

**FIGURE 18-2
Monopsony in a Labour Market**

A monopsonist lowers both the wage rate and the employment below their competitive levels. D and S are the competitive demand and supply curves. In competition, equilibrium is at E_0, the wage rate is w_0, and the quantity of labour hired is q_0. The marginal cost of labour *(MC)* to the monopsonist is above the average cost. The monopsonistic firm will maximize profits at E_1. It will hire only q_1 units of labour. At q_1 the marginal cost of the last worker is just equal to the amount that the worker adds to the firm's revenue, as shown by the demand curve. The wage that must be paid to get q_1 workers is only w_1.

after the union enters the market, let us ask what the union would do if it had the power to set the wage unilaterally. The result will give us insight into the union's objectives in the actual collective bargaining that does occur.

Suppose then that the union can set a wage below which its members will not work. There is now no point in the employer's holding off hiring for fear of driving the wage up or of reducing the quantity demanded in the hope of driving the wage rate down. Here, just as in the case of a wage-setting union in a competitive market, the union presents the employer with a horizontal supply curve (up to the maximum number of workers who will accept work at the union wage). As demonstrated in Figure 18-3, the union can raise wages *and employment* above the monopsonistic level.

Because the union turns the firm into a price taker in the labour market, it can stop a firm from exercising its monopsony power and

FIGURE 18-3
Effects of Union Entry in a Monopsonistic Labour Market

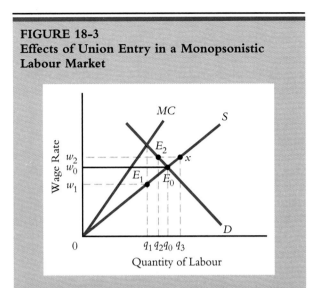

By presenting a monopsonistic employer with a fixed wage, the union can raise both wages and employment over the monopsonistic level. The monopsony position before the union enters is at E_1 (from Figure 18-2), with a wage rate of w_1 and q_1 workers hired. A union now enters and sets the wage at w_0. The supply curve of labour becomes w_0E_0S, and wages and employment rise to their competitive levels of w_0 and q_0 without creating a pool of unemployed workers. If the wage is raised further, say, to w_2, the supply curve will become w_2xS, the quantity of employment will fall below the competitive level, to q_2, and a pool of unsuccessful job applicants of q_2q_3 will develop.

This figure can also be used to illustrate the effect of the government's imposing a minimum wage of w_0 or w_2 on a monopsonistic labour market where the equilibrium wage was initially w_1.

thus raise both wages and employment to the competitive levels.

The union may not be content merely to neutralize the monopsonist's power. It may choose to raise wages further. If it does, the outcome will be similar to that shown in Figure 18-1. If the wage is raised above the competitive level, the employer will no longer wish to hire all the labour that is offered at that wage. The amount of employment will fall, and unemployment will develop. This is also shown in Figure 18-3. Notice, however, that the union can raise wages substantially above the com-

petitive level before employment falls to a level as low as it was in the preunion monopsonistic situation.

So now we know that the employers would like to set the monopsonistic wage and that the union would not want a wage below the competitive wage. The union may target for a still higher wage, depending on how it trades off employment for its members and the wage they earn. If the union is happy with an amount of employment as low as would occur at the monopsonistic wage, it could target for a wage substantially higher than the competitive wage.

Simple demand and supply analysis can take us no further. The actual outcome will, as we have already observed, depend on such other things as what target wage the two sides actually set for themselves, their relative bargaining skills, how each side assesses the costs of concessions, and how serious a strike would be for each.

Minimum Wage Laws

When unions set wages for their members, they are in effect setting a minimum wage. Governments can cause similar effects by legislating specific **minimum wages**, which define the lowest wages that may legally be paid.

In Canada, industries under federal jurisdiction are subject to the Canadian Labour Code, which in 1993 had a minimum wage of $4 per hour. The major coverage, however, is provided by provincial legislation that in 1993 set minimum wages for adult workers ranging from $4.75 per hour in Newfoundland to $6.50 in the Northwest Territories.

For a large proportion of all employment covered by the law, the minimum wage is below the actual market wage. In such cases, the minimum wage is said to be *not binding*. However, some workers are in occupations or industries in which the free market wage rate would be below the legal minimum, and there the minimum wage is said to be *binding* or *effective*.[4]

---

[4]Whether minimum wages are effective is not always easy to determine. For example, one response of employers to minimum wage legislation might be to reduce fringe benefits so that total compensation remains constant.

Although minimum wages are an accepted part of the labour scene, economists view their effects as less obviously beneficial than do many other observers. To the extent that they are effective, they raise the wages of employed workers. However, as our analysis in Chapter 6 indicated, an effective floor price (which is what a minimum wage is) may well lead to a market surplus—in this case, unemployment. Thus, minimum wage will benefit some groups while it hurts others.

The problem is more complicated than the analysis of Chapter 6 would suggest, both because not all labour markets are competitive and because minimum wage laws do not cover all employment. Moreover, some groups in the labour force, especially youth and minorities, are affected more than the average worker.

For simplicity, consider a minimum wage law that applies uniformly to all occupations. The minimum wages will affect only the lowest-paying jobs in the country, which usually require only unskilled labour. In most cases, the workers are not members of unions. Thus, the market structures in which minimum wages are likely to be effective include both those in which competitive conditions pertain and those in which employers exercise monopsony power. The effects on employment are different in the two cases.

Competitive Labour Markets

The consequences for employment of an effective minimum wage are unambiguous when the labour market is competitive. By raising the wage that employers must pay, minimum wage legislation leads to a reduction in the quantity of labour that is demanded and to an increase in the quantity of labour that is supplied. As a result, the actual level of employment falls, and unemployment is generated. This situation is exactly analogous to the one that arises when a union succeeds in setting a wage above the competitive equilibrium wage, as illustrated in Figure 18-1. The excess supply of labour at the minimum wage also creates incentives for people to evade the law by working below the legal minimum wage.

In competitive labour markets, effective minimum wage laws raise the wages of those who remain employed but also create some unemployment.

Monopsonistic Labour Markets

By effectively flattening out the labour supply curve, the minimum wage law can simultaneously increase both wages and employment in monopsonistic labour markets. The circumstances in which this can be done are the same as those in which a union that is facing a monopsonistic employer succeeds in setting a wage above the wage that the employer would otherwise pay, as shown in Figure 18-3. Of course, if the minimum wage is raised above the competitive wage, employment will start to fall, as in the union case. When it is set at the competitive level, however, the minimum wage can protect workers against monopsony power *and* lead to increases in employment.

Overall Effect

Empirical work on minimum-wage laws reflects these mixed theoretical predictions. There is some evidence that those who keep their jobs gain when the minimum wage is raised. There is some evidence that some groups, particularly the young and the unskilled, suffer a decline in employment consistent with raising the wage in a fairly competitive market. At other times and places, there is evidence that both wages earned and employment rise when the minimum wage rises, as is consistent with monopolistic labour markets. In a recent study, the Canadian-born economist David Card, of Princeton University, showed that a substantial rise in the California minimum wage was associated with an increase in wages earned and in employment among teenagers working in fast-food outlets.

Recent empirical work on the subject also tends to suggest that the distributional effects of the minimum wage, like the employment effects, are fairly small. When reviewing the literature on minimum wages, Charles Brown concludes that "the minimum wage is overrated: by its critics as well as its supporters."[5]

During the 1980s, most Canadian provinces allowed the real minimum wage to decline by holding it constant in money terms while the overall price level rose considerably. In the early 1990s, newly elected NDP governments in Ontario and

---

[5]For more information, see Charles Brown, "Minimum Wage Laws: Are They Overrated?" *Journal of Economic Perspectives* (Summer 1988).

British Columbia increased their provinces' minimum wages quite substantially. As time passes, these changes will provide new evidence about the employment effects of minimum wages.

Modern Labour Unions

In the early 1990s, Canadian unions represented only about 28 percent of the workers in the private sector and less than 40 percent of all workers, but union influence is greater than these percentages suggest. One reason is the impact that union wage contracts have on other labour markets. When, for example, the Canadian Auto Workers negotiate a new contract, its provisions set a pattern that directly or indirectly affects other labour markets, both in Ontario and in other provinces. A second reason is the major leadership role that unions have played in the past 50 years in the development of labour market practises and in lobbying for legislation that applies to all workers. Box 18-3 discusses the evolution of unionism in Canada.

Collective Bargaining

The process by which unions and employers (or their representatives) arrive at and enforce their agreements is known as **collective bargaining**. This process has an important difference from the theoretical models with which we began this chapter. There we assumed that the union set the wage and the employer decided how much labour to hire. In collective bargaining, the wage is negotiated. There is usually a substantial range over which an agreement can be reached, and the actual result in particular cases will depend on the strengths of the two bargaining parties and on the skill of their negotiators.[6]

---

[6]In terms of Figure 18-3, it may be that the employer wants the wage to be w_1 and the union wants the wage to be w_2. Depending on each side's market power, the final wage that is agreed on may be anywhere in between.

Wages Versus Employment

Unions seek many goals when they bargain with management. They may push for higher wages, higher fringe benefits, more stable employment, or less onerous working conditions. Whatever their specific goals, unless they face a monopsonist across the bargaining table, they must deal with a fundamental dilemma.

There is an inherent conflict between the level of wages and the size of the union itself.

The more successful a union is in raising wages, the more management will attempt to reduce the size of its work force, substituting capital for labour. This will lead to lower union membership. However, if the union does not provide some wage improvement for its members, they will have little incentive to stay around.

A union that sets wages above the competitive level is making a choice of higher wages for some and unemployment for others. Should the union strive to maximize the earnings of the group that remains employed? If it does, some of its members will lose their jobs, and the union's membership will decline. Should it instead maximize the welfare of its present members? Or should it seek to expand employment opportunities (perhaps by a low-wage policy) so that the union membership grows? Different unions decide these questions differently.

Severe strains developed between Canadian and American members of international unions as a result of different views of how to respond to the difficult economic conditions of the 1980s. Two key differences typified a range of differences in attitudes.

American unions were willing to reopen contracts and accept wage cuts when the alternative seemed to be plant closures or company liquidations. They were also willing to consider schemes designed to move away from the traditional pattern where wages are relatively stable over the cycle while employment does most of the adjusting to fluctuating demand. The alternative is to have wages vary more over the cycle in order to maintain a more stable employment pattern. One way of doing this is to move toward the Japanese arrangement whereby wages are to some extent linked to profits.

Box 18-3

The Historical Development of Canadian Unions

Early Canadian unionization was strongly dominated by the influence of international unions, which had their headquarters and an overwhelming proportion of their membership outside Canada. The creation of Canadian locals of American unions began in the 1860s, and by 1911, the earliest date for which figures are available, international unions had 90 percent of total union membership in Canada.

During the first half of the twentieth century, there was strong pressure, first, toward a single national federation, and second, to achieve autonomy from American unions. The issues became intertwined when conflicts in the United States arose between craft and industrial unions. Until the 1930s, craft unions—which cover persons in one occupation, such as carpenters—were the characteristic form of collective action in the United States. In Canada, meanwhile, trade unionists were attracted to the principle of industrial unions that embraced unskilled workers as well as skilled craftsmen in one industry such as steel making.

Because of the impossibility of establishing bargaining strength by controlling the supply of unskilled workers, the rise of industrial unionism in Canada was associated with political action as an alternative means of improving the lot of the membership. In general, social and political reform were given much more emphasis by Canadian unionists than by their American counterparts. Political action here extended to the support for social democratic political parties: first, the Cooperative Commonwealth Federation (CCF), established in 1932, and later its successor, the New Democratic Party (NDP), formed in 1961.

The late Senator Eugene Forsey, a former director of research for the Canadian Labour Congress, viewed the unification of the bulk of Canadian unions under the CLC in 1956 as the beginning of virtual autonomy for Canadian locals from their U.S. head offices—the CLC has guidelines for the conduct of international unions operating in Canada. Throughout the postwar period, the percentage of total union membership represented by international unions fell: In the mid-1950s, it was about 70 percent, and by 1990, it was only 32 percent.

One factor in the increased share of national unions is the growth of membership in the two unions representing government workers, the Canadian Union of Public Employees and the Public Service Alliance. Another major component of noninternational union membership has arisen out of the distinct aspirations of French-Canadian workers. More recently, the formation of the Canadian Auto Workers, independent of the American Auto Workers, represented a significant further reduction of membership in international unions.

Rapid gains in union membership in Canada occurred in the years during World War II. This led to pressure for the rights of workers to organize and to elect an exclusive bargaining agent. These rights were established by provisions of the Wartime Labour Relations Regulations Act of 1944.

Government intervention in industrial disputes in Canada has a history dating back to the early years of the twentieth century. The earliest legislation applied only to public utilities and coal mining. It provided that before a strike or a lockout could be initiated, the parties were required to submit any dispute to a conciliation board. This system of compulsory conciliation and compulsory delay in work stoppage was extended to a much larger segment of the economy under special emergency powers adopted by the government of Canada during World War II. In the postwar period, jurisdiction over labour policy reverted to the provinces, but the principles established have been carried over into provincial legislation.

Canadian unions have been more inclined to stick with traditional approaches. First, a contract should not be reopened before it expires. Even if the agreed wages threaten to cause plant closures, the sanctity of the contract is a more important principle than the saving of specific jobs. Second, profit sharing means selling out to the bosses. The traditional system should be maintained, in which wages are stable over the cycle and most of the adjustment to variations in demand occurs through variations in employment.

Under the leadership of Bob White, the Canadian Automobile Workers (CAW) split with the United Automobile Workers (UAW) over these and related issues. A separate Canadian union was set up, and its different approach to bargaining soon became apparent.

Since the breakaway, the CAW has been significantly more hostile to changes in work organization than the UAW has been. The CAW's National Policy Statement issued in October 1989 explicitly rejected innovations such as flexible job classifications and supervisor-worker interchanges that appear to have contributed greatly to productivity in the Japanese automobile industry. (Recall the discussion in Box 11-3.) Because the North American automobile industry is under immense challenges from Japanese and other foreign producers, this statement seemed to many observers to be an open invitation to automobile firms to invest in the United States rather than Canada. However, the policy statement and the actual policies adopted by the CAW may differ: Faced with the real possibility of the closure of a major plant in Ste. Therese, Quebec, the union was considerably more flexible about agreeing to a number of changes in work arrangements than its policy statement would have suggested.

Discrimination in Labour Markets

There have been, and continue to be, large differences between the earnings of women and men. If we create an index of median wage and salary earnings with males equal to 100, females equal less than 70. These disparities in earnings have multiple causes, but they raise a concern about the existence of labour market discrimination and the extent to which discriminatory employment practises give rise to the differences in earnings.

A Model of Labour Market Discrimination

To isolate the effects of discrimination, we begin with a simplified picture of a nondiscriminating labour market, and then introduce discrimination. Our discussion is in terms of male versus female, but it applies equally to any form of discrimination in labour markets.

Suppose there are two groups of equal size in a society. One is male; the other, female. Each group has the same proportion who are educated to various levels, each has identical distributions of talent, and so on. Suppose also that there are two occupations. Occupation E (for elite) requires people of above average education and skills, and occupation O (for ordinary) can use anyone, but if wages in the two occupations are the same, employers in occupation O will prefer to hire the above-average worker. There is no discrimination, and the nonmonetary advantages of the two occupations are equal.

The competitive theory of distribution suggests that the wages in E occupations will be bid up slightly above those in O occupations in order that the E jobs attract the workers of above-average skills. Men and women of above-average skill will flock to E jobs, while the others, male and female alike, will have no choice but to seek O jobs. Because skills are equally distributed, each occupation will have half male and half female workers.

Now we introduce discrimination in its most extreme form. All E occupations are hereafter open only to males; all O occupations are open to either males or females. The immediate effect is to reduce by 50 percent the supply of job applicants for E occupations (applicants must be *both* male and above average) and, potentially, to increase by 50 percent the supply of applicants for O jobs (this group includes all women and the below-average men).

Wage Level Effects

Suppose that labour is perfectly mobile among occupations, that everyone seeks the best job that he or she is eligible for, and that wage rates are free to vary so as to equate supply and demand. The analysis is shown in Figure 18-4. Wages rise in E occupa-

FIGURE 18-4
Economic Discrimination: Wage Level Effects

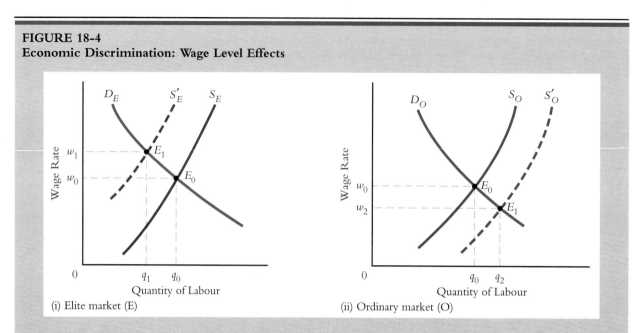

(i) Elite market (E)

(ii) Ordinary market (O)

If market E discriminates against one group and market O does not, the supply curve will shift to the left in E and to the right in O. Market E requires above-average skills, while market O requires only ordinary skills. When there is no discrimination, demands and supplies are D_E and S_E in market E, and D_O and S_O in market O. Initially, the wage rate is w_0 and employment is q_0 in each market. (The actual wage in market E will be slightly higher than the wage in market O.) When all females are barred from E occupations, the supply curve shifts to S'_E, and the wage earned by the remaining workers, all of whom are males, rises to w_1. Females put out of work in the E occupations now seek work in the O occupations. The resulting shift in supply curve to S'_O brings down the wage to w_2 in the O occupations. Because all females are in O occupations, they have a lower wage rate than many males. The average male wage is higher than the average female wage.

tions and fall in O occupations. The take-home pay of those in O occupations falls, and the O group is now approximately two-thirds female.

Discrimination, by changing supply, can decrease the wages and incomes of a group that is discriminated against.

In the longer run, further changes may occur. Notice that total employment in the E industries falls. Employers may find ways to use slightly below-average labour and thus lure the next best qualified males out of O occupations. This will raise O wages slightly, but it will also make these occupations increasingly "female occupations." If discrimination has been in effect for a sufficient length of time, females will learn that it does not pay to acquire above-average skills. Regardless of ability, females are forced by discrimination to work in unskilled jobs.

Employment Effects

For a number of reasons, labour market discrimination may have adverse employment effects that are even more important than effects on wage levels. Labour is not perfectly mobile, wages are not perfectly flexible downward, and not everyone who is denied employment in an E occupation for which she is trained and qualified will be willing to take a "demeaning" O job. We continue the graphical example in Figure 18-5.

If wages do not fall to the market-clearing level, possibly because of minimum wage laws, the increase in supply of labour to O occupations will cause excess supply, which will result in unemployment in O occupations. Since females dominate these occupations, they will bear the brunt of the extra unemployment, as illustrated in Figure 18-5(i).

A similar result will occur if labour is not fully mobile between occupations. For example, many of

FIGURE 18-5
Economic Discrimination: Employment Effects

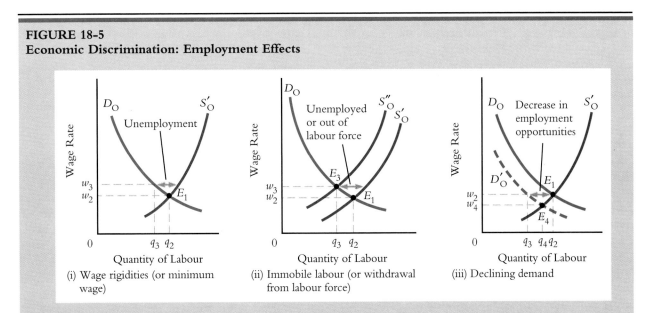

(i) Wage rigidities (or minimum wage)

(ii) Immobile labour (or withdrawal from labour force)

(iii) Declining demand

Increasing supply or decreasing demand in occupations in which those discriminated against are the major sources of labour can increase unemployment. In each part of the diagram the curves D_O and S'_O are those from Figure 18-4(ii); they show the market for O workers after the discriminatory policies are put into effect. Equilibrium is at E_1. In each case the wage w_2 would clear the market and provide employment of q_2.

In part (i), if the wage rate cannot fall below w_3, perhaps because of a minimum-wage law, employment will fall to q_3, and unemployment will occur in the amount shown by the arrows.

In part (ii), if some of the potential workers in the O occupations are unable or unwilling to take employment in O jobs, the supply curve will not be S'_O but S''_O. Equilibrium will be at E_3. Although O wages will rise somewhat to w_3, employment will be only q_3, and a number of workers, shown by the arrows, will not be employed. Whether they are recorded as "unemployed" or as having withdrawn from the labour force will depend on the official definitions.

In part (iii), if demand is declining in O occupations over time, say, from D_O to D'_O, either wages and employment will fall to the new equilibrium E_4 with w_4 and q_4, or wages will be maintained but employment will fall to q_3. The arrows illustrate the latter case, where the fall in employment is q_3q_2.

the O occupation jobs might be in places to which the females are unable or unwilling to move. See Figure 18-5(ii). Potential O workers who cannot move to places where jobs are available become unemployed or withdraw from the labour force. Quite apart from any discrimination, long-term technological changes tend to decrease the demand for less skilled labour of the kind that is required in O occupations. Occupation O then becomes increasingly oversupplied. This possibility is outlined in Figure 18-5(iii).

The kind of discrimination that we have considered in our model is extreme. It is similar to the former South African apartheid system, in which blacks were excluded by law from prestigious and high-paying occupations. In North America, labour market discrimination against a particular group usually occurs in somewhat less obvious ways. First, it may be difficult (but not impossible, as in our model) for members of the group to get employment in certain jobs. Second, members of groups subject to discrimination may receive lower pay for a given kind of work than members of groups not subject to discrimination.

Indeed, the first type of discrimination may encourage the second type! How might this happen? First, if discrimination makes it difficult for a qualified person to get a good job, she may be more willing to accept such a job even if the pay and working conditions are poorer than those given to others in the same job. Even under relatively unfavourable terms, the job will still be better than the alternative (an O job). Second, employers who are seeking to fill E jobs and who have no taste for discrimination nonetheless will be able to hire qualified females at wages that, although higher than O wages, are lower than E wages. As long as there is some discrimination of the first type (in the extreme, apartheid), there will be pressures coming from both the supply and the demand sides of the labour market for discrimination of the second type.

In the long term, these unemployment effects may be increased by sociological and economic forces. Female children of women who are discriminated against may take as role models women who have made a life outside the labour force. Technological changes in the economy tend to decrease the demand for less skilled labour of the kind required in O occupations, which become increasingly oversupplied. This possibility is sketched in Figure 18-5(iii).

These theoretical possibilities have their counterparts in the real world. We shall discuss them briefly.

Female-Male Differentials

Although high unemployment is often a feature of labour market discrimination, it is not the key to female-male differentials. The labour force participation of women more than doubled from 28 percent in 1956 to over 58 percent in 1992. This occurred without any increase in the unemployment rate of females, which is approximately equal to that of males.

Getting jobs is, of course, not the whole story. It has long been clear that women and men are offered, and make, different occupational choices. But even here there is notable progress. Over the past two decades, women have steadily increased their participation in supposedly higher-status occupations, including managerial, sales, scientific, and technical jobs. For example, in 1966, women accounted for 16 percent of the professional labour force; by 1993, that figure had risen to 48 percent.

Despite these rather dramatic changes, average earned income of females in the labour force is well below that of males of similar ages. The female-to-male earnings ratio has narrowed slightly from approximately 0.59 in 1960 to about 0.70 in 1992. The persistence of the remaining salary gap for females is due to a combination of causes in addition to straightforward discrimination: Women are still underrepresented in high-status occupations, pro-

portionately fewer women than men reach higher-paying jobs in the occupations in which both work, and those who do reach higher-paying jobs do so more slowly.

Discrimination within occupations. To what extent do differences in pay levels of men and women *within* an occupation reflect direct discrimination against women, and to what extent do they reflect other sex-linked characteristics, the most important of which is the persistent difference in lifetime patterns of labour force participation? The evidence shows that, on average, women have fewer years of work experience than men of the same age. The average working female is less mobile occupationally and geographically than her male counterpart. These facts reflect, at least in part, *labour market attachment.* For example, many women withdraw from the labour force or work only part time in order to have and raise children.

The causes of gender differences in labour market attachment have attracted attention from both social psychologists and economists. There is ample evidence that *sex-role socialization* is an important factor. To the extent that women and men are socialized to accept the view that women should be the primary caretakers of young children, some social scientists argue that differences in labour market attachment arise from a form of indirect discrimination. However important this may be, it arises from differences in the way in which boys and girls are raised, not from the direct behaviour of the labour market.

The extent of direct discrimination in an occupation may be measured by comparing the pay status of groups with similar characteristics. Studies of the sources of male-female pay differences in Canada have found that just over a third (37 percent) of the differences could be explained by differences in education, work experience, and labour market attachment. A study by professors Shapiro and Stelener shows much the same thing and concludes that from 12.5 to 25 percent of the pay differences are *not* explained by these variables.[7] Analysts attribute this part of male-female pay differentials to direct discrimination.

[7]Much of this literature is summarized in University of Toronto economist Morley Gunderson's "Male-Female Wage Differentials and Policy Responses," *Journal of Economic Literature* 27 (1989): 46-72.

Interoccupational discrimination. Women may tend to be employed in a different set of occupations from men. They were refused admission, or discouraged from seeking entry into, certain occupations in the past; for example, they were urged into nursing rather than medicine, social work rather than law, and secretarial schools rather than managerial training programs. The result of this is called *occupational segregation.* Similarly, girls were raised in a culture in which their education seemed less important than that of their brothers or in which they were trained to think of themselves as potential homemakers were less likely to acquire the skills for many high-paying occupations that were wholly within their capabilities. This is a form of sex-role socialization.

Differences in pay among occupations reflect, as we have seen, differences in supply and demand, including nonmonetary factors. Might they not also reflect discrimination, if one occupation is predominantly female and the other predominantly male? This is certainly possible, and a number of studies have shown that such an effect exists; that is, if one uses the characteristics of workers (education, training, experience, etc.) to explain their wages, the fraction of female workers in the occupation has a significant negative effect. Moreover, this effect exists for both men and women. Men (and women) who work in predominantly female occupations are paid less than men (and women) with the same training and experience in predominantly male occupations. For this reason, many have urged that attention be paid to interoccupational pay differences under the general term *pay equity*. Determining how much observed differences reflect discrimination is extremely difficult, because so many different considerations affect the pay levels of, say, firefighters and librarians.

Government Policies to Redress Discrimination

Governments have long had policies to eliminate discrimination between men and women doing the same job. These policies are relatively easy to administer. They require that a man and a woman doing a job with the same job description must receive the same pay.

A much harder case arises when an attempt is made to remove alleged discrimination between jobs. If one job is staffed primarily with women and another primarily with men, do differences between the wages paid in the two jobs represent differences in market conditions, or are they due to discrimination?

There is no doubt that some discrimination does occur. For example, psychologists have conducted many studies that suggest a bias against women that could easily lead to discriminatory pay differences. In one experiment, department heads were given identical files, one with a male name and the other with a female name. They were 10 percent more likely to select the male for a job offer than the female with the identical resume. In another experiment, female college students were asked to rank paintings on a scale from 1 to 10. The same picture consistently got a higher rating when it had a male name attached than when it was ascribed to a female artist.

Most empirical studies of male-female wage differentials show that many of the differences between jobs are due to differences in such objective factors as educational requirements and years of experience in the work force and on the job. When all such factors have been allowed for, however, there remains a residual that is consistent with some direct sex discrimination.

Much of the persistence of male-female pay differentials results from wages in male-dominated occupations exceeding those in female-dominated ones. As a result, the federal government and many of the provinces have enacted legislation that mandates wage adjustments to eliminate disparities between jobs of "comparable worth" or "equal value." Initially, such policies applied only to public-sector employment, but in 1987, pay equity legislation in Ontario expanded the coverage to the private sector as well.[8]

Comparable worth policy relies on a job evaluation program that measures the *intrinsic* value of different occupations. In practise, this involves assigning "worth points" to various attributes of a given job (typically effort, initiative, skill, training, responsibility, and conditions of work). These points can then be summed to obtain a "total job score"; comparing scores for different jobs allows a comparison of their intrinsic values. Pay equity requires that two jobs of equal value receive equal pay.

---

[8]As of 1993, the Ontario legislation applied only to within-firm comparisons in the private sector, and individual firms were given considerable freedom to design their own evaluation schemes.

Needless to say, pay equity policies have been controversial. Supporters argue that they do not go far enough and that significant differentials will persist even after full implementation. Critics argue that the evaluation schemes are often arbitrary and always imperfect. Simple schemes are easy to administer but give poorer results; more complex schemes are, in principle, more accurate but harder to administer. Implementation problems such as definition of an establishment, determination of criteria to include in the evaluation program and the weights to assign to them, and definition of gender dominance plague most schemes currently in place.

Economists are often concerned that the policies fail to distinguish between equilibrium and disequilibrium differentials as stressed in Chapter 17. They fear that misguided attempts to eliminate equilibrium differentials will lead to the emergence of excess demand in some occupations and excess supply in others, with associated efficiency costs for the economy.

Supporters of pay equity policy often argue that job evaluation and comparison play an important role in any big firm's employment policy, implicitly and often explicitly. Hence, they argue, pay equity legislation merely formalizes in law procedures that already play an important role in labour markets. Economists point out, however, that market-oriented job evaluation policies of individual firms, whether explicit or implicit, have the major advantage of reacting quickly to market forces. Such evaluations are only a guideline to determining wages. If changes occur to make previously determined evaluations no longer consistent with market balance, and surpluses or shortages arise, firms will respond quickly by altering their guidelines and changing relative wages. Legislated comparisons determining wages may cause shortages or surpluses to persist for long periods of time.

A preliminary assessment of pay equity legislation in Canada was put forward by Professor Roberta Robb of Brock University.[9] She identifies three potential costs: economic efficiency losses (including allocation distortions and implementation costs), private costs of employers (including higher wages for some female employees and administration costs), and private costs of employees (including adverse employment effects for females). Potential benefits include increased productivity of females (resulting from the incentive effects of increased earnings) and a reduced male-female wage differential. The latter is viewed as an objective in its own right, and it has been suggested that current legislation may succeed in reducing the differential from its current 40 percent to 25 percent.

Is pay equity "progressive pragmatism," as one supporter put it, or is it "a profoundly flawed concept," as a critic pronounced? The answer will depend on the magnitude of the resource misallocation caused by setting relative wages through a system that does not attempt to balance demand and supply and on one's view of whether this lost efficiency is a price worth paying in the name of equity. As Robb concludes, "This kind of legislation is likely to have a very significant impact on individual perceptions of what women's jobs are worth. This result is clearly important if one believes that part of the role of this policy is to break the cycle of systematically undervaluing women's jobs."

---

[9]"The Costs and Benefits of Canadian Pay Equity Policy" in Richard Chaykowski, ed. *Pay Equity Legislation* (Kingston, Ont.: Queen's University Industrial Relations Centre, 1990).

SUMMARY

1. In a competitive labour market, wages are set by the forces of supply and demand. Differences in wages will arise because some workers have higher skills and abilities than others, because some skills are more valued than others, because some jobs are more onerous than others, because of varying amounts of human capital, and because of discrimination based on such factors as gender and colour.

2. A union entering a competitive market can raise wages, but only at the cost of reducing employment and creating a pool of unem-

ployed who would like to work at the going wage rate but are unable to find employment in that market.

3. A monopsonistic buyer entering a competitive labour market will reduce both the wage and the volume of employment.

4. A union entering a monopsonistic market may increase both employment and wages over some range. If, however, it sets the wage above the competitive level, it will create a pool of workers who are unable to get the jobs they want at the going wage.

5. Governments set some wages above their competitive levels by passing minimum-wage laws. These laws raise the incomes of many employees and cause unemployment for some of those with the lowest levels of skills, but raise both wages and employment in markets that are monopsonistic.

6. Labour markets have developed a wide variety of institutions, including labour unions and employers' associations, which affect wage determination.

7. Unions face a basic conflict between the goals of raising wages and preserving employment opportunities for members and potential members.

8. Discrimination has played a role in labour markets. It affects wages and employment opportunities in part by limiting labour supply in the best-paying occupations and by increasing it in less attractive occupations.

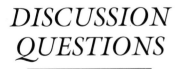

TOPICS FOR REVIEW

Competitive wage differences

Monopsony power

Power of unions

Effects of minimum wages

Collective bargaining

Effects of economic discrimination on wages and employment

Comparable worth

DISCUSSION QUESTIONS

1. A union that has bargaining rights in two plants of the same company in different provinces may insist on equal pay for equal work in the two plants, but not on equal pay for men and women in the same jobs. Can you see any economic reasons for such a distinction?

2. U.S. unions have traditionally supported laws restricting immigration, expelling illegal aliens, and raising the minimum wage and extending its coverage. How do each of these positions benefit or hurt the following groups: (a) consumers, (b) workers as a whole, (c) unionized workers with seniority in their jobs?

3. One critic of pay equity legislation argues that it leads to distortions because it confuses "value determined at the *margin* by supply and demand" with a "job evaluator's concept of the *average* value of the inputs required to do the job." Reread the discussion of the paradox of value in Chapter 8, and then comment on this criticism.

4. "The great increase in the number of women entering the labour force for the first time means that relatively more women than men earn beginning salaries. It is therefore not evidence of discrimination that the average wage earned by females is less than that earned by males." Discuss.

5. The American Cyanamid Corporation once had a policy of removing women of childbearing age from, or not hiring them for, jobs that exposed them to lead or other substances that could damage a fetus. Is this sex discrimination? Whether it is or is not, debate whether this sort of protective hiring rule is something that the government should require, encourage, or prohibit.

6. "One can judge the presence or absence of discrimination by looking at the proportion of the population in different occupations." Does such information help? Does it suffice? Consider each of the following examples. Relative to their numbers in the total population, there are
   a. Too many blacks and too few Jews among professional athletes.
   b. Too few male secretaries.
   c. Too few female judges.

7. Consider the consequences of applying the notion of equal pay for work of equal value to compensation of:
   a. Football coaches and cross-country coaches.
   b. University presidents and network anchors.
   c. Fashion models and poets.
   d. Police in large cities and police in small towns.

8. Compare the following policies designed to reduce pay differentials due to occupational segregation of women in lower-paying jobs.
   a. Making pay adjustments based on an analysis of the purported comparable worth of occupations.
   b. Removing barriers to women's employment in traditionally male jobs.
   c. Setting quotas based on the relevant population statistics for minimum fractions of females in each occupation.

9. Actuaries are among the highest-paid people of all professionals. According to *Forbes* magazine, "The biggest drag on finding new actuaries is the rarefied mathematical talents the job requires. Like fiction writing or figure skating, this is a profession you join not for the money but because you love the work." Compare the market for actuaries with that for insurance agents. How do demand and supply conditions differ? What might account for the high salaries of actuaries?

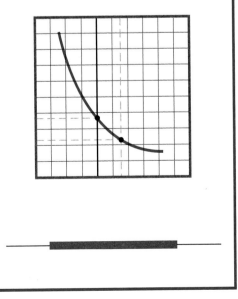

19

Nonrenewable Natural Resources and Capital

In this chapter, we discuss the important case of nonrenewable resources and capital. These are similar factors of production in that they are a stock of valuable things that get used up in the process of producing goods and services. They are different in that capital can be replaced, while nonrenewable natural resources cannot. A new machine can always be created to replace one that wears out. A barrel of oil used represents a permanent reduction in the total stock of oil in the world. No more natural oil can be created to replace what we use.

Resources that can be replaced, either by being made by man, as with machines, or by reproducing themselves, as with people or fish, are called **renewable resources**. Resources that cannot be renewed, as with fossil fuels, are called **nonrenewable or exhaustible resources**.

The Economics of Nonrenewable Resources

The world's minerals and fossil fuels are examples of nonrenewable resources. However, since some of the stock is as yet undiscovered, the *known* supply of each is not fixed over time. New discoveries add to the known stock, and extraction subtracts from it. It is, however, possible to imagine exhausting all of the world's supplies of oil, natural gas, coal, or any one mineral. In this sense, they are nonrenewable.

Are we exhausting our supply of nonrenewable resources too quickly? Some people ask: "Should we not save more of them for our children and grandchildren?" Others are willing to let future generations take care of themselves. "After all," they argue, "they will be richer than we are in any case."

How does the price system regulate the use of a nonrenewable resource? Does it lead to overly rapid exploitation? Does it lead to too much conservation of a resource that may in any case be rendered less useful by future technological change?

Determining the Rate of Extraction

To focus on the basic issues, it is easiest to consider at the outset a nonrenewable resource whose total supply is known. Suppose for the moment that all the petroleum in existence has been discovered so that every unit that is used permanently diminishes the available stock by one unit.

Many different firms own the land that contains the oil supply. They have invested money in discovering the oil, drilling wells, and laying pipelines. Assume that their current extraction costs are virtually zero; all they have to do is turn their taps on, and the oil flows at any desired rate to the petroleum markets.[1]

Optimal Firm Behaviour

What should each firm do? It could extract all of its oil in a great binge of production this year, or it could husband the resource for some future rainy day and produce nothing this year. In practise, it is likely to adopt some intermediate policy, producing and selling some oil this year and holding stocks of it in the ground for extraction in future years. But *how much* should it extract this year and *how much* should it carry over for future years? What will the decision imply for the price of oil over the years?

The firms that own the oil land are holding a valuable resource. Holding it, however, has an opportunity cost: The oil could have been extracted and sold this year, yielding revenue to the firms (and value to consumers) in the same year. A firm will be willing to leave the resource in the ground only if it earns a return equal to what it can earn in other investments. This is measured by the interest rate.

First, suppose the price of oil is expected to rise by less than the interest rate. Oil extracted and sold now will have a higher value than oil left in the ground. Firms will, therefore, extract more oil this year. Because the demand curve for oil has a negative slope, raising the extraction rate will lower this year's price. Production will rise, and the current price will fall until the expected price rise between this year and next year is equal to the interest rate.[2]

The firms will then be indifferent at the margin between producing another barrel this year and holding it for production next year.

Second, suppose that the price is expected to rise by more than the interest rate. Firms will prefer to leave more in the ground, where they earn a higher return than could be earned by selling the oil this year and investing the proceeds at the current interest rate. Thus, firms will cut their rate of production for this year, which will raise this year's price. When the current price has risen so that the gap between the current price and next year's expected price is equal to the interest rate, firms will value equally a barrel of oil extracted and one left in the ground.

In a perfectly competitive industry, the profit-maximizing equilibrium for a nonrenewable resource occurs when the last unit produced now earns just as much for each firm as it would if it had been left in the ground for future use.

To illustrate these important relations, assume that next year's price is expected to be $1.05 and that the rate of interest is 5 percent.

First, suppose the current price is $1.04 per barrel. Clearly, it pays to produce more now, since the $1.04 that is earned by selling a barrel now can be invested to yield approximately $1.09 ($1.04 x 1.05), which is more than the $1.05 that the oil would be worth in a year's time if it is left in the ground. Second, suppose that the current price is $0.90 per barrel. Now it pays to reduce production, since oil left in the ground will be worth 16.66 percent more next year [(1.05/0.90)100]. Extracting it this year and investing the money will only produce a gain of 5 percent. Finally, let the current price be $1.00. Now oil producers make the same amount of money whether they leave $1.00 worth of oil in the ground to be worth $1.05 next year or they sell the oil for $1.00 this year and invest the proceeds at a 5 percent interest rate.

Market Pricing

What we have established so far determines the pattern of prices over time: If stocks are given and unchanging, prices should rise over time at a rate equal to the rate of interest. But what about the

---

[1] It is, of course, a simplification of the real case to assume that current production costs are actually zero. The assumption, however, is not too far from reality in the case of such a resource as oil, where the fixed costs of discovery, extraction (e.g., drilling wells), and distribution (e.g., laying pipelines) account for the bulk of total costs. When the variable extraction costs are nonzero, all statements about prices in the text refer to the margin by which price *exceeds* the current variable costs of extraction.

[2] The discussion is simplified by assuming next year's expected price to be given. The decision to produce more this year may also affect next year's price. If the total supplies are small, next year's expected price may rise. The argument proceeds exactly as in the text, except that the equilibrium gap between two prices is achieved by the present price falling and the expected future price rising rather than by having next year's expected price remaining constant and all the adjustment coming through this year's price.

level of prices? Will they start low and only rise to moderate levels over the next few years, or will they start high and then rise to even higher levels? The answer depends on the total stock of the resource that is available (and, where some new discoveries are possible, on the expected additions to that stock in the future). The scarcer is the resource relative to the demand for it, the higher its market price will be at the outset.

The profile of the resource's price over time is to rise at a rate equal to the rate of interest, while the height of that price profile will depend on the resource's scarcity relative to current demand.

Optimal Social Behaviour

Petroleum is a valuable social resource, and the value to consumers of one more barrel produced now is the price that they would be willing to pay for it, which is the current $1.00 market price of the oil. If the oil is extracted this year and the proceeds are invested at the rate of interest (the proceeds might be used to buy a new capital good), they will produce $1.05 worth of valuable goods next year. If that barrel of oil is not produced this year and is left in the ground for extraction next year, its value to consumers at that time will be next year's price of oil. It is not socially optimal, therefore, to leave the oil in the ground unless it will be worth $1.05 to consumers next year. More generally, society obtains increases in the value of what is available for consumption by conserving units of a nonrenewable resource to be used in future years only if the price of the units is expected to rise at a rate that is at least as high as the interest rate.

This answer to the question "How much of a nonrenewable resource should be consumed now?" was provided many years ago by the U.S. economist Harold Hotelling. His answer is very simple, yet it specifically determines the optimal profile of prices over the years. It is interesting that the answer applies to all nonrenewable resources. It does not matter whether there is a large or a small demand or whether that demand is elastic or inelastic. In all cases the answer is the same:

The rate of extraction of any nonrenewable

resource should be such that its price increases at a rate equal to the interest rate.

For example, if the rate of interest is 4 percent, then the price of the resource should be rising at 4 percent per year. If it is rising by more, there is too much current extraction; if it is rising by less, then there is not enough current extraction. We have already seen that this is the rate of extraction that will be produced by a competitive industry.

The Rate of Extraction

Hotelling's rule does not tell us exactly how many barrels should be produced each year. Instead, it only tells us that the year's extraction rate *should be such that* the market price rises over time at a rate equal to the rate of interest. What then should the actual extraction rate be *if the competitive market fulfills Hotelling's rule for optimal extraction rates?* The answer to this question *does* depend on market conditions. Specifically, it depends on the position and the slope of the demand curve. If the quantity demanded at all prices is small, the rate of extraction will be small. The larger the quantity demanded at each price, the higher the rate of extraction will tend to be.

Now consider the influence of the demand elasticity. A highly inelastic demand curve suggests that there are few substitutes and that purchasers are prepared to pay large sums rather than do without the resource. This will produce a relatively even rate of extraction, with small reductions in each period being sufficient to drive up the price at the required rate. A relatively elastic demand curve suggests that people can easily find substitutes once the price rises. This will encourage a great deal of consumption now and a rapidly diminishing amount over future years, since large reductions in consumption are needed to drive the price up at the required rate.

Figure 19-1 illustrates this working of the price mechanism with a simple example in which the whole stock of oil must be consumed in only two periods, this year and next year. The general point is as follows:

The more inelastic the demand curve, the more even the rate of extraction (and hence the rate of use) will be over the years; the

FIGURE 19-1
The Extraction Rate for a Nonrenewable Resource

(i) Relatively flat demand curve

(ii) Relatively steep demand curve

The shape of the demand curve determines the extraction profile over time. In the example in this figure, the interest rate is assumed to be 10 percent, and there is a fixed supply of 200,000 tons of oil that can be extracted from the ground at zero variable cost. (All costs are fixed costs.) The oil is available for extraction either in the current period or in the next period, after which it spoils.

In part (i) of the figure, the demand curve is relatively flat. The two conditions—that the whole supply be used over two periods and that the price rise by 10 percent between the two periods—dictate that the quantities be 120,000 tons in the first period, with a price of $1.00 per ton, and 80,000 tons in the second period, with a price of $1.10 per ton.

In part (ii), the demand curve is rather steep. The same two conditions now dictate that the quantities be 104,000 tons in the first period, with a price of $1.50 per ton, and 96,000 tons in the second period, with a price of $1.65 per ton.

more elastic the demand curve, the more un-even the rate of extraction will be over the years.

An elastic demand curve will lead to a large consumption now and a rapid fall in consumption over the years. An inelastic demand curve will lead to a smaller consumption now and a less rapid fall in consumption over the years.

Rents to Natural Resources

The incomes earned by the owners of the oil resources are *rents* in the sense defined in Chapter 17: The owners would be willing to produce the oil at any price that covers the direct costs of extraction, which in this example is zero.[3] Although these in-

comes serve no function in getting the product produced, since any nonzero price would do that, they do fulfill the important function of determining the extraction rate, and hence the use of the resource, *over time.* As we have seen, the price profile determines the use of the resource, and hence the amount of resources allocated to its production, *over time.*

The Price System as a Conservation Mechanism

In this discussion, we see the price system playing its now familiar role of coordinator. By following private profit incentives, firms are led to conserve the resource in a manner that is consistent with society's needs.

---

[3]In real cases, the direct cost of extracting the resource is positive, and the rent is the income earned above that amount.

The Role of Rising Prices

From society's viewpoint, the optimal extraction pattern of a totally nonrenewable resource occurs when its price rises each year at a rate equal to the interest rate. If the price is prevented from rising, the resource is depleted much too fast. The rising price fulfills a number of useful functions.

First, the rising price encourages conservation. As the resource becomes scarcer and its price rises, users will be motivated to be more and more economical in its use. Uses with low yields may be abandoned altogether, and uses with high yields will be pursued only as long as their value at the margin is enough to compensate for the high price.

Second, the rising price encourages the discovery of new sources of supply—at least in cases in which the world supply is not totally fixed and already known.

Third, the rising price encourages innovation. New products that will do the same job may be developed, as well as new processes that use alternative resources.

How Might the Price System Fail?

We will discuss three basic ways in which the price system might fail to produce the optimal rate of resource extraction: First, private owners may not have sufficient information to determine the optimal extraction rate; second, deficiencies in property rights may result in firms having incentives to extract the resource too fast; and third, markets may not correctly reflect social values. We look at examples of each of these and ask if they justify government intervention.[4]

Ignorance. Private owners might not have enough knowledge to arrive at the best estimate of the rate at which prices will rise. If they do not know the world stocks of their commodity and the current extraction rate, they may be unable to estimate the rate of the price rise and thus will not know when to raise or lower their current rates of extraction. For example, if all firms mistakenly think that prices will not rise greatly in the future,

they will all produce too much now and conserve too little for future periods.

There is no reason to think that the government could do better, unless it has access to some special knowledge that private firms do not possess. If it does have such knowledge, the government can make it public; further intervention is unnecessary if a competitive industry is maximizing profits on the basis of the best information available to it. In practise, what knowledge does exist about both the proven reserves of nonrenewable resources and their current extraction rates is usually freely and openly available.

Inadequate property rights. Some nonrenewable resources have the characteristics of what is called *common property.* Such property cannot be exclusively owned and controlled by one person or firm. For example, one person's oil-bearing land may be adjacent to another person's, and the underground supplies may be interconnected. In such a case, if one firm holds off producing now, the oil may end up being extracted by the neighbour. In such cases, which are sometimes encountered with petroleum, there is a tendency for a firm to extract the resource too fast, because a firm's oil that has been left in the ground may not be available to that firm at a future date. (Similar issues arise with any common property resource, such as fishing grounds.)

What is being described is a problem of inadequate property rights. Since the resource will be worth more in total value when it is exploited at the optimal extraction rate than when small firms exploit it too quickly, there will be an incentive for individual owners to combine until each self-contained source of supply is owned by only one firm. After that, the problem of overexploitation will no longer arise. Government ownership is not necessary to achieve this result. What is needed, at most, is intervention to ensure that markets can work to provide the optimal size of individual units so that proper extraction management can be applied by the private owners.

Political uncertainty can provide another source of inadequate property rights. For example, the owners of the resource may fear that a future election or a revolution will establish a government that will confiscate their property. They will then be motivated to exploit the resource too quickly, on the grounds that certain revenue now is more valu-

---

[4]This discussion partly anticipates the analysis in Part 7, which investigates market successes and market failures in more general terms.

able than highly uncertain revenue in the future. The current rate of extraction will tend to increase until the expected rate of price rise exceeds the interest rate by a sufficient margin to compensate for the risks of future confiscation of supplies left in the ground.

Unequal market and social values.   Normally, in a competitive world the market interest rate indicates the rate at which it is optimal to discount the future over the present. Society's investments are valuable if they earn the market rate of return and are not valuable if they earn less (because the resources could be used in other ways to produce more value to consumers). In certain circumstances, however, the government may have reasons to adopt a different rate of discount. It is then said that the *social rate of discount*—the discount rate that is appropriate to the society as a whole—differs from the private rate, as indicated by the market rate of interest. In such circumstances, there is reason for the government to intervene to alter the rate at which the private firms would exploit the resource.

Critics are often ready to assume that profit seeking producers will despoil most nonrenewable resources by using them up too quickly. They argue for government intervention to conserve the resource by slowing its rate of extraction. Yet unless the social rate of discount is *less than* the private rate, there is no clear social gain in investing by holding resources in the ground where they only will yield, say, a 2 percent return when, say, 5 percent can be gained on other investments.

Since governments must worry about their short-term popularity and their chances of reelection, there is no presumption that government intervention will slow down the rate of extraction, even if the social discount rate is below the private rate. Instead, governments might extract resources faster than market forces would left to themselves. A good example is provided by the Hibernia oil field that lies off the Newfoundland coast. The costs of developing the field and extracting the oil exceed its market value. It would thus not be developed under free-market conditions. Instead taxpayers' money is being used to produce oil whose market value is less than its costs of production. If left in the ground, the field would one day develop a positive value, if either the price of oil rose or costs of production fell.

Actual Price Profiles

Many nonrenewable resources do not seem to have the steadily rising profile of prices that the theory predicts. The price of petroleum, having been raised artificially by the OPEC cartel, returned in the late 1980s to an inflation-adjusted level that was not far from where it was in 1970 and has remained there ever since. Indeed, it has since been held somewhat above that price only insofar as the producing countries have succeeded in intermittently enforcing some output restrictions. The price of coal has not soared, nor has the price of iron ore. In many cases, the reason lies in the discovery of new supplies, which have prevented the total known stocks of many resources from being depleted. In the case of petroleum, for example, the ratio of known reserves to one year's consumption is no lower now than it was two or even four decades ago. Furthermore, most industry experts believe that large quantities of undiscovered oil still exist under both the land and the sea.

In other cases, the invention of new substitute products has reduced the demand for some of these resources. For example, plastics have replaced metals in many uses, and fiber optics have replaced copper wire in many types of message transmission.

In yet other cases, the reason is to be found in government pricing policy. An important example of this type is the use of *nonrenewable* water for irrigation in much of the United States. Current U.S. policy will have strong effects on Canada, which controls a large *renewable* supply of water from rivers and lakes. Vast underground reserves of water lie in aquifers beneath many areas of the United States. Although these reserves were accumulated over millennia, they are being used up at a rate that will exhaust them in a matter of decades. The water is often supplied by government water authorities at a price that covers only a small part of total cost and that does not rise steadily to reflect the dwindling stocks.

Such a constant-price policy for *any* nonrenewable resource creates three characteristic problems. First, the resource will be exhausted much faster than if price were to rise over time. A constant price will lead to a constant rate of extraction to meet the quantity demanded at that price until the resource is completely exhausted. Second, no signals go out to induce conservation, innovation, and exploration. Third, when the supply of the resource is finally exhausted, the adjustment will have to come all at once. If the price had risen steadily each year under free-market conditions, adjustment would have taken place little by little each year. The controlled price, however, gives no signal of the ever-diminishing stock of the resource until all at once the supplies run out. The required adjustment will then be much more painful than it would have been if it had been spread over time in response to steadily rising prices.

Capital

Capital is a produced factor of production, and hence, it is renewable. The nation's capital stock consists of all those produced goods that are not wanted by consumers but are used in the production of other goods and services. Factories, machines, tools, computers, roads, bridges, and railroads are but a few of the many examples.

We begin our study of capital by exploring an important complication that arises because factors of production are durable—a machine lasts for years, a labourer for a lifetime, and land more or less forever. *It is convenient to think of a factor's lifetime as being divided into the shorter periods that we refer to as production periods, or rental periods.* The present time is the current period. Future time is one, two, three, and so on periods hence.

The durability of factors makes it necessary to distinguish between the factor itself and the flow of services that it provides in a given production period. We can, for example, rent the use of a piece of land for some period of time, or we can buy the land outright. This distinction is just a particular instance of the general distinction between flows and stocks that we first encountered in Chapter 4.

Although what follows applies to any durable factor, applications to capital are of most importance, so we limit the discussion to capital. Box 19-1 discusses some of these issues as they apply to labour.

Two Prices of Capital

If a firm hires the use of a piece of capital equipment for some period of time—for example, one truck for one month—it pays a price for the privilege of using that piece of capital equipment. If the firm buys the truck outright, it pays a different (and higher) price for the purchase. Consider in turn each of these prices.

Rental Price

The *rental price of capital* is the amount that a firm pays to obtain the services of a capital good for a given period of time. The rental price of one week's use of a piece of capital is analogous to the weekly wage rate that is the price of hiring the services of labour.

Just as a profit-maximizing firm operating in competitive markets continues to hire labour until its marginal revenue product (*MRP*) equals its wage, so will the firm go on hiring capital until its *MRP* equals its rental price, which we call *R*. Since in a competitive market, all firms will face the same rental price, all firms that are in equilibrium will have the same *MRP* of capital.

A capital good may also be used by the firm that owns it. In this case, the firm does not pay out any rental fee. However, the rental price is the amount that the firm could charge if it leased its capital to another firm. It is thus the *opportunity cost* to the firm of using the capital good itself. This rental price is the *implicit* price that reflects the value to the firm of the services of its own capital that it uses during the current production period.

Whether the firm pays the rental price explicitly or calculates it as an implicit cost of using its own capital, the rental price of a capital good over the current production period is equal to its marginal revenue product.

Purchase Price

The price that a firm pays to buy a capital good is called the *purchase price of capital.* When a firm buys a capital good outright, it obtains the use of the good's services over the whole of that good's life-

Box 19-1

The Rental and Purchase Price of Labour

If you wish to farm a piece of land, you can buy it yourself, or you can rent it for a specific period of time. If you want to set up a small business, you can buy your office and equipment, or you can rent them. The same is true for all capital and all land; a firm often has the option of buying or renting.

Exactly the same would be true for labour if we lived in a slave society. You could buy a slave to be your assistant, or you could rent the services either of someone else's slave or of a free person. Fortunately, slavery is illegal throughout most of today's world. As a result, the labour markets that we know deal only in the services of labour; we do not go to a labour market to buy a worker, only to hire his or her services.

You can, however, buy the services of a labourer for a long period of time. In professional sports, multiyear contracts are common, and 10-year contracts are not unknown. The late Herbert von Karajan was made conductor for life of the Berlin Philharmonic Orchestra. Publishers sometimes tie up their authors in multibook contracts, and movie and television production firms often sign up their actors on long-term contracts. In all cases of such *personal services contracts,* the person is not a slave, and his or her personal rights and liberties are protected by law. The purchaser of the long-term contract is nonetheless buying ownership of the factor's services for an extended period of time. The price of the contract will reflect the person's expected earnings over the contract's lifetime. If the contract is transferable, the owner can sell these services for a lump sum or rent them out for some period. As with land and capital goods, the price paid for this *stock* of labour services depends on the expected rental prices over the contract period.

time. What the capital good will contribute to the firm is a flow that is equal to the expected marginal revenue product of the good's services over the good's lifetime. The price that the firm is willing to pay is, naturally enough, related to the total value that it places now on this stream of *expected* receipts to be received over future time periods.

The term *expected* emphasizes that the firm is usually uncertain about the prices at which it will be able to sell its outputs in the future. For the sake of simplicity, we assume that the firm knows the future *MRP*s.

Present Value of Future Returns

Consider the stream of future income that is provided by a capital good. How much is that stream worth *now?* How much would someone be willing to pay now to buy the right to receive that flow of future payments? The answer is called the good's *present value.* In general, **present value** *(PV)* refers to the value *now* of one or more payments to be received *in the future.*

Present Value of a Single Future Payment

One period hence.　To learn how to find the present value, we start with the simplest possible case. How much would a firm be prepared to pay *now* to purchase a capital good that will produce a single marginal physical product valued at $100 in one year's time, after which time the good will be useless? One way to answer this question is to discover how much the firm would have to lend out in order to have $100 a year from now. Suppose for the moment that the interest rate is 5 percent, which means that $1.00 invested today will be worth $1.05 in one year's time.[5]

If we use *PV* to stand for this unknown amount, we can write *PV*(1.05) = $100 (the left-hand side of this equation means *PV* multiplied by 1.05). Thus *PV* = $100/1.05 = $95.24. This tells us that the present value of $100, receivable in one year's time, is $95.24 when the interest rate is 5 percent. Anyone who lends out $95.24 for one year at 5 percent interest will receive $95.24 back plus $4.76 in interest, which makes $100 in total. When we calculate this present value, the interest rate is used to *discount* (i.e., reduce to its present value) the $100 to be received one year hence. The maximum price that a firm would be willing to pay for this capital good is $95.24 (assuming that the interest rate relevant to the firm is 5 percent).

To see why, let us start by assuming that firms are offered the capital good at some other price. Say that the good is offered at $98. If, instead of paying this amount for the capital good, a firm lends its $98 out at 5 percent interest, it would have at the end of one year more than the $100 that the capital good will produce. (At 5 percent interest, $98 yields $4.90 in interest, which, together with the principal, makes $102.90.) Clearly, no profit-maximizing firm would pay $98—or, by the same reasoning, any sum in excess of $95.24—for the capital good. It could do better by using its funds in other ways.

Now say that the good is offered for sale at $90. A firm could borrow $90 to buy the capital good and would pay $4.50 in interest on its loan. At the end of the year, the good yields $100. When this is used to repay the $90 loan and the $4.50 in interest, $5.50 is left as profit to the firm. Clearly, it would be worthwhile for a profit-maximizing firm to buy the good at a price of $90 or, by the same argument, at any price less than $95.24.

The actual present value that we have calculated depended on our assuming that the interest rate is 5 percent. What if the interest rate is 7 percent? At that interest rate, the present value of the $100 receivable in one year's time would be $100/1.07 = $93.46.

These examples are easy to generalize. In both cases we have found the present value by dividing

the sum that is receivable in the future by 1 plus the rate of interest.[6] In general, the present value of *R* dollars one year hence at an interest rate of *i* per year is

$$PV = \frac{R}{(1 + i)} \qquad [1]$$

Several periods hence. Now we know how to calculate the present value of a single sum that is receivable one year hence. The next step is to ask what would happen if the sum were receivable at a later date. What, for example, is the present value of $100 to be received *two* years hence when the interest rate is 5 percent? This is $100/(1.05)(1.05) = $90.70. We can check this by seeing what would happen if $90.70 were lent out for two years. In the first year, the loan would earn interest of (0.05)($90.70) = $4.54, and hence after one year the firm would receive $95.24. In the second year, the interest would be earned on this entire amount; interest earned in the second year would equal (0.05)($95.24) = $4.76. Hence, in two years the firm would have $100. (The payment of interest in the second year on the interest income earned in the first year is known as *compound interest*.)

In general, the present value of *R* dollars after *t* years at *i* percent is

$$PV = \frac{R}{(1 + i)^t} \qquad [2]$$

All that this formula does is discount the sum, *R,* by the interest rate, *i,* repeatedly, once for each of the *t* periods that must pass until the sum becomes available. If we look at the formula, we see that the higher *i* or *t* is, the higher is the whole term $(1 + i)^t$. This term, however, appears in the denominator, so *PV* is *negatively* related to both *i* and *t*.

The formula $PV = R/(1 + i)^t$ shows that the present value of a given sum payable in the

---

[5]The analysis in the rest of this chapter assumes *annual* compounding of interest.

[6]Notice that in this type of formula, the interest rate, *i,* is expressed as a decimal fraction where, for example, 7 percent is expressed as 0.07, so (1 + *i*) equals 1.07.

future will be smaller the more distant the payment date and the higher the rate of interest.

A continued stream. Now consider the present value of a stream of receipts that continues indefinitely, as might the *MRP* of a very long-lived piece of capital. At first glance, that *PV* might seem very high, because the total amount received grows without reaching any limit as time passes. The previous section suggests, however, that people will not value the far-distant money payments very highly.

To find the *PV* of $100 a year, payable forever, we ask: How much would you have to invest now, at an interest rate of *i* percent per year, to obtain $100 each year? This is simply $iPV = \$100$, where *i* is the interest rate and *PV* the sum required. Dividing through by *i* shows the present value of the stream of $100 a year forever:

$$PV = \frac{\$100}{i}$$

For example, if the interest rate is 10 percent, the present value would be $1,000. This merely says that $1,000 invested at 10 percent yields $100 per year, forever. Notice that, as in the previous sections, *PV* is negatively related to the rate of interest: The higher the interest rate, the less is the present value of the stream of future payments.

In the text, we have concentrated on finding the present value of amounts available in the future. Box 19-2 reverses the process and discusses the future value of sums available in the present.

Conclusions

From the foregoing discussion, we can put together the following important propositions about the rental and purchase prices of capital.

1. The rental price of capital paid in each period is the flow of net receipts that the capital good is expected to produce during that period, that is, the marginal revenue product of the capital good.
2. The maximum purchase price that a firm would pay for a capital good is the discounted present value of the flow of net receipts, that is,

rental values, that the good is expected to produce over its lifetime.

3. The maximum purchase price that a firm would pay for a capital good is positively associated with its rental price and negatively associated with both the interest rate and the amount of time that the owner must wait for payments to accrue.

Equilibrium of the Firm

An individual firm faces a given interest rate and a given purchase price of capital goods. The firm can vary the quantity of capital that it employs, and, as a result, the marginal revenue product of its capital varies. The law of diminishing returns tells us that the more capital the firm uses, the lower is its *MRP*.

The Decision to Purchase Capital

Consider a firm deciding whether or not to add to its capital stock and facing an interest rate of 10 percent at which it can borrow (and lend) money. The first thing the firm needs to do is to estimate the expected marginal revenue product of the new piece of capital over its lifetime. Then it discounts this at a rate of 10 percent to find the present value of that stream of receipts the machine will create.[7] Let us say it is $5,000.

The present value, by its construction, tells us how much any flow of future receipts is worth now. If the firm can buy the machine for less than its *PV,* this is a good buy. If it must pay more, the machine is not worth its price.

It is always worthwhile for a firm to buy an-

---

[7]Suppose that the machine has an *MRP* of $1,000 each period. First, suppose the machine only lasts this period. The present value is then $1,000. Next suppose it lasts two periods. The *PV* is then $1,000 + $1,000/(1.10) = $1,909.09. If it lasts three periods, the *PV* is $1,000 + $1,000/1.10 + $1,000/(1.10)^2 = $2,735.53, and so on. Each additional period that it lasts produces an *MRP* of $1,000, but at a more and more distant date, so that the *present value* of that period's revenue gets smaller due to more heavy discounting. The details of the calculation do not need to concern us. We only need to know that such a present value can be calculated.

Box 19-2

The Future Value of a Present Sum

In the text, we have concentrated on the present value of amounts to be received in the future. We can, however, turn the question around and ask what is the future value of an amount of money that is available in the present.

Assume that you have $100 available to you today. What will that sum be worth next year? If you lend it out at 5 percent, you will have $105 in one year. Letting PV stand for the sum you have now and FV for the value of the sum in the future, we have $FV = PV(1.05)$ in this case. Writing the interest rate as we have in the text we get:

$$FV = PV(1 + i)$$

If we divide through by $(1 + i)$ we get Equation 1 in the text.

Next, if we let the sum build up by reinvesting the interest each year, we get:

$$FV = PV(1 + i)^t$$

If we divide both sides by $(1 + i)^t$, we get Equation 2 in the text.

This tells us that what we did in the text is reversible. If we have an amount of money today, we can figure out what it will be worth if it is invested at compounded interest for some number of future periods. Similarly, if we are going to have some amount of money at some future date, we can figure out how much we would need to invest today to get that amount at the specified date in the future.

Our argument tells us that the two sums, PV and FV, are linked by the compound interest expression $(1 + i)^t$. To go from the present to the future, we *multiply* PV by the interest expression, and to go from the future to the present we *divide* FV by the interest expression.

The rule of 72 is a convenient way of going from PV to FV by finding out how long it takes for FV to become twice the size of PV at any given interest rate. According to that rule, the time it takes for FV to become twice PV is given approximately by $72/100i$. So, for example, if i is 0.1 (an interest rate of 10 percent) any present sum doubles in value in $72/10 = 7.2$ years.

---

other unit of capital whenever the present value of the stream of future *MRP*s that the capital provides exceeds its purchase price.

The Size of the Firm's Capital Stock

Since the *MRP* declines as the firm's capital stock rises, the firm will eventually reach an equilibrium with respect to the size of its capital stock. The firm will go on adding to its capital until the *present value* of the flow of *MRP*s conferred by the last unit added is equal to the purchase price of that unit.

The equilibrium capital stock of the firm is such that the present value of the stream of net income that is provided by the marginal unit of capital is equal to its purchase price.

Now let the firm be in equilibrium with respect to its capital stock, and ask what would lead the firm to wish to increase that stock. Given the price of the machines, anything that increases the present value of the flow of income that the machines produce will have that effect. Two things will do this job. First, the *MRP*s of the capital may rise.

That would happen if technological changes make capital more productive, so that each unit produces more than before. (This possibility is dealt with later in the chapter.) Second, the interest rate may fall, causing an increase in the present value of any given stream of future *MRP*s. For example, suppose that next year's *MRP* is $1,000. This has a *PV* of $909.09 when the interest rate is 10 percent and $952.38 when the interest rate falls to 5 percent.

So when the interest rate falls, the firm will wish to add to its capital stock. It will go on doing so until the decline in the *MRP*s of successive additions to its capital stock, according to the law of diminishing returns, reduces the present value of the *MRP* at the new, lower rate of interest to the purchase price of the capital.

The size of a firm's desired capital stock increases when the rate of interest falls, and it decreases when the rate of interest rises.

This relationship is shown in Figure 19-2. It can be considered as the firm's demand curve for capital plotted against the interest rate. It shows how the desired stock of capital varies with the interest rate. (It is sometimes called the *marginal efficiency of capital curve*.)

Equilibrium for the Whole Economy

The term **capital stock** refers to some aggregate amount of capital. The *firm's capital stock* has an *MRP*, showing the net increase in the firm's revenue when another unit of capital is added to its existing capital stock. The *economy's capital stock* also has a marginal revenue product. This is the addition to total national output (GDP) that is caused by adding another unit of capital to the economy's total stock. This capital stock also has an average product, which is total output divided by the total capital stock (i.e., the amount of output per unit of capital).

The same analysis that we used for one firm in the previous section applies to the whole economy. The lower the rate of interest, the higher is the desired stock of capital that all firms will wish to hold. Such a curve is shown as the economy's demand curve in Figure 19-3.

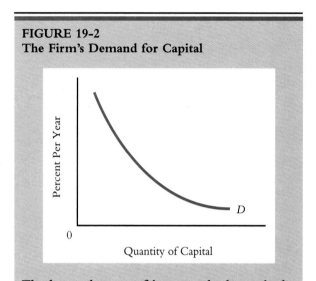

FIGURE 19-2
The Firm's Demand for Capital

The lower the rate of interest, the larger is the firm's desired capital stock. A firm will go on adding to its capital stock until the discounted present value of the stream of marginal revenue products equals the cost of a unit of capital. The lower the interest rate, the higher is the present value of any given stream of marginal revenue products and hence the more capital that the firm will wish to use.

Short-Run Equilibrium

In the short run, the economy's capital stock is given, but for the economy as a whole, the interest rate is variable. Whereas the firm reaches equilibrium by altering its capital stock, the whole economy reaches equilibrium through variations in the interest rate.

For the economy as a whole, the condition that the present value of the *MRP*s should equal the price of capital goods determines the equilibrium interest rate.

Let us see how this comes about. If the price of capital is less than the present value of its stream of future *MRP*s, it would be worthwhile for all firms to borrow money to invest in capital. For the economy as a whole, however, the stock of capital cannot change quickly, so the effect of this demand for borrowing would be to push up the interest

FIGURE 19-3
The Equilibrium Interest Rate

In the short run, the interest rate fluctuates to equate the demand and supply of capital; in the long run, the interest rate falls as more capital is accumulated. The economy's desired capital stock is negatively related to the interest rate, as shown by the curve D. In the short run, the capital is given. When the stock is K_0, the equilibrium interest rate is i_0, because above that rate people will not want to hold all the available capital, and below it, people will want to borrow and add to capital. In the long run, as the capital stock grows to K_1, the equilibrium interest rate falls to i_1.

FIGURE 19-4
The Effect of Changing Technology and Capital Stock

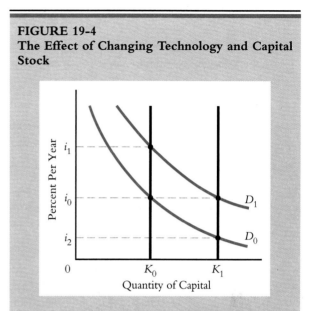

Increases in technological knowledge and the capital stock have opposite effects on the equilibrium interest rate. The original capital stock is K_0, and the original state of technology gives rise to a relation between the desired capital stock and the interest rate D_0. Thus, the equilibrium interest rate is i_0. Technological improvements shift the desired capital stock curve to D_1 and, with a constant stock of capital, would raise the interest rate to i_1. Suppose that in addition, the capital stock increases to K_1. If the curve had remained at D_0, the equilibrium interest rate would have fallen to i_2. In the figure, the two effects exactly offset each other, and i remains unchanged at i_0, where K_1 and D_1 intersect.

rate until the present value of the MRPs equals the price of a unit of capital goods. Conversely, if the price of capital is above its present value, no one would wish to borrow money to invest in capital, and the rate of interest would fall. This is illustrated in Figure 19-3.

Changing Capital and Technology

In an economy with positive saving, more capital is accumulated over time, and the stock of capital grows slowly. As this happens, the MRP falls. This will cause the equilibrium interest rate to fall over time, as is also shown in Figure 19-3.

In the very long run, technology changes. As a result, the capital stock becomes more productive as the old, obsolete capital is replaced by newer, more efficient capital. This shifts the MRP curve outward, which tends to increase the equilibrium interest rate associated with any particular size of the capital stock. The accumulation of capital moves the economy downward to the right along any given MRP curve, and that tends to lower the interest rate associated with any one MRP curve. The net effect on the interest rate of both of these changes may be to raise it, to lower it, or to leave it unchanged, as shown in Figure 19-4. The very-long-run effects of changing technology, combined with a growing capital stock, are studied further in Chapter 38.

SUMMARY

1. The socially optimal rate of exploitation for a completely nonrenewable resource occurs when its price rises at a rate that is equal to the rate of interest. This is also the rate that will be established by a profit-maximizing, competitive industry.

2. Resources for which the demand is highly elastic will have a high rate of exploitation in the near future and a fairly rapid fall-off over time. Resources for which the demand is highly inelastic will have a lower rate of exploitation in the near future and a smaller fall-off over time.

3. Rising prices act as a conservation device by rationing the consumption over time according to people's preferences. As prices rise, conservation, discovery of new sources of supply, and innovation to reduce demand are all encouraged.

4. The price system can fail to produce optimal results if (a) people lack the necessary knowledge, (b) property rights are inadequate to protect supplies left for future use by their owners, or (c) the social rate of discount differs significantly from the market rate.

5. Controlling the price of a nonrenewable resource at a constant level speeds up the rate of exploitation and removes the price incentives to react to the growing scarcity.

6. Because capital goods are durable, it is necessary to distinguish between the stock of capital goods and the flow of services provided by them and thus between their purchase price and their rental price. The linkage between them relies on the ability to assign a present value to future returns. The present value of a future payment will be lower when the payment is more distant and the interest rate is higher.

7. The rental price of capital in each period equals its marginal revenue product in that period. It is the amount that is paid to obtain the flow of services that a capital good provides for a given period. The purchase price is the amount that is paid to acquire ownership of the capital, and in equilibrium it is equal to the present value of the net income stream generated by the capital. This is the present value of capital's future stream of marginal revenue products.

8. An individual firm will invest in capital goods as long as the present value of the stream of future net incomes that are provided by another unit of capital exceeds its purchase price. For a single firm and for the economy as a whole, the size of the total capital stock varies negatively with the rate of interest.

TOPICS FOR REVIEW

Hotelling's rule

The role of rising prices of nonrenewable resources

Rental price and purchase price of capital

Present value

The interest rate and the capital stock

DISCUSSION QUESTIONS

1. Can you think of any resources that are renewable if they are exploited at one rate and nonrenewable if they are exploited at other, higher rates?

2. Some Canadians opposed the 1988 Canada-U.S. Free Trade Agreement because they wished to prohibit the export of Canadian oil and natural gas to the United States and instead to save it for use by future generations of Canadians. Some people in the United States opposed the same agreement because they wished to restrict the import of cheap Canadian natural gas into the United States. What would have been the economic gains and losses resulting from following the courses of action advocated by these groups?

3. Outline some of the main events that would follow if no further significant discoveries of oil were ever made after 1995.

4. Why would Americans be interested in gaining control over Canadian water supplies in the future? Why would the Canadian government have resisted granting such control in the text of the Canada-U.S. free trade agreement? Should the U.S. have asked for it (which it did not, since water was outside of the Agreement, as it is in all free trade agreements and customs unions)?

5. Suppose you are offered, free of charge, either one of each of the following pairs of assets. What considerations would determine your choice?
   a. A perpetuity that pays $20,000 a year forever or an annuity that pays $100,000 a year for 5 years.
   b. An oil-drilling company that earned $100,000 after corporate taxes last year or Canadian Government Bonds that paid $100,000 in interest last year.
   c. A 1 percent share in a new company that has invested $10 million in a new cosmetic that is thought to appeal to middle-income women or a $100,000 bond that has been issued by the same company.

6. How would you go about evaluating the present value of the following?
   a. The existing reserves of a relatively small oil company.
   b. The total world reserves of an exhaustible natural resource whose completely fixed supply is known.
   c. A long-term bond, issued by a very shaky Third World government, in which it promises to pay the bearer $1,000 per year forever.
   d. A lottery ticket that your neighbor bought for $10, which was one of 1 million tickets sold for a drawing that was to be held in one year's time and that was to pay $2 million to the single winning ticket.

7. Explain the economic reasons behind the following headlines taken at different times from the business section of the local press.
   a. Rising interest rates depress bond markets.
   b. Falling interest rates encourage conservation.
   c. Major companies reconsider production plans on rumours of major new oil discoveries.

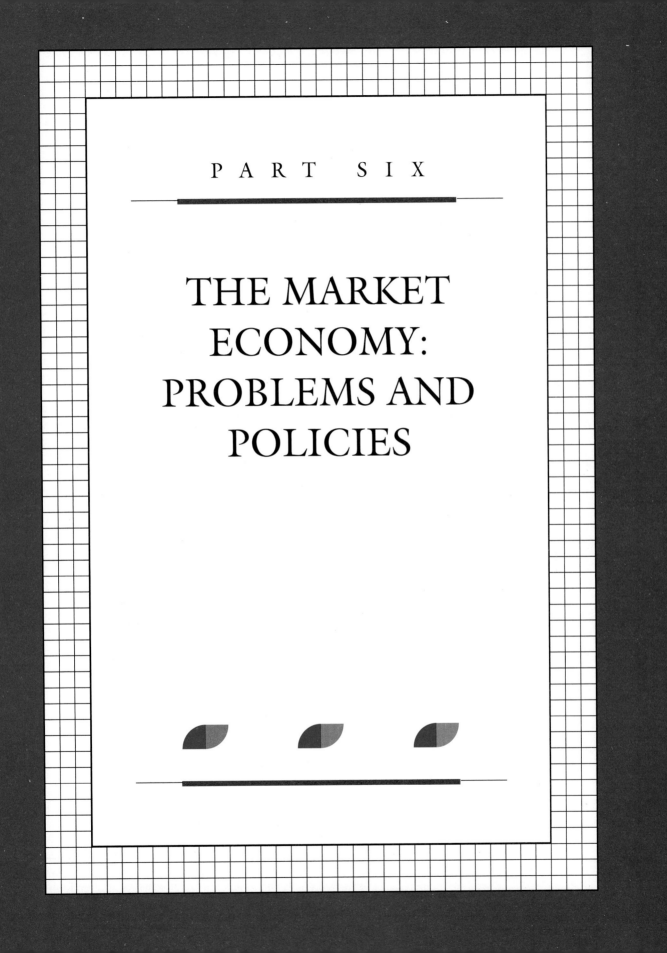

PART SIX

THE MARKET
ECONOMY:
PROBLEMS AND
POLICIES

20

Benefits and Costs of Government Intervention

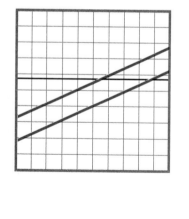

There are two caricatures of the Canadian and the U.S. economies. In one, these countries are the last strongholds of free enterprise, with millions of people in a mad and brutal race for the almighty dollar. In the other, Canadian and U.S. businesspeople, workers, and farmers are seen as strangling slowly in a web of red tape spun by the spider of government regulation. Neither is realistic.

Many aspects of economic life in Canada and the United States are determined by the free-market system. Private preferences, expressed through private markets and influencing private profit-seeking enterprises, determine much of what is produced, how it is produced, and the incomes of productive factors.

But even casual observation makes it clear that public policies and public decisions also play a large role in the economic life of the citizens of Canada and the U.S. populace. Laws restrict what people and firms may do, and taxes and subsidies influence their choices. Much public expenditure is not market determined, and this influences the distribution of national product. Canada and the United States are, in fact, mixed economies.

The general case for some reliance on free markets is that allowing decentralized decision making is more efficient in a number of ways than having all economic decisions made by a centralized planning body. Indeed, much of the political upheaval in Eastern Europe in the last few years has arisen from the very weak performance of planned economies.

The general case for some public intervention is that almost no one wants to let markets decide everything about our economic affairs. Most people's moral and practical sense argues for some state intervention to mitigate the disastrous results that the market deals out to some. Most people believe that there are areas in which markets do not function well and in which state intervention can improve the general social good. For such reasons, there is no known economy in which the people have opted for complete free-market determination of all economic matters and against any kind of government intervention.

The operative choice today is not between an unhampered free-market economy and a fully centralized command economy. It is, instead, about the *mix* of markets and government intervention. The mixture varies greatly among economies and over time. Whether the mixture existing in Canada today could be improved—and, if so, how—is a major political and economic issue.

Even the most passionate advocates of free markets agree that government must provide for enforcement of the rules under which private firms and persons make contracts. Without well-defined property rights, the enforcement of contracts, and a reasonable assurance that goods and services will not be stolen, market economies cannot function. In the modern mixed economy, however, government does a great deal more than create and police the institutions within which the private sector flourishes.

One reason that there are mixed economies lies in what an unkind critic once called the economists' two great insights: *Markets can work, and markets can fail.* A second reason is what the critic might have called the political scientists' two great insights: *Government intervention can work, and government intervention can fail.*

In this chapter we discuss the role of the government in market-based economies, making the case both for and against government intervention. In the succeeding three chapters we look at the principal types of intervention in more detail.

How Markets Coordinate

Any economy consists of thousands upon thousands of individual markets. There are markets for agricultural goods, for manufactured goods, and for consumers' services; there are markets for intermediate goods such as steel and pig iron, which are outputs of some industries and inputs of others; there are markets for raw materials such as iron ore, trees, bauxite, and copper; there are markets for land and for thousands of different types of labour; there are markets in which money is borrowed and in which securities are sold. An economy is not a series of markets functioning in isolation but an interlocking system in which events in one market affect tens of thousands of others.

Any change, such as an increase in demand for a particular product, requires many further changes and adjustments. Should the quantity produced change? If it should, by how much and by what means? Any change in the output of one product will generally require changes in other markets and will start a chain of adjustments. Someone or something must decide what is to be produced, how, and by whom, and what is to be consumed and by whom.

The essential characteristic of the market system is that its coordination occurs in an unplanned, decentralized way. Millions of people make millions of independent decisions concerning production and consumption every day. Most of these decisions are not motivated by a desire to contribute to the social good or to make the whole economy work well but by fairly immediate considerations of self-interest. The price system coordinates these decentralized decisions, making the whole system fit together and respond to the wishes of individual consumers and producers.

The basic insight into how a market system works is that decentralized, private decision makers, acting in their own interests, respond to such signals as the prices of what they buy and sell. Economists have long emphasized price as a signaling device. When a commodity becomes scarce, its free-market price rises. Firms and households that use the commodity are led to economize on it and to look for alternatives. Firms that produce it are led to produce more of it. How the price system informs these decisions has been examined at many places in this book. When a shortage occurs in a market, price rises and profits develop; when a glut occurs, price falls and losses develop. These are *signals*, for all to see, that arise from the overall conditions of total supply and demand. An appreciation for the coordination performed by the price system and an anticipation of some of the problems involved in interfering with it can be found in Box 20-1.

The Role of Profits and Losses

Although the free-market economy is often described as the *price system,* the basic engine that drives the economy is economic profits. Except when there is monopoly or oligopoly, economic profits and losses are symptoms of *disequilibrium,* and they are the driving force in the adaptation of the economy to change.

A rise in demand for a commodity or a fall in production costs creates profits for that commodity's producers. Profits make an industry attractive to new investment. They signal that there are too few resources allocated to that industry. In search of these profits, more resources enter the industry, increasing output and driving down price until profits are driven to zero. A fall in demand or a rise in production costs creates losses. Losses signal the opposite; they imply that an excess of resources is allocated to the industry. Resources will leave the industry until those left behind are no longer suffering losses.

Box 20-1

A View from the Outside of the Inside of Upside Down

The operation of the price system, and the effectiveness with which it helps coordinate decisions, is often taken for granted.* Some insight into its complexity can be gleaned by examining what can happen when governments try to intervene in its operations. In the early 1970s, in an attempt to reduce inflation, the U.S. government under President Richard Nixon tried directly to control the millions of individual prices of goods, services, and factors of production. Here Jackson Grayson, Nixon's "price administrator," tells of some of the problems he encountered:

> One of the main reasons why the policy-making process in general and wage and price controls in particular are inherently difficult is because they are attempting to regulate the most sophisticated information system that the world has ever seen—namely the North American market economy. . . . The information system is the network formed by free people buying and selling, and the signals are the variations in and the levels of wages, prices, interest rates, rents and, unfortunately, taxes. . . .
>
> Most of the products and services that we take for granted in our everyday lives can be taken for granted only because there is a functioning price system. A system that, despite its imperfections, delivers just the right quantity of California lettuce to Montana or Alberta, Canada, and decides the relationship between raw log prices in California and the price of finished lumber in Boston. As we discovered when we tampered with, and effectively suspended, the operation of the price system, we could no longer rely on the system itself and were forced to get more and more involved with what were, before controls, essentially automatic functions.
>
> The problem that policy-makers must cope with, if they are determined to control the system, is the endless detail that is involved in the operation of the system. To control the system and yet keep it running smoothly, the authorities must intercept all of the signals coming from the system (and there are hundreds of millions), interpret them, appropriately change them (assuming they know how) and retransmit them.
>
> What we at the Price Commission continuously found was that everything is related to everything else and there was, accordingly, no such thing as one intervention. We were drawn inevitably and progressively deeper into the system, and the temptation to limit the necessity for our involvement by arbitrarily changing the system was very great. . . .
>
> The difficulty of taking over the wage-price signaling mechanism is indicated by the fact that during the first three weeks of Phase II there were nearly 400,000 inquiries about the program. In terms of getting down to the nitty gritty, had the Dow Chemical Company and the Commission not agreed to an across-the-board increase of 2 percent, we would have had to examine nearly 100,000 submissions on different products for that company alone.

* Excerpted from an article of the same title by Jackson Grayson, Dean of the School of Business, Southern Methodist University, in *The Illusion of Wage and Price Control,* ed. M. Walker (Vancouver: Fraser Institute, 1976).

The importance of profits and losses is that they set in motion forces that tend to move the economy toward a new equilibrium.

Individual households and firms respond to common signals according to their own best interests. There is nothing planned or intentionally coordinated about their actions. Yet when, say, a shortage causes price to rise, individual buyers begin to reduce the quantities that they demand and individual firms begin to increase the quantities that they supply. As a result, the shortage begins to lessen. As it does, price begins to come back down, and profits are reduced. These signals in turn are seen and responded to by firms and households. Eventually, when the shortage has been eliminated, there are no profits to attract further increases in supply. The chain of adjustments to the original shortage is completed.

Notice that in the sequence of signal-response-signal-response, no one has to foresee at the outset the final price and quantity, nor does any government agency have to specify who will increase production and who will decrease consumption. Some firms respond to the signals for more output by increasing production, and they keep on increasing production until the signals get weaker and weaker and finally disappear. Some buyers withdraw from the market when they think that prices are too high, perhaps to return when in their view prices become more reasonable. Households and firms, responding to market signals, not to the orders of government bureaucrats, determine who will increase production and who will limit consumption. No one is forced to do something against his or her best judgement. Voluntary responses collectively produce the end result.

Because the economy is adjusting to shocks continuously, a snapshot of the economy at any given moment reveals substantial positive profits in some industries and substantial losses in others. A snapshot at another moment also will reveal profits and losses, but their locations will be different.

The price system, like an *invisible hand* (Adam Smith's famous phrase), coordinates the responses of individual decision makers who seek only their own self-interests. Because they respond to signals that reflect market conditions, their responses are coordinated without any conscious planning.

Notice that the price system coordinates responses even to prices that are set by monopolistic producers or pegged by government controls. The signal-response process occurs in a price system even when the prices have not been determined in freely competitive markets. The details of the outcomes will be somewhat different under monopoly and oligopoly compared with competition, but when market signals change, the responses will usually be in the same direction. Although monopoly and government controls usually lead to inefficiency

(see Chapter 15), they do not prevent the tendency of prices to rise when things are scarce, nor do they stop the tendency for producers to minimize costs. It is these reactions that are at the heart of a price system's ability to coordinate economic behaviour.

The Case for the Market System

In presenting the case for free-market economies, economists have used two different approaches. One of these may be characterized as the formal defense. It is based upon showing that a free-market economy consisting of nothing but perfectly competitive industries would lead to an optimal allocation of resources. The case was discussed in Chapter 15.

The other approach is at least as old as Adam Smith and is meant to apply to market economies whether they are perfectly competitive or not. It is based on variations and implications of the theme that the market system is an effective coordinator of decentralized decision making. The case is intuitive in that it is not laid out in equations representing a complete, formal model of an economy, but it does follow from some hard reasoning, and it has been subjected to much intellectual probing. What is the nature of this defense of the free market?

Flexible and Automatic Coordination

Defenders of the market economy argue that, compared with the alternatives, the decentralized market system is more flexible and leaves more scope for adaptation to change at any moment in time and for quicker adjustment over time.

Suppose, for example, that the price of oil rises. One household might prefer to respond by maintaining a high temperature in its house and economizing on its driving; another household might do the reverse. A third household might turn down its air conditioning instead. This flexibility can be contrasted with centralized control, which would force the same pattern on everyone, say by fixing the price, by rationing heating oil and gasoline, by regulating permitted temperatures, and by limiting air conditioning to days when the temperature exceeded 27°C.

Furthermore, as conditions change over time, prices in a market economy will change, and decentralized decision makers can react continually. In contrast, government quotas, allocations, and rationing schemes are much more difficult to adjust. As a result, there are likely to be shortages and surpluses before adjustments are made. One great value of the market is that it provides automatic signals *as* a situation develops, so that all of the consequences of some major economic change do not have to be anticipated and allowed for by a body of central planners. Millions of adaptations to millions of changes in tens of thousands of markets are required every year, and it would be a Herculean task to anticipate and plan for them all.

A market system allows for coordination without *anyone* needing to understand how the whole system works. As Professor Thomas Schelling put it:

> The dairy farmer doesn't need to know how many people eat butter and how far away they are, how many other people raise cows, how many babies drink milk, or whether more money is spent on beer or milk. What he needs to know is the prices of different feeds, the characteristics of different cows, the different prices . . . for milk . . ., the relative cost of hired labour and electrical machinery, and what his net earnings might be if he sold his cows and raised pigs instead.[1]

It is, of course, an enormous advantage that all the producers and consumers of a country collectively can make the system operate without any one of them, much less all of them, having to understand how it works. Such a lack of knowledge becomes a disadvantage, however, when people have to vote on schemes for interfering with market allocation.

Stimulus to Innovation and Growth

Technology, tastes, and resource availability are changing all the time, in all economies. Thirty years ago there was no such thing as a personal computer or a digital watch. Front-wheel drive was a curiosity. Students carried their books in briefcases or in canvas bags that were anything but waterproof. Manuscripts only existed as hard copy, not as files in a computer. In order to change one word in a manuscript, one often had to retype every word on a page. Videocassettes did not exist. The next 30 years will surely also see changes great and small. New products and techniques will be devised to adapt to shortages, gluts, and changes in consumer demands, and to exploit new opportunities made available by new technologies. Fiber optics, for example, are likely to change radically the nature of communication, permitting general availability of inexpensive two-way video transmission.

In a market economy, individuals risk their time and money in the hope of earning profits. While many fail, some succeed. New products and processes appear and disappear. Some are fads or have little impact; others become items of major significance. The market system works by trial and error to sort out the successes from the failures and allocates resources to what prove to be successful innovations.

In contrast, planners in more centralized systems have to guess which innovations will be productive and which products will be strongly demanded. Planned growth may achieve wonders by permitting a massive effort in a chosen direction, but central planners also may guess wrong about the direction and put far too many eggs in the wrong basket or reject as unpromising something that will turn out to be vital. Probably the biggest failure of centrally planned economies was their inability to encourage the experimentation and innovation that has proved to be the driving force behind long-run change and growth in all advanced market economies. It is striking that the last decade has seen most centrally planned economies abandon their system in favour of a price system in one fell swoop while the only remaining large planned economy, China, is slowly introducing more and more market determination into most aspects of its economy.

Relative Prices Reflect Relative Costs

A market system tends to drive prices toward the average total costs of production. When markets are close to perfectly competitive, this movement occurs quickly and completely; but even where there is substantial market power, new products and new producers respond to the lure of profits, and their output drives prices down toward the costs of production.

---

[1] Schelling, T.C. *Microeconomics and Macro Behavior* (New York: Norton, 1978).

The advantage of having relative prices reflect relative costs was discussed in Chapter 15. When prices are equal to marginal costs, there will be allocative efficiency, because market choices are then made in the light of opportunity costs.[2] Firms will choose methods that minimize their own cost of producing output, and in so doing will automatically minimize the opportunity cost of the resources that they use. Similarly, when households choose commodity A over commodity B even though A uses resources of twice the total value of the resources used to produce B, they will have to pay the (difference in) price. They will only do so when they value A correspondingly more than B at the margin.

When relative prices reflect relative costs, producers and consumers use the nation's resources in a manner that is consistent with allocative efficiency.

Decentralization of Power

Another important part of the case for a market economy is that it tends to decentralize power and thus requires less coercion of individuals than does any other type of economy. Of course, even though markets tend to diffuse power, they do not do so completely; large firms and large unions clearly have and exercise substantial economic power.

While the market power of large corporations and unions is not negligible, it tends to be constrained both by the competition of other large entities and by the emergence of new products and firms. This is the process of creative destruction that was described by Joseph Schumpeter (see pages 247–248). In any case, say defenders of the free market, even such aggregations of private power are far less substantial than government power.

Governments must coerce if markets are not allowed to allocate people to jobs and commodities to consumers. Not only will such coercion be regarded as arbitrary (especially by those who do not like the results), but the power surely creates major opportunities for bribery, corruption, and allocation

according to the tastes of the central administrators. If, at the going prices and wages, there are not enough apartments or coveted jobs to go around, the bureaucrats can allocate some to those who pay the largest bribe, some to those with religious beliefs, hairstyles, or political views that they like, and only the rest to those whose names come up on the waiting list.

The Case for Intervention

Free markets do all of the good things that we have just discussed and more; yet there are many circumstances in which the free market does not produce the most desirable outcomes. When this happens, economists say that markets have *failed*. The case for intervening in free markets turns in large part on identifying the conditions that lead to **market failure**. Much of the following discussion is devoted to this task.

The word *failure* in this context may convey the wrong impression.

Market failure does not mean that nothing good has happened but rather that the *best attainable outcome* has not been achieved.

The term *market failure* is used to apply to two quite different sets of circumstances. One is the failure of the market system to achieve efficiency in the allocation of society's resources. The other is the failure of the market system to serve social goals other than efficiency, such as a desired distribution of income or the preservation of value systems. We treat each in turn.

Failure to Achieve Efficiency

There are four broad types of phenomena that lead to inefficient market outcomes, called *monopoly power, externalities, collective consumption goods,* and *information asymmetries.*

Monopoly power, externalities, collective consumption goods, and information asym-

---

[2] The mechanism in the text only ensures that prices tend to equal average costs, not marginal costs. Except when there is natural monopoly, long-run average costs will be near long-run marginal costs, and the mechanism in the text will generate allocations that are near to being efficient.

metries cause inefficiency to arise, because in market equilibrium the marginal revenue for the producer is not equal to the marginal cost to society.**

This violates the conditions for allocative efficiency that were discussed in Chapter 15.

Monopoly Power

As we discussed in Chapter 15, firms that face negatively sloped demand curves will maximize profits at an output where price exceeds marginal cost, leading to inefficiency. Although some market power is maintained through artificial barriers to entry, such power can also arise naturally, because in some industries the least costly way to produce a good or a service is to have few producers relative to the size of the market. The standard government remedies are competition policy public ownership and regulation of privately owned firms, which, as discussed in Chapter 15, present problems of their own.

Externalities as a Source of Inefficiency

Costs, as economists define them, involve the value of resources used in the process of production. According to the opportunity-cost principle, value is the benefit that resources would produce in their best alternative use. But who decides what resources are used when and what their opportunity cost is?

Consider the case of a person who is thinking of extending a party for one more hour at 1:00 A.M. For this person, the opportunity cost includes the psychological value of getting an extra hour of sleep, as well as the money cost of whatever will be eaten and drunk, the value of repairs to the apartment, and so forth. However, there is another resource used when the party runs for an extra hour—the neighbours' sleep—and the host need not consider it when she makes her decision to keep the stereo blasting.

Private and social costs.   The difference in the viewpoint of the party thrower and the neighbours illustrates the important distinction between **private cost** and **social cost.** Private cost measures the best alternative use of the resource available to the private decision maker. The party thrower incurs private costs equal to her best alternative use of the resources that go into an extra hour of partying.

The party thrower cannot make any use of the neighbours' sleep and so may value the sleep at zero. The *social cost* includes the private cost but also includes the best use of *all* resources available to society. In this case, social cost includes the cost imposed on the neighbours by an extra hour of partying.

Discrepancies between private and social cost lead to market failure.

The reason for this is that efficiency requires that prices cover social cost, but private producers and consumers, adjusting to private costs, will neglect those elements of social cost that are incurred by others. This is shown in Figure 20-1.

As an example, consider the case of a firm whose production process generates harmful smoke. Individuals who live and work in the neighborhood of the firm bear real costs due to the firm's production. In addition to the disutility of enduring the smoke and of any adverse health effects, they may invest in air conditioners so that they can keep the noxious fumes out. None of the resources that are used to remove the pollution are available to the firm. Therefore, the value of these resources will not be taken into account when the firm decides how much to produce. The element of social cost that the firm is ignoring in its decision is external to its decision-making process.

In general, discrepancies between social and private cost occur when there are **externalities,** which are the costs or benefits of a transaction that are incurred or received by other members of the society but not taken into account by the parties to the transaction. They are also called *third-party effects,* because parties other than the two primary participants in the transaction (the buyer and the seller) are affected. Externalities arise in many different ways, and they may be beneficial or harmful.

When I paint my house, I enhance my neighbours' view and the value of their property. When an Einstein or a Rembrandt gives the world a discovery or a work of art whose worth is far in excess of what he is paid to produce it, he confers an external benefit. Private producers will tend to produce too little of commodities that generate beneficial externalities because they bear all of the costs, while others reap part of the benefits.

Other externalities, such as pollution, are harmful.

FIGURE 20-1
Private and Social Cost

A competitive firm will produce output to the point where its private marginal cost equals the market price. In this case, every unit of output produced imposes *external costs,* equal to the distance between MC_p (private marginal cost—the marginal cost curve that is faced by the firm) and MC_s (social marginal cost).

The profit-maximizing competitive firm chooses to produce q_0, the output where price equals private marginal cost. If the full social cost of production were taken into account, only q^* would be produced. Notice that for each unit of output between q^* and q_0, the cost borne by all members of society exceeds the value to consumers, which is the market price. Over this range, social cost exceeds private revenue, implying allocative inefficiency.

Externalities, whether adverse or beneficial, cause market outcomes to be inefficient, because they cause marginal private revenue to differ from marginal social cost.

The importance of property rights. The economist and Nobel laureate R. H. Coase has argued that when property rights are well defined (e.g., the law is clear on whether a polluter has rights to determine the emissions from a smokestack, or whether a landowner has rights to sue the producer of noxious materials that fall on her land), third parties will be able to negotiate with the producers of externalities in order to ensure that the producers take all relevant valuations of their behaviour into account. To the extent that this view is correct, ex-

ternalities would not be a source of market failure, because social marginal cost and marginal benefit would be included in the supply and demand curves of those engaged in the externality-producing activity. Equilibrium would be efficient, in that social marginal cost and social marginal benefit would be equalized.

The practical application of Coase's insight depends in large part on the number of third parties affected. Where there are millions, as often is the case with air pollution in urban areas, it is hard to see how the negotiations could proceed except with government acting on behalf of the third parties. Where there are only a few, it is quite plausible that careful definition of property rights would be sufficient to permit private markets to deal efficiently with the externality.

Collective Consumption Goods as a Source of Inefficiency

Collective consumption goods are sometimes called **public goods.** The total cost of providing collective consumption goods does not increase as the number of consumers increases. The classic case is national defense. Adding to the population of Canada does not diminish the extent to which each Canadian citizen is defended by a given size and quality of the armed forces. Information is also a public good. Suppose a certain food additive causes cancer. The cost of discovering this needs to be borne only once. The information is then of value to everyone who might have used the additive, and the cost of making the information available to one more consumer is essentially zero. Other public goods include lighthouses, weather forecasts (a type of information), the provision of clean air, and outdoor concerts.

Generally, the private market will not produce efficient amounts of the public good, because once the good is produced, it is either inefficient or impossible to make people pay for its use. Indeed, markets may fail to produce collective consumption goods at all. The obvious remedy in these cases is government provision of the good, paid for by taxes.

How much of a public good should the government provide? It should provide up to the point where the *sum of everyone's individual valuations* of the good is just equal to the marginal cost of providing the good. To see why we must add up everyone's marginal valuation, consider a simple example. Suppose Andy, Bibbiana, Carol, and Dick are all thinking of renting a videotape. Watching the video will be a collective consumption good for the four of them, because the cost will be the same no matter how many of them decide to watch. Suppose each honestly expresses his or her value of watching the tape. Say it is worth $1.00 to Andy, $2.00 each to Bibbiana and Carol, and $0.50 to Dick. If the rental charge for the tape is $5.50 or less, it is worth renting, because the total value to all consumers will be at least equal to the cost.

What if the cost of renting the tape is only $2.75? How should the four decide how to pay for it? One way is to have everyone kick in half of what the tape is worth to them: Andy pays $0.50, Bibbiana and Carol $1.00 each and Dick $0.25 making $2.75 in total. But if this method is adopted, everyone will have an incentive to understate the value that they place on watching the tape, hoping to get the others to pay for their "free ride." This is an example of the *free-rider problem* of paying for public goods.

Inefficient exclusion. Sometimes it is possible to eliminate the free-rider problem by charging a fee for using a public good. In the example above, the videotape rental would have been covered if the group decided to charge each member of the group $1.00 to watch the video. Doing this, however, would have been inefficient. Dick, who would be willing to pay $0.50 to see the video, would be excluded. The marginal benefit from letting Dick see the video is $0.50, and the marginal cost is zero. It is plainly inefficient to exclude him, because $0.50 worth of value is forgone, at no cost, when he is excluded.

Parks, roads, and bridges often are financed through fees or tolls that lead to *inefficient exclusion*. Exclusion in these cases is inefficient for exactly the same reason that it was inefficient to exclude Dick from watching the video in the previous example. Efficiency requires that social marginal cost be equal to social marginal benefit. For an uncongested road, the marginal cost of use is very close to zero. (Gasoline taxes typically cover maintenance costs.) Charging a toll that pays for construction of a road, as is sometimes done on some Canadian freeways and bridges, excludes users who value its use at more than the marginal cost of their using it but less than the toll. (There is also another inefficiency involved

in charging tolls. They are expensive to collect, and, as anyone who has ever driven on busy toll roads or bridges knows, they cause congestion of their own.)

Even where getting around the free-rider problem is technically possible, doing so is usually inefficient. As in cases in which the private market would not produce a public good at all, the obvious remedy is government provision.

Efficient provision of public goods requires that consumers pay the marginal cost of their consumption—zero. Private markets will never provide goods at a price of zero and thus will always underprovide collective consumption goods.

Asymmetric Information as a Source of Inefficiency

The role of information in the economy has received increasing attention from economists in recent years. Information is, of course, a valuable commodity, and markets for information and expertise are well developed, as every college student is aware. Markets for expertise are conceptually identical to markets for any other valuable service. They can pose special problems, however. One of these we have already discussed: Information is often a public good and thus will tend to be underproduced by the private sector, because once the information is known to anyone it is extremely cheap to make it available to others.

Even where information is not a public good, markets for expertise are prone to market failure. The reason for this is that one party to a transaction often can take advantage of special knowledge in ways that change the nature of the transaction itself. The two important sources of market failure that arise when privately held information is bought and sold are *moral hazard* and *adverse selection*.

Moral hazard. In general, we say that there is **moral hazard** when one party to a transaction has both the incentive and the ability to shift costs onto the other party. Moral hazard problems often arise from insurance contracts. The classic example is the homeowner who does not bother to shovel snow from his walk because he knows that his insurance will cover the cost if the mail carrier should twist an ankle. The costs of the homeowner's lax behaviour will be borne largely by others, including the mail carrier, the insurance company, and, indirectly, others who purchase insurance. Individuals and firms who are insured against loss will often take less care to prevent that loss than they would in the absence of insurance. They do so because they do not bear all of the marginal cost imposed by the risk, while they do bear all of the marginal cost of taking action to reduce the risk.

As in all of the cases of market failure that we have considered, the failure arises because the marginal private benefit of an action is not equal to the marginal social cost of that action. The existence of insurance markets, which ideally merely spread existing risk, will also increase the total amount of risk present because of moral hazard.

Insurance is not the only context in which moral hazard problems arise. Another example is professional services. Suppose you ask a dentist whether your mouth needs some expensive work or a lawyer whether you need legal assistance. The dentist and the lawyer both face moral hazard, in that they both have a financial interest in giving you answers that will encourage you to buy their services, and it is difficult for you to find out if their advice is good advice. A similar situation occurs when you ask your mechanic what is wrong with your engine. In all of these cases, one party to the transaction has special knowledge that he or she could use to change the nature of the transaction in his or her favour. As long as the auto mechanic merely is selling her expertise in repairing cars, there is no problem, but when she uses her expertise to persuade the consumer to demand more repairs than are warranted, there is a moral hazard problem. Codes of professional ethics and licensing and certification practises, both governmental and private, are reactions to concerns about this kind of moral hazard.

Adverse selection. Closely related to moral hazard is the problem of **adverse selection**—the tendency of people who are most at risk to buy the most insurance. A person who is suffering from a heart condition may seek to increase his life insurance coverage by purchasing as much additional coverage as is available without a medical examination. People who buy insurance almost always know more about themselves as individual insurance risks than do their insurance companies. The company can try to limit the variation in risk by requiring physical examinations (for life or health insurance) and by

setting up broad categories based on variables, such as age and occupation, over which actuarial risk is known to vary. The rate charged is then different across categories and is based on the average risk in each category, but there will always be much variability of risk *within* any one category.

Those who know that they are well above the average risk for their category are offered a bargain and will be led to take out more car, health, life, or fire insurance than they otherwise would. Their insurance premiums also will not cover the full expected cost of the risk that they are insuring against. Once again, their private cost is less than social cost. On the other side, someone who knows she is a low risk and pays a higher price than the amount warranted by her risk is motivated to take out less insurance than she otherwise would. In this case, her private cost is more than the social cost.

In both cases, resources are allocated inefficiently because the marginal private benefit of the action (taking out insurance) is not equal to the social cost.

More generally, any time either party to a transaction lacks information that the other party has or is deceived by claims made by the other party, market results will tend to be changed, and such changes may lead to inefficiency. Economically (but not legally) it is but a small step from such unequal knowledge to outright fraud. The arsonist who buys fire insurance before setting a building on fire or the businessperson with fire insurance who decides that a fire is preferable to bankruptcy are extreme examples of moral hazard.

Asymmetric information is involved in many other situations of market failure. The *principal-agent problem*, which was discussed in Chapter 16, is an example. In its classic form, the firm's managers act as agents for the stockholders, who are the legal principals of the firm. The managers are much better informed than the principals are about what they actually do and what they could do. Indeed, the managers are hired for their special expertise. Given that it is expensive for the shareholders (principals) to monitor what the managers (agents) do, the managers have latitude to pursue goals other than the firms' profits. The private costs and benefits of their actions thus will be different from the social costs and benefits, with the usual consequences for the efficiency of the market system. Another example of market failure due to asymmetric information is the apparent overdiscounting of the prices of used cars because of the buyer's risk of acquiring a "lemon." (See the discussion of this problem in Box 8-1.)

Other Social Goals

The great strength of the market system is its ability to generate reasonably efficient outcomes in a great many cases, using very decentralized organization. Markets do this well because, most of the time, the information that they need to perform well is derived from individuals' desires to improve their private circumstances. It should not be surprising that markets do not always perform well in fostering broader social goals. Some of these goals (for example, the desire for an "equitable" income distribution) are basically economic. Some, especially notions that people in a given society should have shared values, such as patriotism or a belief in civil liberties, are basically not economic. In either set of cases, however, markets are not very effective, precisely because the goods in question are not of the kind that can be exchanged in decentralized transactions. (Indeed, if we stretch the definition a bit, these are collective consumption goods, and we learned earlier in this chapter that markets tend to underproduce such goods.)

Income Distribution

An important characteristic of a market economy is the *distribution* of the income that it determines. People whose services are in heavy demand relative to supply, such as television anchorpersons and superior football players, earn large incomes, whereas people whose services are not in heavy demand relative to supply, such as Ph.D.s in classics and high school graduates without work experience, earn much less.

The distribution of income produced by the market can be looked at in equilibrium or in disequilibrium. In equilibrium, in an efficiently operating free-market economy, similar efforts of work or investment by similar people will tend to be similarly rewarded everywhere in the economy. Of course, dissimilar people will be dissimilarly rewarded.

In disequilibrium, similar people making similar efforts are likely to be dissimilarly rewarded. People in declining industries, areas, and occupations suffer the punishment of low earnings through no fault of their own. Those in expanding sectors earn the reward of high earnings through no extra effort or talent of their own.

These rewards and punishments serve the important function in decentralized decision making of motivating people to adapt. The advantage of such a system is that individuals can make their own decisions about how to alter their behaviour when market conditions change; the disadvantage is that temporary rewards and punishments are dealt out as a result of changes in market conditions that are beyond the control of the affected individuals.

Moreover, even equilibrium differences in income may seem unfair. A free-market system rewards certain groups and penalizes others. Because the workings of the market may be stern, even cruel, society often chooses to intervene. Should heads of households be forced to bear the full burden of their misfortune if, through no fault of their own, they lose their jobs? Even if they lose their jobs through their own fault, should they and their families have to bear the whole burden, which may include starvation? Should the ill and the aged be thrown on the mercy of their families? What if they have no families? Both private charities and a great many government policies are concerned with modifying the distribution of income that results from such things as where one starts, how able one is, how lucky one is, and how one fares in the labour market.

Often the goal of a more equitable distribution conflicts with the goal of a more efficient economy.

Some of the problems that this can create in policy debates are further discussed in Box 20-2.

Preferences for Public Provision

Police protection, even justice, might be provided by private-market mechanisms. Security guards, private detectives, and bodyguards all provide police-like protection. Privately hired arbitrators, "hired guns," and vigilantes of the Old West represent private ways of obtaining "justice." Yet the members of society may believe that a public police force is *preferable* to a private one and that public justice is preferable to justice for hire. The question of the boundary between public and private provision of

Box 20-2

Distribution Versus Efficiency—The Leaky Bucket

Measures that redistribute income almost invariably also reduce ecomomic efficiency. The late Arthur Okun's image of the leaky bucket summarizes the problem very well. Suppose we have a well-supplied reservoir of water, and we wish to get some water to a household that is not able to come to the reservoir. The only vessel available for transporting the water is a leaky bucket; it works, in that water is deliverable to the intended location, but it works at cost, in that some of the water is lost on the trip. Thus, in order to get a gallon of water to its destination, more than a gallon of water has to be removed from the reservoir. It may be possible to design better or worse buckets, but all of them will leak somewhat.

The analogy to an economy is this: The act of redistribution (carrying the water) reduces the total value of goods and services available to the economy (by the amount of water that leaks on the trip). Getting a dollar to those in need reduces the resources available to everyone else by more than a dollar.

Why is the bucket always leaky? Because there is no way to redistribute income without changing the incentives faced by private households and firms. Generally, a program that takes from the rich and gives to the poor will reduce the incentives of both the rich and the poor to produce income. A policy of subsidizing goods that are deemed to be important—goods such as food, shelter, or oil—will cause the market prices of those goods to be lower than marginal costs, implying that resources used to produce those goods could be used to produce goods of higher value elsewhere in the economy. (This is the basic efficiency argument that we first discussed in Chapter 15.)

Measuring the efficiency costs of redistribution is an important area of economic research. Most economists would agree that programs that directly redistribute income are more efficient (per dollar of resources made available to a given income group) than programs that subsidize the prices of specific commodities. One reason for this is that price subsidies apply even when high-income households purchase the commodities in question.

Redistribution virtually always entails some efficiency cost, and price subsidies are generally less efficient than direct income transfers. This *does not imply* that such programs should not be undertaken. (That buckets leak surely does not imply that they should not be used to transport water, given that we want to transport water and that the buckets we have are the best available tools.) Whatever the social policy regarding redistribution of income, economics has an important role to play in measuring the efficiency costs and distributional consequences of different programs of redistribution. Put another way, it has useful things to say about the design and deployment of buckets.

any number of goods and services became an important topic of debate during the 1980s, and the debate shows no sign of waning. In Canada and Western Europe, the issue is framed as *privatization*. In the formerly Socialist countries of Eastern Europe, the disposition of much of the productive capacity of whole countries is currently under dispute. In all of these cases, part of the debate is about the magnitude of the efficiency gains that could be realized by private organization, and part is about less tangible issues, such as changes in the character and distribution of goods and services that may take place when production is shifted from one sector to the other.

Protecting Individuals from Others

People can use and even abuse other people for economic gain in ways that the members of society find offensive. Child labour laws and minimum standards of working conditions are responses to such actions. Yet direct abuse is not the only example of this kind of market failure. In an unhindered free market, the adults in a household would usually decide how much education to buy for their children. Selfish parents might buy no education, while egalitarian parents might buy the same education for all of their children, regardless of their abilities. The members of society may want to interfere in these choices, both to protect the child of the selfish parent and to ensure that some of the scarce educational resources are distributed according to the ability and the willingness to use them rather than according to a family's wealth. All households are forced to provide a minimum of education for their children, and a number of inducements are offered—through public universities, scholarships, and other means—for talented children to consume more education than they or their parents might choose if they had to pay the entire cost themselves.

Paternalism

Members of society, acting through the state, often seek to protect adult (and presumably responsible) individuals, not from others but from themselves. Laws prohibiting the use of heroin, crack, and other drugs and laws prescribing the installation and use of seat belts are intended primarily to protect individuals from their own ignorance or shortsightedness. This kind of interference in the free choices of individuals is called **paternalism.** Whether such actions reflect the wishes of the majority in the society or whether they reflect the actions of overbearing governments, there is no doubt that the market will not provide this kind of protection. Buyers do not buy what they do not want, and sellers have no motive to provide it.

Protection and paternalism are often closely related to **merit goods.** Merit goods are goods that society deems to be especially important and that those in power feel individuals should be required

or encouraged to consume. Housing, education, and health care are prime examples of merit goods.

Social Obligations

In a free-market system, if you can pay another person to do things for you, you may do so. If you persuade someone else to clean your house in return for $35, presumably both parties to the transaction are better off: You prefer to part with $35 rather than to clean the house yourself, and the person you hire prefers $35 to not cleaning your house. Normally, society does not interfere with people's ability to negotiate mutually advantageous contracts.

Most people do not feel this way, however, about activities that are regarded as social obligations. For example, when military service is compulsory, contracts similar to the one between you and a housekeeper could also be negotiated. Some persons faced with the obligation to do military service could no doubt pay enough to persuade others to do their tour of service for them.[3] By exactly the same argument as we just used, we can presume that both parties will be better off if they are allowed to negotiate such a trade. Yet such contracts are usually prohibited. They are prohibited because there are values to be considered other than those that can be expressed in a market. In times when it is necessary, military service by all healthy males is usually held to be a duty that is independent of an individual's tastes, wealth, influence, or social position. It is felt that everyone *ought* to do this service, and exchanges between willing traders are prohibited.

Military service is not the only example of a social obligation. Citizens cannot buy their way out of jury duty or legally sell their votes to another, even though in many cases they could find willing trading partners.

Even if the price system allocated goods and services with complete efficiency, members of a society might not wish to rely solely on the market if they had other goals that they wished to achieve.

---

[3]During the American Civil War, it was a common practise for a man to avoid the draft by hiring a substitute to serve in his place.

Government Intervention

Private collective action sometimes can remedy the failures of private individual action. (Private charities can help the poor; volunteer fire departments can fight fires; insurance companies can guard against adverse selection by more careful classification of clients.) However, by far the most common remedy for market failure is government intervention.

The previous discussion makes clear that markets sometimes *do* fail, thereby providing potential scope for governments to intervene in beneficial ways. Whether government intervention is warranted in a given case will depend both on the magnitude of the market failure that the intervention is designed to correct and on the costs of the government action itself.

The idea *behind benefit-cost analysis* is simple: Add up the (opportunity) costs of a given policy, then add up the benefits, and do the policy if the benefits outweigh the costs. In practise, benefit-cost analysis can be difficult for three reasons. First, it may be difficult to ascertain what will happen when an action is undertaken. Second, many government actions involve costs and benefits that will take place only in the distant future. Third, some benefits and costs (e.g., the benefits of prohibiting actions that would harm members of an endangered species of animal) are very difficult to quantify. The practise then is to use benefit-cost analysis to measure the things that can be measured and to be sure that the things that cannot be measured are not forgotten when collective decisions are made. By narrowing the range of things that must be determined by informal judgement, benefit-cost analysis plays a useful role.

In this chapter, we have been working toward a benefit-cost analysis of government intervention. We have made a general case against it (free markets are great economizers on information and coordination costs). We have made a general case for it (free markets will fail to produce efficiency when there are public goods, externalities, or information asymmetries and will also not achieve social goals other than economic efficiency). We

now turn to the more specific questions of what governments do when they intervene, what the costs of government intervention are, and under which circumstances government interventions may fail to reduce the degree of failure in some markets.

The Tools of Government Intervention

The legal power of governments to intervene in he workings of the economy is limited only by the Charter of Rights (as interpreted by the courts), the willingness of legislatures to pass laws, and the willingness of the government to enforce them. There are numerous ways in which one or another level of government can prevent, alter, complement, or replace the workings of the unrestricted market economy.

Public provision. National defense, the criminal justice system, the public schools, the highway system, air traffic control, and the national parks are all examples of goods or services that are directly provided by governments in Canada. Public provision is the most obvious remedy for market failure to provide collective consumption goods, but it is also often used in the interest of redistribution (e.g., hospitals) and other social goals (e.g., public schools). In Chapter 22, we shall consider public spending in detail.

Redistribution and social insurance programs. Taxes and spending are often used to provide a distribution of income that is different from that generated by the private market. Government transfer programs affect the distribution of income in this way. In Chapter 22, we will examine the distributive effects of the tax system. Chapter 23 also provides a discussion of the effect of redistributive government spending.

Regulation. Government regulations are public rules that apply to private behaviour. In Chapter 15, we saw that governments regulate private markets in order to limit monopoly power. In Chapter 21, we will focus on regulations designed to deal with environmental quality and with workplace safety. Among other things, government regulations prohibit minors from consuming alcohol, require that children attend school, penalize racial discrimination in housing and labour markets, and require that new automobiles have passive passenger restraints. Government regulation is used to deal with all of the sources of market failure that we have discussed in this chapter; it applies at some level to virtually all spheres of modern economic life.

Structuring incentives. Almost all government actions, including the kinds that we have discussed here, change the incentives facing households and firms. If the government provides a park, people will have a weakened incentive to own large plots of land of their own. Fixing minimum or maximum prices (as we saw in the discussion of rent control and agriculture in Chapter 6) affects privately chosen levels of output.

The government can adjust the tax system to provide subsidies to some kinds of behaviour and penalties to others (see Chapter 22). In some countries, deductible mortgage interest makes owned housing relatively more attractive than other assets that a person might purchase. Such tax treatment sends the household different signals from those sent by the free market. Scholarships to students to become nurses or teachers may offset barriers to mobility into those occupations. Fines and criminal penalties for violating the rules that are imposed are another part of the incentive structure. By providing direct or indirect fines or subsidies, the government can (in principle) correct externalities, induce private production of public goods, change the income distribution, and encourage behaviour that is deemed socially valuable. However, as we shall see, interventions of this kind are not always successful, and they often do as much or even more harm than good.

The government has many tools at its disposal and can use them singly or in combination to address different kinds of market failure.

The Costs of Government Intervention

Consider the following argument: (1) The market system is working imperfectly; (2) government has the legal means to improve the situation; (3) therefore, the public interest will be served by government intervention.

This appealing argument is deficient because it neglects three important considerations. First, government intervention is itself costly in that it uses scarce resources; for this reason alone, not every market failure is worth correcting. Second, government intervention may be imperfect. Just as markets sometimes succeed and sometimes fail, so government intervention sometimes succeeds and sometimes fails. Third, deciding what governments are to do and how they are to do it is difficult and costly.

For the remainder of the discussion in this section, note that the *benefit* of government intervention is the value of the market failures that the intervention will correct. Imagine that such a failure has been identified and evaluated. The question at hand, then, is whether the benefits of the intervention will exceed these costs.

Large potential benefits do not necessarily justify government intervention, nor do large potential costs necessarily make it unwise. What matters is the balance between benefits and costs.

There are several kinds of costs of government intervention.

Direct Resource Costs

Government intervention uses real resources that could be used elsewhere. Civil servants must be paid. Paper, photocopying, and other trappings of bureaucracy, the steel in the navy's ships, the fuel for the army's tanks, and the pilot of the Prime Minister's jet all have valuable alternative uses. The same is true of the accountants who administer the social security system and of the educators who retrain displaced workers.

Similarly, when inspectors visit plants to monitor compliance with government-imposed standards of health, industrial safety, or environmental protection, they are imposing costs on the public in the form of the salaries and expenses of the inspectors. When regulatory bodies develop rules, hold hearings, write opinions, or have their staff prepare research reports, they are incurring costs. The costs of the judges, clerks, and court reporters who hear, transcribe, and review the evidence are likewise costs imposed by government regulation. All these activities use valuable resources that could have provided very different goods and services.

All forms of government intervention use real resources and hence impose direct costs.

This type of cost is fairly easy to identify, as it almost always involves expenditure of public funds. Other costs of intervention are less apparent but no less real.

Costs Imposed Outside the Government

Most government interventions in the economy impose some costs on firms and households. The nature and the size of the extra costs borne by firms and households subject to government intervention vary with the type of intervention. A few examples will illustrate what is involved.

Changes in costs of production. Government safety and emission standards for automobiles have raised the costs of both producing and operating cars. These costs are much greater than the direct budgetary costs of administering the regulations. Taxes used to finance the provision of collective consumption goods must be paid by producers and consumers and often increase the cost of producing or selling goods and services. Less direct, but also important, is the possibility that some kinds of regulation deter potential innovation, because the innovation might not be approved by the regulators. This, too, could increase the costs of production in the very long run.

Costs of compliance. Government regulation and supervision generate a flood of reporting and related activities that often are summarized in the phrase *red tape*. The number of hours of business time devoted to understanding, reporting, and contesting regulatory provisions is enormous. Pay equity, anti-discrimination provisions, occupational safety, and environmental control have all increased the size of nonproduction payrolls. The legal costs alone of a major corporation sometimes can run into tens or hundreds of millions of dollars per year. While all

this provides lots of employment for lawyers and economic experts, it is costly because there are other tasks such professionals could do that would add more to the production of consumer goods and services.

Households also bear compliance costs directly. A recent study found that the time and money cost of filling out individual income tax returns was about 8 percent of the total revenue that is collected. In addition to costs of compliance, there are costs borne as firms and households try to avoid regulation. There will be a substantial incentive to find loopholes in regulations. Resources that could be used elsewhere will be devoted by the regulated to the search for such loopholes and then, in turn, by the regulators to counteracting such evasion.

Rent-seeking. A different kind of problem arises from the mere existence of government and its potential to use its tools in ways that affect the distribution of economic resources. This phenomenon was dubbed "rent-seeking" by American economist Ann Krueger, because private firms, households, and business groups will use their political influence to seek economic rents from the government. These valuable rents can come in the form of favourable regulations, direct subsidies, and profitable contracts. Democratic governments are especially vulnerable to manipulation of this kind, because they respond to well-articulated interests of all sorts.

Rent-seeking is endemic to mixed economies. Because of the many things that governments are called upon to do, they have the power to act in ways that transfer resources among private entities. Because they are democratic, they are responsive to public pressure of various kinds. If a government's behaviour can be influenced, whether by voting, campaign contributions, lobbying, or bribes, real resources will be used in trying to influence government behaviour.

Finally, rent-seeking on the part of the clients and employees of public agencies is one of the reasons often given for the privatization movement that we discussed earlier in this chapter. The argument here is that privatization would limit (although not eliminate) the scope for political influence on behalf of both employees and specific groups of beneficiaries of public services.

Government "Imperfection": Social Choice Theory

Our conceptual benefit-cost analysis of government intervention is almost complete. First, we calculate the social cost of each market failure. Then we make our best estimate of the effect of an intervention designed to correct that failure—in most cases the best that we can do is less than the maximum potential benefit. Then we calculate the costs of the intervention, as outlined in the preceding section. If the benefits exceed the costs, the intervention is warranted. Unfortunately, things are never this simple. For one thing, many of the benefits of government intervention are extremely difficult to quantify. Even in the easy cases, however, where the benefits and the direct costs of intervention can be measured, and the indirect costs are unimportant, governments, like private markets, are imperfect. Often they will fail, in the same sense that markets do, to achieve their potential.

Causes of Government Failure

The reason for government failure is not that public-sector employees are less able, honest, or virtuous than people who work in the private sector. Rather, the causes of government failure are inherent in government institutions, just as the causes of market failure are inherent in the nature of markets. Importantly, some governmental failure is an inescapable cost of democratic decision making. The reasons are studied in a branch of economics called *social choice theory.*

Inefficient public choices. At the core of most people's idea of democracy is that each citizen's vote should have the same weight. One of the insights of social choice theory is that resource allocation, based on the principle of one-person-one-vote, will generally be inefficient because it fails to take into account the *intensity of preferences.* Consider three farmers, A, B, and C, who are contemplating building access roads. Suppose that the road to A's farm is worth $7,000 to A and that the road to B's farm is worth $7,000 to B. (C's farm is on the main road, which already exists.) Suppose that, under the taxing rules in effect, each road would cost A, B, and C each $2,000. It is plainly efficient to build both roads, since each generates net benefits of $1,000

($7,000 gross benefits to the farmer helped, less $6,000 total cost). But each would be defeated 2–1 in a simple majority vote. (B and C would vote against A's road; A and C would vote against B's road.)

Now suppose that we allow A and B to make a deal: "I will vote for your road if you will vote for mine." Although such deals are often decried by political commentators, the deal enhances efficiency: Both roads now get 2–1 majorities, and both roads get built. However, such deals can just as well reduce efficiency. If we make the gross value of each road $5,000 instead of $7,000 and let A and B make their deals, each road will still command a 2–1 majority, but building the roads will now be inefficient. (The gross value of each road is now only $5,000, while the cost is still $6,000.) A and B will be using democracy to appropriate resources from C while reducing economic efficiency. Box 20-3 provides a more general discussion of the difficulties in making social choice by majority vote.

Special interests. The case in the immediately preceding paragraph can be interpreted in a different way. Instead of being the third farmer, C might be all of the other voters in the county. Instead of bearing one third of the costs, A and B each might bear only a small portion of the costs. To the extent that A and B are able to go to the local government and forcefully articulate the benefits that they would derive from the roads, they may be able to use democracy to appropriate resources from taxpayers in general. Much of the concern with the power of special interests stems from the fact that the institutions of representative democracy tend to be responsive to benefits (or costs) that focus on particular, identifiable, and articulate groups. Often, costs that are borne diffusely by taxpayers or voters in general are hardly noticed.

This potential bias applies to regulations as well as to direct government provisions. Chapter 15 discussed a number of cases in which economic regulations are used to benefit the affected industry. Similarly, as we saw in Chapter 6, rent control can be interpreted, at least in part, as benefiting existing tenants at the expense of future potential tenants; the latter group tends to have no political power at all.

Governments as monopolists. Governments face the same problems of cost minimization that private

Box 20-3

Arrow's Impossibility Theorem

Economist and Nobel laureate Kenneth Arrow has shown that it is generally impossible to construct a set of rules for making social choices that is at once comprehensive, democratic, efficient, and consistent. Arrow's theorem has led to decades of work on the part of economists, philosophers, and political scientists, who have tried to find conditions under which democracy can be expected to yield efficient (or otherwise favoured) allocations of resources. The news is generally not good. Unless individual preferences or their distribution in the population meet fairly unlikely criteria, either democracy or efficiency must be sacrificed in the design of social choice mechanisms.

The Arrow theorem can be illustrated by a simple case, depicted in the following table.

Density of trees C	Voter		
	A	B	
Sparse	3	1	2
Medium	1	2	3
Thick	2	3	1

Imagine that we have a society that consists of three voters who are choosing how many trees to plant in the local park. The three possibilities are as follows: (1) Plant very few trees in one corner. This would make the park suitable for frisbee and soccer but not for walks in the woods. (2) Plant trees in moderate density throughout the park. In this case, the park would be nice for playing tag and jogging but not usable for most sports. (3) Plant trees densely everywhere. This would make the park a pleasant place to get away from it all (for whatever reasons) but not a good place to jog in. Voter A loves jogging, hates frisbee and the noise that frisbee players make, and likes walking in the woods. His ranking of the alternatives is 2-3-1. Voter B likes the wide open spaces. His ranking is 1-2-3. Voter C likes to play frisbee, likes solitude even more, and has little taste for a park that provides neither. Her ranking is 3-1-2.

Suppose that the electorate gets to choose between alternatives that are presented two at a time. What does majority rule do? It depends on which two alternatives are presented. In a choice of 1 versus 2, 1 wins, getting votes from B and C. When the choice is between 2 and 3, 2 wins, getting votes from A and B. When 3 is pitted against 1, 3 wins with the support of A and C. Thus, the *social choice mechanism* of *majority rule* is inconsistent. It tells us that 1 is preferred to 2, 2 is preferred to 3, and 3 is preferred to 1. The arbitrary (undemocratic) selection of which set of alternatives to offer to the electorate determines the outcome in spite of a democratic vote.

firms do but often operate in an environment where they are monopoly producers without stockholders. Large governments (provinces, big cities, the federal government) face all of the organizational problems faced by large corporations. They tend to use relatively rigid rules and thus to respond slowly to change. Building codes are an example of this type of problem. Most local governments have detailed requirements regarding the materials that must go into a new house, factory, or office. When technology changes, the codes often lag behind. For example, plastic pipe, which is cheaper and easier to use than steel pipe, was prohibited by building codes for decades after its use became efficient. Similarly, much antipollution regulation specifies the type of control equipment that must be employed. Changes in technology may make a regulation inefficient, but the regulation may stay in place for some time.

Like those of large private enterprises, a government's "organization chart" will often be out of date. For most of this century the Canadian government has regulated freight rates charged by railroads. With the advent of buses and trucks, the government should have turned to developing a healthy *transportation system*. Yet for years the imposed rate structure favoured railroads. The same kind of problem—a misclassification of the relevant economic issue—might well have arisen when the purchasing division in a large corporation, which used typewriters exclusively, was confronted with modern word-processing technology. In the private sector, there are often market forces pushing the corporation into revising its view of the problem at hand. Usually, there is no market mechanism tending to force governments toward the use of relatively efficient rules of thumb and organizational structures. Put in the language of Chapter 16, the scope for satisficing governments to depart from optimal behaviour is generally greater than that for satisficing firms. Put in another way, much government failure arises precisely because governments do not have competitors and are not constrained by the bottom line.

Principal-agent problems in government. Governments face the same kinds of *principal-agent problems* (see Chapter 16) that firms do, but the problem in the case of governments can be more serious for two reasons. First, the possibility of a hostile takeover, although quite powerful as applied to elected officials (they can be removed from office), is very weak as applied to bureaucracies. Second, the principal in the case of government is all of its citizens, and this group will in general be unable to agree on what it is that government *should* do. Stockholders can all agree that the firm should maximize profits. Citizens who vote, by contrast, are not expected to agree on any simple mission for their elected representatives. This lack of agreement makes it that much more difficult for the agents to serve their principals and that much easier for agents who do not perform well to get away with it.

How Much Should Government Intervene?

The theoretical principles for determining the optimal amount of government intervention are individually accepted by almost everyone. What they add up to, however, is more controversial. Moreover, the issue is often framed ideologically: Those on the right wing tend to compare an actual, heavy-handed government with a hypothetical competitive market. Those on the left wing tend to compare "perfect" governmental intervention with the actions of the actual imperfect market.

Evaluating the costs and the effectiveness of government intervention requires a comparison of the private economic system as it is working (not as it might work ideally) with the pattern of government intervention as it is likely to perform (not as it might perform ideally).

The cases that we have made for and against government intervention are both valid, depending on time, place, and the values that are brought to bear. At this point, we turn to the issue of what government actually does, something that will perhaps illuminate the question of what it ought to do. In Chapter 15, we discussed government action that is designed to affect monopoly and competition. In the next three chapters, we shall discuss in some detail three other important types of intervention in the Canadian economy today: environmental and safety regulation, taxation, and public spending.

SUMMARY

1. The various markets in the economy are coordinated in an unplanned, decentralized way by the price system. Profits and losses play a key role in achieving a coordinated market response. Changes in prices and profits, resulting from emerging scarcities and surpluses, lead decision makers to adapt to a change in any one market. Such responses tend to correct the shortages and surpluses as well as to change the market signals of prices and profits.

2. Important features of market coordination include voluntary responses to market signals, the limited information required by any individual, and the fact that coordination will occur under any market structure.

3. A widely held argument in favour of the market system goes beyond its ability to provide automatic coordination. Many believe that its flexibility and adaptability make it the best coordinator and also encourage innovation and growth. The tendency of the market to push relative prices toward the costs of production fosters efficient allocation of resources. Furthermore, the market economy tends to be impersonal, to decentralize power, and to require relatively little coercion of individuals.

4. Markets do not always work perfectly. Four main sources of market failure are (a) externalities arising from differences between private and social costs and benefits, (b) the inability of markets to produce collective consumption goods, (c) information asymmetries, and (d) failure to achieve social goals other than efficiency.

5. Pollution is an example of an externality. An important source of pollution is producers' use of water and air that they do not regard as scarce. Because they do not pay the costs of using these resources, they are not motivated to avoid the costs.

6. National defense is an example of a collective consumption good, often called a public good. Markets fail to produce collective consumption goods because the benefits of such goods are available to people whether they pay for them or not.

7. Information asymmetries cause market failure when one party to a transaction is able to use his or her expertise to manipulate the transaction in his or her own favour. Moral hazard, adverse selection, and principal-agent problems are all consequences of information asymmetries.

8. Changing the distribution of income is one of the roles for government intervention that members of a society may desire. Others include values that are placed on public provision for its own sake, on protection of individuals from themselves or from others, and on recognition of social obligations.

9. Microeconomic policy concerns activities of the government that alter the unrestricted workings of the free-market system in order to affect either the allocation of resources or the distribution of income. Major tools of microeconomic policy include (a) public provision, (b) redistribution, (c) regulation, and (d) structuring incentives. (The first two are the subject of Chapters 22 and 23.) Regulation can take a variety of forms. Incentives can be structured in a number of ways, including the use of fines, subsidies, taxes, and effluent charges (which are discussed in Chapter 21).

10. The costs and benefits of government intervention must be considered in deciding whether, when, and how much intervention is appropriate. Among the costs are the direct costs that are incurred by the government; the costs that are imposed on those who are regulated, direct and indirect; and the costs that are imposed on third parties. These costs are seldom negligible and are often large.

11. The possibility of government failure must be balanced against the potential benefits of removing market failure. It is neither possible nor efficient to correct all market failure; neither is it always efficient to do nothing.

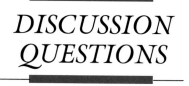

TOPICS FOR REVIEW

Market coordination

Differences between private and social valuations

Market failure

Regulation

Externalities

Collective consumption goods

Information asymmetries

Benefits and costs of government intervention

Rent-seeking

Government failure

DISCUSSION QUESTIONS

1. Should the free market be allowed to determine the price for the following, or should government intervene? Defend your choice for each.
   a. Transit fares.
   b. Plastic surgery for victims of fires.
   c. Garbage collection.
   d. Postal delivery of newspapers and magazines.
   e. Fire protection for churches.
   f. Ice cream.

2. The following activities have known harmful effects. In each case, identify any divergence between social and private costs.
   a. Cigarette smoking.
   b. Driving a car at a speed limit of 100 kmh.
   c. Private ownership of guns.
   d. Drilling for offshore oil.

3. Operators of fishing fleets off the east coast of North America have been complaining that the size of their catches has fallen markedly over the past few years. Suppose there are many boats engaged in commercial fishing. Use the idea of externalities to show that each boat can be expected to fish more than the socially optimal amount.

4. Suppose the facts asserted below are true. Should they trigger government intervention? If so, what policy alternatives are available?
   a. The proportion of total national income taken up in medical and hospital costs in Canada has been rising faster than in any other country except the United States.
   b. The cost of an average one-family house in Vancouver, B.C., is now about $300,000—an amount that is out of the reach of many people.

c. Cigarette smoking reduces life expectancy of the smoker by 8 years.

d. Saccharin in large doses has been found to cause cancer in mice.

5. Consider the possible beneficial and adverse effects of each of the following forms of government intervention.

a. Charging motorists a tax for driving in the downtown areas of large cities and using the revenues to provide peripheral parking and shuttle buses.

b. Prohibiting juries from awarding large malpractise judgements against doctors.

c. Mandating no-fault automobile insurance, in which the automobile owner's insurance company is responsible for damage to his or her vehicle no matter who causes the accident.

d. Requiring automobile manufacturers to warrant the tires on cars that they sell instead of (as at present) having the tire manufacturer be the warrantor.

6. The president of Goodyear Tire and Rubber Company complained that government regulation had imposed $30 million per year in "unproductive costs" on his company, as listed below. How would one determine whether these costs were "productive" or "unproductive"?

a. Environmental regulation, $17 million.

b. Occupational safety and health, $7 million.

c. Motor vehicle safety, $3 million.

d. Personnel and administration, $3 million.

7. Your local government probably provides, among other things, a police department, a fire department, and a public library. What are the market imperfections, if any, that each of these works to correct? Which of these are closest to being collective consumption goods? Which are farthest?

8. Suppose that for $100 a laboratory can accurately assess a person's probability of developing a fairly rare disease that is costly to treat. What would be the likely effects of such a test on health insurance markets?

9. What market failure(s) do public support of higher education seek to remedy? How would you go about evaluating whether the benefits of this support outweigh the costs?

10. What government failure might be involved when professional organizations encourage a provincial government to stiffen the requirements necessary to be licensed to practise a profession? What market failure might such requirements correct? How would you weigh arguments for and against stiffening the requirements?

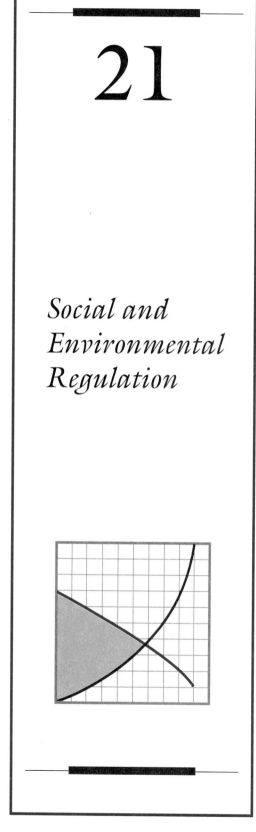

21

Social and Environmental Regulation

In almost everything we do, we are subject to some form of government regulation. The system of criminal law regulates our interactions with people and property. Local zoning ordinances regulate the ways in which the land that we own may be used. Insurance commissions must approve both the insurance contracts that we sign and the rates that are charged. Public utility commissions set rates for electricity, natural gas, local telephone service, and a host of other goods and services. Seat belts, brake lights, turn signals, air bags, internal door panels, bumpers, air conditioners, and catalytic converters are all subjects of regulation in just one industry. The number of electrical outlets per room, the material used for plumbing, and the spacing of the vertical supports in an interior wall are usually dictated by local building codes. The list goes on and on. Governments may have more effect on the economy through regulation than through taxing and spending.

In the previous chapter, we identified a number of types of market failure that might be addressed by government policy. Regulation of economic activity is used to address most of them in one way or another. Market failure arising from *natural monopoly* has led both to public ownership and public regulation of privately owned firms, as discussed in Chapter 15. *Externalities,* especially the negative externalities of industrial pollution, are the motivation for environmental regulation, a major topic of this chapter.

Regulation of advertising and much health and safety regulation are designed to deal with market failures arising from *information asymmetries*. There is no easy way for a consumer to know whether the paint on a child's toy can cause lead poisoning, so a government body regulates the market for children's toys. Occupational licensing is defended on the same grounds; in most provinces, professionals as different as barbers and psychiatrists must undergo specified courses of training before they are allowed to ply their trades. The idea is to prevent "just anyone" from claiming and abusing alleged expertise.

Information about a professional's training is a *public good:* Once the information is available to one consumer, it can be made available to all very cheaply. Occupational licensing is a way to produce this public good—in the form of the familiar diploma that hangs on the wall of the barbershop, physician's office, or repair garage. It is also, unfortunately, an effective way to monopolise a trade or occupation.

Regulations also can be used to change the *distribution of income.* This is the purpose of, among other regulations, rent controls, minimum wages, and agricultural supply management.

Finally, the laws and regulations that enforce private contracts are a pure public good that is essential to the operation of a market economy. Without reliably enforceable contracts, many transactions would be so risky that they would not take place.

The principal topic of this chapter is **social regulation**. Social regulation does not mean the regulation of social behaviour (e.g., dress and speech). Rather, it is the regulation of economic behaviour to advance social goals.

In this chapter, we consider both the market failures that social regulation addresses and the effectiveness and costs of different kinds of regulation in correcting these market failures. We start by extending the analysis of negative externalities in Chapter 20 to the problem of environmental pollution.

The Economics of Pollution and Pollution Control

Pollution is a negative externality. As a consequence of producing or consuming goods and services, "bads" are produced as well. Steel plants produce heat and smoke in addition to steel. Farms produce chemical runoff as well as food. Households produce human waste and garbage as they consume goods and services. In all of these cases, the technology of production and consumption automatically generates pollution. Indeed, there are few human endeavors that do not have negative pollution externalities.

The Economic Rationale for Regulating Pollution

When firms use resources that they do not regard as scarce, they are not motivated to consider the cost of those resources. This is a characteristic of most examples of pollution, including the case that is illustrated in Figure 21-1. When a paper mill produces pulp for the world's newspapers, more people are affected than its suppliers, employees, and customers. Its water-discharged effluent hurts the fishing boats that ply nearby waters, and its smog makes many resort areas less attractive, thereby reducing the tourist revenues that local motel operators and boat renters can expect. The profit-maximizing firm neglects these external effects of its actions because its profits are not affected by them.

Allocative efficiency requires that the price (the

**FIGURE 21-1
Pollution Externalities**

Internalizing an externality can correct market failure. The private marginal cost curve, MC_p, is the conventional marginal cost for a firm that is producing output in a competitive market. The external cost curve EC depicts marginal cost that the firm's production imposes on people other than its owners, employees, and customers. Because the firm is maximizing profits, it will ignore EC and produce output Q_1, where the market price P_m equals private marginal cost. Adding EC and MC_p yields *social marginal* cost, MC_s. The socially optimal level of output is Q_2, where price is equal to MC_s. Here the price is sufficient to pay for the private marginal cost of production, MC_p, *and* to compensate others for the external marginal cost imposed on them, EC.

Suppose that the firm is required to pay a tax of $\$EC$ per unit of output. Its MC_p curve will now become the MC_s curve. The externality will be *internalized*, and the profit-maximizing firm will be motivated to reduce its output to the socially optimal level, Q_2. It does this because, with the tax added to its private marginal cost, Q_2 is the profit-maximizing level of output.

value that consumers place on the marginal unit of output) be just equal to the marginal social cost (the value of resources that society gives up to produce the marginal unit of output). When there are harmful externalities, marginal social cost and *marginal private cost*, the cost borne by the producer, will diverge.

By producing where price equals marginal private cost and thereby ignoring the externality, the firm is maximizing profits but producing too much output. The price that consumers pay just covers the marginal private cost but does not pay for the external damage. The *social benefit* of the last unit of output (the market price) is less than the *social cost* (marginal private cost plus the social cost imposed by the externality). Reducing output by one unit would reduce both social benefit and social cost, but would reduce social cost by more, because social cost is larger. Thus, reducing output by one unit would save economic resources and increase efficiency. The market fails to achieve efficiency because of the externality.

Making the firm bear the entire social cost of its production is called *internalizing* the externality. This will cause it to produce at a lower output. Indeed, at the optimal output, where the externality is completely internalized, consumer prices would just cover all of the marginal social cost of production— marginal private cost plus the externality. We would have the familiar condition for economic efficiency that marginal benefits to consumers are just equal to the marginal cost of producing these benefits. The difference here is that some of the marginal social cost takes the form of an externality.

Suppose that Warthog Industries, Inc., manufactures kitchen cabinets and that residue from painting the cabinets is washed into a stream that runs beside the plant. The stream is part of the municipal water supply, which is treated at a water purification plant before it is sent into people's homes. Suppose that each cabinet produced increases the cost of running the water treatment plant by $0.10. Then, in terms of the previous analysis, the external cost is $0.10 per unit, and *marginal social cost* will be exactly $0.10 above *marginal private cost*.

In practise, the external cost is often quite difficult to measure. This is especially so in the case of air pollution, where the damage is often spread over hundreds of thousands of square miles and can have real but small effects upon millions of people. Another difficulty arises because the cost that is imposed by pollution will generally depend on the mechanisms that are used to undo the damage that it causes. Control mechanisms are themselves costly, and their costs also must be counted as part of the social cost of pollution. Nevertheless, the basic analysis of Figure 21-1 applies to these more difficult cases.

The socially optimal level of output is at the quantity where *all* marginal costs, private plus external, equal the marginal benefit to society.

Notice that the optimal level of output is not the level at which there is *no* pollution. Rather, it is the level at which the beneficiaries of pollution (the consumers and producers of Warthog Industries' kitchen cabinets, in our example) are just willing to pay the marginal social cost that is imposed by the pollution.

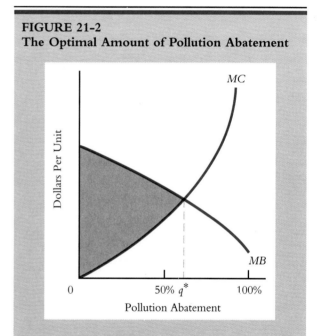

FIGURE 21-2
The Optimal Amount of Pollution Abatement

The optimal amount of pollution abatement occurs where the marginal cost of reducing pollution is just equal to the marginal benefits from doing so. *MB* represents the marginal benefit that is achieved by pollution prevention in some activity. *MC* represents the marginal cost of preventing pollution; it rises sharply as more and more pollution is eliminated. The optimal level of pollution control is q^*, where *MB = MC*. *Notice that not all pollution is eliminated.* For all units up to q^*, the marginal benefits derived from pollution abatement exceed the marginal costs. The total net benefit from the optimal amount of pollution abatement is given by the shaded area— the sum of the difference between marginal benefit and marginal cost at each level of output. Any further reductions in pollution beyond q^* would add more to costs than to benefits.

Unregulated markets tend to produce excessive amounts of environmental damage. Zero environmental damage, however, is neither technologically possible nor economically efficient.

Pollution Control in Theory and Practise

The analysis of how much pollution to prohibit, and how much pollution to allow, is summarized in Figure 21-2, which depicts the benefits and costs of pollution control. It might be thought of as applying, for example, to water pollution in a specific watershed. It is drawn from the perspective of a public authority that has been charged with maximizing social welfare. The downward-sloping curve is the "demand" for *pollution abated* (or prevented). The reason that we conduct the analysis in terms of pollution prevented is that pollution *abatement*, not pollution *creation*, is the service with positive economic value, and we are used to studying the supplies and demands for goods and services with positive values. If no pollution is abated, the watershed will be subject to the amount of pollution that would occur in an unregulated market. The greater the amount of pollution that is prevented, the smaller is the amount of pollution that remains.

The marginal cost of preventing pollution is often small at low levels of abatement while rising steeply after some point. (This is the shape shown in Figure 21-2.) There are two reasons for this shape. First is the familiar logic behind increasing marginal costs. For each firm that pollutes, there will be some antipollution measures that can be taken fairly easily, so the first portion of pollution reduction will be cheap relative to later portions. In addition, pollution reduction of any degree is usually easier for some firms than for others. For example, new facilities usually run cleaner than old ones. Reducing pollution from a factory that was designed in the era of environmental concern may be much easier than obtaining similar reductions from an older factory. After some point, however, the easy plants and the easy fixes are exhausted, and the marginal cost of reducing pollution further rises steeply.

The marginal benefit of pollution reduction in Figure 21-2 is depicted as falling for much the same reason that the typical demand curve slopes downward. Starting at any nonlethal level of pollution, people will derive some benefit from reducing the level of pollution, but the marginal benefit from a given amount of reduction will be lower, the lower is the level of pollution. Put another way, in a very dirty environment, a little cleanliness will be much prized, but in a very clean environment, a little more cleanliness may be of only small additional value.[1]

The optimal amount of pollution reduction occurs where the marginal benefit is equal to the marginal cost—where "supply" and "demand" in Figure 21-2 intersect. In trying to reach this optimum, the pollution control authority faces three serious problems.

First, although Figure 21-2 looks like a supply-demand diagram, we have already seen that the private sector will not by itself create a market in pollution control. Thus, the government must intervene in private-sector markets if the optimal level of control that is shown in Figure 21-2 is to be attained.

The second problem is that the optimal level of pollution abatement generally is not easily known, because the marginal benefit and the marginal cost curves that are shown in Figure 21-2 are not usually observable. In practise, the government must estimate these curves. Accurate estimates are often difficult to obtain, especially when the technology of pollution control is changing rapidly and the health consequences of various pollutants (e.g., chemicals that are new to the marketplace) are not known.

Determining the optimal level of pollution control is often very difficult in practise.

The third problem is that the available techniques for regulating pollution are themselves imperfect. Even when the optimal level of pollution control is known, there are both technical and legal impediments to achieving that level through regulation.

---

[1] In the case of toxic pollutants, the marginal benefit does not decline smoothly. There, the marginal benefit of pollution reduction is small or zero if the level of emissions is above some dangerous threshold and is very large when pollution is reduced below the threshold. The marginal benefit curve in these cases would be strongly kinked at the threshold. The health consequences of most pollution, however, are of a kind that is consistent with the shape of the demand curve that is shown in Figure 21-2.

Direct Controls

Direct controls are the form of environmental regulations used most often. Automobile emissions standards are direct controls that are familiar to most of us. The standards must be met by all new cars that are sold in Canada. They require that emissions per kilometre of a number of noxious chemicals and other pollutants be less than certain specified amounts. The standards are the same no matter where the kilometres are driven. The marginal benefit of reducing carbon monoxide emissions in rural Saskatchewan, where there is relatively little air pollution, is certainly much less than the marginal benefit in Montreal, where there is already a good deal of carbon monoxide in the air. Yet the standard is the same in both places.

Direct controls also often require that specific techniques be used in order to reduce pollution. Thus, coal-fired utility plants were sometimes required to use devices called scrubbers in order to reduce sulphur dioxide emissions, even in cases where other techniques could have achieved the same level of pollution abatement at lower cost.

Another form of direct control is the simple prohibition of certain polluting behaviours. Many cities and towns, for example, prohibit the private burning of leaves and other trash because of the air pollution problem that the burning would cause. A number of communities have banned the use of wood stoves. Similarly, the government gradually reduced the amount of lead allowed in leaded gasoline and then eliminated leaded gasoline altogether.

Problems with direct controls.   Direct controls are likely to be economically inefficient; more pollution can usually be abated by alternative methods at the same economic cost as that imposed by direct controls. Suppose that pollution of a given waterway is to be reduced by a certain amount. Regulators will typically apportion the required reduction among all of the polluters according to some roughly equitable criterion. The regulators might require that every polluter reduce its pollution by the same percentage. Alternatively, every polluter might be required to install a certain type of control device or to ensure that each litre of water that is dumped into the watershed meets certain quality criteria. Although any of these rules might seem reasonable, unless the polluters face identical pollution abatement costs, each of them will be inefficient.

To see this, consider two firms that face different costs of pollution abatement, as depicted in Figure 21-3. Suppose that firm A's marginal cost of pollution abatement is everywhere below firm B's. Such a circumstance is quite likely when one recalls that pollution comes from many different industries. It may be easy for one industry to cut back on the amount that it uses of some pollutant; in another industry, the pollutant may be an integral part of the production process. The most efficient way to reduce pollution would be to have firm A cut back on its pollution until the marginal cost of further reductions is just equal to firm B's marginal cost of reducing its first (and cheapest to forgo) unit of pollution. Once their marginal costs of reducing pollution are equalized, *further* reductions in pollution will be efficient only if this equality is maintained.

To see this, suppose that the marginal costs of abatement are different for the two firms. By reallocating some pollution abatement from the high-marginal-cost firm to the low-marginal-cost firm, total pollution abatement could be kept constant while the real resources used to abate pollution would be reduced. Alternatively, one could hold the resource cost constant and increase the amount of abatement.

Direct pollution controls are usually inefficient in that they do not minimize the cost of a given amount of pollution abatement. This implies that they also do not abate the most pollution possible for a given cost.

When direct controls require that firms adopt specific techniques of pollution abatement, a second type of inefficiency arises. Regulations of this kind tend to change only slowly: The regulators often will mandate today's best techniques tomorrow, even if something more effective has come along.

Both of these sources of inefficiency in direct controls are examples of government failure, as discussed in Chapter 20. In both cases, the government does not do as well as it could in pursuing its important social objectives. In terms of Figure 21-2, government failure adds to the marginal cost of pollution reduction. Thus, the socially optimal level of pollution will be higher, the less efficient is the method used to control pollution.

A final problem that arises with direct controls in practise is that they are expensive to monitor and to enforce. The regulatory agency has to check, fac-

FIGURE 21-3
Potential Inefficiency of Direct Pollution Controls

Requiring equal amounts of pollution abatement from different polluters is likely to be inefficient. Firm A is able to reduce its emissions according to the marginal cost curve MC_A. Firm B, which operates at the same scale but in a different kind of factory, has a higher marginal cost of abatement, MC_B. Suppose that a regulatory authority requires that the two firms reduce pollution by the same amount, Q_R. Firm A will have a marginal cost of pollution abatement of C_A, whereas firm B's marginal cost will be C_B, which is larger than C_A.

To see that this outcome is inefficient, consider what happens if firm A increases its pollution abatement by one unit, while firm B is allowed to pollute one unit more. Total pollution remains the same, but total costs fall. Firm A incurs added costs of C_A, and firm B saves a greater amount, C_B. Because the total amount of pollution is unchanged, the total social cost of pollution and pollution abatement would fall.

tory by factory, farm by farm, how many pollutants of what kinds are being emitted. It also needs a mechanism for penalizing offenders. Accurate monitoring of all potential sources of pollution requires a level of resources that is much greater than has ever been made available to the relevant regulatory agencies. Moreover, the existing system of fines and penalties, in the view of many critics, is not nearly harsh enough to have much effect. A potential polluter, required to limit emissions of a pollutant to so many kilograms or litres per day, will take into account the cost of meeting the standard, the probability of being caught, and the severity of the penalty before deciding how to behave. If the chances of being caught and the penalties for being caught are small, the direct controls may have little effect.

Monitoring and enforcement of direct pollution controls is costly, which reduces the effectiveness of the controls.

Emissions Taxes

An alternative method of pollution control is to levy a tax on emissions at the source. The great advantage of such a procedure is that it internalizes the pollution externality, so that decentralized decisions can lead to efficient outcomes. Again, suppose that firm A can reduce emissions cheaply, while it is more expensive for firm B to reduce emissions. If all firms are required to pay a tax of t on each unit of pollution, profit maximization will lead them to reduce emissions to the point where the marginal cost of further reduction is equal to t. This means that firm A will reduce emissions much more than firm B and that in equilibrium, both will have the same marginal cost of further abatement, which is required for efficiency. This is illustrated in Figure 21-4.

Note that if the regulatory agency is able to obtain a good estimate of the marginal damage that is done by pollution, it could set the tax rate just equal

FIGURE 21-4
A Tax on Pollution

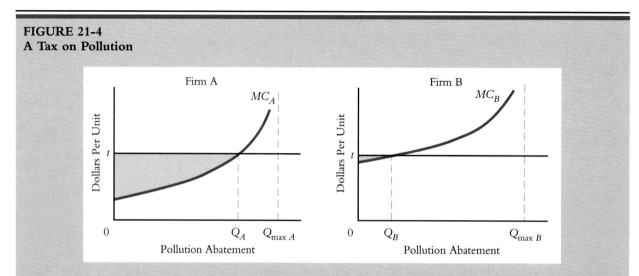

Taxes on pollution can lead to efficient pollution abatement. As in Figure 21-3, firm A faces a lower marginal cost of pollution abatement than does firm B. Suppose that the regulatory authority imposes a tax of t per unit of pollution. Firm A will choose to reduce its pollution by Q_A. Up to this point, the tax saved by reducing pollution exceeds the marginal cost of reducing pollution. If firm A chooses not to abate pollution at all, it would pay t times Q_{max} in pollution taxes, where Q_{max} is the firms' total pollution if it does nothing to prevent pollution. By reducing its pollution to $Q_{max} - Q_A$ (the same thing as abating pollution by Q_A), firm A saves an amount that is given by the shaded area in the panel on the left.

Firm B chooses to abate only a small amount of pollution, Q_B. Any further abatement would require that the firm incur costs along MC_B, which would be greater than the benefits of taxes saved, t.

to that amount. In such a case, polluters would be forced by the tax to internalize the full pollution externality.

A second great advantage of using emissions taxes is that they do not require the regulators to specify anything about *how* polluters should abate pollution. Rather, polluters themselves can be left to find the most efficient abatement techniques. The profit motive will lead them to do so, because they will want to avoid paying the tax.

Emissions taxes can, in principle, perfectly internalize pollution externalities, so that profit-maximizing behaviour on the part of firms will lead them to produce the efficient amount of pollution abatement at minimum cost.

Box 21-1 discusses a simple and increasingly familiar type of pollution tax—charging for household garbage by the bag.

Difficulties in using emissions taxes. Emissions taxes can only work if it is possible to measure emissions accurately. For some types of pollution, this does not pose much of a problem, but for many other types of pollution, good measuring devices that can be installed at reasonable cost do not exist. Obviously, in these cases emissions taxes cannot work. One important example of such a case is automotive pollution. It would be very expensive to attach a reliable monitor to every car and truck and then to assess taxes due based on readings from the monitor. In this case, as in many others, direct controls are the only feasible approach.

When there is good reason to prohibit a pollutant altogether, direct controls are obviously better than taxes. Municipal bans on burning of rubbish fall in this category, as do the occasional emergency bans on some kinds of pollution that are invoked during an air pollution crisis in cities such as Vancouver.

Another problem with emissions taxes involves

Box 21-1

Charging for Emissions at Home

One of the most common forms of pollution is household trash. The economic theory of pollution externalities discussed in the text suggests that a tax on household trash would reduce the volume of pollution. In a number of communities in Canada and the United States, per-bag charges on household trash have led to reductions in the amount of trash generated. The waste that is not going into the costly bags is going into compost heaps and into recycling.

Communities vary in the way that charges are assessed, and in the degree of support that they provide for alternative uses of waste. Typically, the municipal garbage trucks will only pick up trash if the trash bag (or other type of garbage) carries a special sticker. The stickers are sold by the municipal authorities; the fewer a household uses, the less money it spends on having its trash picked up. Fees of $1 to $2 per bag are not uncommon. In one U.S. community, High Bridge, N.J., a fee of $1.25 has led to a reduction of 25 percent in the volume of garbage.

The externality in this case is the use of landfills. Especially in the more populated areas of the country, landfills for solid waste are becoming scarce and, consequently, expensive. By charging residents something for use of the landfill, alternative means of dealing with waste are encouraged, and a solid waste facility of given size can last longer.

Avoiding any burden on the needy is relatively easy to accomplish if that is desired. Tags can be given free to those on welfare, or to those below some minimum income. (But since the charges are usually modest, the policy of granting any exceptions is contentious.)

The problem of finding the optimum charge per bag of garbage poses serious technical difficulties. Also, rather than pay the charge, some households will illegally dump their trash, adding to environmental damage. However, the pollution itself is easy to measure, and it is plain that the optimum charge is more than zero.

---

setting the tax rate. Ideally, the regulatory agency would obtain an estimate of the marginal social damage caused per unit of each pollutant and set the tax equal to this amount. This would perfectly internalize the pollution externality. However, the information that is needed to determine the marginal social damage curves shown in Figures 21-1 and 21-2 is often difficult to obtain. If society is currently far away from the optimum, it may be very difficult to estimate what the marginal social damage will be at the optimum. If the regulatory agency sets the tax rate too high, too many resources will be devoted to pollution control (the equilibrium will be beyond q^* in Figure 21-2). If the tax is set too low, there will be too much pollution. In many practical cases, regulators may have a much better idea of the acceptable level of pollution

than of the tax rate that would lead to that result. Further, when the technology of pollution abatement changes, the tax rate would have to change as well, and governments are often very slow to adjust tax rates.

A potentially serious problem with emissions taxes is that information necessary to determine the optimal tax rate is often unavailable or out of date.

Tradeable Emissions Permits

One great advantage of direct controls is that the regulators can set the standards to limit the total quantity of pollution in a given geographic area. This can be done without knowing the details of either the marginal benefit or the marginal cost curves in Figure 21-2. The great advantage of emissions taxes is that they allow for decentralized decision making, providing firms with an incentive to internalize the negative externality of pollution. *Tradeable emissions permits* can combine both of these advantages, and thus have the potential for being superior to either direct controls or emissions taxes.

In Figure 21-3, we noted that direct pollution controls would generally be inefficient, because the marginal cost curves for pollution abatement would vary across firms. Tradeable permits can solve this problem. To see this, the regulators must first figure out how much pollution to allow. This involves reformulating the regulator's problem. Start with the same conditions as those in Figure 21-3, and permit each firm to pollute exactly the same amount as would be allowed by the direct controls in Figure 21-3. Instead of saying to each firm, "Thou shalt abate pollution by Q_R," however, the regulators say, "Thou shalt not pollute more than you would if you abated by Q_R." The statements are identical in meaning. All that we have done is to describe a glass that is two-thirds empty as being one-third full.

Now suppose that the firms are allowed to buy and to sell **tradeable emissions permits**—rights to pollute. Trades among firms will lead to discovery of the lowest-cost means of achieving the permitted level of pollution.

At the initial permitted amounts of pollution (Q_R), the marginal cost of pollution for firm A is lower than that for firm B. Firm B would be willing to pay up to MC_B for the right to pollute one more unit, and firm A would be willing to sell that right for any amount that exceeded MC_A. Notice that, if such a trade were made, the total amount of pollution would be unchanged, the total cost of abating pollution would fall (by $MC_B \times MC_A$), and both firms would be at least as well off as before. We would thus have a clear efficiency improvement. No one is made worse off, and at least one party is made better off.

Once the firms are allowed to exchange rights to pollute, they will do so until their marginal abatement costs are equalized. At this point, there is no further gain from trading permits. Notice that the new equilibrium is identical to that depicted in Figure 21-4, with the equilibrium *price* of an emissions permit just equal to the emissions *tax* shown in that figure. However, with tradeable permits, regulators do not need to calculate the optimal pol-

lution tax. Given the permitted quantity of pollution, the market in permits will calculate the equivalent to the tax through the voluntary trades of firms.

Tradeable emissions permits can be used to achieve the same allocation of resources as would occur with emissions taxes, with much less information required of the regulatory authorities.

One problem with both pollution taxes and tradeable permits is more political than economic, but it is certainly important in explaining why such policies are not used more often. Opponents of tradeable permits often argue that by providing permits, rather than simply outlawing pollution above some amount, the government is condoning crimes against society. Direct controls, according to this argument, have much greater normative force, because they say that violating the standards is simply wrong. Emissions taxes and markets for pollution make violating the standards just one more element of cost for the firm to consider as it pursues its private goals.

Most economists find arguments of this kind unpersuasive. An absolute ban on pollution is impossible, and in choosing how much pollution to allow, society must trade pollution abatement against other valuable things. Economic analysis has a good deal to say about how a society might minimize the cost of *any* degree of pollution abatement, or maximize the amount of pollution abated for any given cost that the society is willing to bear.

Tradeable emissions permits in practise. Tradeable permits and emissions taxes pose formidable problems of implementation. Some of these involve technical difficulties in measuring pollution and in designing mechanisms to ensure that firms and households comply with regulations. Additionally, the potential efficiency gains arising from tradeable permits cannot be realized if regulatory agencies are prone to change the rules under which trades may take place. This has been a problem in the past, but it is a problem that can be corrected.

Although they have been seriously discussed in Canada, most experimentation with marketable rights to pollute has been done so far in the United States. Even there, many of the schemes have been heavily hedged around by nonmarket conditions.

Both the U.S. Environmental Protection Agency (the EPA) and a number of state regulatory agencies have allowed limited trading of emissions permits for over a decade. A recent study that examined the most important of these programs estimated that they had saved as much as $12 billion in the cost of pollution control, with approximately the same result for environmental quality as the costlier direct controls that they replaced.[2]

Governmental creation of a "market" in "bads" may become one of the most promising strategies for efficiently overcoming the market failure that leads to environmental pollution.

Much environmental pollution is caused by the failure of markets to account for externalities. At the same time, marketlike mechanisms can be effective in internalizing the externalities. Pollution is an example of a problem in which markets themselves can be used to correct market failure. Box 21-2 discusses some of the sources of opposition to using markets to address environmental issues.

Regulation for Health and Safety

The Department of Consumer and Corporate Affairs must approve the marketing of both prescription and nonprescription drugs in Canada. The National Transport Agency requires that automobiles have brake lights and seat belts, and a requirement that new automobiles be equipped with air bags has been a source of controversy for a decade. Consumer and Corporate Affairs can remove dangerous goods from the marketplace. It can also set standards for product safety, such as requiring "dead man" controls that automatically stop engines in lawn mowers when the operator lets go of the handle. It also regulates "truth in advertising." The Workmen's Compensation Board is broadly responsible for health and safety in the workplace. It sets detailed

standards designed to reduce workers' exposure to injury and to health risks, such as asbestos.

What all of these examples have in common is that the market failure they address is in the market for information. A consumer will generally have difficulty determining if a cold remedy has dangerous side effects, what the effect of brake lights is on the chances of having an accident, or how likely a child's pyjamas are to catch fire. An individual worker may be in no position to assess the risks of working on a given machine and may not be able to find out easily whether there are toxic chemicals in the workplace.

Health and Safety Information as a Public Good

In the previous chapter, we saw that information is likely to be underproduced in private markets, because many kinds of information are (nearly) *pure public goods*. Once the flammability of different materials that are used in children's pyjamas is known, making the information available to interested parents can be done at negligible marginal cost. A private firm that develops the information would be unable to recoup its investment. Thus, unless the government intervenes, product information would tend to be either unavailable or available only at inefficiently high prices. Most economists would agree that information about safety in the workplace and product safety is a public good; this provides a rationale for the government either to produce or to require private firms to produce such information.[3]

---

[2]Robert W. Hahn, "Economic Prescriptions for Environmental Problems," *Journal of Economic Perspectives* 3, 2 (Spring 1989), pp. 95–115.

[3]Those who do not agree would rely on the legal system to compel private producers and employers to develop the information. If someone is hurt by an unsafe product, the person can sue the manufacturer for damages. If the manufacturer has provided accurate information about the risks inherent in using the product, the consumer's chance of winning the lawsuit is much reduced. Thus, the manufacturer has an interest in developing accurate information. A similar case can be made regarding worker health and safety. In practise, however, many lawsuits of this kind are defended on the grounds that manufacturers had no knowledge of or reason to be concerned about their products' hazards. That such defenses often succeed suggests that there is an incentive to *fail* to develop relevant information about health and safety.

Box 21-2

Resistance to Market-Based Environmental Policies

Despite the many advantages that can be identified for market-based approaches to the environment, this approach encounters much resistance from firms, ordinary members of the public, and environmentalists. Why?

Producers

Opposition to market-based solutions sometimes comes from management. Several reasons for such opposition may be suggested.

Some firms object to the costs that they are asked to pay in terms of emissions taxes or the purchase prices of pollution rights. However, there is no reason why payments to government under any market-based scheme need to be a tax grab. Taxes need not be in excess of the costs imposed on society by the industry's activities. If government uses the introduction of a market-based scheme to raise *general revenue,* firms can oppose the *extra* tax burden without opposing the market-based scheme itself.

The introduction of market-based measures may signal the end of a free ride that producers have been taking at society's expense. If the firms in an industry were bearing none of the cost of its pollution, almost any antipollution scheme will impose a burden on them—but only to the extent of forcing them to bear the costs of their own activities. The difference between the command solution and the market-based solution, however, is that the former will cost the industry, and hence the average firm in the industry, more than the market solution.

Market-based schemes do not ensure that *all* firms pay less than under a common scheme, only

that the *average* firm does. When some firms pay more, they may oppose the measures out of self-interest or a feeling of injustice that they must pay more than some of their competitors. Of course, command solutions also have differential impacts on firms.

Finally, under market-based schemes, many firms feel a sense of unfairness because their competitors continue polluting while they must clean up. Their complaints ignore the fact that those who continue to pollute have paid for the right to do so, either by paying effluent taxes or by buying pollution rights, and that the complaining firm could do the same if it wished (it does not do so because cleaning up is cheaper for it than paying to pollute, as the neighbors are doing).

This points to a key issue in assessing market-based solutions: Such solutions must not be judged in isolation. Given a government's decision to reduce pollution, the market solution must be compared with its alternatives. When this is done, much of the producer opposition fades away, because most of the reasons for opposition are less in the market-based than in the command solution.

The Public

Opposition from the public can develop for a number of reasons, including the often encountered general hostility to market-based solutions and a preference for government-imposed solutions.

One source of public opposition is a moral reaction to giving anyone a right to pollute. Since it involves human survival, dealing in rights to pollute seems evil to many. This view makes difficult the rational evaluation of alternative plans for dealing with a serious social problem.

A further important source of opposition is found in the market-based solution's characteristic of allowing those who have the highest costs of cleaning up to go on polluting while those with the lowest costs do the cleaning up. Morality may dictate to many observers that the biggest polluters should do the cleaning up. Economists cannot show this reaction to be wrong; they can only point out the cost in terms of the higher prices, lower employment, unnecessary resource use, and less overall pollution abatement that follow from adopting such a moral position.

Environmentalists

Many environmentalists are skeptical about the efficiency of markets. Some do not understand economists' reasoning as to why markets can be, and often are, efficient in their use of resources. Others understand the economists' case but reject it, although few complete the argument by trying to demonstrate that command-type allocation by government will be more effective.

Second, many environmentalists do not like the use of self-interest incentives to solve social issues. Economists who point to the voluminous evidence of the importance of self-interest incentives are often accused of ignoring higher motives such as social duty, self-sacrifice, and compassion. Although such motives are absent from the simple theories that try to explain the everyday behaviour of buyers and sellers (because it has not been found necessary to introduce such motives into these theories), economists since Adam Smith have been aware that these higher motives often do exert strong influences on human behaviour.

Such higher motives are very powerful at some times and in some situations, but they do not govern many people's behaviour in the course of day-to-day living. If we want to understand how people behave in the aftermath of a flood, or an earthquake, or a war, we need motives in addition to self-interest; if we want to understand how people behave day after day in their buying and selling, we need little other than a theory of the self-interested responses to market incentives. Since control of the environment requires influencing the mass of small decisions, as well as a few large ones, the appeal to self-interest is the only currently known way to induce the required behaviour through voluntary actions.

Finally, some people have a somewhat mystical view that resources are above mere monetary calculation and should thus be treated in special ways. The economist can point out that the use of the mystical view to justify departing from solutions based on calculations of market failures (which are measured in terms of failure to provide maximum economic value) ensures that measured material living standards will be lowered. If that is the understood and accepted price of regarding resources as mystical entities, then so be it!

Is Good Information Enough?

In practise, most health and safety regulation goes well beyond the simple provision of information. Rather, firms are required to meet standards of workplace and product safety. Many economists have argued that given good information, private markets will ensure efficient levels of workplace safety. In order to evaluate this argument, we present here a very simple example of what might happen if there were no standards and everyone had accurate information about safety risks. Consider a worker who can take a job at either firm A or firm B. Suppose that the worker knows that accidents at firm A will lead the typical worker to miss two weeks of work per year, whereas the average time lost to injury at firm B is one week per year. There is no compensation paid for the time spent at home due to injury. In order to keep the example simple, suppose lost pay is the only cost of accidents that is borne by workers. (These must be pretty trivial accidents!) Equilibrium in the labour market can only occur if workers at firm A have a higher wage than workers at firm B. Assume that full-time work in both firms is 50 weeks per year. Workers in firm A can expect to be laid up and unable to work for an average of one week per year more than those at firm B. They will thus require a wage that is 50/49 times the wage paid to workers in firm B (assuming that they get no pleasure from spending a week laid up at home).

Notice that in this example, all that is required for equilibrium to occur is that the workers know the probability of accidents at each firm and that markets respond to conditions of demand and supply. No government standard needs to be set. Rather, workers who work in the firm that is less safe will demand a compensating wage differential in order to work there. Thus, the greater the chance of an accident at work, the higher are the wages that a firm must pay. This is illustrated by the upward-sloping curve shown in Figure 21-5. From the perspective of the employer, the curve represents the marginal wage cost (per worker) of increasing the probability of accidents. As accidents become more likely (moving along the horizontal axis), the firm must pay higher wages.

There is also a corresponding marginal benefit curve facing the firm. Returning to our example, suppose that firm A could be made just as safe as firm B if it spent C dollars per year per worker on

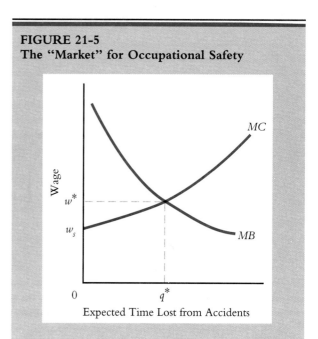

FIGURE 21-5
The "Market" for Occupational Safety

The labour market can induce firms to provide workplace safety. Suppose that a perfectly safe workplace would have to pay a wage of only w_s. As the expected time lost because of accidents increases, the required wage rises in order to compensate workers for the risk of injury. The curve that shows the higher wages is labeled MC, because it gives the (per worker) marginal cost to the firm of letting the workplace become less safe.

The marginal benefit to the firm of reducing safety is given by the MB curve, which shows the *savings* (per worker) that the firm can obtain by reducing safety-related expenditures. At the axis, time that is lost through accidents is zero; the workplace is perfectly safe. The MB curve starts very high, because the cost of making a very safe workplace perfectly safe is likely to be very high. Thus, reducing safety by a small amount from perfect safety would sharply reduce the firm's costs.

Where the two curves intersect, the marginal cost of making the workplace safer is just equal to the marginal benefit from doing so. To the left of q^*, reducing safety in the workplace saves MB and costs only MC.

Given that the MC curve is derived from the preferences of workers who are well informed about workplace risks, the market solution of q^* and w^* will be cost-minimizing for the firm and socially efficient.

improved lighting and more frequent cleanup of potentially hazardous debris on the shop floor. If C is greater than one week's pay, the extra costs would not be worth it. The firm would be spending C per worker per year and saving less than C. If the costs of reducing the probability of lost time at work by one week per worker (C) were less than one week's pay, however, a cost-minimizing firm would incur those costs. In general, the marginal benefit to the firm of increasing the probability of accidents is the saving in safety-related costs. This is shown as the downward-sloping MB curve in Figure 21-5.

In equilibrium, firms will choose a level of safety such that the savings in nonwage costs of reducing safety a little bit is just equal to the increase in the wages that the firm would have to pay. Notice that the optimal rate of accidents, much like the optimal level of pollution, is not zero. Rather, it depends on the cost of reducing the level of accidents.

In the simplified world of Figure 21-5, there is no need for safety standards; if workers are perfectly informed about the risk of accidents (and about the costs that they would bear when accidents occur) and firms minimize costs, the private market will generate efficient solutions. This argument also can be extended to product safety, given the strong assumption that consumers are perfectly informed about the risks inherent in consuming the products that they buy.

With full information, private markets will produce efficient levels of occupational and product safety.

The above analysis is not meant to describe reality. Instead, it provides a benchmark against which to judge the efficiency of government intervention to promote health and safety.

Full information may be impossible to obtain or to evaluate. Our example of firm A and firm B could work quite well for, say, an experienced machinist who is comparing two machine shops. Such a worker will have a good sense of what can be expected on the shop floor and may be able to estimate quite accurately the chances of injury. If the government requires all firms to publish their accident histories every year, the worker can make an informed choice. Such a choice may be impossible, however, when the cause of harm in the workplace

is a chemical that might cause cancer. Evaluation of carcinogens often takes many years; there is likely to be uncertainty in the medical literature; and it is very likely that the typical worker will have a difficult time interpreting the information, even if it is made easily available.

Information about safety risks in offices is also unlikely to be available in all cases. Most white-collar workers have no idea what their buildings are made of, how quickly the buildings would burn, or what kind of emergency lighting would be available in case of a fire. Further, it would not be easy for them to decode the blueprints of different buildings to make informed choices about fire safety.

Similar problems arise with product safety. The typical automobile driver is not able to make informed choices about the benefits of collapsing steering columns, reinforced door panels, or antilock braking systems. A complete maintenance report on each airplane that you fly on would probably be of little help to you in assessing the safety of the airplane. Less dramatically, it would be prohibitively expensive for the government to develop accident data for every consumer product and then to let consumers sift through the information as they decided what to buy.

Safety standards can free workers and consumers from attempting difficult calculations that they are ill equipped to make. When information is costly or impossible to process, standards can enhance efficiency.

Paternalism. One of the most cost-effective regulations in existence involves collapsing steering columns in automobiles. (The idea is that, in the event of a front-end collision, the steering column breaks rather than impaling the driver.) According to a recent estimate, the protection afforded by the collapsing steering column saves about 1,300 lives per year at a cost (in 1985) of $100,000 per life.[4] On pure efficiency grounds, matters might be further improved if automobile manufacturers offered the

---

[4]Between 1985 and 1993, the price level rose by a little more than 30 percent. This means that a regulation that cost about $100,000 to save a life in 1985 would have cost about $130,000 to save a life in 1993. Similarly, a regulation that cost $1.3 million to save a life in 1985 would have cost about $1.7 million in 1993.

collapsing steering column as an option and were required to provide data on the hazards of noncollapsing steering columns. Only very ardent proponents of laissez faire would argue for such a policy.

Another safety regulation requires that children's sleepwear meet a nonflammability standard. (The standard requires that the fabric not burst into flame when it is lit.) This regulation is less cost effective than the requirement of collapsing steering columns. In 1985, the cost *per life saved* was estimated to be about US$1.3 million. Still, few people would wish to permit parents to choose flammable pyjamas at somewhat lower cost. It is hard to think of a government regulation that is more literally paternalistic!

Health and Safety Regulation in Practise

In Chapter 20, we noted that even when there is market failure, the case for government intervention is weakened by the possibility of government failure. Perhaps the most widely cited examples of government failure arise in the area of health and safety regulation.

A notorious example of (temporary) regulatory failure is the short-lived ban on saccharin. Saccharin was banned when huge doses of saccharin caused rats to get cancer. When the required doses were seen to exceed anything humans were likely to take, the ban was lifted. Banning products from the market even when the risk of cancer is very low and the cost of alternative products is high is a questionable policy.

Assessing the risk that a product will cause cancer can be extremely difficult, and scientists' estimates of the risk often change with new information and new studies. For example, dioxin, which was once believed to be among the most toxic of substances produced by industry, is now widely believed to be much less dangerous. At the same time, many scientists are coming to believe that electric blankets once thought totally safe may cause cancer. Uncertainty about the actual risks engendered by the use of different products greatly increases the difficulty of health and safety regulation and increases the economic cost of regulation as well. If regulatory standards and rules could be expected to

stay fixed, businesses could plan and act accordingly. However, new scientific evidence often leads to changes in regulation, which can require that firms change their techniques and their products, adding to the average cost of doing business. There is no obvious solution to this problem.

As with pollution, health and safety regulators often take an engineering approach to their task. Rather than specifying a particular outcome or providing incentives for increased safety, they mandate that certain kinds of equipment be used to perform certain functions. For example, government regulations require that handrails be of a certain height and a certain distance from the wall, and have supports of specified spacing and diameter.

In principle, the case for the engineering approach may be stronger for safety regulation than it is for pollution control, because the alternative of a "safety tax" is generally not feasible. Unfortunately, the problems inherent in all engineering standards—that they may become obsolete and that they may be much more effective in some settings than in others—remain. To the extent possible, efficiency dictates that standards be expressed in terms of required performance rather than required design and materials. The reason for this is that it provides an incentive for firms to find inexpensive ways of meeting the standards, thus reducing the cost of complying with them.

Benefit-Cost Analysis of Social Regulation

The social purpose of health, safety, and pollution regulation is obvious. No one wants unsafe products, hazardous workplaces, and ugly or dangerous environments. However, even for as wealthy a society as Canada in the 1990s, the goals of health and safety cannot be absolute ones. There is no such thing as a completely safe workplace or product; it is impossible to establish that a prescription drug can never be harmful; it is difficult to think of any human activity that does not generate some amount of waste. Given that these problems will always be with us to some degree, the relevant question is *to what degree*. Economics can help provide an answer to the question by evaluating costs as well as benefits—an answer that has been a recurring theme of both this chapter and this book.

For economic efficiency, environmental, health, and safety risks should be reduced to the point where the marginal social cost of further reduction is just equal to the marginal social benefit of further reduction.

Many critics of the economic approach to social regulation rightly point out that these costs and benefits are often very difficult to measure. True as this may be in certain cases, the logic of the benefit-cost criterion still holds. Unless public policies attempt to equate marginal benefits and marginal costs, scarce social resources will be wasted and we will get fewer positive results than could be obtained from the resources that are used.

Cost-effectiveness analysis is a procedure that is much easier to perform than cost-benefit analysis. In cost-effectiveness analysis, the analyst holds constant the *outputs* of a policy and looks for the cheapest (most cost-effective) way of achieving those outputs. Such analysis is particularly useful when it is difficult to measure the value of outputs. A prominent example involves the cost of saving lives. We do not presume to put a dollar value on a human life. Cost-effectiveness analysis, however, tells us that in designing programs to save human lives, we should implement those programs that do so at lowest cost first. If we do not, we will be wasting resources that could be devoted to saving lives and thus will be saving fewer lives than we could.

A recent study of regulations designed to save lives reveals an extraordinary range in the cost per life saved of actual and proposed regulations. The most cost effective is the collapsing steering column, at US$100,000 per life, in 1993. The least cost-effective regulation in place at the time of the study involved the compulsory use of DES in cattle feed to reduce the chances of certain meat-borne diseases. It was calculated to cost US$170 million per life saved, over a thousand times as much.[5] We do not need to put a value on human life to know that there are thousands of ways to spend $170 million and save more than one life. Consider, for example, the hiring of crossing guards who would work during rush hours, policing the most traveled street

corners that do not have crossing guards. Assuming a wage of $17,000 per year per guard (surely high for a part-time job such as this one), 10,000 such guards could be hired for one year. They would surely save more than one life.

The rationale for seeking efficiency in social regulation comes from the same source as the rationale for seeking economic efficiency in other areas. The more efficiently the goals of social regulation are pursued, the more resources will be available to pursue other things of value, and the more benefits can be achieved for any given amount of resource use.

Regulatory Reform

Growing concerns about a variety of perceived problems with Canada's regulatory structure—including obsolescence in the face of rapid changes in technology and world markets, significant compliance costs, and inefficiencies in the regulatory process—have led to a number of developments in Canada.[6] (There have been similar developments in the United States, Europe, and Japan as well.) We have already encountered the deregulation trend in Chapter 15 in the context of competition policy, but the current debate and trend concerning regulation of the economy extends beyond the direct regulation of industry.

Over a decade ago, the Economic Council of Canada published two major reports on regulation: *Responsible Regulation* (1979) presented a critical appraisal of the regulatory process, and *Reforming Regulation* (1981) put forward a number of specific recommendations. In its 1979 report, the council proposed that an extensive consultative process be part of any major government attempt at regulatory change, that any major new regulatory proposals be subjected to formal benefit-cost analysis, and that the government review existing regulations and operations of regulatory agencies on a regular basis.

In its 1981 report, the council made proposals that touched on a wide range of regulated activities—trucking, airlines, telecommunications, agri-

---

[5]John F. Morral III, "A Review of the Record," *Regulation*, November/December 1986, pp. 25–34.

[6]This section draws on a detailed discussion by Professor John Strick of the University of Windsor, *The Economics of Government Regulation: Theory and Canadian Practice* (Toronto: Thompson, 1990).

culture, occupational health and safety, and the environment. The general thrust of its proposals was to "streamline the regulatory process and where possible to reduce the extent of regulation." Increased competition and increased application of market forces and financial incentives were also stressed.

When the Progressive Conservative government took office in 1984, it took up this theme of regulatory reform as a key part of its agenda. In 1986, the government announced its Regulatory Reform Strategy—although it did not endorse comprehensive deregulation, the government committed itself not only to limit the proliferation of new regulations but also "to 'regulate smarter' through greater efficiency, greater accountability, and greater sensitivity to those affected by federal regulations." The strategy invoked a number of principles, including

- Recognition of the role of the marketplace
- Continued use of regulation to achieve social and economic objectives
- Use of benefit-cost analysis to screen new initiatives
- Increased public access and participation in the process

Many of the new procedures found their way into practise, and regulatory hearings have become a regular part of the public policy landscape. Whether the new procedures have in fact met the stated objectives is not yet clear; many critics argue that the new processes, though open, are inefficient. For example, the hearings that finally ended Bell Canada's monopoly on long-distance phone service lasted over 18 months and cost close to $100 million.

Most economists would support the principles of the Regulatory Reform Strategy. Even if it is fully adopted, however, difficult social choices and difficult technical problems, of both measurement and program design, will remain. Moreover, when health, life, and safety are at stake, there are many who will never be comfortable with the results of decentralized decision making, no matter how well informed the parties to private transactions may be. The desire to protect people from the negative consequences of their actions extends well beyond an interest in internalizing externalities or providing efficient levels of information.

Economic analysis can help society to examine the costs and the consequences of social regulation. Most important, it can help regulators to achieve desired consequences at minimum cost and thus reduce the level of government failure. It can help us to decide how best to intervene in the interest of health and safety, but it cannot tell us how much we should intervene.

SUMMARY

1. Almost all economic activity is subject to at least some government regulation. Government regulation is used to deal with every type of market failure—public goods, externalities, natural monopoly problems, information asymmetries, and social values.

2. Most pollution problems can be analysed as negative externalities. Polluting firms and households going about their daily business do harm to the environment and fail to take account of the costs that they impose on others.

3. The economically efficient level of pollution in any activity is generally not zero; it is the level where the marginal cost of further pollution reduction is just equal to the marginal damage done by a unit of pollution. If a firm or a household faces incentives that cause it to internalize fully the costs that pollution imposes, it will choose the economically efficient level of pollution.

4. Pollution can be regulated either directly or indirectly. Direct controls are used most often. Direct controls are often inefficient, be-

cause they require that all polluters meet the same standard regardless of the benefits and costs of doing so. Indirect controls, such as taxes on emissions, are more efficient; ideally, they cause firms to internalize perfectly the pollution externality. Tradeable emissions permits could have the same effect as taxes without requiring regulators to know as much about the technology of pollution abatement.

5. Health and safety regulation covers workplace health and safety and product safety. Some economists have argued that regulation of this kind is unnecessary, because, if people are well informed about health and safety risks, the level of resources devoted to safety and health will be efficient.

6. Full information about health and safety risks is often difficult to obtain or to evaluate. Society may also choose not to permit people to face certain kinds of risks. In either of these cases, health and safety regulation addresses a real market failure. Government failure is common in the areas of health and safety regulation.

7. Cost-effectiveness analysis is a method of evaluating regulations when the benefits are hard to measure. It is particularly helpful for evaluating regulations that are designed to save lives, where the most cost-effective regulation is the one that saves the most lives per dollar of cost.

8. Increased use of benefit-cost and cost-effectiveness analysis could reduce the social costs imposed by social regulation. Alternatively, holding social cost constant, it could increase the benefits from social regulation.

TOPICS FOR REVIEW

Costs and benefits of pollution abatement

Emissions taxes

Direct controls

Efficient level of pollution

Tradeable emissions permits

Regulatory failure

Cost-effectiveness analysis

Regulatory reform

DISCUSSION QUESTIONS

1. Many occupations are licensed, either by governments or by professional organizations. Are economists licensed? Should they be? Why or why not?

2. "Pollution is wrong. When a corporation pollutes, it commits assault on the citizens of the country and it should be punished." Comment on this quotation in light of the discussion in this chapter.

3. Assume that the following statements are true. What do they imply about the argument that health and safety regulations are necessary to promote economic efficiency?

   a. Welders who work on the upper stories of unfinished skyscrapers are paid more than welders who work only indoors.

    b. Following a commercial airplane crash, the stock market value of the airline company involved tends to fall.

    c. Within a city, housing of a given structural quality tends to sell for less, the greater is the health risk that is posed by air quality in the neighbourhood.

    d. For decades, asbestos was widely used as insulation. Installers of asbestos insulation routinely breathed asbestos fiber in concentrations that are now known to be potentially lethal. For some years, asbestos producers were aware that asbestos was dangerous but did not share this information with installers.

    e. Until recently, the upholstery in airline seats emitted lethal fumes when the seats were burning.

4. Consider the following (alleged) facts about pollution control and indicate what, if any, influence they might have on policy determination.

    a. The cost of meeting pollution requirements is about $300 per person per year.

    b. More than one third of the world's known oil supplies lie under the ocean floor, and there is no known blowout-proof method of recovery.

    c. Sulphur removal requirements and strip-mining regulations have led to the tripling of the cost of a ton of coal used in generating electricity.

    d. Every million dollars that is spent on pollution control creates 47 new jobs in the economy.

5. During a Pittsburgh air pollution alert, a 69-year-old retired steelworker was interviewed. He said, "I've got a heart condition myself, and I know that when I look out the window and see the air like it was this morning, I've got to stay inside. Yesterday, I tried to drive to the store, and I couldn't see 50 feet ahead of me, it was so thick, so I just came home. I remember that when I was young, we never thought about pollution. Everybody was working, and everybody had money, and the smokestacks were smoking, and the air was dirty, and we were all happy. I think the best air we ever had in Pittsburgh was during the Depression. That's when nobody was working." Comment on this statement in terms of the issues discussed in this chapter.

6. Suppose you were given the job of drafting a law to regulate water pollution over the entire length of some river.

    a. How would you determine how much total pollution to permit?

    b. What control mechanism would you use to regulate emissions into the river? Why?

    c. Would you impose the same rules on cities as on farms?

    d. Would the answers to any of the preceding questions depend on the quality of information that would be available to you? How and why?

7. Under current regulations, cleaning up all known toxic waste sites would cost between $300 billion and $700 billion. Yet, according to a recent newspaper article, "virtually all of the risk to human health, most analysts agree, could be eliminated for a tiny fraction of these sums." The same article notes that many experts argue that "once [dangerous sites are] identified, the cleanup should be carefully aimed at saving lives rather than restoring land to preindustrial condition." In one site, the former goal could be achieved for $71,000; the latter would cost over $13,000,000.

How would you frame a benefit-cost analysis of different strategies for cleaning up toxic waste?

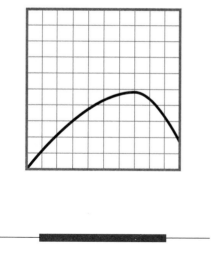

22

Taxation and Public Expenditure

I n Chapter 21, we saw some of the reasons why the scope of government is so extensive. Taxation is needed to raise money for public spending, and it can also play a policy role in its own right. Taxes can affect the distribution of income—some people get taxed more than others. Moreover, by taxing some activities heavily and others lightly or not at all, the tax system can influence the allocation of resources. In some cases, tax policy is carefully designed with such effects in mind; in other cases, the effects are unintentional by-products of policies pursued for other purposes.

In this chapter, we ask how taxation and public expenditure affect the allocation of resources and the distribution of income, and to what extent they are effective tools of public policy. We also consider the question of the allocation of government services and taxes among the various levels of government.

Taxation

There is a bewildering array of taxes. Some, such as income taxes, are highly visible. Others are all but invisible because, for example, they are imposed on producers of raw materials and intermediate products. People and firms are taxed on what they earn, on what they spend, and on what they own. Not only are taxes numerous, but they take a big bite. Personal income taxes take the largest proportion of income, and two thirds of their revenue goes to the Federal government. Aggregate taxes amounted to a little more than 20 percent of Canadian GDP in 1960 and a little less than 40 percent in 1993. The diversity and yield of various taxes are shown in Table 22-1.

Aspects of the Tax System

When the government taxes one group in society more heavily than it taxes another, it influences the distribution of income. The effect of taxes on the distribution of income can be summarized in terms of *progressivity*. A **progressive tax** system takes a larger percentage of income from people the higher their income. A **proportional tax** system takes amounts of money from people in direct proportion to their income. A **regressive tax** system takes a larger percentage of income from people the lower their income.[1]

---

[1]While our interest is ultimately in the progressivity of the tax system as a whole, it will also be useful to identify the progressivity of particular features of the tax system, such as income taxes or sales taxes.

TABLE 22-1 Taxes as a Percentage of Total Canadian Income and Their Division Among Levels of Government, 1991.

	Taxes as Percentage of Canadian Income	Percentage of Taxes Divided		
		Federal	Provincial	Municipal
Personal income taxes	15.9%	62.2	37.8	0
General sales taxes	5.5	47.4	52.5	0.1
Health and social insurance levies	3.7	60.7	39.3	0
Property taxes	3.7	0	8.8	91.2
Corporate income taxes	2.4	67.9	32.1	0
Import duties	0.6	100	0	0
Revenue from natural resource taxes	3.1	1.2	98.0	0
Other	2.6	37.5	60.4	2.0
Total	37.5	50.1	40.5	9.4

Source: Tax Facts Eight, Fraser Institute.

Personal income taxes take the largest bite of income, and two thirds of their revenue goes to the federal government. The first column shows the percentage of Canadian national income taken by various taxes. The next three columns show the percentage division of the revenues from each tax going to each level of government.

A tax system is said to be progressive if it decreases the inequality of income distribution and regressive if it increases the inequality, other things being equal.

The differences can be illustrated by an example. Suppose that we have a very small town with 100 taxpayers, half of whom earn $20,000 a year and half of whom earn $40,000 a year. The town's budget for street repair is $10,000 per year.

Now consider three alternative tax systems. First, if the tax system were simply to assess $100 per year from each taxpayer, the outcome would be regressive: Lower-income taxpayers would be paying 0.5 percent of their incomes, and higher-income taxpayers would be paying only 0.25 percent of theirs. Second, if the repairs were paid for by a proportional tax, everyone would pay 0.33 percent of income: This would amount to $66.67 for the low-income households and $133.33 for the high-income households. Finally, a scheme whereby the first $20,000 of income would be subject to a 0.1 percent tax rate and all income above $20,000 would be subject to a 0.8 percent tax rate would be

progressive. The low-income taxpayers would pay only 0.1 percent of their incomes ($20), while taxes would average 0.45 percent for the high-income group ($180). Note that in all three cases the total tax revenues add up to the requisite $10,000.

Tax expenditures.   Sometimes taxes are used in ways that are similar to spending programs. For example, one way to deal with polluted rivers is to spend public funds to clean them up. An alternative, as we saw in Chapter 21, is to use taxes to penalize polluters or to give tax concessions to firms that install pollution-abating devices. Tax concessions that seek to induce market responses are called **tax expenditures**—tax revenue forgone to achieve purposes that the government believes are desirable.

The difference between a tax expenditure and an ordinary budgetary expenditure is that a tax expenditure reduces the revenue side of the budget instead of increasing the expenditure side. Tax expenditures usually receive little scrutiny from Parliament. Their effects are usually harder to discern and harder to evaluate than those of direct spending programs.

The Canadian Tax System

Taxes are collected by the federal government, by each of the 10 provinces, and by thousands of cities, townships, and villages. The federal government collects about as much revenue as all other governments put together. The provinces, in turn, collect about four times as much as local governments. The federal government gets over 50 percent of its revenues from taxes paid directly by individuals and corporations and over 20 percent from taxes collected on the sale of goods and services (mainly the GST). The provinces get just over 40 percent from income taxes and about 35 percent from sales taxes. The municipalities rely almost exclusively on property taxes for their tax revenues.[2]

Personal Income Taxes

Personal income taxes are paid directly to the government by individuals. The amount of tax any individual pays is the result of a fairly complicated series of calculations. All types of income are included in what is called total income, although certain types of income qualify for total or partial exemption.[3] Then a number of allowable deductions are subtracted from total income to determine taxable income.

Taxes payable are then calculated from a schedule relating taxable income to taxes due. The tax schedule takes into account the facts that the personal tax rate changes as taxable income changes and that gross taxes are reduced by nonrefundable tax credits to determine net taxes. The federal tax rate is graduated in three steps. The positions of the steps change from year to year because they are partially indexed. In 1992, the lowest rate applied to taxable income up to about $28,000, the next rate up to about $56,000, and the top rate applied thereafter.

Since those rates were instituted, both the federal and many provincial governments have added

more progressivity while levying surcharges that kick in at various higher levels of income.

Quebec runs its own income tax system, and the other nine provinces simply use the federal tax base (and federally distributed tax forms) and essentially "top up" federal taxes. Except for Quebec, taxpayers pay a single amount to Revenue Canada, which then distributes the total between the federal government and each province according to the amount collected from residents of that province.

Table 22-2 shows the average and marginal rates paid by a single taxpayer at various income levels and in selected provinces. The figures vary across provinces because different provincial rates are added onto the common federal rate. Average rates of tax rise continually with income as more and more income becomes subject to the top marginal tax rate. Currently in most provinces an *average* rate of 40 percent is reached when income is about $100,000.

The **average tax rate** paid by a taxpayer is his or her total income tax payment divided by total income. The taxpayer's **marginal tax rate** is the amount of tax he or she would pay on an additional dollar of income. As can be seen from Table 22-2, the combined marginal tax rate rises as income rises; this *progressive marginal tax rate* contributes to the progressivity of the income tax system.

A major reform of the personal income tax system occurred in 1987. The theme of the reform was to *broaden the tax base* by eliminating a number of exemptions and deductions and to *lower marginal tax rates*. The new system is considerably simpler, as there are now just three tax brackets. The conversion of the basic personal exemption to a personal tax credit—worth the same to each taxpayer regardless of income level—contributes to rather than detracts from the progressivity of the system. Further, marginal rates have been reduced for most Canadians, and many low-income Canadians now pay no taxes.

Although the changes introduced in 1987 were substantial and were intended to be part of a comprehensive reform of the tax system, the personal income tax system continues to change. A special levy has been introduced on high-income earners, intended to "claw back" social benefits such as family allowances. Also, first the federal and then many provincial governments have introduced "temporary" surtaxes on medium and high incomes to help deal with growing fiscal deficits. These surtaxes

---

[2]Each of the lower levels of government also receives revenue in the form of transfer payments from more senior governments as well as some revenues from other sources such as the profits from provincial liquor monopolies.

[3]Until 1972, most capital gains were tax free in Canada. In 1993, there was a personal lifetime exemption on the first $100,000 for capital gains. Seventy-five percent of all further gains must be counted as part of taxable income.

TABLE 22-2   Personal Income Tax, Marginal Rates for a Single Taxpayer in Selected Provinces, 1991

| Province | *Taxable Income* | | | | |
	10,000	*25,000*	*53,000*	*78,000*	*100,000*
Newfoundland	28.4	28.4	43.4	49.9	49.9
Prince Edward Island	27.7	27.7	42.4	48.7	50.4
Nova Scotia	28.0	28.0	42.8	50.9	50.1
New Brunswick	28.1	28.1	42.9	49.3	51.0
Quebec	32.9	38.1	47.0	51.1	51.1
Ontario	26.9	26.9	41.1	47.8	49.1
Manitoba	30.7	28.8	44.8	51.0	51.0
Saskatchewan	33.4	28.4	44.6	50.9	50.8
Alberta	30.5	26.3	40.9	47.0	47.0
British Columbia	26.6	26.6	40.7	48.3	48.3

Source: The National Finances 1991, Canadian Tax Foundation.

Tax rates vary across provinces due to different provincial add-ons and surtaxes. These rates, which include federal and provincial surtaxes, have been creeping up over the last few years. By 1993, the combined maximum marginal rate exceeded 50 percent in most provinces and approached 55 percent in some.

have brought the top marginal rate over 50 percent in many provinces. In British Columbia, for example, surtaxes took the top rate to 51 percent in 1993 and were scheduled to raise it to 54 percent in 1994. This means that people in the top tax bracket keep 46 cents out of each additional dollar that they earn. The net result of all these changes is that the loopholes have been reduced, effective marginal rates are some of the highest in the industrialised world, and the tax system is becoming more complex. These developments run counter to the principles that guided the attempts at reform in the 1980s. They also raise the question of how high tax rates can become without causing major shrinkages in the tax base as some people emigrate, some move to the underground economy, and some choose leisure over work.

Corporate Taxes

The federal corporate income tax is, for practical purposes, a flat-rate tax on profits as defined by the taxing authorities—which includes the return on capital as well as pure economic profits. In 1993, the rate was 28 percent.

As with the personal income tax, the 1987 reform not only lowered tax rates but also broadened the tax base, and on the whole, the changes tended to raise taxes paid by corporations. Base-broadening was accomplished primarily by eliminating tax concessions, called investment tax credits, that had been used to encourage investment.

There is controversy over how much of the corporate taxation is shifted to consumers rather than being paid by shareholders. (Tax shifting was first discussed in Chapter 6.)

Recently the British Columbia government instituted a corporate wealth tax. This is an annual levy on the value of each firm's assets. It is paid whether the firm makes profits or losses. Such corporate wealth taxes are almost unknown in the industrialised countries, and their introduction in British Columbia was bitterly criticised by the business community and would-be foreign investors, especially in Southeast Asia.

Excise and Sales Taxes

An excise tax is levied on a particular commodity, such as liquor. In many countries, commodities such as tobacco, alcohol, and gasoline are singled out for high rates of excise taxation. Because these commodities usually account for a much greater proportion of the expenditure of lower-income than higher-income groups, the taxes on them are regressive.

A sales tax applies to the sale of all or most goods and services. All provinces except Alberta impose a retail sales tax. Such a tax is mildly regressive, because poorer families tend to spend a larger proportion of their incomes than richer families. For example, suppose there is a 7 percent comprehensive sales tax. A family that earns $25,000 a year and saves nothing will pay 7 percent of its income on sales taxes; a family that earns $70,000 a year and saves $10,000 will pay 6 percent.

Both excise and sales taxes are often referred to as *indirect taxes* **to contrast them with income taxes, which are levied directly on individuals or firms.**

The GST. The goods and services tax (the GST) was introduced amid enormous political controversy. It is effectively a tax on almost all goods and services produced in the country (food and a few other things go untaxed) and was introduced for a number of reasons. First, it removed the bias in the old manufacturer's sales tax (MST), which encouraged imports and discouraged exports. In contrast, the GST taxes imports but exempts exports. Second, it followed the modern trend to tax consumption rather than income. Income taxes hit all income, including savings, while the GST hits only that part of income that is spent. Third, it does not distort the relative prices of goods and services, whereas the old MST raised the price of goods relative to services. Fourth, it followed the trend in almost all other developed nations (except the United States), which levy similar taxes; they are called *value added taxes* (VAT) in Europe.

In practise, the GST works by taxing a firm on the gross value of its output and then allowing a tax credit equal to the taxes paid on the inputs that were produced by other firms. Effectively, this taxes each firm's contribution to the value of final output—its value added. The result is the same as if each good and service bore a 7 percent tax when it was sold to its final user.

The operation of the GST for the case of the stages leading from the mining of iron ore to the manufacture of a washing machine is illustrated in Figure 22-1. Further controversies surrounding the GST are discussed in more detail in Box 22-1.

Being a consumption tax, the unaided GST would be mildly regressive, because the proportion of income saved, and hence not taxed, rises with income. This characteristic was avoided by exempting food and, more importantly, giving low- and middle-income people a refundable tax credit, which for the poor exceeds the value of GST that they would pay even if they spent all of their incomes on taxable commodities.

Property Taxes

Property taxes, based on the value of taxable property, are an important source of revenue for municipalities.

The property tax is the most important tax in Canada that is based on wealth. It is different from any other important tax because taxpayers do not have to buy or sell anything in order to incur a tax liability.

Taxing the value of existing property creates two problems. First, someone has to assess what the property is worth. Because the assessment is only an estimate, it is always subject to challenge. Second, sometimes owners of property that is quite valuable have low incomes and thus have difficulty paying the tax.

The progressivity of the property tax has been studied extensively. It is well known that the rich live in more expensive houses than the poor, but this only establishes that the rich tend to pay more in property tax than the poor. Most studies have shown that the proportion of income spent for housing tends to decrease with income. Many, but not all, public finance experts believe, therefore, that the property tax tends to be mildly regressive in its overall effect.

Evaluating the Tax System

To evaluate the *tax system,* the important question is this: Holding constant the amount of revenue to be raised, what makes one tax system better or worse than another? Economists deal with this question by

FIGURE 22-1
The Operation of a Value Added Tax

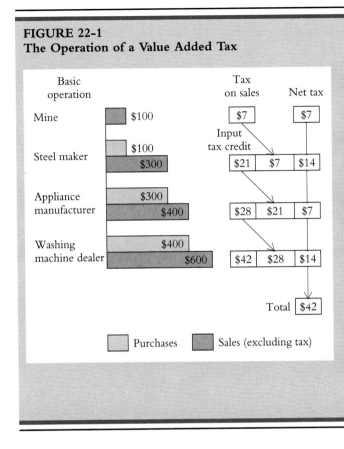

A tax on value added is the same as a tax on the value of total output produced by a firm with a credit allowed for the tax paid by other firms from which it has purchased produced inputs. The example is for the stages involved as iron ore is mined and then sold to a steel maker, the steel then sold to an appliance manfacturer, and a washing machine sold to a retailer and then to a homeowner. The example makes the simplifying assumption that no produced inputs are used in the mining operation; at all further stages, the use of produced inputs makes the firm's value added less than the value of final output at that stage. The steel maker's value added is $200, and its tax is thus $14; this equals $21 on the total value of its output less the $7 credit on the taxes already paid by the mine on the value of the ore. Total taxes paid equal $42, which is 7 percent of the $600 value of the final product (the washing machine); each firm pays 7 percent of its share in creating that $600 value.

---

considering two aspects of taxation—equity and efficiency. We deal with equity first.

Taxes and Equity

Debate about income distribution and tax policy invokes the important but slippery concepts of *equality* and *equity*.

Equality

To tax everyone equally can mean several things. It might mean that everyone should pay the same amount—which would be hard on the unemployed worker and easy on the heiress. It might mean that everyone should pay the same proportion of income, say, a flat 20 percent, whether rich or poor, living alone or supporting eight children, healthy or

suffering from a disease that requires expensive treatment. It might mean that each should pay an amount of tax such that everyone's income after taxes is the same—which would remove any incentive to earn an above-average income. Or it might mean none of these things.

Equity

Equity—fairness—is a normative concept; what one group thinks is fair may seem outrageous to another. Two principles can be helpful in assessing equity in taxation—ability to pay and benefits received.

The ability-to-pay principle.   Most people view an equitable tax system as being based on people's *ability to pay taxes.* In considering equity that is based on ability to pay, two concepts need to be distinguished.

Box 22-1

The Goods and Services Tax

Amidst country-wide criticism and political turmoil in the Senate, the goods and services tax (GST) replaced the federal sales tax (FST) in January 1991. To some extent, this change was an extension of the theme of broadening the tax base and lowering the tax rate that had been featured in the reform of the direct tax system. Under the FST, services were excluded—the tax was also known as the manufacturers' sales tax (MST), since it was levied only on manufactured goods. Further, many industries were exempt, so manufactured goods were treated in a discriminatory fashion. The GST broadened the base to include almost all goods and services produced in Canada (food and some financial services are notable exceptions), and the tax rate was reduced from the 13.5 percent FST rate to 7 percent under the GST.

Much of the rationale for the change stemmed from dissatisfaction with the FST. The narrow base of the FST created distortions by treating various industries differently, leading to an inefficient allocation of resources—there were about 22,000 special provisions for the FST that were the result of industries or firms negotiating special treatment for themselves. Also, the continual erosion of the base

as new industries negotiated special treatment meant that the FST no longer provided a stable revenue source.

In addition to the problems created by the narrow base, economists identified two other undesirable features of the FST. First, it taxed goods produced for export but not imports; this put Canadian industries at a competitive disadvantage both at home and abroad. Second, since many manufactured capital goods are used as inputs by other industries, the FST raised the price of those inputs and thus again damaged the competitiveness of Canadian producers. These two problems were addressed by the *multistage* nature of the GST.

One advantage of using a multistage tax is that it reduces *tax cascading,* which is the term used to describe the fact that under the FST some commodities effectively get taxed more than once. For example, consider the production of a washing machine, illustrated in Figure 22-1. If sales taxes were levied on all transactions, with no offsetting tax credits applied to inputs in the manufacturing process, the ore would be taxed three times: when it was sold to the steel maker, when the steel was sold to the appliance manufacturer, and when the appli-

---

Vertical equity concerns equity across income groups; it focuses on comparisons between individuals or families with different levels of income.

This concept is central to discussions of the progressivity of taxation. Proponents of progressive taxation argue as follows. (1) Taxes should be based on ability to pay. (2) The greater one's income, the greater the percentage of income that is available for goods and services beyond the bare necessities. (3) Thus, the greater one's income, the greater the proportion of income that is available to pay taxes. (4)

Thus, an ability-to-pay standard of vertical equity requires progressive taxation.

Horizontal equity concerns equity within a given income group; fundamentally, it is concerned with establishing just who should be considered equal to whom in terms of ability to pay taxes.

Two households with the same income may have different numbers of children to support. One of the households may have greater dental expenses, leaving less for life's necessities and for taxes. One of ance was sold to the consumer. Analogously, the steel would be taxed twice. The GST eliminates this cascading: Once the tax on the ore is collected when it is sold to the steel maker, its value is not taxed again, since further purchasers are given a tax credit for the tax embodied in their purchases.

The elimination of tax cascading is especially important when considering investment and international trade. When a firm invests in a new machine or builds a new plant, many of its purchases will be subject to sales tax. Under a single-stage tax, this is the end of the story, and the sales tax clearly raises the cost of investment to the firm. With a multistage tax, the firm gets a credit for the taxes already paid on its purchases of goods and machines. This reduces the cost of investment to the firm.

In a detailed study of the GST, the Economic Council of Canada argued that the replacement of the 13.5 percent FST with a GST at a lower rate would have a number of important effects. Since the effective tax on manufactured goods would fall and that on services (for example, restaurant meals and legal advice) would rise, total output of the former would rise relative to the output of the latter. The council also argued that exports would

rise, imports would fall, savings and investment would both rise, and a process of capital upgrading would occur, leading to increased productivity and growth.

In spite of its being an improvement over the FST, the GST proved to be extremely unpopular, partly because most Canadians were unaware of the FST, and its deficiencies. Unlike provincial sales taxes, the FST was "invisible"; it was applied before the retail transaction, and hence its presence was hidden in retail selling prices. Much of the opposition came from small business, farmers, fishermen, and professionals, who feared the burden of record keeping and paperwork that such a complicated system entails. Others feared that once the GST was introduced, governments could easily raise more revenue by increasing the GST rate. October 1993 saw the election of a new liberal government pledged to eliminate the GST. A replacement that raised equal revenue would almost certainly be another similar tax on all output. If the new tax could be integrated with the Provincial sales taxes, large reductions in both the public and the private sectors' costs of administration could be effected.

the households may incur expenses that are necessary for earning income (e.g., requirements to buy uniforms or to pay union dues). There is no objective way to decide how much these and similar factors affect the ability to pay taxes. In practise, the income tax law makes some allowance for some factors that create differences in ability to pay by permitting taxpayers to exempt some of their income from tax. However, the corrections are rough at best. We consider the issue of horizontal equity in more detail in Chapter 23.

The benefit principle. According to the *benefit*

principle, taxes should be paid in proportion to the benefits that taxpayers derive from public expenditure.[4] From this perspective, the ideal taxes are *user charges,* such as those that would be charged if private firms provided the government services. The benefit principle is the basis for the gasoline tax,

[4]It is difficult to see how the benefit principle could be applied to many of the most important categories of government spending. Who gets how much benefit from national defense or from the interest on the national debt? It is even more difficult to imagine applying the benefit principle to programs that redistribute income.

since gasoline usage is closely correlated to the services obtained from using public roads. There is also a special airline ticket excise tax that is used for airport operations, air traffic control, and airport security. Although there are other examples, especially at the local level, the benefit principle has historically played only a minor role in the design of the Canadian tax system.

How Progressive Is the Canadian Tax System?

Although most public controversy over tax equity stresses the progressivity or regressivity of particular taxes, what matters in the end is the overall effect of the whole tax system. For a modern government to raise sufficient funds, many taxes must be used. Also, since each tax has its own loopholes and anomalies, the use of many taxes tends to cover everyone one way or another. Not all of these taxes can be equally progressive, so how rich, middle-income, and poor people are treated relative to each other depends on how the whole system impacts on each group.

The effect of the tax system on the distribution of income depends on the mix of taxes of different kinds. Federal taxes tend to be somewhat progressive; the progressivity of the income tax system and the use of a low-income tax credit more than offset the regressivity of the federal GST. Provincial and municipal governments rely heavily on property and sales taxes and, thus, have tax systems that are probably slightly regressive. Furthermore, income from different sources is taxed at different rates. For example, in the federal personal income tax, income from royalties on oil wells is taxed more lightly than income from royalties on books, and profits from sales of assets (capital gains) are taxed more lightly than wages and salaries. To evaluate progressivity, one needs to know the way in which different levels of income correlate with different sources of income.

Many writers have concluded that overall the tax system has very little net effect on the distribution of income, except for very low- and very high-income persons.

The tax system tends to be roughly proportional for middle-income classes and mildly progressive for low- and high-income persons.

The progressivity of government activity. In evaluating the progressivity of all government activities, how the money is spent is just as important as how it is collected. A regressive tax may nevertheless provide funds for increased welfare payments, and thus the combined effect of the tax system and government spending may be progressive, since it may ultimately redistribute income from higher- to lower-income families.

Efficiency

The tax system influences the allocation of resources by altering such things as the *relative* prices of various goods and factors and the *relative* profitability of various industries.

Although it is theoretically possible to design a neutral tax system—one that leaves all relative prices unchanged—the actual tax system does alter the allocation of resources. The reason for this is that the taxes themselves change the relationship between prices and marginal costs and shift consumption and production toward goods and services that are taxed relatively lightly and away from those that are taxed more heavily. Usually, this alteration of free-market outcomes causes economic inefficiency. In a world without taxes (and without other market imperfections), prices would equal marginal costs, and society's resources could be allocated efficiently.

Of course, in a world without taxes, there would be other problems—it would be impossible to pay for any government programs or public goods desired by society. In practise, then, the relevant objective for tax policy is to design a tax system that minimizes inefficiency, *given the amount of revenue to be raised*. In designing such a tax system, a natural place to start would be with taxes that both raise revenue and enhance efficiency. Examples are the fines and emissions taxes that we discussed in Chapter 21. When taxes are imposed on negative externalities, marginal social benefit is moved closer to marginal social cost, *and* government revenue is raised. Unfortunately, such taxes cannot raise nearly enough revenue to finance all of government expenditure.

In the absence of externalities, a tax normally does two things. It takes money from the taxpayers, and it changes their behaviour. Taxpayers are typically made worse off by both. Economists call the revenue collected the **direct burden** of the tax. The additional costs that result from the induced changes in behaviour is called the **excess burden**. The excess burden is the amount of money that the taxpayers would have to be given, *over and above the tax paid,* in order to be just as well off as they would have been if there were no tax.

An example may help. Suppose that your province imposes a $2 excise tax on the purchase of compact discs. If you still buy your usual five CDs a month, you pay $10 in taxes, and you therefore have to reduce your consumption of other goods by $10. If you were given an additional $10 a month in income, you would be exactly as well off as you were before the tax was imposed. Thus, the total burden on you is equal to the direct burden, $10 a month. There is also no economic inefficiency; the cost of raising $10 a month for the province is just the $10 a month that you pay in taxes.

Suppose that your friend down the block is also a music fan but not quite so fanatical. The tax leads her to cut back on her consumption of CDs from two a month to none. In this case, your friend pays no taxes, but she is clearly worse off. She has given up the satisfaction that she would have derived from two new CDs a month. She would have to be given some amount of money greater than zero (exactly her consumer surplus from buying two untaxed CDs per month) in order to make her as well off as she was before the tax was imposed. In this case, the direct burden is zero (because no tax is paid) but there is an excess burden.

When a tax is imposed, some people behave like the music buff and do not change their consumption of the taxed good at all, others cease consuming the taxed good altogether, and still others simply reduce consumption. There will be an excess burden for those in the latter two groups. This means that the revenue collected will understate the total cost to taxpayers of generating that revenue. Since we are holding constant the total revenue raised, and hence the direct burden, an efficient tax system will be one that minimizes the amount of excess burden.

The excess burden is minimized when taxes are imposed on goods for which the price elasticity of demand is least; the extreme case is illustrated by the music fan, whose price elasticity of demand is zero. A good with perfectly inelastic demand (one that has a vertical demand curve) can be taxed with no excess burden at all. Unfortunately, many of life's necessities (such as food) have very price inelastic demand curves, so a tax system that taxed only goods that had inelastic demand curves would prove to be very regressive. This illustrates an important general point:

Efficiency and equity are often competing goals in the design of tax systems.

Supply-Side Effects of Taxation

In principle, taxes on some activities can be so high that reducing the tax rate would actually increase tax revenue. This is the idea behind the **Laffer curve** shown in Figure 22-2. Its essential feature is that tax revenues reach a maximum at some income tax rate well below 100 percent.

The reasoning behind the general shape of the Laffer curve is as follows. At a zero tax rate, no revenue would be collected. As rates are raised above zero, some revenue will be gained. But as rates approach 100 percent, revenue will again fall to zero because no one would earn taxable income if all of it went to the government. It follows that there must be some tax rate, greater than zero and less than 100 percent, at which tax revenue reaches a maximum. Above that rate, increases in the tax rate reduce tax revenue. Also, there will be a separate Laffer curve for each type of tax. (Strictly speaking, there could be more than one maximum on each curve, but that need not detain us here.)

Just where this maximum occurs—whether at average tax rates closer to 40 or to 70 percent—is currently unknown for either corporate or personal income taxes. The curve does, however, provide an important warning: Governments cannot increase their tax revenues to any desired level simply by increasing their tax rates. Sooner or later, further increases in the rates will lower revenues.

Tax Incidence

One major unresolved question about taxes and resource allocation is empirical: Just how different is the allocation because of tax policy? There is no consensus on this question, because we are not sure who ultimately pays the taxes that are levied. **Tax shifting** is the passing of the burden of the tax from

FIGURE 22-2
A Laffer Curve

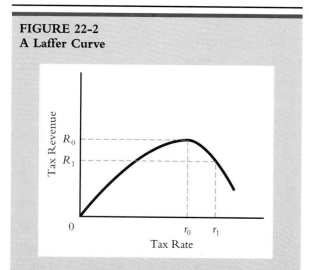

Increases in tax rates beyond some level will decrease rather than increase tax revenue. The curve relates the government's tax revenue to the tax rate. As drawn, revenue reaches a maximum level of R_0 at average tax rate r_0. If the tax rate were r_1, *reducing* it to r_0 would increase revenue to the government from R_1 to R_0.

whoever initially pays it to someone else. **Tax incidence** refers to who ultimately bears the burden of the tax.

When a tax is imposed on a firm, do its owners bear the burden of the tax, or do they pass it on to their consumers in the form of higher prices? The following example shows why this is a difficult question to answer.

Do Landlords or Tenants Pay the Property Tax?

Landlords characteristically protest the crushing burden of property taxes. Tenants often reply that landlords shift the whole burden of the tax to them in the form of higher rents. Both sides cannot be right in alleging that each bears the entire burden of the tax!

To examine the incidence, suppose that a city imposes a property tax and the thousands of landlords in the city decide to raise rents by the full amount of the tax. This scenario is shown graphically in Figure 22-3.

There will be a decline in the quantity of rental accommodations demanded as a result of the price increase. This, with no change in the quantity supplied, will cause a surplus of rental accommodations at the higher prices. Landlords will find it difficult to replace tenants who move out, and the typical unit will remain empty longer between tenancies. Prospective tenants will find alternative sites to choose from and will become very particular about what they expect from landlords.

Some prospective tenants, seeing vacant apartments, will offer to pay rents below the asking rent. Some landlords will accept such offers rather than earn nothing from vacant premises. Once some landlords cut rents, others will have to follow suit or find their properties staying unrented for longer periods of time.

Eventually, rentals will reach a new equilibrium at which the quantity demanded equals the quantity supplied. The equilibrium rental price will be higher than the original before-tax rent but lower than the rent that passes the entire tax on to the tenants.

The incidence of the property tax is shared by landlords and tenants.

Just how it is shared by the two groups will depend on the elasticity of the demand and supply curves.[5] These elasticities will in turn depend on how much and how quickly landlords and tenants react to changes in rents.

Notice that the question of incidence is not answered by knowing who writes the check to pay the tax bill. In many European countries, the tenant rather than the landlord is sent the tax bill and pays the tax directly to the city; even in this case, however, the landlord bears part of the burden. As long as the existence of the tax reduces the quantity of rental accommodations demanded below what it would otherwise be, the tax will depress the amount received by landlords. In this way, landlords will bear part of the burden.

---

[5]We suggest that you draw a series of diagrams with demand and supply curves of different slopes to see how this works. In each case, shift the supply curve up by the same vertical amount—to represent the property tax—and see what proportion of the increase is reflected in the new equilibrium price.

FIGURE 22-3
The Incidence of a Tax on Rental Housing

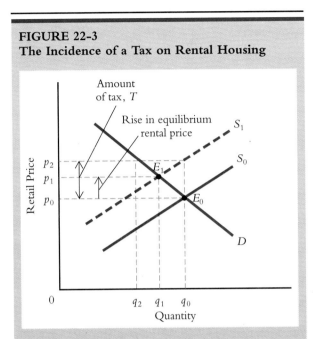

Since the equilibrium rent rises by less than the amount of the tax, landlords and tenants share the burden. The supply schedule S_0 reflects the landlords' willingness to supply rental housing at different levels of rents received. Before the tax, equilibrium is at E_0. When a tax of T is imposed on landlords, the supply curve shifts up by the full amount of the tax to S_1. Suppose that landlords attempt to raise rents by the full amount of the tax, from p_0 to p_2. There will be an excess supply of housing of q_2q_0 at p_2, and rents will fall. At the new equilibrium E_1, with rental price p_1, landlords have succeeded in raising the rental price by p_0p_1, less than p_0p_2, the full amount of the tax. Thus, landlords are paying p_1p_2 of the total tax on each unit that is rented.

Notice also that this result emerges whether landlords and tenants realize it or not. Because rents are changing for all sorts of other reasons, no one will have much idea of what equilibrium rentals would have been in the absence of the tax. It does not do much good just to look at what happens immediately after tax rates are changed, because, as we have already seen, landlords may begin by raising rents by the full amount of the tax. Although they think they have passed the tax on, this creates a disequilibrium. In equilibrium, prices will have risen by less than the full amount of the tax.

Public Expenditure

Public expenditure affects both the distribution of income and the allocation of resources. In recent years, spending by the consolidated public sector—which includes federal, provincial, and municipal governments—has equaled about 45 percent of Canadian GDP. Table 22-3 gives the distribution of consolidated government spending across a number of major *functions.* As can be seen, health care, education, and social welfare are the largest items; collectively, they make up nearly half the total. Transportation and communication and interest on the public debt add up to another 25 percent of the total. The remainder covers everything else, from police protection and sanitation to general administration of government and scientific research. About 40 percent of public expenditure is made by the federal government.

Types of Government Expenditures

Table 22-4 classifies federal and provincial governments by type of expenditure. For each level of government, total expenditures are equal to the sum of program expenditures and debt service payments; program expenditures include purchases of goods and services and various transfer payments. Figure 22-4 shows the changing importance of different types of federal government expenditure programs. On the one hand, federal government purchases of goods and services, which reflect what the government does by way of current production, have been declining steadily. On the other hand, transfer payments to individuals have been rising steadily.

Provision of goods and services. As Table 22-4 indicates, about 20 percent of combined federal and provincial government spending was for the provision of goods and services. Such spending is the dominant type for provincial (and municipal) governments, as it was for the federal expenditure until 1971 (see Figure 22-4 on page 440).

Among the goods and services provided by government are defense, transportation facilities, ed-

TABLE 22-3   Expenditures of All Governments by Function, 1991

Category	Expenditures (billions of dollars)	Percentage distribution	Average annual rate of growth 1979–1989 (percent)
Health	41.5	13.4	11
Social services	67.1	21.7	10
Education	36.7	11.9	8
Transportation and communication	15.1	4.9	6
Interest on the public debt	62.7	20.2	15
All other	86.5	27.9	8.2
Total	309.6	100.0	10

Source: Statistics Canada, 68–512.

Health, social services, and debt service charges were the fastest-growing categories of government expenditure in the 1980s. The table shows combined expenditures for federal, provincial, and municipal governments. The category "All other" includes sanitation and waste removal, natural resources, general government, police and fire protection, recreation, and cultural activities.

ucation, and municipal services. In these activities, the government acts in much the same way a firm acts, using factors of production to produce outputs. By and large, these are outputs of collective consumption goods, goods with strong third-party effects, or services whose benefits are not marketable.

Public opinion polls show that the majority of Canadians support public provision of such services as basic education, hospital care, and medical care. Nonetheless, rising costs of such services are becoming a serious problem.

Transfer payments.   Recall that transfer payments are defined as payments that do not arise out of the production or sale of goods and services. They include welfare and Canada Pension Plan (CPP) payments; intergovernmental transfers, that is, transfers from one level of government to another; and by convention, they also include interest on the national debt. Transfers are also made by provincial and municipal governments. (Private transfer payments, such as private pensions and charitable contributions by individuals and corporations, are not included in Table 22-4.)

Although federal government purchases of goods and services are large ($30 billion in 1991), they have remained roughly constant in real terms since the early 1960s. They have been overtaken by transfer payments as the largest form of federal government expenditure.

Transfer payments have been steadily increasing in importance, and this has led to significant effects on both the distribution of income and the allocation of resources.

Fiscal Federalism

Canada is a federal state with governing powers divided between the central authority and the 10 provinces and three territories. Municipalities provide a third level of government, whose powers are determined by the provincial legislatures. Since revenue sources do not always match revenue needs at each level, *intergovernmental transfers* are required, as shown in Table 22-4. They allow the various func-

TABLE 22-4 **Federal and Provincial Expenditures by Type, 1992**

Type	Federal		Provincial	
	Expenditures (billions of dollars)	Percentage of total	Expenditures (billions of dollars)	Percentage of total
Purchases of goods and services	30.74	18.9	48.5	29.09
Transfers to persons	54.6	33.5	34.5	20.7
Transfers to business	5.2	3.2	7.2	4.3
Interest on the public debt	38.5	23.6	22.9	13.7
Transfers to other levels of government	32.5	19.9	52.7	31.6
Other transfers	1.3	.8	1.0	.6
Total	162.8	100	166.8	100

Source: Statistics Canada, 13–001.

Purchases of goods and services constitute less than one quarter of federal government expenditures and less than one third of provincial government expenditures. The table shows total expenditures by type for each of the federal and provincial governments. Transfer payments constitute the majority of expenditures. For the federal government, transfers to persons plus interest on the debt account for about 57 percent of its total expenditures, while transfers to governments (mostly the provinces) account for another 20 percent. For the provinces, transfers to municipalities account for 32 percent of total expenditures (excluding hospitals).

tions to be distributed among governments in a manner not dictated by revenue sources.

The Intergovernmental Activities

Our discussion in Chapter 21 of reasons for government intervention suggested a number of principles for determining the distribution of activities among levels of government.

Geographic extent of externalities. Because the government of a province or a municipality is unlikely to be responsive to the needs of citizens outside its jurisdiction, public services that involve geographic spillovers may not be provided adequately unless responsibility for them is delegated to a higher level of government. For example, national defense is normally delegated to the central government for this reason. Control of pollution is another obvious case, since contamination of air and water often literally spills over provincial and municipal boundaries. In Canada, the third-party effects in-

volved in both examples are not even confined within national boundaries, as evidenced by ongoing negotiations with the United States over control of acid rain.

At the other extreme is fire protection. If fire protection is to be effective, it is necessary that there be fire stations serving fairly small geographic areas. Accordingly, responsibility for fire stations lies with municipal governments.

Regional differences in preferences. The delegation of some functions to lower levels of government may provide a political process that is more responsive to regional differences in preferences for public versus private goods. Some people may prefer to live in communities with higher-quality schools and police protection, and they may be prepared to pay the high taxes required. Others may prefer lower taxes and lower levels of services. Another important issue at the local level is the extent to which industry should be attracted in order to broaden the property tax base; individual valuations of the social costs in terms of aesthetic or environmental effects

FIGURE 22-4
The Changing Form of Major Federal Expenditures, 1950–1992

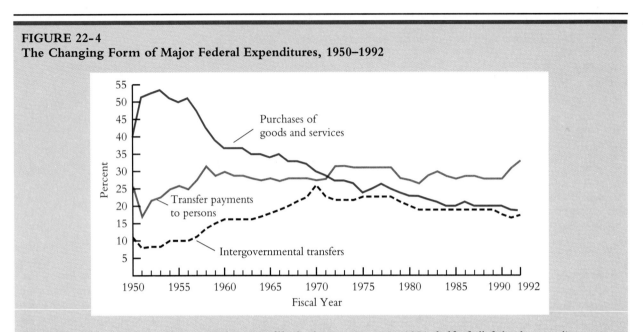

Transfer payments have been growing steadily in importance. In 1951, half of all federal expenditures were for purchases of goods and services. By 1992, the figure was less than 20 percent. Total transfer payments to persons in Canada and to provincial and municipal governments have increased from about 30 percent to over 50 percent of the total. The proportion of government expenditure going as transfers to lower levels of government reached a peak in 1972 and has fallen gradually since then. The three categories of expenditure that are shown in the figure account for over 70 percent of total federal expenditures. The largest item not shown on the figure is net interest on the federal debt. (*Source:* Statistics Canada, 11–210.)

are bound to differ, and different local governments will develop different policies in this regard.

At the provincial level, the distinct aspirations of French Canada are a primary consideration in the distribution of functions between Ottawa and the provinces. Indeed, dissatisfaction with the present arrangements, not only in Quebec but also in other provinces, has been a major political problem in Canada throughout its history.

Redistribution of income. An important activity of government is the redistribution of income by taxing the relatively well off and channeling the funds to citizens in need by means of transfer payments. Both the federal and the provincial governments actively pursue redistributive policies within their jurisdictions.

Administrative efficiency. Administrative efficiency requires that duplication of the services provided at different levels of government be minimized and that related programs be coordinated. On the revenue side, it is desirable that a particular tax be collected by only one level of government. This consideration has led to the negotiation of federal-provincial tax agreements that provide for efficient collection and revenue sharing.

Intergovernmental Transfers

In addition to the federal government and the 10 provincial governments, there are three territories, more than 4,000 municipalities, and thousands of townships in Canada. Moreover, a large number of overlapping counties or districts are responsible for such local authorities as school boards. Each of these governmental units spends public money, and each must get the money in order to spend it. Not all units have access to revenue that matches the division of responsibilities. This provides the first reason for intergovernmental transfers.

A second reason arises from the spillover effects of activities, both public and private, from one region or locality to others. If, for example, most local roads in one municipality get about 20 percent of their use from people who live outside that municipality, a provincial government grant that pays the municipality 20 percent of its road expenditures will internalize the spillover. The analysis, shown in Figure 22-5, is the same as the analysis of externalities presented in Chapter 21. In this case, however, the preferred policy is a subsidy rather than a tax, because the spillover (externality) is a beneficial one. The 20 percent subsidy reduces the marginal cost of building roads and will cause local governments to build more roads.

Another reason for intergovernmental transfers arises from the use of the federal government's *spending power.* For example, Section 36 of the Constitution Act (1982) stipulates that the federal government shares responsibility with the provinces for the pursuit of interpersonal equity. Since many of the policy instruments for addressing equity (e.g., health and education) are the responsibility of the provinces, the only way the federal government can fulfill its responsibility is to collect sufficient taxes and then transfer them to the provinces on the condition that provincial spending in the designated areas satisfy national objectives.

The transfer of funds from higher to lower levels of government has been an important aspect of the Canadian federal system since confederation. Transfers are also the focus of many of the continuing controversies surrounding federal-provincial relations.

The scope and nature of intergovernmental grants have changed dramatically over the years. Federal transfers to provincial governments expanded from $200 million in 1950 to over $24 billion in 1991, a more than 126-fold increase. This represented an increase from 6.8 percent to 19 percent of federal revenues; for the provincial governments, federal transfers as a share of their revenues increased, on average, from 20 percent to over 35 percent. The transfers occur under four basic programs: revenue sharing, equalization payments, con-

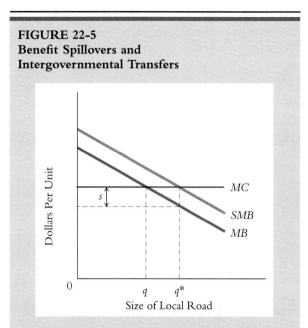

FIGURE 22-5
Benefit Spillovers and Intergovernmental Transfers

Intergovernmental transfers can internalize benefit spillovers. The figure depicts a local government's demand and cost of adding to the size of a road. The MB curve shows the marginal benefit to the residents of the locality. MC is the marginal cost of making the road larger. Left to its own devices, the municipal government will choose a road of size q, where marginal benefit equals marginal cost. This neglects the SMB curve, which adds the demands of *nonresident* users of the road to that of local users, yielding the social marginal benefit. If the provincial government offers a subsidy of s per unit of road built, the local government will choose q^*, where marginal benefit equals the marginal cost it faces, $MC - s$. If s is chosen optimally by the provincial government, this will be the size of road at which social marginal benefit equals social marginal cost.

ditional grants, and established programs financing (EPF). Whereas the revenue-sharing and equalization payments transfers are intended largely for income distribution, the conditional grants and EPF have perhaps their main impact on resource allocation. Federal payments for 1992–1993 under the variety of transfers are shown in Table 22-5.

Revenue sharing. Since the 1940s, most provinces have maintained **tax-rental arrangements**, whereby the federal government collects income

TABLE 22-5   Major Federal Transfers to Provinces 1980–1993

		Established Programs Financing			Canada Assistance Plan		
	Equalization (1)	Cash (2)	Value of Tax Points (3)	Total (4)	Cash (5)	Value of Tax Points (6)	Total (7)
			(dollars per capita) All Provinces				
1980/81	155.5	213.1	194.6	407.7	80.1	12.1	92.2
1982/83	198.1	261.8	241.6	503.3	117.1	14.1	131.2
1984/85	216.4	318.0	265.3	583.2	142.9	15.0	157.9
1986/87	228.5	343.9	315.2	659.1	160.5	17.4	177.9
1988/89	281.3	342.6	378.7	721.3	178.8	20.2	198.9
1990/91	303.6	330.1	427.9	758.0	206.9	23.9	230.8
1992/93	307.3	294.2	458.0	752.2	232.8	25.3	258.1

Source: A Partnership in Trouble, C. D. Howe Institute.

Per capita federal grants to provinces to finance established programs have been declining in nominal dollar terms since 1988–1989. The major federal transfers for program assistance, mainly for education and health, now come from transfers of tax revenues rather than cash grants. Equalization, although now capped, grew slightly through 1992–1993. Both cash and tax transfers for the Canada Assistance Plan continue to grow.

taxes and makes a per capita payment to the provinces for that right. In 1993, with the exception of the Quebec personal income tax and the Ontario and Quebec corporate levies, all income taxes in Canada were collected by the federal government.

Federal income tax rates are set at levels that allow substantial "tax room" to the provinces. Outside Quebec, the provincial income tax is calculated as a percentage of the federal tax payable at rates determined by the individual provinces. A similar arrangement applies to the corporate income tax. The effect of these measures is shown in Table 22-5 under the heading "value of tax points."

Equalization payments. With the object of ensuring that citizens in all regions of the country have access to a reasonable level of public services, **equalization payments** are made out of federal government general revenues to provinces with below-average tax capacity. It is important to note that this is not a revenue-sharing program (provinces with above-average tax capacity do not pay

in), nor is it a conditional grant program. These grants are calculated by a complicated formula that involves, at last count, 29 revenue sources.

Equalization payments are a relatively new phenomenon in Canada, but they have exhibited rapid growth. From their inception with the 1957 Tax-Sharing Act to the time of the 1977 Fiscal Arrangements Act, they expanded from $130 million to $2.2 billion. Table 22-5 shows that equalization payments for 1992–1993 were $600 per person, making a total of over $16 billion.

Canada Assistance Plan (CAP). Under this plan, the Federal government pays half the costs of meeting the basic needs of those persons lacking an adequate income from other sources, as well as half the associated administrative costs. Uniformity of provincial programs is not a requirement. The provinces design and administer their own programs but then only need to meet half the cost themselves. These programs also cover road building, vocational schools, and assistance to needy old people, the disabled, and unemployed persons not eligible for unemployment insurance. In addition, extensive regional development plans have been financed under such sharing agreements, including the building of transportation facilities and other infrastructure, subsidies modernization grants, the relocation of rural populations, and technical assistance.

In the view of Queen's University political economist Peter Leslie:

> The effects of cost sharing have been far-reaching. Without it Canada could not have established a welfare state such as now exists. Cost sharing has, however, infringed on regional provincial autonomy [in major ways].[6]

Established programs financing (EPF). The 1977 Fiscal Arrangements Act placed on a new basis federal financing of three major programs previously treated as conditional grants: hospital insurance, medicare, and postsecondary education. They are referred to as established programs to indicate that their existence is not conditional on federal involvement. Because federal contributions are independent of the costs of the programs, the federal government can control its own contribution. The provinces have gained, for they need not now be confined by narrowly defined federal program conditions.

National standards. Although people often talk as if the federal provincial transfers established national standards, neither the CAP nor the EPF actually set such standards. Support levels under the CAP vary widely across provinces. No conditions whatsoever are set in relation to the transfers linked to postsecondary education. In health care, the only national standards are general principles such as portability among provinces and universality. No federal authority can complain about an alleged inadequacy in some province's health care system. The only rule is that whatever is provided by a province should be universally available within that province.

Cutbacks

Since the mid-1970s, the federal budget has been in chronic deficit. By the mid-1980s, the deficit had

reached the $30 billion mark and was projected to rise even further. In that atmosphere of fiscal concern, the federal government began to look for every possible avenue of expenditure reduction. Not surprisingly, the intergovernmental transfer system came under close scrutiny.

Cutbacks affected all major areas of the system. A ceiling was placed on equalization payments so that they could not grow faster than the GDP. In 1987, the ceiling began to have an effect, reducing equalization payments by about $3 billion from what they otherwise would have been over the next three years.

The EFP programs were first capped in 1983. The growth in transfers (cash plus tax points) under this heading were reduced successively from the rate of GDP growth to GDP growth minus first one, then two, then three percentage points. Finally in 1989–1990, they were fixed in money terms. Since tax-point transfers continue to grow with the GDP, it is estimated that the cash payment component will be phased out completely within this decade.

The CAP was also capped. Since 1990, the rule has been that payments under the CAP to provinces not receiving equalization grants cannot increase by more than 5 percent per year. This was a particularly severe blow to Ontario, which lost $1.1 billion in fiscal year 1991–1992 alone. In 1992–1993, CAP transfers covered a little less than 30 percent of Ontario's expenditures under the CAP programs, whereas the relevant figure was 50 percent as recently as 1989–1990.

In Peter Leslie's words:

> It is quite clear that the present pattern of fiscal arrangements cannot be sustained for long. They are already set to self-destruct. The problem is most obvious in the case of EPF. As the federal government's cash contribution to health care and postsecondary education dwindles, its ability to exercise any policy influence in these areas will also disappear. Opinions on the subject will vary on whether the removal is desirable or not. However, there is no doubt that when it happens—as it will if EPF is allowed to phase itself out—a major feature of Canadian federalism will be phased out with it.[7]

---

[6] Peter M. Leslie, "The Fiscal Crisis of Canadian Federalism," in *A Partnership in Trouble*, C.D. Howe Institute (Toronto: Howe Institute, 1993), p. 26.

[7] Leslie, "Crisis of Federalism," pp. 48–49

Public Expenditure and the Distribution of Income

As Table 22-1 indicates, the federal government raises most of its revenues by income-related taxes. When these federal receipts are transferred back to individuals or to provincial and municipal governments, they have a substantial redistributive effect.

Federal Transfer Payments to Individuals

Transfers to individuals are classified according to four types: demogrants, guaranteed income, social insurance, and social assistance. Old-age security and family allowance payments are in the first group, which includes payments to all persons who meet some minimum requirement such as age or residency; guaranteed income supplements and child tax credits are examples of the second; the Canada Pension Plan and unemployment insurance are examples of the third; and the fourth includes special programs for widows, single parents, and others who have no recourse to other support programs.

Transfers to individuals by the federal government have grown as a proportion of expenditures from about 15 percent in 1930 to about 28 percent by the early 1990s. These transfers are often intended as a form of insurance or as an incentive for individuals to redirect expenditures toward specific items such as housing or health. Many of them are part of income maintenance programs. The net effect of the transfers is to reduce inequality in the distribution of income.[8] The percentage of all personal income received in the form of government transfer payments has increased sharply, from about 9 percent in 1965 to more than 14 percent in 1991.

Though some transfer payments go to people with above-average incomes, most do not.

---

[8]The relative importance of the federal government in making transfers to individuals has been declining since the early 1960s, and that of the provinces has been increasing.

Transfer payments have thus tended to reduce the inequality of the distribution of income.

The Overall Redistributive Effects of Public Expenditures

Since the tax system tends to be roughly proportional in its effect, the overall progressivity of government policies depends on the progressivity of government expenditures. The large and growing role of transfer payments probably assured that starting in the mid-1950s there was some substantial net redistribution of income from high- and middle-income groups to the less well off. But such redistribution has never been massive.

Why does government expenditure not have a bigger effect on income distribution? One view is that government programs overall are less progressive than observers once thought, because some undoubtedly progressive programs are offset by others that are regressive. Another view is that market forces exert steady pressure toward more inequality, which government programs merely offset.

Most economists agree that there is a limit to how much inequality can be eliminated. There is controversy as to how close we are to that limit. And beyond that, there is controversy as to how close it is desirable to get to as much equality as possible, both on ethical grounds of justice and economic grounds of incentives.

Public Expenditure and the Allocation of Resources

Total government expenditures on goods and services increased almost 75-fold over the period 1950-1990, indicating a near doubling in the ratio of government expenditures to total goods and services produced in the economy, from 22 percent to over 45 percent. In the period since 1960, increases in expenditures have been largest in such areas of provincial and municipal responsibility as health and education. As a result, the federal share of total government expenditures has been falling and that of provincial and municipal governments has been rising. For example, the ratio of federal to provincial government spending on goods and services was about 1.7 in 1950; it has fallen steadily ever since, so that by 1991 it was about 0.68, less than half the 1950 value. An even more dramatic picture of the increased decentralization that has occurred is seen by looking at the revenue side: The tax revenue of the federal government is now about equal to that of the provincial governments; in 1950 it was triple!

Two reasons for the changing distribution of government size deserve to be mentioned.

Rising demand for local government services. The services provided by cities have a high income elasticity of demand. As societies become wealthier, their residents want more parks, more police protection, more and better schools and universities, and more generous treatment of their less fortunate neighbors.

Rising relative cost of municipal government services. While average output per hour of work in manufacturing has risen about 50 percent in a decade, the size of the beat covered by a police officer, the number of students taught by each school teacher, the number of families that can be effectively handled by a social worker, or the number of temperatures that can be taken by one hospital nurse have not risen in proportion. Because wage levels tend to rise with national average productivity, the unit costs of services in these public-sector occupations with low productivity growth have risen. The increased demand for government services due to rising national income combined with rising unit costs has put great pressure on governments' fiscal capacity.

Evaluating the Role of Government

Almost everyone would agree that the government has a major role to play in the economy because of the many sources of possible market failure. Yet there is no consensus that the present level and role of government intervention is about right.

Allocation between the public and private sectors. When the government raises money by taxation and spends it on an activity, it increases the spending of the public sector and decreases that of the private sector. Since the public sector and the private sector spend on different things, the government is changing the allocation of resources. Is that good or bad? How do we know if the country has the right balance between the public and private sectors? Should there be more schools and fewer houses or more houses and fewer schools?

For all goods that are produced and sold on the market, the consumer demand has a significant influence on the relative prices and quantities produced and thus on the allocation of the nation's resources. But no market provides relative prices for private houses versus public schools; thus, the choice between allowing money to be spent in the private sector and allowing it to be spent for public goods is a matter to be decided by Parliament and other legislative bodies.

John Kenneth Galbraith's bestseller *The Affluent Society* proclaimed that a correct assignment of marginal utilities would show them to be higher for an extra dollar's worth of expenditure on parks, clean water, and education than for an extra dollar's worth of expenditure on television sets and deodorants. In this view, the political process often fails to translate preferences for public goods into effective action; thus, more resources are devoted to the private sector and fewer to the public sector than would be the case if the political mechanism were as effective as the market.

The alternative view has many supporters, who agree with Professor James Buchanan that society already has gone beyond the point where the value of the marginal dollar spent by government is greater than the value of that dollar left in the hands of households or firms that would have spent it had it not been taxed away. These people argue that because bureaucrats are spending other people's money, they don't care very much about a few million or billion dollars here or there. They have only a weak sense of the opportunity cost of public expenditure and, thus, tend to spend beyond the point where marginal benefits equal marginal costs.

Scope of government activity. One of the most difficult problems for the student of the Canadian economic system is to maintain perspective about the scope of government activity in the market economy. On the one hand, there are literally tens of thousands of laws, regulations, and policies that affect firms and households. Many people believe that significant additional deregulation would be possible and beneficial.

On the other hand, private decision makers still have an enormous amount of discretion about what they do and how they do it. One pitfall is to become so impressed (or obsessed) with the many ways in which government activity impinges on the individual that one fails to see that these only make changes—sometimes large, but often small—in market signals in a system that basically leaves individuals free to make their own decisions. It is in the private sector that most individuals choose their occupations, earn their living, spend their incomes, and live their lives. In this sector too, firms are formed, choose products, live, grow, and sometimes die.

Costs and benefits. A different pitfall is to fail to see that some (perhaps most) of the amounts paid by the private sector to the government as taxes also buy goods and services that add to the welfare of individuals. By and large, the public sector complements the private sector, doing things the private sector would leave undone or would do differently. To recognise this is not to deny that there is often waste, and sometimes worse, in public expenditure.

Yet another pitfall is failing to recognise that the public and private sectors compete in the sense that both make claims on the resources of the economy. Government activities are not without opportunity costs, except in those rare circumstances in which they use resources that have no alternative use.

Equity and efficiency. A related pitfall is to believe that the government's alleged inability to improve efficiency also implies an inability to improve equity. Throughout the world, governments are placing more reliance on markets in order to im-

prove economic efficiency and prospects for growth. Accepting the market for efficiency reasons does not, however, require accepting an increase in the hardships borne by the poor. Promoting social justice through government interventions directed at equity is compatible with promoting efficiency, provided that appropriate means are carefully chosen.

Evolution of policy. Public policies in operation at any time are not the result of a single master plan that specifies precisely where and how the public sector shall seek to complement or interfere with the workings of the market mechanism. Rather, as individual problems arise, governments attempt to meet them by passing ameliorative legislation. These laws stay on the books, and some become obsolete and unenforceable. This is true of systems of law in general.

Many anomalies exist in our economic policies; for example, laws designed to support the incomes of small farmers have created some agricultural millionaires, and commissions created to ensure competition often end up creating and protecting monopolies. Neither individual policies nor whole programs are above criticism.

In a society that elects its policy makers at regular intervals, however, the majority view on the amount and type of government interference that is desirable will have some considerable influence on the interference that actually occurs. Fundamentally, a free-market system is retained because it is valued for its lack of coercion and its ability to do much of the allocating of society's resources better than any known alternative. But we are not mesmerized by it; we feel free to intervene in pursuit of a better world in which to live. We also recognise, however, that sometimes intervention has proved ineffective or even counterproductive.

SUMMARY

1. Although the main purpose of the tax system is to raise revenue, tax policy is potentially a powerful device for income redistribution because the progressivity of different kinds of taxes varies greatly. Personal income tax rates have traditionally been highly progressive, but their effect on progressivity is reduced by other provisions of the tax law. Sales and excise taxes are usually mildly regressive. The regressivity of the GST was removed at lower income levels by refundable tax credits.

2. Tax expenditures are provisions in the tax law that provide favourable tax treatment for certain economic behaviour. Tax ex-

penditures in the income tax reduce the progressivity of the tax system.

3. Evaluating the tax system involves evaluating the efficiency and progressivity of the entire system. For a given amount of revenue to be raised, efficiency and progressivity can be altered by changing the mix of the various taxes used. The total Canadian tax structure is roughly proportional, except for very low- and very high-income groups (where it is mildly progressive). The 1987 tax reforms increased progressivity at low income levels but reduced it at high income levels. Subsequent changes have increased it at the high income level.

4. Evaluating the effects of taxes on resource allocation requires determining tax incidence, that is, determining who really pays the taxes. For most taxes, the incidence is shared. Excise taxes, for example, affect prices and are thus partly passed on to consumers and partly absorbed by producers. The actual incidence depends on such considerations as demand and supply elasticities.

5. A large part of public expenditure is for the provision of goods and services. Other types of expenditures, including subsidies, transfer payments to individuals, and intergovernmental transfers, rose sharply from the 1950s through the 1980s. The four major types of federal-provincial transfers are revenue sharing, equalization payments, conditional grants, and established program financing.

6. The major redistributive activities of the federal government take the form of direct transfer payments to individuals and to provincial and municipal governments for economic welfare payments and regional adjustments. Although the public sector has a tendency to redistribute some income from high- and middle-income groups to the poor, the change in income inequality from decade to decade has been relatively small.

7. Government expenditure of all kinds has a major effect on the allocation of resources. The government determines how much of our total output is devoted to such things as national defence, education, highways, and health care.

8. Intergovernmental transfers that are a response to regional income inequalities affect the allocation of resources.

9. Evaluating public expenditures involves reaching decisions about the absolute merit of government programs (do benefits exceed costs?) and about the relative merit of public and private expenditures.

TOPICS FOR REVIEW

Tax expenditures

Progressive, proportional, and regressive taxes

Vertical and horizontal equity

Tax incidence

Transfer payments to individuals

Intergovernmental transfers

Choosing between private and public expenditures

DISCUSSION QUESTIONS

1. The Canadian taxpayer faces dozens of different taxes with different incidences, different progressivities, and different methods of collection. Discuss the case for and against a single taxing authority that would share the revenue with all levels of government. Why don't governments use a single tax source with the desired amount of progressivity built into it?

2. Consider a change in the tax law that lowers every taxpayer's marginal tax rate, with the maximum rate dropping from 50 percent to 33 percent, but with an increase in the tax base that leaves total tax revenue unchanged.
   a. Is it possible that everyone's average tax *rate* will fall?
   b. Is it possible that everyone's tax *bill* will fall?
   c. Suppose that contributions to universities and colleges are tax deductible under the original tax law but not under the revised one. Would you predict that such contributions would increase, decrease, or remain the same?
   d. If such contributions are fully deductible under both the original and revised tax laws, would the amount of such contributions be expected to increase, decrease, or remain the same?
   e. Consider now taxpayers whose marginal tax rate falls from 50 percent to 33 percent *and* whose tax bills are less after the revision. Repeat the question in *d*.

3. How might each of the following affect the incidence of a real estate property tax imposed on central-city rental property?
   a. The residents of the community are new immigrants who face racial discrimination in neighboring areas.
   b. The city installs a good, cheap, rapid transit system that makes commuting to the suburbs less expensive and more comfortable.
   c. Rent control is imposed; no rent presently being charged may be increased.

4. In reaction to the Conservative government's 1987 conversion of the basic personal exemption and some deductions to tax credits, the *Toronto Star* ran a column, under the sensational headline "Sneaking Some Socialism Through the Back Door," that argued that the proposed changes would "replace measures which allow the rich to shield their income with provisions that raise the income level of the poor." How would the measures proposed accomplish this?

5. In Canada, each individual has a lifetime $100,000 exemption for capital gains income, and subsequent capital gains are taxed at three-quarters the rates applicable to other income. Who benefits from this provision? What are its effects on the distribution of income and the allocation of resources? Should capital gains be treated as income for tax purposes? Should they be taxed at all?

6. "Taxes on tobacco and alcohol are nearly perfect taxes. They raise lots of revenue and discourage smoking and drinking." In this statement, to what extent are the two effects inconsistent? How is the incidence of an excise tax related to the extent to which it discourages use of the product?

7. Suppose that it is agreed to spend $1 billion in programs to provide the poor with housing, better clothing, more food, and better health services.

   a. Argue the case for and against assistance of this kind rather than giving the money to the poor to spend as they think best.

   b. Should federal transfers to the provinces be conditional grants or grants with no strings attached? Is this the same issue raised in a or is it a different one?

8. Develop the case for and against having the federal government (rather than provincial and municipal governments) provide each of the following:

   a. Police protection.
   b. Teachers' salaries.
   c. Highways.
   d. Welfare payments to the poor.

9. Medical and health costs were 4.5 percent of GDP in 1950 and over 10 percent in 1993. Is 10 percent necessarily too much? Is it necessarily a sign that we are providing better health care? How might an economist think about what is the right percentage of GDP to devote to medical care?

23

Canadian Social Policy

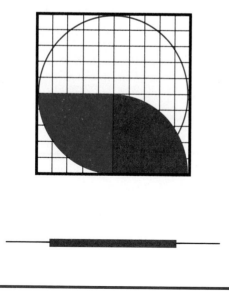

Controversies over Canada's social programs have been major news items in recent years. Canadian governments have been urged to reexamine and redesign these programs with the twin objectives of improving the benefits delivered to the intended beneficiaries and reducing costs wherever possible. The relevant concept of cost is *social cost,* encountered in Chapter 21, which is broader than just the direct cost of financing the programs.

Given the concern over the federal budget deficit that has—counting from 1993—exceeded $25 billion per year for each year of the last decade $30 billion in most and $40 billion in 1993–1994, it is natural that such a large category of spending should come under scrutiny. Assessing program effectiveness and evaluating proposals for reform of Canada's social policies are not, however, simple matters. One-line evaluations, such as "Nothing needs to be changed" or "The whole system needs to be swept away," are too simplistic but all too common. In this chapter, we review some of the issues in the debate over Canada's social programs, arguing the need for a careful approach to reforming it.

Canada's Social Programs in Perspective

Spending by all levels of government on social programs has grown as a share of national income from just over 20 percent in 1950 to about 32 percent in 1993. In addition, there has been a steady increase in the relative importance of spending by the provincial governments; their spending has grown from just over 5 percent in 1950 to about 25 percent in 1993.

The Variety of Social Programs

Some social programs are *universal*, in the sense that they pay benefits to anyone meeting only such minimal requirements as age or residence. These are called **demogrants**. Other programs are selective, in the sense that they pay benefits only to people who qualify by meeting specific conditions. These conditions are usually related to income, in which case the term **income-tested** (or **income-related**) **benefits** is used. Some benefits are taxable, so net after-tax receipts decline as income rises; others are not taxable, so net receipts are independent of income. Some are expenditure programs (including direct transfers to persons), while others are delivered through the tax system in the form of special tax concessions called *tax expenditures*. Some programs are administered by the federal government, some by the provincial governments, and still others by the municipalities.

Table 23-1 gives a breakdown of the more than $63 billion spent by the federal government on all social programs in 1990-1991. The table shows both the division of the $63 billion total into direct spending and tax expenditures as well as the allocation of federal spending across six main categories of social programs.

Fiscal, Economic, and Demographic Setting

Three major challenges must be met by any Canadian social spending policy that is to succeed in future decades. These are the challenges posed by government deficits, technological changes, and demographic trends.[1]

The fiscal challenge. The fiscal challenge to social programs is a serious one. With the federal deficit running at over $40 billion in 1993, and with $50 billion, or 48 percent of total federal program expenditures, being spent each year on social programs and another $14 billion annually in tax expenditures, it is inevitable that social programs be reviewed carefully.

Fiscal constraints are also severe at the provincial level. Health care expenditures alone account for over 30 percent of total provincial expenditures and are rising. In 1993, all of the 10 provinces, some more economically depressed than others, were running budget deficits.

Anyone who would leave social spending untouched while still seeking to reduce the deficit substantially must look to tax increases. However, many critics hold that it would be hard for Canada to increase its already-high tax rates significantly without creating pressures on firms and higher-income individuals to move to the United States.

The need to reduce budget deficits and the desire to avoid tax increases create pressure to

[1] We have adopted this trilogy, and much of the discussion, from T. J. Courchene, *Social Policy in the 1990s: Agenda for Reform* (Toronto: C. D. Howe Institute, 1987). An update appears in Courchene's chapter on social policy in *Getting It Right* (Toronto: C. D. Howe Institute, 1991).

TABLE 23-1 Federal Spending on Social Programs in 1990-1991
(estimated in billions of dollars)

	Direct spending	Tax expenditures[a]	Total
Child benefits	2.7	1.7	4.4
Elderly benefits	17.0	−0.5	16.5
Income security			
Unemployment insurance	12.7	−2.0	10.7
Canada Assistance Plan	4.8	—	4.8
Registered savings plans[b]	—	6.5	6.5
Human resources	5.0	3.0	8.0
Health care	7.0	5.5	12.5
Totals	49.2	14.2	63.4

Sources: Treasury Board and Department of Finance.

[a] Includes federal component only. The provinces also collect revenues on such programs as family allowance, old age security, and unemployment insurance and contribute tax revenues forgone for others, including child and elderly tax credits and registered savings plans.

[b] Registered Retirement Savings Plans and registered pension plans.

Of the more than $63 billion spent on social programs by the federal government in 1990-1991, nearly 80 percent came from direct spending and 20 percent was delivered through the tax system. Child and elderly benefits, each of which include both demogrant and income-tested components, accounted for over $20 billion of the total. Three key programs—unemployment insurance, the Canada Assistance Plan (provincially administered welfare programs), and registered savings plans—accounted for about $22 billion. Human resource development—including contributions to postsecondary education and to labour market schemes—amounted to about $8 billion, and transfers to the provinces for health care accounted for more than $12 billion.

reform social policy to meet its objectives at lower cost.

The adjustment challenge. Many recent studies of the Canadian economy, including those done by the Macdonald Royal Commission, have stressed the fierce competition and the rapid change that characterize today's international trading world.

To improve or even maintain living standards in a competitive and changing world, coun-

tries need to adjust continuously to changing market conditions.

This is especially true for small countries such as Canada that are heavily dependent on international trade. As Queens University economist, Thomas Courchene, puts it:

> The challenge to social policy is twofold: first, to ensure that the incentives within the social policy network will encourage, rather than inhibit, the required adjustment on the economic front; second, to ensure that the social safety net evolves in a manner that reflects the changing needs of citizens as they adapt to the new economic order.

For example, if the economic system requires that people change jobs more frequently than in the past, it is important that pensions be fully portable (that is, that workers be able to take their pension rights with them when they change jobs).

The demographic challenge. Important demographic developments that are already under way imply that social policies designed for the 1960s will not always be well suited to the needs of the 1990s and subsequent decades. Consider just a few of these developments:

1. An increasingly aging population is putting stresses on the health system. Expenditure on health care is large and growing; demographic trends suggest that this growth will continue, and possibly even accelerate, unless changes are made in the current system.
2. The increasingly aging population will also put stress on the pension system. Although the federal government is currently taking in more in pension contributions than it is paying out as benefits, the situation will reverse before the end of the century, after which time the excess of benefits paid over contributions received will grow steadily.
3. A rise in single-parent families, particularly those with women at their head, is causing an increase in the number of working poor whose needs are different from those of the unemployed or the unemployable poor.
4. The rise in two-worker households brings a demand for expanded day-care facilities.

5. Many workers are finding that after 20 or 30 years of working in the same job, their skills become obsolete. Retraining facilities and organized assistance in finding new jobs are needed if such workers are to remain gainfully employed. Otherwise, they face a decade or more of unemployment before they reach normal retirement age.

The Federal-Provincial Perspective

Canada's constitution originally granted all authority in social policy to the provinces. As social policy became increasingly important, agreements between the two levels of government gave the federal government responsibility for a large amount of social spending. In some cases, this involves direct federal spending, as with the old age security and family allowance programs, and in other cases it involves transferring funds to the provincial governments. (The latter were discussed in Chapter 22.) Some federal payments to provinces are then distributed directly to persons; this is the case with the federal government's Canada Assistance Plan, which is used by the provinces to finance their own welfare programs. Other payments, such as those related to health and postsecondary education, are used by the provinces to finance various expenditures.

Although we focus on federal programs in most of this chapter, a number of reasons why the provinces are important players in determining the cost and effectiveness of Canadian social policy warrant mention.

First, as we have already observed, a large amount of federal spending is in the form of transfer payments to the provinces. Though some transfer payments are nominally earmarked for specific purposes (in particular, postsecondary education and health), the provinces are not required to match their spending changes in these areas to changes in federal transfers received. In recent years, growth in provincial spending in these areas, particularly education, has often been less than the growth in transfers from the federal government. Hence, to analyse the efficacy of social programs in these areas, it is not sufficient to focus only on federal transfers. Further, since each province allocates over 60 percent of its spending to social policy, any dramatic change in provincial spending would also represent a significant change in total national spending.

Second, Canada's regional pressures play a major role in shaping federal-provincial fiscal relations. Equalization payments, discussed in Chapter 22, are relevant here. Although they are not considered part of federal social spending, they are a transfer to the provinces whose explicit purpose is to compensate for any shortfall in the fiscal capacity of the relatively poorer provinces to provide a minimum level of government services, primarily social services.

Third, under intense pressure to reduce its budget deficit, the Federal government has been capping, and sometimes even reducing, its transfers to the provinces. The extent of these changes is such that the whole concept of fiscal federalism is threatened. Fiscal federalism was a particularly Canadian vision in which the federal government tried to ensure national standards in areas such as health care for which the provinces had authority. The basic idea was that the federal government contributed a major part of the costs of such programs and used its financial involvement as leverage to ensure common standards. As the Federal contributions are reduced, provincial autonomy is increased. Some see this as a major loss of national commonality, others as a gain in encouraging experimentation.[2]

Finally, since the multitude of federal and provincial social programs overlap in their effects, any program change made by one level of government will have one effect if it is offset by the other level and another effect if it is not offset. For example, when in its May 1985 budget the federal government enriched the child tax credit to increase the after-tax income of very poor families with children, a number of provinces reacted by cutting back on their welfare programs. In those provinces, benefits delivered to the poor were not changed in aggregate, but the burden of financing those benefits was shifted to the federal government, and the distribution of benefits was shifted from families without children to those with children.

Experiences such as this illustrate an important point:

Effective reform of Canadian social policy requires changes that are coordinated and sweeping, not piecemeal. The inherent difficulties of such coordination are aggravated by Canada's adversarial political system and by the never easy and often stormy nature of federal-provincial relations in Canada.

We first wrote the above color passage in 1987, and events since then only serve to underline its message: Every independent body that has studied Canadian social policy has called for major reforms to allow the system to continue to do its job at a cost the tax system can bear; every attempt at reform by the federal government has met with strong resistance from the opposition parties and the provinces.

Issues in Assessing Social Programs

The complex array of Canadian social programs raises several issues that must be addressed before the impact of social policies can be analysed or proposals for their reform assessed.

Policy Interactions

Interactions between schemes are important not only at the federal-provincial level but also within one level of government. For example, the unemployment insurance program clearly interacts with federal job creation and job training programs as well as with other social programs designed to direct resources to needy families and regions.

For a meaningful analysis of the current state of any social program and proposed changes in it, the program must be viewed in the context of the overall system.

Policy Objectives

Given the wide array of programs, each directed at a narrow goal but each interacting with other programs, policy objectives must be clearly understood if policies are to be evaluated intelligently.

Policy evaluation usually involves tradeoffs among objectives.

The need for normative judgements. One major objective of most social policies is to redistribute income away from people least in need toward those

---

[2]This issue is discussed in much more detail in Chapter 37 on government deficits.

most in need. Evaluating need requires making value judgements, which are expressed in the political rather than the economic arena.

Vertical and horizontal equity. As noted in Chapter 22, *vertical equity* concerns equity across income classes, and *horizontal equity* concerns equity within a given income class.

Distribution versus efficiency. A major issue in the design of social policy is the potential conflict between achieving some desired distribution of income and ensuring that the economy operates efficiently so as to produce the maximum possible total income.

When a person who receives income-tested benefits earns enough income to have the benefits reduced, there is an implicit tax-back rate on that income, because the person's disposable income increases by less than the newly earned income. For example, consider a person earning no income and receiving income-tested benefits of $8,000 who takes a part-time job paying $2,000 on which no income tax is payable. However, if her income-tested benefits are reduced by $1,000 as a result of taking the job, her implicit tax rate is 50 percent. If a second person in the same situation has his income-tested benefits reduced by $2,000, he faces an implicit tax rate of 100 percent!

When people pay income taxes and also receive income-tested social benefits, the explicit income tax rate on their income and the implicit tax-back rate on their benefits are said to be *stacked,* and the combined rate is called the effective marginal tax rate. For example, if a person earns an extra dollar and pays 25 cents in income tax while having her benefits reduced by 30 cents, her effective marginal tax rate is 55 percent.

Because of the high tax-back rates that apply to many income-tested benefits, many beneficiaries face very high effective marginal tax rates, even 100 percent or greater! It should come as no surprise that beneficiaries may reject the opportunity to work when their net income would be no more, or even *less,* than their net income when they choose not to work but receive full benefits.

Some of the most serious efficiency effects of the tax and transfer system follow from its creation of high effective marginal tax rates that discourage beneficiaries from actions that would improve the performance of the economy and increase their own self-reliance.

In a background study for the Quebec White Paper of 1984, Bernard Fortin and Henri-Paul Rousseau of Laval University estimated that the average *efficiency cost* of Quebec's tax and transfer system was 27 cents per dollar. This means that, on average, for every dollar of tax revenue raised by the government, 27 cents was lost due to efficiency costs associated with the distortion of incentives by the tax system. More important, they estimated that the marginal *social cost* of the tax and transfer system was 56 cents. This means that for each additional dollar raised from a proportional increase in Quebec taxes, the private sector lost $1.56 in income. Even though the generosity of Quebec's social programs means that their estimates probably overstate the case for Canada as a whole, these calculations show that the economic costs of Canada's social programs are far from trivial. This conclusion is reinforced when we note that the study did not include the direct costs of raising tax revenues, enforcing tax laws, or distributing social benefits.

The social costs arising from disincentives in the tax and transfer system hurt everyone in the economy, including the people the social programs are designed to help.

Open-economy considerations. In a small open economy such as Canada's, a further efficiency issue relates to the international mobility of labour and capital. The issue can be seen by considering a more extreme case that applied for many years in the United Kingdom. In the 1960s and 1970s, marginal rates of income tax, running over 80 percent, encouraged a brain drain of successful people leaving the United Kingdom for lower-tax countries such as the United States. If these high-income earners had remained at home under a regime of, say, 40 to 45 percent maximum income tax rates, then for any given level of tax-financed spending, lower-income persons would have to pay less taxes than when the high-income earners had emigrated.

Similar considerations apply to capital. Is it better to have firms located in one's own country paying 30 or 40 percent income tax or located abroad in order to avoid an 80 percent domestic tax rate and thus paying no domestic taxes? Egalitarianism may argue for the high rates, but the loss of revenue and other benefits from the location of industry at home must be set against any perceived gain in equity. An example of the mobility of capital was provided in the 1980s when the National Energy Policy made foreign oil companies unwelcome in Canada. Within a matter of months, oil exploration companies, many of which were Canadian, packed up their mobile drilling rigs and left Canada for what they saw as more profitable opportunities south of the border.

If Canada lets its rates of taxes and benefits get seriously out of line with those in the United States, it risks suffering a significant brain and capital drain to that country. Thus there are always substantial "harmonization pressures" between Canadian and American policies.

Of course, Canadian policies need not be identical to those in the United States, but if they get out of line in a way that labour and capital regard as undesirable, there is a risk of inducing an emigration of factors that will harm the Canadian economy. Note that these harmonization pressures depend on the international mobility of factors of production, not on the level of tariffs.

Security versus adjustment. An important goal of social policies is to provide a safety net to cushion economic shocks. It is possible to cushion people against shocks without inhibiting adjustment; retraining and relocation grants are examples. It is also possible to cushion them in ways that inhibit adjustment; shoring up declining industries and providing government jobs for declining occupations are examples.

Many economists argue that in today's fiercely competitive world, assistance should be provided to those most hurt by economic shocks but that the assistance should encourage rather than inhibit adaptation.

It is not always easy to stick to this general principle. Many specific interventions that were designed to increase security have reduced adaptability. It is important that such antiadjustment assistance mech-

anisms not be built into the statutory part of the social system.

Intergenerational issues. Many social programs are targeted at retired persons, the older of whom started their working lives during the Great Depression of the early 1930s. There were few pensions then, and saving was difficult, given the prevailing low incomes. Thus, the older segment of those above retirement age tend on average to be low-income persons, and transfers from younger to older citizens reduce income inequalities.

Of course, many of those who were poor when young will remain poor when they are old, but many of those now entering the senior citizens' category are not poor. Because of the high incomes that were earned during the last half of the twentieth century and the generous pension plans that have been established, those now retiring are on average quite well off. Furthermore, the population is slowly aging, and in the early part of the twenty-first century the proportion of the population that is elderly will be much higher than it is today. These considerations suggest the following conclusion:

On grounds of equity and fiscal capacity, help for the elderly needs to be more focused on lower-income groups than it is at present.

We return to this issue later in the chapter.

Universality

Controversy has raged over the universality of Canada's social policies. Supporters feel that many of the programs should be available to all Canadians regardless of their incomes or other circumstances. This is the concept of universality. Critics argue that programs should be made more selective, targeted toward people in real need, as the best way of preserving the high standard of the Canadian system at an affordable cost.

In the 1930s, the idea of universality came to be accepted as the best way of providing security. Generalizing from the experience of the 1930s, economic risks were assumed to be felt by everyone. The need was for mass and guaranteed protection rather than for conditional systems that produced benefits at the whim of the granting body. What was required was a *right* to social security for every citizen.

Universality was also thought to protect against politically motivated tampering. It was argued that if everyone benefited, there would be a powerful constituency to protect the system should any future politician try to dismantle it. A selective system targeted at the poor would be much more vulnerable to such an attack, since the poor have a weaker political voice than the middle class. The importance of this consideration can be seen in the political ease with which American President Ronald Reagan dismantled much of the American antipoverty program in the 1980s—a program directed solely at the poor. The contrast with the outcry when the Canadian Conservative government tried to tamper even slightly with the universal old age pension scheme is striking.

These reasons for universality suggest that this aspect is not likely to be dropped from many of Canada's social welfare schemes. Greater targeting and cost effectiveness are likely to be obtained, however, by ensuring that more of the benefits are taxable, by making greater use of tax credits instead of tax deductions, and by a fuller integration of the tax and transfer system so as to avoid stacking and associated disincentives.

An Outline of Selected Programs

Now we shall look in some detail at the various elements of Canada's existing social programs and at some suggestions for reform.

Human Resource Development Programs

A survey recently published by the Canadian Labour Market and Productivity Centre showed that Canadian business and labour leaders regard the top priority for improving Canada's international competitiveness as training and education. This was ranked above all other factors, including lower in-terest rates, lower government deficit, and increased spending on research and development. Thomas Courchene adds that education and skills development are also key to understanding economic inequality *within* Canada.

Public education, one of the earliest types of social expenditure in Canada, remains one of the most important. It has been supplemented over the years by numerous other programs aimed at developing human resources.

Basic Education

Primary and secondary schools teach literacy and numeracy. These basic skills are needed in order to acquire further marketable skills. Canada has one of the world's highest per capita expenditures on basic education, yet Canadian students do relatively poorly on international comparisons that use standardized tests. Studies show that many Canadian adults (some estimates say as many as one quarter) are functional illiterates—people who cannot comprehend simple written instructions well enough to carry them out. One educational target should be to reduce illiteracy and innumeracy, deficiencies that are lifetime handicaps.

Basic education is supplemented by further education and training. This occurs in postsecondary institutions, technical schools, and universities, as well as in the workplace. At the beginning of the decade, the federal government operated about a dozen nonuniversity job creation and training schemes, enrolling nearly half a million people and costing nearly $2 billion. Although few doubt that these schemes are of great value, the critics have noted many deficiencies in the programs and recommended major changes.

Postsecondary Education

Postsecondary education is a provincial responsibility in Canada. As a result of tax-sharing arrangements discussed in Chapter 22, the federal government makes large but falling grants to the provinces—amounting to about $1.5 billion in 1992—which are nominally geared to financing the necessary expenditures. However, in 1992, several provinces were spending less money on their universities than the federal high-education grants that they received.

In Canada, all universities are public institutions, and university education is heavily subsidized by government, with student fees accounting for only about 15 percent of total costs. Two arguments can be advanced for subsidizing higher education: One is an efficiency argument, and one is redistributional. First, there are externalities for the whole country from higher education. In many cases these externalities cannot be internalized by the students receiving the education, so, left to their own maximizing decisions, students who had to pay the whole cost of their education would choose less than is socially optimal. Second, charging anything like the full cost would make education prohibitively expensive to low- and even middle-income families. Government subsidies help provide training according to ability rather than according to income.

Arguments to reduce the subsidy to higher education, and thus to finance a larger fraction of the costs of running universities from tuition fees, start with the observation that the value of many kinds of education is internalized and recaptured in higher incomes earned by the recipients in their later life. This is particularly true of professional training in such fields as law, medicine, dentistry, higher education, and computer science. Yet students in these fields typically pay a smaller part of their real education costs than students in the arts, where the argument for externalities is greatest. Also, the subsidized education does represent a significant income transfer from taxpayers to students, although the latter have lower incomes than many of the students can expect to earn.

People who worry about the equity issue in this context often argue for a system of student loans, whereby more of the cost of education would be recouped from the students themselves later in their lifetimes. People opposed to loans argue, among other things, that loans will discourage children in lower-income families from continuing on to higher education because, from the vantage point of their family's current low income, the liability to be taken on by the student will seem enormous.

Job Creation Programs

People with few skills and little job experience often find themselves in a Catch-22 situation:

Employers are reluctant to hire inexperienced persons, but the only way to gain experience is to be employed.

To address this problem, the federal government operates a number of job creation programs that attempt to provide the long-term unemployed and new labour market entrants with job experience and basic labour market skills.

People receiving unemployment insurance anywhere in Canada can enroll in job training programs, completing apprenticeship or journeyman requirements while still receiving unemployment insurance benefits. The federal government has recently announced that funds will be set aside for job creation for people on social assistance. The Quebec government is experimenting with a program that gives supplementary benefits to welfare recipients who voluntarily accept on-the-job training. These examples illustrate a major point on which many experts agree:

Unemployment could be reduced and the earning power of the labour force raised if job creation programs were fully coordinated with both the unemployment insurance program and provincial welfare programs, to produce a unified scheme that overcame the serious disincentive effects of those programs.

Income Transfer and Security Programs

Income transfer and security programs provide assistance for people in financial need due to unemployment, injury, or inadequate wages. (The last group constitutes the working poor.) These programs—which comprise the so-called social safety net—include welfare, unemployment insurance, and family benefits. They make payments to approximately 9 million adult Canadians each year and cost the federal government about $20 billion per year.

As is evident from its variety of schemes, the income transfer and security system has many goals. One of the most important is to reduce poverty. Though nothing like the serious problem it was in Canada's past and still is in many other countries, poverty remains a matter of real concern to Canadian policy makers. Not the least cause for concern is that the majority of the poverty that can be eliminated by economic growth may have already been eliminated, meaning that much of the remaining poverty may represent the "hard core" that will persist no matter how wealthy the society becomes and can only be alleviated by active public policy. The problem of poverty is discussed in more detail in Box 23-1 on page 460.

Unemployment Insurance (UI)

Unemployment insurance is the single most costly program administered by the federal government, accounting for over $19 billion of payments in 1992. Originally instituted in 1940 as an insurance scheme against temporary bouts of unemployment, it was extended in scope and generosity by changes instituted in the 1970s. Many of those changes have been the object of criticism, and a few reforms designed to meet some of those criticisms have been effected in the 1990s.

All the studies made of the UI system over the last decade have called for major reforms. They have argued that the system has become overburdened by being used for too many, often conflicting objectives. It should, they argued, be returned to its prime objective of providing insurance against temporary bouts of involuntary unemployment, and other schemes should be used to achieve other objectives. Supporters of the system have fiercely resisted all suggested changes.

UI gives incentives to remain in seasonal jobs and in areas with poor employment prospects and to take UI-financed holidays. Rational people respond by doing so, thus increasing the national unemployment rate.

Saying that the UI system encourages behaviour that increases unemployment and reduces regional mobility does not say that the unemployed themselves are responsible for the "abuses" of the system that lead to these results.

The responsibility lies with the people who designed the incentives and those who strive to preserve them. It is they who can alter the system to make it deliver the intended benefits with fewer incentives for undesired behaviour.

A number of changes have been made during the 1990s. Some respond to the criticisms noted above. For example, rules for qualifying to receive benefits have been tightened, and extended coverage and additional assistance provided for individuals attending approved training courses. Other changes worked in the opposite direction, by expanding coverage into areas some critics had argued were better handled outside of the UI program (for example, expanded parental and sickness benefits). A proposal to deny unemployment insurance to those who quit their jobs voluntarily (unless under specified conditions, such as sexual harassment) caused violent dispute in 1993 and was withdrawn by the government.

Public Assistance Programs

Social assistance for individuals below retirement age, usually called welfare, is mainly a provincial and municipal responsibility in Canada.

Suggested reforms take two main forms. First, remove the disincentives to work implied by the present stacking of reductions in income-tested benefits and income taxes on earnings, as we have already discussed. Second, provide positive incentives to self-help by increasing benefits for recipients who accept work or training for work.

Under the Canada Assistance Plan (CAP), the federal government used to contribute half of the cost of such programs. Since 1990, however, the higher-income provinces (technically those not receiving equalization grants) have had the federal government's contribution limited to an increase of 5 percent per year. Ontario estimated that this cap on the CAP cost it $1.1 billion in the fiscal year 1991—1992. This will put strong pressures on the provincial governments to alter their systems—for better or for worse.

Child Benefits System

Benefits to families with children cost the federal government over $4 billion in 1993. The support system has been evolving quite rapidly over the years. Prior to the last change in 1993, the system had three parts: first, a family allowance that paid money directly to the mother according to the number of children; second, a personal tax credit that depended on both the number of children and the family's income; and third, a refundable tax credit available only to lower income families. It reduced the tax bill by the amount of the credit (in contrast to other measures that reduce taxable income and so are more valuable the higher is one's tax bracket). It was refundable, so that if its value exceeded the amount of tax owing, the balance would be paid out.

In the 1993 budget, the last one by the conservative government, this system was significantly reformed (once again). The existing programs were replaced by a Child Tax Benefit paid monthly, generally to the mother. According to the Minister of Finance, its main features were as follows: first, the three programs are consolidated into one unified benefit of $1,020 per child; second, the basic benefit is increased by $75 for the third and each subsequent child and by $213 for each child under seven where no child care expenses are claimed; third, for low-income families, the benefit will also include a new earned-income supplement of up to $500 per family.

The benefits do not vary with the number of parents or the number of income earners in the family, as did the previous programs. Instead, they vary only with income. Benefits for a two-child family start at $2,040, rise to $2,540 at a family income of $10,000, fall to $1,830 at an income of $30,000, and reach zero at an income of $60,000.

The new child support system is focused on lower income families and is much simpler than the previous mix of programs.

It no doubt points the direction to be taken by many other welfare reforms to come. Indeed, it is probable that no part of the system has settled into its final new shape. Further changes can be expected until the whole system of social expenditures has been rethought from top to bottom.

Day care.   The great rise of two-income families in which both husband and wife work has led to a growth of day-care facilities. Working couples with preschool-age children who cannot afford to pay someone to come to their own home must rely on day-care facilities.

Advocates argue that the state ought to provide such care just as it provides free medical and hospital care. Women's groups also argue that affordable day care is a necessary part of women's liberation. Without it, they say, many women will not be able to support their families or to fulfill their career ambitions by taking on meaningful work outside the home.

Opponents argue on efficiency grounds that if the second income earner cannot earn enough to pay for day care, it is inefficient for that person to work. Total income would be higher if he or she stayed home, freeing the resources that would have been used to keep the family's children in day care. Opponents also argue on equity grounds that there is no reason why two-income parents with children in day care should be subsidized by funds collected from single persons, married couples who elect to have one parent stay at home to look after the children, and two-income families without children of day-care age. Finally, on fiscal grounds, opponents argue that any universal day care scheme would be prohibitively expensive.

An added issue turns on who should provide the day care. Some groups argue that day care should be provided solely by state-run institutions whose employees would be public servants (and members of the powerful public service union, CUPE). Others argue that a state monopoly would discourage experimentation while leading to inflated costs. They accept government regulation of standards and, if desired, some government day care facilities, but they call for private sector provision to be permitted as a check on costs and standards, and as an encouragement to experimentation.

Given the fiscal pressures on the Federal government, most observers agree that a federally funded national day-care plan is a dead issue. However, working couples are allowed to deduct some of their day care expenses from their income for tax purposes. In the 1993 budget, the maximum amount deductible was raised from $4,000 to $5,000 for each eligible child younger than seven years of age or with a serious disability, and to $3,000 for each eligible child who is older than seven but less than 15 years of age.

Proposals for reform.   Most proposals for reform of the family benefits program focus on reducing its demogrant component and redirecting more expenditure to the CTC. Two main faults were alleged with the system as it had evolved up to 1993. Both problems arose because many of the payments worked through the tax system. The first criticism was that the benefits that were tax related were paid once a year, an infrequency that was highly undesirable for low income families. The 1993 budget removed this complaint by having the benefit cheques mailed out monthly, based on calculations made by Revenue Canada on each person's tax return. The second criticism has yet to be addressed. Being based on tax returns, this year's benefits depend on last year's income. This means that the system is in-

Box 23-1

Poverty in Canada

What is poverty, and whom does it affect? One definition says that one lives in poverty if one is poorer than most of one's fellow citizens. Since there will always be a bottom 10 percent of any income distribution who are poorer than the remaining 90 percent, poverty in this sense will always be with us. If a completely relative definition is not very revealing, neither is an unchanging absolute definition. The living standards of Canadians regarded as poor would have looked more than adequate to Canadians of 100 years ago and would look princely to citizens of many countries even today.

To meet both of these concerns, economists define poverty as some given level of income, rather than just in relative terms, but they also recognise that as average living standards rise over time, so will our ideas of what constitutes poverty.

Statistics Canada defines the poverty level as the level of income at which a household spends on average more than 58.5 percent of its income on the three basic necessities of food, shelter, and clothing. For a family of four, the Canadian poverty level in 1991 ranged from $17,539 in rural areas to $25,761 in the largest cities. Although $25,761 will buy enough food, shelter, and clothing for a family of four to get by, it does not provide enough money for the full range of commodities that most of us take for granted, such as having a refrigerator, a TV set that works, constant hot water, and an occasional night out. Many of the poor are understandably upset that they are outsiders looking in on the comfortable way of life shown in ads and on television. "I'd like, just once," one of the poor said to a magazine interviewer, "to buy Christmas presents the children want instead of presents they need."

Who Are the Poor?

According to the criterion just outlined, 12.1 percent of Canadian families and 30.2 percent of unattached individuals were living in poverty in 1991.

There are poor among all ages, races, and educational levels, employed as well as unemployed. Yet some groups have much higher incidences of poverty than others. For example, the table shows that you are more likely to be poor if you live in the Atlantic provinces, if you are a member of a large family, or if you are an unattached individual over 65 years of age.

Poverty is, however, by no means restricted to these groups. More than half the poor families live in urban areas, live in Ontario and the western provinces, have no more than one child, and are headed by persons of working age. Furthermore, about one fourth of those in poverty work full time (the so-called working poor), and over half work at least part time. These facts help to dispose of two superficial caricatures: the slothful father who feigns a disability because he is too lazy to do an honest day's work and the family with so many children that an ordinary decent wage is spread so thin that the entire household is reduced to poverty. Individual households that come close to these extremes can be found, but most poor households do not.

Between 1969 and 1986, the proportion of Canadians living in poverty fell by 35 percent. In part this reflected a variety of government initiatives of the sort discussed in this chapter. But in large measure, it resulted from the growth in average income, which has always been the greatest source of relief from poverty.

It would be a mistake, however, to expect growth to eliminate all poverty. The source of today's poverty problem is no longer low average income but particular groups who are left behind in the general rise in living standards caused by economic growth. It is little consolation—indeed, it must add to the gall—that they are poor in an increasingly affluent society.

There is no single answer to the question of what causes poverty in the midst of plenty. It is partly a result of mental and physical handicaps, partly of low motivation, partly of the raw deal that fate gives to some, partly the result of changing market conditions when industries and occupations can no longer prosper, partly a result of unwillingness or inability to invest in the kind of human capital that does pay off in the long run, and partly the result of the market's valuing the particular abilities an individual does have at such a low price that even in good health and with full-time employment the income that can be earned leaves that person below the poverty line.

Just as there is no single reason for poverty, there is no single cure. Many of the social programs outlined in this chapter attempt to get at various causes. If poverty has fallen over the decades in Canada, the two main reasons are economic growth and social programs that seek to provide assistance for those who cannot help themselves and to assist those who can to learn to do so.

Incidence of Poverty Among Canadian Families by Selected Characteristics, 1991

Characteristics	Percentage of families falling below the poverty line
All families	12.1
Place of residence	
Metropolitan	11.1
Other urban	11.5
Rural	15.5
Region	
Atlantic	16.6
Quebec	14.0
Ontario	10.0
Prairies	13.6
British Columbia	9.2
Number of children under 16 years of age	
0	9.6
1 or 2	20.1
3 or more	27.9
Age of head of family	
Under 25	35.1
25–54	12.3
55–64	11.8
65 and over	6.3
Sex of head of family	
Male	8.7
Female	37.6
Employment status of head of family	
In labour force	8.7
Not in labour force	21.4

Source: Statistics Canada, 13-207.

flexible with respect to (the small but not insignificant) number of families that suffer drastic deteriorations in their economic conditions within one year. As a source of help for newly poor persons, the payments may come too late, even if they are not too little.

Benefits for the Elderly

Over the next decades, a larger and larger fraction of Canadians will be retired, and thus the working people who will be directly or indirectly supporting the retired will constitute a smaller and smaller fraction of the population.

Canada's present youthful age structure may make us think we are richer as a nation than we actually are. When only a small proportion of the population is retired, it is easy to be generous to them, because the burden is spread over so many working persons. However, generous schemes may become difficult to honour when a large proportion of the population is retired, as it will be early in the twenty-first century.

Registered Retirement Savings Plans (RRSP). RRSPs provide an incentive for individuals to provide for their own retirement, either because they are not covered by a company plan or because they wish to supplement their company plan. Funds contributed are deductible from taxable income but become fully taxable when they are withdrawn. It is thus a tax deferral plan, and as such it is more valuable the higher one's current taxable income and the lower one's expected future income. Although RRSPs are often criticised as being a "rich person's tax benefit," it is interesting to note that almost one third of the labour force contributes to such plans, and of those who contribute, about 25 percent have incomes below $20,000.

The Canada Pension Plan (CPP). The CPP provides a basic level of retirement income for all Canadians who have contributed to it over their working lives. (A separate but similar scheme exists in Quebec.) Unlike some private programs, the pension provided by the CPP is portable—changing jobs does not cause any loss of eligibility.

The most important concern about the plan is that it subsidizes the generation currently receiving pensions. Rates were very low when these people were young, and as a result they will receive pensions more than five times as large as what their contributions would actually have bought. This makes the plan a very good deal for those presently retired, but it means that any increase in future benefits will have to be paid for on top of the existing subsidy to those already retired. To make the scheme self-supporting, the government currently plans for contributions nearly to double between 1985 and 2011.

Private-sector pensions. Problems with private-sector pensions include portability, since often some or all eligibility is lost when a worker changes employers; the minimum period of employment needed to qualify, which is often quite long; and vestibility, how soon the pension contributions made by employer and employee belong to the employee.

Recent changes to the Federal Pension Benefits Standards Act have significantly changed the requirements on these matters. This legislation covers approximately 1 million employees under federal labour jurisdiction, and it is also expected to serve as a model for provincial pension reforms. These amendments will permit individuals to accumulate pension credits after only two years of employment and to transfer these benefits easily as they move among jobs. In addition, there is some significant extension of eligibility to part-time workers—an important matter, since part-time work is increasing in many sectors of the economy.

Retirement income security programs. The existing public benefits system for the elderly is in many ways analogous to the child benefits system. There are three programs, each similar to a corresponding program in the child benefits system.

First, a universal benefit, or demogrant, called the old age security (OAS) program, acts much like the family allowance. Under the OAS program, the government sends out monthly benefit cheques to each Canadian over the qualifying age of 65. The OAS and UI are the two most expensive programs administered by the federal government, accounting for about $19 billion each in 1992. However, as we noted in Chapter 22, since 1989, OAS payments to relatively wealthy individuals have been recaptured by means of a tax clawback.

Second, in calculating the personal nonrefundable tax credit, provisions available to the elderly serve to reduce their taxes payable. These include a credit available to anyone 65 or older and a pension income credit that offsets the taxes due on the first $1,000 of pension income.

Third, an income-tested program, called the guaranteed income supplement (GIS), provides benefits targeted to the low-income elderly. (In some provinces this is supplemented by further target assistance.) The GIS provides for most of the progressivity that arises in the elderly benefits system.

As with most social programs, the elderly benefits system started out as a pure income-tested benefit scheme and then evolved its current mixture of universal and income-tested elements. Many currently debated proposals for reform focus on the mix of universal and tested elements. The increased emphasis on universality took place during a period when most elderly people were in lower income categories. Recently, more and more people who have received these payments have been in income brackets that are higher than that of the average taxpayer who has financed them.

One proposal for reform is to follow the United States in gradually raising the eligibility age for full OAS benefits. In the United States, the age is to rise from 65 to 66 between the years 2000 and 2009 and then to 67 between 2017 and 2027.

A second proposal is to reduce (or even eliminate) the special provisions for pension income and age in the calculation of the personal tax credit. Some reform was accomplished in 1987, when these credits replaced analogous tax exemptions that were felt to be regressive in their effects. Many social policy analysts feel that any special provisions are anachronisms. They may have served useful functions when they were introduced, given the low incomes of the elderly and the sparsity of other programs. However, they are anomalies in a world of enriched pensions, health benefits, and OAS and GIS programs.

Health Care

Taking federal and provincial payments into account, Canada's public health care system is the country's single most expensive social policy. In 1989, health expenditures accounted for between 8 and 9 percent of Canadian GDP. This is the second highest proportion of GDP so devoted in all the advanced industrial countries. The annual cost of the part of health care that is paid for by government amounted in that year to over $2,000 for every man, woman, and child in the country—or over $4,000 for every person who pays income taxes. It has also been rising rapidly in recent years.

Most observers agree that some type of expenditure-controlling reform is urgently needed. Unfortunately, agreement stops here. Debate currently rages on what reforms are practicable and acceptable.

One major possibility of cost containment is to move away from the present system of fee for service. In the system used in most of Canada, the physician and the hospital charge a prescribed fee for each service that is performed. Since under any provincial health scheme, the doctor's and hospital's collection rate is 100 percent, there is no reason for the provider of health services to economize on those services. Indeed, much research shows that the rate of elective surgery—operations that are not necessary for survival but may be useful—rises with the ratio of physicians to the population. In areas where there are many physicians, the typical physician has time on his or her hands, and the rate of elective surgery goes up. In areas where doctors are in short supply, much less elective surgery is performed.

This illustrates a general point. The case for the free market is strongest when consumers are the best judges of their own needs. The case for market efficiency is greatly weakened when suppliers can influence the demand for the product they supply. Thus, in the many cases where judgement is needed to decide among several courses of action, all of which have something to recommend them, the evidence is that doctors create their own demand. This does not imply dishonesty on the part of doctors, merely that where judgement calls must be made, the amount of spare time available to doctors will influence their decisions, possibly unconsciously.

Health maintenance organizations (HMOs) provide a possible way around this problem. Large hospitals and large groups of doctors work on what is called a *capitation* basis. This means that the HMO is paid an annual fee for each person registered with it. Since payment is on a per capita basis rather than on a services-rendered basis, there is no incentive to prescribe more care than is needed. The HMO at Sault Ste. Marie, pioneered by the steelworkers' union and their employers, was an early and successful Canadian example of such an organization.

As with all social institutions, there are pros and cons to HMOs. They have their strong supporters and their strong detractors. No doubt their value in holding costs down while maintaining the quality of

Box 23-2

The Rising Cost of Health Care

Almost everyone would agree that in a wealthy society such as Canada, some acceptable level of health care should be available to all citizens by right. Economic analysis shows that these two elements—the belief in the right to free medical care and the concern over its high and rising social cost—are not unrelated.

Explaining the High Cost

Without health insurance, a single major operation or a prolonged illness could impoverish even the most prudent middle-income household. Why has health care become so costly?

Low productivity increases

One reason is that the wages of nurses, laboratory technicians, and other medical service personnel have risen substantially relative to their productivity (the number of temperatures taken, beds made, and meals served per employee do not increase much over time).

Rising quality

A second reason is the steadily rising quality of medical care. Available knowledge and equipment have improved, and it is now possible not only to provide quicker, surer cures for common ailments but also to prevent and treat less common ailments and complications. Moreover, as per capita income has risen, people have been prepared to pay for more and better health. The demand for health care has proved to be income elastic.

Zero marginal cost

Since most insurance and publicly provided medical programs do not include significant *marginal charge* to the patient for the incremental medical or hospital care consumed, an individual has no incentive to economize on the quantity or quality of elective care. In the market system, individuals would choose medical care (as they choose housing) from a wide variety of price-quality alternatives. If patients had to pay their own bills, and if they could make fully informed choices, many might prefer to pay less and not have the best available treatment in all circumstances. But at zero marginal cost, patients will naturally prefer to have the extra benefits of the best possible care, no matter what the extra cost to the insurance company, employer, or government.

Doctors and hospitals can pass along the higher costs of advanced modern techniques to insurers in higher fees, especially if they do not have to worry that those higher fees may cause a reduction in the quantity of their services demanded. They may well reason, "Our job is to give the best treatment; let others worry about the costs."

What Are the Right Quantity and Quality of Medical Care?

No doubt the acceptable minimum level of health care, to be provided by public support if necessary, has risen over time; accordingly, public intervention in the health sector has increased. The issue provokes more emotion than a discussion of housing or clothing. After all, human lives are at stake.

However, much (although, of course, not all) medical and hospital care is elective and has almost nothing to do with life or death. By way of analogy, to say that no one should starve is not to say that all people should receive all the free food they want to eat. Nonvital attention accounts for a large part of our demand for health care. If it is offered at little or no marginal cost to users, it will be consumed beyond the point where marginal benefits are equal to the cost of providing it.

But even where life is at stake, do we really always want the very best? Suppose that the extra cost of the very best at all times does pay off in an increased probability of survival. How much would we pay to have, say, only 9 instead of 10 people in 10,000 die from a particular disease? Surely few would want to spend a billion dollars per life saved; most would say that the opportunity cost was too high. Yet doctors in hospitals often make a different decision implicitly by ordering the best of everything. They then pass the costs on to society as a whole through increased resource allocation to the health sector. The issue is not whether to save lives but the opportunity cost of doing so. Money spent to save lives here is money not available to save lives (or improve the quality of life) elsewhere.

In adopting a policy toward health care, there are at least three separable decisions: how much care to provide, how to allocate the cost of that care, and how to ration the supply. In the market system, prices do all three. When we elect to have the government intervene because we do not like the free-market results, someone has to make these decisions. In health care, as elsewhere, if the price paid by users is kept below the marginal cost of providing the services, the private market will have excess demand. The government must either provide the services demanded directly or subsidize others to do so, or some way must be found to limit the demand to the quantity available. In countries with national health services, rationing is accomplished in part by long lines at doctors' offices and long waits for hospital admissions and in part by a lower average quality of medical services, which then reduces demand.

Controlling the Cost

Neither providers nor patients have sufficient incentive under many present schemes to keep down the costs of medical care. One solution is to place enough of a marginal charge on users that they will ask themselves whether this doctor's visit, this extra day in the hospital, or this use of the most advanced health monitoring system is worth the cost to them.

New institutional arrangements are emerging with incentives to control costs. Ontario and Alberta have experimented, apparently successfully, with privatization of hospital management. Quebec has almost 200 *centres locaux de service communautaires,* which are community run and where physicians are retained on a salaried, not fee-for-service, basis. Ontario has over 60 health service organizations (HSOs) that also retain physicians on a salaried basis. Other developments include capitation arrangements, whereby physicians agree to provide specified levels of care for a fixed fee per patient per year. These institutions all have incentives to keep their costs down.

health services will be debated for a long time to come. Aspects of the health care system and the role of the market in reforming it are discussed further in Box 23-2.

A Final Word

We have seen that Canada's social policy is made up of a complex system of benefits and tax expenditures. There is no doubt that it achieves many of its goals. There is also no doubt that the system could be improved by an integrated set of reforms. As the fiscal problems of high, persistent government deficits continue, many who support the system argue that it must be reformed to become more focused on those in need. They argue that, failing such reform, across-the-board massive reductions may be forced on governments who are being pressed by unsustainably high levels of debt to make major cuts in their deficits. This has already happened, for example, in New Zealand.

Reforming the system is unpopular, because people who run the risk of losing some net benefits tend to be very vocal and to find ready political champions. Other opponents of reform fear that any changes will begin a process of eroding the whole social policy system, which many regard as one of Canada's outstanding accomplishments. It remains to be seen whether any Canadian government will attempt a major overhaul of the system— an overhaul that many observers feel could make the system fairer, less costly, yet more effective but would cause a short-term political outcry.

SUMMARY

1. Canadian governments have been urged to reexamine and redesign social programs with the twin objectives of improving their ability to deliver benefits to the intended beneficiaries and reducing costs wherever possible.
2. Some social programs, called demogrants, are universal, paying benefits to anyone meeting such minimal requirements as residence or age. Other programs are selective, which usually means that they are income tested. Some are taxable and thus provide net receipts that decline as income rises; others are not taxable and thus have net benefits that are independent of income. Some are expenditure programs (including direct transfers to persons), and others are delivered through the tax system in the form of special tax concessions (called tax expenditures). Some programs are administered by the federal government, some by the provincial governments, and still others by the municipalities.
3. Three major challenges must be met by a successful Canadian social spending policy for the 1990s. These are the challenges posed by government deficits, technological changes, and demographic trends. In the absence of major new revenue sources, it is not a question of whether social programs should be rationalized but of how this should be done.
4. Social programs and proposed changes to them must be understood in the context of the overall tax and transfer system.
5. Social policies cannot be evaluated without value judgements about desirable goals and tradeoffs among objectives. In evaluating social policies, attention is paid to vertical and horizontal equity. Because of the high rate at which many income-tested benefits are reduced as income rises, the effective marginal tax rate of many beneficiaries is very high.

6. The effect of the tax and transfer system on the international movement of mobile labour and capital also needs to be considered.

7. Measures designed to increase economic security need to be examined for adverse effects on adjustment to change.

8. Although there has been much concern about preserving the universality of Canada's social welfare system, the facts that many schemes are income tested and that many benefits are taxable mean that the whole system is progressive, with net benefits tending to fall as income rises.

9. The two major categories of programs are human resource development programs—which include postsecondary education, job creation, and unemployment insurance—and income transfer and security programs. This second category includes unemployment insurance, public assistance programs (welfare), child benefits schemes, benefits for the elderly, and health care, which, when provincial and federal expenditures are counted, is the single most expensive social program in the country, accounting for between 8 and 9 percent of total national income.

TOPICS FOR REVIEW

Fiscal, economic, and demographic pressures

Vertical and horizontal equity

Universal versus selective programs

Demogrants

Tax exemptions and tax credits

Adjustment versus security

Disincentives and social costs

DISCUSSION QUESTIONS

1. Discuss the concept of universality as it applies to medical care and the OAP.

2. In a recent conference volume, Queen's University professor Keith Banting wrote the following: "The issue is not whether we want a universal or selective welfare state. Rather the questions are: What is the basic structure of the universal programs which we must maintain, and what is the appropriate supplement of selective programs which can be woven in and around that basic universal structure or framework." Discuss this quotation.

3. Discuss the implications for social policy objectives of basing social programs on family rather than individual income.

4. Is the deduction allowed for contributions to RRSPs regressive?

5. In the February 1986 federal budget, Finance Minister Michael Wilson identified four objectives for reform of social policy:
   - Maintaining universal access
   - Directing more resources to the people most in need
   - Improving opportunities for individuals to become self-reliant
   - Reducing the after-tax value of benefits to higher-income Canadians who do not need assistance

   Examine a couple of existing programs (or recent reforms) in terms of these criteria.

6. How would converting the basic personal income exemption to a tax credit affect the disincentives faced by one spouse entering the labour market? What about when the other spouse is already working and earning a much higher wage?

7. "As currently constituted, the unemployment insurance program has very little to do with either unemployment or insurance." Discuss.

8. Discuss the pros and cons of introducing user fees for hospital and medical care at a rate well below full cost and with exceptions for low-income persons.

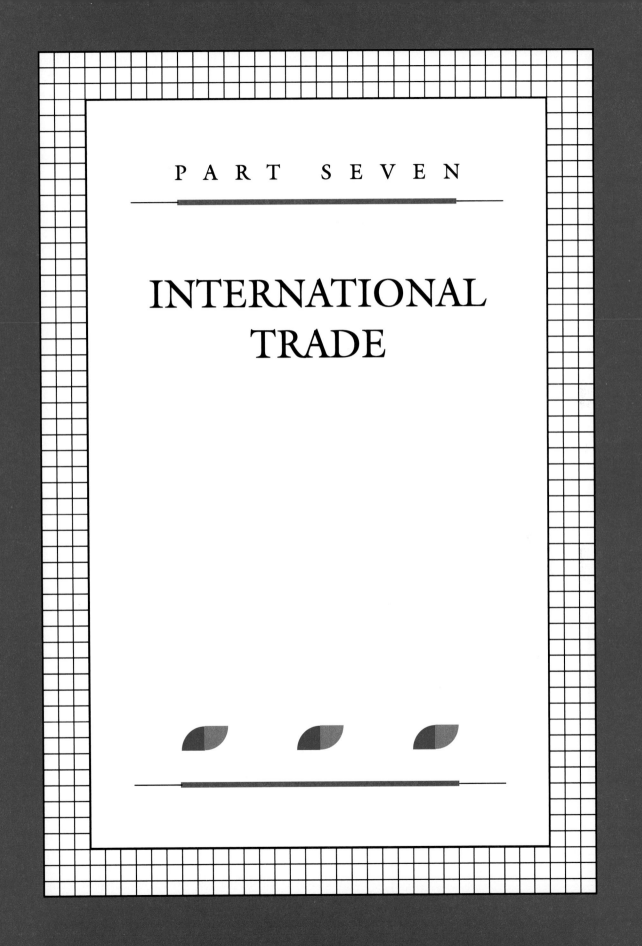

PART SEVEN

INTERNATIONAL TRADE

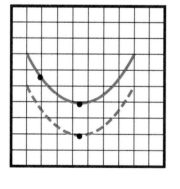

24

The Gains from Trade

Canadians buy Volkswagens, Germans take holidays in Venice, Italians buy spices from Tanzania, Africans import oil from Iraq, Arabs buy Japanese cameras, and the Japanese buy Canadian lumber. *International trade* refers to exchanges of goods and services that take place across international boundaries.

The founders of modern economics were concerned with international trade problems. The great eighteenth-century British philosopher and economist David Hume, one of the first to work out the theory of the price system as a control mechanism, developed his concepts mainly in terms of prices in foreign trade. Adam Smith, in *The Wealth of Nations*, attacked government restriction of trade. David Ricardo, in 1817, developed the basic theory of the gains from trade that is studied in this chapter. The repeal of the Corn Laws—tariffs on the importation of grains into Great Britain—and the transformation of that country during the nineteenth century from a country of high tariffs to one of completely free trade were, to a significant extent, the result of agitation by economists whose theories of the gains from trade led them to condemn tariffs.

In this chapter we explore the fundamental question of what is gained by international trade; in Chapter 25 we will deal with the pros and cons of interfering with the free flow of such trade.

Sources of the Gains from Trade

The increased output realized as a result of trade is called the **gains from trade**. Although politicians often regard foreign trade differently from domestic trade, economists from Adam Smith on have argued that the causes and consequences of international trade are simply an extension of the principles governing domestic trade. What is the advantage of trade among individuals, among groups, among regions, or among countries? The answer is most easily seen by considering the differences between a world with trade and a world without it.

Interpersonal, Interregional, and International Trade

Consider trade among individuals. Without trade, each person would have to be self-sufficient, each would have to produce all the food, clothing, shelter, medical services, entertainment, and luxuries that he or she consumed. A world of individual self-sufficiency would be a world with extremely low living standards.

Trade among individuals allows them to specialize in activities that they can do well and to buy from others the goods and services that they cannot easily produce. A good doctor who is a bad carpenter can provide medical services not only for her own family but also for an excellent carpenter who does not possess either the training or the ability to practise medicine. Thus, trade and specialization are intimately connected. Without trade, individuals must be self-sufficient. With trade, individuals can specialize in what they do well and satisfy other needs by trading.

The same principles apply to regions. Without interregional trade, each region would be forced to be self-sufficient. With trade, each region can specialize in producing commodities for which it has some natural or acquired advantage. Plains regions can specialize in growing grain, mountain regions can specialize in mining and forest products, regions with abundant power can specialize in heavy manufacturing, and regions with highly skilled labour can specialize in knowledge-intensive high-tech goods. Cool regions can produce wheat and other crops that thrive in temperate climates, and hot regions can grow such tropical crops as bananas, sugar, and coffee. The living standards of the inhabitants of all regions will be higher when each region specializes in products in which it has some natural or acquired advantage and obtains other products by trade than when all regions seek to be self-sufficient.

The same principle also applies to nations. Nations, like regions or persons, can gain from specialization and from the international trade that must accompany it. Specialization means that each country produces more of some goods than its residents wish to consume and less of others.

Trade is necessary to achieve the gains that specialization in production makes possible.

This discussion suggests one important possible gain from trade:

By engaging in trade, each individual, region, or nation is able to concentrate on producing goods and services that it produces efficiently while trading to obtain goods and services that it does not produce.

Specialization and trade go hand in hand, because there is no motivation to achieve the gains

from specialization without being able to trade the goods that are produced for goods that are desired. Economists use the term *gains from trade* to embrace the results of both.

We shall examine two sources of the gains from trade. The first source consists of international differences in production costs that give rise to advantages in producing certain goods and disadvantages in producing others. These gains occur even though each country's costs of production are unchanged by the existence of trade. The second source is the reduction in each country's costs of production that results from the greater scale of production that specialization and trade make possible.

Gains from Trade with Given Costs

In order to focus on differences in countries' conditions of production, suppose that there are no advantages arising from either economies of large-scale production or cost reductions that are the consequence of learning new skills. In these circumstances, what leads to gains from trade? To examine this question, we use an example involving only two countries and two products, but the general principles apply as well to the cases of many countries and many commodities.[1]

A Special Case: Absolute Advantage

The gains from trade are clear when there is a simple situation involving absolute advantage. **Absolute advantage** concerns the quantities of a single product that can be produced using the same quantity of resources in two different regions. One region is said to have an absolute advantage over a second region in the production of commodity X when an equal quantity of resources can produce more X in the first region than in the second.

Suppose that region A has an absolute advantage over B in one commodity and that region B has an absolute advantage over A in another. In such a situation, the total production of both regions can be increased (relative to a situation of self-sufficiency) if each specializes in the commodity in which it has the absolute advantage.

Table 24-1 provides a simple example. Total

---

[1]An earlier illustration of the same principle was given in Box 3-1 on page 44.

TABLE 24-1   Gains from Specialization with Absolute Advantage

Part A: Amounts of wheat and cloth that can be produced with one unit of resources in Canada and England

	Wheat (bushels)	Cloth (metres)
Canada	10	6
England	5	10

Part B: Changes resulting from the transfer of one unit of Canadian resources into wheat and one unit of English resources into cloth

	Wheat (bushels)	Cloth (metres)
Canada	+10	− 6
England	− 5	+10
World	+ 5	+ 4

When each country has an absolute advantage in one of the commodities, specialization makes it possible to produce more of both commodities. Part A shows the production of wheat and cloth that can be achieved in each country by using one unit of resources. Canada can produce 10 bushels of wheat or 6 metres of cloth; England can produce 5 bushels of wheat or 10 metres of cloth. Canada has an absolute advantage in producing wheat, and England in producing cloth. Part B shows the changes in production caused by moving one unit of resources out of cloth and into wheat production in Canada and moving one unit of resources in the opposite direction in England. There is an increase in world production of 5 bushels of wheat and 4 metres of cloth; worldwide, there are gains from specialization. In this example, the more resources are transferred into wheat production in Canada and cloth production in England, the larger the gains will be.

world production of both wheat and cloth increases when each country produces more of the good in which it has an absolute advantage. A rise in the production of all commodities entails a rise in average living standards.

The gains from specialization make the gains from trade possible. When specialization occurs, England produces more cloth and Canada more wheat than if they were self-sufficient. Canada is now producing more wheat and less cloth than

Canadian consumers wish to buy, and England is now producing more cloth and less wheat than English consumers wish to buy. If consumers in both countries are to get cloth and wheat in the desired proportions, Canada must export wheat to England and import cloth from England.

A First General Statement: Comparative Advantage

When each country has an absolute advantage over the other in the production of one commodity, the gains from trade are obvious. What, however, if Canada can produce both wheat and cloth more efficiently than England? In essence, this was David Ricardo's question, posed over 175 years ago. His answer underlies the theory of comparative advantage and is still accepted by economists as a valid statement of the potential gains from trade.

To start with, assume that Canadian efficiency increases tenfold above the levels recorded in the example, so that one unit of Canadian resources can produce either 100 bushels of wheat or 60 metres of cloth. English efficiency remains unchanged (see Table 24-2). It might appear that Canada, which is now better at producing both wheat and cloth than England, has nothing to gain by trading with such an inefficient foreign country, but it *does* have something to gain. Table 24-2 shows that it is still possible to increase world production of both wheat and cloth by having Canada produce more wheat and less cloth and by having England produce more cloth and less wheat.

What is the source of this gain? Although Canada has an *absolute* advantage over England in the production of both wheat and cloth, the *margin* of advantage differs in the two commodities. Canada can produce 20 times as much wheat as England by using the same quantity of resources, but only 6 times as much cloth. Canada is said to have a **comparative advantage** in the production of wheat and a comparative disadvantage in the production of cloth. (This statement implies another: England has a comparative disadvantage in the production of wheat, in which it is one twentieth as efficient as Canada, and a comparative advantage in the production of cloth, in which it is only one sixth as efficient.)

A key proposition in the theory of international trade is this:

TABLE 24-2 Gains from Specialization with Comparative Advantage

Part A: Amounts of wheat and cloth that can be produced with one unit of resources in Canada and England

	Wheat (bushels)	Cloth (metres)
Canada	100	60
England	5	10

Part B: Changes resulting from the transfer of one tenth of one unit of Canadian resources into wheat and one unit of English resources into cloth

	Wheat (bushels)	Cloth (metres)
Canada	+10	− 6
England	− 5	+10
World	+ 5	+ 4

When there is comparative advantage, specialization makes it possible to produce more of both commodities. The productivity of English resources is left unchanged from Table 24-1; that of Canadian resources is increased tenfold. England no longer has an absolute advantage in producing either commodity. Total production of both commodities can nonetheless be increased by specialization. Moving one tenth of one unit of Canadian resources out of cloth and into wheat and moving one unit of resources in the opposite direction in England causes world production of wheat to rise by 5 bushels and cloth by 4 metres.

TABLE 24-3 Absence of Gains from Specialization When There Is No Comparative Advantage

Part A: Amounts of wheat and cloth that can be produced with one unit of resources in Canada and England

	Wheat (bushels)	Cloth (metres)
Canada	100	60
England	10	6

Part B: Changes resulting from the transfer of 1 unit of Canadian resources into wheat and 10 units of English resources into cloth

	Wheat (bushels)	Cloth (metres)
Canada	+100	−60
England	−100	+60
World	0	0

Where there is no comparative advantage, no reallocation of resources within each country can increase the production of both commodities. In this example, Canada has the same absolute advantage over England in each commodity (tenfold). There is no comparative advantage, and world production cannot be increased by reallocating resources in both countries. Therefore, specialization does not increase total output.

The gains from trade depend on the pattern of comparative, not absolute, advantage.

A comparison of Tables 24-1 and 24-2 refutes the notion that the absolute *levels* of efficiency of two areas determine the gains from specialization. The key is that the *margin of advantage* that one area has over the other *must differ* between commodities. As long as this margin differs, total world production can be increased when each area specializes in the production of that commodity in which it has a comparative advantage.

Comparative advantage is necessary, as well as sufficient, for gains from trade. This is illustrated in Table 24-3, which shows a case in which Canada

has an absolute advantage in both commodities, but neither country has a comparative advantage in the production of either commodity. Canada is 10 times as efficient as England in the production of wheat and in the production of cloth. Now there is no way to increase the production of both wheat and cloth by reallocating resources. Part B of the table provides one example of a resource shift that illustrates this.

Absolute advantage without comparative advantage does not lead to gains from trade.

A Second General Statement: Opportunity Costs

Much of the foregoing argument uses the concept of a unit of resources. It assumes that units of re-

TABLE 24-4 Opportunity Cost of Wheat and Cloth in Canada and England

	Wheat (bushels)	Cloth (metres)
Canada	0.60 metre cloth	1.67 bushels wheat
England	2.00 metres cloth	0.50 bushel wheat

Comparative advantages can be expressed in terms of opportunity costs that differ between countries. These opportunity costs can be obtained from Table 24-1 or Table 24-2. The English opportunity cost of one unit of wheat is obtained by dividing the cloth output of one unit of English resources by the wheat output. The result shows that 2 metres of cloth must be sacrificed for every extra unit of wheat produced by transferring English resources out of cloth production and into wheat. The other three cost figures are obtained in a similar manner.

sources can be equated across countries, so that statements such as "Canada can produce 10 times as much wheat with the same quantity of resources as England" are meaningful. Measurement of the real resource cost of producing commodities poses many difficulties. If, for example, England uses land, labour, and capital in proportions that are different from those used in Canada, it may not be clear which country gets more output per unit of resource input. Fortunately, the proposition about the gains from trade can be restated without reference to the fuzzy concept of a unit of resources.

To do this, we go back to the examples of Tables 24-1 and 24-2 and calculate the *opportunity cost* of wheat and cloth in the two countries. When resources are fully employed, the only way to produce more of one commodity is to reallocate resources and produce less of the other commodity. Table 24-1 shows that one unit of resources in Canada can produce 10 bushels of wheat *or* 6 metres of cloth. From this it follows that the opportunity cost of producing one unit of wheat is 0.60 unit of cloth, whereas the opportunity cost of producing one unit of cloth is 1.67 units of wheat. These data are summarized in Table 24-4. The table also shows that in England, the opportunity cost of one unit of wheat is 2.0 units of cloth forgone, while the opportunity cost of one unit of cloth is 0.50 unit of wheat. Table

TABLE 24-5 Gains from Specialization with Differing Opportunity Costs

Changes resulting from each country's producing one more unit of a commodity in which it has the lower opportunity cost

	Wheat (bushels)	Cloth (metres)
Canada	+1.0	−0.6
England	−0.5	+1.0
World	+0.5	+0.4

Whenever opportunity costs differ between countries, specialization can increase the production of both commodities. These calculations show that there are gains from specialization, given the opportunity costs of Table 24-4. To produce one more bushel of wheat, Canada must sacrifice 0.6 metre of cloth. To produce one more metre of cloth, England must sacrifice 0.5 bushel of wheat. Making both changes raises world production of both wheat and cloth.

24-2 also gives rise to the opportunity costs in Table 24-4.

The sacrifice of cloth involved in producing wheat is much lower in Canada than in England. World wheat production can be increased if Canada rather than England produces it. Looking at cloth production, we can see that the loss of wheat involved in producing one unit of cloth is lower in England than in Canada. England has the lower (opportunity) cost as a producer of cloth. World cloth production can be increased if England, rather than Canada, produces it. This situation is shown in Table 24-5.

The gains from trade arise from differing opportunity costs in the two countries.

The conclusions about the gains from trade arising from international differences may be summarized as follows:

1. Country A has a comparative advantage over country B in producing a commodity when the opportunity cost (in terms of some other commodity) of production in country A is lower.

This implies, however, that it has a comparative disadvantage in the other commodity.

2. Opportunity costs depend on the relative costs of producing two commodities, not on absolute costs. (Notice that the examples in Tables 24-1 and 24-2 each give rise to the opportunity costs in Table 24-4.)

3. When opportunity costs are the same in all countries, there is no comparative advantage and hence no possibility of gains from specialization and trade. (You can illustrate this for yourself by calculating the opportunity costs implied by the data in Table 24-3.)

4. When opportunity costs differ in any two countries and both countries are producing both commodities, it is always possible to increase total world production and hence total world consumption of both commodities by a suitable reallocation of resources within each country. (This proposition is illustrated in Table 24-5 and Box 24-1.)

Why Opportunity Costs Differ

We have seen that the sources of the gains from trade are comparative advantages, which themselves arise from differences in opportunity costs among nations. Why do different countries have different opportunity costs?

Different factor proportions. The traditional answer to this question was provided early in the twentieth century by two Swedish economists, Eli Heckscher and Bertil Ohlin. According to their theory, differences in factor endowments among nations result in different opportunity costs. For example, a country that is well endowed with fertile land but has a small population will find that land is cheap but labour is expensive. It will therefore produce cheaply such land-intensive goods as wheat and corn, while labour-intensive manufactured goods, such as watches and silicon chips, will be produced at a high cost. The reverse will be true for a second country that is small in size but possessed with abundant and efficient labour. As a result, the first country will have a comparative advantage in land-intensive goods, the second in labour-intensive goods. Another country that is unusually well endowed with energy will have low energy prices and will thus have a comparative advantage in energy-intensive goods, such as chemicals and aluminum.

According to the Heckscher-Ohlin theory, countries have comparative advantages in the production of commodities that are intensive in the use of the factors of production with which their endowments are relatively abundant.

This is often called the *factor endowment theory of comparative advantage.* It assumes that all countries have the same production functions, which implies that equal inputs of factor services will produce equal outputs in all countries. It explains differences in opportunity costs by national differences in the supplies of factors and hence in relative factor prices.

Different climates. Research suggests that this theory explains much, but by no means all, of observed comparative advantages. One obvious additional influence comes from all the natural factors that can be called *climate* in the broadest sense. If we combine land, labour, and capital in the same way in Nicaragua and in Iceland, we will not get the same output of most agricultural goods. Sunshine, rainfall, and average temperature also matter. If we work with wool or cotton in dry and damp climates, we will get different results. (We can, of course, artificially create most climates in a factory, but it is expensive to create what is freely provided elsewhere.)

Climate, interpreted in the broadest sense, undoubtedly helps to determine comparative advantages.

This explanation assumes that climatic conditions cause nations to have *different* production functions so that the same inputs of factor services will produce different outputs in different countries. Countries will tend to have comparative advantages in goods for whose production their climates are particularly favourable.

Box 24-1

The Gains from Trade Illustrated Graphically

Production, Trade, and Consumption Possibilities

The theory of comparative advantage shows that international trade leads to specialization in production and increased consumption possibilities. In this box we show the important propositions in a figure.

The black line in each part of the figure represents the Canadian and the English production possibility boundaries. In the absence of any international trade, these also represent each country's consumption possibilities. The boundaries are drawn as straight lines so that we can concentrate on the simplest possible case, in which opportunity costs are constant (as they are assumed to be in Tables 24-1 to 24-5).

The difference in the slopes of the production possibility boundaries reflects differences in comparative advantage. In each part, the opportunity cost of increasing production of wheat by the same amount (measured by the distance ba) is the amount by which the production of cloth must be reduced (measured by the distance bc). The relatively steep production possibility boundary for Canada thus in-

dicates that the opportunity cost of producing wheat in Canada is less than that in England.

If trade is possible at some terms of trade between the two countries' opportunity costs of production, each country will specialize in the production of the good in which it has a comparative advantage. In each part of the figure, production occurs at U; Canada produces only wheat, and England produces only cloth.

Consumption possibilities are given by the red lines that pass through U in each part of the figure and have a common slope equal to the terms of trade. The slope of this line is intermediate between the slopes of the two countries' own production possibility curves. Consumption possibilities are increased in both countries; consumption may occur at some point, such as d, that involves a combination of wheat and cloth that was not obtainable in the absence of trade. As we have drawn d on each part of the figure, each country consumes more wheat and more cloth than when each was self-sufficient—showing that trade makes it possible for both countries to have more of both commodities.

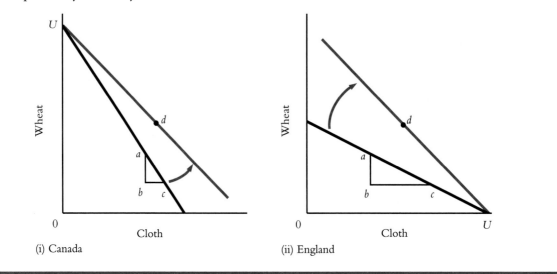

(i) Canada

(ii) England

Gains from Specialization with Variable Costs

So far, we have assumed that unit costs are the same, whatever the scale of output, and have seen that there are gains from specialization and trade as long as there are interregional differences in opportunity costs. If costs vary with the level of output or as experience is acquired via specialization, *additional* sources of gain are possible.

Economies of Scale

Over some range of outputs, unit costs of production usually fall as the scale of output increases. The larger a firm's output, the greater its opportunities to employ efficient, large-scale machinery and to have a detailed division of tasks among its workers. Countries such as Canada, France, and Israel, whose domestic markets are not large enough to exploit all available economies of scale, would find it prohibitively expensive to become self-sufficient. They would have to produce a little bit of everything at very high cost.[2]

Trade allows smaller countries to specialize in producing a limited range of commodities at high enough levels of output that they will reap the available economies of scale.

Economies of scale are illustrated in part (i) of Figure 24-1.

Big countries, such as the United States and Russia, have markets that are large enough to allow the production of most items at home at a scale of output that is great enough to obtain the available economies of scale. For them, the gains from international trade arise mainly from specializing in commodities in which they have a comparative advantage. Yet even for such countries as these, a broadening of their markets permits achieving economies of scale in subproduct lines, such as specialty steels or blue jeans.

The importance of product diversity and specialization in specific subproduct lines has been one of the lessons learned from changing patterns of world trade since World War II. When the European Common Market (now called the European Community or the EC) was set up in the 1950s, economists expected that specialization would occur according to the classical theory of comparative advantage, with one country specializing in cars, another in refrigerators, another in fashion clothes, another in shoes, and so on. This is not the way it has worked out. Today one can buy French, English, Italian, and German fashion goods, cars, shoes, appliances, and a host of other goods in London, Paris, Bonn, and Rome. Ships loaded with Swedish furniture bound for London pass ships loaded with English furniture bound for Stockholm, and so on.

What European free trade did was allow a proliferation of differentiated products, with different countries each specializing in different subproduct lines. Consumers have shown by their expenditures that they value this enormous increase in the range of choice among differentiated products. As Asian countries have expanded into North American markets with textiles, cars, and electronic goods, North American manufacturers have increasingly specialized their production, and we now export textiles, cars, and electronics equipment to Japan while importing similar but differentiated products from Japan.

Learning by Doing

The discussion so far has assumed that costs vary only with the *level* of output. They may also vary with the length of time that a product has been produced.

Early economists placed great importance on a phenomenon that we now call *learning by doing.* They believed that as countries gained experience in particular tasks, workers and managers would become more efficient in performing them. As people acquire expertise, costs tend to fall. There is substantial evidence that such learning by doing does occur in a wide range of industries. It is particularly important in many of today's knowledge-intensive high-tech products.

Learning by doing is a phenomenon quite unlike anything we have studied so far in this book. Care must be taken to distinguish it from the famil-

---

[2]Economies of scale are discussed in Chapter 11. The classic discussion of this effect is quoted in Box 3-2 on page 46.

FIGURE 24-1
Scale and Learning Effects

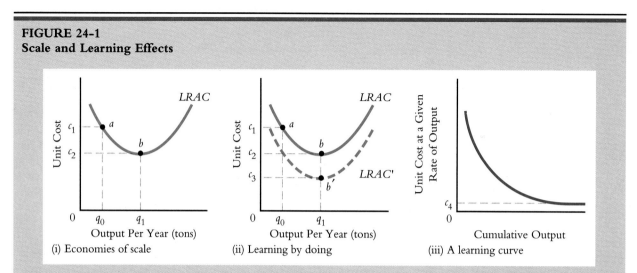

(i) Economies of scale (ii) Learning by doing (iii) A learning curve

Specialization may lead to gains from trade either by permitting economies of scale or by leading to downward shifts of cost curves, or both. Consider a country that wishes to consume the quantity q_0 of some product. Suppose that it can produce that quantity at a unit cost of c_1. Suppose further that the country has a comparative advantage in producing this commodity and can export the quantity q_0q_1 if it produces q_1. This may lead to cost savings in two ways. In part (i), the increased level of production of q_1 compared to q_0 permits it to *move along* its cost curve, *LRAC*, from a to b, thus reaching the *MES* and reducing unit cost to c_2. This is an economy of scale. In part (ii), as workers and management become more experienced, they may discover means of increasing productivity that lead to a downward shift of the cost curve from *LRAC* to *LRAC′*, thus learning by doing. The downward *shift* lowers the cost of producing any rate of output. At output q_1, costs per unit fall to c_3. The movement from a to $b′$ incorporates both economies of scale and learning by doing.

Part (iii) shows a learning curve, which is another way of showing the effects of learning by doing. This curve shows the relation between the costs of *producing a given output per period* and the total output over the whole time during which production has taken place, called *cumulative output*. Growing experience with making the product causes costs to fall as more and more is produced. When all learning possibilities have been exploited, costs reach a minimum level, shown by c_4 in the figure. Moving the rate of output from q_0 to q_1 in part (i) causes the firm to move faster along its learning curve in part (iii).

iar cost curves that relate a firm's costs to its current rate of output.

When learning by doing occurs, the *LRATC* curve shifts downward.

This shift, which is shown in part (ii) of Figure 24-1, means that any given rate of output is associated with a lower average total cost than before. The shift occurs because of increased productivity due to learning from experience gained over all past

production. As a result, costs fall as the total of all cumulative *past* output rises.

This important phenomenon can be shown by a **learning curve**. This curve, which is shown in part (iii) of Figure 24-1, shows how the cost of producing a *given rate of output* falls as the total output accumulates.

An example may help to illustrate learning by doing. Suppose that a firm starts operations on January 1, 1990, producing at a rate of 10,000 units per month. On January 1, 1991, the total of all past output is 120,000 units, and by January 1, 1992, the total is 240,000 units. Now suppose that the unit cost associated with the monthly production of 10,000 units was $5.00 on January 1, 1990, $4.00 on January 1, 1991, and $3.50 on January 1, 1992. This sequence of events allows us to identify three points on the firm's learning curve: The unit cost of producing the given rate of output is $5.00 when past output is zero, $4.00 when past output is 120,000 units, and $3.50 when past output is 240,000 units. The firm has moved along its learning curve. The costs associated with producing 10,000 units a month have fallen as its labour and management have learned from the accumulated experience of producing more and more output.

Now assume that the firm had been able to produce at a faster rate, say, 20,000 units per month. Its unit costs will now fall faster as it moves more quickly down its learning curve. To illustrate the learning effect simply, assume that the average total cost curve is flat for outputs between 12,000 and 24,000 units per month. Thus, unit costs of producing at the higher rate of 24,000 units per month are $5.00 per unit when the firm starts operations on January 1, 1990. However, the firm will move down its learning curve faster as a result of having a higher rate of output. By January 1, 1991, it will have a cumulative past output of 240,000, and its unit costs will have fallen to $3.50, the level it took two years to reach when the firm was producing only 10,000 units a month.

Where learning by doing is important, the higher a firm's current rate of output, the faster its unit costs associated with a *given* rate of output will fall.

This tendency for costs to fall as the total of all past output accumulates confers large advantages on firms that are first into the market with a new product as well as on firms that have a large domestic market that will support a high initial rate of output.

The distinction between economies of large-scale production, which are associated with the *current rate of output,* and learning by doing, which is associated with the *total of all past output,* is illustrated in Figure 24-1. The distinction provides one more example of the difference between a movement along a curve and a shift of a curve.

Recognition of the opportunities for learning

by doing leads to an important implication: Policy makers need not accept *current* comparative advantages as given. Through such means as education and tax incentives, they can seek to develop new comparative advantages.[3] Moreover, countries cannot complacently assume that an existing comparative advantage will persist. Misguided education policies, the wrong tax incentives, or policies that discourage risk taking can lead to the rapid erosion of a country's comparative advantage in a particular product. So, too, can competitive developments elsewhere in the world.

A changing view of comparative advantage. The classical theory of the gains from trade assumes that there are given cost structures, based largely on a country's natural endowments. This leads to a given pattern of international comparative advantage. It leads to the policy advice that a government, interested in maximizing its citizens' material standard of living, should encourage production to be specialized in goods in which it currently has a comparative advantage.

There is today a competing view. In extreme form, it says that comparative advantages certainly exist but are typically acquired, not nature given, *and* they change over time. This view of comparative advantage is *dynamic* rather than static. New industries are seen as depending more on human capital than on fixed physical capital or natural resources. The skills of a computer designer, a videogame programmer, a sound mix technician, or a rock star are acquired by education and on-the-job training (which contribute to the negative slope of their industry's learning curve). Natural endowments of energy and raw materials cannot account for Britain's prominence in modern pop music, the United States' leadership in computer software, or Japan's success in the automobile and silicon-chip industries. When a country such as the United States finds its former dominance (based on comparative advantage) declining in such smokestack industries as automobiles and steel, its firms need not sit idly by. Instead, they can begin to adapt by developing new areas of comparative advantage.

There are elements of truth in both extreme

---

[3]Of course, they might foolishly use the same policies to develop industries in which they do not have, and will never achieve, comparative advantage. See the discussion in Chapter 25.

views. It would be unwise to neglect resource endowments, climate, culture, and social and institutional arrangements. However, it also would be unwise to assume that all sources of comparative advantage are innate and immutable.

To some extent these views are reconciled in the theory of human capital that we discussed in Chapter 18. Comparative advantages that depend on human capital are consistent with the traditional Heckscher-Ohlin theory. The difference is that human capital is acquired by making conscious decisions relating to such matters as education and technical training.

Is comparative advantage obsolete? In the debate preceding the signing of the Canada-U.S. Free Trade Agreement, some opponents argued that the agreement relied on an outdated view of the gains from trade based on comparative advantage. The theory of comparative advantage was said to have been made obsolete by the new theories that we have just discussed.

In spite of such assertions, comparative advantage remains an important economic concept. At any one time, the operation of the price system will result in trade that follows the current pattern of comparative advantage. This is because comparative advantage is reflected in international relative prices, and these relative prices determine what goods a country will import and what it will export. For example, if Canadian costs of producing steel are particularly low relative to other Canadian costs, Canada's price of steel will be low by international standards, and steel will be a Canadian export (which it is). If Canada's costs of producing textiles are particularly high relative to other Canadian costs, Canada's price of textiles will be high by international standards, and Canada will import textiles (which it does—as much as Canadian tariffs and quotas permit). So there is no reason to change the view that Ricardo long ago expounded: *Current* comparative advantage is a major determinant of trade under free-market conditions.

What has changed, however, is economists' views about the *determinants* of comparative advantage. It now seems that current comparative advantage may be more open to change by private entrepreneurial activities and by government policy than used to be thought. Thus, what is obsolete is the belief (to the extent that it was ever held) that a country's current comparative advantages, and

hence its current pattern of imports and exports, must be accepted as given and unchangeable.

The theory that comparative advantage determines trade flows is not obsolete, but the theory that comparative advantage is determined by forces beyond the reach of public policy has been discredited.

It is one thing to observe that governments may be able to influence comparative advantage. It is another thing to conclude that it is advisable for them to try. As we saw in Part 6, the case for a specific government intervention requires that (1) there is scope for governments to improve on the results achieved by the free market, (2) the costs of the intervention be less than the value of the improvement to be achieved, and (3) governments will actually be able to carry out the required interventionist policies (without, for example, being sidetracked by considerations of electoral advantage).

The Terms of Trade

So far we have seen that world production can be increased when countries specialize in the production of the commodities in which they have or can acquire a comparative advantage and then trade with one another. We now ask: How will these gains from specialization and trade be shared among countries? The division of the gain depends on the terms under which trade takes place. The **terms of trade** measure the quantity of imported goods that can be obtained per unit of goods exported and are measured by the ratio of the price of exports to the price of imports.

A rise in the price of imported goods, with the price of exports remaining unchanged, indicates a *fall in the terms of trade*; it will now take more exports to buy the same quantity of imports. Similarly, a rise in the price of exported goods, with the price of imports remaining unchanged, indicates a *rise in the terms of trade*; it will now take fewer exports to buy the same quantity of imports. Thus, the ratio of prices is a measure of the amount of exported goods that are needed to acquire a given quantity of imports.

In the example of Table 24-4, the Canadian domestic opportunity cost of one unit of cloth is 1.67 bushels of wheat. In other words, if in Canada resources are transferred from wheat to cloth, 1.67 bushels of wheat are given up for every metre of cloth gained. However, if Canada can obtain its cloth by trade on more favourable terms, it is worthwhile for the nation to produce and export wheat to pay for cloth imports. Suppose, for example, that international prices are such that 1 metre of cloth exchanges for (i.e., is equal in value to) 1 bushel of wheat. At these prices, Canadians can obtain 1 metre of cloth for 1 bushel of wheat exported. They get more cloth per unit of wheat exported than they can by moving resources out of wheat into cloth production at home. Therefore, the terms of trade favour specializing in the production of wheat and trading wheat for cloth in international markets.

Similarly, in the example of Table 24-4, English consumers gain when they can obtain wheat abroad at any terms of trade that are more favourable than 2 metres of cloth per unit of wheat. If the terms of trade permit exchange of 1 bushel of wheat for 1 metre of cloth, the terms of trade favour English traders' buying wheat and selling cloth in international markets. Here, both England and Canada gain from trade. Each can obtain the commodity in which it has a comparative disadvantage at a lower opportunity cost through international trade than through domestic production. How the terms of trade affect the gains from trade is shown graphically in Box 24-1.

Because actual international trade involves many countries and many commodities, a country's terms of trade are computed as an index number:

$$\text{Terms of Trade} = \frac{\text{index of export prices}}{\text{index of import prices}} \times 100$$

A rise in the index is often referred to as a *favourable* change in a country's terms of trade. A favourable change means that more can be imported per unit of goods exported than previously. For example, if the export price index rises from 100 to 120 while the import price index rises from 100 to 110, the terms-of-trade index rises from 100 to 109. At the new terms of trade, a unit of exports will buy 9 percent more imports than at the old terms.

A decrease in the index of the terms of trade, often called an *unfavourable* change, means that the country can import less in return for any given amount of exports or, what is the same, that it must export more to pay for any given amount of imports. For example, reductions in the international prices of wood and mineral products in the early 1980s hit the Canadian economy particularly hard. The terms of trade turned against Canada as the same amount of exports of mineral and wood products paid for much smaller amounts of imports. Later in the decade, sharp reductions in the international prices of agricultural products, particularly grains, hit the prairie provinces, causing unfavourable changes in their terms of trade.

Many of Canada's exports are heavily concentrated in primary products whose prices tend to vary over the business cycle much more than prices of manufactured goods. Thus, the Canadian terms of trade tend to vary quite significantly over the cycle, turning favourably in boom times and unfavourably in recessions. These swings are often accompanied by swings in optimism and pessimism about the long-run future of the Canadian economy among commentators and policy makers who misinterpret reversible cyclical fluctuations as permanent long-term changes.

SUMMARY

1. One country (or region or individual) has an absolute advantage over another country (or region or individual) in the production of a commodity when it can produce more of the commodity than the other can with the same input of resources in each country.

2. In a situation of absolute advantage, total production of both commodities will be raised if each country specializes in the production of the commodity in which it has the absolute advantage.

However, the gains from trade do not require absolute advantage on the part of each country, only comparative advantage.

3. Comparative advantage is the relative advantage that one country enjoys over another in the production of various commodities. World production of all commodities can be increased if each country transfers resources into the production of the commodities in which it has a comparative advantage.

4. Comparative advantage arises from countries' having different opportunity costs of producing particular goods. This creates the opportunity for all nations to gain from trade.

5. The most important proposition in the theory of the gains from trade is that trade allows all countries to obtain the goods in which they do not have a comparative advantage at a lower opportunity cost than they would face if they were to produce all commodities for themselves. This allows all countries to have more of all commodities than they could have if they tried to be self-sufficient.

6. As well as gaining the advantages of specialization arising from comparative advantage, a nation that engages in trade and specialization may realize the benefits of the economies of large-scale production and of learning by doing.

7. Earlier theories regarded comparative advantage as largely determined by natural resource endowments and climatic factors and thus as difficult to change. Economists now believe that comparative advantage can be acquired and thus can be changed either by private entrepreneurial activity or by government policy.

8. The terms of trade refer to the ratio of the prices of goods exported to the prices of goods imported, which determines the quantities of exports needed to pay for imports. The terms of trade determine how the gains from trade are shared. A favourable change in terms of trade, that is, a rise in export prices relative to import prices, means that a country can acquire more imports per unit of exports.

TOPICS FOR REVIEW

Interpersonal, interregional, and international specialization

Absolute advantage and comparative advantage

Gains from trade: specialization, scale economies, learning by doing, and learning curves

Opportunity cost and comparative advantage

Dynamic comparative advantage

Terms of trade

DISCUSSION QUESTIONS

1. Adam Smith saw a close connection between the wealth of a nation and its willingness "freely to engage" in foreign trade. What is the connection?

2. Suppose that the situation described in the accompanying table exists. Assume that there are no tariffs and no government intervention and that labour is the only factor of production. Let X take different values—say, $10, $20, $40, and $60. In each case, in what

direction will trade have to flow in order for the gains from trade to be exploited?

	Labour cost of producing one unit of	
Country	Artichokes	Bathtubs
Inland	$20	$40
Outland	$15	$X

3. Suppose that Canada had an absolute advantage in all manufactured products. Should it then ever import any manufactured products?

4. Suppose that Canada were to become two separate countries. What predictions would you make about the standard of living compared with what it is today? Does the fact that Canada, the United States, and Mexico are separate countries lead to a lower standard of living in the three countries than if they were united into a new country called Northica?

5. Studies of Canadian trade patterns have shown that high-wage sectors of industry are among the largest and fastest-growing export sectors. Does this contradict the principle of comparative advantage?

6. Predict what each of the following events would do to the terms of trade of the importing country and the exporting country, other things being equal.
   a. A blight destroys a large part of the coffee beans produced in the world.
   b. The Koreans cut the price of the steel they sell to Canada.
   c. General inflation of 10 percent occurs around the world.
   d. Violation of OPEC output quotas leads to a sharp fall in the price of oil.

7. Heavy Canadian borrowing abroad has several times led to a high value of the dollar and thus a rise in the ratio of export prices to import prices. Although this is called a favourable change in the terms of trade, are there any reasons why it may not have been a good thing for the Canadian economy?

8. Discuss the following quotations:
   a. "In today's world of knowledge-intensive production, comparative advantage is more often created than being endowed by nature.
   b. Whether or not specific comparative advantages can be created by good economic policy, they can certainly be destroyed by bad policy.
   c. "In a world of rapid technological change, few comparative advantages are secure over time."

25

The Theory and Practise of Commercial Policy

All governments have policies toward international trade, which are called **commercial policies.** At one extreme is **free trade,** which means an absence of any form of government interference with the free flow of international trade. **Protectionism** refers to any departure from free trade designed to give some protection to domestic industries from foreign competition.

The Theory of Commercial Policy

Today, debates over commercial policy are as heated as they were 200 years ago, when economists were still working out the theory of the gains from trade that we presented in Chapter 24. Should a country permit the free flow of international trade, or should it seek to protect its local producers from foreign competition? Such protection may be achieved either by **tariffs,** which are taxes designed to raise the prices of foreign goods, or by **nontariff barriers (NTBs),** which are devices other than tariffs designed to reduce the flow of imported goods. Examples of NTBs include quotas, voluntary export restrictions, and customs procedures that are deliberately made to be unnecessarily cumbersome. Table 25-1 shows some tariff rates that exist as of 1994. Under a worldwide agreement, known as the Uruguay Round, these tariffs will be reduced by about 30 percent by the end of the century. Under two regional agreements, tariffs will be completely eliminated by 1998 on trade between Canada and the United States, and by early in the next century, on trade between Canada, the United States, and Mexico.

Methods of Protection

Two main types of protectionist policy are illustrated in Figure 25-1. Both cause the price of the imported good to rise and its quantity to fall. They differ, however, in how they achieve these results. The caption to the figure analyses these two types of policy.

Policies That Directly Raise Prices

The first type of protectionist policy directly raises the *price* of the imported commodity. A tariff, also often called an *import duty,* is the most common policy of this type. Other such policies are any rules or regulations that fulfill three conditions: They are costly to comply with; they do not apply to competing, domestically produced commodities; and they are more than is required to meet any purpose other than restricting trade.

TABLE 25-1 Current Tariffs on Industrial Products by Sector: Canada, United States, and All Industrial Countries (*percentage*)[a]

Sector	Canada	United States	All industrial countries
Textiles	16.7	9.2	8.5
Wearing apparel	24.2	22.7	17.5
Leather products	6.3	4.2	3.0
Footwear	21.9	8.8	12.1
Wood products	3.2	1.7	1.9
Furniture and fixtures	14.3		7.3
Paper and paper products	6.7	0.2	4.2
Printing and publishing	1.0	0.7	1.5
Chemicals	7.5	2.4	6.7
Rubber products	6.7	2.5	4.1
Nonmetal mineral products	6.4	5.3	4.0
Glass and glass products	7.2	6.2	7.9
Iron and steel	5.4	3.6	4.4
Nonferrous metals	2.0	0.7	1.6
Metal products	8.5	4.8	6.3
Nonelectrical machinery	4.5	3.3	4.7
Electrical machinery	5.8	4.4	7.1
Transportation equipment	1.6	2.5	6.0
Miscellaneous manufactures	5.4	4.2	4.7
All industries	5.2	4.3	5.8

Source: A. V. Deardorff and R. M. Stern, "Economic Effects of Complete Elimination of Post-Tokyo Round Tariffs," in *Trade Policy in the 1980s*, ed. W. R. Cline (Washington, D.C.: Institute for International Economics, 1983), pp. 674-675.

[a]Weighted by own-country imports, excluding petroleum.

Canada remains a relatively high-tariff country. These Canadian and U.S. tariffs apply to trade with third countries. Tariffs on trade between Canada and the United States are being phased out under the Canada-U.S. Free Trade Agreement over the period 1989-1999. In spite of having cut its tariffs significantly in rounds of GATT negotiations over the past several decades, Canada remains a relatively high-tariff country compared to both the United States, its largest trading partner, and the average of all industrial countries. Note that a few Canadian tariffs are still over 20 percent. The data show tariff rates in effect after the last round of tariff negotiations had been phased in at the end of 1986. They will remain until the Uruguay Round cuts are phased in during the last half of this century.

As shown in part (i) of Figure 25-1, tariffs affect both foreign and domestic producers, as well as domestic consumers. The initial effect is to raise the domestic price of the imported commodity above its world price by the amount of the tariff. Imports fall, and, as a result, foreign producers sell less and so must transfer resources to other lines of production. The price received on domestically produced units rises, as does the quantity produced domestically. On both counts, domestic producers earn more. However, the cost of producing the extra output at home exceeds the price at which it could be purchased on the world market. Thus, the benefit to domestic producers comes at the expense of domestic consumers. Indeed, domestic consumers lose on two counts: First, they consume less of the product because its price rises, and second, they pay a higher price for the amount that they do consume. This extra spending ends up in two places: The extra that is paid on all units produced at home goes to domestic producers, and the extra that is paid on units still imported goes to the government as tariff revenue.

Policies That Directly Lower Quantities

The second type of protectionist policy directly restricts the *quantity* of an imported commodity. A common example is the **import quota,** by which the importing country sets a maximum of the quantity of some commodity that may be imported each year. Increasingly popular, however, is the **voluntary export restriction (VER),** an agreement by an *exporting* country to limit the amount of a good that it sells to the importing country.

The European Community (EC) and the United States have used VERs extensively, and the EC also makes frequent use of import quotas. Japan has been pressured into negotiating several VERs with the EC and the United States in order to limit sales of some of the Japanese goods that have had the most success in international competition. For example, in 1983, the United States and Canada negotiated VERs whereby the Japanese government agreed to restrict total sales of Japanese cars to these two countries for 3 years. When the agreements ran out in 1986, the Japanese continued to restrain their automobile sales by unilateral voluntary action. This episode is further considered in Box 25-1 on page 488.

FIGURE 25-1
Methods of Protecting Domestic Producers

(i) Free trade

(ii) Restricted trade

The same reduction in imports and increase in domestic production can be achieved by using either a tariff or a quantity restriction. In both parts of the figure, D and S are the domestic demand and supply curves, respectively, and p_w is the world price of some commodity that is both produced at home and imported.

Part (i) of the figure shows the situation under free trade. Domestic consumption is q_1, domestic production is q_0, and imports are q_0q_1.

Part (ii) shows what happens when protectionist policies restrict imports to the amount q_3q_2. When this is done by levying a tariff of T per unit, the price in the domestic market rises by the full amount of the tariff to p_d. Consumers reduce consumption from q_1 to q_2 and pay an extra amount, shown by the shaded areas 1, 2, and 4, for the q_2 that they now purchase. Domestic production rises from q_0 to q_3. Since domestic producers receive the domestic price, their receipts rise by the three light-shaded areas, labeled 1, 2, and 3. Area 3 is revenue that was earned by foreign producers under free trade, while areas 1 and 2 are paid by domestic consumers because of the higher prices that they must now pay. Foreign suppliers of the imported good continue to get the world price, so the government receives as tariff revenue the extra amount paid by consumers for the q_3q_2 units that are still imported (shown by the dark shaded area, 4).

When the same result is accomplished by a quantity restriction, the government—through either a quota or a *voluntary export agreement (VER)*—reduces imports to q_3q_2. This drives the domestic market price up to p_d and has the same effect on domestic producers and consumers as the tariff. Since the government has merely restricted the quantity of imports, both foreign and domestic suppliers get the higher price in the domestic market. Thus, foreign suppliers now receive the extra amount paid by domestic consumers (represented by the shaded area labeled 4) for the units that are still imported.

The Case for Free Trade

The case for free trade is based on the analysis presented in Chapter 24, in which we saw that, whenever opportunity costs differ among countries, specialization and trade will raise world living standards. Free trade allows countries to specialize in producing commodities in which they have a comparative advantage.

Free trade allows the maximization of world production, thus making it possible for every household in the world to consume more goods than it could without free trade.

This does not necessarily mean that everyone will be better off with free trade than without it. Protectionism could allow the citizens of some countries to obtain a larger share of a smaller world output, so that they would benefit even though on average everyone would lose. If we ask whether free trade makes it possible to improve everyone's well-being, the answer is yes. But if we ask whether free trade is, in fact, *always* advantageous to *everyone*, the answer is no.

There is abundant evidence to show that significant differences in opportunity costs exist and that large gains are realized from international trade due to these differences. What needs explanation is the fact that trade is not wholly free. Why do tariffs and nontariff barriers to trade continue to exist two centuries after Adam Smith and David Ricardo stated the case for free trade? Is there a valid case for protectionism? Before addressing these questions, let us examine the methods used in protectionist policy.

The Case for Some Protection

The case for protection contains two kinds of arguments. The first concerns national objectives other than national income; the second concerns the desire to increase domestic national income, possibly at the expense of total world income.

Objectives Other Than Maximizing National Income

It is quite possible to accept the proposition that national income is higher with free trade and yet rationally to oppose free trade because of a concern with policy objectives other than maximizing per capita national income.

Noneconomic advantages of diversification. Comparative advantage might dictate that a small country should specialize in producing a narrow range of commodities. Its government might decide, however, that there are distinct social advantages to encouraging a more diverse economy. Citizens would be given a wider range of occupations, and the social and psychological advantages of diversification would more than compensate for a reduction in living standards by, say, 5 percent below what they could be with specialization of production according to comparative advantage.

Risks of specialization. For a very small country, such as Singapore, specializing in the production of only a few commodities—though dictated by comparative advantage—may involve risks that the

country does not wish to take. One such risk is that technological advances may render its basic product obsolete. Everyone understands this risk, but there is debate about what governments can do about it. The pro-tariff argument is that the government can encourage a more diversified economy by protecting industries that otherwise could not compete. Opponents argue that governments, being naturally influenced by political motives, are, in the final analysis, poor judges of which industries can be protected in order to produce diversification at a reasonable cost.

National defense. Another noneconomic reason for protectionism concerns national defense. Such arguments are seldom used in Canada. In the United States, however, it is argued that an experienced merchant marine is needed in case of war and that this industry should be fostered by protectionist policies, even though it is less efficient than that of the foreign competition. The U.S. Jones Act provides this protection by requiring that all cargoes moving between two U.S. ports be carried in U.S. ships.

Protection of specific groups. Although free trade will maximize per capita GDP over the whole economy, some specific groups may have higher incomes under protection than under free trade. An obvious example is a firm or industry that is given monopoly power when tariffs are used to restrict foreign competition. If a small group of firms, and possibly their employees, find their incomes increased by, say, 25 percent when they get tariff protection, they may not be concerned that everyone else's incomes fall by, say, 2 percent. They get a much larger share of a slightly smaller total income and end up better off. If they gain from the tariff, they will lose from free trade.

Conclusion. Although most people would agree that, other things being equal, they would prefer more income to less, a nation may rationally choose to sacrifice some income in order to achieve other goals. Economists can do three things when they are faced with such reasons for imposing tariffs. First, they can see if the proposed tariff really does achieve the goals suggested. Second, they can calculate the cost of the tariff in terms of lowered living standards. Third, they can check policy alternatives to see if there are other means of achieving the stated goal at a lower cost in terms of lost output.

Box 25-1

Import Restrictions on Japanese Cars: Tariffs or Quotas?

In the early 1980s, imports of Japanese cars seriously threatened the automobile industries of the United States, Canada, and Western Europe. While continuing to espouse relatively free trade as a long-term policy, the U.S. and Canadian governments argued that the domestic industry needed short-term protection to tide it over the period of transition as smaller cars became the typical North American vehicle. Voluntary export restrictions (VERs) were reached whereby the Japanese government agreed to organize Japanese auto firms to limit severely the number of Japanese cars that could be exported to the United States and Canada. Over 10 years later, the Japanese still voluntarily restrict their sales of cars to North America.

What does economic theory predict to be the effects of VERs and tariffs? In both cases, imports are restricted, and the resulting scarcity supports a higher market price. With a tariff, the extra market value is appropriated by the government of the importing country—in this case, the U.S. and Canadian governments. With a VER, the extra market value accrues to the goods' suppliers—in this case, the Japanese car makers and their U.S. retailers.

Both cases are illustrated in the accompanying figure. We assume that the North American market provides a small enough part of total Japanese car sales to leave the Japanese willing to supply all the cars that are demanded in the United States and Canada at their fixed list price. This is the price p_0 in both parts of the figure. Given the U.S. demand curve for Japanese cars, D, there are q_0 cars sold before restrictions are imposed.

In part (i), the United States places a tariff of T per unit on Japanese cars, raising their price in the United States to p_1 and lowering sales to q_1. Suppliers' revenue is shown by the light shaded area. Government tariff revenue is shown by the dark shaded area.

In part (ii), a VER of q_1 is negotiated, making the supply curve of Japanese cars become vertical at q_1. The market-clearing price is p_1. The suppliers' revenue is the whole shaded area (p_1 times q_1).

In both cases, the shortage of Japanese cars drives up their price, creating a substantial margin over costs. Under a tariff, the U.S. and Canadian governments capture the margin. Under a VER policy, however, the margin accrues to the Japanese manufacturers.

Although this is a simplified picture, it captures the essence of what actually happened. First, while sellers of North American cars were keeping prices as low as possible, and sometimes offering rebates on slow-selling models, Japanese cars were listed at healthy profit margins. Second, while it was always possible for the buyer of a North American car to negotiate a good discount off the list price, Japanese cars usually sold for their full list price. Third, because Japanese manufacturers were not allowed to supply all of the cars that they could sell in the United States, they had to choose which types of cars to supply. Not surprisingly, they tended to sat-

The Objective of Maximizing National Income

Next we consider five important arguments for the use of tariffs when the objective is to make national income as large as possible.

To alter the terms of trade. Trade restrictions can sometimes be used to turn the terms of trade in favour of countries that produce and export a large fraction of the world's supply of some commodity. They can also be used to turn the terms of trade in favour of countries that constitute a large fraction of the world demand for some commodity that they import.

When the OPEC countries restricted their outisfy fully the demand for their more expensive cars, which have higher profit margins. This change in the product mix of Japanese cars exported to the United States raised the average profit per car exported.

The VERs were thus very costly to North American consumers and an enormous profit boon to Japanese auto manufacturers. Indeed, it was estimated that North American consumers paid about US$150,000 *per year* for each job that was saved in the U.S. and Canadian automobile industries, and that most of this went to Japanese producers! (This cost to consumers per job saved is typical of what is found in many industries where VERs or their equivalents have been used.) Of course, this amount is spread over many consumers, so each does not notice the amount of his or her contribution. Nonetheless, $150,000 per year could do a lot of things, including fully retrain the workers and subsidize their movement to industries and areas where they could produce things that could be sold on free markets without government protection.

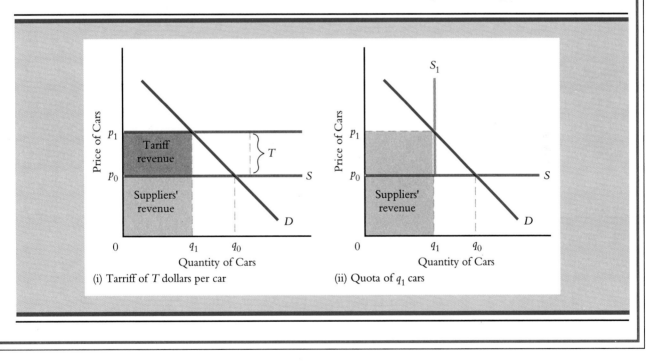

(i) Tarriff of T dollars per car

(ii) Quota of q_1 cars

put of oil in the 1970s, they were able to drive the price of oil up relative to the prices of other traded goods. This turned the terms of trade in their favour: For every barrel of oil exported, they were able to obtain a much larger quantity of imports. When the output of oil grew greatly in the mid-1980s, the relative price of oil fell dramatically, and the terms of trade turned unfavourably to the oil-exporting countries. These are illustrations of how changes in the quantities of exports can affect the terms of trade.

Now consider a country that provides a large fraction of the total demand for some product that it imports. By restricting its demand for that product through tariffs, it can force the price of that product down. This turns the terms of trade in its favour, because it can now get more units of imports per unit of exports.

Both of these techniques lower world output. They can, however, make it possible for a small group of countries to gain, because they get a sufficiently larger share of the smaller world output. However, if foreign countries retaliate by raising their tariffs, the ensuing trade war can easily leave every country with a lowered income.

To protect against "unfair" actions by foreign firms and governments. Tariffs may be used to prevent foreign industries from gaining an advantage over domestic industries through the use of predatory practises that will harm domestic industries and hence lower national income. Two common practises are the payment of subsidies by foreign governments to their exporters and dumping by foreign firms. (Dumping is a tricky concept related to "predatory price behaviour" in the market for exports.) Such practises are called *unfair trade practises,* and the laws that deal with them are called *fair-trade laws* or *trade-remedy laws.* The circumstances under which foreign subsidization and dumping provide a valid argument for tariffs are considered in detail later in this chapter.

To protect infant industries. The oldest valid argument for protectionism as a means of raising living standards concerns economies of scale. It is usually called the **infant industry argument.** If an industry has large economies of scale, costs and prices will be high when the industry is small but will fall as the industry grows. In such industries, the country first in the field has a tremendous advantage. A newly developing country may find that in the early stages of development, its industries are unable to compete with established foreign rivals. A trade restriction may protect these industries from foreign competition while they grow. When they are large enough, they may be able to produce as cheaply as foreign rivals and thus be able to compete without protection.

To encourage learning by doing. Learning by doing, which we discussed in Chapter 24, suggests that the existing pattern of comparative advantage need not be taken as immutable. If a country can learn enough by producing commodities in which it currently is at a comparative disadvantage, it may gain in the long run by specializing in those com-

modities and developing a comparative advantage in them as the learning process helps to lower their costs. Learning by doing is an example of what in Chapter 24 we called *dynamic comparative advantages.* The successes of such *newly industrialised countries* (the so-called NICs) as Hong Kong, South Korea, Singapore, and Taiwan seemed to many observers to be based on acquired skills and government policies that created favourable business conditions. This gave rise to the theory that comparative advantages can change and can be developed by suitable government policies.

Protecting a domestic industry from foreign competition may give its management time to learn to be efficient and its labour force time to acquire needed skills. If so, there may be a long-term payoff to protecting the industry against foreign competition while a dynamic comparative advantage is being developed.

Some countries have succeeded in developing strong comparative advantages in targeted industries, but others have failed. One reason such policies have sometimes failed is that protecting local industries from foreign competition may make the industries unadaptive and complacent. Another reason is that it is difficult to identify now the industries that will be able to succeed in the future. All too often, the protected infant industry grows up to be a weakling that requires permanent tariff protection for its continued existence, or else its rate of learning is slower than for similar industries in countries that do not provide protection from the chill winds of international competition. In these instances, the anticipated comparative advantage never materializes.

To create or to exploit a strategic trade advantage. A major new argument for tariffs or other trade restrictions is to create a strategic advantage in producing or marketing some new product that is expected to generate pure profits. To the extent that all lines of production just cover their full opportunity costs, there is no reason to produce goods other than ones for which a country has a comparative advantage. Some goods, however, are produced in industries containing a few large firms where large scale economies provide a natural barrier to further entry. Firms in these industries can earn extra-high profits over long periods of time. Where such industries are already well established, there is little chance that a new firm will replace one of the existing giants.

The situation is, however, more fluid with new products. The first firm to develop and market a new product successfully may earn a substantial pure profit over all of its opportunity costs and become one of the few established firms in the industry. If protection of the domestic market can increase the chance that one of the protected domestic firms will become one of the established firms in the international market, the protection may pay off. This is the general idea behind the modern concept of strategic trade policy, and it is treated in more detail in the next section.

Strategic Trade Policy and Competitiveness

Implications of high development costs. Many of today's high-tech industries have falling average total cost curves due to their large fixed costs of product development. For a new generation of civilian aircraft, silicon chips, computers, artificial-intelligence machines, and genetically engineered food products, a high proportion of each producer's total costs go to product development. These are fixed costs of entering the market, and they must be incurred before a single unit of output can be sold.

In such industries, the actual costs of producing each unit of an already developed product may be quite small. Even if average variable costs are constant, the large fixed development costs mean that the average total cost curve has a significant negative slope over a large range of output. It follows that the price at which a firm can expect to recover its total cost is negatively related to its expected volume of sales. The larger are the sales that it expects, the lower is the price that it can charge and still expect to recover its full costs.

In such industries, there may be room for only a few firms, and those firms may make large profits. A large number of firms, each of which has a relatively small output, could not recover their fixed costs. A small number of firms, each of which has a high output, can do so. Furthermore, it is possible for these firms to make large profits, whereas the entry of one more firm would cause everyone to suffer losses. In this case, the first firms that become established in the market will control it and will earn the profits.[1]

The production of full-sized commercial jets provides an example of an industry that possesses many of these characteristics. The development costs of a new generation of jet aircraft have risen with each new generation. If the aircraft manufac-

turers are to recover these costs, each of them must have large sales. Thus, the number of firms that the market can support has diminished steadily, until today there is room in the world aircraft industry for only two or three firms that produce a full range of commercial jets.

Argument for subsidies. The characteristics just listed are sometimes used to provide arguments for subsidizing the development of such industries. Suppose, for example, that there is room in the aircraft industry for only three major producers of the next round of passenger jets. If a government subsidizes a domestic firm, this firm may become one of the three that succeed. In this case, the profits that are subsequently earned may more than repay the cost of the subsidy. Furthermore, another country's firm, which was not subsidized, may have been just as good as the three that succeeded. Without the subsidy, however, this firm may lose out in the battle to establish itself as one of the three surviving firms in the market. Having lost this one battle, it loses its entire fight for existence. The firm, and the country's possibility of being represented in the industry, are gone for the foreseeable future.

This example is not unlike the story of the European Airbus. The European producers received many direct subsidies (and they charge that their main competitor, the Boeing 767, received many indirect ones). Whatever the merits of the argument, several things are clear: The civilian jet aircraft industry remains profitable; there is room for only two or three major producers; and one of these would not have been the European consortium if it had not been for substantial government assistance.

Argument for tariffs. The argument for tariffs is that a protected domestic market greatly reduces the risks of product development and allows successful firms to achieve sufficient scale on the domestic

---

[1]The reason for this is found in the indivisibility of product development costs. If, say, $500 million is required to develop a marketable product, a firm that spends only $300 million gets nothing. To see why this creates the potential for profits, assume that the market is large enough for the product to be sold at a price that would cover variable costs of production and also pay the opportunity costs of $1.25 billion worth of capital. Further assume that the capital required for actual production is negligible. In this case, two firms with a total of $1 billion of capital invested in development costs will enter the market and earn large profits. However, if a third firm entered, making the industry's total invested capital $1.5 billion, all three firms would incur losses.

market to be able to sell at competitive prices abroad. The classic example here is the victory in the 1970s of the Japanese semiconductor producers over their U.S. rivals. From the beginning of the industry, U.S. firms held a large competitive edge over all others. Then the Japanese decided to develop their industry. To do so, they shielded their domestic market from penetration by U.S. firms. The Japanese, who at first were well behind the U.S. firms, caught up and were then able to penetrate the open U.S. market. In the end, the Japanese succeeded with the next generation of silicon chips, and the once-dominant U.S. industry suffered greatly. (This does not seem to have stopped the U.S. firms from being successful in the round of competition over the next generation of chips in the 1990s.)

A combination of domestic subsidization and tariff protection allowed the Japanese semiconductor industry to score a major victory in terms of market share over their U.S. competitors. The strategy, however, entailed large costs, both for product development and because of aggressive, below-cost pricing policies. Currently, there is debate as to whether the long-run profits resulting from this policy were sufficient to cover all these costs.

Debate over strategic trade policy. Generalizing from this and similar cases, some economists advocate that Canada and the United States adopt a *strategic trade policy,* which means, for high-tech industries, government protection of the home market and government subsidization (either openly or by more subtle back-door methods) of the product-development stage. These economists say that, if their country does not follow their advice, it will lose out in industry after industry to the more aggressive Japanese and European competition—a competition that is adept at combining private innovative activity with government assistance.

Opponents argue that strategic trade policy is nothing more than a modern version of the age-old, and faulty, justifications for tariff protection. They argue that, once all countries try to be strategic, they will all waste vast sums trying to break into industries in which there is no room for most of them. Canadian and U.S. consumers would benefit most, they say, if their governments let other countries engage in this game. Consumers could then buy the cheap, subsidized foreign products and export traditional, lower-tech products in return. The

opponents of strategic trade policy also argue that democratic governments that enter the game of picking and backing winners are likely to make more bad choices than good ones. One bad choice, with *all* of its massive development costs written off, would require that many good choices also be made, in order to make the equivalent in profits that would allow taxpayers to break even overall.[2]

Advocates of strategic trade policy reply that a country cannot afford to stand by while others play the strategic game. They argue that there are key industries that have major "spillovers" into the rest of the economy. If a country wants to have a high living standard, it must, they argue, compete with the best. If a country lets all of its key industries migrate to other countries, many of the others will follow. The country then risks being reduced to the status of a less-developed nation.

Longer-run considerations. In today's world, a country's products must stand up to international competition if they are to survive. Over time, this requires that they hold their own in competition for successful innovations. Over even so short a period as a decade, firms that do not develop new products (product innovation) and new production methods (process innovation) will fall seriously behind their competitors in many, possibly most, industries. Using case studies covering many countries, economists such as Michael Porter of Harvard have shown that almost all firms that succeed in holding their own in competition based on innovation operate in highly competitive environments.[3]

Protection, by conferring a national monopoly, reduces the incentive for industries to fight to hold their own internationally. Secure in the home market because of the tariff wall, protected industries often become less and less competitive in the international market.

Trade Remedy Laws and Nontariff Barriers

As tariffs were lowered over the years since 1947, countries that wished to protect domestic industries began using, and abusing, a series of trade restric-

---

[2]Let each investment be $100m and, when successful, return $125m, for a 25 percent return. Nine investments cost $900m, and seven successes and two total losses yield $875m. This is an overall loss of $25m on a $900m investment.

[3]Michael Porter, *The Competitive Advantage of Nations* (New York: The Free Press, 1990).

tions that came to be known as nontariff barriers (NTBs). The original purpose of some of these was to remedy certain legitimate problems that arise in international trade. For this reason, they are often called *trade remedy laws*. All too often, however, they are misused to become potent methods of simple protectionism. When this happens they are called measures of *contingent protection*.

Escape clause. One procedure that can be used as an NTB is the so-called escape clause action. A rapid surge of some imports may threaten the existence of domestic producers. These producers may then be given temporary relief to allow them time to adjust. This is done by raising tariff rates on the commodity in question above those set by international agreements. The trouble is that, once imposed, these "temporary" measures are hard to eliminate.

Dumping. When a commodity is sold in a foreign country at a price that is lower than the price in the domestic market, it is called **dumping.** Dumping is a form of price discrimination studied in the theory of monopoly. Most governments have antidumping duties, which protect their own industries against unfair foreign pricing practises.

Dumping, if it lasts indefinitely, can be a gift to the receiving country. Its consumers get goods from abroad at less than their real cost. Dumping is more often a temporary measure, designed to get rid of unwanted surpluses, or a predatory attempt to drive competitors out of business. In either case, domestic producers complain about unfair foreign competition. In both cases, it is accepted international practise to levy *antidumping duties* on foreign imports. These duties are designed to eliminate the discriminatory elements in their prices.

Unfortunately, antidumping laws have been evolving over the last few decades in ways that allow antidumping duties to become barriers to trade and competition, rather than to provide redress for unfair trading practises. Two features of the antidumping system that is now in effect in many countries make it highly protectionist. First, *any* price discrimination is classified as dumping and thus is subject to penalties. Thus, prices in the producer's domestic market become, in effect, minimum prices, below which no sales can be made in foreign markets, whatever the circumstances in the domestic and foreign markets. Second, following a change

in the U.S. law in the early 1970s, many countries' laws now calculate the "margin of dumping" as the difference between the price that is charged in that country's market and the foreign producers' "full allocated cost" (average total cost). This means that, when there is global excess demand so that the profit-maximizing price for all producers is below average total cost (but above average variable cost), foreign producers can be convicted of dumping. This gives domestic producers enormous protection whenever the market price falls temporarily below average total cost.

Countervailing duties. Countervailing duties provide another case in which a trade relief measure can sometimes become a covert NTB. The countervailing duty is designed to act not as a tariff barrier but rather as a means of creating a "level playing field" on which fair international competition can take place. Canadian (and U.S.) firms rightly complain that they cannot compete against the seemingly bottomless purses of foreign governments. Subsidized foreign exports can be sold indefinitely in Canada at prices that would produce losses in the absence of the subsidy. The original object of countervailing duties was to counteract the effect on price of the presence of such foreign subsidies.

If a Canadian or American firm suspects the existence of such a subsidy and registers a complaint, its government is required to make an investigation. For a countervailing duty to be levied, the investigation must find, first, that the foreign subsidy to the specific industry in question does exist and, second, that it is large enough to cause significant injury to competing domestic firms.

There is no doubt that U.S. countervailing duties sometimes have been used to remove the effects of "unfair" competition that are caused by foreign subsidies. The Canadian government complains, however, that countervailing duties are often used as a thinly disguised barrier to trade. At the early stages of the development of countervailing duties, only subsidies whose prime effect was to distort trade were possible objects of countervailing duties. Even then, however, the existence of equivalent domestic subsidies was *not taken into account* when decisions were made to put countervailing duties on subsidized imports. Thus, the United States has some countervailing duties against foreign goods where the foreign subsidy is less than the U.S. subsidy. This does not create a level playing field.

Over time, the type of subsidy that is subject to countervailing duties has evolved until almost any government program that affects industry now risks becoming the object of countervailing duty. Because all governments, including most Canadian provincial and U.S. state governments, have many programs that provide some direct or indirect assistance to industry, the potential for the use of countervailing duties as thinly disguised trade barriers is enormous.

Fallacious Trade-Policy Arguments

We saw in Chapter 24 that there are gains to be had from a high volume of international trade and specialization. Earlier in this chapter, we saw that there can be valid arguments for a moderate degree of protectionism. However, there are also many claims that do not advance the debate. Fallacious arguments are heard on both sides, and they colour much of the popular discussion. These arguments have been around for a long time, but their survival does not make them true. We examine them now to see where their fallacies lie.

Fallacious Protectionist Arguments

A number of fallacious arguments for levying tariffs have held the public's attention for centuries. Their age attests to their ability to persuade voters but not to their validity.

Prevent exploitation.   According to the exploitation theory, trade can never be mutually advantageous; any gain going to one trading partner *must* be at the other's expense. Thus, the weaker trading partner must protect itself by restricting its trade with the stronger partner. However, the principle of comparative advantage shows that it is possible for both parties to gain from trade and thus refutes the exploitation doctrine of trade.

Protect against low-wage foreign labour.   Surely, the argument runs, the products of low-wage countries will drive Canadian products from the market, and the high Canadian standard of living will be dragged down to that of its poor trading partners. Arguments of this sort have swayed many voters through the years. Its latest manifestation is found in the argument that Canada and the United States should not enter a free-trade agreement with Mex-

ico because high-wage Canadian and U.S. producers will be unable to compete against low-wage Mexican producers. In this section, we consider the average effects on the country as a whole. Later, we will consider how tariffs may benefit particular subgroups within a country.

As a prelude to considering such arguments, consider what the argument would imply if it were taken out of the international context and put into a local one, where the same principles govern the gains from trade. Is it really impossible for a rich person to gain from trading with a poor person? Would the local millionaire be better off if she did all her own typing, gardening, and cooking? No one believes that a rich person cannot gain from trading with those who are less rich.

Why, then, must a rich group of people lose from trading with a poor group? "Well," you say, "the poor group will price its goods too cheaply." Does anyone believe that consumers lose from buying in a discount house or a supermarket just because the prices are lower there than at the old-fashioned corner store? Consumers gain when they can buy the same goods at a lower price. If the Indonesians and Mexicans can only pay low wages and thus sell their goods cheaply, Indonesian and Mexican labour *may* suffer, but Canadian consumers will gain because they obtain their goods at a low cost in terms of the goods that must be exported in return. The cheaper our imports are, the better off we are in terms of the goods and services that are available for domestic consumption. In this case, low wages usually means low productivity. Economic forces will usually cause wages to follow productivity relatively closely.

Stated in more formal terms, the gains from trade depend on comparative, not absolute, advantages. World production is higher when any two areas, say, Canada and Mexico, specialize in the production of the goods for which they have a comparative advantage than when they both try to be self-sufficient.

Might it not be possible, however, that Mexico will undersell Canada in all lines of production, leaving Canada even worse off than if it had no trade with Mexico? The answer is no. The reason for this depends on the behaviour of exchange rates, which we shall study in Chapter 39. As we shall see, equality of demand and supply in foreign-exchange markets ensures that trade flows in both directions, so that one country cannot undersell another in all lines of production.

What we shall see in greater detail in Chapter 39 is the following. Imports can be obtained only by spending the currency of the country that makes the imports. Claims to this currency can be obtained only by exporting goods and services or by borrowing. Thus, lending and borrowing aside, imports must equal exports. All trade must be in two directions; countries can buy only if they can also sell.

In the long run, trade cannot hurt a country by causing it to import without exporting.

Trade, then, always provides scope for international specialization, with each country producing and exporting those goods for which it has a comparative advantage and importing those goods for which it does not.

Create domestic jobs and reduce unemployment. It is sometimes said that an economy with substantial unemployment, such as that of Canada in the 1930s or the early 1990s, provides an exception to the case for freer trade. Suppose that tariffs or import quotas cut the imports of Japanese cars, Korean textiles, Italian shoes, and French wine. Surely, the argument maintains, this will create more employment for central Canadian automobile workers, Quebec textile workers, B.C. lumber products, and prairie farm workers. The answer is that it will—initially. But the Japanese, Koreans, Italians, and French can buy from Canada only if they get Canadian dollars from those who have goods in Canada. The decline in their sales of automobiles, textiles, shoes, and wine will decrease their purchases of Canadian cars, clothing, lumber and grain, as well as vacations in Canada. Jobs will be lost in export industries and gained in industries that formerly faced competition from imports. The likely long-term effect is that overall unemployment will not be reduced but will merely be redistributed among industries. Because the export industries that contract tend to be more efficient than the import-competing industries that expand, this policy tends to reallocate resources from more to less efficient lines of production and hence to reduce overall GDP.

Fallacious Free-Trade Arguments

The strength of the genuine arguments for relatively free trade has prevented the use of many fallacious arguments. Nonetheless a number of fallacies are commonly repeated.

Free trade always benefits all groups and all countries. This is not necessarily so. Some groups, particularly workers in protected industries, may gain from protection. If free trade is adopted, these groups may lose even though the average income rises across the whole country. It is even possible that protection can raise average income for a whole country. A large country may gain by restricting trade in order to get a sufficiently favourable shift in their terms of trade. Such countries would lose if they gave up these tariffs and adopted free trade unilaterally.

Infant industries never abandon their tariff protection. We have already studied the argument for temporarily protecting infant industries until they grow large enough to reap economies of large scale production. It is sometimes argued, however, that granting protection to infant industries is a mistake, because these industries seldom admit to growing up and will cling to their protection even when they are fully grown. However, infant industry tariffs are a mistake *only* if these industries never grow up. In this case, permanent tariff protection would be required to protect a weak industry that would never be able to compete on an equal footing in the international market. However, if the industries do grow up and achieve the expected scale economies, the fact that, like any special interest group, they cling to their tariff protection is not a sufficient reason for denying protection to other, genuine infant industries. When economies of scale are realized, the real costs of production are reduced and resources are freed for other uses. Whether or not the tariff or other trade barriers remain, a cost saving has been effected by the scale economies.

Commercial Policy in the World Today

Foreign trade is vastly important in today's globalised world. This trade is aided by a number of institutions and agreements and hindered by a number of protectionist policies that we survey in this section.

The International Agreements on Commercial Policy

Before 1947, any country was free to impose any tariffs on its imports. However, when one country increased its tariffs, the action often triggered retaliatory actions by its trading partners. The 1930s saw a high-water mark of world protectionism, as each country sought to raise its employment by raising its tariffs. The end result was lowered efficiency, less trade, but not more employment. Since that time, much effort has been devoted to reducing tariff barriers, on both a multilateral and a regional basis.

The General Agreement on Tariffs and Trade (GATT)

One of the most notable achievements of the post-World War II era was the creation of the General Agreement on Tariffs and Trade (GATT). The principle of the GATT is that each country agrees not to make unilateral tariff increases. This prevents each country from raising its own tariffs in pursuit of selfish gain and ending in a situation in which all countries lose because all raise their tariffs. The GATT countries then meet periodically to negotiate on matters affecting foreign trade and to agree on across-the-board tariff cuts.

The two most recently completed rounds of GATT agreements have each reduced world tariffs by about one third. The Kennedy Round negotiations were completed in 1967, and new rates were phased in over a five-year period, ending in 1972. The Tokyo Round negotiations were completed in 1979, and the agreed tariff reductions were completed in 1986.

The year 1986 also saw the beginning of a new round of GATT negotiations, called the Uruguay Round. This round addressed five key issues: (1) the growing worldwide use of nontariff barriers to trade; (2) the need to develop rules for liberalizing trade in services, which is the most rapidly growing component of foreign trade; (3) the distorting effect on trade in agricultural products caused by heavy domestic subsidization of agriculture, particularly in the European Community; (4) the need to develop more effective methods of settling disputes that arise from violations of GATT rules; and (5) the desire of developed nations to gain better copyright protection for intellectual property—a desire that pitted the rich, innovating nations against the poorer nations with a self-interest in gaining access to intellectual property on terms as favourable as possible. (Intellectual property is a property right resulting from mental effort, such as discovery, product development, or the creation of a work of art, and resulting in a right of ownership conferred by a document such as a patent or a copyright.)

Negotiations dragged on, missing several deadlines in 1990, 1991, 1992, and 1993. Finally in December 1993, agreement was reached. The successful completion of the Uruguary Round brought important gains on each of the issues listed above.

Regional Agreements

Three standard forms of regional trade-liberalizing agreements are free-trade areas, customs unions, and common markets.

A **free-trade area (FTA)** is the least comprehensive of the three. It allows for tariff-free trade among the member countries, but it leaves each member free to levy its own trade restrictions on imports from other countries. As a result, members must maintain customs points at their common borders to make sure that imports into the free-trade area do not all enter through the member that is levying the lowest tariff on each item. They must also agree on *rules of origin* to establish when a good is made in a member country, and hence is able to pass duty free across their borders, and when it is imported from outside the FTA, and hence is liable to pay duties when it crosses borders within the FTA.

A **customs union** is a free-trade area plus an agreement to establish common barriers to trade with the rest of the world. Because they have a common tariff against the outside world, the members have no need for customs controls on goods moving among themselves or for rules of origin.

A **common market** is a customs union that also has free movement of labour and capital among its members.

Free-trade areas. The first important free-trade area in the modern era was the European Free Trade Association (EFTA). It was formed in 1960 by a group of European countries that were unwilling to join the EC because of its all-embracing character. Not wanting to be left out of the gains from trade, they formed an association whose sole purpose was tariff removal. First, they removed all tariffs on trade among themselves. Then each country signed a free-trade-area agreement with the EC. This makes the EC-EFTA market the largest tariff-free market in the world (over 300 million people). Most of the EFTA countries are now moving to enter the EC some time in the 1990s.

In 1985, the United States signed a limited free-trade agreement with Israel. In 1988, a sweeping agreement was signed between Canada and the United States, instituting free trade on all goods and many services and covering what is the world's largest flow of international trade between any two countries. This agreement is discussed at length later in the chapter. Australia and New Zealand have also entered into an association that removes restrictions on trade in goods and services between the two countries.

In 1991, at Mexico's behest, the United States, Canada, and Mexico began negotiations for a North American Free Trade Area, a so-called NAFTA. The agreement was signed in 1992, ratified by the three countries in 1993, and the first tariff cuts occurred in January 1994. NAFTA is discussed in more detail later in the chapter.

Common markets. The most important example of a common market came into being in 1957, when the Treaty of Rome brought together France, Germany, Italy, Holland, Belgium, and Luxembourg in what was first called the European Common Market (ECM), then renamed the European Economic Community (EEC), and finally just called the European Community (EC). The original six countries were joined in 1973 by the United Kingdom, the Republic of Ireland, and Denmark; Greece entered in 1983, and Spain and Portugal joined in 1986.

This organization is dedicated to bringing about free trade, complete mobility of factors of production, and the eventual harmonization of fiscal and monetary policies among the member countries. Many tariffs on manufactured goods were eliminated, and much freedom of movement of labour and capital was achieved. Then a major push for greatly increased integration resulted in a treaty in 1992. What came to be called "Europe 1992" is a much more fully integrated market than the Europe of a decade earlier. The goal is tariff-free movement of goods and services, complete factor mobility, and, eventually, a single European currency. If that finally happens, Europe will be a more integrated market than is Canada today.

The Crisis in the Multilateral Trading System

At the end of World War II, the United States took the lead in forming the GATT and in pressing for reductions in world tariffs through successive rounds of negotiations. Largely as a result of this U.S. initiative, the world's tariff barriers have been greatly reduced, while the volume of world trade has risen steadily.

The 1980s saw a serious crisis evolve in this multilateral trading system. The most important single force that led to this was a shift in the attitudes of many U.S. citizens toward protectionism. There are at least two key reasons for this shift.

The Growth of Protectionist Sentiment

First, under the impact of the persistent trade deficit, many influential U.S. leaders have become protectionist, a sentiment that has not prevailed to such a degree since the early 1930s. Second, the stiff competition coming from Japanese and European industry has led many U.S. citizens to fear a loss of U.S. competitiveness. Many fear that U.S. industry cannot compete effectively in the free market. This concern leads some to support *managed trade* as a protectionist device.

The growth of protectionist sentiments is not confined to the United States. Similar changes have been occurring in Europe for similar reasons. The great success of Japanese exporters in penetrating the EC market, while helping consumers, has caused trouble for many producers and has led to a search for ways to protect firms in the EC. The EC has made use of quotas, antidumping duties, and VERs. Because fighting an antidumping case can be time consuming and expensive, the mere registering of an antidumping complaint can often lead a foreign firm to raise its prices to the levels that are charged by domestic producers. This has the effect, desired by the domestic producers, of preventing more efficient foreign suppliers from underselling them.

The Pressure to Manage Trade

In the free-market system, competitive prices determine what is imported and what is exported. Under managed trade, the state has a major influence in determining the direction and magnitude of the flow of trade. The voluntary export agreement that we have discussed is a typical example of the tools of managed trade. To fulfill a VER, the government of the exporting country must form its exporting firms into a cartel so that they can divide up the portion of the foreign market that they are allowed to serve, as well as collectively ensuring that they do not violate the export ceiling.

Another current example of the influence of managed trade is the judging of trade balances bilaterally rather than multilaterally. Pressure is being exerted to manage U.S. trade so as to reduce large bilateral imbalances. The essence of the multilateral trading system, however, is that one country does not have to buy the same amount from another country as it sells to it. Enforcing bilateral balances would impose this requirement on each pair of trading countries. Such a requirement makes no more economic sense, however, than requiring that the barber only cut the butcher's hair to the value of the meat that he buys from her, and so on for each supplier with whom the barber deals. To achieve bilateral balances, the state must intervene in the market to regulate exports and imports.

Will the Multilateral Trading System Survive?

The next decade will be critical for the future of the multilateral trading system, which has served the world so well since the end of World War II. The dangers are, first, a growth of regional trading blocs that will trade more with their own member countries and less with others, and second, the growth of state-managed trade. The 1920s and 1930s provide a cautionary tale. Arguments for restricting trade always have a superficial appeal and sometimes have real short-term payoffs. In the long term, however, a major worldwide escalation of tariffs would lower efficiency and incomes and restrict trade worldwide, while doing nothing to raise employment. Both economic theory and the evidence of history support this proposition. Although most agree that pressure should be put on countries that restrict trade, the above analysis suggests that these pressures are best applied using the multilateral institution of the GATT. Unilateral imposition of restrictions in response to the perceived restrictions in other countries can all too easily degenerate into a round of mutually escalating trade barriers.

It is notable that in the United States, one of the staunchest defenders of the free-market system, many voices are being raised to advocate moves that reduce the influence of market forces on international trade and increase the degree of government control over that trade. It is ironic to see enthusiasm for state-managed trade growing just as the former Socialist countries of Eastern Europe have at last agreed that free markets are better regulators of economic activity than is the government. The strength of the movement to manage trade will become clearer during the 1990s.

Canadian Commercial Policy

Foreign trade accounts for a large part of the Canadian economy, as it does for most small high-income countries. In 1992, exports were about 25 percent of Canadian GDP, compared to about 9 percent for the United States. Figure 25-2 shows Canadian exports and imports as a percentage of GDP for the years 1947–1986.

The Canadian economy is heavily dependent on foreign trade and open foreign competition, because exports generate a large part of private-sector Canadian national income.

Canada's climate and resource endowments help to determine its trade patterns. Severe winters cause Canadians to spend money on foreign vacations and on imports of fresh fruits and vegetables. Canada has an abundance of arable land, timber, minerals, and energy in the form of both fossil fuels and hydroelectric power. As a consequence, Canada's exports are heavily concentrated in *primary products* and in manufactured goods that require large amounts of these resources in their production. A further important resource is human capital. The literate, numerate, relatively sophisticated majority of the Canadian population gives Canada a comparative advantage in many skill-intensive commodities.[4]

---

[4]This is one reason why economists worry so much about the current decline in educational standards. If the education of Canadians and Americans who become average members of the labour force declines seriously relative to what is obtained by Europeans and Japanese, Canadian and American comparative advantages will shift toward lower-skill, lower-income-producing activities.

FIGURE 25-2
Exports and Imports as a Percentage of GDP, 1972–1992

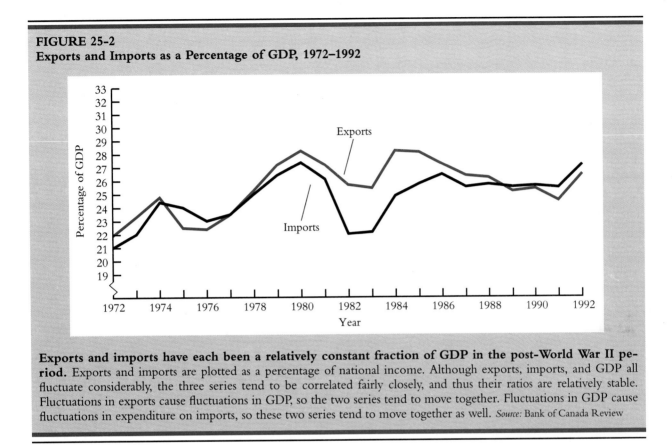

Exports and imports have each been a relatively constant fraction of GDP in the post-World War II period. Exports and imports are plotted as a percentage of national income. Although exports, imports, and GDP all fluctuate considerably, the three series tend to be correlated fairly closely, and thus their ratios are relatively stable. Fluctuations in exports cause fluctuations in GDP, so the two series tend to move together. Fluctuations in GDP cause fluctuations in expenditure on imports, so these two series tend to move together as well. *Source:* Bank of Canada Review

The Historical Background

The Staples Thesis

The central role of primary product exports in Canada's economic development is illustrated by the experience with prairie wheat, which emerged as an important export between the years 1886 and 1914. During this wheat boom period, real GDP increased by 150 percent and population grew from 5.1 to 7.9 million. Much of this growth was tied closely to the wheat sector. For example, over 10,000 miles of railway track were laid in order to transport agricultural products from the prairies to the lakehead at Thunder Bay and to the west coast. With the expansion of the railways came construction of grain elevators and investment in farm equipment and food-processing industries.

Based in part on Canada's experience during the wheat boom, Professors Harold Innis of the University of Toronto and W. A. MacIntosh of Queen's University developed the *staples thesis.* According to this thesis, economic growth in Canada has been tied to a sequence of exports of staple products, primary products for which Canada has had a comparative advantage. The important staple industries in the seventeenth and eighteenth centuries were the fur trade and the east coast fishery; during the nineteenth century, timber and wheat from Upper Canada were the important staples; and in the twentieth century, staples have been prairie wheat, pulp and paper, minerals, and oil and natural gas. These staples have been important not only as exports but also as stimuli to growth in other sectors of the economy.

Reciprocity: 1854–1866

In 1854, British North America and the United States signed a reciprocity treaty, and until 1866, when the treaty was abrogated by the United States, many commodities (including all primary products) crossed the border duty free.

High Tariffs and the National Policy: 1878–1935

After futile attempts to restore free trade with the United States, and partly in response to a major recession, Sir John A. MacDonald introduced his National Policy in 1878. This policy was presented as a program for long-run economic development and included subsidies for building railways, support for farm settlement, and emphasis on the export of a few primary products. However, the cornerstone was increased tariff protection for Canadian manufacturing.

Manufacturing industries in Ontario and Quebec gained from tariff protection, but the remaining provinces, which mainly exported primary goods and imported manufactured goods, lost by it. The National Policy raised the prices of the manufactured goods they bought. They had either to buy expensive, tariff-protected Canadian-produced goods or else pay the tariff-burdened price for imported goods.

Falling Tariffs: 1935 to the Present

The enormous increase in world protectionism in the 1920s and early 1930s demonstrated how vulnerable Canadians were to trade restrictions imposed by other countries. As a result, Canadian policy switched from pursuing trade restrictions to promoting trade liberalization.

This historic shift began with two tariff-reducing treaties negotiated with the United States in 1935 and 1937. It was confirmed in 1947, when Canada became a charter member of the GATT.

As a result of the tariff cuts negotiated between 1935 and 1980, Canadian tariffs have fallen from high to moderate levels. In the process, much Canadian manufacturing has been integrated into the world economy, and Canada has become an exporter of many manufactured goods (while also remaining an important exporter of primary products). Table 25-2 gives some relevant data. At the same time, Canadian exports have become increasingly concentrated in the U.S. market, as shown by Table 25-3.[5]

---

[5]One reason for this shift was the United Kingdom's entry into the European Economic Community in 1973, which ended any major trading relation between Canada and the United Kingdom. Another reason was the success of Canadian business in penetrating the U.S. market, which in the 1980s was the only *growing* market open to international traders. Firms from all over the world tried to sell more in that market, and Canadians succeeded better than almost any other country.

TABLE 25-2   Commodity Composition of Canadian Exports, 1960–1992

	1960	1970	1980	1992
Food and agriculture	18.8	11.4	11.1	9.2
Crude materials	21.2	18.8	19.8	13.0
Fabricated materials	51.9	35.8	39.4	32.4
Manufactured end products	7.8	33.8	29.4	44.3
Special transactions	0.3	0.2	0.3	1.1
Total	100.0	100.0	100.0	100.0

Source: Statistics Canada, *Summary of External Trade.*

Analysis of Canada's trade and industrial performance by the Economic Council of Canada indicated that trade liberalization in the 1970s and 1980s resulted in more trade *within* each industry. As trade barriers have been reduced, both Canadian exports and Canadian imports have increased in virtually all sectors. Whole industries did not disappear in either Canada or the United States. Instead, each industry has specialized in *particular product lines* in each country so that both Canadian *and* American exports have increased in each industry. The shift in *net* export positions has been modest for most industries. This is just as it was in Europe when trade was liberalized after formation of the Common Market, and for just the same reason—because so much of the adjustment was intraindustry. This specialization within industries is particularly important for Canada because of the small size of the Canadian market, which makes it difficult to cover fixed costs when the full range of modern differentiated products is produced by Canadian firms for sale only within Canada. The pioneering analysis of this point was first done by two Canadian economists, Stephen Stykholt and Harry Eastman, and is further explained in Box 25-2 on page 502.

The development of a competitive manufacturing sector in Canada was aided by a sectoral free trade agreement called the Auto Pact. Introduced in 1965, this pact effectively integrated the Canadian and American auto industries. It provided safeguards to prevent the industry from moving to the United States—which proved unnecessary, as Canadian efficiency soon matched and sometimes exceeded U.S. efficiency. Under the pact, the Canadian auto industry grew to be the largest manufacturing industry in central Canada and the largest Canadian ex-

TABLE 25-3 Composition of Canada's Trade, Selected Years *(percentage)*

	Exports			Imports		
	1960	*1983*	*1992*	*1960*	*1983*	*1992*
United States	57	73	77	70	72	65
United Kingdom	17	3	2	11	2	3
Other EC	8	5	5	5	6	7
Japan	3	5	5	2	6	7
All other countries	15	14	11	12	14	18

Source: Statistics Canada, *Summary of External Trade.*

porter. This pact was absorbed within the Canada-U.S. Free Trade Agreement and will become, in somewhat strengthened form, a part of the NAFTA, which is discussed below.

Many Canadian manufacturing industries have developed to the extent that they can export successfully, and several Canadian firms, such as Northern Telecom, Alcan, and Bombardier, have developed into highly successful transnational corporations. Although resource-based industries will continue to be important, Canada's future prosperity is linked more and more to its ability to export manufactured and service-related products. But the world markets for manufactured goods and services are fiercely competitive, and Canada's access to these markets is not assured. Policy makers are concerned not only to gain better access to foreign markets, but simply to preserve existing access.

Throughout the 1980s, growing U.S. protectionism not only threatened the access to the American market of many of Canada's exports, it also threatened to cause an exodus of Canadian capital to the United States. Many successful Canadian exporters were motivated to set up plants in the United States in order to avoid existing U.S. trade barriers and threatened new ones. Such relocations occurred in large numbers throughout the 1980s.

The Canada-U.S. Free Trade Agreement

The Canada-U.S. Free Trade Agreement (FTA) was proposed by many as a natural response to the economic problems described above. On the positive side, it was pointed out that about three quarters of

the trade barriers that existed in 1935 had already been dismantled, while Canadian industry had prospered with steadily increasing employment, exports, and real wages. Business leaders were mainly confident that they could benefit from open global competition without tariff protection. On the negative side, the fear of mounting U.S. protectionism led many to look for ways of preserving Canada's access to its most important foreign market, the United States.

After nearly two years of negotiations, an agreement was signed in October 1987. There followed a year of intense debate in Canada on the economic, social, and political consequences of the proposed FTA. In November 1988, a federal election, fought mainly on the free-trade issue, returned to power the Progressive Conservative Party, which supported the FTA (both the Liberal Party and the NDP opposed it). On January 1, 1989, the first round of tariff cuts took place, and firms began to restructure their investment and other decisions in the expectation of tariff-free flows of all trade across the Canada-United States border before the end of the twentieth century.

The Underlying Principle: National Treatment

The FTA is based on the fundamental principle of *national treatment*, which means that each country treats the other country's goods, firms, and investors when they are within its own borders just as it would its own goods, firms, and investors. This principle, which is also embedded in the GATT, is intended to give *maximum policy independence* to each country while preventing it from using its laws to discriminate on the basis of the nationality of indi-

Box 25-2

Gains from Specialization with Differentiated Products: The Eastman-Stykholt Analyses

Most manufacturing industries produce a wide range of differentiated products. For example, the paper industry produces over 300 types and grades of paper products. Furthermore, technological developments are constantly changing the products that can be produced.

Associated with each differentiated product are heavy fixed costs for product development and sometimes for product-specific machinery. Like all fixed costs, they give rise to a range of falling unit costs as the overheads are spread over more units when output rises. Total unit costs will start to rise only when rising marginal costs of production are strong enough to offset the effect of these falling overheads per unit of output. As a result, associated with each line of differentiated goods there is a minimum efficient scale (MES) that is often quite large.

The consequences of this large MES for firms producing in and serving only the Canadian market were analysed in an important study by professors Harry Eastman and Stephen Stykholt of the Uni-

versity of Toronto. They showed that the Canadian market is often not large enough to allow each differentiated product to be produced at minimum efficient scale as long as each Canadian industry produces the whole range of products for the domestic market alone. Thus, when tariffs protect Canadian firms selling solely for the home market, unit costs are considerably higher than they would be if the market were large enough to allow production to reach MES in each product line, as it often does in the large U.S. markets.

When tariffs are removed, the Canadian firms specialize in a reduced number of product lines, which they produce at their MESs, selling some of the output in the domestic market and exporting the rest. As a result, cost-reducing economies are achieved. Exports of some product lines go up, as do imports of other product lines. So trade increases on an intraindustry basis, and the advantages of efficiency in production are achieved without losing the advantages of diversity in consumption. This specialization in a narrowed range of product lines,

---

viduals and firms. According to the FTA's national treatment clause, all *new* government policies, rules, or regulations that do not directly inhibit trade are permissible as long as they meet a single key test: that they apply with equal force to foreign and to domestic entities. (Existing ones are exempt from the national treatment obligation.) Thus Canadians can have environmental protection laws, social services, or any other laws, rules, and regulations that differ greatly from their U.S. counterparts as long as they apply these equally to both Canadian and foreign firms operating in Canada.

The Specific Terms

The main terms of the free trade agreement were as follows:

1. All tariffs are being removed from all trade between the two countries over the first 10 years.
2. The agreement removes a number of nontariff barriers, such as quotas and some "buy local" government procurement policies. Quotas remained, however, where they were required to support the supply management schemes of the

with the resulting increase in intraindustry trade, is often referred to as *rationalization* of the domestic industry.

Such rationalization has occurred when tariffs have been reduced on Canadian-American trade as a result of successive rounds of negotiations under the GATT. It has often resulted from simple profit-maximizing reactions to changing market circumstances.

The figure illustrates this analysis. It shows the average total cost curve for *one* product type in a firm producing *many* types of some differentiated product. The Canadian demand curve for this product type is D. The lowest price at which costs can be covered is p_C, where sales are q_C.

The U.S. market is so large that firms selling a range of differentiated products in that market can produce an output of each product that is at, or near, the MES of q^*. They thus achieve the price p_{US}.

When Canadian firms gain access to the U.S. market, they specialize in a few product types and produce at a volume sufficient to reach the MES of each. The outputs of each of these product types will be q^* or more. This will allow cost to be covered at the price prevailing in the American market, which is p_{US}.

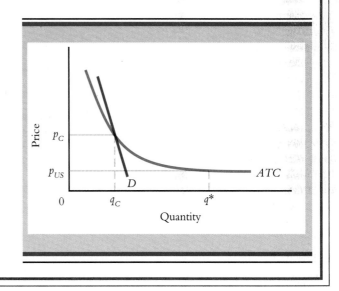

Canadian provincial governments. (See Chapter 6 for a discussion of these schemes.) By providing for a closer (voluntary) harmonization of standards, the FTA seeks to control another potent nontariff barrier.

3. The FTA institutionalizes the present regime of free trade in energy products, although all foreign (including U.S.) takeovers of Canadian energy firms are still subject to government review and approval. It contains a controversial clause that requires energy sharing in times of national shortage. This clause has no effect in normal times, when markets will set the prices and quantities of energy being traded. The clause comes into effect only if the exporting country decides that there is some emergency sufficient to justify introducing production and export controls that interfere with existing commercial contracts. The agreement then requires that exports should be restricted no more than in proportion to restrictions on total output. For example, Canada could not impose a reduction in production of 30 percent and then place the entire reduction on foreign con-

sumers. The clause does *not* require that once some amount of energy is sold to the United States, it must always be sold in the future. If in the normal evolution of the Canadian economy, Canada requires a larger proportion of its energy supplies for home consumption, normal commercial contracts will be negotiated, selling more to home users and less abroad. The only thing that the FTA prevents is *government intervention* to cut off supplies going to the partner country on the grounds of emergency if similar restrictions are not placed on domestic consumers.

4. The FTA allows for freer trade in services by having each country extend the principles of *right of establishment* and *national treatment* to the other country's firms that sell services. This means that firms selling services in one country have the right to establish themselves in the other country and be treated the same as local service firms.

5. The FTA prevents discrimination against each country's investment in the other country by extending the principle of national treatment to all such investment.

6. The FTA provides two dispute settlement mechanisms (DSMs), one for settling disputes related to all aspects of the agreement, the other for dealing with the application of countervailing and antidumping laws in each country.

Evaluation

The FTA caused great debate in the period leading up to its signing, and it still arouses strong passions today. Disagreement raged over its economic, social, and political manifestations. By and large, supporters saw it as primarily an economic agreement, one among many such agreements in place throughout the world, whose impact beyond its beneficial economic effects would be small. By and large, opponents saw it as a broad politicoeconomic agreement that would have profound political and social effects extending well beyond the harmful economic effects they alleged it would have.

Economic effects.   Supporters argued that the FTA is merely a continuation of the Canadian trend toward liberalizing trade that was begun in 1935 and that there was every reason to expect this round of tariff reductions to bring effects similar to those that followed all earlier rounds—a growing number of jobs, growing exports (and imports), growing real incomes, relatively minor adjustment problems, and a growing attractiveness of Canada for foreign investment (since the entire U.S.-Canadian market can be served, duty free, from Canada).

Opponents said that the results of this new round of tariff reduction will be quite different from the results of previous rounds—more jobs destroyed by new import competition than are created by new exports, falling exports and rising imports, falling real incomes, and a flight of foreign capital (now that there is no protected Canadian market to keep foreign firms in Canada, producing solely for domestic demand).

Most of the early debate concerned the jobs alleged to be lost by the Agreement during the transitional phase. Economists, however, have always argued that the long-run effects of trade liberalization have little or nothing to do with the average rate of unemployment.

There is no body of economic theory, and there is no body of established evidence, showing that the average amount of a country's employment or unemployment is related to the height of the country's tariffs and other trade restrictions once a transitional adjustment period is over.

Trade liberalization gives opportunities to specialize in the things one can do best and therefore to earn higher incomes and profits than when one produces inefficiently under tariff protection.

Trade liberalization is about the quality, not the quantity, of jobs.

The issue of transitional job loss is considered further in Box 25-3.

Policy Constraints

Much of the debate over the FTA concerned allegations that Canada has given up too much sovereignty by constraining itself explicitly or implicitly with respect to many economic and social policies that it might want to adopt in the future.

Economic policy.   Does the FTA seriously constrain future Canadian economic policy? It certainly institutionalizes free-market competition in energy between Canada and the United States. Further-

Box 25-3

Employment Effects of the Canada–U.S. FTA

According to economic theory, any effects that tariff reductions have on unemployment will be transitory and will depend on the balance between jobs lost in inefficient, mainly import-competing industries that shrink and jobs gained in efficient, mainly exporting industries that grow. Unfortunately, these short-term effects were obscured by the worldwide recession which began in 1990 and from which Canada began to emerge in 1993—and in which Europe was still mired. Clearly, to discover the short-term job loss and job creation caused by the FTA, we must find its effects *net of the cyclical loss of jobs that would have happened, FTA or no FTA.*

In the midst of a serious recession, it was difficult to estimate how much of the job loss was due to the tariff reduction. If estimating job losses was difficult, then estimating the jobs newly created by the agreement was doubly so.

What was known was that Canada in general, and central Canada in particular, had been very badly hit by a serious worldwide recession. It was also clear that the job losses throughout the country had a number of causes:

- First and foremost was the cyclical loss that would be replaced when the recession ended.
- Second, the Bank of Canada undertook to drive the inflation rate to zero just as the adjustment to the FTA was taking place. This drove both the absolute level of interest rates and the spread against the U.S. rates to high levels.
- Third, partly as a result of high interest rates and partly as a result of the budget deficit that sucked foreign funds into Canada, the Cana-

dian dollar was overvalued throughout the recession, which raised the price of Canadian exports in the United States.
- Fourth, there was the restructuring of the older industries under the impact of a changing and globalising world economy. Much of that restructuring took place south of the border in the previous recession of the early 1980s. There, the old smokestack industries gave way to the rust belt as widespread readjustment occurred. Ontario and Quebec were shielded from that readjustment by a severely undervalued dollar (due to capital movements). As a result, the readjustment did not occur then, nor did it occur during the prolonged recovery that brought prosperity to efficient and inefficient firms alike during the mid and late 1980s. Then came the recession of the early 1990s, which coincided this time with an overvalued Canadian dollar. So all of the structural readjustment that had taken place over 10 years in the U.S. border states took place in Canada during one recession.
- Fifth, there was the ongoing worldwide readjustment of the location of manufacturing industries, particularly those that use mainly unskilled labour, due to the globalising of the economy.

Sorting out the net effect of the adjustment to the FTA on jobs from the major effects of these other forces was a nearly impossible task in the midst of the recession. What is clear is that most of the job losses were due to the non-FTA forces listed above.

more, it would be impossible under the FTA to go back to higher tariffs or increased trade restrictions against the United States. Although the ability to do so is already greatly constrained by Canada's membership in the GATT, the FTA goes further. The FTA also makes it difficult to institute tougher controls on U.S. foreign investment or a revised National Energy Policy. By tying Canada into market competition, the FTA seems beneficial to people who believe that market forces tend to produce good results on balance. By the same token, it seems harmful to those who distrust market forces.

The FTA does nothing, however, to prevent interference by either country's government into market forces by any desired degree as long as the interference is operated on a national treatment basis.

Social policy. A major charge of the agreement's critics was that it will force a harmonization of Canadian social and economic policies with those of the United States. It was argued that the closer competition between firms in the two countries would cause firms in Canada to push for reductions in all social services and tax burdens to their American levels (and that governments would accede to these demands).

Supporters pointed out that the principle of national treatment, which is the guiding principle of the FTA, provides no legal pressure for harmonization of social policies. As for market pressures, they argued that since Canada's distinctive social policies had evolved during the period from 1947 to 1985, when Canada was dismantling most of its tariff protection, eliminating the last of the tariffs would cause no more harmonization pressures than the earlier tariff reductions did. They accepted that harmonization pressures are strong but argued that they are related to the mobility of factors of production rather than to the mobility of goods. Countries must worry, for example, about getting their levels of personal and corporate taxes out of line with other countries for fear of inducing a flight of capital and highly talented labour to the lower-tax jurisdiction. These pressures not to get policies too far out of line, which have always been very strong between Canada and the United States, are caused by the fear of factor movements, and economic theory does not suggest that they will be greater when tariffs are zero than when tariffs were 10 percent.

Political sovereignty. Many people feared increasing dominance of the United States as a result of closer economic ties with that country. Some went so far as to predict the end of Canada as an independent country within 10 years.

Supporters of the FTA argued that other countries had survived free trade arrangements without losing their political sovereignty and that the principle of national treatment was designed to encourage national sovereignty in all areas other than trade restrictions. They also noted that Canada had lived in close proximity with the United States for a long time and that removing the last of the already greatly reduced tariffs was unlikely to have such dramatic political effects.

The Results

Economists who have studied the effects of the Treaty of Rome, which brought the European Community into existence in 1958, agree that the major effects could not be discerned until at least 10 years had passed. Similarly, in spite of the understandable desire of supporters and critics to get strong evidence, many years must go by before the changes due to the FTA can be firmly established. One reason for this is that most of the changes expected from the FTA are not large in relation to other changes that are occurring all the time. For example, the 12 percent rise in the external value of the Canadian dollar from 76.8 U.S. cents to 85.7 U.S. cents that occurred between 1988 and 1991 had the same unfavourable effect over 2 years on the Canadian firms competing against foreign imports as will result from the entire removal of a 10 percent tariff over 10 years.

Nonetheless some changes were observable after only 4 years. A study by the C. D. Howe Institute in 1993 showed that Canadian exports to the United States were expanding much faster than exports to the rest of the world, indicating that the tariff reductions are having their expected effects. Thirty-four Canadian industries had increased market shares in the United States, while only 11 industries had their market shares decline. Most difficulties were being felt in import-competing industries, which is what theory predicts. An agreement such as the FTA brings its advantages by encouraging a movement of resources out of protected but inefficient import-competing industries, which decline, and into efficient export industries, which expand. Furthermore massive productivity increases were being registered by many of the most successful exporting industries.

By general agreement among trade policy experts, the DSM has worked remarkably well. Panel members have reacted as professionals, not as nationals. Cases have been decided on merits, and there have been no serious allegations that decisions were decided on national grounds.

Close to 25 such cases had arisen by 1993, most of them involving appeals against U.S. determinations on countervail and antidumping issues. In cases against the United States, the panel must decide if the U.S. decision is "unsupported by substantial evidence on the record, or otherwise not in accordance with laws." Most interesting to Canadians are the first two cases in which the United States tried to avoid panel decisions. In both cases the panels forced the United States to back down and drop its duties on Canadian goods. Trade specialists agree that Canada could not have achieved these favourable outcomes without the dispute settlement mechanism that the free trade agreement provided.[6]

In the red raspberries case, the U.S. Department of Commerce reacted to a panel referral by simply giving a better explanation of its behaviour and holding to its original determination. The panel then directed the Department to calculate the alleged Canadian dumping in a different way. When it did so, the case for dumping evaporated.

In the frozen pork case, the panel found that the U.S. agency (the International Trade Commission) had reached findings that " rely heavily on or flowed directly from faulty use of statistics." The ITC responded by strengthening the case for its original finding and reasserting that finding. The panel then reported that the ITC's findings were "not supported by substantial evidence." On the urging of the ITC commissioners, and with substantial Congressional pressure, the U.S. government then appealed the decision to the Extraordinary Challenge Committee, which is meant to be invoked only in the most extreme cases. The ECC then unanimously upheld the panel. There can be little doubt that in the absence of the FTA, the decision of the ITC against Canada would have stood. It is even more remarkable that after the panel's decision, heavy American political pressure could not reverse the result.

The NAFTA

In 1992, agreement was reached on a Canada-U.S.-Mexico FTA called the North American Free Trade Agreement (NAFTA).

Contents

The new NAFTA is closely patterned on the existing U.S.-Canada agreement, although it is somewhat more protectionist in a few sectors. Notably, it significantly increases the difficulty for automobiles, textiles, and apparel imported from non-NAFTA countries to compete with similar products produced within the three NAFTA countries. The agreement also exempts Mexico's oil industry from the conditions already agreed upon between Canada and the United States. The reason is that the Mexican industry is shielded from foreign influence by the Mexican constitution. Although a bargaining victory for Mexico, it is not clear that it will gain from excluding foreign influences on competition and innovation in such a key industry.

The agreement also contains an accession clause allowing other countries to enter the FTA. The text itself is longer and more complex than the U.S.-Canada agreement, because it is meant to be able to accommodate all Latin American and Caribbean Basin countries so that it can grow into a full-scale Western Hemispheric Free Trade Agreement (WHFTA). In the United States, the agreement came to Congress under the "fast-track" procedure, by which Congress can only vote to accept or reject the entire agreement but cannot amend it.[7] It was passed by the Congress in November 1993 and the first tariff cuts were made in January 1994.

---

[6]At the time of writing, it looks as though a much more serious case of such U.S. behaviour may arise with respect to the lumber industry.

---

[7]Before the fast-track procedure was introduced, the United States and foreign negotiators working on some treaty would carefully balance their compromises to come to a mutually acceptable package. The agreement then went to the Senate, which could strike down the clauses it did not like—generally those embodying U.S. compromises—and accept those clauses it did like—generally those embodying foreign compromises. Not surprisingly, foreign governments became unwilling to negotiate complex agreements with the United States under such a procedure, and the fast track provided the way of restoring the willingness of foreign countries to negotiate with the United States.

Background of Liberalization

Mexico's willingness to enter a free-trade agreement with the United States is the outcome of the remarkable liberalization of its economy that began in the mid-1980s. For decades, Mexico experimented with policies of high tariffs and quota restrictions designed to build up infant industries, plus heavy domestic subsidization and deficit financing that resulted in inflation rates that often exceeded 10 percent *per month*. Then in the mid-1980s, these policies finally were recognised to be failures, and an outward-looking stance was adopted. Tariffs, often as high as 100 to 200 percent, were slashed unilaterally. Quotas were eliminated on most imports. Subsidies for domestic firms were cut, inflationary financing was brought nearly under control, and a general reliance on the market system over state control was accepted. The effects on the Mexican economy were dramatic. Both exports and imports grew rapidly. To secure its liberalization, to guarantee its access to wider markets, and to make Mexico an attractive place for foreign investment, the government sought the free-trade agreement with the United States. Canada then insisted on joining the negotiations.

The Mexican example of liberalization is being followed by many other countries of Latin America. The decades of inward-looking, state-interventionist policies have been declared failures, and the countries are moving to adopt more market-oriented, outward-looking policies. Imports are no longer restricted, and exports are growing where the countries have comparative advantages rather than where the government subsidizes most. Like Mexico, these countries are seeking to consolidate their outward-looking policies by entering full trade-liberalizing agreements with their neighbours. The first moves have been with immediate neighbours. But now that the NAFTA has gone through, these countries may well join with it to form a wider WHFTA. This lies in the future, but the remarkable movement toward market-oriented policies in Latin American countries makes it a distinct possibility. If the whole hemisphere were to join into one free-trade area, this would create a single market that would contain 1 billion people early in the twenty-first century, and in which goods and services moved tariff free. One of Canada's major motives in joining the U.S.-Mexican talks on free trade was to turn a proposed U.S.-Mexico bilateral FTA into a trilateral NAFTA and so to influence the way in which hemispheric free trade might evolve. This issue is discussed in Box 25-4.

The Critics

Many criticisms have been levied at the NAFTA. Here we mention only a few of the most common.

1. Critics argue that Canada will be swamped by goods produced by cheap Mexican labour. Supporters reply that simple calculation shows that to be a major overstatement of the possibilities. About 1.5 percent of Canadian imports currently come from Mexico, and these are subject to a current average duty of about 7 percent (many Mexican goods now enter duty free). Suppose if Mexican labour gets $2.00 an hour, the tariff then raises the cost of a good that embodies an hour of that labour from $2.00 to $2.14. So supporters of the we-will-be-swamped view must find some mystery as to why Canada is not swamped by cheap Mexican goods now. Be that as it may, consider the tariff elimination. Its removal would take the cost of the same Mexican good from $2.14 back to $2.00. This is a 7 percent reduction in price and the rise in Canadian imports will depend on the Canadian price elasticity of demand for Mexican goods. If that elasticity is unity, the increase in demand will be 7 percent, while if it is five (a far higher figure than has ever been observed over a whole group of imported commodities), the increase will be 35 percent. The resulting rise in Canadian imports from Mexico causes the proportion of Canadian imports coming from that country to rise from 1.5 percent to 1.6 percent in the first case and from 1.5 to 2 percent in the second, more extreme case. (Of course, Canadian exports to Mexico also rise.) Clearly, the picture of a Canadian market swamped by imports from Mexico is not based on an appreciation of current magnitudes or the amounts by which they are likely to change.

2. A second argument of the critics is that a significant portion of our industry will migrate to Mexico. The supporters reply that Mexico cannot absorb that much industry from the United States and Canada. More importantly, they say, migration to Mexico has much to do with globalisation and little to do with tariffs. Indeed, significant amounts of migration have oc-

Box 25-4

Hub and Spoke Versus Plurilateral Regionalism

One model for the evolution of free trade in the Western Hemisphere was the so-called hub and spoke model, in which the United States acted as hub by establishing bilateral agreements with a series of countries that became the spokes. Only the hub country has tariff-free access to *all* spoke country markets, while the spoke countries, including Canada, have tariff-free access to only the United States.

The hub and spoke model is a recipe for American hegemony over the hemisphere.

This arrangement confers an advantage on U.S.-based firms when selling into any spoke country in competition against firms based in other spoke countries. For this reason, it also makes the U.S. hub a more attractive location for investment than any of the spoke countries.

Although there is no evidence that U.S. policy makers actively pursued such a model, it would have been thrust upon them if they accepted the Mexican invitation to negotiate a bilateral FTA.

The alternative model goes by the mouthful name of "plurilateral regionalism." In it, all countries are members of a single FTA in which all have equal access to the markets of all member countries.

Plurilateral regionalism is a recipe for trade among equals.

So a major argument for Canada becoming involved in the negotiations and turning them into a NAFTA was to push hemispheric trade liberalization on the path of plurilateral regionalism rather than a hub and spoke development. That Canada managed to do this was a substantial accomplishment.

Those who argued that the Canada-U.S. Agreement gave the United States too much economic power might have welcomed the NAFTA initiative as diluting the U.S. power, first by adding Mexico, then Chile and possibly others to the FTA. Instead, many of these same critics opposed Canada's involvement in the NAFTA and therefore threw their weight behind the hub and spoke model. This would have made Canada one spoke, while Mexico and other Latin American countries became other spokes, all revolving around a dominant U.S. hub.

curred without a NAFTA. Canada is made more, not less, attractive to investment by being inside, rather than outside, the FTA and the NAFTA—because the more foreign market access we can offer, the more attractive are we as a location for investment.

3. Critics also argue that Canada should not trade with an imperfect democracy such as Mexico. Supporters reply that Canada trades all over the world with many less perfect democracies than Mexico. Indeed, a strong case can be made that democracy thrives on the development of rising

standards of living and a growing middle class. It would be a rash person who would say the best way to encourage Mexican democracy is to restrict trade with Mexico and prevent its living standards from rising through trade.

4. Critics also argue that the ordinary Mexicans will not benefit from NAFTA-induced economic growth, only the rich will. This view does not stand up to investigation. The distribution of income does vary among countries with the same per capita GDPs, but as a general tendency across all countries, the higher the av-

Box 25-5

NAFTA *and the* Environment

A vigorous argument against the NAFTA was mounted by some groups who are concerned with the environment. Some environmental activists accepted the NAFTA and hoped to work within it to raise common environmental standards. Others rejected the NAFTA on the grounds that it will do serious harm to the environment in the United States and Canada. They argue in the following way.

1. Firms will relocate to Mexico to escape the costs of higher standards in Canada and the United States.
2. This will exert pressures on Canada and the United States to lower environmental standards.
3. As a result, NAFTA will be bad for the environment, and this is sufficient cause for rejecting the whole agreement.

Supporters of NAFTA reply as follows.

1. Canada trades with many nations whose environmental standards are lower than the Mexicans'. Indeed, the NDP government in British Columbia has suggested, as an alternative to NAFTA, that British Columbia increases its trade with the countries of Southeast Asia. However, many of these countries are despoiling their environments much more than is Mexico in the very sectors, such as lumber, where Canada is trying to raise its standards.
2. Compliance with environmental standards is not a large proportion of total costs of most industries. Research shows that, typically, environmental measures may raise production costs by from 0.5 to 2.0 percent. These are not the kinds of cost differences that drive decisions on where to invest internationally.
3. Free trade will raise Mexican living standards, and environmental protection has a very high income elasticity. Typically, poor countries want jobs at almost any cost. Only when incomes rise are people willing to sacrifice some income for the environment. So the best way to *lower* Mexican environmental standards and so *increase* the incentives for firms to emigrate to Mexico—to the extent such incentives exist—is to refuse to trade with the Mexicans.
4. After the main NAFTA text was agreed, side agreements were negotiated on the environment and labour practices. The environmental agreement provides significant protection against the use of lax enforcement of environmental laws to attract polluting industries. If NAFTA had not gone forward, these would have been lost. In addition, Mexican growth and industrialisation, which will continue to be strong, would have gone on without any of the constraints on Mexican environmental policies that membership in the NAFTA will impose.

erage GDP, the higher is everyone's income. Citizens of poor countries, such as Bangladesh and India, try to move to richer countries such as Singapore, Malaysia, and Thailand, not the other way around. To say that the best way to help the lower-income people is not to trade with them, and to try to stop their growth of per capita GDP on the grounds that growth only helps the rich, has no support from the facts. All over the world, countries are adopting market-oriented growth policies, and many of them have got onto sustained growth paths. Supporters of NAFTA agree that worldwide poverty is a terrible thing. But, they argue, to try to alleviate it by preventing the worldwide movement to economic liberalization is misguided. There is *no known way* for a country with a low per capita GDP to eliminate widespread poverty other than through economic growth. In today's world, growth without a substantial involvement in trade is virtually impossible.

When all of these arguments have been made for and against, many people react by saying that what really matters is protection of the environment. This key issue is discussed further in Box 25-5.

The Outlook for Canadian Trade

The breakup of the world into a set of trading blocks that do more and more trade within the block and less and less with outside countries would be to the disadvantage of most countries, particularly the smaller ones. Bilateral bargaining between nations tends to involve large countries, with the smaller ones left on the sidelines. For these two reasons, among many others, Canada, as a small trading country, has an enormous stake in the preservation of the liberalized multilateral trading system.

The high stakes ensure that Canadian policy makers will continue to regard the GATT as Canada's best friend in pushing for more liberalized international trade and as its best defense against protectionist pressures. The FTA and the NAFTA, however, also give Canada increased access to what is by far its largest market and shields that access to some extent against growing protectionist sentiment in the United States. These agreements do not provide a perfect shield, but it is difficult to argue that Canadian access to the U.S. market would be better protected without the FTA than with it.

Canada prospers or suffers as its trading sector prospers or suffers. For this reason, maintaining a healthy trading sector will remain, as it has been for decades, a prime concern of Canadian policy makers, who wish to maintain and enhance the country's material prosperity.

SUMMARY

1. Domestic industries may be protected from foreign competition by tariffs and other policies, which affect the prices of imports, or by import quotas and voluntary export agreements, which affect the quantities of imports. Both sets of policies end up increasing prices in the domestic market and lowering the quantities of imports. Both harm domestic consumers and benefit domestic producers of the protected commodity. The major difference is that the extra money paid for imports goes to the government under tariffs and to foreign producers under quantity restrictions.

2. The case for free trade is that world output of all commodities can be higher under free trade than when protectionism restricts regional specialization.

3. Protection can be urged as a means to ends other than maximizing world living standards. Examples of such ends are to produce a diversified economy, to reduce fluctuations in national income, to retain distinctive national traditions, and to improve national defense.

4. Protection also can be urged on the grounds that it may lead to higher living standards for the protectionist country than a policy of free trade would. Such a result might come about by using a monopoly position to influence the terms of trade or by developing a dynamic comparative advantage by allowing inexperienced or uneconomically small industries to become efficient enough to compete with foreign industries.

5. A recent argument for protection is to operate a strategic trade policy whereby a country attracts firms in oligopolistic industries

that, due to scale economies, can earn large profits even in equilibrium.

6. As tariff barriers have been reduced over the years, they have been replaced in part by nontariff barriers. Voluntary export agreements are straightforward restrictions on trade. Antidumping and countervailing duties can provide legitimate restraints on foreign unfair trading practises, but they can also be used as nontariff barriers to trade.

7. Some fallacious protectionist arguments are that (a) mutually advantageous trade is impossible because one trader's gain must always be the other's loss; (b) buying abroad sends our money abroad, while buying at home keeps our money at home; (c) our high-paid workers must be protected against the competition from low-paid foreign workers; and (d) imports are to be discouraged, because they lower national income and cause unemployment.

8. Some fallacious free-trade arguments are that (a) because free trade maximizes world income, it will maximize the income of every individual country and (b) because infant industries seldom admit to growing up and thus try to retain their protection indefinitely, the whole country necessarily loses by protecting its infant industries.

9. The General Agreement on Tariffs and Trade, whereby countries agree to reduce trade barriers through multilateral negotiations and not to raise them unilaterally, has greatly reduced world tariffs since its inception in 1947. The European Free Trade Area and the European Community are regional arrangements for free trade in goods among their members.

10. Since 1935, Canadian trade policy has supported trade liberalization, first with reciprocal agreements with the United States, then through the GATT, and more recently with the Canada-U.S. Free Trade Agreement and the NAFTA.

11. Past reductions in tariffs on Canadian-American trade led mainly to intraindustry specialization, with both countries' imports and exports tending to increase in each industry as firms specialized in particular product lines.

12. The Canada-U.S. Free Trade Agreement provides for the complete elimination of tariffs on all trade in goods between the two countries by 1998, the liberalization of trade in services and some government procurement, and the removal of some nontariff barriers (and mandated major negotiations on other nontariff barriers over a period of five years). It also provides for freer movement of capital between the two countries. It institutionalized free trade in energy and contains a controversial energy-sharing agreement for use in times of energy crisis. A number of sectors, including the Canadian cultural industries—broadly defined to include the mass media—are exempt from the terms of the agreement.

13. The North American Free Trade Agreement incorporates the Canada-U.S. agreement into a more embracing free trade area designed to be capable of extension to include, if they so wish, all of the countries of Latin America and the Caribbean Basin.

TOPICS FOR REVIEW

Free trade and protectionism

Tariff and nontariff barriers to trade

Countervailing and antidumping duties

General Agreement on Tariffs and Trade (GATT)

Common markets, customs unions, and free trade associations

Canada-U.S. Free Trade Agreement (FTA)

National treatment

The North American Free Trade Agreement (NAFTA)

DISCUSSION QUESTIONS

1. It has been calculated that the voluntary export agreement to reduce Japanese car imports into the North American market cost Canadian and American consumers more than $150,000 per year per job saved. Who gained and who lost from this agreement?

2. The policy of "aggressive reciprocity" has recently been urged on the Canadian and the American governments. Under it, every time a foreign government introduced a new barrier to trade, Canada and the United States would reciprocate aggressively by introducing a new barrier of their own. Discuss the likely outcome of such a policy. What are some alternative policies for enhancing world trade?

3. Look at the Canadian tariffs shown in Table 25-1. What economic and political reasons can you see for duties on some commodities being above the average rate of duty charged and for others being below it? What other forms of protectionism could make some duties misleading?

4. Discuss the following statements made during the Canadian free-trade debate. Three of the four can be challenged using points of economic theory.

    a. "Tariff reductions, which should help both countries, disproportionately benefit the United States because average Canadian tariffs are higher."—Jeff Simpson, Toronto Globe and Mail, October 9, 1987.

    b. "The historical records show that the concerns expressed two decades ago about the Auto Pact were not entirely misplaced. In only 9 years of the Pact's 22 years of operation has Canada been in a surplus position in Auto Pact trade."—Glen Williams, Toronto Globe and Mail, November 28, 1987.

    c. "We would like to think we are about to get the best of both worlds—Canadian stability and a more caring society, combined with U.S. markets—but what if instead, we get their crime rates, health programs, and gun laws and they get our markets, or what is left of them?"—Margaret Atwood, testimony to Parliamentary committee on free trade, November 4, 1987.

    d. "The complete removal of tariffs doesn't help Canadian exporters as much as the devaluation of our dollar, because the key to breaking into the U.S. market is to be able to flog it with cheaper goods than they have at home."—Edgar Benson, former Liberal minister of finance, *Toronto Star*, October 10, 1987.

5. Some Canadians opposed a Canadian free trade agreement with Mexico on the grounds that Canadian firms could not compete with the goods produced by cheap Mexican labour, which, at the 1993 exchange rate, was earning about C$2.00 per hour in the highest wage sectors. Comment on the following points in relation to the above argument:

   a. Many Mexican goods already enter Canada free of tariffs, and where tariffs are levied, the average Canadian rate is less than 10 percent.

   b. Not only are Mexican wages low, but the average productivity of Mexican workers is also low.

   c. The theory of the gains from trade says that rich, high-productivity countries can profitably trade with poor, low-wage countries.

   d. A situation in which Mexico undersold all Canadian tradeable goods and services could not be one of international trade equilibrium.

   e. Technological change is rapidly reducing the proportional of total costs accounted for by wages; in many industries that use high-tech production methods, this proportion is already well below 20 percent.

6. Many opponents of the Canada-U.S. FTA, and of the NAFTA, worried that it would cause an exodus of Canadian based-firms to Mexico. Assume you are advising a foreign firm that is considering investing in North America to serve the whole North American market. Under which set of arrangements would Canada be most and least attractive as a location (other things being equal)? Which can be decided by Canadian policy makers and which are beyond their control?

   a. There are no agreements between Canada, United States or Mexico (The status quo in 1985).

   b. The only agreement is the Canada-U.S. FTA (the status quo in 1990).

   c. The United States has separate bilateral agreements with Canada and with Mexico (what would have happened under Mexico's original suggestion, or if Canada rejected the NAFTA while the United States and Mexico accepted it).

   d. The only agreement is a bilateral one between the United States and Mexico (what would happen if Canada rejected the NAFTA and abrogated its agreement with the United States.)

   e. There is a single NAFTA agreement among the three countries (what will happen if all three countries accept the NAFTA).

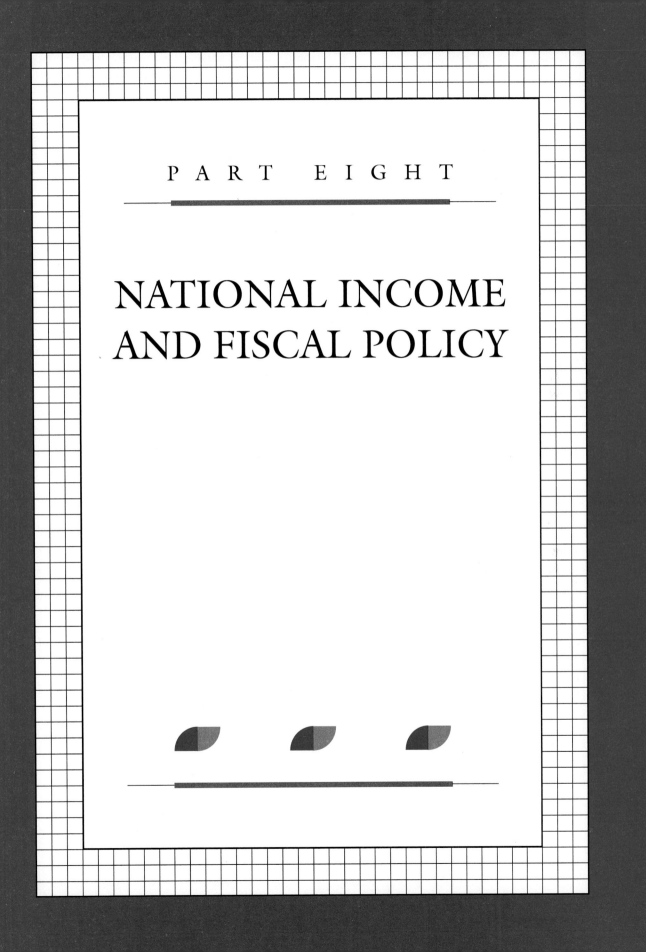

P A R T   E I G H T

NATIONAL INCOME AND FISCAL POLICY

26

An Introduction to Macroeconomics

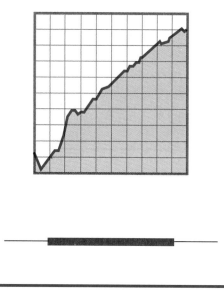

I nflation, unemployment, recession, and economic growth are everyday words. Governments worry about how to prevent recessions, reduce inflation, increase competitiveness, and stimulate growth. Households are anxious to avoid the unemployment that comes with recessions, to protect themselves against the hazards of inflation, and to obtain the rising incomes that usually accompany economic growth. Firms are concerned about how inflations, recessions, and foreign competition affect their profits.

Each of the concerns just mentioned plays a major role in macroeconomics.

What Is Macroeconomics?

Macroeconomics is the study of how the economy behaves in broad outline without dwelling on much of its interesting, but sometimes confusing, detail. As was noted in Chapter 3, macroeconomics is largely concerned with the behaviour of economic *aggregates*, such as total consumption, total investment, and total exports, and the average price of all goods and services. These aggregates result from activities in many different markets and from the behaviour of different decision makers in households, governments, and firms. In contrast, *microeconomics* deals with the behaviour of individual markets, such as those for wheat, coal, or strawberries, and with the detailed behaviour of individual decision makers, such as firms and households.

In macroeconomics, we add the value of wheat, coal, strawberries, haircuts, and appendectomies to the value of all other goods and services produced and study the movement of aggregate *national product*. We also average the prices of all commodities consumed and discuss the *price level* for the entire economy. While these measures suppress much important detail, they allow us to view the big picture. In macroeconomics, we look at the broad range of opportunities and difficulties facing the economy as a whole. When national product rises, the output of most commodities and the incomes of most people usually rise with it. When the price level rises, virtually everyone in the economy is forced to make adjustments. When the unemployment rate rises, workers are put at an increased risk of losing their jobs and suffering losses in their incomes. These movements in economic aggregates are strongly associated with the economic concerns of most individuals: the health of the industries in which they work and the prices of the goods they purchase. These associations are why macroeconomic aggregates get air time on the evening news; understanding them is one important reason why we study macroeconomics.

Major Macroeconomic Issues

Business cycles. The economy tends to move in a series of ups and downs, called *business cycles*, rather than in a steady pattern. The 1930s saw the greatest worldwide economic depression in the twentieth century, with almost one fifth of the Canadian labour force unemployed for an extended period. In contrast, the 25 years following World War II was a period of sustained economic growth, with only minor interruptions caused by modest recessions. Then the business cycle returned in more serious form in the 1980s. The beginning and the end of that decade witnessed the two worst worldwide recessions since the 1930s. What fueled the recovery of the mid-1980s? Why did another severe recession occur in 1990–1992? Why was the recovery that started in early 1993 so slow in developing momentum?

Overall living standards. As we saw in Chapter 1, both total and per capita output have risen for many decades in most industrial countries. These long-term trends have meant rising average living standards. Since the early 1970s, however, average living standards have grown much less rapidly than during the preceding decades of the twentieth century. Indeed, in the United States, the *real wage*, the quantity of goods and services that can be purchased by the average hourly money wage, was lower in 1991 than it was in 1973. In Canada, where real wages grew just over 40 percent over the decade 1950–1959 and just under 40 percent in the subsequent decade, real wages grew on average by a mere 2 percent over the entire decade from 1980–1989. Although long-term growth gets less play on the evening news than does the current inflation rate or unemployment rate, it is the predominant determinant of the economic prospects facing a society from decade to decade and generation to generation. Among the most important issues in macroeconomics is discovering the causes of the slowdown in worldwide growth rates that began in the 1970s and continued into the 1990s and finding out what, if anything, governments do about it.

Inflation and recession. From 1950 to 1970, an inflation rate of 4 percent was regarded as unacceptably high. By contrast, in the mid-1980s, the government claimed credit for having *reduced* inflation to 4 percent! Was the Bank of Canada pursuing good or bad policy when it announced late in the 1980s that it intended to drive the Canadian inflation rate to zero?

Earlier in the century, alternating bouts of inflationary boom and deflationary recession caused many headaches for policy makers. Booms still tend to be accompanied by inflationary pressures, but it can no longer be assumed that recessions will bring deflations. Why were the recessions of the 1970s and early 1980s accompanied not only by their familiar companion, high unemployment, but also by an unexpected fellow traveler, rapid inflation? Will **stagflation**—simultaneous high unemployment and rapid inflation—return? Or will the relatively low inflation rates of the early 1990s persist?

Government budget deficits. In earlier times, booms tended to be accompanied by *budget surpluses*, governments spending less than their current tax receipts, while recessions were accompanied by *budget deficits*, governments spending more than current tax receipts. Starting in the mid-1970s, the federal budget went into growing deficit, which persisted through good times and bad. The Conservative government that was elected in 1984 had a mandate to lower the deficit but, although it stopped the deficit's rapid growth, the government was unable or unwilling to reduce it. These deficits had to be financed by government borrowing, which raised the national debt. Just as the ratio of federal debt to national product—the so-called *debt/GDP ratio*—seemed to have been stabilized at around 0.60, the provincial governments fell into chronic deficit, which drove the overall government debt/GDP ratio close to 0.90 by 1993. This made public debt average over $20,000 for every Canadian citizen or over $80,000 for a family of four. This is a burden of debt that only a few advanced countries have exceeded during peacetime. How will Canadians be affected by this unprecedented amount of peacetime government debt?

Key Macroeconomic Phenomena

The current macroeconomic state of the nation can be fairly fully described by the level and rate of

FIGURE 26-1
The Circular Flow of Income and Expenditure

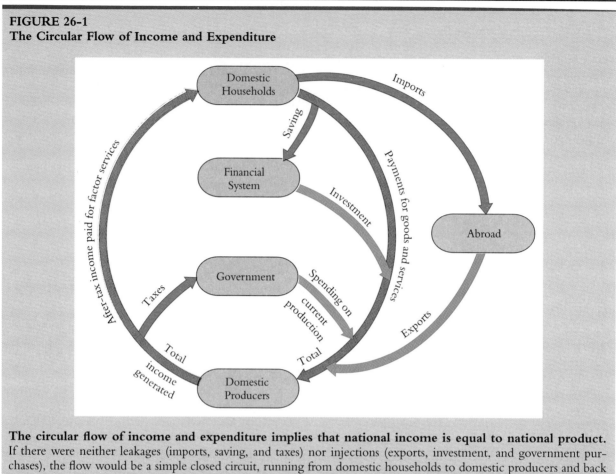

The circular flow of income and expenditure implies that national income is equal to national product.
If there were neither leakages (imports, saving, and taxes) nor injections (exports, investment, and government purchases), the flow would be a simple closed circuit, running from domestic households to domestic producers and back to households. Injections (shown in green) and leakages (also called withdrawals and here shown in blue) complicate the picture but do not change the basic result: Domestic production creates a claim on the value of that production; when all of the claims are added up, they must be equal to the value of all of the production.

growth of total and per capita output, the amount of employment and the unemployment rate, the inflation rate, the interest rate, the external value of the Canadian dollar, and the balance of trade. We hear about each of these indicators on the nightly news and read about them in newspapers; politicians give campaign speeches about them; economists theorize about them. In this chapter, we discuss each of these variables, with an emphasis on why and how they affect our economic welfare. In Chapter 27, we expand the discussion to consider how the macroeconomic variables are measured. The remainder of this book is largely about the causes and consequences of changes in each of these variables.

Output and Income

The most comprehensive measure of a nation's overall level of economic activity is the value of its total production of goods and services, called *national product*. Since all the value that is produced must ultimately belong to someone in the form of a claim on that value, the national product is equal to the total income claims generated by the production of goods and services. Hence, when we study national product, we are also studying *national income*.

Figure 26-1, which reproduces Figure 3-2 (on page 54), depicts national income and expenditure as a circular flow. For the nation as a whole, all of the value that is produced must ultimately belong to someone in the form of a claim on that value. Much of it goes as wages, interest, profits, and rents to compensate the labour, capital, and land used to produce the output. The rest is accounted for by sales taxes that accrue to governments and belong to the citizens whom those governments represent. Thus, the national product is equal to the total income claims generated by the production of goods and services.

There are several related measures of a nation's total output and total income. Their various definitions, and the relationships among them, are discussed in detail in the next chapter. In this chapter, we use the generic term *national income* to refer to both the value of total output and the value of the income claims generated by the production of that output.

Aggregating Total Output

To measure total output, quantities of a variety of goods are *aggregated*. To construct such totals, we add up the *values* of the different products. We cannot add tons of steel to loaves of bread, but we can add the money value of steel production to the money value of bread production. Hence, by multiplying the physical output of a good by its price per unit and then summing this value for each good produced in a nation, we can calculate the quantity of total national output *measured in dollars*.

Real and Nominal Values

The total that was just described gives the *money value* of national output, often called **nominal national income**. A change in this measure can be caused by a change in either the physical quantities or the prices on which it is based. Economists wish to determine the extent to which any change is due to changes in quantities or to changes in prices. To do this, they distinguish between changes in **real national income**, which occur only when the *quantities* of goods and services change, and changes in the *price level*. In order to measure real national income, economists must determine what would have happened to national income if prices had remained constant. To do this, they value all the quantities produced in each year at a constant set of prices that prevailed in some arbitrarily chosen *base period*. Thus real national income measures the total

value of all individual outputs, where each output is valued, not at current prices, but at a set of prices that prevailed in some base period.

Nominal national income is often referred to as *money national income* or *current-dollar national income*. Real national income is often called *constant-dollar national income*. Denoted by the symbol Y, real national income tells us the value of current output measured at constant prices—the sum of the individual quantities, each valued at prices that prevailed in the base period. Comparing real national incomes of different years provides a measure of the change in the quantity of output that has occurred during the intervening period.

Since its calculation holds prices constant, real national income changes only when quantities change.

Since our interest is primarily in the *real* output of goods and services, we shall use the terms *national income* and *national output* to refer to *real national income* and *real national output*, unless otherwise specified. (An example, illustrating the important distinction between real national income and money national income, is given in Box 27-2 on page 556.)

National Income: The Historical Experience

One of the most commonly used measures of national income is called *gross domestic product*, or GDP. This can be measured in either real or nominal terms; we focus here on real GDP. The details of its calculation will be discussed in Chapter 27. *In this chapter, we use the terms national income and GDP interchangeably to refer to the nation's total income and its total product.*

Part (i) of Figure 26-2 shows real GDP produced by the Canadian economy since 1930; part (ii) shows its annual percentage change for the same period. The GDP series in Figure 26-2(i) shows two kinds of movement.

Long-term growth. The major movement in GDP is an upward trend that increased real output more than sevenfold in the half century from 1939 to 1989. Because the trend has generally been upward in the modern era, it is referred to as *economic growth*. Long-term growth in real national income is reflected in the upward trend in real GDP.

FIGURE 26-2
Canadian Real National Income and Growth Rate, 1930–1992

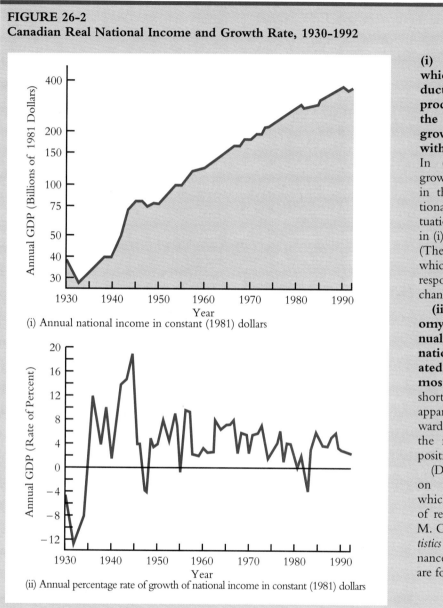

(i) Annual national income in constant (1981) dollars

(ii) Annual percentage rate of growth of national income in constant (1981) dollars

(i) Real national income, which measures the total production of goods and services produced in the economy over the period of a year, has grown steadily since 1930, with only a few interruptions. In (i), we see the long-term growth of the economy reflected in the upward trend of real national income. Shorter-term fluctuations are obscured by this trend in (i) but are highlighted in (ii). (The figure uses a semilog scale in which equal vertical distances correspond to equal percentage changes.)

(ii) Real growth in the economy, as measured by the annual rate of change of real national income, has fluctuated considerably but has been mostly positive. In (ii), the short-term fluctuations are readily apparent, but the long-term upward trend still shows up because the majority of observations are positive.

(Data prior to 1947 are based on GNP, thereafter on GDP, which is now the standard measure of real national income.) (*Sources:* M. C. Urquhart, ed., *Historical Statistics of Canada;* Department of Finance, *Economic Review,* 1993 data are for June.)

The growth in real per capita GDP is the basis of the enormous increase in living standards that Canadians have enjoyed throughout the twentieth century.

Short-term fluctuations. A second feature of the real GDP series is the short-term fluctuations around the trend, often described as cyclical fluctuations. Overall growth so dominates the real GDP series that the fluctuations are hardly visible in Fig-

ure 26-2(i). However, as can be seen in part (ii) of the figure, cyclical fluctuations in real GDP have been significant in the past.

The cyclical behaviour of real national income is reflected in the annual fluctuations in the growth rate of real GDP.

The **business cycle** refers to these short-term fluctuations as the continual ebb and flow of business

FIGURE 26-3
A Stylized Business Cycle

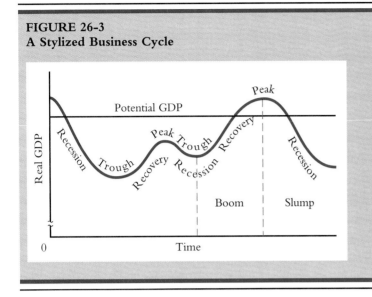

Although the phases of business fluctuations are described by a series of commonly used terms, no two cycles are the same. Starting from a lower turning point, a cycle goes through a phase of recovery, or expansion, reaches an upper turning point, and then enters a period of recession. Cycles differ from one another in the severity of their troughs and peaks and in the speed with which one phase follows another. Sometimes, the entire rising half of the cycle is loosely referred to as a *boom* and the entire falling half is called a *slump*.

activity that occurs around the long-term trend after seasonal adjustments have been made.[1]

Figure 26-3 shows stylized cycles that illustrate some useful terms. It is important to realize, however, that no two cycles are exactly the same. There are variations in duration and magnitude. Some expansions are long and drawn out, as was the one that began in 1983; others come to an end before high employment of labour and industrial capacity is reached. Nonetheless, although they are neither smooth nor regular, fluctuations are systematic enough that it is useful to identify common factors in the four phases. Some of the most important of these are outlined in Box 26-1.

Potential Income and the GDP Gap

Actual national income represents what the economy does, in fact, produce. An important related concept is **potential national income**, which measures what the economy could produce if all resources—land, labour, and productive capacity—were fully employed at their normal levels of utilization. This concept is usually referred to as potential income but is sometimes called *high-employment income.*[2] We give it the symbol Y^* to distinguish it from actual national income, which is indicated by Y.

What is variously called the **output gap** or the **GDP gap** measures the difference between what would have been produced if potential or high-employment national income had been produced and what is actually produced, as measured by the current GDP. The gap is calculated by subtracting actual national income from potential income $(Y^* - Y)$.

When potential income exceeds actual income, the gap measures the market value of goods and services that *could have been produced* if the economy's resources had been fully employed but that actually went unproduced. The goods and services that are not produced when the economy is operating below Y^* are permanently lost to the economy. Because these losses occur when employable resources are unused, they are often called the *deadweight loss* of unemployment. When the economy is operating

---

[1]When economists wish to analyze monthly or quarterly data, they often make a *seasonal adjustment* to remove fluctuations that can be accounted for by the regular seasonal pattern evident in many economic series. For example, logging activity tends to be low in the winter months and high in the summer months, whereas sales of fuel oil tend to have the reverse seasonal pattern. Retail sales are highest in December.

[2]In everyday usage, the words *real* and *actual* have similar meanings. In national-income theory, however, their meanings are quite distinct. *Real* national income is distinguished from *nominal* national income, and *actual* national income is distinguished from *potential* national income. The latter both refer to real measures, so that the full descriptions are, in fact, actual real national income and potential real national income.

Box 26-1

The Terminology of Business Cycles

Trough

A trough is characterized by high unemployment and a level of demand that is low in relation to the economy's capacity to produce. There is thus a substantial amount of unused productive capacity. Business profits are low; for some individual companies, they are negative. Confidence about economic prospects in the immediate future is lacking, and, as a result, many firms are unwilling to risk making new investments.

Recovery

The characteristics of a recovery, or expansion, are many: Run-down equipment is replaced; employment, income, and consumer spending all begin to rise; and expectations become more favourable as a result of increases in production, sales, and profits. Investments that once seemed risky may be undertaken as the climate of business opinion starts to change from one of pessimism to one of optimism. As demand rises, production can be increased with relative ease merely by reemploying the existing unused capacity and unemployed labour.

Peak

A peak is the top of a cycle. At the peak, existing capacity is utilized to a high degree; labour shortages may develop, particularly in categories of key

skills; and shortages of essential raw materials are likely. As shortages develop in more and more markets, a situation of general excess demand develops. Costs rise, but since prices rise also, business remains profitable.

Recession

A **recession**, or contraction, is a downturn in economic activity. Common usage defines a recession as a fall in the real GDP for two quarters in succession. Demand falls off, and, as a result, production and employment also fall. As employment falls, so do households' incomes. Profits drop, and some firms encounter financial difficulties. Investments that looked profitable with the expectation of continually rising demand now appear unprofitable. It may not even be worth replacing capital goods as they wear out, because unused capacity is increasing steadily. In historical discussions, a recession that is deep and long lasting is often called a **depression**.

Booms and Slumps

Two nontechnical but descriptive terms are often used. The whole falling half of the cycle is often called a *slump*, and the whole rising half is often called a *boom*. These are useful terms to use when we do not wish to be more specific about the economy's position in the cycle.

below its potential level of output—that is, when Y is less than Y^*—the output gap is called a **recessionary gap**.

In booms, actual national income may *exceed* potential income, causing the output gap to become negative. Actual income can exceed potential income because potential income is defined for a *normal rate of utilization* of factors of production, and there are many ways in which these normal rates can be exceeded temporarily. Labour may work

longer hours than normal; factories may operate an extra shift or not close for routine repairs and maintenance. Although these expedients are only temporary, they are effective in the short term. When actual income exceeds potential income, there is generally upward pressure on prices. For this reason, when Y exceeds Y^*, the output gap is called an **inflationary gap**.

Figure 26-4(i) shows potential income for the years 1967 through 1992. The rising trend reflects

FIGURE 26-4
Potential National Income and the Output Gap, 1970-1992

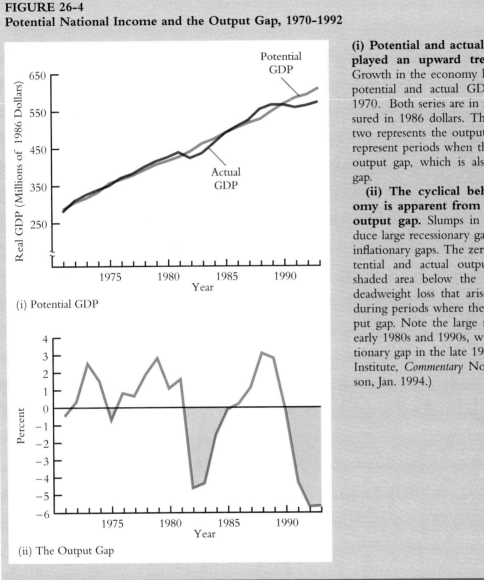

(i) Potential GDP

(ii) The Output Gap

(i) Potential and actual GDP have both displayed an upward trend in recent years. Growth in the economy has been such that both potential and actual GDP have doubled since 1970. Both series are in real terms and are measured in 1986 dollars. The distance between the two represents the output gap. The shaded areas represent periods when there has been a positive output gap, which is also called a recessionary gap.
(ii) The cyclical behaviour of the economy is apparent from the behaviour of the output gap. Slumps in economic activity produce large recessionary gaps, and booms produce inflationary gaps. The zero line indicates that potential and actual output are the same. The shaded area below the zero line indicates the deadweight loss that arises from unemployment during periods where there is a recessionary output gap. Note the large recessionary gaps in the early 1980s and 1990s, with an intervening inflationary gap in the late 1980s. (*Source:* C.D. Howe Institute, *Commentary* No. 56, by William Robson, Jan. 1994.)

the growth in the productive capacity of the Canadian economy over this period. The figure also shows actual real national income (reproduced from Figure 26-2), which has kept approximately in step with potential income. The distance between the two, which is the GDP gap, is plotted in part (ii) of Figure 26-4. Fluctuations in economic activity are apparent from fluctuations in the size of the gap. The deadweight loss from unemployment over any time span is indicated by the overall amount of the

gap over that time span. It is shown in part (ii) of Figure 26-4 by the shaded area between the curve and the zero line, which represents the level at which actual output equals potential output.

Why National Income Matters

National income is an important measure of economic performance in both the short run and the long run. Short-run movements in the business cycle receive the most attention in politics and in the press, but most economists agree that long-term growth, the rate of change of *potential income*, is in many ways the more important of the two.

Short-term fluctuations. Recessions cause unemployment and lost output. When actual income is below potential income, there is economic waste and human suffering as a result of a failure to use the economy's resources (including its human resources) at their normal intensity of use.

Booms, although associated with high employment and high output, can bring problems of their own. When actual national income exceeds potential income, strong inflationary pressure usually results, causing serious concern for any government that is committed to keeping the inflation rate low.

When we study short-term fluctuations, it is convenient to regard potential income, Y^*, as constant. Since it changes very slowly, little harm is done by assuming it to be constant as long as our purpose is to study short-term fluctuations around Y^*.

Long-term growth. In the long term, the course of real output is dominated by the growth in potential income, while fluctuations around potential income are relatively unimportant. When studying long-term trends, we cannot therefore regard Y^* as fixed.

The long-run trend in real national income per capita is the principal determinant of long-term improvements in a society's overall standard of living. When income per person grows, each generation can expect, on average, to be substantially better off than preceding ones. For example, if real income per capita grows at the relatively modest rate of 1.5 percent per year, the average person's lifetime income expectancy will be *twice* that of his or her grandparents.

In the long run, national income can grow for two reasons. One is growth in the amount of output produced per hour of work. It is this growth, the growth of *labour productivity*, that has generally eliminated the low living standards that prevailed at the start of the Industrial Revolution in the mid-eighteenth century. A second source of growth in income arises from changes in the amount of labour supplied. If the population grows (or the existing population works more hours), more output will be produced. The difference between these two sources of growth is important. When productivity increases, more output is obtained for a given amount of effort. When the total amount of work increases, more output is obtained by using more resources. Income rises, but the amount of income per person need not rise.

In the Canadian economy, much of the growth in income during the 1970s and 1980s was due to increases in the total number of hours worked. A relatively small part of that growth, compared to the trend of the rest of the century, could be attributed to growth in labour productivity. This reduction in productivity growth has created new interest in the sources of economic growth, a subject that is one of the major themes in our discussion of macroeconomics.

Although economic growth makes people better off on average, it does not necessarily make every individual better off. Some people are harmed by the economic change that accompanies growth, although most people benefit.

It is also important to remember that national income is far from a perfect measure of economic well-being, in part because it fails to measure many things, such as leisure time, that matter to people. Chapter 27 contains a detailed discussion of how economists measure national income and an evaluation of the strengths and weaknesses of those measures.

Employment, Unemployment, and the Labour Force

National income and *employment* (and, hence, *unemployment*) are closely related. If more is to be produced, either more workers must be used in production or existing workers must produce more. The first change means a rise in employment and actual national income; the second means a rise in labour productivity and in potential as well as actual income. In the short run, when the economy's potential income is fixed, the only way to produce more output is to employ more workers. Trend increases in productivity are a major source of economic growth, but their main effects are felt over longer periods of time.

The Canadian **labour force** is the total number of adults (aged 15 and over) who are either employed or unemployed. The **employed** denotes the number of adult workers who hold jobs. The **unemployed** denotes the number of adult workers who are not employed but are actively searching for a job. The **unemployment rate**, usually rep-

Box 26-2

How Accurate Are the Unemployment Figures?

No measurement of unemployment is completely accurate. The unemployment figures that are calculated by Statistics Canada, however, have a number of shortcomings that reveal much about the concept of unemployment itself.

Measured unemployment may overstate or understate the number of people who are involuntarily unemployed. On the one hand, measured unemployment overstates true unemployment by including people who are voluntarily out of work. For example, unemployment compensation provides protection against genuine hardship, but it also induces some people to stay out of work and collect unemployment benefits for as long as the benefits last. Such people have, in fact, voluntarily withdrawn from the labour force, although, in order to remain eligible for unemployment payments, they must make a show of looking for a job by registering at the local unemployment service office. Such people usually are included in the ranks of the unemployed because, for fear of losing their benefits, they tell the person who surveys them that they are actively looking for a job.

On the other hand, the measured figure understates involuntary unemployment by omitting some people who would accept a job if one were available but who did not actively look for one during the week in which the data were collected. For example, people who have not found jobs after searching for a long time may become discouraged and stop seeking work. Such people have withdrawn voluntarily from the labour force and will not be recorded as unemployed. They are, however, unemployed in the sense that they would willingly accept a job if one were available. People in this category are referred to as *discouraged workers*. They have voluntarily withdrawn from the labour market because they believe that they cannot find a job under current conditions.

In addition, there are part-time unemployed people. If some people are working 6 hours instead of 8 hours per day because there is insufficient demand for the product that they help to make, then these workers are suffering 25 percent unemployment even though none of them are reported as unemployed. Twenty-five percent of that group's potential labour resources are going unused. Involuntary part-time work is a major source of unemployment of labour resources that is not reflected in the overall unemployment figures that are reported in the press.

The official figures for unemployment are useful, particularly because they tell us the *direction* of changes in unemployment. It is unlikely, for example, that the figures will be rising when unemployment is really falling. For all of the reasons that we have just discussed, however, they can at times give under- or overestimates of the total number of persons who would be genuinely willing to work if they were offered a job at the going rate of pay.

---

resented by the symbol U, is unemployment expressed as a percentage of the labour force.

$$U = \frac{\text{umemployed}}{\text{labour force}} \times 100 \text{ percent}$$

The number of unemployed persons in Canada is estimated from a sample survey conducted each month by Statistics Canada. Persons who are currently without a job but who say they have searched actively for one during the sample period are recorded as unemployed. The total number of estimated unemployed is then expressed as a percentage of the labour force (employed plus unemployed) to obtain the figure for percentage unemployment. Some problems connected with this measurement are discussed in Box 26-2.

Consideration of employment and unemployment suggests another concept, that of *full employment* or *high employment*. One confusing thing about full employment is that it does *not* mean an absence of unemployment. This is why the concept is now often called *high employment*, although the long history of the use of the term *full employment* in economics guarantees that it will be heard for some time to come. There are two main reasons why full employment is always accompanied by some unemployment.

First, there is a constant turnover of individuals in given jobs and a constant change in job opportunities. New members enter the work force; some people quit their jobs; others are fired. Although the number of vacant positions may equal the number looking for such positions, it takes time for these people to find jobs. So, at any point in time, there is unemployment due to the normal turnover of labour. Such unemployment is called **frictional unemployment**.

Second, because the economy is constantly changing and adapting, at any moment in time there will always be some mismatching between the characteristics of the labour force and the characteristics of the available jobs. This is a mismatching between the structure of the supplies of labour and the structure of the demands for labour. The mismatching may occur, for example, because labour does not have the skills demanded or because labour is not in the part of the country where the demand is located. Unemployment that occurs because of a mismatching of the characteristics of the supply of labour and the demand for labour, even when the overall demand for labour is equal to the overall supply, is called **structural unemployment**. We will have more to say about these two types of unemployment in Chapter 36.

High or full employment is said to occur when the only existing unemployment is frictional and structural. At less than full employment, other types of unemployment are present as well. One major reason for lapses from full employment lies with the business cycle. During recessions, unemployment rises above the minimum avoidable amount of frictional and structural unemployment. This excess amount is called **cyclical unemployment** (or, sometimes, *deficient-demand unemployment*).

The measured unemployment rate when the economy is at full employment is often called the **natural rate of unemployment** or the **NAIRU**.[3] Estimates of this rate are difficult to obtain and are often a source of disagreement among economists. Nevertheless, such estimates are a useful benchmark against which economists can gauge the current performance of the economy, as measured by the actual unemployment rate. Estimates indicate that the natural rate of unemployment rose throughout the 1970s from around 5.5 percent to a high of around 7.5 percent in the late 1970s, and it has now fallen to between 5 and 6 percent. (We shall discuss the reasons for these changes in Chapter 36.)

Unemployment: The Historical Experience

Figure 26-5(i) shows the trends in the labour force, employment, and unemployment since 1930. Despite booms and slumps, employment has grown roughly in line with the growth in the labour force and the total population. In the 1980s, however, the labour force and employment grew faster than the total population in response to the increasing participation of youths and women in the labour force.

Although the long-term growth trend dominates the employment figures, some unemployment is always present. Figure 26-5(ii) shows that the short-term fluctuations in the unemployment rate have been quite marked. The unemployment rate has been as low as 1.4 percent in 1944 and as high as 19.3 percent in 1933; in the post-World War II period, the unemployment rate fell as low as 3.4 percent in 1956 and rose as high as 12.6 percent in 1982.

The high unemployment rate of the Great Depression in the early 1930s tends to dwarf the fluctuations in unemployment that have occurred since then. Nonetheless, the fluctuations in unemployment in recent decades have been neither minor nor unimportant.

Unemployment can rise either because employment falls or because the labour force rises. In recent decades, the number of people entering the labour force has exceeded the number leaving it. The resulting rise in the labour force has meant that unemployment has sometimes grown even in periods when employment was also growing.

---

[3] *NAIRU* is an acronym for "non-accelerating inflationary rate of unemployment." The reasons for the use of this term will become clear in Chapter 36.

FIGURE 26-5
Canadian Labour Force, Employment, and Unemployment, 1930–1992

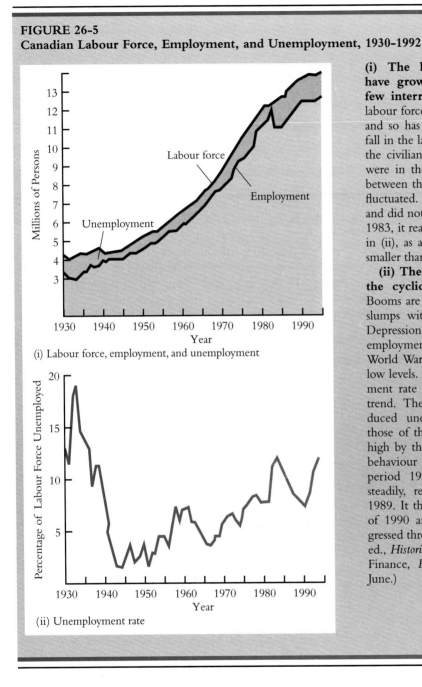

(i) Labour force, employment, and unemployment

(ii) Unemployment rate

(i) The labour force and employment have grown since the 1930s with only a few interruptions. The size of the Canadian labour force has more than doubled since 1930, and so has the number of the employed. The fall in the labour force in the early 1940s was in the civilian labour force. The missing workers were in the military. Unemployment, the gap between the labour force and employment, has fluctuated. It reached a peak of 800,000 in 1933 and did not reach that level again until 1977. In 1983, it reached 1.5 million, although as we see in (ii), as a fraction of the labour force, this is smaller than the 1933 figure.

(ii) The unemployment rate responds to the cyclical behaviour of the economy. Booms are associated with low unemployment, slumps with high unemployment. The Great Depression of the 1930s produced record unemployment rates for an entire decade. During World War II, unemployment rates fell to very low levels. Since 1945, however, the unemployment rate has demonstrated a gradual upward trend. The recession of the early 1980s produced unemployment rates second only to those of the 1930s; these rates were extremely high by the standards of the postWorld War II behaviour of the Canadian economy. Over the period 1983-1986, the rate fell slowly but steadily, reaching 7.5 percent at the end of 1989. It then rose dramatically in the recession of 1990 and fell slowly as the recovery progressed through 1993. (*Sources:* M. C. Urquhart, ed., *Historical Statistics of Canada;* Department of Finance, *Economic Review;* 1993 data are for June.)

Why Unemployment Matters

The social and political significance of the unemployment rate is enormous. The government is blamed when it is high and takes credit when it is low. Few macroeconomic policies are planned without some consideration of how they will affect it. No other summary statistic, with the possible exception of the inflation rate, carries such weight as a source of both formal and informal policy concern as the percentage of the labour force unemployed.

Unemployment causes economic waste and human suffering. The economic waste is obvious. Human effort is the least durable of economic commodities. If a fully employed economy with a constant labour force has 14 million people who are willing to work in 1993, their services must be either used in 1990 or wasted. When the services of only 12.6 million are used because 10 percent of the labour force is unemployed, one year's potential output of 1.4 million workers is lost forever. In an economy in which there is not enough output to meet everyone's needs, many people feel that any waste of potential output is undesirable and that large wastes are tragic.

Severe hardship can be caused by prolonged periods of unemployment. A person's spirit can be broken by a long period of desiring but being unable to find work. Research has shown that crime, divorce, and general social unrest tend to be positively associated with long-term unemployment.

In the not-so-distant past, only private charity or help from friends and relatives stood between the unemployed and starvation. Today, welfare and unemployment insurance have softened those effects, particularly when unemployment is for short periods, as is often the case. However, when an economic slump is deep and prolonged, as in the early 1980s and the early 1990s, people begin to exhaust their unemployment insurance and must fall back on savings, welfare, or charity.

Inflation and the Price Level

Everyone knows what inflation is. Most people complain about its effects when the inflation rate is high and worry that it is just around the corner when the inflation rate is low. Inflation means that prices in general are going up—not just the price of gasoline, blue jeans, or chewing gum, but the price of almost everything.

To study inflation, economists use two concepts. The first is the *price level*, which refers to the average level of all prices in the economy and is indicated by the symbol P. The second is the *rate of inflation*, which is the rate at which the general price level is rising.

In order to measure the price level, economists construct a *price index*, which averages the prices of different commodities according to how important they are. The best-known price index in Canada is the **Consumer Price Index (CPI)**, which measures the average cost of the goods and services that are bought by the average Canadian consumer.

The CPI expresses the price level at any time in relation to what a given bundle of commodities

(those consumed by the average Canadian urban resident) cost in a base period. The base period in use in 1993 was 1986, for which the value of the index is set to 100. Thus, when we read that the CPI for February 1993 had a value of 130, we know that a bundle of goods and services that cost $100 during 1986 would have cost $130 if purchased in February 1993. Generally, price indexes compare the cost of a given bundle of goods and services purchased at different times.[4]

Because the CPI is based on consumption for the average household, it does not measure accurately the change in the cost of living for each and every household. Rich, poor, young, old, single, married, urban, and rural households typically consume goods in different proportions. An increase in air fares, for example, will raise the cost of living of a frequent traveler but not affect that of a nontraveling household.

The more an individual household's consumption pattern conforms to that of the typical pattern used to create a price index, the better the index will reflect changes in that household's cost of living.

By allowing us to compare the general price level at different times, a price index such as the CPI also allows us to measure the rate of inflation. For example, the value of the CPI in February 1993 was 130.0 and in February 1992 was 127.1. The *rate of inflation* during that one-year period, expressed in percentage terms, would be the change in the price level divided by the initial price level, times 100: $[(130 - 127.1)/127.1] \times 100 = 2.28$ percent.

When time periods are not exactly one year apart, changes in price levels are usually converted to *annual rates*, the average year-to-year percentage change in prices over the period measured. For example, the CPI in September 1992 was 128.4, and in December 1992, it was 129.4. During the three months separating September and December, the CPI rose by 0.78 percent. If the CPI had grown at 0.78 per three months for a whole year, the percentage increase over the year would have been 3.16. Thus, over the period from September 1991

---

[4]Details on how the CPI is constructed are provided in the appendix to this chapter.

to December 1992, we say that the CPI was growing at an annual rate of 3.16 percent. **[31]**

Inflation: The Historical Experience

Figure 26-6 shows the CPI and the inflation rate (measured by the annual rate of change in the CPI) from 1930 to 1992. What can we learn from this figure?

First, we learn that the price level is constantly changing. Second, we learn that in only two years since the end of the Second World War in 1945 did the price level fall; in all other years, the inflation rate was positive. The cumulative effect of this sequence of small but repeated price increases is quite dramatic; in 1980, the price level was six times higher than it was in 1930.

Third, we learn that whereas the long-term increasing trend stands out when we look at the price level, the short-term fluctuations stand out when we look at the inflation rate. The sharp year-to-year swings in the inflation rate have sometimes been dramatic. The increases in the inflation rate to double-digit levels in 1974 and again in 1979 were associated with major shocks to the world prices of oil and foodstuffs, and the declines in inflation that followed were delayed responses to major recessions. (Note that even when the inflation rate *falls,* as it did in 1982, for example, the price level continues to rise as long as inflation remains *positive.*) At the end of the 1980s, the rate began to tumble, and in 1992, it was at a low of 1.2 percent, a figure that has not been experienced since the early 1950s.

Why Inflation Matters

Money is the universal yardstick in our economy. We measure economic values in terms of money, and we use money to conduct our economic affairs. Things as diverse as wages, bank balances, the value of a house, and a university's endowment all are stated in terms of money. We value money, however, not for itself but for what we can purchase with it. The terms **purchasing power of money** and *real value of money* refer to the amount of goods and services that can be purchased with a given amount of money. A change in the price level affects us because it changes the real value of money.

The purchasing power of money is negatively related to the price level.

For example, if the price level doubles, a dollar will buy only one half as much, whereas if the price level halves, a dollar will buy twice as much. Figure 26-6 shows that inflation has reduced the purchasing power of money over each of the last five decades.

If inflation reduces the real value of a given sum of money, it also reduces the real value of anything else whose price is *fixed* in money terms. Thus, the real value of a money wage, a savings account, or the balance that is owed on a student loan is reduced by inflation.

A fully anticipated inflation. It is possible to imagine an inflation that has no real effects of any kind. What is required for this to happen is, first, that everyone who is making any sort of financial arrangement knows what the inflation rate will be over the life of the arrangement and, second, that *all* financial obligations be stated in real terms. The real behaviour of the economy would then be exactly the same with or without an inflation. Say, for example, that both sides of a wage contract agree that wages should go up by 3 percent in real terms. If the inflation rate is expected to be zero, they would agree to a 3 percent increase in money wages. If a 10 percent inflation is expected, however, they would agree to a 13 percent increase in money wages. Ten percent would be needed to maintain the purchasing power of the money wages that would be paid, and 3 percent would be needed to bring about the desired increase in purchasing power.[5]

Similarly, a loan contract would specify that the amount repaid on the loan be increased over the amount borrowed by the rate of inflation. Thus, if $100 is borrowed and the price level rises by 10 percent, then $110 would have to be returned (quite apart from any interest that might be paid on the loan). This would ensure that the real value of what is borrowed stays equal to the real value of what is returned.

Taxes would also have to be adjusted. For example, the personal exemption on the income tax (the amount of income that each person can exempt from taxation) would have to be increased by

---

[5]This is approximately correct, as discussed further in Math Note 32.

FIGURE 26-6
The Canadian Price Level and Inflation Rate, 1930–1992

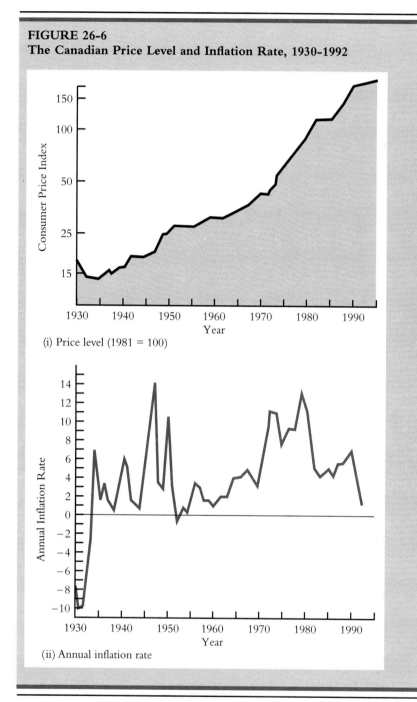

(i) Price level (1981 = 100)

(ii) Annual inflation rate

(i) The overwhelming trend movement in the price level since 1930 has been upward. The data reflect the Consumer Price Index from 1930 to 1990, with 1981, as the base year, equal to 100. They are plotted on a semilog scale on which equal vertical distances represent equal percentage changes. Any acceleration in the rate of increase in the price level shows up as increasing steepness of the curve.

(ii) The rate of inflation has varied from −10 percent to +14 percent since 1930. Prices fell dramatically at the onset of the Great Depression. They rose sharply during and after World War II and during the Korean War. For about a decade thereafter, no trend in the inflation rate was discernible. Starting in the mid-1960s, however, inflation experienced a strong upward trend, interrupted by short-term fluctuations. In 1983, inflation fell to its lowest level since the early 1970s, and it averaged around 4 to 5 percent through most of the 1980s. Then after a short rise at the end of the long expansion in 1989–1990, it tumbled to the 1–2 percent range in the early 1990s. (*Sources:* M. C. Urquhart, ed., *Historical Statistics of Canada;* Department of Finance, *Economic Review;* 1993 data are for June.)

10 percent to keep the real value of the exemption constant, given a 10 percent inflation rate.

The result of all this would be a 10 percent increase in everyone's money incomes and money assets, combined with a 10 percent increase in all money prices and all money liabilities. Nothing real would have changed. People's higher money incomes would buy the same amount as before, and the real value of their assets and liabilities would be unchanged.

Once everything has adjusted, any one price level works as well as any other price level.

This is just what we should expect, since it would indeed be magic if altering the number of zeros that we use when stating monetary values could change anything real.[6]

A completely unanticipated inflation. At the opposite extreme from a fully anticipated inflation is a completely unanticipated inflation. No one sees it coming; no one is prepared to offset its consequences. The real value of all contracts that are specified in money terms will change unexpectedly. Who will gain and who will lose?

An unexpected inflation benefits anyone who has an obligation to pay out money and harms anyone who is entitled to receive money.

For example, consider a wage contract that specifies a wage increase of 3 percent on the assumption that the price level will remain constant. Both employers and employees expect that the purchasing power of wages paid will rise by 3 percent as a result of the new contract. Now assume, however, that the price level unexpectedly rises by 10 percent over the life of the wage contract. The 3 percent increase in money wages now means a reduction in the purchasing power of wages of about 7 percent. Employers selling goods whose prices rise at the average rate gain because their wage payments represent a smaller part of the value of their output than they had expected. Workers lose because their wages represent a smaller receipt of purchasing power than they had expected.

People who have borrowed money will pay back a smaller real amount than they borrowed. By the same token, people who have lent money will receive back a smaller real amount than they lent. Say, for example, that Gerry lends Helen enough money to buy a medium-sized car, and the price level subsequently doubles. When Helen pays back the money that she borrowed, Gerry finds himself with only one half of the amount now required to buy the car.

Wage earners and lenders will be able to adjust to the new price level when they make new contracts, but some people will be locked into their old money contracts for the rest of their lives. The extreme case is suffered by those who live on fixed money incomes. For example, pensions that are provided by the private sector often promise to pay a certain number of dollars per year for life. On retirement, this sum may look adequate, even generous. Twenty years later, however, inflation may have reduced its purchasing power to the poverty level. A family that retired on a fixed money income in 1973 would have found the purchasing power of that income reduced year by year, until in 1993, it would have been only 30 percent of its original value. To understand the impact of this, imagine being told that, for every dollar that you now spend, only 30 cents can be spent in the future.

Intermediate cases. There are several reasons why virtually all real inflations fall somewhere between the two extremes (fully anticipated or complete surprise) that we have just discussed.

First, the inflation rate is usually variable and seldom foreseen exactly, even though its general course may be anticipated. Thus, the actual rate will sometimes be higher than expected—to the benefit of those who have contracted to pay money. At other times, the inflation rate will be lower than expected—to the benefit of those who have contracted to receive money. Given the lack of certainty, different people will have different expectations.

Because it is hard to foresee accurately, inflation adds to the uncertainties of economic life. Highly variable inflation rates cause great uncertainty.

Second, even if the inflation rate is foreseen, all adjustments to it cannot occur at the same speed. As a result, inflation redistributes income, and it does so in a haphazard way. Those whose money incomes adjust more slowly than prices are rising will lose; those whose money incomes keep ahead of the inflation will gain.

---

[6]For those of you who have studied microeconomics, this is another way of stating the point that *only relative prices matter* for resource allocation. If all prices rise by 10 percent, or by any other uniform percentage, relative prices are unchanged. The same relation holds in an open economy, where in the face of an alteration in the domestic price level, the exchange rate changes to keep relative international prices and asset values unchanged.

Third, even if the inflation rate is foreseen, the full set of institutions that would be needed for everyone to avoid its consequences does not exist. For example, many private pension plans are stated in money terms. Employees have little choice but to take the only plan that their employers make available to them. Thus, even when inflation is foreseen, some people will wind up living on fixed nominal incomes and thus will see their real incomes erode over time.

Fourth, much of the tax system is defined in nominal money terms, causing its effects to vary with the price level. For example, machinery and equipment owned by businesses wear out with use. The tax code allows for this by permitting firms to deduct *depreciation allowances* from their income for tax purposes. The depreciation allowances are usually calculated as a certain fraction of the original purchase price of the machinery or equipment. If there has been a rapid inflation, the allowed depreciation may be much less than the real depreciation. This makes capital more expensive for firms and tends to reduce investment (and, as we shall see, economic growth).

Indexing.   Some of the effects of inflation can be avoided by indexing. **Indexing** means linking the payments that are made under the terms of a contract to changes in the price level. For example, a retirement pension might pay the beneficiary $15,000 per year starting in 1996, and it might specify that the amount paid will increase each year in proportion to the increase in the CPI. Thus, if the CPI turns out to rise by 10 percent between 1996 and 1997, the pension that is payable in 1997 would rise by 10 percent, to $16,500. If the CPI rose only 5 percent, the pension would also rise by 5 percent, to $15,750. In either case, indexing would hold the real purchasing power of the pension constant.

Indexing is potentially valuable as a defense against unforeseen changes in the price level, as a method of reducing uncertainty, and as a way of adapting institutions so that contracts can be made in real terms. In practise, however, indexing is used much less than it might be. Most of the tax code is no longer fully indexed, and the vast majority of contracts are written in nominal terms, putting them at risk for the consequences of unanticipated inflation.

The Interest Rate

If a bank lends you money, it will usually ask you to agree to a schedule for repayment. Furthermore, it will charge you interest for the privilege of borrowing the money. If, for example, you are lent $1,000 today, repayable in one year's time, you may also be asked to pay $10 per month in interest. This makes $120 in interest over the year, which can be expressed as an interest rate of 12 percent per annum [(120/1,000) × 100 percent].

The **interest rate** is the price that is paid to borrow money for a stated period of time and is expressed as a percentage amount per dollar borrowed. For example, an interest rate of 12 percent per year means that the borrower must pay 12 cents per year for every dollar that is borrowed.

Just as there are many prices of goods, so there are many interest rates. The bank will lend money to an industrial customer at a lower rate than it will lend money to you—there is a lower risk of not being repaid. The rate charged on a loan that is not to be repaid for a long time will usually differ from the rate on a loan that is to be repaid quickly.

When economists speak of *the* interest rate, they mean a rate that is typical of all the various interest rates in the economy. Dealing with one interest rate suppresses much interesting detail. However, interest rates generally move together, so following the movement of one rate allows us to consider changes in the level of interest rates in general. The *prime rate* of interest, the rate that banks charge to their best business customers, may be thought of as *the* interest rate, since, when the prime rate changes, most other rates change in the same direction.

Interest Rates and Inflation

How does inflation affect the rate of interest? In order to begin developing an answer, imagine that your friend lends you $100 and that the loan is repayable in one year. The amount that you pay her for making this loan, measured in money terms, is the nominal interest rate. If you pay her $108 in one year's time, $100 will be repayment of the amount of the loan (which is called the principal) and $8 will be payment of the interest. In this case, the nominal interest rate is 8 percent [(8/100 × 100 percent].

How much purchasing power has your friend gained or lost by making this loan? As we have already noted in our discussion of the consequences of inflation, the answer will depend on what happens to the price level during the year. Intuitively, the more the price level rises, the worse your friend will do, and the better the transaction will be for you. This result occurs because the more the price level rises, the less valuable are the dollars that you use to repay the loan. The real rate of interest measures the real return on a loan, in terms of purchasing power.

If the price level remains constant over the year, then the real rate of interest that your friend earns would also be 8 percent, because she can buy 8 percent more goods and services with the $108 that you repay her than with the $100 that she lent you. However, if the price level rises by 8 percent, the real rate of interest would be zero, because the $108 that you repay her buys the same quantity of goods as the $100 that she originally gave up. If she is unlucky enough to lend money at 8 percent in a year in which prices rise by 10 percent, the real rate of interest that she earns is minus 2 percent. The repayment of principal and nominal interest of 8 percent will purchase 2 percent less, in goods and services, than the amount originally lent.

If lenders and borrowers are concerned with real costs, measured in terms of purchasing power, the nominal rate of interest will be set at the real rate to which they agree as a return on their money plus an amount to cover any expected rate of inflation. Consider a one-year loan that is meant to earn a real return to the lender of 5 percent. If the expected rate of inflation is zero, the nominal interest rate set for the loan will be 5 percent. If a 10 percent inflation is expected, the nominal interest rate will be 15 percent.

To provide a given expected real rate of interest, the nominal interest rate must be set at the desired real rate of interest plus the expected annual rate of inflation. [32]

The extra amount to cover the inflation is often called the *inflationary* premium. Thus, the nominal interest rate equals the real interest rate plus the inflationary premium.

Because they often overlook this point, many people are surprised at the high nominal rates of interest that exist during periods of rapid inflation. For example, when the nominal interest rates rose drastically in 1980, many commentators expressed shock at the "unbearably" high rates. Most of them failed to notice that with inflation running at about 12 percent, an interest rate of 15 percent represented a real rate of only 3 percent. Had the Bank of Canada given in to the pressure to hold interest rates to the more "reasonable" level of 10 percent, it would have been imposing a *negative* real rate of interest. The purchasing power that lenders would get back, including interest, would be less than the purchasing power of the amount that was originally lent.

The burden of borrowing depends upon the real, not the nominal, rate of interest.

For example, a nominal interest rate of 8 percent, combined with a 2 percent rate of inflation, is a much greater real burden on borrowers than a nominal rate of 16 percent, combined with a 14 percent rate of inflation. As discussed in more detail in Box 26-3, lenders often suffer from a similar confusion.

Figure 26-7 shows the nominal and the real rate of interest paid on short-term government borrowing since 1950. Interest rates were both high and volatile during the early part of the 1980s. During the latter part of the 1980s, rates fell somewhat and became somewhat less variable. During late 1991 and early 1992, both real and nominal interest rates fell, with real interest rates reaching their lowest levels in over a decade.

Why Interest Rates Matter

As we shall see in Chapter 33, real interest rates help to determine the amount of total investment expenditure. When real interest rates are high, it is costly to borrow, and there is less real investment than when interest rates are low. The greater is investment expenditure, the greater will be potential GDP in the future. Thus, real interest rates, through their effect on investment, affect long-term growth and *future* living standards. Changes in investment can also cause swings in the business cycle. A slowdown in investment expenditure can trigger a slump; conversely, when investment increases sharply, GDP generally follows. Thus, via their effect on invest-

Box 26-3

Does a Fall in Inflation Hurt Lenders?

In the early 1990s, the Canadian inflation rate fell to very low levels, and nominal interest rates followed. Many retired persons complained that their incomes had fallen because their money held in government bonds produced a lower cash flow. Their mistake was in regarding the whole nominal interest as current income. By spending the inflationary premium, these persons were allowing the real purchasing power of their capital, and the real income it generates, to be reduced by the inflation rate. For example, a couple who spent the whole nominal interest earnings in the face of a 5 percent inflation would find their real income halved in just over 14 years. To preserve the real value of capital and income, the inflationary premium needs to be saved and added to the sum lent out, thus keeping its real value constant.

To illustrate this, consider a retired person who has $200,000 invested in government bonds that earn 10 percent nominal interest in the face of a 5 percent inflation. If the person regards the entire $20,000 as income and spends it, the real purchasing power of this cash flow will fall by 5 percent per year. At the end of 20 years, the prices of everything he buys will have risen by 2.65 times, and he will be able to buy only about 38 percent ([1/2.65]100) as much as 20 years ago. Also, the real value of the $200,000 he passes on to his heirs will be only 38 percent of its original real value. He will have consumed all of his income and much of his wealth.

A second person who "saves" half of her interest earnings and spends the other half will maintain her real wealth and income over the 20 years. At the end of 20 years, the nominal value of her wealth will be $530,000; her nominal interest earnings will be $53,000 per year, which will have the same purchasing power as the original $200,000 (since $53,000/2.65 = $20,000).

The second person has correctly regarded only the real return of $10,000 in the first year as income and the other $10,000 as an inflationary premium to compensate for the loss of real value of her capital.

Now assume that the inflation rate falls to zero while the nominal interest rate falls to 5 percent. The first investor has only $10,000 to spend each year and complains bitterly that his income has been cut in half. What has really happened is that he has stopped consuming his capital because the real value of his $200,000 will now be unchanged when he spends all his interest earnings. He can, if he wishes, return to his former real position in which the inflation rate was 5 percent and he spent all of his interest earnings of $20,000. All he needs to do is to spend his interest earnings *and* spend 5 percent of his capital each year. At the end of 20 years, his capital will have shrunk to a nominal value of $76,000. Having only $76,000 and an unchanged price level is identical in terms of real purchasing power to having $200,000 and a price level that has risen by 2.65.

When the inflation rate falls to zero, the second investor now spends all her interest earnings of $10,000. She no longer needs to save and add to the nominal value of her capital because its real value is no longer being eroded by inflation. She correctly perceives that her real income is unchanged by the fall in inflation and the nominal interest rate. Measured in purchasing power, her expenditure and the value of her capital is unchanged from year to year.

Failure to understand these basic but subtle relations have led many a retired person slowly but surely down the path to poverty when inflation rates are even moderately high.

FIGURE 26-7
Real and Nominal Interest Rates, 1950–1992

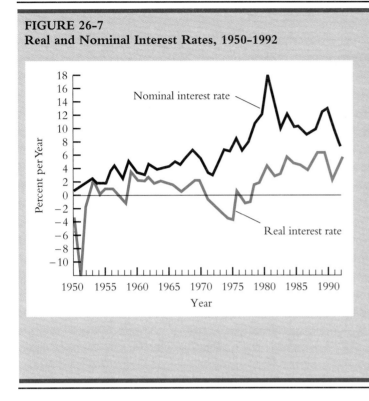

The inflationary trend in the postwar era has meant that the real interest rate has almost always been less than the nominal interest rate. The data for the nominal interest rate show the average rate of interest on three-month Treasury bills in each year from 1950. The real interest is calculated as the nominal interest rate minus the actual rate of inflation over the same period. For the most part, the real interest rate has been below 3 percent throughout the period. Through much of the 1970s, the real interest rate was negative, indicating that the inflation rate exceeded the nominal interest rate. The 1980s saw real interest rates rise to heights that were unprecedented in the past. In the middle of the decade, as inflation moderated, both real and nominal interest rates fell, only to rise again. The success of the Bank's anti-inflation policies in the early 1990s brought rates down to levels not seen since the 1960s.

ment, real interest rates also affect unemployment and output in the short run. In addition, interest rates are an important determinant of the standard of living of many retired people who live on pensions or savings. For them, the higher are real interest rates, the higher will be the level of their real incomes.

The International Economy

The two important indicators of the Canadian position in the international economy are the *exchange rate*, which measures the international value of the dollar, and the *balance of payments*, which records virtually all international economic transactions.

The Exchange Rate

If you are going on a holiday to Mexico, you will need Mexican pesos to pay for your purchases. Most banks, as well as any foreign exchange bureau, will make the necessary exchange of currencies for you. They will sell you pesos in return for your dollars. If you get 2,500 pesos for each dollar that you give up,

the two currencies are trading at a rate of $1 = 2,500 pesos or, what is the same thing, 1 peso = 0.0004 dollars.

The exchange rate refers to the rate at which different currencies are traded for each other.

In particular, the **exchange rate** between the Canadian dollar and any foreign currency is the quantity of Canadian dollars that is needed to buy one unit of that currency. For example, at the beginning of April 1993, it cost 1.26 Canadian dollars to buy 1 U.S. dollar. The exchange rate was 1.26. Put the other way round, one Canadian dollar was worth 0.79 U.S. dollars. This latter figure is often referred to as the *external value of the Canadian dollar*. Note that the exchange rate is negatively related to the external value of the Canadian dollar. A rise in the exchange rate means that it takes more C$s to buy a unit of foreign exchange, so each C$ is worth less in terms of foreign exchange.

A rise in the exchange rate is the same thing as a fall in the external value of the domestic currency.

Box 26-4

The Exchange Rate and the External Value of the Currency

To illustrate these important relations, we concentrate on the rates that are most familiar to all of us, those between the Canadian dollar and the U.S. dollar. Recall once again the critical definitions, all looked at from the point of view of the C$. The *exchange rate* is the number of C$s needed to buy US$1. The *external value* of the C$ is the number of US$s you can get for C$1.

Suppose you are told that the cost of US$1 is C$1.25. That is the exchange rate, but what is the external value of the C$? What we know is

$$US\$1 = C\$1.25$$

Dividing through by 1.25 tells us that

$$US\$1/1.25 = C\$1$$

which, doing the division, is

$$US\$0.80 = C\$1$$

This shows that the exchange rate and the external value of the currency are the reciprocals of each other. It follows that they move in opposite directions. Thus, when the exchange rate appreciates, the external value of the C$ depreciates; when the exchange rate depreciates, the external value of the C$ appreciates.

Now suppose you go into the bank to discover that the exchange rate has risen to 1.333. This tells you that you now have to pay C$1.33 for every U.S. dollar you buy. It is clear that the C$ is now *less* valuable, since you have to pay more of them to buy the same US$. To see this, calculate the external value of the C$ as 1/1.333 = 0.75. So the C$ is now only worth 75 U.S. cents.

It may sound confusing that a fall in the external value of the C$ is shown by a rise in the exchange rate, while a rise in the external value of the C$ is shown by a fall in the exchange rate. This, however, is no more confusing than that when all prices go up, the value of money goes down. All you need to remember is that the exchange rate tells how many C$s are needed to buy one US$, and the higher that number, the less is each C$ worth.

These relations can be confusing, and they are illustrated further in Box 26-4.

The term **foreign exchange** refers to foreign currencies or claims to foreign currencies, such as bank deposits, checks, and promissory notes, that are payable in foreign money. The **foreign exchange market** is the market where foreign exchange is traded—at prices expressed by the exchange rates.

The value of the Canadian dollar can be looked at in two ways. The *internal value of the dollar* refers to its power to purchase goods in Canadian domestic markets. We have already seen that the price level and the internal value of the dollar are negatively related: The higher the price level, the lower the purchasing power of a dollar. The *external value of the dollar* refers to its power to purchase foreign currencies. This external value is negatively related to the exchange rate, which, as you will recall, measures the dollar cost of a unit of foreign exchange. The lower the dollar's external value (that is, the less foreign currency it will buy), the higher the exchange rate (that is, the greater the number of Canadian dollars that must be used to purchase a unit of foreign exchange).

Figure 26-8 shows two indicators of the Canadian exchange rate since 1971. The first is the Canadian dollar price of one U.S. dollar; the second

FIGURE 26-8
Canadian Dollar Exchange Rates, 1971-1992

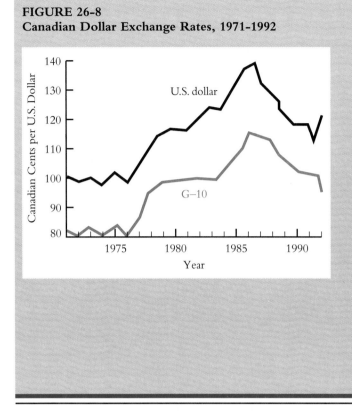

The exchange rate rose steadily from the mid-1970s through the mid-1980s; from 1986 through mid-1990 it fell. The black line shows the Canada-U.S. exchange rate, defined as the Canadian currency price, measured in cents, of one U.S. dollar. That price rose steadily from about $1.00 in 1976 to almost $1.40 in 1986; the rise in the price of U.S. dollars meant that the external value of the Canadian dollar was falling. From 1986 through mid-1990, the price of U.S. dollars fell continually, indicating a rising external value of the Canadian dollar. Then in 1992 (and 1993), the exchange rate rose once again, lowering the external value of the Canadian dollar.

The colored line shows the Canadian dollar exchange rate in terms of a weighted average of the currencies of 10 major industrial countries, known as G-10. It is expressed as an index, with 1981 set equal to 100. This weighted average shows a similar pattern of a rising price of foreign exchange from 1976 through 1986 and a falling price from 1986 through mid-1990. (*Sources: Bank of Canada Monthly Review*, various issues.)

is an index of the weighted-average Canadian dollar price of the currencies of a group of 10 major industrial countries, called the G-10. Since the United States is such a major trading partner for Canada, the U.S. dollar gets a strong weight in the index, and the two series give a very similar picture.

For the first half of the 1970s, the external value of the Canadian dollar was relatively stable, fluctuating only moderately and not showing any trend. From 1976 through 1986, the external value of the Canadian dollar declined sharply, as both measures of the exchange rate rose over that period.

From 1986 through mid-1990, the external value of the Canadian dollar strengthened, as both measures of the exchange rate fell; by mid-1990, both were back to approximately their 1980 levels. As the 1990s started, the strong external value of the Canadian dollar was a major point of controversy; Bank of Canada Governor John Crow argued that it was a necessary by-product of his commitment to fighting inflation, while many Canadian manufacturers said that it was destroying the competitiveness of Canadian industry by making foreign imports into Canada too cheap and making Cana-

dian exports too expensive on world markets. The external value of the dollar remained high until mid-1992, when the exchange rate finally rose to values exceeding 1.25. This increased the competitiveness of Canadian exports. We shall study these important events in more detail in Chapters 39 and 40.

The balance of payments. In order to know what is happening to the course of international trade and international capital movements, governments keep an account of the transactions among countries. These accounts are called the **balance-of-payments accounts**. They record all international payments that are made for the buying and selling of both goods and services, as well as financial assets such as stocks and bonds.

Figure 26-9 shows one part of the balance of payments that is most often the subject of controversy. This is the balance of payments on the *traded goods and services*. This covers all trade in visible goods and in services. The balance is the difference between the value of Canadian exports and the value of Canadian imports. As can be seen from

FIGURE 26-9
Canadian Imports, Exports, and Balance of Trade, 1970–1992

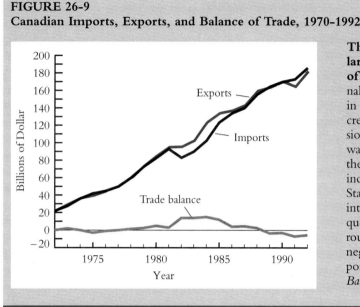

Though imports and exports are each quite large and have grown steadily, the balance of trade stays roughly in balance. The nominal value of imports and of exports rose steadily in the 1970s and 1980s, due both to price increases and to quantity increases. The sharp recession that Canada experienced in the early 1980s was accompanied by a sharp fall in imports, and the subsequent recovery was spurred in part by increased export sales (primarily to the United States). As a result, the balance of trade moved into a surplus in the 1980s, although it subsequently returned to its historical norm of being roughly in balance. There was a relatively large negative balance in 1991, due to the fall in exports caused by a severe U.S. recession. (*Sources: Bank of Canada Monthly Review,* various issues.)

Figure 26-9, Canadian exports and imports both rose steadily in the 1970s and 1980s, and the balance of trade fluctuated slightly but remained at or near a roughly balanced position.[7]

Cycles and Trends

Why are the price level, national income, employment, and the value of the dollar what they are today? What causes them to change? These are some of the questions that macroeconomics seeks to answer.

Before we begin to study these questions, it is useful to emphasise a distinction that has been made repeatedly in this chapter—the distinction between *cycles* and *trends*. Both are crucial to understanding the economy and evaluating its ability to provide goods, services, and opportunities.

Long-term trends. The study of economic trends is the study of the economy over extended periods of time. Here, we are primarily concerned with understanding the sources of long-term growth and the development of public policies that affect economic growth. Recent economic history has made the study of trends especially important. From the end of World War II until the late 1960s, output per hour of work in Canada grew at a rate of nearly 4 percent a year. Since 1970 it has grown at a rate of somewhat less than 1 percent a year. These differences matter: With productivity growing at 4 percent a year, living standards double every 18 years. At an annual growth of 1 percent a year, living standards double only every 72 years. The trend in productivity and the trend in potential GDP that are determined by productivity growth and population growth are the key objects of study for the long term.

In studying long-term trends, it is appropriate to ignore deviations from trend.

For trend analysis, this simplification does not cost us much, because over the long haul, actual GDP moves quite closely with potential GDP. And, over long time periods, we are most interested in

---

[7] In former times, when trade was mostly in goods, the figures were usually given only for trade in goods, often referred to as trade under the *merchandise account.* Today, services account for an important and growing amount of exports and imports, so it is more appropriate to consider imports and exports of both goods and services. In this book, "imports," "exports," and "the trade balance" always refer to trade in goods and services.

the evolution of the economy's *capacity* to produce (i.e., its potential output).

Short-term fluctuations.   While trends greatly affect economic welfare over the long haul, at any given time what matters more is how the economy is doing relative to its *current* potential. To examine this, we study business cycles, shorter-term fluctuations away from trend growth. These fluctuations are important: When the economy is operating well below its potential, unemployment is high, with its accompanying human suffering and economic waste. When the economy is operating above its potential, inflationary pressures are strong, with their accompanying economic distortions.

Changes in productivity and in the labour force dominate the long-term trends of output and employment, but productivity and the labour force generally change only slowly.

In studying short-term movements, it is appropriate to ignore long-term trends.

This is done with respect to national income by treating both the labour force and productivity as constant. Under these assumptions, a rise in output means a rise in employment and a fall in unemployment: Output is positively associated with employment and negatively associated with unemployment. Taking productivity and the labour force as constant not only greatly simplifies our discussion but also reasonably approximates reality when we are dealing with the *short-term* behaviour of the economy.

SUMMARY

1. Macroeconomics examines the behaviour of such broad aggregates and averages as the price level, national income, potential national income, the GDP gap, employment, and unemployment.

2. The value of the total production of goods and services in a nation is called national product. Since production of output generates income in the form of claims on that output, the total is also referred to as *national income*. One of the most commonly used measures of national income is gross domestic product (GDP).

3. Nominal national income evaluates output in current prices. Real national income evaluates output in base period prices. Changes in real national income reflect changes in quantities of output produced.

4. Fluctuations of national income around its potential level are associated with the business cycle. Recoveries pass through peaks and become recessions, which in turn pass through troughs to become recoveries. Although these movements are systematic rather than random, they are by no means completely regular.

5. Potential real national income measures the capacity of the economy to produce goods and services when factors of production are employed at their normal intensity of use. The GDP gap is the difference between potential and actual real national income. A positive GDP gap is called a *recessionary gap* while a negative GDP gap is called an *inflationary gap*.

6. The unemployment rate is the percentage of the labour force not employed but actively searching for a job. The labour force and employment have both grown steadily for the past half century. The unemployment rate fluctuates considerably from year to year. Unemployment imposes serious costs on the economy in the form of economic waste and human suffering.

7. The price level is measured by a price index, which measures the cost of a set of goods in one year relative to their cost in an (arbitrary) base year.

8. The inflation rate measures the rate of change of the price level. Although it fluctuates considerably, the inflation rate has been positive in almost all years, which means that the price level has displayed a continual upward trend since 1929.

9. Other important macroeconomic variables include nominal and real interest rates; exchange rates, which refer to the cost of Canadian dollars in terms of foreign currency; and the balance of payments, which is a record of all international transactions made by Canadian firms, households, and governments.

10. The dominant historical trends of the economy are growth of real output, employment, and the price level, over the long term. This growth has never been entirely smooth; there have always been fluctuations in output, unemployment, and the price level around their trend growth rates. The study of growth is simplified by ignoring these fluctuations and focusing on the broad trends. The study of the fluctuations is simplified by assuming that trends are zero, so that all changes are fluctuations.

TOPICS FOR REVIEW

National product and national income

Real and nominal national income

Potential and actual national income and the GDP gap

Employment, unemployment, and labour force

The price level and rate of inflation

The effects of anticipated and unanticipated inflation

The exchange rate and the external value of the currency

The real and nominal interest rates

The balance of payments

DISCUSSION QUESTIONS

1. Classify the issues raised in the following newspaper headlines as microeconomic, macroeconomic, or both.
   a. "Lettuce crop spoils as strike hits B.C. lettuce producers."
   b. "Analysts fear rekindling of inflation as economy recovers toward full employment."
   c. "Index of industrial production falls by 4 points."
   d. "Price of bus rides soars in Centerville as city council withdraws transport subsidy."
   e. "A fall in the unemployment rate signals the beginning of the end of the recession in the Edmonton area."
   f. "Silicon chip technology brings falling prices and growing sales of microcomputers."
   g. "Rising costs of imported raw materials cause most Canadian manufacturers to raise prices."

2. Most of the films on the list of 10-biggest-ever money makers have been made in the recent past. Does this mean that the most popular films are the most recent ones?

3. Between 1979 and 1986, employment in Canada grew by over 10 percent, from 10.4 million to 11.6 million. However, over that same period, unemployment grew from 836,000 to 1.2 million, and the unemployment rate rose from 7.4 percent to 9.6 percent. How do you reconcile these apparently conflicting statistics? Which do you think gives the most accurate description of developments in the economy?

4. During the economic recovery from 1983 through 1990, GDP at current prices grew at an average rate of 3.1 percent per year. To what extent does this imply an improvement in the economic circumstances of the average Canadian? What would we need to know in order to distinguish the effects on (a) a bank manager in Halifax, (b) an autoworker in Oshawa, (c) a pensioner living in retirement in Victoria, British Columbia, and (d) an oil field rigger living in Alberta?

5. Discuss the following statements about unemployment.
   a. "Unemployment is a personal tragedy and a national waste."
   b. "No one needs to be unemployed these days; just look at the help-wanted ads in the newspapers and the signs in the stores."
   c. "Unemployment insurance is a boondoggle for the lazy and unnecessary for the industrious."

6. If the inflation rate was predicted to be 10 percent next year, why would most people be unwilling to lend money at 5 percent interest? Say that 5 percent was all they could get, and they had money they didn't want to spend for a year. Would they do better just to hold the money? What could they do that would be better than lending their money at 5 percent?

7. What might lie behind the allegation that "inflation is legalized government robbery" and the reply that "inflation only hurts the ignorant, because no one with reasonable foresight needs to lose through inflation?"

8. In the good old days at the turn of the century, you could buy a drink for 5 cents and a full meal for 25 cents. Were they, then, good old days of high purchasing power for the average person?

9. Is a widow who lives entirely off her holding of government bonds better off if the inflation rate is 10 percent and the interest rate 14 percent or if the rates tumble to 1 percent and 6 percent respectively? What if the second set of rates is 1 percent and 5 percent, and she is subject to an average rate of tax of 30 percent on her interest earnings?

APPENDIX TO CHAPTER

26

How the CPI Is Constructed

Two important questions must be answered when any price index is constructed. First, what group of prices should be used? This depends on the index. The Consumer Price Index (CPI), which is calculated by Statistics Canada, covers prices of commodities that are commonly bought by households. Changes in the CPI are meant to measure changes in the typical household's *cost of living*. (Other indexes, such as the wholesale price index, cover the prices of different groups of commodities.)

Second, how should the movements in consumer prices be added up and summarized in one price index? If all prices change in the same proportion, this would not matter: a 10 percent rise in every price would mean a 10 percent rise in the average of all prices, no matter how the average was constructed. However, different prices usually change in different proportions. It then matters how much importance we give to each price change. Changes in the price of bread, for example, are much more important to the average consumer than changes in the price of caviar. In calculating a price index, each price is given a *weight* that reflects its importance.

Let us see how this is done for the CPI. Government statisticians periodically survey a representative group of households. This shows how consumers spend their incomes. The average bundle of goods that is bought is determined, along with the proportion of expenditure that is devoted to each good. These proportions become the weights attached to the individual prices in calculating the CPI. As a result, the CPI weights rather heavily the prices of commodities on which consumers spend much of their income and weights rather lightly the prices of commodities on which consumers spend only a little of their income. Table 26A-1 provides a simple example of how these weights are calculated.

Once the weights are chosen, the average price can be calculated for each period. This is done, as shown in Table 26A-2, by multiplying each price by its weight and summing the resulting figures. However, a single average price is not informative. Suppose, for example, you were told that the average price of all goods that were bought by consumers last year was $89.35. "So what?" you might well ask, and the answer would be, "So, not very much; by itself, this tells you nothing useful." Now suppose you are told that this year's average price for the same set of consumers' purchases is $107.22. Now you know that, on average, prices paid by consumers have risen sharply over the year. In fact, the increase is 20 percent.[1]

The average for each period is divided by the value of the average for the base period and multiplied by 100. The resulting series is called an index number series; by construction, the base period value in this series equals 100. If prices in the next period average 20 percent higher, the index number for that period will be 120. A simple example of how these calculations are carried out is given in Table 26A-2.

Price indexes are constructed by assigning weights to reflect the importance of the individual items being combined. The value of the index is set equal to 100 in the base period.

Table 26A-2 shows the calculation of what is called a *fixed-weight index*. The weights are the proportion of income that is spent on the three goods in the base year. These weights are then applied to the prices in each subsequent year. The value of the index in each year measures exactly how much the base-year bundle of goods would cost at that year's

---

[1] The change is $17.87, which is 20 percent of the initial average price of $89.35

TABLE 26A-1   Calculation of Weights for a Price Index

Commodity	Price	Quantity	Expenditure price × quantity	Proportional weight
A	$5	60	$300	0.50
B	1	200	200	0.33
C	4	25	100	0.17
Total			$600	1.00

The weights are the proportions of total expenditure that are devoted to each commodity. This simple example lists the prices of three commodities and the quantities bought by a typical household. Multiplying price by quantity gives expenditure on each, and summing these gives the total expenditure on all commodities. Dividing expenditure on each good by total expenditure gives the proportion of total expenditure that is devoted to each commodity, as shown in the last column. These proportions become the weights for the price indexes that are calculated in Table 26A-2.

prices.[2] Fixed-weight indexes are easy to interpret, but problems arise with a fixed-weight index because consumption patterns change over the years. The fixed weights represent with decreasing accuracy the importance that consumers *currently* place on each of the commodities.

The CPI used to be calculated using fixed weights that were changed only every decade or so. Recently, however, there has been a change in this procedure. The survey of consumers' expenditure is updated every year and the weights used to calculate the CPI are revised every three years. This avoids the problem of the fixed-weight index becoming steadily less representative of current expenditure patterns.

[2]To verify this, calculate the total expenditure required to buy 60 units of commodity A, 200 units of commodity B, and 25 units of commodity C in each of the three years for which price data are given in Table 26A-2. Divide the resulting amounts by $600, multiply by 100, and you will get exactly the index values shown in the table.

TABLE 26A-2   Calculation of a Price Index

Commodity	Weight	Price 1980	Price 1985	Price 1990	Price × weight 1980	Price × weight 1985	Price × weight 1990
A	0.50	$5.00	$6.00	$14.00	$2.50	$3.00	$7.00
B	0.33	1.00	1.50	2.00	0.33	0.495	0.66
C	0.17	4.00	8.00	9.00	0.68	1.36	1.53
Total	1.00				$3.51	$4.855	$9.19

$$\text{Index} \quad 1980 \quad \frac{3.51}{3.51} \cdot 100 = 100$$

$$1985 \quad \frac{4.855}{3.51} \cdot 100 = 138.3$$

$$1990 \quad \frac{9.19}{3.51} \cdot 100 = 261.8$$

A price index expresses the weighted average of prices in the given year as a percentage of the weighted average of prices in the base year. The prices of the three commodities in each year are multiplied by the weights from Table 26A-1. Summing the weighted prices for each year gives the average price in that year. Dividing the average price in the given year by the average price in the base year and multiplying by 100 gives the price index for the given year. The index is, of course, 100 when the year is also taken as the given year, as is the case for 1980 in this example.

Measuring the Rate of Inflation

At the beginning of 1993, the CPI was 129.6 (1986 = 100). This means that at the beginning of 1993, it cost just under 30 percent more to buy a representative bundle of goods than it did in the base period. In other words, there was a 29.6 percent *increase* in the price level over that period as measured by the CPI. The *percentage change* in the cost of purchasing the bundle of goods that is covered by any index is thus the level of the index minus 100.

The *inflation rate* between any two periods of time is measured by the percentage increase in the relevant price index from the first period to the second period. In the rare event of a drop in the price level, we speak of a *deflation*. When the amount of the rise in the price level is being measured from the base period, all that needs to be done is to subtract the two indexes, as we have just done. When two other periods are being compared, we must be careful to express the change as a percentage of the index in the first period.

If we let P_1 indicate the value of the price index in the first period and P_2 its value in the second period, the inflation rate is merely the difference between the two, expressed as a percentage of the value of the index in the first period:

$$\text{Inflation rate} = \frac{(P_2 \times P_1)}{P_1} \times 100$$

(When P_1 is the base period, its value is 100, and the expression shown above reduces to $P_2 - P_1$.) In other cases, the full calculation must be made. For example, the index went from 126.7 in January 1992 to 129.6 in January 1993, indicating a rate of inflation of 2.31 percent over the year. The rise of 2.9 points in the index is a 2.31 percent rise over its initial value of 126.7.

If the two values being compared are not a year apart, it is common to convert the result to an *annual rate*. For example, the CPI was 135.2 in April 1991 and 135.6 in May 1991. This is an increase of 0.295 percent over the month [(0.4/135.2) × 100]. It is also an *annual rate* of approximately 3.55 percent (0.295 percent × 12) over the year.[3] This means that *if* the rate of increase that occurred between April and May 1991 did persist for a year, the price level would rise by approximately 3.55 percent over the year.

------

[3]We say *approximately* because a 0.295 percent rise each month that is *compounded* for 12 months will give rise to an increase over the year that is greater than 3.55 percent. The appropriate procedure is to increase the index in January by 0.295 twelve times rather than just to multiply it by 12. The two results are the difference between simple and compound interest rates. **[31]**

27

Measuring Macroeconomic Variables

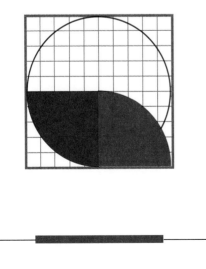

Our ultimate goal is to understand the type of macroeconomic events that were outlined in Chapter 26. Our first step is to look in some detail at the measurement and interpretation of variables relating to national output and national income.[1] We need to study national output and national income in order to develop the concepts used in macroeconomic theory and also to be able to interpret measures that play a prominent role in everyday discussion.

National Output Concepts

We are concerned in this chapter with measuring the nation's output and the income that is generated by its production. We start by asking what we mean by output.

Value Added as Output

It may seem strange to ask what we mean by output. Surely the town bakery knows what it produces, and if General Motors does not know its own output, what does it know? If each firm knows the value of its total output, all the national income statisticians have to do is to add up each separate output value to get the nation's output—or is that all?

The reason why getting a total for the nation's output is not quite so simple as it seems is that one firm's output is another firm's input. The local baker uses flour that is the output of the flour milling company, and the flour milling company in turn uses wheat that is the farmer's output. What is true in bread production is true of most commodities.

Production occurs in stages: Some firms produce outputs that are used as inputs by other firms, and these other firms in turn produce outputs that are used as inputs by yet other firms.

If we merely added up the market values of all outputs of all firms, we would obtain a total that was greatly in excess of the value of the economy's actual output.

The local baker provides an example. If we added the total value of the sales of the wheat farmer, the miller, and the baker, we would be counting the value of the wheat

---

[1] We saw in Chapter 26 how the important labour force variables are measured. Measurements of the other important macroeconomic phenomena discussed in that chapter follow directly from measurement of income and output, which is the main subject of this chapter.

three times, the value of the milled flour twice, and the value of the bread once.

The errors that would arise in estimating the nation's output by adding all sales of all firms is called **double counting**. *Multiple counting* would be a better term, since if we added up the values of all sales, the same output would be counted every time it was sold from one firm to another.

The problem of double counting is solved by distinguishing between two types of output. **Intermediate goods and services** are outputs of some firms that are in turn inputs for other firms. **Final goods and services** are goods that are not, in the period of time under consideration, used as inputs by other firms. The term **final demand** refers to the purchase of final goods and services for consumption, for investment (including inventory accumulation), for use by governments, and for export. It does not include goods and services that are purchased by firms and used as inputs for producing other goods and services during the period under consideration.

If the sales of firms could be readily separated into sales for final use and sales for further processing by other firms, measuring total output would still be straightforward. It would equal the value of all *final goods and services* produced by firms, excluding all intermediate goods and services. However, when Stelco sells steel to the Ford Motor Company, it does not care, and usually does not know, whether the steel is for final use (say, construction of a new warehouse) or for use as an intermediate good in the production of automobiles.[2] The problem of double counting must therefore be resolved in some other manner.

To avoid double counting, statisticians use the important concept of *value added*. Each firm's value added is the value of its output minus the value of the inputs that it purchases from other firms (which were in turn the outputs of those other firms). Thus a steel mill's value added is the value of its output minus the value of the ore that it buys from the mining company, the value of the electricity and fuel oil that it uses, and the values of all other inputs that it buys from other firms. A bakery's value

added is the value of the baking products that it produces minus the value of the flour and other inputs that it buys from other firms.

The total value of a firm's output is the gross value of its output. The firm's value added is the net value of its output. It is this latter figure that is the firm's contribution to the nation's total output. It is what its own efforts add to the value of what it takes in as inputs.

Value added is useful in avoiding the statistical problem of double counting; it is the correct measure of each firm's own contribution to total output, the amount of market value that is produced by that firm.

The concept of value added is further illustrated in Box 27-1. In this simple example, as in all more complex cases, the value of total output of final goods is obtained by summing all the individual values added.

The sum of all values added in an economy is a measure of the economy's total output. This measure of total output is called gross domestic product (GDP). It is a measure of all final output that is produced by all productive activity in the economy.

Table 27-1 gives the GDP by major industry groups for the Canadian economy in 1992.

National-Income Accounting: Gross Domestic Product

The measures of national income and national product that are used in Canada derive from an accounting system called the National Income and Product Accounts (NIPA). The accounts, produced by Statistics Canada, provide a framework for studying national income. The National Income and Product Accounts are not simply collections of economic data. They have a logical structure, based on the simple yet important idea that whenever national product is produced, it generates an equivalent amount of national income.

---

[2]Even if we use our earlier example of bread, a bakery cannot be sure that its sales are for final use, since the bread may be further "processed" by a restaurant prior to its final sale to a customer for eating.

Box 27-1

Value Added Through Stages of Production

Because the output of one firm often becomes the input of other firms, the total value of goods sold by all firms greatly exceeds the value of the output of final products. This general principle is illustrated by a simple example in which firm R starts from scratch and produces goods (raw materials) valued at $100; the firm's value added is $100. Firm I purchases raw materials valued at $100 and produces semimanufactured goods that it sells for $130. Its value added is $30, because the value of the goods is increased by $30 as a result of the firm's activities. Firm F purchases the semimanufactured goods for $130, works them into a finished state, and sells the final products for $180. Firm F's value added is $50. The value of the final goods, $180, is found either by counting only the sales of firm F or by taking the sum of the values added by each firm. This value is much smaller than the $410 that we would obtain if we merely added up the market value of the commodities sold by each firm.

	Firm R	Firm I	Firm F	All firms
Transactions at Three Different Stages of Production				
A. Purchases from other firms	$ 0	$100	$130	$230 Total interfirm sales
B. Purchases of factors of production (wages, rent, interest, profits)	100	30	50	180 Total value added
A + B = value of product	$100	$130	$ 50	$410 Total value of all sales

Look again at Figure 26-1, page 518, which shows the circular flow of expenditure and income. The right half of the figure focuses on expenditures to purchase the nation's output in product markets, and the left half focuses on factor markets through which the receipts of producers are distributed to factors of production.

Corresponding to the two halves of the circular flow are two ways of measuring national income: by determining the value of what is produced and by determining the value of the incomes generated by production. Both measures yield the same total, which is called **gross domestic product (GDP).**[3] When it is calculated by adding up the total expenditure for each of the main components of final output, the result is called *GDP on the expenditure side.* When it is calculated by adding up all the incomes generated by the act of production, it is called *GDP on the income side.*

The conventions of double-entry bookkeeping require that all value produced must be accounted for by a claim that someone has to that value. Thus, the two values calculated from the income and the expenditure sides are identical conceptually and differ in practise only because of errors of measurement. Any discrepancy arising from such errors is then reconciled, so that one common total is given as *the* measure of GDP. Both calculations are of interest, however, because each gives a different and useful breakdown. Also, having two independent ways of measuring the same quantity, in this case the sum of values added in the economy, provides a

[3]Each of these totals must also equal the sum of values added in the economy, as discussed in the preceding section.

TABLE 27-1 Real Gross Domestic Product, 1992

	Billions of 1986 dollars	Percent of GDP
Value added by sector		
Agriculture, fishing, and forestry	14.4	2.9
Mines, quarries, and oil wells	20.5	4.1
Manufacturing	85.4	17.0
Construction	28.9	5.8
Electric power, gas, and water utilities	16.6	3.3
Transportation, storage, and communication	43.2	8.6
Retail and wholesale trade	59.6	11.9
Financial, insurance, and real estate	84.8	16.8
Community, business, and personal services	114.4	22.8
Nonbusiness sector	34.1	6.8
GDP (at factor cost)	501.9	100.0
Plus: Indirect taxes less subsidies	186.4	
GDP (at market prices)	688.3	

Source: Statistics Canada, 11-003E; 15–001.

GDP, a measure of total output produced in Canada, can be decomposed into the contribution to that total by each of a number of sectors. GDP at factor cost equals the sum of values added of each sector. As can be seen, manufacturing is the largest sector, contributing 17 percent. To convert *GDP at factor cost* to *GDP at market prices*, we have to add indirect taxes net of subsidies to the former.

useful check on statistical procedures and on unavoidable errors in measurement.

GDP From the Expenditure Side

GDP for a given year is calculated from the expenditure side by adding up the expenditures needed to purchase the final output produced in that year. Total expenditure on final output is the sum of four broad categories of expenditure: consumption, investment, government, and net exports. In the following chapters, we will discuss in considerable detail the causes and consequences of movements in each of these four expenditure categories. Here, we define what they are and how they are measured. Throughout, it is important to remember that the classification is exhaustive: The terms are defined in such a way that *all* expenditure on final output falls into one of the four categories.

Consumption Expenditure

Consumption expenditure includes expenditure on all goods and services produced and sold to their final users during the year. It includes services, such as haircuts, medical care, and legal advice; nondurable goods, such as fresh meat, clothing, cut flowers, and fresh vegetables; and durable goods, such as cars, television sets, and air conditioners. We denote actual measured consumption expenditure by the symbol C^a.

Investment Expenditure

The next category of total expenditure is called **investment expenditure**, which is defined as expenditure on the production of goods not for present consumption. Investment expenditure is in three categories: expenditure on inventories; expenditure on capital goods, such as factories, machines, and warehouses; and expenditure on the construction of residential housing. The goods that are created by this expenditure are called **investment goods**.

Investment creates goods to add to the nation's total stock of capital. So net investment—total new investment *minus* depreciation—is the *addition to* the nation's total stock of capital.

Inventories. Almost all firms hold stocks of their inputs and their own outputs. These stocks are called **inventories.** Inventories of inputs and unfinished materials allow firms to maintain a steady stream of production in spite of short-term fluctuations in the deliveries of inputs bought from other firms. Inventories of outputs allow firms to meet orders in spite of temporary fluctuations in the rate of output or sales.

An accumulation of inventories counts as current investment, because it represents goods produced but not used for current consumption. A drawing down of inventories, often called a *decumulation*, counts as disinvestment, because it represents a reduction in the stock of finished goods that are available for future use.

Additions to inventories are a part of the economy's production of investment goods. These goods are included in the national-income accounts at market value, which includes the wages and other costs that the firm incurred in producing them and the profit that the firm will make when they are sold. Thus, in the case of inventories of a firm's own output, the expenditure approach measures what will have to be spent to purchase the inventories when they are sold rather than what has so far been spent to produce them.

Plant and equipment. All production uses capital goods, which are manufactured aids to production, such as tools, machines, and factory buildings. The economy's total quantity of capital goods is called the **capital stock**. Creating new capital goods is an act of investment and is called *business fixed investment*, or the shortened form, **fixed investment**.

Residential investment. A house or an apartment building is a durable asset that yields its utility over a long period of time. This meets the definition of investment that we gave earlier, so housing *construction* is counted as investment expenditure rather than as consumption expenditure. When a family purchases a house from the builder, the ownership of an already produced asset is transferred, and that transaction is not a part of national income.

Gross and net investment. The total investment expenditure is called **gross investment**. Gross investment is divided into two parts: replacement investment and net investment. **Replacement investment** is the amount of investment that just maintains the level of existing capital stock. Replacement investment is called the **capital consumption allowance** or simply **depreciation**. Gross investment minus replacement investment is **net investment**. Positive net investment increases the economy's total stock of capital, while replacement investment keeps the existing stock intact by replacing what has been used up.

All of gross investment is included in the calculation of national income. This is because all investment goods are part of the nation's total output, and their production creates income (and employment) whether the goods produced are a part of net investment or are merely replacement investment. Actual total investment expenditure is denoted by the symbol I^a.

Government Purchases of Goods and Services

When governments provide goods and services that households want, such as roads and air traffic control, it is obvious that they are adding to the sum total of valuable output in the same way as do private firms that produce the trucks and airplanes that use the roads and air lanes. With other government activities, the case may not seem so clear. Should expenditures by the federal government to send a peace keeper to Bosnia, or to pay a civil servant to refile papers from a now defunct department, be regarded as contributions to national income? Some people believe that many (or even most) activities in Ottawa or in City Hall are wasteful, if not downright harmful. Others believe that governments produce many of the important things of life, such as education and pollution control.

National-income statisticians do not speculate about which government expenditures are worthwhile. Instead, they include all government purchases of goods and services as part of national income. (Government expenditure on investment goods is included as government expenditure rather than investment expenditure.) Just as the national product includes, without distinction, the outputs of both gin and Bibles, it also includes helicopters and the upkeep of parks, along with the services of federal judges, senators, and even Revenue Canada investigators. Actual government purchases of goods and services is denoted by the symbol G^a.

Government output typically is valued at cost rather than at the market value. In many cases, there is really no choice. What, for example, is the market value of the services of a court of law? No one knows. We do know, however, what it costs the government to provide these services, so we value them at their cost of production.

Although valuing at cost is the only possible way to measure many government activities, it does have one curious consequence. If, due to an increase in productivity, one civil servant now does what two used to do, and the displaced worker shifts to the private sector, the government's measured contribution to national income will register a decline. On the other hand, if two workers now do what one worker used to do, the government's measured contribution will rise. Both changes could occur even though the services the government actually provides have not changed. This is an inevitable but curious consequence of measuring the value of the government's output by the cost of the factors, mainly labour, that are used to produce it.

It is important to recognise that only government expenditures *on currently produced goods and services* are included as part of GDP. A great deal of government expenditure is not a part of GDP. For example, when a government agency makes Canada Pension Plan payments to a retired person, the government is not purchasing any currently produced goods or services from the retired. The payment itself adds neither to employment of factors nor to total output. The same is true of payments on account of unemployment insurance, welfare, and interest on the national debt (which transfers income from taxpayers to holders of government bonds). All such payments are examples of **transfer payments**, which are government expenditures that are not made in return for currently produced goods and services. They are not a part of expenditure on the nation's total output and therefore are not included in GDP.[4]

Thus, when we refer to government purchases

as part of national income or use the symbol G^a, we include all government expenditure on currently produced goods and services, and we *exclude* all government transfer payments. (The term *government outlays* is often used to describe all government spending, including transfer payments.)

Net Exports

The fourth category of aggregate expenditure, one that is very important to the Canadian economy, arises from foreign trade. How do imports and exports influence national income?

Imports. A country's GDP is the total value of final commodities produced in that country. If your cousin spends $12,000 on a car that was made in Japan, only a small part of that value will represent expenditure on Canadian production. Some of it represents payment for the services of the Canadian dealers and for transportation; the rest is the output of Japanese firms and expenditure on Japanese products. If you take your next vacation in Italy, much of your expenditure will be on goods and services produced in Italy and thus will contribute to Italian GDP.

Similarly, when a Canadian firm makes an investment expenditure on a Canadian-produced machine tool that was made partly with imported raw materials, only part of the expenditure is on Canadian production; the rest is expenditure on the production by the countries that are supplying the raw materials. The same is true for government expenditure on such things as roads and dams; some of the expenditure is for imported materials, and only part of it is for domestically produced goods and services.

Consumption, investment, and government expenditures all have an import content. To arrive at total expenditure on Canadian output, we need to subtract from total Canadian expenditure any expenditure on imports of goods and services, which is given the symbol IM^a.

Exports. If Canadian firms sell goods or services to German households, the goods and services are a part of German consumption expenditure but also constitute expenditure on Canadian output. Indeed, all goods and services that are produced in Canada and sold to foreigners must be counted as part of Canadian production and income; they are pro-

---

[4]Of course, the recipients of transfer payments often choose to spend their money on consumption. Such expenditure then counts as consumption, and thus as part of GDP, in the same way as any other consumption expenditure.

duced in Canada, and they create incomes for the Canadian residents who produce them. They are not purchased by Canadian residents, however, so they are not included as part of C^a, I^a, or G^a. Therefore, to arrive at the total value of expenditure on Canadian domestic product, it is necessary to add in the value of Canadian exports. Actual exports of goods and services are denoted by the symbol X^a.

It is customary to group actual imports and actual exports together as **net exports**. Net exports are defined as total exports of goods and services minus total imports of goods and services ($X^a - IM^a$), which we will also denote NX^a. When the value of Canadian exports exceeds the value of Canadian imports, the net export term is positive. When, as in recent years, the value of imports exceeds the value of exports, the net export term becomes negative.

Total Expenditures

Gross domestic product from the expenditure side is the sum of the four expenditure categories that we have just discussed. These data are shown in Table 27-2 for Canada in 1992.

GDP, calculated from the expenditure side, is the sum of consumption, investment, government, and net export expenditures on currently produced goods and services.

GDP From the Income Side

The production of a nation's output generates income. Labour must be employed, land must be rented, and capital must be used. The calculation of GDP from the income side involves adding up factor incomes and other claims on the value of output until all of that value is accounted for. We have already noted that because all value produced must be owned by someone, the value of production must equal the value of income claims generated by that production.

Factor Payments

National-income accountants distinguish four main components of factor incomes: wages, rent, interest, and profits.

TABLE 27-2   Components of GDP From the Expenditure Side, 1992

Expenditure category	Billions of dollars	Percentage of GDP
Consumption	419.9	61.1
Government	164.1	23.9
Investment	109.2	15.9
Net exports	−3.9	−0.6
Statistical discrepancy	−2.3	−0.3
	687.0	100.0

Source: Statistics Canada, 11-010.

GDP measured from the expenditure side of the national accounts gives the size of the major components of aggregate expenditure. Consumption is by far the largest expenditure category, equal to over 60 percent of GDP. Government accounted for almost 25 percent and investment about 15 percent. Whereas exports and imports are both quite large (each about 25 percent of GDP), net exports are quite small; in 1992 they represented a mere 0.3 percent of GDP. Notice that the statistical discrepancy is almost as large as the measured trade balance (net exports).

Wages. Wages and salaries (which national-income accountants call *compensation to employees*, but which are usually just called *wages*) are the payment for the services of labour. Wages include take-home pay, taxes withheld, social security, pension fund contributions, and other fringe benefits. In total, wages represent that part of the value of production that is attributable to labour.

Rent. Rent is the payment for the services of land and other factors that are rented. A major problem arises with housing. For the purposes of national-income accounting, home owners are viewed as renting accommodations from themselves. The amount of rent in the GDP thus includes payments for rented housing plus "imputed rent" for the use of owner-occupied housing.[5]

---

[5]The concepts of rent, interest, and profits that are used in macroeconomics do not correspond exactly to the concepts with the same names that are used in microeconomics, but the details of the differences need not detain us.

Interest. Interest includes interest that is earned on bank deposits, interest that is earned on loans to firms, and miscellaneous other investment income.

Profits. Some profits are paid out as **dividends** to owners of firms; the rest are retained for use by firms. The former are called *distributed profits*, and the latter are called *undistributed profits* or *retained earnings*. Both distributed and undistributed profits are included in the calculation of GDP. For accounting purposes, total profits are reported in two separate categories—corporate profits and incomes of unincorporated businesses (mainly small businesses, farmers, partnerships, and professionals).

Profits and interest together represent the payment for the use of capital—interest for borrowed capital and profits for capital contributed by the owners of firms.

Net Domestic Income at Factor Cost. The sum of the four components of factor incomes—wages, rent, interest, and profits—is called **net domestic income at factor cost**. It represents the share of total production that goes as income to the factors of production, labour, land, and capital; the rest is capital consumption and net business taxes.

Nonfactor Payments

Factor incomes do not account for all of GDP. We now consider claims on the total value of GDP that do not belong to factors of production.

Indirect business taxes net of subsidies. We now distinguish between total income valued *at factor cost* and total income valued *at market prices*. The difference between the two is created by two payments: indirect business taxes and those of subsidies.

If, for example, a good's market price of $10 includes $1 in taxes on output and sales, only $9 is available as income to factors of production. One dollar's worth of market value represents the government's claim on that value. When adding up income claims to determine GDP, it is therefore necessary to include that part of the total market value of output that is the government's claim exercised through its taxes on goods and services. These claims include provincial sales taxes and the federal goods and services tax (GST) or any tax that replaces it.

Subsidies. It is also necessary to subtract government subsidies on goods and services, since these payments allow incomes to *exceed* the market value of output. Suppose, for example, that a municipal bus company spends $150,000 producing bus rides and covers its costs by selling $140,000 in fares and obtaining a $10,000 subsidy from the local government. The total income that the company generates from its production is $150,000, but the total market value of its output is only $140,000, with the difference made up by the subsidy. To get from total income to total output, we must subtract the amount of the subsidy.

Net domestic product at market prices. Adding indirect business taxes to the four components of factor incomes and subtracting subsidies gives **net domestic product at market prices**. Taxes and subsidies often are combined into a single term, called *indirect taxes net of subsidies*.

Net domestic product equals the sum of wages, rent, interest, profits, and indirect taxes net of subsidies.

Depreciation. Another component on the income side that is not a factor payment arises from the distinction between net and gross investment. Depreciation, or capital consumption, is the value of capital that has been used up in the process of producing final output. It is part of gross profits, but, being that part needed to replace capital used up in the process of production, it is not part of net profits. Hence, depreciation is not income earned by any factor of production. Instead, it is value that must be reinvested just to maintain the existing stock of capital equipment.

Total Product

Adding depreciation to net domestic product gives gross domestic product.

From the income side, GDP is the sum of the factor incomes that are generated in the process of producing final output *plus* indirect taxes net of subsidies *plus* depreciation.

The various components of the income side of the GDP in the Canadian economy in 1992 are

TABLE 27-3 Components of GDP From the Income Side of Accounts, 1992

	Billions of dollars	Percentage of GDP
Compensation to employees	393.4	57.3
Corporate profits (before taxes)	33.4	4.9
Net interest	52.6	7.7
Rental income	37.1	5.4
Net domestic income at factor cost	517.0	75.3
Net indirect taxes	86.0	12.5
Net domestic income at market prices	603.0	87.8
Capital consumption allowance	82.0	11.9
Statistical discrepancy	2.0	0.3
GDP at market prices	687.0	100.0

Source: Statistics Canada, 11-010.

GDP measured from the income side of the accounts gives the size of the major components of the income that is generated by producing the nation's output. The largest category, equal to 57 percent of GDP, was compensation to employees, which includes wages and salaries plus employers' contributions to unemployment insurance, pensions, and similar schemes. The sum of compensation to employees, corporate profits, interest, and rental income equals net domestic income at factor cost. Adding net indirect taxes yields net domestic income at market prices. Adding the capital consumption allowance, which is the part of the earnings of businesses that is needed to replace capital used up during the year, and allowing for the statistical discrepancy yields GDP at market prices.

shown in Table 27-3. Note that one of the terms in the table is called *statistical discrepancy*; this is a "fudge factor" to make sure that the independent measures of income and product come to the same total. Statistical discrepancy is a clear indication that national income and product accounting is not error free.

Income Produced and Income Received

GDP provides a measure of total output produced in Canada and of the total income generated as a result of that production. However, the total income

received by Canadians differs from GDP for two reasons. Some Canadian production creates factor earnings for foreigners who have previously invested in Canada or who sell services to producers in Canada; on this account, income received by Canadians will be less than Canadian GDP. Second, many Canadians earn income as a result of foreign investments and of factor services sold abroad; on this account, income received by Canadians will be greater than Canadian GDP.

While the GDP measures the output, and hence the income, that is *produced* in Canada, the **gross national product, the GNP**, measures the income that is *received* in Canada. To arrive at GNP from GDP, it is necessary to add incomes generated by foreign production but earned by Canadian residents and subtract incomes generated by Canadian production but earned by foreign residents.

Total output produced in the economy, measured by GDP, differs from total income received by Canadians, measured by GNP, due to net foreign factor payments.

Reconciling GDP with GNP. Table 27-4 shows the reconciliation of GDP with GNP. Recall that GNP measures income received by Canadian residents, whereas GDP measures output produced in Canada. Since Canada has had a long history of importing capital from abroad, Canadian factor payments made to foreigners exceed Canadian factor payments received from foreigners, and hence Canadian GDP exceeds Canadian GNP. (This does not mean that the net effects of Canada's foreign borrowing has been to reduce incomes of Canadians; most estimates show that foreign investment has contributed more to GDP than it has to the repatriation of factor payments and hence has increased GNP.)

Other Income Concepts

GDP and GNP are the most comprehensive concepts of outputs and income. The next most comprehensive concept is net domestic product. As we saw in building up the income approach, this is GDP minus the capital consumption allowance. Net domestic product is thus a measure of the net out-

TABLE 27-4   Reconciling GDP with GNP

	Billions of dollars
GDP at market prices (from Table 27-3)	687.3
Plus: Investment income received from foreigners	7.7
Less: Investment income paid to foreigners	
GNP at market prices	32.6
	662.4

Source: Statistics Canada, 11-010.

GNP, income owned or received by Canadians, is equal to GDP, income produced in Canada, plus factor income received from foreigners, less factor income paid to foreigners. Since Canada has traditionally experienced significant net foreign investment, investment income paid to foreigners is large, and hence net international factor payments for Canada are negative. As a result, GNP is less than GDP.

put of the economy after deducting from gross output the amount needed to maintain intact the existing stock of capital. It is the maximum amount that could be consumed without actually running down the economy's capital stock.

Personal income is income that is earned by or paid to individuals before allowing for personal income taxes on that income. Some personal income goes for taxes, some goes for savings, and the rest goes for consumption. A number of adjustments to net domestic product are required to arrive at personal income. The most important are (1) subtracting *indirect business taxes net of subsidies,* which are the part of the market value of output that goes directly to governments (this, as we have seen, gives net domestic income at factor cost); (2) subtracting profits retained by corporations; (3) subtracting income taxes paid by businesses; and (4) adding transfer payments to households. The first three are parts of the value of output not paid to households; the fourth is paid to households and thus is income that households have available to spend or to save, even though the payments are not part of GNP.

Disposable personal income is the amount of current income that households have available for spending and saving; it is personal income minus personal income taxes.

Disposable personal income is GNP *minus* any part of it that is not actually paid to households *minus* personal income taxes paid by households plus transfer payments received by households.

The relationships among these various measures are shown in Table 27-5.

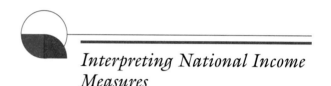

Interpreting National Income Measures

The information provided by national income data is useful, but unless it is carefully interpreted, it can be misleading. Furthermore, each of the specialized measures gives different information. Thus, each may be the best statistic for studying a particular range of problems. Any statistical measure will be determined partly by some arbitrary decisions that might have been decided in another way. The most important matters of interpretation will be dealt with now.

Real and Nominal Measures

In Chapter 26, we distinguished between real and nominal measures of national income and output. We learned in that chapter that when we add up money values of outputs, expenditures, or incomes, we end up with what are called *nominal values.* Suppose that we found that a measure of nominal GDP had risen by 70 percent between 1980 and 1990. If we wanted to compare *real GDP* in 1990 to that in 1980, we would need to determine how much of that 70 percent nominal increase was due to increases in prices and how much was due to increases in quantities produced. Although there are many possible ways of doing this, the basic principle is always the same. It is to compute the value of output, expenditure, and income in each period by using a common set of *base period prices.* When this is done, we speak of real output, expenditure, or income as being measured in *constant dollars.*

GDP valued at current prices is a nominal

TABLE 27-5 Various National Income Measures, 1992

	Billions of dollars
Gross domestic product at market prices	688
Less: Net foreign investment income	− 24
Gross national product at market prices	664
Less: Capital consumption allowance	− 82
Net domestic product at market prices	582
Less: Indirect taxes net of subsidies	− 85
Net domestic income at factor cost	497
Less: Retained earnings and business taxes	− 44
Plus: Government transfer payments to households	+101
Personal income	560
Less: personal income taxes	−101
Disposable personal income	459

Source: Statistics Canada 11-010.

Each of the six related national income measures focuses on a different aspect of the national output. Gross domestic product measures total output produced in Canada. Gross national product measures the market value of total income received by Canadians. Net domestic product measures the net value of national income after an allowance for maintaining the capital stock. Net domestic income at factor cost converts market price values to factor costs by adjusting for government indirect taxes net of subsidies. Personal income measures income earned or received by Canadians before personal income taxes. Disposable income measures Canadians' after-tax income; it is the amount they have available to spend or to save. Notice that transfer payments accounted for more than 20 percent of total personal income.

measure. GDP valued at base period prices is a real measure.

Any *change* in nominal GDP reflects the combined effects of changes in quantities and changes in prices. However, when real income is measured over different periods by using a common set of base period prices, changes in real income reflect only changes in real output.

The Implicit Deflator

If nominal and real GDP change by different amounts over some time period, this must be be-

cause prices have changed over that period. Comparing what has happened to nominal and real GDP over the same period implies the existence of a price index measuring the change in prices over that period. We say "implies," because no price index was used in calculating real and nominal GDP. However, an index can be inferred by comparing these two values. Such an index is called an *implicit price index* or an *implicit deflator.* It is defined as follows:

Implicit deflator

$$= \frac{\text{GDP at current prices}}{\text{GDP at base period prices}} \times 100\%$$

The implicit deflator is the most comprehensive index of the price level, because it covers all the goods and services that are produced by the entire economy. Although some other indexes use fixed weights, implicit deflators are variable-weight indexes. They use the current year's "bundle" of production to compare the current year's prices with those prevailing in the base period. Thus, the 1994 deflator uses 1994 output weights, and the 1995 deflator uses 1995 output weights. Box 27-2 illustrates the calculation of real and nominal national income and an implicit deflator for a simple hypothetical economy that produces only wheat and steel.

A change in any nominal measure of national income can be split into a change due to prices and a change due to quantities. For example, in 1992, Canadian nominal GDP was 1.6 percent higher than in 1991. This increase was due to a 0.70 percent increase in prices and a 0.9 percent increase in real GDP. Table 27-6 gives nominal and real income and the implicit deflator for selected years since 1940.

Total Values and Per Capita Values and Productivity

The rise in real GDP during this century has had two main causes: an increase in the amounts of land, labour, and capital used in production and an increase in output per unit of input. In other words, more inputs have been used, and each input has become more productive. For some purposes, such as assessing a country's potential military strength or

Box 27-2

Calculation of Nominal and Real National Income

To see what is involved in calculating nominal national income, real national income, and the implicit deflator, an example may be helpful. Consider a simple hypothetical economy that produces only two commodities, wheat and steel. Table 1 gives the basic data for output and prices in the economy for two years.

TABLE 1   Data for a Hypothetical Economy

	Quantity produced		Prices	
	Wheat (bushels)	Steel (tons)	Wheat (dollars per bushel)	Steel (dollars per ton)
Year 1	100	20	10	50
Year 2	110	16	12	55

Table 2 shows nominal national income, calculated by adding the money values of wheat output and of steel output for each year. In year 1, the value of both wheat and steel production was $1,000, so nominal income was $2,000. In year 2, wheat output rose to $1,320, and steel output fell to $880. Since the rise in value of wheat was greater than the fall in value of steel, nominal income rose by $200.

TABLE 2   Calculation of Nominal National Income

Year 1 $(100 \times 10) + (20 \times 50) = \$2,000$
Year 2 $(110 \times 12) + (16 \times 55) = \$2,200$

Table 3 shows real national income, calculated by valuing output in each year by year 2 prices; that

is, year 2 becomes the base year for weighting purposes. In year 2, wheat output rose, but steel output fell. Using year 2 prices, the value of the fall in steel output between years 1 and 2 exceeded the value of the rise in wheat output, and real national income fell.

TABLE 3   Calculation of Real National Income Using Year 2 Prices

Year 1 $(100 \times 12) + (20 \times 55) = \$2,300$
Year 2 $(110 \times 12) + (16 \times 55) = \$2,200$

In Table 4, the ratio of nominal to real national income is calculated for each year and multiplied by 100. This ratio implicitly measures the change in prices over the period in question and is called the *implicit deflator* or *implicit price index*. The implicit deflator shows that the price level increased by 15 percent between year 1 and year 2.

TABLE 4   Calculation of Implicit Deflator

Year 1 $(2,000 \div 2,300) \times 100 = \ \ 86.96$
Year 2 $(2,200 \div 2,200) \times 100 = 100.00$

In Table 4, we used year 2 as the base year for comparison purposes, but we could have used year 1. The implicit deflator would then have been 100 in year 1 and 115 in year 2, and the increase in price level would still have been 15 percent. Or, the base year could be some earlier year. No matter what year is picked as the year in which the index had a value of 100, however, the change in the implicit deflator between year 1 and year 2 is 15 percent.

TABLE 27-6   GDP in Current and Constant Dollars

Year	(1) GDP in billions of current dollars	(2) GDP in billions of 1986 dollars	(3) Implicit national income deflator (1986 = 100)
1935	4,301	51,202	8.4
1945	11,863	82,381	14.4
1955	29,250	149,234	19.6
1965	57,523	202,964	28.3
1975	171,540	320,035	53.6
1980	309,891	381,992	81.1
1985	477,988	438,450	109.0
1990	667,843	502,691	133.5
1992	687,334	502,097	137.1

Source: M. C. Urquhart, ed., *Historical Statistics of Canada;* Statistics Canada, 11-010.

Current-dollar GDP tells us about the money value of output; constant-dollar GDP tells us about changes in physical output. GDP in current dollars gives the total value of all final output in any year, valued in the selling prices of that year. GDP in constant dollars gives the total value of all final output in any year, in this case, 1986.

The ratio of *GDP in current dollars* to *GDP in constant dollars* times 100 is the implicit GDP deflator. (It is in effect a price index with current year quantity weights.)

the total size of its market, we want to measure total output. For other purposes, such as studying changes in living standards, we require per capita output, which is obtained by dividing total output by the population. Per capita GDP gives a measure of how much output there is on average for each person in the country.

GDP divided by the number of persons employed tells us the average output per employed worker. This is one measure of labour productivity. GDP divided by the total number of hours worked measures output per hour of labour input and provides a second measure of labour productivity.

Until recently, it did not matter much whether we looked at per capita GDP or one of the productivity measures such as GDP per hour worked, because the growth in per capita output has largely been due to growth in labour productivity. Starting about 1975, although per capita output continued to rise, much of the increase could be accounted for by increases in the amount of labour supplied. There was a slowdown in productivity growth, accompanied by a marked increase in both the number of workers and hours of work relative to the population.

The divergence between the growth of output per capita and the growth of labour productivity means the increases in output per capita overstate

increases in economic welfare. When output grows while inputs stay constant, the average person will be unambiguously better off. When output grows because more people are working more, the average person may be no better off than before. Because of this, productivity measures are generally the best measures of the ability of an economy to produce goods and services that raise average living standards.

What National Income Does Not Measure

National income measures the flow of economic activity in organized markets in a given year. But much economic activity takes place outside of the markets that the national-income accountants survey. Although these activities are not typically included in GDP or GNP, they nevertheless use real resources and satisfy real wants and needs.

Illegal activities. GDP does not measure illegal activities, even though many of them are ordinary business activities that produce goods and services sold on the market and that generate factor incomes. Many forms of illegal gambling, prostitution, and drug trade come into this category. To gain an accurate measure of the *total* demand for factors of production in the economy, of *total* marketable output, or of incomes generated, we should include these activities, whether or not we as individuals approve of them. The omission of illegal activities is no trivial matter. The drug trade alone is a multibillion-dollar business.[6]

Unreported activities. A significant omission from the measured GDP is the so-called underground economy. The transactions that occur in the underground economy are perfectly legal in themselves; the only illegality involved is that such transactions are not reported for tax purposes. One example of this is the carpenter who repairs a leak in your roof and takes payment in cash or in kind in order to avoid taxation. Because such transactions go unreported, they are omitted from GDP.

The growth of the underground economy is encouraged by the rising rates of taxation and is facilitated by the rising importance of services in the nation's total output. The higher the tax rates, the more there is to be gained by going underground. It is also much easier for a carpenter to pass unnoticed by government authorities than it is for a manufacturing establishment.

Estimates of the Canadian underground economy vary widely, but all show its importance growing rapidly in recent years. The estimates vary from the low of 3–5 percent given by Statistics Canada to the high of 15 given by professor Reuven Brenner of McGill University. In other countries, the figures are even higher. The Italian underground economy, for example, has been estimated at close to 25 percent of that country's total GDP!

Nonmarketed activities. If a home owner hires a firm to do some landscaping, the value of the landscaping enters into GDP; if the home owner does the landscaping herself, the value of the landscaping is omitted from GDP. Other nonmarketed activities include, for example, the services of those who do housework at home, any do-it-yourself activity, and voluntary work such as canvassing for a political party, helping to run a volunteer day-care centre, or leading a Boy Scout troop.

One important nonmarketed activity is leisure itself. If a lawyer voluntarily chooses to work 2,200 hours a year instead of 2,400 hours, measured national income will fall by the attorney's wage rate times 200 hours. Yet the value to the lawyer of the 200 hours of new leisure, which is enjoyed outside of the marketplace, must exceed the lost wages, so total economic welfare has risen rather than fallen. Until recently, one of the most important ways in which economic growth benefited people was by permitting increased amounts of time off work. Because the time off is not marketed, its value does not show up in measures of national income.

Economic bads. When an electricity generating station sends sulphur dioxide into the atmosphere, leading to acid rain and environmental damage, the value of the electricity sold is included as part of GDP, but the value of the damage done by the acid rain is not deducted. Similarly, the gasoline that we use in our cars is part of national income, but the damage done by burning that gasoline is not deducted. To the extent that economic growth brings with it increases in pollution, congestion, and other disamenities of modern living, national income measures will overstate the value of the growth. They measure the increased economic output and income, but they fail to deduct for the increased "bads" that generally accompany economic growth.

Do the Omissions Matter?

GDP does a reasonable job of measuring the flow of goods and services through the market sector of the economy. Usually, an increase in GDP implies greater opportunities for employment for those households who sell their labour services in the market. Unless the importance of unmeasured economic activity changes rapidly, *changes* in GDP will do an excellent job of measuring *changes* in economic activity and economic opportunities. However, when the task at hand is measurement of the overall flow of goods and services available to satisfy people's wants, regardless of the source of the goods and services, then the omissions that we have discussed above become undesirable and potentially serious. Still, in the relatively short-term, changes in

---

[6]Some illegal activities do get included in national income measures, although they are generally misclassified by industry. The income is included because people sometimes report their earnings from illicit activities as part of their earnings from legal activities. They do this to avoid the fate of Al Capone, a famous Chicago gangster in the 1920s and 1930s, who, having avoided conviction on many counts, was finally caught for tax evasion.

Box 27-3

GDP *and Economic Growth*

GDP is not a very good indicator of the long-term growth in welfare that accompanies long-term economic growth. The reason is that so many of the major benefits that growth provides are imperfectly measured or not measured at all by the GDP. This can be dramatically illustrated by looking at some of the most important changes that accompanied the first Industrial Revolution.

1. In early eighteenth-century Europe, average life expectancy was around 30 years; in France, one in five children were dead by the end of the first year of life, and 50 percent of registered children were dead by age 10! Life expectancy rose dramatically after the Industrial Revolution.

2. Industrialisation reduced famine and hunger. Not only did the average food intake rise, its year to year *variation* fell. It is of little consolation to a peasant that the average food consumption is above the subsistence level over the decades if fluctuations in harvests periodically drive it below the subsistence level, thus causing starvation.

3. Technological changes that accompanied the Industrial Revolution virtually eliminated many terrible diseases that had been common until that time, such as plague, tuberculosis, cholera, dysentery, smallpox, and leprosy.

4. The urbanisation that accompanied industrialisation increased literacy and education and broadened experience. Before then, poverty and a rural, peasant existence, with little or no communication between the village and the outside world, tended to be associated with superstition and very narrow experience.

5. Privacy became possible when people moved from the peasant dwelling, where the entire family lived, ate, and slept in one room, to multiroom urban sites.

6. The introduction of a market economy greatly increased the mobility of persons among jobs. In the rural societies, there were few options for employment, and customary behaviour—doing what one's parents did—dominated job selection.

7. The Industrial Revolution was based on mass production of goods sold mainly to low- and middle-income people. These changed the *quality* of consumption. For example, instead of wooden clogs, people adopted leather shoes; instead of rough, homespun cloth, people had factory-made shirts and skirts; instead of mud floors and thatched roofs, people had wooden floors and rain-proof roofs; instead of all living in one room, parents had a room separate from their children. These things may seem trivial to us today, but they changed the way of life of ordinary people. Throughout the late eighteenth century and all of the nineteenth century, a succession of new products continued to alter the way ordinary people lived until, by the mid-twentieth century, the ordinary working person had a structurally different way of life from his or her counterpart in the mid-eighteenth century. Statistics, however, are the same if a doubling of GDP takes the form of twice as much of the same, or of new things that enhance the quality of life. The effect on living standards is, however, much greater when new commodities replace older ones rather than just more of the same becoming available.

Sources: J. Blum, *Our Forgotten Past: Seven Centuries of Life on the Land, (London: Thames and Hudson, 1982).* F. Braudel, *Structures of Everyday Life, 15th–18th Century* (New York: Harper and Row, 1981). N. Rosenberg and L. E. Birdzell, Jr., *How the West Grew Rich* (New York: Basic Books, 1986).

GDP will usually be good measures of the direction, if not the exact magnitude, of changes in economic welfare.

The omissions cause serious problems when national income measures are used to compare living standards in structurally different economies. Generally, the nonmarket sector of the economy is larger in rural than in urban settings and in less developed than in more developed economies. Be cautious, then, when interpreting data from a country with a very different climate and culture. When you hear that the per capita GDP of Nigeria is about C$1,100 per year, you should not imagine living in Fredericton on that income. The limitations of the GDP are further considered in Box 27-3.

Is There a Best Measure of National Income?

To ask which is *the* best income measure is like asking which is *the* best carpenter's tool. The answer depends on the job to be done. The decision concerning which measure to use will depend on the problem at hand, and solving some problems may require information provided by several different measures, or information not provided by any conventional measures. If we wish to predict households' consumption behaviour, then disposable income may be the measure that we need to use. If we wish to account for changes in employment, then constant-dollar GDP may be the measure that we want. For an overall measure of economic welfare, we may need to supplement or modify conventional measures of national income, none of which measure *the quality of life*.

Even as economists do develop new measures for some purposes, it is unlikely that GDP (and its relatives) will be discarded. Economists and policy makers who are interested in changes in market activity and in employment opportunities for factors of production will continue to use GDP and other related measures, because they are the ones that come closest to telling them what they need to know.

SUMMARY

1. Each firm's contribution to total output is equal to its value added, which is the gross value of the firm's output minus the value of all intermediate goods and services—that is, the outputs of other firms—that it uses. Goods that count as part of the economy's output are called final goods; all others are called intermediate goods. The sum of all the values added produced in an economy is the economy's total output, which is called gross domestic product (GDP).

2. Gross domestic product (GDP) can be calculated in three different ways: (i) as the sum of all values added by all producers of both intermediate and final goods, (ii) as the expenditure needed to purchase all final goods and services produced during the period, and (iii) as the income claims generated by the total production of goods and services. The first method uses the census of industry; the other two use the expenditure and income sides of the national accounts. By standard accounting conventions, these three aggregations define the same total.

3. From the expenditure side of the national accounts, $GDP = C^a + I^a + G^a + (X^a \times M^a)$. C^a comprises consumption expenditures of households. I^a is investment in plant and equipment, residential construction, and inventory accumulation. Gross investment can be split into replacement investment (necessary to keep the stock of capital intact) and net investment (net additions to the stock of capital). G^a is government purchases of goods and services. ($X^a \times$

IM^a) represents net exports, or exports minus imports; it will be negative if imports exceed exports.

4. GDP measured from the income side adds up all claims to the market value of production. Wages, rent, interest, profits, depreciation (or capital consumption allowance), and indirect business taxes net of subsidies are the major categories.

5. GDP measures production that is located in Canada, and gross national product (GNP) measures income accruing to Canadian residents. The difference is due to the balance between Canadian claims to incomes that are generated abroad and foreign claims to incomes that are generated in Canada.

6. Real measures of national income are calculated to reflect changes in real quantities. Nominal measures of national income are calculated to reflect changes in both prices and quantities. Any change in nominal income can be split into a change in real income and a change due to prices. Appropriate comparisons of nominal and real measures yield implicit deflators.

7. Several related but different income measures are used in addition to GDP. Net domestic product measures total output after deducting the capital consumption allowance. Personal income is income actually earned by households before any allowance for personal taxes. Disposable personal income is the amount actually available to households to spend or to save, that is, income minus taxes.

8. GDP and related measures of national income must be interpreted with their limitations in mind. GDP excludes production resulting from activities that are illegal, that take place in the underground economy, or that do not pass through markets. Moreover, GDP does not measure everything that contributes to human welfare.

9. Notwithstanding its limitations, GDP remains a useful measure of the total economic activity that passes through the nation's markets and for explaining changes in the employment opportunities facing households who sell their labour services on the market.

TOPICS FOR REVIEW

Value added

GDP as the sum of all values added

Intermediate and final goods

GDP from the expenditure and income sides

GNP

Disposable income

Implicit deflator

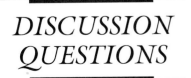

DISCUSSION QUESTIONS

1. If Canada and the United States were to join together as a single country, what would be the effect on their total GDP (assuming that output in each country is unaffected)? Would any of the components in their GDPs change significantly?

2. In 1986, Statistics Canada switched from reporting national income in terms of GNP to reporting it in terms of GDP. How do

these two measures differ? Do you think GDP is a better or worse measure of national income than GNP? Does your answer depend on the purpose the measure is being used for?

3. "Every time you rent a U-Haul, brick in a patio, grow a vegetable, fix your own car, photocopy an article, join a food co-op, develop your own film, sew a dress, stew fruit, or raise a child, you are committing a productive act, even though these activities are not reflected in the gross domestic product." To what extent are each of these things "productive acts"? Are any of them included in GDP? If they are excluded, does the exclusion matter?

4. In measuring GDP from the expenditure side, which of the following expenditures are included? Why?
   a. Expenditures on automobiles by consumers and by firms.
   b. Expenditures on food and lodging by tourists and by businesspeople on expense accounts.
   c. Expenditures on new machinery and equipment by firms.
   d. The purchase of one corporation by another corporation.
   e. Increases and decreases in business inventories.
   f. Purchase of a second-hand automobile.

5. What would be the effect of the following events on the measured value of Canada's real GDP? Speculate on the effects of each event on the true well-being of Canadians.
   a. Destruction of thousands of homes and stores by flood water.
   b. Complete cessation of all imports from Europe.
   c. An increase in the amount of acid rain that falls.
   d. An increase in the amount of spending on devices that reduce pollution at a major hydroelectricity plant.

6. Consider the effect on measured GDP and on economic well-being of each of the following:
   a. Reduction in the standard work week from 40 hours to 30 hours.
   b. Hiring of all welfare recipients as government employees.
   c. Increase in the salaries of priests and ministers as a result of increased contributions of churchgoers.

7. Use the table that appears on the endpapers at the back of this book to calculate the percentage increase over the most recent two decades of each of the following magnitudes. Can you account for the relative size of these changes?
   a. GDP in current dollars.
   b. GDP in constant dollars.
   c. Disposable income in constant dollars.
   d. Disposable income per capita in constant dollars.

8. A recent newspaper article reported that Switzerland was considered the "best" place in the world to live. In view of the fact that Switzerland does not have the highest per capita income in the world, how can it be ranked as the "best"?

9. Some scientific evidence suggests that the burning of fossil fuels is causing general "global warming," which may pose considerable long-term risk to economic and social well-being. In the current national accounts, value added in the production and use of fossil

fuel adds to the GDP. What does this suggest about GDP as a measure of economic welfare?

10. One way of estimating the size of the underground economy is to see the amount of cash Canadians are carrying relative to the total value of GDP. Why would a rapid rise in the ratio of cash held by the public to GDP indicate a rise in the underground economy? Why do you think that ratio has risen steadily since the introduction of the GST and the rises in rates of personal income tax in the 1990s?

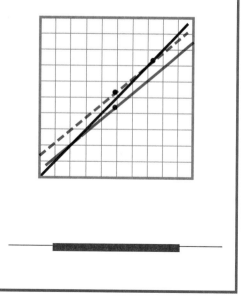

28

National Income and Aggregate Expenditure I: Consumption and Investment

I n Chapters 26 and 27, we encountered a number of important macroeconomic variables. We described how they are measured and how they have behaved over the past half century or so. We now turn to a more detailed study of what *causes* these variables to behave as they do. In particular, we study the forces that determine national income (and hence employment and unemployment) and the price level.

National income and the price level are determined simultaneously. To understand how they are determined, it is easier first to study them one at a time. So in this chapter and the next, we simplify matters by studying the determination of national income *under the assumption that the price level is constant.* The simplified analysis that we explore now will be an important step toward understanding how prices *and* incomes are determined together, which is the subject of Chapters 30 and 31.

Our ability to explain the behaviour of national income depends on our understanding of what determines the amount that households and firms spend and why they change their spending. For this reason, we begin with an examination of the *expenditure decisions* of households and firms.

What Determines Desired Expenditure?

Before we can answer the question posed in the heading, we must deal with a few important preliminaries.

Some Important Preliminaries

From actual to desired expenditure. In Chapter 27 we discussed how national-income statisticians divide actual GDP, calculated from the expenditure side, into its components: consumption, investment, government, and net exports.

In this chapter and the next, we are concerned with a different concept. It is variously called *desired, planned,* or *intended* expenditure. Of course, all people would like to spend virtually unlimited amounts, if only they had the resources. Desired expenditure does not refer, however, to what people would like to do under imaginary circumstances; it refers to what people want to spend out of the resources that are at their command. The *actual* values of the various categories of expenditure are indicated by C^a, I^a, G^a, and $(X^a\text{-}IM^a)$. We use the same letters without the superscript a to indicate the *desired* expenditure in the same categories: C, I, G, and $(X\text{-}IM)$.

Everyone with income to spend makes expenditure decisions. Fortunately, it is unnecessary for our purposes to look at each of the millions of such individual decisions. Instead, it is sufficient to consider four main groups of decision makers: domestic households, firms, governments, and foreign purchasers of domestically produced commodities. The actual purchases made by these four groups account for the four main categories of expenditure that we have studied in the previous chapter: consumption, investment, government, and net exports. Their desired expenditures, made up of desired consumption, desired investment, desired government purchases, and desired exports, account for total desired expenditure. (To allow for the fact that many of the commodities desired by each group will have an import content, we subtract expenditure on imports.) The result is total desired expenditure on domestically produced goods and services, called **aggregate expenditure,** *AE:*

$$AE = C + I + G + (X - IM)$$

Desired expenditure need not equal actual expenditure, either in total or in any individual category. For example, firms may not plan to invest in inventory accumulation this year but may do so unintentionally. If they produce goods to meet estimated sales, but demand is unexpectedly low, the unsold goods that pile up on their shelves are undesired and unintended inventory accumulation. In this case, actual investment expenditure, I^a, will exceed desired investment expenditure, I.

National-income accounts measure actual expenditures in each of the four categories: consumption, investment, government, and net exports. National-income theory deals with desired expenditures in each of these four categories.

Autonomous and induced expenditure. In what follows, it will be useful to distinguish between *autonomous* and *induced* expenditure. Components of aggregate expenditure that do *not* depend on national income are called **autonomous expenditures.** Autonomous expenditures can and do change, but such changes do not occur systematically in response to changes in national income.[1]

Components of aggregate expenditure that *do* change in response to changes in national income are called **induced expenditures.** As we will see, the induced response of aggregate expenditure to a change in national income plays a key role in the determination of equilibrium national income.

A simple model. To develop a theory of national-income determination, we need to examine the determinants of each component of desired aggregate expenditure. In this chapter, we focus on desired consumption and desired investment. Consumption is the largest single component of aggregate expenditure, and, as we will see, it provides the single most important link between desired aggregate expenditure and national income. Investment is national income that is not used either for current consumption or by governments, and it is an important determinant of potential income in the future.

We will discuss net exports and government expenditure in detail in Chapter 29. These two components of aggregate expenditure are essential to understanding how national income is determined and are important in their own right. However, our purpose here is to develop the simplest model of a national economy that can show how desired spending and actual national income are determined together.

The basic structure of the model is most easily seen if things are kept as simple as possible. For this reason, we consider a **closed economy,** an economy that has no international trade. This economy also has no government, no undistributed profits (i.e., all profits are paid out to the owners of firms), and a constant price level. Although this is about as simple as an economy can get, it allows us to discover the principles of national income and expenditure determination that apply directly to the more realistic complete models that we study in subsequent chapters. For now, however, imagine a remote island populated by rugged individualists.

Desired Consumption Expenditure

We are now ready to study the determinants of desired expenditure flows. We start with consumption.

Households can do one of two things with their disposable income: spend it on consumption or save

---

[1]This distinction was first discussed in Chapter 2. See page 28.

it. **Saving** is all disposable income that is not consumed.

By definition, there are only two possible uses of disposable income: consumption or saving. So when the household decides how much to put to one use, it has automatically decided how much to put to the other use.

What determines the division between the amount that households decide to spend on goods and services for consumption and the amount that they decide to save? The factors that influence this decision are summarized in the consumption function and the saving function.

The Consumption Function

The **consumption function** relates the total desired consumption expenditure of all households to the factors that determine it. It is, as we shall see, one of the central relationships in macroeconomics.

Although we are ultimately interested in the relationship between consumption and national income, the underlying behaviour of households depends on the income that they actually have to spend—their disposable income. Under the simplifying assumptions that we have made in this chapter, there are no taxes and no undistributed profits. All income that is generated is received by households. Therefore, disposable income, which we denote by Y_d, is equal to national income, Y. (Later in our discussion, Y and Y_d will diverge, because taxes are a part of national income that is not at the disposal of households.)

Consumption and Disposable Income

It should not surprise us to hear that a household's expenditure is related to the amount of income that it has at its disposal. There is, however, more than one way in which this relationship could work. To see what is involved, consider two quite different households.

The first household is headed by the proverbial prodigal son. It spends everything it receives and puts nothing aside for a rainy day. When overtime results in a large paycheck, the household goes on a binge. When it is hard to find work during periods of slack demand, the household's paycheck is small and its members cut their expenditures correspondingly. This household's expenditure each week is thus directly linked to each week's take-home pay, that is, its current disposable income.

The second household is a prudent planner. It thinks about the future as much as the present, and it makes plans that stretch over its lifetime. It puts money aside for retirement and for the occasional rainy day when disposable income may fall temporarily—it knows that it must expect alternating bouts of good and bad times. It also knows that it will need to spend extra money while the family is being raised and educated and that its income will probably be highest later in life when the children have left home and the parents have finally reached the peaks of their personal careers. This household may borrow to meet higher expenses earlier in life, paying back out of the higher income that the household expects to attain later in life. A temporary, unexpected windfall of income may be saved. A temporary, unexpected shortfall may be cushioned by spending the savings that were put aside for just such a rainy day. In short, this household's current expenditure will be closely related to its expected *lifetime income*. Fluctuations in its *current income* will have little effect on its current expenditure, unless such fluctuations also cause the household to change its expectations of lifetime income, as would be the case, for example, if an unexpected promotion came along.

John Maynard Keynes, the famous English economist who developed the basic theory of macroeconomics—and, incidentally, gave his name to "Keynesian economics"—inhabited his theory with prodigal sons. For them, current consumption expenditure depended only on current income. To this day, a consumption function based on this assumption is called a *Keynesian consumption function* by most economists.

Later, two U.S. economists, Franco Modigliani and Milton Friedman, both of whom were subsequently awarded the Nobel Prize in economics, analysed the behaviour of prudent households. Their theories, which Modigliani called the *life-cycle theory* and which Friedman called the *permanent-income theory,* explain some observed consumer behaviour that cannot be explained by the Keynesian consumption function.

However, the differences between the theories of Friedman and Modigliani, on the one hand, and Keynes, on the other, are not as great as it might seem at first sight. To see why this is so, let us return to our two imaginary households and see why their actual behaviour may not be quite so divergent as we have described it.

Even the household that is headed by the prodigal son may be able to do some smoothing of expenditures in the face of income fluctuations. Most households have some money in the bank and some ability to borrow, even if it is just from friends and relatives. As a result, every income fluctuation will not be matched by an equivalent expenditure fluctuation.

In contrast, although the prudent household wants to smooth its pattern of consumption completely, it may not have the borrowing capacity to do so. Its bank may not be willing to lend money for consumption when the security consists of nothing more than the expectation that the household's income will be much higher in later years. This may mean that the household's consumption expenditure fluctuates more with its current income than it would wish.

This suggests that the consumption expenditure of both types of households will fluctuate to some extent with their current disposable incomes and to some extent with their expectations of future disposable income. Moreover, in any economy, there will be households of both types, both spendthrifts and planners, and aggregate consumption will be determined by a mix of the two types. As we develop our basic theory, we will often find it useful to make the simplifying assumption that consumption expenditure is primarily determined by current disposable income. That is, we will often use a Keynesian consumption function and then indicate how things change if we consider more sophisticated theories of consumer spending.

The term *consumption function* describes the relationship between consumption and the variables that influence it; in the simplest theory, consumption is primarily determined by current disposable income.

When a household's income is zero, it will still (via begging, borrowing, or drawing down savings) consume some minimal amount. This level of consumption expenditure is *autonomous,* because it persists even when there is no income. The higher a household's income, the more it will want to consume. This part of consumption is *induced*; that is, it varies with disposable income and hence, in our simple model, with national income.

Consider the schedule relating disposable income to desired consumption expenditure for a hypothetical economy that appears in the first two columns of Table 28-1. In this example, autonomous consumption expenditure is $100 billion, whereas induced consumption expenditure is 80 percent of disposable income. In what follows, we use this hypothetical example to illustrate the various properties of the consumption function.

Average and marginal propensities to consume. To discuss the consumption function concisely, economists use two technical expressions.

The **average propensity to consume (APC)** is total consumption expenditure divided by total disposable income: $APC = C/Y_d$. The third column of Table 28-1 shows the APC calculated from the data in the table. Note that APC falls as disposable income rises.

The **marginal propensity to consume (MPC)** relates the *change* in consumption to the *change* in disposable income that brought it about. MPC is the change in disposable income divided into the resulting consumption change: $MPC = \Delta C/\Delta Y_d$ (where the Greek letter Δ, delta, means "a change in"). The last column of Table 28-1 shows the MPC that corresponds to the data in the table. Note that, by construction, the MPC is constant. **[33]**

The slope of the consumption function. Part (i) of Figure 28-1 shows a graph of the consumption function, derived by plotting consumption against income using data from the first two columns of Table 28-1. The consumption function has a slope of $\Delta C/\Delta Y_d$, which is, by definition, the marginal propensity to consume. The positive slope of the consumption function shows that the MPC is positive; increases in income lead to increases in expenditure.

Using the concepts of the average and marginal propensities to consume, we can summarize the properties of the short-term consumption function as follows:

1. There is a break-even level of income at which APC equals unity. Below this level, APC is greater than unity; above it, APC is less than unity.
2. MPC is greater than zero but less than unity for all levels of income.

**TABLE 28-1 The Calculation of Average Propensity to Consume *(APC)* and Marginal Propensity to Consume *(MPC) (billions of dollars)*

Disposable income (Y_d)	Desired consumption (C)	$APC = C/Y_d$	ΔY_d (change in Y_d)	ΔC (change in C)	$MPC = \Delta C/\Delta Y_d$
$ 0	$ 100	—			
100	180	1.800	$ 100	$ 80	0.80
400	420	1.050	300	240	0.80
500	500	1.000	100	80	0.80
1,000	900	0.900	500	400	0.80
1,500	1,300	0.867	500	400	0.80
1,750	1,500	0.857	250	200	0.80
2,000	1,700	0.850	250	200	0.80
3,000	2,500	0.833	1,000	800	0.80

APC measures the proportion of disposable income that households desire to spend on consumption; *MPC* measures the proportion of any increment to disposable income that households desire to spend on consumption. The data are hypothetical. We call the level of income at which desired consumption equals disposable income the break-even level; in this example it is $500 billion. *APC,* calculated in the third column, exceeds unity—that is, consumption exceeds income—below the break-even level. Above the break-even level, *APC* is less than unity. It is negatively related to income at all levels of income. The last three columns are set between the lines of the first three columns to indicate that they refer to changes in the levels of income and consumption. *MPC,* calculated in the last column, is constant at 0.80 at all levels of Y_d. This indicates that in this example $0.80 of *every* additional $1.00 of disposable income is spent on consumption, and $0.20 is used to increase saving.

The 45° line. Figure 28-1(i) contains a line that is constructed by connecting all points where desired consumption (measured on the vertical axis) equals disposable income (measured on the horizontal axis). Because both axes are given in the same units, this line has a positive slope of unity; that is, it forms an angle of 45° with the axes. The line is therefore called the **45° line.**

The 45° line makes a handy reference line. In part (i) of Figure 28-1, it helps to locate the break-even level of income at which consumption expenditure equals disposable income. The consumption function cuts the 45° line at the break-even level of income, in this instance $500 billion. (The 45° line is steeper than the consumption function because the *MPC* is less than unity.)

The Saving Function

Households decide how much to consume and how much to save. As we have said, this is a single decision: how to divide disposable income between consumption and saving. It follows that, once we know the dependence of consumption on dispos-

able income, we also automatically know the dependence of saving on disposable income. (This is illustrated in Table 28-2.)

There are two saving concepts that are exactly parallel to the consumption concepts of *APC* and *MPC*. The **average propensity to save (APS)** is the proportion of disposable income that households want to save, derived by dividing total desired saving by total disposable income, $APS = S/Y_d$. The **marginal propensity to save (MPS)** relates the change in total desired saving to the *change* in disposable income that brought it about: $MPS = \Delta S/\Delta Y_d$.

There is a simple relationship between the saving and the consumption propensities. *APC* and *APS* must sum to unity, and so must *MPC* and *MPS*. Because income is either spent or saved, it follows that the fractions of incomes consumed and saved must account for all income ($APC + APS = 1$). It also follows that the fractions of any increment to income consumed and saved must account for all of that increment ($MPC + MPS = 1$). **[34]**

Calculations from Table 28-2 will allow you to confirm these relationships in the case of the exam-

FIGURE 28-1
The Consumption and Saving Functions

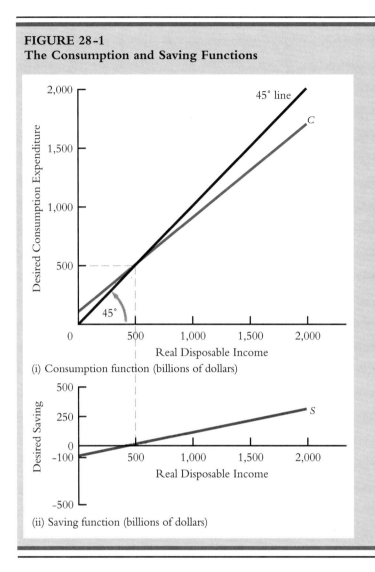

(i) Consumption function (billions of dollars)

(ii) Saving function (billions of dollars)

Both consumption and saving rise as disposable income rises. Line C in part (i) relates desired consumption expenditure to disposable income by using the hypothetical data from Table 28-1. Its slope, $\Delta C/\Delta Y_d$, is the marginal propensity to consume *(MPC)*. The consumption line cuts the 45° line at the break-even level of disposable income, $500 billion in this case. Note that the level of autonomous consumption is $100 billion.

Saving is all disposable income that is not spent on consumption $(S = Y_d - C)$. The relationship between desired saving and disposable income is derived in Table 28-2, and it is shown in part (ii) by line S. Its slope, $\Delta S/\Delta Y_d$, is the marginal propensity to save *(MPS)*. The saving line cuts the horizontal axis at the break-even level of income. The vertical distance between C and the 45° line in part (i) is by definition the height of S in part (ii); that is, any given level of disposable income must be accounted for by the amount consumed plus the amount saved. Note that the level of autonomous saving is $-$$100 billion. This means that at zero income, a household will draw down existing assets by $100 a year.

ple given. *MPC* is 0.80 and *MPS* is 0.20 at all levels of income, while, for example, at an income of $2,000 billion, *APC* is 0.85 and *APS* is 0.15.

Figure 28-1(ii) shows the saving schedule given in Table 28-2. At the break-even level of income, where desired consumption equals disposable income, desired saving is zero. The slope of the saving line $\Delta S/\Delta Y_d$ is equal to the *MPS*.

Wealth and the Consumption Function

The Keynesian consumption function that we have been analysing can easily be combined with the more recent "permanent-income" theories of con-

sumption. According to the permanent-income theories, households save in order to accumulate wealth that they can use during their retirement (or pass on to their heirs). Suppose that there is an unexpected rise in wealth. This will mean that less of current disposable income needs to be saved for the future, and it will tend to cause a larger fraction of disposable income to be spent on consumption and a smaller fraction to be saved. Thus, the consumption function will be shifted upward and the saving function downward, as shown in Figure 28-2. A fall in wealth increases the incentive to save in order to restore wealth. This shifts the consumption function downward and the saving function upward.

TABLE 28-2 Consumption and Saving Schedules *(billions of dollars)*

Disposable income	Desired consumption	Desired saving
$ 0	$ 100	$−100
100	180	−80
400	420	−20
500	500	0
1,000	900	+100
1,500	1,300	+200
1,750	1,500	+250
2,000	1,700	+300
3,000	2,500	+500
4,000	3,300	+700

Saving and consumption account for all household disposable income. The first two columns repeat the data from Table 28-1. The third column, desired saving, is disposable income minus desired consumption. Consumption and saving both increase steadily as disposable income rises. In this example, the break-even level of disposable income is $500 billion.

Desired Investment Expenditure

Investment expenditure is the most volatile component of GDP, and changes in investment expenditure are strongly associated with economic fluctuations. For example, the Great Depression witnessed a dramatic fall in investment. Total investment fell from almost double the amount that was needed to replace the capital goods that were being used up in the process of producing GDP in 1929 to less than one sixth the amount that was needed just to keep the stock of capital intact in 1932. Less dramatically, at the trough of the recession of the early 1990s, investment expenditure was 10 percent less than what it had been 3 years earlier.

Investment and the Real Interest Rate

Other things being equal, the higher is the real interest rate, the higher is the cost of borrowing money for investment purposes and the less is the amount of desired investment expenditure. This relationship is most easily seen if we disaggregate in-

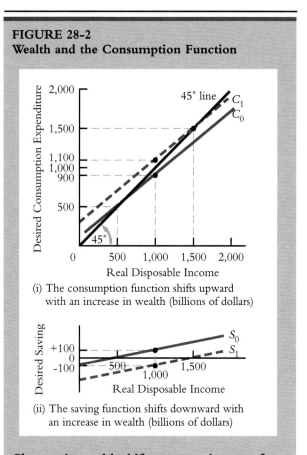

FIGURE 28-2
Wealth and the Consumption Function

(i) The consumption function shifts upward with an increase in wealth (billions of dollars)

(ii) The saving function shifts downward with an increase in wealth (billions of dollars)

Changes in wealth shift consumption as a function of disposable income. In part (i), line C_0 reproduces the consumption function from Figure 28-1 (i). An increase in the level of wealth raises desired consumption at each level of disposable income, thus shifting the consumption line up to C_1. In the figure, the consumption function shifts up by $200, so with disposable income of $1,000, for example, desired consumption *rises* from $900 to $1,100. As a result of the rise in wealth, the break-even level of income rises to $1,500.

The saving function in part (ii) shifts down by $200, from S_0 to S_1. Thus, for example, at a disposable income of $1,000, saving *falls* from +$100 to −$100.

vestment into its major parts: inventories, business fixed investment, and residential housing.

Inventories. Inventory changes represent only a small percentage of private investment in a typical year, but their average size is not an adequate measure of their importance. They are one of the more volatile elements of total investment and therefore have a major influence on shifts in investment expenditure.

When a firm ties up funds in inventories, those same funds cannot be used elsewhere to earn income. As an alternative to holding inventories, the firm could lend the money out at the going rate of interest. Thus, the higher the real rate of interest, the higher will be the opportunity cost of holding an inventory of a given size; the higher that opportunity cost, the smaller are the inventories that will be desired.

The higher is the real rate of interest, the lower is the desired stock of inventories. Changes in the rate of interest cause temporary bouts of investment (or disinvestment) in inventories.

Residential housing construction. Expenditure on residential housing is also volatile. Between 1972 and 1992, it varied between 4.8 and 7.6 percent of all noninventory private investment in Canada and between 4.5 and 7.5 percent of GDP. Because expenditures for housing construction are both large and variable, they exert a major impact on the economy.

Most houses are purchased with money that is borrowed by means of mortgages. Interest on the borrowed money typically accounts for over one half of the purchaser's annual mortgage payments; the remainder is repayment of the original loan, called the principal. Because interest payments are such a large part of mortgage payments, variations in interest rates exert a substantial effect on the demand for housing.

The importance of interest rates was borne out by experiences from 1979 to 1982, when mortgage rates rose from less than 11 percent to just over 15 percent and housing starts fell from 1,194,000 units in 1979 to a mere 661,000 in 1982. (Because inflation fell from 1980, the increased nominal interest rates also meant increased real rates.) The construction industry itself and its major suppliers, such as the cement and the lumber industries, felt the blow of a dramatic fall in demand. Conversely, during the mid-1980s, interest rates fell sharply, and there was a boom in the demand for new housing; that boom

persisted until late 1988, when interest rates started to rise again.

Expenditure for residential construction tends to vary negatively with interest rates.

Plant and equipment. Investment in plant and equipment is the largest component of domestic investment. Over one half is financed by firms' retained profits (profits that are *not* paid out to their shareholders). This means that current profits are an important determinant of investment.

The rate of interest is also a major determinant of investment in plant and equipment. As became abundantly clear during the early 1980s, high interest rates greatly reduced the volume of investment as more and more firms found that their expected profits from investment did not cover the interest on borrowed investment funds. Other firms that had cash on hand found that purchasing interest-earning assets provided a better return than investment in plant and equipment; for them, the increase in real interest rates meant that the opportunity cost of investing in plant and equipment had risen.

Expectations and Business Confidence

Investment takes time. When a firm invests, it increases its future capacity to produce output. If the new output can be sold profitably, the investment will prove to be a good one. If the new output does not generate profits, the investment will be a bad one. When the investment is undertaken, the firm does not know if it will turn out well or badly—it is betting on a favourable future that cannot be known with certainty.

When firms see good times ahead, they will want to invest so as to reap future profits. When they see bad times, they will not invest, because, given their expectations, there will be no payoff to doing so.

Investment depends in part on firms' forecasts of the future state of the economy.

Investment as Autonomous Expenditure

We have seen that investment is influenced by many things. For the moment, we treat investment as autonomous, meaning only that it is uninfluenced by changes in national income. This allows us to study, first, how national income is determined when there is an unchanged amount of desired investment expenditure and, second, how alterations in the amount of desired investment cause changes in equilibrium national income. (In later chapters, we will link changes in national income to changes in investment via induced changes in interest rates.)

The Aggregate Expenditure Function

The aggregate expenditure function relates the level of desired real expenditure to the level of real income. Generally, total desired expenditure on the nation's output is the sum of desired consumption, investment, government, and net export expenditures. In the simplified economy of this chapter, aggregate expenditure is just equal to $C+I$.

$$AE = C + I$$

Table 28-3 shows how the AE function can be calculated, given the consumption function of Tables 28-1 and 28-2 and a constant level of desired investment of $250 billion. In this specific case, all of investment expenditure is autonomous, as is the $100 billion of consumption that would be desired at zero national income. Total autonomous expenditure is thus $350 billion—induced expenditures are just equal to induced consumption, which is equal to $0.8Y$. Thus, desired aggregate expenditure, whether thought of as $C + I$ or as autonomous plus induced expenditure, can be written as $AE = \$350$ billion $+ 0.8Y$. This aggregate expenditure function is illustrated in Figure 28-3.

The propensity to spend out of national income. The fraction of any increment to national income that will be spent on purchasing domestic output is called the economy's **marginal propensity to spend.** The marginal propensity to spend is measured by the change in aggregate expenditure di-

TABLE 28-3 The Aggregate Expenditure Function in a Closed Economy with No Government *(billions of dollars)*

National income (Y)	Desired consumption expenditure (C = 100 + 0.8Y)	Desired investment expenditure (I = 250)	Desired aggregate expenditure (AE = C + I + G + [X− IM])
$ 100	$ 180	$250	$ 430
400	420	250	670
500	500	250	750
1,000	900	250	1,150
1,500	1,300	250	1,550
1,750	1,500	250	1,750
2,000	1,700	250	1,950
3,000	2,500	250	2,750
4,000	3,300	250	3,550

The aggregate expenditure function is the sum of desired consumption, investment, government, and net export expenditures. In this table, government and net exports are assumed to be zero, investment is assumed to be constant at $250 billion, and desired consumption is based on the hypothetical data given in Table 28-2. The autonomous components of desired aggregate expenditure are desired investment and the constant term in desired consumption expenditure. The induced component is the second term in desired consumption expenditure $(0.8Y)$.

The marginal response of consumption to a change in national income is 0.8, the marginal propensity to consume. The marginal response of desired aggregate expenditure to a change in national income, $\Delta AE/\Delta Y$, is also 0.8, because all induced expenditure in this economy is consumption expenditure.

vided by the change in income, or $\Delta AE/\Delta Y$, the slope of the aggregate expenditure function. In this book, we will denote the marginal propensity to spend by the symbol z, which will typically be a number greater than zero and less than one.

Similarly, the **marginal propensity not to spend** is the fraction of any increment to national income that does not add to desired aggregate expenditure. This is denoted $(1-z)$—if z is the part of

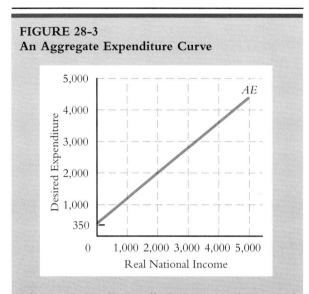

FIGURE 28-3
An Aggregate Expenditure Curve

The aggregate expenditure curve relates total desired expenditure to national income. The AE curve in the figure plots the data from the first and the last columns of Table 28-3, which are repeated in Table 28-4. Its intercept (which in this case is $350) shows autonomous expenditure, which in this case is the sum of autonomous consumption of $100 and investment of $250. Its slope (which in this case is 0.8) shows the marginal propensity to spend.

a dollar of incremental income that is spent, $(1-z)$ is the part that is not spent.[2]

In the example given in Table 28-3, z, the marginal propensity to spend, is 0.8. If national income increases by a dollar, 80 cents will go into increased spending. Twenty cents [one dollar times 0.2, the value of $(1-z)$] will go into increased saving and will not be spent.

The marginal propensity to spend, which we have just defined, should not be confused with the marginal propensity to consume, which we defined earlier in the chapter. The marginal propensity to spend is the amount of extra total expenditure induced when *national income* rises by $1, while the

marginal propensity to consume is the amount of extra consumption expenditure induced when households' *disposable income* rises by $1. In the simple model of this chapter, the marginal propensity to spend is equal to the marginal propensity to consume, and the marginal propensity not to spend is equal to the marginal propensity to save. [In later chapters, when we add government and the international sector, the marginal propensity to spend differs from the marginal propensity to consume. Both here and in later chapters, it is the more general measures z and $(1-z)$ that are important for determining equilibrium national income.]

Determining Equilibrium National Income

We are now ready to see what determines the *equilibrium* level of national income. Recall from Chapter 4 that equilibrium is a state of balance between opposing forces. When something is in equilibrium, there is no tendency for it to change; forces are acting on it, but they balance out, and the net result is *no change*. Any conditions that are required for something to be in equilibrium are called its *equilibrium conditions*.

Table 28-4 illustrates the determination of equilibrium national income for our simple hypothetical economy. Suppose that firms are producing a final output of $1,000 billion, and thus national income is $1,000 billion. According to the table, at this level of income, aggregate desired expenditure is $1,150 billion. If firms persist in producing a current output of only $1,000 billion in the face of an aggregate desired expenditure of $1,150 billion, one of two things must happen.[3]

One possibility is that households, firms, and governments will be unable to spend the extra $150 billion that they would like to spend, so lines or waiting lists of unsatisfied customers will appear. These will send a signal to firms that they can increase their sales if they increase their production. When the firms increase production, national income rises. Of course, the individual firms are in-

---

[2]More fully, these terms would be called the marginal propensity to spend *on national income* and the marginal propensity not to spend *on national income*. The marginal propensity not to spend $(1-z)$ is often referred to as the *marginal propensity to withdraw*. Not spending part of income amounts to a *withdrawal* or a *leakage* from the circular flow of income, as illustrated in Figure 26-1 on page 518.

[3]A third possibility, that prices could rise, is ruled out by assumption in this chapter.

TABLE 28-4   The Determination of Equilibrium National Income *(billions of dollars)*

National income (Y)	Desired aggregate expenditure (AE = C + I)	
$ 100	$ 430	Pressure on income to rise ↓
400	670	
500	750	
1,000	1,150	
1,500	1,550	
1,750	1,750	Equilibrium income ↑
2,000	1,950	
3,000	2,750	
4,000	3,550	Pressure on income to fall

National income is in equilibrium where aggregate desired expenditure equals national income. The data are copied from Table 28-3. When national income is below its equilibrium level, aggregate desired expenditure exceeds the value of current output. This creates an incentive for firms to increase output and hence for national income to rise. When national income is above its equilibrium level, aggregate desired expenditure is less than the value of current output. This creates an incentive for firms to reduce output and hence for national income to fall. Only at the equilibrium level of national income is aggregate desired expenditure exactly equal to the value of the current output.

terested only in their own sales and profits, but their individual actions have as their inevitable consequence an increase in GDP.

The second possibility is that all spenders will spend everything that they wanted to spend. Then, however, expenditure will exceed current output, which can happen only when some expenditure plans are fulfilled by purchasing inventories of goods that were produced in the past. In our example, the fulfilment of plans to purchase $1,150 billion worth of commodities in the face of a current output of only $1,000 billion will reduce inventories by $150 billion. As long as inventories last, more goods can be sold than are currently being produced.[4]

[4]Notice that in this example, actual national income is equal to $1,000. Desired consumption is $900 and desired investment is $250, but the reduction of inventories of $150 is unplanned negative investment; thus, actual investment is only $100.

Eventually, inventories would run out. But before this happens, firms will increase their outputs as they see their inventories being depleted. Extra sales can then be made without a further depletion of inventories. Once again, the consequence of each individual firm's behaviour, in search of its own individual profits, is an increase in national income. Thus, the final response to an excess of aggregate desired expenditure over current output is a rise in national income.

At any level of national income at which aggregate desired expenditure exceeds total output, there will be pressure for national income to rise.

Next, consider the $4,000 billion level of national income in Table 28-4. At this level, desired expenditure on domestically produced goods is only $3,550 billion. If firms persist in producing $4,000 billion worth of goods, $450 billion worth must remain unsold. Therefore, inventories must rise. However, firms will not allow inventories of unsold goods to rise indefinitely; sooner or later, they will reduce the level of output to the level of sales. When they do, national income will fall.

At any level of income for which aggregate desired expenditure is less than total output, there will be a pressure for national income to fall.

Finally, look at the national-income level of $1,750 billion in Table 28-4. At this level, and only at this level, aggregate desired expenditure is equal to national income. Purchasers can fulfill their spending plans without causing inventories to change. There is no incentive for firms to alter output. Because everyone wishes to purchase an amount equal to what is being produced, output and income will remain steady; they are in equilibrium.

The equilibrium level of national income occurs where aggregate desired expenditure equals total output.

This conclusion is quite general and does not depend on the numbers that are used in the specific example. Appendix B to Chapter 29 shows this by giving a more general derivation of equilibrium national income.

FIGURE 28-4
Equilibrium National Income

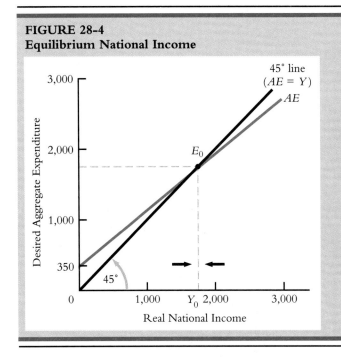

Equilibrium national income occurs at E_0, where the desired aggregate expenditure line intersects the 45° line. If real national income is below Y_0, desired aggregate expenditure will exceed national income, and production will rise. This is shown by the arrow to the left of Y_0. If national income is above Y_0, desired aggregate expenditure will be less than national income, and production will fall. This is shown by the arrow to the right of Y_0. Only when real national income is Y_0 will desired aggregate expenditure equal real national income.

Figure 28-4 shows the determination of the equilibrium level of national income. In that figure, the line labeled AE graphs the aggregate expenditure function given by the first and last columns of Table 28-3 and also shown in Table 28-4. The line labeled 45° line $(AE = Y)$ graphs the equilibrium condition that aggregate desired expenditure equals national income. Since in equilibrium the variables measured on the two axes must be equal, the line showing this equality is a 45° line. Anywhere along that line, the value of desired expenditure, which is measured on the vertical axis, is equal to the value of real national income, which is measured on the horizontal axis.[5]

Graphically, equilibrium occurs at the level of income at which the aggregate desired expenditure line intersects the 45° line. This is the level of income where desired expenditure is just equal to total national income and therefore is just sufficient to purchase total final output.

Now we have explained the equilibrium level of national income that arises at a *given price level*. In the next section, we shall study the forces that cause equilibrium income to change. We shall see that shifts in desired consumption and investment expenditure can cause major swings in national income.

---

[5]Because it turns up in many different guises, the 45° line can cause a bit of confusion until one gets used to it. The main thing about it is that it can be used whenever the variables plotted on the two axes are measured in the same units, such as dollars, and are plotted on the same scale. In that case, equal distances on the two axes measure the same amounts. One inch may, for example, correspond to $1,000 on each axis. In such circumstances, the 45° line joins all points where the values of the two variables are the same. In Figures 28-1 and 28-2, the 45° line shows all points where *desired consumption expenditure* equals *real disposable income* because these are the two variables that are plotted on the two axes. In Figure 28-4 and all those that follow it, the 45° shows all points at which *desired total expenditure* equals *real national income* because those are the variables that are measured on the two axes of these figures.

Changes in National Income

Because the AE function plays a central role in our explanation of the equilibrium value of national income, you should not be surprised to hear that shifts in the AE function play a central role in explaining why national income changes. (Remember that we continue to assume that the price level is constant.) To understand this influence, we must recall an important distinction first encountered in

FIGURE 28-5
Movements Along and Shifts of the *AE* Function

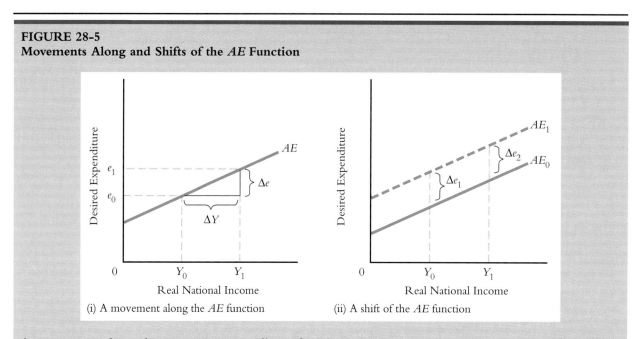

(i) A movement along the *AE* function   (ii) A shift of the *AE* function

A movement along the aggregate expenditure function occurs in response to a change in income; a shift of the *AE* function indicates a different level of desired expenditure at each level of income. In part (i), a change in income of ΔY, from Y_0 to Y_1, changes desired expenditure by Δe, from e_0 to e_1. In part (ii), a shift in the expenditure function from AE_0 to AE_1 raises the amount of expenditure associated with *each* level of income. At Y_0, for example, desired aggregate expenditure is increased by Δe_1; at Y_1 it is increased by Δe_2. (If the aggregate expenditure line shifts parallel to itself, $\Delta e_1 = \Delta e_2$.) (Notice that from here on we drop aggregate from the vertical axis label and write Desired Expenditure. The term aggregate is always understood even when we omit it to save space.)

Chapter 4—the distinction between *shifts* in a curve and *movements along* a curve.

Suppose desired aggregate expenditure rises. This may be a response to a change in national income, or it may be the result of an increased desire to spend at each level of national income. A change in national income causes a *movement along* the aggregate expenditure function. An increased desire to spend at each level of national income causes a *shift in* the aggregate expenditure function. Figure 28-5 illustrates this important distinction.

Shifts in the Aggregate Expenditure Function

For any specific aggregate expenditure function, there is a unique level of equilibrium national income. If the aggregate expenditure function shifts,

the equilibrium will be disturbed, and national income will change. Thus, if we wish to find the causes of changes in national income, we must understand the causes of shifts in the *AE* function.

The aggregate expenditure function shifts when one of its components shifts, that is, when there is a shift in the consumption function, in desired investment expenditure, in desired government expenditure on goods and services, or in desired net exports. In this chapter, we consider only shifts in the consumption function and in desired investment expenditure. Both of these are changes in desired aggregate expenditure at every level of income.

Upward Shifts

What will happen if households permanently increase their levels of consumption spending at each level of disposable income, or if the Ford Motor Company increases its rate of annual investment in order to expand its capacity to produce? (In considering these questions, remember that we are dealing with continuous flows measured as so much per period of time. An upward shift in any expenditure function means that the desired expenditure associated with each level of national income rises to and stays at a higher amount.)

Because any such increase in desired expenditure shifts the entire aggregate expenditure function upward, the same analysis applies to each of the changes mentioned. Two types of shift in AE occur. First, if the same addition to expenditure occurs at all levels of income, the AE curve shifts parallel to itself, as shown in part (i) of Figure 28-6. Second, if there is a change in the propensity to spend out of national income, the slope of the AE curve changes, as shown in part (ii) of Figure 28-6. (Recall that the slope of the AE curve is z, the marginal propensity to spend.) A change such as the one illustrated would occur if consumers decided to spend more of every dollar of disposable income.

Figure 28-6 shows that upward shifts in the aggregate expenditure function increase equilibrium national income. After the shift in the AE curve, income is no longer in equilibrium at its original level, because at that level desired expenditure exceeds national income. Equilibrium national income now occurs at the higher level indicated by the intersection of the new AE curve with the 45° line, along which aggregate expenditure equals real national income.

Downward Shifts in Expenditure Functions

What happens to national income if there is a decrease in the amount of consumption or investment expenditure desired at each level of income? These changes shift the aggregate expenditure function downward. A constant reduction in desired expenditure at all levels of income shifts AE parallel to itself. A fall in the marginal propensity to spend out of national income reduces the slope of the AE function. When we use the saving-investment relation, we must note that a downward shift in the consumption function causes an upward shift in the saving function, reducing the equilibrium level of income, at which saving equals investment.

The Results Restated

We have derived two important general propositions of the elementary theory of national income.

1. A rise in the amount of desired aggregate expenditure that is associated with each level of national income will increase equilibrium national income.

2. A fall in the amount of desired aggregate expenditure that is associated with each level of national income will lower equilibrium national income.

The Multiplier

We have learned how to predict the direction of the changes in national income that occur in response to various shifts in the aggregate expenditure function. We would like also to predict the *magnitude* of these changes.

Economists need to know the *size* of the effects of changes in expenditures. During a recession, the government sometimes takes measures to stimulate the economy. If these measures have a larger effect than estimated, demand may rise too much, and full employment may be reached with demand still rising. (We will see in Chapter 30 that this outcome will have an inflationary impact on the economy.) If the government greatly overestimates the effect of its measures, the recession will persist longer than is necessary. In this case, there is a danger that the policy will be discredited as ineffective, even though the correct diagnosis is that too little of the right thing was done.

Definition. A measure of the magnitude of changes in income is provided by the *multiplier*. We have just seen that a shift in the aggregate expenditure curve will cause a change in equilibrium national income. Such a shift could be caused by a change in any autonomous component of aggregate expenditure, for example, an increase or decrease in desired investment. An increase in desired aggregate expenditure increases equilibrium national income by a multiple of the initial increase in autonomous expenditure. The **multiplier** is the ratio of the change in income to the change in expenditure, that is, the change in national income *divided by* the change in autonomous expenditure that brought it about.

Why the multiplier is greater than unity. What will happen to national income if Bombardier de-

FIGURE 28-6
Shifts in the *AE* Curve

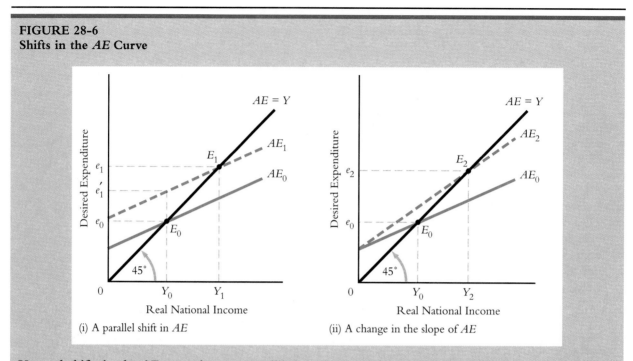

(i) A parallel shift in *AE*   (ii) A change in the slope of *AE*

Upward shifts in the AE curve increase equilibrium income; downward shifts decrease equilibrium income. In parts (i) and (ii), the aggregate expenditure curve is initially AE_0 with national income Y_0.

In part (i), a parallel upward *shift* in the *AE* curve from AE_0 to AE_1 means that desired expenditure has increased by the same amount at each level of national income. For example, at Y_0 desired expenditure rises from e_0 to e_1 and therefore exceeds national income. Equilibrium is reached at E_1, where income is Y_1 and expenditure is e_1. The increase in desired expenditure from e'_1 to e_1, represented by a *movement along AE_1*, is an induced response to the increase in income from Y_0 to Y_1.

In part (ii), a nonparallel upward shift in the *AE* curve, say, from AE_0 to AE_2, means that the marginal propensity to spend at each level of national income has increased. This leads to an increase in equilibrium national income. Equilibrium is reached at E_2, where the new level of expenditure e_2 is equal to income Y_2. Again, the initial *shift* in the *AE* curve induces a *movement along* the new *AE* curve.

Downward shifts in the *AE* curve, from AE_1 to AE_0 or from AE_2 to AE_0, lead to a fall in equilibrium income to Y_0.

cides to spend an extra $100 million each year on new factories? Initially, the new construction will create $100m worth of new national income per year and a corresponding amount of employment for households and firms on which the initial $100m is spent, but this is not the end of the story. The increase in national income of $100m will cause an increase in disposable income, which will cause an induced rise in consumption expenditure.

Electricians, masons, and carpenters—who gain new income directly from the building of the factory—will spend some of it on food, clothing, entertainment, cars, television sets, and other commodities. When output expands to meet this demand, employment will increase in all the affected industries. New incomes will then be created for workers and firms in these industries. When they, in turn, spend their newly earned incomes, output and employment will rise further. More income will be created, and more expenditure will be induced. Indeed, at this stage we might wonder whether the increases in income will ever come to an end. To deal with this concern, we need to consider the multiplier in somewhat more precise terms.

The simple multiplier defined. Consider an increase in autonomous expenditure of ΔA, which

FIGURE 28-7
The Simple Multiplier

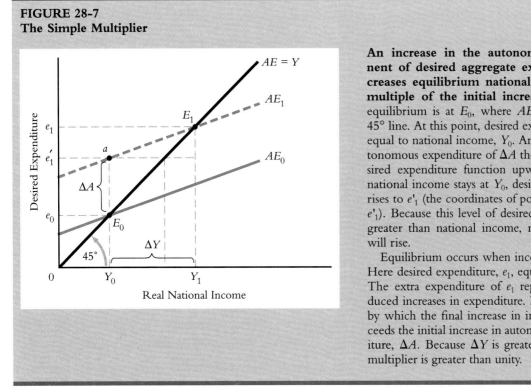

An increase in the autonomous component of desired aggregate expenditure increases equilibrium national income by a multiple of the initial increase. The initial equilibrium is at E_0, where AE_0 intersects the 45° line. At this point, desired expenditure, e_0, is equal to national income, Y_0. An increase in autonomous expenditure of ΔA then shifts the desired expenditure function upward to AE_1. If national income stays at Y_0, desired expenditure rises to e'_1 (the coordinates of point a are Y_0 and e'_1). Because this level of desired expenditure is greater than national income, national income will rise.

Equilibrium occurs when income rises to Y_1. Here desired expenditure, e_1, equals income, Y_1. The extra expenditure of e_1 represents the induced increases in expenditure. It is the amount by which the final increase in income, ΔY, exceeds the initial increase in autonomous expenditure, ΔA. Because ΔY is greater than ΔA, the multiplier is greater than unity.

might be, say, $100m per year. Remember that ΔA stands for *any* increase in autonomous expenditure; this could be an increase in investment or in the autonomous component of consumption. The new autonomous expenditure shifts the aggregate expenditure function upward by that amount. National income is no longer in equilibrium at its original level, because desired aggregate expenditure now exceeds income. Equilibrium is restored by a *movement along* the new AE curve.

The **simple multiplier** measures the change in equilibrium national income that occurs in response to a change in autonomous expenditure *at a constant price level*. We refer to it as "simple" because we have simplified the situation by assuming that the price level is fixed. Figure 28-7 illustrates the simple multiplier and makes clear that it is greater than unity. Box 28-1 provides a numerical example.

The Size of the Simple Multiplier

The size of the simple multiplier depends on the slope of the AE function, that is, on the marginal propensity to spend, z. This is illustrated in Figure 28-8.

A high marginal propensity to spend means a steep AE curve. The expenditure induced by any initial increase in income is large, with the result that the final rise in income is correspondingly large. By contrast, a low marginal propensity to spend means a relatively flat AE curve. The expenditure induced by the initial increase in income is small, and the final rise in income is not much larger than the initial rise in autonomous expenditure that brought it about.

The larger the marginal propensity to spend, the steeper is the aggregate expenditure function and the larger is the multiplier.

The precise value of the simple multiplier can be derived by using elementary algebra. (The derivation is given in Box 28-2, on page 582.) The result is that the simple multiplier, which we call K, is

$$K = \frac{\Delta Y}{\Delta A} = \frac{1}{1 - z}$$

Box 28-1

The Multiplier: A Numerical Example

Consider an economy that has a marginal propensity to spend out of national income of 0.80. Suppose that autonomous expenditure increases by $100m per year, because a large corporation spends an extra $100m per year on new factories. National income initially rises by $100m, but that is not the end of it. The factors of production involved in factory building that received the first $100m spend $80 million. This second round of spending generates $80 million of new income. This new income, in turn, induces $64 million of third-round spending, and so it continues, with each successive round of new income generating 80 percent as much in new expenditure. Each additional round of expenditure creates new income and yet another round of expenditure.

The table carries the process through 10 rounds. Students with sufficient patience (and no faith in mathematics) may compute as many rounds in the process as they wish; they will find that the sum of the rounds of expenditures approaches a limit of $500 million, which is five times the initial increase in expenditure.[35] The graph of the cumulative expenditure increases shows how quickly this limit is approached.

The multiplier is thus 5, given that the marginal propensity to spend is 0.8. Had the marginal propensity to spend been lower, say, 0.667, the process would have been similar, but it would have approached a limit of three instead of five times the initial increase in expenditure.

Round of spending	Increase in expenditure (millions of dollars)	Cumulative total (millions of dollars)
Initial increase	100	100.0
2	80	180.0
3	64	244.0
4	51.2	295.2
5	41.0	336.2
6	32.8	369.0
7	26.2	395.2
8	21.0	416.2
9	16.8	432.8
10	13.4	446.2
11 to 20 combined	47.9	494.1
All others	5.8	500.0

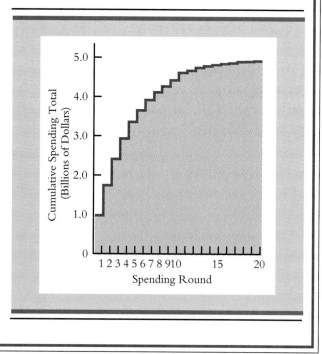

FIGURE 28-8
The Size of the Simple Multiplier

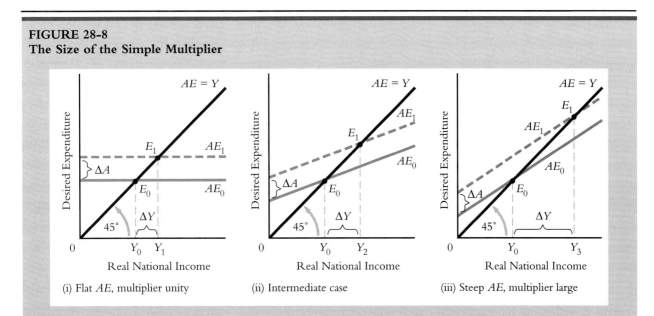

(i) Flat AE, multiplier unity   (ii) Intermediate case   (iii) Steep AE, multiplier large

The larger the marginal propensity to spend out of national income (z), the steeper is the AE curve and the larger is the multiplier. In each part of the figure, the initial aggregate expenditure function is AE_0, equilibrium is at E_0, with income Y_0. The AE curve than shifts upward to AE_1 as a result of an increase in autonomous expenditure of ΔA. ΔA is the same in each part. The new equilibrium is at E_1.

In part (i), the AE function is horizontal, indicating a marginal propensity to spend of zero $(z = 0)$. The change in income, ΔY, is only the increase in autonomous expenditure, because there is no induced expenditure by those who receive the initial increase in income. The simple multiplier is then unity, its minimum possible value.

In part (ii), the AE curve slopes upward but is still relatively flat $(z$ is low). The increase in national income to Y_2 is only slightly greater than the increase in autonomous expenditure that brought it about.

In part (iii), the AE function is quite steep $(z$ is high). Now the increase in income to Y_3 is much larger than the increase in autonomous expenditure that brought it about. The simple multiplier is quite large.

where z is the marginal propensity to spend out of national income. (As we have seen, z is the slope of the aggregate expenditure function.)

As we saw earlier, the term $(1 - z)$ stands for the marginal propensity not to spend out of national income. For example, if 0.80 of every $1.00 of new national income is spent $(z = 0.80)$, then $0.20 is the amount not spent. The value of the multiplier is then calculated as $K = 1/(0.20) = 5$.

The simple multiplier equals the reciprocal of the marginal propensity not to spend.

From this we see that, if $(1-z)$ is small (that is, if z is large), the multiplier will be large (because extra income induces much extra spending). What if $(1-z)$ is large? The largest possible value of $(1-z)$ is

unity, which arises when z equals zero, indicating that none of any additional national income is spent. In this case, the multiplier itself has a value of unity; the increase in equilibrium national income is confined to the initial increase in autonomous expenditure. There are no induced additional effects on spending, so national income only increases by the original increase in autonomous expenditure. The relation between $(1-z)$ and the size of the multiplier is illustrated in Figure 28-8.

To estimate the size of the multiplier in an actual economy, we need to estimate the value of the marginal propensity not to spend out of national income in that economy, that is, $(1-z)$. Evidence suggests that Canadian value is much larger than the 0.2 that we used in our example, in large part because there are a number of elements of national in-

Box 28-2

The Multiplier: An Algebraic Approach

Basic algebra is all that is needed to derive the exact expression for the multiplier. Readers who feel at home with algebra may want to follow this derivation. Others can skip it and rely on the graphical and numerical arguments that have been given in the text.

First, we derive the equation for the AE curve. Aggregate expenditure is divided into autonomous expenditure, A, and induced expenditure, N. In the simple model of this chapter, A is just equal to investment plus autonomous consumption. N is just equal to induced consumption.*

Thus, we can write

$$AE = N + A \qquad [1]$$

Because N is expenditure on domestically produced output that varies with income, we can write

$$N = zY \qquad [2]$$

where z is the marginal propensity to spend out of national income. (z is a positive number between zero and unity. In the simple model of this chapter, with no government and no foreign sector, it is equal to the marginal propensity to consume.) Substituting Equation 2 into Equation 1 yields the equation of the AE curve.

$$AE = zY + A \qquad [3]$$

Now we write the equation of the 45° line,

$$AE = Y \qquad [4]$$

which states the equilibrium condition that desired aggregate expenditure equals national income. Equations 3 and 4 are two equations with two unknowns, AE and Y. To solve them, we substitute Equation 3 in Equation 4 to obtain

$$Y = zY + A \qquad [5]$$

Subtracting zY from both sides yields

$$Y - zY = A \qquad [6]$$

Factoring out Y yields

$$Y(1 - z) = A \qquad [7]$$

Dividing through by $1-z$ yields

$$Y = \frac{A}{(1 - z)} \qquad [8]$$

This tells us the equilibrium value of Y in terms of autonomous expenditures A and the propensity not to spend out of national income $(1-z)$. Now consider a one-dollar increase in A. The expression $Y = A/(1-z)$ tells us that if A changes by one dollar, the change in Y will be $1/(1-z)$ dollars. Generally, for a change in autonomous spending of ΔA, the change in Y, which we call ΔY, will be

$$\Delta Y = \frac{\Delta A}{(1 - z)} \qquad [9]$$

Dividing through by ΔA gives the value of the multiplier, which we designate by K:

$$K = \frac{\Delta Y}{\Delta A} = \frac{1}{(1 - z)} \qquad [10]$$

---

* When we add imports and government in the next chapter, N will include induced imports, and A will include government spending and exports. The derivation here is quite general, however. All that matters is that desired aggregate expenditure can be divided into one class of expenditure, N, that varies with income and another class, A, that does not.

come that are "not spent" that we have not yet discussed. In addition to saving, which we have discussed, these "withdrawals" from the circular flow of income include income taxes and import expenditures. For the Canadian economy in the 1990s, this leads to a realistic estimate of something around 0.65 for $(1-z)$. Thus, the simple Canadian multiplier is closer to 1.5 than to 5, as in the example.

The simple multiplier is a useful starting point for understanding the effects of expenditure shifts on national income; however, as we shall see in subsequent chapters, many complications will arise.

SUMMARY

1. Desired aggregate expenditure includes desired consumption, desired investment, and desired government expenditures, plus desired net exports. It is the amount that economic agents want to spend on purchasing the national product. In this chapter, we consider only consumption and investment.

2. A change in disposable income leads to a change in consumption and saving. The responsiveness of these changes is measured by the marginal propensity to consume (MPC) and the marginal propensity to save (MPS), which are both positive and sum to one, indicating that all disposable income is either spent on consumption or saved.

3. A change in wealth tends to cause a change in the allocation of disposable income between consumption and saving. The change in consumption is positively related to the change in wealth, while the change in saving is negatively related to this change.

4. Investment depends, among other things, on real interest rates and business confidence. In our simple theory, investment is treated as autonomous.

5. In the simple theory of this chapter, investment expenditures and the constant term in the consumption function are both autonomous expenditures. The part of consumption that responds to income is called induced expenditure.

6. At the equilibrium level of national income, purchasers wish to buy an amount equal to what is being produced. At incomes above equilibrium, desired expenditure falls short of national income, and output will sooner or later be curtailed. At incomes below equilibrium, desired expenditure exceeds national income, and output will sooner or later be increased.

7. In a closed economy with no government, desired saving equals desired investment at equilibrium national income.

8. Equilibrium national income is represented graphically by the point at which the aggregate expenditure curve cuts the 45° line, that is, where total desired expenditure equals total output. This is the same level of income at which the saving function cuts the investment function.

9. With a constant price level, equilibrium national income is increased by a rise in either the desired consumption or the desired investment expenditure that is associated with each level of the national income. Equilibrium national income is decreased by a fall in these desired expenditures.

10. The magnitude of the effect on national income of shifts in autonomous expenditure is given by the multiplier. It is defined as $K = \Delta Y/\Delta A$, where ΔA is the change in autonomous expenditure.

11. The simple multiplier is the multiplier when the price level is constant. It is equal to $1/(1-z)$, where z is the marginal propensity to spend out of national income. Thus, the larger z is, the larger is the multiplier. It is a basic prediction of national income theory that the simple multiplier, relating $1 worth of spending on domestic output to the resulting increase in national income, is greater than unity.

TOPICS FOR REVIEW

Desired expenditure

Consumption function

Average and marginal propensities to consume and to save

Aggregate expenditure function

Marginal propensities to spend and not to spend

Equilibrium national income at a given price level

Saving-investment balance

Shifts of and movements along expenditure curves

Effect on national income of changes in desired expenditures

The simple multiplier

The size of the multiplier and slope of the AE curve

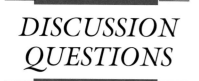

DISCUSSION QUESTIONS

1. Relate the following newspaper headlines to shifts in the C, S, I and/or AE functions and to changes in equilibrium national income.
   a. "Revival of consumer confidence leads to increased spending."
   b. "High interest rates discourage new house purchases."
   c. "Concern over future leads to a reduction in inventories."
   d. "Accelerated depreciation allowances in the new federal budget sets off boom on equipment purchases."

2. Interpret each of the following statements either in terms of the shape of a consumption function or the values of MPC and APC.
   a. "Tom Green has lost his job, and his family is existing on its past savings."
   b. "The Grimsby household is so rich that they used all the extra income they earned this year to invest in a wildcat oil-drilling venture."
   c. "We always thought Harris was a miser, but when his wife left him, he took to wine, women, and song."
   d. "The inflation has made the Schultzes feel so poor that they are adding an extra $100 a week to their account at the savings bank."

e. "The last stock market crash led young Ross to cancel two planned trips abroad, even though his job as a broker was never at risk."

3. Why might an individual's marginal propensity to consume be higher in the long run than in the short run? Why might it be lower? Is it possible for an individual's average propensity to consume to be greater than unity in the short run? In the long run? Can a country's average propensity to consume be greater than unity in the short run? In the long run?

4. Explain carefully why national income changes when desired aggregate expenditure does not equal national income. Sketch scenarios that fit the cases of too much and too little desired expenditure.

5. Explain how a sudden, unexpected fall in consumer expenditure would initially cause an increase in investment expenditure by firms.

6. Explain how an increase in desired saving would reduce equilibrium income.

7. What relationship is suggested by the following newspaper headline: "Auto sales soar as recovery booms?"

8. Locate at least two current press stories that suggest shifts in the *AE* curve.

29

National Income and Aggregate Expenditure II: An Open Economy with Government

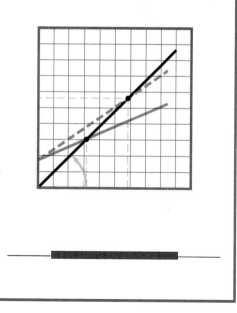

In Chapter 28, we developed a highly simplified model of national income determination in a closed economy with fixed prices. The economy that we live in and wish to study is both more interesting and more complicated. Unlike the economy of Chapter 28, it has a government (in fact, several levels of government), and it engages in foreign trade. In this chapter, we add a government and a foreign sector to our simple model. Adding the government sector allows us to study *fiscal policy*, the ability of the government to use its taxing and spending powers to affect the level of national income. In Chapter 30, we will expand the model further to explain the price level.

As we proceed, it is important to remember that the key elements of our theory of income determination are unchanged. The most important of these, which will remain true even after incorporating government and the foreign sector, are restated here.

1. Aggregate desired expenditure can be divided into autonomous expenditure and induced expenditure. Induced expenditure is expenditure that depends on the level of national income.
2. The equilibrium level of national income is the level at which the sum of autonomous and induced desired expenditure is equal to the level of national income. Graphically, this is where the aggregate expenditure line intersects the 45° line.
3. The simple multiplier measures the change in equilibrium national income that takes place in response to a unit change in autonomous domestic expenditure, with the price level held constant.

Government: Spending and Taxes

Government spending and taxing policies affect equilibrium national income in two important ways. First, government purchases are part of autonomous expenditure. Second, in deriving disposable income, taxes must be subtracted from national income, and government transfer payments must be added. Because disposable income determines consumption expenditure, the relationship between desired consumption and national income becomes somewhat more complicated when a government is added.

A government's plans for taxes and spending define its *fiscal policy*, which has important effects on the level of national income in both the short and the long run. Our discussion of fiscal policy begins in this chapter and continues in Chapter 31 and in Chapter 37.

Government Spending

In Chapter 27, we distinguished between *government purchases* of goods and services and government *transfer payments*. The distinction bears repeating here. Government purchases are part of GDP. When the government hires a bureaucrat, buys a paper clip, or purchases fuel for the navy, it is directly adding to the demands on the economy's current output of goods and services. Thus, desired government purchases, G, are part of aggregate expenditure. (For now, we assume that the government simply chooses a level of desired purchases and is able to spend that amount. Later, we will look at the determinants of desired government purchases in more detail.)

The other part of government spending, transfer payments, also affects desired aggregate expenditure, but only indirectly. Consider Canada Pension (CPP) payments. In and of themselves, these government expenditures place *no* demand on the nation's production of goods and services. However, when recipients spend part of their pensions on consumption, an indirect effect on aggregate expenditure results—transfer payments lead to higher consumption, which is, of course, part of aggregate expenditure and of GDP. (To the extent that recipients of transfers save the money, there is no increased demand for national output.)

Government transfer payments affect aggregate expenditure only through the effect that these payments have on *disposable* income. Transfer payments increase disposable income, and increases in disposable income, via the consumption function, increase desired consumption expenditure.

Tax Revenues

Tax revenues may be thought of as negative transfer payments in their effect on desired aggregate expenditure. Tax payments reduce disposable income relative to national income; transfers raise disposable income relative to national income. For the purpose of calculating the effect of government policy on desired consumption expenditure, it is the net effect of the two that matters.

We define **net taxes** to be total tax revenues received by the government minus total transfer payments made by the government, and we denote net taxes as T. (For convenience, when we use the term "taxes," we will mean net taxes unless we explicitly state otherwise.) Since transfer payments are smaller than total taxes, net taxes are positive, and disposable income is substantially less than national income. (It was first under about 70 percent of GDP in 1992.)

The Budget Balance

The **budget balance** is the difference between total government revenue and total government expenditure, or, equivalently, it equals net taxes minus government purchases, $T - G$. When revenues exceed expenditure, the government is running a **budget surplus.** When expenditures exceed revenues, as they have for two decades, the government is running a **budget deficit.**[1] When the two amounts are equal, the government has a **balanced budget.** When the budget is in deficit, the government is adding to the national debt since it must borrow to cover its deficit. When the budget is in surplus, the government is reducing the national debt since the surplus funds are used to pay off old debt.

Tax and Expenditure Functions

We treat government expenditure as autonomous. The government decides how much it wishes to spend and holds to these plans whatever the level of national income. We also treat *tax rates* as autonomous. The government sets its tax rates and does not vary them as national income varies. This, however, implies that *tax revenues* are induced. As national income rises, a tax system with given rates will yield more revenue. For example, when income rises, people will pay more income tax in total even though income tax rates are unchanged.

Table 29-1 and Figure 29-1 illustrate these assumptions with a specific example. They show the size of the government's surplus when its desired purchases (G) are constant at $170 billion and its net tax revenues are equal to 10 percent of national income. Notice that the government budget surplus increases with national income. This relationship occurs because net tax revenues rise with income but, by assumption, government purchases do not. The slope of the budget surplus function is just

---

[1] When the government runs a budget deficit, it must borrow the excess of spending over revenues. It does this by issuing *and selling government bonds.* When the government runs a surplus, it uses the excess revenue to purchase outstanding government bonds. The stock of outstanding bonds is termed the *national debt.* Deficits and the national debt are the principal topics of Chapter 37.

TABLE 29-1   The Budget Surplus Function
(billions of dollars)

National income (Y)	Government purchases (G)	Net Taxes (T = 0.1Y)	Government Surplus (T − G)
500	170	50	−120
1,000	170	100	−70
1,750	170	175	5
2,000	170	200	30
3,000	170	300	130
4,000	170	400	230

The budget surplus is negative at low levels of national income and becomes positive at sufficiently high levels of national income. The table shows that the size of the budget surplus increases with national income, given constant expenditure and taxing rules. For example, when national income rises by $1,000 billion, the deficit falls or the surplus rises by $100 billion.

FIGURE 29-1
Budget Surplus Function

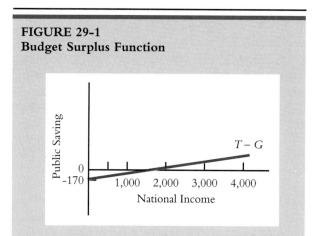

The budget surplus increases as national income increases. This figure plots the $T − G$ column from Table 29-1. Notice that the slope of the surplus function is equal to the income tax rate of 0.1.

equal to the income tax rate. The *position* of the surplus function is determined by fiscal policy, as we discuss later in this chapter.[2]

Provincial and Municipal Governments

Most of our discussion of government spending and taxing is focused on the federal government, which generally has far more discretion over its fiscal policy than do provincial and local governments. However, it is important to remember that in Canada, provincial and municipal governments account for *more* purchases of goods and services than does the federal government, while the federal government raises about the same amount of tax revenue as do the provincial and municipal governments combined.

When measuring the overall contribution of the public sector to aggregate expenditure and to national saving, all levels of government must be included. Thus, G and T in the national income accounts measure purchases by all governments and net taxes collected by all governments.

Net Exports

Although rich in natural resources, Canada also imports many raw materials and energy products. Canadian households typically consume a wide range of imported goods, such as Japanese cars and American refrigerators. Canada also exports a wide variety of products to the rest of the world, including grains, commuter jets, and computer software. Foreign trade accounts for about 25 percent of Canadian national income, and U.S.-Canadian trade is the largest two-way flow of trade between any two countries in the world today.

The Net Export Function

In Chapter 26, we noted that we use the terms *imports* and *exports* to refer to goods and services. Services are a growing part of international trade; consultants, architects, product designers, lawyers,

---

[2]The numerical example used here is designed only to illustrate the principles of income determination developed in this chapter. To avoid the appearance of direct applicability of overly simplified models, we have deliberately chosen not to use "realistic" numbers. (In any case numbers that are "realistic" today may be "unrealistic" in three years time.) In our example, equilibrium national income works out to be $2 trillion, which is above the 1992 Canadian figure of nearly C$700 billion and below the 1992 U.S. figure of US$6 trillion

accountants, bankers, and insurance firms, along with many other service activities, all sell much of their output to residents of foreign countries. In our theory, we are interested in the amount of trade that responds quickly to changes in national incomes, price levels, and exchange rates. Thus, our theory covers goods *and traded* services when it refers to imports and exports.

Exports depend on spending decisions made by foreign households that purchase Canadian goods and services. Typically, therefore, exports will not change as a result of changes in Canadian national income. They are exogenous expenditure from the point of view of Canadian national income.

Imports, however, depend on the spending decisions of Canadian households. All categories of expenditure have an import content; Canadian-made cars, for example, use large quantities of imported components in their manufacture. Thus, imports rise when the other categories of expenditure rise. Because consumption rises with income, imports of foreign-produced consumption goods and materials that go into the production of domestically produced consumption goods also rise with income.

Desired net exports are negatively related to national income because of the positive relationship between desired imports and national income.

This negative relationship between net exports and national income is called the *net export function.* Data for a hypothetical economy with constant exports and with imports that are 10 percent of national income are given in Table 29-2 and illustrated in Figure 29-2. In this example, exports form the autonomous component and imports form the induced component of the desired net export function.[3]

Shifts in the Net Export Function

We have seen that the net export function relates net exports $(X - IM)$, which we also denote NX, to

---

[3]The formulation in the table implicitly assumes that all imports are for final consumption; imports rise when income rises, but imports do not change when *other* categories of autonomous expenditure change. This simplification will prove useful in our development of the determination of equilibrium income and does not affect the essentials of the theory. Appendix A to this chapter shows how to allow for an import content to *all* expenditure flows.

TABLE 29-2   A Net Export Schedule
(billions of dollars)

National income (Y)	Exports (X)	Imports (IM = 0.1Y)	Net export
1,000	240	100	140
2,000	240	200	40
2,400	240	240	0
3,000	240	300	−60
4,000	240	400	−160
5,000	240	500	−260

Net exports fall as national income rises. The data are hypothetical. They assume that exports are constant and that imports are 10 percent of national income. In this case, net exports are positive at low levels of national income and negative at high levels of national income.

national income. It is drawn on the assumption that everything that affects net exports, except domestic national income, remains constant. The major factors that must be held constant are foreign national income, relative international price levels, and the exchange rate. A change in any of these factors will affect the amount of net exports that will occur at each level of Canadian national income and hence will shift the net export function.

Notice that anything that affects Canadian exports will change the values in the export column in Table 29-2 and so will shift the net export function parallel to itself, upward if exports increase and downward if exports decrease. Also, notice that anything that affects the proportion of income that Canadian consumers wish to spend on imports will change the values in the import column in Table 29-2, and thus will change the slope of the net export function by making imports more or less responsive to changes in domestic income. What factors will cause such shifts?

Foreign income. An increase in foreign income, other things being equal, will lead to an increase in the quantity of Canadian goods demanded by foreign countries, that is, to an increase in Canadian exports. The increase is in the constant, X, of the net export function, causing NX to shift upward, parallel to its original position. A fall in foreign income leads to a parallel downward shift in the net export function.

FIGURE 29-2
The Net Export Function

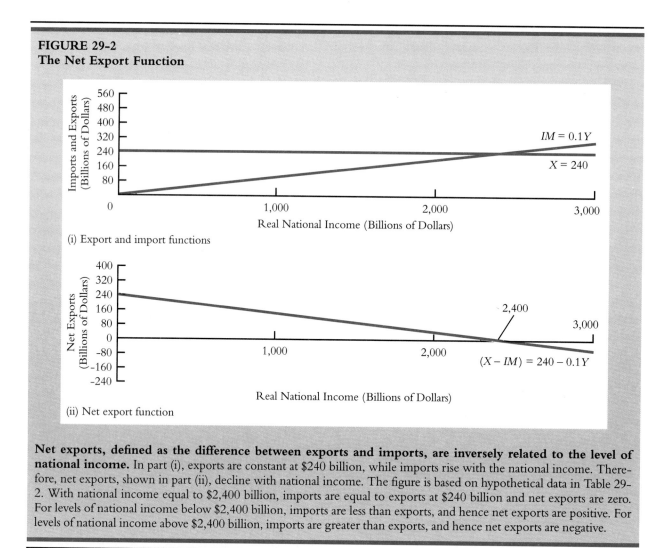

(i) Export and import functions

(ii) Net export function

Net exports, defined as the difference between exports and imports, are inversely related to the level of national income. In part (i), exports are constant at $240 billion, while imports rise with the national income. Therefore, net exports, shown in part (ii), decline with national income. The figure is based on hypothetical data in Table 29-2. With national income equal to $2,400 billion, imports are equal to exports at $240 billion and net exports are zero. For levels of national income below $2,400 billion, imports are less than exports, and hence net exports are positive. For levels of national income above $2,400 billion, imports are greater than exports, and hence net exports are negative.

Relative international prices. Any change in the average prices of Canadian goods relative to those of foreign goods will cause both imports and exports to change. This will shift the net export function.

Consider first a rise in Canadian prices relative to prices in foreign countries. On the one hand, foreigners now see Canadian goods as more expensive relative both to goods produced in their own country and to goods imported from countries other than Canada. As a result, Canadian exports will fall. On the other hand, Canadians will see imports from foreign countries become cheaper relative to the prices of Canadian-made goods. As a result, they will buy more foreign goods, and Canadian imports will rise. Both of these shifts cause the net export function to shift downward and change its slope, as shown in Figure 29-3.

Second, consider the opposite case of a fall in Canadian prices relative to prices of foreign-made goods. On the one hand, Canadian exports will now look cheaper in foreign markets relative both to their home-produced goods and to goods imported from countries other than Canada. As a result, Canadian exports rise. On the other hand, the same change in relative prices—Canadian-made goods become cheaper relative to foreign-made goods—causes Canadian imports to fall. Thus, the net export function shifts upward, as shown in Figure 29-3.

To apply these results, we need only to note those things that will cause relative international prices to change. The two important causes are international differences in inflation rates and changes in exchange rates.

FIGURE 29-3
Shifts in the Net Export Function

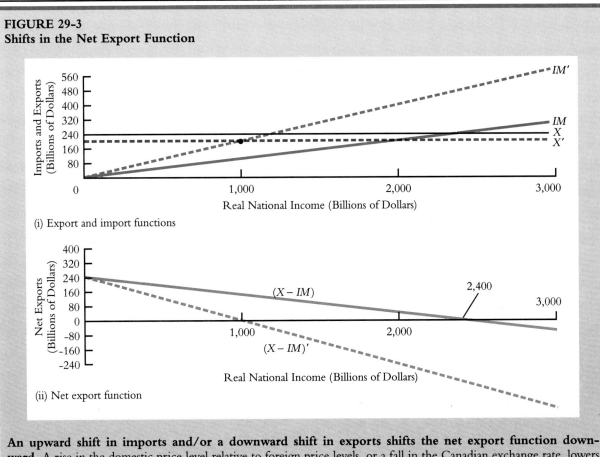

(i) Export and import functions

(ii) Net export function

An upward shift in imports and/or a downward shift in exports shifts the net export function downward. A rise in the domestic price level relative to foreign price levels, or a fall in the Canadian exchange rate, lowers exports from X to X'I and raises the import function from IM to IM'. This shifts the net export function downward from (X − IM) to (X − IM)'. Starting from the primed functions, a fall in the domestic price level relative to foreign price levels, or a rise in the C$ exchange rate, raises exports to X and lowers the import function to IM, raising the net export function to (X − IM). (In the figure, imports are 10 percent of Y along IM and are assumed to rise to 20 percent of Y when Canadian goods become more expensive relative to foreign goods, while exports fall from 240 to 200.)

Consider inflation rates first. Canadian prices will rise relative to foreign prices if the Canadian inflation rate is higher than the inflation rates in other major trading countries. In contrast, Canadian prices will fall relative to foreign prices if the Canadian inflation rate is lower than the rates in other major trading countries. Since most of Canada's trade is with the United States, the most important single comparison is between the inflation rates in Canada and the United States.

Now consider the exchange rate. A rise in the Canadian dollar exchange rate means that foreigners must pay less of their money to buy one Canadian

dollar, while Canadian residents must pay more Canadian dollars to buy a unit of any foreign currency. For example, if the exchange rate goes from 1.20 to 1.35, Canadians have to pay 15 cents more for every U.S. dollar's worth of U.S. goods that they buy. In contrast, U.S. residents now have to pay only 74 cents (1/1.35) to get a C$ to buy a Canadian good, whereas before they had to pay 83 cents (1/1.20).[4] As a result, the price of foreign goods in

---

[4]If you have forgotten these relations between the exchange rate and the amounts of one currency that must be paid to buy another currency, you should review Box 26-4 on page 536.

terms of Canadian dollars rises, and the price of Canadian goods in terms of foreign currency falls. This reduction in the relative price of Canadian goods will cause a shift in expenditure away from foreign goods and toward Canadian goods. Canadian residents will import less at each level of Canadian national income, and foreigners will buy more Canadian exports. The net export function thus shifts upward.

A fall in the Canadian dollar exchange rate has the opposite effect, causing substitution of foreign for Canadian goods in both foreign and Canadian markets, thus shifting the net export function downward.

The results of this important chain of reasoning are summarized below.

1. **Canadian prices rise relatively to foreign prices if either the Canadian inflation rate exceeds the rate in other major trading countries or if the Canadian dollar exchange rate falls. This discourages exports and encourages imports, causing the net export function to shift downward.**
2. **Canadian prices fall relative to foreign prices if either the Canadian inflation rate is less than the rates in other major trading countries or if the Canadian dollar exchange rate rises. This encourages exports and discourages imports, causing the net export function to shift upward.**

Equilibrium National Income

We are now ready to see how equilibrium national income is determined in our new model that includes a government and a foreign sector. In Chapter 28, we determined equilibrium national income by finding the level of national income where desired aggregate expenditure is equal to national income. The addition of government and the foreign sector changes the calculations that we must make but does not alter the basic principles that are involved. Our first step is to derive a new aggregate expenditure function that incorporates the effects of government and foreign trade.

Relating Desired Consumption to National Income

Our theory of national-income determination re-

quires that we relate each of the components of aggregate expenditure to the level of national income. When there are taxes, the relationship between consumption and national income involves both the relation between consumption and disposable income and the relation, via taxes, of disposable income and national income.

Continuing the example begun earlier, assume that disposable income is always 90 percent of national income.[5] Whatever the relationship between C and Y_d, we can always substitute $0.9Y$ for Y_d. Thus, if changes in consumption were always 80 percent of changes in Y_d, changes in consumption would always be 72 percent (80 percent of 90 percent) of changes in Y. **[36]**

Table 29-3 illustrates how we can write desired consumption as a function of Y as well as of Y_d. We can then derive the marginal response of consumption to changes in Y by determining the proportion of any change in *national income* that goes to a change in desired consumption.

The marginal response of consumption to changes in national income ($\Delta C/\Delta Y$) is equal to the marginal propensity to consume out of disposable income ($\Delta C/\Delta Y_d$) multiplied by the fraction of national income that becomes disposable income ($\Delta Y_d/\Delta Y$).

We now have a function that shows how desired consumption expenditure varies as *national income* varies, including the effects of taxes and transfer payments. This function is part of the aggregate expenditure function.

The Aggregate Expenditure Function

As in Chapter 28, in order to determine equilibrium national income, we start by defining the aggregate expenditure function,

$$AE = C + I + G + NX$$

Table 29-4 on page 594 illustrates the calculation of the aggregate expenditure function. It shows a schedule of desired expenditure for each of the components of aggregate expenditure, and it shows total desired *aggregate* expenditure at each level of national income. Figure 29-4 on page 593 shows this aggregate expenditure function in graphical form.

---

[5]In this case, T, desired net taxes, would be given by the function $T = 0.1 Y$.

TABLE 29-3 Consumption as a Function of Disposable Income and National Income *(billions of dollars)*

(1) National income (Y)	(2) Disposable income ($Y_d = 0.9Y$)	(3) Desired consumption ($C = 100 + 0.8Y_d$)
100	90	172
1,000	900	820
2,000	1,800	1,540
3,000	2,700	2,260
4,000	3,600	2,980

If desired consumption depends on disposable income, which in turn depends on national income, desired consumption can be written as a function of either income concept. The data are hypothetical. Column 2 shows deductions of 10 percent of any level of national income to arrive at disposable income. Deductions of 10 percent of Y imply that the remaining 90 percent of Y becomes disposable income. Column 3 shows consumption as $100 billion plus 80 percent of disposable income.

By relating columns 2 and 3, one sees consumption as a function of disposable income. By relating columns 1 and 3, one sees the derived relationship between consumption and national income. In this example, the change in consumption in response to a change in disposable income (i.e., the MPC) is 0.8, and the change in consumption in response to a change in national income is 0.72.

FIGURE 29-4
An Aggregate Expenditure Curve

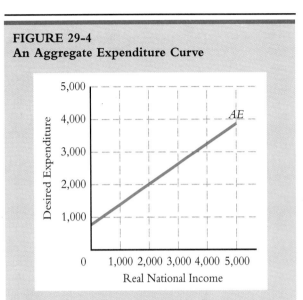

The aggregate expenditure curve relates total desired expenditure to national income. The *AE* curve in the figure plots the data from the first and the last columns of Table 29-4. Its intercept shows $760 billion of autonomous expenditure ($100 billion autonomous consumption plus $250 billion investment plus $170 government, plus $240 billion autonomous net exports). Its slope is the marginal propensity to spend (which, following the calculations in Table 29-4 on page 594, is 0.62 in this case).

The Marginal Propensity to Spend

As in Chapter 28, the slope of the aggregate expenditure function is the *marginal propensity to spend* on national income (z). With the addition of taxes and net exports, however, the marginal propensity to spend is no longer equal to the marginal propensity to consume.

Suppose that the economy produces $1.00 of extra income and that the response to this is governed by the relationships in Tables 29-1 and 29-2, as summarized in Table 29-4. Since $0.10 is collected by the government as net taxes, $0.90 is converted into disposable income, and 80 percent of this amount ($0.72) becomes consumption expenditure. However, import expenditure also rises by $0.25, so expenditure on domestic goods, that is, aggregate expenditure, rises by only $0.47. Thus, z, the marginal propensity to spend, is 0.47

(0.47/1.00). What is not spent on domestic output includes the $0.10 in taxes, the $0.18 of disposable income that is saved, and the $0.25 of import expenditure, for a total of $0.53. Hence, the marginal propensity not to spend, $1 - z$, is $1 - 0.47 = 0.53$.

Determining Equilibrium National Income

The logic of national income determination in our (now more complicated) hypothetical economy is exactly the same as in the closed economy without government discussed in Chapter 28. We have added two new components of aggregate expenditure, G and $(X - IM)$. We have also made the calculation of desired consumption expenditure more complicated; taxes must be subtracted from national income in order to determine disposable income. However, *equilibrium national income is still the level of national income at which desired aggregate expenditure equals national income.*

The aggregate expenditure function can be used directly to determine equilibrium national in-

TABLE 29-4 The Aggregate Expenditure Function *(billions of dollars)*

National income (Y)	Desired consumption expenditure (C = 100 + 0.72Y)	Desired investment expenditure (I = 250)	Desired government expenditure (G = 170)	Desired net export expenditure (X − IM = 240 − 0.10Y)	Desired aggregate expenditure (AE = C + I + G + [X − IM])
100	172	250	170	230	822
400	388	250	170	200	1,008
500	460	250	170	190	1,070
1,000	820	250	170	140	1,380
2,000	1,540	250	170	40	2,000
3,000	2,260	250	170	−60	2,620
4,000	2,980	250	170	−160	3,240
5,000	3,700	250	170	−260	3,860

The aggregate expenditure function is the sum of desired consumption, investment, government, and net export expenditures. The table is based on the hypothetical data given in Tables 29-1, 29-2, and 29-3. The autonomous components of desired aggregate expenditure are desired investment, desired government purchase, desired export expenditures, and the constant term in desired consumption expenditure. These sum to $760 billion in the given example. The induced components are the second term in desired consumption expenditure (0.72Y) and desired imports (0.10Y).

The marginal response of consumption to a change in national income is 0.72, calculated as the product of the marginal propensity to consume (0.8) times the fraction of national income that becomes disposable income (0.9). The marginal response of desired aggregate expenditure to a change in national income, $\Delta AE/\Delta Y$, is 0.62.

come. In Table 29-4, the equilibrium is $2,000 billion. When national income is equal to $2,000 billion, it is also equal to desired aggregate expenditure.

Suppose that national income is less than its equilibrium amount. The forces leading back to equilibrium are exactly the same as those described on pages 573–575 of Chapter 28. When households, firms, foreign demanders, and governments try to spend at their desired amounts, they will try to purchase more goods and services than the economy is currently producing. Thus, some of the desired expenditure must either be frustrated or take the form of purchases of inventories of goods that were produced in the past. As firms see that they are (or could be) selling more than they are producing, they will increase production, thereby increasing the level of national income.

The opposite sequence of events occurs when national income is greater than the level of aggregate expenditure desired at that income. Now the total of household consumption, business investment, government purchases, and net foreign demand on the economy's production is less than national output. Firms will be unable to sell all of their output. Their inventories will be rising, and they will not permit this to happen indefinitely.

They will seek to reduce the level of output until it equals the level of sales, and national income will fall.

Finally, when national income is equal to desired aggregate expenditure ($2,000 billion in Table 29-4), there is no pressure for output to change. Consumption, investment, government purchases, and net exports just add up to national product. Firms are producing exactly the quantity of goods and services that purchasers want to use, given the level of income.

Graphical exposition. Figure 29-5 illustrates the determination of equilibrium and the behaviour of the economy when it is not in equilibrium. (The discussion parallels that of Figure 28-4.) The line labeled *AE* is simply the aggregate expenditure function shown in Figure 29-4. The slope of *AE* is the marginal propensity to spend (as always, in models where consumption is the only induced expenditure flow). Recall that *AE* is a depiction of the behaviour of desired purchases in the economy. It shows how much national product people wish to purchase at each level of national income.

The line labeled *AE = Y* (the 45° line) depicts the equilibrium condition that desired aggregate ex-

FIGURE 29-5
Equilibrium National Income

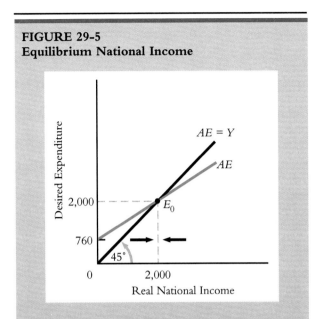

Equilibrium national income occurs at E_0, where the desired aggregate expenditure line intersects the 45° line. Here, the aggregate expenditure line is taken from Figure 28-3; autonomous expenditure is $760, and the slope of AE is 0.62. If real national income is below $2,000, desired aggregate expenditure will exceed national income, and production will rise. This is shown by the arrow to the left of $Y = \$2,000$. If national income is above $2,000, desired aggregate expenditure will be less than national income, and production will fall. This is shown by the arrow to the right of $Y = \$2,000$. Only when real national income is $2,000 will desired aggregate expenditure equal real national income.

penditure be equal to actual national income. Any point on this line *could* be an equilibrium, but only one is. Equilibrium occurs where behaviour (as depicted by the AE function) is consistent with equilibrium (as depicted by $AE = Y$). At the equilibrium level of income, desired expenditure is just equal to national income and is therefore just sufficient to purchase total national output.

Shifts in Aggregate Expenditure

Shifts in any of the components of planned aggregate expenditure will cause changes in equilibrium

national income. In Chapter 28, we investigated the consequences of shifts in the consumption function and in the investment function. Here we take a first look at fiscal policy—the effects of government spending and taxes. We also consider shifts in the net export function. First, we take account of the fact that the simple multiplier is reduced by the presence of taxes and the marginal propensity to import.

The simple multiplier revisited. In Chapter 28, we saw that the *simple multiplier*, the amount by which equilibrium national income changes when autonomous expenditure changes by a dollar, was equal to $1/(1 - z)$. In the example considered throughout Chapter 28, z, the marginal propensity to spend, was equal to 0.8, and the multiplier was equal to 5, or $1/(0.2)$. In the example that we have developed in this chapter, with a marginal propensity to import of 0.25 and a marginal income tax rate of 0.1, the marginal propensity to spend is 0.47. Ten percent of a one-dollar increase in autonomous spending goes to taxes, leaving 90 cents of disposable income. With a marginal propensity to consume of 0.8, 72 cents is spent. Of this, 25 cents is spent on imports, leaving a total of 47 cents to be spent on domestically produced consumption goods. Thus, $(1 - z)$ is (0.53), and the simple multiplier is $1/(0.53) = 1.89$.

Net Exports and Equilibrium National Income

Earlier in this chapter, we discussed the determinants of net exports and of shifts in the net export function. As with the other elements of desired aggregate expenditure, if the net export function shifts upward, equilibrium national income will rise; if the net export function shifts downward, equilibrium national income will fall.

Autonomous net exports. Net exports have both an autonomous component and an induced component. Generally, exports themselves are autonomous with respect to domestic national income. Foreign demand for Canadian goods and services depends on foreign income, on foreign and Canadian prices, and on the exchange rate, but it does not depend on Canadian income. Export demand could also change because of a change in tastes. Suppose that foreign consumers develop a taste for Canadian-made designer clothing and desire to consume $500 million more per year of such goods than they had in the past. The net export function (and the aggregate expenditure function) will shift up by $500 million, and equilibrium national income will increase by $500 million times the multiplier.

Induced net exports. The Canadian demand for imports depends, in part, on Canadian income. The greater is domestic income, the greater will be Canadian demand for goods and services in general, including those produced abroad. Because imports are subtracted to obtain net exports (net exports equal $X - IM$), the marginal propensity to import (m) is subtracted from the marginal propensity to spend, z. Thus, the greater is the marginal propensity to import, the lower will be the marginal propensity to spend, and the lower will be the multiplier, $1/(1 - z)$.

Fiscal Policy

Fiscal policy involves the use of government spending and tax policies to influence total desired expenditure and by shifting the AE curve, to alter national income. Alterations in fiscal policy will normally alter the government's deficit or surplus.

Financial Implications of Deficits and Surpluses

When the government runs a deficit by spending more than it raises, where does the money come from? When the government runs a surplus by raising more than it spends, where does the money go? The difference between expenditure and current revenue shows up as changes in the government's debt.

A deficit requires an increase in borrowing, for which there are two main sources: the central bank and the private sector. When the government borrows from the private sector, this action merely shifts funds between the two sectors. When the government "borrows" from the central bank, however, the central bank creates new money. Since the central bank can create as much money as it likes,

there is no limit to what the government can "borrow" from it.

Because a deficit must be covered by borrowing, a deficit adds to the national debt, which represents the sum of all past borrowing minus all past repayments. In contrast, a surplus is used to retire existing debt and thus causes a reduction in the total national debt.

Since government expenditure increases aggregate desired expenditure and taxation decreases it, the *directions* of the required changes in spending and taxation are generally easy to determine once we know the direction of the desired change in national income. But the *timing, magnitude,* and *mixture* of the changes pose more difficult issues.

Any policy that attempts to stabilize national income at or near any desired level (usually potential national income) is called **stabilization policy.** Here, we deal only with the basic ideas of stabilization through fiscal policy. In Chapter 31, we return to discuss some of its complications after we have developed the needed theory.

The basic idea of stabilization policy follows from what we have already learned. A reduction in tax rates or an increase in government expenditure shifts the AE curve upward, causing an increase in equilibrium national income. An increase in tax rates or a decrease in government expenditure shifts the AE curve downward, causing a decrease in equilibrium income.

If the government has some target level of GDP, it can use its tax and expenditures as instruments to push the economy toward that target. First, suppose the economy is in a serious recession. The government would like to increase national income. The appropriate fiscal tools are to raise expenditures and/or to lower tax rates. Second, suppose the economy is "overheated." In the next two chapters, we will study what this means in detail. In the meantime, we observe that an overheated economy has such a high level of national income that shortages are pushing up prices and causing inflation. Without worrying too much about the details, just assume that the current level of national income is higher than the target income that the government judges to be appropriate. What should the government do? The fiscal tools at its command are to lower government expenditure and to raise tax rates, both of which have a depressing effect on national income.

Now let us look in a little more detail at how this works out.

Changes in Government Purchases

Suppose that while holding tax rates constant, the government decides to reduce its spending on industry, science, and technology, saving $1 billion a year in spending. Planned government purchases (G) would fall by $1 billion at every level of income, shifting AE downward by the same amount. How much would equilibrium income change? This can be calculated using the multiplier. Government purchases are part of autonomous expenditure, so a *change* in government purchases of ΔG will lead to a *change* in equilibrium national income of the multiplier times ΔG. In this example, equilibrium income would fall by $1 billion times the simple multiplier.

Increases in government purchases would have the opposite effect. If the government were to spend $2 billion on new highways, equilibrium national income would rise by $2 billion times the simple multiplier.

An increase in expenditures with tax rates constant will have an expansionary effect on national income and will increase the budget deficit. Decreases in G are contractionary and reduce the deficit.

Changes in Tax Rates

If tax rates change, the relationship between disposable income and national income changes. As a result, the relationship between desired consumption expenditure and national income also changes. For any given level of national income, there will be a different level of disposable income and thus a different level of consumption, as illustrated in Table 29-5. Consequently, a change in tax rates will also cause a change in z, the marginal propensity to spend out of national income.

Consider a decrease in tax rates. If the government holds its expenditure constant and decreases its rate of income tax so that it collects $0.05 less out of every dollar of national income, then disposable income rises in relation to national income. Thus, consumption also rises at every level of national income. This results in a (nonparallel) upward shift of the AE curve, that is, an increase in the slope of the curve, as shown in Figure 29-6. The result of this shift will be a rise in equilibrium national income, as is also shown in Figure 29-6.

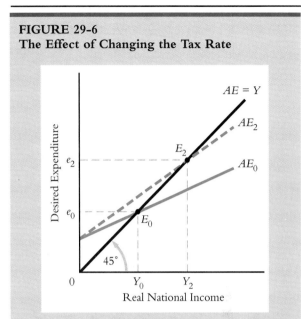

FIGURE 29-6
The Effect of Changing the Tax Rate

Changing the tax rate changes equilibrium income by changing the slope of the AE curve. A reduction in tax rates pivots the AE curve from AE_0 to AE_2. The new curve has a steeper slope, because the lower tax rate withdraws a smaller amount of national income from the desired consumption flow. Equilibrium income rises from Y_0 to Y_2, because at every level of national income, desired consumption, and hence aggregate expenditure, is higher.

If we take AE_2 and Y_2 to be the initial equilibrium, an increase in tax rates will reduce the slope of the AE curve, thereby reducing equilibrium income, as shown by AE_0 and Y_0.

A rise in taxes has the opposite effect. A rise in tax rates with expenditure constant causes a decrease in disposable income, and hence consumption expenditure, at each level of national income. This results in a (nonparallel) downward shift of the AE curve and thus decreases the level of equilibrium national income, as illustrated in Figure 29-6.

Increases in tax rates have a contractionary effect on the economy and reduce the deficit; decreases in rates are expansionary and increase the deficit.

Tax rates and the multiplier. Earlier in this chapter, we recalled that the *simple multiplier* is equal to the reciprocal of one minus the marginal propensity

TABLE 29-5   Tax Changes Shift the Function Relating Consumption to National Income
(billions of dollars)

(1) National income (Y)	Disposable income equal to 80 percent of national income (tax rate = 0.2)		Disposable income equal to 90 percent of national income (tax rate = 0.1)	
	(2) Disposable income ($Y_d = 0.8Y$)	(3) Consumption ($C = 100 + 0.8Y_d$)	(4) Disposable income ($Y_d = 0.9Y$)	(5) Consumption ($C = 100 + 0.8Y_d$)
100	80	164	90	172
500	400	420	450	460
1,000	800	740	900	820

The consumption function shifts if the relationship between disposable and national income changes. The table is based on the simplified hypothetical consumption function from Table 28-1 combined with the assumption that Y_d is a constant fraction of Y. Initially, $Y_d = 0.8Y$, yielding the schedule relating consumption to national income that is given in columns 1 and 3 and is described by the equation $C = 100 + 0.64Y$. Income-tax rates are then decreased so that 90 percent of national income becomes disposable income. Column 4 indicates the Y_d that corresponds at the decreased tax rate to each level of Y shown in column 1. With an unchanged consumption function, consumption at the new tax rate is given by column 5. Columns 1 and 5 give the new schedule relating consumption to *national income*, described by the equation $C = 100 + 0.72Y$.

to spend. That is, the multiplier equals $1/(1 - z)$, where z is the marginal propensity to spend out of national income. The simple multiplier tells us how much equilibrium national income changes when autonomous expenditure changes by a dollar and there is no change in prices.

When tax rates change, the multiplier also changes. Suppose that the *MPC* is 0.8 and the tax rate *falls* by $0.05 per dollar of national income. This would increase the marginal propensity to spend by $0.04 per dollar of national income. (Disposable income would rise by $0.05 per dollar at each level of national income, and consumption would rise by the marginal propensity to consume, 0.8, times $0.05, which is $0.04.) The increase in the value of z, the marginal propensity to spend, would cause the multiplier to rise, making equilibrium income more responsive to changes in autonomous expenditure from any source.

The lower is the income tax rate, the larger is the simple multiplier.

Figure 29-6 illustrates the effect of tax rates on the multiplier and also illustrates the effect of a change in tax rates on equilibrium income: When the tax rate falls, disposable income rises at each level of income. According to the consumption function, the increase in disposable income causes desired consumption to rise as well, rotating the *AE* curve upward. The new, steeper *AE* curve intersects the 45° line at a higher level of income. Similarly, when the tax rate rises, the process is reversed.

Balanced Budget Changes

Another policy available to the government is to make a balanced-budget change by altering spending and taxes equally. Say the government increases tax rates enough to raise an extra $1 billion that it then uses to purchase goods and services. Aggregate expenditure would remain unchanged if, and only if, the $1 billion that the government takes from the private sector would otherwise have been spent on that sector. If so, the government's policy would reduce private expenditure by $1 billion and raise its own spending by $1 billion. Aggregate demand, and hence national income and employment, would remain unchanged.

But this is not the usual case. When an extra $1 billion in taxes is taken away from households, they usually reduce their spending on domestically produced goods by less than $1 billion. If the marginal propensity to consume out of disposable income is, say, 0.75, consumption expenditure will fall by only $750 million. If the government spends the entire $1 billion on domestically produced goods, aggregate expenditure will increase by $250 million. In this case the balanced budget increase in government expenditure has an expansionary effect because it shifts the aggregate expenditure function upward and hence shifts the *AD* curve to the right.

A balanced budget increase in government expenditure will have a mild expansionary effect on national income, and a balanced budget decrease will have a mild contractionary effect.

The **balanced budget multiplier** measures these effects. It is the change in income divided by the balanced budget change in government expenditure that brought it about. Thus if the extra $1 billion of taxes causes national income to rise by $500 million, the balanced budget multiplier is 0.5; if income rises by $1 billion, it is 1.0.

When expenditure is increased with no corresponding increase in tax rates, we say it is deficit financed.

Now compare the sizes of the multipliers for a balanced budget and a deficit-financed increase in government spending. With a deficit-financed increase in expenditure, there is no increase in tax rates and hence no consequent decrease in consumption expenditure to offset the increase in government expenditure. With a balanced budget increase in expenditure, however, the offsetting increase in tax rates and decrease in consumption does occur. Thus the balanced budget multiplier is much lower than the multiplier that relates the change in income to a deficit-financed increase in government expenditure with tax rates constant.

Lessons and Limitations

In this and the preceding chapter, we have discussed the determination of the four categories of aggregate expenditure and seen how they simultaneously determine equilibrium national income. The basic approach, which is the same no matter how many categories are considered, was first presented in Chapter 28 and has been recapitulated and extended in this chapter. The appendix to this chapter provides an algebraic exposition of the model.

Any factor that shifts one or more of the components of desired aggregate expenditure will change equilibrium national income, *at a given price level*.

In the following chapters we augment the income-expenditure model by allowing the price level to change, in both the short run and the long run. When prices change, real income will change by amounts different from those predicted by the simple multiplier. We shall see that changes in desired aggregate expenditure generally change both prices *and* real national income. This is why the simple multiplier, derived under the assumption that prices do not change, is too simple.

However, there are three ways in which the simple income-aggregate expenditure model developed here remains useful, even when prices are incorporated. First, the simple multiplier will continue to be a valuable starting place in calculating actual changes in national income in response to changes in autonomous expenditure. Second, no matter what the price level, the components of aggregate expenditure add up to national income in equilibrium. Third, no matter what the price level, desired aggregate expenditure must equal national income in equilibrium.

SUMMARY

1. Government spending is part of autonomous aggregate expenditure. Taxes minus transfer payments are called net taxes and affect aggregate expenditure indirectly. Taxes reduce disposable income, whereas transfers increase disposable income. Disposable income, in turn, determines desired consumption, according to the consumption function.

2. The budget balance is defined as government revenues minus government expenditures. When the result is positive, the budget is in surplus; when it is negative, the budget is in deficit.

3. Since desired imports increase as national income increases, desired net exports decrease as national income increases, other things being equal. Hence, the net export function is negatively sloped.

4. As in Chapter 28, national income is in equilibrium when desired aggregate expenditure, $C + I + G + (X - IM)$, equals national income.

5. Equilibrium national income is negatively related to the amount of tax revenue that is associated with each level of national income. The size of the multiplier is negatively associated with the income tax rate.

6. The government's plans are summarized by the government surplus function, which relates the level of the surplus (or deficit) to national income. Fiscal policy determines the position of the budget surplus function. The level of national income then determines the size of the actual deficit or surplus.

TOPICS FOR REVIEW

Taxes and net taxes

The budget balance

The budget surplus function

The net export function

The marginal propensity to spend

Calculation of the simple multiplier

Fiscal policy and equilibrium income

DISCUSSION QUESTIONS

1. State the implied impact on the *AE* curve and hence on equilibrium national income that relates to each of the following headlines.
   a. "Armed forces cut sharply."
   b. "Russia agrees to buy more Canadian wheat."
   c. "Major Canadian companies expected to cut capital outlays."
   d. "Provincial governments increase personal income-tax rates."
   e. "The United States imposes import restrictions on Canadian lumber products."

2. Massive and growing public debt has forced the federal and most provincial governments to try to reduce their budget deficits irrespective of the state of the economy. What fiscal measures would reduce their deficits? Why might a reduction of 10 percent in government expenditure accomplish much less than a 10 percent decrease in the deficit, at least in the first instance? What effect will this overriding need to cut deficits have for fiscal policy. What state of the economy would turn this deficit reducing stance into good fiscal policy by accident?

3. Between 1984 and 1993 the federal government's estimates of its own deficit in each coming year have usually been less than the estimates made by private sector economists. Much of the discrepancy seems to be accounted for by assumptions about the state of

the economy over the coming year. How do assumptions about the economy affect estimates of the budget deficit? Given these systematic differences, were the Feds likely to have been more or less optimistic about the state of the economy than private sector economists? Look at the data and see who was closer to being right.

4. During the recession of 1990–1991, net exports fell. Is this consistent with Canadian imports depending on Canadian income while Canadian exports are constant? Is it consistent with Canadian exports being autonomous because they depend on U.S. income? (Approximately 75 percent of Canadian exports go the United States). What do you think happened to U.S. income and the Canadian exchange rate?

5. The government allows contribution to a registered retirement savings plan (up to a given percentage of income) to be deducted from gross income when calculating taxable income. What is the effect of this on personal saving?

6. U.S. state governments are prohibited by law from running budget deficits. Compare this with Canadian provincial governments. What effect do such laws in the United States and their absence in Canada have on the shape of the government budget surplus functions in the two countries?

7. Classify each of the following government activities as government purchase (G) or transfer program (T).
   a. Welfare payments for the poor.
   b. Payments to teachers in public schools.
   c. Payments to teachers at military colleges.
   d. Payments on account of hospital and medical care.
   e. Public Health Service vaccination programs.

8. In the Federal election of 1993, the victorious Liberals promised to spend more money in their first year in order to increase national income and employment. They also said very little about their plans, if any, to reduce the budget deficit from its figure of over $35 billion. Look at the subsequent record of the government, which will be established after this book is published, to see what their actual fiscal policy has been.

APPENDIX A TO CHAPTER

29

Import Content of Autonomous Expenditure

To simplify the treatment in the text, we assumed that all imports were embodied in consumption goods. Some of them may be final consumption goods, such as Japanese cars, and others may be foreign-made components of consumption goods assembled in Canada—such as hard disks made in Singapore and incorporated into a Canadian computer. Formally, what we have assumed is that consumption is the only expenditure flow with any import content.

This simplifies the treatment by relating imports to national income but not to changes in autonomous expenditure. To understand the workings of the national income model, this is a useful simplification but it can be misleading. In this appendix, we consider the effects of dropping this simplification. The appendix is mainly for those who may be worried by the assumption used in the text.

Import Content of Expenditure Flows

In practise, all categories of expenditure have an import content. Consider, first, an additional $100 million of domestic investment expenditure. When such expenditure goes to building factories, many of the materials used in the factory will be imported. Thus, the expenditure on domestically produced goods and services rises by less than $100 million, while new imports account for the rest. The same is true of all other categories of expenditure. If the government embarks on a new road building program, only part of the expenditure will be a net addition to the domestic circular flow while the rest will leak out as expenditure on imports of many road-building materials. Even exports have a large import content. When Canadian firms sell an extra $100 million of new exports, this represents an injection of less than $100 million into the Canadian circular flow. The rest will be expenditures on imports of such things as components

made in Taiwan and Indonesia that end up in the exported good.

Since we assumed in the text that only consumption expenditure had any import content, none of the categories of autonomous expenditure had any such content. The results derived in the text are exactly correct for this case. To apply it to the real world, we need to look in more detail at the import content of each expenditure flow.

Aggregate Expenditure and Import Content

The aggregate expenditure function is

$$Y = C + I + G + (X - IM).$$

We handle the import content of consumption by allowing both C and IM to depend on Y. Letting c and m be the marginal propensities to spend and to import, we rewrite the above equation as:

$$Y = cY + I + G + (X - mY).$$

Now we allow for the import content of autonomous expenditure by separating it out in each case:

$$Y = cY + (I - I_m) + (G - G_m) \\ + [(X - X_m) - mY],$$

where I_m, G_m and X_m are the import contents of investment expenditure, government expenditure, and exports.

There are two ways to handle the analysis from here on. First, we can deal with the terms in the parentheses, which means that each injection is defined as net of its import content. This was the approach taken by Professor James Meade in his famous treatises written earlier in this century. The main problem with this approach is that the magnitudes net of import content are not easy to relate to the published statistics. It is also not easy to use a model defined in these terms to deal with the effects of changes in autonomous expenditure on the trade balance.

Second, we can deal with gross spending in each category and gather up all the import-content terms into a single term for autonomous imports:

$$Y = cY + I + G + [X - (Z + mY)]$$

where Z is the autonomous component of imports equal to $I_m + G_m + X_m$. The main problem with this approach is that every time any element of autonomous expenditure changes, Z also changes by the import content of that autonomous expenditure.

In more advanced work, some decision must be made on how to handle the import contents of all expenditure flows when a model is constructed. In elementary treatments, it is simpler to avoid these complex problems of modeling by making the simplifying assumption used in the text that only consumption expenditure has an import content.

Multipliers of Less than Unity

For most purposes of understanding the basic working of the model of the determination of national income, the assumption used in the text is harmless. The one place in which it can be misleading, however, is in making us think that the multiplier is larger than it really is. Indeed, once an import content to autonomous expenditure flows is admitted, there is no need for the multiplier to exceed unity *where the change in injections is measured to include its import content.*

Consider, for example, a situation in which the government increases expenditure by $1 billion on projects that have an import content of 50 percent (not an impossibly high figure in Canada). This means that the initial injection into the domestic circular flow is only $500 million—the rest goes to imports. If the multiplier is 1.8, the final change in national income will be $900, which is less than the original increase in government expenditure!

The above result does not contradict the theory. The theory refers to an injection into the *domestic circular flow,* which is clearly the *domestic content* of any increased expenditure. Once the import content is admitted, the theory predicts that the multiplier must exceed unity when applied to the domestic content of any injection of new expenditure but not to the gross amount.

APPENDIX B TO CHAPTER

29

The Income-Expenditure Model Treated Algebraically

We start with the definition of desired aggregate expenditure:

$$AE = C + I + G + (X - IM) \qquad [1]$$

For each component of *AE,* we write down a behavioural function.

$$C = a + bY_d \text{ (consumption function)} \qquad [2]$$

where *a* is autonomous consumption spending and *b* is the marginal propensity to consume.

$$I = I_0 \qquad [3]$$
$$G = G_0 \qquad [4]$$
$$X = X_0 \qquad [5]$$
$$IM = mY \text{ (import function)} \qquad [6]$$

where *m* is the marginal propensity to import. (Obviously, the "behavioural" functions for investment, government purchases, and exports are very simple: These are all assumed to be independent of the level of national income.)

Before deriving aggregate expenditure, we need to determine the relationship between national income *(Y)* and disposable income *(Y_d)*, because it is Y_d that determines desired consumption expenditure. Y_d is defined as income after net tax collections, where net tax collections are total tax collections minus government transfer payments. (Government transfers to households have exactly the same effect as tax reductions. They put money in the hands of the private sector without directly using goods and services.) In Chapter 29 we examined a very simple linear income tax of the form $T = tY$. More generally, we might imagine autonomous net taxes T_0 and induced net taxes tY, so

the tax function is given by:

$$T = T_0 + tY \qquad [7]$$

Taxes must be subtracted from national income to obtain disposable income,

$$Y_d = Y - T_0 - tY = Y(1 - t) - T_0 \qquad [8]$$

Substituting Equation 8 into the consumption function allows us to write consumption as a function of national income.

$$C = a - bT_0 + b(1 - t)Y \qquad [9]$$

Notice that autonomous consumption now has two parts, *a* and $-bT_0$, where the latter term is the effect of autonomous taxes on consumption.

Now we can add up all of the components of desired aggregate expenditure, substituting Equations 3, 4, 5, 6, and 9 into Equation 1:

$$AE = a - bT_0 + b(1 - t)Y + I_0 + G_0$$
$$+ X_0 - mY \qquad [10]$$

In equilibrium, aggregate expenditure must equal income, so, as an equilibrium condition,

$$AE = Y \qquad [11]$$

Substitute [11] into [10]:

$$Y = a - bT_0 + b(1 - t)Y + I_0$$
$$+ G_0 + X_0 - mY \qquad [12]$$

Group all the terms in *Y* on the right-hand side, and subtract them from both sides:

$$Y = Y[b(1 - t) - m] + a - bT_0 + I_0 + G_0 + X_0 \tag{13}$$

$$Y - Y[b(1 - t) - m] = a - bT_0 + I_0 + G_0 + X_0 \tag{14}$$

Notice that $[b(1 - t) - m]$ is exactly the marginal propensity to spend out of national income, defined earlier as z. When national income goes up by a dollar, only $1 - t$ dollars go into disposable income, and only b of that gets spent on consumption. Additionally, m gets spent on imports, which are not expenditure on national income. Thus, $b(1 - t) - m$ gets spent on domestic output.

Substituting $z = b(1 - t) - m$ and solving Equation 14 for equilibrium Y yields

$$Y = \frac{a - bT_0 + I_0 + G_0 + X_0}{1 - z} \tag{15}$$

Notice that the numerator of Equation 15 is autonomous expenditure, A (see Box 28–2). Thus, Equation 15 can be rewritten as

$$Y = \frac{A}{1 - z} \tag{16}$$

Notice also that if autonomous expenditure rises by some amount ΔA, Y will rise by $\Delta A/(1 - z)$. Thus, the simple multiplier is $1/(1 - z)$.

The Algebra Illustrated

The numerical example that was carried through Chapters 28 and 29 can be used to illustrate the preceding exposition. In that example, the behavioural equations are

$$C = 100 + 0.8Y_d \tag{17}$$

$$I = 250 \tag{18}$$

$$G = 170 \tag{19}$$

$$X - IM = 240 - 0.1Y \tag{20}$$

$$T = 0.1Y \tag{21}$$

T_0 is 0, so, from Equation 8, disposable income is given by $Y(1 - t) = 0.9Y$. Substituting this into Equation 17 yields

$$C = 100 + 0.72Y_d$$

as in Equation 9.

Now, recalling that in equilibrium $AE = Y$, we add up all the components of AE and set the sum equal to Y, as in Equation 12:

$$Y = 100 + 0.72Y + 250 + 170 + 240 - 0.1Y \tag{22}$$

Collecting terms yields

$$Y = 760 + 0.62Y \tag{23}$$

Subtracting $0.62Y$ from both sides gives

$$0.38Y = 760 \tag{24}$$

and dividing through by 0.38, we have

$$Y = 760/0.38 = 2,000 \tag{25}$$

This can also be derived by using Equation 16. Autonomous expenditure is 760, and z, the marginal propensity to spend out of national income, is 0.62. Hence, $(1 - z)$ is 0.38. Thus, from Equation 16, equilibrium income is $760/(0.38) = 2,000$, which is exactly the equilibrium we obtained in Table 29-4.

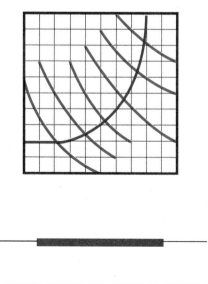

30

National Income and the Price Level in the Short Run

In the preceding two chapters, we have developed a model of income determination in an economy with constant prices. In a real economy, of course, prices are changing all the time. On the supply side, the prices of imported materials used by firms and households change frequently and sometimes dramatically, as when oil prices soared during 1973–1974 and 1979–1980. On the demand side, a boom in the United States increases Canadian exports to the United States. As we discussed in Chapter 29, a domestic tax cut can lead to an increase in spending; the event actually occurred in the United States in the early 1980s.

Virtually all shocks to the economy affect *both* national income *and* the price level; that is, they have both real and nominal effects, at least initially. To understand these effects, we need to drop the assumption that the price level is constant and also to develop some further tools, called the *aggregate demand curve* and *aggregate supply curve*.

We make the transition to a variable price level in two steps. First, we study the consequences for national income of *exogenous* changes in the price level—changes that happen for reasons that are not explained by our model of the economy. Then we use our model to *explain* movements in both national income *and* the price level.

Exogenous Changes in the Price Level

What happens to equilibrium national income when the price changes for some exogenous reason, such as a rise in the price of imported raw materials? To find out, we need to understand how the change affects desired aggregate expenditure.

Shifts in the AE Curve

There is one key result that we need to establish: A rise in the price level *shifts* the aggregate expenditure curve downward, while a fall in the price level *shifts* it upward. In other words, the price level and desired aggregate expenditure are negatively related to each other. A major part of the explanation lies with how the change in the price level affects desired consumption expenditure and desired net exports.[1]

---

[1]The effect on investment expenditure is also important, and it works in the same direction as the change in consumption and net exports. This is discussed in Chapter 33.

Changes in Consumption

The link between a change in the price level and changes in desired consumption is provided by wealth. It is in two parts. The first part is provided by the effect of changes in the price level on the wealth of the private sector.

Much of the private sector's total wealth is held in the form of assets with a fixed nominal money value. One obvious example is money itself—cash and bank deposits. Other examples include many kinds of debt, such as treasury bills and company bonds.[2] When a bill or a bond matures, the owner is repaid a stated sum of money. What that money can buy—its real value—depends on the price level. The higher the price level, the less the given sum of money can purchase. For this reason, a rise in the domestic price level lowers the real value of all assets that are denominated in money units. How does this affect individuals?

An individual who holds a bond has loaned money to the individual who issued it. When the real value of the asset falls, the individual who holds it has her wealth reduced. However, the individual who issued the bond has his real wealth increased. This is because the face value of the bond represents less purchasing power as a result of the rise in the price level. So the individual who has to repay the bond will part with less purchasing power to do so and so has more wealth.

A change in the price level affects the wealth of holders of assets denominated in money terms in exactly the opposite way as it affects the wealth of those who issued the asset.

Inside assets. An *inside asset* is one that is issued by someone (an individual or a firm) in the private sector and also held by someone in the private sector. It follows that for inside assets, a rise in the price level lowers the real wealth of an asset holder but raises the real wealth of the asset issuer, who will have to part with less purchasing power when the bond is redeemed. With inside assets, therefore, the wealth changes are exactly offsetting. A rise in the price level lowers the real wealth of the person who owns any asset that is denominated in money but it raises the real wealth of the person who must redeem the asset.

Outside assets. *Outside assets* are those held by someone in the domestic private sector but issued by some entity outside of that sector. In practise, this usually means the government or any foreign issuer. In this case, the only private-sector wealth holders to experience wealth changes when the price level changes are the holders of the outside assets. There are no offsetting private-sector wealth changes for the issuers of the assets, since they are not in the private sector. It follows that a change in the price level does cause a change in net private wealth held in outside assets denominated in nominal money units. A rise in the price level lowers the real wealth of holders of these assets.[3]

A change in the price level causes no net change in the wealth of the private sector with respect to inside assets, but it does cause a change with respect to outside assets, since the issuers are not in the private sector.

The second link in the chain running from changes in the price level to changes in desired consumption is provided by the relationship between wealth and consumption that we stressed in Chapter 28 (see Figure 28-2 on page 570). Whenever households suffer a decrease in their wealth, they increase their saving so as to restore their wealth to the level that they desire for such purposes as retirement. At any level of income, an increase in desired saving, of course, implies a reduction in desired consumption. Conversely, whenever households get an increase in their wealth, they reduce their saving and consume more, causing an upward shift in the function that relates desired consumption expenditure and national income.

A rise in the domestic price level lowers the real value of total private-sector wealth by lowering the real value of outside assets de-

---

[2] These and other credit instruments are discussed in detail in Box 32-2, on page 662. In the meantime, all you need to know is that a bill is evidence of a short-term loan, typically of 3 months' duration, while a bond is evidence of a longer-term loan that may run for 1–2 to 20–25 years.

[3] We are assuming that taxpayers do not include in their wealth calculations the real value of future tax liabilities. Taxpayers must pay taxes to service the national debt, and when a rise in the price level lowers its real value, it also lowers the real value of future tax liabilities by exactly the same amount. For the moment we ignore this possible offsetting change, which we briefly discuss in Chapter 37.

nominated in money units. This leads to a fall in desired consumption and this, in turn, implies a downward shift in the aggregate expenditure curve. A fall in the domestic price level leads to a rise in wealth and desired consumption and thus to an upward shift in the aggregate expenditure curve.

We have concentrated here on the direct effect of the change in wealth on desired consumption expenditure. There is also an indirect effect that operates through the interest rate. Although this effect is potentially very powerful, we cannot study it until we have studied the macroeconomic role of money and interest rates. Further discussion of this point must therefore be postponed until Chapter 33.[4]

Changes in Net Exports

When the domestic price level rises, Canadian goods become more expensive relative to foreign goods. As we saw in Chapter 29, this change in relative prices causes Canadian consumers to reduce their purchases of Canadian goods, which now have become relatively more expensive, and to increase their purchases of foreign goods, which now have become relatively less expensive. At the same time, consumers in other countries reduce their purchases of the now relatively expensive Canadian goods. We saw in Chapter 29 that these changes can be summarized as a downward shift in the net export function.

A rise in the domestic price level shifts the net export function downward, which means a downward shift in the aggregate expenditure curve. A fall in the domestic price level

---

[4]Here is a brief summary of what is involved. When the price level rises, firms and households need to cover their increased money expenses between one pay day and the next. This means that they need to hold more money on average. The increased demand for money bids up the price that must be paid to borrow money (the interest rate). Firms that borrow money to build plants and to purchase equipment and households that borrow money to buy consumer goods and housing respond to rising interest rates by choosing to spend less on a host of items, such as capital goods, housing, automobiles, and many other durable goods. This means that there is a decrease in the aggregate demand for the nation's output.

shifts the net export function and the aggregate expenditure curves upward.

In simple language, if Canadian goods and services become more expensive, less of them will be bought by foreigners, so total desired expenditure on Canadian output will fall; if Canadian goods and services become cheaper, more will be bought, and total desired expenditure on them will rise.[5]

Changes in Equilibrium Income

Because it causes downward shifts in both the net export function and the consumption function, a rise in the price level causes a downward shift in the aggregate desired expenditure curve, as shown in Figure 30-1. This figure also allows us to reconfirm what we already know from Chapter 29: When the *AE* curve shifts downward, the equilibrium level of national income falls.

Because a rise in the domestic price level causes the aggregate expenditure curve to shift downward, it reduces equilibrium national income.

Now suppose that there is a fall in the price level. Because this is the opposite of the case that we have just studied, we can summarize the two key effects briefly. First, Canadian goods become relatively cheaper internationally, so net exports rise. Second, the purchasing power of some existing assets that are denominated in money terms is increased, so households spend more. The resulting increase in desired expenditure on Canadian goods causes the *AE* curve to shift upward and hence raises equilibrium national income. This is also shown in Figure 30-1.

Because a fall in the domestic price level causes the aggregate expenditure curve to shift upward, it increases equilibrium national income.

---

[5]This assumes that the price elasticity of demand for traded goods exceeds unity. This standard assumption in the study of international trade is discussed further in Chapter 39.

FIGURE 30-1
Aggregate Expenditure and the Price Level

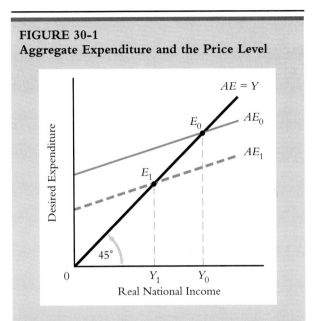

Changes in the price level cause the AE curve to shift and thus cause equilibrium national income to change. At the initial price level, the AE curve is given by the solid line AE_0, and hence equilibrium national income is Y_0. An increase in the price level reduces desired aggregate expenditure and thus causes the AE curve to shift downward to the dashed line, AE_1. As a result, equilibrium national income falls to Y_1.

Starting with the dashed line, AE_1, a fall in the price level increases desired aggregate expenditure, shifting the AE curve up to AE_0 and raising equilibrium national income to Y_1.

The Aggregate Demand Curve

We now know from the behaviour underlying the aggregate expenditure curve that the price level and real national income are negatively related to each other; that is, a change in the price level changes equilibrium national income in the opposite direction. This negative relationship can be shown in an important new concept, called the *aggregate demand curve*.

Recall that the AE curve relates national income to desired expenditure for a given price level, plotting income on the horizontal axis. The **aggregate demand (AD) curve** relates equilibrium national income to the price level, again plotting

income on the horizontal axis. Because the horizontal axes of both the AE and the AD curves measure real national income, the two curves can be placed one above the other so that the level of national income on each can be compared directly. This is shown in Figure 30-2.

Now let us see how the AD curve is derived. Given a value of the price level, equilibrium national income is determined in part (i) of Figure 30-2 at the point where the AE curve crosses the 45° line. In part (ii) of Figure 30-2, the combination of the equilibrium level of national income and the corresponding value of the price level is plotted, giving one point on the AD curve.

When the price level changes, the AE curve shifts, for the reasons just seen. The new position of the AE curve gives rise to a new equilibrium level of national income that is associated with the new price level. This determines a second point on the AD curve, as shown in part (ii) of Figure 30-2.

Any change in the price level leads to a new AE curve and hence to a new level of equilibrium income. Each combination of equilibrium income and its associated price level becomes a particular point on the AD curve.

Note that, because the AD curve relates equilibrium national income to the price level, changes in the price level that cause *shifts in* the AE curve cause *movements along* the AD curve. A movement along the AD curve thus traces out the response of equilibrium income to a change in the price level.

The aggregate demand curve shows for each price level the associated level of equilibrium national income for which aggregate desired expenditure equals total income.

The Slope of the AD Curve

Figure 30-2 provides us with sufficient information to establish that the AD curve is negatively sloped.

1. A rise in the price level causes the aggregate expenditure curve to shift downward and hence leads to a movement upward and to the left along the AD curve, reflecting a fall in the equilibrium level of national income.

FIGURE 30-2
The *AD* Curve and the *AE* Curve

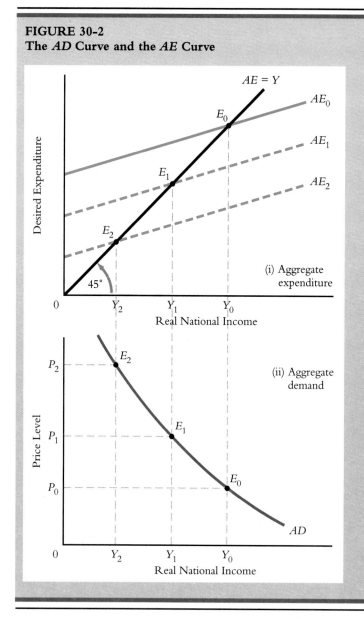

(i) Aggregate expenditure

(ii) Aggregate demand

Equilibrium income is determined by the *AE* curve for each given price level; the level of income and its associated price level are then plotted to yield a point on the *AD* curve. When the price level is P_0, the *AE* curve is AE_0, and hence equilibrium national income is Y_0, as shown in part (i). (This reproduces the initial equilibrium from Figure 30-1.) Plotting Y_0 against P_0 yields the point E_0 on the *AD* curve in part (ii).

An increase in the price level to P_1 causes AE_0 in part (i) to shift downward to AE_1 and thus causes equilibrium national income to fall to Y_1. Plotting this new, lower level of national income, Y_1, against the higher price level, P_1, yields a second point, E_1, on the *AD* curve in part (ii). A further increase in the price level to P_2 causes the *AE* curve in part (i) to shift downward further, to AE_2, and thus causes equilibrium national income to fall further, to Y_2. Plotting Y_2 against P_2, yields a third point, E_2, on the *AD* curve in part (ii).

Thus, a change in the price level causes a shift in the *AE* curve in part (i) and a movement along the *AD* curve in part (ii).

2. A fall in the price level causes the aggregate expenditure curve to shift upward and hence leads to a movement downward and to the right along the *AD* curve, reflecting a rise in the equilibrium level of national income.

In Chapter 4, we saw that demand curves for individual goods such as carrots and automobiles are negatively sloped. However, the reasons for the negative slope of the *AD* curve are different from the reasons for the negative slope of individual demand curves that are used in microeconomics; this important point is discussed further in Box 30-1.

Points off the *AD* Curve

The *AD* curve depicts combinations of national income and the price level that give equilibrium between aggregate desired expenditure and actual output in the sense that aggregate desired expenditure equals actual output. These points are said to be *consistent* with expenditure decisions.

Box 30-1

The Shape of the Aggregate Demand Curve

In Chapter 4, we studied the demand curves for individual products. It is tempting to think that the properties of the aggregate demand curve arise from the same behaviour that gives rise to those individual demand curves. Unfortunately, life is not so simple. Let us see why we cannot take such an approach.

If we assume that we can obtain a negatively sloping aggregate demand curve in the same manner that we derived negatively sloping individual market demand curves, we would be committing the fallacy of composition. This is to assume that what is correct for the parts must be correct for the whole.

Consider a simple example of the fallacy. An art collector can go into the market and add to her private collection of nineteenth-century French paintings provided only that she has enough money. However, the fact that any one person can do this does not mean that everyone could do so simultaneously. The world's stock of nineteenth-century French paintings is fixed. All of us cannot do what any one of us with enough money can do.

How does the fallacy of composition relate to demand curves? An individual demand curve describes a situation in which the price of one commodity changes while the prices of all other commodities and consumers' money incomes are constant. Such an individual demand curve is neg-

atively sloped for two reasons. First, as the price of the commodity rises, each consumer's given money income will buy a smaller *total* amount of goods, so a smaller quantity of each commodity will be bought, other things being equal. Second, as the price of the commodity rises, consumers buy less of it and more of the now relatively cheaper substitutes.

The first reason has no application to the aggregate demand curve, which relates the total demand for all output to the price level. All prices and total output are changing as we move along the *AD* curve. Because the value of output determines income, consumers' money incomes will also be changing along this curve.

The second reason does apply, but in a limited way, to the aggregate demand curve. A rise in the price level entails a rise in *all* domestic commodity prices. Thus, there is no incentive to substitute among domestic commodities whose prices do not change relative to each other. However, it does give rise, as we saw earlier in this chapter, to some substitution between domestic and foreign goods and services. Domestic goods and services rise in price relative to imported goods and services, and the switch in expenditure will lower desired aggregate expenditure on domestic output and hence will lower equilibrium national income.

The national income given by any point on the aggregate demand curve is such that, *if* **that level of output is produced, aggregate desired expenditure at the *given price level* will exactly equal the output.**

Points to the left of the *AD* curve show combinations of national income and the price level that cause aggregate desired expenditure to exceed out-

put. There is thus pressure for income to rise, because firms could sell more than current output. Points to the right of the *AD* curve show combinations of national income and the price level for which aggregate desired expenditure is less than current income. There is thus pressure for income to fall, because firms will not be able to sell all of their current output. These relationships are illustrated in Figure 30-3.

FIGURE 30-3
The Relationship Between the *AE* and *AD* Curves

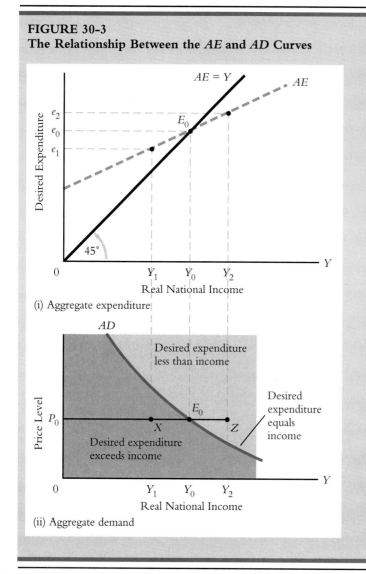

(i) Aggregate expenditure

(ii) Aggregate demand

The *AD* curve plots the price level against the level of national income consistent with expenditure decisions at that price level. With the price level P_0, equilibrium national income is Y_0, shown by the intersection of *AE* and the 45° line at E_0 in part (i) and by the point E_0 on the *AD* curve in part (ii).

With the price level constant at P_0, consider a level of national income of Y_1, which is less than Y_0. As can be seen in part (i), if national income were equal to Y_1, desired aggregate expenditure would be e_1, which is greater than Y_1. Hence, Y_1 is not an equilibrium level of national income when the price level is P_0, and the combination (P_0, Y_1) is not a point on the *AD* curve in part (ii), as shown by point *X*.

Now consider a level of national income of Y_2, which is greater than Y_0. As can be seen in part (i), if national income were equal to Y_2, desired aggregate expenditure would be e_2, which is less than Y_2. Hence, Y_2 is not an equilibrium level of national income when the price level is P_0, and the combination (P_0, Y_2) is not a point on the *AD* curve in part (ii), as shown by point *Z*.

Repeating the same analysis for each given price level tells us that, for all points to the left of the *AD* curve (dark-shaded area), income is tending to rise, because desired expenditure exceeds income, whereas, for all points to the right of the *AD* curve (light-shaded area), income is tending to fall, because desired aggregate expenditure is less than income.

Shifts in the *AD* Curve

Because the *AD* curve plots equilibrium national income as a function of the price level, anything that alters equilibrium national income *at a given price level* must shift the *AD* curve. In other words, any change (other than a change in the price level) that causes the *aggregate expenditure curve* to shift will also cause the *AD* curve to shift. (Recall that a change in the price level causes *a movement along* the *AD* curve.) Such a shift is called an *aggregate demand shock.*

For example, in the early 1980s, changes in the U.S. tax laws led to an increase in the amount of U.S. consumption expenditure associated with each level of U.S. national income. This was an expansionary demand shock that shifted the U.S. *AD* curve to the right. It spilled over into Canada in terms of a shift in the Canadian export function. Increased U.S. expenditure on consumption meant more expenditure on imports that directly and indirectly enter into consumption. So Canada also received an aggregate demand shock. This was ultimately due to U.S. policy but was transmitted through a rise in U.S. consumption expenditure to a rise in U.S. imports to a rise in Canadian exports and then to Canadian aggregate demand.

Using our new concepts, the conclusions on page 577 now can be restated as follows:

A rise in the amount of desired consumption, investment, government, or net export expenditure that is associated with each level of national income shifts the *AD* curve to the right. A fall in any of these expenditures shifts the *AD* curve to the left.

The Simple Multiplier and the *AD* Curve

We saw in Chapter 29 that the simple multiplier measures the magnitude of the *change* in equilibrium national income in response to a change in autonomous expenditure when the price level is constant. It follows that this multiplier gives the magnitude of the *horizontal* shift in the *AD* curve in response to a change in autonomous expenditure. This is shown in Figure 30-4.

The simple multiplier measures the horizontal shift in the *AD* curve in response to a change in autonomous expenditure.

If the price level remains constant and firms are willing to supply everything that is demanded at that price level, the simple multiplier will also show the change in equilibrium income that will occur in response to a change in autonomous expenditure.

Equilibrium National Income and Price Level

So far we have explained how the equilibrium level of national income is determined *when the price level is taken as given* and how that equilibrium changes as the price level is changed exogenously. We are now ready to take an important further step: adding an *explanation* for the behaviour of the price level. To do this, we need to take account of the supply decisions of firms.

The Aggregate Supply Curve

Aggregate supply refers to the total output of goods and services that firms wish to produce, assuming that they can sell all that they wish to sell. Aggregate supply thus depends on the decisions of firms to use workers and all other inputs in order to produce goods and services to sell to households, governments, and other firms, as well as for export.

An *aggregate supply curve* relates aggregate supply to the price level. It is necessary to define two types of such curves. The **short-run aggregate supply (SRAS) curve** relates the price level to the quantity that firms would like to produce and to sell *on the assumption that the prices of all factors of production remain constant.* The *long-run aggregate supply (LRAS) curve*, which we will define more fully in the next chapter, relates the price level to desired sales after the economy has fully adjusted to that price level. For the remainder of this chapter, we confine our attention to the *SRAS* curve.

The Slope of the Short-Run Aggregate Supply Curve

To study the slope of the *SRAS* curve, we need to see how costs are related to output and then how prices and outputs are related.

Costs and output. Suppose that firms wish to increase their outputs above current levels. What will this do to their costs per unit of output—often called their **unit costs**? *The short-run aggregate supply curve is drawn on the assumption that the prices of all factors of production that firms use, such as labour, remain constant.* This does not, however, mean that unit costs will be constant. As output increases, less efficient standby plants may have to be used, and less efficient workers may have to be hired, while existing workers may have to be paid overtime rates for additional work. For these and other similar reasons, unit costs will tend to rise as output rises, even when input prices are constant.[6]

---

[6]Readers who have studied microeconomics will recognise the law of diminishing returns as one reason why costs rise in the short run as firms squeeze more output out of a fixed quantity of capital equipment.

FIGURE 30-4
The Simple Multiplier and Shifts in the *AD* Curve

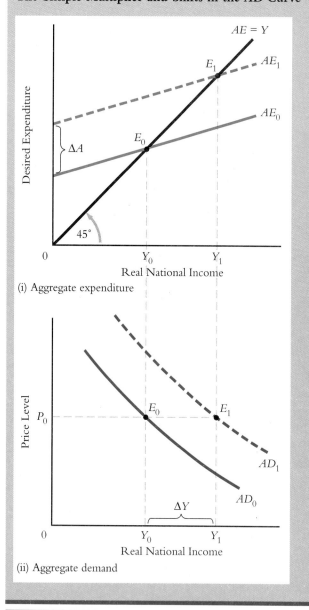

(i) Aggregate expenditure

(ii) Aggregate demand

A change in autonomous expenditure changes equilibrium national income for any given price level, and the simple multiplier measures the resulting horizontal shift in the aggregate demand curve. The original desired expenditure curve is AE_0 in part (i). Equilibrium is at E_0, with national income Y_0 at price level P_0. This yields point E_0 on the curve AD_0 in part (ii).

The AE curve in part (i) then shifts upward from AE_0 to AE_1, due to an increase in autonomous expenditure of ΔA. Equilibrium income now rises to Y_1, with the price level still constant at P_0. Thus, the AD curve in part (ii) shifts to the right to point E_1, indicating the higher equilibrium income Y_1, associated with the same price level P_0. The magnitude of the shift, ΔY, is given by the simple multiplier.

A fall in autonomous expenditure can be analysed by shifting the AE curve from AE_1 to AE_0, which shifts the AD curve from AD_1 to AD_0 at the price level of P_0. The equilibrium value of national income falls from Y_1 to Y_0.

Unit costs and output are positively related.

Prices and output. To consider the relationship between price and output, we need to consider firms that sell in two distinct types of markets: those in which firms are price takers and those in which firms are price setters. Some industries, including

those that produce most basic industrial materials and some energy products, contain many individual firms. In these cases, each one is too small to influence the market price, which is set by the overall forces of demand and supply. Each firm must accept whatever price is set on the open market and adjust its output to that price. The firms are said to be *price takers* and *quantity adjusters*. When the market price changes, these firms will react by altering their production.

Because their unit costs rise with output, price-taking firms only produce more if price rises and will produce less if price falls.

Many other industries, including most of those that produce manufactured products, contain so few firms that each can influence market prices. Most such firms sell products that differ from one another, although all are similar enough to be thought of as the single commodity produced by one industry. For example, no two kinds of automobiles are the same, but all automobiles are sufficiently alike so that we have no trouble talking about the automobile industry and the commodity, automobiles. In such cases, each firm must quote a price at which it is prepared to sell each of its products; that is, the firm is a *price setter*. If the demand for the output of price-setting firms increases sufficiently to take their outputs into the range in which their unit costs rise (e.g., because overtime is worked and standby plants are brought into production), these firms will not increase their outputs unless they can pass at least some of these extra costs on through higher prices. When the demand falls, they will reduce output, and competition among them will tend to cause a reduction in prices whenever their unit costs fall.

Price-setting firms will increase their prices when they expand output into the range in which unit costs are rising.

This is the basic behaviour of firms in response to the changes in demand and prices when factor prices are constant, and it explains the slope of the *SRAS* curve, such as the one shown in Figure 30-5.

The actions of both price-taking and price-setting firms cause the price level and total output to be positively associated with each other; the graphical expression of this relationship is the positively sloped short-run aggregate supply curve.

Shifts in the *SRAS* Curve

Shifts in the *SRAS* curve, which are shown in Figure 30-6, are called *aggregate supply shocks*. Two

FIGURE 30-5
A Short-Run Aggregate Supply Curve

The *SRAS* curve is positively sloped. The positive slope of the *SRAS* curve shows that with the prices of labour and other inputs given, total desired output and the price level will be positively associated. Thus, a rise in the price level from P_0 to P_1 will be associated with a rise in the quantity of total output supplied, from Y_0 to Y_1.

Notice that the slope of the *SRAS* curve is fairly flat at low levels of income and very steep at higher levels. Box 30-3 provides a detailed explanation of this characteristic shape. Briefly, at low levels of income, where there is excess capacity in the economy, output can be increased with little change in cost. As the economy approaches potential income (somewhere between Y_0 and Y_1 in the figure), it becomes very difficult to increase real output in response to demand changes, and increased demand will mainly generate higher prices.

sources of aggregate supply shocks are of particular importance: changes in the price of inputs and increases in productivity.

Changes in input prices. Factor prices are held constant along the *SRAS* curve, and when they change, the curve shifts. If factor prices rise, firms will find the profitability of their current production reduced. For any given level of output to be produced, an increase in the price level will be required. If prices do not rise, firms will react by decreasing production. For the economy as a whole, this means that there will be less output at each price level than before the increase in factor prices.

**FIGURE 30-6
Shifts in the *SRAS* Curve**

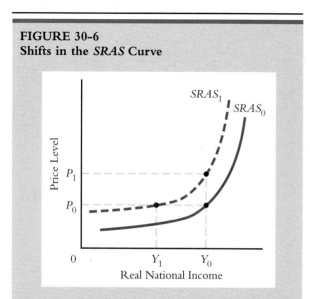

A shift to the left of the *SRAS* curve reflects a decrease in supply; a shift to the right reflects an increase in supply. Starting from P_0, Y_0 on $SRAS_0$, suppose there is an increase in input prices. At price level P_0 only Y_1 would be produced. Alternatively, to get output Y_0 would require a rise to price level P_1. The new supply curve is $SRAS_1$, which may be viewed as being above and to the left of $SRAS_0$. An increase in supply, caused, say, by a decrease in input prices, would shift the *SRAS* curve downward and to the right, from $SRAS_1$ to $SRAS_0$.

Thus, if factor prices rise, the *SRAS* curve shifts upward. (Notice that when a positively sloped curve shifts upward, indicating that any given quantity is associated with a higher price level, it also shifts to the left, indicating that any given price level is associated with a lower quantity.)

Similarly, a fall in factor prices causes the *SRAS* curve to shift downward (and to the right). This increase in supply means that more will be produced and offered for sale at each price level.[7]

Increases in productivity. If labour productivity rises, meaning that each worker can produce more,

the unit costs of production will fall as long as wage rates do not rise sufficiently to offset the productivity rise fully. Lower costs generally lead to lower prices. Competing firms cut prices in attempts to raise their market shares, and the net result of such competition is that the fall in production costs is accompanied by a fall in prices.

Because the same output is sold at a lower price, this causes a downward shift in the *SRAS* curve. This shift is an increase in supply, as illustrated in Figure 30-6.

A rightward shift in the *SRAS* curve, brought about, for example, by an increase in productivity with no increase in factor prices, means that firms will be willing to produce more national income with no increase in the price level. This result has been the object of many government policies that seek to encourage increases in productivity.

A change in either factor prices or productivity will shift the *SRAS* curve, because any given output will be supplied at a different price level than previously. An increase in factor prices or a decrease in productivity shifts the *SRAS* curve to the left; an increase in productivity or a decrease in factor prices shifts it to the right.

Macroeconomic Equilibrium

We have now reached our objective: We are ready to see how both real national income and the price level are simultaneously determined by the interaction of aggregate demand and aggregate supply.

The equilibrium values of national output and the price level occur at the intersection of the *AD* and *SRAS* curves, as shown by the pair Y_0 and P_0 that arise at point E_0 in Figure 30-7. We describe the combination of national income and price level that is on both the *AD* and the *SRAS* curves as a *macroeconomic equilibrium,* and its determination in Figure 30-7 should be studied carefully at this point.

To see why the pair of points, (Y_0, P_0), is the only macroeconomic equilibrium, first consider what Figure 30-7 shows would happen if the price level were below P_0. At this lower price level, the desired output of firms, as given by the *SRAS* curve, is less than desired aggregate expenditure at that level of output. The excess desired aggregate

---

[7]Note that, for either the *AD* or the *SRAS* curve, a shift to the right means an increase, and a shift to the left means a decrease. Upward and downward shifts, however, have different meanings for the two curves. An upward shift of the *AD* curve reflects an increase in aggregate demand, but an upward shift in the *SRAS* curve reflects a decrease in aggregate supply.

FIGURE 30-7
Macroeconomic Equilibrium

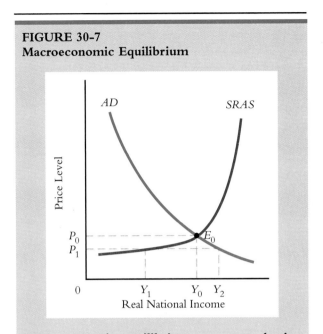

Macroeconomic equilibrium occurs at the intersection of the AD and SRAS curves and determines the equilibrium values for national income and the price level. Given the AD and SRAS curves in the figure, macroeconomic equilibrium occurs at E_0, with national income equal to Y_0 and the price level equal to P_0. At P_0 the desired output of firms, as given by the SRAS curve, is equal to the level of national income that is consistent with expenditure decisions, as given by the AD curve.

If the price level were equal to P_1, less than P_0, the desired output of firms, given by the SRAS curve, would be Y_1. However, at P_1, the level of output that is consistent with expenditure decisions, given by the AD curve, would by Y_2, greater than Y_1. Hence, when the price level is P_1, or any other level less than P_0, the desired output of firms will be less than the level of national income that is consistent with expenditure decisions.

Similarly, for any price level above P_0, the desired output of firms, given by the SRAS curve, would exceed the level of output that is consistent with expenditure decisions, given by the AD curve.

The only price level where the supply decisions of firms are consistent with desired expenditure is a macroeconomic equilibrium. At P_0, firms wish to produce Y_0. When they do so, they generate a national income of Y_0; when income is Y_0, decision makers wish to spend exactly Y_0, thus purchasing the nation's output. Hence, all decisions are consistent with each other.

expenditure will cause prices to be bid up, and national income will increase along the SRAS curve. Hence, there can be no macroeconomic *equilibrium* when the price level is below P_0.

Similarly, Figure 30-7 shows that, when the price level is above P_0, the behaviour underlying the SRAS and AD curves is not consistent. In this case, producers will wish to supply more than the level of output that is demanded at that price level. If firms were to produce their desired levels of output, desired expenditure would not be large enough to purchase everything that would be produced.

Only at the combination of national income and price level given by the intersection of the SRAS and AD curves are spending (demand) behaviour and supply behaviour consistent.

When the price level is less than its equilibrium value, expenditure behaviour is consistent with a level of national income that is greater than the desired output of firms. When the price level is greater than its equilibrium value, expenditure behaviour is consistent with a level of national income that is less than the desired output of firms.

Macroeconomic equilibrium thus requires that two conditions be satisfied. The first is familiar to us because it comes from Chapters 28 and 29: At the prevailing price level, desired aggregate expenditure must be equal to national income, which means that households are just willing to buy all that is produced. The AD curve is constructed in such a way that this condition holds everywhere on it. The second requirement for equilibrium is introduced by consideration of aggregate supply: At the prevailing price level, firms must wish to produce the prevailing level of national income, no more and no less. This condition is fulfilled everywhere on the SRAS curve. Only where the two curves intersect are both conditions fulfilled simultaneously.

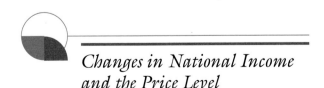

Changes in National Income and the Price Level

The aggregate demand and aggregate supply curves now can be used to understand how various shocks to the economy change both national income and the price level.

A shift in the *AD* curve is called an **aggregate demand shock.** A *rightward* shift in the *AD* curve is an *increase* in aggregate demand; it means that, at all price levels, expenditure decisions will now be consistent with a *higher* level of real national income. Similarly, a *leftward* shift in the *AD* curve is a *decrease* in aggregate demand; it means that, at all price levels, expenditure decisions will now be consistent with a *lower* level of real national income.

A shift in the *SRAS* curve is called an **aggregate supply shock.** A *rightward* shift in the *SRAS* curve is an *increase* in aggregate supply; at any given price level, *more* real national income will be supplied. A *leftward* shift in the *SRAS* curve is a *decrease* in aggregate supply; at any given price level, *less* real national income will be supplied.[8]

What happens to real national income and to the price level when one of the aggregate curves shifts?

A shift in either the *AD* or the *SRAS* curve leads to changes in the equilibrium values of the price level and real national income.

Box 30-2 deals with the special case of a perfectly elastic *SRAS* curve. In that case, the aggregate supply curve determines the price level by itself, while the aggregate demand curve then determines real national income by itself.

Aggregate Demand Shocks

Figure 30-8 shows the effects of an increase in aggregate demand. This increase could have occurred because of, say, increased investment or government spending; it means that more national output would be demanded at any given price level. For now, we are not concerned with the source of the shock; we are interested in its implications for the price level and real national income. As is shown in the figure,

[8]The distinction between movements along and shifts of curves that we encountered in Chapter 4 and again in Chapter 29 is also relevant here. A *movement along* an aggregate demand curve is called a "change in the quantity demanded," whereas a *shift* in an aggregate demand curve is called a "change in demand." A similar distinction applies to the supply curve.

**FIGURE 30-8
Aggregate Demand Shocks**

Shifts in aggregate demand cause the price level and real national income to move in the same direction. An increase in aggregate demand shifts the *AD* curve to the right, say, from AD_0 to AD_1. Macroeconomic equilibrium moves from E_0 to E_1. The price level rises from P_0 to P_1 and real national income rises from Y_0 to Y_1, reflecting a movement along the *SRAS* curve.

A decrease in aggregate demand shifts the *AD* curve to the left, say, from AD_1 to AD_0. Equilibrium moves from E_1 to E_0. Prices fall from P_1 to P_0, and real national income falls from Y_1 to Y_0, again reflecting a movement along the *SRAS* curve.

following an increase in aggregate demand, both the price level and real national income rise.

Figure 30-8 also shows that both the price level and real national income fall as the result of a decrease in demand.

Aggregate demand shocks cause the price level and real national income to change in the same direction; both rise with an increase in aggregate demand, and both fall with a decrease in aggregate demand.

An aggregate demand shock means that there is a shift in the *AD* curve (for example, from AD_0 to AD_1 in Figure 30-8). Adjustment to the new equilibrium following an aggregate demand shock involves a movement along the *SRAS* curve (for example, from point E_0 to point E_1).

Box 30-2

The Keynesian SRAS Curve

In this box, we consider an extreme version of the *SRAS* curve that is horizontal over some range of national income. It is called the Keynesian short-run aggregate supply curve, after John Maynard Keynes, who in his famous book *The General Theory of Employment, Interest and Money* (1936) pioneered the study of the behaviour of economies under conditions of high unemployment.

The behaviour that gives rise to the Keynesian *SRAS* curve can be described as follows. When real national income is below potential national income, individual firms are operating at less than normal-capacity output, and they hold their prices constant at the level that would maximize profits if production were at normal capacity. They then respond to demand variations below that capacity by altering output. In other words, they will supply whatever they can sell at their existing prices as long as they are producing below their normal capacity. This means that the firms have horizontal supply curves and that their output is *demand determined*.[*]

Under these circumstances, the economy has a horizontal aggregate supply curve, indicating that

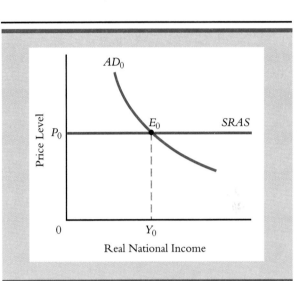

---

[*] The evidence is strong that firms, particularly in the manufacturing sector, do behave like this in the short run. One possible explanation for this is that changing prices frequently is too costly, so firms set the best possible (profit-maximizing) prices when output is at normal capacity and then do not change prices in the face of short-term fluctuations in demand.

any output up to potential output will be supplied at the going price level. The amount that is actually produced is then determined by the position of the aggregate demand curve, as shown in the figure. Thus, we say that real national income is demand determined. If demand rises enough so that firms are trying to squeeze more than normal output out of their plants, their costs will rise, and so will their prices. Thus, the horizontal Keynesian *SRAS* curve applies only to national incomes below potential income.

The Multiplier When the Price Level Varies

We saw earlier in this chapter that the simple multiplier gives the extent of the horizontal shift in the *AD* curve in response to a change in autonomous expenditure. If the price level remains constant and *if* firms are willing to supply all that is demanded at

the existing price level, then the simple multiplier gives the increase in equilibrium national income.

Now that we can use aggregate demand and aggregate supply curves, we can answer a more interesting question: What happens in the more usual case in which the aggregate supply curve slopes upward? In this case, a rise in national income caused by an increase in aggregate demand will be associated with a rise in the price level. However, we have seen that a rise in the price level (by reducing net exports and by lowering the real value of household wealth) shifts the AE curve downward, which lowers equilibrium national income, other things being equal. The outcome of these conflicting forces is easily seen using aggregate demand and aggregate supply curves.

As can be seen in Figure 30-8, when the $SRAS$ curve is positively sloped, the change in national income that has been caused by a change in autonomous expenditure is no longer equal to the size of the horizontal shift in the AD curve. A rightward shift of the AD curve causes the price level to rise, which in turn causes the rise in national income to be less than the horizontal shift of the AD curve. Part of the expansionary impact of an increase in demand is dissipated by a rise in the price level, and only part is transmitted to a rise in real output. Of course, there still is an increase in output, so a multiplier still may be calculated, but its value is not the same as that of the simple multiplier.

When the $SRAS$ curve is positively sloped, the multiplier is smaller than the simple multiplier.

Why is the multiplier smaller when the $SRAS$ curve is positively sloped? The answer lies in the behaviour that is summarized by the AE curve. To understand this, it is useful to think of the final change in national income as occurring in two stages, as shown in Figure 30-9.

First, with prices remaining constant, an increase in autonomous expenditure shifts the AE curve upward and therefore shifts the AD curve to the right. This is shown by a shift upward of the AE curve in part (i) of the figure and a shift to the right of the AD curve in part (ii). The horizontal shift in the AD curve is measured by the simple multiplier, but this cannot be the final equilibrium position, because firms are unwilling to produce enough to satisfy the extra demand at the existing price level.

Second, we take account of the rise in the price level that occurs owing to the positive slope of the $SRAS$ curve. As we have seen, a rise in the price level, via its effect on net exports and on wealth, leads to a downward shift in the AE curve. This second shift of the AE curve partially counteracts

the initial rise in national income and so reduces the size of the multiplier. The second stage shows up as a downward shift of the AE curve in part (i) of Figure 30-9 and a movement upward and to the left along the AD curve in part (ii).

The Importance of the Shape of the $SRAS$ Curve

We now have seen that the shape of the $SRAS$ curve has important implications for how the effects of an aggregate demand shock are divided between changes in real national output and changes in the price level. Figure 30-10, on page 622, highlights this by considering AD shocks in the presence of an $SRAS$ curve that exhibits three distinct ranges. Box 30-3 explores some possible reasons for such an increasing slope of the $SRAS$ curve.

Over the *flat* range, from 0 to Y_0, any change in aggregate demand leads to no change in prices and, as seen earlier, a response of output equal to that predicted by the simple multiplier.

Over the *intermediate* range, along which the $SRAS$ curve is positively sloped, from Y_1 to Y_4, a shift in the AD curve gives rise to appreciable changes in both real income and the price level. As we saw earlier in this chapter, the change in the price level means that real income will change by less in response to a change in autonomous expenditure than it would if the price level were constant.

Over the *steep* range, for output above Y_4, very little more can be produced, however large the demand is. This range deals with an economy near its capacity constraints. Any change in aggregate demand leads to a sharp change in the price level and to little change in real national income. The multiplier in this case is nearly zero.

How do we reconcile what we have just discovered with the analysis of Chapters 28 and 29, where shifts in AE *always* change national income? The answer is that each AE curve is drawn on the assumption that there is a constant price level. A rise in AE shifts the AD curve to the right. However, a steep $SRAS$ curve means that the price level rises significantly, and this shifts the AE curve downward, offsetting some of its initial rise.

This interaction is seen most easily if we study the extreme case, shown in Figure 30-11, on page 623, in which the $SRAS$ curve is vertical. An increase in autonomous expenditure shifts the AE curve upward, thus raising the amount demanded. However, a verti-

FIGURE 30-9
The *AE* Curve and the Multiplier When the Price Level Varies

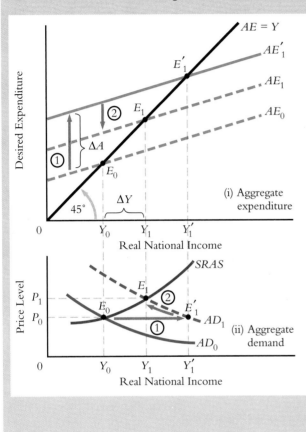

(i) Aggregate expenditure

(ii) Aggregate demand

An increase in autonomous expenditure causes the *AE* curve to shift upward, but the rise in the price level causes it to shift part of the way down again. Hence, the multiplier effect on income is smaller than when the price level is constant. Originally, equilibrium is at point E_0 in both part (i) and part (ii), with real national income at Y_0 and price level at P_0. Desired aggregate expenditure then shifts by ΔA to AE'_1, taking the aggregate demand curve to AD_1. These shifts are shown by arrow 1 in both parts. If the price level had remained constant at P_0, the new equilibrium would have been E'_1 and real income would have risen to Y'_1. The amount $Y_0Y'_1$ is the change called for by the simple multiplier.

Instead, however, the shift in the *AD* curve raises the price level to P_1, because the *SRAS* curve is positively sloped. The rise in the price level shifts the aggregate expenditure curve down to AE_1, as shown by arrow 2 in part (i). This is shown as a movement along the *AD* curve, as indicated by arrow 2 in part (ii). The new equilibrium is thus at E_1. The amount Y_0Y_1 is ΔY, the actual increase in real income, whereas the amount $Y_1Y'_1$ is the shortfall relative to the simple multiplier due to the rise in the price level.

The multiplier, adjusted for the effect of the price increase, is the ratio of $\Delta Y/\Delta A$ in part (i).

cal *SRAS* curve means that output cannot be expanded to satisfy the increased demand. Instead, the extra demand merely forces prices up, and, as prices rise, the *AE* curve shifts downward once again. The rise in prices continues until the *AE* curve is back to where it started. Thus, the rise in prices offsets the expansionary effect of the original shift and, as a result, leaves both real aggregate expenditure and equilibrium real income unchanged.

The discussion of Figures 30-10 and 30-11 illustrates a general proposition:

The effect of any given shift in aggregate demand will be divided between a change in real output and a change in the price level, depending on the conditions of aggregate supply. The steeper is the *SRAS* curve, the greater is the price effect, and the smaller is the output effect.

For reasons discussed in Boxes 30-2 and 30-3 (on pages 619 and 624), many economists think that the *SRAS* curve is shaped like that in Figure 30-10, that is, relatively flat for low levels of income and becoming steeper as the level of national income increases. This shape of the *SRAS* curve implies that at low levels of national income (well below potential), shifts in aggregate demand primarily affect output, and at high levels of national income (above potential), shifts in aggregate demand primarily affect prices.

Of course, as we have noted already, treating wages and other factor prices as constant is appropriate only when the time period under considera-

FIGURE 30-10
The Effects of Increases in Aggregate Demand

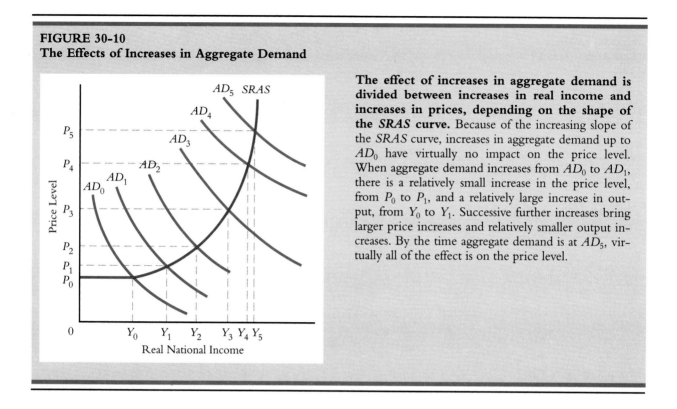

The effect of increases in aggregate demand is divided between increases in real income and increases in prices, depending on the shape of the *SRAS* curve. Because of the increasing slope of the *SRAS* curve, increases in aggregate demand up to AD_0 have virtually no impact on the price level. When aggregate demand increases from AD_0 to AD_1, there is a relatively small increase in the price level, from P_0 to P_1, and a relatively large increase in output, from Y_0 to Y_1. Successive further increases bring larger price increases and relatively smaller output increases. By the time aggregate demand is at AD_5, virtually all of the effect is on the price level.

tion is short. Hence, the *SRAS* curve is used only to analyse short-run, or *impact*, effects. In the next chapter, we shall see what happens in the *long run* when factor prices respond to changes in national income and the price level. First, however, our analysis of the short run needs to be rounded out with a study of aggregate supply shocks.

Aggregate Supply Shocks

A decrease in aggregate supply is shown by a shift to the left in the *SRAS* curve and means that less national output will be supplied at any given price level. An increase in aggregate supply is shown by a shift to the right in the *SRAS* curve and means that more national output will be produced at any given price level.

Figure 30-12, on page 623, illustrates the effects on the price level and real national income of aggregate supply shocks. As can be seen from the figure, following the decrease in aggregate supply, the price level rises and real national income falls. This combination of events is called *stagflation*, a rather inelegant word that has been derived by combining *stagnation* (a term that is sometimes used to mean less than full employment) and *inflation*.

Figure 30-12 also shows that an increase in aggregate supply leads to an increase in real national income and a decrease in the price level.

Aggregate supply shocks cause the price level and real national income to change in opposite directions: With an increase in supply, the price level falls and income rises; with a decrease in supply, the price level rises and income falls.

An aggregate supply shock means that there is a shift in the *SRAS* curve (for example, from $SRAS_0$ to $SRAS_1$ in Figure 30-12). Adjustment to the new equilibrium following the shock involves a movement along the *AD* curve (for example, from E_0 to E_1).

Oil prices have provided three major examples of aggregate supply shocks in recent decades. The

FIGURE 30-11
Demand Shocks When the *SRAS* Curve Is Vertical

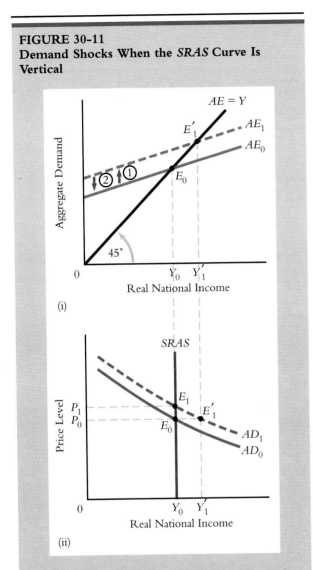

(i)

(ii)

FIGURE 30-12
Aggregate Supply Shocks

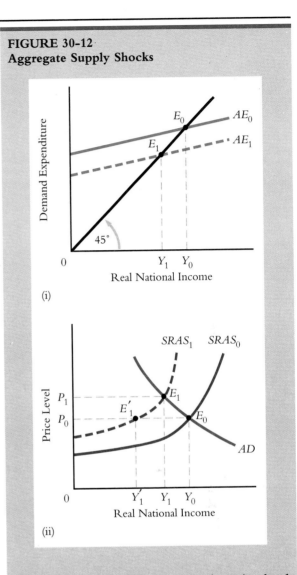

(i)

(ii)

If the *SRAS* curve were vertical, the effect of an increase in autonomous expenditure would be solely a rise in the price level. An increase in autonomous expenditure shifts the *AE* curve upward from AE_0 to AE_1, as shown by arrow 1 in part (i). Given the initial price level P_0, equilibrium would shift from E_0 to E'_1 and real national income would rise from Y_0 to Y'_1 (Primes are used on these variables because these results cannot persist; real national income cannot rise to Y'_1.) However, the price level does not remain constant. This is shown by the *SRAS* curve in part (ii). Instead, the price level rises to P_1. This causes the *AE* curve to shift back down all the way to AE_0, as shown by arrow 2 in part (i), and equilibrium income stays at Y_0. In part (ii) the new equilibrium is at E_1, with income at Y_0, which is associated with the new price level, P_1.

Shifts in aggregate supply cause the price level and real national income to move in opposite directions. The original equilibrium is at E_0, with national income of Y_0 appearing in both parts of the figure. The price level is P_0 in part (ii), and, at that price level, the desired aggregate expenditure curve is AE_0 in part (i).

An aggregate supply shock now shifts the *SRAS* curve in part (ii) to $SRAS_1$. At the original price level of P_0, firms are now only willing to supply Y'_1. The fall in supply, with no corresponding fall in demand, causes a shortage that leads to a rise in the price level along $SRAS_1$. The new equilibrium is reached at E_1, where the *AD* curve intersects $SRAS_1$. At the new, and higher, equilibrium price level of P_1, the *AE* curve has fallen to AE_1, as shown in part (i), which is consistent with equilibrium national income of Y_1.

Box 30-3

More on the Shape of the SRAS *Curve*

The *SRAS* curve relates the price level to the quantity of output that producers are willing to sell. Notice two things about the shape of the *SRAS* curve in Figure 30-5 on page 615: It has a positive slope, and the slope increases as output rises.

Positive Slope

The most obvious feature of the *SRAS* curve is its positive slope, indicating that a higher price level is associated with a higher volume of real output, other things being equal. Because the prices of all of the factors of production are being held constant along the *SRAS* curve, why is the curve not horizontal, indicating that firms would be willing to supply as much output as might be demanded with no increase in the price level?

The answer is that, even though *input prices* are constant, *unit costs of production* eventually rise as output increases. Thus, a higher price level for increasing output—rising short-run aggregate supply—is necessary to compensate firms for rising costs.

The preceding paragraph addresses this question: What has to happen to the price level if national output increases, with the price of factors of production remaining constant? Alternatively, one could ask: What will happen to firms' willingness to supply output if product prices rise with no increase in factor prices? Production becomes more profitable, and since firms are interested in making profits, they will usually produce more.[*] Thus, when the price level of final output rises while factor prices are held constant, firms are motivated to in-

crease their outputs. This is true for the individual firm and also for firms in the aggregate. This increase in the amount produced leads to an upward slope of the *SRAS* curve.

Thus, whether we look at how the price level will respond in the short run to increases in output or how the level of output will respond to an increase in the price level with input prices being held constant, we find that the *SRAS* curve has a positive slope.

Increasing Slope

A less obvious but in many ways more important property of a typical *SRAS* curve is that its slope *increases* as output rises. It is rather flat to the left of potential output and rather steep to the right. Why? Below potential output, firms typically have unused capacity—some plant and equipment are idle. When firms are faced with unused capacity, only a small increase in the price of their output may be needed to induce them to expand production—at least up to normal capacity.

Once output is pushed far beyond normal capacity, however, unit costs tend to rise quite rapidly. Many higher-cost expedients may have to be adopted. Standby capacity, overtime, and extra shifts may have to be used. Such expedients raise the cost of producing a unit of output. These higher-cost methods will not be used unless the selling price of the output has risen enough to cover them. The further output is expanded beyond normal capacity, the more rapidly unit costs rise and hence the larger is the rise in price that is needed to induce firms to increase output even further.

This increasing slope is sometimes called the *first important asymmetry* in the behaviour of aggregate supply. (The second, "sticky wages," will be discussed in the next chapter.)

---

[*] Those who have studied microeconomics already can understand this in terms of perfectly competitive firms being faced with higher prices and thus expanding output *along* their marginal cost curves until marginal cost is once again equal to price.

economy is especially responsive to changes in the market for oil, because, in addition to being used to produce energy, oil is an input into plastics, fertilizers and many other materials that are widely used in the economy. Massive increases in oil prices during 1973–1974 and 1979–1980 caused leftward shifts in the *SRAS* curve. National income fell while the price level rose, causing stagflation. During the mid–1980s, oil prices fell substantially. This shifted the *SRAS* curve to the right, increasing national income and putting downward pressure on the price level.

We can see now how a rightward shift in the *SRAS* curve, which is brought about by an increase in productivity or a fall in input prices without a fully offsetting increase in factor prices, raises real national income and lowers the price level.

SUMMARY

1. The *AE* curve shows desired aggregate expenditure for each level of income at a particular price level. Its intersection with the 45° line determines equilibrium national income for that price level, on the assumption that firms will produce everything that they can sell at the going price level. Equilibrium income then occurs where desired aggregate expenditure equals national income (output). A change in the price level is shown by a *shift* in the *AE* curve: upward when the price level falls and downward when the price level rises. This leads to a new equilibrium level of national income.

2. The *AD* curve plots the equilibrium level of national income that corresponds to each possible price level. A change in equilibrium national income following a change in the price level is shown by a *movement along* the *AD* curve.

3. A rise in the price level lowers exports and lowers consumers' spending (because it decreases consumers' wealth). Both of these changes lower equilibrium national income and cause the aggregate demand curve to have a negative slope.

4. The *AD* curve shifts when any element of autonomous expenditure changes, and the simple multiplier measures the magnitude of the shift. This multiplier also measures the size of the change in real equilibrium national income when the price level remains constant *and* firms produce everything that is demanded at that price level.

5. The short-run aggregate supply (*SRAS*) curve, drawn for given factor prices, is positively sloped, because unit costs rise with increasing output and because rising product prices make it profitable to increase output. An increase in productivity or a decrease in factor prices shifts the curve to the right. A decrease in productivity or an increase in factor prices has the opposite effect.

6. Macroeconomic equilibrium refers to equilibrium values of national income and the price level, as determined by the intersection of the *AD* and *SRAS* curves. Shifts in the *AD* and *SRAS* curves, called aggregate demand shocks and aggregate supply shocks, change the equilibrium values of national income and the price level.

7. When the *SRAS* curve is positively sloped, an aggregate demand shock causes the price level and national income to move in the same direction. When the *SRAS* curve is flat, shifts in the *AD*

curve primarily affect real national income. When the *SRAS* curve is steep, shifts in the *AD* curve primarily affect the price level.

8. An aggregate supply shock moves equilibrium national income along the *AD* curve, causing the price level and national income to move in opposite directions. A leftward shift in the *SRAS* curve causes a stagflation—rising prices and falling national income. A rightward shift causes an increase in real national income and a fall in the price level. The division of the effects of a shift in *SRAS* between a change in national income and a change in the price level depends on the shape of the *AD* curve.

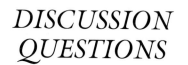

TOPICS FOR REVIEW

Effects of a change in the price level

Relationship between the *AE* and *AD* curves

Negative slope of the *AD* curve

Positive slope of the *SRAS* curve

Macroeconomic equilibrium

Aggregate demand shocks

The multiplier when the price level varies

Aggregate supply shocks

Stagflation

DISCUSSION QUESTIONS

1. Indicate whether each of the following events is the *cause* or the *consequence* of a shift in aggregate demand or supply. If it is a cause, what do you predict will be the effect on the price level and on real national income?
   a. Unemployment decreased in 1994.
   b. OPEC raised oil prices in 1980.
   c. OPEC was forced to accept lower oil prices in 1985.
   d. In the early 1970s, Canada experienced a rapid inflation under conditions of approximately full employment.
   e. In France in 1981, income and employment continued to fall while the price level was relatively stable.
   f. The end of the Cold War led to large decreases in defense spending in many countries.
   g. Canadian exports fell in response to a high value of the Canadian dollar in 1990–1991 and then rose as the C$ fell in value in 1992–1993.
   h. Most provinces raised their personal income tax rates in the early 1990s.
   i. Inflationary pressures receded during the recession of 1990–1992.
   j. The federal and the provincial governments took measures to reduce their budget deficits in the mid 1990s.

2. Explain the following as consequences of shifts in either the aggregate demand curve or the aggregate supply curves, or both. Pay attention to the initial position before the shift(s) occur.

    a. Output and unemployment rise while prices hold steady.

    b. Prices soar, but employment and output hold steady.

    c. Inflation accelerates even as the recession in business activity deepens.

3. During 1979 through 1980, the British government greatly reduced income taxes but restored the lost government revenue by raising excise and their equivalent of the GST. This led to a short burst of extra inflation and a fall in employment. Explain this in terms of shifts in the aggregate demand or aggregate supply curves, or both.

4. What would happen to employment and income if, in an attempt to lower Canadian unemployment, the federal government increased import barriers? What would happen if all countries did the same?

5. Show the effects on the price level and output of income tax cuts that make people work more in an economy that is experiencing an inflationary gap.

6. Following are the combinations of output and price level, given by indexes for GDP and the CPI, respectively, for some recent years. Treat each pair as if it is the intersection of an *AD* and an *SRAS* curve. Plot these and indicate in each case the direction of shift of the *SRAS* or *AD* curve that could have caused them. Why might you be uncertain about some of the shifts.

	CPI (1986 = 100)	GDP (millions of 1986 dollars)
1980	67.2	425
1981	75.5	440
1982	83.7	426
1983	88.5	439
1984	92.4	467
1985	96.0	489
1986	100.0	506
1987	104.4	527
1988	108.6	553
1989	114.0	566
1990	119.5	563
1991	126.2	553
1992	128.1	558

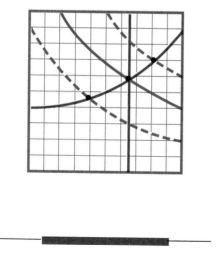

31

National Income and the Price Level in the Long Run

Every worker knows that the best time to ask for a raise is during a boom, when the demand for labour is high. Workers also know that it is difficult to get significant wage increases during a recession, when high unemployment signals a low demand for labour. Every businessperson knows that the cost of many materials tends to rise rapidly during business expansions and to fall—often dramatically—during recessions. In short, factor prices change with economic conditions, and we need to allow for these effects. It is high time, therefore, to go beyond the assumption of fixed factor prices that we used to study the initial effects of aggregate demand and aggregate supply shocks in Chapter 30. To do this, we need to see what happens in a longer-term setting, when changes in national income *induce* changes in factor prices. Once we have completed this task, we can use our model of the macro-economy to investigate the causes and consequences of business cycles and continue our exploration of fiscal policy.

Induced Changes in Factor Prices

We must begin by reconsidering two key concepts that we first encountered in Chapter 26: potential income and the output (or GDP) gap.

Another Look at Potential Income and the GDP Gap

Recall that potential income is the total output that can be produced when all productive resources—labour and capital equipment in particular—are being used at their *normal rates of utilization.* When a nation's actual national income diverges from its potential income, the difference is called the GDP or output gap. (See Figure 26-4 on page 523.)

Although growth in potential income has powerful effects from one decade to the next, its change from one year to the next is small enough to be ignored when studying the year-to-year behaviour of national income and the price level. Therefore, in this discussion, we will continue with the convention, first adopted in Chapter 26, of ignoring the small changes in potential income caused by year-to-year changes in productivity. This means that variations in the output gap are determined solely by variations in actual national income around a given potential national income.

Figure 31-1 shows actual national income being determined by the intersection of the *AD* and *SRAS* curves. Potential income is constant, and it is shown by identical vertical lines in the two parts of the figure. In part (i), the *AD* and *SRAS* curves intersect to produce an equilibrium

FIGURE 31-1
Actual Income, Potential Income, and the Output Gap

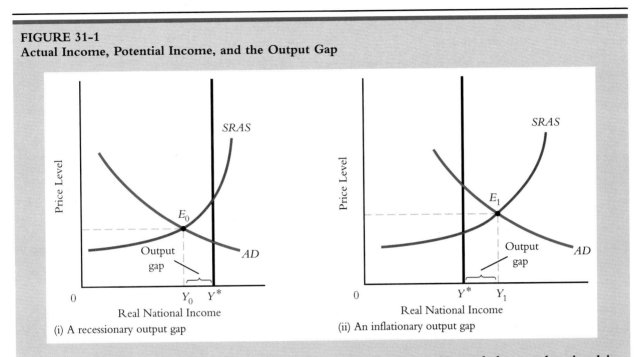

The output gap is the difference between potential national income, $Y*$, and the actual national income, Y. Potential national income is shown by a vertical line because it refers to a given, constant level of real national income. Actual national income is determined by the intersection of the aggregate demand (AD) and short-run aggregate supply (SRAS) curves.

In part (i), the positions of AD and SRAS curves result in a recessionary gap: Equilibrium is at E_0, so actual national income is given by Y_0, which is less than potential income. The output gap is thus $Y* - Y_0$.

In part (ii), the positions of the AD and SRAS curves result in an inflationary gap. Although potential income is unchanged at $Y*$, equilibrium is now at E_1, so actual national income is given by Y_1, which is greater than potential income. The output gap is $Y* - Y_1$.

national income that falls short of potential income. The result is called a *recessionary gap*, because recessions often begin when actual income falls below potential income. In part (ii), the AD and SRAS curves intersect to produce an equilibrium national income that exceeds potential income, resulting in an *inflationary gap*. The way in which an inflationary output gap puts upward pressure on prices will become clear in the following discussion.

Factor Prices and the Output Gap

The output gap provides a convenient measure of the pressure of demand on factor prices. When national income is high relative to potential income, demand for factors will also be high. When national income is low relative to potential income, demand for factors will be correspondingly low. This rela-

tionship is true of all factors. The discussion that follows is simplified, however, by focusing on one key factor, labour, and on its price, the wage rate.

When there is an inflationary gap, actual income exceeds potential, and the demand for labour services will be relatively high. When there is a recessionary gap, actual income is below potential and the demand for labour services will be relatively low.

Each of these situations has implications for wages. Before turning to a detailed analysis, we first consider a benchmark for the behaviour of wages. Earlier, we referred to average costs per unit of output as *unit costs*; to focus on labour costs, we now use average wage costs per unit of output, which we refer to as *unit labour costs*.

Upward and downward wage pressures. In this section, we consider the *upward* and *downward* pressures on wages that are associated with various output gaps. Inflationary gaps will exert upward pressure on wages, and recessionary gaps will exert downward pressure on wages. To what do the upward and downward pressures relate? One answer would be that upward pressure means that wages would rise, and downward pressure means that wages would fall. However, most wage bargaining starts from the assumption that, other things being equal, workers will get the benefit of increases in their own productivity by receiving higher wages. Thus, when national income is at its potential level, so that there are neither upward nor downward pressures on wages caused by output gaps, wages will tend to be rising at the same rate as productivity is rising.[1] When wages and productivity change proportionately, *unit labour costs* remain unchanged. For example, if each worker produces 4 percent more and earns 4 percent more, unit labour costs will remain constant. This, then, is the benchmark:

When there is neither excess demand nor excess supply in the labour market, wages will tend to be rising at the same rate as labour productivity; as a result, unit labour costs will remain constant.

Note that, with unit labour costs remaining constant, there is no pressure coming from the labour market for the *SRAS* curve to shift and hence no pressure for the price level to rise or to fall.

In comparison with this benchmark, upward pressure on wages means that there is pressure for wages to rise faster than productivity is rising. Thus, unit labour costs will also be rising. For example, if money wages rise by 8 percent while productivity rises by only 4 percent, labour cost per unit of output will be rising by about 4 percent. In this case,

the *SRAS* curve will be shifting to the left, reflecting upward pressure on wages coming from the labour market.

Downward pressure on wages means that there is pressure for wages to rise slower than productivity is rising. When this occurs, unit labour costs will be falling. For example, if productivity rises by 4 percent while money wages rise by only 2 percent, labour costs per unit of output will be falling by about 2 percent. In this case, the *SRAS* curve will be shifting to the right, reflecting downward pressure on wages coming from the labour market.

Actual GDP exceeds potential GDP. Sometimes the *AD* and *SRAS* curves intersect where actual output exceeds potential, as illustrated in part (ii) of Figure 31-1. Firms are producing beyond their normal capacity output, so there is an unusually large demand for all factor inputs, including labour. Labour shortages will emerge in some industries and among many groups of workers, particularly skilled workers. Firms will try to bid workers away from other firms in order to maintain the high levels of output and sales made possible by the boom conditions.

As a result of these tight labour-market conditions, workers will find that they have considerable bargaining power with their employers, and they will put upward pressure on wages relative to productivity. Firms, recognizing that demand for their goods is strong, will be anxious to maintain a high level of output. Thus, to prevent their workers from either striking or quitting and moving to other employers, firms will be willing to accede to some of these upward pressures.

The boom that is associated with an inflationary gap generates a set of conditions—high profits for firms and unusually large demand for labour—that exerts upward pressure on wages.

Potential GDP exceeds actual GDP. Sometimes the *AD* and *SRAS* curves intersect where actual output is less than potential, as illustrated in part (i) of Figure 31-1. In this situation, firms are producing below their normal capacity output, so there is an unusually low demand for all factor inputs, including labour. The general conditions in the market for labour will be the opposite of those that occur when actual output exceeds potential. There will be labour surpluses in some industries and among some

---

[1] Ongoing inflation would also influence the normal pattern of wage changes. Wage contracts often allow for changes in prices that are expected to occur during the life of the contract. (Of course, if wages merely rise to keep pace with product prices, there is no effect on unit labour costs; labour cost per dollar's worth of output will be constant.) For now we make the simplifying assumption that the price level is expected to be constant; hence, changes in money wages also are expected to be changes in real wages. The distinction between changes in money wages and real wages, and the important role played by expectations of price level changes, will be discussed in Chapter 32.

groups of workers. Firms will have below-normal sales and not only will resist upward pressures on wages but also will tend to offer wage increases below productivity increases and may even seek reductions in money wages.

The slump that is associated with a recessionary gap generates a set of conditions—low profits for firms, unusually low demand for labour, and a desire on the part of firms to resist wage demands and even to push for wage concessions—that exerts downward pressure on wages and unit labour costs.

Adjustment asymmetry. At this stage, we encounter an important asymmetry in the economy's aggregate supply behaviour. Boom conditions, along with severe labour shortages, cause wages, unit labour costs, and the price level to rise rapidly. When there is a large excess demand for labour, wage (and price) increases often run well ahead of productivity increases. Money wages might be rising by 10 or 15 percent, while productivity might be rising at only 2 or 3 percent. Under such conditions, unit labour costs will be rising rapidly.

The experience of many developed economies suggests, however, that the downward pressures on wages during slumps often do not operate as quickly as do the upward pressures during booms. Even in quite severe recessions, when the price level is fairly stable, money wages may continue to rise, although their rate of increase tends to fall below that of productivity. For example, productivity might be rising at, say, 1.5 percent per year while money wages are rising at 0.5 percent. In this case, unit labour costs are falling, but only at about 1 percent per year, so the rightward shift in the *SRAS* curve and the downward pressure on the price level are correspondingly slight. Money wages may actually fall, reducing unit wage costs even more, but the reduction in unit labour costs in times of the deepest recession has never been as fast as the increases that have occurred during several of the strongest booms.

Both upward and downward adjustments to unit labour costs do occur, but there are differences in the speed at which they typically operate. Excess demand can cause unit labour costs to rise very rapidly; excess supply often causes unit labour costs to fall more slowly.

In Chapters 35 and 36, we explore the consequences of this asymmetry for the relationship between unemployment and inflation, which is one of the most important relationships in macroeconomics.[2]

Inflationary and recessionary gaps. Now it should be clear why the output gaps are named as they are. When actual national income exceeds potential national income, there will normally be rising unit costs, and the *SRAS* curve will be shifting upward. This, in turn, will push the price level up. Indeed, the most obvious event accompanying these conditions is likely to be a significant inflation. The larger is the excess of actual income over potential income, the greater will be the inflationary pressure. The term *inflationary gap* emphasizes this salient feature, when output exceeds potential output.

When actual output is less than potential output, as we have seen, there will be unemployment of labour and other productive resources. Unit labour costs will fall only slowly, leading to a slow downward shift in the *SRAS* curve. Hence, the price level will be falling only slowly, so that *unemployment* will be the output gap's most obvious result. The term *recessionary gap* emphasizes this salient feature that high rates of unemployment occur when actual output falls short of potential output.

The induced effects of output gaps on unit labour costs and the consequent shifts in the *SRAS* curve play an important role in our analysis of the long-run consequences of aggregate demand shocks, to which we now turn.

The Long-Run Consequences of Aggregate Demand Shocks

We can now extend our study to cover the longer-run consequences of aggregate demand shocks, when incorporating changes in factor prices. We need to examine separately the effect of aggregate demand shocks on factor prices for expansionary and for contractionary shocks, since the behaviour of unit costs is not symmetrical for the two cases.

---

[2]This is the second asymmetry in aggregate supply that we have encountered. The first refers to the changing slope of the *SRAS* curve, as discussed in Box 30-3.

FIGURE 31-2
Demand-Shock Inflation

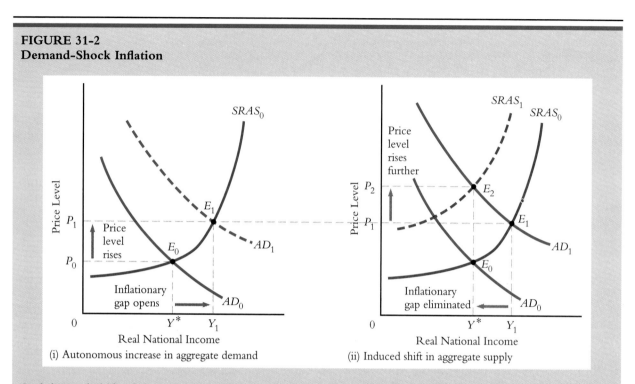

(i) Autonomous increase in aggregate demand (ii) Induced shift in aggregate supply

A rightward shift of the *AD* curve first raises prices and output along the *SRAS* curve. It then induces a shift of the *SRAS* curve that further raises prices but lowers output along the *AD* curve. In part (i), the economy is in equilibrium at E_0, at its level of potential output, Y^*, and price level P_0. The *AD* curve then shifts to AD_1. This moves equilibrium to E_1, with income Y_1 and price level P_1, and opens up an inflationary gap of $Y^* - Y_1$.

In part (ii), the inflationary gap results in an increase in wages and other input costs, shifting the *SRAS* curve leftward. As this happens, income falls and the price level rises along AD_1. Eventually, when the *SRAS* curve has shifted to $SRAS_1$, income is back to Y^* and the inflationary gap has been eliminated. However, the price level has risen to P_2.

Expansionary Shocks

Suppose that the economy starts with a stable price level at full employment, so actual income equals potential income, as shown by the initial equilibrium in part (i) of Figure 31-2.

Now suppose that this happy situation is disturbed by an increase in autonomous expenditure, perhaps caused by a sudden boom in investment spending. Figure 31-2(i) shows the effects of this aggregate demand shock in raising both the price level and national income. Now actual national income exceeds potential income, and there is an inflationary gap.

We have seen that an inflationary gap causes wages to rise faster than productivity, which in turn causes unit costs to rise. The *SRAS* curve shifts to

the left as firms seek to pass on their increases in input costs by increasing their output prices. For this reason, the initial increases in the price level and in real national income shown in part (i) of Figure 31-2 are *not* the final effects of the demand shock. As seen in part (ii) of the figure, the upward shift of the *SRAS* curve causes a further rise in the price level, but this time the price rise is associated with a fall in output.

The cost increases (and the consequent upward shifts of the *SRAS* curve) continue until the inflationary gap has been removed, that is, until income returns to Y^*, its potential level. Only then is there no abnormal demand for labour, and only then do wages and unit costs, and hence the *SRAS* curve, stabilize.

This important expansionary demand-shock sequence can be summarized as follows:

1. Starting from full employment, a rise in aggregate demand raises the price level and raises income above its potential level as the economy expands along a given *SRAS* curve.
2. The expansion of income beyond its normal capacity level puts pressure on factor markets; factor prices begin to increase faster than productivity, shifting the *SRAS* curve upward, such that prices are higher at every level of output.
3. The shift of the *SRAS* curve causes national income to fall along the *AD* curve. This process continues *as long as* actual income exceeds potential income. Therefore, actual income eventually falls back to its potential level. The price level is, however, now higher than it was after the initial impact of the increased aggregate demand, but inflation will have come to a halt.

The ability to wring more output and income from the economy than its underlying potential output (as in point 2) is only a short-term possibility. National income greater than Y^* sets into motion inflationary pressures that tend to push national income back to Y^*.

There is an automatic adjustment mechanism that eventually eliminates any inflation caused by a one-time demand shock by returning output to its potential level and thus removing the inflationary gap.

Contractionary Shocks

Let us return to that fortunate economy with full employment and stable prices. It appears again in part (i) of Figure 31-3, which is similar to part (i) of Figure 31-2. Now assume that there is a *decline* in aggregate demand, perhaps due to a major reduction in investment expenditure.

The first effects of the decline are a fall in output and some downward adjustment of prices, as shown in part (i) of the figure. As output falls, unemployment rises. The difference between potential output and actual output is the recessionary gap that is shown in Figure 31-3.

Flexible wages. What would happen if severe unemployment caused wage rates to fall rapidly rela-

tive to productivity? Say, for example, that with productivity rising by 1 percent per year, money wages fell by 4 percent. Unit costs would then *fall* by 5 percent. Falling wage rates would lower unit costs, causing a rightward shift of the *SRAS* curve. As shown in part (ii) of Figure 31-3, the economy would move along its fixed *AD* curve, with falling prices and rising output until full employment was restored at potential national income Y^*. We conclude that if wages were to fall rapidly whenever there was unemployment, the resulting fall in the *SRAS* curve would restore full employment.

Flexible wages that fell rapidly during periods of unemployment would provide an automatic adjustment mechanism that would push the economy back toward full employment whenever output fell below potential.

Box 31-1 takes up the interesting case of how the adjustment mechanism might work if the aggregate demand shock were anticipated in advance.

Sticky wages. Boom conditions, along with severe labour shortages, do cause wages to rise rapidly, shifting the *SRAS* curve upward. However, as we noted earlier when we encountered the second asymmetry of aggregate supply behaviour, experience suggests that wages typically do not fall rapidly in response to recessionary gaps and their accompanying unemployment. It is sometimes said that wages are "sticky" in a downward direction. This does not mean that wages never fall. In recession, money wages often rise more slowly than productivity and some money wages even fall. But the gap between money wage changes and productivity changes is typically quite small during recessions. This means that unit labour costs will fall only slowly. This, in turn, means that the downward shifts in the *SRAS* curve occur slowly, and the adjustment mechanism that depends on these shifts will operate slowly.

The weakness of the adjustment mechanism does not mean that slumps must always be prolonged. Rather, this weakness means that speedy recovery back to full employment must be generated mainly from the demand side. If the economy is to avoid a lengthy period of recession or stagnation, the force leading to recovery usually must be a rightward shift of the *AD* curve rather than a downward drift of the *SRAS* curve. The possibility that government *stabilization policy* might accom-

FIGURE 31-3
Demand-Shock Deflation with Flexible Wages

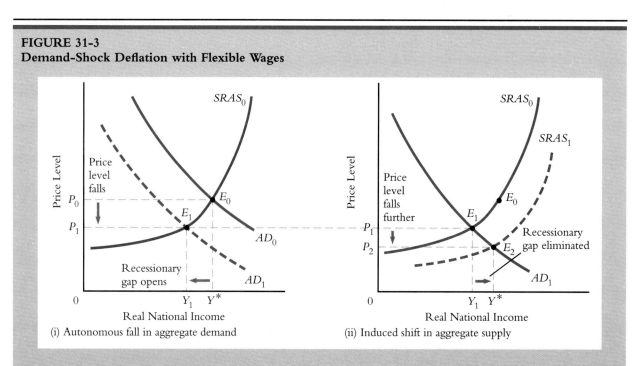

(i) Autonomous fall in aggregate demand

(ii) Induced shift in aggregate supply

A leftward shift of the *AD* curve first lowers prices and output along the *SRAS* curve and then induces a (slow) shift of the *SRAS* curve that further lowers prices but raises output along the *AD* curve. In part (i), the economy is in equilibrium at E_0, at its level of potential output, Y^*, and price level P_0. The *AD* curve then shifts to AD_1, moving equilibrium to E_1, with income Y_1 and price level P_1, and opens up an recessionary gap of $Y^* - Y_1$.

Part (ii) shows the adjustment back to full employment that occurs from the supply side of the economy. The fall in wages shifts the *SRAS* curve to the right. Real national income rises, and the price level falls further along the *AD* curve. Eventually, the *SRAS* curve reaches $SRAS_1$, with equilibrium at E_2. The price level stabilizes at P_2 when income returns to Y^*, eliminating the recessionary gap.

---

plish this is one of the more important and contentious issues in macroeconomics, one that we will return to often throughout the remainder of this book.

The *SRAS* curve shifts to the left fairly rapidly when national income exceeds Y^*, but it shifts to the right only slowly when national income is less than Y^*.

The asymmetry. This difference in speed of adjustment is a consequence of the important asymmetry in the behaviour of aggregate supply that was noted earlier in this chapter. This asymmetry helps to explain two key facts about our economy. First, unemployment can persist for quite long periods without causing decreases in unit costs and prices of

sufficient magnitude to remove the unemployment. Second, booms, along with labour shortages and production beyond normal capacity, do not persist for long periods without causing increases in unit costs and the price level.

The Long-Run Aggregate Supply (LRAS) Curve

The adjustments to expansionary and contractionary shocks that we have just discussed suggests an important concept: the **long-run aggregate supply (LRAS) curve.** This curve relates the price level to real national income after wage rates and all other input costs have been fully adjusted to

Box 31-1

Anticipated Demand Shocks

Suppose that the increase in aggregate demand that is illustrated in Figure 31-2 was widely anticipated well before it occurred. For example, an approaching election might lead to the widespread belief that the government would stimulate the economy in order to improve its electoral chances.

Further, suppose that most employers and employees believe that one of the effects of the demand stimulation will be an inflation. Workers might press for wage increases to prevent the purchasing power of their earnings from being eroded by the coming price increases. Firms would believe that demand for their products was likely to rise, enabling them to raise their selling prices. They might therefore be persuaded to grant wage increases now and pass these on to consumers in terms of higher prices.

A demand stimulus that was widely expected to occur and whose inflationary effects were widely understood could lead to upward pressure on wages, even without the opening of any inflationary gap.

If this were to occur, the leftward shift in the *SRAS* curve that is depicted in part (ii) of Figure 31-2 could occur quickly, perhaps accompanying, or even preceding, the rightward shift in the *AD* curve in part (i). Given *perfect* anticipation of the effects of the demand stimulus, and *full* adjustment to it in advance, the equilibrium would go straight from E_0 to E_2. The intermediate position, E_1, with its accompanying inflationary gap (with national income in excess of potential income), would be completely bypassed.

A similar story might be told for an anticipated fall in aggregate demand. The effects of an unanticipated fall are shown in the two parts of Figure 31-3. However, if the fall were widely anticipated and its effects were generally understood, firms might reduce their wage offers and workers might accept the decreases because they expect prices to fall as well. In this case, it is conceivable that the economy could bypass the recessionary stage and go straight to a lower price level at an unchanged level of real national income.

This possibility, that anticipated demand shocks might have no real effects on real national income and hence on unemployment, plays a key role in some important controversies concerning the effectiveness of government policies. We shall study these in detail in Chapter 37.

In the meantime, we may notice that the complete absence of effects on aggregate output in the transitionary period requires that everyone has full knowledge both of the exact amount of the stimulus that the government will induce and of the new equilibrium values of the relevant prices and wages. In other words, everyone knows what the new equilibrium will be and goes directly to it. Generally, people do not have such perfect knowledge and foresight, so there is some groping toward the equilibrium, and hence some effects on aggregate output, until the final equilibrium set of wages and prices is reached.

---

eliminate any unemployment or overall labour shortages.[3]

---

[3]Students who have studied microeconomics will notice that this use of the term *long run* is different from its meaning in macroeconomics. Note, however, the key similarity that the long run has more flexibility for adjustment than does the short run.

Shape of the LRAS *curve.* Once all the adjustments that are required have occurred, the economy will have eliminated any excess demand or excess supply of labour. In other words, full employment will prevail, and output will necessarily be at its potential level, Y^*. It follows that the aggregate supply curve, becomes a vertical line at Y^*, as shown in Figure 31-4. The *LRAS* curve is sometimes called

FIGURE 31-4
The Long-Run Aggregate Supply (LRAS) Curve

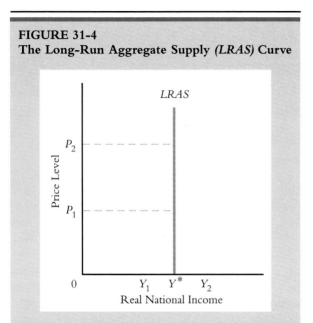

The long-run aggregate supply curve is a vertical line drawn at the level of national income
that is equal to potential income, **Y***. It is a vertical line, because the total amount of goods that the
economy produces when all factors are efficiently
used at their normal rate of utilization does not vary
with the price level. If the price level were to rise
from P_1 to P_2 *and* wages and all other factor prices
were to rise by the same proportion, the total desired
output of firms would remain at Y^*.

If income were Y_1, which is less then Y^*, wages
would be falling and the *SRAS* curve would be shifting rightward; hence, the economy would not be on
its *LRAS* curve. If income were Y_2, which is greater
than Y^*, wages would be rising and the *SRAS* curve
would be shifting leftward; hence, again, the economy
would not be on its *LRAS* curve.

the classical aggregate supply curve because the classical economists were mainly concerned with the
behaviour of the economy in long-run equilibrium.

Notice that the vertical *LRAS* curve does not
represent the same thing as the vertical portion of
the *SRAS* curve (see Figure 30-10). Over the vertical range of the *SRAS* curve, the economy is at its
utmost limit of productive capacity, when no more
can be squeezed out, as might occur in an all-out
war effort. The vertical shape of the *LRAS* curve is
due to the workings of an adjustment mechanism
that brings the economy back to its potential out-

put, even though output may differ from potential
for considerable periods of time. It is called the
long-run aggregate supply curve, because it arises as
a result of adjustments that take a substantial amount
of time.

Along the *LRAS* curve, all the prices of all outputs and all inputs have been fully adjusted to eliminate any excess demands or supplies. Proportionate
changes in money wages and the price level (which,
by definition, will leave real wages unaltered) will
also leave equilibrium employment and total output
unchanged. In the next section, we will ask what
does change when we move from one point on the
LRAS curve to another.

Long-Run Equilibrium

Figure 31-5 shows the equilibrium output and the
price level as they are determined by the intersection of the *AD* curve and the vertical *LRAS* curve.
Because the *LRAS* curve is vertical, shifts in aggregate demand change the price level but not the level
of equilibrium output, as shown in part (i). By contrast, a shift in aggregate supply changes both output
and the price level, as shown in part (ii). For example, a rightward shift of the *LRAS* curve increases
national income and leads to a fall in the price level.

With a vertical *LRAS* curve, in the long run,
total output is determined solely by conditions of supply, and the role of aggregate demand is simply to determine the price level.

What does change when the economy moves
from one point on the LRAS curve, such as E_0 in
part (i) of Figure 31-5, to another point, such as E_1?
Although *total output* and *total desired expenditure* do
not change, *their compositions* do change. The higher
is the price level, the lower is household wealth (for
a given nominal stock of assets) and hence the lower
is consumption. (Recall from Chapter 28 that the
lower is wealth, the higher is saving and hence the
lower is consumption.) Also, the higher is the price
level, the lower are exports and the higher are inputs and, hence, the lower are net exports.

Say the economy starts at a point on the SRAS
curve and an increase in government expenditure
then creates an inflationary gap. Money wages and
the price level rise until the gap is removed. At the

new long run equilibrium, the higher level of government spending is exactly offset by lower consumption and net exports, leaving total output unchanged. A similar analysis holds for an increase in investment. In the new-long run equilibrium, the higher level of investment spending will be exactly offset by lower consumption spending and net exports.

The vertical _LRAS_ curve shows that, given full adjustment of input prices, potential income, _Y*_, is compatible with any price level, although its composition among consumption, investment, government, and net exports may be different at different price levels.

In Chapter 33, we will discover circumstances under which a rise in the price level has _no real effects_, so that not only are total income and total expenditure the same at all points on the _LRAS_ curve, but its composition among _C, I, G_ and _(X−IM)_ is also the same.

National Income in the Short and Long Run

We have now identified two distinct equilibrium conditions for the economy.

1. In the short run, the economy is in equilibrium at the level of income and prices where the _SRAS_ curve intersects the _AD_ curve.
2. In the long run, the economy is in equilibrium at potential income, the position of the vertical _LRAS_ curve. The price level is that at which the _AD_ curve intersects the _LRAS_ curve.

When the economy is in long-run equilibrium, it is also in short-run equilibrium.

The _position_ of the _LRAS_ curve is at _Y*_, which is determined by past economic growth. Deviations of actual income from potential income—output gaps—are generally associated with business cycles. Changes in total real output (and hence in employ-

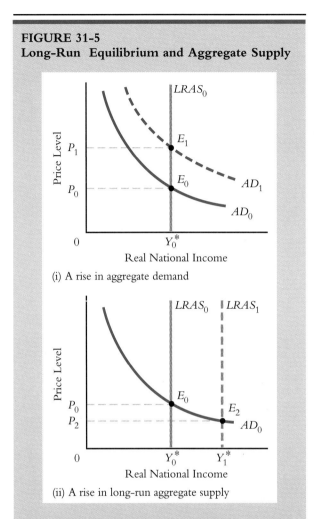

FIGURE 31-5
Long-Run Equilibrium and Aggregate Supply

(i) A rise in aggregate demand

(ii) A rise in long-run aggregate supply

When the _LRAS_ curve is vertical, aggregate supply determines the long-run equilibrium value of national income at _Y*_. Given _Y*_, aggregate demand determines the long-run equilibrium value of the price level. In both parts of the figure, the initial long-run equilibrium is at E_0, so the price level is P_0 and national income is Y^*_0.

In part (i), a shift in the _AD_ curve from AD_0 to AD_1, with the _LRAS_ curve remaining unchanged, moves the long-run equilibrium form E_0 to E_1. This raises the price level from P_0 to P_1 but leaves national income unchanged at Y^*_0 in the long run.

In part (ii), a shift in the _LRAS_ curve from $LRAS_0$ to $LRAS_1$, with the aggregate demand curve remaining constant at AD_0, moves the long-run equilibrium from E_0 to E_2. This raises national income from Y^*_0 to Y^*_1 but lowers the price level from P_0 to P_2.

FIGURE 31-6
Three Ways of Increasing National Income

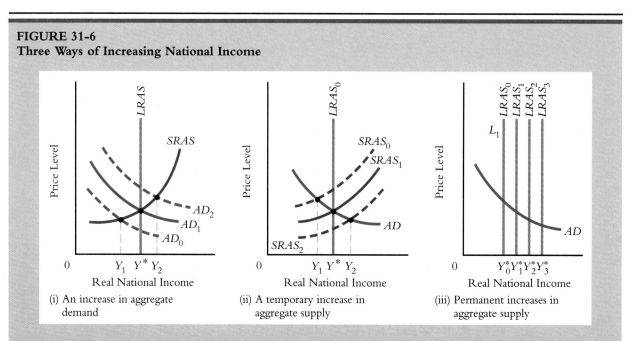

(i) An increase in aggregate demand

(ii) A temporary increase in aggregate supply

(iii) Permanent increases in aggregate supply

National income will increase in response to an increase in aggregate demand or an increase in aggregate supply. The increase will be permanent if the *LRAS* curve shifts, but if the *LRAS* curve does not shift, any divergences of income from potential will be only temporary; the output gap that is created will set in motion the wage adjustments that we studied earlier in this chapter. In part (i) of the figure the *AD* curve shifts to the right. If the initial level of income is Y_1, then the shift from AD_0 to AD_1 eliminates the recessionary gap and raises national income to Y^*. If the initial level of income is Y^*, then the shift from AD_1 to AD_2 raises national income to Y_2 and thereby opens up an inflationary gap.

In part (ii) the *SRAS* curve shifts to the right. If the initial level of income is Y_1, then the shift from $SRAS_0$ to $SRAS_1$ eliminates the recessionary gap and raises national income to Y^*. If the initial level of income is Y^*, then the shift from $SRAS_1$ to $SRAS_2$ raises national income to Y_2 and thereby opens up an inflationary gap.

In the cases shown in parts (i) and (ii), any increase in income beyond potential is temporary, since, in the absence of any additional shocks, the inflationary gap will cause wages and other factor prices to rise; this will cause the *SRAS* curve to shift upward and, hence, national income to converge to Y^*.

In part (iii) the *LRAS* curve shifts to the right, causing potential income to increase. Whether or not actual income increases immediately depends on what happens to the *AD* and *SRAS* curves. Since, in the absence of other shocks, actual income eventually converges to potential income, a rightward shift in the *LRAS* curve eventually leads to an increase in actual income. If the shift in the *LRAS* curve is recurring, then national income will grow continually.

ment, unemployment, and living standards) may take place due either to growth or to the business cycle.

This discussion suggests a need to distinguish three ways in which GDP can be increased. These are illustrated in Figure 31-6.

Increases in aggregate demand.   As shown in part (i) of Figure 31-6, an increase in aggregate demand will yield a one-time increase in real GDP. If that increase occurs when there is a recessionary gap, it pushes GDP toward potential income and thus

short-circuits the working of the automatic adjustment mechanism that eventually would have achieved the same outcome by depressing wages and other costs. (The operation of this adjustment mechanism is discussed in detail earlier in this chapter; see especially pages 630–631.)

If the demand shock pushes GDP beyond potential income, the rise in GDP above potential income will only be temporary; the inflationary gap will cause wages and other costs to rise, shifting the *SRAS* curve to the left. This drives GDP back toward potential, so that the only lasting effect is on the price level. Box 31-2 gives a number of reasons why we might expect the effect of demand shocks on GDP to be cyclical, that is, to cause GDP to move first one way, then the other.

Increases in aggregate supply. Increases in aggregate supply will also lead to an increase in GDP. Here it is useful to distinguish between two possible kinds of increases that might occur—those that leave the *LRAS* curve unchanged and those that shift it.

Part (ii) of Figure 31-6 shows the effects of a temporary increase in aggregate supply. This will shift the *SRAS* curve to the right but will have no effect on the *LRAS* curve or, hence, on potential income. The shock will thus cause GDP to rise relative to potential, but the increase will be soon reversed—in this case, possibly even before any significant impact on wages and other costs can be detected.

Part (iii) of Figure 31-6 shows the effects of permanent increases in aggregate supply that shift the *LRAS* curve. A once-and-for-all increase, due, say, to a labour-market policy that reduces the level of structural unemployment, will lead to a one-time increase in potential GDP. A recurring increase that is due, say, to population growth, capital accumulation, or ongoing improvements in productivity causes a continual rightward shift in the *LRAS* curve, giving rise to a continual increase in the level of potential GDP.

Economic Growth

A gradual but continual rise in potential GDP, or what we have called *economic growth*, is the main source of improvements in the standard of living over the long term.

Eliminating a severe recessionary gap will cause a once-and-for-all increase in national income of perhaps 4 percent, while eliminating structural unemployment will raise it by somewhat less. However, a growth rate of 3 percent per year raises national income by 10 percent in 3 years and *doubles* it in 24 years and *quadruples* it in 48 years.

In any given year, the position of the *LRAS* curve is at potential GDP, Y^*. The "long run" to which the *LRAS* curve refers is thus one in which the resources available to the economy do not change, but in which all markets reach equilibrium. Economic growth moves the *LRAS* curve to the

right, year by year. Here, there is no long run in which everything settles down, because growth is a continuing process. Rather, the movement in *LRAS* is a continuing movement in Y^*.

Cyclical Fluctuations

Figure 31-6 allows us to distinguish the causes of trend growth in potential GDP, which is the gradual rightward shifting of the *LRAS* curve, from the causes of cyclical fluctuations, which are deviations from that trend.

Cyclical fluctuations in GDP are caused by shifts in the *AD* and *SRAS* curves that cause actual GDP to deviate temporarily from potential GDP.

These shifts, in turn, are caused by changes in a variety of factors, including interest rates, exchange rates, consumer and business confidence, and government policy. Although the resulting deviations of actual from potential GDP are described as "temporary," recall from the discussion above that the automatic adjustment mechanism may work slowly enough that the deviations can persist for some time, perhaps several years.

Figure 31-7 shows three different economic series. Each of these, as well as dozens of others that might be studied, tells us something about the general variability of the economy. Some move more than others, and no two move exactly together; yet all exhibit a cyclical pattern, and they tend to move approximately together.

Figure 31-8 on page 642 relates three key parts of aggregate expenditure to total income. Fluctuations in both investment and exports show a pattern similar to the fluctuations in GDP. This is consistent with their being part of the cause of the GDP fluctuations. In contrast, fluctuations in government expenditure do not show any clear association with fluctuations in GDP.

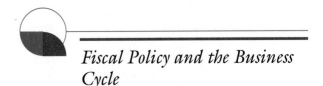

Fiscal Policy and the Business Cycle

In Chapter 29, we briefly introduced the basic concepts of fiscal and stabilization policies. The latter

Box 31-2

Demand Shocks and Business Cycles

Aggregate demand shocks are a major source of fluctuations in GDP around Y^*. As we have seen, an expansionary demand shock, starting from a position of full employment, will lead to an increase in output, followed by a fall in output accompanied by an increase in prices as the adjustment mechanism restores the economy to equilibrium. Depending on the nature and magnitude of the shock, the adjustment will take many months, often stretching into one or two years.

Suppose that the government increases spending on roads or that economic growth in the United States leads to an increase in demand for Canadian exports. No matter what the source of growth in demand, the economy will not respond instantaneously. In many industries, it takes weeks or months, or even longer, to bring new or mothballed capacity into production and to hire and train new workers. The multiplier process itself also takes time, as households and firms respond to the change in income that results from an initial increase in autonomous spending.

Because of these lags in the economy's response, changes in demand give rise to changes in output that are spread out over a substantial period of time. An increase in demand may lead to a gradual in-

crease in output that builds up over several months. Then, as output does change, the adjustment mechanism comes into play. As an inflationary gap opens up, wages and costs start to rise, shifting the *SRAS* curve to the left.

Thus, a once-and-for-all positive demand shock gives rise to a *cyclical* output response, with GDP first rising because of the rightward shift in the *AD* curve and then falling because of the upward shift in the *SRAS* curve. A negative demand shock is likely to play out even more slowly because of the asymmetry of response. Again, however, the behaviour of output will be cyclical: Starting from potential output, GDP will fall over a period of time, because of a leftward shift in the *AD* curve, and then rise slowly as the adjustment mechanism shifts *SRAS* to the right.

Each major component of aggregate expenditure, consumption, investment, net exports, and government purchases is subject to continual random shifts, which are sometimes large enough to disturb the economy significantly. Adjustment lags convert such shifts into cyclical oscillations in national income.

---

attempts to stabilize national income at or near some desired level (usually potential national income). In the remainder of this chapter, we further study taxing and spending as tools of fiscal stabilization policy. In Chapter 37, after we have discussed money and the banking system, we will return to the subject in more detail.

Since government expenditure increases aggregate demand and taxation decreases it, the *direction* of the required changes in spending and taxation is generally easy to determine once we know the direction of the desired change in national income. However, the *timing*, *magnitude*, and *mixture* of the changes pose more difficult issues.

There is no doubt that the government can

exert a major influence on national income. Prime examples are the massive increases in military spending during major wars. Canadian federal expenditure during World War II rose from 12.2 percent of GDP in 1939 to 41.8 percent of GDP in 1944. At the same time, the unemployment rate fell from 11.4 percent to 1.4 percent. Economists agree that the increase in government spending helped to bring about the rise in GDP and the associated fall in unemployment. Similar experiences occurred during the rearmament of most European countries before, or just following, the outbreak of World War II in 1939 and in the United States during the Vietnam War in the late 1960s and early 1970s.

FIGURE 31-7
Three Indicators of Changes in Economic Activity, 1962–1989

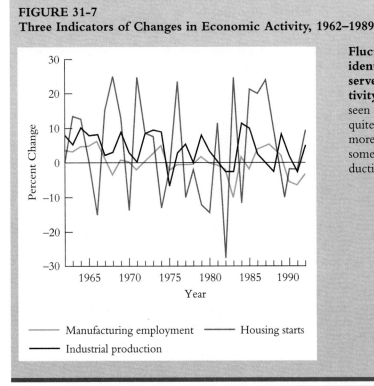

Fluctuations follow similar, but by no means identical, patterns for various series that can serve as indicators of aggregate economic activity. The cyclical pattern of fluctuations is easily seen in all three series, although the amplitudes are quite different. Housing starts tend to fluctuate more, and employment in manufacturing fluctuates somewhat less, than the series for industrial production. (*Source:* Statistics Canada, 11-030E.)

Fiscal policy can be used in an attempt to stablize the economy at its potential income. In the heyday of fiscal policy, from about 1945 to about 1970, many economists were convinced that the economy could be stabilized adequately just by varying the size of the government's taxes and expenditures. That day is past. Today, most economists are aware of the many limitations of fiscal policy.

The Basic Theory of Fiscal Stabilization

A reduction in tax rates, an increase in government expenditure or, to a lesser extent, a balanced increase in both taxes and expenditure will shift the *AD* curve to the right, causing an increase in GDP. An increase in tax rates, a cut in government expenditure or to a lesser extent, a balanced decrease in both taxes and expenditure, will shift the *AD* curve to the left, causing a decrease in GDP. (See Figure 30-8 for a detailed discussion.)

A more detailed look at how fiscal stabilization works will provide a useful review. It will also help to show some of the complications that arise in making fiscal policy.

A recessionary gap. The removal of a recessionary gap is illustrated in Figure 31-9. There are two possible ways in which the gap may be removed.

First, the recessionary gap may eventually drive wages and other factor prices down by enough to shift the *SRAS* curve to the right and thereby reinstate high employment and potential income (at a lower price level). The evidence, however, is that this process takes a substantial period of time.

Second, the *AD* curve could shift to the right, restoring the economy to full employment and potential income (at a higher price level). The government can cause such a shift by using expansionary fiscal policy. The advantage of using fiscal policy is that it may substantially shorten what would otherwise be a long recession. One disadvantage is that the use of fiscal policy may stimulate the economy just before private-sector spending recovers on its own. As a result, the economy may overshoot its potential output, and an inflationary gap may open up. In this case, fiscal policy that is intended to

FIGURE 31-8
Changes in GDP and Selected Components, 1950–1989

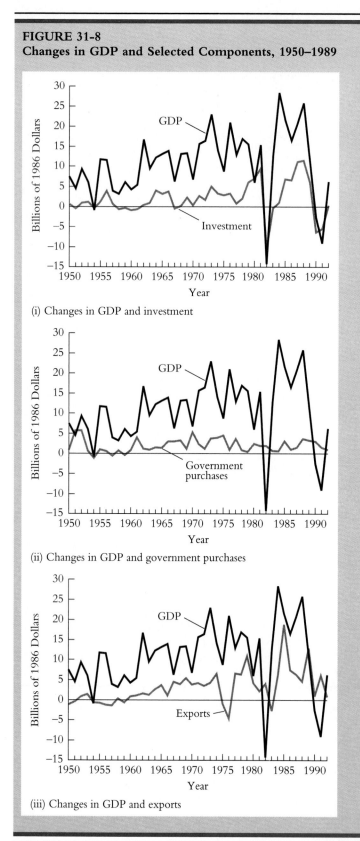

(i) Changes in GDP and investment

(ii) Changes in GDP and government purchases

(iii) Changes in GDP and exports

Changes in GDP have been closely related to investment expenditures and exports. Part (i) shows that changes in GDP and changes in investment are closely correlated, tending to rise and fall together. For example, the recessions in the mid-1970s, and the early 1980s and 1992–1991 were all accompanied by sharp drops in investment spending, and the recovery from each of these recessions was accompanied by sustained increases in investment spending.

Part (ii) shows that changes in government purchases are quite small over the period shown and consequently are not an important contributor to fluctuations in GDP.

Part (iii) shows that changes in exports are closely correlated with changes in GDP. For example, the recession in the early 1980s witnessed a dramatic fall in exports, and the subsequent recovery in GDP was accompanied by a sharp rise in exports. Note the exception in 1990-1991 when exports continued to rise in the face of a severe recession. (*Source:* Statistics Canada, 13-531, 13-201, 11-030E.)

FIGURE 31-9
Removal of a Recessionary Gap

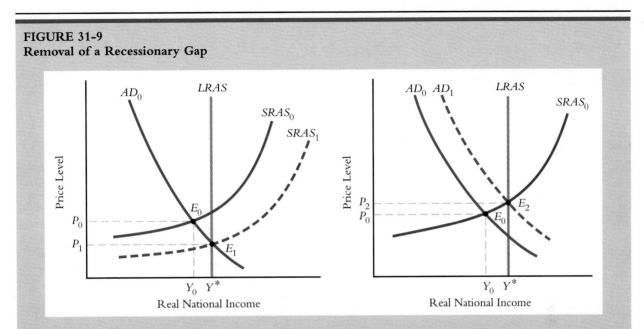

A recessionary gap may be removed by a (slow) rightward shift of the *SRAS* curve, a natural revival of private-sector demand, or a fiscal policy-induced increase in aggregate demand. Initially, equilibrium is at E_0, with national income at Y_0 and the price level at P_0. The recessionary gap $Y^* - Y_0$.

As shown in part (i), the gap might be removed by a shift in the *SRAS* curve to $SRAS_1$. The increase in aggregate supply could occur as a result of reductions in wage rates and other input prices. The shift in the *SRAS* curve causes a movement down and to the right along AD_0. This movement establishes a new equilibrium at E_1, achieving potential income, Y^*, and lowering the price level to P_1.

As shown in part (ii), the gap might also be removed by a shift of the *AD* curve to AD_1. This increase in aggregate demand could occur either because of a natural revival of private-sector expenditure or because of a fiscal policy-in-duced increase in expenditure. The shift in the *AD* curve causes a movement up and to the right along $SRAS_0$. This movement shifts the equilibrium to E_2, raising income to Y^* and the price level to P_2.

promote economic stability can actually cause instability.

An inflationary gap.   Figure 31-10 shows how an inflationary gap can be removed either from the de-mand or from the supply side.

First, wages and other factor prices may be pushed up by the excess demand. The *SRAS* curve will therefore shift to the left, eventually eliminating the gap, reducing income to its potential level, and raising the price level.

Second, the *AD* curve can shift to the left, restoring equilibrium GDP. The government, by raising taxes or cutting spending, can induce such a shift, reducing aggregate demand sufficiently to re-move the inflationary gap. The advantage of this ap-proach is that it avoids the inflationary increase in

prices that accompanies the first method. One dis-advantage is that if private-sector expenditures fall due to natural causes, national income may be pushed below potential, thus opening up a reces-sionary gap.

A key proposition.   This discussion suggests that, in circumstances in which the automatic adjustment mechanisms either fail to operate quickly enough or give rise to undesirable side effects such as rising prices, there is a potential stabilizing role for fiscal policy.

Government taxes and expenditures shift the *AD* curve and hence can be used to remove persistent GDP gaps.

FIGURE 31-10
Removal of an Inflationary Gap

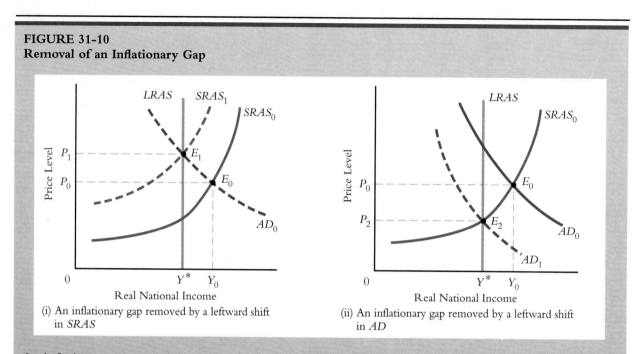

(i) An inflationary gap removed by a leftward shift in *SRAS*

(ii) An inflationary gap removed by a leftward shift in *AD*

An inflationary gap may be removed by a leftward shift of the *SRAS* curve, a reduction in private-sector demand, or a policy-induced reduction in aggregate demand. Initially, equilibrium is at E_0, with national income at Y_0 and the price level at P_0. The inflationary gap is $Y^* - Y_0$.

As shown in part (i), the gap might be removed by a shift in the *SRAS* curve to $SRAS_1$. The decrease in aggregate supply could occur as a result of increases in wage rates and other input prices. The shift in the *SRAS* curve causes a movement up and to the left along AD_0. This movement establishes a new equilibrium at E_1, reducing income to its potential level, Y^*, and raising the price level to P_1.

As shown in part (ii), the gap might also be removed by a shift of the *AD* curve to AD_1. This decrease in aggregate demand could occur either because of a fall of private spending or because of contractionary fiscal policy. The shift in the *AD* curve causes a movement down and to the left along $SRAS_0$. This movement shifts the equilibrium to E_2, lowering income to Y^* and the price level to P_2.

The Paradox of Thrift

As we discovered in Chapter 29, government tax revenues are related to the performance of the economy; they are high during booms and low during slumps. Thus, if a government follows a balanced budget policy, its fiscal policy becomes **pro-cyclical.** It will restrict its spending during a recession because its tax revenue is low, and it will increase its spending during a recovery when its tax revenue is rising. In other words, it rolls with the economy, raising and lowering its spending in step with everyone else, exactly counter to the theory of fiscal stabilisation that we just discussed.

The theory of national income determination predicts that an increase in saving (which implies a reduction in consumption expenditure) will shift the *AD* curve to the left and hence *reduce* the equi-

librium level of income in the short run. The contrary case, a general decrease in thrift and increase in expenditure, shifts the *AD* curve to the right and hence increases national income in the short run. This prediction is known as the *paradox of thrift.*[4]

The policy implication of this prediction is that substantial unemployment can be combated by encouraging governments, firms, and households to spend more, *not* to save more. In times of unemployment and depression, frugality will only make things worse. This prediction goes directly against the idea that we should tighten our belts when

[4]The prediction is not actually a paradox. Rather, the prediction is a straightforward implication of the theory of income determination. The expectations that lead to the "paradox" are based on the fallacy of composition: the belief that what is true for the parts is necessarily true for the whole.

times are tough. The notion that it is not only possible but also acceptable to spend one's way out of a depression touches a sensitive point with people raised on the belief that success is based on hard work and frugality and not on prodigality; as a result, the idea often arouses great hostility.

Applications. As is discussed in Box 31-3, the implications of the paradox of thrift were not generally understood during the Great Depression, and most governments followed procyclical spending policies in order to balance their budgets. When Milton Friedman said, "We are all Keynesians now," he was referring to (among other things) the general acceptance of the view that the government's budget is much more than just the revenue and expenditure statement of a very large organization. Whether we like it or not, the sheer size of the government's budget inevitably makes it a powerful tool for influencing the economy.

Limitations. The paradox of thrift concentrates on shifts in aggregate demand that have been caused by changes in saving (and hence spending) behaviour. Hence, it applies only in the short run, when the *AD* curve plays an important role in the determination of national income.

In the long run, when the economy is on its *LRAS* curve, and hence aggregate demand is not important for the determination of real national income (see Figure 31-5), the paradox of thrift does not apply. The more people and governments save, the larger is the supply of funds available for investment. The more people invest, the greater is the growth of potential income. Increased potential income causes the *LRAS* curve to shift to the right.

These longer-term effects were discussed briefly earlier in this chapter (pages 631–634) and are taken up in detail in Chapter 38 in the discussion of economic growth. In the meantime, we concentrate on the short-run demand effects of saving and spending.

The paradox of thrift is based on the short-run effects of changes in saving and investment on aggregate demand.

Automatic Stabilizers

In Chapter 29, we introduced the *budget surplus function.* The *discretionary* fiscal policy that we have been discussing in this chapter involves *shifts* in the budget surplus function. Expansionary policies, whether increases in purchases or decreases in net taxes, reduce the budget surplus (increase the deficit) at every level of national income, shifting the *AD* curve to the right. Contractionary policies increase the surplus (reduce the deficit) at every level of income, shifting the *AD* curve to the left.

Even when the government does not undertake to stabilize the economy via discretionary fiscal policy, the upward slope of the budget surplus function means that there are fiscal effects that cause the budget to act as an *automatic stabilizer* for the economy.

The budget surplus increases as income increases because tax revenues rise, and some transfer payments, especially unemployment insurance and welfare payments, fall. Thus, net taxes move in the same direction as national income. (Unless there are changes in policy, government purchases are generally unaffected by cyclical movements in the economy.) With procyclical net tax revenues, disposable income moves in the same direction as national income but does not move by as much. The government keeps a share of the increased national income when national income rises. When national income falls, the fall in net taxes makes disposable income fall by less.

In Chapter 29, for example, we assumed that the net income tax rate was 10 percent of national income. This implies that a $1 rise in autonomous spending would increase disposable income by only $0.90, dampening the multiplier effect of the initial increase. Generally, the wedge that income taxes place between national income and disposable income reduces the marginal propensity to spend out of national income, thereby reducing the size of the multiplier. The lower the multiplier, the less will equilibrium national income tend to change for a given change in autonomous expenditure. The effect is to stabilize the economy, reducing the fluctuations in national income that are caused by changes in autonomous expenditure. Because no policies need to be changed in order to achieve this result, the properties of the government budget that cause the multiplier to be reduced are called **automatic fiscal stabilizers.**

Limitations of Discretionary Fiscal Policy

According to the discussion of the previous few pages, returning the economy to high employment

Box 31-3

Fiscal Policy and the Great Depression

Failure to understand the implication of the paradox of thrift led many countries to adopt policies during the Great Depresion that were disastrous. Failure to understand the role of built-in stabilizers has also led many observers to conclude, erroneously, that fiscal expansion had been tried in the Great Depression but had failed. Let us see how these two misperceptions are related.

The Paradox of Thrift in Action

In Canada, Prime Minister R. B. Bennett said in 1932, in the worst recession in recorded history, "We are now faced with the real crisis in the history of Canada. To maintain our credit we must practise the most rigid economy and not spend a single cent." His government that year brought down a budget based on the principle of trying to balance revenues and expenditures, and it included *increases* in tax rates.

U.S. President Franklin D. Roosevelt, in his first inaugural address (1933), urged: "Our great primary task is to put people to work... [This task] can be helped by insistence that the federal, state and local governments act forthwith on the demand that their costs be drastically reduced... There must be a strict supervision of all banking and credits and investments."

Across the Atlantic, King George V told the British House of Commons in 1931, "The present condition of the national finances, in the opinion of His Majesty's Ministers, calls for the imposition of additional taxation and for the effecting of economies in public expenditure."

As the paradox of thrift predicts, these policies reduced aggregate demand and hence tended to worsen, not cure, the Depression.

Interpreting the Deficit in the 1930s

Government deficits did increase in the 1930s, but they were not the result of a program of deficit-financed public expenditure. They were the result of the fall in tax yields brought about by the fall in national income as the economy sank into depression. The various governments did not advocate a program of massive deficit-financed spending to shift the *AD* curve to the right. Instead, they hoped that a small amount of government spending plus numerous policies designed to stabilize prices and to restore confidence would lead to a recovery of private investment expenditure that would substantially shift the aggregate demand curve. To have expected a massive revival of private investment expenditure as a result of the puny increase in aggregate demand instituted by government now seems hopelessly naïve.

When we judge these policies from the viewpoint of modern multiplier theory, their failure is no mystery. Indeed, Professor E. Cary Brown of MIT, after a careful study, concluded, "Fiscal policy seems to have been an unsuccessful recovery device in the 'thirties—not because it did not work, but because it was not tried."

The performance of the North American economies from 1930 to 1945 is quite well explained by national income theory. It is clear that the governments did not effectively use fiscal measures to stabilize their economies. War cured the Depression because war demands made acceptable a level of government expenditure sufficient to remove the recessionary gap. Had the Canadian and American administrations been able to do the same, they might have ended the waste of the Depression many years sooner.

would simply be a matter of cutting taxes and raising government spending in some combination. Why did so many economists believe that such policies would be "as likely to harm as help"? Part of the answer is that the execution of discretionary fiscal policy is anything but simple.[5]

Lags. To change fiscal policy requires making changes in taxes and government expenditures. The changes must be agreed upon by the cabinet and passed by parliament. The political stakes in such changes are generally very large; taxes and spending are called "bread and butter issues" precisely because they affect the economic well-being of almost everyone. Thus, even if economists agreed that the economy would be helped by, say, a tax cut, politicians would likely spend a good deal of time debating *whose* taxes should be cut by *how much.* The delay between the initial recognition of a recession or inflation and the enactment of legislation to change fiscal policy is called a **decision lag.**

Once policy changes are agreed upon, there is still an **execution lag**, adding time between the enactment and the implementation of the change. Furthermore, once policies are in place, it will usually take still more time for their economic consequences to be felt. Because of these lags, it is quite possible that by the time a given policy decision has any impact on the economy, circumstances will have changed such that the policy is no longer appropriate. Figure 31-11 illustrates the problems that can arise in these circumstances.

To make matters even more frustrating, tax measures that are known to be temporary are generally less effective than measures that are expected to be permanent. If households know that a given tax cut will only last for a year, they may recognise that the effect on their long-run consumption possibilities is small and may adjust their short-run consumption relatively little.

The more closely household consumption expenditure is related to lifetime income rather than to current income, the smaller will be

---

[5]Another part of the answer has to do with the long-term consequences of budget deficits. This subject is taken up in Chapter 37. Also, as we shall see in Chapter 40, international considerations may reduce (but not eliminate) fiscal policy's effectiveness as a stabilization tool.

FIGURE 31-11
Effects of Fiscal Policies That Are Not Reversed

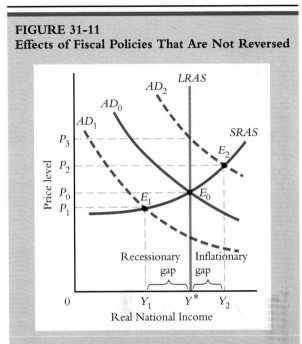

Fiscal policies that are initially appropriate may become inappropriate when private expenditure shifts. The normal level of the aggregate demand function is assumed to be AD_0, leaving income normally at Y^* and the price level at P_0. Suppose a slump in private investment shifts aggregate demand to AD_1, lowering national income to Y_1 and causing a recessionary gap of $Y^* - Y_1$.

The government now introduces fiscal expansion to restore aggregate demand to AD_0 and national income to Y^*. Suppose that private investment then recovers, raising aggregate demand to AD_2. If fiscal policy can be quickly reversed, aggregate demand can be returned to AD_0 and income stabilized at Y^*. If the policy is not quickly reversed, equilibrium will be at E_2 and an inflationary gap $Y^* - Y_2$ will open up. This gap will cause wages to rise and thus shift the SRAS curve leftward and eventually restore Y^* at price level P_3.

Now suppose that starting from equilibrium E_0, a persistent investment boom takes AD_0 to AD_2. In order to stop the price level from rising in the face of the newly opened inflationary gap, the government introduces fiscal restraint, thereby shifting aggregate demand back to AD_0. Further assume, however, that the investment boom then comes to a halt, so that the aggregate demand curve shifts downward to AD_1. Unless the fiscal policy can be rapidly reversed, a recessionary gap will open up and equilibrium income will fall to Y_1.

the effects on current consumption of tax changes that are known to be of short duration.

The role of discretionary fiscal policy. All of these difficulties suggest that attempts to use discretionary fiscal policy to fine tune the economy are fraught with difficulties. **Fine-tuning** refers to the use of fiscal and monetary policy to offset virtually all fluctuations in private sector spending and so hold national income at, or very near, its potential level at all times. However, neither economic nor political science has yet advanced far enough to allow policy makers to undo the consequences of every aggregate demand shock. On the other hand, many economists would still argue that when a recessionary gap is large enough and persists for long enough, gross tuning may be appropriate. **Gross-tuning** refers to the occasional use of fiscal and monetary policy to remove large and persistent GDP gaps. Advocates of gross tuning hold that fiscal policy can and should be used to return the economy to full employment when a GDP is large and

persistent. Other economists believe that fiscal policy should not be used for economic stabilization under any circumstances. Rather, they would argue, tax and spending behaviour should be the outcome of public choices regarding the long-term size and financing of the public sector and should not be altered for short-term considerations. We return to these debates in Chapters 37 and 38.

To get ahead of our story, the desirability of using fiscal policy to stabilize the economy depends a great deal on the speed with which the adjustment mechanism returns the economy to potential income. If the adjustment mechanism works quickly, there is no role for discretionary fiscal policy. If the adjustment mechanism works slowly, there may well be a role for policies that can be used to shift aggregate demand. Fiscal policy is one such policy. Monetary policy, which we take up in the next three chapters, is another. Only when we have completed our study of the way in which money and monetary institutions fit into the overall macroeconomy can we fully outline the choices available to governments wishing to stabilize their economies.

SUMMARY

1. Potential income is treated as given and is represented by a vertical line at Y^*. The output gap is equal to the horizontal distance between Y^* and the actual level of income, as determined by the intersection of the AD and $SRAS$ curves.

2. An expansionary demand shock creates an inflationary gap causing wages to rise faster than productivity. Unit costs rise, shifting the $SRAS$ curve to the left and resulting in a higher level of prices, with output eventually falling back to its potential level.

3. A contractionary demand shock creates a recessionary gap. Wages fall relative to productivity, shifting the SRAS curve to the right. Since factor prices tend to be sticky, the automatic adjustment process tends to be slow, and a recessionary gap tends to persist for some time.

4. The long-run aggregate supply ($LRAS$) curve relates the price level and national income after all wages and other costs have been adjusted fully to long-run equilibrium. The $LRAS$ curve is vertical at the level of potential income, Y^*. As a result, output in the long run is determined by the position of the $LRAS$ curve, and the only long-run role of the AD curve is to determine the price level. Economic growth determines the position of the $LRAS$ curve.

5. GDP can increase (or decrease) for any of three reasons: a change in aggregate demand; a change in short-run aggregate supply; or a change in long-run aggregate supply, which is called economic growth. The first two changes are typically associated with business cycles.

6. Demand shocks are an important source of business cycles. As the shock works its way through the economy and the adjustment mechanism comes into play, GDP will often exhibit a cyclical (up and down, or down and up) pattern.

7. In principle, fiscal policy can be used to stabilize the position of the *AD* curve at or near potential GDP. To remove a recessionary gap, governments can shift *AD* to the right by cutting taxes and increasing spending. To remove an inflationary gap, governments can pursue the opposite policies.

8. When the economy is in a recessionary gap, increases in desired savings on the part of firms, households, and governments are likely to lead to further reductions in GDP, and may lead to reductions in actual saving. This phenomenon is often called "the paradox of thrift." In the long run, with the economy at Y^*, the paradox does not obtain, and increased thrift will lead to increased economic growth.

9. Because government tax and transfer programs tend to reduce the size of the multiplier, they act as automatic stabilizers. When national income changes, in either direction, disposable income changes by less because of taxes and transfers.

10. Discretionary fiscal policy is subject to decision lags and execution lags that limit its ability to take effect quickly. Some economists argue that these limitations are so severe that fiscal policy should never be used for stabilization because it will do more harm than good. Others argue that the automatic adjustment mechanism works so slowly that fiscal policy can play an important role in stabilizing the economy.

TOPICS FOR REVIEW

The output gap and the labour market

Inflationary gap

Recessionary gap

Asymmetry of wage adjustment

Changes in aggregate demand and induced wage changes

Wages, productivity, and unit costs

The Automatic adjustment mechanism

Long-run aggregate supply (*LRAS*) curve

Economic stabilization

Decision lags and execution lags

Automatic stabilizers

DISCUSSION QUESTIONS

1. "Starting from a full-employment equilibrium, an increase in government spending can produce more output and employment at the cost of a once-and-for-all rise in the price level."

   "Increased spending can never lead to a permanent increase in output above its full employment level."

   Discuss these two statements in terms of short- and long-run aggregate supply curves.

2. Identify the effects of each of the following events on the *SRAS* and the *LRAS* curves.

   a. Increase in the price of imported raw materials that are used in key manufacturing industries.

   b. Increase in the price of imported consumption goods such as coffee or bananas.

   c. Increased restrictions on pollution emissions in an attempt to combat acid rain.

   d. Projections of reduced federal government deficits over the next 5 years.

   e. An improved economic outlook leading to an investment boom.

   f. Increased labour force participation rate of key sectors of the population.

3. Interpret each of the following news items in terms of *AD* and *SRAS* curves. (Assume that the statements are correct for purposes of drawing your curves.)

   a. "Management representative says union wage demands are irresponsible in the face of current high unemployment rates."

   b. "Government spokesman says that although the recovery is expected to be vigorous, it will witness only modest reductions in the unemployment rate."

   c. "Wage increases have failed to keep up with inflation during the current boom."

   d. "Innovations in microelectronic technology will lead to an increase in both national output and unemployment."

4. Comment on the following newspaper headline: "More growth seen as cure for inflation."

5. Politicians are sometimes accused of adopting policies that bring "short-term gain at the cost of long-term pain," while statesmen offer "short-term pain to buy long-term gain." What policies that shift aggregate demand or aggregate supply curves might come under one or the other of these descriptions?

6. About 25 percent of Canadian national income is generated through exports, of which about 75 percent go to the United States. Why do Canadians worry that "when the United States gets an (economic) cold, Canada may get (economic) pneumonia"? Why does Canada often experience "export-led recoveries" from severe recessions?

7. If downward flexibility of money wages would allow the automatic adjustment mechanism to eliminate recessionary gaps

quickly, why do workers usually resist wage cuts during times of economic slump?

8. Since different series behave differently, does it make sense to talk about a business cycle? Predict the comparative behaviour of the following pairs of series in relation to fluctuations in GDP.

   a. Purchases of food and purchases of consumer durables.
   b. Tax receipts and business failures.
   c. Unemployment and birth rates.
   d. Employment in Ontario and employment in Alberta.

   Check your predictions against the facts for the last decade.

9. Which of the following would be built-in stabilizers?

   a. UI payments.
   b. Cost-of-living escalators in government contracts and pensions.
   c. Income taxes.
   d. Free further education for unemployed workers after 6 months of unemployment, provided that they are under 30 years old and have had 5 or more years of full-time work experience since high school.

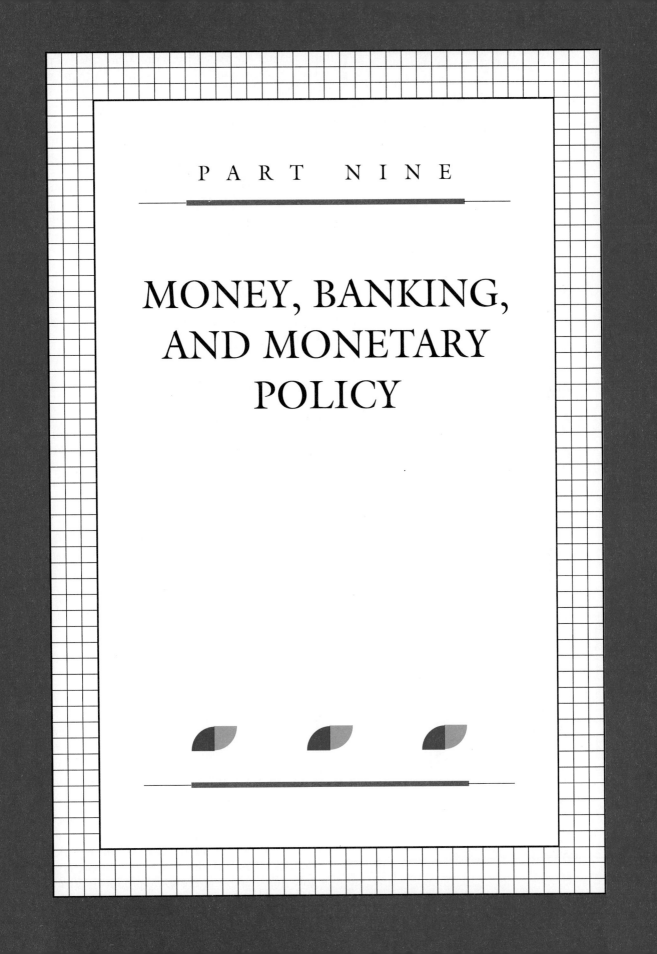

PART NINE

MONEY, BANKING, AND MONETARY POLICY

32

The Nature of Money and Monetary Institutions

I n this chapter, we ask: What is the significance of money to the economy, and how did it come to play its present role? Many people believe that money is one of the more important things in life, and that there is never enough of it. Yet economists argue that increasing any country's money supply would not make its average citizen better off. Although money allows those who have it to buy someone else's output, the total amount of goods and services available for everyone to buy depends on the total output produced, not on the total amount of money that people possess. In the terminology of Chapter 31, an increase in the quantity of money will not increase the level of potential national income, Y^*.

The Classical View

In the eighteenth and nineteenth centuries, economists explained the independence of Y^* from monetary factors in terms of an economic theory that distinguished sharply between the "real sector of economy" and the "monetary sector." This approach led to a view of the economy that is now referred to as the *classical dichotomy*.

According to these so-called classical economists, the allocation of resources, and hence the determination of real national income, is determined in the real sector. Further, they argued that it is *relative prices,* including the level of wages relative to the price of commodities, that matter for this process.

According to the classical economists, the allocation of resources and the determination of real national income depends only on relative prices.

These early economists argued that the price *level* is determined in the monetary sector of the economy. If the quantity of money were doubled, *other things being equal,* the prices of all commodities and money income would double. Relative prices would remain unchanged, and the real sector would be unaffected.

According to the classical economists, an increase in the money supply leads to a proportionate increase in all money prices, with no change in the allocation of resources or the level of real national income.

The doctrine that the quantity of money influences the level of money prices but has no effect on the real part of the economy is called the **neutrality of money.** Because early economists believed that the most important questions—How much does the economy produce? What share of it does each group in the society get?—were answered in

FIGURE 32-1
Index of Canadian Wholesale Prices, 1867-1992

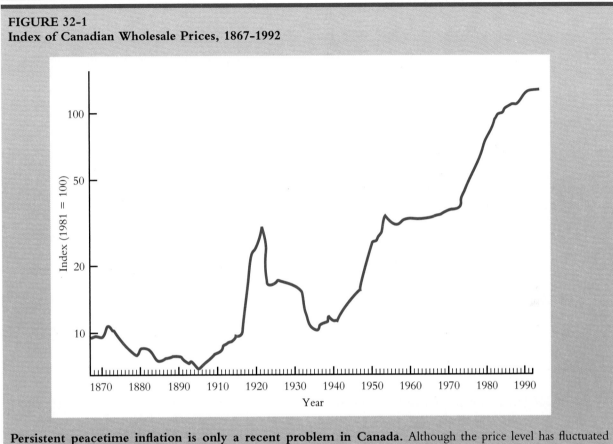

Persistent peacetime inflation is only a recent problem in Canada. Although the price level has fluctuated throughout Canadian history, no long-term trend was visible during the period from confederation to 1940. From the time of World War II to the present, the price level has shown a consistent upward trend. (*Source:* Statistics Canada, Industrial Price Index, 62-0112.)

the real sector, they spoke of money as a veil behind which occurred the real events that affected material well-being.

The Modern View

Most modern economists still accept the insights of the early economists that relative prices are a major determinant of the allocation of resources and that the quantity of money has a lot to do with determining the absolute level of prices. They accept the neutrality of money in long-run equilibrium, when all the forces causing change have fully worked themselves out. However, they do not accept the neutrality of money when the economy is adjusting to the various factors that cause it to change, that is,

when the economy is not in a state of long-run equilibrium. Thus, they reject the classical dichotomy as a description of the day-to-day behaviour of the economy.

Money and the price level. Modern economists stress that there is a strong link between money and the price level, especially over long periods of time, when the conditions of long-run equilibrium are apt to be most relevant. In Chapter 26 (see pages 528–532), we discussed the price level and inflation, and we presented some evidence from the Canadian experience over the past half century or so.

Figure 32-1 gives a longer-run perspective. It shows the course of wholesale prices in Canada

FIGURE 32-2
A Price Index of Consumables in Southern England, 1275-1959

Over the past seven centuries, long periods of stable prices have alternated with long periods of rising prices. This remarkable price series shows an index of the prices of food, clothing, and fuel in southern England from 1275 through 1959. The trend line shows that the average change in prices over the whole period was 0.5 percent per year. The shaded areas indicate periods of unreversed inflation. The series also shows that even the perspective of a century can be misleading, because long periods of stable or gently falling prices tended to alternate with long periods of rising prices. (*Source: Lloyds Bank Review*, No. 58, October 1960.)

since confederation. Despite the large fluctuations that occurred during the nineteenth century, the price trend during that period was neither upward nor downward. In contrast, the twentieth century has seen large fluctuations *and* a distinct rising trend in the price level.

Although admittedly a long time, even two centuries may still not be enough to give us a clear perspective of very-long-term price fluctuations. Figure 32-2 shows the course of the price level in southern England over seven centuries. It shows that there was an overall inflationary trend but that it was by no means evenly spread over the centuries.

The Nature of Money

Money affects the price level in the long run, and both the price level and the level of real income in the short run. But what exactly is money? More folklore and general nonsense are believed about money than about any other aspect of the economy. In this section we describe the functions of money and briefly outline its history.

What Is Money?

In economics, **money** has usually been defined as any generally accepted medium of exchange. A **medium of exchange** is anything that will be widely accepted in a society in exchange for goods and services. Although its medium-of-exchange role is its most important one, money can also serve other roles:

Money acts as a medium of exchange and can also serve as a store of value and a unit of account.

Different kinds of money vary in the degree of efficiency with which they fulfill these functions. As we shall see, different definitions of the money supply stress different functions of money.

A medium of exchange. If there were no money, goods would have to be exchanged by barter (one good being swapped directly for another). We discussed this cumbersome system in Chapter 3. The major difficulty with barter is that each transaction requires a *double coincidence of wants;* anyone who specialized in producing one commodity would have to spend a great deal of time searching for satisfactory transactions.

The use of money as a medium of exchange alleviates this problem. People can sell their output for money and subsequently use the money to buy what they wish from others.

The double coincidence of wants is unnecessary when a medium of exchange is used.

By facilitating transactions, money makes possible the benefits of specialization and the division of labour, which in turn contribute to the efficiency of the economic system. It is not without justification that money has been called one of the great inventions contributing to human freedom and well-being.

To serve as an efficient medium of exchange, money must have a number of characteristics. It must be readily acceptable. It must have a high value relative to its weight (otherwise it would be a nuisance to carry around). It must be divisible, because money that comes only in large denominations is useless for transactions with only a small value. Finally, it must be difficult, if not impossible, to counterfeit.

A store of value. Money is a convenient way to store purchasing power; goods may be sold today, and money may be stored until it is needed. To be a satisfactory store of value, however, money must have a relatively stable value. A rise in the price level means a decrease in the purchasing power of money. When the price level is stable, the purchasing power of a given sum of money is also stable; when the price level is highly variable, this is not so, and the usefulness of money as a store of value is undermined. Over the past two decades, Canadian inflation has been high enough and variable enough to diminish money's usefulness as a store of value.[1] However, Canadian inflation rates have been modest compared to those in some other countries; an extreme example is discussed in Box 32-1.

Although in a noninflationary environment, money can serve as a satisfactory store of accumulated purchasing power for a single individual, even in those circumstances it cannot do so for the society as a whole. A single individual can accumulate dollars, and when the time comes to spend them, he or she will be able to command the current output of others. All of society cannot do this. If all individuals were to save their money and then retire simultaneously to live on their savings, there would be no current production to purchase and consume.

The society's ability to satisfy wants depends on goods and services being available; if some of this want-satisfying capacity is to be stored up for the whole society, some goods that could be produced today must be saved for future periods.

A unit of account. Money also may be used purely for accounting purposes without having a physical existence of its own. For instance, a government store in a truly communist society might say that everyone had so many "dollars" to use each month. Goods could then be assigned prices and each consumer's purchases recorded, the consumer being allowed to buy until the allocated supply of dollars was exhausted. These dollars need have no existence other than as entries in the store's books, yet they would serve as a perfectly satisfactory unit of account.

Whether they could also serve as a medium of exchange between individuals depends on whether the store would agree to transfer dollar credits from one customer to another at the customer's request. Banks will transfer dollars credited to deposits in this way, and thus a bank deposit can serve as both a unit of account and a medium of exchange. Notice that the use of *dollars* in this context suggests a further sense in which money is a unit of account. People think about values in terms of the monetary unit with which they are familiar.

A related function of money is that it can be used as a *standard of deferred payments.* Payments that are to be made in the future, on account of debts and so on, are reckoned in money. Money's ability to serve as a *unit of account over time* in this manner is much diminished by inflation.

The Origins of Money

The origins of money go far back in antiquity. Most primitive tribes are known to have made some use of it.

---

[1]See, for example, Figure 26-6 on page 530. The experience of inflation is discussed in more detail in Chapter 35.

Box 32-1

Hyperinflation

Can the price level ever rise so rapidly that money loses its usefulness either as a medium of exchange or as a store of value? The answer appears to be that occasionally, this does happen. Inflation rates of 50, 100, and even 200 percent or more per year have occurred year after year in many countries and have proven to be manageable as people adjust their contracts in real terms. Although there are strains and side effects, the evidence shows such situations to be possible without causing money to become useless.

Does this mean that there is no reason to fear that rapid inflation will turn into hyperinflation that will destroy the value of money completely? The historical record is not entirely reassuring. There have been a number of cases in which prices began to rise at an ever-accelerating rate until a nation's money ceased to be a satisfactory store of value, even for the short period between receipt and expenditure, and hence ceased also to be useful as a medium of exchange.

The index of wholesale prices in Germany during and after World War I is given in the table. The index shows that a good purchased with one 100-mark note in July 1923 would have required *ten million* 100-mark notes for its purchase only four months later! Although Germany had experienced substantial inflation during World War I, averaging more than 30 percent per year, the immediate post war years of 1920 and 1921 gave no sign of an explosive inflation. Indeed, during 1920, price stability was experienced, but in 1922 and 1923 the price level exploded. On November 15, 1923, the mark was officially repudiated, its value wholly destroyed. How could this happen?

When an inflation becomes so rapid that people lose confidence in the purchasing power of their currency, they rush to spend it. People who have goods become increasingly reluctant to accept the rapidly depreciating money in exchange. The rush to spend money accelerates the increase in prices until people finally become unwilling to accept money on any terms. What was once money ceases to be money.

The price system can then be restored only by repudiation of the old monetary unit and its replacement by a new unit. This destroys the value of

Metallic Money

All sorts of commodities have been used as money at one time or another, but gold and silver proved to have great advantages. They were precious because their supplies were relatively limited, and they were in constant demand by the wealthy for ornament and decoration. Thus, these metals tended to have a high and stable price. Further, they were easily recognised, they were divisible into extremely small units, and they did not easily wear out.

Precious metals came to circulate as money and to be used in many transactions.

Before the invention of coins, it was necessary to carry the metals in bulk. When a purchase was made, the requisite quantity of the metal was carefully weighed on a scale. The invention of coinage eliminated the need to weigh the metal at each transaction, but it created an important role for an authority, usually a monarch, who made the coins. They contained a given amount of precious metal for value and some base metal for durability. The ruler then affixed his or her seal, guaranteeing the amount of precious metal that the coin contained. This was clearly a great convenience, as long as traders knew that they could accept the coin at its "face value." The face value was nothing more than a statement that a certain weight of precious metal was contained therein.

However, coins often could not be taken at their face value. A form of counterfeiting—clipping

Date		German wholesale price index (1913 = 1)
January	1913	1
January	1920	13
January	1921	14
January	1922	37
July	1922	101
January	1923	2,785
July	1923	74,800
August	1923	944,000
September	1923	23,900,000
October	1923	7,096,000,000
November	1923*	750,000,000,000

*The mark was repudiated on November 15, 1923.

monetary savings and of all contracts specified in terms of the old monetary unit.

Until recently, there were only about a dozen documented hyperinflations in world history, among them the collapse of the continental during the American Revolution, the ruble during the Russian Revolution, the drachma during and after the German occupation of Greece in World War II, the pengo in Hungary during 1945 to 1946, and the Chinese national currency during 1946 to 1948. Every one of these hyperinflations was accompanied by great increases in the money supply; new money was printed to give governments purchasing power that they could not or would not obtain by taxation. Further, every one occurred in the midst of a major political upheaval in which grave doubts existed about the stability and the future of the government itself. Recent upheavals in Eastern Europe have produced additional, more recent cases. For example, in 1983 the rate of inflation in Yugoslavia was 4,000 percent per year.

Is hyperinflation likely in the absence of civil war, revolution, or collapse of the government? Most economists think not. Further, it is clear that high inflation rates over a period of time do not mean the inevitable or even likely onset of hyperinflation, however serious the distributive and social effects of such rates may be.

a thin slice off the edge of the coin and keeping the valuable metal—became common. This, of course, served to undermine the acceptability of coins—even if they were stamped. To get around this problem, the idea arose of minting the coins with a rough edge. The absence of the rough edge would immediately indicate that the coin had been clipped. This practise, called *milling,* survives on some coins as an interesting anachronism to remind us that there were days when the market value of the metal in the coin was equal to the face value of the coin.

Not to be outdone by the cunning of their subjects, some rulers were quick to seize the chance of getting something for nothing. The power to mint placed rulers in a position to work a *really profitable fraud.* They often used some suitable occasion—a marriage, an anniversary, an alliance—to remint the coinage. Subjects would be ordered to bring their coins into the mint to be melted down and coined afresh with a new stamp. Between the melting down and the recoining, however, the rulers had only to toss some further inexpensive base metal in with the molten gold. This *debasing* of the coinage allowed the ruler to earn a handsome profit by minting more new coins than the number of old ones collected, and putting the extras in the royal vault.

The result of debasement was inflation. The subjects had the same number of coins as before and hence could demand the same quantity of goods. When rulers paid their bills, however, the recipients of the extra coins could be expected to spend them. This caused a net increase in demand, which in turn bid up prices.

Debasing the coinage was a common cause of increases in prices.

It was the experience of such inflations that led early economists to stress the link between the quantity of money and the price level.

Gresham's law. The early experience of currency debasement led to the observation known as **Gresham's law,** after Sir Thomas Gresham, an advisor to the Elizabethan court, who coined the phrase "bad money drives out good."

When Queen Elizabeth I came to the throne of England in the middle of the sixteenth century, the coinage had been severely debased. Seeking to help trade, Elizabeth minted new coins that contained their full face value in gold. However, as fast as she fed these new coins into circulation, they disappeared. Why?

Suppose that you possessed one new and one old coin, each with the same face value, and had a bill to pay. What would you do? Clearly, you would use the debased coin to pay the bill and keep the undebased one. (You part with less gold that way.) Suppose that you wanted to obtain a certain amount of gold bullion by melting down the gold coins (as was frequently done). Which coins would you use? Clearly, you would use new, undebased coins because you would part with less "face value" that way. The debased coins would thus remain in circulation, and the undebased coins would disappear.

Gresham's insights have proven helpful in explaining the experience of a number of modern high-inflation economies. For example, in the 1970s, inflation in Chile raised the value of the metallic content in coins above their face value. Coins quickly disappeared from circulation as private citizens sold them to entrepreneurs who melted them down for their metal. Only paper currency remained in circulation and was used even for tiny transactions such as purchasing a pack of matches. Gresham's law is one reason why modern coins, unlike their historical counterparts, are now merely tokens that contain a metallic value that is only a minute fraction of their face value.

Paper Money

The next important step in the history of money was the evolution of paper currency, one source of which was goldsmiths. They were artisans who worked with gold and required secure safes. The public began to deposit their gold for safekeeping. Goldsmiths would give their depositors receipts promising to hand over the gold on demand. When any depositor wished to make a large purchase, she could go to her goldsmith, reclaim some of her gold, and hand it over to the seller of the goods. If the seller had no immediate need for the gold, he would carry it back to the goldsmith for safekeeping.

If people knew the goldsmith to be reliable, there was no need to go through the cumbersome and risky business of physically transferring the gold. Buyers needed only to transfer the goldsmith's receipt to sellers, who would accept it as long as they were confident that the goldsmith would pay over the gold whenever it was needed. If the seller wished to buy a good from a third party, who also knew the goldsmith to be reliable, this transaction could also be effected by passing the goldsmith's receipt from the buyer to the seller. The convenience of using pieces of paper instead of gold is obvious.

When it first came into being, paper money represented a promise to pay so much gold on demand. In this case, the promise was made first by goldsmiths and later by banks. Such paper money was *backed* by precious metal and was *convertible on demand* into this metal. In the nineteenth-century private banks commonly issued paper money, called **bank notes,** nominally convertible into gold.

Fractionally backed paper money. Early on, many goldsmiths and banks discovered that it was not necessary to keep an ounce of gold in the vaults for every claim to an ounce circulating as paper money.

At any one time, some of the bank's customers would be withdrawing gold, others would be depositing it, and most would be trading in the bank's paper notes without any need or desire to convert them into gold.

As a result, the bank was able to issue more money redeemable in gold than the amount of gold that it held in its vaults. This was good business, because the money could be invested profitably in interest-earning loans to households and firms. To this day, banks have many more claims outstanding against them than they actually have in reserves available to pay those claims. We say that the currency issued in such a situation is *fractionally backed* by the reserves.

The major problem with a fractionally backed convertible currency was maintaining its convertibility into the precious metal by which it was backed. The imprudent bank that issued too much paper money would find itself unable to redeem its currency in gold when the demand for gold was even slightly higher than usual. It would then have to suspend payments, and all holders of its notes would suddenly find that the notes were worthless. The prudent bank that kept a reasonable relationship between its note issue and its gold reserve would find that it could meet a normal range of demand for gold without any trouble.

Even prudent banks were not immune from sudden rushes to withdraw funds. If the public lost confidence and demanded redemption of its currency *en masse,* the banks would be unable to honor their pledges. The history of nineteenth- and early twentieth-century banking on both sides of the Atlantic is full of examples of banks that were ruined by "panics," or sudden runs on their gold reserves. When this happened, the banks' depositors and the holders of their notes would find themselves with worthless pieces of paper.

Fiat Money

As time went on, note issue by private banks became less common, and central banks took control of the currency. In time, *only* central banks were permitted to issue notes. Originally, the central banks issued currency that was fully convertible into gold. In those days, gold would be brought to the central bank, which would issue currency in the form of "gold certificates" that asserted that the gold was available on demand. The gold supply thus set some upper limit on the amount of currency.

However, central banks, like private banks before them, could issue more currency than they had in gold, because in normal times, only a small fraction of the currency was presented for payment at any one time. Thus, even though the need to maintain convertibility under a gold standard put an upper limit on note issue, central banks had sub-

stantial discretionary control over the quantity of currency outstanding.

During the period between World Wars I and II, almost all of the countries of the world abandoned the gold standard; their currencies were thus no longer convertible into gold. Money that is not convertible by law into anything valuable derives its value from its acceptability in exchange. **Fiat money** is widely acceptable because it is declared by government order, or *fiat,* to be legal tender. **Legal tender** is anything that by law must be accepted when offered either for the purchase of goods or services or to discharge a debt.

Today almost all currency is fiat money.

Today, a few countries preserve the fiction that their currency is backed by gold, but no country allows its currency to be converted into gold on demand. Gold backing for Canadian currency was eliminated in 1940, although note issues continued to carry the traditional statement "will pay to the bearer on demand" until 1954. Today's Bank of Canada notes simply say, "This note is legal tender." It is, in other words, fiat money pure and simple.

Fiat money is valuable because it is accepted in payment for the purchase of goods or services and for the discharge of debts.

Many people are disturbed to learn that present-day paper money is neither backed by nor convertible into anything more valuable—that it consists of nothing but pieces of paper whose value derives from common acceptance and from confidence that it will continue to be accepted in the future. Many people believe that their money should be more substantial than this. Yet money is, in fact, nothing more than pieces of paper.

If fiat money is acceptable, it is a medium of exchange. Further, if its purchasing power remains stable, it is a satisfactory store of value. And if both of these things are true, it will also serve as a satisfactory unit of account.

Modern Money

By the twentieth century, private banks had lost the authority to issue bank notes. Yet, as we shall see, they did not lose the power to create money. A

Box 32-2

Terminology of a Modern Financial System

Throughout this and subsequent chapters, we will encounter many different types of financial assets, or *securities*. One important distinction is between equity and debt. In short, equity represents ownership, whereas debt represents a loan.

Equity refers to assets such as *stocks* or *shares* that represent evidence of part ownership of a firm, and hence provide a claim on the earnings of that firm; the return on equity depends upon the performance of the firm. Equity is also often called *real capital*, or just *capital*; unless the context makes it clear, care must be taken to distinguish the use of the term *real capital* to refer to the actual plant, equipment, and machinery that constitute a firm's physical assets, and the use of the term to refer to the financial assets that represent a claim on the earnings of that firm.

Debt refers to assets issued by firms and governments that promise to repay the amount borrowed, almost always at some specified future date. This amount is called the *principal* (sometimes the face value or the redemption value of the asset). The time at which the loan will be repaid is called the asset's maturity date. The time until the maturity date is called the **term to maturity**, or simply the **term**, of the asset. A very few bonds, called *perpetuities*, pay interest forever and never repay the principal.

Many debt instruments, often called bonds, promise to pay a stated sum of money as interest each year as well as to repay the principal on the maturity date. Unless the bond is issued by a firm that goes bankrupt and cannot meet its obligations, the return on debt does not depend upon the earnings of the firm—the interest must be paid whether the firm is profitable or not and thus represents a prior claim on the firm's earnings before any payment to equity holders is made.

A second major type of debt instrument is called a *bill*. Bills promise a single payment (combining interest and principal) that will usually be made in less than one year. As well as borrowing by selling bonds, the government also borrows substantial sums by issuing bills which are called **treasury bills**. The price paid for a bill is less than the amount the bill promises to pay; this is referred to as the *discount*. The difference between the purchase price and the payment represents the interest on the bill. So if a ninety day, $1,000 bill sells for $980, the interest is 2 percent over a three-year period or 8 percent a year.

A key feature of most financial assets is that their ownership is transferable, and hence they can be bought and sold in financial markets. As with anything else that is bought and sold, the price of financial assets fluctuates in response to shifts in supply and demand. In the next chapter (see especially

number of terms that will be encountered as we discuss modern money and the institutions related to it are discussed in Box 32-2.

Deposit Money

As with gold transfers, this is a tedious procedure. It is more convenient to have the bank transfer claims to money on deposit. As soon as cheques, which are written instructions to the bank to make a transfer, became widely accepted in payment for commodities and debts, bank deposits became a form of money called deposit money. **Deposit money** is defined as money held by the public in the form of deposits in commercial banks that can be withdrawn on demand. These are also called **demand deposits**.[2]

Box 33-1) we will look more carefully at the determination of the price of financial assets. In particular we will examine the relationship between the price paid for an asset and the *yield* it earns. To anticipate that discussion, we will see that when the price of an asset that promises to pay a certain income stream in the future changes, the yield on that asset changes in the opposite direction. *The more one pays to obtain a claim on a given income stream, the lower the yield on one's investment, and vice versa.*

One important characteristic of financial assets is their *riskiness*, which refers to the possibility that the future payments will not be made or not be made in full. Typically, investors are thought to be *risk averse*, so the riskier an asset is, the higher the yield it will have to offer in order to induce investors to buy it.

Another important characteristic of financial assets is their *liquidity*, which refers to their usefulness as a ready means of payment. Money can always be used as a means of payment and hence is a perfectly liquid asset. Other financial assets can be sold in the market and hence are convertible into cash, so they appear to be just as liquid as money. However, the markets for some assets are such that they cannot always be instantly sold, or at least not at anything other than a "bargain-basement" price (often called the liquidation value); to receive the price that is justified by the asset's risk and return, some time and expense must be incurred. Further, because the market price of an asset will fluctuate when interest rates change, there is always some uncertainty about what the market value of a particular asset will be at some future date, even when there is no uncertainty about the future payments it will generate. This uncertainty reduces the liquidity of an asset. As we shall see in Box 33-1, the longer is an asset's term to maturity, the greater is the potential range of fluctuations in its market price. As a result, *longer-term assets are less liquid than are short-term assets.*

A bank deposit is, from this perspective, just one very short term and highly liquid asset, and hence it is often called *deposit money*. When the bank receives a deposit, the deposit creates an *asset* for the bank in the form of the increased funds held. It also creates an obligation on the part of the bank in that it must stand ready to turn the funds over to the depositor, either on demand or after the period of time set out in the terms of the deposit. From the bank's viewpoint, the obligation created by the deposit is a *liability*, and, as we shall see, it is common to speak of a bank's *deposit liabilities*. This can be confusing until you realize that the deposit liability is just the counterpart to the asset that the bank holds as a result of the individual having made the deposit.

Cheques are in some ways the modern equivalent of old-time bank notes issued by commercial banks. The passing of a bank note from hand to hand transferred ownership of a claim against the bank. Similarly, a cheque on a deposit account is an order to the bank to pay the designated recipient, rather than oneself, money credited to the account. Cheques, unlike bank notes, do not circulate freely

[2]For many years, government regulations created a sharp distinction among the various types of financial intermediaries by limiting the types of transactions each could engage in. The past decade has seen a sweeping deregulation of the financial system, so that many of these traditional distinctions no longer apply. Thus, when we speak of commercial banks, that term can be taken to extend to other financial intermediaries that create deposit money, including savings banks, credit unions, and savings and loan associations.

from hand to hand; thus cheques themselves are not currency. The balance in the demand deposit *is* money; the cheque transfers money from one person to another. Because cheques are easily drawn and deposited and because they are relatively safe from theft, they are widely used. In 1992, approximately 7.5 billion cheques were drawn in Canada. During the last two decades, the number of cheques drawn increased by about 7 percent per year.

Thus, when chartered banks lost the right to issue notes of their own, the form of bank money changed, but the substance did not. Today, banks have money in their vaults (or on deposit with the central banks) just as they always did. Once it was gold; today it is the legal tender of the times—fiat money. It is true today, just as in the past, that most of the bank's customers are content to pay their bills by passing among themselves the bank's promises to pay money on demand. Only a small proportion of the transactions made by the bank's customers is made in cash.

Bank deposits are money. Today, just as in the past, banks can create money by issuing more promises to pay (deposits) than they have cash reserves available to pay out.

The Banking System

Many types of institutions make up a modern banking system such as exists in Canada today. The **central bank** is the government-owned and -operated institution that serves to control the banking system. Through it, the government's monetary policy is conducted. In Canada, the central bank is the Bank of Canada, also referred to as the Bank.

Financial intermediaries are privately owned institutions that serve the general public. They are called intermediaries because they stand between savers, from whom they accept deposits, and investors, to whom they make loans. In this chapter, we focus on an important class of financial intermediaries, the *commercial banks*; in Canada, the most important of these are the *chartered banks*.

Central Banks

All advanced free market economies have, in addition to commercial banks, a central bank. Many of the world's early central banks were private, profit-making institutions that provided services to ordinary banks. Their importance, however, caused them to develop close ties with government. Central banks soon became instruments of the government, though not all of them were publicly owned. The Bank of England (the "Old Lady of Threadneedle Street"), one of the world's oldest and most famous central banks, began to operate as the central bank of England in the seventeenth century, but it was not "nationalized" until 1947.

The similarities in the functions performed and the tools used by the world's central banks are much more important than the differences in their organization. Although our attention is given to the operations of the Bank of Canada, its basic functions are similar to those of the Bank of England, the Bank of Greece, or the Federal Reserve System in the United States.

Organization of the Bank of Canada

The Bank of Canada is a publicly owned corporation; all profits accruing from its operations are remitted to the government of Canada. The responsibility for the Bank's affairs rests with a board of directors composed of the governor, the senior deputy governor, the deputy minister of finance, and 12 directors. The governor is appointed by the directors, with the approval of the cabinet, for a 7-year term.

The organization of the Bank of Canada is designed to keep the operation of monetary policy free from day-to-day political influence. Thus, the Bank is not responsible to Parliament for its day-to-day behaviour in the way that the Department of Finance is for the operation of fiscal policy. Nonetheless, the governor of the Bank and the minister of finance consult regularly. Furthermore, in the case of fundamental disagreement over policy, the governor must resign or acquiesce to the cabinet's desired policy as enunciated by the minister.[3]

---

[3]In 1962, when James Coyne was governor, such a fundamental disagreement arose and Coyne was eventually forced to resign. This established the precedent that the final responsibility for monetary policy lies with the government, not the governor.

TABLE 32-1   Assets and Liabilities of the Bank of Canada, January 1993 *(millions of dollars)*

Assets		Liabilities	
Government of Canada securities	21,332	Notes in circulation	23,165
Advances to banks	497	Government of Canada deposits	11
Foreign-currency assets	200	Deposits of chartered banks	740
Other assets	2,624	Foreign-currency liabilities	290
Total	24,653	Other liabilities and capital	447
		Total	24,653

Source: Bank of Canada Review, Spring 1993

The balance sheet of the Bank of Canada shows that it serves as banker to the chartered banks and the government and as issuer of our currency; it also suggests the Bank's role as regulator of money markets and the money supply. The principal liabilities of the Bank are the basis of the money supply. Bank of Canada notes are currency, and the deposits of the chartered banks give them the reserves they use to create deposit money. The Bank's holdings of Government of Canada securities arise from its operations designed to regulate the money supply and financial markets.

Basic Functions of the Bank

A central bank serves four main functions: as a banker for private banks, as a bank for the government, as the controller of the nation's supply of money, and as a supporter of financial markets. The first three functions are revealed by a study of Table 32-1, which shows the balance sheet of the Bank of Canada.

Banker to the chartered banks. The central bank accepts deposits from the chartered banks and will, on order, transfer them to the account of another bank. In this way, the central bank provides the chartered banks with the equivalent of a chequing account and with a means of settling debts to other banks. The deposits of the chartered banks with the central bank appear in Table 32-1. Notice that the cash reserves of the chartered banks deposited with the central bank are *liabilities* of the central bank, because it promises to pay them on demand.

Historically, one of the earliest services provided by central banks was that of "lender of last resort" to the banking system. Central banks would lend money to private banks that had sound investments (such as government securities and safe loans to individuals) but were in urgent need of cash. If such banks could not obtain ready cash, they might be forced into insolvency, because they could not meet the demands of their depositors, in spite of their being basically sound. Today's central banks continue to be the lender of last resort.

U.S. banks borrow extensively from the Federal Reserve System in order to maintain their reserves, but the corresponding institutional arrangement that Canadian banks use is somewhat more complicated. Some Bank of Canada holdings of government securities, shown in Table 32-1, are held under **purchase and resale agreements (PRA)**. Rather than rely on loans from the Bank of Canada, the chartered banks meet their immediate cash requirements by varying the amount of **day-to-day loans** they make available to a group of investment dealers who carry inventories of government of Canada securities. When necessary, these dealers can obtain financing from the Bank of Canada under PRA; that is, they can sell securities to the Bank of Canada and agree to buy them back at a later date. Thus, when the chartered banks reduce their day-to-day loans, they induce an increase in PRA. The result is the same as if the banks had borrowed from the Bank of Canada directly.

Banker to the government. Governments, too, need to hold their funds in an account into which they can make deposits and on which they can write cheques. The government of Canada keeps its chequing deposits at the Bank of Canada, replenishing them from much larger accounts kept at the chartered banks. When the government requires more money, it too needs to borrow, and it does so by printing bonds. Most are sold directly to the public, but occasionally, the government raises funds by selling securities (mostly short term) to the central bank, which "buys" them by crediting the government's account with a deposit for the amount of the purchase. In July 1992, the Bank of Canada held over $21 billion in government of Canada securities.

Controller and regulator of the money supply.

One of the most important functions of a central bank is to control the money supply. From Table 32-1, it is clear that the overwhelming proportion of a central bank's liabilities (its promises to pay) are either notes (money) or the reserves of the chartered banks, which underlie the deposits (money) of households and firms.

The central bank can change the levels of its assets and liabilities in many ways, and as its liabilities rise and fall, so does the money supply. Suppose, for example, that the central bank buys $100 million worth of newly printed bonds from the government of Canada. The bank's assets (government bonds) rise by $100 million, and so do its liabilities (government of Canada deposits). The government has an extra $100 million of purchasing power to spend. As easy as printing money, you say. Indeed, it is the same thing.

Regulator and supporter of money markets.

Central banks usually assume a major responsibility to support the country's financial system and to prevent serious disruption by wide-scale panic and resulting bank failures. Various institutions are in the business of borrowing on a short-term basis and lending on a long-term basis. To some extent, the chartered banks do this when they take in deposits and lend money for various terms. But trust and mortgage loan companies are the major institutions for this kind of transaction. They receive deposits from the public and lend the money on long-term mortgages.

Large, unanticipated increases in interest rates tend to squeeze these institutions. The average rate they earn on their investments rises only slowly as old contracts mature and new ones are made, but they must either pay higher rates to hold on to their deposits or accept wide-scale withdrawals that could easily bring about insolvency. To prevent such financial disasters, central banks often buy and sell government bonds either to slow the rate of change in interest rates or to narrow the range over which the rates are allowed to fluctuate.

Conflicts among functions.

The several functions of the central bank are not always compatible. For example, in pursuit of an anti-inflationary policy, the Bank may cause interest rates to rise. The resulting squeeze makes life uncomfortable for banks and other financial institutions and makes borrowing expensive for the government. If the Bank chooses to ease those problems, say, by lending money to chartered banks, it is relaxing its anti-inflationary policy.

The Bank must strive to balance conflicting objectives. We discuss a number of aspects of this conflict in Chapter 34. However, at this stage, we note that many critics think that the Bank does not always succeed in finding the right balance between its conflicting objectives.

The Canadian Banking System

All Canadian banks owned in the private sector, that is, all banks except the Bank of Canada, are referred to as **commercial banks**. The Canadian banking system is controlled by the provisions of the Bank Act, first passed in 1935 and revised several times since. Under the Bank Act, charters can be granted to financial institutions to operate as banks, and until 1980, there were only a few chartered banks, most of which were very large and each of which operated under identical regulatory provisions.

The 1980 revisions to the Bank Act allowed foreign banks to commence operations in Canada, although it severely limited the scale and scope of their activity. Subsequent revisions have altered some of these restrictions and made it easier to obtain new banking charters, but the revisions have maintained the distinction between these newer institutions and banks operating under what are essentially the pre-1980 provisions of the Bank Act. The original provisions, in slightly modified form, are now known as Schedule A of the Bank Act; the foreign banks and the new, smaller domestic banks operate under Schedules B and C. The term **chartered banks** is usually reserved for the Schedule A banks.

The chartered banks have common attributes: They hold deposits for their customers; they permit certain deposits to be transferred by cheque from an individual account to other accounts held in any bank branch in the country; they make loans to households and firms; they invest in government securities.

Banks are not the only financial institutions in the country. Many other privately owned, profit-seeking institutions, such as trust companies and credit unions, accept savings deposits and grant loans for specific purposes. Finance companies make loans to households for practically any purpose—sometimes at very high effective interest rates. The post office and the telegraph system will transfer money, and credit card companies will extend credit so that purchases can be made on a buy-now, pay-later basis.

The commercial banks are subject to federal regulations and until recently were required to hold reserves with the Bank of Canada against their deposit liabilities. Other institutions do not face reserve requirements, but most are subject to various federal and provincial regulations concerning ownership and control and the types of financial activities they are allowed to engage in. Thus, there are differences among all types of financial institutions, not just between banks and others.

The chartered banks have historically been such a stable and dominant group that the terms *chartered banks* and *banking system* have been considered virtually synonymous. However, recent events may serve to break this identification. First, there have been dramatic changes in the makeup of the chartered banks—in 1985, two relatively new regionally based chartered banks failed, and since then, banks have merged in two instances and two Canadian banks were taken over by foreign banks. Second, the federal government and several provincial governments have recently proposed extensive changes in regulations, including the abolition of reserve requirements for the chartered banks, that would further blur the distinction between the chartered banks and other financial institutions. Third, there have been sweeping changes *internationally* in the structure and functioning of financial markets; some of these developments are discussed further in Box 32-3.

Interbank activities. Chartered banks have a number of interbank cooperative relationships. For example, banks often share loans. Even the biggest bank cannot meet all the credit needs of a giant corporation, and often a group of banks will offer a "pool loan," agreeing on common terms and dividing the loan up into manageable segments.

Another form of interbank cooperation is the bank credit card. Visa and MasterCard are the two most widely used credit cards, and each is operated by a group of banks.

Probably the most important form of interbank cooperation is cheque clearing and collection. Bank deposits are an effective medium of exchange only because banks accept each other's cheques. If a depositor in the Bank of Montreal writes a cheque to someone who deposits it in the Toronto Dominion Bank, the Bank of Montreal now owes money to the Toronto Dominion Bank. This creates a need for the banks to present cheques to each other for payment.

There are millions of such transactions in the course of a day, and they result in an enormous sorting and bookkeeping job. Multibank systems make use of a **clearing house** where interbank debts are settled. At the end of the day, all the cheques drawn by the Bank of Montreal's customers and deposited in the Toronto Dominion Bank are totaled and set against the total of all the cheques drawn by the Toronto Dominion's customers and deposited in the Bank of Montreal. It is necessary only to settle the difference between the two sums. The actual cheques are passed through the clearing house back to the bank on which they were drawn. Both banks are then able to adjust the individual accounts by a set of book entries. A flow of cash between banks is necessary only when there is a net transfer of cash from the customers of one bank to those of another. This flow of cash is accompanied by a transfer of deposits held by the chartered banks with the Bank of Canada.

Profit seeking. Banks are private firms that start with invested capital and seek to "earn money" in the same sense as firms making neckties or bicycles. A chartered bank provides a variety of services to its customers: a safe place to store money, the convenience of demand deposits that can be transferred by personal cheque, a safe and convenient place to earn a modest but guaranteed return on savings, and often financial advice and estate management services. The bank earns some revenue by charging for these services, but such fees are a small part of the bank's total earnings. The largest part (typically about five sixths) of a bank's earnings is derived from the bank's ability to invest profitably the funds placed with it.

Box 32-3

The Globalisation of Financial Markets

Technological innovations in communication and the desire to avoid onerous government regulations have led to a globalisation of the financial service industry over the past two decades. Computers, satellite communication systems, reliable telephones with direct worldwide dialing, electronic mail, and fax machines—all coming into widespread use only within the past decade—have put people in instantaneous contact anywhere in the world.

As a result of these new technologies, borrowers and lenders can learn about market conditions and then move their funds instantly in search of the best loan rates. Large firms need transaction balances only while banks in their area are open. Once banks close for the day in each centre, the firms will not need these balances until tomorrow's reopening; thus, the funds can be moved to another market, where they are used until it closes. They are then moved to yet another market. Funds are thus free to move from London to New York to Tokyo and back to London on a daily rotation. This is a degree of global sophistication that was inconceivable before the advent of the computer, when international communication was much slower and costlier than it now is. To facilitate the movement in and out of various national currencies, increasing amounts of

bank deposits are denominated in foreign rather than domestic currencies.

One of the first developments in this movement toward globalisation was the growth of the foreign currency markets in Europe in the 1960s. At first the main currency involved was the U.S. dollar, and hence *Eurodollar* markets were the first to develop. Today, the *Eurobond* market is an international market where bonds of various types, denominated in various national currencies, are issued and sold to customers located throughout the world. The customers are mainly public corporations, international organizations, and multinational enterprises. The *Eurocurrency* market is a market for short-term bank deposits and bank loans denominated in various currencies.

The original attraction of the Eurodollar market was the freedom from the restrictions placed by the Federal Reserve on American commercial banks. By operating in offshore markets, banks were able to cut unit costs by dealing in large volume at the wholesale level. They could then offer rates that were higher for lenders and lower for borrowers than those prevailing in the United States.

The progressive worldwide lifting of interest-rate ceilings and other capital market restrictions

---

Table 32-2 is the combined balance sheet of the chartered banks in Canada. The bulk of a bank's liabilities are deposits owed to its depositors. The principal assets of a bank are the *securities* it buys (including government bonds), which pay interest or dividends, and the *loans* it makes to individuals and to businesses. A bank loan is a liability to the borrower (who must pay it back) but an asset to the bank. The bank expects not only to have the loan repaid but also to receive interest that more than compensates for the paperwork involved and the risk of nonpayment.

Banks attract deposits by paying interest to depositors and by providing them, for a fee that does not cover the banks' full cost, with services such as

clearing cheques and providing regular monthly statements. Banks earn profits by lending and investing money deposited with them for more than they pay their depositors in terms of interest and other services provided.

Competition for deposits. Competition for deposits is active among banks and between banks and other financial institutions. Financial deregulation, which removed restrictions on the activities of various financial institutions, has contributed to this competition. Interest paid on deposits, special high-interest certificates of deposit (CDs), advertising, personal solicitation of accounts, giveaway programs that occurred in the 1980s led to a further globalisation of financial markets. Although this removed some of the original reasons for their growth, the Euromarkets prospered. First, they allowed banks to avoid the remaining domestic regulations. Second, the advantage of having an international market dealing in many different national currencies was sufficient to sustain the markets.

The increasing sophistication of information transfer also led to a breakdown of the high degree of specialization that had characterized financial markets in earlier decades. When information was difficult to obtain and analyse, an efficient division of labour called for a host of specialist institutions, each with expertise in a narrow range of transactions. As a result of the new developments in communication technology, economies of large scale led to the integration of various financial operations within one firm. For example, in many countries, banks have moved into the markets where securities are traded, while many security-trading firms have begun to offer a range of banking services. As the scale of such integrated firms increases, they find it easier to extend their operations geographically as well as functionally.

It has often been difficult for government regulations to keep up with these rapid changes. Governments that relaxed their regulations first in face of the evolving realities often allowed their financial institutions to gain important advantages in international competition. The U.K. government has been quick to react to these developments, and as a result, London has retained its strong position in the international financial world. The Canadian government also reacted relatively quickly by allowing banks to expand their functions into areas formerly barred to them and allowing foreign banks increased access to the Canadian market. In contrast, the U.S. government has been slow to adapt. For example, it still limits interstate banking and prevents U.S. banks from extending their operations beyond the ones traditionally reserved for banks. As a result, the U.S. banks have lost out heavily to European and Japanese banks.

The kinds of government intervention into domestic capital markets and government control over international capital flows that characterized the 1950s and 1960s is no longer possible. International markets are just too sophisticated. Globalisation is here to stay, and by removing domestic restrictions and exchange controls, governments in advanced countries are only bowing to the inevitable.

---

for new deposits to existing accounts, and improved services are all forms of competition for funds.

Reserves

All bankers would as a matter of convenience and prudence keep sufficient cash on hand to be able to meet depositors' day-to-day requirements for cash.

The Need for Reserves

Just as the goldsmiths of old discovered that only a fraction of the gold they held was ever withdrawn at any given time, and just as banks of old discovered that only a small fraction of convertible bank notes was actually converted, so too have modern banks known that only a small fraction of their deposits will be withdrawn in cash at any one time.

The reserves needed to assure that depositors can withdraw their deposits on demand will be quite small in normal times.

In abnormal times, however, nothing short of 100 percent might do the job if the commercial banking system had to stand alone. A major bank failure that caused a general loss of confidence in

TABLE 32-2   Consolidated Balance Sheet of Canadian Chartered Banks, January 1993 *(billions of dollars)*

Assets		Liabilities	
Reserves (including deposits with Bank of Canada)	5.3	Demand deposits	22.6
Loans (determined in Canadian dollars)	309	Savings deposits	223.9
Government of Canada securities	34.9	Time deposits	90.7
Foreign-currency assets	211.6	Foreign-currency liabilities	226.9
Other assets	89.5	Other liabilities	
Total	650.3	Capital account	106.2
		Total	650.3

Source: Bank of Canada Review, Spring 1993.

Reserves are only a small fraction of deposit liabilities. If all the banks' customers who held demand deposits tried to withdraw them in cash, the banks could not meet this demand without liquidating $15 billion of other assets. This would be impossible without assistance from the Bank of Canada.

banks' ability to redeem their deposits, could lead to a run on banks as depositors rushed to withdraw their money. Faced with such a panic, banks would have to close.

Sufficient liquidity to meet abnormal situations can be provided by the central bank.

Because it controls the supply of bank reserves, the central bank can provide all the reserves that are needed to meet any abnormal situation. It can do this in two ways. First, it can lend reserves directly to the chartered banks, using as collateral bank assets that are sound but not easy to liquidate quickly. Second, it can enter the open market and buy all the securities that the commercial banks need to sell. Once the public finds that deposits can be turned into cash, the panic will usually subside, and any further drain of cash out of banks will cease.

The possibility of panic withdrawals is also greatly diminished by the provision of government deposit insurance, which guarantees that depositors will get their money back even if a bank fails completely. Most depositors will not withdraw their money as long as they are *certain* they can get it when they need it.

Although deposit insurance confers a number of benefits on the operation of the financial system, it has also been subject to considerable criticism in recent years. This is taken up in Box 32-4.

Target Reserves

We have seen that banks hold reserves in order to meet temporary cash drains that arise when a bank's payments exceed its receipts. Receipts occur when the bank's customers deposit either cash or cheques drawn on other banks; payments are required either when cheques drawn by the bank's customers are deposited in other banks or when customers make cash withdrawals. A bank with no access to reserves will be unable to meet even a temporary cash drain and will be forced to suspend payments. This is something that banks must avoid at almost any cost.

A bank's **reserve ratio** is the fraction of its deposit liabilities that it *actually holds* as reserves, either as cash or as deposits with the central bank. A bank's **target ratio** is the fraction of its deposits it *wishes to hold* as reserves.

In the past, legal requirements imposed by the Bank Act have required the chartered banks to hold reserves. These requirements were thought necessary to ensure the stability of the banking system. The reserves that the Bank Act required the banks to hold were called **required reserves**.

Starting in the early 1980s, Canadian banks argued that the legal requirement to hold some of their assets as non-interest-bearing reserves placed them at a disadvantage relative to their competitors that were not subject to such requirements. The competitors included Canadian nonbank financial

Box 32-4

Deposit Insurance and the Financial System

Deposit insurance assures depositors that their funds are secure whatever the fate of their deposit institution. This is a great boon for depositors, but experience has shown that it is a double-edged sword.

On the one hand, deposit insurance provides security to depositors. This is a good thing in itself. It also helps to stabilise the economy in times of financial distress by preventing large losses of wealth when financial institutions fail.

On the other hand, deposit insurance creates an incentive for financial intermediaries to pursue riskier investments than they would if depositors had to worry about losing their deposits should the institution fail. Because of deposit insurance, depositors have no reason to select deposit institutions according to the riskiness of their investments. They are free instead to select the institution that pays the highest interest without worrying about the associated risk.

Deposit insurance is thus an example of an important class of government institutions that create situations whereby *heads the private investor wins and tails the taxpayer loses.* Financial institutions take in depositors' insured funds; if the owners place them in risky ventures that pay off, the owners get the profits; if the owners place the funds in ventures that fail often enough to bring down the whole institution, the taxpayers must meet the bill by repaying those who provided the capital (the depositors).

Canadian financial institutions have occasionally failed, including two western banks in the mid-1980s. When those institutions went under, depositors were repaid by the Canadian Federal Deposit Insurance Corporation (FDIC). Although the legal ceiling on deposit insurance was $60,000, deposits in excess of that amount were also repaid, using taxpayer money. This created the precedent that ceilings on deposit insurance were not to be taken seriously. Any amount would be likely to be repaid. Hence, no investor need worry about the financial probity of the investments made by the institutions in which his or her money was deposited.

Two types of reforms are possible. One type would keep deposit insurance and provide the necessary accompanying regulations; the other would take deregulation to its logical conclusion of ending deposit insurance.

The implications of deposit insurance for the investment behaviour of financial intermediaries suggests that if deposit insurance is to be maintained, other regulations concerning capital requirements and investment standards need to be applied. In addition, the deposit insurance system might be reformed in order to relate the cost of insurance for a particular institution to the risks implied by that institution's asset position.

Many economists believe that if deregulation of financial institutions is regarded as desirable, it should be accompanied by a removal of deposit insurance, so that the people who use the funds will be accountable to those who provide them.

institutions, such as trust companies, and some foreign commercial banks. Globalisation of financial markets had brought domestic financial institutions into direct competition with foreign ones, and continuing deregulation of financial markets had enhanced the competition between banks and non-bank financial institutions. After much deliberation, the government responded to these complaints by phasing out all legal reserve requirements early in the 1990s.

We can imagine two situations under a regime of zero required reserves. In the first, the commercial banks are on their own (the situation before central banks were instituted). They can count on no other institution to help them in time of need. In this case, the target reserves needed to meet any normal cash drain would be a significant fraction of the bank's total liabilities—indeed, nothing short of 100 percent reserves would guarantee solvency in the face of a major run by the bank's depositors.

In the second situation, a central bank is present, to come to the commercial banks' assistance when they are caught short of reserves due to a temporary adverse payments balance. Now the banks can carry less reserves than in the first situation. How few reserves they will carry will depend on the cost of getting assistance from the central bank when they are caught short of reserves. This is the system the Bank now operates. The commercial banks have no required reserves but they must worry about running out of reserves because the support given them by the Bank of Canada comes at a substantial cost.

Look again at Table 32-2, and observe that the banking system's cash reserves are less than 1 percent of its liabilities. If the holders of even 5 percent of its deposits demanded cash, the banks would have been unable to meet the demand without outside help. Reserves can be as low as they are because the banks know that the Bank of Canada will help them out in time of temporary need.

We will study how the Bank of Canada can influence the money supply under a zero required reserve system after we have examined how the money supply is itself determined. Our analysis of the money supply process is based on the following behaviour of the chartered banks:

Chartered banks will wish to maintain some target level of reserves determined by their target ratio of reserves to deposits. In the past, this target ratio was legally imposed; today, it is determined by the banks themselves.

Any reserves in excess of target reserves are called *excess reserves*. All that matters for what follows is that there is some target reserve ratio, no matter how small.

Money Creation by the Banking System

The fractional reserve system provides the leverage that permits commercial banks and other financial institutions to create money. The process is important and needs to be examined in some detail.

Some Simplifying Assumptions

To focus on the essential aspects of how banks create money, assume that banks can invest in only one kind of asset, loans, and that there is only one kind of deposit, a demand deposit.

Two other assumptions are provisional. When we have developed the basic ideas concerning the bank's creation of money, these assumptions will be relaxed.

1. *Fixed reserve ratio.* It is assumed that all banks have the same target reserve ratio. In our numerical illustration, we shall assume that this ratio is 20 percent (i.e., 0.20); that is, $1 of reserves are desired to be held for every $5 of deposits. Thus, we assume that all banks want to invest any reserves that they have in excess of their target reserves; this implies that they always believe that there are profitable investments—loans, in our example—to be made when they have excess reserves.

2. *No cash drain from the banking system.* It is assumed that the public holds a fixed amount of

TABLE 32-3   Initial Balance Sheet of the Canadian Immigrants Bank of Commerce (*thousands of dollars*)

Assets		Liabilities	
Cash and other reserves	200	Deposits	1,000
Loans	900	Capital	100
Total	1,100	Total	1,100

The CIBC has a reserve of 20 percent of its deposit liabilities. The chartered bank earns money by finding profitable investments for much of the money deposited with it. In this balance sheet, loans are its earning assets.

currency in circulation. Thus, changes in the money supply will take the form of changes in deposit money.

The Creation of Deposit Money

A hypothetical bank's balance sheet is shown in Table 32-3. The hypothetical Canadian Immigrants Bank of Commerce (CIBC) has assets of $200 of reserves (all figures are in thousands of dollars), held partly as cash on hand and partly as deposits with the central bank, and $900 of loans outstanding to its customers. Its liabilities are $100 to those who initially contributed capital to start the bank and $1,000 to current depositors. The bank's target ratio of reserves to deposits is $200/1,000 = 0.20$, exactly equal to its minimum requirement.

A Single New Deposit

An immigrant arrives in the country and opens an account by depositing $100 with the CIBC. This is a wholly new deposit for the bank, and it results in a revised balance sheet (Table 32-4). As a result of the immigrant's new deposit, both cash assets and deposit liabilities have risen by $100. More important, the CIBC's ratio of reserves to deposits has increased from 0.20 to 0.27 ($300/1,100$). The bank now has $80 in excess reserves; with $1,100 in deposits, its required reserves are only $220.

The CIBC will now lend the $80 excess reserves that it is holding. Table 32-5 shows the posi-

---

TABLE 32-4 Balance Sheet of CIBC After an Immigrant Deposits $100
(thousands of dollars)

Assets		Liabilities	
Cash and other reserves	300	Deposits	1,100
Loans	900	Capital	100
Total	1,200	Total	1,200

The immigrant's deposit raises deposit liabilities and cash assets by the same amount. Since both cash and deposits rise by $100, the cash reserve ratio, formerly 0.20, increases to 0.27. The bank has more cash than it needs to provide a 20 percent reserve against its deposit liabilities.

TABLE 32-5 CIBC Balance Sheet After a New Loan and Cash Drain of $80
(thousands of dollars)

Assets		Liabilities	
Cash and other reserves	220	Deposits	1,100
Loans	980	Capital	100
Total	1,200	Total	1,200

The bank lends its surplus cash and suffers a cash drain. The bank keeps $20 as a reserve against the immigrant's new deposit of $100. It lends $80 to a customer who writes a cheque to someone who deals with another bank. When the cheque is cleared, the CIBC suffers an $80 cash drain. Comparing Tables 32-3 and 32-5 shows that the bank has increased its deposit liabilities by the $100 deposited by the new immigrant and increased its assets by $20 of cash reserves and $80 of new loans. It has also restored its reserve ratio of 0.20.

---

tion after this has been done and after the proceeds of the loan have been withdrawn to be deposited to the account of a customer of another bank. The CIBC once again has a 20 percent reserve ratio.

So far, of the $100 initial deposit in the CIBC, $20 is held by the CIBC as reserves against the deposit and $80 has been lent out in the system. However, other banks have received new deposits of $80 stemming from the loans made by the CIBC; persons receiving payment from those who borrowed the $80 from the CIBC will have deposited those payments in their own banks. Note that while the banking system suffers no cash drain (i.e., all the money lent out is returned to the banking system as deposits), the CIBC does suffer a cash drain (i.e., most of the money lent out is not redeposited at the CIBC).

The banks that receive deposits from the proceeds of the CIBC's loan are sometimes called *next-generation banks* or, more specifically according to the situation, *second-generation, third-generation,* and so on. In this case, the second-generation banks receive new deposits of $80, and when the cheques clear, they have new reserves of $80. Because they require only $16 in additional reserves to support the new deposits, they have $64 of excess reserves. They now increase their loans by $64. After this money is spent by the borrowers and has been deposited in other, third-generation banks, the balance

TABLE 32-6 Changes in the Balance Sheets of Second-Generation Banks *(thousands of dollars)*

Assets		Liabilities	
Cash and other reserves	+16	Deposits	+80
Loans	+64		
Total	+80	Total	+80

Second-generation banks receive cash deposits and expand loans. The second-generation banks gain new deposits of $80 as a result of the loan granted by the CIBC, which is used to make payments to customers of the second-generation banks. These banks keep 20 percent of the cash they acquire as their reserve against the new deposit, and they can make new loans using the other 80 percent. When the customers who borrowed the money make payments to the customers of third-generation banks, a cash drain occurs.

sheets of the second-generation banks will have changed, as in Table 32-6.

The third-generation banks now find themselves with $64 of new deposits. Against these, they

need hold only $12.80 in cash, so they have excess reserves of $51.20 that they can immediately lend out. Thus begins a long sequence of new deposits, new loans, new deposits, and new loans. The stages are shown in Table 32-7. The series in the table should look familiar, for it is the same convergent process we met when dealing with the multiplier in Chapter 28.

If v is the reserve ratio, the ultimate effect on the deposits of the banking system of a new deposit will be $1/v$ times the new deposit.[4] **[37]** The banking system has created new deposits and thus new money, although each banker can honestly say, "All I did was invest my excess reserves. I can do no more than manage wisely the money I receive." At the end of the process depicted in Table 32-7, the change in the combined balance sheets of all the banks in the system is shown in Table 32-8.

---

[4]The "multiple expansion of deposits" that has just been worked through applies in reverse to a withdrawal of funds. Deposits of the banking system will fall by $1/v$ times any amount withdrawn from the bank and not redeposited at another.

TABLE 32-7 Sequence of Loans and Deposits After a Single Initial Deposit *(thousands of dollars)*

Bank	New deposits	New loans	Addition to reserves
CIBC	100.00	80.00	20.00
Second-generation bank	80.00	64.00	16.00
Third-generation bank	64.00	51.20	12.80
Fourth-generation bank	51.20	40.96	10.24
Fifth-generation bank	40.96	32.77	8.19
Sixth-generation bank	32.77	26.22	6.55
Seventh-generation bank	26.22	20.98	5.24
Eighth-generation bank	20.98	16.78	4.20
Ninth-generation bank	16.78	13.42	3.36
Tenth-generation bank	13.42	10.74	2.68
Total first 10 generations	446.33	357.07	89.26
All remaining generations	53.67	42.93	10.74
Total for banking systems	500.00	400.00	100.00

The banking system as a whole can create deposit money whenever it receives new reserves. The table shows the process of the creation of deposit money on the assumptions that all the loans made by one set of banks end up as deposits in another set of banks (the next-generation banks), that the target reserve ratio *(v)* is 0.20, and that there are no excess reserves. Although each bank suffers a cash drain whenever it grants a new loan, the system as a whole does not, and in a series of steps it increases deposit money by $1/v$, which in this example is five times the amount of any increase in reserves that it obtains.

TABLE 32-8 The Combined Balance Sheets of All the Banks in the System Following the Multiple Expansion of Deposits *(thousands of dollars)*

Assets		Liabilities	
Cash and other reserves	+100	Deposits	+500
Loans	+400		
Total	+500	Total	+500

The reserve ratio is returned to 0.20. The entire initial deposit of $100 ends up as reserves of the banking system. Therefore, deposits rise by (1/0.2) times the initial deposit, that is, by $500.

Many Deposits

A more realistic picture of deposit creation is one in which new deposits accrue simultaneously to all banks, perhaps because of changes in the monetary policy of the government. (We shall study monetary policy in detail in Chapter 34.)

Say, for example, that the community contains 10 banks of equal size and that each receives new deposits of $100 in cash. Now each bank is in the position shown in Table 32-4, and each can begin to expand deposits based on the $100 of excess reserves. (Each bank does this by granting loans to customers.)

Because each bank does one tenth of the total banking business, an average of 90 percent of any newly created deposit will find its way into other banks as the customer pays other people in the community by cheque. This will represent a cash drain from the lending bank to the other banks. However, roughly 10 percent of each new deposit created by each of the other nine banks should find its way into this bank. All banks receive new cash and all begin creating deposits simultaneously.

The expansion can go on with each bank watching its own ratio of cash reserves to deposits, expanding deposits as long as the ratio exceeds 1:5 and ceasing when it reaches that figure. The process will come to a halt when each bank has created $400 in additional deposits, so that for each initial $100 cash deposit, there is now $500 in deposits backed by $100 in cash.

The general rule, if there is no cash drain, is that a banking system with a reserve ratio of v can change its deposits by $1/v$ times any change in reserves.

Variable Reserve Ratios and Cash Drains

The two simplifying assumptions made earlier can now be relaxed.

Variable reserve ratio. If banks do not choose to invest excess reserves, the multiple expansion discussed will not occur. Turn back to Table 32-4. If the CIBC had been content to hold 27 percent reserves, it might well have done nothing more. Other things being equal, banks will choose to invest excess reserves because of the profit motive. But there may be times when they believe that the risk is too great. It is one thing to be offered a good rate of interest on a loan, but if the borrower defaults on the payment of interest and principal, the bank will be the loser. Similarly, if the bank expects interest rates to rise in the future, it may hold off making loans now, so that it will have reserves available to make more profitable loans after the interest rate has risen.

Deposit creation does not happen automatically; it depends on decisions of bankers. If banks do not choose to use excess reserves to expand their loans, there will be no expansion of deposits.

The money supply is thus at least partly determined by the chartered banks in response to such forces as changes in the level of economic activity or in interest rates. However, the upper limit of deposits is determined by the banks' willingness to hold reserves and by the reserves available to them, both of which are under the influence of the Bank of Canada.

Cash drain. Normally, firms and households keep some *fraction* of their money holding in cash. If, for example, this amount is, 5 percent, then of

TABLE 32-9 The Combined Balance Sheets of All the Banks in the System Following the Multiple Expansion of Deposits with a Cash Drain *(thousands of dollars)*

Assets		Liabilities	
Cash and other reserves	+80	Deposits	+400
Loans	+320		
Total	+400	Total	+400

The reserve ratio is 0.20 and cash drain is 0.05. Only $80 of the initial deposit of $100 ends up as reserves of the banking system. Therefore, deposits rise by (1/0.2) times the $80, that is, by $400.

every new $100 that is created, $95 will be held as deposits while $5 will be held as cash. In that case, an extra $100 in money supply will not all stay in the banking system; some will remain on deposit and the rest will be added to cash in the hands of the public. In such a situation, any multiple expansion of bank deposits will be accompanied by a cash drain to the public that will reduce the maximum expansion below what it was when the public was content to hold all its new money as bank deposits.

The story of deposit creation when all banks receive new deposits and there is a cash drain to the public goes like this. Each bank starts creating deposits and suffers no significant cash drain to other banks. But because approximately 5 percent of newly created deposits are withdrawn to be held as cash, each bank suffers a cash drain to the public. The expansion continues, each bank watching its own ratio of cash reserves to deposits, expanding deposits as long as the ratio exceeds 1:5 and ceasing when it reaches that figure. Because the expansion is accompanied by a cash drain, it will come to a halt with a smaller deposit expansion than in the case of no cash drain.[5]

Table 32-9 shows the consolidated balance sheets of the banking system after the deposit expansion arising from an initial injection of $100

---

[5]It can be shown algebraically that the percentage of cash drain must be added to the reserve ratio to determine the maximum possible expansion of deposits. **[38]**

when there is a cash drain. As shown, since there is a cash drain of $20, reserves rise by only $80 and deposits rise by only $400.

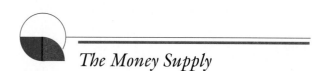

The Money Supply

The total stock of money in the economy at any moment is called the **money supply** or the **supply of money**. Economists use several alternative definitions for the money supply, most of which are regularly reported in the *Bank of Canada Review*. Typically, the definitions involve the sum of currency in circulation plus some types of deposit liabilities of financial institutions; definitions vary in terms of what deposits are included. Different definitions become more or less useful as the importance of different types of deposits changes.

Kinds of Deposits

Most of the deposits held by the average person are either demand deposits or savings deposits.

Over the last 10-15 years, banks have evolved a bewildering array of different types of deposits. From our point of view, the most important distinction is between deposits that can be transferred by cheque, called "chequable," and those that cannot, called "nonchequable." Chequable deposits are media of exchange; nonchequable ones are not.

Until recently, the distinction lay between demand deposits, which earned little or no interest but were chequable, and savings deposits, which earned a higher interest return but were nonchequable.

Today, however, it is so easy to transfer funds from some deposits that are technically nonchequable to chequable deposits that the distinction is quite blurred at the margin. The deposit that is genuinely tied up for a period of time now takes the form of a **term deposit**, which has a specified withdrawal date, a minimum of 30 days into the future, and which pays a much reduced interest rate in the event of early withdrawal. Term and other nonchequable deposits pay significantly higher interest rates than do chequable deposits.

TABLE 32-10   Canadian Money Supply, January 1993 (billions of dollars)

Currency	22.1
+Demand deposits	20.8
=M1	42.9
+Personal savings deposits and nonpersonal notice deposits	262.6
=M2	305.5
+Nonpersonal fixed-term deposits and foreign-currency deposits	67.4
=M3	372.9

Source: Bank of Canada Review, Spring, 1993.

The money supply can be defined in a variety of ways: M1, M2, and M3 figures are all published regularly by the Bank of Canada. M1 is the narrowly defined money supply that includes items that serve directly as media of exchange. M2 includes additional categories of bank deposits that serve the store-of-value function and can be readily converted into demand deposits or currency. M3 adds in bank term deposits that cannot be converted easily, because the funds must remain on deposit for a fixed term, and foreign-currency deposits, whose value in terms of Canadian dollars varies with the exchange rate. (A series called M2+ adds to M2-related deposits with trust companies, credit unions, and Quebec savings institutions called *caisses populaires*.)

Definitions of the Money Supply

Different definitions of the money supply include different types of deposits. The narrowly defined money supply, called **M1**, includes currency and deposits that are themselves usable as media of exchange. Broader definitions, such as **M2** and **M3**, include savings accounts and term deposits. These are liquid assets that serve the temporary store-of-value function and are in practise quickly convertible into a medium of exchange at a known price ($1 on deposit in a savings account is always convertible into a $1 demand deposit or $1 in cash).

Table 32-10 shows the principal elements in these definitions of the money supply. The details of the differences are not important at this stage; what matters is that broadly defined, money comprises a spectrum of closely related financial assets that their holders regard as highly substitutable for each other.

Near Money and Money Substitutes

Over the past two centuries, what has been accepted by the public as money has expanded from gold and silver coins to include first bank notes and then bank deposits subject to transfer by cheque. Until recently, most economists would have agreed that money stopped at that point. No such agreement exists today, and an important debate centres on the definition of money appropriate to present circumstances.

If we concentrate only on the medium-of-exchange function of money, there is little doubt about what is money in Canada today. Money consists of notes, coins, and deposits subject to transfer by cheque or cheque-like instruments. No other asset constitutes a generally accepted medium of exchange.

The problem of deciding what is money arises because some media of exchange—currency, which carries no interest yield, and demand deposits, whose interest yield tends to be quite low—may provide relatively poor ways to meet the store-of-value function (see Table 32-11). Assets that earn a higher-interest return will do a better job of meeting this function of money than currency or demand deposits. At the same time, however, these other assets are less capable of filling the medium-of-exchange function.

Near Money

Assets that fulfill adequately the store-of-value function and are readily converted into a medium of exchange but are not themselves a medium of exchange are sometimes called **near money**. Deposits at a trust company are a characteristic form of near money. When you have such a deposit, you know exactly how much purchasing power you hold (at current prices), and, given modern banking practises, you can turn your deposit into a medium of exchange—cash or a chequing deposit—at a moment's notice. Furthermore, your deposit will earn some interest during the period that you hold it.

Why then does not everybody keep his or her money in such deposits instead of in demand deposits or currency? The answer is that the inconvenience of continually shifting money back and forth may outweigh the interest that can be earned. One week's interest on $100 (at 10 percent per year) is

TABLE 32-11 The Dollar as a Store of Value Since 1962

$1 put aside in	Had the purchasing power 5 years later of	Its average annual loss of value over the 5-year period was
1962	$0.86	2.9%
1967	0.79	4.6
1972	0.47	14.0
1977	0.37	18.0
1982	0.76	4.7
1987	0.81	4.1

The dollar has become an increasingly less satisfactory store of value since the 1960s. The second column shows the purchasing power, measured by the Consumer Price Index, of $1 five years after it was saved (assuming that it earned no interest). In order for it to have maintained its real purchasing power, it would have had to earn the annual after-tax percentage return shown in the last column. The increase in the required return explains the growing use of near money and money substitutes that (unlike currency and demand deposits) earn interest.

only about 20 cents, not enough to cover car fare to the bank or the cost of mailing a letter. For money that will be needed soon, it would hardly pay to shift it to a term deposit.

In general, whether it pays to convert cash or chequable deposits into higher interest-earning term deposits for a given period will depend on the inconvenience and other transactions costs of shifting funds and on the amount of interest that can be earned.

There is a wide spectrum of assets in the economy that pay interest and also serve as reasonably satisfactory temporary stores of value. The difference between these assets and savings deposits is that their capital values are not quite as certain as those of demand and term deposits. If I elect to store my purchasing power in the form of a treasury bill that matures in 30 days, its price on the market may change between the time I buy it and the time I want to sell it, say, 10 days later. If the price changes, the purchasing power available to me changes. But because of the short horizon to maturity, the price will not change very much. (After all, the government will pay the face value in a few weeks.) Such a security is thus a reasonably satisfactory short-run store of purchasing power. Indeed, any readily saleable capital asset whose value does not fluctuate significantly with the rate of interest will satisfactorily fulfill this short-term store-of-value function.

Money Substitutes

Things that serve as temporary media of exchange but are not a store of value are sometimes called **money substitutes**. Credit cards are a prime example. With a credit card, many transactions can be made without either cash or a cheque. The evidence of credit, the credit slip you sign and hand over to the store, is not money, because it cannot be used to make other transactions. The credit card serves the short-run function of a medium of exchange by allowing you to make purchases, even though you have no cash or bank deposit currently in your possession. But this is only temporary; money remains the final medium of exchange for these transactions when the credit account is settled.

Conclusion

Since the eighteenth century, economists have known that the amount of money in circulation is an important economic variable. As theories became more carefully specified in the nineteenth and early twentieth centuries, they included a variable called the "money supply." But for theories to be useful, we must be able to identify real-world counterparts of these theoretical magnitudes.

What is an acceptable enough medium of exchange to count as money has changed and will continue to change over time. New monetary assets are continually being developed to serve some, if not all, the functions of money, and they are more or less readily convertible into money. There is no single, timeless definition of what is money and what is only near money or a money substitute. Indeed, as we have seen, our monetary authorities use several definitions of money, and these definitions change from year to year.

SUMMARY

1. Early economists regarded the economy as being divided into a real sector and a monetary sector. The real sector is concerned with production, allocation of resources, and distribution of income, determined by relative prices. The level of prices at which all transactions take place is determined by the monetary sector, that is, by the demand for and supply of money. With the demand for money being constant, an increase in the money supply would cause all equilibrium money prices to increase, but relative prices, and hence everything in the real sector, would be left unaffected.

2. Traditionally in economics, money has referred to any generally accepted medium of exchange. The major functions of money are to act as a medium of exchange, a store of value, and a unit of account.

3. Money arose because of the inconvenience of barter, and it developed in stages from precious metal, to metal coinage, to paper money convertible to precious metal, to token coinage and paper money fractionally backed by precious metals, to fiat money, and to deposit money. .

4. The Bank of Canada, a publicly owned corporation, is Canada's central bank. It serves as the banker to the chartered banks and to the federal government, regulator of financial markets, and controller of the money supply.

5. Commercial banks are profit-seeking institutions that allow their customers to transfer demand deposits from one bank to another by means of cheques. They create and destroy money as a by-product of their commercial operations—by making or liquidating loans and various other investments.

6. Because most customers are content to pay their accounts by cheque rather than by cash, banks need only small reserves to back their deposit liabilities. When the banking system receives a new cash deposit, it can create new deposits to some multiple of this amount. The exact amount depends on the reserves the banks hold, the amount of cash drain to the public, and whether the banks choose to hold excess reserves.

7. The money supply—the stock of money in the country at a specific moment—can be defined in various ways. M1 is currency plus demand deposits plus chequable substitutes, the narrowest definition now in use. M3, the widest commonly used definition, adds in all time and savings deposits.

8. Near money includes interest-earning assets that are convertible into money on a dollar-for-dollar basis but that are not currently included in the definition of money. Money substitutes, such as credit cards, temporarily serve as a medium of exchange but are not money.

TOPICS FOR REVIEW

Real and monetary sectors of the economy

Functions of money

Gresham's law

Fully backed, fractionally backed, and fiat money

Creation and destruction of deposit money

Target reserve ratio and excess reserves

The money supply

Near money and money substitutes

DISCUSSION QUESTIONS

1. "The love of money is the root of all evil" (I Timothy 6:10). If a nation were to become a theocracy in which money was illegal, would you expect the level of national income to be affected? How about the productivity of labour?

2. Consider each of the following with respect to its potential use as a medium of exchange, a store of value, and a unit of account. Which would you think might be regarded as money?
   a. A $100 Bank of Canada note.
   b. An American Express credit card.
   c. A painting by Picasso.
   d. A treasury bill payable in 3 months.
   e. A savings account with a trust company in London, Ontario.
   f. One share of General Motors stock.
   g. A lifetime pass to the Art Gallery of Ontario.

3. When the Austrian government minted a new 1,000-shilling gold coin—worth $78 face value—the 2.5-cm-diameter coin came into great demand among jewelers and coin collectors. By law, the number of such coins to be minted each year is limited. Lines of people eager to get the coins formed outside the government mint and local banks. "There is exceptional interest in the new coin," said a Viennese banker. "It's a numismatic hit and a financial success." It has disappeared from circulation, however. Explain why.

4. When the rate of exchange was near par, so that the value of $1 Canadian was within 3 cents of $1 U.S., American and Canadian coins circulated side by side, exchanging at their face values. Use Gresham's law to predict which coinage disappeared from circulation in Canada when the Canadian dollar fell to $0.75 U.S. Why did a 3-cent differential not produce this result?

5. Some years ago a strike closed all banks in Ireland for several months. What do you think happened during the period?

6. During hyperinflation in several foreign countries after World War II, American cigarettes were sometimes used in place of money. What made them suitable?

7. Assume that on January 1, 1994, a family had $25,000 that it wished to hold for use one year later. Use library sources to calculate which of the following would have been the best store of value over that period. Will the best store of value over that period necessarily be the best over the next 24 months?
   a. The dollar.
   b. A succession of treasury bills.
   c. Stocks whose prices moved with the Toronto Stock Exchange Industrial 300 average.
   d. A Labatts 11 3/4 percent 2005 bond.
   e. Gold.
   f. Silver.

8. If all depositors tried to turn their deposits into cash at once, they would find that there are not sufficient reserves in the system to allow all of them to do this at the same time. Why then do we not still have panicky runs on the banks? Would a 100 percent reserve requirement be safer? What effect would such a reserve requirement have on the banking system's ability to create money? Would it preclude any possibility of a panic?

9. What would be the effect on the money supply of each of the following?
   a. Declining public confidence in the banks.
   b. A desire on the part of banks to increase their levels of reserves.
   c. Monopolising of the banking system into a single superbank.
   d. Increased use of credit cards.
   e. Transfer of deposits from banks to new nonbank institutions.

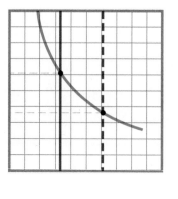

33

The Role
of Money in
Macroeconomics

A t one time or another, most of us have known the surprise of opening our wallets and discovering that we had either more or less money than we thought. There can be pleasure in deciding how to spend an unexpected windfall in the first case, just as there can be pain in deciding which expenditure to eliminate in the second.

What determines how much money people hold in their wallets and in the bank? What happens when people find themselves holding more, or less, money than they wish to? These turn out to be key questions for our study of the influence of money on output and prices.

Financial Assets

At any moment, households have a stock of wealth that they hold in many forms. Some of it is money in the bank or in the wallet; some may be in treasury bills and bonds; and some may be in stocks and shares.[1]

To simplify our discussion, we will group wealth into just two categories, which we will call money and bonds. By *money* we mean M2, as defined in Chapter 32; it includes all assets that serve as a medium of exchange, that is, paper money, coins, and deposits on which cheques may be drawn. By *bonds* we mean all other forms of wealth; they include interest-earning financial assets *plus* claims on real capital.[2]

Given our simple division of assets into two basic types, wealth owners have a single decision to make: how to divide their wealth holdings between bonds and money. As a first step in studying this decision, we must ask how the value of a bond is related to the interest rate.

The Rate of Interest and Present Value

We have seen that a bond is a financial asset that promises to make one or more specified payments at specified dates in the future. The **present value (PV)** of a bond, or of any asset, refers to the value now of the future payment or payments to which the asset establishes a claim. It is the amount it would be worth paying now to buy the claim to the future payments the asset will yield.

Present value depends on the rate of interest, because when we calculate present value, the interest rate is used to *discount* the future payments. This relationship between the

---

[1]At this time, you may find it helpful to review the discussion of the various types of financial assets in Box 32-2 on pages 662–663.

[2]This simplification can take us quite a long way. However, for some problems it is necessary to treat debt and claims on capital as distinct assets, in which case at least three categories—money, debt (bonds), and equity (stocks)—are used.

rate of interest and present value can be seen by considering two extreme examples.

A single payment one year hence.   We start with the simplest case. How much would someone be prepared to pay *now* to purchase a bond that will produce a single payment of $100 in one year's time?

Suppose that the interest rate is 5 percent, which means that $1.00 invested today will be worth $1.05 in one year's time. Now ask how much someone would have to lend out in order to have $100 a year from now. If we use PV to stand for this unknown amount, we can write $PV(1.05) = \$100$ (which means PV *multiplied by* 1.05). If we divide both sides of this equation by 1.05, we get $PV = \$100/1.05 = \$95.24$.[3] This tells us that the present value of $100 receivable in one year's time is $95.24; anyone who lends out $95.24 for one year at 5 percent interest will get back the $95.24 plus $4.76 in interest, which makes $100.

What if the interest rate had been 7 percent? At that interest rate, the present value of the $100 receivable in one year's time would be $100/1.07 = $93.46, which is less than the present value when the interest rate was 5 percent.

A perpetuity.   Now consider another extreme case—a perpetuity that promises to pay $100 per year to its holder *forever.* The *present value* of the perpetuity depends on how much $100 per year is worth, and this again depends on the rate of interest.

A bond that will produce a stream of income of $100 per year forever is worth $1,000 at 10 percent interest, because $1,000 invested at 10 percent per year will yield $100 interest per year forever. However, the same bond is worth $2,000 when the interest rate is 5 percent per year, because it takes $2,000 invested at 5 percent per year to yield $100 interest per year. The lower the rate of interest obtainable on the market, the more valuable is a bond paying a fixed amount of interest.

A general statement.   Similar relations apply to bonds that involve more than a single payment but that are not perpetuities. Although in such cases the calculation of present value is more complicated, the same negative relationship between the interest rate and present value still holds.

---

[3]Notice that in this type of formula, the interest rate is expressed as a decimal fraction where, for example, 5 percent is expressed as 0.05, so $(1 + i)$ equals 1.05.

The present value of any asset that yields a given stream of money over time is negatively related to the interest rate.

Further details on the calculation of present value are given in Box 33-1.

Present Value and Market Price

Present value is important because it establishes the market price for an asset.

The present value of an asset is also the amount that someone would be willing to pay now to secure the right to the future stream of payments conferred by ownership of the asset.

To see this, return to our example of a bond that promises to pay $100 one year hence.

When the interest rate is 5 percent, the present value is $95.24. To see why this is the maximum that anyone would pay for this bond, suppose that some sellers offer to sell the bond at some other price, say, $98. If, instead of paying this amount for the bond, a potential buyer lends its $98 out at 5 percent interest, he or she would have at the end of one year more than the $100 that the bond will produce. (At 5 percent interest, $98 yields $4.90 in interest, which when added to the principal makes $102.90.) Clearly, no well-informed individual would pay $98—or by the same reasoning any sum in excess of $95.24—for the bond.

Now suppose that the bond is offered for sale at a price less than $95.24, say, $90. A potential buyer could borrow $90 to buy the bond and would pay $4.50 in interest on the loan. At the end of the year, the bond yields $100. When this is used to repay the $90 loan and the $4.50 in interest, $5.50 is left as profit. Clearly, it would be worthwhile for someone to buy the bond at the price of $90 or, by the same argument, at any price less than $95.24.

This discussion should make clear that the present value of an asset determines its market price. If the market price of any asset is greater than the present value of the income stream that it produces, no one will want to buy it, and the market price will fall. If the market value is below its present value, there will be a rush to buy it, and the market price will rise. This discussion leads to the following conclusion:

Box 33-1

Calculating Present Value

An asset held now will generate returns in the future. What that stream of future income is worth now is called the asset's *present value*. In general, present value (PV) refers to the value *now* of one or more payments to be received in the future.

This box provides some details concerning the calculation of present value that will prove helpful for understanding the material in the text. If you have studied microeconomics first, some of this material may be familiar from Chapter 19.

Present Value of a Single Future Payment

One period hence. The numerical examples given in the text are easy to generalize. In calculating the present value of a payment one year hence, we divided the sum that is receivable in the future by 1 plus the rate of interest. In general, the present value of R dollars one year hence at an interest rate of i per year is

$$PV = \frac{R}{(1+i)}$$

Several periods hence. What happens to our calculation if the bond still offered a single future payment but the payment were receivable at a later date than one year from now? What, for example, is the present value of $100 to be received *two* years hence if the interest rate is 5 percent? This is

$100/(1.05)(1.05) = $90.70.* We can check this by seeing what would happen if $90.70 were lent out for two years. In the first year, the loan would earn an interest of $(0.05)($90.70) = 4.54, and hence after one year, the lender would receive $95.24. In the second year, the interest would be earned on this entire amount; interest earned in the second year would thus equal $(0.05)($95.24) = 4.76. Hence, in two years, the lender would have $100. (Payment of interest in the second year on the interest income earned in the first year is called *compound interest*.)

In general, the present value of R dollars after t years at i percent is

$$PV = \frac{R}{(1+i)^t}$$

This formula simply discounts the sum, R, by the interest rate, i, repeatedly—once for each of the t periods that pass until the sum becomes available. If we look at the formula, we see that the higher i or t is, the higher the whole term $(1+i)^t$. This term, however, appears in the denominator, so that PV is *negatively* related to both i and t.

---

*As noted in the text, in this type of formula the interest rate is expressed as a decimal fraction. For example, 5 percent is expressed as 0.05, so $(1+i)$ equals 1.05.

In a free market, the equilibrium price of any asset will be the present value of the income stream that it produces.

The Rate of Interest and Market Price

The discussion above leads us to three important propositions. The first two stress the negative relationship between interest rates and asset prices:

1. **If the rate of interest falls, the value of an asset producing a given income stream will rise.**
2. **A rise in the market price of an asset producing a given income stream is equivalent to a decrease in the rate of interest earned by the asset.**

Thus, a promise to pay $100.00 one year from now is worth $92.59 when the interest rate is 8 percent

The formula $PV = R/(1 + i)^t$ shows that the present value of a given sum payable in the future will be smaller the more distant the payment date and the higher the rate of interest.

Present Value of a Sequence of Payments

Suppose now that we wish to calculate the present value of a bond that promises a sequence of payments for a given number of periods. Let R_1, R_2, R_3, and so on represent the payment promised after period 1, period 2, period 3, and so on, and let the last period for which a payment is promised be period T.

The present value of a bond that produces a sequence of payments is just the sum of the present values of each of the payments.

If we also suppose that the interest rate remains constant at i percent, this can be written as follows:

$$PV = \frac{R_1}{(1+i)} + \frac{R_2}{(1+i)^2} + \frac{R_3}{(1+i)^3} + \ldots + \frac{R_T}{(1+i)^T}$$

Present Value of a Perpetual Stream of Payments

Now consider the value that a buyer would place on a $100 perpetuity, that is, on a bond that pro-duces a stream of payments of $100 a year forever. To find the present value of $100 payable every year in the future, we ask how much money would have to be invested now at an interest rate of 10 percent per year to obtain $100 every year in the future. This present value is simply $0.1(PV) = \$100$, where PV is the sum required. In other words, $PV = \$100/0.1 = \$1,000$. This tells us that $1,000 invested at 10 percent interest forever would yield a constant stream of income of $100 per year; put the other way round, when the interest rate is 10 percent, the present value of $100 per year forever is $1,000.

To generalize for any interest rate, we merely write i for the interest rate and R for the revenue to be received each year. Now we wish to find the amount PV that, invested at i, will yield R per year forever. This is $i(PV) = R$, or

$$PV = \frac{R}{i}$$

Here, as before, PV is related to the rate of interest: The higher the interest rate, the less the (present) value of any stream of future receipts will be, and hence the lower the price that anyone would be prepared to pay to purchase the bond.

and only $89.29 when the interest rate is 12 percent: $92.59 at 8 percent interest ($92.59 × 1.08) and $89.29 at 12 percent interest ($89.29 × 1.12) are both worth $100.00 in one year's time.

The third proposition focuses on the term to maturity of the bond:

3.   **The sooner the maturity date of a bond, the less the bond's value will change with a change in the rate of interest.**

To see this last proposition, consider an extreme case. The present value of a bond that is redeemable for $1,000 in one week's time will be very close to $1,000 no matter what the interest rate is. Thus, its value will not change much, even if the rate of interest leaps from 5 percent to 10 percent during that week.

As a second example, consider two bonds, one that promises to pay $100 next year and one that promises to pay $100 in 10 years. A rise in the interest rate from 8 to 12 percent will lower the value of $100 payable in one year's time by 3.6 percent, but it will lower the value of $100 payable in 10 years' time by 37.9 percent.[4]

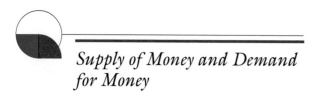

Supply of Money and Demand for Money

The Supply of Money

The money supply is a stock. (It is so many billions of dollars, *not* a flow of so much per unit of time; the distinction was discussed in Box 4-1 on page 60.) In January 1993, M2 was approximately $307 billion.

We saw in Chapter 32 that deposit money is created by the commercial banking system, but only within limits set by their reserves. In Chapter 34, we will see how the reserves of the banking system are controlled by the Bank of Canada. This implies that ultimate control of the money supply is also in the hands of the Bank. In this chapter, we simply *assume* that the money supply can be controlled by the Bank.

The Demand for Money

The amount of wealth that everyone in the economy wishes to hold in the form of money balances is called the **demand for money.** Because, as we assumed at the beginning of this chapter, households are choosing how to divide their given stock of wealth between money and bonds, if we know the demand for money, we also know the demand for bonds. With a *given level of wealth,* a rise in the demand for money necessarily implies a fall in the demand for bonds. If, for example, people wish to hold $1 billion more money, they must wish to hold $1 billion less of bonds. It also follows that if households are in equilibrium with respect to their money holdings, they are also in equilibrium with respect to their bond holdings.

When we say that on January 1, 1993, the quantity of money demanded was $307 billion, we mean that on that date the public wished to hold money balances that totaled $307 billion; but why do firms and households wish to hold money balances at all? There is a cost to holding any money balance. The money could have been used to purchase bonds, which earn higher interest than does money.[5]

The opportunity cost of holding any money balance is the extra interest that could have been earned if the money had been used instead to purchase bonds.

In terms of the distinction between the real and nominal rates of interest that were noted in Chapter 26, the nominal rate of interest is the opportunity cost of holding money. However, because in this chapter we make the simplifying assumption that there is no ongoing inflation, the nominal and real rates of interest are the same; both are measured by the market rate of interest.

Clearly, money will be held only when it provides services that are valued at least as highly as the opportunity cost of holding it. Three important services that are provided by money balances give rise to three motives for holding money: the transactions, precautionary, and speculative motives. We examine each of these in detail.

The Transactions Motive

Most transactions require money. Money passes from households to firms to pay for the goods and

---

[4]The example assumes annual compounding. The first case is calculated from the numbers of the previous example: (92.58 − 89.29)/92.58. The 10-year case uses the formula: Present value = principal/$(1+r)^n$, which gives $46.30 at 8 percent and $28.75 at 12 percent. The percentage fall in value is thus (46.30 − 28.75)/46.30 = 0.379.

[5]As we saw in Chapter 32 (see especially Table 32-10), M2 includes some interest-bearing deposits. This complicates, but does not fundamentally alter, the analysis of the demand for money. In particular, it means that the opportunity cost of holding those interest-bearing components of M2 is not the *level* of interest rates paid on bonds but the *difference* between the rate paid on bonds and the rate paid on M2 assets. Because the interest earned on deposits tends to fluctuate less than rates on marketable securities, the difference tends to move with the level of interest rates in the economy, rising when rates rise and falling when rates fall. For simplicity, we talk of the demand for money responding to the *level* of interest rates, although in reality it is the *difference* between the interest rates on bonds and on money that is the opportunity cost of money.

services produced by firms; money passes from firms to households to pay for the factor services supplied by households to firms. Money balances that are held to finance such flows are called **transactions balances.**

In an imaginary world in which the receipts and disbursements of households and firms are perfectly synchronized, it would be unnecessary to hold transactions balances. If every time a household wanted to spend $10 it received $10 as part payment of its income, no transactions balances would be needed. In the real world, however, receipts and disbursements are not perfectly synchronized.

Consider the balances that are held because of wage payments. Suppose, for purposes of illustration, that firms pay wages every Friday and that households spend all their wages on the purchase of goods and services, with the expenditure spread out evenly over the week. Thus, on Friday morning firms must hold balances equal to the weekly wage bill; on Friday afternoon households will hold these balances.

Over the week, households' balances will be drawn down as a result of purchasing goods and services. Over the same period, the balances held by firms will build up as a result of selling goods and services until, on the following Friday morning, firms will again have amassed balances equal to the wage bill that must be met on that day.

The transactions motive arises because payments and receipts are not synchronized.

What determines the size of the transactions balances to be held? It is clear that in our example, total transactions balances vary with the value of the wage bill. If the wage bill doubles for any reason, the transactions balances held by firms and households for this purpose will also double. As it is with wages, so it is with all other transactions: The size of the balances held is positively related to the value of the transactions.

Next, we ask how the total value of transactions is related to national income. Because of the double counting problem, which we first discussed in Chapter 27, the value of all transactions exceeds the value of the economy's final output. When the miller buys wheat from the farmer and when the baker buys flour from the miller, both are transactions against which money balances must be held,

although only the value added at each stage is part of national income.

Generally, there will be a stable, positive relationship between transactions and national income. A rise in national income also leads to a rise in the total value of all transactions and hence to an associated rise in the demand for transactions balances. This allows us to relate transactions balances to national income. **[39]**

The larger is the value of national income, the larger is the value of transactions balances that will be held.

The Precautionary Motive

Many goods and services are sold on credit. The seller can never be certain when payment will be made, and the buyer can never be certain of the day of delivery and thus when payment will fall due. As a precaution against cash crises, when receipts are abnormally low or disbursements are abnormally high, firms and households carry money balances. **Precautionary balances** provide a cushion against uncertainty about the timing of cash flows. The larger such balances are, the greater is the protection against running out of money because of temporary fluctuations in cash flows.

The seriousness of the risk of a cash crisis depends on the penalties for being caught without sufficient money balances. A firm is unlikely to be pushed into insolvency, but it may incur considerable costs if it is forced to borrow money at high interest rates in order to meet a temporary cash crisis.

The precautionary motive arises because households and firms are uncertain about the degree to which payments and receipts will be synchronized.

The protection provided by a given quantity of precautionary balances depends on the volume of payments and receipts. A $100 precautionary balance provides a large cushion for a household whose volume of payments per month is $800 and a small cushion for a firm whose monthly volume is $25,000. Fluctuations of the sort that create the need for precautionary balances tend to vary directly with the size of the firm's cash flow. To provide the same degree of protection as the value of transactions rises, more money is necessary.[6]

The precautionary motive, like the transactions motive, causes the demand for money to vary positively with the money value of national income.

The Speculative Motive

Firms and households hold some money in order to provide a hedge against the uncertainty inherent in fluctuating prices of other financial assets. Money balances held for this purpose are called **speculative balances.** This motive was first analysed by Keynes, and the classic modern analysis was made by Professor James Tobin, the 1981 Nobel Laureate in Economics.

When a household or a firm holds money balances, it foregoes the extra interest income that it could earn if it held bonds instead. However, market interest rates fluctuate, and so do the market prices of existing bonds (their present values depend on the interest rate). Because their prices fluctuate, bonds are a risky asset. Many households and firms do not like risk; they are said to be *risk averse.*[7]

In choosing between holding money or holding bonds, wealth holders must balance the extra interest income that they could earn by holding bonds against the risk that bonds carry. At one extreme, if a household or a firm holds all its wealth in the form of bonds, it earns extra interest on its entire wealth, but it also exposes its entire wealth to the risk of changes in the price of bonds. At the other extreme, if the household or firm holds all its wealth in the form of money, it earns less interest income, but it does not face the risk of unexpected changes in the price of bonds. Wealth holders usually do not take either extreme position. They hold part of their wealth as money and part of it as bonds; that is, they *diversify* their holdings.

Influence of wealth. Suppose that Ms. B. Smart elects to diversify her wealth by holding 5 percent

of her wealth in money and the other 95 percent in bonds. If her wealth is $50,000, her demand for money will be $2,500. If her wealth increases to $60,000, her demand for money will rise to $3,000.

The speculative motive implies that the demand for money varies positively with wealth.

Although an individual's wealth may rise or fall rapidly, the total wealth of a society changes only slowly. For the analysis of short-term fluctuations in national income, the effects of changes in wealth are fairly small, and we shall ignore them for the present. Over the long term, however, variations in wealth can have a major effect on the demand for money.

Influence of interest rates. Wealth that is held in cash or deposits earns little or no interest; hence, the reduction in risk involved in holding money carries a cost in terms of forgone interest earnings. The speculative motive leads households and firms to add to their money holdings until the reduction in risk obtained by the last dollar added is just balanced (in each wealth holder's view) by the cost in terms of the interest forgone on that dollar.

When the rate of interest falls, the opportunity cost of holding money falls. This leads to more money being held both for the precautionary motive (to reduce risks caused by uncertainty about the flows of payments and receipts) and for the speculative motive (to reduce risks associated with fluctuations in the market price of bonds). When the rate of interest rises, the cost of holding money rises. This leads to less money being held for speculative and precautionary motives.

The precautionary and speculative motives both cause the demand for money to be negatively related to the rate of interest.

Real and Nominal Money Balances

In referring to the demand for money, it is important to distinguish real from nominal values. Real values are measured in purchasing power units; nominal values are measured in money units.

First, consider the demand for money in real terms. This demand is the number of units of purchasing power that the public wishes to hold in the form of money balances. For example, in an imagi-

---

[6]Institutional arrangements affect precautionary demands. In the past, for example, a traveler would have carried a substantial precautionary balance in cash, but today a credit card covers most unforeseen expenses that may arise during traveling.

[7]For those who have studied microeconomics, recall that a person is risk averse when he or she prefers a certain sum of money to an uncertain outcome in which the expected value is the same.

nary one-product wheat economy, this would be measured by the number of bushels of wheat that could be purchased with the money balances held. In a more complex economy, it could be measured in terms of the number of "baskets of goods" represented by a price index, such as the CPI, that could be purchased with the money balances held. When we speak of the demand for money in real terms, we speak of the amount demanded in constant dollars:

The real demand for money is the nominal quantity demanded divided by the price level.

For example, in the decade from 1980 to 1990, the nominal quantity of M1 balances held in Canada increased by 67 percent from $23.6 billion to $39.5 billion. Over the same period, however, the price level, as measured by the CPI, rose by about 77 percent. This tells us that the real quantity of M1 actually fell slightly, from $23.7 billion to about $22.3 billion, measured in constant 1980 dollars.

From real demand to nominal demand. Our discussion has identified the determinants of the demand for real money balances as real national income, real wealth, and the interest rate. Notice that the real demand for money depends on, among other things, real national income; it is not influenced by the price level.

Now suppose that with the interest rate, real wealth, and real national income being held constant, the price level doubles. Because the demand for real money balances will be unchanged, the demand for nominal balances must double. If the public previously demanded $30 billion in nominal money balances, it will now demand $60 billion. This keeps the real demand unchanged at $60/2 = $30 billion. The money balances of $60 billion at the new, higher price level represents exactly the same purchasing power as $30 billion at the old price level.

Other things being equal, the nominal demand for money balances varies in proportion to the price level; when the price level doubles, desired nominal money balances also double.

This is a central proposition of the quantity theory of money, which is discussed further in Box 33-2.

Total Demand for Money

Figure 33-1 summarizes the influences of national income, the nominal rate of interest, and the price level, the three variables that account for most of the short-term variations in the nominal quantity of money demanded. The function relating money demanded to the rate of interest is often called the **liquidity preference (LP) function.** It is also called the **demand for money function.**

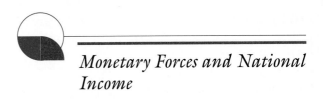

Monetary Forces and National Income

We are now in a position to examine the relationship between monetary forces, on the one hand, and the equilibrium values of national income and the price level, on the other. The first step in explaining this relationship is a new one: the link between monetary equilibrium and aggregate demand. The second is familiar from earlier chapters: the effects of shifts in aggregate demand on equilibrium values of national income and the price level.

Monetary Equilibrium and Aggregate Demand

Monetary equilibrium occurs when the demand for money equals the supply of money. In Chapter 4, we saw that in a competitive market for some commodity, such as carrots, the price will adjust so as to ensure equilibrium. The rate of interest does the same job with respect to money demand and money supply.

The Liquidity Preference Theory of Interest

Figure 33-2 shows how the interest rate equates the demand for money with its supply. When a single household or firm finds that it has less money than it wishes to hold, it can sell some bonds and add the proceeds to its money holdings. This transaction simply redistributes given supplies of bonds and money among individuals; it does not change the total supply of either money or bonds.

Box 33-2

The Quantity Theory of Money

The quantity theory of money can be set out in terms of four equations. Equation 1 states that the demand for money balances depends on the value of transactions as measured by nominal income, which is real income multiplied by the price level:

$$M^D = kPY \qquad [1]$$

Equation 2 states that the supply of money, M, is set by the central bank:

$$M^S = M \qquad [2]$$

Equation 3 states the equilibrium condition that the demand for money must equal the supply:

$$M^D = M^S \qquad [3]$$

Substitution from Equations 2 and 3 into Equation 1 yields:

$$M = kPY \qquad [4]$$

The original classical quantity theory is a long-run theory. It assumes that k is a constant given by the transactions demand for money and that Y is constant at $Y*$, so that we are dealing with a vertical *LRAS* curve. In these circumstances, increases or decreases in the money supply lead to proportional increases or decreases in prices.

Often the quantity theory is presented by using the *equation of exchange:*

$$MV = PY \qquad [5]$$

where V is the **velocity of circulation,** defined as national income divided by the quantity of money:

$$V = \frac{PY}{M} \qquad [6]$$

Velocity may be interpreted as showing the average amount of "work" done by a unit of money. If annual national income is $400 billion and the stock of money is $100 billion, on average, each dollar's worth of money is used four times to create the values added that compose the national income.

There is a simple relationship between k and V. One is the reciprocal of the other, as may be seen immediately by comparing Equations 4 and 6. Thus, it makes no difference whether we choose to work with k or V. Further, if k is assumed to be constant, this implies that V must also be treated as being constant.

An example may help to illustrate the interpretation of each. Suppose the stock of money that people wish to hold equals one fifth of the value of total transactions. Thus, k is 0.2 and V, the reciprocal of k, is 5. If the money supply is to be one fifth of the value of annual transactions, each dollar must be "used" on average five times.

The modern version of the quantity theory does not assume that k and V are exogenously fixed. However, it does argue that they will not change in response to a change in the quantity of money. When Y is held at its potential level $Y*$, the price level once again alters in the same proportion as does the quantity of money.

FIGURE 33-1
The Demand for Money as a Function of Interest Rates, Income, and the Price Level

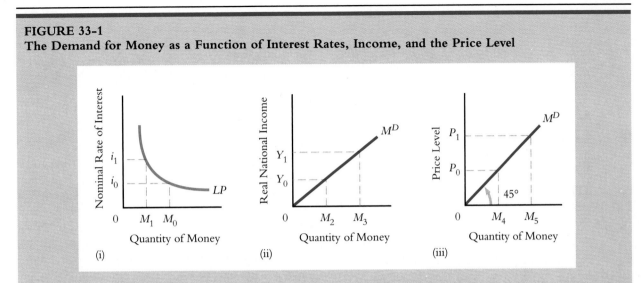

(i)   (ii)   (iii)

The quantity of money demanded varies negatively with the nominal rate of interest and positively with both real national income and the price level. In part (i) the demand for money is shown varying negatively with the interest rate along the liquidity preference function. When the interest rate rises from i_0 to i_1, households and firms reduce the quantity of money demanded from M_0 to M_1.

In part (ii) the demand for money varies positively with national income. When national income rises from Y_0 to Y_1, households and firms increase the quantity of money demanded from M_2 to M_3.

In part (iii) the demand for money varies in proportion to the price level. When the price level doubles from P_0 to P_1, households and firms double the quantity of money demanded from M_4 to M_5.

Now suppose that all of the firms and households in the economy have excess demands for money balances. They all try to sell bonds to add to their money balances, but what one person can do, all persons cannot do. At any moment, the economy's total supply of money and bonds is fixed; there is just so much money and there are just so many bonds in existence. If everyone tries to sell bonds, there will be no one to buy them, and the price of bonds will fall.

We saw earlier (see the numbered color passage on page 684) that a fall in the price of bonds means a rise in the rate of interest. As the interest rate rises, people economize on money balances, because the opportunity cost of holding such balances is rising. This is what we saw in Figure 33-1(i), where the quantity of money demanded falls along the liquidity preference curve in response to a rise in the rate of interest. Eventually, the interest rate will rise enough that people will no longer be trying to add to their money balances by selling bonds. At that point, there is no longer an excess supply of bonds, and the interest rate will stop rising. The demand for money again equals the supply.

Suppose also that firms and households hold larger money balances than they would like. A single household or firm would purchase bonds with its excess balances, achieving monetary equilibrium by reducing its money holdings and by increasing its bond holdings. However, just as in the previous example, what one household or firm can do, all cannot do. At any moment, the total quantity of bonds is fixed, so everyone cannot simultaneously add to personal bond holdings. When all households enter the bond market and try to purchase bonds with unwanted money balances, they bid up the price of existing bonds, and the interest rate falls. Hence, households and firms become willing to hold larger quantities of money; that is, the quantity of money demanded increases along the liquidity preference curve in response to a fall in the rate of interest. The rise in the price of bonds continues until firms and households stop trying to convert bonds into money. In other words, it continues until everyone is content to hold the existing supply of money and bonds.

FIGURE 33-2
The Liquidity Preference Theory of Interest

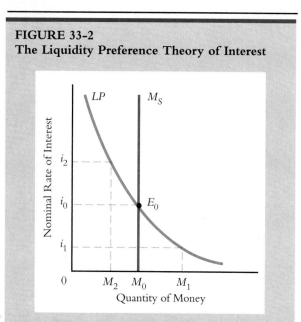

The interest rate rises when there is an excess demand for money and falls when there is an excess supply of money. The fixed quantity of money, M_0, is shown by the completely inelastic supply curve, M_s. The demand for money is LP; its negative slope indicates that a fall in the rate of interest causes the quantity of money demanded to increase. Equilibrium is at E_0, with a rate of interest of i_0.

If the interest rate is i_1, there will be an excess demand for money of M_0M_1. Bonds will be offered for sale in an attempt to increase money holdings. This will force the rate of interest up to i_0 (the price of bonds falls), at which point the quantity of money demanded is equal to the fixed available quantity of M_0. If the interest rate is i_2, there will be an excess supply of money M_2M_0. Bonds will be demanded in return for excess money balances. This will force the rate of interest down to i_0 (the price of bonds rises), at which point the quantity of money demanded has risen to equal the fixed supply of M_0.

Monetary equilibrium occurs when the rate of interest is such that the demand for money equals its supply.

The determination of the interest rate, depicted in Figure 33-2, is often called the *liquidity preference theory* of interest and sometimes the *portfolio balance theory.*

As we shall see, a monetary disturbance—a change in either the demand for money or the supply

of money—will lead to a change in the interest rate. However, as we saw in Chapter 28, investment and hence desired aggregate expenditure, is sensitive to changes in the interest rate. Here, then, is a link between monetary factors and real expenditure flows.

The Transmission Mechanism

The mechanism by which changes in the demand for and supply of money affect aggregate demand is called the **transmission mechanism.** The transmission mechanism operates in three stages: The first is the link between monetary equilibrium and the interest rate, the second is the link between the interest rate and investment expenditure, and the third is the link between investment expenditure and aggregate demand.

From monetary disturbances to changes in the interest rate. The interest rate will change if the equilibrium depicted in Figure 33-2 is disturbed by a change in either the supply of money or the demand for money. For example, as shown in Figure 33-3(i), an increase in the supply of money, with an unchanged liquidity preference function, will give rise to an excess supply of money at the original interest rate. As we have seen, an excess supply of money will cause the interest rate to fall. As also shown in Figure 33-3(i), a decrease in the supply of money will cause the interest rate to rise.

As shown in Figure 33-3(ii), an increase in the demand for money, with an unchanged supply of money, will give rise to an excess demand for money at the original interest rate and will cause the interest rate to rise. As also shown in part (ii) of Figure 33-3, a decrease in the demand for money will cause the interest rate to fall.

Monetary disturbances, which can arise from changes in either the demand for or the supply of money, cause changes in the interest rate.

From changes in the interest rate to shifts in aggregate expenditure. The second link in the transmission mechanism relates interest rates to expenditure. We saw in Chapter 28 that investment, which includes expenditure on inventory accumulation, residential construction, and business fixed investment, responds to changes in the real rate of interest. Other things being equal, a decrease in the

FIGURE 33-3
Monetary Disturbances and Interest Rate Changes

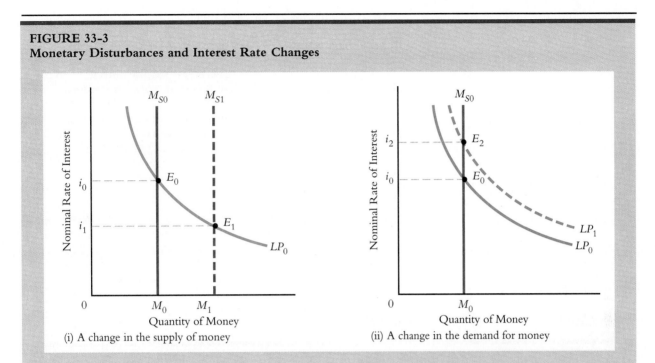

(i) A change in the supply of money   (ii) A change in the demand for money

Shifts in the supply of money or in the demand for money cause the equilibrium interest rate to change. In both parts of the figure the money supply is shown by the vertical curve M_{S0}, and the demand for money is shown by the negatively sloped curve LP_0. The initial equilibrium is at E_0, with corresponding interest rate i_0.

In part (i) an increase in the money supply causes the money supply curve to shift to the right, from M_{S0} to M_{S1}. The new equilibrium is at E_1, where the interest rate is i_1, less than i_0. Starting at E_1, with M_{S1} and i_1, it can be seen that a decrease in the money supply to M_{S0} leads to an increase in the interest rate from i_1 to i_0.

In part (ii) an increase in the demand for money causes the LP curve to shift to the right from LP_0 to LP_1. The new equilibrium occurs at E_2, and the new equilibrium interest rate is i_2, greater than i_0. Starting at E_2, we see that a decrease in the demand for money from LP_1 to LP_0 leads to a decrease in the interest rate from i_2 to i_0.

real rate of interest makes borrowing cheaper and generates new investment expenditure.[8] This negative relationship between investment and the rate of interest is called the **marginal efficiency of investment *(MEI)* function** or sometimes the **investment demand function.**

The first two links in the transmission mechanism are shown in Figure 33-4. We concentrate for the moment on changes in the money supply, although, as we have seen already, the process can also be set in motion by changes in the demand for money. In part (i), we see that a change in the money supply causes the rate of interest to change in the opposite direction. In part (ii), we see that a change in the interest rate causes the level of investment expenditure to change in the opposite direction.[9] Therefore, changes in the money supply cause investment expenditure to change in the same direction.

An increase in the money supply leads to a fall in the interest rate and an increase in investment expenditure. A decrease in the

---

[8]In Chapter 28, we saw that purchases of durable consumer goods also respond to changes in the real interest rate. In this chapter, we concentrate on investment expenditure, which may be taken to stand for *all* interest-sensitive expenditure, and we maintain our simplifying assumption that expected inflation is zero, so that the real and nominal interest rates are equal.

[9]Recall that we have assumed that real and nominal interest rates are the same. Generally, as long as inflation expectations are constant, the change in the nominal interest rate determined in part (i) of Figure 33-4 is equal to the change in the real interest rate in part (ii).

FIGURE 33-4
The Effects of Changes in the Money Supply on Investment Expenditure

(i) Money demand and supply

(ii) The marginal efficiency of investment

Increases in the money supply reduce the rate of interest and increase desired investment expenditure. Equilibrium is at E_0, with a quantity of money of M_0 (shown by the inelastic money supply curve M_{S0}), an interest rate of i_0, and an investment expenditure of I_0 (point A). The Fed then increases the money supply to M_1 (shown by the money supply curve M_{S1}). This lowers the rate of interest to i_1 and increases investment expenditure by ΔI to I_1 (point B). A reduction in the money supply from M_1 to M_0 raises interest rates from i_1 to i_0 and lowers investment expenditure by ΔI, from I_1 to I_0.

money supply leads to a rise in the interest rate and a decrease in investment expenditure.

From shifts in aggregate expenditure to shifts in aggregate demand. Now we are back on familiar ground. In Chapter 30, we saw that a shift in the aggregate expenditure curve leads to a shift in the *AD* curve. This is shown again in Figure 33-5.

A change in the money supply, by causing a change in desired investment expenditure and hence a shift in the *AE* curve, causes the *AD* curve to shift. An increase in the money supply causes an increase in investment expenditure and therefore an increase in aggregate demand. A decrease in the money supply causes a decrease in investment expenditure and therefore a decrease in aggregate demand.

The transmission mechanism connects monetary forces and real expenditure flows. It works from a change in the demand for or the supply of money to a change in bond prices and interest rates, to changes in investment expenditure, and to a shift in the aggregate demand curve.

This is illustrated in Figure 33-6 for the case of an expansionary monetary shock, that is, a shift in money demand or in money supply that tends to increase aggregate demand. Details on how the openness of the economy affects the transmission mechanism are presented in Box 33-3.

Aggregate Demand, the Price Level, and National Income

We have just seen that a change in the money supply shifts the aggregate demand curve. If we want to know what it does to real national income and to the price level, we need to know the slope of the aggregate supply curve. This step, which is familiar from earlier chapters, is reviewed in Figure 33-7 on page 698.[10]

---

[10]Because the demand for money in general will depend on the level of national income, as shown in Figure 33-1(ii), our analysis at this stage is incomplete. The induced change in equilibrium national income will lead to a shift in the liquidity preference function in Figure 33-2. For simplicity, we assume that the demand for money function does not shift in response to a change in national income.

FIGURE 33-5
The Effects of Changes in the Money Supply on Aggregate Demand

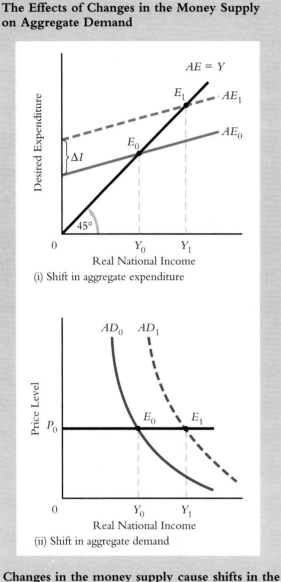

(i) Shift in aggregate expenditure

(ii) Shift in aggregate demand

Changes in the money supply cause shifts in the aggregate expenditure and aggregate demand functions. In Figure 30-4 an increase in the money supply increased desired investment expenditure by ΔI. In part (i) the aggregate expenditure function shifts up by ΔI (which is the same as ΔI in Figure 33-4), from AE_0 to AE_1. At the fixed price level P_0, equilibrium income rises from Y_0 to Y_1, as shown by the horizontal shift in the aggregate demand curve from AD_0 to AD_1 in part (ii).

When the supply of money falls (from M_{S1} to M_{S0} in Figure 33-4), investment falls by ΔI, thereby shifting aggregate expenditure from AE_1 to AE_0. At the fixed price level P_0, this reduces equilibrium income from Y_1 to Y_0.

The key result is that the increase in equilibrium real income is less than the horizontal shift in the AD curve. This is true because part of this shift is dissipated by a rise in the price level: Because the AD curve is negatively sloped, the rise in the price level means that the rise in real output is smaller than the horizontal shift of the AD curve.[11]

---

[11]If you draw the graph, you will see that if the AD curve were vertical, the rise in the price level would not diminish the effect on real output; real output would rise by an amount equal to the horizontal shift of the AD curve.

FIGURE 33-6
Transmission Mechanism for an Expansionary Monetary Shock

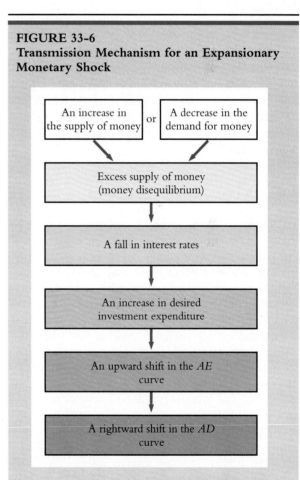

An increase in the supply of money or a decrease in the demand for money leads to an increase in aggregate demand. The excess supply of money following an expansionary monetary disturbance leads to a fall in the interest rate and an increase in investment. This causes an upward shift in the AE curve and thus a rightward shift in the AD curve.

Box 33-3

The Transmission Mechanism in an Open Economy

The text focuses on the interest rate as the channel through which the effects of monetary policy are transmitted to the economy. However, as we have observed in earlier chapters, the "openness" of the economy to international trade and to capital flows introduces two additional complications.[1] First, the effects of monetary contraction or expansion are weakened, because Canadian interest rates are closely linked to interest rates in the rest of the world; this restricts the scope for domestic interest rates to change in response to monetary policy. Second, there is an added channel through which the effects of monetary policy are transmitted to real aggregate demand. This is through changes in the C$ exchange rate.

The Link Between Interest Rates and the External Value of the Dollar

If Canadian interest rates rise relative to those in other countries, the demand for dollar assets will also rise. Canadian residents will be less inclined to invest in assets of other countries, and foreign demand for high-yielding Canadian assets will increase. In order to invest in these assets, foreigners need to buy dollars, and their demand for these dollars on the foreign exchange market will cause the exchange rate to fall.

Low Canadian interest rates have the opposite effect. Canadian residents will want to invest in foreign assets, and foreigners will be less anxious to invest in Canadian assets. Foreigners will demand fewer dollars, and people in Canada will be selling more dollars in order to obtain foreign currencies to invest in higher-yielding foreign assets. This will cause the exchange rate to rise.

[1] These issues are discussed in more detail in Chapter 40.

Other things being equal, the higher Canadian interest rates are, the lower will be the exchange rate, and the lower Canadian interest rates are, the higher will be the exchange rate.

This *negative* relationship between the interest rate and the exchange rate is often featured in newspaper and television discussions. For example, a fall in the exchange rate, say, from 1.25 to 1.17 will often be the result of a rise in Canadian interest rates relative to those in the United States.

The Impact of Changes in the Money Supply

Suppose that in order to stimulate the economy, the Bank of Canada increases the money supply. The initial effects will be exactly the same as in the closed economy analysed in the text. Banks will find that they have excess reserves and will want to make more loans and expand their deposits; households and firms will want to add to their holdings of interest-earning assets. Their combined actions will cause Canadian interest rates to fall.

It is at this point that open economy forces come into play. As Canadian interest rates fall, foreigners and Canadian residents will start to sell Canadian assets in order to purchase foreign assets that now earn interest rates higher than those prevailing in Canada.

Because people are selling Canadian dollar assets, the fall in Canadian interest rates is mitigated. In this way, Canadian interest rates are constrained by those abroad; the availability of interest-earning assets in foreign currencies that investors think are substitutes for Canadian securities implies that Canadian interest rates do not move as much in response to changes in the money supply as they would in a closed economy.

People who have sold their dollar assets will now wish to sell dollars in order to buy foreign exchange, which they will use to purchase foreign assets. This causes the exchange rate to rise.[2]

An increase in the money supply will lead to a fall in domestic interest rates and a rise in the exchange rate. A decrease in the money supply will have the opposite effects, resulting in an increase in interest rates and fall in the exchange rate.

The Transmission Mechanism

How are impacts on the interest rate and the external exchange rate transmitted into changes in the level of economic activity? The reduced response of interest rates to monetary policy implies less effect, for a given change in the money supply, on interest-sensitive expenditures. However, the induced changes in the exchange rate add a new channel by which monetary policy is transmitted to the economy. As we saw in Chapter 29, a depreciation of the dollar, other things being equal, makes Canadian-produced goods more competitive on world markets and thus increases exports and decreases imports.

Because an increase in the money supply leads to a rise in the exchange rate, it stimu-
lates net exports and thereby raises aggregate demand. Similarly, a decrease in the money supply will lower aggregate demand, because it leads to a fall in the exchange rate and hence to a fall in net exports.

The operation of this channel of the transmission mechanism can be seen in terms of the definition of aggregate demand:

$$AD = C + I + G + (X - IM)$$

In a closed economy, monetary policy operates through changes in the interest rate influencing investment expenditure (I) as well as any interest-sensitive consumption expenditures (C); in the open economy, that channel is weakened, but the effects on aggregate demand are reinforced through the effects of changes in the exchange rate on net exports ($X - IM$).

Though the channels are different, the ability of monetary policy to affect national income remains. In the rest of this chapter, we maintain the closed economy analysis for simplicity; we return to the open economy issues in Chapters 39 and 40.

---

[2]Equilibrium will occur when the dollar has depreciated so much that people expect it to appreciate later (i.e., the exchange rate "overshoots" its long-run value), and that expected appreciation compensates investors for the lower nominal interest rate on Canadian bonds. This theory is discussed in more detail later in Chapter 40.

FIGURE 33-7
The Effects of Changes in the Money Supply

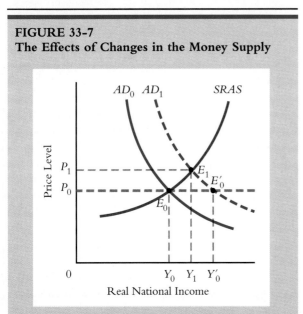

A change in the money supply leads to a change in national income that is smaller than the horizontal shift in the AD curve. An increase in the money supply causes the AD curve to shift to the right, from AD_0 to AD_1. With the price level being held constant, national income would rise from Y_0 to Y'_0. With the upward-sloping $SRAS$ curve, income only rises to Y_1 while the price level rises as well—to P_1.

The Slope of the AD Curve Revisited

We can now use the transmission mechanism to add to the explanation (given in Chapter 30) of the negative slope of the AD curve, that is, to explain why the equilibrium national income that makes desired expenditure equal to GDP is negatively related to the price level. In Chapter 30, when we explained the negative slope of the AD curve, we mentioned three reasons: the wealth effect, the substitution of domestic for foreign goods, and the indirect effect operating through interest rates. Now that we have developed a theory of money and interest rates, we are able to understand the indirect effect that works through the transmission mechanism.

The essential feature of this indirect effect is that a rise in the price level raises the money value of transactions. This leads to an increased demand for money, which brings the transmission mechanism into play. People try to sell bonds to add to their money balances, but, collectively, all they

succeed in doing is forcing up the interest rate. The rise in the interest rate reduces investment expenditure and so reduces equilibrium national income.

This effect is important because, empirically, the interest rate is the most important link between monetary factors and real expenditure flows. This reason for the negative slope of the AD curve is discussed in more detail in the appendix to this chapter.

More on the Adjustment Mechanism

In Chapter 31 (see pages 631–633), we saw that there is an adjustment mechanism in the economy that eventually stops any inflation caused by a one-time demand shock. As shown in part (ii) of Figure 31-2, this mechanism operates by the increase in price causing a movement up and to the left along the AD curve, thus returning output to its potential level and removing the inflationary gap.

In this chapter, we introduced an additional reason for the AD curve to be negatively sloped. The *transmission mechanism* implies that a rise in the price level leads to a rise in interest rates and a fall in investment expenditure. This additional effect reinforces the adjustment mechanism discussed in Chapter 31. An increase in the price level following a demand shock still leads to a movement up and to the left along the AD curve; in the expanded model of this chapter, some of the reduction in aggregate expenditure is now accounted for by a fall in investment.

We can now restate the basic proposition from Chapter 31, *and identify an important qualification.*

A sufficiently large rise in the price level will eliminate any inflationary gap, *provided that the nominal money supply remains constant.*

The adjustment operates through the transmission mechanism linking money to the price level. This mechanism is the reason that the price level and the money supply have been linked for so long in economics; it is also the reason for the qualification about the money supply remaining constant. Many things can cause the price level to rise for some time. Yet whatever the reason for the rise, unless the money supply is expanded, the increase in the price level sets up forces that will remove the initial inflationary gap and so bring demand inflation to a halt.

Frustration of the adjustment mechanism. The self-correcting mechanism for removing an inflationary gap can be frustrated indefinitely if the money supply is increased at the same rate that prices are rising. Say the price level is rising by 10 percent per year under the pressure of a large inflationary gap. Demand for nominal money balances will also be rising by about 10 percent per year. Now suppose that the Bank of Canada increases the money supply by 10 percent per year. No excess demand for money will develop, because the extra money needed to meet the rising demand will be forthcoming. The real interest rate will not rise, and the inflationary gap will not be reduced on this account. This process is analyzed in Figure 33-8.

If the money supply increases at the same rate as the price level rises, the real money supply and hence the real interest rate will remain constant, and the adjustment mechanism will be frustrated.

Inflation is said to be *validated* when the money supply is increased as fast as the price level, so that the adjustment mechanism is frustrated. Validated inflation can go on indefinitely, although, as we shall see in Chapter 35, not at a constant rate.

A recessionary gap. In principle, the adjustment mechanism will also operate to eliminate a recessionary gap. If the recessionary gap were to lead to a fall in wages and other factor prices, the *SRAS* curve would then shift to the right, causing the price level to fall. A fall in the money value of transactions leads to a fall in the quantity of money demanded. People try to turn their money balances into bonds, bidding up their price, which means a fall in the interest rate. This causes investment expenditure to rise, expanding national income along the *AD* curve. However, as we saw in Chapter 31, many economists argue that wages are slow to fall in the face of a recessionary gap. (This was referred to as the second asymmetry of aggregate supply; see the discussion surrounding Figure 31-3.) In this circumstance the adjustment mechanism will not be effective in causing national income to return quickly to its potential level. This is one reason why many economists argue that aggregate demand should be stimulated in the face of a persistent recessionary gap, either through fiscal policy, which we studied in Chapter 31, or through monetary policy. However, this view is challenged by other economists; we will study this debate in Chapter 34.

FIGURE 33-8
Frustration of the Adjustment Mechanism

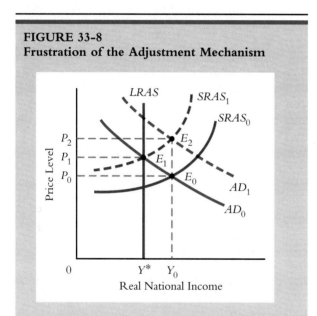

An inflationary gap can persist indefinitely if the money supply increases as fast as the price level. Suppose that the economy is at E_0, with income Y_0 and price level P_0. Because potential income is $Y*$, there is an inflationary gap of $Y*Y_0$. The price level now rises, which tends to shift the economy upward along any given *AD* curve, thereby tending to reduce the excess aggregate demand. However, the Bank increases the money supply, so that the *AD* curve shifts outward, thereby tending to increase excess aggregate demand. If the two forces just balance each other, by the time the price level has risen to P_2, the curve will have shifted to AD_1, leaving the inflationary gap unchanged, with equilibrium at E_2.

The Strength of Monetary Forces

How much will a given change in the money supply cause national income to change? Because a change in the money supply affects national income by causing the *AD* curve to shift, we know from the analysis developed earlier in this chapter (which in turn built on that in Chapter 31) that it is important to distinguish between the effects on national income in the long run and in the short run.

Long-Run Effects on National Income

We have seen that the adjustment mechanism operates to ensure that, regardless of the size of the money supply, real national income eventually converges to its potential level. The operation of this adjustment mechanism following an increase in the money supply is illustrated in Figure 33-9.

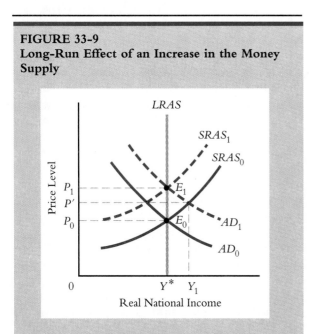

FIGURE 33-9
Long-Run Effect of an Increase in the Money Supply

Real National Income

An increase in the money supply leads to a rightward shift in the AD curve, but because it has no effect on potential income, in the long run it has no effect on national income and results only in a change in the price level. The economy is initially in equilibrium at E_0, with price level P_0 and real national income $Y*$. An increase in the money supply causes the AD curve to shift rightward from AD_0 to AD_1. National income rises to Y_1, and the price level rises to P'. The inflationary gap of $Y*Y_1$ sets the adjustment mechanism in action, driving up wages and causing the SRAS curve to shift up and to the left. The process comes to a halt when national income has returned to its potential level, $Y*$, thus eliminating the inflationary gap, and the price level has risen to P_1.

Although a change in the money supply causes the AD curve to shift, it has no effect on the level of national income in the long run.

Figure 33-9 essentially reproduces the analysis of part (i) of Figure 31-5 on page 637. It also shows that the only long-run effect of a shift in the AD curve following a change in the money supply is a change in the price level, while total national income remains unchanged. We saw in Chapter 31 that when the AD curve shifts because of a change in some exogenous expenditure flow, such as investment or government expenditure, the composition of national income changes. However, when the AD curve shifts because the money supply changes, the results are somewhat different. Because there is no change in any desired expenditure flow at potential national income, the inflationary gap pushes up all money wages and all money prices until not only is total income returned to its potential level, but so is each component of aggregate expenditure. Now the movement from one point on the LRAS curve to another represents solely a change in the price level with no change in any real expenditure flow.

When the price level and the quantity of money are both changed in the same proportion all points on the LRAS curve represent the same national income and the same composition of that total.

This result is often referred to as the *neutrality of money*, as discussed at the beginning of Chapter 32, and it is at the heart of the quantity theory of money, discussed in Box 33-2.

Short-Run Effects on National Income

We now focus on the effects of a change in the money supply on the short-run equilibrium level of national income. As shown in Figure 33-7, this will depend on both aggregate demand and aggregate supply.

The Role of Aggregate Demand

The size of the shift in the AD curve in response to an increase in the money supply depends on the size of the increase in investment expenditure that is stimulated. This, in turn, depends on the strength of the two key linkages that make up the transmission mechanism.

The first consideration is how much interest rates fall in response to the increase in the money supply. *The more interest-sensitive the demand for money, the less interest rates will have to fall to induce firms and households to hold the increase in the money supply.*

The second consideration is how much investment expenditure increases in response to the fall in interest rates. *The more interest-sensitive investment expenditure is, the more it will increase in response to any given fall in the interest rate.*

It follows that the size of the shift in aggregate demand in response to a change in the money supply depends on the shapes of the demand for money and marginal efficiency of investment curves. The influence of the shapes of the two curves is shown in Figure 33-10 and may be summarized as follows:

FIGURE 33-10
Two Views on the Strength of Monetary Changes

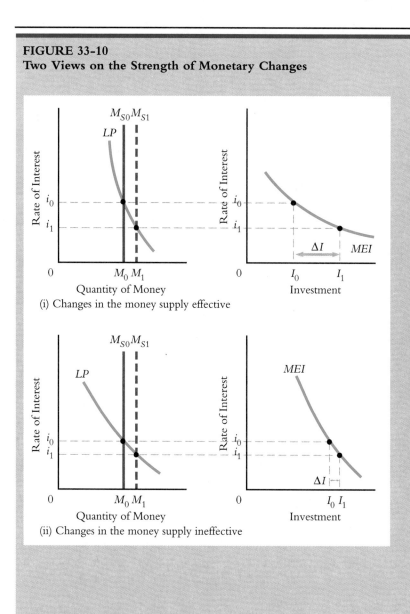

(i) Changes in the money supply effective

(ii) Changes in the money supply ineffective

The strength of the effect of a change in the money supply on investment and hence on aggregate demand depends on the interest elasticity of both the demand for money and desired investment expenditure. Initially, the money supply is M_{S0}, and the economy is in equilibrium, with an interest rate of i_0 and investment expenditure of I_0.

In both parts of the figure the central bank expands the money supply from M_{S0} to M_{S1}. The rate of interest falls froms i_0 to i_1, as shown in each of the left panels. This causes an increase in investment expenditure of ΔI, from I_0 to I_1, as shown in each of the right panels.

In part (i) the demand for money is highly interest-inelastic, so the increase in the money supply leads to a large fall in the interest rate. Further, desired investment expenditure is highly interest-elastic, so the large fall in interest rates also leads to a large increase in investment expenditure. Hence, in this case the change in the money supply will be effective in stimulating aggregate demand.

In part (ii) the demand for money is more interest-elastic, so the increase in the money supply leads to only a small fall in the interest rate. Further, desired investment expenditure is interest-inelastic, so the small fall in interest rates also leads to only a small increase in investment expenditure. Hence, in this case the change in the money supply will not be effective in stimulating aggregate demand.

1. The steeper (less interest sensitive) the *LP* function, the greater the effect a change in the money supply will have on interest rates.

2. The flatter (more interest sensitive) the *MEI* function, the greater the effect a change in the interest rate will have on investment expenditure and hence the larger will be the shift in the *AD* curve.

The combination that produces the largest shift in the *AD* curve for a given change in the money supply is a steep *LP* function and a flat *MEI* function. This combination is illustrated in Figure 33-10(i). It accords with the view that monetary policy is relatively effective as a means of influencing the economy—a view associated with the so-called monetarists. The combination that produces the smallest shift in the *AD* curve is a flat *LP* function and a steep *MEI* function. This combination is illustrated in Figure 33-10(ii). It accords with the view that monetary policy is relatively ineffective—a view associated with some so-called Keynesians. (We shall encounter the differences between monetarists and Keynesians again in Chapter 34.)

The Role of Aggregate Supply

As we saw in Chapter 31, the response of real national income and the price level to any given shift in the *AD* curve depends on the behaviour of aggregate supply. Two aspects of this behaviour are relevant.

The slope of the SRAS *curve.* As shown in Figure 30-10, the steeper the *SRAS* curve is, the larger will be the change in the price level and the smaller will be the change in real national income following a shift in the *AD* curve. Many economists think that when the level of real national income is near (or above) its capacity level, the *SRAS* curve is very steep.

When the economy is operating near or above its capacity level of output, increases in aggregate demand (including those caused by increases in the money supply) will lead to small increases in real national income but will have a substantial effect on the price level.

Shifts in the SRAS *curve.* As we saw in Figure 31-2, shifts in the *SRAS* curve can offset the expansionary effects of an increase in aggregate demand. In that figure, such shifts were induced by changes in factor prices that occurred in response to an inflationary gap. Some economists think that such offsetting shifts in the *SRAS* curve can occur even without the emergence of an inflationary gap if the *AD* shock is caused by an increase in the money supply that is *anticipated*. (This view is related to the views discussed in Box 31-1 on page 635, where we examined the possibility that expectations effects can cause the *SRAS* curve to shift following an anticipated shift in the *AD* curve.)

Figure 33-9 can also be used to illustrate the case of an increase in the money supply that is perfectly foreseen by workers and employers alike. The monetary disturbance shifts the *AD* curve rightward. Workers, knowing that the prices of goods that they buy are going to rise, demand increases in wages to compensate. Employers, knowing that the price of their output is going to rise, grant the wage increases. Thus, the *SRAS* curve immediately shifts leftward; this *expectations effect* means that the adjustment mechanism operates very quickly, thus reducing the effect of a monetary disturbance on real national income.

How far does the *SRAS* curve shift in anticipation of a future shock? In the extreme case where there is no disagreement about the extent or the implications of the initial monetary disturbance and no contractual or institutional forces that would cause wages to adjust slowly to changes in the economy, wages would rise immediately to offset the price increase completely. Real wages would thus remain unchanged, as would real output. Hence, the *SRAS* curve must shift enough to offset completely the expansionary effects on real national income, as shown in the figure.

It is conceivable that in the case of a perfectly anticipated monetary disturbance, all the effects fall immediately on money wages and prices anticipated, and none fall on real wages or real national output.

Of course, most monetary disturbances are, at best, imperfectly foreseen, and typically there is considerable uncertainty about the exact nature and implications of any particular disturbance. Further, responses take time. Hence, an outcome in which the effects on real national income are completely offset is extreme, and any monetary disturbance can be expected to have at least some temporary real effects. However, the expectations effects complicate the analysis of monetary disturbances and create problems for economists who are trying to understand the implications of current monetary events or to advise governments on the use of monetary policy. We will encounter this issue repeatedly in the next few chapters as we study monetary policy and other macroeconomic problems and controversies.

SUMMARY

1. For simplicity, we divide all forms in which wealth is held into money, which is a medium of exchange, and bonds, which earn a higher interest return than money and can be turned into money by being sold at a price that is determined on the open market.

2. The price of bonds varies negatively with the rate of interest. A rise in the interest rate lowers the prices of all bonds. The longer its term to maturity, the greater the change in the price of a bond will be for a given change in the interest rate.

3. The value of money balances that the public wishes to hold is called the *demand for money*. It is a stock (not a flow), measured as so many billions of dollars.

4. Money balances are held, despite the opportunity cost of bond interest forgone, because of the transactions, precautionary, and speculative motives. They have the effect of making the demand for money vary positively with real national income, the price level, and wealth, and negatively with the nominal rate of interest. The nominal demand for money varies proportionally with the price level.

5. When there is an excess demand for money balances, people try to sell bonds. This pushes the price of bonds down and the interest rate up. When there is an excess supply of money balances, people try to buy bonds. This pushes the price of bonds up and the rate of interest down. Monetary equilibrium is established when people are willing to hold the fixed stocks of money and bonds at the current rate of interest.

6. A change in the real interest rate causes desired investment to change along the demand for investment function. This shifts the aggregate desired expenditure function and changes the level of national income at which desired expenditure equals total output. This means that the aggregate demand curve shifts.

7. Points 5 and 6 together describe the transmission mechanism that links money to national income. A decrease in the supply of money shifts the aggregate demand curve to the left. An increase in the supply of money tends to shift the aggregate demand curve to the right.

8. The negatively sloped aggregate demand curve indicates that the higher the price level, the lower the level of national income at which desired expenditure equals output. The explanation lies in part with the effect of money on the adjustment mechanism: Other things being equal, the higher the price level, the higher the demand for money and the rate of interest, the lower the aggregate expenditure function, and thus the lower the income that causes desired expenditure to equal actual output.

9. The adjustment mechanism that causes the aggregate demand curve to have a negative slope means that a sufficiently large rise in the price level will eliminate any inflationary gap. However, this mechanism can be frustrated if the Bank of Canada validates the price rise by increasing the money supply.

10. Changes in the money supply affect national income via shifts in the *AD* curve; hence, they have no effect on national income in the long run.

11. The steeper the *LP* curve and the flatter the marginal efficiency of investment curve, the greater the effect a given change in the money supply will have on aggregate demand. The steeper the *SRAS* curve or the faster wages adjust, the smaller the transitory effect of a given shift in the *AD* curve on national income. If the change in the money supply were widely foreseen and its effects understood, the *SRAS* curve might shift very quickly so as to reduce even further any effects on real national income.

TOPICS FOR REVIEW

Interest rates and bond prices

Transactions, precautionary, and speculative motives for holding money

Liquidity preference (*LP*) function

Monetary equilibrium

Transmission mechanism

Marginal efficiency of investment (*MEI*) function

Money and the adjustment mechanism

The strength of monetary forces

DISCUSSION QUESTIONS

1. "Central banker says using monetary policy to lower interest rates now would only cause inflation to rise and lead to higher interest rates in the future." Explain how this might be so.

2. "Bond prices pressed downward by news of M1's sharp rise, economy's rebound." Does this *Wall Street Journal* headline necessarily contradict our theory about the postulated positive relationship between money supply and bond prices?

3. Historically, construction of new houses has been one of the most interest-sensitive categories of spending. In 1989, the financial press carried a number of stories suggesting that because of financial deregulation and innovations in housing finance, this interest sensitivity had apparently decreased. If this were true, what would be the implications for monetary policy?

4. Describing a possible future "cashless society," a public report recently said, "In the cashless society of the future, a customer could insert a plastic card into a machine at a store and the amount of the purchase would be deducted from his "bank account" in the computer automatically and transferred to the store's account. No cash or cheques would ever change hands." What would such a "debit card" do to the various motives for holding money balances? What functions would remain for com-

mercial banks and for the central bank if money, as we now know it, disappeared in this fashion? What benefits and disadvantages can you see in such a scheme?

5. What motives do you think explain the following holdings?
   a. Currency and coins in the cash register of the local supermarket at the start of each working day.
   b. The payroll account of the Ford Motor Company in the local bank.
   c. Term deposits that mature after one's retirement.
   d. Government bonds held by private individuals.

6. What would be the effects on the economy if Parliament were to vote a once-and-for-all universal social dividend of $5,000 paid to every Canadian over the age of 15, to be financed by the creation of new money?

7. In 1989, economists Christina and David Romer produced a study of post–World War II policies of the U.S. Federal Reserve Board. They examined six episodes in which the Fed tightened monetary policy to reduce inflation and found that each time, following the tightening of monetary policy, the unemployment rate rose sharply and industrial production fell. Further, they estimated that these effects persist, so that unemployment is at its peak $2\frac{1}{2}$ years after the policy is initiated, and "there is only a limited tendency for economic activity to return to its previous path subsequently." Interpret these results in terms of the theoretical framework developed in this chapter.

8. Suppose that you alone know that the Bank of Canada is going to engage in policies that will decrease the money supply sharply, starting next month. How might you make speculative profits by purchases or sales of bonds now?

9. What would happen if, starting from a situation of a 10 percent rate of inflation and of monetary expansion, the Bank of Canada cut the rate of monetary expansion to 5 percent?

10. Trace the full sequence of events by which the adjustment mechanism would work if, in the face of a constant money supply, workers and firms insisted on actions that raised prices continually at a rate of 10 percent per year. "Sooner or later in this situation, something would have to give." What possible things could "give"? What would be the consequence of each "giving"?

APPENDIX TO CHAPTER

33

The Slope of the Aggregate Demand Curve

The AD curve relates the price level to the equilibrium level of real national income. Its negative slope means that the higher the price level, the lower is the equilibrium national income. A major reason for this negative slope is the transmission mechanism.

Let us look at this process in detail. Although the argument contains nothing new, it does require that you follow carefully through several steps.

We start with an initial equilibrium position, corresponding to a given price level P_0, shown by the 0 subscripts in the two figures. Figure 33A-1, which reproduces the relationships depicted in Figure 33-4, shows the determination of the interest rate by the conditions of monetary equilibrium in part (i); that in turn determines the level of desired investment spending by the marginal efficiency of investment schedule in part (ii). Figure 33A-2, which reproduces the relationships depicted in Figure 33-5, shows the AE curve, drawn for that level of investment spending, and the determination of equilibrium national income in part (i); that level of national income is then plotted against the price level to give point A on the AD curve in part (ii).

A rise in the price level raises the money value of transactions and increases the quantity of money demanded at each possible value of the interest rate. As a result, the liquidity preference function shifts

Figure 33A-1
Changes in the Price Level: Interest Rates and Investment

(i) Monetary equilibrium

(ii) Marginal efficiency of investment

Changes in the price level influence the demand for money and hence cause the level of interest rates and desired investment spending to change. In part (i) the money supply is fixed at M_0. Initially money demand is given by LP_0, equilibrium is at E_0, and the interest rate is i_0. Given that interest rate, desired investment spending is I_0, as shown in part (ii) by the MEI schedule.

An increase in the price level causes an increase in the demand for money, and hence the LP curve shifts upward to LP_1. Equilibrium is at E_1, the interest rate rises to i_1, and desired investment spending falls by ΔI_1 to I_1. A further increase in the price level causes a further increase in the demand for money, to LP_2. Equilibrium is at E_2, the interest rate rises to i_2, and desired investment spending falls by ΔI_2 to I_2.

FIGURE 33A-2
Changes in the Price Level: Aggregate Expenditure and National Income

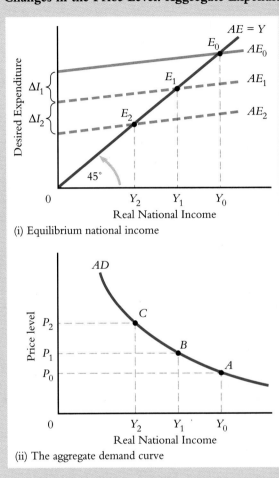

(i) Equilibrium national income

(ii) The aggregate demand curve

Changes in the price level lead to changes in desired aggregate expenditure and hence in the equilibrium level of national income. Equilibrium national income is determined in part (i). At a given initial price level—hence with an initial level of desired investment spending of I_0 from Figure 33A-1—desired aggregate expenditure is shown by AE_0. Equilibrium is at E_0, and equilibrium national income is Y_0. In part (ii) Y_0 is plotted against P_0 to give point A on the AD curve.

An increase in the price level causes a decrease of ΔI_1 in the level of desired investment spending, as determined in Figure 33A-1 and shown in part (i) here. Thus, the AE curve shifts down to AE_1. Equilibrium is at E_1, and equilibrium national income falls to Y_1. In part (ii) the higher price level P_1 is plotted against the lower equilibrium level of income Y_1 as point B on the AD curve.

A further increase in the price level causes a further decrease of ΔI_2 in desired investment spending, as determined in Figure 33A-1 and shown in part (i) here. Thus, the AE curve shifts downward to AE_2. Equilibrium is at E_2, and equilibrium national income falls to Y_2. In part (ii) the higher price level P_2 is plotted against the lower equilibrium level of income Y_2 as point C on the AD curve.

upward, raising the interest rate and reducing the level of desired investment expenditure, as shown in Figure 33A-1. The reduction in investment spending in turn causes the AE curve to shift downward, leading to a reduction in the equilibrium level of national income, as shown in part (i) of Figure 33A-2. The combination of the higher price level and the lower equilibrium level of national income can be plotted as another point, say, point B, on the AD curve in part (ii).

Changes in the price level lead to changes in the interest rate and hence in desired aggregate expenditure and the equilibrium level of national income; other things being equal, the higher the price level, the lower is the equilibrium level of national income.

The negative relationship between the price

level and equilibrium real income shown by the AD curve occurs because, other things being equal, a rise in the price level raises the quantity of money demanded. Notice the qualification "other things being equal." It is important for this process that the nominal money *supply* remain constant. The adjustment mechanism operates because the demand for money increases when the price level rises while the money supply remains constant. The attempt to add to money balances by selling bonds is what drives the interest rate up and reduces desired expenditure, thereby reducing equilibrium national income. (This argument is conducted in terms of the nominal supply of and demand for money. Arguing in terms of the real demand and supply of money leads to identical results.) **[40]**

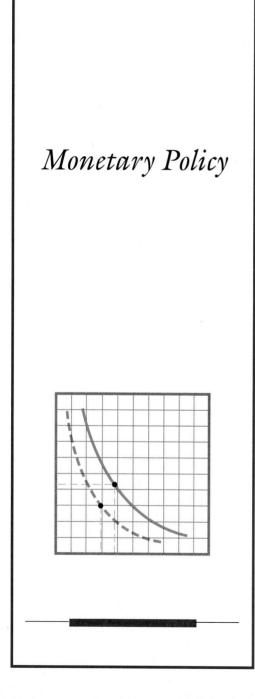

34

Monetary Policy

The Bank of Canada conducts monetary policy in order to influence such key macroeconomic variables as real national income, employment and unemployment, inflation, interest rates, and the exchange rate. The primary way in which it exerts influence on these variables is through influencing the reserves of the banking system and, through them, the supply of money.

Later in this chapter, we study in detail how the Bank conducts its monetary policy. We begin, however, by examining how the Bank controls the money supply.

The Bank of Canada and the Money Supply

Deposit money is the most important part of the money supply. Demand deposits at the chartered banks account for over 50 percent of M1, the narrowest definition of money. Chequable deposits in those institutions account for over 25 percent of M2, the broader measure. As we have seen, the ability of banks to create deposit money depends on their reserves.

The ability of the central bank to affect the money supply is critically related to its ability to affect the reserves of the banking system.

Constant target reserve ratio. In the following sections, we shall discuss two ways in which the central bank affects the reserves of the banking system and hence can influence the money supply. In Chapter 32, we identified the *target reserve ratio* of the commercial banks as the ratio of reserves they wished to hold relative to their deposit liabilities. At this stage of our discussion of open market operations, we suppose that the target reserve ratio is constant.

Open-Market Operations

One important tool that the Bank of Canada uses for influencing the supply of money is the purchase or sale of government securities on the open market. These actions are known as **open-market operations.** Just as there are stock markets, there are active and well-organized markets for government securities. Anyone, including the Bank of Canada, can enter this market to buy or sell negotiable government securities at whatever price supply and demand establishes. These purchases and sales will alter the reserves of the entire banking system in the manner we discuss below.

At the start of 1993, the Bank of Canada held more than $21 billion in government securities. In a typical year, the Bank of Canada may make a *net* addition of $1–2 billion worth to these holdings. During the year, however, its *total* purchases and sales on the open market amount to many times this amount. What is the effect of these purchases and sales?

Purchases on the open market.   When the Bank of Canada buys a treasury bill or a bond from a household or a firm, it pays for the bond with a cheque drawn on itself and payable to the seller. The seller deposits this cheque in a bank, which then presents the cheque to the Bank of Canada for payment. The Bank of Canada then makes a book entry, increasing the deposit of the bank at the central bank.

Table 34-1 shows the changes in the balance sheets of the several parties involved in a Bank of Canada purchase of $100,000 in government securities from a household. At the end of these transactions, the central bank has acquired a new asset in the form of a security and a new liability in the form of a deposit by the bank. The seller has reduced its security holdings and increased its deposits. The bank has increased its deposit liabilities and its reserves by the amount of the transaction. Typically, when the central bank buys securities on the open market, the entire banking system gains new reserves.

Given a constant target reserve ratio, after the transactions shown in Table 34-1 are completed, the banks have excess reserves, that is, reserves over and above those needed to maintain their target reserve ratio. Thus, they are in a position to expand their loans and deposits. Indeed, after the household deposits the proceeds of its sale of the security in its bank account, its bank is placed in the same position as the bank in Table 32-4 on page 673 that received the new deposit from the immigrant.

When the central bank buys securities on the open market, the reserves of the banks are increased. These banks can then expand deposits, thereby increasing the money supply.

Sales on the open market.   When the Bank of Canada sells a security to a household or firm, it receives in return the buyer's cheque drawn against a deposit in a bank. The central bank presents the cheque to the commercial bank for payment. Payment is made by a book entry that reduces the bank's deposit at the central bank.

The changes in this case are the opposite of those shown in Table 34-1. The central bank has reduced its assets by the value of the security it sold and reduced its deposit liabilities to the banks. The household or firm has increased its holdings of securities

TABLE 34-1 Balance Sheet Changes Caused by an Open-Market Purchase from a Household *(thousands of dollars)*

Private households		
Assets		Liabilities
Bonds	−$100	No change
Deposits	+ 100	

Commercial banks		
Assets		Liabilities
Reserves (deposits with central bank)	+$100	Demand deposits +$100

Central bank		
Assets		Liabilities
Bonds	+$100	Deposits of chartered banks +$100

The money supply is increased when the Bank of Canada makes an open-market purchase from the nonbank private sector. When the Bank of Canada buys a $100,000 bond from a household, the household gains money and gives up a bond. The commercial banks gain a new deposit of $100,000 and thus new reserves of $100,000. Commercial banks can now engage in a multiple expansion of deposit money of the sort analyzed in Chapter 32.

and reduced its deposit with a bank. The bank has reduced its deposit liability to the household or firm and reduced its reserves (on deposit with the central bank) by the same amount. In each case, the asset change is balanced by a liability change.

Given a constant target reserve ratio, the bank finds that by suffering an equal reduction in its reserves and its deposit liabilities, its actual ratio of reserves to deposits falls below its target ratio.[1] Banks

---

[1]Consider a bank with $10 million in deposits backed by $1 million cash in fulfillment of a 10 percent target reserve ratio. As a result of the Bank of Canada's open market sales of $100,000 in bonds, the bank loses $100,000 of deposits and reserves. Reserves are now $900,000, while deposits are $9.9 million, and the reserve ratio has fallen to 9.09 percent.

Box 34-1

More on Contractionary Monetary Policy

This box looks at two additional issues that arise with a contractionary monetary policy.

Can the Bank of Canada Always Find Buyers for Securities?

One way in which the Bank pursues a contractionary monetary policy is to sell government securities, thus reducing the reserves available to the banking system. What if the public does not wish to buy the securities that the Bank wishes to sell? Can the Bank force them to do so?

The answer is that there is always a price at which the public will buy. The Bank must be prepared in its open market operations to lower the price of securities as far as necessary in order to sell them. This fall in price is, as we have seen, the same thing as an increase in the interest rate. If the Bank wishes to pursue a contractionary policy by selling government securities, it will have to accept that interest rates must rise.

Do Reserves and the Money Supply Actually Fall?

In every year since 1950, real growth and inflation have ensured that nominal national income has risen. As a result, the demand for money has grown.

In every year in the period, the nominal money supply has grown, reflecting the Bank's decision to supply additional reserves to the banking system to meet the growing demand for money. Does this mean that the Bank has never followed a contractionary monetary policy?

The answer is no. When real income growth and inflation result in a continually growing nominal national income, the stance of monetary policy depends upon the rate at which the money supply is allowed to grow *relative* to the rate of growth of the demand for money. A contractionary monetary policy occurs when the growth in the money supply is held below the rate of growth in the demand for money; it does not require a fall in the absolute size of the money supply.

For example, if nominal national income and the demand for money are both growing at 10 percent per year, the Bank of Canada can follow a contractionary policy if it limits the rate of growth of reserves and the money supply to 7 percent. This would create an excess demand for money, causing interest rates to rise. The higher interest rates, in turn, would feed through the transmission mechanism to slow the growth in spending and, hence, slow the growth in real income or inflation, or both.

---

whose actual reserve ratios are pushed below their target ratios will take steps to restore their reserve ratios. The necessary reduction in deposits can be accomplished by not granting new loans when old ones are repaid or by selling (liquidating) existing investments. (If the central bank requires that the banks maintain some minimum reserve ratio and their actual ratio falls below this, they *must* take immediate steps. In the short term, they may borrow from the Bank of Canada to increase their reserve holdings.)

When the central bank sells securities on the open market, the reserves of the commercial banks are decreased. These banks can in turn contract deposits, thereby decreasing the money supply.

Although the process just described reflects the mechanics of an open-market sale, it does not accurately portray some of the subtleties involved in how the Bank of Canada pursues a tight monetary policy. These are discussed further in Box 34-1.

Shifting Government Deposits

As the government's fiscal agent, the Bank of Canada manages a large amount of government funds. It maintains government accounts on its own books, into which funds are deposited and from which funds are withdrawn. In addition, it manages some government accounts with the chartered banks. Alterations in the amount held in these accounts will affect the reserves of the chartered banks.

A major tool the Bank of Canada uses in its day-to-day operations involves shifting government deposits between itself and the chartered banks.

When the Bank of Canada transfers government deposits, it influences the reserves of the banking system relative to its target level of reserves, thereby inducing an expansion or contraction of the money supply. Suppose, for example, that the Bank of Canada were to transfer $100 million from the government's account at the Bank to the government's account with a chartered bank. The transactions involved are illustrated in Table 34-2. From the government's view, nothing substantial has changed, since its deposits with one financial institution will have fallen, but its deposits with another have risen by the same amount. However, the chartered bank in question will find that its deposit liabilities and reserves will each have risen by $100 million, and hence its ratio of reserves to deposits will have risen. With an unchanged target reserve ratio, the bank will have excess reserves. As with the situation following a Bank of Canada purchase of government securities on the open market, the chartered bank will be in the position shown by Table 32-4 on page 673. It will wish to loan out some of its excess reserves, thus setting in motion an expansion of deposits.

When the central bank transfers government deposits to the chartered banks, the reserves of the chartered banks are increased. These banks can then expand deposits, thereby increasing the money supply.

The first effect is on the reserves of the chartered banks. However, as the deposit money that these banks create from their new reserves spreads out to

TABLE 34-2 Balance Sheet Changes Caused by a Transfer of Government Deposits from the Bank of Canada to a Chartered Bank (millions of dollars)

Chartered bank		
Assets	Liabilities	
Reserves +$100	Government deposits	+$100

Bank of Canada		
Assets	Liabilities	
	Government deposits	−$100
	Chartered bank deposits	+$100

A transfer of government deposits from the Bank of Canada to a chartered bank leads to an increase in the money supply. When the Bank of Canada transfers $100 of government deposits to a chartered bank, the chartered bank's account with the Bank of Canada is credited with a deposit of $100. Thus, the decrease in the Bank of Canada's deposit liabilities to the government is exactly balanced by the increase in its deposit liabilities to the chartered bank. The chartered bank's increase in its deposit liabilities to the government is balanced by the increase in its reserves on deposit with the Bank of Canada. Since its deposits and its reserves have risen by the same amount, it is in the same excess reserve situation as the bank whose balance sheet is shown in Table 32-4 on page 673 and the potential is created for multiple expansion of deposit money as analyzed in Chapter 32.

second- and third-generation banks, the reserves of the whole banking system are affected.

A transfer of government deposits from the chartered banks to the Bank of Canada has the opposite effect. The reserves and deposit liabilities of the banking system fall by the same amount, thus driving the actual reserve ratio below the target reserve ratio. Banks will now have insufficient reserves and will begin to call in existing loans and stop making new ones, setting in motion a process of deposit contraction.

When the central bank transfers government deposits from the chartered banks, the re-

serves of the chartered banks are decreased. These banks will then contract deposits, thereby decreasing the money supply.

Implications for the Money Supply

Notice in Table 32-1 on page 665 that the Bank of Canada's holdings of government securities and its deposit liabilities to the government are both large. Either through open-market operations or switching those government deposits, the Bank can change the reserves of the chartered banks sharply.

Open-market operations and control of government deposits give the central bank a potent weapon for affecting the size of chartered bank reserves and thus for affecting the money supply.

Changing the target reserve ratio. Changes in the money supply in response to Bank of Canada actions to change bank reserves are not automatic but depend on the response of the commercial banks to the changes in their reserve positions. In the preceding discussion, we assumed that the banks maintained a constant target reserve ratio and hence that changes in their actual reserve ratio would set in motion expansion or contraction of deposits. However, the target reserve ratio, and hence the reserves that the banks wish to hold, may vary with economic conditions. For example, banks may wish to hold larger reserves in times of business recession (when there is a low demand for loans and low interest rates) than they do in periods of boom (when the demand for loans is great and interest rates are high).

Changes in the banks' target reserves can lead to a change in the money supply without any actions on the part of the central bank. And if the central bank increases the reserves of the banking system at the same time as the banks decide to hold more, the increase in reserves will not lead to an increase in the money supply.

The significance of a variable target reserve ratio is that it weakens the link between the creation of reserves by the Bank of Canada and money creation. But it does not destroy the link, since, other things being equal, an increase in reserves will lead to some undesired excess reserves and hence to some deposit creation, and a decrease in reserves will lead to a shortage of reserves and hence to some deposit contraction.

Increasing the reserves of the banking system makes it *possible* for the banks to expand the money supply, and an increase in reserves by the central bank will generally lead to some deposit creation and hence to an increase in the money supply.

Moral Suasion

The term *moral suasion* is generally used to describe attempts by the central bank to enlist the cooperation of private financial institutions in the pursuit of some objective of monetary policy. In a country such as Canada, where there are only a few banks, the central bank can easily communicate its view to the chartered banks. In some cases moral suasion involves general discussions aimed at improving understanding of the current financial situation and the objectives of policy. In other cases, specific requests have been issued to the banks. For example, on a number of occasions in the 1980s, the Bank of Canada attempted to restrain the growth of term deposits by requesting the observance of ceilings either on the interest rates offered or on the volume of deposits. In the new regime of zero required reserves, the Bank is expected to influence the commercial banks by directly altering their liquidity while not expecting them to act against their own self-interest.

Changes in the Bank Rate

Under the pre-1990 system, whereby the chartered banks were required to hold some required reserves, they were able to borrow reserves from the Bank of Canada if their reserve holdings fell short of their required reserves. The rate of interest at which the Bank of Canada makes loans to the chartered banks is called the **bank rate.** In principle, a higher bank rate would have induced the banks to hold more reserves in view of the higher cost of borrowing they would have incurred if they suffered a loss of cash and were forced to seek a loan from the Bank to meet their reserve requirements.

Prior to March 1980, the bank rate was simply set by the Bank of Canada. Changes in the rate had an "announcement effect"—such changes were widely interpreted as a signal of changes in the stance of monetary policy, which would cause market interest rates quickly to move in the same direction. Since March 1980, the bank rate itself has become a "market rate." *It is now set automatically at a premium of one quarter of a percentage point over the average rate determined in the weekly Thursday auction of 3-month treasury bills.*

Most observers believed that market rather than policy determination of the bank rate would lessen its role by eliminating the announcement effect. However, the financial press now gives even more attention to changes in the bank rate, which seems to have increased its importance as a signal about monetary policy. The reason is that the Bank of Canada is a major participant in the market for treasury bills, and its purchases or sales designed to alter bank liquidity also influence the treasury bill rate, and through it, the bank rate. Hence the bank rate now signals *actual* rather than *intended* monetary policy.

Monetary Policy with Zero Required Reserves

According to the Bank's new regime brought in near the beginning of the decade, there are no legally required reserves for the banks. As we observed in Chapter 32, banks would still need to hold quite large reserves if they did not have a central bank to fall back on. Today, however, they know that as long as their balance sheets show them to be solvent, the Bank of Canada will provide them with whatever liquidity they require.

The catch is that the Bank provides the needed cash at a significant cost, a cost that works out to be twice the bank rate. The first cost arises because any cash drain that a bank cannot meet from its own reserves must be covered by a loan from the Bank of Canada, which charges the bank rate. The added penalty then arises from the *nonnegative legal reserve requirement.* Each bank is required to hold reserves that average either zero or a positive amount over the averaging period of roughly 4 weeks. So when the bank has a negative balance of $10 million for one day covered by a loan from the Bank, it must hold positive reserves of $10m for at least one other day during the averaging period. When it holds these positive reserves, it loses the interest it could have earned by lending out $10m instead of holding the money in idle reserves. So the interest cost is incurred twice, once when money is borrowed to cover the cash drain and once when zero-interest

earning reserves are held to offset the negative reserves implied by that borrowing.

As a result, banks target to hold some positive level of reserves that will make the return on the last dollar loaned out equal to the benefit of the last dollar added to reserves. This benefit depends on two things. The first is the probability of running out of reserves, which is negatively related to the size of reserves. The second is the penalty of having to borrow from the Bank to cover a deficiency of reserves, which is twice the bank rate times the amount borrowed.

Monetary policy now works in the same way as described in the earlier sections. When the Bank buys bills in the open market, the commercial banks find themselves with excess reserves. They will expand their loans until the excess reserves drain away. When the Bank sells bills, the commercial banks find themselves short of reserves and hence suffer increased risk of being forced to borrow reserves from the Bank. They will cut down on their loans in an attempt to restore their reserves.[2]

Effects of Changes in the Money Supply: A Review

We have now seen how the Bank of Canada can alter the money supply. Before turning to a more detailed discussion of the Bank's operating procedure and the policy choices it faces, we review the analysis in Chapter 33 of the effects of changes in the money supply.

Suppose that initially the economy is in equilibrium at less than potential income. The Bank then buys bills on the open market, increasing the reserves of the banking system and putting downward pressure on interest rates (which is the same as up-

---

[2]Under the new system, reserves tend to be a fraction of 1 percent of all deposit liabilities. Does this mean that the money multiplier exceeds 100? The answer is no. The reason is the money drain to the public caused by an expansion of the money supply. If, for example, the public wishes to hold 10 percent of all its money in cash, 10 percent of any newly created deposit money will be drained away by cash withdrawals. Thus a deposit expansion of 10 times any new reserves will cause all of those reserves to be drained off as cash held by the public.

FIGURE 34-1
Monetary Policy and Macroeconomic Equilibrium

Monetary policy influences aggregate demand through the transmission mechanism, and macroeconomic equilibrium determines the price level P and the level of real ouput Y. Monetary equilibrium requires that the interest rate be such that the money supply equal the quantity of money demanded; for a given money supply this gives rise to the liquidity preference theory of interest, as illustrated in Figure 33-2.

Monetary equilibrium is linked to the determination of aggregate demand via the transmission mechanism, as illustrated in Figure 33-6: Changes in the money market give rise to the changes in interest rates and hence, via the transmission mechanism, to changes in desired aggregate expenditure.

Aggregate demand and short-run aggregate supply together determine the equilibrium values for the price level P and real national income Y. Changes in aggregate demand thus give rise to changes in P and Y; the exact combination of changes in P and Y depends on the slope of the SRAS curve, as shown in Figure 33-7.

ward pressure on the price of bonds). This leads to an increase in the money supply and a fall in interest rates. As a result, there is an increase in desired investment expenditure, which in turn shifts the aggregate demand curve rightward, thus raising equilibrium national income. This process is shown in Figures 33-4 and 33-5 on pages 694 and 695.

When the Bank sells bonds, this reduces the reserves of the banking system and puts upward pressure on interest rates. The money supply falls, and interest rates rise. The increased interest rate causes a reduction in investment expenditure. This in turn shifts the aggregate demand curve leftward and lowers equilibrium income.

Monetary policy works through the transmission mechanism to shift the aggregate demand curve and so to change equilibrium national income. An increase in the money supply is expansionary; a decrease is contractionary.

As a result, changes in the money supply will cause real national income and the price level to change in the same direction, as shown in Figure 33-7 on page 698.

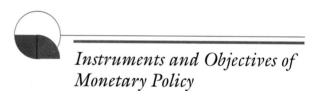

Instruments and Objectives of Monetary Policy

Policy Variables

The Bank of Canada's twin policy variables are real national income and the price level. Recall from Chapter 30 that monetary policy operates by influencing aggregate demand; the resulting link between the Bank's monetary actions and the determination of the price level and real national income is summarized in Figure 34-1.

Nominal national income as a policy variable in the short run. We also saw in Chapter 33 that the short-run effects of a shift in the AD curve are divided between the price level and real output in a manner determined by the slope of the $SRAS$ curve. However, the Bank has no control over this slope. Thus, although the Bank cares about the separate reactions of the price level and of real output, there is little that it can do in the short run to control them independently. For any price level response that is achieved, the real output consequence must be accepted. Alternatively, for any real output response that is achieved, the price level consequence must be accepted.

Monetary policy is not capable of pursuing two objectives of pushing the price level (P) and national income (Y) toward independently determined targets.

For this reason, central banks often focus on nominal national income (PY) as the target for monetary policy in the short run.

The price level as the policy variable in the long run. We have seen that in the long run, when the level of wages is fully adjusted to the price level, the *LRAS* curve is vertical and hence the major impact of monetary policy will be on the price level.

Although monetary policy influences both real output and the price level in the short run, its main effects in the long run are on the price level.

Policy Instruments

Having selected its policy variables and formulated targets for their behaviour, the Bank of Canada must decide how to achieve these targets. Because the Bank can control neither income nor the price level directly, it must employ its *policy instruments*, which it does control directly, to influence aggregate demand in the desired manner.

The primary instruments used by the Bank of Canada to conduct monetary policy are open-market operations and switching government deposits at the chartered banks.

Open-market operations and transfers change the size of the Bank of Canada's monetary liabilities, which are the sum of currency in circulation plus reserves of the chartered banks (see Tables 32-1 and 32-2 on pages 665 and 670). Chartered bank reserves are held on deposit with the Bank of Canada, and are the Bank's liability, because they can be redeemed on demand. The Bank's monetary liabilities, as we saw in Chapter 33, form the *base* on which chartered banks can expand and create deposits. For this reason, its liabilities are often referred to as the **monetary base.**

Intermediate Targets

Major changes in the direction or method of monetary policy are usually made only infrequently. Decisions regarding the implementation of policy must, however, be made almost daily. Given the values that the Bank of Canada wishes its policy variables to take on, and given the current state of the economy, are purchases or sales on the open market called for? How big a purchase? How big a sale? At what interest rate? Such questions must be answered continually in the Bank's day-to-day operations.

Daily information about the policy variables, however, is rarely available. Inflation and unemployment rates are available only on a monthly basis and with a considerable lag. National income figures are available even less frequently; they appear on a quarterly basis. Thus, the policy makers do not know exactly what is happening to the policy variables when they make decisions regarding their policy instruments.

How, then, does the Bank of Canada make decisions? Central banks have typically used *intermediate targets* to guide them when implementing monetary policy in the very short run. To serve as an intermediate target, a variable must satisfy two criteria. First, information about it must be available on a frequent basis, daily if possible. Second, its movements must be closely correlated with those of the policy variable, so that changes in it can reasonably be expected to indicate that the policy variable is also changing.

The two most commonly used intermediate targets have been the money supply and the interest rate. However, these two variables are not independent of each other; recall that the demand for money function relates the quantity of money demanded to the rate of interest. This relationship and its implications for the Bank's choice of intermediate targets are reviewed in Figure 34-2.

The Bank of Canada cannot expect to be able to use its open-market operations to influence both the interest rate and the money supply independently.

Hence, it is important that the Bank not choose a target for one that is inconsistent with the other. By

FIGURE 34-2
Alternative Intermediate Targets

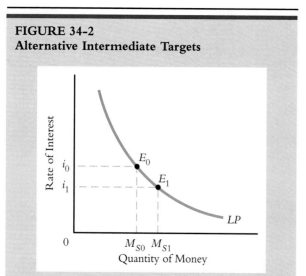

The liquidity preference function relates the money supply to the interest rate, and hence the central bank cannot choose independent targets for the two. The demand for money is given by the negatively sloped liquidity preference function, *LP*, reproduced from Figure 33-2.

If the Bank chooses a target of M_{S0} for the money supply, it must accept that the interest rate will be i_0 because that is the interest rate consistent with the chosen target for the money supply; it cannot expect to be able to achieve a money supply of M_{S0} and an interest rate of i_1.

If the Bank chooses a target of i_0 for the interest rate, it must accept that the money supply will be M_{S0} because that is the money supply consistent with the chosen target for the interest rate; it cannot expect to be able to achieve an interest rate of i_0 and a money supply of M_{S1}.

the same token, because the two are closely related, it might appear not to matter much which one is used.

For example, if the Bank wishes to remove an inflationary gap by reducing aggregate demand, it will sell securities and thus drive their prices down and interest rates up. These open-market sales will also contract the money supply. It is largely immaterial whether the Bank seeks to force interest rates up or to contract the money supply; doing one accomplishes the other. Similarly, driving interest rates down by means of open-market purchases of government securities will tend to expand the money

supply as the public gains money in return for the securities that it sells to the Bank.

In spite of what we have just said, whether the Bank uses interest rates or the money supply as its intermediate target can have some important effects in the short run.

Choice of intermediate targets. Over the years, there has been controversy over the intermediate target that the Bank should rely on most. In the earlier part of the postwar period, many central banks relied mainly on interest rates.

Many economists, and particularly monetarists, criticised the use of interest rates as an intermediate target. These economists pointed out that since interest rates tended to vary directly with the business cycle, rising on the upswing and falling on the downswing, it was difficult for the central bank to determine the impact of its monetary policy by observing the interest rate alone. They cited historical examples in which central banks wished to restrain a boom and were convinced that they were doing so because interest rates were rising sharply, only to later determine that the high demand for money due to the strong expansion was pushing up interest rates. During such periods, the money supply grew substantially, so that contrary to the signals from the rising interest rate, monetary policy had been stimulative—resulting in a cumulative inflationary impact.

These criticisms, and the experience with focusing on interest rates, led to changes in intermediate targets.

In the 1970s, many central banks, including the Bank of Canada, turned to focusing on the money supply as their intermediate target.

At the outset, the measure that was used for this purpose was the narrowly defined money supply, M1. However, it soon became clear that problems also arose when the Bank focused exclusively on M1 as its intermediate target.

Changes in the money supply are reliable indicators of the direction of monetary policy *only* if the demand for money is relatively stable. Experience of the past two decades suggests that the demand for any particular monetary aggregate can change quite substantially and that the Bank often discovers this only after a considerable period of time. Very often, the shifts are out of one type of financial instrument into another; if only the former is included in the monetary aggregate being monitored, then it appears that monetary policy is becoming tighter when, in fact, all that is happening is a substitution of one type of asset for another. The Bank's response to the problems caused by shifts of this type was to again change its intermediate targets.

In the early 1980s, dissatisfaction with M1 as an intermediate target led the Bank of Canada, and many other central banks, to monitor several monetary aggregates rather than just one.

Other experience suggests that there are times when the current state of monetary policy needs to be gauged by measures other than money supply magnitudes. For example, slow growth in all measures of the money supply suggested that monetary policy was fairly tight during the last half of the 1970s. However, decreases in the demand for money that were not fully appreciated at the time meant that the money supply was growing quite rapidly relative to demand, and hence monetary policy was much more expansionary than was thought at the time. More attention to interest rates would have given an important signal of this, because throughout this period interest rates were quite low; in fact, short-term real interest rates were negative.[3] Figure 34-3 illustrates the general lesson.

Lags and the Controversy over Monetary Policy

In Chapter 33 (see the discussion surrounding Figure 33-10 on page 701) we encountered one difference between two groups of macroeconomists who were involved in a debate that was prominent in the 1960s and 1970s. *Monetarists* argued that monetary

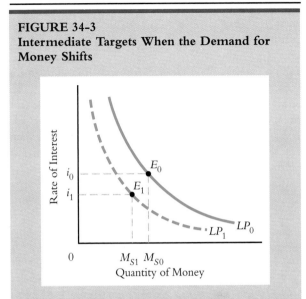

FIGURE 34-3
Intermediate Targets When the Demand for Money Shifts

Shifts in the liquidity preference function change the relationship between the money supply and the interest rate. The demand for money is initially given by the negatively sloped liquidity preference function, LP_0, reproduced from Figure 33-1(i). It then shifts to the left to the dashed liquidity preference function LP_1.

Suppose that, following the shift, equilibrium moves from E_0 to E_1 so the money supply falls from M_{S0} to M_{S1} and the interest rate falls from i_0 to i_1. If the Bank focuses on the fall in the money supply, it will draw the conclusion that monetary policy has tightened. If it focuses on the fall in the interest rate, it will draw the conclusion that monetary policy has eased. In effect, the money supply has fallen less than the demand for money.

policy was potentially very powerful in the sense that a given change in the money supply would give rise to a substantial increase in aggregate demand, whereas *Keynesians* were associated with the view that monetary policy was much less powerful.

However, the debate between the monetarists and the Keynesians involved more than just the *size* of the effect of a change in the money supply on national income; it also focused on the question of whether active use of monetary policy in an attempt to stabilise output and the price level was likely to be successful, or whether it would instead lead to an increase in fluctuations in those variables. This aspect of the debate centres on the role of *lags*.

[3]This means that the rate of inflation exceeded short-term interest rates, so that in terms of purchasing power, lenders were paying borrowers for the privilege of lending money to them! The distinction between nominal and real interest rates is stressed in Chapter 26; see Figure 26-7 on page 535.

Experience has shown that lags in the operation of policy can cause stabilisation policy to be destabilising. In Chapter 31, we discussed how decision and implementation lags might limit the extent to which active use of fiscal policy can be relied upon to stabilize the economy. Although both of these sources of lags are much less relevant for monetary policy, the full effects of monetary policy nevertheless occur only after quite long-time lags. *Execution lags*, lags that occur after the decision has been made to implement the policy, can have important implications for the conduct of monetary policy.

Sources of Execution Lags

1. Open-market operations affect the reserves of the banks. The full increase in the money supply occurs only when the banks have granted enough new loans and made enough investments to expand the money supply by the full amount that is permitted by existing reserve ratios. This process can take quite a long time.
2. Dividing all assets into just two categories, money and bonds, is useful for showing the underlying forces at work in determining the demand for money. In fact, however, there is a whole series of assets, including currency and demand deposits, term deposits, treasury bills, short-term bonds, long-term bonds, and equities. When households find themselves with larger money balances than they require, a chain of substitution occurs, and households try to hold less money and more interest-earning assets. The resulting fall in interest rates, in turn, affects interest-sensitive expenditures. These adjustments can take considerable time to work out.
3. It takes time for new investment plans to be drawn up, approved, and put into effect. It may take a year or more before the full increase in investment expenditure occurs in response to a fall in interest rates.
4. The increased investment expenditures set off the multiplier process that increases national income. This, too, takes some time to work out.

Furthermore, although the end result is fairly predictable, the speed with which the entire expansionary or contractionary process works itself out can vary in ways that are hard to predict. Similar considerations apply to contractionary monetary policies that seek to shift the aggregate expenditure function downward.

Monetary policy is capable of exerting expansionary and contractionary forces on the economy, but it operates with a time lag that is long and variable.

Implications of Execution Lags

To see the significance of execution lags for the conduct of monetary policy, assume that the lag is 18 months. If on December 1, the Bank of Canada decides that the economy needs a stimulus, it can increase the money supply within days, and by the end of the year a significant increase may be registered.

However, because the full effects of this policy take time to work out, the policy may prove to be destabilising. By the fall, a substantial inflationary gap may have developed because of cyclical forces unrelated to the Bank's monetary policy. However, the full effects of the monetary expansion that was initiated 9 months earlier are just being felt, so an expansionary monetary stimulus is adding to the existing inflationary gap.

If the Bank now applies the monetary brakes by contracting the money supply, the full effects of this move will not be felt for another 18 months. By that time, a contraction may have already set in because of the natural cyclical forces of the economy. If this is so, the delayed effects of the monetary policy may turn a minor downturn into a major recession.

The long execution lag of monetary policy makes monetary fine-tuning difficult; the policy may have a destabilizing effect.

If the execution lag were known with certainty, it could be built into the Bank's calculations, but the fact that the lag is highly variable makes this nearly impossible. Of course, when a persistent gap has existed and is predicted to continue for a long time, monetary policy may be stabilizing even when its effects occur after a long time lag.

A Monetary Rule?

Monetarists have persistently criticised the Bank for fine-tuning, and the poor record of monetary policy as a short-run stabilizer has lent force to their criticisms. Monetarists argue that (1) monetary policy is a potent force of expansionary and contractionary pressures; (2) monetary policy works with lags that are both long and variable; and (3) the Bank is, in fact, given to sudden and sharp reversals of its policy stance. Consequently, (4) monetary policy has sometimes had a destabilizing effect on the economy, the policy itself accentuating rather than dampening the economy's natural cyclical swings.

Monetarists argue from this position that the stability of the economy would be much improved if the Bank stopped trying to stabilize it. What then should the Bank do? Because growth of population and of productivity leads to a rising level of output, the Bank ought to expand the money supply year in and year out at a constant rate that is equal to the rate of growth of real income. When the growth rate shows signs of long-term change, the Bank can adjust its rate of monetary expansion. It should not, however, alter this rate with a view to stabilising the economy against short-term fluctuations.

Many other economists think that an appropriate monetary fine-tuning policy can, *in principle*, reduce cyclical fluctuations below what they would have been under a constant-rate rule. However:

The experience of the 1970s convinced many that whatever may be true of *the best conceivable* monetary policy, the Bank's *actual* policy made cyclical fluctuations larger than they would have been under a constant-rate rule.

Subsequent experience has shown, however, that the demand for money sometimes can shift quite substantially. A stable money supply rule in the face of demand instability guarantees monetary shocks, rather than monetary stability. This undermines confidence in the appropriateness of a monetary rule. The daunting challenge that faces central banks in this situation is to offset such shifts in the demand for money while not overreacting and thereby destabilizing the economy. It is also recognised that attempts to use monetary policy to *fine-tune* the economy remain fraught with dangers.

Monetary Policy in Action

This section deals briefly with a few key episodes in recent Canadian monetary history. This is not done just to teach history for its own sake, but because the lessons of past experience and past policy mistakes, interpreted through the filter of economic theory, provide our best hope for improving our policy performance in the future.

Throughout the 1950s and 1960s, the Bank of Canada used interest rates as its main intermediate target. Although it was frequently difficult to judge the stance of monetary policy by observing interest rates, in some instances the stance was clear. For example, there is little doubt that monetary policy was contractionary in 1968 and 1969, when the Bank tried to insulate Canada from rising U.S. inflation.[4] There is also little doubt that monetary policy was quite expansionary in the early 1970s. In 1974, Canadian inflation was close to the double-digit level *before* the first OPEC shock that sent oil prices, and then the general price level, soaring.

By the mid 1970s there was a wide consensus that using interest rates as the main intermediate target was inappropriate, and central banks around the world began to focus instead on monetary aggregates.

Monetary Gradualism: 1975–1980

In 1975, the Bank of Canada announced its policy of "monetary gradualism." This involved gradually reducing the rate of growth of the money supply (narrowly defined as M1) in an effort to reduce the inflation rate slowly. A target range for money supply growth was publicly announced and periodically revised downward.

---

[4]The attempt was frustrated by the Bank's commitment to a fixed rate of exchange between the Canadian dollar and the U.S. dollar. As we shall see in Chapter 40, monetary policy cannot simultaneously control the money supply and the exchange rate.

The Bank was quite successful at keeping actual money growth inside the target range, although there was considerable movement within that range. But after some reduction during the early periods of gradualism, the inflation rate accelerated, and by the end of the decade, it was not far below the rate prevailing when the policy was introduced in 1975.

The restraint sought through gradual reduction in the rate of growth of the money supply was offset by shifts in the demand for money.

These shifts resulted from a series of spectacular institutional changes induced by the high inflation rate. The changes showed just how adaptive financial systems can be to changes in the needs of their users and in the information and technology available to them. (Many of these changes were noted in Chapter 33.) Firms learned how to reduce their M1 balances by careful cash management and were often able to lend their operating balance on an overnight basis, thus earning interest on funds that would otherwise have been idle. Banks introduced automatic transfer systems, where money could be held in interest-earning accounts and transferred to chequing accounts only when needed. As a result of such changes, the private-sector demand for M1 balances often fell faster than the supply was being restricted by the bank. Thus, M1 control did not always create the desired conditions of tight money.

In 1982, the Bank of Canada formally abandoned monetary targeting, although it remained committed to trying to control the economy through aggregate demand. It stated, however, that no observed relation between M1 or any other monetary magnitude, on the one hand, and national income, on the other hand, was stable enough to make complete reliance on monetary aggregates useful.

Monetary Stringency: 1981–1983

The early 1980s saw an extremely restrictive monetary policy, with interest rates rising to unprecedented levels; the rate on 90-day government treasury bills reached over 18 percent, as shown in

Figure 34-4. Over a period of 18 months, inflation fell from around 10 percent to around 4 percent. The cost was a very severe recession.

In 1980, the Canadian and the U.S. central banks had embarked on a policy of monetary restraint aimed at fighting inflation. Interest rates rose, helping to choke off the recovery that had just started. The subsequent rise in rates in early 1982 fed the downturn and helped make it the most serious recession since the 1930s.

These high interest rates, and the recession they wrought, were more severe than might have been expected from the relatively moderate slowdown in the rate of growth of the money supply induced by the central banks.

An unanticipated surge in the demand for money led to a much tighter monetary policy than the Bank had intended.

This unplanned tight monetary policy did not occur because money supply targets were missed, but because money demand rose. (This was the opposite of the shift in the demand for money that disrupted Canadian monetary gradualism in the 1970s.) By June 1982, M1 was back in its target range. The serious weakness in the economy and the "room for monetary ease" created by the return of M1 to its target range led to a loosening of monetary policy in the second half of 1982.

Low Inflation and Economic Recovery: 1983–1987

In early 1983, a sustained recovery began, and by mid-1987, national income had moved back toward potential. Much of the growth was centred in the export-oriented manufacturing industries in Ontario and Quebec. Although painfully slow for Canadians who remained unemployed, the first 4 years of the recovery saw a record 890,000 jobs created and cumulative output growth of 15.7 percent.

The main challenge for monetary policy in this period was to create sufficient liquidity to accommodate the recovery without trigger-

FIGURE 34-4
Short-Term Interest Rates, Canada and the United States, 1979–1990

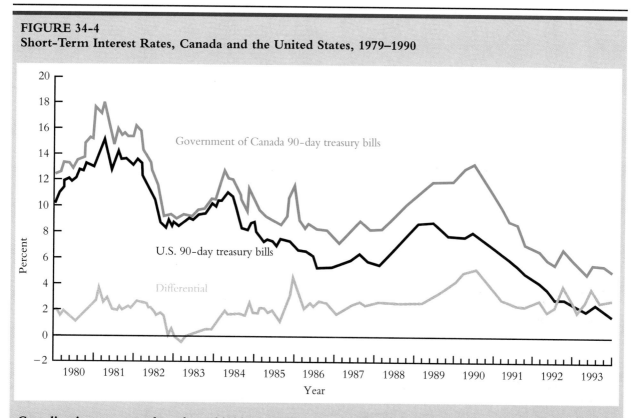

Canadian interest rates have been highly variable over the period shown. They rose with the rising inflation from 1980 to mid-1981. They then fell as inflation fell through most of the 1980s. Starting in 1988, the rates rose steadily under the impact of the Bank of Canada's tough anti-inflation policy. Finally, as the inflation rate tumbled in mid-1992, interest rates, which began to decline in 1990, finally in 1993 reached levels lower than had been seen since the 1960s.

Historically, Canadian interest rates have usually been higher than U.S. rates, the margin typically being between 1 1/2 and 2 1/2 percentage points. In the late 1980s the Bank's anti-inflation policy, which was not matched in the United States by the Fed, drove the differential to unprecedented heights which reached over 5 percentage points at the end of 1990.

ing a return to the high inflation rates that prevailed at the start of the decade.

In spite of much debate and uncertainty, the Bank handled this so-called reentry problem quite well. The Bank allowed a short but rapid burst of growth in the nominal money supply, thus generating the desired increase in real money balances. Once the new level of real balances was achieved, money growth was cut back to a rate consistent with low inflation, allowing for the underlying rate of growth in real income. The trick with this policy was that to avoid triggering expectations of renewed inflation, the Bank had to generate a one-shot increase in the level of the money supply without creating the impression that it was raising the long-term rate of growth of the money supply.

In late 1983 and early 1984, when growth in monetary aggregates first started to surge, many voiced the fear that the Bank was being overly expansionary and was risking a return to higher inflation. As the reentry problem came to be more widely understood and as inflationary pressures failed to reemerge, these criticisms subsided, and the consensus appeared to be that the Bank had done a commendable job of handling the reentry problem.

Continued Recovery and Rising Inflation: 1987–1990

By mid-1987, many observers began to worry that Canadian policy makers were too complacent in accepting the 4 percent range that Canadian inflation settled into. Further, there was concern that inflationary pressures were starting to build; monetary aggregates were growing quickly, real output growth was strong, the unemployment rate was falling, and inflation was rising.

In 1987, many economists argued that if monetary policy were not tightened, Canada would experience gradually increasing inflation until once again a severe monetary restriction would be necessary.

The Bank of Canada apparently agreed with these views. In January 1988, Governor John Crow announced that "price stability" was the Bank's long-term objective for monetary policy.

Specifically, he said that "monetary policy should be conducted so as to achieve a pace of monetary expansion that promotes stability in the value of money. This means pursuing a policy aimed at achieving and maintaining stable prices."[5] This explicit adoption of a zero inflation target and rejection of a short-run income stabilisation target set off a heated debate about the appropriate stance for monetary policy.

The debate was fueled by Crow's decision to give a high profile to his policy by repeatedly articulating and defending it in speeches and public appearances.

The policy of going for zero inflation aroused instant controversy. Some critics said that zero inflation was unobtainable. Others said the costs of reaching it would be too large in terms of several years of recessionary gaps. Supporters said that the long-term gains from having a stable price level with a secure and certain value of money would greatly exceed the costs of getting there.

The controversy reached new heights when in 1990 the country entered, along with much of the rest of the world, a sustained recession. Maintaining the policy of tight money with high interest rates seemed perverse to many when the economy was already suffering from too little aggregate demand to sustain potential output.

Furthermore, the high Canadian interest rates attracted foreign funds. Foreigners who wished to buy Canadian bonds needed Canadian dollars, and their demands forced the exchange rate down. This increased the price of Canadian exports while reducing the price of Canadian imports. This put Canadian export and import-competing industries at a competitive disadvantage, further increasing the unemployment that had been generated by the worldwide recession.

In spite of heavy political pressure to lower interest rates, and of criticism from many economists who might have supported a move to zero inflation in less depressed times, the Bank stood by its policy. It continued to operate a tight monetary policy. The result was an unprecedented differential between Canadian and U.S. interest rates, and a low exchange rate, which hurt the international competitiveness of Canadian goods.

The inflation rate slowly responded by falling from the peak of just over 6 percent that it had sustained in the first half of 1990. By the middle of 1992, the rate had fallen about 1 percent. Nominal interest rates also followed the inflation rate downward, as did the Canadian dollar. By mid-1993, the inflation rate stood at just over 2 percent. The exchange rate of 1.28 was 4 percent *above* the rate of 1.23 that Statistics Canada estimated would equalize the purchasing powers of the Canadian and U.S. dollars. (This meant that, on average, the exchange rate was giving Canadian goods a slight competitive advantage against U.S. goods.) Furthermore, the short-term interest rate had fallen to just over 5 percent, and the differential between Canadian and U.S. rates had fallen to a low level. Figure 34-4 tells the story in detail.

Much of the little inflation that did occur in early 1993 was beyond the Bank's reach, since it came in the government sector, being due to rises in prices resulting from rising taxes on goods and services as well as price rises in regulated industries.

Clearly, the Bank had succeeded in coming close to its target of zero inflation. Controversy continued, however, on two issues. First, was the

---

[5]John W. Crow, "The Work of Canadian Monetary Policy," speech given at the University of Alberta, January 18, 1988; reprinted in *Bank of Canada Review,* February 1988. A detailed analysis of this policy is presented in Richard G. Lipsey (ed.), *Zero Inflation* (Toronto: C. D. Howe Institute, 1990).

result worth the price of a deeper, possibly more prolonged recession than might have occurred if the Bank had been willing to accept 3–4 percent inflation? Second, would the low inflation rate be sustainable once the recovery took the economy back toward potential income? If the inflation rate were to rise to 4 percent during the post-1993 recovery, then the verdict might well be that the cost of temporarily reducing the rate to zero was not worth the transitory gains. The durability of the low inflation rate achieved at such significant costs will be easier to appraise three years from now than it is at the time of writing (late-1993).

The Lessons

The study of the recent past provides a number of important lessons that, if properly understood, should help to guide policy in the future. First, the economy is too complex in its behaviour for a simple money supply rule to provide the best monetary policy. Second, monetary policy can alter between being restrictive and expansive for reasons that *are* related to shifts in the private sector's demand for money and that *are not* related to the Bank's monetary policy. Third, to judge the stance of current monetary policy, the Bank needs to monitor a number of variables, including the various measures of the money supply, real and nominal interest rates, and the exchange rate. Fourth, contrary to what was once widely believed, monetary policy is an extremely potent tool for influencing aggregate demand. It may be difficult to predict in advance how fast and how strongly a given policy will operate, but if the Bank is prepared to be restrictive enough, it can reduce the inflation rate to low levels. There is room for debate about whether the result is worth the cost, but there should be no debate about the ability of the Bank to operate a very restrictive or a very expansive monetary policy, and hence to alter the inflation rate over a wide range of values.

SUMMARY

1. The major tool the Bank of Canada uses to control the supply of money is control of reserves of the banking system through open-market operations and by switching government deposits between itself and the chartered banks. Purchases of bonds on the open market or switching government deposits to the chartered banks increases the reserves of the banking system. Sales on the open market or withdrawing government deposits from the chartered banks reduces bank reserves.

2. The Bank now operates a system of zero required reserves, which means that each bank's reserves must average to zero or a positive amount over the averaging period of approximately 4 weeks. Commercial banks wish to hold some positive reserves, because if they are forced by inadequate reserves to borrow from the Bank of Canada, they pay a price through direct interest costs and forgone interest earnings that is twice the bank rate.

3. The Bank's policy variables are national income and the rate of inflation. To influence these, the Bank works through policy instruments that it can control and that will in turn influence its policy variables. Intermediate targets are used to guide decisions about policy instuments.

4. In its open-market operations the Bank must choose between the interest rate and the money supply as the intermediate target. To reduce national income, the Bank sells bonds on the open market, thereby reducing bank reserves, driving up the rate of interest, and shifting the aggregate demand curve to the left. To increase national income, the Bank buys bonds on the open

market, thereby increasing reserves, driving down the rate of interest, and shifting the aggregate demand curve to the right.

5. In 1988, the Bank announced a policy of "price stability," and by 1992, the rate had fallen to around 1 percent. Controversy concerned two issues. First, was the cost in terms of lost output, heavy unemployment and a temporary reduction in international competitiveness worth the benefit in terms of long-term stable currency? Second, could the low inflation rate be sustained?

6. One lesson for the experience of monetary policy is that the stance of monetary policy depends on fluctuations in both the demand for and the supply of money. Although the Bank can exert a strong influence on money supply, it has less control over money demand. For this reason, monetary policy cannot be reduced to any simple rule.

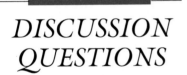

TOPICS FOR REVIEW

Open-market operations

Shifting government deposits

The bank rate

Policy variables, policy instruments, and intermediate targets

Variability of monetary policy and monetary rules

Appropriateness of monetary targets when money demand is shifting

DISCUSSION QUESTIONS

1. During the recovery of the Canadian economy from 1983 to 1985, two different views were often expressed. Some analysts said that adherence to a long-run constant growth rate rule for monetary aggregates was particularly important, lest inflationary expectations be rekindled by an overly fast rate of monetary expansion. Others said that encouraging the recovery required a temporary burst of monetary expansion. Discuss these two views.

2. The U.S. Federal Reserve Board runs a facility in Culpeper, Virginia, that costs $1.8 million per year to maintain and to guard against robbery, according to Senator William Proxmire of Wisconsin. Inside this "Culpeper switch," a dugout in the side of a mountain, the government has hidden $4 billion in new currency for the purpose, it says, of "providing a hedge against any nuclear attack that would wipe out the nation's money supply." Comment on the sense of this policy.

3. Describe the chief weapons of monetary policy available to the Bank of Canada, and indicate whether—and if so, how—they might be used for the following purposes:

    a. To create a mild tightening of bank credit.

    b. To signal that the Bank of Canada favours a sharp curtailment of bank lending.

    c. To permit an expansion of bank credit with existing reserves.

    d. To supply banks and the public with a temporary increase of currency for Christmas shopping.

4. It is often said that an expansionary monetary policy is like "pushing on a string." What is meant by this statement? How does this contrast with a contractionary monetary policy?

5. In what situations might the following pairs of objectives come into conflict?
   a. Lowering the cost of government finance and using monetary policy to change aggregate demand.
   b. Ending a deep recession and maintaining a currently achieved target for monetary growth.
   c. Maintaining stable interest rates and controlling inflation.
   d. Stimulating the economy and supporting the value of the dollar on foreign exchange markets.

6. In 1988, the Bank of Canada announced that it was committed to achieving "price stability," but it did not commit itself to a particular target growth rate for any monetary aggregate that would be consistent with achieving its price stability target. Why do you think it failed to make such a commitment? Write a brief report either defending or criticising the Bank's strategy.

7. In 1993, with 11 percent unemployment, a slow recovery just underway and inflation in the 1 to 2 percent range, the Bank permitted a rapid expansion of M1. Was this inflationary? Why might the Bank have adopted this policy?

8. At our time of writing in December 1993, the new Liberal minister of finance was being urged to reappoint Bank of Canada governor John Crow when his current term expires early in 1994. Economists from the banking community predicted that not appointing Crow would hurt the government's credibility on anti-inflation policy, leading to a sharp rise in Canadian interest rates that would cost the government extra billions in serving its massive national debt. What did the finance minister do? Was there any discernable effect on Canadian interest rates? If so, how long did it appear to last?

34

Securities Markets (Stock Markets)

Stock market values sometimes display cumulative upward movements or cumulative downward movements. The first are called *bull markets,* and the second are called *bear markets.* Most people also know that the Great Depression of the 1930s was preceded by the stock market crash of 1929, which caused what is still the largest percentage loss of stock values ever to be suffered by investors worldwide.

There is clearly some association between fluctuations in the stock market and those in the economy, but is there a causal connection? Do stock market booms help to cause business cycle booms, and do stock market slumps help to cause business cycle slumps? Before we can answer these questions, we need to learn a bit about such markets.

The Function of Securities Markets

When a household buys shares that have been newly issued by a company, it becomes one of the firm's owners. If, at some future date, the household wishes to cease being a shareholder in the firm, the firm will generally *not* repurchase the shares, except in the rare event that the firm is liquidated. If the household wishes to get its money back, it can do so only by persuading someone else to buy its shares in the company.

When a household buys a bond from a company, it becomes one of the firm's creditors. It cannot get its money back from the company before a specified date. For example, if you bought a 2010 bond in 1990, the bond would be redeemed by the company (i.e., the loan would be paid back) only in 2010. If you wished to get your money back sooner, all you could do would be to sell the bond to someone who was willing to become one of the company's creditors.

An organized market in which stocks and bonds are bought and sold is called a *securities market.* Securities markets that deal in shares, or equities, are known as **stock markets.** Two of the best known stock markets are the Toronto Stock Market and New York Stock Exchange. The trading of *existing* shares on the stock market indicates that ownership is being transferred; it does not indicate that companies are raising new money from the public, although firms also do raise funds by issuing new shares.

Securities markets are important because they allow people to put their savings into stocks and bonds that are not directly or quickly redeemable by their issuer.

For example, if I want to invest in a particular stock that I think will earn an attractive yield, I may do so, even though I know that I will want my money back after only a year. I can be confident that I will be able to sell the security a year from now. Nevertheless, although securities markets provide for the quick sale of stocks and bonds, they do not guarantee the price at which stocks and bonds can be sold. The price at any time is the one that equates the demand and supply for a particular security, and rapid fluctuations in stock prices are common.

Prices on the Stock Market

Figure 34A-1 shows the wide swings in a well-known index of stock market prices, the Dow-Jones industrial average. The most recent swing in the period covered in the figure began from a trough in May 1984, when the Dow was about 1100. The index then rose steadily until September 1986, when it reached a value of 1919, a rise of 75 percent in just 28 months. After a significant fall of about 8 percent in September 1986, it then rose spectacularly, reaching 2722 in August 1987. It then started to fall, gradually at first, and then on October 19, 1987—Black Monday—it fell by over 20 percent to 1738. It then climbed fairly steadily, and by early 1989 it had almost reattained its August 1987 peak.[1] It continued to rise steadily through September 1990, when it again fell, although this time by much less than in 1987. From then until early 1992, the Dow rose steadily, reaching over 4000; once again, many commentators were predicting that the Dow was overvalued and were anticipating a downward correction.

From September 1986 to mid-1992, the Dow went through a series of sharp swings, first rising by almost 40 percent in 12 months, then falling by almost 40 percent in the next 2 months, and then rising again by over 50 percent in the next 16 months.

Causes of Stock Market Swings

What causes such rapid gains and losses, and what do they have to do with business cycles?

When investors buy a company's stocks, they are buying rights to share in the stream of dividends to be paid out by that company. They are also buying an asset that they can sell in the future for a gain or a loss.

The value of that stock thus depends on two factors: first, what people expect the stream of future dividend payments to be, and, second, what price people expect to receive when the stocks are sold. (If the price rises, the owner earns a *capital gain;* if the price falls, the owner suffers a *capital loss.*) Both influences make dealing in stocks an inherently risky operation. Will the company in which people are investing pay high dividends in future years? Will the company's value rise so that these people can sell their shares for more than what they bought them for? Although dividend policies of

FIGURE 34A-1
Fluctuations in the Dow-Jones Index of Stock Prices, 1960–1991

Stock market fluctuations are very sharp and irregular, and the decade has witnessed a sharp net increase. The figure shows quarterly figures for the Dow-Jones industrial average of 30 industrial stocks. The index grew steadily from 1962 to 1966 and then displayed very little trend over the next 15 years. Over that period the index did, however, fluctuate sharply; it is these fluctuations that make large speculative gains and losses possible. Three notable falls in the index occurred during the economic downturns in 1969, 1974, and 1981. Although the index was at approximately the same level in 1980 as it was in 1965, the Consumer Price Index had risen by a factor of about 2.6, causing many commentators to believe that the market was "undervalued."

The market fell during the 1981 recession, but the economic recovery that started in 1982 was accompanied by a dramatic sustained increase in the Dow-Jones. From mid-1986 through mid-1992, the index roughly doubled, although that period also witnessed three significant downturns—a relatively minor one in September 1986, a dramatic one in October 1987, and one in September 1990.

---

[1]Commentators are often careless about making the key distinction between the *number of points* by which the index changes over some period and the *percentage* change in that index over the same period. For example, the fall of 984 points from August to October 1987 is the largest fall ever in terms of points. This represented a fall of 36 percent from the August peak of 2722 points. Although this number is significant, it remains dwarfed by the loss that everyone hopes never will be repeated: Over 80 percent of the value of stocks was lost over the 4-year period from 1929 to 1933!

most established companies tend to be fairly stable, stock prices are subject to wide swings.

The Influence of Present and Future Business Conditions

Many influences affect stock market prices; these include the state of the business cycle and the stance of government policies.

Cyclical forces. If investors expect a firm's earnings to increase, the firm will become more valuable and the price of its stock will rise. Such influences cause stock prices to move with the business cycle, being high when current profits are high and low when current profits are low. These influences also cause stock prices to vary with a host of factors that influence expectations of future profits. A poor crop, destruction of trees by acid rain, an announcement of new defense spending, a change in the foreign-exchange value of the dollar, and a change in the political complexion of the administration can all affect profit expectations and hence stock prices.

Policy factors. We shall see later in this book that changes in monetary policy can cause changes in interest rates. Such changes, or just the expectation of them, will have effects on stock prices. Say, for example, that interest rates rise rapidly. Investors will see that they can now earn an increased amount by holding government bonds. As a result, they will wish to alter their investment portfolios to hold more bonds and fewer stocks. Everyone cannot do this, however, because only so many stocks and bonds are available to be held at any given time. As all investors try to sell their stocks, prices fall. The fall will stop only when the expected rate of return to investment in stocks, based on their lower purchase price, makes stocks as attractive as bonds. Then investors will no longer try to shift out of stocks *en masse*.

Speculative Booms

In addition to responding to a host of factors that reasonably can be expected to influence the earnings of companies, stock prices often develop an upward or downward movement of their own, propelled by little more than speculation that feeds on itself.

In major stock market booms, people begin to expect rising stock prices and hurry to buy while stocks are cheap. This action bids up the prices of shares and creates the capital gains that justify the original expectations. Such a situation is an example of *self-realizing expectations.* Investors get rich on paper, in the sense that the market value of their holdings rises. Money making now looks easy to others, who also rush in to buy stocks, and new

purchases push up prices still further. At this stage attention to current earnings all but ceases. If a stock can yield, say, a 50 percent capital gain in one year, it does not matter much if the current earnings represent only a small percentage yield on the purchase price of the stocks. Everyone is "making money," so more people become attracted to the get-rich-quick opportunities. Their attempts to buy pushed prices up still further. In such speculative booms, current earnings represent an ever-diminishing percentage yield on the current price of the stocks.

Capital gains can be so attractive that investors may buy stocks on margin, that is, borrow money to buy them, using the stocks themselves as security for the loans. In doing this, many investors may be borrowing money at a rate of interest that is considerably in excess of the yield from current dividends. Even if $50,000 is borrowed at 10 percent (interest payments are $5,000 per year) to buy stocks and yields a current dividend return of only 4 percent (dividend receipts are $2,000 per year), the investor's logic says "never mind," for the stocks can be sold in a year or so for a handsome capital gain that will more than repay the $3,000 of interest not covered by dividends. Some people have the luck or good judgment to sell out near the top of the market, and they actually make money. Others wait eagerly for ever greater capital gains, and in the meantime they get richer and richer—on paper.

Eventually, something breaks the period of unrestrained optimism. Some investors may begin to worry about the very high prices of stocks in relation not only to current yields but also to possible future yields, even when generous allowances for growth are made. Or it may be that the prices of stocks become depressed slightly when a sufficiently large number of persons try to sell out in order to realize their capital gains. As they offer their securities on the market, they cannot find purchasers without some fall in prices. Even a modest price fall may be sufficient to persuade others that it is time to sell. However, every share that is sold must be bought by someone. A wave of sellers may not find new buyers at existing prices, causing prices to fall. Panic selling may now occur.

A household that borrowed $50,000 to buy stocks near the top of the market may find the paper value of its holdings sliding below $50,000. How will it repay its loan? Even if it does not worry about the loan, its broker will. The household may sell now before it loses too much, or its broker may "sell the customer out" to liquidate the loan. All this causes prices to fall even further and provides another example of self-realizing expectations. If enough people think that prices are going to come down, their attempt to sell out at the present high prices will create the fall in prices, the expectations of which caused the selling.

This is a very simple and stylized description of a speculative cycle, yet it describes the basic elements of market booms and busts that many believe have recurred throughout stock market history. It happened in the Jay Cooke panic of 1873 and in the Grover Cleveland panic of 1893. The biggest boom of all began in the mid-1920s and ended on Black Tuesday, October 29, 1929. The collapse was dramatic, with stocks losing about one-half of their value in about two months. Nor did it stop there. For four years stock prices continued to decline, until the average value of stock sold on the New York Stock Exchange had fallen from its 1929 high of $89.10 per share to $17.35 per share by late 1933. It also happened, although less dramatically, in the booms and busts of the 1970s and 1980s, discussed earlier in this section.

Speculative behaviour means that stock market prices do not always just reflect the fundamentals that underlie the expected profitability of companies; in this sense, the stock market is sometimes said to be over- or undervalued. However, the extent of the over- or undervaluation is difficult to determine, and hence it is hard to predict when, and by how much, prices will "correct." For example, consider the long upswing that more than doubled stock prices in just over three years between early 1984 and October 1987. At the time the United States enjoyed a very strong recovery, and the rising stock prices no doubt reflected the resulting favourable profit outlook of companies. However, many doubted that the full increase was justified by underlying business opportunities and hence felt that there may have been a speculative component to the rise in stock values. These people argued that the dramatic fall that occurred on Black Monday represented a "correction" that removed much of the speculative component from the prices. Of course, this is easy to say after the fact. If any of us had known in advance when and by how much prices would correct, we would have been able to make a huge profit.

Stock Market Swings: Cause or Effect of Business Cycles?

Stock markets tend often to lead, and sometimes to follow, booms and slumps in business activity. In both cases the causes usually run from real business conditions, whether actual or anticipated, to stock market prices. This is the dominant theme: the stock market as a reflector.

Stock market fluctuations are more typically a consequence than a cause of the business cycle.

It is also possible for the stock market to be a causal factor in the business cycle. The value of the stock market influences the wealth of households, which ultimately own the market, either directly or through their pension funds. Thus, stock prices can be expected to influence their consumption spending. (Recall the wealth effect from Chapter 28; see Figure 28-2.) Firms also use the stock market to issue new shares in order to finance investment spending; when stock market prices are low, they find this an unattractive way to raise new money and thus may choose to cancel, or at least postpone, investments. As a result, many people believed that the dramatic fall in stock value in the October 1987 crash would cause households to curtail their consumption spending in response to their perceived fall in wealth. On this basis many forecasters predicted that the stock market fall of Black Monday would lead to a serious downturn in economy. After the event, such gloom-and-doom forecasts turned out to be inaccurate; apparently, people did not perceive the fall in the stock market as an indication that their permanent incomes or wealth had fallen dramatically, and hence they did not reduce their consumption spending.

In many cases the stock market and the business cycle both reflect the common influence of other factors. For example, stock markets often react to changes in interest rates that may be caused by government policy; as we have seen, such interest rate changes can also play a causal role in cyclical fluctuations in the economy. Typically, the stock market responds more quickly than does the economy to such influences, and for this reason many observers look to it as a "leading indicator" of likely future economic developments.

The relationship between the stock market and the economy is further complicated by the existence of occasional speculative booms and busts. There are often real economic forces influencing expectations of stock prices, but, at least for a while, the prices may become dominated by speculative psychology. Unfortunately, speculative behaviour causes the stock market to react to many events that turn out to have little or no enduring implications for the economy. As one wag put it, the stock market has predicted seven out of the last two recessions!

Stock Markets: Investment Marketplaces or Gambling Casinos?

Stock markets fulfill many important functions. It is doubtful that the great aggregations of capital that are needed to finance modern firms could be raised under a private-ownership system without them. There is no doubt, however, that they also provide an unfortunate attraction for many naive investors, whose get-rich-quick dreams are more often than not destroyed by the fall in prices that follows the occasional speculative booms that they help to create.

To some extent public policy has sought to curb the excesses of stock market speculation through supervision of security issues. Public policy seeks, among other things, to prevent both fraudulent or misleading information and trading by "insiders" (those in a company who have confidential information). Moreover, the regulators can limit the ability of speculators to trade on margin.

All in all, the stock market is both a real marketplace and a place to gamble. As in all gambling situations, players who are less well informed and less clever than the average player tend to be losers in the long term.

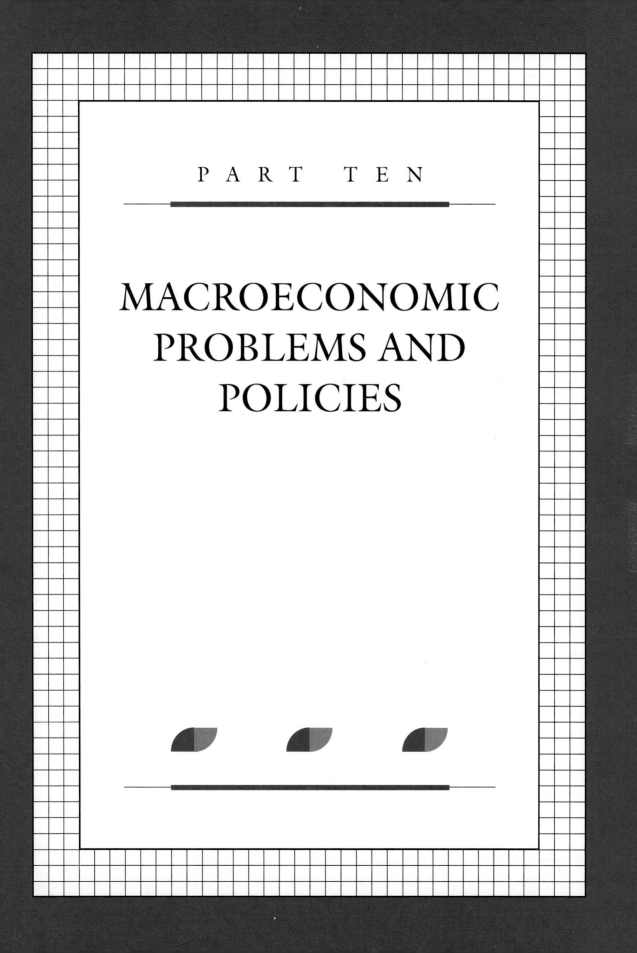

PART TEN

MACROECONOMIC PROBLEMS AND POLICIES

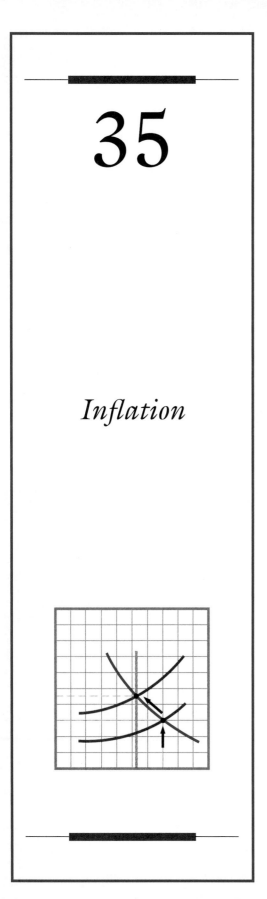

35

Inflation

If you look back at Figure 26-6, on page 530 you will see that for 20 years following World War II, inflation remained low. The only exceptions were the "bubbles" immediately following World War II and the Korean War. During the second half of the 1960s, the inflation rate slowly inched upward and reached the double-digit range in the mid-1970s. By then, inflation had been declared public enemy number one. Even more worrisome, it fell only slightly during the late 1970s, in the face of a concerted anti-inflationary policy that included statutory control of wages and prices and an apparently restrictive monetary policy. It rose again to the double-digit level in 1980, and remained quite stubbornly high during the recession of 1981–1982. At last, in 1983, inflation fell dramatically to around 4 percent, where it remained through 1987. Although this was an improvement over the double-digit inflation rates experienced earlier, 4 percent was, historically, a high inflation rate to be experienced at the end of a serious recession. Then, during the latter half of 1988, the rate crept up to over 5 percent, where it stayed through 1989 and the early part of 1990. The Bank of Canada's attempt to push inflation down—first back to the 4 percent level, where it had been stabilized for years, and then over the longer term to about one percent—caused renewed controversy about the methods, the costs, and the benefits of controlling inflation.

In Chapter 26, we examined the costs of inflation. We now need to ask further questions about inflation. What are its causes? What are the costs of reducing it? Can inflation be prevented from rising into the double-digit range again? Can inflation ever be eliminated altogether?

Causes and Consequences of Inflation

An inflationary shock is anything that tends to increase the price level; a deflationary shock is anything that tends to decrease it. We start by making three important distinctions concerning these shocks.

1. Inflations or deflations that are caused by shifts in aggregate demand—which are referred to as demand shocks—must be distinguished from inflations or deflations that are caused by shifts in aggregate supply—which are referred to as supply shocks.
2. Isolated once-and-for-all shocks must be distinguished from repeated shocks. The former cause temporary bouts of inflation as the price level moves from one equilibrium level to another. The latter cause continuous, or sustained, inflations.

3. Increases in the price level that occur even though the money supply is constant must be distinguished from those that occur when the money supply is increasing. When an increase in the money supply accompanies inflationary shocks, the resulting inflation is said to be *validated* by the monetary expansion.

In this book, we use the term *inflation* as it is commonly used in ordinary speech to mean any rise in the price level. We then make the distinction between once-and-for-all and continuing rises in the price level (discussed in point 2 above) by referring to temporary or once-and-for-all inflation, on the one hand, and to continuing or sustained inflation, on the other.[1]

We first studied inflationary shocks in Part 8. At that time, it was enough to say that an inflationary gap implies excess demand for labour, low unemployment, upward pressure on wages, and hence an upward-shifting *SRAS* curve. Understanding the forces that cause wage rates to change, and knowing when these changes do and do not cause the *SRAS* curve to shift, are keys to understanding inflation.

Why Wages Change

We saw in Chapter 31 that increases in wage rates do not necessarily cause unit costs to rise, because these costs depend on the relationship between the price of labour and labour productivity (i.e., output per unit of labour input). For example, if wage rates and productivity both rise by 3 percent, each unit of labour costs 3 percent more but also produces 3 percent more. As a result, labour costs per unit of output remain unchanged. What matters then is the relation between changes in money wages and changes in productivity. We use the words "changes in money wages *relative to productivity*" to refer to *the percentage change in money wages minus the percentage change in productivity*; the result measures the change in unit costs of production.

Two main forces that can cause unit wage costs to change systematically are demand for labour and expectations.[2] Much of what we say in the case of demand is a recapitulation of material first presented in Chapter 31, but the points are important enough to bear repeating.

Labour Demand

In Chapter 31, we stated three propositions about how changes in money wages relative to productivity were influenced by the relation between aggregate demand and aggregate supply:

1. The excess demand for labour that is associated with an inflationary gap puts upward pressure on money wages relative to productivity. Money wages rise more rapidly than productivity is rising.
2. The excess supply of labour associated with a recessionary gap puts downward pressure on money wages relative to productivity. Money wages rise more slowly than productivity is rising, and they may even fall.
3. The absence of either an inflationary or a recessionary gap means that demand forces do not exert any pressure on money wages either to rise or to fall relative to productivity.

The NAIRU. We saw in Chapter 26 that when current national income is at its potential level ($Y = Y*$), unemployment is not zero. Instead, there may be a substantial amount of frictional and structural unemployment caused, for example, by the movement of people between jobs. Recall that the rate of unemployment that exists when national

---

[1]Some economists reserve the term *inflation* for sustained changes in the price level, using other words, such as a rise in the price level, to refer to once-and-for-all changes. As long as one understands the distinction, the choice of words is not a substantial matter.

[2]Changes in wages relative to productivity may be affected by other forces that are associated with neither excess demand nor expectations of inflation—such as government guidelines, union power, and employers' optimism. These forces can be positive, pushing wages higher than they otherwise would go, or negative, pushing wages lower than they otherwise would go. Since there are many such forces that tend to act independently of one another, they may be regarded as *random shocks.* Although they may occasionally have significant effects in any one year, over a longer period of time, positive shocks in some years will tend to be offset by negative shocks in other years so that, in total, they contribute little to the long-term trend of the price level. For this reason, they can be ignored in an introductory study.

TABLE 35-1   The Characteristics of Various Output Gaps

Recessionary gaps	Potential income	Inflationary gaps
$Y < Y*$	$Y = Y*$	$Y > Y*$
$U > \text{NAIRU } (U*)$	$U = \text{NAIRU } (U*)$	$U < \text{NAIRU } (U*)$
$\dot{W} < \dot{g}$	$\dot{W} = \dot{g}$	$\dot{W} > \dot{g}$
$\dot{c} < 0$	$\dot{c} = 0$	$\dot{c} > 0$

Unit costs fall during recessionary gaps and rise during inflationary gaps. During a recessionary gap, income is less than potential, the unemployment rate exceeds the NAIRU ($U*$), money wages rise (indicated by $\dot{W}$) at a lower rate than does productivity (indicated by $\dot{g}$), and the change in unit costs is negative—that is unit costs fall. During an inflationary gap, income exceeds potential, the unemployment rate is less than NAIRU, money wages rise at a faster rate than productivity, and unit costs rise. When income is at its potential level, unemployment is at the NAIRU, money wages change at the same rate as productivity, and unit costs remain constant.

income is at its potential level is called the *NAIRU* (and is designated by the symbol $U*$).[3] It follows from this definition that when current national income exceeds full-employment income ($Y > Y*$), current unemployment will be less than the *NAIRU* ($U < U*$). When current national income is less than full-employment income ($Y < Y*$), current unemployment will exceed the *NAIRU* ($U > U*$).[4]

We have seen that wages and unit costs react to various pressures of demand. These demand pressures can now be stated either in terms of the relation between actual and potential income or the relation between actual unemployment and the NAIRU. This is done in Table 35-1.

The effect of the demand for labour on wages can be shown by what is called a *Phillips curve*, which is discussed in Box 35-1 on page 736.

Expectational Forces

A second force that can influence wages is *expectations.* Suppose, for example, that both employers and employees expect a 4 percent inflation next year. Workers will start negotiations from a base of a 4 percent increase in money wages, which would hold their *real wages* constant. Firms also may be inclined to begin bargaining by conceding at least a 4 percent increase in money wages relative to productivity, because they expect that the prices at which they sell their products will rise by 4 percent. *Starting from that base,* workers will attempt to obtain some desired increase in their real wages. At this point, such factors as profits and bargaining power become important.

The general expectation of some specific inflation rate creates pressure for wages to rise by that rate relative to productivity and, hence, for unit costs to rise at that rate.

The key point is that money wages can be rising relative to productivity even if no inflationary gap is present. As long as people expect prices to rise, their behaviour will put upward pressure on money wages, causing unit costs to rise, thus shifting the *SRAS* curve upward.

The formation of expectations. The foregoing discussion suggests that the manner in which people form their expectations about the future course of inflation may have an important effect on that inflation. Generally, we can distinguish two main patterns: One is to look backward to past experience;

---

[3]As we noted earlier, these initials stand for *nonaccelerating inflationary rate of unemployment.* The reason for using this mouthful to describe the amount of unemployment associated with $Y*$ will be explained later in the chapter.

[4]The NAIRU is sometimes called the *natural rate of unemployment,* but NAIRU is now the more common usage.

the other is to look at current circumstances for a clue as to what may happen in the near future.

The first type of expectations can be called *backward looking.* People look to the past to predict what will happen in the future. The simplest possible form of such expectations is to expect the past to be repeated in the future. According to this view, if inflation has been 10 percent over the last 2 years, people will expect it to be 10 percent next year. This expectation, however, is excessively naive. Everyone knows that the inflation rate does change, and, therefore, that the past cannot be a perfectly accurate guide to the future.

A less naïve version would have people revise their expectations in light of the mistakes that they made in estimating inflation in the past. For example, if you thought that this year's inflation rate was going to be 10 percent but it turned out to be only 6 percent, you might revise your estimate of next year's rate down somewhat from 10 percent. Perhaps you might not go all the way to 6 percent; you might split the difference and estimate next year's rate to be 8 percent.

These are just simple illustrations of the many ways in which people can base their predictions of the future on the immediate past.

Backward-looking expectations tend to change slowly because some time must pass before a change in the actual rate of inflation provides enough past experience to cause expectations to adjust.

The second main type of expectations is composed of those that look to current conditions to estimate what is likely to happen in the future. One version of this type assumes that people look to the government's current macroeconomic policy to form their expectations of future inflation. They are assumed to understand how the economy works, and they form their expectations by predicting the outcome of the policies now being followed. In an obvious sense, such expectations are *forward looking.*

A strong version of forward looking expectations is called **rational expectations.** Rational expectations are not necessarily always correct; instead, *the rational expectations hypothesis assumes that people make the best possible use of all the available infor-* *mation, which implies that they will not continue to make persistent, systematic errors in forming their expectations.* Thus, if the economic system about which they are forming expectations remains stable, their expectations will be correct *on average.* Sometimes, next year's inflation rate will turn out to be above what people expected it to be; at other times, it will turn out to be below what people expected it to be. On average over many years, however, the actual rate will not, according to the rational expectations theory, be consistently under- or overestimated.

Rational expectations have the effect of speeding up the adjustment of expectations. Instead of being based on past inflation rates, expected inflation is based on the anticipation of the outcome of existing and expected economic conditions and government policies.

Assuming that expectations are solely backward looking seems overly naïve. People do look ahead and assess future possibilities rather than just blindly reacting to what has gone before. Yet the assumption of "rational" forward looking expectations that predict the expected inflation rate correctly, or nearly correctly, much of the time requires that both labour and management have a degree of understanding about the detailed effects of government policy on inflation that few economists would claim to have.

Of course, people will not make the same error of consistently underpredicting (or overpredicting) the inflation rate for decades, but evidence suggests that they can do so for substantial periods, especially when they do not fully understand the causes of current inflation. Every past period of inflation has led to intense debate among economists about its causes, cures, and probable future course. If professionals are uncertain, it would be surprising if wage and price setters made correct predictions on average over any short period of time.

Many observers suspect that the process of wage setting combines rational, forward looking expectations with expectations based on the experience of the recent past. Depending on the circumstances, expectations will sometimes tend to rely more on past experience and at other times more on present events whose effects are expected to influence the future.

Box 35-1

The Phillips Curve and the Shifting SRAS Curve

In the early 1950s, Professor A. W. Phillips of the London School of Economics was conducting path-breaking research on macroeconomic policy. In his early models, he related the rate of inflation to the difference between actual and potential income, $Y*$. Later, he investigated the empirical underpinnings of this equation by studying the relationship between the rate of increase of wage costs and the level of unemployment. He studied these variables because unemployment data were available as far back as the mid-nineteenth century, whereas very few data on output gaps were available when he did his empirical work. In 1958, he reported that a stable relationship had existed between these two variables for 100 years in the United Kingdom. This relationship came to be known as the Phillips curve. The **Phillips curve** provided an explanation, rooted in empirical data, of the speed with which wage changes shifted the SRAS curve by changing unit labour costs.

The Phillips curve can be translated into one that relates wage changes to output gaps by noting that unemployment and the gaps are negatively related. A recessionary gap is associated with high unemployment, and an inflationary gap is associated with low unemployment. Thus, the Phillips curve can also be drawn with national income on the horizontal axis, as in the accompanying figures.

Both figures show the same information. Inflationary gaps (which correspond to low unemployment rates) are associated with *increases* in wages relative to productivity, whereas recessionary gaps (which correspond to high unemployment rates) are associated with *decreases* in wages relative to productivity. (For simplicity, we assume zero productivity growth in this box.)

The Phillips curve must be clearly distinguished from the SRAS curve. The SRAS curve has the *price level* on the vertical axis, whereas the Phillips curve has the *rate of wage inflation* on the vertical axis. Therefore, the Phillips curve tells us how fast the SRAS curve is shifting when actual income does not equal potential income.

Only when $Y = Y*$ is the SRAS curve not shifting because of demand pressures. Aggregate demand for labour then equals aggregate supply; the only unemployment is thus frictional and structural. There is then neither upward nor downward pressure of demand on wages. Thus, the Phillips curve cuts the axis at potential income $Y*$ and at the corresponding level of unemployment $U*$. This is how Phillips drew his curve.

The Phillips curve soon became famous. It provided a link between national-income models and labour markets. This link allowed macroeconomists to drop the uncomfortable assumption, which they had often been forced to use in many of their earlier

Overall Effect

The overall change in wage costs relative to productivity is a result of the two basic forces that we have just studied:[5]

Percentage increase in money wages = Demand effect + Expectational effect

It is important to realize that what happens to wage costs is the net effect of both of these forces. Consider two examples.

First, suppose that, with productivity unchanged, both labour and management expect 3

---

[5]Recall from footnote 2 that we are ignoring a host of other nonsystematic causes.

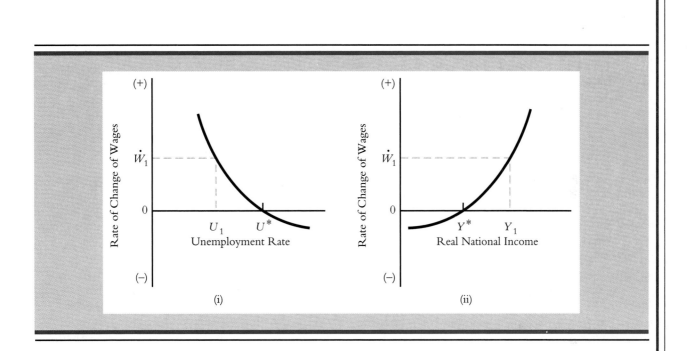

formal models, that money wages were rigidly fixed and neither rose nor fell as national income varied. By relating money wages to national income, the Phillips curve determines (in conjunction with productivity changes) the speed at which the SRAS curve shifts.

Consider, for example, the situation that is shown in Figure 35-2, where the level of income determined by the AD and SRAS curves is Y_1. Plotting Y_1 on the Phillips curve in part (i) of the accompanying figure tells us that wage costs will be rising at $\dot{W}_1$. Then the SRAS curve in Figure 35-2 will be shifting upward by that amount. The same information can be seen in part (ii) of the accompanying figure, where a national income of Y_1 in part (ii) corresponds to unemployment of U_1 in part (i).

percent inflation next year and are willing on this account to allow money wages to increase by 3 percent. Doing so would leave the relationship between wages and other prices unaltered. Suppose as well that at the current level of national income, there is a significant inflationary gap with an associated labour shortage. The demand pressure causes wages to rise by an additional 2 percentage points.

The final outcome is that wages rise by 5 percent, the net effect of a 3 percent increase due to expectations and a 2 percent increase due to demand forces.

For the second example, assume again that, with productivity constant, expected inflation is 3 percent but that this time there is a recessionary gap at the current level of national income. The associated heavy unemployment exerts downward pressure on wage bargains. Hence, the demand effect now works to moderate wage increases, say, to the extent of 2 percentage points. Wages rise by 1 percent, the net effect of a 3 percent increase due to expectations and a 2 percent decrease due to demand forces.

From Wages to the SRAS Curve

We have already established in Chapter 31 that *shifts* in the SRAS curve depend on what happens to unit costs. (Recall that for *movements along* a given SRAS curve, wage rates and other input prices are constant.)

We have just seen that inflationary gaps and expectations of inflation put pressure on wage rates to rise relative to productivity and, hence, on the SRAS curve to shift upward. Recessionary gaps and expectations of deflation put pressure on wage rates to fall relative to productivity and, hence, on the SRAS curve to shift downward. What happens to the SRAS curve in any one year is the net effect of these two forces.

The net effect of the two forces acting on unit costs—demand and expectations—determines what happens to the SRAS curve.

We are now ready to examine the causes and consequences of inflationary shocks. We begin with an economy in long-run equilibrium: The price level is stable, and national income is at its potential level. We then study the economy as it is buffeted by different types of shocks. Figure 35-1 provides a guide to the various cases that we will consider; it should be used as a reference as the discussion proceeds.

Demand Shocks

An inflation that is caused by general excess demand in the markets for final output and for factors of production is variously called a *demand-shock inflation*, a *demand-side inflation*, or more simply, *demand inflation*. Demand inflation occurs when a rightward shift in the AD curve causes aggregate demand to

exceed aggregate supply at full-employment income. The initial shift in the AD curve could have been caused by a reduction in taxes; by an increase in such autonomous expenditure items as investment, government, and net exports; or by an increase in the money supply.[6]

Major demand shock inflations occurred in Canada during and after the First and Second World Wars, in the early 1970s, and in the early 1980s. We shall see that in the latter two periods, these inflations were exacerbated by severe supply shocks. Demand inflations almost always occur in times of major wars, when heavy demand for military output and monetary expansion creates general excess demand throughout the economy. They also sometimes occur at the top of strong peacetime upswings, as rising output causes excess demand to develop simultaneously in the markets for labour, intermediate goods, and final output.

To begin our study of demand inflation, suppose that an initial equilibrium is disturbed by a rightward shift in the aggregate demand curve. This shift causes the price level and output to rise, as shown in Figure 30-8 on page 618 and summarized under "initial effects" of a demand shock in Figure 35-1.

It is important next to distinguish between the case in which the Bank of Canada validates the demand shock and the case in which it does not.

No monetary validation. The case of no monetary validation is also covered in Figure 31-2 on page 632, and its results are summarized as Case 1 in Figure 35-1. Because the initial rise in AD takes output above the full-employment level, an inflationary gap opens up. The pressure of excess demand soon causes wages to rise relative to productivity, shifting the SRAS curve upward and to the left. As long as the Bank holds the money supply constant, the rise in the price level moves the economy upward and to the left along the fixed AD curve, reducing the inflationary gap. Eventually, the gap is eliminated, and equilibrium is established at a higher but stable price level, with income at its potential level. In this case, the initial period of infla-

---

[6]As we saw in Chapter 33, an increase in the money supply works through the transmission mechanism—higher price of bonds, lower interest rates, increased investment expenditure—to shift the AD curve to the right.

FIGURE 35-1
The Effects of Inflationary Shocks

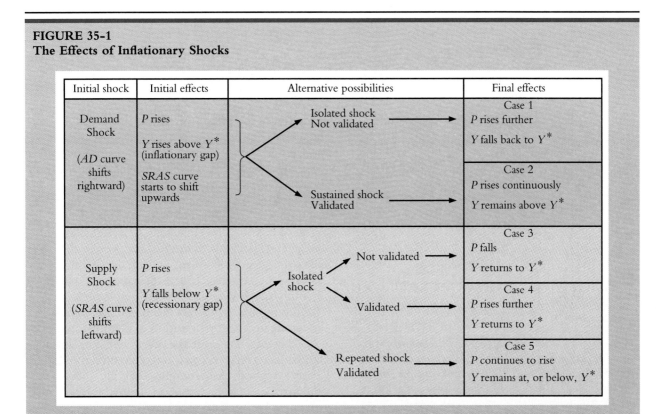

Demand and supply shocks have different final effects, depending on whether or not they are isolated or sustained and are validated or nonvalidated. This figure summarizes the analysis of each of the five cases given in the text. It should be referred to after reading the text discussion of each of the cases. All comparisons assume that income is initially at its potential level and that the price level is stable.

The initial effects of a demand shock are to raise national income and the price level. If the shock is isolated, the price level continues to rise until income falls back to its potential level (Case 1). If the shock is sustained and validated (validation turns an isolated shock into a sustained shock), the price level continues to rise, while income stays above its potential level (Case 2).

The initial effects of a supply shock are to raise the price level but to reduce national income. Once the shock is over, income will return to its potential level, with a lowered price level if there is no validation (Case 3) and with a higher price level if there is validation (Case 4). If the shock is sustained and validated, the price level can continue to rise with or without a persistent recessionary gap (Case 5).

tion is followed by further inflation that lasts only until the new equilibrium is reached.

Monetary validation. Next, suppose that after the demand shock has created an inflationary gap, the Bank increases the money supply whenever output starts to fall. This case takes us beyond our discussions in earlier chapters. It is analyzed in Figure 35-2, and its results are summarized as Case 2 in Figure 35-1.

Two forces are now brought into play. Spurred by the inflationary gap, the wages increase relative to productivity causing the *SRAS* curve to shift to the left. Fueled by the expansionary monetary policy, the *AD* curve shifts to the right. As a result of both of these shifts, the price level rises, but national income need not fall. Indeed, if the shift in the *AD* curve exactly offsets the shift in the *SRAS* curve, national income and the inflationary gap will remain constant.

FIGURE 35-2
A Validated Demand-Shock Inflation

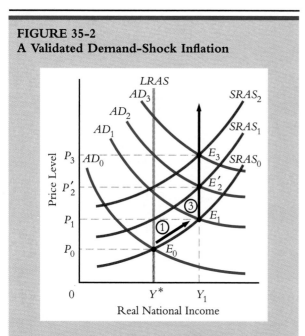

Monetary validation causes the *AD* curve to shift rightward, offsetting the leftward shift in the *SRAS* curve and thereby leaving an inflationary gap in spite of the ever-rising price level. As in Figure 31-2, an initial demand shock shifts equilibrium from E_0 to E_1, taking income to Y_1 and the price level to P_1. The resulting inflationary gap then causes the *SRAS* curve to shift to the left. This time, however, the money supply is increased, shifting the *AD* curve to the right. By the time the aggregate supply curve has reached $SRAS_1$, the aggregate demand curve has reached AD_2. Now instead of being at E_2 as in Figure 31-2, equilibrium is at E_2'. Income remains constant at Y_1, leaving the inflationary gap constant at $Y^* Y_1$, while the price level rises to P_2'.

The persistent inflationary gap continues to push the *SRAS* curve to the left, while the continued monetary validation continues to push the *AD* curve to the right. By the time the aggregate supply reaches $SRAS_2$, the aggregate demand has reached AD_3. The price level has risen still further to P_3, but because of the frustration of the adjustment mechanism, the inflationary gap remains unchanged at $Y^* Y_1$. As long as this monetary validation continues, the economy moves along the vertical path of arrow 3.

Validation of an initial demand shock turns what would have been a transitory inflation into a sustained inflation fueled by monetary expansion. The subsequent shifts in the *AD*

curve that perpetuate the inflation are caused by monetary forces.

Supply Shocks

Any rise in the price level originating from increases in costs *that are not caused by excess demands in the markets for factors of production* is variously called a *supply-shock inflation,* a *supply-side inflation,* or sometimes a *cost-push inflation.*

Starting with income at its potential level of Y^*, examples of a supply-side shock are a rise in the costs of imported raw materials, or a rise in domestic wage costs per unit of output, or a rise in the GST. The rise in wage costs may occur, as we saw above, because of generally held expectations of inflation. If both employers and employees expect an inflation, money wages are likely to rise in relation to productivity in anticipation of that inflation.

These shocks cause the *SRAS* curve to shift upward. They may or may not also shift the *LRAS* curve. Suppose, for example, that the shock takes the form of a large increase in money wages relative to productivity. This shock will raise costs of production, and hence the price level needed to sustain any given output will be higher. As a result, the *SRAS* curve will shift upward. However, this price change will not affect the economy's capacity to produce output when all resources are fully employed at normal levels of capacity. This type of shock, called a *nominal shock,* tends to leave the economy's potential income unchanged and, therefore, does not shift the *LRAS* curve.

Now suppose, in contrast, that the shock comes in the form of rising prices of energy and other raw materials brought about because more and more labour and capital are needed to produce a given output from depleting stocks. This is an example of a *real shock.* Firms are not just paying more money for the same inputs and outputs; instead more real inputs are required to produce the same domestic outputs. Shocks of this sort reduce the economy's capacity to produce—potential output is reduced, causing the *LRAS* curve to shift to the left.[7]

---

[7]Other real supply-side shocks, such as improvements in technology, shift the *LRAS* and the *SRAS* curves to the right. Since this chapter is concerned with inflation, we do not consider such shocks until Chapter 38.

Adverse aggregate supply shocks always shift the *SRAS* curve to the left; if they are real shocks, they will also shift the *LRAS* curve to the left.

In the following discussion, we deal with supply-side shocks that shift the *SRAS* curve to the left but leave the *LRAS* curve unchanged.[8]

Initial Effects

The initial effects of any leftward shift in the *SRAS* curve are that the equilibrium price level rises while the equilibrium output falls. The rise in the price level shows up as a temporary burst of inflation. These effects were first discussed in Figure 30-12 on page 623. Although we now wish to go beyond that earlier discussion, we will begin by repeating it in Figure 35-3, which compares the original equilibrium with the equilibrium after the supply shock. (Figure 35-1 summarizes these results as the initial effects of a supply shock.)

What happens next depends both on whether the shock is an isolated event or one of a series of recurring shocks and on how the Bank reacts. If the Bank responds by increasing the money supply, it validates the supply shock; if it holds the money supply constant, the shock is not validated.

Isolated Supply Shocks

Suppose that the leftward shift in the *SRAS* curve is an isolated event, perhaps caused by a once-and-for-all increase in the cost of imported raw materials. How does monetary policy affect the economy's response to such an isolated supply shock?

No monetary validation. The possibility of a non-validated isolated supply shock is summarized as Case 3 under "final effects" in Figure 35-1. The leftward shift in the *SRAS* curve in Figure 35-3 causes the price level to rise and pushes income below its full-employment level, opening up a re-

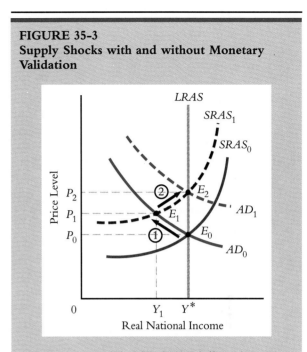

FIGURE 35-3
Supply Shocks with and without Monetary Validation

Inflationary supply shocks initially raise prices while lowering income. A supply shock causes the *SRAS* curve to shift leftward from $SRAS_0$ to $SRAS_1$, as shown by arrow 1. Equilibrium is established at E_1.

If there is no monetary validation, the unemployment would put downward pressure on wages and other costs, causing the *SRAS* curve to shift slowly back to the right, to $SRAS_0$. Prices would fall and output would rise until the original equilibrium was restored.

If there is monetary validation, the *AD* curve shifts from AD_0 to AD_1, as shown by arrow 2. This reestablishes full-employment equilibrium at E_2 but with a higher price level, P_2.

---

[8]Other cases can be handled easily by shifting the *LRAS* curve to the left. In such cases, when the analysis in the text tells us that the long-run position is restored, it will not be at its preshock level of income but, rather, at a lower one that is consistent with the new leftward-shifted *LRAS* curve.

cessionary gap. Pressure mounts for money wages and other factor costs to fall relative to productivity.

As long as money wages rise less rapidly than productivity is rising, unit costs will fall. Consequently, the *SRAS* curve shifts rightward, increasing equilibrium income while reducing the price level. The *SRAS* curve will continue to shift, stopping only when national income is returned to its potential level. If potential income is unaffected by the shock, then the *SRAS* curve will shift back to its initial position (i.e., $SRAS_0$ in Figure 35-3). Equilibrium income is returned to Y^*, and the price level is returned to its initial value of P_0. Thus, the period of inflation accompanying the original supply shock is eventually followed by a period of deflation that continues until long-run equilibrium is reestablished at the intersection of the *AD* and *LRAS* curves.

A major concern in this case is the speed of the adjustment, which in earlier chapters we referred to as the second asymmetry of aggregate supply. If unit labour costs do not fall rapidly in the face of excess supply in the labour market, the adjustment back to full employment can take a very long time. Assume, for example, that the original shock raised prices and money costs by 10 percent. To reverse this shock, unit costs must fall by 10 percent. If money wages stay constant while productivity rises by 2 percent each year, it will take nearly 5 years to complete the adjustment.

Whenever unit costs fall only slowly in the face of excess supply, the recovery back to full employment from a nonvalidated supply-shock inflation will take a long time.

Concern that such a lengthy adjustment will occur is the motive that often lies behind the strong pressure on the Bank of Canada to validate supply shocks.

Monetary validation. Now let us see what happens if the money supply is changed in response to the isolated supply shock. Suppose that the Bank decides to validate the supply shock, because it believes that relying on cost deflation to restore full employment would force the economy to suffer an extended slump. The monetary validation shifts the aggregate demand curve to the right and causes both the price level and output to *rise*. As the recessionary gap is eliminated, the price level rises further, rather than falling back to its original value, as it did when the supply shock was not validated. These effects are also illustrated in Figure 35-3, and they are summarized under Case 4 in Figure 35-1.

Monetary validation of an isolated supply shock causes the initial rise in the price level to be followed by a further rise, resulting in a higher price level than would occur if the recessionary gap were relied on to reduce costs and prices.

The most dramatic example of an isolated supply-shock inflation came in the wake of the first OPEC oil-price shock. In 1974, the countries who were members of the Organization of Petroleum Exporting Countries (OPEC) agreed to restrict output. Their action caused a dramatic increase in the prices of petroleum and many petroleum-related products, such as fertilizer and chemicals. The resulting increase in industrial costs shifted *SRAS* curves upward in all industrial countries. The Bank of Canada validated the supply shock with large increases in the money supply, while the U.S. central bank, the Fed, did not. As the theory predicts, Canada experienced a large increase in its price level but almost no recession, while the United States experienced a much smaller increase in its price level but a severe recession.

Repeated Supply Shocks

Now assume that the economy is buffeted by a series of repeated supply shocks. One example would be a repeated rise in the prices of all imported raw materials and energy products for several successive years. A second example could come from wages in the case studied earlier, where persistent expectations of continued inflation cause wages to rise period by period. Since it turns out to be important to our later analysis, we take the second case, in which wages rise relative to productivity, because both employers and employees expect further inflation. This rise in wages shifts the *SRAS* curve upward.

No monetary validation. Suppose that the Bank does not validate these repeated supply shocks and instead holds the money supply constant. The initial effect of the leftward shift in the *SRAS* curve is to open up a recessionary gap, as shown by arrow 1 in Figure 35-3. If wages continue to rise, subjecting the economy to further supply shocks, prices continue to rise and output continues to fall. Eventually, the tradeoff between higher wages and unemployment will become obvious to everyone. On the one hand, workers will realize that higher wages come at the cost of falling employment, and they will cease pressing for wage increases. On the other hand, employers will realize that they cannot simply pass on increased wages in the form of increased prices without suffering further decreases in sales, and they will become less willing to grant such increases in wages, even if they expect the inflation to continue for some time. Thus, a nonvalidated supply-shock inflation is self-limiting, because the rising recessionary gap that it causes tends to restrain further wage increases.

Because repeated nonvalidated supply shocks must come to an end, their results are identical to those of a single isolated supply shock. Whether the recessionary position shown by E_1 in Figure 35-3 is the result of a single isolated supply-side shock or of a series of repeated shocks, the end result is the same: The price level is higher and national income is lower than in the economy's initial preshock equilibrium.

What happens next is also just a repeat of what we have already studied for an isolated shock. When the persistent unemployment eventually erodes inflationary expectations, wages will fall relative to productivity, thus reversing the supply shock. Eventually, full employment will be restored, and the price level will return to its original value. This is Case 3 in Figure 35-1.

Nonvalidated supply-shock inflations caused by expectations of further inflation have natural correctives created by the rising recessionary gap. But these correctives may take a long time to operate, and hence a wage-cost push can cause a long and sustained stagflation, combining inflation with rising unemployment.

Monetary validation. Now suppose that the Bank validates the initial supply shock with an increase in the money supply, thus shifting the aggregate demand curve to the right, as shown in Figure 35-4.

In the new full-employment equilibrium, both money wages and prices have risen. Workers are no better off than they were originally, although those who remained in jobs were temporarily better off in the transition after wages had risen (taking equilibrium to E_1 in Figure 35-4) but before the price level had risen (taking equilibrium to E_2). The rise in wages has been offset by a rise in prices.

There is no reason for employers and employees to expect that the inflation will stop here. Insofar as expectations are backward looking, people have the experience of past inflation to go on. Insofar as expectations are forward looking, there is no reason for people to see current monetary policy stopping inflation unless, first, the Bank emphasizes that what

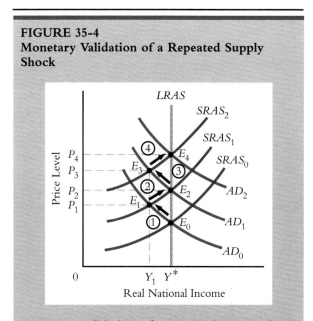

FIGURE 35-4
Monetary Validation of a Repeated Supply Shock

Monetary validation of a repeated supply shock causes continuous inflation in the absence of excess demand. The initial equilibrium is at E_0. A supply shock then takes equilibrium to E_1, just as in Figure 35-3. This is the stagflation phase of rising prices and falling output; it is indicated by arrow 1.

The Bank then validates the supply shock by increasing the money supply, taking the AD curve to AD_1 and equilibrium to E_2. This is the expansionary phase of rising prices and output (arrow 2).

A second supply shock, followed by monetary validation, takes equilibrium to E_3 (arrow 3) and then to E_4 (arrow 4). As long as the supply shocks and monetary validation continue, inflation continues.

it has just done is a once-and-for-all monetary accommodation and, second, the Bank is believed by wage and price setters.

The stage is now set for wages and prices to rise further when the economy is hit with another supply shock. If the Bank again validates the shock with an appropriate increase in the money supply, full employment is restored, but at the cost of a further round of inflation. If this process goes on repeatedly, it causes a continual supply-shock inflation. The wage-cost push tends to cause stagflation, with rising prices and falling output. Monetary validation tends to reinforce the rise in prices but to offset the fall in output. The results are summarized as Case 5 in Figure 35-1.

Two things are required for this type of supply-shock inflation to be sustained over a long time. First, continued increases in money wages must occur, even in the absence of excess demand for labour and goods. In some countries, powerful unions can cause such increases. This may never have been the case in the United States, and many believe it is no longer a serious possibility in Canada. What can cause continued wage increases today, however, is expectations of continued inflation.

First, as discussed earlier, if everyone expects some specific inflation rate, say 4 percent, workers may ask for a 4 percent increase in money wages just to hold their own against the expected inflation, and employers may grant the increases, expecting to be able to pass the extra costs on through increased prices. The result is self-fulfilling expectations. Because everyone expects the inflation rate, their actions in expectation of that rate bring that rate about. Second, the central bank must validate the resulting inflation by increasing the money supply, thereby preventing the unemployment that would otherwise occur. The process set up by this sequence of wage-cost increases and monetary validation is often called a *wage-price spiral*.

Is Monetary Validation of Supply Shocks Desirable?

Once started, a wage-price spiral can be halted only if the Bank stops validating the supply shocks that are causing the inflation. The longer it waits to do so, the more firmly held will be the expectations that it will continue its policy of validating the shocks. These entrenched expectations may cause wages to continue rising even after validation has ceased. Because employers expect prices to rise, they go on granting wage increases. If expectations are entrenched firmly enough, the wage push can continue for quite some time, in spite of the downward pressure caused by the rising unemployment associated with the growing recessionary gap.

Because of this possibility, many economists argue that the wage-price spiral should not be allowed to begin. One way to ensure that it does not is to refuse to validate any supply shock whatsoever.

To some economists, caution dictates that no supply shocks should be validated, lest a wage-price spiral be set up. Other economists are willing to risk validating obviously isolated shocks in order to avoid the severe, though transitory, recessions that otherwise accompany them.

Inflation as a Monetary Phenomenon

A long-standing debate among economists concerns the extent to which inflation is a monetary phenomenon. Does it have purely monetary causes—changes in the demand or the supply of money? Does it have purely monetary consequences—only the price level is affected? One slogan that states an extreme position on this issue was made popular many years ago by Milton Friedman: "Inflation is *everywhere* and *always* a monetary phenomenon." To consider these issues, let us summarize what we have learned already. First, look at the causes.

1. On the demand side, anything that shifts the *AD* curve to the right will cause the price level to rise. This includes such expenditure changes as upward shifts in the consumption, investment, government expenditure, or net export functions, and such monetary changes as an increase in the money supply or a decrease in money demand. On the supply side, anything that increases costs of production will shift the *SRAS* curve to the left and cause the price level to rise.
2. Such inflations can continue for some time without being validated by increases in the money supply.
3. The price level increases must *eventually* come to a halt, unless monetary expansion occurs.

Points 1 and 2 provide the sense in which, looking at causes, a temporary burst of inflation need not be a monetary phenomenon. It need not have monetary causes, and it need not be accompanied by monetary expansion. Point 3 provides the sense in which, looking at causes, *sustained* inflation must be a monetary phenomenon. If a rise in prices is to continue indefinitely, it must be accompanied by continuing increases in the money supply (or decreases in money demand). This is true regardless of the cause that set the inflation in motion. Of course, something that cannot continue indefinitely might continue for a very long time, so there is still plenty of room for disagreement over the mix of monetary and nonmonetary causes in any observed inflation.[9]

Second, let us summarize the consequences of inflation, assuming that actual national income was initially at its potential level.

4. In the short run, demand-shock inflation tends to be accompanied by an increase in national income above its potential level.
5. In the short run, supply-shock inflation tends to be accompanied by a decrease in national income below its potential level.
6. When all costs and prices are adjusted *fully* (so that the relevant supply-side curve is the *LRAS* curve), shifts in either the *AD* or *SRAS* curve leave national income unchanged and affect only the price level.

Points 4 and 5 provide a sense in which, looking at consequences, inflation is not, in the short run, a purely monetary phenomenon. Point 6 provides the sense in which, looking at consequences, inflation is a purely monetary phenomenon from the point of view of long-run equilibrium.

There is still plenty of room for debate, however, on how long the short run will last. Most economists believe that the short run can be long enough for inflation to have major real effects. Indeed, if the inflation is sustained, many of its real effects may persist indefinitely. For example, distortions caused by many aspects of the tax system being defined in money rather than real terms will persist as long as inflation continues, even if it proceeds at a steady and fully expected rate.

We have now reached three important conclusions:

1. Without monetary validation, demand shocks cause temporary bursts of inflation that are accompanied by inflationary gaps. The gaps are removed as rising costs push the *SRAS* curve to the left, returning national income to its potential level, but at a higher price level.

2. Without monetary validation, supply shocks cause temporary bursts of inflation that are accompanied by recessionary gaps (stagflation). The gaps are eventually removed as wages fall relative to productivity, restoring equilibrium at potential income and at the initial price level.
3. With continuing validation, inflation initiated by either supply or demand shocks can continue indefinitely; an ever-increasing money supply is necessary for sustained inflation.

Sustained Inflation[10]

Why has the Canadian economy undergone several periods of sustained inflation—sometimes rapid, as in the 1970s and early 1980s, and sometimes more gradual, as in the late 1980s and early 1990s? Can sustained inflation continue indefinitely at a more or less constant rate? What are the costs and benefits of reducing or eliminating a sustained inflation? Is zero inflation a viable policy target in the long run?

Accelerating Inflation

To study one of the most serious problems associated with a sustained inflation, we take up the story where we left it on page 740 at the end of the section discussing the monetary validation of a demand shock inflation. When the Bank engages in such validation, the *AD* and *SRAS* curves will both be shifting upward, allowing the price level to rise with no necessary reduction in the inflationary gap. This is the situation shown in Figure 35-2.

What now happens to the rate of inflation is predicted by the **acceleration hypothesis**, which holds that when the central bank engages in whatever rate of monetary expansion is needed to hold the inflationary gap constant, the actual inflation rate will accelerate. The Bank may start by validating a 3 percent inflation, but soon 3 percent will become 4 percent, and if the Bank insists on validating 4 percent, the rate will become 5 percent,

---

[9]The statement that inflation is everywhere and always a monetary phenomenon depends on a restricted and specific definition of the term *inflation*. To justify the statement, a temporary burst of inflation with nonmonetary causes must be called *a rise in the price level*, and the term *inflation* must be reserved for increases in the price level that are sustained long enough so that they must be accompanied by monetary expansion.

[10]The rest of this chapter can be omitted without loss of continuity.

and so on without limit, until the Bank finally stops its validation.

There are several steps in the reasoning behind this acceleration hypothesis. The first concerns the development of inflationary expectations.

Expectational effects. To illustrate the importance of expectations in accelerating a sustained inflation, assume that the inflationary gap shown in Figure 35-2 creates sufficient excess demand to push up wages 2 percent per year faster than productivity is rising. The demand effect in the equation on page 736 is thus 2 percent. As a result, unit costs and hence the *SRAS* curve will also tend to be rising at 2 percent per year.

When the inflation has persisted for some time, people will come to expect that the monetary validation, and hence the inflation, will continue. Once this happens, the expectation of 2 percent inflation will tend to push up wages and unit costs by that amount *in addition to* the demand pressure. As the demand effect on wages is augmented by the expectational effect, the *SRAS* curve will begin to shift upward more rapidly. When expectations are for a 2 percent inflation and demand pressure is also pushing wages up by 2 percent, the overall effect will be a 4 percent increase in wages, unit costs, and the *SRAS* curve.

Sooner or later, however, the 4 percent inflation will come to be expected, and the expectational effect will rise to 4 percent. This, added to the demand component, will create an inflation rate of 6 percent. And so this spiral will go on. As long as there is a demand effect arising from an inflationary gap, and as long as actual inflation is equal to the demand effect plus the expectational effect, the inflation rate cannot stay constant because expectations will always be revised upward toward the actual inflation rate.[11]

More rapid monetary validation required. The second step in the argument is that, if the Bank of Canada still wishes to hold the level of output constant, it must increase the rate at which the money supply is growing. This action is necessary because in order to hold national income constant, the *AD* curve must be shifted at an increasingly rapid pace to offset the increasingly rapid shifts in the *SRAS* curve, which are driven by the continually rising rate of expected inflation.

An increasing rate of inflation. The third step in the argument is that the rate of inflation must now be increasing because of the increasingly rapid upward shifts in both the *AD* and *SRAS* curves. The rise in the actual inflation rate will in turn cause an increase in the expected inflation rate. This will then cause the actual inflation rate to increase, which will in turn increase the expected inflation rate, and so on. The net result is a *continually increasing rate of inflation.*[12] The tendency for inflation to accelerate is discussed further in Box 35-2 on page 748.

According to the acceleration hypothesis, as long as an inflationary gap persists, expectations of inflation will be rising, which will lead to increases in the actual rate of inflation.

A Sustained, Constant Rate of Inflation

The discussion of accelerating inflation implies that a sustained inflation at a constant rate is possible only when national income is at its potential level, so that there is no demand component to inflation. In that case, all inflation is expectational. If the inflation is fully expected, the actual and the expected rates must be equal. Provided that there is no demand component, the inflation can go on forever at a constant rate, validated by a constant rate of mon-

---

[11]This can easily be seen if we write the actual inflation rate (which we call A) as the sum of the demand effect (which we call D) and the expectations effect (which we call E): $A = D + E$. If we have a positive actual rate, A, and a positive demand rate, D, the expected rate cannot equal the actual rate. Instead, it must be less than the actual rate by the amount of the demand effect: $E = A - D$. Thus, it is not possible to find a steady inflation rate in which expectations are fulfilled in the face of an inflationary gap. Correct expectations means $E = A$, and this is inconsistent with any positive D.

[12]Now we see the reason for the name *NAIRU*. At any level of unemployment less than the *NAIRU*, national income is above $Y*$, and the inflation rate tends to accelerate. So the *NAIRU* is the lowest level of unemployment (highest level of income) consistent with a nonaccelerating rate of inflation.

etary expansion.[13] This case is considered in more detail in Box 35-3 on page 750.

Breaking a Sustained Inflation

An economy may be undergoing a sustained inflation in either of two situations. First, income may exceed its potential level, producing an inflationary gap with the resulting demand inflation fully validated by the Bank. Such a situation is shown in Figure 35-2. Second, there may be a validated pure expectational inflation with the income at or a bit below its potential income.

Costs

In either situation, reducing the inflation takes time and involves major costs. The technique is for the Bank to stop validating the inflation. It does this by lowering the rate of growth of the money supply below the rate of growth of money demand, thus creating an excess demand for money. This action forces up interest rates and lowers real aggregate demand, reducing any existing inflationary gap. We shall soon see that it is usually necessary for the Bank to go further, creating a substantial recessionary gap that persists until the inflation is eliminated.

The process involves many costs. The recessionary gap hurts all those who suffer from recessions, including the unemployed and the owners of firms who lose profits and risk bankruptcy. Unemployed resources mean lost output and, hence, lower real national income than would otherwise be produced. The temporary rise in interest rates hurts borrowers, including people with mortgages and firms with large loans. Among these groups who are most exposed, and may lose their wealth, are young households with large mortgages and small firms that have taken on large debts to finance expansions.

Reducing a sustained inflation is thus a classic case of a policy that brings short-term pain for long-term gain. Inevitably the question arises: Are the future benefits worth the immediate costs?

Reducing a sustained inflation quickly incurs high costs for a short period of time; reducing it slowly incurs lower costs but for a longer period of time.

The process of reducing a sustained inflation can be divided into three phases.

Phase 1: Removing the Monetary Validation

The first phase consists of slowing the rate of monetary expansion below the current rate of inflation, thereby slowing the rate at which the AD curve is shifting upward. The simplest case is when the Bank adopts a "cold turkey approach," in which the rate of monetary expansion is cut to zero, so that the upward shift in the AD curve is halted abruptly.[14] This case implies a large and rapid increase in both nominal and real interest rates.

At this point a controversy often breaks out—as it did in the early 1980s and early 1990s—over the effects that the increase in the interest rate has on inflation. One group will point out that the rise in the interest rate increases business costs and that passing on the extra costs through higher prices adds to inflation. They will condemn the Bank's tight monetary policy as inflationary. A second group will argue that the rising interest rate signifies a slowdown in the rate of monetary expansion without which inflation cannot be curbed.

The first group is correct in pointing out that the rise in interest rates may cause a one-time increase in the price level. The rise in interest costs may shift the SRAS curve upward, just as a rise in wage costs does. This rise in interest costs, however, has only a *one-time effect* on the price level. The first group is wrong, therefore, in asserting that the Bank's policy of driving up interest rates is contributing to a long-term increase in the rate of inflation.

---

[13]The relation developed in the previous footnote can be used to explain why a constant rate of inflation that persists must be a purely expectational inflation. Actual inflation is the sum of expected and demand inflation: $A = D + E$. If the rate of inflation is to be constant, expected inflation must not be changing. This will only happen when expectations are being fulfilled—which means that expected and actual inflation are equal, so $E = A$. This can only be true when D is zero. But D can only be zero at potential income, where there is neither an inflationary nor a deflationary gap.

---

[14]The more "realistic" case in which the Bank withdraws its monetary validation over a more extended period of a few years is essentially the same, although its details are more complex to work out.

Box 35-2

The Phillips Curve and Accelerating Inflation

As discussed in Box 35-1, Phillips was interested in studying the short-run behaviour of an economy subjected to cyclical fluctuations. Other economists, however, treated the curve as establishing a long-term tradeoff between inflation and unemployment.

Let the government stabilise income at Y_1 (and thus unemployment at U_1), as shown in the accompanying figures. To do this, it must validate the ensuing wage inflation, which is indicated by W_1 in the figure. The government thus seems to be able to choose among particular combinations of inflation and unemployment, with lower levels of unemployment being attained at the cost of higher rates of inflation.

In the 1960s, Phillips curves were fitted to the data for many countries, and governments made decisions about where they wished to be on the tradeoff between inflation and unemployment. Then in the late 1960s, in country after country, the rate of wage and price inflation associated with any given level of unemployment began to rise. Instead of being stable, the Phillips curves began to shift upward. The explanation lay primarily in a shifting relationship between the pressure of demand and wage increases due to expectations, as discussed in the text.

It was gradually understood that the original Phillips curve concerned only the influence of demand and left out inflationary expectations. This omission proved to be important and unfortunate. An increase in expected inflation shows up as an upward shift in the original Phillips curve that was drawn in Box 35-1. The importance of expectations can be shown by drawing what is called an **expectations-augmented Phillips curve**, as shown here. The heights of the Phillips curves above the axis at $Y*$ and at $U*$ show the expected inflation rate. These distances represent the amount that wages will rise when neither excess-demand nor excess-supply pressures are being felt in labour markets. The actual wage increase is shown by the augmented curve, with the increase in wages exceeding expected inflation whenever $Y > Y*$,$(U < U*)$ and falling short of expected inflation whenever $Y < Y*(U > U*)$.

The demand component shown by the simple Phillips curve tells us by how much wage changes will deviate from the expected inflation rate.

Now we can see what was wrong with the idea of a stable inflation-unemployment tradeoff. Targeting a particular income Y_1 or unemployment U_1 in the figures is fine as long as no inflation is *expected*, but once some particular rate of inflation comes to be expected, people will demand that much just to hold their own. The Phillips curve will shift upward to the position shown in the figures. Now there is inflation $\dot{W}_2$ because of the combined effects of expectations and excess demand.

However, this higher rate is above the expected rate. Once this higher rate comes to be expected, the Phillips curve will shift upward once again.

The second group is correct in saying that the rise in the interest rate is a necessary part of an anti-inflationary policy. As long as the price level continues to rise, the rise in the interest rate reduces aggregate desired expenditure, taking equilibrium national income upward along a fixed AD curve—it therefore provides a *permanent reduction* in the inflationary gap.

Now suppose that the Bank resists the pleas to hold down interest rates. It continues with its "no validation" policy. The AD curve stops shifting, but, under the combined influence of the present infla-

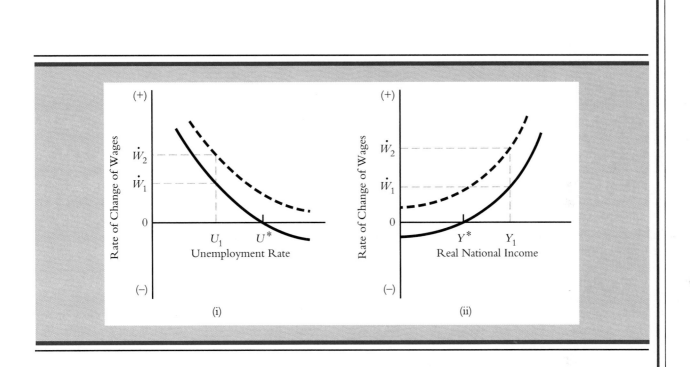

The **expectations-augmented Phillips curve shows that the actual rate of inflation exceeds the expected rate whenever there is an inflationary gap.**

Sooner or later, such a situation will cause inflationary expectations to be shifted upward. As a result, the inflation rate associated with any given level of Y or U rises over time. This is the phenomenon of accelerating inflation that is discussed in the text.

The shifts in the Phillips curve are such that most economists agree that in the long run, when inflationary expectations have fully adjusted to actual inflation, there is no tradeoff between inflation and unemployment. That is, they believe that the long-run Phillips curve is a vertical line at the NAIRU.

tionary gap and expectations of continued inflation, wages continue to rise. Thus, the $SRAS$ curve continues to shift upward. Eventually, the inflationary gap will be removed, as shown in part (i) of Figure 35-5.

If demand were the only influence on wages, that would be the end of the story. At $Y = Y*$ there would be no upward demand pressure on wages and other costs. Unit costs would stop rising, the $SRAS$ curve would be stabilized, and the economy would remain at full employment with a stable price level.

Box 35-3

Constant Inflation

When national income is at its potential level, there is neither an inflationary nor a recessionary gap. In this case, there is no demand effect operating on wage changes. Leaving random shocks aside, the only force operating on wages is expectations. Say, for example, that both workers and employers expect 4 percent inflation and that employers are prepared to raise wages by 4 percent per year to keep wages in line with everything else. Wages will rise by 4 percent per year, and the *SRAS* curve will shift upward by that amount each year. If the Bank validates the resulting inflation, the *AD* curve will also shift upward by that amount.

This case is illustrated in the accompanying figure. Expectations of a constant rate of inflation cause wages, unit costs, and the *SRAS* curve to shift upward at a uniform rate from $SRAS_0$ to $SRAS_1$, to $SRAS_2$, and so on. Monetary validation is causing the *AD* curve to shift upward at the same time from AD_0 to AD_1, to AD_2, and so on. As a result, national income remains at $Y*$, with unemployment at the NAIRU and a steady inflation rate that takes the price level from P_0 to P_1, to P_2, and so on. Equilibrium follows the arrow from E_0 to E_1, to E_2, and so on. In this situation, wage costs are rising due to expectations of inflation, and these expectations are being fulfilled.

Steady inflation at potential income results when the rate of monetary growth, the rate

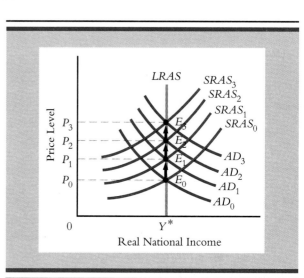

of wage increase, and the expected rate of inflation are all consistent with the actual inflation rate.

The key point about a pure expectational inflation at a constant rate is that there is no demand effect operating on wage bargains. Wages rise at the expected rate of inflation, just enough to preserve the existing relationship between wages and all other prices. The labour shortages that accompany an inflationary gap are absent, as are the labour surpluses that accompany a recessionary gap.

Phase 2: Stagflation[15]

Governments around the world have often wished that things were really so simple. However, wages depend not only on current excess demand but also

on inflationary expectations. Once inflationary expectations have been established, it is not always easy to get people to revise them downward, even in the face of announced changes in monetary policies. Thus, the *SRAS* curve continues to shift upward, causing the price level to continue to rise and income to fall.

Expectations can cause inflation to persist after its original causes have been removed.

---

[15]If the economy began with a purely expectational inflation, with national income at or below full employment, what we call Phase 2 would be the first phase. However, the rest of the story is the same whether the starting point is a demand inflation or a pure expectational inflation.

FIGURE 35-5
Eliminating Entrenched Inflation

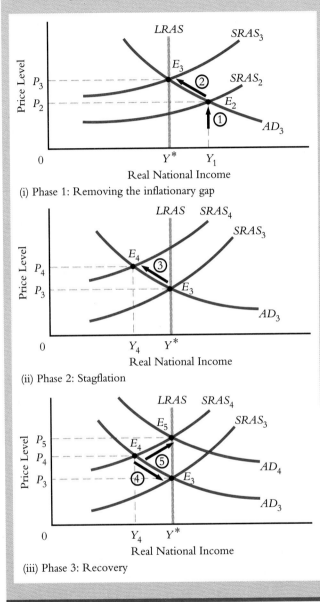

(i) Phase 1: Removing the inflationary gap

(ii) Phase 2: Stagflation

(iii) Phase 3: Recovery

(i) Phase 1: The elimination of entrenched inflation begins with a demand contraction to remove the inflationary gap. Fully validated inflation of the type shown in Figure 35-2 is taking the economy along the path shown by arrow 1 here. When the curves reach $SRAS_2$ and AD_3, the Bank stops expanding the money supply, thus stabilizing aggregate demand at AD_3. Wages continue to rise, taking the $SRAS$ curve leftward. The economy moves along arrow 2, with income falling and the price level rising. When aggregate supply reaches $SRAS_3$, the inflationary gap is removed, income is Y^*, and the price level is P_3.

(ii) Phase 2: Expectations and wage momentum lead to stagflation, with falling output and continuing inflation. The economy moves along the path shown by arrow 3. The driving force is now the $SRAS$ curve, which continues to shift, because inflationary expectations cause wages to continue to rise. The recessionary gap grows as income falls. Inflation continues, but at a diminishing rate. If wages stop rising when income has reached Y_4 and the price level has reached P_4, the stagflation phase is over, with equilibrium at E_4.

(iii) Phase 3: After expectations are reversed, recovery takes income to Y^*, and the price level is stabilized. There are two possible scenarios for recovery. In the first, the recessionary gap causes wages to fall (slowly), taking the $SRAS$ curve back to $SRAS_3$ (slowly), as shown by arrow 4. The economy retraces the path originally followed in part (ii) back to E_3. In the second scenario, the Bank increases the money supply sufficiently to shift the AD curve to AD_4. The economy then moves along the path shown by arrow 5. This restores potential income at the cost of further temporary inflation that takes the price level to P_5. Full employment and a stable price level are now achieved.

What was initially a demand and expectational inflation due to an inflationary gap becomes a pure expectational inflation.

This is Phase 2, shown in part (ii) of Figure 35-5.

The ease with which the Bank can end such an inflation, and the costs of doing so, both depend on how easy it is to change these expectations of continued inflation. This change is more difficult to the extent that expectations are backward looking, and easier to the extent that expectations are forward looking.

To the extent that people look mainly to past inflation rates to determine their expectations of the future, they will be slow to change their expectations. As the actual rate falls below their expected rate, a long time will be required for the downward adjustment to take place. The longer a given rate has persisted, the more firmly will expectations that the rate will persist be built into people's behaviour. An inflation that has persisted long enough to create firmly established expectations that it will continue is sometimes called an *entrenched inflation*.

To the extent that expectations are adjusted to current events, people will take notice of the Bank's changed behaviour and revise their expectations of future inflation downward in the light of the new monetary policy. *If* people fully understand the Bank's policies as soon as they are implemented, *if* they have full confidence that the Bank will stick to its policies, *if* they know exactly how much time will be required for the Bank's policies to have effect, and *if* they adjust their expectations exactly in line with this knowledge, then there is little need for any recessionary gap to develop. Once the inflationary gap has been removed, expectations will immediately be revised downward, so there will then be no pressure on unit costs to rise because of either demand or expectational forces. The inflation will be eliminated at almost no cost.

How long the inflation persists after the inflationary gap has been removed depends on how quickly expectations of continued inflation are revised downward. This revision will be faster the more are expectations based on a rational understanding of the Bank's current policies, the stronger is the belief that these policies will be adhered to in the future, and the better is the public's knowledge of how the economy will react to the anti-inflationary policies.

The emerging recessionary gap has two effects. First, there is rising unemployment. Thus, the demand influence on wages relative to productivity becomes negative. Second, as the recession deepens and monetary restraint continues, people revise their expectations of inflation downward. When they have no further expectations of inflation, there are no further increases in wages relative to productivity, and the *SRAS* curve stops shifting. The stagflation phase is over. Inflation has come to a halt, but a large recessionary gap now exists. At this point, nominal interest rates will fall, because they no longer need to include an inflationary premium. Furthermore, the Bank can allow real interest rates

to fall, since it no longer wishes to exert contractionary pressure on the economy.

As we note later in this chapter, the evidence from the Canadian economy is that Phase 2 is normally accompanied by large recessionary gaps and significant amounts of lost output before the inflation is checked.

Phase 3: Recovery

The final phase is the return to full employment. When the economy comes to rest at the end of the stagflation, the situation is exactly the same as when the economy is hit by an isolated supply shock (see Figure 35-3). The move back to full employment can be accomplished in either of two ways. First, the recessionary gap can be relied on to reduce unit costs, thus shifting the *SRAS* curve downward. Second, the money supply can be increased to shift the *AD* curve to a level that is consistent with full employment. These two possibilities are illustrated in part (iii) of Figure 35-5.

Some economists worry about waiting for costs and prices to fall, because they fear that the process will take a very long time. Others worry about a temporary burst of monetary expansion, because they fear that expectations of inflation may be rekindled when the Bank increases the money supply. If inflationary expectations are revived, the Bank will then have an unenviable choice. Either it must let another severe recession develop to break these new inflationary expectations, or it must validate the inflation in order to reduce unemployment. In the latter case, the Bank is back where it started, with validated inflation on its hands and with diminished credibility.[16]

Anti-Inflation Policy in Canada

In this final section, we continue the discussion of Canadian anti-inflation policy begun in Chapter 34. We are now able to make it more explicit by using the tools developed earlier in this chapter. As with previous chapters, we are not covering history for

---

[16] This is the so-called reentry problem that was discussed in Chapter 34.

its own sake. Instead, we are studying the lessons of the past where they are relevant to current policy issues. We begin our study with the inflation of the 1970s.

The early 1970s witnessed quite expansionary fiscal and monetary policies. The money supply was expanded rapidly, and an inflationary gap opened up as national income exceeded potential income. As a result, inflation began to rise. Expansion continued until early 1974, and inflation rose throughout that period. Then a recession set in. As a recessionary gap began to open up, the normal expectation was that inflation would diminish. Just then, however, the first OPEC shock hit. The prices of oil and the myriad petroleum-related products soared. This supply shock sent inflation into the double-digit range. The result was stagflation.

Wage and Price Controls and Monetary Gradualism: 1975–1980

Canadian policy makers interpreted the stagflation as accelerating wage-push inflation in a time of world recession. Having failed in an attempt to secure agreement of labour in a voluntary incomes policy, the government decided to impose wage and price controls. An Anti-Inflation Board was set up and given power to control wages and prices for 3 years. At roughly the same time, the Bank of Canada adopted a policy of "monetary gradualism" by announcing its intention to reduce gradually the rate at which the money supply was growing.

Whether by accident or by design, the two policies made a coherent package. The monetary policy was meant to reduce the speed with which the AD curve was shifting upward. Wage-price controls were meant to reduce the speed with which the $SRAS$ curve was shifting upward. If the upward rush of the two curves could be slowed at the same rate, the inflation rate could be reduced without having to endure the stagflation phase (Phase 2 in Figure 35-5), which occurs when the rise of the AD curve is checked faster than that of the $SRAS$ curve.

At first, all seemed to go well. The inflation rate fell in successive years starting in 1975. Then in 1979 and in 1980, a new setback appeared in the form of a substantial supply-side shock. The cause was a large increase in the world price of oil, due to a second round of OPEC output restrictions. There was also an AD shock caused by sharp reductions in the demand for M1 balances due to the monetary innovations discussed in Chapter 34. The result was that money became more plentiful *relative to demand*. Thus, instead of operating its intended contractionary monetary policy, the Bank was presiding over an expansionary policy. This experience was discussed in the section on monetary gradualism on page 719. So there were both adverse AD and $SRAS$ shocks. As a result, the 1980 inflation rate was once again as high as it had been just before wage-price controls were introduced.

As we have noted earlier, the propositions that a loose monetary policy stimulates the economy and leads to inflation and that a tight monetary policy does the opposite remained valid. The key conclusions illustrated by the failure of monetary gradualism in the 1970s are that demand-side measures can be offset by unfavourable supply-side shocks and that it is not always possible to identify a tight or loose policy solely by the rate of growth of the money supply.

Stabilizing Inflation: 1981–1988

By the beginning of the 1980s, rapid inflation seemed firmly entrenched, and a major controversy arose over how to reduce it. Most people agreed on the goal of returning to a much lower inflation rate, but there was disagreement as to the means of achieving that goal.

Monetarists advocated breaking the inflation with monetary restraint in the manner analyzed earlier in this chapter. Since they felt that there would be a short Phase 2, they were willing to rely exclusively on monetary policy to bring about the transition from a high to a low inflationary environment.

Keynesians agreed that a low rate of monetary growth was a necessary condition for returning to a low rate of inflation. However, because they felt that Phase 2 would be long—some talked in terms of 5 to 10 years—they were reluctant to use monetary policy alone during the transition. As a result, many Keynesians advocated using wage-price controls once again in conjunction with a restrictive monetary policy. Such controls, which are an exam-

Box 35-4

Incomes Policies

In the past, Keynesian economists have often recommended the use of incomes policies as an anti-inflationary device. There is a wide range of such policy measures. Voluntary guidelines for wage and price increases can be set, as they were in the United States under the Kennedy administration in the 1960s. The government may consult labour and business leaders with a view to moderating their wage demands and price hikes, as has often been done in European countries. More drastically, compulsory controls may be imposed on wage, price, and profit increases. A proposal commonly made in the 1970s and early 1980s was for a **tax-related incomes policy (TIP)**, which would operate through the tax system to provide penalties for "excessive" wage and price hikes and rewards for moderate ones.

Incomes policies might be used for three quite distinct purposes: (1) to suppress demand inflation, (2) to break expectational inflation, and (3) to control permanent wage-cost push inflation. We discuss the first two purposes in this box and the third in the text.

Demand Inflation

One reason that incomes policies have a bad reputation throughout the world is that they have often been used, as they were in the United States during Richard Nixon's presidency, in a futile attempt to stop demand inflation. To see why such an attempt is futile, consider the situation shown at E_0 in Figure 30-8 on page 618. If nothing else is done, the inflationary gap will cause the price level to rise to P_1. Wage and price controls could be used to hold the price level at P_0, but once the controls are removed, the excess demand will cause prices to rise.

The conclusion that using incomes policy in an attempt to control demand inflation will be ineffective (while the cost in terms of social stress and economic disruption can be enormous) is borne out not only by the U.S. experience of the early 1970s but by the experience of Britain and a number of other European countries as well.

Expectational Inflation

When entrenched inflation exists, incomes policies may help to break expectations. If successful, incomes policies will greatly reduce the stagflation phase. This could happen if, once Phase 1 is over and the inflationary gap has been eliminated, incomes policies were used to stop wages and prices from rising because of the expectational effect. The *SRAS* curve would not continue to shift upward and thereby open up a recessionary gap. Once expectations have adjusted to the new anti-inflationary monetary policy and to the existing stable price level, the controls could be removed. Phase 2 in Figure 35-5 would have been eliminated, leaving

---

ple of a broader class of policies, called incomes policies, are further discussed in Box 35-4.

The Reduction of Inflation: 1981–1984

In 1981, the Bank of Canada chose to follow the United States in adopting a highly restrictive monetary policy. Serious recession, falling sales, and falling profits eventually moderated wage increases. When it came, the fall in inflation was dramatic: from a peak of 13 percent in mid-1981 to around 5 percent by early 1984.

By 1984, the restrictive policies had succeeded in reducing inflation to a level not seen since the early 1960s, but it had also produced a major recession with all its attendant costs, including unemployment, lost output, business bankruptcies, and foreclosed mortgages.

the economy with stable prices and full employment without having had to suffer the prolonged recession typical of Phase 2.

The sequence of events seems almost too good to be true. The stagflation phase is eliminated, and the economy goes directly from Phase 1, with an inflationary gap, to the final equilibrium at $Y*$. If such a policy had been tried, as many advocated during the early 1980s, *and if it had worked*, the recession of the early 1980s, with all of its consequent unemployment and lost output, would have been avoided.

Controls were used when an Anti-Inflation Board (the AIB) formed part of a package to counter the double-digit inflation of the 1974–1975 period. Detailed studies by several Canadian economists have shown that the AIB probably reduced the rate of inflation by about 2 percentage points. It did this by helping to break generally held expectations that the inflation would not respond rapidly to monetary restraint. This means that it helped to shorten, even if not to eliminate, the recessionary Phase 2.

What Can We Conclude?

Opponents of incomes policies believe that the costs of using incomes policies will exceed the alleged benefits. First, they argue that the benefits, in terms of shortening the stagflation phase, would be small, because the policies would not be wholly successful in restraining wage and price increases. Second, they argue that the costs, in terms of direct administrative burdens and indirect frustration of the workings of the price system, would be large.

Although most international experience is with incomes policies used in futile attempts to control demand inflation, the evidence about the costs of using such policies may be relevant, even where the objective is not futile. The evidence suggests that when prices are set by government administrators rather than market forces, the allocation of resources becomes increasingly arbitrary, with serious consequences for the efficient working of the economic system. There is nothing in theory or evidence, however, to conclusively rule out the possibility that a short period of incomes policy, combined with a severely restrictive monetary policy, may shorten Phase 2 sufficiently to make the benefits of a smaller loss of output exceed the costs of temporarily distorting the pattern of wages and prices.

The results came out somewhere between the extremes that had been predicted. Thus, as so often happens with great debates, neither the extreme pessimists nor the extreme optimists were right. The truth lay somewhere in between. Whatever the reasons, during the early 1980s, inflation fell faster than many Keynesians had expected, and the slump was deeper and more prolonged than many monetarists had expected.

A Stable Inflation Rate: 1985–1988

For several years following 1984, the Canadian inflation rate stabilized at a figure around 4 percent, and it was a time of low inflation in the world as a whole. There was no reason for the inflation rate to rise, since there was no inflationary gap in the Canadian economy. The inflation seemed purely expectational: People expected a 4 percent inflation rate, and the Bank validated that rate through monetary expansion.

But since there clearly was a recessionary gap, why did inflation not fall further? The answer here seems to be that the weak demand forces that work toward deceleration when there is excess supply were swamped by the forces of expectational inflation and random shocks.

A Policy of Price Stability

In 1988, a long period of expansion was bringing the Canadian economy close to its potential national income. The inflation rate began to creep upward, going over 5 percent in 1989 and reaching 6 percent for a few months in 1990.

Fearing an erosion of its hard-won gains in reducing inflation earlier in the decade, the Bank of Canada reacted by adopting a restrictive monetary policy. Interest rates were driven up, and as discussed on page 722, the Canadian dollar rose, putting tradeable goods producers under heavy competitive pressure. The country's economic expansion proved remarkably resilient. The inflationary gap and the high inflation rate persisted for over a year, in spite of very high interest rates and a strong Canadian dollar. Finally, by the middle of 1990, the inflation rate began to fall appreciably. By autumn, it had returned to the 4 percent plateau from which it had accelerated two years earlier. The Bank, however, persisted in its tight policy.

Recession and Tight Money

By late 1990, the economy was clearly into a recession and many who supported the Bank's longer-term policy called for a little fine-tuning. They felt that the Bank could mitigate the recession by easing up on its tight monetary policy, returning to it once the next recovery had begun. The Bank responded by reiterating the policy of driving the inflation rate close to zero over a period of a few years, without concern for the short-term state of the economy. The Bank, therefore, ignored the growing recessionary gap and continued its tight monetary policy.

For technical reasons to do with bias in index numbers, the CPI would probably show an inflation rate of between 1/2 and 1 percent even if the price level was in fact constant.[17] Thus the Bank's objective of zero actual inflation translated into a measured inflation rate of less than 1 percent.

This policy sparked enormous controversy. Some critics felt that the costs of reducing the inflation rate below 4 percent would be excessive. They preferred to have the economy adjust to that rate rather than undergo the costs of reducing the rate to 2 percent, let alone to zero. Other critics, while accepting zero inflation as the ultimate goal, argued that the policy should not be pursued when the economy was already in the midst of a serious recession.

Supporters pointed out that 4 percent inflation cut the purchasing power of money in half in about 18 years and that 4 percent was a high inflation rate by the standards as far back as records go. (See the series going back to the thirteenth century in England in Figure 33-2 on page 656.) They therefore argued that zero was the best long-run goal. To the critics who said, "yes, but not now," the supporters replied that reducing entrenched inflation is always costly, and there will always be strong arguments for not incurring these costs at present. They felt that the commitment to zero inflation must be honoured and the costs accepted, since the longer that attempt was postponed the greater would be the costs of finally reducing inflation. The reason why the costs might grow over time is that inflationary expectations might become more firmly entrenched and the Bank's commitment to zero inflation less and less credible. For both these reasons, the longer the attempt was postponed, the more severe the recession that would have to be endured to finally get the rate down to zero.

In the event, the Bank stuck to its policy in spite of strong criticism from most politicians, many businesspersons, and some economists. The recession was indeed severe, Canadian interest rates stayed well above U.S. rates, and the C$ remained high on foreign exchange markets, putting Canadian exporters at a competitive disadvantage. However, the inflation rate responded as theory predicts, and by the end of 1992, it fell below 1 percent. The Bank was able to declare victory (at least for the time being). Monetary policy was eased somewhat, causing interest rates and the C$ to fall sharply.

---

[17] These technical reasons are many and varied. For example, price indexes have difficulty coping with quality increases. When prices rise, this may be partly to cover a rise in quality and only partly to cover a pure price increase per unit of real service delivered.

Is Price Stability Possible in the Long-Term?

The Bank's zero-inflation policy rekindled a debate that had recurred at various times in the past: *Is full employment compatible with a stable price level?*

As long as the *SRAS* curve shifts only because of demand and expectational (plus random shock) effects, as we assumed earlier in this chapter, the answer is yes, full employment *is* compatible with stable prices. What worries some observers, however, is the possibility of a cost push that pushes wages up faster than productivity, once the fear of unemployment is reduced by the continued achievement of potential income. As far back as the 1940s, many Keynesians were worried that once the government was committed to maintaining full employment, much of the discipline of the market would be removed from wage bargains. The scramble of every group trying to get ahead of every other group would lead to wage-cost push inflation. The commitment to full employment would then lead to validating increases in the money supply.

There is evidence that something like this has happened periodically over the past 40 years in Britain and in many of the countries of continental Europe. Most economists are more skeptical that it has been a serious force in the United States, while the Canadian case is less clear. Some observers still worry that full employment and a low, stable inflation rate may in the end prove incompatible in Canada. They argue for some permanent form of incomes policy. (See Box 35-4.)

Some economists follow this line of reasoning and argue that although zero inflation may be achieved for short periods of time, there will always be a tendency for the price level to rise when the economy remains at or near its potential income. They argue that a positive inflation rate in the range of 3–5 percent should be accepted by the Bank as the inevitable price of achieving "full employment." They argue further that a sustained commitment to stable prices will condemn the economy to operate on average well below its level of potential income. They believe that at or even near potential income, wage-push inflation becomes strong. As inflation begins to develop, the Bank will quickly adopt a contractionary monetary policy that will cut off expansions before they are fully developed. They believe that the only way to reconcile high employment with zero inflation is by using some form of the incomes policies discussed in Box 35-4.

Those who support the zero inflation policy argue as follows. The best way to ensure that the two objectives of stable prices and high employment can be obtained most of the time is for governments to make clear that a stable price level, rather than full employment, is their overriding commitment; whenever the two come into short-run conflict, price stability will be given priority over full employment! They argue that once this message has been accepted by the public, there will be two benefits. First, wage-cost push inflation may not occur, even at full employment. Second, incipient inflation of the supply- or demand-shock variety will be easy to quell with only minor recessions, because inflationary expectations will never have a chance to become strongly entrenched. In this environment, major policy-induced recessions would not be required to control an outbreak of inflation. Paradoxically, by abandoning its full-employment commitment, the government might make the maintenance of something close to full employment much more likely—at least, that is how the argument goes.

Conclusion

Throughout the history of economics, inflation has been recognised as a harmful phenomenon. This view was given renewed strength as a result of the worldwide experiences of high inflation rates since the 1960s. The resolve is there, at least in advanced industrial countries, to prevent another outbreak of rapid inflation and, should one occur for reasons of unavoidable supply-side shocks, to prevent it from continuing long enough to become firmly entrenched in people's expectations. The resolve is, however, much weaker among the general public, as revealed by the strong criticisms of the Bank's attempts at the turn of the decade to push inflation back to its 1980s plateau of 4 percent.

It is clear from experience that reducing the inflation rate by any significant amount usually has costs in terms of reduced output and increased unemployment. It is also clear from past policy debates that every time the Bank undertakes to do this, controversy will break out, whatever the current inflation rate. One side will argue that any reduction in the inflation rate is too costly and the other side will argue that these consequences must be accepted as the price of keeping some control over the inflation rate. Otherwise, the rate would slowly ratchet up under the impacts of supply- and demand-side shocks that the Bank was never allowed to counter because of fear of the short-run costs of doing so.

It remains to be seen which side will dominate policy in the 1990s: those who would resist, even at major cost, any tendency for the inflation rate to rise and would try to hold it at or near zero, or those who are unwilling to accept the costs of strong anti-inflation policies as the price of achieving zero inflation. Either way, the outcome of the debate will affect us all.

SUMMARY

1. Sustained price inflation will be accompanied by a closely related growth in wages and other factor costs, so that the *SRAS* curve is shifting upward. Forces that influence shifts in the *SRAS* curve can be divided into two main components: demand and expectations.

2. The influence of demand can be expressed in terms of inflationary and recessionary gaps, which relate national income to potential income, or in terms of the difference between the actual rate of unemployment and the NAIRU.

3. With constant productivity, expectations of inflation tend to cause wage settlements that preserve the expected real wage and hence lead to nominal wage increases equal to the expected price level increases. Expectations can be based on past experience of inflation and/or on expectations of the outcome of current economic policies.

4. The initial effects of inflationary demand shocks are a rise in the price level and a rise in national income. If the inflation is unvalidated, income returns to its potential level, while the price level rises further. Monetary validation allows a demand inflation to proceed without reducing the inflationary gap.

5. If the Bank of Canada validates a continuing demand inflation, seeking to hold the inflationary gap constant, the actual rate of inflation will tend to accelerate.

6. The initial effects of inflationary supply shocks are a rise in the price level and a fall in national income. If the inflation is unvalidated, national income will slowly return to its potential level as the price level slowly falls to its preshock level. Monetary validation allows a sustained cost-push inflation to continue in spite of a persistent recessionary gap.

7. If the Bank of Canada wishes to stop a sustained inflation, it must reduce its rate of monetary expansion, raising interest rates and reducing aggregate desired expenditure, and eventually eliminating any inflationary gap. Although the rise in interest rates may cause a once-and-for-all upward shift in the *SRAS* curve, the rise is a necessary part of an anti-inflationary policy that slows the rate of growth of the money supply, thereby stopping the outward shift of the *AD* curve.

8. The process of stopping a sustained inflation can be divided into three phases. Phase 1 consists of ending monetary validation and

allowing the upward shift in the *SRAS* curve to remove any inflationary gap that does exist. In Phase 2, a recessionary gap develops as expectations of further inflation cause the *SRAS* curve to continue to shift upward even after the inflationary gap is removed. The recession that characterizes this phase will be deeper and last longer when there is a large backward-looking component to expectations than when expectations are mainly forward looking. In Phase 3, the economy returns to full employment, sometimes aided by a once-and-for-all monetary expansion that raises the *AD* curve to the level consistent with potential income at the present price level.

TOPICS FOR REVIEW

Temporary and sustained inflation

Monetary validation of demand and supply shocks

Expectational inflation

The NAIRU

Accelerating inflation

Breaking a sustained inflation

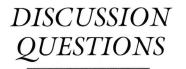

DISCUSSION QUESTIONS

1. Discuss the following statements, all of which were made in a debate about the Bank's policy of zero inflation, organized by the C. D. Howe Institute in Toronto.

    a. "Thus, we have a picture of the central bank putting workers out of work and businesses out of business to influence wage settlement discussions. Truly a ludicrous situation!"

    Doug Peters, T. D. Bank

    b. "With unemployment at 8 percent and inflation at 5 percent, the former is too high and the latter is too low."

    Pierre Fortin, UQAM

    c. "We live in a monetary economy . . . if the price system is to function efficiently and the economy is to achieve its full potential, monetary policy must preserve the value of money . . . Inflation does not make the system work better."

    Paul Jenkins, Bank of Canada

    d. "Those of us who have not forgotten the great social cost—in terms of unemployment, human misery, and lost output—of bringing the inflation rate down from its two digit levels in the early 1980s have reason to be thankful that the Bank has not given in to the siren calls for made-in-Canada interest rates or for accepting the primacy of employment over inflation as a policy goal. If it had, it would have found within a year or two that made-in-Canada, low interest rates rapidly would have become made-in-Canada high interest rates, and that employment is always the big loser when an accelerating inflation rate becomes too high for it to be ignored any longer."

    R.G. Lipsey, Simon Fraser University

2. On what source or sources of inflation do the following statements focus attention?

   a. "The one basic cause of inflation is the government's spending more than it takes in. The cure is a balanced budget."

   b. "Wage bargains currently being negotiated in the public sector will soon cause inflation to accelerate."

   c. "Canadians have become so accustomed to 4 percent inflation that it would be difficult for the Bank of Canada to induce the transition to 1 or 2 percent inflation."

   d. "As the Canadian business expansion continued, inflationary pressures seemed to be building up across the country."

   e. "Every time the Bank of Canada has made a determined attempt to reduce inflation drastically, it has succeeded within 1–3 years."

   f. "Heavy borrowing by the German government to finance investment in former East Germany fuels inflation, causing the Bundesbank (the German central bank) to push up interest rates in response."

3. "What this country needs is sound money and plenty of it" — quoted from an anonymous source by Doug Purvis in his essay in the C. D. Howe Institute's publication *Zero Inflation*. Why do you think Purvis argued that there was a contradiction between maintaining a sound money and having a large supply of it?

4. In the run-up to the 1993 federal election, when the Canadian inflation rate had been stabilised at about 1 1/2 percent, both the Liberals and the NDP argued that Canadian interest rates and the external value of the Canadian dollar were too high. What monetary policies would be required to drive the nominal Canadian interest rate severely downward? What does theory predict would be the consequences for the Canadian inflation rate and nominal interest rates over a 2-year period? What would happen to the exchange rate, Canadian, and would this help the competitiveness of Canadian exports? Check up on the monetary policy that was followed during 1994-1995 and on the course of Canadian nominal and real interest rates during the same period.

5. When the entrenched inflation of the early 1980s was broken, the economies of many industrial countries came to rest with a relatively low inflation rate and high unemployment. People who feared the outbreak of inflation opposed even a temporary increase in the rate of monetary expansion. Use aggregate demand and aggregate supply analysis to show why some people felt that a *temporary* burst of monetary expansion might bring increases in employment without increases in inflation.

6. What theory or theories of inflation are suggested by each of the following quotations?

   a. Canadian newspaper headline in 1986: "February producer prices steady—fall in energy costs largest in 6 years."

   b. Newspaper editorial in Manchester, England: "If American unions were as strong as those in Britain, American inflationary experience would have been as disastrous as Britain's."

    c. Study issued in 1980 by the Worldwatch Institute: "The nation's spiraling inflation reflects a global depletion of physical resources and therefore cannot be cured by traditional fiscal and monetary tools."

    d. Article in the London *Economist*: "Oil price collapse will reduce today's inflation rate."

    e. A Canadian newspaper article in October 1990: "The combination of the Kuwaiti crisis and an emerging recession is a sure recipe for worldwide stagflation."

7. Discuss the apparent conflict between the following views. Can you suggest how they might be reconciled using aggregate demand and aggregate supply analysis?

    a. "A rise in interest rates is deflationary, since breaking entrenched inflation with a tight monetary policy usually requires that interest rates rise steeply."

    b. "A rise in interest rates is inflationary, since interest is a major business cost and, as with other costs, a rise in interest will be passed on by firms in terms of higher prices."

8. Whatever its initiating causes, inflation cannot persist unless it is validated by increases in the money supply. Why is this so? Does it not imply that control of inflation is merely a matter of not allowing the money supply to rise faster than the rate of increase of real national income?

9. It has been estimated that reducing inflation by 1 percentage point requires a 4-percentage-point reduction of national income for one year. Use *AD* and *SRAS* curves to show why this might be so. Why might the cost in terms of lost income vary from one inflationary period to another? Are there reasons to think that the cost might be higher the longer the inflation has persisted? What might the Bank do to reduce the cost?

36

Employment and Unemployment

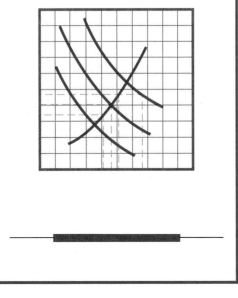

When national income changes, the volumes of employment and unemployment change as well. Figure 26-5 on page 527 shows the course of employment and unemployment in Canada. Unemployment, which is the main subject of this chapter, follows a cyclical path, rising during periods of recession and falling in periods of business expansion. The unemployment rate does not, however, show any significant long-term trend over time.

In macroeconomics, we distinguish between the NAIRU, which you will recall is the rate of unemployment that occurs when national income is at its potential ($Y*$), and the rate of cyclical unemployment, which is the unemployment associated with fluctuations of national income around its potential. The unemployed are those who are without jobs and are actively searching for jobs. We sometimes measure the unemployed as numbers of persons and sometimes as *rates,* expressed as percentages of the total labour force.

After a preliminary look at employment, we study cyclical unemployment. Then we consider the NAIRU in much more detail, asking such questions as: What types of unemployment make up the NAIRU? Why does the NAIRU change? Can government policy do anything to reduce the NAIRU?

Employment and Unemployment in Canada

Considered over the long term, the most striking features revealed by Figure 26-5 are trend increases in both total employment and the total labour force. Over the decades, the economy has generated a net increase in new jobs fast enough to employ the rising number of potential workers. As a result, the unemployment *rate*—which is the difference between the labour force and employment, expressed as a percentage of the labour force—has *not* risen decade by decade.

The unemployment rate does fluctuate from year to year, because changes in the labour force are not exactly matched by changes in employment.

Changes in Total Employment

On the supply side, the labour force has expanded virtually every year since the end of the Second World War in 1945. The causes have included a rising population, which causes increased entry into the labour force of people born in Canada 15 to 25 years previously; increased labour force participation by various groups, especially women; and immigration of working-age persons.

On the demand side, many existing jobs are destroyed every year, and many new jobs are created. Economic growth causes some sectors of the economy to decline and others to expand. Jobs are lost in the sectors that are contracting. Jobs are created in the expanding sectors. Additionally, even in stable industries, many firms die and many new firms are born. The net increase in employment is the difference between all the jobs that are lost and all those that are created.

In most years, enough new jobs have been created both to replace the old jobs that are destroyed and to provide jobs for the increased numbers in the labour force. The result has been a net increase in employment in almost all years.

In mild recessions, often called "growth recessions," the unemployment rate increases because the net creation of new jobs, though positive, falls below the net increase in the size of the labour force. Only in relatively severe recessions does the actual number of jobs decrease.

Changes in Unemployment

In the early 1980s, worldwide unemployment rose to high levels. The unemployment rate remained high in many advanced industrial countries and only began to come down, and then very slowly, during the latter half of the decade. Canadian experience reflected these international developments rather closely. From a high of 11.8 percent in 1983, the Canadian unemployment rate fell to 7.5 percent in 1989, a point very close to the NAIRU. It then rose through most of 1990 and 1991, reaching 11.8 percent in November 1992 and then falling very slowly through 1993.

Consequences of Unemployment

Unemployment is a social "bad" just as much as output is a social "good." The harm caused by un-

employment is measured in terms of the output lost to the whole economy and the harm done to the individuals who are unemployed.

Lost output. Every unemployed person is someone willing and able to work but unable to find a job. The unemployed are valuable resources whose potential output is wasted. The output counterpart of unemployment is the recessionary gap—potential GDP that is not produced. According to an empirical relation sometimes called Okun's law, for every percentage point that unemployment rises above the NAIRU, output falls by about 2.5 percentage points below potential. In a world of scarcity with many unsatisfied wants, this loss represents a serious waste.

Personal costs. Many social policies designed to alleviate the short-term economic consequences of unemployment have been instituted since the 1930s. Being unemployed, even for some substantial period of time, is no longer the economic disaster that it once was. But the effects of long-term high unemployment, in terms of the disillusioned who have given up trying to make it within the system and who contribute to social unrest, should be a matter of serious concern to the haves as well as the have-nots. The case for concern about high unemployment has been eloquently put by Princeton economist Alan Blinder:

> A high-pressure economy provides opportunities, facilitates structural change, encourages inventiveness and innovation, *and* opens doors for society's underdogs. . . . All these promote the social cohesion and economic progress that make democratic mixed capitalism such a wonderful system when it works well. A low-pressure economy slams the doors shut, breeds a bunker mentality that resists change, stifles productivity growth, and fosters both inequality and mean-spirited public policy. All this makes reducing high unemployment a political, economic, and moral challenge of the highest order.[1]

Kinds of Unemployment

For purposes of study, the unemployed are classified in various ways. They can be grouped by personal

---

[1] Alan S. Blinder, "The Challenge of High Unemployment," *American Economic Review*, 78, 2 (1988), p. 1.

characteristics, such as age, sex, degree of skill or education, or ethnic group. They can also be classified by geographical location, by occupation, by the duration of unemployment, or by the reasons for their unemployment.

In this chapter, we are concerned mainly with the reasons for unemployment. Although it is not always possible to say why a particular person does not have a job, it is often possible to gain some idea of the total number of people unemployed for each major cause.

In Chapter 26 (see Box 26-2 on page 525), we noted that the recorded figures for unemployment may significantly understate or overstate the numbers who are actually willing to work at the existing set of wage rates. We noted that overstatement arises because the measured figure for unemployment includes people who are not interested in work but who say they are in order to collect unemployment benefits. We also noted that understatement arises because people who would like to work but have ceased to believe that suitable jobs are available voluntarily withdraw from the labour force. Although these people are not measured in the survey of unemployment (which requires that people actively look for work), they are unemployed in the sense that they would accept a job if one were available at going wage rates. People in this category are referred to as **discouraged workers.** They have voluntarily withdrawn from the labour market, not because they do not want to work, but because they believe that they cannot find a job given current labour market conditions.

In Chapter 26, we also distinguished three types of unemployment: *cyclical, frictional,* and *structural.* Both frictional and structural unemployment exist even when national income is at its potential level, and hence there is neither a recessionary gap nor an inflationary gap. Together, these two types of unemployment make up the NAIRU. We first study cyclical unemployment and then the NAIRU.

Cyclical Unemployment

As we saw in Chapter 26, the term *cyclical unemployment* refers to unemployment that occurs whenever total demand is insufficient to purchase all of the economy's potential output, causing a recessionary gap in which actual output is less than potential. Cyclical unemployment can be measured as the number of persons currently employed minus the number of persons who would be employed at potential income. *When cyclical unemployment is zero, the number of unfilled jobs currently available is equal to the number of persons unemployed.* In this situation, all existing unemployment is either structural or frictional, and the rate of unemployment is the NAIRU.

National income theory seeks to explain cyclical unemployment.

People who are cyclically unemployed are normally presumed to be **involuntarily unemployed** in the sense that they are willing to work at the going wage rate, but jobs are not available. The persistence of cyclical unemployment poses a challenge to economic theory.

To see what is involved in this challenge, suppose that aggregate demand is fluctuating, causing national income to fluctuate around its potential level. This fluctuation will cause the demands for labour in each of the economy's labour markets to fluctuate as well, rising in booms and falling in slumps. If all of the labour markets had fully flexible wage rates, wages would fluctuate to keep quantity demanded in each individual market equal to quantity supplied in that market. We would observe cyclical fluctuations in employment and in the wage rate but no changes in unemployment. Again, if labour markets had fully flexible wage rates, the demand for labour would fall in recessions, and wage rates would fall as well. On the one hand, some people would withdraw from the labour force, being unwilling to work at the lower wage. On the other hand, firms would reduce the number they employ by less than they would have if the wage rate had not changed. The labour market would then reach equilibrium at a lower wage and a lower volume of employment but with no involuntary unemployment. In booms, the demand for labour would rise, causing the wage rate to rise. This would attract more workers into the labour force while reducing the quantity of labour demanded by firms below what it would have been if wage rates had not changed.

Employment and the labour force would vary procyclically (i.e., rising in booms and falling in

FIGURE 36-1
Employment and Wages in a Single Competitive Labour Market

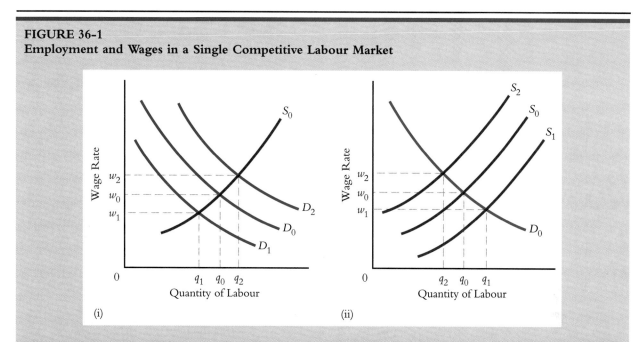

In a perfectly competitive labour market, wages and employment fluctuate in the same direction when demand fluctuates and in opposite directions when supply fluctuates; in both cases there is no involuntary unemployment. The figure shows a single perfectly competitive market for one type of labour. In part (i), the demand curves D_1, D_2, and D_0 are the demands for this market when there is a slump, a boom, and when aggregate income is at its potential level. As demand rises from D_1 to D_0 to D_2, wages rise from w_1 to w_0 to w_2, and employment rises from q_1 to q_0 to q_2. At no time, however, is there any involuntary unemployment.

In part (ii), the supply of labour fluctuates from S_1 to S_0 to S_2, and wages fluctuate from w_1 to w_0 to w_2. In this case, wages fall when employment rises, and vice versa, but again there is no involuntary unemployment.

slumps), but there would be no significant amounts of involuntary unemployment. The behaviour just outlined is shown for a typical labour market in Figure 36-1.

The hypothetical situation we have just described is not what we actually observe. Instead, we see cyclical fluctuations, not only in employment, but also in unemployment. Furthermore, the changes in wage rates that do occur are insufficient to equate demand and supply, as is shown in Figure 36-2. Unemployment exceeds the NAIRU in slumps and is below it in booms. Although wages do tend to vary over the cycle, the fluctuations are not sufficient to remove all cyclical variations in unemployment. Why is this so?

Two types of explanation have been advanced over the years. The line of explanation that we consider first is associated with those who are sometimes called *new classical* economists. The ex-

planation assumes that labour markets are always in equilibrium in the sense that quantity demanded is continually equated with quantity supplied.

New Classical Theories

One new classical explanation of cyclical fluctuations in employment assumes that they are caused by fluctuations in the willingness of people to supply their labour, as shown in part (ii) of Figure 36-1. If the supply curves of labour fluctuate cyclically, this will lead to cyclical variations in employment. This explanation of cyclical behaviour in the labour market has two problems. First, the wage will tend to rise in slumps and fall in booms, which is not what we observe. Second, there will still be no systematic cyclical *unemployment*, since labour markets always clear, leaving everyone who wishes to work actually working. Supply-induced fluctuations in

FIGURE 36-2
Unemployment in a Single Labour Market with Sticky Wages

When the wage rate does not change enough to equate quantity demanded and quantity supplied at all times, there will be unemployment in slumps and labour shortages in booms in each individual labour market. When demand is at its normal level, D_0, the market is cleared with wage rate w_0, employment is q_0, and there is no unemployment. In a recession, demand falls to D_1, but the wage only falls to w_1'. As a result, q_1 labour is demanded, and q_1' is supplied. Employment is determined by the quantity demanded at q_1. The remainder of the supply for which there is no demand, $q_1 q_1'$, is unemployed. In a boom, demand rises to D_2, but the wage rate only rises to w_2'. As a result, the quantity demanded is q_2', whereas only q_2 is supplied. Employment rises to q_2, which is the amount supplied. The rest of the demand cannot be satisfied, making excess demand for labour of $q_2 q_2'$.

employment form part of the basis of what is called real business cycle theory, which is discussed in Box 36-1 on page 768.

A second line of explanation lies in errors on the part of workers and employers in predicting the course of the price level over the business cycle. To see the argument, start by assuming that each of the economy's markets is in equilibrium, that there is full employment, that prices are stable, and that the actual and the expected rates of inflation are zero. Now suppose the government increases the money supply by 5 percent. People find themselves with unwanted money balances, which they seek to spend. For simplicity, assume that the increased money supply leads to an increase in desired expenditure on all commodities; the demand for each commodity shifts to the right, and all prices rise (since they are competitively determined). Individual decision makers see their selling prices go up and mistakenly interpret the increase as a rise in their own relative price. The reason is that they expect the overall inflation rate to be zero. Firms will produce more, and workers will work more; both groups think they are getting an increased *relative* price for what they sell. Thus, total output and employment rise.

When both groups eventually realize that their own relative prices are in fact unchanged, output and employment fall back to their initial levels. The extra output and employment occur only while people are being fooled. When they realize that *all* prices have risen by 5 percent, they revert to their initial behaviour. The only difference is that now the price level has risen by 5 percent, leaving relative prices unchanged.

A similar argument shows that an unanticipated decrease in the money supply would cause output to fall below its full-employment level.

All new classical explanations assume that labour markets clear, and then they look for reasons why employment fluctuates. They all imply, therefore, that people who are not working have voluntarily withdrawn from the labour market for one reason or another; there is no involuntary unemployment.

New Keynesian Theories

Many economists find new classical explanations implausible. They believe that people correctly read market signals but react in ways that do not cause markets to be in equilibrium at all times. These economists believe that many who are recorded as unemployed are involuntarily unemployed *in the sense that they would accept an offer of work in jobs for which they are trained, at the going wage rate, if such an offer were made.* These economists concentrate their efforts on explaining why wages do not fluctuate in labour markets so as to eliminate involuntary unemployment.

Theories that attempt to explain involuntary unemployment examine the forces that determine how quickly wages in actual labour markets respond to changes in economic conditions. If wages do not respond quickly to shifts in supply and demand, quantity supplied and quantity demanded may *not* be equated for extended periods of time. Labour markets will then display unemployment during recessions and excess demand during booms. This is shown for one typical labour market in Figure 36-2.

These theories start with the everyday observation that wage rates do not change every time demand or supply shifts. When unemployed workers are looking for jobs, they do not knock on employers' doors and offer to work at lower wages than are being paid to current workers; instead, they answer want ads and hope to get the jobs offered, but often are disappointed. Nor do employers, seeing an excess of applicants for the few jobs that are available, go to the current workers and reduce their wages until there is no one who is looking for a job; instead, they pick and choose until they fill their needs and then hang a sign saying "No Help Wanted."[2]

Long-term relationships. One set of theories, associated with the work of Arthur Okun and Robert Hall, among others, explains the familiar observations made in the preceding paragraph as results of the advantages to both workers and employers of relatively long-term, stable employment relationships. Workers want job security in the face of fluctuating demand. Employers want workers who understand the firm's organization, production, and marketing plans. Under these circumstances, both parties care about things in addition to the wage rate, and wages become somewhat insensitive to fluctuations in current economic conditions. Wages are, in effect, regular payments to workers over an extended employment relationship rather than a device for fine-tuning the current supplies and demands for labour. Given this situation, the tendency is for employers to "smooth out" the income of employees by paying a steady money wage and letting profits and employment fluctuate to absorb the effects of temporary increases and decreases in demand for the firm's product.

A number of labour-market institutions work to achieve these results. For example, many long-term contracts provide for a schedule of money wages over a period of several years. Another example is fringe benefits, such as pensions and health care, which tend to bind workers to particular employers. Another example is pay that rises with years of service. This helps to bind the employee to the company, whereas seniority rules for layoffs bind the employer to the long-term worker.

These things tend to be the glue that leads to long-term employment, despite the known fact that the output attributable to workers rises rapidly as they gain experience, reaches a peak, and then falls off as their age advances. Under gradually rising wages, experienced workers tend to get less than the value of the output that they produce at earlier ages and more as they near retirement.[3] But over the long pull, they are paid, on average, the value of their output to the firm, just as microeconomic theory predicts (see Chapter 17). Between the impact of wages that rise with employee age and the impact of dismissal during recessions in ascending order of seniority, employers and employees are held to each other, allowing payment of a more or less steady wage in spite of fluctuating economic circumstances.

In such labour markets, the wage rate does not fluctuate to clear the market. Wages are written over what has been called the long-term "economic climate" rather than the short-term "economic weather." Because wages are thus insulated from short-term fluctuations in demand, any market

---

[2]This observation concerns cyclical variations in the demand for labour. It does not conflict with the different observation that, when firms get into long-term competitive trouble, workers sometimes reopen contracts and agree to wage cuts in order to save the firm and their jobs.

[3]The relevant microeconomic concept is the value of labour's marginal product.

Box 36-1

Real Business Cycle Theory

As Professor Alan Stockman of the University of Rochester states, "The purpose of real business cycle (RBC) theory is to explain aggregate fluctuations in business cycles without reference to monetary policy."*

Real business cycle research has evolved from an attempt to explain cyclical fluctuations in the context of models in which equilibrium prevails at all times. In this sense, the models can be seen as a further extension of the traditional monetarist and new classical approaches. The researchers' desire to model *equilibrium* outcomes reflects their belief that the channels through which monetary policy affects real outcomes in the traditional macro model are not clearly understood. The focus on *real* disturbances reflects their skepticism about the evidence on the strength of those monetary effects in both the traditional macro model and in the new classical models.

The view of the business cycle found in RBC models is that fluctuations in national income are caused by fluctuations in the vertical *LRAS* curve. In contrast, the traditional theory of fluctuations is based on fluctuations in the *AD* curve.

The explanation of cyclical fluctuations that arises in RBC models is based on the role of supply shocks originating from sources such as oil price changes, technical progress, and changes in tastes.

In this view, unemployment is always equal to the NAIRU, and it is the NAIRU itself that fluctuates.

Key Propositions and Criticisms

The RBC approach is controversial. The major claims in favour of it include the following:

1. It has been able to explain the recent behaviour of the economy quite well statistically, while disavowing any role for aggregate demand fluctuations in the business cycle.
2. It suggests that an integrated approach to understanding cycles and growth may be appropriate, since both reflect forces that affect the *LRAS* curve. The distinction it makes is that some shocks are temporary (and thus have cyclical effects) and that some are permanent (and therefore affect the economy's growth).
3. It provides valuable insights into how shocks, regardless of their origin, spread over time to the different sectors of the economy. By abstracting from monetary issues, it is possible to address more details concerning technology and household choice involving intertemporal tradeoffs among consumption, labour supply, and leisure.
4. It has focused on integrating the explanation of a number of facts that other approaches have

clearing that occurs does so through fluctuations in the volume of employment rather than in wages. Of course, wages must respond to permanent shifts in market conditions, for example, the permanent and unexpected decline in the demand for the output of a particular industry.

Efficiency wages. The idea of the efficiency wage forms the core of another strand of thinking about

why wages do not readily fall in response to excess supply in labour markets. For any of a number of reasons, employers may find that they get more output per dollar of wages paid (i.e., a more efficient work force) when they pay labour somewhat more than the minimum amount that would induce workers to work for them.

Suppose that it is costly for employers to monitor workers' performance on the job, so that some ignored, such as seasonal and cyclical fluctuations, consumption varying less than output over the business cycle, and procyclical movements of hours worked and of average labour productivity.

Critics of the approach focus on some implausible results, express concern about its assumed underlying behaviour, and argue that the phenomena mentioned in point 4 have already been given satisfactory explanations. More importantly, they are skeptical about a model in which monetary forces are completely ignored. For example, they point out that RBC models are unable to provide insights into the correlation between money and output that is at the heart of the traditional macro model. Furthermore, RBC models are unable to provide insights into empirical regularities involving nominal variables, such as prices that apparently vary less than quantities and nominal prices that vary procyclically.

Policy Implications

Because the approach gives no role to aggregate demand in influencing business cycles, it provides no role for stabilization operating through monetary and fiscal policies. However, the models predict that the use of such demand management policies can be harmful.

The basis for this prediction is the proposition in RBC models that cycles represent *efficient* responses to the shocks that are hitting the economy. Policy makers may mistakenly interpret cyclical fluctuations as deviations from full-employment equilibrium that are caused by fluctuations in aggregate demand. The policy makers may try to stabilize output and thereby distort the maximizing decisions made by households and firms. In turn, this distortion will cause the responses to the real shocks (as opposed to nominal, monetary shocks) to be inefficient.

Although only a minority of economists espouse these models as complete or even reasonable descriptions of the business cycle, and thus only a minority take seriously the strict implications for policy, many accept the view that real disturbances can play an important role in business cycles.

*Alan C. Stockman, "Real Business Cycle Theory: A Guide, an Evaluation, and New Directions," *Federal Reserve Bank of Cleveland Monthly Review*, 1988, pp. 24 – 47.

workers will be able to shirk duties with a low probability of being caught.[4] Given prevailing labour-market institutions, it is generally impossible for employers to levy fines on employees for shirking on the job. The employees could just leave

their jobs rather than pay the fines. Further, if the workers can easily find new jobs that are just as good, firing is not much of a threat. However, if there is a group of potential employees who are currently unemployed and would like to work at the going wage, the threat of firing workers in order to discipline them is much enhanced. Under these conditions, employees who are fired will be made worse off by being fired precisely because it is

[4]This is an example of the principal-agent problem in microeconomics, discussed in Chapter 16.

difficult to find other work at the wage they were receiving.

Efficiency wage theory says that firms may find it advantageous to pay high enough wages so that working is a clearly superior alternative to being laid off. This will improve the quality of workers' output without firms' having to spend heavily to monitor workers' performance.

Economists such as George Akerlof of the University of California have observed that workers who believe that they are well treated work harder than those who believe that they are treated badly. This gives a reason for paying an efficiency wage—provided that the increased output from treating workers well covers the increased cost of doing so.

A variant of efficiency wage theory seeks to explain why firms do not cut wages during recessions. If workers feel unfairly treated when their wages are reduced, wage reductions (at least in response to moderate recessions) may cost firms more (in lost output from unhappy employees) than they save in reduced wages.[5] If so, real wages may not fall rapidly enough to eliminate cyclical and real-wage unemployment.

The basic message of new Keynesian theories of unemployment is that competitive labour markets cannot be relied on to eliminate unemployment by equating current demand for labour with current supply, and, as a result, unemployment will rise and fall as the demand for labour rises and falls over the cycle.

The NAIRU

We now turn to a consideration of the NAIRU, which, as we have seen, is composed of frictional and structural unemployment.

---

[5]See Daniel Kahneman, Jack Knetsch, and Richard Thaler, "Fairness as a Constraint on Profit Seeking," *American Economic Review,* 76 (1986), pp. 728 – 741, for an interesting discussion, by a psychologist and two economists, of ways in which notions of fairness can influence decisions on economic matters.

Frictional Unemployment

As we saw in Chapter 26, *frictional unemployment* results from the normal turnover of labour. An important source of frictional unemployment is young people who enter the labour force and look for jobs. Another source is people who leave their jobs. Some may quit because they are dissatisfied with the type of work or their working conditions; others may be fired. Whatever the reason, they must search for new jobs, which takes time. Persons who are unemployed while searching for jobs are said to be frictionally unemployed, or, alternatively, in *search unemployment.*

The normal turnover of labour would cause frictional unemployment to persist, even if the economy were at potential income and the structure of jobs in terms of skills, industries, occupations, and location were unchanging.

Is Frictional Unemployment Voluntary?

Some frictional unemployment is clearly voluntary. For example, a worker may know of an available job but may not accept it so she can search for a better one. The new classical view regards all frictional unemployment as voluntary. Critics of that view argue that many frictionally unemployed workers are involuntarily unemployed, because they lost their jobs through no fault of their own (e.g., their factories may have closed down) and because they have not yet located one of the jobs they believe to be available *somewhere* and for which they believe they are qualified. The principle here is that because knowledge of labour market opportunities takes time and money to acquire, frictional unemployment will persist, and it will be involuntary in the sense that people who currently have not located a job will find one after further search.

Structural Unemployment

Structural adjustments can cause unemployment. When the pattern of demand for goods changes, the pattern of the demand for labour changes. Until labour adjusts fully, *structural unemployment* develops. Such unemployment may be defined as unemployment caused by a mismatch between the structure of the labour force—in terms of skills, occupations, industries, or geographical locations—and the structure of the demand for labour.

Natural Causes

Changes that accompany economic growth shift the structure of the demand for labour. Demand rises in such expanding areas as British Columbia and falls in declining areas such as Newfoundland and parts of southern Ontario. Demand rises for workers with certain skills, such as computer programming and electronics engineering, and falls for workers with other skills, such as stenography, assembly line work, and middle management. According to a 1992 Federal government report: "a gradual but significant shift toward high-skilled jobs has taken place. The evolutionary shift toward service-sector employment and the restructuring within all industries in response to technological change has favoured workers with more years of schooling." To meet changing demands, the structure of the labour force must change. Some existing workers can retrain and some new entrants can acquire fresh skills, but the transition is often difficult, especially for experienced workers whose skills become economically obsolete. Structural unemployment occurs when such adjustments are slow enough that severe pockets of unemployment develop in areas, industries, and occupations in which the demand for factors of production is falling faster than the supply.

One of the more dramatic recent structural changes in the economy has been in the organization of the firm. Manufacturing firms used to be organized much like an army, with a pyramidal command structure. Most key strategic decisions were made near the top and lesser ones concerning implementation at lower levels. This structure required an array of middle-level managers who passed information upward to the top level and downward to the production level and who made various secondary decisions themselves. Recent changes pioneered among Japanese firms have led to a much looser organization with much more local autonomy among the subsections of the firm. As a

result, large numbers of middle managers' jobs have been made redundant. They find themselves on the labour market at middle age, with many of their skills rendered obsolete.[6]

Increases in international competition can have effects similar to those of economic growth and change. As the geographical distribution of world production changes, so does the composition of production and of labour demand in any one country. Labour adapts to such shifts by changing jobs, skills, and locations, but until the transition is complete, structural unemployment exists.

Structural unemployment will increase if there is either an increase in the speed at which the structure of the demand for labour is changing or a decrease in the speed at which labour is adapting to these changes.

Policy Causes

Government policies can influence the speed with which labour markets adapt to changes. Some countries, such as the United Kingdom and Canada, have adopted policies that discourage movement among regions, industries, and occupations. These policies tend to raise structural unemployment. Others, such as Sweden, have done the reverse and have encouraged workers to adapt to change. Partly for this reason, Sweden's unemployment rates were well below the European and North American norms during the 1980s.

Policies that discourage firms from replacing labour with machines may protect employment over the short term. If, however, such policies lead to the decline of an industry because it cannot compete effectively with innovative foreign competitors, serious structural unemployment can result in the long run.

Minimum-wage laws can cause structural unemployment by pricing low-skilled labour out of the market. As explained in Chapter 18, effective

---

[6]These changes are discussed in detail in such books as Robert Reich, *The Work of Nations* (New York: Knopf, 1991) and James Womack, Daniel Jones, and Daniel Roos, *The Machine That Changed the World* (New York: Maxwell MacMillan, 1990), both of which can be read without an in-depth knowledge of economic theory.

minimum-wage laws have two results when they are imposed on competitive markets: They reduce the employment of the unskilled while raising the wages of those who retain their jobs. In most Canadian provinces, until recently, minimum wages were too low to have significant effects on wage rates and employment. In the early 1990s, however, the NDP governments of Ontario and British Columbia raised their minimum wages quite significantly. In a few years' time, research will show whether or not the rise in unskilled unemployment predicted by economic theory actually took place.

Minimum wage laws may also affect the distribution of income. A recent study by Steven Davis of the National Bureau of Economic Research shows that overall wage inequality increased during the 1980s in Australia, Canada, Germany, Japan, Sweden, the United Kingdom and the United States. Among the advanced countries, wage inequality was stable only in France and the Netherlands. The French experience is interesting. Among the top half of income earners, wage inequality increased, just as it did in other countries. This tendency was offset, however, by diminished inequality among the bottom half. Large increases in the minimum wage raised wages of the unskilled relative to the others and resulted in an overall stable measure of inequality.

Is Structural Unemployment Voluntary?

According to the new classical view, all structural unemployment is voluntary. Say, for example, that there is an excess supply of skilled auto workers and an excess demand for unskilled dishwashers. If an unemployed auto worker does not take one of the available jobs as a dishwasher, he is voluntarily deciding to stay unemployed in the hopes of finding a job that uses his skills.

Critics reply: "But what if it is the other way round?" What if, as is often the case, there is an excess supply of unskilled workers and an excess demand for those with skills? The unemployed dishwasher cannot accept a job as a computer programmer; his skills do not equip him for this. This mismatching between the skills of those unemployed and the skills required by the available jobs cannot easily be removed by individual actions of the unemployed dishwashers, nor can it be blamed on their union, since they have none. It can, however, be removed eventually by education that allows the dishwasher, or his daughter, to become a computer programmer.

The Relationship Between Frictional and Structural Unemployment

As with many distinctions, the one between structural and frictional unemployment becomes blurred at the margin. In a sense, structural unemployment is really long-term frictional unemployment. Consider a change that requires labour to move from one sector to another. If the reallocation occurs quickly, we call the unemployment *frictional;* if the reallocation occurs slowly, we call the unemployment *structural*.

The major characteristic of both frictional and structural unemployment is that there are as many unfilled vacancies as there are unemployed persons.

In the case of pure frictional unemployment, the job vacancy and the searcher are matched. The only problem is that the searcher has not yet located the vacancy. In the case of structural unemployment, the job vacancy and the searcher are mismatched in one or more relevant characteristics, such as occupation, industry, location, or skill requirements.

Experience

In practise, structural and frictional unemployment cannot be separated, and they are shown together by the amount and nature of unemployment when income is at its potential level.

As of 1993, the last year for which income was close to potential was 1989. Although data for later years are available, this peak year of the economic expansion represents the best one in which to find characteristics of structural plus frictional unemployment.

Figure 36-3 shows that education confers a twin advantage. As we saw earlier, not only does one's income expectancy rise with education, but the probability of suffering unemployment falls dramatically. Among both men and women, high school dropouts have the highest unemployment

FIGURE 36-3
Unemployment by Educational Experience

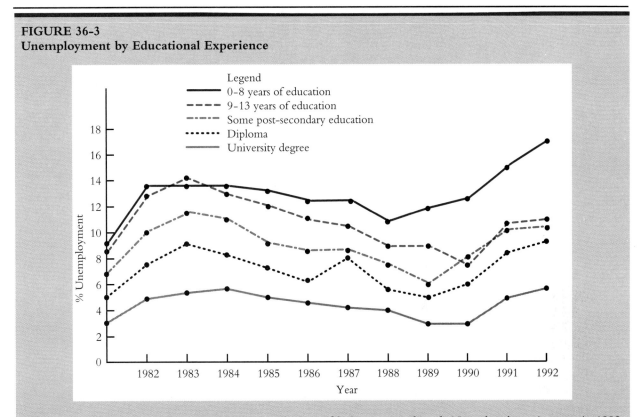

Legend
— 0-8 years of education
--- 9-13 years of education
-·-·- Some post-secondary education
······ Diploma
—— University degree

The more education one has, the lower the chance of being unemployed. Note that the series stops in 1992 which was a period of high unemployment at the end of the 1990–1992 recession. Although there is a strong cyclical component to all unemployment, the tendency for unemployment to fall as education rises shows clearly in the data. As well as having high recorded unemployment levels, those with very low educational standards tend to have the lowest participation rates. Thus, many in the 0-8 group who are not recorded as being unemployed because they have dropped out of the labour force, would accept a job if one were available. (*Source:* Statistics Canada, 71-001.)

rates, high school graduates the next highest, and college graduates the lowest.

Figure 36-4 shows that unemployment is very high among the young. This unemployment is partly frictional, in that young people tend to change jobs more often than older people, and partly structural, in that the demand for less experienced and less trained workers has been falling relative to the demand for more experienced and better trained workers. Married men tend to have the best experience with respect to unemployment, whereas women who maintain families fare relatively poorly—in contrast to women in general, who do almost as well as men in general.

Finally, as Figure 36-5 shows, unemployment rates vary significantly across provinces, tending to

be lowest in the prairie provinces and highest in Atlantic Canada.

Why Does the NAIRU Change?

We have noted that structural unemployment can increase because the pace of change accelerates or the pace of adjustment to change slows down. An increase in the rate of growth, for example, usually speeds up the rate at which the structure of the demand for labour is changing. The adaptation of labour to the changing structure of demand may be slowed by such diverse factors as a decline in education and new regulations that make it harder for

FIGURE 36-4
Unemployment by Age and Sex, March 1993

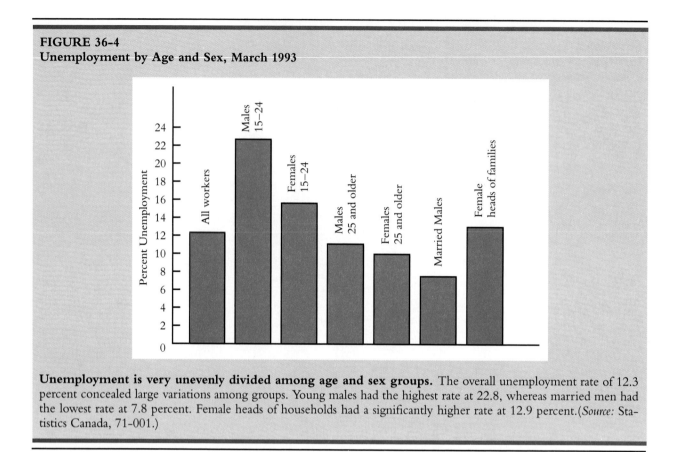

Unemployment is very unevenly divided among age and sex groups. The overall unemployment rate of 12.3 percent concealed large variations among groups. Young males had the highest rate at 22.8, whereas married men had the lowest rate at 7.8 percent. Female heads of households had a significantly higher rate at 12.9 percent.(*Source:* Statistics Canada, 71-001.)

workers in a given occupation to take new jobs in other areas or occupations. Any of these changes will cause the NAIRU to rise. Changes in the opposite direction will cause the NAIRU to fall.

Demographic Changes

Because people usually try several jobs before settling into one for a longer period of time, young or inexperienced workers have higher unemployment rates than experienced workers. The proportion of inexperienced workers in the labour force rose significantly as the baby boom generation of the 1950s entered the labour force in the 1970s and 1980s, along with an unprecedented number of women who elected to work outside the home. It is estimated that these demographic changes added nearly a percentage point to the NAIRU. Since birthrates were low in the 1960s, and a further increase in the percentage of women entering the labour force is unlikely, some demographically induced fall in this

type of unemployment has been occurring recently and will continue over the 1990s.

Although the NAIRU, and youth unemployment in particular, should fall as the baby boom generation passes on to middle age, many observers worry about the long-term consequences for some individuals. Learning through on-the-job experience is a critical part of developing marketable labour skills, and those who suffered prolonged unemployment during their teens and twenties have been denied that experience early in their working careers. These workers may have little option later in life but to take temporary jobs at low pay and with little future job security.

The large increase in female participation rates and the related increase in the number of households with more than one income earner have also affected the NAIRU. In 1960, only 30 percent of women 20 years and older were in the labour force; in 1972, the figure was 38 percent; by 1993, it had jumped to 52 percent. When both husband and wife work, it is possible for one to support both,

FIGURE 36-5
Unemployment by Region, March 1993

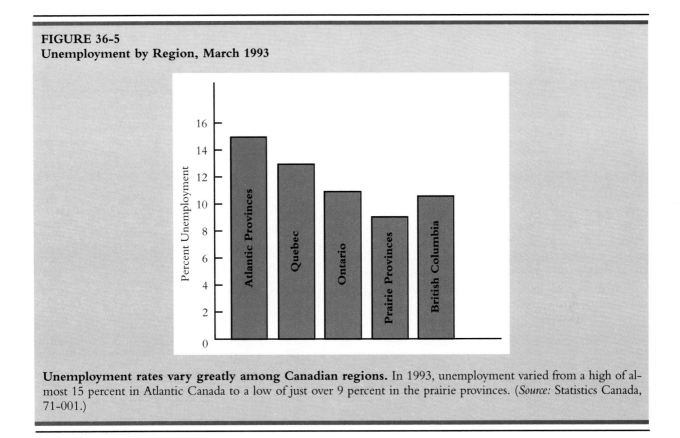

Unemployment rates vary greatly among Canadian regions. In 1993, unemployment varied from a high of almost 15 percent in Atlantic Canada to a low of just over 9 percent in the prairie provinces. (*Source:* Statistics Canada, 71-001.)

while the other looks for "a really good job" rather than accepting the first job offer that comes along. This can increase recorded unemployment while not inflicting hardship on those involved.

Wage and Price Rigidity

Some research suggests that the speed with which wages and prices adjust to changing market conditions may have slowed in the 1970s and 1980s. Anything that slows the speed of adjustment to the economy's ever-changing conditions will create a larger pool of structural unemployment. The decline of unions and the willingness of many workers to accept wage cuts when their employers get into serious difficulties may increase wage flexibility in the future—particularly compared to many European countries, where wage structures are relatively insensitive to shorter-term fluctuations in business conditions. If so, this should reduce the NAIRU.

Hysteresis

Recent models of unemployment show that the size of the NAIRU can be influenced by the *size* of the actual current rate of unemployment.[7] Such models get their name from the Greek word *hysteresis,* implying "lagged effect."

One mechanism that can lead to hysteresis in labour markets has already been noted. It arises from the importance of experience and on-the-job training. Suppose, for example, that a period of recession causes a significant group of new entrants to the labour force to have unusual difficulty in obtaining their first jobs. As a result, the unlucky group will be slow to acquire the important skills that workers generally learn in their first jobs. When demand increases again, this group of work-

---

[7]See, for example, Olivier Blanchard and Lawrence Summers, "Hysteresis and the European Unemployment Problem," *NBER Macroeconomics Annual* (1986), pp. 15–78.

ers will be at a disadvantage relative to workers with normal histories of experience, and the unlucky group may have unemployment rates that will be higher than average. Thus, the NAIRU will be higher than it would have been, had there been no recession.

Another force that can cause such effects is emphasized by commentators in Western Europe, which has a heavily unionized labour force. In times of high unemployment, people who are currently employed (insiders) may use their bargaining power to ensure that their own status is maintained and prevent new entrants to the labour force (outsiders) from competing effectively. In an *insider-outsider* model of this type, a period of prolonged high unemployment—whatever its initial cause—will tend to become "locked in." If outsiders are denied access to the labour market, their unemployment will fail to exert downward pressure on wages, and the NAIRU will tend to rise.

Increasing Structural Change

The amount of resource reallocation across industries and areas increased in the mid-1970s, slackened in the mid-1980s, and accelerated in the early 1990s. In part, this is the result of the increasing integration of the Canadian economy with the rest of the world and the globalisation of world markets. Most observers feel that this integration has been beneficial overall. One less fortunate consequence, however, is that Canadian labour markets are increasingly affected by changes in demand and supply conditions anywhere in the world—changes that require adjustments throughout the world's trading nations.

The following structural changes have created a continuing need for rapid adjustments over the past few decades:

■ Increases in the demand for food because of the failure of agricultural industries in Eastern Europe

■ Increases in the supply of agricultural products owing to the green revolution in less developed countries and heavy agricultural subsidization in the European Community (EC) of Western Europe

■ Enormous OPEC-induced increases in the price of oil in the 1970s and early 1980s, fol-

lowed by almost equally precipitous declines in the mid-1980s that carried through into the 1990s

■ The rise of Japanese industrial power, including its challenge to the integrated U.S.-Canada auto industry

■ The communication revolution, leading to the decentralization of industry, with components produced in various countries and assembled in others

■ Robotization, which increased industrial productivity and reduced the demand for assembly-line workers

■ The growth of knowledge-intensive industries that require highly educated work forces and that can be freely movable geographically

■ Globalisation of competition, with fewer and fewer domestic markets that are sheltered by natural or artificial barriers

■ Changes in the organization of firms

■ The decline of employment in manufacturing

■ The enormous growth in service employment

Although evidence is difficult to obtain, some observers argue that the increasing pace and the changing nature of technological change since the mid-1970s has contributed to an increase in the level of structural unemployment.

Future Outlook

Certain factors may work to reduce NAIRU in the future. First, the proportion of youths and women newly entering the labour force will diminish as the baby boom generation ages and the female participation rate stabilizes. Second, educational systems in some provinces are being revamped to give students better job-related training. Third, governments may become more aware of the importance of structural changes in the economy and of the need for policies to encourage rather than inhibit adaptability and flexibility in the economy. In spite of these favourable tendencies, however, structural unemployment could rise if the demand for unskilled workers declines fast enough as a result of ongoing technological change. This could lead to increased structural unemployment among the young, the unskilled, and those with only high school educations.

Reducing Unemployment

Other things being equal, all governments would like to reduce unemployment. The questions are: "Can it be done?" and "If so, at what cost?" Some points of caution concerning policies directed at structural unemployment and other consequences of structural change are given in Box 36-2.

Cyclical Unemployment

We do not need to say much more about cyclical unemployment, because its control is the subject of stabilization policy, which we have studied in several earlier chapters. A major recession that occurs because of natural causes can be countered by monetary and fiscal policy to reduce cyclical unemployment.

There is controversy about how much the government can and should do in this respect. Advocates of stabilization policy call for some combination of expansionary fiscal and monetary policies to reduce such gaps, at least when they last for sustained periods of time. Advocates of a hands-off policy say that normal market adjustments can be relied on to remove such gaps and that well-intentioned government policy will only make things worse. They call for setting simple rules for monetary and fiscal policy that would make discretionary stabilization policy impossible. This matter was discussed in detail at the end of Chapter 34.

Whatever may be argued in principle, policy makers have not yet agreed to abandon such stabilization measures in practise. However, the persistent slump that beset the Canadian economy in 1990–1992 was the first since World War II that was not countered by monetary and fiscal policy designed to provide stimulus for the recovery phase. On the fiscal side, government deficits that had persisted over booms and slumps had led to such an accumulation of government debt that the policy of long-term debt reduction took precedence over short-term stabilization policy. On the monetary side, the Bank of Canada had adopted long-term

price stability as its overriding goal and abandoned any attempt at short-term stabilization.

The mid-1970s and late 1980s saw the emergence of *policy-induced* cyclical unemployment. It occurred when the government's anti-inflation policy led to drastic contractionary policies that opened up large recessionary gaps. As we saw in Chapter 35, a temporary bout of cyclical unemployment was the price of reducing inflation.

Frictional Unemployment

The turnover that causes frictional unemployment is an inevitable part of the functioning of the economy. To the extent that it is caused by ignorance, increasing the knowledge of workers about market opportunities may help. But such measures have a cost, and that cost has to be balanced against the benefits.

Some frictional unemployment is an inevitable part of the learning process. New entrants have to try jobs to see which are suitable, and that leads to a high turnover rate among the young and hence high frictional unemployment.

Unemployment insurance is one method of helping people cope with unemployment. Certainly, it has reduced significantly the human costs of the bouts with unemployment that are inevitable in a changing society. Nothing, however, is without cost. Although unemployment insurance alleviates the suffering caused by some kinds of unemployment, it can itself contribute to unemployment in that it encourages search unemployment, as we have already observed.

Supporters of unemployment insurance emphasize its benefits. Critics emphasize its costs. As with any policy, a rational assessment of the value of unemployment insurance requires a balancing of its undoubted benefits against its undoubted costs. Many Canadian citizens believe that when this calculation is made, the benefits greatly exceed the costs, although many also recognise the scope for reform of certain aspects of the program. An active policy debate concerns recommendations to return unemployment insurance (UI) to its stated purpose while reducing its use for a number of other purposes, such as regional support, and providing welfare for those who can never achieve employment

Box 36-2

*Industrial Change: An Economist's Cautionary Tale**

The audience hushed as the members of the government's investigating commission filed into the room. The chief forecasting wizard (behind his back, some called him the economic soothsayer) began his report: "I have identified beyond reasonable doubt the underlying trends now operating," he declared to the expectant audience. "The nation's leading industry, industry X, is in a state of decline. From its current position of employing close to 50 percent of our work force, it will, within the duration of one lifetime, employ only 3 percent."

"Over 40 percent of the nation's jobs destroyed within one lifetime!" proclaimed the newspaper headlines.

"Where can new jobs possibly come from at so rapid a pace?" asked a labour leader.

"The government must protect industry X; we just cannot let all these jobs go down the tubes," argued an employer.

"Perhaps we should identify and promote new 'sunrise industries,'" said a senior bureaucrat. Indeed, it had been widely believed that a new high-tech product, product Z, would become the wave of a future new transportation revolution. A call went out for subsidies and tax breaks to back its development.

"Is there any hope that the private sector might provide the new jobs?" someone asked.

"Possibly," said a junior economist, more out of desperation than hope, "the new product Y that is being produced by a few people in backyard sheds might grow to be a significant employer."

He was immediately pounced on by a pride of self-proclaimed realistic thinkers. "Product Y! It's noisy, it's smelly, and it's a plaything for the rich. Surely *it* will never provide significant employment."

All of the economic facts in the above tale are true; only the government commission and the policy initiatives are fictitious.

The country was Canada. The time was 1900. Industry X, the employer of close to 50 percent of the work force, was agriculture. Product Z, the sunrise industry, was the large, powered, lighter-than-air craft known as the zeppelin. Product Y, the scorned plaything of the rich, was the automobile.

The decline of some traditional industries is always a cause for concern. Some of them are suffering a temporary decline, and some are declining permanently. In either event, the hardships on those losing their jobs are severe. The tale just told has a serious message. Here are a few of the lessons that can be gained from comparing the Canadian economy in 1900 and in 1990.

First, the economy is constantly changing. Indeed, the motto of any market economy could be that "nothing is permanent." New products appear continually; others disappear. At the early stage of a new product, total demand is low, costs of production are high, and many small firms are each trying to get ahead of their competitors by finding the twist that appeals to consumers or finding the technique that slashes costs. Sometimes, new products

---

for more than the minimum period needed to qualify for UI.

Reforming unemployment insurance. Many provisions have been advocated over the years to the UI scheme to focus it more on those in general

need and to reduce its effect of raising the unemployment rate. For example, workers who voluntarily quit their jobs should not be eligible for UI.[8]

---

[8]Such a provision needs, and normally has, safeguards to cover voluntary separation *with cause*—such as sexual harassment.

never get beyond that phase; they prove to be passing fads. Others, however, do become items of mass consumption.

Successful firms in growing industries buy up, merge with, or otherwise eliminate their less successful rivals. Simultaneously, their costs fall, owing to scale economies. Competition drives prices down along with costs. Eventually, at the mature stage, a few giant firms often control the industry. They become large, conspicuous, and important parts of the nation's economy. Sooner or later, new products arise to erode the position of the established giants. Demand falls off, and unemployment occurs as the few firms run into financial difficulties.

A large, sick, declining industry may appear to many as a national failure and a disgrace. At any moment, however, firms can be found in all phases—from small firms in new industries to giant firms in established or declining industries. Large, declining industries are as much a natural part of a healthy, changing economy as large, stable industries and small, growing ones.

Second, the policy of shoring up the declining industries of the 1990s could be just as destructive to our living standards as the policy of protecting the agricultural sector from decline in 1900 would have been. (Policies that ease the human cost of the adjustment are not, however, in this category.)

Third, to tell where the new employment will come from requires the kind of crystal ball that our young economist would have needed in 1900 to stick by his wild guess of identifying the new plaything of the rich as the massive automobile industry of 30 years later. Economists are continually being asked: "Where will the new employment come from?" The answer "We don't know" is *wrongly* taken to mean "It won't come." In the past, the new jobs have come, and we see no new, identifiable forces that would prevent their coming in the future. For example, in the course of the current recovery, many people gaining employment are starting in *new* jobs—jobs with firms and in locations that did not exist or would not have been predicted even 5 years ago.

Fourth, picking winners and backing them with government policy is dangerous. All too easily, it can become a waste of public funds while inhibiting the development of the real winners. People risking their own money and diversifying risks over many ventures are probably a better route to employment creation than governments that risk taxpayers' money, mesmerized by fads and fashion.

Fifth, the industrial policy that is needed is one that encourages private initiatives and risk taking. Small businesses are often, if not always, the route to the creation of new employment. Risk taking and the growth of small firms should not be discouraged by such things as complicated regulatory rules and tax laws.

They should also be actively seeking employment and must not turn down a suitable offer. These changes have been introduced in many countries, but so far have been resisted successfully in Canada.

More recently, *experience rating* has sought to distribute the costs more in proportion to the benefits. The old system, under which all firms paid the same UI tax, implicitly subsidized those who caused most unemployment and taxed most heavily those who caused least unemployment. Under experience rating, firms with histories of sizable layoffs pay more than those with better layoff records.

Structural Unemployment

The reallocation of labour among occupations, industries, skill categories, and regions that gives rise to structural unemployment is an inevitable part of growth. There are two basic approaches to reducing structural unemployment: First, try to arrest the changes that accompany growth, and, second, accept the changes and try to speed up the adjustments. Throughout history, labour and management have advocated, and governments have tried, both approaches.

Resisting change. Since the Industrial Revolution, workers have often resisted the introduction of new techniques to replace the older techniques at which they were skilled. This is understandable. New techniques often destroy the value of the knowledge and experience of workers skilled in the displaced techniques. Older workers may not even get a chance to start over with the new technique. Employers may prefer to hire younger persons who will learn the new skills faster than older workers who are set in their ways of thinking. From society's point of view, new techniques are beneficial, because they are a major source of economic growth. From the point of view of the workers they displace, new techniques can be a disaster.

Here are two characteristic ways in which economic change has been resisted. First, a declining industry may be supported with public funds. If the market would support an output of X, but subsidies are used to support an output of $2X$, jobs are provided for, say, half the industry's labour force, who would otherwise become unemployed and have to find jobs elsewhere. Second, change may be accepted but agreement reached to continue to employ workers who would otherwise be made redundant by the new technology. Both these policies are attractive to the people who would otherwise become unemployed. It may be a long time before they can find other jobs, and when they do, their skills may not turn out to be highly valued in their new occupations.

Over the long term, however, such policies run into increasing difficulties. Agreements to hire unneeded workers raise costs and can hasten the decline of an industry threatened by competitive products. An industry that is declining because of economic change becomes an increasingly large burden on the public purse, as economic forces become less and less favourable to its success. Sooner or later, public support is withdrawn, and an often precipitous decline then ensues.

In assessing the remedies for structural unemployment, it is important to realize that although they are not viable in the long run for the entire economy, they may be the best alternatives for the affected workers during their lifetimes.

There is often a genuine conflict between the private interest of workers threatened by structural unemployment, whose interests lie in preserving existing jobs, and the social interest served by economic growth, which raises living standards.

Aiding adjustments to change. Another policy to deal with structural change is to accept the decline of industries and the loss of specific jobs that go with it, and try to reduce the cost of adjustment for those affected. Retraining and relocation grants make movement easier and reduce structural unemployment without inhibiting economic change and growth.

A number of policies have been introduced in Canada. These have focused on two sources of adjustment problems. One is imperfections in capital markets that make it difficult for workers to borrow funds in order to retrain or relocate. The other is the lack of good information about current and future job prospects.

A major aspect of labour market policies is education. Between 1960 and 1990, university enrollment rose from 107,000 to 514,000, and community college enrollment increased from 50,000 to 315,000. Over the same period, the number of persons undertaking technical training increased from fewer than 5,000 to over 350,000, partly under the stimulus of the Adult Occupational Training Act of 1967.

Policies to improve the flow of information include the creation of job banks and information centres and initial steps toward a nationwide computerized information system called Jobscan. Job creation programs, such as the Local Employment Assistance Programme, Canada Community Services Projects, New Technology Employment Programme, and Summer Canada are also major labour market policies aimed at structural unemployment.

A number of programs that aid adjustment in a variety of ways exist under the National Training Act and the Labour Adjustment Benefits Act. The Canadian Mobility Programme, which finances relocation and travel assistance, spends about $8 million annually and each year helps about 5,000 workers relocate permanently and another 20,000 temporarily. Women's employment counseling centres serve 5,000 women entering or reentering the work force each year. Other services meet the special needs of such groups as the physically disabled, criminal offenders, and youths.

In 1985, the Conservative government introduced the Canadian Job Strategy. This strategy involved federal expenditures of about $1.4 billion annually toward six programs, the biggest of which were Job Development, Job Entry, and Skill Shortages. These programs were meant to be directed to groups such as women, aboriginal peoples, and disabled persons who were perceived as being "disadvantaged" in labour markets. The funds are allocated on a regional basis. The $1.4 billion does not, however, all represent new expenditures, as a number of existing labour market adjustment programs—including the Industry and Labour Adjustment Program and the Canadian Industrial Renewal Program—were discontinued.

As global economic competition becomes more and more severe and as new knowledge-driven methods of production spread, the ability to adjust to economic change will become increasingly important.[9] Countries that succeed in the global mar-

ketplace, while also managing to maintain humane social welfare systems, will be those that best learn how to *cooperate* with change. This will mean avoiding economic policies that inhibit change while adopting social policies that reduce the human cost of adjusting to change. This is an enormous challenge for future Canadian economic and social policies.

Conclusion

Over the years, unemployment has been regarded in many different ways. Harsh critics see it as proof that the market system is badly flawed. Reformers regard it as a necessary evil of the market system and a suitable object for government policy to reduce its incidence and its harmful effects. Others see it as being created, to a significant extent, by some perverse incentives arising from policies designed to help the unemployed.

Most government policy has followed a middle route. Fiscal and monetary policies have sought to reduce at least the most persistent of recessionary gaps, and a host of labour market policies have sought to reduce the incidence of frictional and structural unemployment. Such social policies as unemployment insurance have sought to reduce the sting of unemployment for the many who were thought to suffer from it for reasons beyond their control.

---

[9]This was one of the main themes emphasized by the Macdonald Commission on Canada's Economic Prospects, whose report was published in 1985.

SUMMARY

1. Canadian employment and the Canadian labour force have increased along a strong upward trend throughout all of this century. The rate of unemployment has varied cyclically while showing no strong upward trend.

2. Looking at causes, it is useful to distinguish among several kinds of unemployment: (a) cyclical unemployment, which is caused by too low a level of aggregate demand; (b) frictional unemployment, which is caused by the length of time that it takes a new entrant to find a first job and existing workers to move from job to job as a result of normal labour turnover; and (c) structural unemployment, which is caused by the need to reallocate resources among occupations, regions, and industries as the structure of demands

and supplies change. Together, frictional unemployment and structural unemployment make up the NAIRU, which is then expressed as a percentage of the total labour force.

3. There is debate among economists regarding the causes of cyclical unemployment. New classical theories look to explanations that allow the labour market to be cleared continuously. Such theories can explain cyclical variations in employment but do not predict a large group of workers who would like to work at the going wage rates but for whom jobs are not available. Recent neo-Keynesian theories have focused on the long-term nature of employer-worker relationships and on the possibility that it is efficient for employers to pay wages that are above the level that would clear the labour market.

4. The NAIRU will always be positive, because it takes time for labour to move between jobs both in normal turnover and in response to changes in the structure of the demand for labour. Government policies can also influence the NAIRU.

5. Unemployment insurance helps to alleviate the human suffering that is associated with inevitable unemployment. It also increases unemployment by encouraging voluntary search unemployment.

6. Cyclical unemployment can be reduced by raising aggregate demand. Frictional and structural unemployment can be reduced by making it easier to move between jobs, by slowing down the rate of change in the economy, and by raising the cost of staying unemployed. However, in a growing, changing economy populated by people who wish to change jobs for many reasons, it is neither possible nor desirable to reduce unemployment to zero.

TOPICS FOR REVIEW

Cyclical unemployment

Frictional unemployment

Structural unemployment

Efficiency wages

Hysteresis

The components of the NAIRU

Determinants of the size of the NAIRU

Policies to reduce the NAIRU

Policies to reduce cyclical unemployment

DISCUSSION QUESTIONS

1. Interpret the following statements from newspapers in terms of types of unemployment:
   a. "Recession hits local factory; 2,000 laid off."
   b. "A job? I've given up trying," says a mother of three.
   c. "We closed down because we could not meet the competition from Taiwan," says a local manager.
   d. "When they raised the minimum wage, I just could not afford to keep all of these retired policemen on my payroll as security guards," says the owner of a local shopping centre.

    e. "Slack sales put local foundry on short time."

    f. "Of course, I could take a job as a dishwasher, but I'm trying to find something that makes use of my high school training," says a local teenager in our survey of the unemployed.

    g. "Retraining main challenge in increased use of robots."

    h. "Modernization and tariff cuts may reduce textile employment."

    i. "Uneven upturn: Signs of recovery in Ontario, but B.C. and the Atlantic provinces still in depression."

2. Discuss the following recommendations made by the Economic Council of Canada in 1990.

    a. "We recommend that reform of the federal government's labour market strategy move in the direction of supporting skill development and employability as the primary objective."

    b. "We recommend that the federal government increase the UI funds available for retraining and relax the eligibility restrictions for training under the UI program."

    c. "We recommend that the federal government allocate increased funds to the Industrial Adjustment Service to be used as 'seed money' for the development of sector-specific human-resource plans in industries that have chosen to initiate such plans."

    d. "We support the adoption of legislation in all jurisdictions that will provide for the inclusion of part-time employees with an ongoing employer attachment, on a prorated basis, in all employee-benefit programs normally available to full-time employees."

    e. "Governments should be alert to the possibility that labour market trends may necessitate further rethinking of the overall approach to retirement income security in the 1990s."

3. Discuss the following views:

    a. "Canadian workers should resist automation, which is destroying their jobs," says a labour leader.

    b. "Given the fierce foreign competition, it's a case of automate or die," says an industrialist.

4. Use the latest *Bank of Canada Review* to compare the percentage of total unemployment across provinces and age groups, in the last year available, with the figures for earlier years given in Figures 36-4 and 36-5. Can you think of any reasons why the figures have changed?

5. What theories can you suggest to explain why unemployment rates stay persistently above average for youths and below average for males over 25?

6. In the 1993 election campign, the Liberals promised to create new jobs by having the federal, provincial, and municipal governments combine to spend $6 billion on infrastructure. What was the value of Canadian GDP at the time? How much do you think unemployment was likely to fall if the entire $6 billion was borrowed, or if it came by reducing other expenditures, or if it was raised through taxes?

    Check what actually happened. Did the extra expenditure occur? If so how was it financed?

7. At a time when the Canadian unemployment rate stood at close to 10 percent, the press reported, "Skilled labour shortage plagues many firms—newspaper ads often draw few qualified workers; wages and overtime are up." What type of unemployment does this suggest is important?

8. What differences in approach toward the problem of unemployment are suggested by the following facts?

   a. In the 1960s and 1970s, Britain spent billions of dollars on subsidizing firms that would otherwise have gone out of business, in order to protect the jobs of the employees.

   b. Sweden has been a pioneer in spending large sums to retrain and to relocate displaced workers.

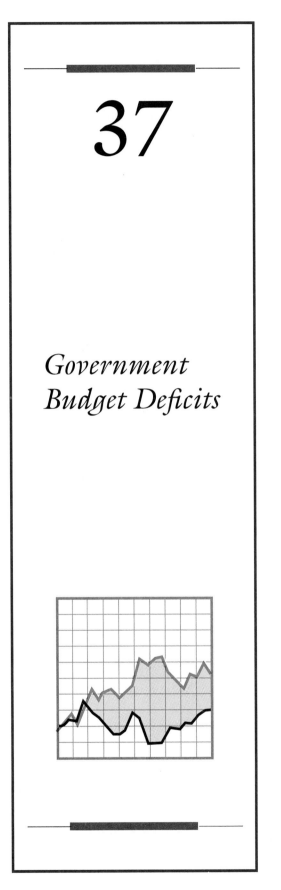

37

Government Budget Deficits

The federal government's budget deficit soared from $8 billion in 1979 to over $31 billion in 1985. With some ups and downs, it remained at historically high levels over the next several years, then soared to a new record high of $34.6 billion in 1992 and topped $35 billion in 1993.

Background to Deficits and Debt

No single measure associated with the government has ever been the focus of so much attention and controversy in the media, on the campaign trail, and in coffee shops and bars across the nation. During the 1980s and early 1990s, strong views about the deficit and its potential effects were not hard to come by. One extreme was that the deficit was a "time bomb ticking away, threatening the prosperity of all Canadians." At the other extreme was the view that the only threat the deficit posed arose from the effects of severe policy actions taken on the advice of deficit alarmists.

In the 1990s, the focus of attention shifted from the federal deficit to those of the provinces. Soaring provincial deficits took over from the federal deficit as the prime contributor to a rising level of total Canadian public debt. In 1992, all provinces had significant deficits that in many cases were also rising.

Many Canadians had been concerned about the size of the deficit for over a decade. Yet it persisted at record levels. Why are government budget deficits so large? Why do Canadians worry about them? Are they really such a big problem?

When looking at deficits and other related figures, we can start by looking at raw data. For example, the federal deficit was about $4 billion in 1975 and about $28 billion in 1990, making an increase of 700 percent.

The problem with such simple comparisons is that they take no account of the size of the economy. Some deficits that would be unmanageable for a small economy, such as New Zealand, would be quite acceptable for the larger Canadian economy. Similarly, a deficit that seemed crushing in Canada in 1890 might seem trivial in Canada in 1990, because real Canadian GDP is many times larger now than it was then.

The size of the GDP is a good approximation of the country's taxable capacity: the higher the GDP, the more tax revenue will be yielded by a given set of tax rates. For this reason, it is usually helpful to judge the importance of the deficit and other related financial data by expressing them as percentages of the nation's GDP.

Facts About Deficits

The federal deficit. The recent emergence of record federal budget deficits is shown in Figure 37-1. Part (i) shows total federal spending (on goods and services and transfers) and total federal revenues since 1967 as a percentage of GDP. Part (ii) shows the deficit, again measured as a percentage of GDP—this is the shaded area between the two lines in part (i).

Persistent deficits began in the mid-1970s. From 1975 to 1980, federal expenditures were a relatively constant fraction of GDP, while federal tax revenues fell sharply. This is the basis for the Department of Finance's view that discretionary tax cuts introduced in the 1970s were initially responsible for rapid growth in the deficit. Other analysts, however, argue that it was the failure to constrain expenditures in the face of the tax cuts that is responsible and that there was also a switch toward delivering some transfers through tax concessions rather than direct expenditure.

The increase in the deficit that occurred from 1981 to 1983 reflects the combined effects of the severe recession in 1982, some mild discretionary fiscal expansion, and increased interest payments on the government's debt. This last was due both to the sharp rise in interest rates that occurred and to the cumulative effect of the persistent deficits on the size of the government debt.

After 1982, the deficit increased dramatically as a share of GDP. Then, after falling slightly during the last stages of the expansion in the late 1980s, it rose to record heights in the recession of 1990-1992.

Provincial deficits. Until the late 1980s, provincial and municipal governments had experienced relatively small budget imbalances. Hence, most of the concern about budget deficits in Canada has been focused on the federal government. In fact, throughout the 1970s and early 1980s, the total government deficit was smaller than the federal government deficit, reflecting the combined surpluses of the other two levels of government. Since 1986, however, the total government deficit has been larger than the federal deficit.

In 1986, a time of national economic expansion, all 10 provincial governments were running deficits. Although deficits had been the order of the day in certain provinces, they had traditionally been offset by surpluses in other provinces. In 1986, a deficit even emerged in Alberta, which had typically been a surplus province due to large oil revenues. Alberta began running deficits in response to locally depressed economic conditions brought about by adverse shocks to the agricultural and energy sectors. Most worrying was the deficit in Ontario, a province that had been experiencing a sustained economic expansion since 1983. By 1990, several provinces had their credit ratings downgraded, which meant higher interest had to be paid on the outstanding debt. The bonds of more than one province were getting close to a "junk bond rating," at which many institutional investors were legally barred from holding the bonds. In 1992, all 10 provinces were once again running deficits.

Sources of provincial deficits. Some provinces, such as Newfoundland and Saskatchewan, fell into chronic deficit because their economies were in chronic difficulties, leading to shrinking tax bases. Other provinces had encountered buoyant conditions in the 1980s but had ignored the basic advice of Keynesians' countercyclical fiscal policy—a policy that most of them espoused.

Although Keynesian fiscal policy calls for accepting deficits in recessions for their built-in stabilising effects, the problem was that the other half of the Keynesian advice, to run surpluses in booms, had not been followed. All through the expansion of the 1980s, provincial revenues grew rapidly, especially in Ontario and British Columbia. Instead of getting into a surplus position that would allow for the application of Keynesian policies during the next recession, the provinces increased expenditure along with their rising revenues. Many of the increases were statutory and hence difficult to reduce when revenues fell, as inevitably they would when the next recession came. So when the recession did occur in 1990, the provinces found themselves in an exposed fiscal position. Although many tried to ignore their deficits during the first year of the recession, they were forced to deal with them as financial markets began expressing concern about their creditworthiness, and as interest payments began to take up a rising proportion of their total expenditures. As a result, many provincial governments that espoused Keynesian policies found themselves in the perverse position of trying to cut expenditure and increase tax rates during a recession, because they

FIGURE 37-1
Federal Revenues, Expenditures, and Budget Balances, 1967-1989
(Percentage of GDP, National Accounts Basis)

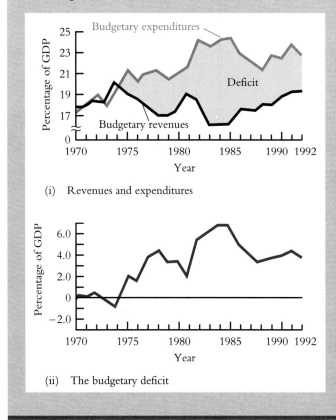

(i)   Revenues and expenditures

(ii)   The budgetary deficit

The deficit has grown sharply in recent years, reflecting rapid increases in expenditures relative to revenues. The graphs in (i) show expenditures and revenues of the federal government, both as a percentage of national income. The difference is the federal deficit, shown in (ii).

From 1967 through 1973, expenditures grew steadily while revenue fluctuated around a rising trend; as a result, the budget balance fluctuated between deficit and surplus positions but showed no clear trend. Persistent deficits emerged in the next five years as expenditures remained roughly constant while revenues fell.

In the 1980s the deficit increased dramatically. In the early part of the decade, the growth in the deficit reflected the effects of the recession; cyclical adjustment grew sharply in this period. Revenues fell sharply and have recovered only slowly since. Expenditures rose rapidly, in part reflecting the operation of automatic stabilizers. More recently, government restraint curtailed growth in program spending, but this was more than offset by the rapid growth in interest payments on the national debt, so that, as shown, total expenditure continued to rise. Since 1988 the deficit has fallen as a percentage of GDP. (*Source*: Department of Finance. *Budget Papers*, 1993.)

had not been willing to do just that during the preceding period of expansion.

From Deficits to the National Debt

The national debt is the total debt owed by all the governments of Canada; it represents the *cumulative* effect of all past deficits and surpluses. When a government runs a deficit in any one year, it must borrow and therefore add to the total debt that it owed at the start of the year. When it runs a surplus, it pays off some of its past borrowing and therefore reduces its total debt.

A deficit increases the national debt; a surplus reduces it.

As we shall see, much of the concern about government budget deficits arises from their cumulative ef-

fect on the national debt and on the government's interest obligations.

Facts About the Debt

Federal debt.   At the end of 1992, the federal government's debt was over $380 billion, which represents more than $14,000 for every man, woman, and child in the country, or $56,000 for a family of four. About 15 percent of the debt was held by the government itself and by the Bank of Canada; interest payments on this part of the debt are only bookkeeping transactions.[1] The other 85 percent is held privately by Canadians and foreigners.

---

[1]The Bank of Canada buys government bonds in the course of operating monetary policy (see Chapter 34). Government departments sometimes acquire government bonds with funds that they do not need for relatively short periods of time.

FIGURE 37-2
Relative Significance of the National Debt, 1938–1992

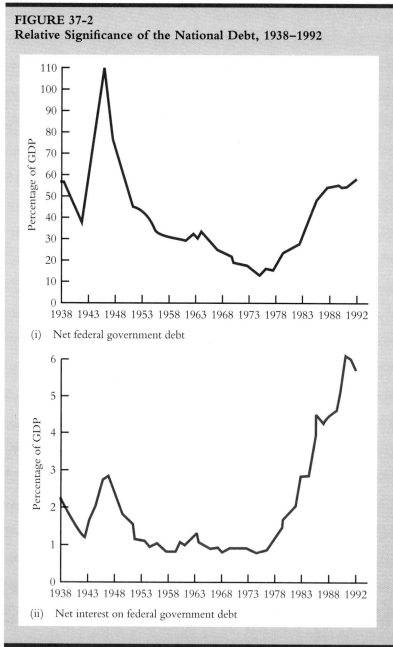

(i)   Net federal government debt

(ii)   Net interest on federal government debt

After falling for 30 years, the national debt and interest payments have both risen as a share of national income since 1975. Net federal government debt is plotted in (i), net interest payments made by the federal government in (ii), both expressed as a percentage of GDP. The national debt, after rising sharply through World War II, was a declining fraction of GDP until 1975. Since 1975 there has been a continuing rise, increasing quite sharply in the past few years. In 1992 the ratio reached 59.2 percent.

Interest payments on the national debt have followed a similar pattern; since interest rates rose in the late 1970s and early 1980s, the upturn in interest payments was sharper and occurred sooner than with the debt. The same was true at the end of the 1980s. Although Federal debt continued to climb through 1992, interest payments fell as a percentage of GDP due to a sharp fall in interest rates. (*Source*: Department of Finance, *Quarterly Economic Review*.)

The national debt represents money that the federal government has borrowed by selling treasury bills and government bonds to Canadian and foreign households, firms, and institutional investors.

In this sense, the national debt is owed by all of us to some of us and to foreigners.

As with deficits, in evaluating the national debt and the government's interest payments on it, it is useful to consider them *relative* to the size of the economy. Worries about the debt arise primarily when the debt grows faster than the economy; it is really the *debt-to-GDP ratio* that matters. A national debt of $400 billion clearly has different implications when GDP is $50 billion than when it is $500 billion.

Figure 37-2 shows historical data for the debt and interest payments on it as a proportion of GDP. Part (i) shows that federal debt as a proportion of GDP started to fall at the end of World War II and continued to fall until 1975. The debt rose relative to GDP after 1977, and by 1989 it had reached almost 54 percent of GDP. That figure is still much less than it was at the postwar peak, when it exceeded 100 percent. Nevertheless, the trend is worrisome and the ratio is high for peacetime periods.

Interest payments. Consider next the interest payments on the federal debt, often called the *debt service payments,* shown in Figure 37-2(ii). The current ratio of nearly 6 percent is high by historical standards.

It is useful to examine the deficit by looking at the interest payments on the national debt separately from other government expenditures, called program expenditures. The difference between the government's program expenditures and its revenues is called its *primary deficit.* The total deficit is equal to the primary deficit plus the government's debt service payments.

Since fiscal year 1989-1990, debt service payments have exceeded the total federal deficit, indicating that the government's *primary budget balance* (which excludes debt service payments) has been in surplus.

Another perspective on debt service payments is their share of government revenues and expenditures. In 1991-1992, the debt service payments of $65 billion represented 20 percent of total federal government spending and over 22 percent of total revenues. Both are very high by historical standards; for example, they are more than double the corresponding fractions in 1970.

Combined debt. Early in the 1990s, the federal debt seemed likely to stabilize at around 60 percent of GDP. Although that was a high figure, many expressed satisfaction that its growth had at least been arrested. At the same time, however, provincial deficits began to soar. Much of the cause was the severe recession that had temporarily reduced the tax base, although there seemed to be some longer-run forces also acting in the same direction.

Figure 37-3 shows the build-up of the combined federal and provincial debt since 1960. By 1992, it had reached nearly 90 percent of GDP. Figure 37-4 shows the breakdown of the current debt among the provinces as a percentage of GDP.

Evaluating the Deficit

To judge the importance of the deficit, economists look at several different forces that influence it. This allows them to define several different deficits whose separate behaviours shed light on the deficit as a whole.

The most serious problem in judging either the long-run importance of the deficit or how well it is doing its job as a short-term built-in stabilizer arises from the fact that the deficit is partly determined exogenously by the government's fiscal policy and partly endogenously by the state of the economy. Let us see why this is so.

Government tax revenues are related to the performance of the economy. For a given tax rate, tax revenues will rise when income rises and fall when income falls. Because government purchases are relatively insensitive to the level of national income, the budget surplus will rise (the budget deficit will fall) as income rises. This relationship is given by the *budget surplus function.* This function is illustrated both in Figure 29-1 on page 588, and in Figure 37-5 by the curves labeled $B = T - G$, where B stands for budget surplus.

With a given spending and taxing policy, as national income changes, the budget surplus changes in the same direction.

When the government sets tax rates and makes its plans for spending, it determines the position of the budget surplus function. The higher the net tax rate, the higher and steeper will be the curve in Figure 37-5. (Recall that the net tax rate includes taxes net of transfer payments; typically, tax revenues rise

FIGURE 37-3
Total Public Net Debt as a Percentage of GDP (Public Accounts Basis)

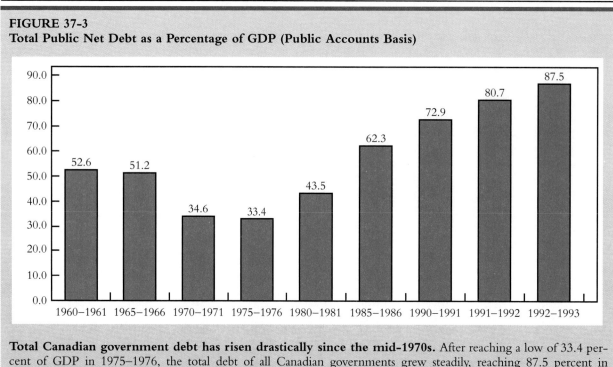

Total Canadian government debt has risen drastically since the mid-1970s. After reaching a low of 33.4 percent of GDP in 1975–1976, the total debt of all Canadian governments grew steadily, reaching 87.5 percent in 1992–1993. (*Source*: Department of Finance, Ottawa, 1993.)

FIGURE 37-4
Canada's Government Debt-to-GDP Ratio (Fiscal Year 1992–1993)
(Federal and Provincial Net Debt: percentage of GDP)

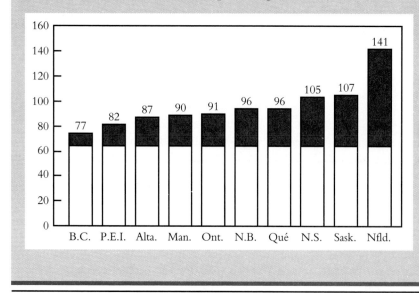

Provincial debts contribute significantly to the total Canadian national debt. The chart shows each province's share of federal debt as 64 percent of GDP. It then adds the province's debt to make a combined total of debt as a proportion of GDP, that runs from 77 percent for British Columbia to 141 percent for Newfoundland. (*Source*: Department of Finance, Ottawa, 1993.)

FIGURE 37-5
The Budget Surplus (Deficit) Function

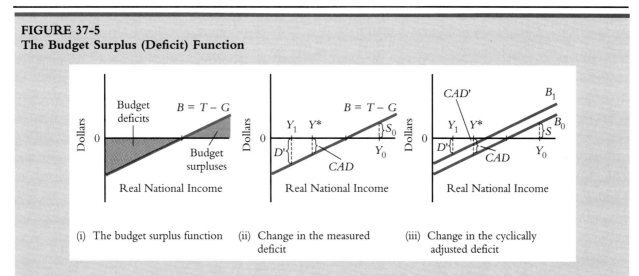

(i) The budget surplus function

(ii) Change in the measured deficit

(iii) Change in the cyclically adjusted deficit

The budget surplus can change either because of a change in fiscal policy or because of a change in national income. Parts (i) and (ii) illustrate the same budget surplus function, showing that the budget surplus increases (budget deficit falls) as national income rises.

Part (ii) defines the cyclically adjusted surplus (or deficit) (CAS or CAD) as the budget balance that obtains at potential national income, $Y*$. In the example, the CAD is a deficit, as it is for current fiscal policy in Canada. At a sufficiently high income, Y_0, the actual budget would be in surplus by an amount S_0. At incomes lower than $Y*$, such as Y_1, the actual budget would be in deficit by D', more than the amount of the CAD. Throughout the curve in part (ii), fiscal policy is unchanged. The deficit and surplus change only because national income changes.

Part (iii) shows how the actual deficit (or surplus) might move in a different direction from the CAD or CAS. Suppose the economy starts at Y_0, with fiscal policy given by B_0. If fiscal policy is made more restrictive, through some combination of higher taxes and lower government purchases, the budget balance will now behave according to B_1. At the same time, if income should fall to Y_1, the budget surplus of S will turn into a deficit of D'. By looking at the actual budget balance, one would see the budget move from surplus to deficit, suggesting, incorrectly, that the fiscal policy had become more stimulative of the economy. Focusing on the CAD, however, the level of budget balance at $Y*$, makes it clear that B_1 is more restrictive than B_0—the CAD is smaller at $Y*$ (and at every level of income) with the fiscal policy given by B_1.

---

and transfer payments fall as income rises.) The lower the level of planned government purchases, the higher will be the budget surplus function. The higher is the budget surplus function, the higher will be the surplus (the lower the deficit) *at any given level of national income.*

Fiscal policy determines the *position* of the budget surplus (or deficit) function.

The actual budget surplus (or deficit). Tax rates were higher in 1992 than in 1991, yet the budget deficit *grew* by $4 billion. Does this imply that the tax increases failed to reduce the deficit? No. The budget deficit grew between 1991 and 1992 because the economy went deeper into recession. Thus, while the tax increases shifted the budget surplus function up, the economy moved to the left along the new, higher curve. The net effect was an increase in the deficit. Part (iii) of Figure 37-5 illustrates how this outcome could happen.

The actual level of the budget surplus (or deficit) depends on both fiscal policy, which determines the location of the budget surplus function, *and* the level of national income, which determines a specific point on the budget surplus function.

TABLE 37-1   Actual and Cyclically Adjusted Federal Government Budget Balances, 1970-1992 (*billions of dollars, National Accounts basis*)

Year	Actual budget deficit*	Cyclical adjustment	Cyclically adjusted budget deficit*
1970	−0.3	−0.3	−0.6
1971	0.1	−0.2	−0.1
1972	0.5	−0.2	0.3
1973	−0.4	0.5	0.1
1974	−1.3	−0.3	−1.6
1975	3.8	−1.0	2.8
1976	3.3	0.2	3.5
1977	7.3	0.2	7.5
1978	10.9	0.1	11.0
1979	9.4	0.4	9.8
1980	10.7	−0.3	10.4
1981	7.3	0.6	7.9
1982	20.3	−4.3	16.0
1983	25.0	−3.6	21.4
1984	30.0	−0.8	29.2
1985	31.4	0.8	32.2
1986	23.6	1.1	24.7
1987	20.7	2.0	22.7
1988	19.1	3.9	23.0
1989	21.2	3.0	24.2
1990	25.5	−0.5	25.0
1991	29.8	−6.0	23.8
1992	25.5	−7.7	17.8

Source: Department of Finance, *Economic and Fiscal Reference Tables,* August 1993.

The cyclical adjustment shows the amount of the deficit caused by the existing output gap. When there is a recessionary gap, with actual output below potential, the adjustment is negative, making the cyclically adjusted deficit smaller than the actual deficit. This was the situation during the period 1982–1986, for example. When there is an inflationary gap, with actual output above potential, the adjustment is positive, making the cyclically adjusted deficit greater than the actual deficit. This was the situation during the period 1987–1990, for example.

Variations in the cyclically adjusted deficit give an indication of variations in the fiscal stance. For example, fiscal policy became more restrictive in 1981, when the CAD fell from $10.3 to $7.4 billion, and more expansionary in 1989, when the CAD rose from $24.2 to $27.5 billion. Note that the CAD was reduced dramatically from 1990 to 1992 but the actual deficit remained high due to the severe recession.

*A minus sign indicates a surplus.

The cyclically adjusted surplus (or deficit). Because it depends in part on the level of national income, the actual budget deficit is a poor measure of either the effect of fiscal policy on the economy or of the long-term deficit problem. For example, if national income fell by enough, the budget deficit could increase at the same time that fiscal policy became more restrictive. In order to measure the fiscal stance independently of the level of national income, it is necessary to develop a measure of the budget balance that is also independent of the level of national income.

Economists have developed the concept of the **cyclically adjusted surplus (CAS)** and **cyclically adjusted deficit (CAD)**. These are also known as the *structural surplus (or deficit),* defined as the budget surplus (or deficit) that *would obtain if the economy were operating at potential national income.*[2]

Fixing the level of income at which the deficit is measured removes the changes in the actual deficit that are caused by changes in income. The structural deficit measures the position of the budget surplus function, which is solely determined by fiscal policy.

The behaviour of the *CAD* in recent years is shown in Table 37-1. Parts (ii) and (iii) of Figure 37-5 illustrate how the *CAD* can be used to judge the stance of fiscal policy. The higher is the structural deficit, the higher is the government's net contribution to aggregate expenditure at that level of income.

Why Worry About Deficits?

So much for the size of deficits and their appropriate measurement. The next question is: Should we worry about them?

[2]The concept used to be called the *full employment surplus.* The change from *full employment* to *cyclically adjusted* came during the 1970s, when the amount of unemployment that is associated with potential income rose so much that referring to it as *full employment* became embarrassing. The change from *surplus* to *deficit* in common usage took place between the 1960s, when many economists were concerned that high surpluses exerted a depressing effect on GDP, and the 1980s, when nearly everyone became concerned about large deficits.

Postponed Tax Liability

Assume the government decides to make $1b of new expenditure. It can raise tax rates until its revenues rise by $1b, and the matter ends there. Or it can borrow $1b. As long as that debt exists, the interest on it is the cost of postponing the payment of $1b. If the debt is retired, $1b of tax revenue is used at that time to pay for the original expenditure. As Milton Friedman likes to put it: There is no free lunch. Government expenditure must be paid for; either it is paid for by current tax payments, or the liability is passed on to the future. The current cost of passing the tax liability on is the current interest bill that must be paid on the debt incurred to finance the expenditure.

Debt is a postponed tax liability, and the interest paid on that debt is the cost of postponing the liability.

Ricardo Neutrality

Some economists have argued that deficits and public debt have no important effects on the economy. The logic underlying this belief, which is called the *Ricardian neutrality proposition.*

The basic idea of this proposition is that well-informed taxpayers can arbitrage the government's decision on how it is to finance its current expenditure. They do this by borrowing or lending to offset the government's actions. To see how this works, consider once again the government's decision to spend an additional $1b for one year.

First, say the government decides to borrow the funds. If taxpayers would have preferred to pay now, they can buy the bonds floated by the government. The interest they earn on the bonds will yield the income they need to pay the extra taxes required to finance the interest charges on the government's new debt. If the government ever decides to raise taxes to pay off the debt, the taxpayers can cash in their bonds to meet their new tax liabilities.

Second, say that the government decides to raise taxes by $1b, but taxpayers would prefer to postpone payment. They borrow on the bond market to pay their current taxes.

Thus, as long as everyone knows what is going on, the private sector can determine whether the government's $1b of expenditure is paid for now or in the future, whatever financing method the government adopts.

This argument requires, among other things, that those in the private sector understand that government borrowing represents a tax liability that belongs to them or their heirs; that they can borrow all they wish on capital markets; and that postponed liabilities are not so large as to undermine the belief that future taxes can support them.

To understand this last point, assume that both the government and taxpayers want to postpone the payments needed to finance a continuing flow of government expenditure, so they borrow to meet current expenditures. If the borrowing continues, the national debt can grow without limit, and, if it grows faster than the economy, the debt-to-GDP ratio also grows without limit. Sooner or later, lenders will begin to fear that the postponed tax liabilities are becoming too large to service. They will become unwilling to lend further, and a fiscal crisis will occur.

Most observers believe that Canada is still some way from a lender-imposed crisis, although several provinces have had their credit ratings downgraded, giving early warning signs that they cannot go on borrowing indefinitely. Figure 37-6 gives some indication of where Canadian debt stands in comparison with the other major industrial countries.

A less formal argument that the national debt is of no concern to the nation as a whole, since it is something that we as citizens owe to ourselves, is discussed in Box 37-1 on page 796.

Effects of Deficits

For most economists, the relevant question is not whether deficits have effects, but the form and magnitude of those effects.

One way in which deficits influence the economy is through their short-run stabilizing or destabilizing effects.

This stabilization role was emphasized in Chapter 31.

Figure 37-5 shows the complications that arise when using the current deficit to judge the stance

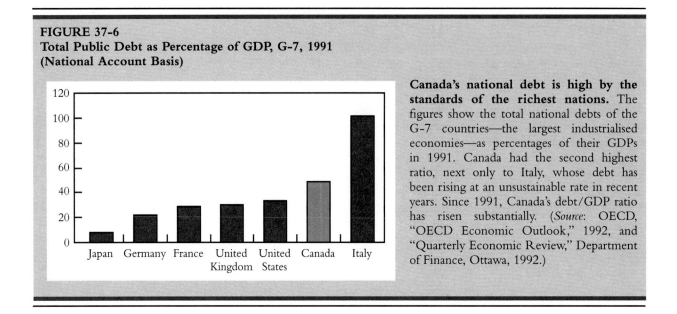

FIGURE 37-6
Total Public Debt as Percentage of GDP, G-7, 1991
(National Account Basis)

Canada's national debt is high by the standards of the richest nations. The figures show the total national debts of the G-7 countries—the largest industrialised economies—as percentages of their GDPs in 1991. Canada had the second highest ratio, next only to Italy, whose debt has been rising at an unsustainable rate in recent years. Since 1991, Canada's debt/GDP ratio has risen substantially. (*Source*: OECD, "OECD Economic Outlook," 1992, and "Quarterly Economic Review," Department of Finance, Ottawa, 1992.)

of fiscal policy for stabilization purposes. The persistence in Canada of a large *cyclically adjusted deficit* (*CAD*), along with a large actual deficit and a rising debt-to-GDP ratio, reinforces the concerns that many economists have about the deficit.

A second way in which deficits can influence the economy is through their potential to affect income and welfare adversely in the long run.

People worry about the long-run effects of persistent deficits for many reasons. We will look at several.

Will a Deficit Cause Inflation?

Neither economic theory nor the available evidence suggests that deficits by themselves are sufficient to cause inflation. The worry that persistent deficits may cause inflation arises out of the fear that a persistent deficit will eventually cause the Bank of Canada to increase the money supply, which, as we saw in Chapter 35, is a necessary condition for a sustained inflation. This possibility applies only to the federal debt, since only the federal government can order the Bank of Canada to create new money to pay its interest bills.

To date, however, this has not been a problem, as the deficit has been financed by government borrowing in private-sector capital markets; only if it

were financed by selling bonds to the Bank would the growth rate in the money supply be increased. (When this happens, the Bank *creates* the money to finance the deficit by giving the government new deposits in return for its new bonds.) If this increase in the money supply is too rapid, then—as we saw in Chapter 35—it will cause inflation.

Deficits financed by the continual creation of new money cause continual inflation; deficits financed by private-sector borrowing do not.

Will the Deficit Crowd Out Private Investment?

People fear that deficit spending may lead to a more or less equivalent reduction in private-sector investment spending. Government borrowing to finance its deficit can absorb a significant proportion of private savings. In 1990, for example, the federal deficit was nearly two thirds of total private-sector savings by households and firms. The fear is that heavy government borrowing drives up the interest rate, and the higher interest rate reduces private investment expenditure.

If government borrowing to finance the deficit drives up the interest rate, some private investment expenditure will be crowded out.

This effect can be seen by referring to the definition of aggregate expenditure as the sum of consumption, investment, and government expenditure plus net exports:

$$AE = C + I + G + (X - IM) \qquad [1]$$

The argument is that, other things being equal, the rise in interest rates caused by a government deficit will lead to a fall in investment spending, I, and thus to a fall in desired aggregate expenditure, AE.

This effect is more likely when the economy is close to full employment. When there is a large recessionary gap, the rise in income will increase the volume of savings (as households move along their savings functions, as shown in Figure 28-1 on page 569). In this case, the new savings generated by the rise in income help to finance the deficit so that less crowding out of existing private-sector borrowing need occur.

Will the Deficit Crowd Out Net Exports?

In a relatively small trading country such as Canada, a budget deficit tends to crowd out exports rather than private investments. This phenomenon is analysed more fully in Chapter 40. In the meantime, however, we can see how it works in broad outline.

The government borrowing to finance a large budget deficit tends to push up interest rates. But as soon as Canadian rates rise significantly above those in the rest of the world, funds flow into Canada, attracted by the relatively higher rates to be earned on funds lent in Canada.

In an open economy such as Canada's, instead of driving up interest rates sufficiently to crowd out private investment, the government budget deficit tends to attract foreign capital.

The rush to buy Canadian dollars in order to invest in Canada depresses the exchange rate. This reduces Canadian exports and encourages Canadian imports.

A persistent government budget deficit lowers the exchange rate and causes net exports to fall.

This type of crowding out can also be seen in terms of Equation 1, where now it is $X - IM$ that falls.

Will the Debt Harm Future Generations?

To the extent that government borrowing to finance current expenditures crowds out private investment, there will be a smaller stock of capital to pass on to future generations. Less capital means less output; this is the long-term burden of the debt.

Despite large deficits, investment was sustained at high levels throughout the 1980s. Does this mean that we do not need to worry about a burden arising from the large deficits? Unfortunately, the answer is no. Because private investment has been maintained, foreign lenders have supplied much of the funds.[3] Thus, while future generations of Canadians may well inherit a capital stock that is not significantly reduced as a result of the deficit, they will inherit an increased stock of foreign liabilities. Either way, their wealth will have been reduced relative to what it would have been without the deficits.

Payments of interest and dividends on liabilities owed abroad will lower GNP (income owned by Canadian residents) in relation to GDP (output produced in Canada), since some income generated by the output will accrue to foreign residents. These payments will also lower GNP relative to what it would have been without the deficits.

Borrowing from abroad entails a transfer of purchasing power to domestic residents when the borrowing occurs and a transfer back to foreign residents when interest payments and repayments of principal occur.

Also, future generations have to either repay the debt or continue to pay interest on it. They are thus either paying the tax bill for things their parents and grandparents received from the government, or they are paying the interest cost of postponing the bill to a yet later date. If their parents and grandparents saved to offset the deficit (as in the Ricardo effect),

---

[3]As we shall see in Chapter 39, the capital inflows from abroad are matched by a deficit on the current account, and the association of the current account deficit with the government budget deficit has become known as the *twin-deficits problem*.

Box 37-1

Does the National Debt Matter?

The Owe-It-To-Ourselves View

A few economists have argued that since the national debt simply involves a debt of some Canadians payable to other Canadians, it imposes no net burden on the country. Of course, these economists recognise that the debt is a burden to taxpayers in general, who must ultimately provide the funds for the government to make interest payments on the debt. But, the owe-it-to-ourselves argument holds, that burden is exactly offset by the interest payments that are made to Canadians who own government bonds.

The owe-it-to-ourselves view thus argues that the major effect of the national debt is that interest payments on it merely redistribute income from the general taxpayer toward bondholders. Since government bonds are widely held, being a major component of most public and private pension funds, the argument holds that even this redistribution of income is not a serious matter.

This contention raises several issues.

Crowding Out

First, suppose that the basic facts alleged in the owe-it-to-ourselves view are true—that is, that virtually all Canadian government debt is in fact held by Canadians. Even in this case, it does not follow that there is no net burden to the Canadian economy arising from the government debt.

Economic theory and evidence suggest that government bonds are held instead of claims on income streams produced by real capital. That is, if the debt did not exist, people would still wish to hold assets to provide income in the future; in the absence of the government debt, they would have invested in corporations engaged in producing goods and services. Thus, the bonds, which on net contribute nothing to the economy but merely redistribute income from one group to another, crowd out investment in real capital that would have created wealth and income for Canadians.

Furthermore, taxes must be levied to pay the interest on the national debt. High tax rates can become counterproductive in driving people and capital either abroad or into the underground economy. This can have serious effects on the economy.

Finally, if the debt gets so large that lenders fear the tax base cannot support it, they will demand large risk premiums that put further pressure on the tax system and can, as they have with some other governments, lead to a fiscal crisis in which further money cannot be borrowed at an acceptable rate.

International Capital Mobility

The basic contention that the debt is merely owed to ourselves is not completely true. Though the majority of Canadian government bonds are held by Canadian citizens, government bonds are also sold on international markets, and a rising proportion, over 25 percent in 1993, is held by foreigners. Ac-

later generations inherit the wealth to offset their extra tax burden. If, however, previous generations took what the government had to offer without offsetting it with extra savings, as surely many people have done, then these later generations will be stuck with the bill for what their predecessors received from the government.

Does the Size of the Debt Hamper Economic Policy?

In 1989, over 30 percent of all tax revenues went to pay interest on the national debt! In 1992, although the debt was larger, interest on it only took up about 22 percent of all tax revenues, due to cordingly, the interest payments on these bonds, which must be financed by Canadian taxpayers, accrue to foreign nationals.

The fact that some Canadian government debt is held abroad is enough to upset the owe-it-to-ourselves view. But the situation is even more complicated—and more damaging to this view.

Suppose that a Canadian corporation wishes to float a new debt issue in order to finance a new factory. Although it might normally expect to sell a large fraction of the new bonds on the Canadian market, the volume of the Canadian government's sales of bonds to finance its budget deficit may force the Canadian corporation to sell much of its debt abroad. Given the total amount of debt issued by Canadian governments, there are not enough Canadian savings to finance the borrowing requirements of both the government and the private sector. It is thus inevitable that many new issues of stocks and bonds are sold to foreigners.

Again, there will be a burden to the national debt, not in the form of a reduced capital stock in Canada, but in the form of reduced income and wealth for Canadians. Foreign nationals will now own claims to the income from the new Canadian investment projects, and some of the income from these Canadian projects will accrue to those foreign nationals who acquired these financial claims.

In this case, the burden to the national debt arises *indirectly* because of the need that it creates for Canadian firms to finance their investment by selling bonds and equities abroad. Once this indirect effect is recognised, simply looking at the share of foreign ownership of the national debt does not give a good indication of how much is owed to ourselves and how much is actually owed to foreign nationals.

What Limits the Acceptable Size of the Deficit?

If the owe-it-to-ourselves view were correct, there should be no limit to an acceptable level of government debt. Surely, the politicians would like that, as it would allow them to avoid many of the hard decisions involved in restraining expenditures and raising taxes. However, since the debt represents postponed tax liabilities, a debt that grows faster than GDP will eventually exceed the capacity of taxpayers to finance the growing interest bill that is the current cost of postponing these liabilities. When this happens, a crisis will suddenly stop further borrowing. Drastic spending cuts and tax increases will have to be imposed rapidly. Such a crisis has already hit New Zealand, which tumbled from the world's third highest living standard to the twenty-third highest in the course of a very few years and in the process was forced to reduce its whole income support system drastically.

the fall in interest rates. In both cases, the magnitude of the interest obligation put a severe strain on all government policies. Three ways in which it does this deserve mention.

First, to meet growing interest payments, expenditure on many existing programs must be cut, and many desirable new programs cannot be adopted. During the first 6 years of the Conservative government's tenure, program expenditure fell as a fraction of GDP, but most of the saving went to pay the rising interest bill on the national debt rather than to cutting the deficit.

Second, fiscal stabilization policy is made difficult. According to the theory of stabilization policy, the government should run a surplus or a small deficit in boom times and a large deficit during slumps. (Built-in stabilizers will do much of the job automatically *if* the government's fiscal position is satisfactory on average over the cycle.) The persistent deficits over the past few years have meant that to some extent, governments have been stimulating the economy during a boom. Even more worrisome, in order to eliminate their deficits and control the growth of debt, governments have had to go on trying to cut their deficits even when a severe slump exists.

Third, the fiscal deficit greatly complicates the Bank of Canada's anti-inflationary policy.

Because the government's deficits were stimulating the economy, the Bank had to drive interest rates up sufficiently to counteract that stimulus and then even further to get the desired contractionary pressures.

Because of this, since the mid-1980s, many economists have been publicly urging the government to alter the balance between fiscal and monetary policies. A major reduction in the budget deficit would be contractionary, and this would allow a less restrictive monetary policy, with its accompanying lower interest rates. If desired, the two effects could be adjusted so as approximately to offset each other, so that aggregate demand would be unaffected.

Proposals to Control the Deficit

As we have seen, government deficits contribute to aggregate demand and hence can, during a recession, play a useful role in dampening cyclical fluctuations in the economy. As we have also seen, government deficits contribute to increases in the national debt and hence, persistent deficits can, in the long term, lead to a reduction in living standards of the average Canadian. This conflict between the short-term stabilization role of deficits and the long-term adverse effects of a large public debt has been a subject of constant debate.

Views range from those who dismiss the long-run costs of the national debt and hence are not concerned about the deficit to those who wish to eschew the short-term stabilization role for the deficit entirely and impose a virtual straitjacket on the government, requiring it always to balance its

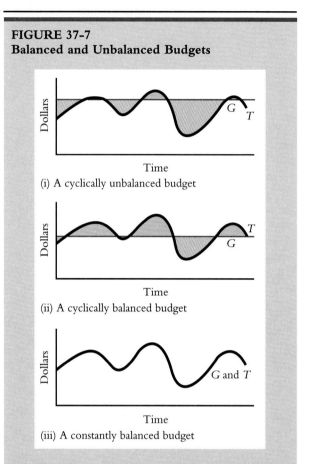

FIGURE 37-7
Balanced and Unbalanced Budgets

(i) A cyclically unbalanced budget

(ii) A cyclically balanced budget

(iii) A constantly balanced budget

An annually (constantly) balanced budget is a destabilizer; a cyclically balanced budget is a stabilizer. The flow of tax receipts, T, is shown varying over the business cycle, while in (i) and (ii) government expenditure, G, is shown at a constant rate.

In (i) deficits (red areas) are common and surpluses (blue areas) are rare because the average level of expenditure exceeds the average level of taxes. Such a policy will tend to stabilize the economy against cyclical fluctuations, but the average fiscal stance of the government is expansionary. This has been the characteristic Canadian budgetary position over the past several decades.

In (ii) government expenditure has been reduced until it is approximately equal to the average level of tax receipts. The budget is now balanced cyclically. The policy still tends to stabilize the economy against cyclical fluctuations because of deficits in slumps and surpluses in booms. However, the average fiscal stance is neither strongly expansionary nor strongly contractionary.

In (iii) a balanced budget has been imposed. Deficits have been prevented, but government expenditure now varies over the business cycle, which tends to destabilize the economy by accentuating the cyclical swings in aggregate expenditure.

budget. We now look at some of the specific proposals that have been put forward; some of the general options are illustrated in Figure 37-7.

An annually balanced budget? Much current rhetoric of fiscal restraint calls for a balanced budget. In the United States, the Gramm-Rudman-Hollings bill, passed in late 1985, mandated expenditure cuts in order to eliminate the federal deficit by 1993. It failed to do so, and much of the deficit reduction that it did achieve came from "window dressing." This term refers to such dodges as shifting expenditures to accounts that are not covered in the budget and once-and-for-all shifts of tax revenue to get them into an earlier year.

An annually balanced budget would be extremely difficult, perhaps impossible, to achieve. With fixed tax rates, tax revenues fluctuate as national income fluctuates. Much government expenditure is fixed by past commitments, and most of the rest is hard to change quickly.

But suppose that an annually balanced budget, or something approaching it, were feasible. What would its effects be? Would they be desirable?

We saw earlier that a large government sector whose expenditures on goods and services are not very sensitive to the cyclical variations in national income is a major built-in stabilizer. To insist that annual government expenditure be tied to annual tax receipts would be to abandon the present built-in stability provided by the government. Government expenditure would then become a major *destabilizing* force. Tax revenues necessarily rise in booms and fall in slumps; an annually balanced budget would force government expenditure to do the same. Changes in national income would then cause induced changes not only in household consumption expenditure but also in government expenditure. This would greatly increase the economy's marginal propensity to spend and hence increase the value of the multiplier. This would serve as a *built-in destabilizer*!

An annually balanced budget would accentuate the swings in national income that accompany changes in such autonomous expenditure flows as investment and exports.

A cyclically balanced budget. An alternative policy, one that would prevent continual deficits (and could also inhibit the growth in the size of the government sector), would be to balance the budget over the business cycle. This would be more feasible than the annually balanced budget, and it would not make government expenditure a destabilizing force.

Although more attractive in principle than the annually balanced budget, a cyclically balanced budget carries problems of its own. Government might well spend in excess of revenue in one year, leaving the next government the obligation to spend less than current revenue in following years. Could such an obligation to balance over a period of several years be made binding? What one government commits itself to in one year does not necessarily restrict what it (or its successor) does the next year.

Perhaps even more of a problem is that there is always room for some disagreement about the current state of the business cycle. A requirement to balance the budget over the business cycle can only be implemented on the basis of some forecast of future economic conditions. Forecasting of the level of economic activity is imperfect, to say the least, and there will be genuine disagreement among economists about what stage of the business cycle the economy is in and where the economy is headed. Compounding the difficulty that rises from such uncertainty is the fact that politicians will have a stake in the economic forecast. Those who favour increased government spending will tend to argue that *this* year is an unusually bad one, and the deficits of this year can be made up by the surpluses in (better) years to come. On the other side, some will always tend to find this year to be unusually good, a time to run surpluses against the hard times to follow.

Though a budget balanced over the course of the business cycle is in principle an acceptable way of reconciling short-term stabilization and long-term prudence, the business cycle may not be well enough defined to make the proposal operational.

Allowing for growth. A further problem is that the goal of budget *balance*, whether applied annually or over the cycle, is in fact stricter than is required to avoid a rising debt-to-GDP ratio. Growth in GDP (due either to growth in real output or to inflation) means that some growth in the debt, and hence a (small) deficit, is consistent with a stable debt-to-GDP ratio.

For economists who think of a stable debt-to-GDP ratio as the appropriate indicator of fis-

Box 37-2

Debt, Deficits, and Sustainability

One way of checking whether concern about persistent government budget deficits is justified is to ask whether the current fiscal plan is *sustainable*. A sustainable fiscal plan is one that will not lead to unlimited growth in the debt-to-GDP ratio.

An unsustainable fiscal plan leads to a debt, and hence to interest payments, which are an ever-increasing fraction of GDP. If the current fiscal plan is unsustainable, the government will eventually have to introduce some fiscal correction; otherwise, its deficit would eventually absorb all of the tax revenues in interest payments on the debt.

To examine this issue more fully, we need to introduce a fundamental equation that describes the evolution of the debt-to-GDP ratio over time. To do this, we let B stand for the size of the government debt, Y for national income as measured by GDP, and b for the ratio of the two; that is, $b = B/Y$, the debt-to-GDP ratio. Next let b' stand for the change in the debt-to-GDP ratio over time. A positive value for b' means that the ratio is increasing, and a negative value for b' means that the ratio is decreasing.

Using basic calculus, b' can be expressed as the sum of the two terms on the right side of Equation 1.[45]

$$b' = (g-t) + (i-n)b$$

The first term on the right-hand side is called the *primary deficit* and it shows the difference between government program expenditure g and government tax revenue t, each measured as a fraction of GDP. The second term is the debt-to-GDP ratio b multiplied by the difference between the interest rate i and the rate of growth of GDP, n.

To see the role of these two terms, we consider each in isolation. First, suppose that the primary deficit is zero (i.e., that $g = t$); the equation shows that in this case, the change in the debt-to-GDP ratio is equal to the term $(i-n)b$. This tells us that there are two competing pressures on b'. Interest payments (ib) have to be financed by issuing new debt, so there is upward pressure of this amount on b. This tends to make b' positive. However, since we are concerned with the ratio of debt to GDP, growth in GDP serves to reduce the ratio; this term ($-nb$) puts downward pressure on the ratio and hence tends to make b' negative. Thus, whether the ratio rises or falls (that is, whether b' is positive or negative) depends on whether the interest rate i is greater than or less than the growth rate n.

Now suppose that the interest rate i is just equal to the growth rate n. This makes the second term in the equation zero, so the change in the ratio is equal to $g-t$. Now we see that a primary deficit (program spending, g, greater than tax revenue, t) will cause the debt-to-GDP ratio to rise over time (b' positive), since financing the primary deficit requires that more debt be issued. A primary surplus (g less than t) means that the government can gradually retire debt, and thus the debt-to-GDP ratio will fall over time (b' negative).

We can now examine the conditions that must be satisfied if the "deficit" is to be sustainable. There are two cases, depending on the relation between the interest rate, i, and the growth rate, n.

First, consider the case where the interest rate i is less than the growth rate n. In this case, even if there is a primary deficit (g greater than t) that makes b' positive, the ratio will eventually stabilize, since b' will eventually turn down. Initially, the primary deficit, the $g-t$ term, will cause the debt-to-GDP ratio b to grow. However, this growth in b

increases the weight given to the second term in the equation, which is negative. As this second term grows in absolute size, the rate at which the debt grows, given by b', falls. Eventually, b' will reach zero, and hence the ratio b will be constant.*

Second, consider the case where the interest rate, i, is greater than the growth rate, n. In this case, the second term in the equation is positive. For b' to be zero in this case requires a primary surplus, so that the negative value of $g - t$ offsets the positive value of $(i - n)b$.

A further difficulty arises in this second case because it involves an inherent instability. Any increase in b, say, due to a temporary primary budget deficit, will tend to make b' positive and thus cause further increases in b. This is because the initial rise in b increases the weight given to the second term in the equation (where the interest payment effect, ib, outweighs the growth effect, nb.) In order to limit this self-reinforcing and potentially explosive effect, the government would have to undertake discretionary fiscal actions to create a primary surplus, so that the negative effects of the first term again offset the positive effects of the second term.

In its budgets and other public documents throughout the late 1980s and early 1990s, the Canadian government repeatedly focused on the implications of current and projected fiscal measures for the evolution of the debt-to-GDP ratio. The April 1989 budget, for example, stated explicitly, "The focus of the government's fiscal strategy is to

stabilize and then reduce the size of the federal debt relative to GDP." In terms of the equation, this means lowering b' first to zero and then to below zero.

The government also noted that this objective had been difficult to achieve, since the interest rate had exceeded the economy's growth rate in every year since 1981 (i.e., the second term in the equation was positive). Early in the decade, there had also been a significant primary deficit (i.e., the first term in the equation was also positive), and as a result the debt-to-GDP ratio grew rapidly. A key part of the government's fiscal strategy was to reduce the primary deficit, and it fell from a peak of 5 percent in 1984 to a position of balance by 1988 and in 1989 turned to a surplus where it has remained since then. However, the debt-to-GDP ratio continued to grow, since the positive effect of the interest-growth differential (the second term) outweighed the negative effect of the primary surplus (the first term). Had the 1989-1990 primary surplus been attained earlier in the decade, when the debt was a smaller fraction of GDP, the debt ratio would have started to fall some time ago.

The government's strategy to halt the growth in the debt ratio relied on three developments. First, the primary surplus had to be increased further. Second, as the strategy started to work and the growth in the debt ratio slowed, it was hoped that interest rates would fall. Third, the government projected increased economic growth as a result of some of its policies, such as free trade with the United States, deregulation, and privatization, and the replacement of the manufacturer's sales tax with the GST. (The hoped-for rise in n would serve to reduce the magnitude of the second term in the equation.

The value at which b will be stabilized is found by setting $b' = 0$ in the equation, and then solving for b. This particular value, which we label $b*$, is given by $b = -(g - t)/(i - n)$. If i and n can be taken as given, the government can choose the "steady state" debt ratio $b*$ by choosing the appropriate value of $g - t$.

cal prudence, *budget balance* means a deficit such that the debt grows at the same rate as nominal GDP.

Debt Reduction

When the Progressive Conservatives formed the government in 1984, they made reduction of the large and growing budget deficit a major policy commitment. The main objective of the government's fiscal plan was first to stabilize the debt-to-GDP ratio at a level below 60 percent and then to have the ratio slowly fall to a lower level. Although the budget deficits were not reduced as much as had been hoped, they were stabilized in the neighbourhood of $30 billion per year. The continued growth of the GDP held the federal debt-to-GDP ratio at just below 60 percent, although total federal and provincial debt continued to rise through 1993. Box 37-2 discusses the conditions under which the debt-to-GDP ratio can be stabilized and the conditions under which it will grow without limit.

The existing combined federal-provincial debt-to-GDP ratio of close to 90 percent was generally believed to be too large. It means, among other things, that government revenues are heavily committed to paying interest on the national debt and that there is little room for new fiscal initiatives. A large debt also makes the deficit highly sensitive to swings in the interest rate.

Many critics called for much larger reductions in the budget deficit. However, as long as the rate of growth of the debt could be held below the rate of growth of GDP, the crucial debt-to-GDP ratio would fall. This would reduce the burden of the debt as measured by the proportion of national income needed to be raised in taxes just to service that debt.

Evaluation. In a study written for the Macdonald Commission in the mid-1980s, Professors Neil Bruce and Douglas Purvis, then of Queen's University, addressed the issue of fiscal prudence by evaluating the government's medium-term fiscal plan.

Bruce and Purvis defined the *imprudent deficit* as the part of projected deficits that contributes to growth in the debt-to-GDP ratio above some target level. Thus, they allow for trend growth in the economy and for projected inflation. Their calculation showed the imprudent deficit to be significant. They concluded that there was cause for concern

about the long-term implications of projected deficits and that some concerted but systematic phasing in of budget cuts was in order. Further, they argued that even though the actual cuts could be implemented gradually, the process had to be started quickly, so that the programs for reestablishing fiscal prudence would be flexible enough that the short-term objectives of fiscal stabilization need not be abandoned. Their advice was not followed, and neither the federal nor the provincial governments were in a position to operate fiscal stabilization during the deep recession of 1990-1992.

The need for fiscal prudence is accepted by virtually everyone. How to evaluate it and enforce it, however, is still subject to controversy. Indeed, there is serious doubt that the idea of a balanced budget over any time period is operational.

Many economists believe that a superior alternative to insisting on a precise balance is to pay attention to the balance without making a fetish of never adding to the national debt.

The Political Economy of the Debt

Almost all economists accept that if the debt got so large that it could not be serviced without either putting a crushing burden on taxpayers or forcing the government to create new money to service it, there would be serious problems. But some think we are still a long way from that point. To them, the overriding principle is that the debt should be allowed to vary according to the needs of stabilization policy.

An alternative view is what has come to be called *fiscal conservatism*. The main premise of fiscal conservatives is that governments are not passive agents who do what is necessary to create full employment and maximize social welfare. Instead, governments are composed of individuals—elected officials, legislators, and civil servants—who, like everyone else, seek mainly to maximize their own well-being. Their welfare is best served by a big role for government and by a satisfied electorate. Thus, they tend to favour spending and to resist tax increases. This creates a persistent tendency toward deficits that is quite independent of any consideration of a sound fiscal policy.

The debate reflects deeply held views about the role of government, the nature and motivation of public officials, and the desirability of stabilization. Keynesians are more likely to emphasize the potential benefits from active fiscal policy and to regard substantial government intervention as essential to an effective and humane society. Fiscal conservatives are likely to see public intervention, however well motivated, as probably inept and ultimately destabilizing.

The deficits of the past decade have also received enough public attention so that the majority of both Keynesians and fiscal conservatives consistently argue that the deficit must be reduced. In spite of the fact that deficit reduction is politically uncontroversial in principle, it has proved very difficult to effect in practise. This is not entirely surprising. As we have seen, most of the harm that will arise from deficits will only appear over the very long term, in the form of reduced living standards in the future. To do something about deficits, politicians must raise taxes and cut spending today, imposing real costs on today's voters, when the uncertain benefits of those actions will only be reaped in the relatively distant future.

SUMMARY

1. The recent record of persistent, large government budget deficits has attracted enormous attention and generated heated debate over the policy options. In order to put the growth of the deficit in perspective, it is useful to measure it relative to GDP. After roughly balancing, on average, for the 1960s and early 1970s, the government budget deficit rose from less than 1 percent of GDP at the start of the decade to over 6 percent in 1984 and remained high through the remainder of the 1980s and early 1990s.

2. Deficits influence the economy through their short-run stabilizing or destabilizing role and through their potential to affect income and welfare adversely in the long run. The latter effects arise from the build-up of the debt-to-GDP ratio.

3. Over the decades, Canadian national debt and debt service payments have risen and fallen as a percentage of national income, but since the mid-1970s, they have shown an upward trend. Recent increases in these ratios reflect the cumulative effects of persistently large federal deficits dating back to the mid-1970s and provincial deficits since the mid-1980s. Persistent deficits are a cause for concern for several reasons, including inflation, crowding out of investment and net exports, and reducing national income in the long run.

4. An annually balanced budget would be unfeasible; even if it were possible, it would destabilize the economy. A cyclically balanced budget would act as a stabilizer and would also curb the growth of the government sector.

5. In a growing economy, the concept of budget balance allows for a small but positive deficit, such that the stock of debt grows at the same rate as nominal GDP.

6. Keynesians tend to take a relatively sanguine view of the effect of active fiscal policy on the national debt. As long as the national debt does not grow rapidly as a proportion of national income, they view its short-term fluctuations as a stabilizing device and its long-term upward trend as a reasonable price to pay for economic stability.

7. Fiscal conservatives mistrust government and view insistence on a balanced budget as the only effective means of curtailing reckless government spending that wastes scarce resources and feeds the fires of inflation.

TOPICS FOR REVIEW

Short-run and long-run effects of deficits

The relationship between deficits and the national debt

Debt service payments

Debt-to-GDP ratio

Cyclically balanced budget

Keynesian and fiscal conservative views of debt

DISCUSSION QUESTIONS

1. In 1990, the Canadian economy slid into a recession, while the deficit and, in particular, debt service payments continued at record levels. The first development led many people to call for fiscal stimulus, while the second development led to calls for fiscal restraint. Write a brief analysis of the bases for these competing views; then review the record to see what was actually done and why.

2. In the light of federal and provincial fiscal policies since the Federal election of October 1993, discuss the following summary of a workshop on Canada's fiscal outlook held by the C. D. Howe Institute in January 1993.

    ". . . Canada is fast approaching a crisis point, where continued heavy borrowing may not be possible. . . . The problem's low position on the public and political agenda prompted considerable pessimism about whether it would be addressed in time.

    The group canvassed a variety of options for redressing the fiscal balances of Canadian governments, ranging from elimination of overlap to wholesale cuts in transfers. There was little support for major tax increases. . . .

    One message, however, emerged clearly from the workshop. The damage to Canadians' living standards of a fiscal retrenchment forced by an abrupt end to investors' willingness to buy Canadian debt would be far greater than that of a timely, controlled budget-balancing process. It has never been more urgent for Canadian governments to act vigorously in addressing this serious—and seriously neglected—problem."

3. Evaluate each of the following proposals to "control the deficit" in order to avoid the long-run burden of the debt.
    a. Maintaining a zero cyclically adjusted deficit.
    b. Keeping the debt-to-GDP ratio constant.
    c. Limiting government borrowing in each year to some fixed percentage of national income in that year.

4. Judith Maxwell, former chairperson of the now disbanded Economic Council of Canada, warned in 1991 that "when interest rates are higher than the economic growth rate, the ratio of debt to GDP acquires dangerous upward momentum." Discuss why this is so. Does the current Canadian situation reflect this combination?

5. What problems for budgetary control are posed by the fact that economic forecasting is imperfect? How might these problems be minimized?

6. How does the decision of whether to raise taxes or issue bonds in order to finance the unusually high government expenditures incurred during a war influence who pays for the war?

7. In 1993, John Crow, governor of the Bank of Canada, expressed concern about the persistent government deficit and the growing level of debt in the economy. Why should this concern him?

8. In 1989, the U.S. Congressional Budget Office director, Robert Reischaner, said: "We have a long way to go before the [government budget] deficit is brought down to a level where Americans should feel comfortable." Arguing that the borrowing caused by the deficit erodes living standards for future generations, "How well do you want your children and grandchildren to live?" he asked. Write a critique either supporting or challenging Reischaner's views.

9. What will well-informed taxpayers do in each of the following four situations after the government decides to spend an additional sum for one period?

   a. Both the government and the taxpayers wish to pay now.

   b. Both wish to postpone payment.

   c. The government wishes to postpone but taxpayers want to pay now.

   d. The government wants to pay now but taxpayers wish to postpone payment.

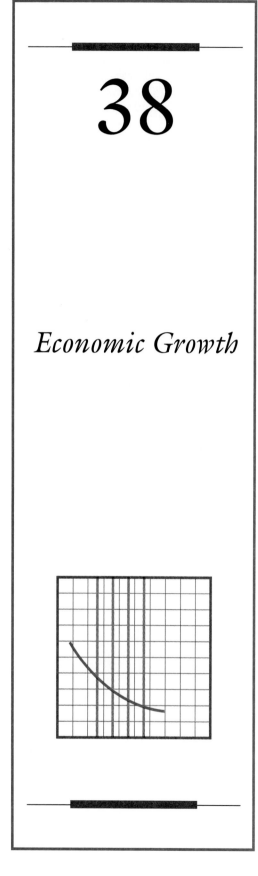

38

Economic Growth

E conomic growth is the single most powerful engine for generating long-term increases in living standards. What happens to our material living standards over time depends primarily on the growth in national income (as measured, for example, by the GDP) in relation to the growth in population.

The Nature of Economic Growth

We saw in Chapter 1 that in the first 7 decades of the twentieth century, per capita GDP rose steadily, while its distribution became somewhat less unequal. As a result, most Canadians became materially better off decade by decade, and children were typically substantially better off than their parents had been at the same age. In the 1970s, however, the engine of growth faltered. Growth rates of GDP fell, and the distribution of income stopped becoming less unequal. As a result, the real incomes of many Canadian families remained relatively constant. Although they still live in one of the richest societies in all of human history, many spoke of the end of the North American dream that each generation could expect to be much better off than its predecessors. The change in attitudes and perceptions brought about in the minds of ordinary middle-class citizens by the mere slowdown of rapid growth shows how important was the part that steady growth had played in people's minds, hearts, and dreams over the decsades.

Shifts in Aggregate Demand and Aggregate Supply

In earlier chapters, we outlined the effects of shifts in aggregate demand and aggregate supply. Economic growth concerns sustained shifts in aggregate supply; hence, many of the points made in earlier chapters in the context of one-time shifts bear repeating in this new context.

Figure 38-1, which is similar to Figure 31-6 on page 638, illustrates some important causes of rising national income.[1] If there is a recessionary gap, policies that increase aggregate demand will yield a once-and-for-all increase in national income. Once potential income is achieved, however, further increases in aggregate demand yield only transitory increases in real income but lasting increases in the price level.

---

[1]The figures are not identical because they emphasize slightly different points.

FIGURE 38-1
Ways of Increasing National Income

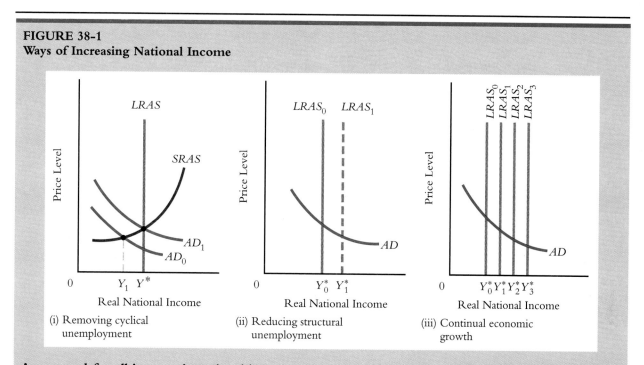

A once-and-for-all increase in national income can be obtained by raising aggregate demand to remove a recessionary gap or by shifting the *LRAS* curve, say, by cutting structural unemployment. Continual increases in national income are possible through continued economic growth, which shifts the *LRAS* curve. In part (i), with the aggregate demand curve at AD_0, there is a recessionary gap of $Y_1 Y*$. An increase in aggregate demand from AD_0 to AD_1 achieves a once-and-for-all increase in national income from Y_1 to $Y*$.

In part (ii), potential output rises from Y_0* to Y_1* due to measures that reduce structural unemployment. The *LRAS* curve shifts from $LRAS_0$ to $LRAS_1$ because people who were formerly unemployed due to having the wrong skills or being in the wrong place are now better suited for employment.

In part (iii), increases in factor supplies and productivity lead to increases in potential income. This *continually* shifts the long-run aggregate supply curve outward. In successive periods, it moves from $LRAS_0$ to $LRAS_3$, taking potential income from Y_0* to Y_1* to Y_2*, and so on, as long as growth continues.

Policies that reduce structural unemployment can also increase the employed labour force and thus increase potential income. The resulting increase in income might not be very large, but social benefits would result from the reduction in unemployment, especially in the long-term unemployment that occurs when people are trapped in declining areas, industries, or occupations. The increase, however, is once-and-for-all, as the total number of unemployed falls to a new, lower level. Similar results come from measures that increase economic efficiency. A once-and-for-all increase in potential output occurs as a given employed labour force works more efficiently.

Over the long haul, the main cause of rising national income is *economic growth*—the increase in po-

tential income due to changes in factor supplies (labour and capital) and in the productivity of factors (output per unit of factor input). As we observed in Chapter 31, the removal of a serious recessionary gap or the elimination of all structural unemployment might cause a once-and-for-all increase in national income by, at the very most, 6 percent. However, a growth rate of 3 percent per year raises national income by 6 percent in 2 years and *doubles* it in about 24 years and quadruples it in 48 years. Even a 1 percent growth rate doubles income over one normal lifetime of about 70 years.

Growth is a much more powerful method of raising living standards than is the removal of recessionary gaps, structural unemployment,

TABLE 38-1   The Cumulative Effect of Growth

| Year | Rate of growth per year | | | | |
	1%	2%	3%	5%	7%
0	100	100	100	100	100
10	110	122	135	165	201
30	135	182	246	448	817
50	165	272	448	1,218	3,312
70	201	406	817	3,312	13,429
100	272	739	2,009	14,841	109,660

Small differences in growth rates make enormous differences in levels of potential national income over a few decades. Let potential national income be 100 in year 0. At a rate of growth of 3 percent per year, it will be 135 in 10 years, 448 after 50 years, and over 2,000 in a century. The compounding of sustained rates of growth is a powerful force!

or inefficiencies, *because growth can go on indefinitely.*

Table 38-1 illustrates the cumulative effect of what seem to be very small differences in growth rates. Notice that if one country grows faster than another, the gap in their respective living standards will widen progressively. If, for example, countries A and B start from the same level of income and if country A grows at 3 percent per year while country B grows at 2 percent per year, A's per capita income will be twice B's in 72 years. You may not think that it matters much whether the economy grows at 2 percent or 3 percent per year, but your children and grandchildren will! **[41]**

Economic Growth, Efficiency, and Redistribution

Observing that economic growth is the most important force for raising living standards over the long term in no way implies that policies designed to increase economic efficiency or to redistribute income are unimportant.

Reducing inefficiency. If, at any moment in time, national income could be increased by removing

certain inefficiencies, such gains would be valuable. After all, any increase in national income is welcome in a world where many wants go unsatisfied. Furthermore, inefficiencies may themselves serve to reduce the growth rate. For example, the supply management policies that raise the prices of poultry and eggs, which can be criticised for violating efficiency conditions in the food market, can also be criticised for hurting the international competitiveness of canned food industries by raising the cost of some of their major inputs.

Redistribution. Economic growth has made the poor vastly better off than they would have been if they had lived 100 years ago. Yet that is little consolation when they see that they cannot afford many things that are currently available to citizens with higher incomes. After all, people compare themselves with others in their own society, not with their counterparts at other times or in other places. Because many people care about relative differences among individuals, governments continue to have policies to redistribute income and to make such basic services as education and hospital care available to everyone, at least to some minimum acceptable standard.

Interrelations among the goals. Economists once assumed that the goals of redistributing income, increasing efficiency, and ensuring growth could each be treated independently of each other. It is now understood that distribution, efficiency, and growth are interrelated. For example, policies that create extreme inefficiencies or a distribution of income unrelated to the market value of work can adversely affect the growth rate. It follows that policies designed to reduce inefficiencies or redistribute income need to be examined carefully for any effects that they may have on growth, while policies designed to affect growth need to be examined for their effects on economic efficiency and income distribution. A policy that reduces growth *may* be a bad bargain, even if it increases the immediate efficiency of the economy or creates a more equitable distribution of income.

Consider a hypothetical redistributive policy that raises the share of GDP going to poorer people by 5 percent but lowers the rate of economic growth from 2 to 1 percent. In 10 years, those who gained from the policy would be no better off than if they had not received the redistribution of income while the growth rate had remained at 2 percent (and, of course, everyone who did not gain from the redistribution would be worse off). After 20 years, those who had gained from the redistribution would have 5 percent more of a national income that was 12 percent smaller than it would have been if the growth rate had remained at 2 percent.

Conversely, a policy that creates a more equitable distribution of income at only a small cost in terms of a lower growth rate may be judged an acceptable tradeoff. Deciding among such competing policy goals requires value judgements that take us beyond economics. Economists play an important part, however, in establishing these interrelationships. Misguided policies are likely to be followed if policy makers think that measures adopted to get closer to any one of these goals will have no effect on the others.

Of course, not all redistribution policies have unfavourable effects on the growth rate. Some may have no effect, and others—by raising the health and educational standards of ordinary workers—may raise the growth rate.

Saving, Investment, and Growth

Both saving and investment affect real national income. To understand their influence, it is critical to distinguish between their short-run and long-run effects.

Short-Run and Long-Run Effects of Investment

The theory of income determination that we studied in Part 8 is a short-run theory. It takes potential income as constant and concentrates on the effects of shifts in aggregate demand brought about by changes in various types of expenditure, including investment. These shifts cause actual national income to fluctuate around a given potential income. This short-term viewpoint is the focus of Figure 38-1(i).

In the long run, by adding to the nation's capital stock, investment raises potential income. This effect is shown by the continuing shift of the *LRAS* curve in Figure 38-1(iii).

The theory of economic growth is a long-run theory. It concentrates on the effects of investment in raising potential national income and ignores short-run fluctuations of actual national income around potential income.

The contrast between the short- and long-run aspects of investment is worth emphasizing. In the short run, any activity that puts income into people's hands will raise aggregate demand. Thus, the short-run effect on national income is the same whether a firm "invests" in digging holes and refilling them or in building a new factory. The long-run growth of potential income, however, is affected only by the part of investment that adds to a nation's productive capacity, that is, by the factory but not by the refilled hole.

Similar observations hold for public-sector expenditure. Any expenditure will add to aggregate demand and raise national income if there are unemployed resources, but only some expenditures increase potential income. Although public investment expenditure on such things as roads and health may increase potential national income, expenditure that shores up a declining industry in order to create employment may have an adverse effect on growth of potential income. The latter expenditure may prevent the reallocation of resources in response to shifts both in the pattern of world demand and in the country's comparative advantage. Thus, in the long run, the country's capacity to produce commodities that are demanded on world markets may be diminished.

Short-Run and Long-Run Effects of Saving

The short-run effect of an increase in saving is to reduce aggregate demand. If, for example, households elect to save more, then they spend less. The resulting downward shift in the consumption function lowers aggregate demand and thus lowers equilibrium national income.

In the longer term, however, higher savings are necessary for higher investment. Firms usually reinvest their own savings, and the savings of households pass to firms, either directly through the purchase of stocks and bonds or indirectly through financial intermediaries. In the long run, the higher the level of savings, the higher the level of investment—and, due to the accumulation of more and better capital equipment, the higher the level of investment, the higher the level of real income. A high-saving economy accumulates assets faster, and thus grows faster, than does a low-saving economy.

In the long run, there is no paradox of thrift; societies with high savings rates have high investment rates and, other things being equal, high growth rates of real income.

Benefits and Costs of Growth

We start by looking at the benefits of growth, and then we consider the costs. Boxes 38-1 and 38-2 outline some of the popular arguments on both sides of the growth debate.

Benefits of Growth

Growth and Living Standards

We have already observed that in the long term, economic growth is the primary engine for raising general living standards. For those who share in it, growth is a powerful weapon against poverty. A family that is earning $25,000 today can expect an income of about $30,500 within 10 years (in constant dollars) if it shares in a 2 percent growth rate, and $37,000 if that rate is 4 percent.

The transformation of the lifestyle of ordinary workers in advanced industrial nations, including Canada, between 1870 and 1970 provides a notable example of the escape from poverty that growth makes possible. Much of the concern today over economic problems facing Canadian families stems from the decline of growth that occurred after 1970. Partly because growth has slowed and partly because the distribution of income has changed unfavourably to them, the incomes of the many working families have remained nearly constant over the last two decades.

Growth and Income Redistribution

Not everyone benefits equally from growth. Many of the poorest are not even in the labour force and thus are unlikely to share in the higher wages that, along with profits, are the primary means by which the gains from growth are distributed. For this reason, even in a growing economy, redistribution policies will be needed if poverty is to be averted.

A rapid growth rate makes the alleviation of poverty easier politically. If existing income is to be redistributed, someone's standard of living will actually have to be lowered. However, when there is economic growth and when the increment in income is redistributed (through government intervention), it is possible to reduce income inequalities without actually having to lower anyone's income. It is much easier for a rapidly growing economy to be generous toward its less fortunate citizens—or neighbours—than it is for a static economy.

Growth and Life Style

A family often finds that a big increase in its income can lead to a major change in the pattern of its consumption—that extra money buys important amenities of life. In the same way, the members of society as a whole may change their consumption patterns as their average income rises. Not only do markets in a country that is growing rapidly make it profitable to produce more cars, but also the government is led to construct more highways and to provide more recreational areas for its newly affluent and mobile citizens. At yet a later stage, a concern about litter, pollution, and ugliness may become important, and their correction may then begin to account for a significant fraction of GDP. Such "amenities" usually become matters of social concern only when growth has ensured the provision of the basic requirements for food, clothing, and housing of a substantial majority of the population.

Costs of Growth

Other things being equal, most people would probably regard a fast rate of growth as preferable to a slow one, but other things are seldom equal.

The Opportunity Cost of Growth

In a world of scarcity, almost nothing is free. Growth requires heavy investments of resources in capital goods, as well as in activities such as education. Often these investments yield no immediate return in terms of goods and services for consumption; thus, they imply that sacrifices have been made by the current generation of consumers.

Growth, which promises more goods tomorrow, is achieved by consuming fewer goods today. For the economy as a whole, this sacri-

Box 38-1

An Open Letter to the Ordinary Citizen from a Supporter of the "Growth Is Good" School

Dear Ordinary Citizen:

You live in the world's first civilization that is devoted principally to satisfying *your* needs rather than those of a privileged minority. Past civilizations have always been based on leisure and high consumption for a tiny upper class, a reasonable living standard for a small middle class, and hard work with little more than subsistence consumption for the great mass of people.

The continuing Industrial Revolution is based on mass-produced goods for you, the ordinary citizen. It ushered in a period of sustained economic growth that has dramatically raised consumption standards of ordinary citizens. Reflect on a few examples: travel, live and recorded music, art, good food, inexpensive books, universal literacy, and a genuine chance to be educated. Most important, there is leisure to provide time and energy to enjoy these and thousands of other products of the modern industrial economy.

Would any ordinary family seriously prefer to go back to the world of 150 or 500 years ago in its same relative social and economic position? Surely the answer is no. However, for those with incomes in the top 1 or 2 percent of the income distribution, economic growth has destroyed much of their privileged consumption position. They must now vie with the masses when they visit the world's beauty spots and be annoyed, while lounging on the terrace of a palatial mansion, by the sound of charter flights carrying ordinary people to inexpensive holidays in far places. Many of the rich complain bitterly about the loss of exclusive rights to luxury consumption, and it is not surprising that they find their intellectual apologists. Whether they know it or not, the antigrowth economists are not the social revolutionaries that they think they are. They say that growth has produced pollution and wasteful consumption of all kinds of frivolous products that add nothing to human happiness. However, the democratic solution to pollution is not to go back to where so few people consume luxuries that pollution is trivial but rather to learn to control the pollution that mass consumption tends to create.

It is only through further growth that the average citizen can enjoy consumption standards (of travel, culture, medical and health care, etc.) now available only to people in the top 25 percent of the income distribution—which includes the intellectuals who earn large royalties from the books that they write in which they denounce growth. If you think that extra income confers little real benefit, just ask those in the top 25 percent to trade incomes with average citizens.

Ordinary citizens, do not be deceived by disguised elitist doctrines. Remember that the very rich and the elite have much to gain by stopping growth and even more by rolling it back, but you have everything to gain by letting it go forward.

Onward!

A. N. Optimist

---

fice of current consumption is the primary cost of growth.

An example will suggest the magnitude of this cost. Suppose that a hypothetical economy has full employment and is experiencing growth at the rate of 2 percent per year. Its citizens consume 85 percent of the GDP and invest 15 percent. They know that, if they immediately decrease their consumption to 77 percent of GDP, they will produce more

Box 38-2

An Open Letter to the Ordinary Citizen from a Supporter of the "Growth Is Bad" School

Dear Ordinary Citizen:

You live in a world that is being despoiled by a mindless search for ever-higher levels of material consumption at the cost of all other values. Once upon a time, men and women knew how to enjoy creative work and to derive satisfaction from simple activities. Today, the ordinary worker is a mindless cog in an assembly line that turns out more and more goods that the advertisers must work overtime to persuade the worker to consume.

Statisticians count the increasing flow of material output as a triumph of modern civilization. You arise from your electric-blanketed bed, clean your teeth with an electric toothbrush, open a can of the sad remnants of a once-proud orange with an electric can opener, and eat your bread baked from superrefined and chemically refortified flour; you climb into your car to sit in vast traffic jams on exhaust-polluted highways.

Television commercials tell you that by consuming more you are happier, but happiness lies not in increasing consumption but in increasing the ratio of *satisfaction of wants* to *total wants*. Since the more you consume, the more the advertisers persuade you that you want to consume, you are almost certainly less happy than the average citizen in a small town in 1900, whom we can visualize sitting on the family porch, sipping lemonade, and enjoying the antics of the children as they jump rope with pieces of old clothesline.

Today, the landscape is dotted with endless factories that produce the plastic trivia of the modern industrial society. They drown you in a cloud of noise, air, and water pollution. The countryside is despoiled by strip mines, petroleum refineries, acid rain, and dangerous nuclear power stations, producing energy that is devoured insatiably by modern factories and motor vehicles. Worse, our precious heritage of natural resources is being rapidly depleted.

Now is the time to stop this madness. We must stabilise production, reduce pollution, conserve our natural resources, and seek justice through a more equitable distribution of existing total income.

A long time ago, Malthus taught us that if we do not limit population voluntarily, nature will do it for us in a cruel and savage manner. Today, the same is true of output: If we do not halt its growth voluntarily, the halt will be imposed on us by a disastrous increase in pollution and a rapid exhaustion of natural resources.

Citizens, awake! Shake off the worship of growth, learn to enjoy the bounty that is yours already, and reject the endless, self-defeating search for increased happiness through ever-increasing consumption.

Upward!

I. Realvalues

capital and thus shift at once to a 3 percent growth rate. The new rate can be maintained as long as they keep saving and investing 23 percent of the national income. Should they do it?

Table 38-2 illustrates the choice in terms of time paths of consumption. Using the assumed figures, it takes 10 years for the actual amount of consumption to catch up to what it would have been had no reallocation been made. In the intervening 10 years, a good deal of consumption is lost, and the cumulative losses in consumption must be made up before society can really be said to have broken even. It takes an additional 9 years before total consumption over the whole period is as large is it

TABLE 38-2 The Opportunity Cost of Growth

Year	(1) Level of consumption at 2% growth rate	(2) Level of consumption at 3% growth rate	(3) Cumulative gain (loss) in consumption
0	85.0	77.0	(8.0)
1	86.7	79.3	(15.4)
2	88.5	81.8	(22.1)
3	90.3	84.2	(28.2)
4	92.1	86.8	(33.5)
5	93.9	89.5	(37.9)
6	95.8	92.9	(40.8)
7	97.8	95.0	(43.6)
8	99.7	97.9	(45.4)
9	101.8	100.9	(46.3)
10	103.8	103.9	(46.2)
15	114.7	120.8	(28.6)
20	126.8	140.3	19.6
30	154.9	189.4	251.0
40	189.2	255.6	745.9

Transferring resources from consumption to investment goods lowers current income but raises future income. The example assumes that income in year zero is 100 and that consumption of 85 percent of national income is possible with a 2 percent growth rate. It is further assumed that to achieve a 3 percent growth rate, consumption must fall to 77 percent of income. A shift from column 1 to column 2 decreases consumption for 10 years but increases it thereafter. The cumulative effect on consumption is shown in column 3; the gains eventually become very large.

would have been if the economy had remained on the 2 percent path. **[42]**

Over a longer period, however, the payoff from the growth policy becomes enormous. Forty years on, the national income in the more rapidly growing economy is 35 percent higher than in the slower growing economy. The total difference in consumption over those 40 years has become three times the annual amount of consumption in the faster growing society at year 40.

Social and Personal Costs of Growth

A growing economy is a changing economy. Innovation renders some machines obsolete and also leaves some people partly obsolete. No matter how well trained workers are at age 25, in another 25 years many will find that their skills are at least partly obsolete. A rapid growth rate requires rapid adjustments, which can cause much upset and misery to the people who are affected by it.

It is often argued that costs of this kind are a small price to pay for the great benefits that growth can bring. Even if this is true in the aggregate, these personal costs are very unevenly borne. Indeed, many of those for whom growth is most costly (in terms of lost jobs) share least in the fruits that growth brings.

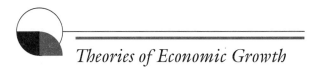

Theories of Economic Growth

In this section, we study some of the new theories that seek to explain economic growth. This is an exciting area. Ideas are changing rapidly as research of both a theoretical and an empirical nature expands our knowledge of the growth process.

Research suggests that four of the most important determinants of growth of total output are:

1. *Growth in the labour force* such as occurs when the population grows or participation rates[2] rise
2. *Investment in human capital* such as comes from formal education and on-the-job experience
3. *Investment in physical capital* such as factories, machines, and transportation and communication facilities
4. *Technological change* brought about by innovation that introduces new products, new ways of producing existing products, and new forms of business organization

The Aggregate Production Function

To study how these four forces operate, we first write a simple expression for the relation between the total amounts of labour (L) and capital (K) employed and the nation's total output, its GDP:

$$GDP = f(L, K)$$

---

[2]Recall that the participation rate is the proportion of the total population that is in the labour force.

This is called the **aggregate production function.** It is aggregate because it relates the economy's total output, its GDP, to the total amount of the two main factors that are used to produce that output.[3] (A micro-production function, such as is discussed in Chapters 10 and 11, relates the output of one firm or one industry to the factors of production employed by that firm or industry.) The function, indicated by the letter *f*, shows the relation between the inputs of *L* and *K* and the output of GDP. The production function tells us how much GDP will be produced for given amounts of labour and capital employed. For example, the function may tell us that when 200 million units of labour and 300 million units of capital are used, the GDP will be 2,450 million. **[43]**

We may now use this aggregate production function to discuss some theories of economic growth.

---

[3]Basic growth theory emphasizes the production of manufactured goods and services where, in contrast to agriculture, land is rarely a limiting factor. All the relatively small amounts of land that are needed can be obtained and, hence, nothing significant is lost by ignoring land in the analysis of an industrialised economy—although this could not be done for an agricultural economy.

Neoclassical Growth Theory

One branch of neoclassical theory deals with growth when the stock of technological knowledge remains unchanged. There are no innovations: no new ways of making things and no new products. As a result, the relation between inputs and output, as shown by the production function, does not change. The key aspects of what is called the neoclassical model are that the aggregate production function displays *decreasing returns* when either factor is increased on its own, and *constant returns* when both factors are increased together (and in the same proportion).

Decreasing Returns to a Single Factor

To start with, suppose that the population of the country grows while the stock of capital remains constant. More and more people go to work using a fixed quantity of capital. The amount that each new unit of input adds to total output is called its *marginal product*. The operation of the famous **law of diminishing returns** tells us that the employment of equal additional amounts of labour will eventually add less to total output than the previous unit. In other words, sooner or later each additional unit of labour will encounter a diminishing marginal product. Table 38-3 and Figure 38-2 illustrate this

---

TABLE 38-3   Diminishing Returns Illustrated

(1) Units of fixed factor	(2) Units of variable factor	(3) Units of total output	Average product of labour (column 3 ÷ column 2)	Marginal product of labour (change in column 3)
9	1	12.0	12.0	12.0
9	2	17.0	8.5	5.0
9	3	20.8	6.9	3.8
9	4	24.0	6.0	3.2
9	5	26.8	5.4	2.8
9	6	29.4	4.9	2.6
9	7	31.9	4.6	2.5
9	8	34.0	4.2	2.1
9	9	36.0	4.0	2.0
9	10	37.9	3.8	1.9

With one input held constant, the marginal and average products of the variable input eventually decline. Column 3 shows total output as more and more of the variable factor is used in combination with a fixed quantity of a fixed factor. **[44]** The average product, which is total product divided by the number of units of the variable factor, declines continuously. The marginal product, which is the increase in total product as successive units of the variable factor are added, also declines continuously.

Constant Returns to Scale

The other main property of the neoclassical aggregate production function is called **constant returns to scale**. This rule says that if the amounts of both labour and capital are both changed in equal proportion, the total output will also change in that proportion. For example, 10 percent increases in the amounts of both labour and capital used will lead to a 10 percent increase in GDP.

Sources of Growth in the Neoclassical Model

Now consider each of the sources of growth listed above. To begin with, we let each source operate with the others held constant.

Labour force growth. In the long term, we can associate labour force growth with population growth (although in the short term, the labour force can grow if participation rates rise even though the population remains constant). As more labour is used, there will be more output and, consequently, growth in total GDP. The law of diminishing returns tells us that, sooner or later, each further unit of labour to be employed will cause smaller and smaller additions to GDP. Eventually, not only will the marginal product of labour be falling, but the average product will fall as well. Beyond that point, although economic growth continues in the sense that total output is growing, living standards are falling in the sense that average GDP per head of population is falling. If we are interested in growth in living standards, we are concerned with increasing GDP *per person*. Whenever diminishing average returns applies, increases in population on their own are accompanied by falling living standards.[5]

Human capital. Capital often means physical capital, the plants and equipment that embody current technological knowledge. Another kind of capital is also of great importance to the growth process. This is human capital, the knowledge and skills embodied in people.

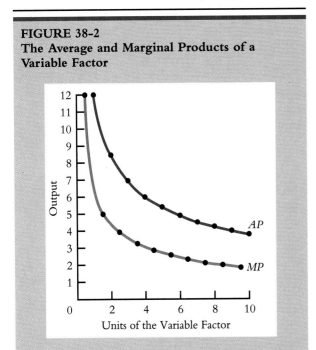

FIGURE 38-2
The Average and Marginal Products of a Variable Factor

The average and marginal products of any variable factor decline as successive units of that factor are added to a fixed amount of another factor. This figure plots the data from Table 38-3. It shows the marginal and average products of the variable factor declining as more and more units of that factor are used. The marginal products are plotted between the units of the variable factor, since they apply to a change from one amount to the next.

---

famous relation, which is referred to as *diminishing returns to a single factor.*

The law of diminishing returns applies to any factor that is varied while the other factors are held constant. Thus, successive amounts of capital added to *a fixed supply of labour* will also eventually add less and less to GDP.

According to the law of diminishing returns, the increment to total production will eventually fall steadily whenever equal increases of a variable factor of production are combined with another factor of production whose quantity is fixed.[4]

---

[4]In some production functions, marginal product may rise at first and only begin to decline after a certain critical amount of the variable factor is used. In the neoclassical, constant-returns functions, however, marginal product declines from the outset, as shown in the figures.

[5]In the neoclassical model, diminishing returns sets in from the outset, so that there is no range over which population increases cause rising marginal or average product of labour. The issue of when diminishing returns sets in need not concern us here, since all that matters for the text discussion is that increases in any one factor, other things held constant, must encounter diminishing returns sooner or later.

Human capital has several aspects. One involves improvements in the health and longevity of the population. Of course, these are desired as ends in themselves, but they also have consequences for both the size and the productivity of the labour force. There is no doubt that improvements in the health of workers have increased productivity per worker-hour by cutting down on illness, accidents, and absenteeism.

A second aspect of the quality of human capital concerns technical training—from learning to operate a machine to learning how to be a scientist. This training depends on the current state of knowledge, and advances in knowledge allow us not only to build more productive physical capital but also to create more effective human capital. Training is clearly required if a person is to operate, repair, manage, or invent complex machines. More subtly, there may be general social advantages to an educated population. Productivity improves with literacy. The longer a person has been educated, the more adaptable, and thus the more productive in the long run, that person is in the face of new and changing challenges.

A third aspect of human capital is its contribution to growth and innovation. Not only can current human capital embody in people the best current technological knowledge, but, by training potential innovators, it leads to advances in our knowledge and hence contributes to growth.

Physical capital.   Increases in the amount of capital on their own affect GDP in a manner similar to population growth alone. Eventually, each successive unit of capital will add less to total output than each previous unit of capital.

There is, however, a major contrast with the case of labour growth, because it is output per person that determines living standards, not output per unit of capital. Thus, as capital increases, living standards increase, because output is rising while the population is constant. Indeed, per capita output can be increased by adding more capital as long as its marginal product exceeds zero. However, since the increases in output are subject to diminishing returns, successive additions to the economy's capital stock bring smaller and smaller increases in per capita output.

In the neoclassical model, the operation of diminishing returns means that capital accumulation on its own brings smaller and smaller increases in per capita GDP.

Balanced growth.   Now consider what happens if labour and capital grow at the same rate. In this case, the neoclassical assumption of constant returns to scale means that GDP grows in proportion to the increases in inputs. As a result, per capita output (GDP/L) remains constant. Thus, growth in labour and capital leads to growth in total GDP but unchanged per capita GDP.

This "balanced growth path" is not, however, the kind of growth that concerns those interested in living standards. It is just more of the same: larger and larger economies, with more capital and more labour doing exactly what the existing capital and the existing labour were already doing. There is nothing new.

Growth and living standards.   In this neoclassical model with constant technology, the only way for growth to add to living standards is for the per capita capital stock to increase. The law of diminishing returns dictates, however, that the rise in living standards brought about by successive equal increases in capital will inexorably diminish. Raising living standards becomes more and more difficult as capital accumulation continues.

The Solow Residual

In 1957 Robert Solow, who subsequently won the Nobel Prize in economics for his path-breaking work in growth and other fields of economics, decided to see what the data could tell him about the type of growth model we have just been discussing.

He took U.S. data from 1909 to 1949, using measures of the total labour force, the total capital stock, and GDP, and applied it to the neoclassical production function given earlier in this section.[6] He made two important discoveries.

First, only about half of the growth in *total GDP* could be accounted for by growth in the inputs of labour and capital. Second, less than 20 percent of the growth in *GDP per person employed* could be accounted for by the growth in the capital stock. The growth in GDP that could *not* be accounted for by increased use of capital and labour came to be called the *Solow residual.* It was assumed to be caused by technical change coming from innovation (although other influences on labour and capital not

---

[6]This was done by using standard statistical techniques to fit the production function to the data.

incorporated in Solow's measurements also turned out to have significant effects).

In the neoclassical model, technological change can be regarded as shifting the production function so that the same amount of labour and capital produce more GDP. This result is depicted in Figure 38-3 by rightward shifts in the *MP* curves of labour and capital: The same amount of input produces more output. **[45]**

Technological Change

New knowledge and inventions can contribute markedly to the growth of potential national income, even without capital accumulation. To illustrate this point, assume that the proportion of a society's resources that is devoted to the production of capital goods is just sufficient to replace capital as it wears out. Thus, if the old capital is merely replaced in the same form, the capital stock will be constant, and there will be no increase in the capacity to produce. However, if there is a growth of knowledge, so that, as old equipment wears out, it is replaced by different, more productive equipment, national income will be growing.

Increases in productive capacity that are created by installing new and better capital goods are called **embodied technical change.** The historical importance of embodied technical change is clear: The assembly line and automation transformed most manufacturing industries, the airplane revolutionized transportation, and electronic devices now dominate the information-technology industries. These innovations, plus less well-known but no less profound ones—for example, improvements in the strength of metals, the productivity of seeds, and the techniques for recovering basic raw materials from the ground—create new investment opportunities.

Less obvious but nonetheless important changes occur through **disembodied technical change,**

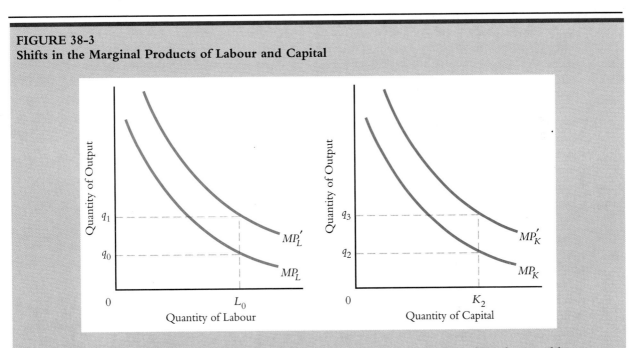

FIGURE 38-3
Shifts in the Marginal Products of Labour and Capital

Technological change shifts the marginal product curves such that each unit of the factor adds more to the total product than previously. The original marginal product curves are MP_L and MP_K. Technological change then alters the production function to allow any given amount of labour and capital to produce more. The marginal product of labour for a given amount of capital shifts to MP'_L. The marginal product of each unit of labour therefore rises. For example, whereas the unit L_0 previously had a marginal product of q_0, its marginal product is now q_1. Likewise, the marginal product curve of capital for a given amount of labour shifts from MP_K to MP'_K. Now each quantity of capital has a higher marginal product than it had previously. For example, the unit K_2, which formerly had a marginal product of q_2, now has a marginal product of q_3.

that is, changes in the organization of production that are not embodied in particular capital goods. Examples are improved techniques of management, design, marketing, organization of business activity, and feedback from user experience to product improvement.

Most innovations involve both embodied and disembodied changes. They cause continual changes in the techniques of production and in the nature of what is produced. Looking back over the past century, firms produce very few products today in the same way that they did in the past, and much of what is produced and consumed is in the form of new or vastly improved products. Major innovations of the twentieth century include the development of such key products as the telephone, television, the mass-produced automobile, the airplane, plastics, coaxial cable, xerography, the electron microscope, the computer, the transistor, and the silicon chip. It is hard for us to imagine life without them.

The modern understanding that technological innovation is at the heart of the growth process has led to two important developments in many economists' views on growth. The first is that technological change is largely endogenous to the economic system. The second is that investment that increases the capital stock may encounter increasing rather than diminishing returns. These insights have led to new growth theories that go far beyond the neoclassical growth model.

Endogenous Growth

In the neoclassical model, innovation shifts the production function but is itself unexplained (it is assumed to be measured by the unexplained residual—the amount of income growth that cannot be accounted for by anything else). This view holds that technological change is *exogenous*. It has profound effects on economic variables, such as GDP, but it is not influenced by economic causes. It just happens.

Yet microeconomic research by many scholars over the last several decades has established that technological change is responsive to such economic signals as prices and profits; in other words, it is *endogenous* to the economic system. Much of the earliest work on this issue was done in Europe by scholars associated with the Science Policy Research Unit (SPRU) in Sussex, England. The most influential overall single study, however, was by the American professor Nathan Rosenberg, whose path-breaking book *Inside the Black Box* argued this case in great detail.

Technological change stems from research and development and from innovating activities that put the results of R&D into practise. These are costly and highly risky activities, undertaken largely by firms and usually in pursuit of profit. Not surprisingly, these activities respond to economic incentives. If the price of some particular input such as petroleum or skilled labour goes up, R&D and innovating activities will work to alter the production function to economize on these inputs. This process is not a substitution of less expensive inputs for more expensive ones within the confines of known technologies; rather, it is the development of new technologies in response to changes in relative prices. Rosenberg shows, first, that R&D designed to apply known basic principles is responsive to economic signals, and, second, that *basic research* itself is responsive. One reason for the latter is that the basic research agenda is strongly influenced by practical issues of the day. For example, basic research in solid state physics became popular, and was heavily funded, only after the development of the transistor.

There are many important implications of this new understanding that, to a great extent, growth is achieved through costly, risky, innovative activity that occurs to a significant extent in response to economic signals. We will now discuss some of these implications.

The Complexity of the Innovation Process

The pioneering theorist of innovation, Joseph Schumpeter, developed a model in which innovation flowed in one direction, from a pure discovery "upstream," to more applied R&D, then to working machines, and finally to output "downstream."

In contrast, modern research shows that innovation involves a large amount of "learning by doing" at all of its stages.[7] What is learned "downstream" then modifies what must be done "upstream." The best innovation-managing systems encourage feedback from the more applied steps to the purer researchers and from users to designers.

---

[7]This phenomenon, whereby costs per unit of output fall steadily over time as firms learn how to manage new technologies, is discussed in more detail in Chapter 24.

This interaction is illustrated by the differences between the Japanese automobile manufacturers and their North American competitors in the handling of new models. North American design has traditionally been centralized: Design production teams develop the overall design and then instruct their production sections what to do, as well as asking for bids from parts manufacturers to produce according to specific blueprints. As a result, defects in the original design are often not discovered until production is under way, causing many costly delays and rejection of parts already supplied. Japanese firms involve their design and production departments and their parts manufacturers in all stages of the design process. Parts manufacturers are not given specific blueprints for production but, rather, are given general specifications and asked to develop their own detailed designs. As they do so, they learn. They then feed information about the problems they are encountering back to the main designers while the general outlines are not yet finalized. As a result, the Japanese usually design a new product faster, at less cost, and with far fewer problems when production is finally put into place.[8]

The Location of Innovation

Innovation typically takes place in different parts of the producer-user chain in different industries—as shown, for example, by the research of Eric von Hippel of MIT. In some industries, manufacturers make most of the product innovations. In other industries, users make most of them.

Unless these differences are appreciated, public policy designed to encourage innovation can go seriously astray. An example is provided by von Hippel in the following words:

> Consider the current concern of U.S. policymakers that the products of U.S. semiconductor process equipment firms are falling behind the leading edge. The conventional assessment of this problem is that these firms should somehow be strengthened and helped to innovate so that U.S. semiconductor equipment users (makers of semiconductors) will not also fall behind. But investigation shows that most process equipment innovations in this field are, in

fact, developed by equipment *users*. Therefore, the causality is probably reversed: U.S. equipment builders are falling behind because the U.S. user community they deal with is falling behind. If this is so, the policy prescription should change: Perhaps U.S. equipment builders can best be helped by helping U.S. equipment users to innovate at the leading edge once more.[9]

The message for policy makers is important: An understanding of the details of the innovating process in each industry is needed if successful innovation-encouraging policies are to be developed.

Costly Diffusion

The *diffusion* of technological knowledge from those who have it to those who want it is not costless (as it was assumed to be in Schumpeter's model). Firms need research capacity just to adopt the technologies developed by others. Some of the knowledge needed to use a new technology can only be learned through experience by plant managers, technicians, and operators (such knowledge is called *tacit*). We often tend to think that once a production process is developed, it can easily be copied by others. Indeed, some advanced economic theories use the hypothesis of replication, which holds that any known process can be replicated in any new location by using the same factor inputs and management as are used in the old location. In practise, however, the diffusion of new technological knowledge is not so simple.

For example, Richard Nelson of Columbia University and Sidney Winter of the General Accounting Office in Washington, D.C., have argued that most industrial technologies require technology-specific organizational skills that can be "embodied" neither in the machines themselves, nor in instruction books, nor in blueprints. Acquiring tacit knowledge requires a deliberate process of building up new skills, work practises, knowledge, and experience:

> As an initial perspective on the problem, we would not recommend the [hypothesis of replication] . . . but the following account from Polayni: ". . . even in modern industries the indefinable knowledge is still an essential part of technology. I have myself watched in Hungary a new, imported machine for blowing electric lamp bulbs, the exact counterpart of

---

[8] A detailed account of this issue can be found in James Womack, Daniel Jones, and Daniel Roos, *The Machine That Changed the World* (New York: Ransom Associates, 1990). North American firms have recently begun to adopt some of these Japanese practises.

[9] Eric von Hippel, *The Sources of Innovation* (New York: Oxford University Press, 1988), pp. 9-10.

which was operating successfully in Germany, failing for a whole year to produce a single flawless bulb[!]" . . . [T]he creation of productive organizations is *not* a matter of implementing fully explicit blueprints by purchasing homogeneous inputs on anonymous markets; a firm that is already successful in a given activity is a particularly good candidate for being successful with new capacity of the same sort.[10]

The fact that diffusion is a costly, risky, and time-consuming business explains why new technologies take considerable time to diffuse, first through the economy of the originating country and then through the rest of the world. If diffusion were simple and virtually costless, the puzzle would be why technological knowledge and best industrial practises did not diffuse very quickly. As it is, decades can pass before a new technological process is diffused everywhere that it could be employed.

Market Structure and Innovation

Because it is highly risky, innovation is encouraged by an environment in which there is strong rivalry and discouraged by monopoly practises. Rivalry among three or four large firms often produces much innovation, but a single firm, especially if it serves a secure home market protected by trade barriers, seems much less inclined to innovate.[11]

Government interventions that are designed to encourage innovation often allow the firms in an industry to work together as one. Unless great care is exercised, and unless sufficient foreign competition exists, the result may be a national monopoly that will discourage risk taking rather than encourage it, as is the intention of the policy.

The United Kingdom provides many examples of this mistaken view of policy. For example, British policy in the 1960s

operated under the faulty theory that encouraging British companies to merge would create world-class competitors. Consolidation of steel, automobiles, machine tools, and computers all led to notable failures. A program of research support for industry. . . proved disastrous. The British government tried to choose promising technologies and gave direct grants to firms to develop them. Most of the choices were failures. [In contrast]. . . unusually low levels of regulation in some service industries have avoided disadvantages faced by other nations and allowed innovation and change. . . in auctioneering. . . trading and insurance. British firms in these industries have been among the most innovative in the world.[12]

Culture and Innovation

Innovation is a highly risky business with results that are very hard to predict. One researcher called innovators "maniacs with a vision." In other words, although innovation does respond to economic incentives, it is not such a simple matter as calculating which of several established techniques to adopt when building a new factory. The nature of innovation may therefore be influenced by many forces, such as national character, religion, and the country's social attitude toward failure. For example, in English-speaking countries, a failure or two on the way to becoming a millionaire is usually taken to be one of the normal risks of business. In other countries, such as Germany and Japan, however, failure in business has serious adverse social consequences. As a result, the climate for new, start-up businesses seems to be more favourable in the United States than in Germany and Japan.

Shocks and Innovation

One interesting consequence of endogenous technical change is that shocks that would be unambiguously adverse to an economy operating with fixed technology can sometimes provide a spur to innovation that proves a blessing in disguise. A sharp rise

---

[10]Richard Nelson and Sidney Winter, *An Evolutionary Theory of Economic Change* (Cambridge, MA: Harvard University Press, 1982), p. 119.

[11]This is an important theme in much contemporary research, supported by evidence from such authors as Alfred D. Chandler, Jr. (*Scale and Scope: The Dynamics of Industrial Capitalism*, Cambridge, MA: Harvard University Press, 1990), David Mowrey and Nathan Rosenberg (*Technology and the Pursuit of Economic Growth*, Cambridge, England: Cambridge University Press, 1989), and Michael Porter (*The Competitive Advantage of Nations*, New York: Free Press, 1990). Although the ideas of Joseph Schumpeter lie behind much of modern growth theory, this emphasis on competitive behaviour seems on the surface to conflict with his ideas. The apparent conflict arises because the theories available to Schumpeter in his time offered only two market structures, perfect competition and monopoly. He chose monopoly as the structure more conducive to growth on the grounds that monopoly profits would provide the incentive to innovate, and innovation itself would provide the mechanism whereby new entrants could compete with established monopolies. (He called this latter process "creative destruction.") Modern economists, faced with a richer variety of theoretical market structures, find that competition among oligopolists is usually more conducive to growth-enhancing technological change than is monopoly.

[12]Porter, *The Competitive Advantage of Nations*, p. 507.

in the price of one input can raise costs and lower the value of output per person for some time. But it may lead to a wave of innovations that reduce the need for this expensive input and, as a side effect, greatly raise the productivity of labour.[13]

Sometimes, individual firms will respond differently to the same economic signal. Sometimes, those who respond by altering technology will do better than those who concentrate their efforts on substituting within the confines of known technology. For example, in *The Competitive Advantage of Nations*, Michael Porter tells the story of the consumer electronics industry, in which U.S. firms moved their operations abroad to avoid high and rigid labour costs. They continued to use their existing technology and went where labour costs were low enough to make that technology pay. Their Japanese competitors, however, stayed at home. They innovated away most of their labour costs and then built factories in the United States to replace the factories of U.S. firms that had gone abroad!

Innovation as a Competitive Strategy

Managing innovation better than one's competitors is one of the most important objectives of modern firms that wish to survive. Firms often fail because they do not keep up with their competitors in the race to develop new and improved products and techniques of production and distribution.[14] Success in real-world competition often depends more on success in managing innovation than on success in adopting the right pricing policies or in making the right capacity decisions from already-known technological possibilities.

Increasing Returns Theories

We saw earlier that neoclassical theories assume that investment is always subject to diminishing returns.

New growth theories emphasize the possibility of *increasing returns to investment*. A number of sources of increasing returns have been noted. These fall under the general categories of fixed costs and ideas.

Fixed Costs

1. Investment in the early stages of development of a country, state, or town may create new skills and attitudes in the work force that are then available to all subsequent investors, whose costs are therefore lower than those encountered by the initial investors.
2. Each new investor may find the environment more and more favourable to its investment because of the infrastructure that has been created by those who came before.
3. The first investment in a new product will encounter countless problems both of production and of product acceptance among customers that, once overcome, cause fewer problems to subsequent investors.

All of these cases, and many more that could be mentioned, are examples of a single phenomenon:

Many investments require fixed costs, the advantages of which are then available to subsequent investors; hence, the investment costs for "followers" can be substantially less than the investment costs for "pioneers."[15]

More generally, many of the sources of increasing returns are variations on the following general theme: Doing something really new is difficult, both technically and in terms of customer acceptance, whereas making further variations on an accepted and developed new idea becomes progressively easier.

We have already seen one reason for this rule: The costly knowledge developed by early pioneers often becomes available to followers at a much lower cost. A second reason concerns customers. When a new product is developed, customers will often resist adopting it, both because they may be conservative and because they know that new products usually have teething troubles. Customers also need time to learn how best to use the new product—they need to do what is called "learning by

---

[13]This is why in microeconomics we study three runs: the short run, the long run, and the very long run. Often, the very-long-run response to a change in relative prices is much more important than either the short-run response, limited by fixed capital, or the long-run response, limited by existing technology.

[14]The book *Made in America: Regaining the Competitive Edge*, by Michael Dertouzos, Richard Lester, and Robert Solow (Cambridge, MA: MIT Press, 1989), gives a series of case studies where these are the reasons why U.S. firms have lost out to the Japanese and why in other cases U.S. firms have done better than their Japanese competitors.

[15]The general phenomenon discussed here has been the subject of intense study since the early 1970s.

using." The first firms in the field with a truly new idea, such as personal computers, usually meet strong customer resistance, but this resistance erodes over time.

Slow acceptance of new products by customers is not necessarily irrational. When a sophisticated new product comes on the market, no one is sure if it will be a success, and the first customers to buy it take the risk that the product may subsequently turn out to be a failure. They also incur the costs of learning how to use it effectively. Many potential users take the not unreasonable attitude of letting others try a new product, following only after the product's success has been demonstrated. This makes the early stages of innovation especially costly and risky.

These points lead to the following overall result:

For many reasons, successive increments of investment associated with a new set of innovations often yield a range of increasing returns, as costs that are incurred in earlier investment expenditure provide publicly available knowledge and experience and as customer attitudes and abilities become more receptive to new products.

The implications of these ideas have been the subject of intense study ever since they were first embedded in modern growth models by Paul Romer of the University of California and Robert Lucas of the University of Chicago.[16] Probably the most important contrast between these new theories and the neoclassical theory concerns investment and income. In the neoclassical model, diminishing returns to capital implies a limit to the possible increase of per capita GDP. In the new models, investment alone can hold a constant population on a "sustained growth path" in which per capita GDP increases without limit, provided that the investment embodies the results of continual advances in technological knowledge.

Ideas

An even more fundamental change in the new theories is the shift from the economics of goods to the economics of ideas. The economics of ideas is profoundly different from the economics of physical goods, and the differences are only just beginning to be appreciated.

Physical goods, such as factories and machines, exist in one place at one time. The nature of this existence has two consequences. First, when physical goods are used by someone, they cannot be used by someone else. Second, if a given labour force is provided with more and more physical objects to use in production, sooner or later diminishing returns will be encountered.

Ideas have different characteristics. First, once someone develops ideas, they are available for use by everyone. Ideas can be used by one person without reducing their use by others. For example, if one firm uses a truck, another firm cannot use it at the same time, but one firm's use of a revolutionary design for a new suspension on a truck does not prevent other firms from using that design as well. Ideas are not subject to the same use restrictions as goods.

Second, ideas are not necessarily subject to decreasing returns. As our knowledge increases, each increment of new knowledge does not inevitably add less to our productive ability as did each previous increment. A year spent improving the operation of semiconductors may be more productive than a year spent improving the operation of vacuum tubes (the technology used before semiconductors).

The evidence from modern research is that new technologies are usually absolutely factor saving—in other words, they use less of all inputs per unit of output. Furthermore, there is no evidence that from decade to decade the factor saving associated with increments of new knowledge is diminishing.

Modern growth theories stress the importance of ideas in producing what can be called knowledge-driven growth. New knowledge provides the input that allows investment to produce increasing rather than diminishing returns. Since there are no practical boundaries to human knowledge, there need be no immediate boundaries to finding new ways to produce more output using less of all inputs.[17]

Classical and neoclassical growth theories gave economics the name "dismal science" by emphasizing diminishing returns under conditions of given technology. The modern growth theories are more optimistic, because they emphasize the unlimited potential of

---

[16]As with so many innovations, these new views have many historical antecedents, including a classic article in the 1960s by Nobel prize winner Kenneth Arrow of Stanford University.

[17]Possibly, at some distant date, we may know everything there is to know, but if it ever comes, that date is clearly a long, long way in the future.

knowledge-driven technological change to economize on all resource inputs and because they display increasing returns to investment with constant population.

Insofar as these new ideas are true, however, they refer to long-term trends. The dynamics of market systems cause growth rates to vary from decade to decade for reasons that are not fully understood. Over the long haul, however, there seems no reason to believe that equal increments of human effort must inevitably be rewarded by ever-diminishing increments to material output.

Further Causes of Growth

So far, we have looked at increases in labour and capital and at innovation as causes of growth. Contemporary studies suggest that other causes of growth are also important. The influence of these other causes appears as shifts in the production function, so that any given number of hours of labour operating with a given amount of capital produce more and more output as time passes.

Institutions

Almost all aspects of a country's institutions can foster or deter the efficient use of a society's natural and human resources. Social and religious habits, legal institutions, and traditional patterns of national and international trade are all important. So, too, is the political climate.

Historians of economic growth, such as Paul David and Nathan Rosenberg, attribute much of the growth of Western economies in the postmedieval world to the development of *new institutions*, such as the joint-stock company and limited liability. Many students of modern growth suggest that institutions are as important today as they were in the past. They suggest that the societies that are most successful in developing the new institutions that are needed in today's knowledge-intensive world of globalised competition will be the ones at the forefront of economic growth.

The Role of the Government

Governments play an important role in the growth process.

First, the government needs to provide the framework for the market economy that is given by such things as well-defined property rights secure from arbitrary confiscation, security and enforcement of contracts, law and order, a sound money, and the basic rights of the individual to locate, sell, and invest where and how he or she decides.

Second, governments need to provide infrastructure. For example, transportation and communication networks are critical to growth in the modern globalised economy. Some of the facilities, such as roads, bridges, and harbors, are usually provided directly by governments. Others, such as telecommunication, rail, and air services, can be provided by private firms, but government regulations and competition policy may be needed to prevent the emergence of growth-inhibiting monopolies in these areas.

Education and health (especially for the disadvantaged) are important forms of expenditure. Creating the appropriate factors of production is critical to creating comparative advantages in products that can be exported. This requires general education, trade schools, and other appropriate institutions for formal education as well as policies to increase on-the-job training within firms.

Other possible government policies include favourable tax treatment of saving, investment and capital gains; R&D tax incentives and funding assistance; and policies to encourage some fraction of the large pools of financial capital held by pension funds and insurance companies to be used to finance innovation.

Finally, emphasis can be placed on poverty reduction for at least two reasons. First, poverty can exert powerful antigrowth effects. People in poverty will not develop the skills to provide a productive labour force, and they may not even respond to incentives that are provided. Malnutrition in early childhood can affect a person's capacities for life. Second, although economic growth tends to reduce the incidence of poverty, it does not eliminate it.

Growth and Competitiveness in Advanced Industrial Economies

Recent shifts in apparent competitive advantage among industrial nations have aroused an active debate about the sources of continued growth in advanced industrial countries. In particular, many North American industries worry about losing their competitive edge to firms in Japan and the newly industrialised countries of East Asia. An entire new field of study has developed, focusing on competitiveness in advanced industrial countries and the relation between competitiveness and economic growth.

The modern industrial world is dominated by a number of characteristics.

1. Transnational corporations control much of the world's productive capacity and most international investment flows. They can locate their production of individual components of any one commodity wherever costs are lowest.[18]
2. This leads to globalised competition among transnational firms, whereby firms owned in one country compete with firms owned in many other countries.
3. In contrast, significant amounts of innovative activity are undertaken by individual entrepreneurs. As their firms succeed, they look to becoming globally competitive. At this point, it is often more profitable to sell the firm, with its ideas, to an established transnational rather than to incur the enormous cost of developing a global marketing organization to sell the firm's product.
4. Much modern production—both in transnational corporations and in small, innovating firms—is knowledge intensive; it will go where the human capital is and where that capital is supplied at the lowest cost. Traditional natural resource motivations for industrial location are becoming less and less important in many lines of production.
5. In today's rapidly changing, globally competitive world, each firm's competitive advantage increasingly depends on its ability to innovate at a rate sufficiently rapid to stay on the cutting edge of product and production process development.

For these and many more reasons, governments of many advanced nations, including Canada and the United States, are asking themselves what is needed to sustain competitive advantage and thereby sustain economic growth in a rapidly evolving world. Some consensus views have emerged:

1. Market incentives must be stressed—subsidization and other traditional supports too often end up supporting industries that cannot compete over the long term.
2. Government policies that inhibit competitiveness need to be revised. For example, protection of domestic firms against competition coming from highly innovative foreign firms can slow down the domestic rate of innovation and cause domestic firms to fall further and further behind their foreign rivals.
3. "Climate-type" encouragement to innovative activity is valuable. These include broad incentives, such as encouraging both R&D and overall savings, as well as altering education to produce more people trained to provide a comparative advantage in knowledge-intensive industries. (Comparative advantage is briefly discussed in Box 3-1 on pages 44–45 and in detail in Chapter 24.)
4. To the extent that future production will be knowledge intensive, comparative advantage in advanced, high-value-added, high-wage industries may be determined by educational systems.[19] Indeed, evidence given by such labour economists as the Canadian-born economist David Card of Princeton University suggests that return to education has been rising rapidly in recent years. There are strong arguments in favour of educational reform that will better equip workers with newly required skills while reducing functional illiteracy and the lack of numerical skills.

Debate continues over more specific policies. Should North American governments pick specific industrial winners and back them? The majority opinion among economists is that they should not, for two reasons. First, there is no evidence that North American civil servants risking taxpayers' money will make more successful investments than private investors risking their own money. Second, when given the chance to exercise discretion, North American governments often make decisions

---

[18]See Box 9-2 and Chapter 16, pages 307–313, for further discussions of the importance of transnationals.

[19]The firm's value added is what it has available to pay taxes and remunerate its factors of production. Firms that produce low value added per worker can only pay low wages per worker.

directed toward winning the next election rather than maximizing economic advantage.[20]

If governments are not to back winning firms, should they instead back winning activities? They could, as Canada currently does, give tax advantages to R&D. The case for encouraging more R&D than the market would provide lies with what in microeconomics are called externalities. In our earlier discussion of increasing returns in the growth process, we saw that the results of early R&D are often available at a lower cost to firms that enter the market at a later date. As a result, the initial firms cannot fully appropriate in their own profits the value of knowledge that they create with their R&D. To the extent that the value of their R&D is not translated into their own private profits, firms will invest in less R&D than is socially desirable. Hence, a case exists for government encouragement of R&D. The form of this encouragement should not be support for particular R&D ventures, which requires the government to act as an entrepreneur, but rather a reduction in the cost of all R&D, so that the private cost to the firm reflects only the benefits it is able to appropriate for itself and not the benefits it is freely providing to others.

A more vexing problem involves foreign government interventions into the processes of growth, competition, and innovation—such as direct subsidies to specific innovating firms—that have been rejected by the domestic government. If some foreign governments are engaging in a host of such interventionist industrial policies, can North American governments afford to leave all such activity to market forces? It is all very well to say that the market is the best arbitrator of success or failure, but *if* other governments are playing an interventionist game, won't firms in countries with noninterventionist policies be outcompeted by subsidized firms in the interventionist countries? Does this not provide a reason for the Canadian and U.S. governments to copy the behaviour of interventionist governments, in order to put its entrepreneurial players on a level playing field with those in the interventionist coun-

tries? Possibly it does. Lester Thurow of MIT is a strong advocate of this position.

Yet if direct, detailed government intervention is counterproductive, the argument that "what one country does, others must do in self-defense" could easily lead to a high level of unproductive worldwide intervention.[21] This is a major unsettled issue that is strongly debated in Canada and the United States today.

Are There Limits to Growth?

Many opponents of growth argue that sustained world growth is undesirable; some argue that it is impossible. A current bumper sticker reads "Economic growth a cancer on society." Of course, all terrestrial things have an ultimate limit. Astronomers predict that the solar system itself will die when the sun burns out in another 5 billion or so years. To be of practical concern, a limit must be within our planning horizons.

Resource Exhaustion

The years since World War II have seen a rapid acceleration in the consumption of the world's resources, particularly fossil fuels and basic minerals. World population has increased from under 2.5 billion to nearly 6 billion in that period; this increase alone has intensified the demand for the world's resources. Furthermore, the single fact of population growth greatly understates the pressure on resources. As economic development spreads to more and more countries, living standards are rising, in some cases at a rapid rate. As people attain higher incomes, they consume more resources. So not only are there more people in the world, but many of those people are consuming increasing quantities of resources.

Present technology and resources could not possibly support the present population of the world

---

[20]It is worth noting, as further discussed in Chapter 41, that many of the newly industrialised Asian economies have successfully run quite interventionist science and innovation policies. One possible explanation for their success is that their political process does not divert such policies from their growth-creating objectives as much as happens in vote-conscious, openly democratic governments.

[21]This is similar to the problem that arises with tariffs. Everyone agrees that a high level of world tariffs is harmful to all the world's trading nations. Yet one country can sometimes gain a selfish advantage by levying tariffs. If one country does so, others are likely to follow in self-defense. The net result can be rounds of tariff increases that end up lowering all countries' living standards. See Chapter 25 for further discussion.

Box 38-3

The Brundtland Commission and "Sustainable Development"

Since 1980, there has been a major increase in public awareness of the environmental problems faced by all nations. Problems such as global warming, ozone depletion, soil erosion, and acid rain have risen to the top of the political agenda around the world. As barges laden with toxic waste are shunted about in search of a country that is willing to accept their cargo, policy makers have come to recognise that even problems that once were considered to be purely local in nature, such as garbage disposal, have become international in scope.

In 1983, the United Nations created the World Commission on Environment and Development (called the Brundtland Commission after its chairman, Gro Harlem Brundtland) to examine global environmental and development problems and design solutions. In its 1987 report, *Our Common Future*, the Brundtland Commission outlined a broad agenda for integrating economic development and environmental policy. The commission stressed the view that economic growth and environmental protection are interdependent: Growth cannot long continue at the present rate of environmental degradation.

The report introduced the concept of *sustainable development*, defined as "development that meets the needs of the present without compromising the ability of future generations to meet their own needs."

The idea that economic growth is limited by "nature" is not new. In the early 1970s, the Club of Rome focused on the limits to growth arising from the supply of natural resources: It extrapolated from the shortages in oil, caused by the formation of OPEC and the attendant price increases, that industrialised countries faced an imminent absolute limit to growth. This prediction was refuted by experience, as higher prices for fuel led to increases in both total supply and the efficiency with which it has been used.

The bounds to growth envisioned by the Brundtland Commission are not absolute but rather a function of the "present state of technology" and the capacity of the "biosphere to absorb the effects of human activity." The environment imposes limits to the growth that can occur with any specific technology, because it is the fundamental capital upon which economic development is based. As technology and economic organization improve, the stream of wealth that flows from this stock of "environmental capital" can continue to increase. The concept of sustainable development stresses the role of the environment as capital that, if exhausted, cannot be replaced.

Regardless of whether an institution is a government agency, a small firm, or a transnational corporation, the Brundtland Commission's message applies: All institutions that affect the environmental base of the economy must respect the needs of future generations.

According to the commission, governments need to expand their role in the collection and the dissemination of information and, where possible, should produce an annual account of the nation's environment and resource base "to complement the traditional annual fiscal budget and economic development plans." Recall from Chapter 27 that the national income accounts measure *net* national income by subtracting depreciation of capital from *gross* national product. The Brundtland Commission's recommendations involve expanding this concept to subtract some measure of the deterioration of the environment in calculating the level and rate of growth of net national income. The idea is that the environment is part of our capital, and when we degrade it, we reduce our ability to generate real income in the future, as occurs when a machine used for producing consumer goods depreciates.

Some of the Brundtland Commission's recommendations require increased government involvement in economies in order to produce and enforce environmental regulations. Although it recognises the value of economic incentives in generating the cost reductions that flow from more efficient use of resources, the commission also feels that there are limits to the ability of competitive industry to reduce waste voluntarily: "Regulations imposing uniform performance standards are essential to ensure that industry makes the investments necessary to reduce pollution and waste and to enable them to compete on an even footing." (In microeconomic terms, this is seen as an intervention, justified by market failure, and a distinction between private and social costs, as discussed in Chapters 20 and 21.)

In other cases, what is required is *less* government intervention, and the report calls on governments to examine whether existing policies and subsidies contribute to resource-efficient practises. For example, agricultural policy that protects farmers in industrialised countries is criticised for being "studded with contradictions that encourage the degradation of the agricultural resource base and, in the long run, do more harm than good to the agri-cultural industry." The solution lies in "reducing incentives that force overproduction and noncompetitive production in the developed market economies and enhancing those that encourage food production in developing countries."

More specific recommendations are made for reforming international organizations, in which an "extensive institutional capacity exists that could be redirected towards sustainable development"; thus, most of the proposed changes "will not require additional financial resources but can be achieved through a reorientation of existing mandates, programmes, and budgets and a redeployment of existing staff." The efficacy of existing institutions is reduced by their "fragmented" nature and a "weakness of coordination." Key to these reforms is the requirement that sustainable development be made central to the mandate of all international bodies such as UN agencies, the IMF, and the World Bank. The United Nations Environment Program (established in 1972) should be strengthened to become a clearing house for information and to become the "principal advocate" for cooperation on environmental issues. The funding of nongovernmental organizations (NGOs) should be increased, and these groups should be more fully integrated into intergovernmental organizations, as NGOs can "often provide an efficient and effective alternative to public agencies."

Our Common Future is a hopeful document, but its hope is tempered with the realization that unless major conservation initiatives are acted on quickly, the current serious rate of environmental degradation will soon start to harm the health and welfare of all of us.

at a standard of living equal to that of today's average North American family. For example, the demand for oil would increase more than tenfold. It is evident that resources are insufficient to accomplish this rise in living standards with present technology.

Most economists, however, agree that absolute limits to growth, based on the assumptions of constant technology and fixed resources, are not relevant. As modern growth theory stresses, technology changes continually, as do stocks of resources. For example, 40 years ago, few would have thought that the world could produce enough food to feed its present population of nearly 6 billion people, let alone the 10 billion at which the population is projected to stabilise sometime in the midtwenty-first century. Yet this task now seems feasible. Famines do occur, but they are often the result of government policy during a civil war, as in Ethiopia and the Sudan, or of climatic changes plus poor land conservation policies, as in the Sahel region of central Africa and the southern slopes of the Himalaya Mountains.

There will never be full protection from the vagaries of nature, nor from willful or ignorant mismanagement. However, in the early 1990s, the developed world struggles not with a food shortage, but with a food glut. Farm support policies in the European Community turned the countries of Europe into food exporters rather than food importers, as they had been in past centuries. These subsidies greatly hurt agricultural producers in countries that would export agricultural produce if free-market prices prevailed. A mere 3 percent of U.S., Canadian, and European labour applied to limited farmland with modern technology is producing more food than the world markets can consume. The problem in the early 1990s is how to reduce subsidized production, not how to produce more.[22]

It is possible that, 50 years from now, the global energy problem will be as much a thing of the past as the *global* food shortage problem is today. Technology could by then have produced a cheap, nonpolluting energy source (possibly based on solar energy or nuclear fusion).

Furthermore, research into technological change shows that the typical process (as opposed to product) innovation uses less of all inputs per unit of output. Thus, technological change is part of the solution, not part of the problem. The problem is too many people aspiring to levels of consumption that cannot be sustained with *existing technologies.*

The future is always uncertain, and it is instructive to recall how many things that we accept as commonplace today would have seemed miraculous a mere 25 years ago.

Yet there is surely cause for concern. Although many barriers can be overcome by technological advances, such achievements are not instantaneous and are certainly not automatic. There is a critical problem of timing: How soon can we discover and put into practise the knowledge required to solve the problems that are made ever more imminent by the growth in the population, the affluence of the rich nations, and the aspirations of the billions who now live in poverty?

There is no guarantee that a whole generation will not be caught in transition between technologies, with enormous social and political consequences. One positive outgrowth of concern over environmental issues is the recent attention given to the concept of "sustainable development," discussed further in Box 38-3.

Renewable Resources

One possible limitation to growth relates to renewable resources. The demands placed on them threaten to destroy their natural recuperative cycle. Throughout history, for example, fishermen were a small part of the predatory process. Now the demands of nearly 6 billion people have made fish a scarce resource, threatening to destroy the fish-generating capacity of many oceans. In the Mediterranean, many species of fish that were once eaten as staple food by ordinary people are now consumed almost exclusively by well-off tourists.

Pollution

A further problem is how to cope with pollution. Air, water, and earth are polluted by a variety of natural activities, and through billions of years, the environment has coped with these. The earth's natural processes had little trouble coping with the pol-

---

[22]Although globally there is enough food for everyone, severe problems arise when primarily agricultural economies suffer drought and other natural disasters, or wars and other man-made disasters. The problem, then, is not to produce more food worldwide but to be sure that it is available where it is needed.

lution generated by its 1 billion inhabitants in 1800. But the nearly 6 billion people who now exist put demands on pollution-abatement systems that threaten to become unsustainable. Smoke, sewage, chemical waste, hydrocarbon emissions, spent nuclear fuel, and a host of other pollutants threaten to overwhelm the earth's natural regenerative processes.

Conscious management of pollution and renewable resources was unnecessary when the world's population was 1 billion people, but such management has become a pressing matter of survival now that nearly 6 billion people are seeking to live in the same space and off the same resources.

Conclusion

The world faces many problems. Starvation and poverty are the common lot of citizens in many countries and are not unknown in countries such as Canada and the United States, where average living standards are high. Growth has raised the average citizens of advanced countries from poverty to

plenty in the course of two centuries—a short time in terms of human history. Further growth is needed if people in less developed countries are to escape material poverty, and further growth would help advanced countries to deal with many of their pressing economic problems.

Rising population and rising per capita consumption, however, put pressure on the world's natural ecosystems, especially through the many forms of pollution. Further growth must be sustainable growth, which in turn must be based on idea-driven technological change. Past experience suggests that new technologies will use less of all resources per unit of output. But if they are to dramatically reduce the demands placed on the earth's ecosystems, price and policy incentives will be needed to direct technological change in more "environmentally friendly" ways. Just as present technologies are much less polluting than the technologies of 100 years ago, the technologies of the twenty-first century must be made much less polluting than today's.

There is no guarantee that the world will solve the problems of sustainable growth, but there is nothing in modern growth theory and existing evidence to suggest that such an achievement is impossible.

SUMMARY

1. Real national income can be increased on a once-and-for-all basis from the demand side by removing recessionary gaps and from the supply side by reducing structural unemployment and economic inefficiencies. Sustained increases, however, are due mainly to economic growth, which continuously pushes the *LRAS* curve outward, thereby increasing potential income.
2. Investment has short-term effects on national income through aggregate demand and long-term effects through growth in potential national income. Saving reduces consumption and aggregate demand and therefore reduces national income in the short run, but in the long run, saving finances the investment that leads to growth in potential income.
3. The most important benefit of growth lies in its contribution to the long-run struggle to raise living standards and to escape poverty. Growth also facilitates the redistribution of income among people.
4. Growth, though often beneficial, is never costless. The opportunity cost of growth is the diversion of resources from current consumption to capital formation. For individuals who are left behind in a rapidly changing world, the costs are higher and more personal.
5. The neoclassical model displays diminishing returns when one factor is increased on its own and constant returns when all fac-

tors are increased together. In a balanced growth path, labour, capital, and national income all increase at a constant rate, leaving living standards unchanged.

6. When the neoclassical model was related to actual data, much of the observed growth in national income could not be explained by the growth in labour and capital. The unexplained growth, called the residual, was ascribed to technological change.

7. Modern growth theory treats technological change as an endogenous variable that responds to market signals. The diffusion of technology is also endogenous. It is costly and often proceeds at a relatively slow pace.

8. Some modern growth theories display increasing returns as investment increases on its own. This investment confers externalities such that successive increments of investment may add constant or even successively *increasing* amounts to total output.

9. Recently, the advanced industrial countries have become increasingly concerned with maintaining their international competitiveness in order to continue their economic growth. Globalised competition and the increasing pace of technological change, particularly of the knowledge-driven variety, have made countries acutely aware of how easy it is to lose one's position at or near the forefront of the innovating nations.

10. The critical importance of increasing knowledge and new technology to the goal of sustaining growth is highlighted by the great drain on existing natural resources that has resulted from the explosive growth of population and output in recent decades. Without continuing technological change, the present needs and aspirations of the world's population cannot come anywhere close to being met.

11. Rising population and rising real incomes place pressure on resources. Although resources will not be exhausted in general, particular resources, such as petroleum, will be. Furthermore, resources that renewed themselves without help from humans when the world's population was 1 billion people can easily be exhausted unless they are consciously conserved now that the world's population exceeds 6 billion. This enormous increase in population has similar effects on pollution: The earth's environment could cope naturally with much of human pollution 200 years ago, but the present population is so large that pollution has outstripped nature's coping mechanisms.

TOPICS FOR REVIEW

Short-run and long-run effects of investment and saving

Cumulative nature of growth

Benefits and costs of growth

The neoclassical aggregate production function

Balanced growth

Endogenous technical change

Increasing returns to investment

Embodied and disembodied technical change

The economics of goods and of ideas

Resource depletion and pollution

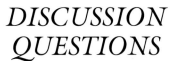

DISCUSSION QUESTIONS

1. Economic growth is often studied in macroeconomic terms, but in a market economy, who makes the decisions that lead to growth? What kinds of decisions and what kinds of actions cause growth to occur? How might a detailed study of individual markets be relevant to understanding economic growth?

2. Discuss the following quote from a newspaper article that appeared in the summer of 1989: "Economics and the environment are not strange bedfellows. Environment-oriented tourism is one creative way to resolve the conflict between our desire for a higher standard of living and the realization that nature cannot absorb everything we throw at it. The growing demand for eco-tourism has placed a premium on the remaining rain forests, undisturbed flora and fauna, and endangered species of the world."

3. Use a UN publication to discover the per capita GDP in the world today. If growth were stopped everywhere, could output be redistributed to raise living standards in the poorer countries near to those currently enjoyed in the developed countries? Would a massive redistribution of income among nations be politically and economically feasible?

4. *Family Weekly* recently listed among "inventions that have changed our lives" microwave ovens, digital clocks, bank credit cards, freeze-dried coffee, tape cassettes, climate-controlled shopping malls, automatic toll collectors, soft contact lenses, tubeless tires, and electronic word processors. Which of these would you hate to do without? Which, if any, will have a major impact on life in the twenty-first century? If there are any that you believe will not, does this mean that they are frivolous and unimportant?

5. The Overseas Development Council recently introduced "a new measure of economic development based on the physical quality of life." Its index, called PQLI, gives one-third weight to each of the following indicators: literacy, life expectancy, and infant mortality. While countries such as the United States and Canada rank high on either the PQLI or on an index of per capita real national income, some relatively poor countries, such as Sri Lanka, rank much higher on the PQLI index than much richer countries such as Algeria and Kuwait. Discuss the merits or deficiencies of this measure.

6. "The case for economic growth is that it gives man greater control over his environment, and consequently increases his freedom." Explain why you agree or disagree with this statement by Nobel laureate W. Arthur Lewis.

7. Consider a developed economy that decides to achieve a zero rate of growth for the future. What implications would such a "sta-

tionary state" have for the processes of production and consumption and for human inventive activity?

8. Suppose that solar energy becomes the dominant form of energy in the twenty-first century. What effects will this have on the growth rates of Africa and Northern Europe?

9. Discuss the following newspaper headlines in terms of the sources, costs, and benefits of growth.
   a. "Stress addiction: 'Life in the fast lane' may have its benefits."
   b. "Education: An expert urges multiple reforms."
   c. "Industrial radiation risk higher than thought."
   d. "Developments in the field of management design are looking ahead."
   e. "Ford urged by federal safety officials to recall several hundred thousand of its 1981-1982 front-drive vehicles because of alleged fire hazards."

10. Dr. David Suzuki, an opponent of further economic growth, has recently argued that, despite the fact that "in the twentieth century the list of scientific and technological achievements has been absolutely dazzling, the costs of such progress are so large that negative economic growth may be right for the future." Policies to achieve this include "rigorous reduction of waste, a questioning and distrustful attitude towards technological progress, and braking demands on the globe's resources." Identify some of the benefits and costs of economic growth, and evaluate Dr. Suzuki's position. What government policies would be needed to achieve his ends?

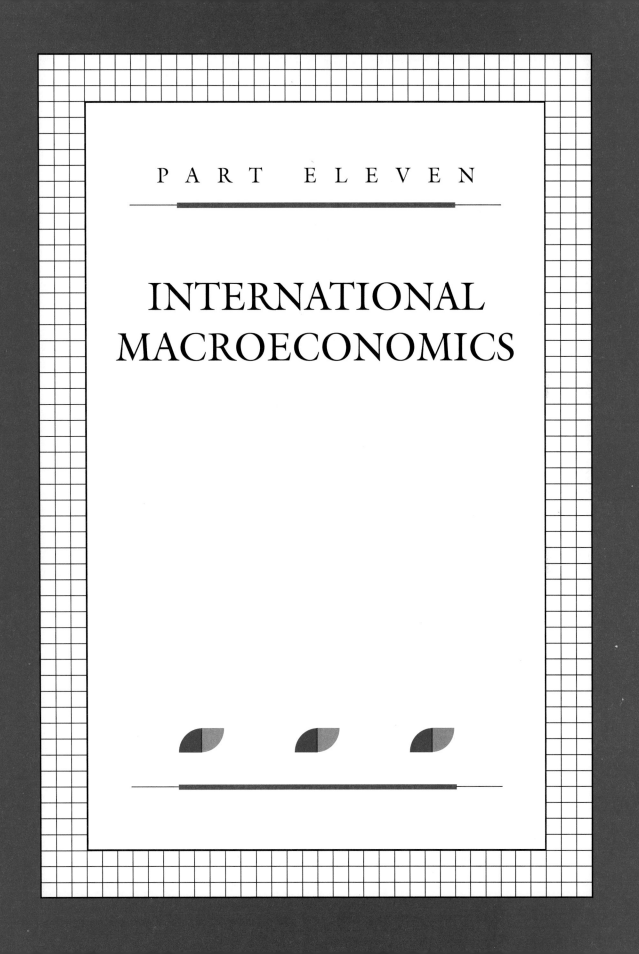

PART ELEVEN

INTERNATIONAL MACROECONOMICS

39

Exchange Rates and the Balance of Payments

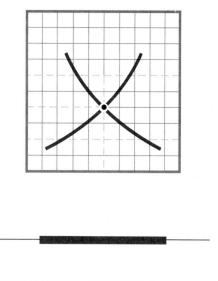

The value of the Canadian dollar on foreign exchange markets matters to many people. It affects the decisions of a Japanese firm wanting to sell cars in Canada, a Canadian person wanting to buy a German government bond, a French exporter selling kitchen appliances to Canada, a Canadian firm hoping to sell commuter airplanes to American feeder airlines, and exporters of Canadian wood and mineral products in markets where prices are quoted in U.S. dollars. It also matters to Canadian tourists cashing their Canadian dollar traveler's cheques in Miami, London, Athens, or Bangkok. It even matters to Canadians who have neither bought nor sold foreign currency or even heard of the exchange rate. This is because the exchange rate helps to determine the cost of imported goods as well as the amount of employment offered by firms that sell on foreign markets or compete with imports for sales in the Canadian market.

The discussion in this chapter brings together material on three topics studied elsewhere in this book: the theory of supply and demand (Chapter 4), the nature of money (Chapter 32), and international trade (Chapter 24).

We shall examine the simple case of a *small open economy (SOE),* an economy that can exert no influence on the world prices of traded goods. The quantities it exports and imports are small in relation to the total volume of world trade in these commodities, so its exporters and importers must buy and sell at prices that are established in world markets. For many Canadian commodities, such as wheat, forest products, and minerals, this is the correct assumption. For Canada as a whole, this is a useful simplification.

A small open economy faces international terms of trade that are fixed in world markets and hence beyond its control.

The Determination of Exchange Rates

Our first task in this chapter is to study how exchange rates are determined and how they equilibrate the flows of payments that arise from trade and capital movements.

The Nature of Foreign Exchange Transactions

We have seen that money, which consists of any accepted medium of exchange, is vital in any economy that relies on specialization and exchange. Yet money as we know it is a *national* matter, closely controlled by national governments. If you live in Sweden, you will earn kronor and spend kronor; if you run a business in Austria, you borrow schillings and meet your payroll with schillings. The currency of a country is acceptable within the borders of that country, but it will not usually be accepted by households and firms in another country. The Stockholm bus company will accept kronor for a fare but not Austrian schillings. The Austrian worker will not take Swedish kronor for wages but will accept schillings.

The situation is similar in Canada, except that our proximity to the United States leads many Canadian sellers to accept U.S. dollars over the counter. Because U.S. dollars are so well known and so common, Canadian merchants are willing to accept them and then do what the customer would otherwise have had to do: take the U.S. money to the bank and exchange it for Canadian money. For international transactions, however, this is the rare exception rather than the rule.

When Canadian producers sell their products, they require payment in Canadian dollars. They must meet their wage bills, pay for their raw materials, and reinvest or distribute their profits. There is no problem when they sell to Canadian purchasers. However, when they sell their goods to Japanese importers, either the Japanese must exchange their yen to acquire dollars to pay for the goods, or the Canadian producers must accept yen. They will accept yen only if they know that they can exchange the yen for the dollars that they require. The same holds true for producers in all countries: They must eventually receive payment for the goods that they sell in terms of the currency of their own country.

Trade between nations would be greatly hampered if it were not possible to exchange the currency of one nation for that of another.

The Exchange Rate

We studied the exchange rate in Chapter 26. The material on pages 535–538 and Box 26–4 should be reviewed carefully at this time. Take care, the relation between the exchange rate and the value of the domestic currency on the foreign exchange market, called the *external value of the currency,* can be confusing and should be committed to memory. We summarize it below:

The exchange rate is the amount of domestic currency needed to buy a unit of foreign currency. It is negatively related to the external value of the domestic currency. An appreciation in the exchange rate is a depreciation of the external value of the domestic currency, and a depreciation in the exchange rate is an appreciation of the external value of the domestic currency.

The Mechanism of Foreign Exchange Transactions

Let us see how foreign exchange transactions are carried out. Suppose that a Canadian firm wishes to purchase a British sports car to sell in Canada. The British firm that made the car requires payment in pounds sterling. If the car is priced at £15,000, the Canadian firm will go to its bank, purchase a cheque for £15,000, and send the cheque to the British seller. Let us suppose this requires that the firm pay $25,000.[1] The British firm deposits the cheque in its bank. (The exchange rate in this transaction is 1.667, because it costs $1.667 to buy one British pound sterling; the external value of the Canadian dollar measured in sterling is £0.60, because one Canadian dollar will buy that amount of sterling.)

Now assume that in the same period, a British wholesale firm purchases 25 Canadian refrigerators to sell in Britain. If the refrigerators are priced at $1,000 each, the Canadian seller will have to be paid $25,000. To make this payment, the British importing firm goes to its bank, writes a cheque on its account for £15,000, and receives a cheque drawn on a Canadian bank for $25,000. The cheque is sent to Canada and deposited in a Canadian bank.

The effects of the two transactions are shown in Table 39-1. The transactions balance, and there is no net change in international liabilities. No money need pass between British and Canadian banks; each bank merely increases the deposit of one domestic customer and decreases the deposit of another. Indeed, as long as the flow of payments between the

---

[1]Banks charge a commission for making currency exchanges, but for simplicity, we shall ignore this and assume that parties can exchange moneys back and forth at the going exchange rate.

TABLE 39-1   Changes in the Balance Sheets of Two Banks as a Result of International Payments

U.K. Bank			Canadian Bank		
Assets	*Liabilities*		*Assets*	*Liabilities*	
No Change	(1) Deposits of car exporter	+£15,000	No change	(1) Deposits of car importer	−$25,000
	(2) Deposits of refrigerator importer	−£15,000		(2) Deposits of refrigerator exporter	− $25,000
	Net change	0		Net change	0

International transactions involve a transfer of deposit liabilities among banks. The table records two separate international transactions at an exchange rate of £1.00 = $1.66 Canadian: (1) a Canadian purchase of a British car for £15,000 (= $25,000) and (2) a British purchase of Canadian refrigerators for $25,000 (= £15,000). The Canadian's import of a car reduces deposit liabilities to Canadian residents and increases deposit liabilities to British residents. The Britisher's import of refrigerators does the opposite. When several transactions are equal in value, there is only a transfer of deposit liabilities among individuals within a country. The Canadian refrigerator manufacturer received (in effect) the dollars the Canadian car purchaser gave up to get a British-made car.

---

two countries is equal (Canadians pay as much to British residents as British residents pay to Canadians), all payments can be managed as in the example, and there will be no need for a net payment from British banks to Canadian banks.

All these calculations involve comparing magnitudes measured in different currencies. These comparisons are done using exchange rates. We now turn to an analysis of how such exchange rates are determined.

Our next step in studying how exchange rates are determined is to look at the link between exchange rates and the prices of a country's imports and exports.

Exchange Rates Changes and Foreign Trade

A small open economy faces prices of internationally traded goods that are fixed in foreign currency. The exchange rate translates these into domestic prices. If, for example, the price of wheat is US$3.00 a bushel on international wheat markets, the Canadian dollar price that is earned by Canadian wheat exporters depends on the exchange rate. When the rate is C$1.20 to the U.S. dollar, the Canadian domestic price of wheat is C$3.60. This is because the US$3.00 earned from the foreign sale of a bushel of wheat is converted into C$3.60 when

it is sold on the foreign exchange market at a rate of C$1.20 for every U.S. dollar sold.

In Figures 4A-1 and 4A-2 (page 80) we showed how imports and exports were determined in a small open economy facing given world prices for traded goods. We drew the domestic demand and supply curves plotted against domestic prices. We then used the world price, *stated in units of domestic currency,* to determine the quantity of imports and exports of a product. To do this, we needed an exchange rate to convert world prices into local currency, although we did not say so at the time. Since the exchange rate, e, is the number of units of domestic currency needed to buy one unit of foreign currency, the domestic price of traded goods, p_d, is the *world* price of traded goods expressed in foreign currency, p_f, multiplied by the exchange rate:

$$p_d = ep_f$$

To repeat the example given earlier, when the international price of wheat is US$3.00 per bushel and the exchange rate is 1.20, the Canadian dollar price of wheat is US$3.00 per bushel times 1.20, which is C$3.60 per bushel.

It is now a simple matter to see the effect of a change in the exchange rate on the domestic prices of traded goods. Say that the Canadian exchange rate depreciates so that it takes only C$1.10 to buy one U.S. dollar. The domestic price of a bushel of wheat that costs US$3.00 is now only C$3.30, since

C$3.30 is all the Canadian dollars that can be bought with US$3.00. (The formula $p_d = ep_f$ gives the right answer, since 1.10 times US$3.00 per bushel equals C$3.30 per bushel.) As a second example, say that the Canadian exchange rate appreciates so that it now takes C$1.40 to buy one U.S. dollar. Now the Canadian dollar price of wheat rises to $4.20, since that is the number of Canadian dollars that US$3.00 will buy on the foreign exchange market.

A depreciation of the exchange rate lowers the Canadian domestic prices of internationally traded goods; an appreciation raises them.

To study the effects of changes in the exchange rate further, we return to the example given in the appendix to Chapter 4, a country that is exporting wheat and importing cloth.

First consider an appreciation of the exchange rate. A 10 percent appreciation, for example, would mean that the domestic currency prices of the two goods must rise by 10 percent. Look first at the export good, wheat. Since the sale of a unit of wheat abroad still yields the same amount of foreign exchange, it now yields 10 percent more in terms of domestic currency. Domestic purchasers too will have to pay 10 percent more, for if the domestic price did not rise, producers would sell only in the export market. Similarly, the purchase of cloth still requires the same amount of foreign currency, but 10 percent more of the domestic currency must be paid to obtain the required amount of foreign currency. Thus, the domestic currency price of imported cloth also rises by 10 percent.

The effects of these price changes are illustrated in Figures 39-1 and 39-2. In the market for wheat, the increase in the domestic price causes the quantity supplied domestically to rise and the quantity demanded domestically to fall. As a result, the quantity of wheat exported, which is equal to the excess of the quantity supplied domestically over the quantity demanded domestically, *rises* (see Figure 39-1). In the market for cloth, the increase in the domestic price also causes the quantity supplied domestically to increase and the quantity demanded domestically to fall. Since domestic demand exceeded domestic supply in the initial situation, this response *reduces* the excess demand. As

a result, the quantity of cloth imported *decreases* (see Figure 39-2).

For a small country, an appreciation of the exchange rate causes the domestic prices of traded goods to rise, thereby increasing the quantity supplied and decreasing the quantity demanded domestically. Therefore, the volume of exports rises while the volume of imports falls.

As a result of these changes, net exports, $X - IM$, rise. Since net exports are a component of aggregate demand, the depreciation increases the country's aggregate demand. This in turn tends to increase equilibrium national income.

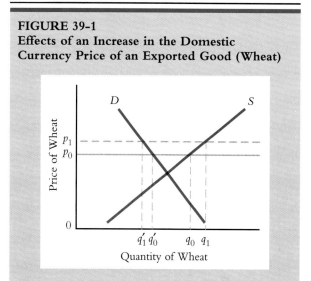

FIGURE 39-1
Effects of an Increase in the Domestic Currency Price of an Exported Good (Wheat)

An increase in the domestic currency price of export goods leads to an increase in the volume of exports. Exports of wheat are determined by the domestic excess supply of the tradeable good at the domestic price. (The domestic price is the world price adjusted by the exchange rate.) D and S are the domestic demand and supply schedules. If the world price expressed in domestic currency is p_0, quantity q_0 will be produced, of which q_0' will be consumed domestically and $q_0'q_0$ will be exported. An appreciation of the exchange rate or an increase in the world price causes the domestic currency price to rise to p_1. As a result, domestic consumption falls to q_1', quantity supplied rises to q_1, and exports rise to $q_1'q_1$.

FIGURE 39-2
Effects of an Increase in the Domestic Currency Price of an Imported Good (Cloth)

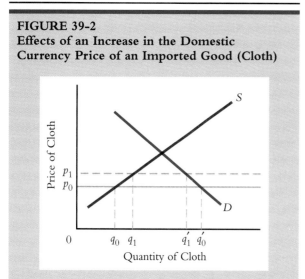

An increase in the domestic currency price of import goods leads to a decrease in the volume of imports. Imports of cloth are determined by the domestic excess demand for cloth at the domestic price. (The domestic price is the world price adjusted by the exchange rate.) D and S are the domestic demand and supply schedules. If the world price expressed in domestic currency is p_0, quantity q_0' will be consumed, of which q_0 will be produced domestically and $q_0'q_0$ will be imported. An appreciation of the exchange rate or an increase in the world price causes the domestic currency price to rise to p_1. As a result, quantity supplied rises to q_1, domestic consumption falls to q_1', and imports fall to $q_1'q_1$.

Next, consider a depreciation of the exchange rate. This will *lower* the domestic prices of traded goods. For both cloth and wheat, this leads to a reduction in the quantity supplied domestically and an increase in the quantity demanded domestically. The quantity of cloth that is imported now rises, while the quantity of wheat that is exported falls. This is also shown in Figures 39-1 and 39-2.

For a small country, a depreciation of the exchange rate causes the domestic prices of traded goods to fall, thereby decreasing the quantity supplied and increasing the quantity demanded domestically. Therefore, the volume of exports falls while the volume of imports rises.

As a result of these changes, net exports fall. This causes a decrease in aggregate demand and hence a fall in equilibrium national income.

The Exchange of Currencies

For simplicity, we shall consider an example involving trade between Canada and the United States and the determination of the exchange rate between their two currencies, the Canadian dollar and the U.S. dollar. The two-country example simplifies things, but the principles apply to all foreign transactions. *Thus, in our example, U.S. dollars stand for foreign exchange in general, and the Canadian dollar price of one U.S. dollar stands for foreign exchange rates in general.*

We can relate our example to the demand and supply analysis of Chapter 4. To do so, we need only recognise that *in the market for U.S. dollars,* the holders of Canadian dollars who want U.S. dollars are *demanders* of U.S. dollars, and the holders of U.S. dollars who want Canadian dollars are *suppliers* of U.S. dollars. We could also look at the same transaction in terms of the market for Canadian dollars: The holders of Canadian dollars who want U.S. dollars are suppliers of Canadian dollars, and the holders of U.S. dollars who want Canadian dollars are demanders of Canadian dollars. Both views are different ways of looking at the same transactions.

Because one currency is traded for another on the foreign exchange market, an offer to buy Canadian dollars implies a willingness to sell foreign exchange, and an offer to sell Canadian dollars implies a desire to buy foreign exchange.

Consider a simple example. When the exchange rate is 1.2, a U.S. importer who offers to buy C$6.00 with U.S. dollars must be offering to sell US$5.00. Similarly, a Canadian importer who offers to sell C$6.00 for U.S. dollars must be offering to buy US$5.00. As this example illustrates, a theory of the exchange rate between Canadian and U.S. dollars can deal with *either* the demand for and the supply of Canadian dollars *or* the demand for and the supply of U.S. dollars; both sets of demands and supplies need not be considered. We shall con-

Supply of Foreign Exchange

U.S. dollars are supplied on the foreign exchange market to finance purchases made by foreigners from Canadian residents. In addition to the purchase of Canadian exports, such as wheat, there are purchases of assets previously owned or newly issued by Canadian firms and governments. Such purchases give rise to *capital flows.* These play an important role in exchange markets, and we study them in detail later in this chapter; for the present, we continue to focus on imports and exports of goods and services.

Our representative Canadian export is wheat. We saw in Figure 39-1 that a rise in the Canadian exchange rate leads to an increase in the *quantity* of wheat exports. Since in our simplified model, the *U.S. dollar price* of wheat is set on the international wheat market and is unaffected by any changes in the exchange rate, the total U.S. dollar value of Canadian wheat exports must rise. Foreign purchasers must be spending more U.S. dollars to buy Canadian wheat, and these U.S. dollars go to purchase the Canadian dollars needed to pay Canadian sellers for this wheat. It follows that an appreciation of the exchange rate will increase the supply of U.S. dollars offered on the foreign exchange market.

By the same argument, a fall in the exchange rate leads to a decrease in the quantity of wheat exports. Since these are sold at an unchanged U.S. dollar price, the U.S. dollar value of Canadian sales of wheat must fall. Thus, a fall in the exchange rate will decrease the supply of U.S. dollars offered on the foreign exchange market.

The foregoing analysis tells us the sign of the slope of the supply curve of U.S. dollars on the foreign exchange market, since it shows that the exchange rate and the quantity of U.S. dollars offered to buy Canadian exports are positively related.

The supply curve of U.S. dollars on the foreign exchange market is positively sloped when plotted against the dollar exchange rate.

The common sense of this result is that since Canadian exports of wheat are sold at a given U.S. dollar price, anything that increases the quantity of their sales must increase the total value of U.S. dollars spent on them. This spending takes the form of offering U.S. dollars on the foreign exchange mar-

---

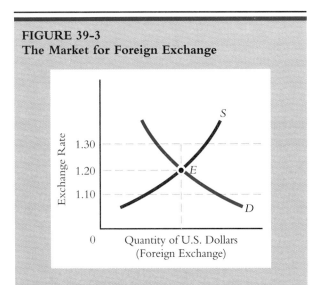

FIGURE 39-3
The Market for Foreign Exchange

The equilibrium exchange rate is the price that equates the demand and supply of foreign exchange. In this example, the U.S. dollar stands for all foreign exchange, and the exchange rate is the number of Canadian dollars required to buy one U.S. dollar. The *S* curve is the supply of U.S. dollars to the foreign exchange market to be used to make purchases in Canada. The *D* curve is the demand for U.S. dollars on the foreign exchange market to be used to make purchases in the United States. The quantity of U.S. dollars demanded is equal to the quantity supplied at an exchange rate of 1.20. When the exchange rate is low, say, 1.10, there is an excess demand for U.S. dollars, which bids the price up. When the exchange rate is high, say, 1.30, there is an excess supply of U.S. dollars, which bids the price down.

---

centrate on the demand, supply, and price of U.S. dollars.

Figure 39-3 plots the *quantity of U.S. dollars* on the horizontal axis and the exchange rate, the *price of one U.S. dollar* measured in Canadian dollars, on the vertical axis. Moving down the vertical scale to *lower exchange rates,* the foreign currency (U.S. dollars) becomes *cheaper*; its external value is depreciating on the foreign exchange market while the external value of the Canadian dollar is *appreciating.* Moving up the scale to higher exchange rates, the foreign currency (U.S. dollars) becomes *more expensive,* so its external value is appreciating, while the external value of the Canadian dollar is depreciating.

ket to buy the Canadian dollars needed to pay Canadian exporters.

Demand for Foreign Exchange

In our two-country example, the demand for U.S. dollars on the foreign exchange market is merely the opposite side of the supply of Canadian dollars. Who wants to sell Canadian dollars for foreign exchange? In our example, Canadians seeking to purchase the representative U.S. export, cloth, will require foreign exchange to make their purchases. Hence they will wish to supply Canadian dollars in exchange for U.S. dollars.[2]

When the exchange rate rises, the Canadian price of U.S. cloth rises. As we saw in Figure 39-2, Canadians will import less of the now more expensive U.S. cloth. Since the U.S. dollar price of cloth is unchanged, buying less cloth means needing fewer U.S. dollars to pay for it. Thus, the Canadian demand for U.S. dollars falls.

Now consider the opposite case, in which the exchange rate depreciates. American cloth exports to Canada become cheaper, and more will be sold. Since the U.S. dollar price of cloth is unchanged, buying more means spending more U.S. dollars. Thus, there is an increase in the amount of U.S. dollars demanded on the foreign exchange market.

Together, these two reactions tell us the sign of the slope of the demand curve for U.S. dollars.

The demand curve for U.S. dollars on the foreign exchange market is negatively sloped when plotted against the exchange rate.

Equilibrium Exchange Rates

The exchange rate between Canadian and U.S. dollars is set on a competitive market by the forces of demand and supply. (Even when the Bank of Canada intervenes to influence the exchange rate, it does so by adding its own demand or supply to what is coming from the private sector.) For this reason, the text deals with the case of rates that are determined on free markets. The opposite extreme, where the rate is pegged by the central bank, is found in some other countries and did exist in some past periods in Canada. It is briefly described in Box 39-1 on page 842.

_____

[2]A demand for U.S. dollars may also result from capital flows if Canadians seek to buy U.S. assets. As with the supply of U.S. dollars to purchase Canadian assets, we neglect this until later in the chapter.

Assume that the current exchange rate is so low (say, 1.05 in Figure 39-3) that the quantity of U.S. dollars demanded exceeds the quantity supplied. U.S. dollars will be in scarce supply. Some people who require U.S. dollars to make payments to the United States will be unable to obtain them, and the price of U.S. dollars—the exchange rate—will be bid up.

As the exchange rate rises, the domestic market price of Canadian imports rises; hence the quantity of imports falls, as does the quantity of U.S. dollars demanded on the foreign exchange market to pay for these imports. This is a movement along the demand curve, D, in Figure 39-3. However, the appreciation of the exchange rate also leads to a rise in the dollar price of Canadian exports and a resulting increase in the quantity sold abroad. Thus, the amount of U.S. dollars offered to buy more Canadian exports at an unchanged U.S. dollar price must rise. This is a movement along the supply curve, S, in Figure 39-3. Thus, a rise in the exchange rate reduces the quantity of U.S. dollars demanded and increases the quantity of U.S. dollars supplied. Where the two curves intersect, quantity demanded equals quantity supplied, and the foreign exchange market is in equilibrium.

What happens if the price of foreign exchange is too high? The quantity of U.S. dollars demanded will be less than the quantity of U.S. dollars supplied. With U.S. dollars in excess supply, some people who wish to convert U.S. dollars into Canadian dollars will be unable to do so. The price of U.S. dollars will fall, fewer U.S. dollars will be supplied, more will be demanded, and equilibrium will be reestablished.

In the foreign exchange market, as in other competitive markets, the forces of demand and supply establish an equilibrium exchange rate at which quantity demanded equals quantity supplied.

Changes in Exchange Rates

What causes exchange rates to vary? The simplest answer to this question is changes in demand or supply in the foreign exchange market. Anything that shifts the demand curve for U.S. dollars to the right or the supply curve for U.S. dollars to the left leads to a rise in the exchange rate. Anything that

FIGURE 39-4
Changes in Exchange Rates

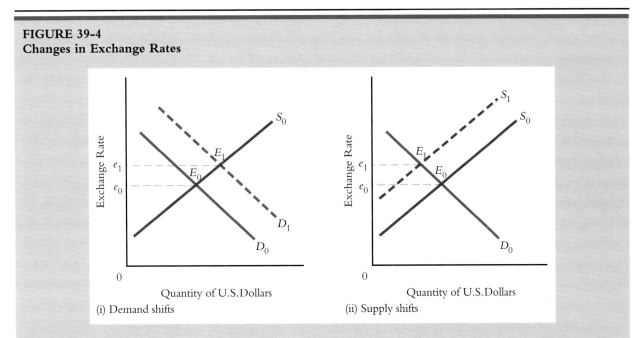

(i) Demand shifts

(ii) Supply shifts

An increase in the demand for U.S. dollars or a decrease in their supply will cause the exchange rate to appreciate; a decrease in the demand or an increase in supply will cause it to depreciate. The initial demand and supply curves are D_0 and S_0, equilibrium is at E_0, with an exchange rate of e_0. An increase in the demand for dollars, as shown by a rightward shift in the demand curve from D_0 to D_1 in part (i), or a decrease in the supply of dollars, as shown by a leftward shift in the supply curve from S_0 to S_1 in part (ii), will cause the exchange rate to appreciate. In both parts, the new equilibrium is at E_1, and the appreciation is shown by the rise in the exchange rate from e_0 to e_1.

A decrease in the demand for U.S. dollars, as shown by a leftward shift in the demand curve from D_1 to D_0 in part (i), or an increase in the supply of U.S. dollars, as shown by a rightward shift in the supply curve from S_1 to S_0 in part (ii), will cause the exchange rate to depreciate. The equilibrium shifts from E_1 to E_0, and the depreciation is shown by the fall in the exchange rate from e_1 to e_0 in both parts.

shifts the demand curve for U.S. dollars to the left or the supply curve for U.S. dollars to the right leads to a fall in the exchange rate. These results, which are shown in Figure 39-4, are nothing more than a restatement of the laws of demand and supply, applied now to the market for foreign exchange.

The trick in applying demand and supply theory to the foreign exchange market is knowing what causes the demand and supply curves to shift. There are many causes, some of them transitory and some persistent, and we shall study several of the most important.

Foreign Inflation

What happens when the rest of the world experiences inflation while our domestic economy does not? Domestic costs and the prices of domestic (nontraded) goods remain unchanged. However, world prices of all traded goods rise. As a result, at the initial exchange rate, the domestic prices of all traded goods rise.

We saw in Figures 39-1 and 39-2 that the rise in the world prices of exported and imported goods leads domestic firms to increase the quantities of their exports while decreasing the quantities of their imports. These changes cause shifts in the demand and supply curves in the foreign exchange market. More Canadian exports sold at a higher world price mean more foreign exchange offered in return for Canadian dollars. The supply curve of foreign exchange shifts right, as shown in Figure 39-5. Fewer imports purchased at higher foreign prices means less spent on imports—at least as long as the per-

Box 39-1

Managing Fixed Exchange Rates

Canada has been on a flexible, market-determined exchange rate throughout most of the period since the end of the Second World War. There were, however, two periods in the 1940s and the 1960s when it operated under fixed rates. The rest of the world operated under fixed rates from 1945 until the early 1970s under the Bretton Woods monetary system. Since that system broke down in the early 1970s, most advanced countries operate under flexible exchange rate regimes. The countries of the European Community (with the exception of the United Kingdom) operate a mixed system, in which they fix the rates between their own currencies, which fluctuate as a block against other currencies. Finally, many of the less developed countries operate under regimes of fixed exchange rates.

The figure shows how a central bank operates such a regime. Assume for purposes of illustration that the Bank of Canada fixed the exchange rate between the narrow limits of, say, C$1.23 to C$1.27 to the U.S. dollar. The Bank then stabilizes the exchange rate in the face of seasonal, cyclical, and other fluctuations in demand and supply, entering the market to prevent the rate from going outside the permitted band on either side of the par value. At the price of 1.23, the Bank offers to buy dollars, for permitted purposes, in unlimited amounts; at the price of 1.27, the Bank offers to sell U.S. dollars

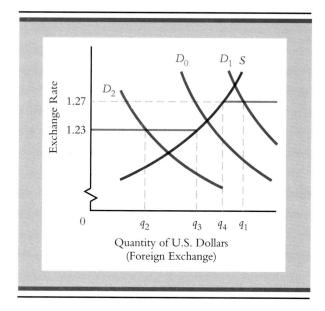

in unlimited amounts. When the Bank buys foreign exchange, its exchange reserves rise; when it sells foreign exchange, its reserves fall.

1. If the demand curve cuts the supply curve in the range 1.23 to 1.27, then the Bank need not intervene in the market.

---

centage fall in the quantity demanded exceeds the percentage rise in the price.[3] The demand curve for

foreign exchange thus shifts leftward, as shown in Figure 39-5.

Now, at the original exchange rate, there is an excess supply of foreign exchange, and the market exchange rate falls to a new equilibrium level.

Other things being equal, foreign inflation will lead to a depreciation of the Canadian exchange rate.

[3]This is true as long as the elasticity of demand for imports is greater than unity—the fall in the volume of imports will then swamp the rise in price, and hence fewer dollars will be spent on them. This elasticity condition is related to a famous long-standing issue in international economics. In what follows, we adopt the standard case of the condition's being met. In a more general form, it is called the *Marshall-Lerner condition* after two famous economists who first studied the problem.

2. If the demand curve shifts to D_1, then the Bank must sell dollars from its reserves to the extent of q_4q_1 in order to prevent the price of dollars from rising above 1.27.

3. If the demand curve shifts to D_2, the Bank must buy dollars to the extent of q_2q_3 and add them to the exchange rate reserves in order to prevent the price of dollars from falling below 1.23.

If, *on the average,* the demand and supply curves intersect in the range 1.23 to 1.27, then the exchange reserves will be relatively stable, with the Bank buying dollars when the demand is abnormally low and selling them when the demand is abnormally high. Over a long period, the average level of reserves will then be fairly stable.

If conditions change (e.g., there is more rapid inflation in one country than in the other), the exchange reserves will rise or fall more or less continuously. Say that the *average* level of demand becomes D_1, with fluctuations on either side of this level. The average drain on reserves will then be q_4q_1 per period. *This situation cannot continue indefinitely.* The Bank has two alternatives: It can change the fixed exchange rate so that the band of permissible prices straddles the equilibrium price, or it can try to shift the curves so that the intersection is in the band 1.23 to 1.27. To accomplish this, it must restrict demand for foreign exchange: It can impose import quotas and foreign-travel restrictions, or it can seek to increase the supply of dollars by encouraging exports.

The Bank can induce movements of short-term capital to assist in its policy of fixing the exchange rate in spite of fluctuations in the demand for and supply of foreign exchange. Assume, for example that in the figure, the demand for dollars is D_1 and the supply S, so that there is a potential deficit of q_4q_1 per period. The Bank can raise the short-term rate of interest and attract short-term capital. This shifts the supply of dollars to the right. If the curve is shifted to cut D_1 vertically above q_1, the inflow of short-term capital just covers the potential shortfall, and the exchange reserves are not run down. *Provided the Bank guessed correctly* that the demand was *abnormally* high, the policy will work. If the demand now falls to produce a free-market rate within the permitted range, the Bank can lower interest rates, as it no longer needs to attract short-term capital to cover the excess demand for foreign exchange at the maximum permitted exchange rate.

Domestic Inflation

Suppose now that foreign prices of tradeable goods are constant but there is domestic inflation. This means increases in domestic wages, in other domestic costs of production, and in the prices of domestic goods and services (things such as haircuts and restaurant meals that are not traded internationally). As a result of the rise in costs, the domestic supply curves for traded goods (both imports and exports) will shift leftward. As a result of the rise in prices of nontraded goods, the domestic demand curves for traded goods will shift rightward. This is because at any given exchange rate, traded goods are now cheaper relative to nontraded goods, so more will be demanded and less will be supplied. As a result of these various changes, the quantity of imports will rise and the quantity of exports will fall. This situation is shown in Figure 39-6 on page 845.

At any given exchange rate, these changes in

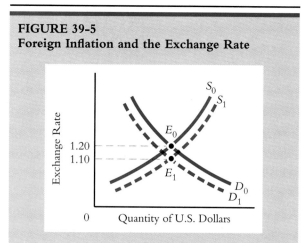

FIGURE 39-5
Foreign Inflation and the Exchange Rate

Foreign inflation will increase the supply of foreign exchange and decrease the demand, thus causing a fall in the exchange rate. The initial demand and supply curves are shown by the solid curves (labeled D_0 and S_0), and the initial equilibrium is at E_0. Now suppose that foreign inflation occurs. This raises the foreign price of all tradeable goods. At any given exchange rate, this will cause an increase in the Canadian dollar price of traded goods, and as we saw in Figure 39-1 and 39-2, the quantity of Canadian exports will increase and the quantity of Canadian imports will decrease as a result. The increase in Canadian exports gives rise to an increase in the supply of U.S. dollars, as shown by the shift in the supply curve from S_0 to S_1. The decrease in Canadian imports gives rise to a decrease in the demand for U.S. dollars, as shown by the shift in the demand curve from D_0 to D_1. As a result, the exchange rate falls from 1.20 to 1.10.

the quantities of imports and exports will cause the supply and demand of foreign exchange to change. The decrease in exports will cause the quantity of U.S. dollars supplied to the foreign exchange market to decrease. The increase in imports will cause the quantity of U.S. dollars demanded in the foreign exchange market to increase. As a result, the equilibrium exchange rate rises; that is, the external value of the Canadian dollar falls.

Other things being equal, a localized Canadian inflation will lead to a rise in the exchange rate.

Inflation in All Countries

Now consider a case in which the domestic country experiences exactly the same rate of inflation as the rest of the world. Now the demand and supply curves for traded goods in Figure 39-5 shift upward as before, but so does the world price of imports and exports. (The rise in the world price is not shown in the figure.) The two shifts offset each other: The upward shifts in the demand and supply curves reduce exports and increase imports, while the upward shift in world prices increases exports and reduces imports. With equal rates of inflation in Canada and the rest of the world, the prices of non-traded Canadian goods remain unchanged *relative to* internationally traded goods at the original exchange rate. There is no reason to expect any change in any country's demand for imports or its supply of exports at the original exchange rate. Hence, there is no change in the demand for and supply of foreign exchange.

The effects of equal rates of inflation in all trading countries offset each other, leaving unchanged both the incentive to import and to export and the equilibrium exchange rate.

Unequal Inflation

The results we have just seen show that the *relative rates of inflation* between any two trading countries is an important determinant of the exchange rate between their two currencies. Differences in the inflation rates will cause changes in imports and exports and hence changes in quantities demanded and supplied on the foreign exchange market. Thus, the exchange rate between the two currencies will change. An important general conclusion follows from a simple extension of the cases just studied:

If the price level of one country is rising relative to that of another country, its exchange rate will be appreciating.

Capital Movements

Capital flows influence exchange rates. For example, an increased Canadian desire to invest in assets in the United States will cause holders of Canadian

FIGURE 39-6
Domestic Inflation and International Trade

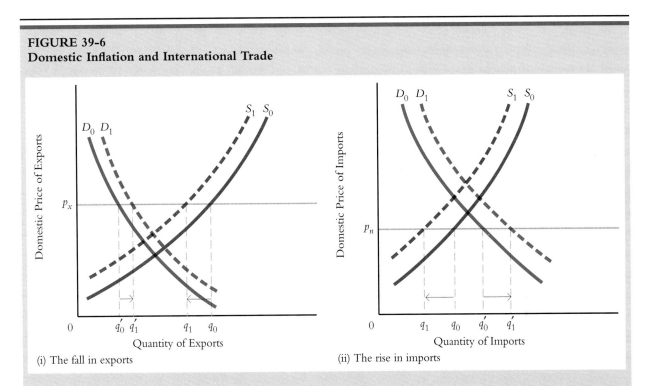

(i) The fall in exports   (ii) The rise in imports

Domestic inflation unmatched in the rest of the world increases the domestic demand for traded goods and reduces the domestic supply; as a result, the quantity of exports falls and the quantity of imports rises. The initial supply and demand curves are shown by the solid lines D_0 and S_0 in both parts of the figure. In each market, the initial quantity supplied is given by q_0 and the initial quantity demanded by q_0'. Initial exports are given in (i) by $q_0'q_0$ and initial imports in (ii) by q_0q_0'.

Domestic inflation causes the demand curves for each traded good to shift rightward from D_0 to D_1 and the supply curve for each to shift leftward from S_0 to S_1. As a result, quantity demanded rises from q_0' to q_1' and quantity supplied falls from q_0 to q_1.

In the market for exports, where domestic supply initially exceeded demand, the inflation thus causes exports to fall, from $q_0'q_0$ to $q_1'q_1$. (In turn, this means that the supply of U.S. dollars in the foreign exchange market falls, as shown by a shift from S_1 to S_0 in Figure 39-5.)

In the market for imports, where domestic demand initially exceeded supply, the inflation thus causes Canadian imports to rise, from $q_0'q_0$ to $q_1'q_1$ (In turn, this means that the demand for U.S. dollars on the foreign exchange market rises, as shown by a shift from D_1 to D_0 in Figure 39-5.)

dollars to demand the U.S. dollars needed to buy U.S. assets. This shifts the demand curve for U.S. dollars to the right, causing the exchange rate to appreciate. The reverse would happen if Americans wished to invest in Canada: The increased supply of U.S. dollars would depreciate the exchange rate.

A movement of investment funds has the effect of depreciating the exchange rate of the **capital-importing country and appreciating the exchange rate of the capital-exporting country.**

This statement is true for all capital movements, short term or long term. Since the motives that lead to large capital movements are usually different in the short and long terms, each must be considered separately.

Short-term capital movements. A major incentive for short-term capital flows is international differences in interest rates. If one major country's short-term rate of interest rises above the rates in most other countries, there will tend to be a large inflow of short-term capital into that country to take advantage of the differential. The extra supply of foreign exchange will tend to depreciate the exchange rate. Conversely, if the short-term interest rate falls, there will be a movement of short-term funds out of the country. The increased demand for foreign exchange will appreciate the exchange rate.

A second motive for short-term capital movements is speculation about a country's exchange rate. If foreigners expect the Canadian exchange rate to depreciate, they will rush to buy assets that pay off in Canadian dollars. The supply of foreign currency to the foreign exchange market pushes the exchange rate down, thus realizing the expectations of this change. Conversely, if foreigners expect the Canadian exchange rate to appreciate, they will be reluctant to hold Canadian securities. They will seek to sell Canadian dollars, demanding U.S. dollars in exchange. This pushes the exchange rate up, thus producing the expected change. This is another example of the phenomenon of *self-realizing expectations* that we have encountered at several earlier points in this book.

Long-term capital movements. Long-term capital movements are largely influenced by long-term expectations about various countries' profit opportunities and exchange rates. A U.S. firm will be more willing to invest in Canada than in the United States if it expects the Canadian investment to earn more *U.S. dollars* than an investment in the United States. This could happen if the Canadian investment earned greater profits (translated into U.S. dollars) than the U.S. investment at the current exchange rate. It could also happen if the profits were the same, translated at the current exchange rate, but the U.S. firm expected future depreciation of the Canadian exchange rate.

Structural Changes

Structural change is an omnibus term for changes in costs of production, the invention of new products, or anything else that affects the pattern of comparative advantage. For example, if the quality of Canadian products does not improve as rapidly as does the quality of U.S. products, consumer demand (at fixed prices) will shift slowly away from the Canadian products and toward U.S. products. On the foreign exchange market, there will be a steady increase in the demand for U.S. dollars combined with a steady decrease in the supply of U.S. dollars as both Canadians and Americans buy fewer Canadian and more U.S. goods. As a result, the exchange rate will appreciate.

The Behaviour of Exchange Rates

The long-term trend of exchange rates is dominated by changes in relative international price levels. In the short term, however, exchange rates show much more volatility than can be explained by movements in relative price levels. Let us look first at long-term trends, then at short-term volatility.

Long-Term Trends

According to the **purchasing power parity (PPP)** theory, a currency will tend to have the same purchasing power when it is spent in its home country as it would have if it were converted to foreign exchange and spent in the foreign country. This implies that over the long term, the average value of the exchange rate between two currencies depends on their relative purchasing power.

If, at existing values of relative price levels and the exchange rate, a currency has a higher purchasing power in its own country, it is said to be *undervalued*—a term that refers to the external value of the currency. There is then an incentive to sell foreign exchange and buy the domestic currency in order to take advantage of its higher purchasing power in the domestic economy. This will put downward pressure on the exchange rate (and hence raise the currency's external value).

Similarly, if a currency has a lower purchasing power in its own country, it is said to be *overvalued*. There is then an incentive to sell the domestic currency and buy foreign exchange in order to take advantage of the higher purchasing power abroad. This will put upward pressure on the exchange rate, which lowers the currency's external value.

The PPP exchange rate is determined by relative price levels in the two countries.

An example may help. Suppose that the same bundle of goods costs US$100 in the United States and C$120 in Canada. The PPP exchange rate is now 1.20. At that rate, the U.S. bundle will sell for $120 in Canada while the Canadian bundle will sell for $100 in the United States. Next, assume that the Canadian price level rises by 20 percent, while the U.S. price level rises by only 5 percent over the same period. As a result, the prices of the bundle rise to US$105 in the United States and C$144 in Canada. The PPP value of the Canadian exchange rate then appreciates by approximately 15 percent to 1.371. This rate reflects the 15 percent rise in the Canadian price level relative to the U.S. price level. Now the U.S. bundle costs (1.05)(1.371) = $1.44 in Canada, while the Canadian bundle costs (144)(1.371) = $105 in the United States.

The PPP exchange rate adjusts so that the relative price of the two nations' goods (measured in the same currency) is unchanged, because the change in the relative values of two currencies compensates exactly for differences in national inflation rates.

If the actual exchange rate changes along with the PPP rate, the competitive positions of producers in the two countries will be unchanged. Firms that are located in countries with high inflation rates will still be able to sell their outputs on international markets, because the exchange rate adjusts to offset the effect of the rising domestic prices.

Short-Term Fluctuations

The exchange rate between Canadian dollars and other major currencies, in particular the US$, has followed the PPP rate over the long term. However, large fluctuations have occurred around the PPP rate.

Many economists used to argue that speculators would stabilize the actual value of exchange rates within a narrow band around the PPP value. The argument was that, because everyone knew the normal value was the PPP rate, speculators who were seeking a profit when the rate deviated from its PPP level would quickly force the rate back to that level. To illustrate, suppose the PPP rate of the Canadian dollar is 1.25 and that the exchange rate falls to $1.15 (i.e., the external value of the C$ rises from US$0.80 to US$0.87). Speculators would rush to buy U.S. dollars (and sell Canadian dollars) at C$1.15 per U.S. dollar, expecting to sell U.S. dollars for Canadian dollars later when the rate returned to its PPP level of $1.25. This very action would raise the demand for the US$ and help push the exchange rate back toward its PPP level.

Such speculative behaviour would stabilize the exchange rate near its PPP value, *if* speculators could be sure that the deviations would be small and short lived. However, flexible exchange rates have actually produced wide swings around the PPP rate, some of which lasted for long periods. Whatever the original causes of these wide and persistent swings, they serve to reduce the stabilizing potential of speculation. For example, if the C$ rose above its PPP value of 1.25, speculators would know that it might go higher and stay there for quite a while before returning to the PPP rate. In that case, it might be worth speculating that the exchange rate would be, say, 1.35 next week rather than the rate of 1.25 at some time in the indefinite future.

The wide swings in exchange rates that have occurred imply that speculative buying and selling cannot be relied on to hold exchange rates close to their PPP values.

These wide fluctuations have mainly been caused by large international movements in short-term capital. When short-term capital floods into Canada, large supplies of foreign exchange come on the market seeking to be traded for Canadian dollers, to invest in such short-term Canadian assets as treasury bills. This depreciates the exchange rate. When short-term capital flows out of Canada, there is a large demand for foreign exchange, which appreciates the Canadian exchange rate.

Exchange Rate Overshooting

Differences in interest rates between countries, due to differences in monetary and fiscal policies as well as other factors, can trigger large capital flows as investors seek to place their funds where returns are highest. These capital flows in turn will result in swings in the exchange rate between the two countries. Some economists argue that this is the fundamental reason for the wide fluctuations in exchange rates that have been observed.

To illustrate, in the early 1990s, the Bank of Canada operated a tight monetary policy, in order to restrain Canadian inflation. As we saw in Chapter 34, this led to an increase in Canadian interest rates. Canadian interest rates rose 3–4 percentage points above those in the United States.

The interest rate differential induced capital to flow into Canada. Canadian and foreign investors alike sold assets denominated in U.S. dollars and sought to buy Canadian dollar assets that earned higher interest. Before they could do this, however, they had to supply U.S. dollars to the foreign exchange market (seeking Canadian dollars in return). The increased supply depreciated the C$ exchange rate.

A tight monetary policy will lead to higher interest rates, a capital inflow, and a depreciation of the Canadian exchange rate.

As long as the return on Canadian assets is above that on foreign assets, the capital inflows will continue, as will the downward pressure on the exchange rate. When will the process stop? It will stop only when the expected returns on Canadian and foreign assets are again roughly equalized. The key is that the expected return includes not only the interest earnings but also the gains or losses that might arise because of changes in the exchange rate during the period of the investment. A foreign investor holding a Canadian asset will receive Canadian dollars when the asset is sold, and will at that time want to exchange Canadian dollars for foreign exchange. If the exchange rate has appreciated by then, that will be a source of loss that has to be balanced against the interest income in assessing the net return on holding the asset.

Equilibrium occurs when the depreciation of the Canadian exchange rate is large enough that investors expect a future appreciation that just offsets the interest premium from investing funds in Canadian dollars.

Suppose, for example, that investors believe that the PPP rate is 1.25, but as they rush to buy dollars to take advantage of higher Canadian interest rates, they push the exchange rate to, say, 1.05. They do not believe this rate will be sustained and, instead, expect it to rise in the future. If foreign investors expect the exchange rate to rise at 4 percent per year, they will be indifferent between lending

money in Montreal at 7 percent and doing so in New York at 3 percent. The extra 4 percentage points per year of interest that they earn in Montreal is exactly offset by the 4 percentage points that they expect to lose when they turn their money back into their own currency.

Any policy that raises domestic interest rates above world levels will cause the exchange rate to depreciate enough to create an expected future appreciation that will be sufficient to offset the interest differential.

If interest differentials are to persist, the exchange rate must change relative to its equilibrium or PPP value; this is often referred to as *overshooting* of the exchange rate.

One implication of this theory is that a central bank that is seeking to use its monetary policy to attain its domestic policy targets may have to put up with large fluctuations in the exchange rate. In the example, the high Canadian interest rates that were the result of a restrictive monetary policy in 1989–1992, caused a depreciation of the Canadian exchange rate. The overshooting of the C$ below its PPP exchange rate put export and import-competing industries under temporary but severe pressure from foreign competition, because Canadian goods became expensive relative to imported goods. The resulting fall in demand for Canadian goods helped to open up a recessionary gap, thus providing a further mechanism by which the restrictive monetary policy was transmitted to the rest of the Canadian economy. This was discussed in Box 33-3 on page 696.

The overvaluation of the Canadian dollar in the early 1990s caused the recession to be particularly severe in Canada, and Canadian export and import-competing industries suffered to some extent. Not surprisingly, this spurred many calls for protectionist measures to save jobs, such as withdrawing from the Canada-U.S. Free Trade Agreement (FTA). However, when Canadian interest rates fell in 1992–1993, the value of the C$ also fell drastically, removing all the competitive disadvantage and leaving the exchange rate about 2–4 percent *higher* than Statistics Canada estimated its PPP rate to be. Furthermore, the complaints from industry appeared to have overestimated the losses due to the low exchange rate. Subsequent research showed that all through the period, Canadian exports to the United

States rose steadily, showing that the beneficial effects of falling U.S. tariffs due to the FTA were stronger than the harmful effects of an exchange rate that was below its PPP rate.

The Balance of Payments

To know what is happening to the course of international trade, governments keep track of the transactions among countries. The record of such transactions is kept in the *balance-of-payments accounts.*

The Payments Accounts

Each transaction, such as a shipment of exports or the arrival of imported goods, is classified according to the payments or receipts of foreign exchange that would typically arise from it. Tables 39-2 and 39-3 show the major items in the Canadian balance-of-payments accounts for 1992.

Current Account

The **current account,** which is shown for 1992 in Table 39-2, records transactions arising from trade in goods and services and from income accruing to capital owned in one country and invested or lent out in another. The current account is divided into two main sections.

The first of these is the **trade account.** The trade account is in turn made up of two subsections. The **merchandise account** records payments and receipts arising from the import and export of tangible goods, such as computers, cars, wheat, and shoes. Canadian imports require the use of foreign exchange and hence are entered as debit items on the visible account; Canadian exports earn foreign exchange and hence are recorded as credit items. The second subsection of the trade account records payments arising from trade in services, covering items such as insurance, shipping, consultants' fees, and tourism.

The second main section of the current account covers investment income plus transfers, such as payments made by people working in Canada to their families who live abroad. Investment income

TABLE 39-2	Canadian Balance of International Payments, 1992 (billions of dollars)

Current Account		
Merchandise Trade		
Exports	157.5	
Imports	−148.1	
Balance		9.4
Traded Services		
Exports	24.6	
Imports	−38.0	
Balance		−13.4
Balance of trade		−4.0
Investment Income		
Receipts	7.7	
Payments	−32.6	
Balance		−24.9
Net transfers		0.2
Balance on current account		−28.7

The Canadian current account was in deficit by almost $29 billion in 1992. Canada had a surplus on merchandise trade and a deficit on traded services, making a small overall deficit on the balance of trade. This was augmented by a large deficit on investment income (interest and dividends) of almost $25 billion. As long as the large government budget deficit creates large foreign borrowing, this deficit on investment income will grow.

covers international payments of interest, dividends, and profits that are made for capital used in one country but owned by residents of another country.[4] We refer to this as the *investment income* account.

As shown in Table 39-2, Canadian merchandise exports were $157.5 billion in 1992, and Canadian merchandise imports were $148.1 billion; thus, the merchandise account balance had a surplus of $9.4 billion. As can also be seen in the table, the traded service account had a net deficit of $13.4 billion, making an overall deficit on the balance of trade of $4 billion. Net investment income and other transfers showed an enormous deficit of $25 billion. This largely represents interest on Canadian debt held by foreigners. Much of this foreign-held debt is the direct or indirect effect of the budget deficits of Cana-

[4]The symbols X and IM as used in this book refer to exports and imports of both tangible goods and services but do not include payments of interest, dividends, and profits.

TABLE 39-3 Canadian Balance of International Payments, 1992 (billions of dollars)

Capital Account

Canadian Capital Exports		
Direct investment abroad	−3.3	
Portfolio investment	−4.9	
Total		−8.2
Canadian Capital Imports		
Direct foreign investment in Canada	4.7	
Purchases of Canadian stocks	1.0	
Net purchases of Canadian bonds	18.2	
Total		23.9
Short-term capital net		4.6
Statistical discrepancy		1.4
Balance on Private Transactions		21.7
Addition to official reserves		7.0
Balance on capital account		28.7

The Canadian capital account was in surplus, indicating large capital imports in 1992. Canadian direct investment abroad was almost equal to foreign direct investment in Canada. A large imbalance occurred, however, in bond transactions, where foreigners purchased $18.2 billion more of Canadian bonds than Canadians did of foreign bonds. This was a major way in which the large Canadian government budget deficits were financed. Overall, there was a net inflow of almost $22 billion of private sector capital. Also, the Bank of Canada accumulated $7 billion worth of foreign exchange, making the overall surplus $28.7 billion, equal to the deficit on current account.

dian governments, as well as the foreign borrowing of such crown corporations as the provincial hydro authorities.

Overall, the current account showed a deficit of nearly $29 billion. This deficit represented a net demand for foreign exchange of $29 billion; the way in which such funds are obtained is often referred to as *financing* the current account deficit.

Capital Account

The second main division in the balance of payments is the **capital account**, which records transactions related to international movements of financial capital. Canadian investment in foreign assets, called a *capital outflow* or a *capital export*, uses foreign exchange and so is entered as a debit item in the

Canadian payments accounts.[5] Foreign investment in Canadian assets, called a *capital inflow* or a *capital import*, earns foreign exchange and so is entered as a credit item.

As shown in Table 39-3, Canadians increased their direct and portfolio investments abroad by $8.2 billion in 1992, resulting in a capital outflow of that amount, while foreigners increased their corresponding investments in Canada by $23.9 billion, resulting in a capital inflow of that amount. Paralleling what was said earlier about interest payments to foreigners, by far the largest item in the capital account is net purchases of Canadian bonds by foreigners. The net surplus on capital account was $21.7. What this means is that Canadians were increasing their net foreign indebtedness to cover their net national dissaving.

Short-term and long-term capital flows. Figures for capital movements are sometimes divided into two categories that distinguish between movements of short-term and long-term capital. Short-term capital is money that is held in the form of highly liquid assets, such as bank accounts and short-term treasury bills. If a nonresident merchant buys dollars and places them in a deposit account in Montreal, this represents an inflow of short-term capital into Canada, and it will be recorded as a credit item on short-term capital account. Long-term capital represents funds coming into Canada (a credit item) or leaving Canada (a debit item), to be invested in less liquid assets, such as long-term bonds, or in physical capital, such as a new automobile assembly plant.

Portfolio investment and direct investment. The two major types of capital movements are *direct investment* and *portfolio investment*. **Direct investment** relates to changes in nonresident ownership of domestic firms and resident ownership of foreign firms. Thus, one form of direct investment in

---

[5] It may seem odd that whereas a merchandise export is a credit item on the current account, a capital export is a debit item on the capital account. To understand this terminology, consider the export of Canadian funds for investment in a German bond. The capital transaction involves the purchase, and hence the *import*, of a German bond, and this has the same effect on the balance of payments as the purchase, and hence the import, of a German good. Both items involve payments to foreigners, and both use foreign exchange. Both are thus debit items in Canadian balance-of-payments accounts.

Canada is capital investment in a branch plant or a subsidiary corporation in Canada in which the investor has voting control. Another form is a takeover, in which a controlling interest in a firm, previously controlled by residents, is acquired by foreigners. **Portfolio investment,** on the other hand, is investment in bonds or a minority holding of shares that does not involve legal control.

Movement of Official Reserves

The final section in the balance-of-payments account represents transactions in the *official reserves* that are held by a country's central bank, and is referred to as *movements of official reserves* or, sometimes, as *payments on the official settlements account.* These transactions reflect the financing of the balance on all other parts of the accounts. The central banks of most countries hold financial reserves that they use to operate in the foreign exchange market. Some of these reserves are held in gold, some in foreign currencies or claims on them, and some in an international currency, called *special drawing rights* or *SDRs.*

The Bank of Canada, operating on behalf of the government, often intervenes in the market for foreign exchange to influence the Canadian dollar's exchange rate. For example, to prevent the value of the exchange rate from rising, the Bank must sell gold or foreign exchange (and accept Canadian dollars in return). It can do so only if it holds reserves of gold or foreign exchange (or can borrow from other central banks). When the Bank wishes to stop the exchange rate from depreciating, it enters the market and buys foreign exchange (supplying Canadian dollars in return). It then adds the foreign exchange to its reserves.

The final item in the capital account, shown in Table 39-3, is a selling of foreign exchange reserves by the Bank of Canada to the tune of $7 billion. This is by far the highest figure over the last several decades. This means that the Bank financed 25 percent of Canada's 1992 current account deficit by running down its reserves to supply foreign exchange to the market. The net effect was to stop the exchange rate from rising as a result of the private sector's excess demand for foreign exchange. Had the Bank not intervened so massively, the exchange rate would have risen considerably. This is quite an unusual amount of intervention by the Bank of Canada, and it was associated with its anti-inflation-

ary policy.[6] In a typical year, the Bank's intervention is less than $1 billion. This implies that the exchange rate will average quite close to the free market rate that would have been established in the absence of any Bank purchases or sales of foreign exchange.

Overall, the total balance on capital account is equal in size and opposite in sign to the overall balance on current account.

The Meaning of Payments Balances and Imbalances

We have seen that the payments accounts show the total of receipts of foreign exchange (credit items) and payments of foreign exchange (debit items) in each category of payment. It is also common to calculate the *balance* on separate items or groups of items. The concept of the balance of payments is used in a number of ways. These can be confusing, so we must approach this issue in steps.

The Balance of Payments Must Balance Overall

Notice two things about the payments accounts. First, they record *actual payments*, not *desired payments.* Second, they record *all payments*, whatever the reason for which they were made.

It is quite possible that at the existing exchange rate between Canadian dollars and U.S. dollars, holders of U.S. dollars want to purchase more Canadian dollars than holders of Canadian dollars want to sell in exchange for U.S. dollars. In this situation, the quantity of Canadian dollars demanded exceeds the quantity supplied. However, holders of U.S. dollars cannot actually buy more Canadian dollars than holders of Canadian dollars actually sell; every U.S.$ that is bought must have been sold by someone, and every C$ that is sold must have been bought by someone.

---

[6]Selling foreign exchange, like selling treasury bills, is an open market operation that reduces bank liquidity. This measure thus contributed to the Bank's tight monetary policy, but at the cost of putting added pressure on Canadian producers of tradeable goods, since the exchange rate was kept lower than it otherwise would have been.

Box 39-2

Why Total Payments Always Balance: An Illustration

Trade Between Two Countries

Suppose that the sole international transaction made this year by a small country called Myopia was an export to Canada of Myopian coconuts worth $1,000. Further suppose that the Myopian central bank issues a local currency, the stigma, but does not operate in the foreign exchange market. Finally, suppose that Myopia's self-sufficient inhabitants want no imports. Surely, then, you might think Myopia has an overall favourable balance of $1,000, which is a current account receipt, C_R, with no balancing item on the payments side.

To see why this is wrong, we ask what the exporter of coconuts did with the dollars he received. If he deposited them in a Toronto bank, this represents a capital export from Myopia. Myopians have accumulated claims on foreign exchange, which they hold in the form of a deposit with a foreign bank. Thus there are two entries in the Myopian accounts—one a credit item for the export of coconuts (C_R = $1,000) and the other a debit item for the export of capital (K_P = $1,000).

The fact that the same agent made both transactions is irrelevant. Although the current account shows a credit balance, the capital account exactly balances this with a debit item. Hence, looking at the *balance of payments as a whole*, the two sides of the account are equal. The balance of payments has balanced—as always it must.

Consider now a slightly more realistic case. If the coconut exporter wants to turn his $1,000 into Myopian stigmas so that he can pay his coconut pickers in local currency, he must find someone who wishes to buy his Canadian dollars in return for Myopian currency. But we have assumed that no one in Myopia wants to import, so no one wants to sell Myopian currency for current account reasons. Assume, however, that a wealthy Myopian landowner would like to invest $1,000 in Toronto by buying shares in a Canadian firm. To do so he needs $1,000. The coconut exporter can sell his $1,000 to the landowner in return for stigmas. Now he can pay his local bills. The landowner sells his stigmas to the exporter in return for dollars. Now he can buy the Canadian shares.

It follows that if we add up all the receipts arising from (1) payments received by Canadian residents on account of Canadian exports of goods and services, (2) capital imports, and (3) purchase of foreign exchange or gold by the Bank of Canada, these must be exactly equal to all payments made by holders of dollars arising from (1) Canadian imports of goods and services, (2) exports of capital, and (3) sale of foreign exchange or gold by the Bank.

This relation is so important that it pays us to write it out in symbols. We let C, K, and B stand for current account, capital account, and movements of official reserves, respectively, and use P for payments (debit items) and R for receipts (credit items). Now we can write

$$C_R + K_R + B_R = C_P + K_P + B_P \qquad [1]$$

All this tells us is that if we add up across all transactions, payments must equal receipts in total.

Although the relation given in the equation is necessarily true, it often worries students who feel that it need not be true. To help clarify the issue, some apparent exceptions are considered in Box 39-2.

Payments on Specific Parts of the Accounts Need Not Balance

Although the overall total of payments must equal the overall total of receipts, the same zero balance

Once again, the Myopian balance of payments will show two entries, equal in size but opposite in sign. The credit item for the export of coconuts (the sale of coconuts that earned foreign exchange) and the debit item for the export of capital (the purchase of the Canadian shares that used foreign exchange) balance each other out.

Trade Involving Many Countries

In the example, Myopia had what is called a bilateral payments balance with Canada which means that the payments and receipts flowing between them are equal. If there were only two countries in the world, their overall payments would have to be in bilateral balance; that is, one country's payments to the other would be equal to its receipts from the other. This is not true when there are more than two countries.

Suppose that one year later, Myopia again sells $1,000 worth of coconuts to Canada but that the landowner does not wish to invest further in Canada. Now suppose, however, that the Myopian people wish to buy 200,000 yen worth of parasols from Japan. (Assume also that on the foreign exchange market, $1.00 Canadian trades for 200 yen.) Finally, assume that a Japanese importer wishes to buy $1,000 worth of Canadian skateboards.

What in effect happens is that the Myopian coconut exporter sells his $1,000 to the Japanese skateboard importer for 200,000 yen, which the coconut dealer then sells to the Myopian parasol importer in return for Myopian stigmas. (In the real world, the exchanges are usually made through financial institutions, but the text describes what happens in effect.) Now the Myopian payment statistics will show a $1,000 bilateral payment surplus with Canada—receipts of $1,000 from Canada on account of coconut exports and no payments to Canada—and a bilateral deficit with Japan of 200,000 yen—$1,000 of payments to Japan on account of parasol imports and no receipts from Japan. But when both countries are considered, Myopia's *multilateral payments* are in balance.

does not have to hold on subsections of the overall accounts. We now look at the balances on parts of the accounts, first in relation to particular countries and then in relation to particular subsectors of the account.

Country balances. When all foreign countries are taken together, each country's overall payments must balance, but one country can have bilateral surpluses or deficits with other individual foreign countries or groups of countries. In general, the **multilateral balance of payments** refers to the balance between one country's payments to and receipts from the rest of the world. When all items are considered, every country must have a zero multilateral payments balance with the rest of the world, although it can have bilateral surpluses or deficits with individual countries. This important principle is illustrated in the second part of Box 39-2.

Subsection balances. The balance on visible, or merchandise, account refers to the difference between the value of Canadian exports of goods and the value of imports of goods. A surplus occurs when exports of goods exceed imports of goods; a deficit occurs when imports exceed exports. The balance on invisibles refers to the difference between the value of receipts on invisibles and the value of payments for invisibles. The **current account balance** is the sum of the balances on the visible and invisible accounts. It gives the balance between payments and receipts on all income-related items.

As a carryover from a long-discredited eighteenth-century economic doctrine called mercantilism, a credit balance on current account (receipts exceeding payments) is called a **favourable balance of payments**, and a debit balance (payments exceeding receipts) is called an **unfavourable balance of payments.**

Mercantilists, both ancient and modern, hold that the gains from trade arise from having a favourable balance of trade. This misses the whole point of the principle of comparative advantage discussed in Chapter 24. That principle shows that countries can gain from a *balanced increase* in trade between themselves because of the opportunity it provides for each country to specialize according to its comparative advantage. The modern resurgence of mercantilist views is discussed in Box 39-3.

The balance on capital account gives the difference between receipts of foreign exchange and payments of foreign exchange arising out of capital movements. A surplus ("favourable") balance on capital account means that a country is a *net importer of capital*; a deficit ("unfavourable") balance means that the country is a *net exporter of capital.*

Notice that a deficit on capital account, which is referred to as an unfavourable balance, merely indicates that a country is investing abroad. Investing abroad and accumulating assets that will earn income in the future may be desirable. So once again, we observe that there is nothing necessarily unfavourable about having an "unfavourable" balance on any of the payments accounts.

The Relations of Various Balances

Two important points require notice. First, since overall payments must balance, the terms *balance-of-payments deficit* and *balance-of-payments surplus* refer to the balance on *some part* of the payments accounts. Second, because of the necessity for the balance of payments to balance overall, a deficit on any one part of the accounts implies an offsetting surplus on the rest of the accounts.

Two important applications of this second point will be considered. The first concerns the balances on current and capital accounts, and the second concerns the use of official reserves and the balances on the remainder of the overall accounts.

The current and capital account balances. To help clarify the relation between current and capital balances, suppose that the Bank of Canada holds its official reserves constant.

Now any deficit or surplus on current account must be matched by an equal and opposite surplus or deficit on capital account. For example, if a country has a credit balance on current account, the foreign exchange earned must appear as a debit item in the capital account. The foreign exchange may be used to buy foreign assets or merely stashed away in foreign bank accounts. In either case, there is an outflow of capital from Canada. It is recorded as a debit item, because it uses foreign exchange.

We can see this clearly if we return to Equation 1. Since F_R equals F_P, by our assumption about the Bank's behaviour, we can eliminate these terms from each side of the equation to get:

$$C_R + K_R = C_P + K_P \qquad [2]$$

Now subtract C_P and K_R from both sides of the equation to get

$$C_R - C_P = K_P - K_R \qquad [3]$$

This expresses in equation form what we have just stated in words: A surplus on current account must be balanced by a deficit on capital account (i.e., an outflow of capital), and a deficit on current account must be matched by a surplus on capital account (i.e., an inflow of capital).

One important implication relates to capital transfers. A country that is importing capital has a surplus on capital account and so it *must* have a deficit on current account. This is the position that the United States was in during all of the 1980s and that Canada was in during the latter part of the decade. Because of the borrowing requirements of a large government budget deficit, there was a capital inflow into these countries. This inflow made a current account deficit inevitable. As long as the capital inflow persisted, no policy measure could remove the current account deficit. It has also been the position throughout much of Canada's history when the country has been a net importer of capital.

Box 39-3

The Volume of Trade, the Balance of Trade, and the New Mercantilism

Media commentators, political figures, and much of the general public often judge the national balance of payments as they would the accounts of a single firm. Just as a firm is supposed to show a profit, the nation is supposed to secure a balance-of-payments surplus, with the benefits derived from international trade measured by the size of that surplus.

This view is related to the exploitation doctrine of international trade. Since one country's surplus is another country's deficit, one country's gain, judged by its surplus, must be another country's loss, judged by its deficit.

People who hold such views today are echoing an ancient economic doctrine called *mercantilism*. The mercantilists were a group of economists who preceded Adam Smith. They judged the success of trade by the size of the trade balance. In many cases this doctrine made sense in terms of their objective, which was to use international trade as a means of building up the political and military power of the state rather than raising the living standards of its citizens. A balance-of-payments surplus allowed the nation (then and now) to acquire foreign exchange reserves. (In those days, the reserves took the form of gold. Today, they are a mixture of gold and claims on the currencies of other countries.) These reserves could then be used to pay armies, composed partly of foreign mercenaries; to purchase weapons from abroad; and to finance colonial adventures.

People who advocate this view in modern times are called *neomercantilists*. Insofar as their object is to increase the power of the state, they are choosing means that could achieve their ends. Insofar as they are drawing an analogy between what is a sensible objective for a business interested in its own material welfare and what is a sensible objective for a government interested in the material welfare of its citizens, their views are erroneous, for the analogy is false.

If we take the view that the object of economic activity is to promote the welfare and living standards of ordinary citizens rather than the power of governments, the mercantilist focus on the balance of trade makes no sense. The law of comparative advantage shows that average living standards are maximized by having individuals, regions, and countries specialize in the things they can produce comparatively best and trading to obtain the things they can produce comparatively worst. The more specialization, the more trade.

In this view, the gains from trade are to be judged by the volume of trade. A situation in which there is a *large volume of trade* but each country has a *zero balance of trade* can thus be regarded as quite satisfactory. Furthermore, a change in commercial policy that results in a balanced increase in trade between two countries will bring gain, because it allows for specialization according to comparative advantage, even though it causes no change in either country's trade balance.

To the business interested in private profit and to the government interested in the power of the state, it is the balance of trade that matters. To the person interested in the welfare of ordinary citizens, it is the volume of trade that matters.

It follows that when we are evaluating any new initiative such as the Canada-U.S. Free Trade Agreement, we need to look at its effects on the volume, not the balance, of trade. A large and equal increase in both exports and imports following the agreement would indicate substantial mutual gains for trade in both countries. A negligible increase in imports and exports would suggest that the agreement was failing to produce the anticipated benefits.

This issue is considered in more detail in Chapter 40.[7]

Use of official reserves. When people speak of a country as having an overall balance-of-payments deficit or surplus, they are usually referring to the *balance of all accounts excluding the use of official reserves.* A balance-of-payments surplus means that the central bank is adding foreign exchange reserves to its holdings; a balance-of-payments deficit means that the central bank is reducing its reserves.

If the central bank does not operate in the foreign exchange market, there can be no overall balance-of-payments deficit or surplus on current plus capital account. Suppose that holders of Canadian dollars are trying to buy more foreign exchange than holders of foreign currencies wish to sell in return for dollars. There will be an excess supply of dollars and an excess demand for foreign exchange.

The dollar will depreciate on the foreign exchange market until demand equals supply. At this point, both desired and actual international payments are in balance.

Whenever exchange rates are completely free to vary, balance-of-payments deficits and surpluses are eliminated through exchange rate adjustments.

Given that the Bank of Canada does not intervene over the long run to hold the C$ away from its equilibrium exchange rate, Canada does not have a long-term, overall balance-of-payments problem. The balance-of-payments deficits that do concern many people relate to the current account. They worry, for example, about the overall balance-of-trade deficit. That, however, is one part of the current account counterpart of the capital account surplus. Concern might be better directed at the capital account surplus, which means large capital inflows, only part of which is in response to favourable investment opportunities in Canada. The rest goes to finance the large government budget deficit. It is money that Canadians are borrowing abroad to finance large excesses of current government spending over current tax income.

---

[7]Commentators sometimes assume that the capital inflow must be to buy new government debt directly. The shortfall between the government's borrowing requirements plus private requirements for funds on the one hand and Canadian savings on the other had to be covered by foreign capital. In practise, much of the foreign capital was invested in the Canadian private sector, leaving the Canadian public to buy Canadian government debt. Thus, the government debt helped to increase foreign ownership of Canadian private-sector debt and equity.

 SUMMARY

1. International trade is greatly facilitated because it is possible to exchange the currency of one country for that of another. The exchange rate between two currencies is the amount of the home currency that must be paid to purchase one unit of a foreign currency. A fall in the exchange rate is the same thing as a rise in the external value of a country's currency and vice versa.
2. The determination of exchange rates in the free market is simply an application of the laws of supply and demand studied in Chapter 4; the item being bought and sold is foreign exchange.
3. The supply of foreign exchange arises from Canadian exports of goods and services and from long-term and short-term capital flows into Canada. The demand for foreign exchange arises from Canadian imports of goods and services and from capital flows out of Canada.
4. An appreciation of the exchange rate raises the domestic price of traded goods, whose prices are fixed in foreign currency. This increases the quantities of such goods supplied domestically and reduces the quantity demanded. As a result, the volume of exports rises, and with it, the supply of foreign exchange. Also, the vol-

ume of imports falls, and with it, the demand for foreign exchange. Thus, the supply curve for foreign exchange is positively sloped and the demand curve for foreign exchange is negatively sloped when the quantities demanded and supplied are plotted against the exchange rate.

5. The exchange rate will appreciate when there is a shift to the right of the demand curve for foreign exchange or a shift to the left of the supply curve. Shifts in the opposite directions will depreciate the exchange rate. Shifts are caused by such things as changes in the prices of imports and exports, the rates of inflation in different countries, capital movements, and structural changes.

6. The long-term value of the exchange rate tends to follow the purchasing power parity rate and hence to change with changes in *relative* international price levels.

7. The exchange rate tends to be quite volatile over the short-term. It is strongly influenced by movements of short-term capital. These are in turn strongly influenced by relative international interest rates and expectations of future changes in exchange rates.

8. Actual transactions among the firms, households, and governments of various countries are reported in the balance-of-payments accounts. Any transaction that uses foreign exchange is recorded as a debit item and any transaction that produces foreign exchange is recorded as a credit item. The sum of all credit items necessarily equals the sum of all debit items, since the foreign exchange that is bought must also have been sold.

9. Major categories in the balance-of-payments account are the trade in goods (merchandise) and services and capital service items and transfers, which make up the current account; the capital account; and movements of official reserves. Ignoring changes in official reserves, a balance on current account must be matched by a balance on capital account of equal magnitude but opposite sign.

10. A country that is importing capital records a surplus on capital account that must be matched by a deficit on current account.

11. There is nothing inherently good or bad about deficits or surpluses on current and capital accounts. Evaluating them requires knowing the circumstances that brought them about.

TOPICS FOR REVIEW

Foreign exchange and exchange rates

Appreciation and depreciation

Sources of the demand for and supply of foreign exchange

Effects on exchange rates of capital flows, inflation, interest rates, and expectations about future exchange rates

Balance of trade and balance of payments

Current and capital accounts

Mercantilist views on the balance and volume of trade

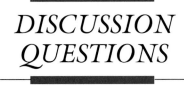

DISCUSSION QUESTIONS

1. What is the probable effect of each of the following on the exchange rate between the Canadian and U.S. dollars?
   a. The quantity of Canadian oil exports is greatly increased.
   b. Canada's inflation rate rises well above the U.S. inflation rate.
   c. Falling unit labour costs in Canada increase the competitiveness of Canadian exports in world markets.
   d. The federal government greatly increases its foreign borrowing in order to finance its deficit in the face of falling domestic savings.
   e. A major boom occurs with rising employment.
   f. The Bank of Canada drives up interest rates sharply in pursuit of its anti-inflation policy.
   g. Canadian consumers increase their purchases of Japanese cars in preference to North American models.

2. For over a decade, Canada has had to sell bonds and bills abroad to finance its excess of government plus investment spending over tax revenue plus private-sector saving.
   a. What are the implications for the capital and the current accounts?
   b. Why, when this dissaving first appeared, was the main current account effect on the balance of *trade*?
   c. Why, over time, would the main current account effect switch to the investment-income side of the current account (interest payments)?
   d. Assess a situation in which the balance on capital account due to net foreign borrowing is exactly equal to (but opposite in sign) the balance of net interest payments on the current account.

3. In the mid-1980s, money wages rose substantially faster in Canada than in the United States. Many Canadians expressed the fear that the rapidly rising wages would price them out of U.S. markets. Would this fear be well founded if the Canada-U.S. exchange rate were fixed? Is it well founded when, as was the case, the external value of the Canadian dollar was free to vary on the open market?

4. Indicate whether each of the following transactions increases the demand for foreign exchange on the foreign exchange market, the supply of foreign exchange, or neither. What will happen to the C$ exchange rate?
   a. IBM moves $10 million from bank accounts in Canada to banks in Paris to expand operations in France.
   b. The Canadian government extends a grant of $3 million to the government of Peru, which Peru uses to buy farm machinery from a Winnipeg firm.
   c. Canadian investors, responding to higher profits of American rather than Canadian corporations, buy stocks through the New York Stock Exchange.
   d. Several countries stop interest payments on their large debts to Canadian and American banks.
   e. Lower interest rates in Montreal than in New York encourage British firms to borrow in the Montreal money market, converting the proceeds into sterling for use at home.

5. What must be the balance of payments on current account when Canada is a major importer of foreign capital? Does it matter if this capital is used to build productive facilities, as it largely was in the late 1970s, or to finance an excess of government spending for current purposes over government tax revenue, as it largely was in the late 1980s?

6. In the mid-1980s, the United States became a major importer of capital, partly to finance the large internal budget deficit and partly because the American boom and the European slump made the United States a highly attractive place in which to invest foreign funds. Predict the effects of this large capital inflow on the U.S. dollar exchange rate and on the balance of payments on current account. Would these developments have anything to do with the upsurge of protectionist sentiment in the U.S. Congress during the latter part of the 1980s?

7. Outline the reasoning behind the following 1993 newspaper headline: "U.S. dollar tumbles as British interest rates weaken."

8. Update Tables 39–2 and 39–3 and comment on the changes that have occurred.

40

Macroeconomic Policy in an Open Economy

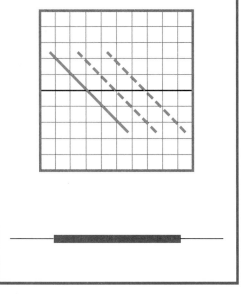

I n the early 1990s, the Canadian economy slid into a deep recession as the external value of the Canadian dollar soared. How were these two events related? In the 1990s, large government budget deficits were accompanied by large current account deficits. Why did economists refer to these as the *twin deficits*? Was the current account deficit the inevitable consequence of the government budget deficit?

In this chapter, we explore these and other issues that arise in an *open* economy. When we focus on *open-economy* issues, new complications arise. These include the behaviour of the exchange rate and its influence on the balance of trade and national income, the nature and extent of foreign borrowing, and the impact on the economy of changes in the terms of trade or in foreign national income, interest rates, and inflation. As we shall also see, the response of the economy to economic policies may be altered in an open economy, as opposed to the closed-economy response emphasized so far in this book.

In the first section of this chapter, we focus on the relationships among the balance of trade, aggregate demand, and national income, and on the role of the exchange rate. We then turn to a discussion of the implications of international movements of capital, or *capital mobility*.

The Balance of Trade and National Income

Suppose that there are no international capital flows in the world economy, so that the only international activities involve the exchange of goods and services across national boundaries. What are the implications of this international trade for the determination of national income and for the role of economic policies?

We start by comparing the basic macroeconomic equilibrium condition for a closed economy with that for an open economy. In each case, we also use the equilibrium condition (in which national income equals desired aggregate expenditure) to analyse the multiplier, relating changes in equilibrium national income to changes in autonomous expenditure. When we consider the multiplier in an open economy, we distinguish between an open economy that maintains a fixed exchange rate and one that has a flexible exchange rate.

In studying national income under these various circumstances, we find that changes in the price level arising as a result of movements along a positively sloped aggregate supply curve complicate but do not change the basic results.[1] Thus, for simplicity, we focus our discussion on shifts in the AD curve *with a given price level*; in terms of the terminology in Chapters 28 and 29, we will focus on the size of the *simple* multiplier.

A Closed Economy

For a closed economy (that is, an economy that does not engage in international trade), the only sources of demand are domestic expenditure: consumption (C), investment (I), and government (G). Thus the equilibrium condition is that in which real national income equals the sum of these three expenditure categories:

$$Y = C + I + G \qquad [1]$$

We saw in Chapter 30 that this equation underlies the aggregate demand *(AD)* curve; see Figure 30-2 on page 610. Recall in particular that the *simple* multiplier gives the size of the horizontal shift in the *AD* curve following a change in autonomous spending. The simple multiplier is equal to $1/(1-z)$, where z is the marginal propensity to spend. As we saw in Chapter 30, for our closed economy, z is equal to $b(1-t)$, where b is the marginal propensity to consume and t is the marginal tax rate.

We want to study what happens when the government changes its fiscal and monetary policies. A simple case of an expansionary fiscal policy is when the government increases its purchases (G rises). A simple case of an expansionary monetary policy is when the Bank of Canada increases the money supply. As we saw in Chapter 34, this sets in motion the transmission mechanism; the interest rate falls, and hence interest-sensitive expenditures (as represented by I) *increase*. Thus, expansionary fiscal and monetary policies both lead to a rightward shift in the *AD* curve and hence to an increase in national income, as illustrated in part (i) of Figure 40-1 by the shift from AD_0 to AD_{closed}.

---

[1]Because the *SRAS* curve does not shift following a change in autonomous spending, the size of the resulting change in national income will be directly related to the size of the shift in the *AD* curve. (This issue is discussed further in Box 40-1 on page 864.)

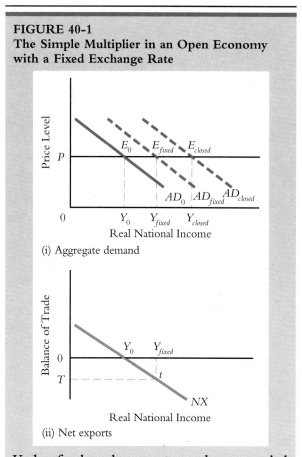

FIGURE 40-1
The Simple Multiplier in an Open Economy with a Fixed Exchange Rate

(i) Aggregate demand

(ii) Net exports

Under fixed exchange rates and zero capital mobility, the simple multiplier is smaller than it would be in a closed economy; the responsiveness of net exports to national income provides an automatic stabilizer. In part (i), aggregate demand is initially given by the negatively sloped line AD_0, and the price level is P. Equilibrium is at E_0 and the equilibrium level of national income is Y_0. An increase in autonomous spending then shifts the *AD* curve to the right; the size of the horizontal shift is given by the simple multiplier. In a closed economy, the *AD* curve shifts to AD_{closed}, the new equilibrium is at E_{closed}, and the new equilibrium level of national income is Y_{closed}.

In an open economy with fixed exchange rates and no capital mobility, the simple multiplier is smaller. The *AD* curve shifts by less, to AD_{fixed}; the new equilibrium is at E_{fixed} and the new equilibrium level of national income is Y_{fixed}, less than Y_{closed}.

In part (ii), the balance of trade is shown by the negatively sloped line NX. At the initial equilibrium level of national income, there is a zero balance of trade; the rise in income to Y_{fixed} in the open-economy fixed-exchange-rate case causes a movement along NX to t, and there is a balance-of-trade deficit of T.

An Open Economy with a Fixed Exchange Rate

Now consider an open economy (that is, one that engages in international trade). For the moment, we suppose that the government adjusts its official financing transactions so as to maintain a fixed exchange rate in the manner discussed in Box 39-1 on page 842. As we saw in Chapter 39, this means that the balance of payments can take on a value different from zero; because we have also simplified our analysis at this stage by supposing that there are no international capital movements, the balance of payments is equal to the balance of trade.

In Chapter 29, we saw that incorporating exports (X) and imports (IM) into the analysis results in the equilibrium condition:

$$Y = C + I + G + (X - IM) \qquad [2]$$

The inclusion of the balance of trade or net export term, $(X - IM)$, in the determination of desired aggregate expenditure has two important implications.

Automatic stabilizer. Because imports rise with national income, the simple multiplier is reduced; that is, there is a smaller horizontal shift in the AD curve following an increase in autonomous spending than would occur in a closed economy. Recall that the simple multiplier is given by $1/(1-z)$ where z is the marginal propensity to spend; in an open economy, the marginal propensity to spend is reduced because of *marginal propensity to import*. This reduction in z increases the denominator $(1-z)$ and thus reduces the size of the multiplier. The simple open-economy multiplier is shown in part (i) of Figure 40-1 as the shift from AD to AD_{fixed}, which is smaller than the closed-economy multiplier shown by the shift from AD_0 to AD_{closed}.[2]

As we saw in Chapter 31, anything that reduces the size of the multiplier, and thus reduces the sensitivity of national income to autonomous changes in spending, is called an *automatic stabilizer.*

Under fixed exchange rates, net exports act as an automatic stabilizer.

The source of the difference between the closed and open economy multipliers is shown in part (ii) of Figure 40-1. In an open economy, the increase in national income following an increase in G causes a movement along the net export function. Thus, following the shock there is a deterioration in the balance of trade as a result of the increase in imports. From Equation 2, we can see that the fixed exchange rate multiplier is smaller because an increase in I or G is partially offset by a decrease in $(X - IM)$.[3]

Export multiplier. Equation 2 shows (as we discussed in Chapter 29) that in an open economy a change in the level of exports will cause national income to change. A change in the level of exports can occur for many reasons, including a change in the terms of trade (i.e., a change in the value of a country's exports relative to its import goods) or a change in the level of economic activity in a country's trading partners. These will lead to a shift in the AD curve and hence to a change in the equilibrium level of national income.

Under fixed exchange rates, changes in exports cause changes in aggregate demand and equilibrium national income.

This is often referred to as the *export multiplier.* The importance of the export multiplier is that it links the levels of economic activity of trading partners. For example, a boom in one country is transmitted to its trading partners via increased demand for the second country's exports.

The operation of the export multiplier is shown in Figure 40-2. As shown in part (i), a change in exports (X) leads to a shift in the AD curve. As shown in part (ii), it will also lead to a *larger* shift in the net export function; in contrast to the effects of an increase in domestic spending, a rise in exports will lead to a balance-of-trade *surplus* rather than a balance-of-trade deficit. **[46]**

---

[2]The simple open-economy multiplier is $1/[1 - b(1 - t) + m]$, where m is the *marginal propensity to import*. Because m is positive, the denominator is increased, and hence the simple open-economy multiplier is smaller than the simple closed-economy multiplier $1/[1 - b(1 - t)]$.

[3]The change in the balance of trade accompanying the change in national income may be undesirable. Thus, under fixed exchange rates, there is a potential conflict for domestic policy makers between their objectives in terms of domestic (or *internal*) policy variables and international (or *external*) ones.

FIGURE 40-2
The Export Multiplier

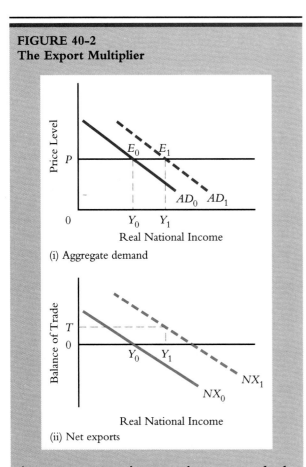

(i) Aggregate demand

(ii) Net exports

An autonomous increase in exports leads, under fixed exchange rates, to an increase in equilibrium national income and to a balance-of-trade surplus.

Initially, aggregate demand is given by AD_0 in part (i), and the net export function is given by NX_0 in part (ii). The price level is P, equilibrium is at E_0, equilibrium national income is Y_0, and there is a zero balance of trade.

Following an autonomous increase in exports, the aggregate demand curve shifts to the right to AD_1 in part (i), and the net export function shifts to the right to NX_1 in part (ii). The new equilibrium is at E_1, with equilibrium national income rising to Y_1. Because the shift in NX is larger than the shift in the AD curve, at the new equilibrium level of income there is a balance-of-trade surplus of T.

In Figures 40-1 and 40-2, the shifts in the AD curves are superimposed on a given price level. A more complete analysis would take account of the effects of a positively sloped $SRAS$ curve; as noted before, this complicates but does not change the

basic results. For those who wish to work through this more complicated case, the analysis is presented in Box 40-1.

Flexible Exchange Rates

The automatic stabilizer role provided by the balance of trade and the potential for the export multiplier to transmit disturbances from one economy to another are key aspects of a fixed exchange rate system. As such, they may be relevant to the historical analysis of periods earlier in this century when the world was essentially on fixed exchange rates, and to a study of the economies of particular provinces within Canada or of countries that are part of the European Exchange Rate Mechanism.

However, in order to study the economies of countries such as Canada and the United States and most other industrialised countries outside of Europe, it is important to examine flexible exchange rates.

As we saw in Chapter 39, a flexible exchange rate means that official financing transactions are zero, so the balance of payments must be zero. In the simplified model of this section, where there are no international capital flows, this means that the balance of trade must be zero. As we will see, this has dramatic implications for open-economy multiplier analysis.

Automatic stabilizer. Look again at Figure 40-1, which shows the situation following an increase in autonomous spending. (In this section, we restrict our attention to the implications for changes in *domestic* spending, G or I; we return to the implications of changes in export spending, X, later.) Following an increase in autonomous domestic spending, aggregate demand and national income have increased, *and* the increase in income has caused a balance-of-trade deficit; this analysis is reproduced in parts (i) and (ii) of Figure 40-3.

Under flexible exchange rates, the balance-of-trade deficit following an increase in domestic spending cannot be sustained.[4] The increased demand for imports resulting from the stimulus to ag-

---

[4]In fact, it would never occur. There would be a tendency for a deficit to emerge, and this would set in motion the reactions discussed in the rest of this section.

Box 40-1

Aggregate Supply and the Open-Economy Multiplier

In this box, we consider the implications of incorporating a positively sloped *SRAS* curve into the analysis of the open-economy multiplier of Figure 40-1.

The basic analysis is presented in the figure. Because the *SRAS* curve does not shift in response to the change in autonomous spending, the change in national income is directly related to the shift in the *AD* curve. Hence, the results from the fixed-price-level analysis of Figure 40-1 appear to carry through to this case.

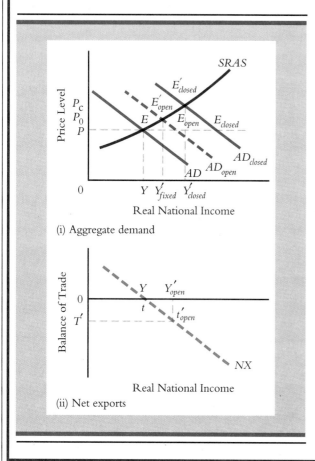

(i) Aggregate demand

(ii) Net exports

One complication is that the slopes of the *AD* and *SRAS* curves might change in the open-economy case. This is difficult to analyse, which is the reason we have focused on the fixed-price case in the text.

The effect of the openness of the economy on the slope of the *SRAS* curve is likely to be minor and, in any event, secondary to our discussion. For simplicity, we do not consider it further.

The implications of changes in the domestic price level effects on *AD* are perhaps more central. When national income *and the price level* change in response to a change in autonomous spending, the components of aggregate demand—*C, I,* and *(X − IM)*—will be affected by the change in the price level. As a result:

The change in national income following a change in autonomous expenditure is smaller because of the positively sloped *SRAS* curve; the rise in the price level leads to a reduction in aggregate demand.

But this is true in both the closed economy and the open economy. Further, the presence of the positively sloped *SRAS* curve does not alter the relative change in national income in the two cases—the multiplier is still smaller in the open economy than in the closed economy.

In the open economy, the rise in national income following an increase in *G* or *I* also leads to a balance-of-trade deficit. From the discussion in Chapter 39, it might appear that the *NX* curve in part (ii) of the figure should shift as a result of the effect of the change in the price level on exports and imports. However, this effect can be incorporated in the slope of the *NX* curve (which changes the magnitude of the slope but not the sign), so that the *NX* curve does *not* shift in response to changes in autonomous spending. **[47]**

FIGURE 40-3
The Simple Multiplier in an Open Economy with a Flexible Exchange Rate

(i) Aggregate demand

Price Level axis, with P, E_0, E_1, E_{closed}, and AD_0, AD_1, AD_{closed}; Real National Income axis with 0, Y_0, Y_1, Y_{closed}.

(ii) Net exports

Balance of Trade axis with 0; Real National Income axis with Y_0, Y_1, Y_{closed}; curves NX_0, NX_1, NX_2.

Under flexible exchange rates and zero capital mobility, the balance of trade is always zero, and hence the open-economy multiplier is identical to the closed-economy multiplier. There is no automatic stabilizer role provided by net exports. In part (i), aggregate demand is initially given by the negatively sloped line AD_0, and the price level is P. Equilibrium is at E_0, and the equilibrium level of national income is Y_0. In part (ii), the balance of trade is shown by the negatively sloped line NX_0, there is a zero balance of trade.

An increase in autonomous spending then shifts the AD curve to the right; at the initial exchange rate, the shift is the same as that shown in Figure 40-1 for a fixed exchange rate; this is shown in part (i) by the shift to AD_1. Thus, at the initial exchange rate, national income would rise to Y_1 and there would be a balance-of-trade deficit. The resulting rise in the exchange rate causes the NX curve to shift to the right, say to NX_1. This in turn causes the AD curve to shift to the right, thus increasing national income and opening up another trade account deficit. This in turn causes a further rise in the exchange rate.

At the new equilibrium, income and the exchange rate must be such that the balance of trade is zero. This occurs when the AD curve shifts by the amount it would shift in a closed economy, that is, to AD_{closed}, so that the new equilibrium is at E_{closed} and the new equilibrium level of national income is Y_{closed}. The exchange rate must rise by enough that there is a zero balance of trade at that level of income; that is, so that the NX curve shifts to NX_2.

gregate demand means that there is an excess demand for foreign currencies in the foreign exchange market as Canadian residents try to buy foreign exchange with which to buy imports. (Equivalently we could have said that there is an excess supply of C$.) As a result, the C$ exchange rate appreciates.

The appreciation of the exchange rate will lead to an increase in exports as Canadian-produced goods become more competitive on world markets, and to a decrease in imports as imported goods become more expensive.[5] This in turn leads to a shift up and to the right of the net export function; the appreciation of the exchange rate means that at any level of national income, net exports are higher. This is shown in part (ii) of Figure 40-3.

How much does the exchange rate appreciate, and how much does the net export function shift?

As we saw in Chapter 39, the exchange rate must appreciate by enough to ensure that the market for foreign exchange clears, which means that net exports are zero. Thus, if national income were to remain constant at its new level (Y_1 in Figure 40-3), the answer would be that the net export function would shift by enough to make the balance of trade zero at that new level of national income. The exchange rate would appreciate by the amount necessary to cause just that shift in the net export function.

However, there is a complication. The improvement in the balance of trade following the appreciation leads to a further increase in aggregate demand. (See Equation 2 above.) This, of course, leads to a further increase in national income, which in turn causes a movement along the new net ex-

[5]We continue to suppose that the elasticity condition in footnote 3 in Chapter 39 is met.

port function. This deterioration in the balance of trade then gives rise to a further appreciation of the exchange rate.

This process comes to a halt when the new level of national income and the new exchange rate are compatible with equilibrium in the market for domestic output (as required by Equation 2) and the balance of trade is zero (as required by the flexible exchange rate in the absence of international capital flows). It might appear that finding the new equilibrium, and assessing the final multiplier impact of the increase in autonomous spending, will be difficult. But further examination of Equation 2 reveals a surprising and simple answer.

Because the balance of trade is zero before and after the increase in autonomous spending, national income behaves as if there were no foreign sector.

This means that the AD curve shifts until it is coincident with the closed economy curve AD_{closed} in Figure 40-1, and the equilibrium level of income is equal to Y_{closed}, the level that would have occurred in the closed economy. This is illustrated in part (i) of Figure 40-3. The NX curve shifts so that the balance of trade is zero when income is at its new equilibrium level. This is illustrated in part (ii) of Figure 40-3.

With zero capital mobility and flexible exchange rates, the simple multiplier in an open economy is the same as that for a closed economy.

This means that the expansion of imports associated with the increased income resulting from an increase in domestic autonomous spending does not provide an additional automatic stabilizer for the economy (as it did under fixed exchange rates). This is true because the exchange rate appreciation that accompanies the expansion of income serves to maintain a zero balance of trade. That is, the appreciation leads to increases in exports and decreases in imports that exactly offset the increase in imports resulting from the expansion of income.

Export multiplier.   Now consider the effects of an increase in exports resulting, say, from a boom in one of the country's trading partners. The effects under fixed exchange rates, shown in Figure 40-2,

are an increase in national income and a balance of trade *surplus.*

Again, the nonzero balance of trade is not sustainable under flexible exchange rates. In this case, the surplus leads to an appreciation of the dollar and a deterioration of the balance of trade; the fall in net exports in turn reduces aggregate demand, causing the AD curve to shift to the left. The fall in national income associated with the reduction in aggregate demand causes a trade account surplus and thus leads to a further appreciation of the dollar.

Once again, the solution to this apparently complicated interaction can be seen quite simply by reference to Equation 2, and again the answer is a surprising one.

Because the balance of trade is zero before and after the increase in exports, national income behaves as if there were no foreign sector.

In terms of Figure 40-2, the appreciation causes the NX and the AD curves to shift to the left until they have been restored to their original positions.

With zero capital mobility and flexible exchange rates, the export multiplier is zero.

The initial autonomous increase in X is offset by a combination of a decline in X and an increase in IM due to the appreciation of the dollar. As a result, the trade account remains in balance and there is no net change in desired aggregate expenditure or, hence, in national income.

The insulation properties of a flexible exchange rate.   These results led many economists to argue that a flexible exchange rate would *insulate* an economy from foreign disturbances that cause the demand for the home economy's exports to change. Thus, a flexible rate was often said to cushion the domestic economy against cyclical variations in economic activity in other countries.

Suppose, for example, that the United States goes into a recession. The decline in U.S. income will lead to a reduction in demand for goods exported from Canada. The fall in exports will reduce income in Canada through the multiplier effect. However, if the value of the C\$ is allowed to respond to market forces, the exchange rate will appreciate, because the trade account deficit reflects an excess demand for U.S. dollars on the market for foreign exchange. This rise in the C\$ exchange rate will stimulate demand for Canadian exports and encourage the substitution of Canadian goods for imports. Thus, the appreciation will provide a stimulus to demand in Canada that will, at least partially, offset the depressing effect of the U.S. recession.

This insulation property, and the proposition that flexible exchange rates increase the multiplier for changes in domestic expenditure (thus enhancing the effectiveness of domestic stabilization), provided the basis on which many economists advocated flexible exchange rates. However, as we shall see in the next section of this chapter, these results depend crucially on the simplifying assumption that there is no capital mobility.

International Capital Mobility

We are now ready to consider the important complications caused by the existence of large international flows of capital. We study three main issues, first, the so called twin deficit issue, second, how capital flows affect the efficiency of fiscal and monetary policy and, third, the alleged insulating properties of flexible exchange rates.

The Twin Deficits

Three important links are poorly understood by most policy makers and many policy critics. These are links between government deficits, the deficit on current account (the twin deficits) and the inflow of foreign capital (which shows up as a surplus on capital account).

To examine these links we need to develop a few new relations which are only small variations on what we already know. In Chapter 27, we saw that the GDP was all income generated by Canadian production, while the GNP was all Canadian income irrespective of where it was generated. To go from the GDP to the GNP we first add receipts by Canadian residents of investment income generated abroad (plus transfers from abroad). We call this R_F. Second, we subtract all income generated in

Canada but paid to residents of foreign countries. We call this P_F. In symbols:

$$GNP = GDP + (R_F - P_F) \qquad [1]$$

Next, we rewrite [1] giving the major categories of expenditure and using Y for GNP:

$$Y = C + I + G + (X - IM) + R_F - P_F \qquad [2]$$

This tells us that when *net* receipts from abroad are zero (i.e., $R_F = P_F$), the GDP equals the GNP. However when net receipts are negative, as they are in Canada today (i.e., $R_F < P_F$), the GNP is less than the GDP.

Next, to get things in a more revealing form, we note that consumption expenditure is equal to GNP minus savings and taxes. What does not go in taxes and is not saved is spent on consumption:

$$C = Y - (S + T) \qquad [3]$$

Now it is a simple matter to substitute [3] into [2] and regroup the terms to obtain:

$$(S + T) - (I + G) = (X - IM) + (R_F - P_F) \qquad [4]$$

The simple steps in getting [4] are given in the footnote.[6]

The terms on the left side of [4] measure what is called *net national saving* when the value is positive and *net national dissaving* when the value is negative. The value tells us the balance between the amount spent on private investment and government on the one hand and the amount of tax revenue and private savings on the other hand. If the balance is zero, there is just enough S and T to finance the spending on I and G. If, however, the balance is negative, as it has been for more than two decades in Canada, there are not enough domestic funds to finance the two expenditures of I and G, *and the balance must come from abroad.*

---

[6]Substituting [3] into [2] gives:
$$Y = Y - S - T + I + G + (X - IM) + (R_F - P_F)$$
Canceling out the Ys and moving the next four terms to the left hand side of the equation, and grouping them into two pairs for convenience yields:
$$(S + T) - (I + G) = (X - IM) + (R_F - P_F)$$
which is equation [4] in the text.

The right hand terms in [4] make up the balance of payments on current account. The first two give the balance of trade while the second two give the balance on investment account (interest, dividends, transfers etc.).

So we can rewrite [4] in words:

Net national savings =
current account balance   [5]

remembering that the current account balance is itself made up of the balance on the trade, and the balance on the investment income account.

A country such as Canada that has large net national dissavings *must* have a corresponding deficit on the current account in the balance of payments.

Notice that it is not the government budget deficit on its own that matters. If there are sufficient private savings to finance the budget deficit as well as all private investment, there will be no foreign repercussions.

The above follows mechanically from our equations. Before going into the economic behaviour that lies behind these relations, we need to add one more link.

Equation [3] in Chapter 39 (see page 854) tells us that changes in official reserves aside, the balances on current and capital accounts must be equal and opposite in sign. This allows us to add our final link to [5] to get the relation given in [6].

Net Ntl Savings = balance on current a/c
              = − balance on capital a/c   [6]

So when net national savings are negative, there must be a negative balance on current account (the twins) and also a positive balance on capital account—which, as we say in Chapter 39, means a flow of foreign capital coming into Canada.

What economic behaviour brings these things about? Start with a country more or less in balance on all three accounts. Then let it cut taxes and raise government expenditure to create high net national dissavings. There are now insufficient domestic funds to finance investment and government expenditure. The shortage of funds will bid up the domestic interest rate and attract foreign capital. But to bring their capital in, foreigners need to sell foreign

exchange in return for domestic currency which depresses the exchange rate. This in turn discourages exports and encourages imports opening up a balance of trade deficit. This is the position the United States has been in for about the last 10 years.

A large increase in the government deficit causes an inflow of foreign capital and tends to be matched at the outset by a large increase in the trade deficit.

Notice that the foreign investors need not buy the government debt. They may buy private sector bonds and equities leaving domestic savers to buy the government debt. All we know is that the net national dissavings must be matched by an inflow of foreign capital. How that is distributed between financing the deficit and financing private investment will depend on many influences not covered by the simple theory we are considering here.

As time passes, the stock of foreign capital will build up and payments of investment income to owners in foreign countries will rise. As this happens, the balance of trade deficit will be slowly replaced by a growing deficit on the investment income account. The way this works is that more and more dollars are sold to transfer Canadian interest and dividends into the currencies of the foreign investors. This increased demand for foreign exchange appreciates the exchange rate, encouraging exports and discouraging imports. Commentators may take satisfaction at the declining trade deficit but if the net national dissavings persist, the trade deficit is being replaced by the investment income deficit. The net exports are going to pay interest to foreigners on past borrowings.

This is roughly the current Canadian position. Our net national dissavings have lasted longer and been a larger proportion of GDP than in the United States. Our trade account (goods and services) shows a small deficit, while our investment account shows a very large deficit—about two thirds of the federal government's budget deficit.

Over time, persistent net national dissavings will tend to be accompanied by a falling deficit on trade and a rising deficit on the investment account (Canadian interest and dividends going to foreign destinations).

This disturbing trend cannot be reversed without attacking the net national dissavings that are its root cause. Until Canadian $(S+T)$ and $(G+I)$ are brought much closer together than they are today, Canada will continue to import large quantities of foreign capital that will be held in the form of public and private sector debt and equities. As this continues the stock of foreign capital will grow, as will the amount of Canadian production that must be exported to pay interest and dividends to foreigners.

Fiscal and Monetary Policy

As we saw in Chapter 39, capital flows are influenced by domestic interest rates. An increase in Canadian interest rates will attract an inflow of short-run capital. A fall in Canadian interest rates will have the opposite effect, as capital moves elsewhere to take advantage of the now relatively higher foreign rates. (Although long-term capital flows are typically less sensitive to interest rate differentials than short-term flows, they also show some response.)

When foreign investors buy securities that are issued by Canadian corporations or governments, or when they invest in Canadian industry, the capital inflow causes an increase in the demand for Canadian dollars in the foreign exchange market. Conversely, the acquisition of foreign assets by Canadian citizens represents a capital outflow and causes an increase in the supply of Canadian dollars in the foreign exchange market.

As we shall now see, this interest responsiveness of international capital flows affects the mechanism by which monetary and fiscal policies influence the economy and thus alters the effectiveness of those policies. The operation of these policies can not only differ sharply from the closed-economy results emphasized earlier in this book, but they can also differ from the simplified open-economy results with no international capital mobility that we have studied so far in this chapter. We continue to focus on the flexible exchange rate case.

Capital mobility complicates the analysis in the first part of this chapter in two related ways. First, the balance of payments is no longer equal to the balance of trade; it is equal to the sum of the balances on the current and capital accounts. Second, the effect of a domestic demand disturbance on the balance of payments, and hence on the exchange

rate, depends on not only its impact on national income but also its impact on interest rates.

Here we focus on the different effects of monetary and fiscal policy when there are international capital flows and a flexible exchange rate. The key to this difference is something we have already encountered earlier in this book—the different effects the two policies have on interest rates.

In a closed economy, monetary and fiscal policies that have the same influence on income have opposite effects on interest rates.

We saw in Chapter 34 that expansionary monetary policy exerts its influence on income primarily by reducing interest rates and thus stimulating interest-sensitive expenditure. We saw in Chapter 37 that fiscal-policy-induced increases in national income are accompanied by increases in interest rates. (See page 794.)

Because monetary and fiscal policies have opposite effects on interest rates, it is important to distinguish between them when considering an open economy with interest-sensitive international capital flows.

Fiscal policy and the capital account. The effects of fiscal policy on the capital account of an open economy are related to the interest rate effects that it would have in a closed economy. Expansionary fiscal policy, for example, pushes interest rates up; in an open economy, this leads to a capital inflow as foreign and domestic investors seek to sell foreign assets and buy higher-yield Canadian assets. In summary:

An expansionary fiscal policy will put upward pressure on interest rates and lead to an inflow of foreign capital, thereby moving the capital account toward a surplus. A contractionary fiscal policy will have the opposite effects.

Monetary policy and the capital account. Because monetary policy influences interest rates in a closed economy, it will also influence the capital account in an open economy:

An expansionary monetary policy will put downward pressure on interest rates and lead to an outflow of capital, thereby moving the

capital account toward a deficit. A contractionary monetary policy will have the opposite effects.

The Effectiveness of Fiscal Policy

Suppose that the government seeks to remove a recessionary gap by expansionary fiscal policy. An increase in government expenditures or a reduction in taxes, or both, will increase income through the multiplier effect and reduce the size of the gap. As we saw earlier in this chapter, this also will cause a movement along the net export function, leading to a deterioration of the trade account.

In the absence of capital mobility, the deterioration of the trade account leads to a depreciation of the dollar; the resulting increase in net exports reinforces the fiscal stimulus and thus increases the size of the fiscal multiplier. With the introduction of capital mobility, we need to consider the impact of the fiscal stimulus on the capital account of the balance of payments.

Capital flows and the crowding-out effect. In a closed economy, a fiscal stimulus causes domestic interest rates to rise. This causes interest-sensitive private expenditures to fall, thus partially offsetting the initial expansionary effect of the fiscal stimulus. As we saw in Chapter 37, this *crowding-out effect* plays an important role in the analysis of fiscal policy in a closed economy.

In an open economy, the crowding-out effect involves an additional channel because of induced effects of international capital flows on net exports. Higher domestic interest rates will induce a capital inflow; if—as is likely—this capital inflow is larger than the balance-of-trade deficit induced by the expansion of national income, it will cause the domestic currency to appreciate.[7] This will depress demand by discouraging exports and by encouraging the substitution of imports for domestically produced goods. The initial expansionary effect of the fiscal stimulus will be offset to a considerable extent

by the effects of currency appreciation; crowding out of fiscal policy will be achieved in part by decreased net exports.

Under flexible exchange rates and capital mobility, there will be a crowding out of net exports that will reduce the effectiveness of fiscal policy.

It is possible for the crowding-out effect of fiscal policy to be mitigated by an accommodating monetary policy. Suppose that, in response to the increase in the demand for money induced by the fiscal expansion, the Bank of Canada increases the money supply so as to maintain domestic interest rates at their initial level. There will then be no capital inflow and no tendency for the currency to appreciate. Equilibrium national income will increase, just as in the zero capital mobility.

The Effectiveness of Monetary Policy

Suppose that the Bank seeks to stimulate demand through an expansionary monetary policy. It buys bonds in the open market, thereby increasing commercial bank reserves and the money supply and reducing interest rates. This stimulates interest-sensitive expenditure and leads to an increase in national income. With zero capital mobility, as shown earlier in this chapter, the increase in national income leads to a balance-of-trade deficit, a depreciation of the Canadian dollar, and a further increase of aggregate demand and national income.

When capital is mobile internationally, lower interest rates will cause an outflow of capital and thus a deficit on the capital account. This will reinforce the deficit on the trade account and will reinforce the pressures for the C$ to depreciate, stimulating exports and reinforcing the expansion in national income. Income and employment will be stimulated not only by the fall in interest rates, but also by the increased demand for domestically produced goods that has been brought about by a depreciation of the currency. The initial monetary stimulus will be *reinforced* by the effects of currency depreciation.

Under flexible exchange rates, monetary policy is a powerful tool for influencing national income and employment. Because capital flows are interest sensitive, a depreciation of

---

[7] It is theoretically possible that the increase in the current account deficit will exceed the increase in the capital inflow so that the overall balance of payments moves into deficit. However, the rapid integration of world capital markets in recent years has made capital flows very sensitive to interest rates, so the case treated in the text is the more likely one.

the currency is an additional channel through which an increase in the money supply stimulates aggregate demand.

The Insulation Properties of Flexible Exchange Rates Revisited

We have seen that international capital mobility enhances the effectiveness of monetary policy under flexible exchange rates but mitigates the effectiveness of fiscal policy. Consider the implications for the effects of an export boom; recall that, in the absence of capital mobility, flexible exchange rates insulate the economy from the effects of such a boom because the export multiplier is zero.

The initial effect of an increase in exports on national income and the balance of trade is as shown in Figure 40-2; national income rises and there is a balance-of-trade surplus. The rise in national income causes an increase in the demand for money, an increase in the domestic interest rate, and hence a capital inflow. This reinforces the pressures caused by the trade account surplus for the currency to appreciate, and therefore to offset the expansionary impact of the export boom.

Capital mobility does not upset the ability of flexible exchange rates to insulate an open economy from the effects of shifts in the demand for its exports.

Suppose, however, that the boom in the foreign country also gave rise to an increase in foreign interest rates. This would lead to a capital outflow from Canada as funds moved in response to the higher foreign interest rates, and hence to a *depreciation* of the Canadian dollar. The depreciation in turn would lead to an improvement in the balance of trade and an increase in national income.

International capital mobility, by linking domestic and foreign interest rates, provides a channel by which business cycles tend to be correlated across countries.

This accords with the experience of the international economy over the past two decades, when the widespread adoption of flexible exchange rates has witnessed a continued correlation of booms and recessions in the major industrial economies.

Canadian Policy

Canadian monetary policy, although nominally under control of the independent Bank of Canada, is actually the responsibility of the Federal government. This principle was firmly established many years ago during the so-called Coyne affair. Having the Bank nominally autonomous shields it partially from political pressure. In practise, however, both monetary and fiscal policy should be seen as being determined by the Federal government.

Canadian macro policy has several times encountered some of the issues we have discussed in this chapter. We take up the story at the beginning of the 1980s.

1980–1983: Imported Monetary Restraint

In the early 1980s, Canadian monetary policy and exchange-rate management were made difficult by the high average level, and volatile behaviour, of U.S. interest rates. A rise in the U.S. interest rate tends to cause outflows of short-term capital from Canada and a resulting appreciation of the exchange rate. This can be avoided only if Canadian interest rates are allowed to rise to match the rates in the United States. Intermediate positions allow for some rise in the exchange rate and some rise in Canadian interest rates.

In 1980, U.S. interest rates rose dramatically. Canadian rates also rose, but by less than those in the United States. The resulting interest differential caused funds to move from Canada to the United States and, as a result, the exchange rate rose somewhat. When another round of U.S. interest rate increases occurred in 1981, Canadian interest rates were allowed to rise along with U.S. rates, and the exchange rate remained relatively stable.

Although nominal interest rates in the United States fell in 1983, real interest rates remained high.

The Bank of Canada walked a middle ground between high Canadian real interest rates and appreciation of the exchange rate. Though the exchange rate rose slowly but steadily from 1982 on, it was widely agreed that monetary policy in Canada was tighter than it would have been in the absence of the very tight U.S. monetary policy. By not allowing the full adjustment to be taken on the exchange rate, the Bank of Canada imported some of the tight U.S. monetary policy in terms of high Canadian interest rates. This caused a substantial fall in inflation in the 1982–1984 period, but also made the 1982 recession more severe than it might otherwise have been.

1984–1987: Recovery and Stable Inflation

During the period 1984–1987, the Bank of Canada was able to reap the benefits of the monetary tightness that it had pursued in the first years of the decade. The economy experienced a sustained recovery, inflation remained stable in the 4 percent range, and interest rates fell dramatically. As a result, the central focus of monetary policy was the reentry problem discussed in Chapter 34—the Bank managed to accommodate the growth in the demand for money while not rekindling inflation. The exchange rate did not play a central role in the overall design or execution of monetary policy in this period, although exchange rate fluctuations were large.

1987–1991: Anti-Inflation and a Falling Exchange Rate

In 1987, the Bank's new governor, John Crow, announced the policy, already discussed in Chapters 34 and 35, of gradually reducing the rate of inflation from its plateau of around 4 percent to zero. Unfortunately, at the same time, the economy was developing an inflationary gap as a result of the longest sustained expansion since World War II. By early 1990, the inflation rate had crept up to over 6 percent.

Containing the rising inflation and reducing the rate toward zero required a tight monetary policy.

Interest rates were driven to unprecedented margins over U.S. rates. At several times during the period, Canadian rates were 4 percentage points above corresponding U.S. rates, and once the margin exceeded 5 percentage points! Attracted by the high interest rates, short-term investment funds flooded into Canada, depreciating the exchange rate to a value well below its PPP rate. Exporters complained of their difficulties in selling profitably in the United States and of the high cost of funds at home. The Bank argued that, although unfortunate, these pressures were the inevitable consequences of the need to fight inflation. Critics argued that the cure was worse than the disease and called for the Bank to accept the higher inflation rate as the cost of letting the dollar and interest rates fall significantly. In a subsequent study made by the C. D. Howe Institute, Canadian exports to the United States were found to have risen all through that period. Evidently the stimulus of falling American tariffs brought about by the Canada-U.S. Free Trade Agreement was stronger than the depressing effects of the overvalued Canadian dollar. In contrast, there were few increases in exports to other countries where there were no tariff cuts. The high Canadian dollar also seemed, according to a Bank of Canada study made in 1993, to have had some effect in forcing Canadian firms to adopt productivity-increasing measures to stay competitive in foreign markets.

1992–?: Price Stability

By late 1992, the battle against inflation had been won—at least for the time being. The measured Canadian inflation rate was in the range of 1–2 percent. Interest rates were allowed to tumble. The exchange rate rose as some funds that had been attracted by the high rates now departed. The stimulus to exports of the higher exchange rate was welcomed, as were lower interest rates for domestic Canadian borrowers. At the time of writing in late 1993, the inflation rate and interest rates are low by historical standards, and the exchange rate is sitting in the range of 1.26–1.30, which Statistics Canada estimated to be about 4 percent above its PPP rate. (Put the other way round, the external value of the C$ was in the range of US$0.77–US$0.79, which was a bit below the PPP value.)

In spite of all the criticism levied against them, Governor Crow's policies had been successful in eliminating inflation, while no permanent damage seemed to have been done to Canada's export industries. Debate no longer centred over whether the Bank could achieve its objectives but over whether the price was worth it in terms of a recession made longer and deeper by the zero-inflation policy. Supporters of the Bank argued that the price actually paid was quite small since, being a worldwide phenomenon, most of the recession would have occurred whatever the Bank had done.

SUMMARY

1. Under fixed exchange rates and zero capital mobility, the responsiveness of imports to national income reduces the size of the autonomous spending multiplier and thus acts as an automatic stabilizer. In this case, national income and the balance of trade surplus move in opposite directions; increases in national income are accompanied by a deterioration in the balance of trade.

2. Under fixed exchange rates and zero capital mobility, changes in the demand for exports lead to a change in equilibrium national income; this is called the export multiplier. In this case, national income and the balance of trade surplus move in the same direction; increases in national income are accompanied by an improvement in the balance of trade.

3. Under flexible exchange rates and zero capital mobility, the balance of trade is zero, so net exports do not influence desired aggregate expenditure. As a result, the economy behaves as if there were no international trade; there is no automatic stabilizer role played by imports, and the export multiplier is zero. The latter is argued to mean that flexible exchange rates insulate the domestic economy from foreign disturbances.

4. International capital mobility means that capital flows, and hence the capital account balance, depend on interest rates. This means that the capital account is influenced by both fiscal and monetary policy, because both influence domestic interest rates. Capital mobility also means that the current account balance can be different from zero; the current account deficit will equal net capital inflows.

5. Under a flexible exchange rate, fiscal policy will be offset by a crowding out of net exports, unless it is accompanied by an accommodating monetary policy that prevents changes in interest rates and the exchange rate.

6. Under a flexible exchange rate, monetary policy is effective in influencing national income. When capital flows are highly interest elastic, the main channel by which an increase in the money supply increases demand for domestically produced goods is through a depreciation of the exchange rate, which in turn leads to an increase in net exports.

7. Tight monetary policy during 1980–1981 had the predicted effects of high interest rates, a strong Canadian dollar, a severe recession, and a reduction in inflation. The same pattern occurred in the early 1990s, when the Bank of Canada drove the measured inflation rate down to around 1 percent at the cost of a higher interest rate, a higher C\$, and a deeper recession than if the 4 percent in-

flation rate had been accepted. The policy succeeded, and debate turned around whether or not the benefits had been worth the costs.

TOPICS FOR REVIEW

Net exports as an automatic stabilizer

Export multiplier

Flexible exchange rates and insulation of the domestic economy

Fiscal and monetary policy and capital flows

Fiscal and monetary policy under flexible exchange rates

Twin deficits

DISCUSSION QUESTIONS

1. Explain how a country can influence the external value of its currency by (a) direct intervention in the foreign exchange market, (b) fiscal policy, and (c) monetary policy.

2. In 1989 and 1990, the Bank of Canada was trying to remove an inflationary gap while Canadian exporters were complaining that the high external value of the Canadian dollar was preventing them from reaping the advantages of the new Canada-U.S. Free Trade Agreement. What classic policy conflict was the Bank encountering? What change in the policy mix was called for to remove the conflict? Why do you think that change did not occur? What alternatives did the Bank have, given that it could control only the monetary policy lever?

3. Suppose that the government deficit remains high but that the rising Canadian national debt and the fear of inflation cause a sharp fall in the desire on the part of foreigners to hold the debt of Canadian government. Outline the key macroeconomic effects of this shift. What policies might you recommend to deal with these consequences?

4. Consider the question posed by economist Fred Bergsten in a monograph that was published in 1988, *America in the World Economy: A Strategy for the 1990s.* What would be the implications for the current account position and policies of Canada (and other countries) if the U.S. current account deficit had shrunk from $155 billion in 1987 to $5 billion by 1992?

5. Consider the following two potential sources of depreciation of the C$ exchange rate: (a) contractionary monetary policy followed by the Bank and (b) foreign inflation. Explain how each could cause the rate to fall. What are the differences for the economy? How would you distinguish between the two?

6. In a speech in December 1980, the governor of the Bank of Canada stated that "the rapid run-up of U.S. short-term [interest] rates is bound to have a major impact on Canada through increases in interest rates [in Canada] or through a fall in the foreign exchange value of the Canadian dollar, or some combination of the two." Why must one of these responses have occurred? What policies could the Bank of Canada have followed in order to influence which of the possible responses occurred? Which would have been preferable?

Mathematical Notes

1. The rule of 72 is an approximation, derived from the mathematics of compound interest. Any variable X with an initial value of X_0 will have the value $X_t = X_0 e^{rt}$ after t years at a continuous growth rate of r percent per year. Because $X_t/X_0 = 2$ requires $r \times t = 0.69$, a "rule of 69" would be correct for continuous growth. The rule of 72 was developed in the context of compound interest, and if interest is compounded only once a year, the product of r times t for X to double is approximately 0.72.

2. Because one cannot divide by zero, the ratio $\Delta Y/\Delta X$ cannot be evaluated when $\Delta X = 0$. However, as ΔX *approaches* zero, the ratio $\Delta Y/\Delta X$ increases without limit:

$$\lim_{\Delta X \to 0} \frac{\Delta Y}{\Delta X} = \infty$$

3. Many variables affect the quantity demanded. Using functional notation, the argument of the next several pages of the text can be anticipated. Let Q^D represent the quantity of a commodity demanded and

$$T, \overline{Y}, N, Y^*, p, p_j$$

represent, respectively, tastes, average household income, population, income distribution, the commodity's own price, and the price of the jth other commodity.

The demand function is

$$Q^D = D(T, \overline{Y}, N, Y^*, p, p_j), \quad j = 1, \ldots, n$$

The demand schedule or curve is given by

$$Q^D = q(p) \,|\, T, \overline{Y}, N, Y^*, p_j$$

where the notation means that the variables to the right of the vertical line are held constant.

This function is correctly described as the demand function with respect to price, all other variables being held constant. This function, often written concisely as $q = q(p)$, shifts in response to changes in other variables. Consider average income: if, as is usually hypothesized, $\partial Q^D / \partial \overline{Y} > 0$, then increases in average income shift $q = q(p)$ rightward and decreases in average income shift $q = q(p)$ leftward. Changes in other variables likewise shift this function in the direction implied by the relationship of that variable to the quantity demanded.

4. The axis reversal arose in the following way. Marshall theorized in terms of "demand price" and "supply price," these being the prices that would lead to a given quantity being demanded or supplied. Thus

$$p^d = D(q) \tag{1}$$
$$p^s = S(q) \tag{2}$$

and the condition of equilibrium is

$$D(q) = S(q)$$

When graphing the behavioural relationships expressed in Equations 1 and 2, Marshall naturally put the independent variable, q, on the horizontal axis.

Leon Walras, whose formulation of the working of a competitive market has become the accepted one, focused on quantity demanded and quantity supplied *at a given price*. Thus

$$q^d = q(p)$$
$$q^s = s(p)$$

and the condition of equilibrium is

$$q(p) = s(p)$$

Walras did not use graphical representation. Had he done so, he would surely have placed p (his independent variable) on the horizontal axis.

Marshall, among his other influences on later generations of economists, was the great popularizer of graphical analysis in economics. Today, we use his graphs, even for Walras's analysis. The axis reversal is thus one of those historical accidents that seem odd to people who did not live through the "perfectly natural" sequence of steps that produced it.

5. Quantity demanded is a simple, straightforward but frequently misunderstood concept in everyday use, but it has a clear mathematical meaning. It refers to the dependent variable in the demand function from note 3:

$$Q^D = D(T, \overline{Y}, N, Y^*, p, p_j)$$

It takes on a specific value whenever a specific value is assigned to each of the independent variables. The value of Q^D changes whenever the value of *any* independent variable is changed. Q^D could change, for example, from 10,000 tons per month to 20,000 tons per month as a result of a *ceteris paribus* change in any one price, in average income, in the distribution of income, in tastes, or in population. It could also change as a result of the net effect of changes in all of the independent variables occurring at once. Thus, a change in the price of a commodity is a sufficient reason for a change in Q^D but not a necessary reason.

Some textbooks reserve the term *change in quantity demanded* for a movement along a demand curve, that is, a change in Q^D as a result of a change in p. They then use other words for a change in Q^D caused by a change in the other variables in the demand function. This usage is potentially confusing, because it gives the single variable Q^D more than one name.

Our usage, which corresponds to that in more advanced treatments, avoids this confusion. We call Q^D *quantity demanded* and refer to *any* change in Q^D as a *change in quantity demanded*. In this usage, it is correct to say that a movement along a demand curve is a change in quantity demanded, but it is incorrect to say that a change in quantity demanded can occur only because of a movement along a demand curve (because Q^D can change for other reasons, for example, a *ceteris paribus* change in average household income).

6. Continuing the development of note 3, let Q^S represent the quantity of a commodity supplied and C, X, p, w_i represent, respectively,

producers' goals, technology, the products' own prices, and the price of the ith input.

The supply function is

$$Q^S = S(G, X, p, w_i), \quad i = 1, 2, \ldots, m$$

The supply schedule or curve is given by

$$Q^S = s(p)\Big|G, X, w_i$$

This is the supply function with respect to price, all other variables being held constant. This function, often written concisely as $q = s(p)$, shifts in response to changes in other variables.

7. Continuing the development of notes 3 through 6, equilibrium occurs where $Q^D = Q^S$. *For specified values of all other variables,* this requires that

$$q(p) = s(p) \tag{1}$$

Equation 1 defines an equilibrium value of p; hence, although p is an *independent* variable in each of the supply and demand functions, it is an *endogenous* variable in the economic model that imposes the equilibrium condition expressed in Equation 1. Price is endogenous because it is assumed to adjust to bring about equality between quantity demanded and quantity supplied. Equilibrium quantity, also an endogenous variable, is determined by substituting the equilibrium price into either $q(p)$ or $s(p)$.

Graphically, Equation 1 is satisfied only at the point where demand and supply curves intersect. Thus, supply and demand curves are said to determine the equilibrium values of the endogenous variables, price and quantity. A shift in any of the independent variables held constant in the q and s functions will shift the demand or supply curves and lead to different equilibrium values for price and quantity.

8. The definition in the text uses finite changes and is called *arc elasticity*. The parallel definition using derivatives is

$$\eta = \frac{dq}{dp} \times \frac{p}{q}$$

and is called *point elasticity*. Further discussion appears in the appendix to Chapter 5.

9. The propositions in the text are proved as follows. Letting *TR* stand for total revenue, we can write

$$TR = pq$$

It follows that the change in total revenue is

$$dTR = qdp + pdq \qquad [1]$$

(Recall that total revenue of the firm and total expenditure by consumers are identical, so the following applies equally to total expenditure.) Multiplying and dividing both terms on the right-hand side of Equation 1 by $p \cdot q$ yields

$$dTR = \left(\frac{dp}{p} + \frac{dq}{q} \right) pq$$

Because *dp* and *dq* are opposite in sign, one positive and one negative, *dTR* will have the same sign as the term in parentheses on the right-hand side that dominates, that is, on which proportionate change is largest.

A second way of arranging Equation 1 is to divide both sides by *dp* to give

$$\frac{dTR}{dp} = q + p \frac{dq}{dp} \qquad [2]$$

From the equation in note 7, however,

$$q\eta = p \frac{dq}{dp} \qquad [3]$$

which we can substitute in Equation 1 to obtain

$$\frac{dTR}{dp} = q + q\eta = q(1 + \eta) \qquad [4]$$

Because η is a negative number, the sign of Equation 4 is negative if the absolute value of η exceeds unity (elastic demand) and positive if it is less than unity (inelastic demand).

Total revenue is maximized when dTR/dp is equal to zero, and as can be seen from Equation 4, this occurs when elasticity is equal to -1.

10. The relationship of the slope of the budget line to relative prices can be seen as follows. In the two-commodity example, a change in expenditure (ΔE) is given by the equation

$$\Delta E = p_C \Delta C + p_F \Delta F \qquad [1]$$

Along a budget line, expenditure is constant; that is, $\Delta E = 0$. Thus, along such a line,

$$p_C \Delta C + p_F \Delta F = 0 \qquad [2]$$

whence

$$-\frac{\Delta C}{\Delta F} = \frac{p_F}{p_C} \qquad [3]$$

The ratio $-\Delta C/\Delta F$ is the slope of the budget line. It is negative because, with a fixed budget, to consume more *F* one must consume less *C*. In other words, Equation 3 says that the negative of the slope of the budget line is the ratio of the absolute prices (i.e., the relative price). Although prices do not show directly in Figure 7–1, they are implicit in the budget line: Its slope depends solely on the relative price, while its position, given a fixed money income, depends on the absolute prices of the two goods.

11. Because the slope of the indifference curve is negative, it is the absolute value of the slope that declines as one moves downward to the right along the curve. The algebraic value, of course, increases. The phrase *diminishing marginal rate of substitution* thus refers to the absolute, not the algebraic, value of the slope.

12. The distinction made between an incremental change and a marginal change is the distinction for the function $Y = Y(X)$ between $\Delta Y/\Delta X$ and the derivative dY/dX. The latter is the limit of the former as ΔX approaches zero. Precisely this sort of difference underlies the distinction between arc and point elasticity, and we shall meet it repeatedly—in this chapter in reference to marginal and incremental *utility* and in later chapters with respect to such concepts as marginal and incremental *product, cost,* and *revenue.* Where *Y* is a function of more than one variable—for example, $Y = f(X, Z)$—the marginal relationship between *Y* and *X* is the partial derivative $\partial Y/\partial X$ rather than the total derivative.

13. The hypothesis of diminishing marginal utility requires that we can measure utility of consumption by a function $U = U(X_1, X_2, \ldots, X_n)$ where $X_1 \ldots, X_n$ are quantities of the n goods consumed by a household. It really embodies two utility hypotheses: first, $\partial U/\partial X_i > 0$, which says that for some levels of consumption, the consumer can get more utility by increasing consumption of the commodity; second, $\partial^2 U/\partial X^2_i < 0$, which says that the marginal utility of additional consumption is declining.

14. *Marginal product,* as defined in the text, is really *incremental product.* More advanced treatments distinguish between this notion and *marginal product* as the limit of the ratio as ΔL approaches zero. Marginal product thus measures the rate at which total product is changing as one factor is varied and is the partial derivative of the total product with respect to the variable factor. In symbols,

$$MP = \frac{\partial TP}{\partial L}$$

15. We have referred specifically both to diminishing *marginal* product and to diminishing *average* product. In most cases, eventually diminishing marginal product implies eventually diminishing average product. That is, however, not necessary, as the accompanying figure shows.

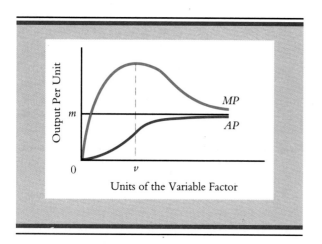

Units of the Variable Factor

In this case, marginal product diminishes after v units of the variable factor are employed.

Because marginal product falls toward, but never quite reaches, a value of m, average product rises continually toward, but never quite reaches, the same value.

16. Let q be the quantity of output and L the quantity of the variable factor. In the short run,

$$TP = q = f(L) \qquad [1]$$

We now define

$$AP = \frac{q}{L} = \frac{f(L)}{L} \qquad [2]$$

$$MP = \frac{dq}{dL} \qquad [3]$$

We are concerned about the relationship between these two. Where average product is rising, at a maximum, or falling is determined by its derivative with respect to L:

$$\frac{d\frac{q}{L}}{dL} = \frac{L\frac{dq}{dL} - q}{L^2} \qquad [4]$$

This may be rewritten

$$\frac{1}{L}\left(\frac{dq}{dL} - \frac{q}{L}\right) = \frac{1}{L}(MP - AP) \qquad [5]$$

Clearly, when MP is greater than AP, the expression in Equation 5 is positive and thus AP is rising. When MP is less than AP, AP is falling. When they are equal, AP is at a stationary value.

17. The text defines *incremental cost.* Strictly, marginal cost is the rate of change of total cost, with respect to output, q. Thus, $MC = dTC/dq$. From the definitions, $TC = TFC + TVC$. Fixed costs are not a function of output. Thus we may write $TC = K + f(q)$, where $f(q)$ is total variable costs and K is a constant. From this, we see that $MC = df(q)/dq$. MC is thus independent of the size of the fixed costs.

18. This point is easily seen if a little algebra is used:

$$AVC = \frac{TVC}{q}$$

but

$$TVC = L \times w$$

and

$$q = AP \times L$$

where L is the quantity of the variable factor used and w is its cost per unit. Therefore,

$$AVC = \frac{L \times w}{AP \times L} = \frac{w}{AP}$$

Because w is a constant, it follows that AVC and AP vary inversely with each other, and when AP is at its maximum value, AVC must be at its minimum value.

19. A little elementary calculus will prove the point:

$$MC = \frac{dTC}{dq} = \frac{dTVC}{dq}$$
$$= \frac{d(L \times w)}{dq}$$

If w does not vary with output,

$$MC = \frac{dL}{dq} \times w$$

However, referring to note 16, Equation 3, we see that

$$\frac{dL}{dq} = \frac{1}{MP}$$

Thus,

$$MC = \frac{w}{MP}$$

Because w is fixed, MC varies negatively with MP. When MP is a maximum, MC is a minimum.

20. As we saw in note 17, $MC = dTVC/dq$. If we take the integral of MC from zero to q_0 we get

$$\int_0^{q_0} MCdq = TVC_{q_0} + K$$

The first term is the area under the marginal cost curve; the constant of integration, K, is fixed cost.

21. Strictly speaking, the marginal rate of substitution refers to the slope of the tangent to the isoquant at a particular point, whereas the calculations in Table 11A–1 refer to the average rate of substitution between two distinct points on the isoquant. Assume a production function

$$Q = Q(K, L) \quad [1]$$

Isoquants are given by the function

$$K = I(L, \overline{Q}) \quad [2]$$

derived from Equation 1 by expressing K as an explicit function of L and Q. A single isoquant relates to a particular value $(\overline{Q})$ at which Q is held constant. Define Q_K and Q_L as an alternative, more compact notation for $\partial Q/\partial K$ and $\partial Q/\partial L$, the marginal products of capital and labour. Also, let Q_{KK} and Q_{LL} stand for $\partial^2 Q/\partial K^2$ and $\partial^2 Q/\partial L^2$, respectively. To obtain the slope of the isoquant, totally differentiate Equation 1 to obtain

$$dQ = Q_K dK + Q_L dL$$

Then, because we are moving along a single isoquant, set $dQ = 0$ to obtain

$$\frac{dK}{dL} = -\frac{Q_L}{Q_K} = MRS$$

Diminishing marginal productivity implies Q_{LL}, $Q_{KK} < 0$, and, hence, as we move down the isoquant of Figure 11A–1, Q_K is rising and Q_L is falling, so the absolute value of MRS is diminishing. This is called the *hypothesis of a diminishing marginal rate of substitution*.

22. Formally, the problem is to maximize $Q = Q(K, L)$ subject to the budget constraint

$$p_K K + p_L L = C$$

To do this, form the Lagrangean

$$Q(K, L) - \lambda(p_K K + p_L L - C)$$

The first-order conditions for finding the saddle point on this function are

$$Q_K - \lambda p_K = 0; \quad Q_K = \lambda p_K \tag{1}$$

$$Q_L - \lambda p_L = 0; \quad Q_L = \lambda p_L \tag{2}$$

$$-p_K K - p_L L + C = 0 \tag{3}$$

Dividing Equation 1 by Equation 2 yields

$$\frac{Q_K}{Q_L} = \frac{p_K}{p_L}$$

That is, the ratio of the marginal products, which is (-1) times the *MRS*, is equal to the ratio of the prices, which is (-1) times the slope of the isocost line.

23. Marginal revenue is mathematically the derivative of total revenue with respect to output, dTR/dq. Incremental revenue is $\Delta TR/\Delta q$. However, the term *marginal revenue* is used loosely to refer to both concepts.

24. For notes 24 through 26, it is helpful first to define some terms. Let

$$\pi_n = TR_n - TC_n$$

where π_n is the profit when n units are sold.

   If the firm is maximizing its profits by producing n units, it is necessary that the profits at output q_n be at least as large as the profits at output zero. If the firm is maximizing its profits at output n, then

$$\pi_n \geq \pi_0 \tag{1}$$

   The condition says that profits from producing must be greater than profits from not producing. Condition 1 can be rewritten as

$$TR_n - TVC_n - TFC_n$$
$$\geq TR_0 - TVC_0 - TFC_0 \tag{2}$$

However, note that by definition

$$TR_0 = 0 \tag{3}$$

$$TVC_0 = 0 \tag{4}$$

$$TFC_n = TFC_0 = K \tag{5}$$

where K is a constant. By substituting Equations 3, 4, and 5 into Condition 2, we get

$$TR_n - TVC_n \geq 0$$

from which we obtain

$$TR_n \geq TVC_n$$

This proves Rule 1.

   On a per unit basis it becomes

$$\frac{TR_n}{q_n} \geq \frac{TVC_n}{q_n} \tag{6}$$

where q_n is the number of units produced.

   Because $TR_n = q_n p_n$, where p_n is the price when n units are sold, Equation 6 may be rewritten as

$$p_n \geq AVC_n$$

25. Using elementary calculus, we may prove Rule 2.

$$\pi_n = TR_n - TC_n$$

each of which is a function of output q. To maximize π, it is necessary that

$$\frac{d\pi}{dq} = 0 \tag{1}$$

and that

$$\frac{d^2\pi}{dq^2} < 0 \tag{2}$$

From the definitions,

$$\frac{d\pi}{dq} = \frac{dTR}{dq} - \frac{dTC}{dq} = MR - MC \tag{3}$$

From Equations 1 and 3, a necessary condition for attaining a maximum π is $MR - MC = 0$, or $MR = MC$, as is required by Rule 2.

26. To prove that for a negatively sloped demand curve, marginal revenue is less than price, let $p = p(q)$. Then

$$TR = pq = p(q) \times q$$

$$MR = \frac{dTR}{dq} = q\frac{dp}{dq} + p$$

For a negatively sloped demand curve, dp/dq is negative by definition, and thus MR is less than price for positive values of q.

27. The equation for a negatively sloped straight-line demand curve with price on the vertical axis is

$$p = a + bq$$

Total revenue is price times quantity:

$$TR = pq = aq + bq^2$$

Marginal revenue is

$$MR = \frac{dTR}{dq} = a + 2bq$$

Thus the MR curve and the demand curve are both straight lines, and the slope of the MR curve ($2b$) is twice that of the demand curve (b).

28. A monopolist selling in two or more markets will set its marginal cost equal to marginal revenue in each market. Thus, the condition $MC = MR_1 = MR_2$ is a profit-maximizing condition for a monopolist that is selling in two markets. In general, equal marginal revenue will mean unequal prices, because the ratio of price to marginal revenue is a function of elasticity of demand: The higher is the elasticity, the lower is the ratio. Thus, equal marginal revenues imply a higher price in the market with the less elastic demand curve.

29. The marginal revenue produced by the factor involves two elements: first, the additional output that an extra unit of the factor makes possible, and, second, the change in price of the product that the extra output causes. Let Q be output, R revenue, and L the number of units of labour hired. The contribution to the revenue of additional labour is $\partial R/\partial L$. This, in turn, depends on the contribution of the extra labour to output $\partial Q/\partial L$ (the marginal product of the factor) and $\partial R/\partial Q$ (the firm's

marginal revenue from the extra output). Thus,

$$\frac{\partial R}{\partial L} = \frac{\partial Q}{\partial L} \cdot \frac{\partial R}{\partial Q}$$

We define the left-hand side as marginal revenue product, MRP. Thus,

$$MRP = MP \cdot MR$$

30. The proposition that the marginal labour cost is above the average labour cost when the average is rising is essentially the same proposition proved in math note 16. Nevertheless, let us do it again, using elementary calculus.

   The quantity of labour depends on the wage rate: $L = f(w)$. Total labour cost is wL. Marginal cost of labour is $d(wL)/dL = w + L(dw/dL)$. Rewrite this as $MC = AC + L(dw/dL)$. As long as the supply curve is positively sloped, $dw/dL > 0$; therefore, $MC > AC$.

31. If prices grow at a rate of 0.87 percent per calendar quarter, prices in any given quarter will be 1.0087 times their level in the previous quarter. Start with a price level of P_0. One quarter later, the price level will be $P_0 \times 1.0087$; the following quarter it will be $P_0 \times 1.0087 \times 1.0087$. In general, for any growth rate per unit of time, g, and starting value, P_0, the price level at time t, P_t, will be $P_0 \times (1 + g)^t$. This is the formula for *compound* growth at rate g per unit of time. Thus, $P_t = (1.0087)^4 = 1.0353$, and prices will have risen by 3.53 percent. For small values of g, $(1 + g)^t$ will be very close to $(1 + tg)$. In this example, $1 + tg = 1 + 4(1.0087) = 1.0348$. But as g gets larger, so does the difference. For example, if prices are growing at 2 percent per month, the annual growth will be $(1.02)^{12} = 1.268$, yielding a growth rate of 27 percent per year. This is considerably more than 24 percent, which is just the monthly rate times 12. Generally, annual rates of growth are calculated by compounding rates of growth that are measured over shorter or longer periods than one year.

32. The statement in the text is an acceptable approximation at the levels of interest and inflation typically encountered in advanced coun-

tries. To derive the precise relation we reason as follows: Let r be the real rate of interest, i the nominal rate and p the rate of inflation over the contract period (say one year). All rates are expressed as ratios, not percentages. Now the nominal sum returned when the loan is repaid is $1 + i$, and the real value of that sum is $(1 + r) = (1 + i)/(1 + p)$. Cross multiplying and expanding the brackets gives: $1 + p + r + rp = 1 + i$, which simplifies to $i = r + p + rp$, or $r = 1 - p - rp$. The text statement ignores the cross term rp. For an extreme rate of inflation of 20 percent (0.02) and a real interest rate of 10 percent (0.01), the error in ignoring rp is only 0.0002, i.e., 2 one-hundredths of 1 percent.

33. In the text, we define MPC as an incremental ratio. For mathematical treatment, it is sometimes convenient to define all marginal concepts as derivatives: $MPC = dC/dY_d$, $MPS = dS/dY_d$, and so on.

34. The basic relationship is

$$Y_d = C + S$$

Dividing through by Y_d yields

$$Y_d/Y_d = C/Y_d + S/Y_d$$
$$1 = APC + APS$$

Next, take the first difference of the basic relationship to get

$$\Delta Y_d = \Delta C + \Delta S$$

Dividing through by ΔY_d gives

$$\Delta Y_d/\Delta Y_d = \Delta C/\Delta Y_d + \Delta S/\Delta Y_d$$
$$1 = MPC + MPS$$

35. The total expenditure over all rounds is the sum of an infinite series. If we let A stand for the initiating expenditure and z for the marginal propensity to spend, the change in expenditure is ΔA in the first round, $z\Delta A$ in the second, $z(z\Delta A) = z^2\Delta A$ in the third, and so on. This can be written as

$$\Delta A(1 + z + z^2 + \cdots + z^n)$$

If z is less than 1, the series in parentheses converges to $1/(1 - z)$ as n approaches infinity. The change in total expenditure is thus $\Delta A/(1 - z)$. In the example in Box 28-1, $z = 0.80$; therefore, the change in total expenditure is five times ΔA.

36. This involves using functions of functions. We have $C = C(Y_d)$ and $Y_d = f(Y)$. So, by substitution, $C = C[f(Y)]$. In the linear expressions that are used in the text, $C = a + bY_d$, where b is the marginal propensity to consume, $Y_D = hY$, so $C = a + bhY$, where bh is thus the marginal response of C to a change in Y.

37. This is easily proved. In equilibrium, the banking system wants sufficient deposits (D) to establish the target ratio (v) of deposits to reserves (R). This gives $R/D = v$. Any change in D of size ΔD has to be accompanied by a change in R of ΔR of sufficient size to restore v. Thus $\Delta R/\Delta D = v$, so $\Delta D = \Delta R/v$, and $\Delta D/\Delta R = 1/v$.

This can be shown also in terms of the deposits created by the sequence in Table 37–7. Let v be the reserve ratio and $e = 1 - v$ be the excess reserves per dollar of new deposits. If X dollars are initially deposited in the system, the successive rounds of new deposits will be $X, eX, e^2X, e^3X, \ldots$. The series

$$X + eX + e^2X + e^3X + \cdots$$
$$= X[1 + e + e^2 + e^3 + \cdots]$$

has a limit

$$X\frac{1}{1 - e} = X\frac{1}{1 - (1 - v)} = \frac{X}{v}$$

This is the total new deposits created by an injection of \$$X$ of new reserves into the banking system. For example, when $v = 0.20$, an injection of \$100 into the system will lead to an increase of \$500.

38. Suppose that the public wishes to hold a fraction, c, of deposits in cash, C. Now suppose that X dollars are injected into the system. Ultimately, this money will be held either as reserves by the banking system or as cash by the public. Thus we have

$$\Delta C + \Delta R = X$$

From the banking system's reserve behaviour, we have $\Delta R + v\Delta D$, and from the public's cash behaviour, we have $\Delta C = c\Delta D$. Substituting into the above equation, we get the result that

$$\Delta D = \frac{X}{v + c}$$

From this we can also relate the change in reserves and the change in cash holdings to the initial injection:

$$\Delta R = \frac{v}{v + c} X$$

$$\Delta C = \frac{c}{v + c} X$$

For example, when $v = 0.20$ and $c = 0.05$, an injection of \$100 will lead to an increase in reserves of \$80, an increase in cash in the hands of the public of \$20, and an increase in deposits of \$400.

39. The argument is simply as follows, where prime marks stand for the first derivatives:

$$M^D = F_1(T), \qquad F'_1 > 0$$

$$T = F_2(Y), \qquad F'_2 > 0$$

where T is transactions and Y is national income.

Therefore,

$$M^D = F_1(F_2(Y))$$

$$= H(Y), \qquad H' > 0$$

where H is the function of the function combining F_1 and F_2.

40. Let $L(Y, r)$ give the real demand for money measured in purchasing power units. Let M be the supply of money measured in nominal units and P an index of the price level, so that M/P is the real supply of money. Now the equilibrium condition requiring equality between the demand for money and the supply of money can be expressed in real terms as

$$L(Y, r) = \frac{M}{P} \qquad [1]$$

or by multiplying through by P in nominal terms as

$$PL(Y, r) = M \qquad [2]$$

In Equation 1, a rise in P disturbs equilibrium by lowering M/P, and in Equation 2, it disturbs equilibrium by raising $PL(Y, r)$.

41. The relations involved here are discussed in math note 1 above.

42. The time taken to break even is a function of the *difference* in growth rates, not their level. Thus, had 4 percent and 5 percent, or 5 percent and 6 percent been used in the example, it still would have taken the same number of years. To see this quickly, recognize that we are interested in the ratio of two growth paths: $e^{r_1 t}/e^{r_2 t} = e^{(r_1 - r_2)t}$.

43. A simple example of a production function is GDP $= z(LK)^{1/2}$. This equation says that to find the amount of GDP produced, multiply the amount of labour by the amount of capital, take the square root, and multiply the result by the constant z. This production function has positive but diminishing returns to either factor. This can be seen by evaluating the first and second partial derivatives and showing the first derivatives to be positive and the second derivatives to be negative. For example, $\partial \text{GDP}/\partial K = (\frac{1}{2}zL^{1/2})/(K^{1/2}) > 0$ and $\partial^2 \text{GDP}/\partial K^2 = (-\frac{1}{2}zL^{1/2})/K^{3/2} < 0$. The production function also displays constant returns to scale, as can be seen by multiplying both L and K by the same constant, λ, and seeing that this multiplies the whole value of the function, that is, the value of GDP, by λ: $z(\lambda L \lambda K)^{1/2} = z(\lambda^2 LK)^{1/2} = \lambda z(LK)^{1/2} = \lambda(\text{GDP})$.

44. The figures are derived from the production function, output $= 4(KL)^{1/2}$, in which both factors have the same average and marginal products.

45. In the neoclassical production function, which allows for growth, we have

$$GDP = z(L^\alpha K^{1-\alpha})$$

The parameter z is a constant that relates given inputs of L and K to a specific GDP. Increases in factor productivity cause z to rise, so that given amounts of L and K are associated with higher GDP. Exogenous technical progress at a constant rate can be shown as

$$GDP_t = z^t(L_t^\alpha K_t^{1-\alpha})$$

where z grows at a constant rate as time passes.

46. The shift in the AD curve, and hence the change in national income, is given by the simple multiplier, which in this case is $1/[1 - b(1 - t) + m]$, times the change in exports, dX.

The shift in the NX curve is given by the solution for dY in the condition $dX - mdY = 0$, which is $1/m$ times dX. Because $1/m$ is larger than $1/[1 - b(1 - t) + m]$, the shift in NX is larger than the shift in AD.

The change in net exports, dNX, is given by the change in exports, dX, minus the change in imports, dIM. The latter is equal to the marginal propensity to import, m, times the change in national income, dY. Thus

$$dNX = dX - [m/[1 - b(1 - t) + m]]dX$$

Because $m/[1 - b(1 - t) + m]$ is less than one, dNX is positive.

47. Net exports equals exports minus imports.

$$NX = X - IM \qquad [1]$$

Exports depend on foreign income, Y^f, and on the terms of trade.

$$X = X_0 + m^f Y^f - b^f\left(\frac{P}{eP^f}\right) \qquad [2]$$

where X_0 is autonomous exports, m^f is the foreign marginal propensity to import, b^f is the response of exports to a change in relative prices, P is the domestic price level, e is the exchange rate, and P^f is foreign prices. Imports depend on domestic income and the terms of trade.

$$IM = M_0 + mY + b\left(\frac{P}{eP^f}\right) \qquad [3]$$

Combining Equations 1, 2, and 3, we can write

$$NX = (X_0 - M_0) + m^f Y^f - mY - c\left(\frac{P}{eP^f}\right) \qquad [4]$$

where $c = b + b^f$. In Chapter 29, we consider this relationship in isolation, and hence the slope of the NX curve when it was drawn against national income was taken to be $dNX/dY = -m$, where the other variables in Equation 4 were held constant. Now we have to take into account the fact that P changes as Y changes.

Writing the $SRAS$ curve as

$$P = g(Y), \qquad g' > 0 \qquad [5]$$

and substituting Equation 5 into Equation 4, we eliminate P to yield

$$NX = (X_0 - M_0) + mY^f - mY - c\left(\frac{g(Y)}{eP^f}\right) \qquad [6]$$

The slope of the NX curve is now given by

$$\frac{dNX}{dY} = -(m + u') < 0 \qquad [7]$$

where $u = cg'/eP^f > 0$. Hence as Y rises, NX falls, both because of the marginal propensity to import and because of substitution away from domestic goods as P rises.

Glossary

absolute advantage When a given amount of resources can produce more of some commodity in one country than in another.

absolute price The amount of money that must be spent to acquire one unit of a commodity. Also called *money price*.

acceleration hypothesis The hypothesis that when national income is held above potential, the persistent inflationary gap will cause inflation to accelerate, and when national income is held below potential, the persistent recessionary gap will cause inflation to decelerate.

actual GDP The gross domestic product that the economy, in fact, produces.

administered price A price set by the conscious decision of the seller rather than by impersonal market forces.

ad valorem tariff An import duty that is a percentage of the price of the imported product.

ad valorem tax See *excise tax*.

adverse selection Self-selection, within a single risk category, of persons of above-average risk.

AE See *aggregate expenditure*.

agents Decision makers, including households, firms, and government bodies.

aggregate demand Total desired purchases by all the buyers of an economy's output.

aggregate demand (AD) curve A curve showing the combinations of real national income and the price level that makes aggregate desired expenditure equal to national income; the curve thus relates the total amount of output that will be demanded to the price level of that output.

aggregate demand shock A shift in the aggregate demand curve.

aggregate expenditure (AE) Total desired expenditure on final output of the economy; $AE = C + I + G + (X - M)$, representing the four major components of aggregate desired expenditure.

aggregate expenditure (AE) function The function that relates aggregate desired expenditure to national income.

aggregate production function The relation between the total amount of each factor of production employed in the nation and the nation's total output, its GDP.

aggregate supply Total desired sales of all the producers of an economy's output.

aggregate supply (AS) curve See *short-run aggregate supply curve* and *long-run aggregate supply curve*.

aggregate supply shock A shift in the aggregate supply curve.

allocation efficiency A situation in which no reorganization of production or consumption could make everyone better off (or, as it is sometimes stated, make at least one person better off while making no one worse off).

allocation of resources See *resource allocation*.

arc elasticity A measure of the average responsiveness of quantity to price over an interval of the demand curve. For analytical purposes it is usually defined by the formula

$$\eta = \frac{\Delta q / q}{\Delta p / p}$$

An alternative formula often used where computations are involved is

$$\eta = \frac{(q_2 - q_1)/(q_2 + q_1)}{(p_2 - p_1)/(p_2 + p_1)}$$

where p_1 and q_1 are the original price and quantity and p_2 and q_2 are the new price and quantity. With negatively sloped demand curves, elasticity is a negative number. The above expressions are therefore usually multiplied by -1 to make measured elasticity positive.

automatic fiscal stabilizers See *automatic stabilizers*.

automatic stabilizers Anything that automatically lessens the magnitude of the fluctuations in national income caused by changes in autonomous expenditures, such as investment.

autonomous expenditure In macroeconomics, elements of expenditure that do not vary systematically with other variables, such as national income and the interest rate, but are determined by forces outside of the theory.

autonomous variable See *exogenous variable*.

average cost (AC) See *average total cost*.

average fixed cost (AFC) Total fixed costs divided by the number of units of output.

average product (AP) Total product divided by the number of units of the variable factor used in its production.

average propensity to consume (APC) The proportion of income devoted to consumption; total consumption expenditure divided by total disposable income ($APC = C/Y_d$).

average propensity to save (APS) The proportion of disposable income devoted to saving; total saving divided by total disposable income ($APS = S/Y_d$).

average revenue (AR) Total revenue divided by quantity sold; this is the market price when all units are sold at one price.

average tax rate The ratio of total taxes paid to total income earned.

average total cost (ATC) Total cost of producing a given output divided by the number of units of output; it can also be calculated as the sum of average fixed costs and average variable costs. Also called *cost per unit, unit cost, average cost.*

average variable cost (AVC) Total variable costs divided by the number of units of output. Also called *direct unit cost, avoidable unit cost.*

balanced budget A situation in which current revenue is exactly equal to current expenditures.

balanced budget multiplier The change in income divided by the tax-financed change in government expenditure that brought it about.

balance-of-payments accounts A summary record of a country's transactions that involve payments or receipts of foreign exchange.

balance of trade The difference between the value of exports and the value of imports of visible items (goods).

bank notes Paper money issued by commercial banks.

bank rate The rate of interest at which the Bank of Canada makes loans to the chartered banks, often interpreted as a signal about the stance of monetary policy.

barter A system in which goods and services are traded directly for other goods and services.

beggar-my-neighbor policies Policies designed to increase a country's prosperity (especially by reducing its unemployment) at the expense of reducing prosperity in other countries (especially by increasing their unemployment).

benefit–cost analysis A technique for evaluating government policies. The sum of the opportunity cost to all parties is compared with the value of the benefits to all parties.

black market A situation in which goods are sold illegally at prices that violate a government price ceiling.

bond An evidence of debt carrying a specified amount and schedule of interest payments and (usually) a date for redemption of its face value.

boom A period in the business cycle characterized by high demand and increasing production at a level that exceeds potential GDP.

break-even price The price at which a firm is just able to cover all of its costs, including the opportunity cost of capital.

budget balance The difference between total government revenue and total government expenditures.

budget deficit Any shortfall of current revenue below current expenditure.

budget line Graphical representation of all combinations of commodities or factors that a household or firm may obtain if it spends a specified amount at fixed prices of the commodities or factors. Also called *isocost line.*

budget surplus Any excess of current revenue over current expenditure.

business cycle Fluctuations of national income around its trend value, after seasonal fluctuations have been removed, and that follow a wavelike pattern.

buyout When a group of investors buys up a controlling interest in a firm.

C See *consumption expenditure.*

capacity The level of output that corresponds to the firm's minimum short-run average total cost.

capital A factor of production consisting of all manufactured aids to further production, including plant, equipment, and inventories.

capital account A part of the balance-of-payments accounts that records payments and receipts arising from the import and export of long-term and short-term financial capital.

capital consumption allowance An estimate of the amount by which the capital stock is depleted through its contribution to current production. Also called *depreciation.*

capital–labour ratio A measure of the amount of capital per worker in an economy.

capital stock The aggregate quantity of capital goods.

cartel An organization of producers who agree to act as a single seller in order to maximize joint profits.

ceiling price See *price ceiling.*

central bank A bank that acts as banker to the commercial banking system and often to the government as well. In the modern world, usually a government-owned and -operated institution that controls the banking system and is the sole money-issuing authority.

centrally planned economy See *command economy.*

certificate of deposit (CD) A negotiable time deposit carrying a higher interest rate than that paid on ordinary time deposits.

ceteris paribus Literally, "other things being equal"; usually used in economics to indicate that all variables except the ones specified are assumed not to change.

change in demand An increase or decrease in the quantity demanded at each possible price of the commodity, represented by a shift in the whole demand curve.

change in quantity demanded An increase or decrease in the specific quantity bought, represented by a change from one point on the demand curve to another point, either on the original demand curve or on a new one.

change in quantity supplied An increase or decrease in the specific quantity supplied, represented by a change from one point on a supply curve to another point, either on the original supply curve or on a new one.

change in supply An increase or decrease in the quantity supplied at each possible price of the commodity, represented by a shift in the whole supply curve.

chartered bank A privately owned, profit-seeking institution that provides a variety of financial services, such as accepting deposits from customers, which it agrees to transfer when ordered by a cheque, and making loans and other investments.

clearing house An institution where interbank indebtedness, arising from transfer of cheques between banks, is computed, offset against each other, and net amounts owing are calculated.

closed economy An economy that has no foreign trade.

collective bargaining The process by which unions and employers arrive at and enforce agreements.

collective-consumption goods Goods or services that, if they provide benefits to anyone, can, at little or no additional cost, provide benefits to a large group of people, possibly everyone in the country. Also called *public goods.*

collusion An agreement among sellers to act jointly in their common interest, for example, by agreeing to raise prices. Collusion may be overt or covert, explicit or tacit.

combine laws Laws that prevent firms either from combining into one unit or acting cooperatively so as to behave monopolistically.

command economy An economy in which the decisions of the government (as distinct from households and firms) exert the major influence over the allocation of resources.

commercial bank Privately owned, profit-seeking institution that provides a variety of financial services, such as accepting deposits from customers, which it agrees to transfer when ordered by a cheque, and making loans and other investments.

commercial policy A government's policy involving restrictions placed on international trade.

commodities Marketable items produced to satisfy wants. Commodities may be either *goods,* which are tangible, or *services,* which are intangible.

common market A customs union with the added provision that factors of production can move freely among the members.

comparative advantage The ability of one nation (region or individual) to produce a commodity at a lesser opportunity cost of other products forgone than another nation.

comparative statics Short for comparative static equilibrium analysis; the derivation of predictions by analyzing the effect of a change in some exogenous variable on the equilibrium position.

competition policy Policies designed to prohibit the acquisition and exercise of monopoly power by business firms.

complement Two commodities are complements when they tend to be used jointly with each other. The degree of complementarity is measured by the size of the negative cross elasticity between the two goods.

concentration ratio The fraction of total market sales (or some other measure of market occupancy) controlled by a specific member of the industry's largest firms, four-firm and eight-firm concentration ratios being most frequently used.

conglomerate merger See *merger.*

constant-cost industry An industry in which costs of the most efficient size firm remain constant as the entire industry expands or contracts in the long run.

constant-dollar GDP Gross national product valued in prices prevailing in some base year; year-to-year changes in constant-dollar GDP reflect changes only in quantities produced. Also called *real GDP.*

constant returns to scale A situation in which output increases in proportion to inputs as the scale of production is increased. A firm in this situation, and facing fixed factor prices, is a *constant-cost firm.*

Consumer Price Index (CPI) A measure of the average prices of commodities commonly bought by households; compiled monthly by the Bureau of Labour Statistics.

consumers' surplus The difference between the total value that consumers place on all units consumed of a commodity and the payment that they must make to purchase that amount of the commodity.

consumption The act of using commodities, either goods or services, to satisfy wants.

consumption expenditure In macroeconomics, household expenditure on all goods and services.

Represented by the symbol C as one of the four components of aggregate expenditure.

consumption function The relationship between total desired consumption expenditure and all the variables that determine it; in the simplest cases, the relationship between consumption expenditure and disposable income and consumption expenditure and national income.

contestable market A market is perfectly contestable if there are no sunk costs of entry or exit, so that *potential* entry may hold profits of existing firms to low levels—zero in the case of perfect contestability.

cooperative solution A situation in which existing firms coorperate to maximize their joint profits.

corporation A form of business organization in which the firm has a legal existence separate from that of the owners, and ownership and financial responsibility are divided, limited, and shared among any number of individual and institutional shareholders.

cost (of output) To a producing firm, the value of inputs used to produce output.

cost–effectiveness analysis Analysis of program costs with the purpose of finding the least-cost way to achieve a given result. See also *benefit-cost analysis.*

cost minimization An implication of profit maximization that the firm will choose the method that produces specific output at the lowest attainable cost.

CPI See *Consumer Price Index.*

cross elasticity of demand (η_{xy}) A measure of the responsiveness of the quantity of a commodity demanded to changes in price of a related commodity, defined by the formula

$$\eta_{xy} = \frac{\text{percentage change in quantity} \atop \text{demanded of one good } X}{\text{percentage change in price} \atop \text{of another good } Y}$$

crown corporation Business concerns owned by government; also known as *public enterprises.*

current account A part of the balance-of-payments accounts that records payments and receipts arising from trade in goods and services and from interest and dividends that are earned by capital owned in one country and invested in another.

current account balance The balance of payments on current account; the sum of the balances on the visisble and the invisible accounts.

current-dollar GDP Gross national product valued in prices prevailing at the time of measurement; year-to-year changes in current-dollar GDP reflect changes both in quantities produced and in market prices. Also called *nominal GDP.*

customs union A group of countries who agree to have free trade among themselves and a common set of barriers against imports from the rest of the world.

cyclical unemployment Unemployment in excess of frictional and structural unemployment; it is due to a shortfall of actual national income below potential national income. Sometimes called *deficit demand unemployment.*

cyclically adjusted deficit (*CAD*) (or surplus (*CAS*)) An estimate of the government budget deficit (expenditure minus tax revenue), not as it actually is but as it would be if national income were at its potential level. The cyclically adjusted surplus (*CAS*) is the negative of the *CAD.*

day-to-day loan A loan made by a chartered bank to an investment dealer. Such loans make up part of the *secondary reserve* of the chartered banks.

debt Generally, amounts owed to one's creditors. From a firm's point of view, that portion of its money capital that is borrowed rather than subscribed by shareholders.

decision lag The period of time between perceiving some problem and reaching a decision on what to do about it.

decreasing returns A situation in which output increases less than in proportion to inputs as the scale of a firm's production increases. A firm in this situation, with fixed factor prices, is an *increasing cost firm.*

deflation A reduction in the general price level.

deflationary gap See *recessionary gap.*

demand The entire relationship between the quantity of a commodity that buyers wish to purchase per period of time and the price of that commodity.

demand curve The graphical representation of the relationship between the quantity of a commodity that buyers wish to purchase per period of time and the price of that commodity, other things being equal.

demand deposit A bank deposit that is withdrawable on demand (without notice of intention to withdraw) and transferable by means of a cheque.

demand for money The total amount of money balances that the public wishes to hold for all purposes.

demand for money function The relation between the quantity of money demanded and the variables that influence it, specifically the level of income and the rate of interest.

demand inflation Inflation arising from excess

aggregate demand, that is, when national income exceeds potential income.

demand schedule A table showing for selected values the relationship between the quantity of a commodity that buyers wish to purchase per period of time and the price of that commodity, other things being equal.

demogrants Social benefits paid to anyone meeting only minimal requirements such as age or residence; in particular, *not* income-tested.

deposit money Money held by the public in the form of demand deposits with commercial banks.

depreciation (of capital) See *capital consumption allowance.*

depreciation (of a currency) A fall in the external value of domestic currency in terms of foreign currency; that is, a fall in the exchange rate.

depression A persistent period of very low economic activity with very high unemployment and high excess capacity.

derived demand The demand for a factor of production that results from the demand for the products that it is used to make.

developed countries The higher-income countries of the world, including the United States, Canada, most of the countries of Western Europe, Japan, Australia, and South Africa.

developing countries The lower-income countries of the world, most of which are in Africa, Asia, and Latin America. Also called *underdeveloped, less developed,* and the *South.*

differentiated product A group of commodities that are similar enough to be called the *same* product but are dissimilar enough so that all of them do not have to be sold at the same price.

diminishing marginal rate of substitution The hypothesis that the marginal rate of substitution changes systematically as the amounts of two commodities being consumed vary.

direct burden Amount of money for a tax that is collected from taxpayers.

discount rate (1) In banking, the rate at which the central bank is prepared to lend reserves to commercial banks. (2) More generally, the rate of interest used to discount a stream of future payments to arrive at their present value.

discouraged workers People who would like to work but have ceased looking for a job and hence have withdrawn from the labour force, because they believe that no jobs are available for them.

discretionary fiscal policy Fiscal policy that is a conscious response (not according to any predetermined rule) to each particular state of the economy as it arises.

disembodied technical change Technical change that raises output without the necessity of building new capital to embody new knowledge.

disequilibrium The absence of equilibrium. A market is in disequilibrium when there is either excess demand or excess supply.

disequilibrium price A price at which quantity demanded does not equal quantity supplied.

disposable personal income (Y_d) GNP minus any part of it not actually paid to households minus personal income taxes paid by households plus transfer payments to households; personal income *minus* personal income taxes.

dividends Profits paid out to shareholders of a corporation.

division of labour The breaking up of a production process into a series of specialized tasks, each done by a different worker.

double counting In national income accounting, adding up the total outputs of all the sectors in the economy so that the value of intermediate goods is counted in the sector that produces them and every time they are purchased as an input by another sector.

dumping In international trade, the practise of selling a commodity at a lower price in the export market than in the domestic market for reasons that are not related to differences in costs of servicing the two markets.

duopoly An industry that contains only two firms.

durable good A good that yields its services over an extended period of time. Often divided into the subcategories *producers' durables* (e.g., machines, equipment) and *consumers' durables* (e.g., cars, appliances).

economic efficiency The least costly method of producing any output.

economic growth Increases in real, or constant-dollar, potential GDP.

economic profits or losses The difference between the revenues received from the sale of output and the opportunity cost of the inputs used to make the output. Negative economic profits are economic losses. Also called *pure profits* or *pure losses,* or simple *profits* or *losses.*

economic rent The surplus of total earnings over what must be paid to prevent a factor from moving to another use.

economies of scale Reduction of costs per unit output resulting from an expansion in the scale of a firm's operations so that more of all inputs are being used.

economies of scope Economies achieved by a firm that is large enough to engage efficiently in multiproduct production and associated large-scale distribution, advertising, and purchasing.

economy A set of interrelated production and consumption activities.

effective rate of tariff The tax charged on any imported commodity expressed as a percentage of the value added by the exporting industry.

elastic demand The situation in which, for a given percentage change in price, there is a greater percentage change in quantity demanded; elasticity greater than unity.

elasticity of demand (η) A measure of the responsiveness of quantity of a commodity demanded to a change in market price, defined by the formula

$$\eta = \frac{\text{percentage change in quantity demanded}}{\text{percentage change in price}}$$

With negatively sloped demand curves, elasticity is a negative number. The above expression is therefore multiplied by -1 to make measured elasticity positive. Also called *demand elasticity, price elasticity.*

elasticity of supply (η_S) A measure of the responsiveness of the quantity of a commodity supplied to a change in the market price, defined by the formula

$$\eta_S = \frac{\text{percentage change in quantity supplied}}{\text{percentage change in price}}$$

embodied technical change Technical change that is intrinsic to the particular capital goods in use, and hence that can be utilized only when new capital, embodying the new techniques, is built.

employment The number of adult workers who hold jobs.

endogenous expenditure See *induced expenditure.*

endogenous variable A variable that is explained within a theory.

ends The goals we seek to attain.

entry barrier Any natural barrier to the entry of new firms into an industry, such as a large minimum efficient scale for firms, or any firm-created barrier, such as a patent.

envelope Any curve that encloses, by being tangent to, a series of other curves. In particular, the *envelope cost curve* is the *LRAC* curve, which encloses the *SRATC* curves by being tangent to each without cutting any of them.

equalization payments Transfers of tax revenues from the federal government to the low-income

provinces to compensate them for their lower potential per capita tax yields.

equilibrium condition A condition that must be fulfilled if some market or sector of the economy, or the whole economy, is to be in equilibrium.

equilibrium differential A difference in factor prices that would persist in equilibrium, without any tendency for it to be removed.

equilibrium price The price at which quantity demanded equals quantity supplied.

equity capital Funds provided by the owners of a firm the return on which depends on the firm's profits.

excess burden The value to taxpayers of the changes in behaviour that are induced by taxes; the amount that taxpayers would be willing to pay, over and above the direct burden of taxes, to abolish the taxes.

excess capacity The amount by which actual output falls short of capacity output (which is the output that corresponds to the minimum short-run average total cost).

excess capacity theorem The property of long-run equilibrium in monopolistic competition that firms produce on the falling portion of their average total cost curves, so that they have excess capacity measured by the gap between present output and the output that coincides with minimum average total cost.

excess demand A situation in which, at the given price, quantity demanded exceeds quantity supplied. Also called a *shortage.*

excess reserves Reserves held by a commercial bank in excess of the legally required minimum.

excess supply A situation in which, at the given price, quantity supplied exceeds quantity demanded. Also called a *surplus.*

exchange rate The price in terms of one currency at which another currency, or claims on it, can be bought and sold.

excise tax A tax on the sale of a particular commodity; may be a *specific tax* (fixed tax per unit of commodity) or an *ad valorem tax* (fixed percentage of the value of the commodity).

execution lag The time that it takes to put policies in place after the decision has been made.

exhaustible resource See *nonrenewable resource.*

exogenous expenditure See *autonomous expenditure.*

exogenous variable A variable that influences endogenous variables but is itself determined by factors outside the theory.

expectational inflation Inflation that occurs because decision makers raise prices (so as to keep their relative prices constant) in the expectation that the price level is going to rise.

expectations-augmented Phillips curve The relationship between unemployment and the rate of increase of money wages or between national income and the rate of increase of money prices that arises when the demand and expectations components of inflation are combined.

external economies of scale Scale economies that cause the firm's costs to fall as *industry output* rises but that are external to the firm and so cannot be obtained by the firm's increasing its own output.

external value of the dollar The value of the dollar expressed in terms of foreign currencies; changes in the dollar's external value are measured by changes in the exchange rate.

externalities Effects, either good or bad, on parties not directly involved in the production or use of a commodity. Also called *third-party effects.*

factor markets Markets in which the services of factors of production are sold.

factor mobility The ease with which factors can be transferred between uses.

factor services The services of factors of production that are used to produce outputs.

factors of production Resources used to produce goods and services to satisfy wants; frequently divided into the basic categories of land, labour, and capital.

falling-cost industry An industry in which the lowest costs attainable by a firm fall as the scale of the industry expands.

favourable balance of payments A credit balance on some part of the international payments accounts (receipts exceed payments); often refers to a favourable balance on current plus capital account (that is, everything except the official settlements account).

FDI See *foreign direct investment.*

fiat money Paper money or coinage that is neither backed nor convertible into anything else but is decreed by the government to be accepted as legal tender and is generally accepted in exchange for goods and services and for the discharge of debts.

final demand Demand for the economy's final output.

final goods and services Goods and services that are not used as inputs by other firms, but are produced to be sold for consumption, investment, government, or exports during the period under consideration.

financial capital See *money capital.*

fine tuning The attempt to maintain national income at or near its full-employment level by means of frequent changes in fiscal or monetary policy.

firm The unit that employs factors of production to produce goods and services.

fiscal policy The use of the government's tax and spending policies in an effort to influence the behaviour of such macro variables as the GDP and total employment.

fixed cost A cost that does not change with output. Also called *overhead cost, unavoidable cost.*

fixed exchange rate An exchange rate that is maintained within a small range around its publicly stated par value by the intervention of a country's central bank in foreign market operations. Also called a *pegged rate.*

fixed factor An input that cannot be increased beyond a given amount in the short run.

fixed investment Investment in plant and equipment.

flexible exchange rate An exchange rate that is left free to be determined by the forces of demand and supply on the free market, with no intervention by the monetary authorities. Also called *floating exchange rate.*

floating exchange rate See *flexible exchange rate.*

foreign direct investment (FDI) Nonresident investment in the form of a takeover or capital investment in a domestic branch plant or subsidiary corporation in which the investor has voting control. See also *portfolio investment.*

foreign exchange Actual foreign currencies or various claims on them, such as bank balances or promises to pay, that are traded for each other on the foreign exchange market.

foreign exchange market The market where different national monies, or claims to these monies, are traded against each other.

45° line In macroeconomics, the line that graphs the equilibrium condition that aggregate desired expenditure should equal national income ($AE = Y$).

fractional reserve system A banking system in which commercial banks are required to keep only a fraction of their deposits in cash or on deposit with the central bank.

free good A commodity for which the quantity supplied exceeds the quantity demanded at a price of zero; therefore, a good that does not command a positive price in a market economy.

free-market economy An economy in which the decisions of individual households and firms (as distinct from the government) exert the major influence over the allocation of resources.

free trade The absence of any form of government intervention in international trade, which implies that imports and exports must not be subject to special taxes or restrictions levied merely because of their status as "imports" or "exports."

free-trade area An agreement among two or more countries to abolish tariffs on all, or most, of the trade among themselves, while each remains free to set its own tariffs against other countries.

frictional unemployment Unemployment caused by the time that is taken for labour to move from one job to another.

full employment See *high employment*.

function Loosely, an expression of a relationship between two or more variables. Precisely, Y is a function of the variables $X_1, \ldots, X_n$ if, for every set of values of the variables $X_1, \ldots, X_n$, there is associated a unique value of the variable Y.

functional distribution of income The distribution of total national income among the major factors of production.

G See *government purchases*.

gains from trade The increased output due to the specialization according to comparative advantage that is made possible by trade.

GDP deflator See *implicit GDP deflator*.

GDP gap See *output gap*.

Giffen good An inferior good for which the negative income effect outweighs the substitution effect, so that the demand curve is positively sloped.

goods Tangible commodities, such as cars or shoes.

goods markets Markets in which outputs of goods and services are sold. Also called *product markets*.

government All public officials, agencies, and other organizations belonging to or under the control of state, local, or federal governments.

government purchases Includes all government expenditure on currently produced goods and services and does not include government transfer payments. Represented by the symbol G as one of the four components of aggregate expenditure. Also called *government expenditure*.

Gresham's law The theory that "bad," or debased, money drives "good," or undebased, money out of circulation, because people keep the good money for other purposes and use the bad money for transactions.

gross domestic product (*GDP*) The total value of all output produced and income generated by economic activity within a country; equal to the sum of all values added in the economy or, what is the same thing, the values of all final goods produced in the economy. Measured from the expenditure side of the national accounts, it is the sum of consumption, investment, government expenditure on final output, and net exports; measured from the income side of the national accounts, it is the sum of factor incomes, plus depreciation, plus indirect taxes net of subsidies. It can be valued at *current prices* to get *nomianl GDP*, which is also called *GDP at current,* or *market, prices*; or it can be valued at base-year prices to get *real GDP*, which is also called *GDP at constant prices*. See also *gross national product*.

gross investment The total value of all investment goods produced in the economy during a stated period of time.

gross national product (GNP) The total value of output received by residents of a country; it differs from GDP by the addition of incomes earned abroad and the subtraction of incomes produced at home but earned by foreign residents. See also *gross domestic product*.

gross national product at market prices See *gross national product*.

gross tuning The use of macroeconomic policy to stabilize the economy such that large deviations from high employment do not occur for extended periods of time.

high employment Employment that is sufficient to produce the economy's potential output; at high employment, all remaining unemployment is frictional and structural.

high-employment GDP (Y^*) See *potential GDP*.

high-employment national income (Y^*) See *potential GDP*.

homogeneous product In the eyes of purchasers, every unit of the product is identical to every other unit.

household All of the people who live under one roof and who make, or are subject to others making for them, joint financial decisions.

human capital The capitalized value of productive investments in persons; usually refers to value derived from expenditures on education, training, and health improvements.

hypothesis of diminishing returns See *law of diminishing returns*.

I See *investment expenditure*.

IM A country's total expenditure on imports.

implicit GDP deflator An index number derived by dividing GDP, measured in current dollars, by GDP, measured in constant dollars, and multiplying by 100. In effect, a price index, with current-year quantity weights, measuring the average change in price of all the items in the GDP. Also called *gross product domestic deflator*.

import quota A limit set by the government on the quantity of a foreign commodity that may be shipped into that country in a given time period.

imputed costs The costs of using factors of production already owned by the firm, measured by the earnings they could have received in their best alternative use.

income-consumption line (or curve) (1) A curve showing the relationship for a commodity between quantity demanded and income, *ceteris paribus*; (2) a curve drawn on an indifference curve diagram and connecting the points of tangency between a set of indifference curves and a set of parallel budget lines, showing how the consumption bundle changes as income changes, with relative prices being held constant.

income effect The effect on quantity demanded of a change in real income.

income elasticity of demand A measure of the responsiveness of quantity demanded to a change in income, defined by the formula

$$\eta_Y = \frac{\text{percentage change in quantity demanded}}{\text{percentage change in income}}$$

incomes policy Any direct intervention by the government to influence wage and price formation.

income-tested benefits Social benefits paid to recipients who qualify because their income falls below some critical level; in particular, more targeted than demogrants. Also called *income-related benefits*.

increasing returns A situation in which output increases more than in proportion to inputs as the scale of a firm's production increases. A firm in this situation, with fixed factor prices, is a *decreasing cost* firm.

index number An average that measures change over time of such variables as the price level and industrial production; conventionally expressed as a percentage relative to a base period, which is assigned the value 100.

indexing The linking of money payments to changes in the price level designed to hold the real value of payments constant.

indifference curve A curve showing all combinations of two commodities that give the household an equal amount of satisfaction and between which the household is thus indifferent.

indifference map A set of indifference curves based on a given set of household preferences.

induced expenditure In macroeconomics, elements of expenditure that are explained by variables within the theory. In the aggregate desired expenditure function, it is any component of expenditure that is related to national income. Also called *endogeneous expenditure*.

industry A group of firms that produce a single product or group of related products.

inelastic demand The situation in which, for a given percentage change in price, there is a smaller percentage change in quantity demanded; elasticity less than unity.

infant industry argument for tariffs The argument that new domestic industries with potentials for economies of scale, or learning by doing, need to be protected from competition from established, low-cost foreign producers, so that they can grow large enough to achieve costs as low as those of foreign producers.

inferior good A good for which income elasticity is negative.

inflation A rise in the average level of all prices. Sometimes restricted to prolonged or sustained rises.

inflationary gap A situation in which actual national income exceeds potential income.

information asymmetries Sources of market failure that arise when one party to a transaction has more information relevant to the transaction than does the other party.

infrastructure The basic installations and facilities (especially transportation and communication systems) on which the commerce of a community depends.

injections Income earned by domestic firms that does not arise out of the spending of domestic households and income earned by domestic households that does not arise out of the spending of domestic firms.

innovation The introduction of an invention into methods of production.

inputs Intermediate products and factor services that are used in the methods of production.

interest The payment for the use of borrowed money.

interest rate The price paid per dollar borrowed per period of time, expressed either as a proportion (e.g., 0.06) or as a percentage (e.g., 6 percent). Also called the *nominal interest rate* to distinguish it from the *real rate of interest*.

intermediate goods and services All outputs that are used as inputs by other producers in a further stage of production.

internal economies of scale Scale economies that result from the firm's own actions and hence are available to it by raising its own output.

internal value of the dollar The purchasing power of the dollar measured in terms of domestic goods and services; changes in the internal value of the dollar are measured in an index of U.S. prices.

internalization A process that results in a producer or consumer taking account of a previously external effect.

invention The discovery of something new, such as a new production technique or a new product.

inventories Stocks of raw materials, goods in process, and finished goods, held by firms to mitigate the effect of short-term fluctuations in production or sales.

investment expenditure Expenditure on the production of goods not for present consumption.

investment goods Goods that are produced not for present consumption; i.e., capital goods, inventories, and residential housing.

invisible account A form of balance-of-payments

account that records payments and receipts arising out of trade in services and payments for the use of capital. Also called *service account*.

invisibles All those items of foreign trade that are intangible; services as opposed to goods.

involuntary unemployment Unemployment due to the inability of qualified persons who are seeking work to find jobs at the going wage rate.

isoquant A curve showing all technologically efficient factor combinations for producing a specified amount of output.

isoquant map A series of isoquants from the same production function, each isoquant relating to a specific level of output.

Keynesians A label attached to economists who hold the view, derived from the work of John Maynard Keynes, that active use of monetary and fiscal policy can be effective in stabilizing the economy. Often the term encompasses economists who advocate active policy intervention in general.

Keynesian short-run aggregate supply curve A horizontal aggregate supply curve, indicating that, when national income is below potential, changes in national income can occur with little or no accompanying changes in prices.

kinked demand curve A demand curve facing an oligopolistic firm that assumes its competitors will match its price reductions but will not respond to its price increases. At the firm's current price-output combination, its demand curve is kinked and its marginal revenue curve is discontinuous.

***k* percent rule** The proposition that the money supply should be increased at a constant percentage rate year in and year out, irrespective of cyclical changes in national income.

labour A factor of production consisting of all physical and mental efforts provided by people.

labour force The total number of persons employed in both civilian and military jobs, plus the number of persons who are unemployed.

labour force participation rate The percentage of the population of working age that is actually in the labour force (i.e., either working or seeking work).

labour union See *union*.

Laffer curve A graph relating the revenue yield of a tax system to the marginal or average tax rate imposed.

laissez faire Literally, "let's do"; a policy advocating the minimization of government intervention in a market economy.

land A factor of production consisting of all gifts of nature, including raw materials and "land," as understood in ordinary speech.

law of demand The assertion that market price and quantity demanded in the market vary inversely with one another, that is, that demand curves are negatively sloped.

law of diminishing returns The hypothesis that, if increasing quantities of a variable factor are applied to a given quantity of fixed factors, the marginal product and average product of the variable factor will eventually decrease. Also called *hypothesis of diminishing returns, law of variable proportions*.

law of variable proportions See *law of diminishing returns*.

learning curve A curve showing how a firm's costs of producing at a given rate of output fall as the total amount produced increases over time as a result of accumulated learning of how to make the product efficiently using given equipment.

legal tender Anything that by law must be accepted for the purchase of goods and services or in discharge of a debt.

less-developed countries (LDCs) The lower-income countries of the world, most of which are in Asia, Africa, and South and Central America. Also called *underdeveloped countries, developing countries,* the *South*.

leveraged buyout (LBO) A buyout of a firm largely financed by borrowed money.

life-cycle theory A hypothesis that relates the household's actual consumption to its expected lifetime income rather than (as in early Keynesian theory) to its current income.

lifetime income See *permanent income*.

limited liability The limitation of the financial responsibility of an owner (shareholder) of a corporation to the amount of money that the shareholder has actually invested in the firm by purchasing its shares.

limited partnership A form of business organization in which the firm has two classes of owners: general partners, who take part in managing the firm and who are personally liable for all of the firm's actions and debts, and limited partners, who take no part in the management of the firm and who risk only the money that they have invested.

liquidity preference (LP) function The function that relates the demand for money to the rate of interest.

logarithmic scale A scale in which equal proportional changes are shown as equal distances (for example, 1 inch may always represent doubling of a variable, whether from 3 to 6 or 50 to 100). Also called *log scale, ratio scale*.

long run A period of time in which all inputs may be varied, but the basic technology of production cannot be changed.

long-run aggregate supply (LRAS) curve A curve

showing the relationship between the price level of final output and the total quantity of output supplied when all markets have fully adjusted to the existing price level; a vertical line at $Y = Y^*$.

long-run average cost (LRAC) curve The curve relating the least-cost method of producing any output to the level of output when all inputs can be varied.

long-run industry supply (LRS) curve A curve showing the relationship between the market price and the quantity supplied by a competitive industry when all the firms in that industry are in full, long-run equilibrium.

Lorenz curve A graph showing the extent of departure from equality of income distribution.

M1 Currency plus demand deposits plus other checkable deposits.

M2 M1 plus money market mutual fund balances, money market deposit accounts, savings accounts, and small-denomination time deposits.

M3 M2 plus large-denomination time deposits (CDs), term repurchase agreements, and money market mutual funds held by institutions.

macroeconomics The study of the determination of economic aggregates, such as total output, total employment, the price level, and the rate of economic growth.

marginal cost (MC) The increase in total cost resulting from raising the rate of production by one unit. Mathematically, the rate of change of cost with respect to output. Also called *incremental cost*.

marginal cost pricing Setting price equal to marginal cost so that buyers are just willing to pay for the last unit bought the amount that it cost to make the unit.

marginal efficiency of capital (MEC) The marginal rate of return on a nation's capital stock. The rate of return on one additional dollar of net investment, that is, an addition of one dollar's worth of new capital to capital stock.

marginal efficiency of investment (MEI) function The function that relates the quantity of investment to the rate of interest.

marginal physical product (MPP) see *marginal product*.

marginal product (MP) The change in quantity of total output that results from using one unit more of a variable factor. Mathematically, the rate of change of output with respect to the quantity of the variable factor. Also called *incremental product* or *marginal physical product (MPP)*.

marginal-productivity theory of distribution The theory that factors are paid the value of their marginal products so that the total earnings of each type of factor of production equals the value of the marginal product of that factor multiplied by the number of units of that factor that are employed.

marginal propensity not to spend The fraction of any increment to national income that is not spent on domestic production ($1 \times \Delta AE/\Delta Y$).

marginal propensity to consume (MPC) The change in consumption divided by the change in disposable income that brought it about; mathematically, the rate of change of consumption with respect to disposable income ($MPC = \Delta C/\Delta Y_d$).

marginal propensity to save (MPS) The change in total desired saving related to the change in disposable income that brought it about ($\Delta S/\Delta Y_d$).

marginal propensity to spend The fraction of any increment to national income that is spent on domestic production; it is measured by the change in aggregate expenditure divided by the change in income ($\Delta AE/\Delta Y$).

marginal rate of substitution (MRS) (1) In consumption, the slope of an indifference curve, showing how much more of one commodity must be provided to compensate for the giving up of one unit of another commodity if the level of satisfaction is to be held constant. (2) In production, the slope of an isoquant, showing how much more of one factor of production must be used to compensate for the use of one less unit of another factor of production if production is to be held constant.

marginal revenue (MR) The change in a firm's total revenue resulting from a change in its rate of sales by one unit. Mathematically, the rate of change of revenue with respect to output. Slso called *incremental revenue*.

marginal revenue product (MRP) The addition of revenue attributable to the last unit of a variable factor ($MRP = MP \times MR$). Mathematically, the rate of change of revenue with respect to quantity of the variable factor.

marginal tax rate The amount of tax that a taxpayer would pay on an additional dollar of income; that is, the fraction of an additional dollar of income that is paid in taxes.

marginal utility The additional satisfaction obtained by a consumer from consuming one unit more of a good or service; mathematically, the rate of change of utility with respect to consumption.

market Any situation in which buyers and sellers can negotiate the exchange of a commodity or group of commodities.

market-clearing price Price at which quantity demanded equals quantity supplied, so that there are neither unsatisfied buyers nor unsatisfied sellers, that is, the equilibrium price.

market economy A society in which people specialize in productive activities and meet most of their material wants through exchanges voluntarily agreed upon by the contracting parties.

market failure Failure of the unregulated market system to achieve optimal allocation efficiency or social goals because of externalities, market impediments, or market imperfections.

market for corporate control An interpretation of conglomerate mergers, leveraged buyouts, and hostile takeovers as mechanisms that place the firm in the hands of those who are able to generate the most value product.

market rate of interest The actual interest rate in effect at a given moment.

market sector That portion of an economy in which commodities are bought and sold and in which producers must cover their costs from sales revenue.

market structure All those features of a market that affect the behaviour and performance of firms in that market, such as the number and size of sellers, the extent of knowledge about each other's actions, the degree of freedom of entry, and the degree of product differentiation.

means The methods of achieving our goals.

median The value within any set of data at which half of the observations are greater and half are less. Thus, half of a population earns income above the median income, and half earns income below the median.

medium of exchange Anything that is generally acceptable in return for goods and services sold.

merchandise account See *trade account*.

merger The purchase of either the physical assets or the controlling share of ownership of one firm by another. In a *horizontal* merger both firms are in the same line of business; in a *vertical* merger one firm is a supplier of the other; if the two are in unrelated industries, it is a *conglomerate* merger.

merit goods Goods such as housing and medical care that are deemed to be especially important.

microeconomic policy Activities of governments designed to alter resource allocation and/or income distribution.

microeconomics The study of the allocation of resources and the distribution of income as they are affected by the workings of the price system and by government policies.

minimum efficient scale *(MES)* The smallest output at which long-run average cost reaches its minimum because all available economies of scale in production and/or distribution have been realized. Also called *minimum optimal scale*.

minimum wages Legally specified minimum rate of pay for labour in covered occupations.

mixed economy An economy in which some decisions about the allocation of resources are made by firms and households and some by the government.

monetarists A label attached to economists who stress monetary causes of cyclical fluctuations and inflations and who believe that an active stabilization policy is not normally required.

monetary base The sum of currency in circulation plus reserves of the commercial banks, equal to the monetary liabilities of the central bank.

monetary equilibrium A situation in which the demand for money equals the supply of money.

monetary policy An attempt to influence the economy by operating on such monetary variables as the quantity of money and the rate of interest.

money Money acts as a medium of exchange and can also serve as a store of value and a unit of account.

money capital Money that a firm raises to carry on its business, including both equity capital and debt. Also called *financial capital*.

money income Income measured in monetary units per period of time.

money rate of interest See *interest rate*.

money substitute Something that serves as a temporary medium of exchange but is not a store of value.

money supply The total quantity of money in an economy at a point in time. Also called *the supply of money*.

monopolist A firm that is the only seller in some market.

monopolistic competition (1) A market structure of an industry in which there are many firms and freedom of entry and exit but in which each firm has a product somewhat differentiated from the others, giving it some control over its price; (2) More recently, any industry in which more than one firm sells differentiated products.

monopoly A market containing a single firm.

monopsony A market situation in which there is a single buyer.

moral hazard A situation in which an individual or a firm takes advantage of special knowledge while engaging in socially uneconomic behaviour.

multilateral balance of payments The balance of payments between one country and the rest of the world taken as a whole.

multiplier The ratio of the change in national income to the change in autonomous expenditure that brought it about.

NAIRU (Short for *nonaccelerating inflationary rate of unemployment*.) The rate of unemployment associated with potential national income and at which a steady, nonaccelerating or nondecelerating inflation can be sustained indefinitely. Also called *the national rate of unemployment.*

Nash equilibrium In the case of firms, an equilibrium that results when each firm in an industry is currently doing the best that it can, given the current behaviour of the other firms in the industry.

national asset formation The sum of investment and net exports.

national debt The current volume of outstanding federal government debt.

national income In general, the value of total output and the value of the income that is generated by the production of that output.

national saving The sum of public saving and private saving. All of national income that is not spent on government purchases or private consumption.

natural monopoly An industry characterized by economies of scale sufficiently large that one firm can most efficiently supply the entire market demand.

natural rate of unemployment See *NAIRU.*

natural scale A scale in which equal absolute amounts are represented by equal distances.

near money Liquid assets that are easily convertible into money without risk of significant loss of value and can be used as short-term stores of purchasing power, but are not themselves media of exchange.

negative income tax (NIT) A tax system in which households with incomes below taxable levels receive payments from the government that are based on a percentage of the amount by which their income is below the minimum taxable level.

negotiable order of withdrawal (NOW) A chequelike device for transferring funds from one person's time deposit to another person.

net domestic income at factor cost The sum of the four components of factor incomes (wages, rent, interest, and profits).

net domestic product Gross domestic product less capital consumed in the production of GDP.

net domestic product at market prices The sum of wages, rent, interest, profits, and indirect taxes minus subsidies.

net exports (*NX*) The value of total exports minus the value of total imports. Represented by the expression $(X - IM)$ as a component of aggregate expenditure, where X is total exports and IM is total imports.

net investment Gross investment minus replacement investment.

net taxes Taxes minus transfer payments.

neutrality of money The doctrine that the money supply affects only the absolute level of prices and has no effect on relative prices and hence no effect on the allocation of resources or the distribution of income.

newly industrialised economies (NIEs) Countries that have industrialised and grown rapidly over the past 30 years to achieve per capita incomes roughly half of those achieved in the United States. Also called *newly industrialised countries* (NICs).

nominal interest rate See *interest rate.*

nominal national income Total national income measured in dollars; the money value of national income. Also called *money national income* or *current-dollar national income.*

nominal rate of tariff The tax charged on any imported commodity.

noncooperative equilibrium An equilibrium reached when firms calculate their own best policy without considering competitor's reactions.

nonmarket sector The portion of the economy in which goods are provided freely so that producers must cover their costs from sources other than sales revenue.

nonrenewable resource Any productive resource that is available as a fixed stock that cannot be replaced once it is used.

nonstrategic behaviour Behaviour that does *not* take account of the reactions of rivals to one's own behaviour.

nontariff barriers Restrictions, other than tariffs, designed to reduce the flow of imported goods.

normal good A good for which income elasticity is positive.

normal profits The opportunity cost of capital and risk taking just necessary to keep the owners in the industry. Normal profits are usually included in what economists, but not businesspersons, call *total costs.*

normative statement A statement about what ought to be—in an ethical sense—as opposed to what actually is, in a positive sense.

oligopoly An industry that contains two or more firms, at least one of which produces a significant portion of the industry's total output.

open market operations The purchase and sale on the open market by the central bank of securities (usually short-term government securities).

opportunity cost The cost of using resources for a certain purpose, measured by the benefit given up by not using them in their best alternative use.

organization theory A set of hypotheses that predicts that the substance of the decisions of a firm is affected by its size and form of organization.

output gap Potential national income minus actual national income. Also called the *GDP gap.*

outputs The goods and services that result from the process of production.

Pareto-efficiency   See *Pareto-optimality.*

Pareto-optimality   A situation in which it is impossible by reallocation of production or consumption activities to make all consumers better off without simultaneously making others worse off (or, as it is sometimes put, to make at least one person better off while making no one else worse off). Also called *Pareto-efficiency.*

partnership   A form of business organization in which the firm has two or more joint owners, each of whom takes part in the management of the firm and is personally responsible for all of the firm's actions and debts.

paternalism   Intervention in the free choices of individuals by others (including governments) to protect them against their own ignorance or folly.

pegged rate   See *fixed exchange rate.*

per capita output   GDP divided by total population.

perfect competition   A market structure in which all firms in an industry are price takers and in which there is freedom of entry into and exit from the industry.

permanent income   The maximum amount that a household can consume per year into the indefinite future without reducing its wealth. (A number of similar, but not identical, definitions are in common use.) Also called *lifetime income.*

permanent-income theory   A hypothesis that relates actual consumption to permanent income rather than (as in the original Keynesian theory) to current income.

personal income   Income earned by, or paid to, individuals before allowance for personal income taxes on that income.

Phillips curve   Originally, a relationship between the percentage of the labour force unemployed and the rate of change of money wages. Now often drawn as a relationship between the percentage of the labour force employed and the rate of price inflation or between actual national income and the rate of price inflation.

point elasticity   A measure of the responsiveness of quantity to price at a particular point on the demand curve. The formula for point elasticity of demand is

$$\eta = \frac{\Delta q}{\Delta p} \times \frac{p}{q}$$

With negatively sloped demand curves elasticity is a negative number. Sometimes the above expression is multiplied by -1 to make elasticity positive.

point of diminishing average productivity   The level of output at which average product reaches a maximum.

point of diminishing marginal productivity   The level of output at which marginal product reaches a maximum.

portfolio investment   Foreign investment in bonds or a minority holding of shares that does not involve legal control. See also *foreign direct investment.*

positive statement   A statement about what actually is (was or will be), as opposed to what ought to be in an ethical sense.

potential GDP (Y*)   The real gross domestic product that the economy could produce if its productive resources were fully employed at their normal levels of utilization. Also called *potential national income, national income, high-employment GDP, high-employment national income.*

potential national income   See *potential GDP.*

poverty gap   The number of dollars per year required to raise everyone's income that is below the poverty level to that level.

poverty level   The official government estimate of the annual family income that is required to maintain a minimum adequate standard of living.

precautionary balances   Money balances held for protection against the uncertainty of the timing of cash flows.

present value (PV)   The value now of one or more payments to be received in the future; often referred to as the *discounted present value* of future payments.

price ceiling   A government-imposed maximum permissible price at which a commodity may be sold.

price-consumption line   A line connecting the points of tangency between a set of indifference curves and a set of budget lines where one absolute price is fixed and the other varies, money income being held constant.

price controls   Government policies that attempt to hold the price in a particular market at a disequilibrium value.

price discrimination   The sale by one firm of different units of a commodity at two or more different prices for reasons not associated with differences in cost.

price elasticity of demand   See *elasticity of demand.*

price floor   A government-imposed minimum permissible price at which a commodity may be sold.

price index   A number that shows the average of some group of prices; expressed as a percentage of the average ruling in some base period. Price indexes can be used to measure the price level at a given time relative to a base period.

price level   The average level of all prices in the economy, usually expressed as an index number.

price makers   Firms that administer their prices. See *administered price.*

price taker   A firm that can alter its rate of production and sales without significantly affecting the market price of its product.

price theory The theory of how prices are determined; competitive price theory concerns the determination of prices in competitive markets by the interaction of demand and supply.

principal-agent problem The problem of resource allocation that arises because contracts that will induce agents to act in their principals' best interests are generally impossible to write or too costly to monitor.

principle of substitution Methods of production will change if relative prices of inputs change, with relatively more of the cheaper input and relatively less of the more expensive input being used.

private cost The value of the best alternative use of resources used in production as valued by the producer.

private saving Saving on the part of households—that part of disposable income that is not spent on consumption.

private sector The portion of an economy in which goods and services are produced by nongovernmental units, such as firms and households.

procyclical Movements of economic variables in the same direction as the business cycle—up in booms and down in slumps.

producers' surplus The difference between the total amount that producers receive for all units sold of a commodity and the total variable cost of producing the commodity.

product differentiation The existence of similar but not identical products sold by a single industry, such as the breakfast food and the automobile industries.

production The act of making commodities—either goods or services.

production efficiency Production of any output at the lowest attainable cost for that level of output.

production function A functional relation showing the maximum output that can be produced by each and every combination of inputs.

production possibility curve A curve that shows which alternative combinations of commodities can just be attained if all available resources are used; it is thus the boundary between attainable and unattainable output combinations. Also called the *production possibility boundary*.

productivity Output produced per unit of some input; frequently used to refer to *labour productivity*, measured by total output divided by the amount of labour used.

product markets Markets in which outputs of goods and services are sold. Also called *goods markets*.

profit (1) In ordinary usage, the difference between the value of outputs and the value of inputs. (2) In microeconomics, the difference between revenues received from the sale of goods and the value of inputs, which includes the opportunity cost of capital; also called *pure profits* or *economic profits*. (3) In macroeconomics, profits exclude interest on borrowed capital but do not exclude the return on owner's capital.

progressive tax A tax that takes a larger percentage of income the higher the level of income.

proportional tax A tax that takes a constant percentage of income at all levels of income and is thus neither progressive nor regressive.

protectionism Any government policy that interferes with free trade in order to give some protection to domestic industries against foreign competition.

proxy An order from a stockholder that passes the right to vote to a nominee, usually an existing member of the board of a firm.

public goods See *collective-consumption goods*.

public saving Saving on the part of governments. Public saving is exactly equal to government budget surpluses, or government revenues less government expenditures.

public sector The portion of an economy in which goods and services are produced by the government or by government-owned agencies and firms.

purchase and resale agreement (PRA) An arrangement by which the Bank of Canada makes short-term advances as a lender of last resort to investment dealers. Government securities are sold to the Bank with an agreement to repurchase them.

purchasing power of money The amount of goods and services that can be purchased with a unit of money. The purchasing power of money varies inversely with the price level. Also called *value of money*.

purchasing power parity (PPP) exchange rate The exchange rate between two currencies that adjusts for relative price levels.

quantity demanded The amount of a commodity that households wish to purchase in some time period.

quantity supplied The amount of a commodity that producers wish to sell in some time period.

rate of inflation The percentage rate of increase in some price index from one period to another.

rate of return The ratio of net profits earned by a firm to total invested capital.

rational expectations The theory that people understand how the economy works and learn quickly from their mistakes, so that, while random errors may be made, systematic and persistent errors are not made.

ratio scale See *logarithmic scale*.

real capital The physical assets that a firm uses to conduct its business, composed of plant, equipment, and inventories. Also called *physical capital*.

real GDP See *constant-dollar GDP*.

real income Income expressed in terms of the purchasing power of money income, that is, the quantity of goods and services that can be purchased with the money income; it can be calculated as money income deflated by a price index.

real national income (Y) National income measured in constant dollars, so that it changes only when quantities change.

real rate of interest The money rate of interest corrected for the change in the purchasing power of money by subtracting the inflation rate.

recession In general, a downturn in the level of economic activity.

recessionary gap A positive output gap; that is, a situation in which actual national income is less than potential income. Also called a *deflationary gap*.

regressive tax A tax that takes a lower percentage of income the higher the level of income.

relative price The ratio of the money price of one commodity to the money price of another commodity; that is, a ratio of two absolute prices.

renewable resources Productive resources that can be replaced as they are used up, as with physical capital; distinguished from nonrenewable resources, which are available in a fixed stock that can be depleted but not replaced.

rent seeking Behaviour in which private firms and individuals try to use the powers of the government to enhance their own economic well-being.

replacement investment The amount of investment that is needed to maintain the existing capital stock intact.

required reserves The reserves that a bank must, by law, keep either in currency or in deposits with the central bank.

reserve ratio The fraction of its deposits that a commercial bank holds as reserves in the form of cash or deposits with a central bank.

resource allocation The allocation of an economy's scarce resources of land, labour, and capital among alternative uses.

retained earnings See *undistributed profits*.

rising-cost industry An industry in which the minimum cost attainable by a firm rises as the scale of the industry expands.

satisficing A hypothesized objective of firms to achieve levels of performance deemed satisfactory rather than to *maximize* some objective.

saving See *private saving, public saving, national saving*.

scarce good A commodity for which the quantity demanded exceeds the quantity supplied at a price of zero; therefore, a good that commands a positive price in a market economy.

scatter diagram A graph of statistical observations of paired values of two variables, one measured on the horizontal and the other on the vertical axis. Each point on the coordinate grid represents the values of the variables for a particular unit of observation.

search unemployment Unemployment caused by people continuing to search for a good job rather than accepting the first job that they come across after they become unemployed.

sectors Parts of an economy.

securities market See *stock market*.

sellers' preferences Allocation of commodities in excess demand by decisions of those who sell them.

service account See *invisible account*.

services Intangible commodities, such as haircuts or medical care.

shareholders See *stockholders*.

short run A period of time in which the quantity of some inputs cannot be increased beyond the fixed amount that is available.

short-run aggregate supply (SRAS) curve A curve showing the relation between the price level of final output and the quantity of output supplied on the assumption that all factor prices are held constant.

short-run equilibrium Generally, equilibrium subject to fixed factors or other things that cannot change over the time period being considered. For a competitive firm, the output at which market price equals marginal cost; for a competitive industry, the price and output at which industry demand equals short-run industry supply and all firms are in short-run equilibrium. Either profits or losses are possible.

short-run supply curve A curve showing the relationship between quantity supplied and market price, with one or more fixed factors; it is the horizontal sum of marginal cost curves (above the level of average variable costs) of all firms in a perfectly competitive industry.

shut-down price The price that is equal to a firm's average variable costs, below which it will produce no output.

simple multiplier The ratio of the change in equilibrium national income to the change in autonomous expenditure that brought it about, *calculated for* a constant price level.

single proprietorship A form of business organization in which the firm has one owner, who makes all the decisions and is personally responsible for all of the firm's actions and debts.

size distribution of income The distribution of

income among households, without regard to source of income or social class of households.

slope The ratio of the vertical change to the horizontal change between two points on a curve.

social benefit The contribution that an activity makes to the society's welfare.

social cost The value of the best alternative use of resources available to society as valued by society. Also called *social opportunity cost.*

social regulation The regulation of economic behaviour to advance social goals when competition and economic regulation will fail to achieve those goals.

special drawing rights (SDRs) Financial liabilities of the IMF held in a special fund generated by contributions of member countries. Members can use SDRs to maintain supplies of convertible currencies when these are needed to support foreign exchanges.

specialization of labour The specialization of individual workers in the production of particular goods and services, rather than producing everything that they consume.

specific tariff An import duty of a specific amount per unit of the product.

specific tax See *excise tax.*

speculative balances Money balances held as a hedge against the uncertainty of the prices of other financial assets.

stabilization policy Any policy designed to reduce the economy's cyclical fluctuations and thereby to stabilize national income at, or near, a desired level.

stagflation The coexistence of high rates of unemployment with high, and sometimes rising, rates of inflation.

stockholders The owners of a corporation who have supplied money to the firm by purchasing its shares. Also called *shareholders.*

stock market An organized market where stocks and bonds are bought and sold. Also called *securities market.*

strategic behaviour Behaviour designed to take account of the reactions of one's rivals to one's own behaviour.

structural unemployment Unemployment due to a mismatch between characteristics required by available jobs and characteristics possessed by the unemployed labour.

substitute Two commodities are substitutes for each other when both satisfy similar needs or desires. The degree of substitutability is measured by the magnitude of the positive cross elasticity between the two.

substitution effect A change in the quantity of a good demanded, which results from a change in its relative price, eliminating the effect on real income of the change in price.

supply The entire relationship between the quantity of some commodity that producers wish to make and sell per period of time and the price of that commodity, other things being equal.

supply curve The graphical representation of the relationship between the quantity of some commodity that producers wish to make and sell per period of time and the price of that commodity, other things being equal.

supply of effort See *supply of labour.*

supply of labour The total number of hours of work that the population is willing to supply. Also called the *supply of effort.*

supply of money See *money supply.*

supply schedule A table showing for selected values the relationship between the quantity of some commodity that producers wish to make and sell per period of time and the price of that commodity, other things being equal.

tacit collusion Collusion that takes place with no explicit agreements. See also *collusion.*

takeover When one firm buys another firm.

takeover bid See *tender offer.*

tariff A tax applied on imports.

tax expenditures Tax provisions, such as exemptions and deductions from taxable income and tax credits, that are designed to induce market responses considered to be desirable. They are called *expenditures* because they have the same effect as directly spending money to induce the desired behaviour.

tax incidence The location of the burden of a tax; that is, the identity of the ultimate bearer of the tax.

tax-related incomes policy (TIP) Tax incentives for labour and management to encourage them to conform to wage and price guarantees.

tax-rental arrangements An agreement by which the federal government makes a per capita payment to the provinces for the right to collect income taxes.

tax shifting The passing of the burden of a tax from whomever pays it to someone else.

technical change See *technological change.*

technological change Any change in the available techniques of production. Also called *technical change.*

tender offer An offer to buy directly, for a limited period of time, some or all of the outstanding common stock of a corporation from its stockholders at a specified price per share, in an attempt to gain control of the corporation. Also called *takeover bid.*

term See *term to maturity.*

term deposit An interest-earning bank deposit, legally subject to notice before withdrawal (in practise the notice requirement is not normally enforced) and until recently not transferable by cheque. Also called *savings deposits* and *time deposits.*

term to maturity The period of time from the present to the redemption date of a bond. Also called simply the *term.*

terms of trade The ratio of the average price of a country's exports to the average price of its imports, both averages usually being measured by index numbers; it is the quantity of imported goods that can be obtained per unit of goods exported.

theory of games The theory that studies rational decision making in situations in which one must anticipate the reactions of one's competitors to the moves one makes.

time series A series of observations on the values of a variable at different points in time.

time-series data A set of measurements or observations made repeatedly at successive periods (or moments) of time.

total cost (*TC*) The total cost to the firm of producing any given level of output; it can be divided into total fixed costs and total variable costs.

total fixed cost (*TFC*) All costs of production that do not vary with level of output. Also called *overhead cost* or *unavoidable cost.*

total product (*TP*) Total amount produced by a firm during some time period.

total revenue (*TR*) Total receipts from the sale of a product; price times quantity.

total utility The total satisfaction resulting from the consumption of a given commodity or group of commodities by a consumer in a given period of time.

total variable cost (*TVC*) Total costs of production that vary directly with level of output. Also called *direct cost* or *avoidable cost.*

tradeable emission permits Government-granted rights to emit specific amounts of specified pollutants that private firms may buy and sell among themselves.

trade account A section of the balance-of-payments accounts that records payments and receipts arising from the import and export of tangible goods. Also called the *visible account* and the *merchandise account.*

transactions balances Money balances held to finance payments because payments and receipts are not perfectly synchronized.

transactions costs Costs incurred in effective market transactions (such as negotiation costs, billing costs, and bad debts).

transfer payment A payment to a private person or institution that does not arise out of current productive activity; typically made by governments, as in welfare payments, but also made by businesses and private individuals in the form of charitable contributions.

transmission mechanism The channels by which a change in the demand or supply of money leads to a shift of the aggregate demand curve.

transnational corporations (TNCs) Firms that have operations in more than one country. Also called *multinational enterprises (MNEs).*

treasury bill The conventional form of short-term government debt. A promise to pay a certain sum of money at a specified time in the future (usually 90 days to 1 year from date of issue). Although treasury bills carry no fixed interest payments, holders earn an interest return because they purchase them at a lower price than their redemption value. Also called *treasury note.*

two-part tariff A method of charging for a good or a service, usually a utility such as electricity, in which the consumer pays a flat access fee and a specified amount per unit purchased.

undistributed profits Earnings of a firm that are not distributed to shareholders as dividends but are retained by the firm. Also called *retained earnings.*

unemployed (*U*) The number of persons 16 years of age and older who are not employed and are actively searching for a job.

unemployment rate Unemployment expressed as a percentage of the labour force.

unfavourable balance of payments A debit balance on some part of the international payments accounts (payments exceed receipts); often refers to the balance on current plus capital account (that is, everything except the official settlements account).

union An association of workers authorized to represent them in bargaining with employers. Also called *trade unions, labour unions.*

unit costs Costs per unit of output, equal to total variable cost divided by total output. Also called *average variable cost.*

utility The satisfaction that a consumer receives from consuming a commodity.

value added The value of a firm's output minus the value of the inputs that it purchases from other firms.

value of money See *purchasing power of money.*

variable Any well-defined item, such as the price of a commodity or its quantity, that can take on various specific values.

variable cost A cost that varies directly with changes in output. Also called *direct cost, avoidable cost.*

variable factor An input that can be varied by any desired amount in the short run.

velocity of circulation (V) National income divided by quantity of money.

very long run A period of time that is long enough for the technological possibilities available to a firm to change.

visible account See *trade account.*

visibles All those items of foreign trade that are tangible; goods as opposed to services.

voluntary export restriction (VER) An agreement by an exporting country to limit the amount of a good exported to another country.

wage and price controls Direct government intervention into wage and price formation with legal power to enforce the government's decisions on wages and prices.

wage-cost push inflation An increase in the price level caused by increases in labour costs that are not themselves associated with excess aggregate demand for labour.

wealth The sum of all the valuable assets owned minus liabilities.

withdrawals Income earned by households and not passed on to firms in return for goods and services purchased, and income earned by firms and not passed on to households in return for factor services purchased.

X Exports; the value of all domestic production sold abroad.

X-inefficiency The use of resources at a lower level of productivity than is possible, even if they are allocated efficiently, so that the economy is at a point inside its production possibility boundary.

X–IM See *net exports.*

Index

Page numbers in this index that are followed by *t, f,* and *n* denote tables, figures, and notes, respectively.

Ability-to-pay principle, and tax system, 431–433
Absolute advantage
  definition of, 471
  example of, 44, 471–472, 472*t*
Absolute price, 75, 129. *See also* Money price
AC (average cost). *See* Average total cost
Acceleration hypothesis, 745–746
  and Phillips curve, 748–749
Actual expenditure, and desired expenditure, 564–565
Actual GDP, 521, 521*n*
AD curve. *See* Aggregate demand curve
Adjustment, versus security, and social policy, 455
Adjustment asymmetry, in aggregate supply behaviour, 631, 634
Adjustment challenge, to social policy, 451–452
Adjustment mechanism, 698–699, 699*f*
Administered price, 263
Administrative efficiency, of government, 440
Adult Occupational Training Act of 1967, 780
Ad valorem tax. *See* Excise tax
Adverse selection, 167, 393
Advertising costs, as entry barrier, 276, 277*f*
AE. *See* Aggregate expenditure
AFC. *See* Average fixed cost
Affluent Society, The (Galbraith), 445
Age, unemployment by, 773, 774*f*
Agents, 44
Aggregate demand, 51
  increases in, and GDP, 638*f*, 638–639
  and monetary equilibrium, 689–694
  and price level/national income, 694–699, 698*f*
  role in money supply, 700–702, 701*f*
  shifts in, 806–808, 807*f*
    and aggregate expenditure shifts, 694, 695*f*
Aggregate demand curve, 609–613
  and aggregate expenditure curve, 609, 610*f*, 611, 612*f*
  definition of, 609
  points off, 610–611
  shape of, 611
  shifts in, 612–613, 614*f*
  simple multiplier and, 613, 614*f*
  slope of, 609–610, 610*f*, 698, 706*f*–707*f*, 706–707

Aggregate demand shock, 618–622
  definition of, 618
  long-run consequences of, 631–637
Aggregated total output, 519
Aggregate expenditure, 565
  and import content, 602–603
  and national income
    consumption and investment, 564–585
    in open economy with government, 586–605
  and price level, 608, 609*f*
  shifts in, 595–599
    and aggregated demand shifts, 694, 695*f*
    from interest rate changes, 692–694, 694*f*
Aggregate expenditure curve, 592, 593*f*
  and aggregate demand curve, 609, 610*f*, 611, 612*f*
  shifts in, 606–608
Aggregate expenditure function, 572*t*, 572–573, 573*f*, 602
  calculation of, 592, 593*t*
  equilibrium national income determined with, 593–594, 594*t*
  shifts in, 575–577, 576*f*, 578*f*
Aggregate production function, 813–814
Aggregate supply, 51, 613, 624, 631, 634
  increases in, and GDP, 638*f*, 639
  and long-run equilibrium, 636–637, 637*f*
  and open-economy multiplier, 864
  role in money supply, 702–703
  shifts in, 806–808, 807*f*
Aggregate supply curve, 613–616. *See also* Short-run aggregate supply curve
  definition of, 613
  long-run, 613, 634–636, 636*f*
Aggregate supply shock, 622–625, 623*f*
  definition of, 618
Agricultural goods
  domestic sales only, 119
  excess supply of, 113
  export of, at world market prices, 118*f*, 118–119
  lagging demand for, 113
  orderly marketing schemes, 122–123
  prices above equilibrium, 119–122, 120*f*
Agriculture
  Canadian policy, 122–123
  income supplements, 123
  long-term trends in, 113–116
  problems of, in free-market price system, 112–123
  productivity, growth of, 113

quotas, 120–122, 121*f*
short-term fluctuations in, 116*f*–117*f*, 116–118
stabilization, in theory, 118–122
subsidies, 120
AIB. *See* Anti-Inflation Board
Airline regulation, 296–297
Akerlof, George, 164, 770
Allocation. *See also* Resource allocation
  of commodities in short supply, 108
  between public and private sector, 445–446
Allocative efficiency, 285–287, 286*f*, 407
  elabouration of, 288–292
  in monopoly, 288, 290–292, 291*f*
  in perfect competition, 287–290, 290*f*
Analytic statements, 26
Announcement effect, 712
Anticombine laws, 298
Antidumping duties, 493
Anti-Inflation Board, 753, 755
Anti-inflation policy, Canadian, 752–758, 777, 872
AP. *See* Average product
APC. *See* Average propensity to consume
APS. *See* Average propensity to save
AR. *See* Average revenue
Arc elasticity, 98
  as point elasticity approximation, 98–101, 99*f*–101*f*
Arrow, Kenneth, 401
AS curve. *See* Aggregate supply curve
Ash, Timothy Garton, 11
Assembly line, 206–208, 268
Assets
  durable, costs of, 178
  financial, 682–686
    features of, 662–663
  inside, 607
  outside, 607
  resaleable, 178
Assumptions, 29
Asymmetric information, as source of inefficiency, 389–390, 392–394, 406
ATC. *See* Average total cost
Australia-New Zealand-U.S. free trade agreement, 497
Auto industry, Canadian and American, integration of, 500–501
Automatic stabilizers, 645
  under fixed exchange rates, 862, 863*f*
  under flexible exchange rates, 863–866, 865*f*

Automobile(s), Japanese, import restrictions on, 488–489
Automobile emissions standards, 410
Autonomous consumption, 567
Autonomous expenditure, 565
    import content of, 602–603
    investment as, 571–572
Autonomous net exports, 595–596
Autonomous variable. *See* Exogenous variable
Auto Pact, 500–501
AVC. *See* Average variable cost
Average(s), calculation of price elasticity with, 86
Average cost. *See* Average total cost
Average cost curve, long-run, 200
    shape of, 200–202, 201*f*
    and short-run average total cost curve, relationship between, 200–203, 203*f*–204*f*
Average cost pricing, 293
    example of, 294–295
Average fixed cost, 189
Average household income, and shifts in demand, 63, 64*t*, 64*f*
Average product, 185
    diminishing, 185*t*, 187
Average product curve, 186*f*, 186–187, 190
Average propensity to consume, 567, 568*t*
Average propensity to save, 568
Average revenue, 221
    for monopoly firm, 241–242, 242*t*, 243*f*
Average revenue curve, 241
Average tax rate, 428
Average total cost, 189
    short-run, 192
Average total cost curve, short-run, and long-run average cost curve, relationship between, 200–203, 203*f*–204*f*
Average variable cost, 189
    short-run, 191*f*, 191–192

Backward merger, 304
Bain, Joe, 273
Balanced budget
    annually, 799
    changes in, 598–599
    cyclically, 799
    definition of, 587
Balanced budget multiplier, 599
Balanced growth path, 816
Balance of payments, 849–856
    Canadian, 537–538, 538*f*
    definition of, 535
    favourable, 854
    multilateral, 853
    overall balance of, 851–852
    specific account balances, 852–854
    unfavourable, 854
Balance-of-payments accounts, 537, 849–851
Balance-of-payments deficit, 854
Balance-of-payments surplus, 854
Balance of trade, 855
    and national income, 860–867
Baldwin, John, 262
Bank(s). *See also* Central bank; Chartered banks
    balance sheet, example of, 672*t*–673*t*, 673

commercial
    definition of, 664, 666
    reserve requirements for, 667
next-generation, 673
profit seeking by, 667–668
second-generation, 673, 674*t*
third-generation, 673–674
Bank Act, 666, 670
Bank deposits, 662–664
Banking system, 664–672
    Canadian, 666–669
    versus chartered banks, 667
    money creation by, 672–676
Bank notes, 660–661
Bank of Canada, 664, 666. *See also* Central bank
    anti-inflation policies, 754–755
    assets and liabilities of, 665, 665*t*
    bank rate, 712–713
    contractionary monetary policy, 710
    fixed exchange rates, 842–843
    foreign exchange intervention, 851
    government security holdings, 665, 711*t*, 711–713, 787
    monetary gradualism, 719–720, 753
    monetary stringency, 720, 721*f*
    and money supply, 708–714
    open-market operations, 708–710, 709*t*
    organization of, 664
    policy objectives and instruments, 715–717
    price stability policy, 722–723, 756–757, 872–873
    reserves, 672
    tight monetary policy, 871–872
Bank of England, 664
Bank rate, 712–713
Bank reserves, 669–672
    need for, 669–670
    target, 670–672
Bargain-basement price, 663
Barter, 43, 43*n*
Base period, 519
Base period prices, 554
Baumol, William, 266, 277
Bear markets, 726
Behaviour
    competitive, 219
        types of, 273
    cooperative, types of, 272–273
    of exchange rates, 846–849
    of firms
        aspects of, 264–265
        and market structure, 218–220
        and nonrenewable resources, 368
    household consumption, 128–158
        under uncertainty, 163–167
    human, predictability of, 27–28
    long-run, in oligopoly, 275–279
    nonstrategic, 268
    social, and nonrenewable resources, 369
    strategic, 268–270, 272
Benefit(s). *See also specific benefit*
    for elderly, 444, 455, 462–463
    income-tested, 450
Benefit-cost analysis, 397
    of government intervention, 397–402
    of social regulation, 420–422
Benefit principle, and tax system, 433–434

Bennett, R. B., 646
Bills, treasury, 307, 662
Birdzell, L. E., 173
Black market, 107*f*, 108–109
    definition of, 108
Black Monday, 727, 729
Black Tuesday, 729
Blank, Rebecca, 15
Blinder, Alan, 763
Bonds, 173, 587*n*, 682, 796–797
    junk, 305–306
Boom, 522
Bottom line, 49
Brand proliferation, 276
Break-even price, 230
Brenner, Reuven, 558
Brown, Charles, 356
Brown, E. Cary, 646
Brownfield investment, 307
Bruce, Neil, 802
Brundtland, Gro Harlem, 826
Brundtland Commission, 826–827
Buchanan, James, 445
Budget, balanced
    annually, 799
    changes in, 598–599
    cyclically, 799
    definition of, 587
Budget balance
    definition of, 587, 802
    primary, 789
Budget deficit. *See also* Government budget deficit
    definition of, 587
Budget line, 128–130, 129*f*
    definition of, 128–129
    shifts in, 130–132
Budget surplus. *See also* Government budget surplus
    definition of, 587
Budget surplus function, 587–588, 588*t*, 588*f*, 645, 789–791, 791*f*
Bull markets, 726
Bureau of Competition Policy, 299
Business conditions, influence on stock markets, 727–730
Business confidence, and investment expectations, 571
Business cycles, 517, 520–521, 521*f*
    and fiscal policy, 639–648
    terminology of, 522
    theory of, 768–769
Business fixed investment, 549
Business organization, forms of, 170–173
Business taxes, indirect, 552, 554
Buyers, discrimination among, 253–254
Buyout(s), 303–307
    definition of, 303
    leveraged, 305–307
        definition of, 305

CAD. *See* Cyclically adjusted deficit
Canada
    agricultural policy in, 122–123
    anti-inflation policy in, 752–758, 777, 872
    auto industry in, integration with American auto industry, 500–501
    balance of payments, 537–538, 538*f*, 849, 849*t*

banking system, 666–669
capital account, 850, 850*t*
chartered banks, combined balance sheet of, 668, 670*t*
combine laws in, 297–298
commercial policy in, 498–511
  historical background of, 499–501
dollar overvaluation in, 848–849
economic structure of, 258–263
employment and unemployment in, 762–764
exchange rate, 536–537, 537*f*, 872
exports, 498, 499*f*
  commodity composition of, 500, 501*t*
foreign investment in and by, 308, 310
  attitudes toward, 309–310
  debate over, 310–313
GDP, 519, 520*f*, 546, 548*t*
imports, 498, 499*f*
income distribution in, 322, 323*t*, 324*f*
industrial concentration in, 260–261
inflation
  historical experience, 529, 530*f*
  stable rate of, 755–756, 872
international economic position, indicators of, 535–538
manufacturing in, concentration in, 262*t*, 262–263
monetary history, 719–723
monetary policy, 871–873
money supply, 677, 677*t*, 708–714
national debt, 793, 794*f*
poverty in, 460–461
public policy in, toward monopoly and competition, 292–299
recession, 756
recovery in, 872
regulatory reform in, 421–422
social policy in, 450–468
  federal spending on, 451, 451*t*
social programs of, outline of, 456–466
tariffs in, 500
tax system in, 428–430, 434
trade
  composition of, 500, 501*t*
  outlook for, 511
transnational corporations in, 310
unemployment in, historical experience of, 526, 527*f*
unionism in, 357–359
  historical development of, 358
wholesale price index, 655*f*, 655–656
Canada Assistance Plan, 442–443, 458
Canada Community Services Projects, 780
Canada Pension Plan, 438, 444, 462, 587
Canada-U.S. Free Trade Agreement, 310, 312, 480, 501–507, 509, 511, 848–849, 855, 872
  employment effects of, 505
  evaluation of, 504
  policy constraints of, 504–506
  results of, 506–507
  underlying principle of, 501–502
Canada-U.S.-Mexico free trade agreement. *See* North American Free Trade Agreement
Canadian Automobile Workers, 359
Canadian Federal Deposit Insurance Corporation, 671

Canadian Immigrants Bank of Commerce, balance sheet, 672*t*–673*t*, 673
Canadian Industrial Renewal Program, 781
Canadian Job Strategy, 781
Canadian Labour Congress, 358
Canadian Labour Market and Productivity Centre, 456
Canadian Mobility Programme, 781
Canadian Union of Public Employees, 358
Canadian Wheat Board, 122–123
CAP. *See* Canada Assistance Plan; Common Agricultural Policy (European Community)
Capacity
  definition of, 192
  excess, 192, 266
Capital, 176, 325, 373–379. *See also* Human capital
  definition of, 662
  demand for, 378, 378*f*
  and equilibrium of firm, 376–378
  equity, 173
  and factor mobility, 333–335
  financial (money), 173
  purchase price of, 373–374
  real (physical), 173, 662, 816
  rental price of, 373
Capital account, 850–851
  Canadian, 850, 850*t*
  and fiscal policy, 869
  and monetary policy, 869–870
Capital account balances, 854–856
Capital consumption allowance, 549
Capital gains, 173, 727–728
  taxes on, 428*n*, 434
Capital import, 850
Capital inflow, 850
Capital-labour ratio, 198
  equilibrium, 199
Capital loss, 727
Capital mobility, 850, 860
  and crowding-out effect, 870
  and exchange rates, 844–846
  international, 796–797, 867–871
Capital stock
  definition of, 378, 549
  of economy, 378
  of firm, size of, 377–378
  and technological change, 379, 379*f*
Capitation basis, 463
Card, David, 356, 824
Cartel(s)
  definition of, 249, 252
  as monopolies, 247–250
  as oligopolies, 272–273
  problems facing, 249–250, 251*f*
Cartelization, effects of, 249, 249*f*
CAS. *See* Cyclically adjusted surplus
Cash drain, from banking system, 672–673, 675–676, 676*t*
CAW. *See* Canadian Automobile Workers
CCF. *See* Cooperative Commonwealth Federation
CDs. *See* Certificates of deposit
Ceiling price. *See* Price ceilings
Central bank, 664–666. *See also* Bank of Canada
  definition of, 664

functions of, 665–666
Centralization, of decision making, 7–8
Centrally planned economy. *See* Command economy
Centres locaux de service communautaires, 465
Certificates of deposit, 668
Ceteris paribus, 59, 62, 74–75
Chandler, Alfred D., Jr., 269–270
Change. *See also* Technological change
  in demand, 65
  in quantity demanded, 65
  in quantity supplied, 70
  resistance to, and structural unemployment, 780
  in supply, 70
Chartered banks
  attributes of, 666–667
  versus banking system, 667
  Canadian, combined balance sheet of, 668, 670*t*
  central bank as banker to, 665
  definition of, 664
  interbank activities of, 667
  target reserves, 670–672
Cheating, covert, in oligopoly, 273, 275
Cheque clearing/collection, 667
Child benefits system, 458–462
Child labour laws, 396
Child Tax Benefit, 444, 459
Choice(s), 3–5
  of factor mix, 198–199
  of firms, 183–185, 208–209
    long-run, graphical representation of, 212–216
    short-run, 185–187
  household, 128–141
  public, inefficient, and government failure, 400
CIBC. *See* Canadian Immigrants Bank of Commerce
Circular flow of income, 51–54, 52*f*, 54*f*
Classical dichotomy, 654–655
Classical theories, of cyclical unemployment, 765*f*, 765–766
Clearing house, 667
Climate
  and comparative advantage, 475
  economic, 767
Closed economy, 565, 861
Club of Rome, 826
Coase, Ronald H., 171, 391
Coinage, 658–660
Collective bargaining, 346, 354, 357
Collective consumption goods. *See also* Public good(s)
  as source of inefficiency, 389–392
Collusion, 272
  tacit, 272
Combine laws, 297–298
Combines Investigation Act, 298
  Amendments of 1976, 298
  Amendments of 1986, 298–299
Command economy, 7–8
  definition of, 48
  failure of, 9–11
  versus market economy, 9–11
  private-ownership, 9
  public-ownership, 9

Commercial bank
  definition of, 664, 666
  reserve requirements for, 667
Commercial policy, 484–514. *See also*
      Protectionism; Trade policy
  Canadian, 498–511
    historical background of, 499–501
  definition of, 484
  international agreements on, 496–497.
      See also specific agreement
    in practise, 495–498
  theory of, 484–495
Commodities, 3. *See also* Goods; Services
  complement, 64
    and demand elasticity, 94
  definition of, and demand elasticity,
      87–89
  exported, 80, 80*f*
  imported, 80*f*, 81
  in short supply, allocation of, 108
  substitute, 63
    and demand elasticity, 87, 94
Common Agricultural Policy (European
      Community), 120
Common market, 497
  definition of, 496
Common property, and resource extraction,
      371
Comparative advantage
  changing view of, 479–480
  definition of, 472
  dynamic, 479, 490
  example of, 44–45, 472–473, 473*t*
  factor endowment theory of, 475
  principle of, 42
  versus social advantage, 487
  viability of, 480
Comparative statics, 72
Compensation to employees. *See* Wage(s)
Competition. *See also* Monopolistic
      competition; Perfect competition
  versus cooperation, 272–275
  and economic growth, in advanced
      industrial economies, 823–825
  globalisation of, 260–261, 824
  government intervention in, 297–299
  imperfect
    market structures under, 263–265
    patterns of, 258–283
  for market shares, 273
  monopolistic, 219
  versus monopoly, 244
  nonprice, 264
  protection against, 296–297
  public policy toward, 284–302
  and strategic trade policy, 491–492
  very-long-run, and oligopoly, 273, 279
Competition policy, 292
Competition Tribunal, 298–299
Competitive advantage, and innovation,
      824
Competitive Advantage of Nations, The
      (Porter), 821
Competitive behaviour, 219
  types of, 273
Competitive markets, 218–240
  labour, 356
  structure of, 218–219
  wage differentials in, 348–350

Competitive strategy, innovation as, 821
Complements, 64
  and demand elasticity, 94
Compliance, with resource regulations, costs
      of, 399
Concentration, industrial, 259–263
Concentration ratio, 259–260
Confirmation, of theory, 30
Conglomerate merger, 304
  dismantling of, 305–306
Consistency assumption, 138
Conspicuous consumption goods, 138–139
Constant cost, 201*f*, 202
Constant-cost industry, 232
Constant dollar, 554
Constant-dollar GDP, 519, 555, 557*t*
Constant inflation, 746–747, 750
Constant returns to scale, 202, 815
Constant target reserve ratio, 708
Consumer(s)
  households as, 45
  and producers, interactions between,
      51–53, 52*f*
Consumer price, 104
Consumer Price Index, 528–529, 756
  construction of, 542–544, 543*t*
Consumer rationality, assumption of,
      159–160
Consumers' surplus, 141–143, 160, 289,
      289*f*
  definition of, 142
  example of, 141*t*, 141–143
  for individual, 142*f*, 142–143
  for market, 142*f*, 143
Consumption
  autonomous, 567
  changes in, and price level, 607
  conspicuous, 138–139
  definition of, 3
  desired, and national income, 592, 593*t*
  and disposable income, 566–567, 568*t*,
      573
  final, services for, 17–18, 546
  induced, 567
  and national income/aggregate
      expenditure, 564–585
Consumption behaviour, household,
      128–158
Consumption expenditure, 548
  desired, 564–569
Consumption function, 566–567
  slope of, 567, 569*f*
  wealth and, 569, 570*f*
Consumption schedule, 568–569, 570*t*
Contestable market, 277–279
  perfect, 278
Contingent protection, 493
Contractionary monetary policy, 710
Contractionary shocks, 633–634, 634*f*
Cooperation
  versus competition, 272–275
  explicit, in oligopoly, 272–275
  tacit, and oligopoly, 273
Cooperative behaviour, types of, 272–273
Cooperative Commonwealth Federation,
      358
Cooperative solution, 270
Coordinate graphing, of relations among
      variables, 36–41, 36*f*–41*f*

Coordination
  in centrally planned economies, failure of,
      10
  of market system, process of, 385–387
Coordination-ownership mix, 9
Corn Laws, repeal of, 470
Corporate control, market for, 303–304
Corporate taxes, 429
Corporate wealth tax, 429
Corporation. *See also* Firm(s); Industry;
      Transnational corporations
  advantages of, 172–173
  crown, 292
  definition of, 170–172
  modern, rise of, 173
  ownership of, separation from control,
      314–315
  structure of, 172
Cost(s). *See also* Opportunity cost
  advertising, as entry barrier, 276, 277*f*
  concepts, 189–191
  constant, 201*f*, 202
  decreasing, in long run, 200–202
  definition of, 176
  of durable assets, 178
  efficiency, of tax and transfer system,
      454
  factor, net domestic income at, 552
  of firms, 176–179
    short-run variation in, 188–193
  fixed, 821–822
    average, 189
    total, 189
  given, gains from trade with, 471–475
  of government intervention, 398–399
  historical, 178
  imputed, 177–179
  increasing, in long run, 202
  of inflation reduction, 747
  of living, 542
  marginal, 189–191, 289*n*
    and output, 613–614
  overhead, 189
  personal
    of economic growth, 813
    of unemployment, 763
  private, 390, 391*f*
    marginal, 407–408
  product development, 202, 491, 491*n*
  production, 202
  real, 114
  relative
    of municipal government services, 445
    and relative prices, 388–389
  set-up, 246
    as entry barrier, 276–277, 277*f*
  in short run, 183–195
  for single-price monopolist, in short run,
      241–243
  social, 390, 391*f*
    of economic growth, 813
    marginal, 408
    versus social benefit, 408
    of tax and transfer system, 454
  sunk, 178–179, 189
    of entry, 278
  total, 189
    average, 189
    short-run, 192

transactions, 315
unavoidable, 189
unit, 613, 629
variable
average, 189
short-run, 191f, 191–192
gains from specialization with, 477–480
total, 189
short-run, 191f, 192
Cost curves. *See also* Long-run cost curves; Short-run cost curves
marginal, 191f, 192
shifts in, 203
Cost-effectiveness analysis, 421
Cost minimization
conditions for, 214–215
definition of, 198
failure of, 315
and profit maximization, 198–199
Cost pricing
average, 293
example of, 294–295
marginal, 293, 294f
Cost-push inflation. *See* Supply-shock inflation
Counterfeiting, 658–659
Countervailing duties, 493–494
Courchene, Thomas, 452
Coyne affair, 871
CPI. *See* Consumer Price Index
CPP. *See* Canada Pension Plan
Craft methods, 206
Created entry barriers, 246–247
Creative destruction, 247–248, 279–280
Credit cards, 667, 678
Cross elasticity of demand, 92–94
Cross-sectional data, 41
Cross subsidization, 296
Crow, John, 722–723
Crowding-out effect, and capital mobility, 870
Crown corporation, 292
Culture, and innovation, 820
Currency
exchange of, 838–840, 839f. *See also* Exchange rates; Foreign exchange
external value of, exchange rate and, 536
Current account, 849
Current account balance, 853–856
Current-dollar GDP, 519, 555, 557t
Current income, 566
Curved lines, and their slopes, 37, 39f
Customs union, definition of, 496
Cutbacks, and federal deficit, 443
Cycles, 538–539
Cyclically adjusted deficit, 791f, 792, 792t, 794
Cyclically adjusted surplus, 791f, 792, 792t
Cyclically balanced budget, 799
Cyclical unemployment, 526, 764–770, 765f–766f
definition of, 764
reduction of, 777

Davis, Steven, 772
Day-care plan, federally funded, 459
Day-to-day loan, 665
Deadweight loss

of monopoly, 291, 291f
of unemployment, 521
Debasement, of coinage, 659–660
Debt, 173. *See also* National debt
definition of, 662
Debt financing, 173–174
Debt/GDP ratio, 517, 799–801
Debt service payments, 788f, 789
Decision lag, 647
Decision makers, 44–47
Decision making
centralization of, 7–8
time horizons for, 183–184. *See also* Long run; Short run; Very long run
Declining-cost industry, 233
Decreasing returns
in long run, 202
to single factor, 814t, 814–815, 815f
Decumulation, 549
Defense, national, 487
Deficient-demand unemployment, 526
Deficit(s)
balance-of-payments, 854
budget. *See also* Government budget deficit
definition of, 587
twin, 860, 867–869
Deflation, 544, 732
demand-shock, with flexible wages, 634, 634f
Deflationary gap. *See* Recessionary gap
Deindustrialisation
of employment, 17
and growth of service sector, 352–353
Demand, 58–66. *See also* Aggregate demand
in action, 103–126
adjustment of, long-run, and oligopoly, 274
for agricultural goods, 113
for capital, 378, 378f
change in, 65
definition of, 62
derived, 325, 331
effective, 59
elastic, 84, 94
excess, 70–71
factor, 325–326
elasticity of, 328–330
when firms are not price takers, 347
final, 546
for firm in perfect competition, 220–223, 221f
for foreign exchange, 840
inelastic, 84, 94
agricultural fluctuations with, 116f, 116–118
for insurance, 163–165
for labour, 733–734
law of, 59n, 61, 72–74, 73f, 137
for local government services, 445
output, elasticity of, 329–330
under perfect competition, 222–223
and price, 59–61
price determination by, 70–75, 71t, 72f
price elasticity of, 82–90, 83f
definition of, 84
for rental accommodations, and rent controls, 111
Demand curve, 36, 61. *See also* Aggregate

demand curve
derivation of
and household choices, 134, 135t, 136f
and indifference theory, 150–154, 151f–152f
example of, 61–62, 62t, 62f
for factors of production
of firm, 326–330, 327f
of industry, 328
of household, derivation of, 158
individual, 139–140
market, 140–141
for monopoly firm, 241
under perfect competition, 221, 221f
perfectly inelastic, 139–141
shape of
effects of, 82–83, 83f
and price elasticity, 85, 87f–88f, 98–100, 99f–100f
shifts in, 62–64, 63f–65f, 64t
and laws of supply and demand, 72–74, 73f
versus movements along, 64–66, 66f
slope of, 83–84, 138–139
and household choices, 135–136, 137f
and indifference theory, 152, 152f
negative, 136, 138–139, 141
positive, 137–141
Demand deposit, 662, 708
Demand elasticity, 84. *See also* Price elasticity of demand
calculation of, 84, 85t
cross, 92–94
and demand curve, 85, 87f–88f
determinants of, 87–90, 89t
of firm, calculation of, from market elasticity, 223
income, 90–92, 94
determinants of, 91t, 91–92
graphical representation of, 92, 93f
long-run and short-run, 89–90, 90f
and sales tax incidence, 104–105, 105f
terminology, 94
and total value, 161–162, 162f
Demand for money, 686–689
nominal, 689
real, 689
total, 689, 691f
Demand for money function, 689, 691f
Demand inflation, 632, 632f, 738
reduction of, with incomes policies, 754
Demand schedule, 61
and equilibrium price, 70, 71t
example of, 61, 62t, 62f
Demand shock(s), 51, 732, 738
aggregate, 618–622
definition of, 618
long-run consequences of, 631–637
anticipated, 635
and business cycle, 640
monetary validation of, 738–740, 739f–740f
Demand-shock deflation, with flexible wages, 634, 634f
Demand-shock inflation. *See* Demand inflation
Demand theory, 159–169
applications of, 160–163
and unrealistic rationality, 159–160

Demogrants, 444, 450
Demography
  and social policy, 452
  and unemployment, 774–775
Department of Commerce (U.S.), 507
Department of Consumer and Corporate
  Affairs, 298, 415
Deposit(s)
  bank competition for, 668–669
  demand, 662, 708
  government, shifting, 711t, 711–713
  kinds of, 676–677
  term, 676
Deposit insurance, and financial system, 671
Deposit liability, 663
Deposit money, 662–664, 708
  creation of, 673–675, 673t–675t
  definition of, 663
Depreciation, 178, 549, 552. See also Capital
    consumption allowance
  straight-line, 178
Depreciation allowances, 532
Depression, 522, 646
Deregulation, 297
Derived demand, 325, 331
Desired consumption, and national income,
    592, 593t
Desired expenditure
  from actual expenditure to, 564–565
  consumption, 564–569
  determinants of, 564–573
  investment, 570–572
Developing countries, 174
  foreign investment in, 308–310
Differentiated product, 263
Diffusion, cost of, 819–820
Diminishing average productivity, point of,
    185
Diminishing average returns, law of, 187
Diminishing marginal productivity, point of,
    186
Diminishing marginal rate of substitution,
    hypothesis of, 147–148, 148t
Diminishing marginal utility, hypothesis of,
    155
Diminishing returns
  and elasticity of factor demand, 329
  law of, 186–188, 814t, 814–815, 815f
  significance of, 187
Direct burden, 435
Direct investment, 850–851
Discount
  definition of, 662
  social rate of, 372
Discouraged workers, definition of, 764
Discretionary fiscal policy, 645
  limitations of, 645–648
Discrimination. See also Price discrimination
  gender, 350, 362–364
  in labour markets, 359–364, 360f–361f
Disembodied technological change,
    817–818
Disequilibrium price, 105–106, 106f
  definition of, 71
  differentials, 337
Disposable income, consumption and,
    566–567, 568t, 573
Dispute settlement mechanisms, 504, 507
Distributed profits, 552

Distribution. See also Income distribution
  versus efficiency, and social policy, 454
Diversification
  of holdings, 688
  noneconomic advantages of, 487
Dividends, 172, 552
Division of labour, 43, 46, 187
  and oligopoly, 268–269
Dollar
  constant, 554
    GDP in, 519, 555, 557t
  current, GDP in, 519, 555, 557t
  external value of, 536
    and interest rate, 696
  internal value of, 536
  overvaluation of, 848–849
  as store of value, 678, 678t
Domestic income, net, at factor cost, 552
Domestic industry, rationalization of, 503
Domestic inflation, and exchange rates,
    843–844, 845f
Domestic jobs, creation of, and
    protectionism, 495
Domestic product, net, at market price, 552
Double coincidence of wants, 656–657
Double counting, 546
Dow-Jones industrial average, 726–727, 727f
DSMs. See Dispute settlement mechanisms
Dumping, 490, 493
Duopoly, 270
Durable assets, costs of, 178
Durable good, 109
Duties
  antidumping, 493
  countervailing, 493–494
  import, 484
Dynamic comparative advantage, 479, 490

East India Company, 173
Eastman, Harry, 500, 502
Eastman-Stykholt analyses, 502–503
EC. See European Community
ECC. See Extraordinary Challenge
    Committee
ECM. See European Common Market
Economic activity
  changes in, indicators of, 639, 641f
  effects of free trade agreements on, 504
Economic bads, and GDP, 558
Economic climate, 767
Economic Council of Canada, 123, 298,
    352–353, 421, 433, 500
Economic efficiency, 197, 284–292
Economic growth, 639, 806–832
  allowance for, and budget balance, 799
  balanced, 816
  benefits of, 810
  and competitiveness, in advanced
      industrial economies, 823–825
  costs of, 810–813
  cumulative effect of, 808, 808t
  definition of, 807
  effects on production possibility boundary,
      6f, 6–7
  and efficiency, 808–809
  endogenous, 818–821
  and GDP, 559
  and increasing returns theories, 821–823
  limits to, 825–829

long-term, 519–520
nature of, 806–810
and redistribution, 808–809
role of government in, 823
role of institutions in, 823
and saving/investment, 809–810
theories of, 813–823
Economic policy
  and free trade agreement, 504–506
  and globalisation, 261
  government, 292
  national, and globalisation, 261
  and size of government budget deficit,
      796–798
Economic problems, key, 6–7
Economic profits. See also Profit(s)
  calculation of, 179, 180f
  definition of, 179
Economic rent, 339–342
  definition of, 340
Economics
  definition of, 3–7
  of ideas, 822–823
  as social science, 23–41
  and society, 2–22
  value-free, possibility of, 33
Economic systems
  alternative, 7–12
  command (centrally planned). See
      Command economy
  definition of, 7
  market. See Market economy
  mixed, 8, 48
  traditional, 7
  types of, 7–9
Economies of scale, 200, 477, 478f
  external, 233
  internal, 233
  and oligopoly, 268–269
  unexploited, 264–265
Economies of scope, and oligopoly, 269
Economists, disagreements among, reasons
    for, 24
Economy. See also specific type
  benefits to, from takeovers, 305
  capital stock of, 378
  definition of, 48
  equilibrium of, 378–379
  functioning of, oligopoly and, 279–280
  modern, aspects of, 13–19
  sectors of, 48–49
Education
  and comparative advantage, 824
  and labour market policies, 780
  postsecondary, 456–457
  public, 396, 456
  unemployment by, 772, 773f
  wage differentials arising from, 349–350
EEC. See European Economic Community
Effective demands, 59
Efficiency. See also Allocative efficiency;
      Productive efficiency
  concepts of, 197
  versus distribution, and social policy, 454
  economic, 197, 284–292
  and economic growth, 808–809
  engineering, 197
  failure to achieve, 389–394
  government, 440, 446

versus income distribution, 395
in monopoly, 288
in oligopoly, 288
Pareto, 285
in perfect competition, 287–288
of tax system, 434–435
technical, 197, 285n
Efficiency cost, of tax and transfer system, 454
Efficiency wages, 768–770
EFTA. See European Free Trade Association
Elastic demand, 84, 94
Elastic income, 91, 94
Elasticity, 82–102. See also Demand
    elasticity; Price elasticity; Supply
    elasticity
    arc, 98
        as point elasticity approximation,
        98–101, 99f–101f
    of factor demand, 328–330
    formal analysis, 98–102
    and marginal revenue, for single-price
        monopolist, 243, 244f
    numerical, interpretation of, 84–85, 85t
    of output demand, 329–330
    point, 98
        precise definition, 101–102, 102f
    symbolic representation of, 98, 98n
    terminology, 94
    unit, 85, 94
Elderly, benefits for, 444, 455, 462–463
Embodied technological change, 817
Emissions permits, tradeable, 413–415
Emissions taxes, 411–413, 412f
Employed, definition of, 524
Employers' associations, 346
Employment, 762–784. See also Labour;
    Unemployment; Wage(s)
    Canadian, 762–764
    creation of, and protectionism, 495
    deindustrialisation of, 17
    effects of free trade agreement on, 505
    full, 526, 757
    high, 526
    and labour market discrimination,
        360–362, 361f
    long-term relationships in, 767–768
    in modern economy, 13
    national income and, 524–528
    versus wages, 357–359
Endogenous expenditure. See Induced
    expenditure
Endogenous growth, 818–821
Endogenous technological change, 204
Endogenous variable, 28–29
Ends
    debates over, 12
    definition of, 12
    examples of, 12
Engineering efficiency, 197
Entry
    effect on long-run equilibrium, 228–230
    freedom of, 204
    importance of, 252
    new, and oligopoly, 274
    potential, 277–279
    sunk costs of, 278
Entry-attracting price, 228–229, 230f
Entry barriers, 246–247
    and cartelization, 250

created, 246–247
definition of, 246
under imperfect competition, 265
importance of, 275–279
natural, 246, 276
significance of, 247
Envelope, 203, 204f
Environment, and North American Free
    Trade Agreement, 510
Environmental degradation, in centrally
    planned economies, 11
Environmental policies, 406–425
    market-based, resistance to, 416–417
Environmental Protection Agency (EPA),
    415
EPF. See Established programs financing
Equality, and taxes, 431
Equalization payments, 442
Equal net advantage, 338
Equation of exchange, 690
Equilibrium. See also Firm(s), equilibrium of
    of economy, 378–379
    exchange rate, 840
    of household, 148–150, 150f
        alternative interpretation of, 157–158
        and utility maximization, 156–157
    in long run, and aggregate supply,
        636–637, 637f
    macroeconomic, 616–617, 617f
        and monetary policy, 714f, 714–715
    monetary
        and aggregate demand, 689–694
        definition of, 689
    Nash, 271f, 271–272
    noncooperative, 270
    perfectly competitive, effects of
        cartelization on, 249, 249f
    prices above, for agricultural goods,
        119–122, 120f
    zero-profit, 229
Equilibrium condition, 71, 573
Equilibrium differential, 337
Equilibrium interest rate, 379, 379f
Equilibrium national income, 592–595
    changes in, 608, 609f
    determination of, 573–575, 574t, 575f,
        593–595, 595f
    and net exports, 595–596
    and price level, 613–617
Equilibrium price
    definition of, 71
    and demand and supply schedules, 70, 71t
    determination of, 71–72, 72f
    short-run, 227
Equipment, investment in, 549, 571
Equity
    definition of, 662
    government, 446
    horizontal, 454
    pay, 338, 363
        government policies on, 363–364
    and taxes, 431–434
    vertical, 454
Equity capital, 173
Equity financing, 173
Error control, in theory testing, 32
Escape clause, 493
Established programs financing, 441, 443
Eurobond market, 668–669

Eurocurrency market, 668–669
Eurodollar market, 668–669
European Airbus, 491
European Common Market, 477, 497
European Community, 120, 477, 485,
    496–497, 506
European Economic Community, 497, 500n
European Free Trade Association, 496–497
Eventually diminishing returns, law of, 187
Excess burden, 435
Excess capacity, 192
Excess capacity theorem, 266
Excess demand, 70–71
Excess reserves, 672
Excess supply, 71
Exchange rates, 535–538. See also Foreign
    exchange
    behaviour of, 846–849
    Canadian, 536–537, 537f, 872
    changes in, 840–846, 841f
        and foreign trade, 836–838, 837f–838f
    definition of, 535, 835
    determination of, 834–849
    equilibrium, 840
    and external value of currency, 536
    fixed
        management of, 842–843
        open economy with, 861f, 862–863
            simple multiplier in, 861, 861f
    flexible, 863–867, 871
    government intervention in, 851
    overshooting of, 847–849
    purchasing power parity, 846–847
Excise tax, 429–430
Exclusion, inefficient, 392
Execution lag, 647, 718
Exhaustible resources. See Nonrenewable
    resources
Exit
    effect on long-run equilibrium, 228–230
    freedom of, 204
Exit-inducing price, 229
Exogenous changes
    in price level, 606–613
    technological, 818
Exogenous expenditure. See Autonomous
    expenditure
Exogenous variable, 28–29
Expansionary shocks, 632f, 632–633
Expectational inflation, 746
    reduction of, with incomes policies,
        754–755
Expectations, 734–735
    backward looking, 735
    forward looking, 735
    investment, and business confidence, 571
    rational, 735
    self-realizing, 728
Expectations-augmented Phillips curve,
    748–749
Expectations effect, 702
Expenditure. See also Aggregate expenditure;
    Autonomous expenditure; Desired
    expenditure; Total expenditure
    consumption, 548
    induced, 565
    investment, 548–549
    public, 437–445, 438t
    tax, 427, 450

Expenditure flows, import content of, 602
Expenditure functions, of government,
    587–588, 588t, 588f
Expenditure side, GDP on, 548–551
    definition of, 547
Experience, and unemployment, 772–773,
    773f–775f
Experience rating, 779
Explicit cooperation, in oligopoly, 272–275
Exploitation theory, of protectionism, 494
Export(s), 588–589. See also Net export(s)
    agricultural, at world market prices, 118f,
        118–119
    Canadian, 498, 499f
        commodity composition of, 500, 501t
    determination of, 79–80, 80f
    and GDP, 550–551
Export demand, for agricultural goods, 113
Export multiplier
    under fixed exchange rates, 862, 863f
    under flexible exchange rates, 866
External economies of scale, 233
Externalities
    definition of, 390
    geographic extent of, 439
    internalization of, 408
    pollution, 407, 407f
    as source of inefficiency, 389–391, 406
External value of dollar, 536
Extraordinary Challenge Committee, 507
Extraterritoriality, 312

Factor cost, net domestic income at, 552
Factor demanded, quantity of, 325–326
Factor earnings, division of, 340f, 340–341
    determinants of, 341–342
Factor endowment theory of comparative
    advantage, 475
Factor markets, 47, 51–52
    operation of, 336f, 336–342
Factor mix, choice of, 198–199
Factor mobility, 333–336
    factor price differentials and, 337–338
Factor payments, 551–552
Factor price(s)
    changes in
        induced, 628–631
        and long-run supply curve, 232
    and cost curves, 203
    and output gap, 629–631
Factor price differentials, 336–338
    disequilibrium, 337
    equilibrium, 337
    and factor mobility, 337–338
    policy issues and, 338–339
Factor pricing, 324
Factor proportions, different, and differing
    opportunity costs, 475
Factor services, definition of, 176
Factors of production, 176. See also Capital;
    Labour; Land; Resource(s)
    basic, 325
    definition of, 3
    demand curve for
        of firm, 326–330, 327f
        of industry, 328
    demand for, 325–326
        elasticity of, 328–330
        when firms are not price takers, 347

fixed, definition of, 184
    hired, 177
    importance of, 329
    purchased, 177
    supply of, 330–336
        to individual firms, 336
        for particular use, 333–336
        total, 332–333
    variable, 330
        definition of, 184
Fair game, 164
Fair-trade laws, 490
Family allowance payments, 444, 459–462
FAO. See Food and Agricultural
    Organization (United Nations)
Farming. See Agriculture
Fast-track procedure, 507, 507n
Favourable balance of payments, 854
FDI. See Foreign direct investment
Federal debt. See National debt
Federal deficit. See Government budget
    deficit
Federal Deposit Insurance Corporation
    (FDIC), 671
Federal Pension Benefits Standards Act, 462
Federal-provincial perspective, on social
    policy, 452–453
Federal Reserve System, 664–665, 668
Fiat money, 661
Final demand, 546
Final goods and services, 546
Financial assets, 682–686
    features of, 662–663
Financial capital, 173
Financial intermediaries, definition of, 664
Financial markets, globalisation of, 668–669
Financial system
    and deposit insurance, 671
    modern, terminology, 662–663
Financing
    debt, 173–174
    equity, 173
    of firms, 173–174
Fine tuning, 648
FIRA. See Foreign Investment Review
    Agency
Firm(s). See also Corporation; Industry
    behaviour of
        aspects of, 264–265
        and market structure, 218–220
        and nonrenewable resources, 368
    capacity of, 192, 266
    capital stock of, size of, 377–378
    choices open to, 183–185, 208–209
        long-run, graphical representation of,
            212–216
        short-run, 185–187
    competition by, intervention to prevent,
        297–299
    costs of, 176–179
        short-run variation in, 188–193
    as decision makers, 46–47
    definition of, 46–47
    demand curve for factors, 326–330, 327f
    demand elasticity, calculation of, from
        market elasticity, 223
    in economic theory, 174–179
    equilibrium of
        and capital, 376–378

long-run, 199, 228–237
    conditions for, 230–231, 231f
    and monopolistic competition, 266
    under monopoly, 246
    versus short-run, 230, 231f
    and technological change, 234, 235f
short-run, 223–228, 225f–226f
    versus long-run, 230, 231f
    and monopolistic competition, 266
    under monopoly, 244–245, 245f
financing of, 173–174
goals of, 313–317
individual, supply of factors to, 336
input decisions made by, analysis of,
    212–216
monopoly, 241, 245
    demand curve for, 241
motivation of, 47, 175–176
oligopoly caused by, 269
in perfect competition, demand and
    revenue for, 220–223, 221f, 224t,
    224f
price selection by, 263–264
price-taking
    in long-run equilibrium, 230
    revenue concepts for, 221–223, 224t,
        224f
    rules for, 225–226
production decisions for, 224–225
product selection by, 263
profitability of, in short run, 227–228, 29f
profit-maximizing, rules for, 224–226
purpose of, 171
response to declining demand, 235
role of, 170–182
start-up, 259
supply curve for, 226, 227f
turnover of, 259
First-come, first-served principle, 108
Fiscal Arrangements Act of 1977, 443
Fiscal challenge, to social programs, 451
Fiscal conservatism, 802
Fiscal federalism, 438–443
Fiscal plan, sustainability of, 800–801
Fiscal policy, 586–588, 596–599
    and business cycle, 639–648
    changes in, 647
    definition of, 596
    discretionary, 645
        limitations of, 645–648
    effectiveness of, 870
    and Great Depression, 646
    and international capital mobility,
        869–871
    procyclical, 644
Fiscal stabilization, theory of, 641–648
Fiscal stabilizers. See Automatic stabilizers
Fixed cost, 821–822
    average, 189
    total, 189
Fixed exchange rate, open economy with,
    861f, 862–863
    simple multiplier in, 861, 861f
Fixed exchange rates, management of,
    842–843
Fixed factor, definition of, 184
Fixed investment, 549
Fixed prices. See Price controls
Fixed reserve ratio, 672

Fixed-weight index, 542–543
Flexible exchange rate, 863–867, 871
Flexible manufacturing, 43, 206, 208
Flexible wages, 633, 634f
Floating exchange rate. See Flexible exchange rate
Flow variables, 60
Food and Agricultural Organization (United Nations), 90
Ford, Henry, 16
Forecasting, 8
Foreign direct investment, 175, 307
Foreign exchange. See also Exchange rates
    definition of, 536
    demand for, 840
    supply of, 839–840
Foreign exchange market, 48, 668–669, 838–840, 839f
    definition of, 536
Foreign exchange transactions
    mechanism of, 835–836, 836t
    nature of, 834–836
Foreign firms/governments, unfair actions by, protection against, 490
Foreign income, and net export function, 589
Foreign inflation, and exchange rates, 841–842, 844f
Foreign investment, 307–313
    in and by Canada, 308, 310
        attitudes toward, 309–310
        debate over, 310–313
    dependence on, and globalisation, 19
    in developing countries, 308–310
    and globalisation, 19
    and government budget deficit, 795–797
Foreign Investment Review Agency, 309
Foreign labour, protection against, 494–495
Foreign trade. See International trade
Forsey, Eugene, 358
45° line, 568
Forward merger, 304
Fossil fuels. See Nonrenewable resources
Fractionally backed paper money, 660–661
Freedom of entry and exit, 204
Free good, 162–163
Free-market economy, 8
    case for, 387–389
    definition of, 48
    role of profits and losses in, 180
    social obligations in, 396
Free-market price system
    agricultural problems in, 112–123
    versus centrally planned economies, 11
    and resource allocation, 114–115
Free-rider problem, 392
Free trade
    case for, 486–487
    European, 477, 496–497
    fallacious arguments concerning, 495
    hub and spoke model of, versus plurilateral regionalism, 509
Free-trade area, 496–497. See also specific agreement
Frictional unemployment, 526, 764, 770
    reduction of, 777–779
    and structural unemployment, relationship between, 772
Friedman, Milton, 566

Frozen pork case, 507
Frozen prices. See Price controls
FST (federal sales tax). See Sales tax
FTA. See Canada-U.S. Free Trade Agreement; Free-trade area
Full-cost pricing, 316
Full employment, 526, 757
Full employment surplus, 792n
Function, 30
Functional distribution of income, 322–325, 323t
    definition of, 322
Future generations, and government budget deficit, 795–796
Future returns, present value of, 374–377

Gains from trade, 470–483
    and differing opportunity costs, 473–475, 474t
    with given costs, 471–475
    graphical illustration of, 476
    sources of, 470–480
    and specialization, 471–473, 472t–473t, 502–503
Galbraith, John Kenneth, 445
Game theory, of oligopoly, 270–272, 271f
GATT. See General Agreement on Tariffs and Trade
GDP. See Gross domestic product
Gender
    and labour market discrimination, 362–364
    unemployment by, 773, 774f
    wage differentials arising from, 350
General Agreement on Tariffs and Trade, 496–498, 500, 503, 506, 511
    Kennedy Round, 496
    Uruguay Round, 122, 484, 496
General partners, 172
General Theory of Employment, Interest and Money, The (Keynes), 619
Germany, hyperinflation in, after World War I, 658
Giffen, Robert, 137
Giffen goods, 137–138
GIS. See Guaranteed income supplement
Globalisation, 18–19
    of competition, 260–261, 824
    of financial markets, 668–669
    of production, 260–261
GNP. See Gross national product
Gold certificates, 661
Good Jobs, Bad Jobs (Economic Council of Canada), 352
Goods
    collective consumption, as source of inefficiency, 389–392
    conspicuous consumption, 138–139
    definition of, 3
    durable, 109
    final, 546
    free, 162–163
    Giffen, 137–138
    government purchases of, 549–550
    inferior, 63n, 91, 94
    intermediate, 546
    investment, 548
    merit, 396
    normal, 63n, 91, 94

public, 406
    health and safety information as, 415–420
    pure, 415
    public provision of, 437–438, 439t
    scarce, 162–163
    subsidies on, 552
Goods and services tax, 430, 430f, 432, 434, 552
Goods markets, 51–52
Gorecki, Paul, 262
Gottschalk, Peter, 15
Government
    activity
        progressivity of, and tax system, 434
        scope of, 445–446
    central bank as banker to, 665–666
    as decision maker, 47
    definition of, 47
    direct control by
        of natural monopoly, 292–295
        of oligopoly, 295–297
    efficiency of, 440, 446
    failure, causes of, 400–402
    imperfection, 400–402
    as monopolist, 400–401
    motivation of, 47
    open economy with, aggregate expenditure and national income in, 586–605
    outlays, 550
    provincial/municipal
        deficits, 786–787
        services, 445
        spending and taxation, 588
    role of
        in economic growth, 823
        evaluation of, 445–446
    spending and taxation, 586–588
        and economic performance, 789
    support of declining industries by, 235–237
Government budget deficit, 517, 785–805. See also National debt
    actual, 791, 791f, 792t
    annually balanced, 799
    background of, 785–792, 787f
    control of, 798f, 798–802
    and cutbacks, 443
    cyclically adjusted, 791f, 792, 792t, 794
    effects of, 791f, 793–794
    evaluation of, 789–792
    financial implications of, 596
    importance of, 792–803
    political economy of, 802–803
    provincial, 786–787
    in 1930s, interpretation of, 646
Government budget surplus, 517, 587
    actual, 791, 791f, 791, 792t
    cyclically adjusted, 791f, 792, 792t
    financial implications of, 596
Government-controlled prices, 105–109
Government deposits, shifting, 711t, 711–713
Government expenditure. See Public expenditure
Government intervention
    in agriculture, 118–122
    amount of, determination of, 402

Government intervention (*continued*)
  benefit-cost analysis of, 397–402
  case for, 389–396
  in competition, 297–299
  costs of, 398–399
  to encourage innovation, 820, 825
  in foreign exchange markets, 851
  in industrial disputes, 358
  in intergovernmental activities, 439–440
  in intergovernmental transfers, 440–443, 441f, 442t
  in market-wage determination, 346
  prevention of, by free trade agreement, 504
  and resource allocation, 114–115
  tools of, 397–398
Government marketing boards, 122
Government policy. *See also specific policy*
  to redress gender discrimination, 363–364
  structural unemployment caused by, 771–772
Government purchases
  changes in, 597
  of goods and services, 549–550
Government regulation, 397
Gramm-Rudman-Hollings bill, 799
Graphing
  of gains from trade, 476
  of income elasticity of demand, 92, 93f
  of relations among variables, 36–41, 36f–41f
  utility, 156
Grayson, Jackson, 386
Great Depression, 646
Green, Christopher, 260
Greenfield investment, 307
Greenhouse effect, economic consequences of, 3
Gresham's law, 660
Gross domestic product, 519, 546–554. *See also* National income
  actual, 521, 521n
    exceeding potential GDP, 630
  Canadian, 519, 520f, 546, 548t
  constant-dollar, 519, 555, 557t
  current-dollar, 519, 555, 557t
  cyclical fluctuations in, 639, 641f–642f
  definition of, 547
  and economic growth, 559
  on expenditure side, 548–551
    definition of, 547
  and exports/imports, 550–551
  high-employment. *See* Potential national income
  on income side, 551–553, 553t
    definition of, 547
  long-term growth in, 519–520
  nominal, measurement of, 554–555
  potential, exceeding actual GDP, 630–631
  real, measurement of, 554–555
  reconciliation with GNP, 553, 554t
  short-term fluctuations in, 520f, 520–521
  size of, and country's taxable capacity, 785
Gross domestic product deflator. *See* Implicit deflator
Gross domestic product gap. *See* Output gap
Gross investment, 549
Gross national product, 553

  reconciliation with GDP, 553, 554t
Gross tuning, 648
Group behaviour, versus individual behaviour, 27
Grover Cleveland panic of 1893, 729
Growth. *See also* Economic growth
  market, stimulus to, from market system, 388
  productivity, significance of, 205
Growth is bad school, 812
Growth is good school, 811
GST. *See* Goods and services tax
Guaranteed income, 444
Guaranteed income supplement, 463

Hall, Robert, 316, 767
Hanratty, Maria, 15
Health care, rising cost of, 464–465
Health care system, public, 463
Health information, as public good, 415–420, 418f
Health maintenance organizations, 463
Health regulations, 415–420
Health service organizations, 465
Heckscher, Eli, 475
Heckscher-Ohlin theory, 475
High employment, 526. *See also* Full employment
High-employment national income. *See* Potential national income
Hired factors of production, 177
Historical cost, 178
HMOs. *See* Health maintenance organizations
Homogeneous labour, one wage for, 348
Homogeneous product, 220, 265
Horizontal equity, 454
Horizontal merger, 303–304
Hostile takeover, 304
  defense against, 306–307
Hotelling, Harold, 369
Hours worked, and labour supply, 332–333
Household. *See also* Individual(s)
  average income of, and shifts in demand, 63, 64t, 64f
  choices, 128–141
  consumption behaviour of, 128–158
    under uncertainty, 163–167
  as decision makers, 45–46
  demand curve of, derivation of, 158
  equilibrium of, 148–150, 150f
    alternative interpretation of, 157–158
    and utility maximization, 156–157
  income change reaction, 149, 151f
  motivation of, 46, 132
  price change reaction, 149–150, 151f
  resource allocation within, 45n
Household trash, and pollution control, 413
Housing
  investment in, 308, 549, 571
  shortage of, and rent controls, 111, 112f
How the West Grew Rich (Rosenberg & Birdzell), 173
HSOs. *See* Health service organizations
Hub and spoke model, of free trade, versus plurilateral regionalism, 509
Hudson's Bay Company, 173
Human behaviour, predictability of, 27–28
Human capital, 815–816

  comparative advantage dependent on, 479–480
  definition of, 348
  wage differentials arising from, 348–350
Human resource development programs, 456–457
Hume, David, 470
Hunter-gatherer societies, 42, 42n
Hydro authorities, provincial, average cost pricing by, 294–295
Hyperinflation, 658–659
Hypothesis, 29–30
  of diminishing returns. *See* Diminishing returns, law of
  rejection or acceptance of, 32–33
Hysteresis, 775–776

Ideas, economics of, 822–823
Ignorance, and resource extraction, 371
Illegal activities, and GDP, 557–558
Imperfect competition
  market structures under, 263–265
  patterns of, 258–283
Imperial Oil, 298, 304
Implicit deflator, 555, 557t
  calculation of, 556
Import(s), 588–589
  Canadian, 498, 499f
  determination of, 79, 80f, 81
  and GDP, 550
Import content, of autonomous expenditure, 602–603
Import duty, 484
Import quota, 485
Import restrictions, on Japanese cars, 488–489
Impossibility theorem, 401
Imprudent deficit, 802
Imputed costs, 177–179
Incentives
  misplaced, in centrally planned economies, 10–11
  structuring, government, 398
Income. *See also* National income
  change in, household reaction to, 149, 151f
  circular flow of, 51–53, 52f
  concepts, 553–554
  current, 566
  disposable, consumption and, 566–567, 568t, 573
  elastic, 91, 94
  factor, components of, 551–552
  foreign, and net export function, 589
  guaranteed, 444
  household, average, and shifts in demand, 63, 64t, 64f
  inelastic, 91, 94
  lifetime, 566
  money, 131
    changes in, 130, 130f
  net domestic, at factor cost, 552
  personal, 554
    disposable, 554
  real, 131
    and relative prices, 131–132
  redistribution of, 397, 440
    and economic growth, 810
  regional equalization of, 338–339

Income-consumption line (curve), 92, 93f, 149, 151f
Income distribution, 14–16
  versus efficiency, 395
  functional, 322–325
    definition of, 322
  government regulation affecting, 397, 406
  and market failure, 394
  and minimum-wage laws, 772
  and public expenditure, 444
  and shifts in demand, 64
  size, 322–325
Income effect, 132f, 132–136
  definition of, 133
  example of, 133, 134f, 135t
  and indifference theory, 152–154, 153f
  and wage rate, 334
Income elasticity of demand, 90–92, 94
  determinants of, 91t, 91–92
  graphical representation of, 92, 93f
Income-expenditure model
  algebraic approach to, 604–605
  of consumption and investment, 564–585
  in open economy with government, 586–605
Income produced, 553
Income received, 553
Income side, GDP on, 551–553, 553t
  definition of, 547
Income supplements, agricultural, 123
Income taxes, personal, 428–429, 429t
Income-tested benefits, 450
Income transfer and security programs, 457–466
Incomes policy, 754–755
Increasing returns
  in long run, 200–202
  theories of, 821–823
Incremental cost. See Marginal cost
Incremental product. See Marginal product
Incremental revenue. See Marginal revenue
Incremental utility, 155n
Index. See also Price index
  fixed-weight, 542–543
Indexing, 532
Indifference curve, 146–148, 147f
Indifference map, 148, 149f
Indifference theory, 146–154
Indirect taxes, 430
Individual(s). See also Household(s)
  consumers' surplus for, 142f, 142–143
  federal transfer payments to, 444
  protection of, 396
Individual behaviour, versus group behaviour, 27
Individual demand curve, 139–140
Induced consumption, 567
Induced expenditure, 565
Induced net exports, 596
Industrial change, and unemployment, 778–779
Industrial concentration, 259–263
Industrialisation, 559
Industry. See also Corporation; Firm(s)
  constant-cost, 232
  control over, loss of, and foreign investment, 311–312
  declining, 234–237
  declining-cost, 233

definition of, 219
  demand curve for factors, 328
  domestic, rationalization of, 503
  infant, protection of, 490, 495
  key, loss of, and foreign investment, 312
  monopoly, 245
  nationalized, 296
  regulated, 296
  supply curve for, 226–228, 228f
    long-run, 232–233, 233f
Industry and Labour Adjustment Program, 781
Inefficiency
  examples of, 284–285
  in monopoly, 288
  in perfect competition, 287–288
Inefficient exclusion, 392
Inefficient public choices, and government failure, 400
Inelastic demand, 84, 94
  agricultural fluctuations with, 116f, 116–118
Inelastic income, 91, 94
Inelastic supply, agricultural fluctuations with, 117f, 117–118
Infant industry argument, 490, 495
Inferior goods, 63n, 91, 94
Inflation, 517, 732–761
  accelerating, 745–746
    and Phillips curve, 748–749
  Canadian
    historical experience, 529, 530f
    policy against, 752–758, 777, 872
    stable rate of, 755–756, 872
  causes and consequences of, 732–745
  completely unanticipated, 531
  constant, 746–747, 750
  definition of, 733, 733n
  demand, 632, 632f, 738
    reduction of, with incomes policies, 754
  and economic recovery, 720–723, 751f, 752
  effects of, avoidance of, 532
  and exchange rates, 841–844, 844f–845f
  expectational, 746
    reduction of, with incomes policies, 754–755
  fall in, effects on lenders, 534
  fully anticipated, 529–531
  and government budget deficit, 794
  interest rates and, 532–533
  intermediate, 531–532
  as monetary phenomenon, 744–745
  ongoing, and wage changes, 630n
  and price level, 528–532, 530f
  prices and, 74–75
  rate of, 6, 528
    measurement of, 544
    stable, 755–756
  reduction of, 386
    by Bank of Canada, 754–755
  significance of, 529–532
  stabilization of, 753–755
  supply-shock, 740
  sustained, 744–752
    reduction of, 747–752, 751f
  validation of, 699, 733
Inflationary gap, 522, 629, 631

removal of, 643, 644f, 698–699
Inflationary premium, 533
Inflationary shock, definition of, 732
Information asymmetries, as source of inefficiency, 389–390, 392–394, 406
Information centres, 780–781
Infrastructure, investment in, 308
Injections, into circular flow of income, 53–54, 54f
Innis, Harold, 499
Innovation. See also Technological change
  as competitive strategy, 821, 824
  and culture, 820
  definition of, 205
  location of, 819
  and market structure, 820
  process of, 208, 492, 818–819
  product, 208, 492
  and shocks, 820–821
  stimulus to, from market system, 388
  and strategic trade policy, 492
  in very long run, and oligopoly, 274–275
Input(s)
  classification of, 176
  decisions about
    firm's, analysis of, 212–216
    and output decisions, 324–325
  definition of, 69, 176
  improved, 208
  prices of, and supply, 69
Input prices, changes in, and SRAS curve, 615–616
Inside assets, 607
Insider trading, 306n
Inside the Black Box (Rosenberg), 818
Institutions, role in economic growth, 823
Insurance
  demand for, 163–165
  deposit, and financial system, 671
  market for, 163–167
  social, 397, 444
  supply of, 165–167
  unemployment, 444, 457–458, 777–779
Interbank activities, of chartered banks, 667
Interest, 552
  liquidity preference theory of, 689–692, 692f
Interest payments, on national debt, 788f, 789
Interest rate, 532–535
  changes in
    aggregate expenditure shifts from, 692–694, 694f
    monetary disturbances from, 692, 693f
  definition of, 532
  and demand for money, 688
  equilibrium, 379, 379f
  and external value of dollar, 696
  and inflation, 532–533
  market, 684–686
  nominal, 533, 535f
  and present value, 682–683
  real, 533, 535f
    investment and, 570–571
  significance of, 533–535
Intergenerational issues, in social policy, 455
Intergovernmental activities, 439–440
Intergovernmental transfers, 438–439, 439t, 440–443, 441f, 442t

Intermediate goods and services, 546
Intermediate products, 176
Intermediate targets, of monetary policy, 715–717, 716f–717f
Internal economies of scale, 233
Internalization, of externalities, 408
Internal value of dollar, 536
International agreements, on commercial policy, 496–497. *See also specific agreement*
International capital mobility, 796–797, 867–871
International economy, Canadian position in, indicators of, 535–538
International prices, relative, and net export function, 590–592, 591f
International trade, 79–81, 470–471
  definition of, 470
  and exchange rate changes, 836–838, 837f–838f
  and globalisation, 18–19
International Trade Commission (U.S.), 507
Interpersonal trade, 470–471
Interregional trade, 470–471
Intervention. *See* Government intervention
Invention, definition of, 205
Inventories, 549, 570–571
Investment. *See also* Foreign investment
  as autonomous expenditure, 571–572
  brownfield, 307
  direct, 850–851
  and economic growth, 809–810
  expectations, and business confidence, 571
  fixed, 549
  greenfield, 307
  gross, 549
  long-run policies for, in natural monopoly, 293–294
  and national income/aggregate expenditure, 564–585
  in plant and equipment, 549, 571
  portfolio, 307, 850–851
  private, and government budget deficit, 794–795
  and real interest rate, 570–571
  replacement, 549
  residential, 549, 571
Investment Canada, 309
Investment demand function, 693, 694f
Investment expenditure, 548–549
  desired, 570–572
Investment goods, 548
Investment income account, 849
Involuntarily unemployed, definition of, 764
Isocost line, 128, 214, 214f
Isoquant(s), 212–216
  definition of, 212
  single, 212t, 212–213, 213f
Isoquant map, 213–214, 214f–215f
Israel-U.S. free trade agreement, 497
ITC. *See* International Trade Commission (U.S.)

Japanese cars, import restrictions, 488–489
Japanese semiconductor industry, 492
Jay Cooke panic of 1873, 729
Job(s). *See* Employment; Labour; Unemployment; Wage(s)

Job banks, 780–781
Job creation programs, 457, 780
Jobscan, 780
Job structure, change in, 16–18, 17f
Jones Act (U.S.), 487
Junk bonds, 305–306

Kahn, Alfred, 278
Kennedy Round (GATT), 496
Key industries, loss of, and foreign investment, 312
Key money, 110
Keynes, John Maynard, 566, 619, 688
Keynesian(s)
  countercyclical fiscal policy, 786–787
  incomes policies, 754–755
  monetary policy views of, 717
  wage-price controls, 753–754
Keynesian consumption function, 566–567, 569
Keynesian short-run aggregate supply curve, 619
Keynesian theories, of cyclical unemployment, 766f, 766–770
Krueger, Ann, 399

Labour, 176, 325. *See also* Employment; Unemployment; Wage(s)
  demand for, 733–734
  division of, 43, 46, 187
    and oligopoly, 268–269
  and factor mobility, 335–336
  foreign, protection against, 494–495
  homogeneous, one wage for, 348
  rental and purchase price of, 374
  specialization of, 42–43
  supply of, 332–334
Labour Adjustment Benefits Act, 781
Labour costs, unit, 629–631
Labour force
  definition of, 332, 524
  growth of, 815
  nonagricultural, structure of, change in, 16–18, 17f
Labour force participation rate, 332
Labour markets
  competitive, 356
  discrimination in, 359–364, 360f–361f
  globalisation of, 18
  monopsonistic, 351–356, 354f–355f
  policies, and education, 780
  and wage rates, 346–355
Labour productivity, 524
  in modern economy, 13–14, 15f–16f
Labour unions. *See* Union(s)
Laffer curve, 435, 436f
Lags, 647f, 647–648
  and monetary policy controversy, 717–719
Lancaster, Kelvin, 266
Land, 176, 325
  and factor mobility, 335
Landlords, and property tax incidence, 436, 437f
Large numbers, law of, 27–28
Large volume of trade, 855
Latin America, trade liberalization in, 508
Law(s), 61
  of demand, 59n, 61, 72–74, 73f, 137

of diminishing average returns, 187
of diminishing marginal utility, 155
of diminishing returns, 186–188, 814t, 814–815, 815f
of eventually diminishing returns, 187
of large numbers, 27–28
minimum wage, 355–357
of one price, 79
of supply, 61, 72–74, 73f
LBO. *See* Leveraged buyout
LDCs. *See* Less developed countries
Leakages, from circular flow of income, 53, 54f
Lean production, 43, 206–208
Learning by doing, 42, 477–480, 490
Learning curve, 42, 478f, 478–479
Least-cost method of output, determination of, 214–215, 215f
Legal tender, 661
Lemieux, Mario, 190
Lender of last resort, 665
Leslie, Peter, 443
Less developed countries, 174
  foreign investment in, 308–310
Leveraged buyout, 305–307
  definition of, 305
Liability(ies)
  of central bank, 665
  definition of, 663
  limited, 172
  tax, postponed, and government budget deficit, 793
  unlimited, 172
Licensing, entry barriers created by, 246
Life-cycle theory, 566
Life style, and economic growth, 810
Lifetime income, 566
Limited liability, 172
Limited partnership, 172
Liquidation value, 663
Liquidity, definition of, 663
Liquidity preference function, 689, 691f
Liquidity preference theory of interest, 689–692, 692f
Living standards, 517
  and economic growth, 810–811, 816
  in modern economy, 13–16
Loans, day-to-day, 665
Local Employment Assistance Programme, 780
Long run. *See also* Very long run
  agricultural trends in, 113–116
  behaviour in, in oligopoly, 275–279
  choices for firms in, graphical representation of, 212–216
  definition of, 184
  demand adjustment in, and oligopoly, 274
  demand elasticity in, 89–90, 90f
  industry supply curve in, 232–233, 233f
  investment in
    and economic growth, 809–810
    in natural monopoly, 293–294
  monetary forces in, and national income, 700, 700f
  monetary policy variables in, 715
  national income in, 628–639, 638f
  price level in, 628–651
  production in, 196–203
  rent controls in, 111, 112f

supply curves in, versus short run, 226–227
supply elasticity in, 95
Long-run aggregate supply (LRAS) curve, 613, 634–636, 636f
Long-run average cost (LRAC) curve, 200
shape of, 200–202, 201f
and short-run average total cost curve, relationship between, 200–203, 203f–204f
Long-run cost curves, 200–203
and short-run costs, relationship between, 202–203
Long-run equilibrium. *See also* Firm(s), equilibrium of
and aggregate supply, 636–637, 637f
Long-run industry supply (LRS) curve, 232–233, 233f
Lorenz curve, 323, 324f
Losses
definition of, 179
role of
in free-market system, 180
in market coordination, 385–387
LP function. *See* Liquidity preference function
Lucas, Robert, 822
Lumonics, 309–310
Luxuries, definition of, 161

M1, 677, 708, 716, 719
M2, 677, 682, 708
M3, 677
MacDonald, John A., 500
Macdonald Royal Commission, 451, 802
MacIntosh, W. A., 499
Macroeconomic equilibrium, 616–617, 617f
and monetary policy, 714f, 714–715
Macroeconomic policy, in open economy, 860–874
Macroeconomics, 516–544
definition of, 7, 49–50, 516
major issues, 517
overview of, 51–54
phenomena, 517–539
role of money in, 682–707
Macroeconomic variables, measurement of, 545–563
Majority rule, social choice mechanism of, 401
Malthus, Thomas, 187
Managed trade, 497–498
Management, supply, agricultural, 120, 121f, 122
Manufacturer's sales tax, 430, 432
Manufacturing
flexible, 43, 206, 208
services in, growth of, 17
Marginal cost, 189–191, 289n
Marginal cost curves, 191f, 192
Marginal cost pricing, 293, 294f
Marginal efficiency of investment function, 693, 694f
Marginal physical product, 185, 325, 347
Marginal private cost, 407–408
Marginal product, 185–186, 325, 814–815, 815t
diminishing, 185t, 187
shifts in, 817, 817f

Marginal product curve, 186f, 186–187, 190
Marginal propensity not to spend, 572–573, 573n
Marginal propensity to consume, 567, 568t
Marginal propensity to import, 862, 862n
Marginal propensity to save, 568
Marginal propensity to spend, 593, 594t, 861
on national income, 572, 573n
Marginal propensity to withdraw, 573n
Marginal rate of substitution
definition of, 147
diminishing, hypothesis of, 147–148, 148t
Marginal revenue, 221–223
for monopoly firm, 241–242, 242t, 243f
for single-price monopolist, and elasticity, 243, 244f
Marginal revenue product, 326, 347, 373
and demand curve for factors, 327f, 328
physical component of, 326–327, 327f
value component of, 327f, 327–328
Marginal social cost, 408
Marginal tax rate, 428
progressive, 428
Marginal utility
definition of, 155
diminishing, hypothesis of, 155
theory of, 155–158
Marginal value, 160
Margin of advantage, 473
Market(s). *See also* Labour markets
black, 107f, 108–109
common, 496–497
consumers' surplus for, 142f, 143
contestable, 277–279
perfect, 278
for corporate control, 303–304
definition of, 48, 219
discrimination among, 253
elasticity of demand, calculation of firm's demand elasticity from, 223
factor, 47, 51–52
operation of, 336f, 336–342
financial, globalisation of, 668–669
foreign. *See also* International trade
dependence on, and globalisation, 19
foreign exchange, 48, 668–669, 838–840, 839f
definition of, 536
globalisation of, 18–19
goods, 51–52
growth, stimulus to, from market system, 388
inefficient, 389–394
for insurance, 163–167
money, control and regulation of, by central bank, 666
origin of, 42, 48
securities, 726–730
Market demand curves, 140–141
Market economy, 8
versus command economy, 9–11
definition of, 42
modern, origins of, 13
and ongoing change, 16–18
overview of, 42–56
private-ownership, 9
public-ownership, 9
resource allocation in, 43, 114–115
Market failure, 11

definition of, 389
from natural monopoly, 406
and social goals, 394–396
types of, 389–396
Marketing boards, government, 122
Market mechanism, under oligopoly, 279
Market power, degree of, 204
Market price
and interest rate, 684–686
net domestic product at, 552
and nonrenewable resources, 368–369
and present value, 683–684
Market rate of interest, 684–686
Market sector, 49
Market shares, competition for, and oligopoly, 273
Market structure
competitive, 218–240
wage differentials in, 348–350
definition of, 218
and firm behaviour, 218–220
under imperfect competition, 263–265
and innovation, 820
perfectly competitive, 219
significance of, 219–220
wage differentials arising from, 350–355
Market success, 11
Market supply curves. *See* Supply curve(s)
Market system
case for, 387–389
coordination of, process of, 385–387
Market value
and resource extraction, 372
versus total value, 160, 161f
Markham, Jesse, 280
Marshall, Alfred, 59n, 137, 259, 329, 331, 339n
Marx, Karl, 322
Mass-production methods, 206–208
Maximization of net advantage, 337–338
MC. *See* Marginal cost
McLuhan, Marshall, 260
McVey, John, 262
Meade, James, 602
Means, 12
Medium of exchange, money as, 656–657
MEI function. *See* Marginal efficiency of investment function
Mercantilism, 855
Merchandise account, 849
Merger(s), 303–307
backward, 304
under civil law, 299
conglomerate, 305
dismantling of, 305–306
definition of, 303
forward, 304
horizontal, 303–304
types of, 303–304
vertical, 304
Merit goods, 396
MES. *See* Minimum efficient scale
Metallic money, 658–660
Mexico, free trade agreement, with Canada and United States. *See* North American Free Trade Agreement
Microeconomics
definition of, 6, 49–50
overview of, 50–51

Milling, 659
Minerals. *See* Nonrenewable resources
Minimum efficient scale, 230, 246, 502
Minimum wage, definition of, 355
Minimum-wage laws, 355–357
  structural unemployment caused by, 771–772
Mixed economy, 8
  definition of, 48
Modern view, 655–656
Modigliani, Franco, 566
Monetarists, 717, 719
Monetary base, 715
Monetary disturbances, from interest rate changes, 692, 693f
Monetary equilibrium
  and aggregate demand, 689–694
  definition of, 689
Monetary forces
  and national income, 689–699
    in long run, 700, 700f
    in short run, 700–703, 701f
    strength of, 699–703
Monetary gradualism
  Canadian, 719–720
  and wage/price controls, 753
Monetary institutions, nature of, 654–681
Monetary phenomenon, inflation as, 744–745
Monetary policy, 708–730
  in action, 719–723
  Canadian, 871–873
  contractionary, 710
  controversy over, and lags, 717–719
  effectiveness of, 870–871
  influence on stock markets, 728
  instruments and objectives of, 714–717
  intermediate targets of, 715–717, 716f–717f
  and international capital mobility, 869–871
  and macroeconomic equilibrium, 714f, 714–715
  with zero required reserves, 713
Monetary restraint, imported, 871–872
Monetary stringency, Canadian, 720, 721f
Monetary validation
  of accelerating inflation, 746
  of demand shocks, 738–740, 739f–740f
  and inflation reduction, 747–749, 751f
  of supply shocks, 741f, 741–744, 743f
Money, 682
  creation of, by banking system, 672–676
  definition of, 656–657
  demand for, 686–689
  deposit, 662–664, 708
    creation of, 673–675, 673t–675t
    definition of, 663
  fiat, 661
  macroeconomic role of, 682–707
  metallic, 658–660
  modern, 661–664
  nature of, 654–664
  near, 677–678
  neutrality of, 654–655
  origins of, 657–661
  paper, 660–661
  and price level, 655–656, 655f–656f
  purchasing power of, 529
  purpose of, 43
  quantity theory of, 690
  real value of, 529
  tight, 756
Money balances
  nominal, 688–689
  real, 688–689
Money capital, 173
Money flows, 51, 53n, 53–54, 54f
Money income, 131
  changes in, 130, 130f
Money markets, control and regulation of, by central bank, 666
Money national income, 519
Money price, 75, 129
  proportional changes in, 130–131
Money rate of interest. *See* Interest rate
Money substitutes, 678
Money supply, 676–678, 686
  Canadian, 677, 677t, 708–714
  changes in, 710
    impact of, 694, 696–697, 698f, 700, 700f, 713–714
  control and regulation of, by central bank, 666
  definition of, 676
  and government deposits, 712
Monopolist, 241
  government as, 400–401
  multiprice, 250–255
  single-price, 241–247
Monopolistic competition, 219, 265–268
  versus oligopoly, 268
  theory of, 265–268
Monopolistic practises, 288, 292
Monopoly, 219, 241–257
  cartel as, 247–250
  versus competition, 244
  deadweight loss of, 291, 291f
  definition of, 241
  efficiency and inefficiency in, 287–288, 290–292, 291f
  versus monopsony, 354–355
  natural, 246
    direct control of, 292–295
    market failure arising from, 406
  versus oligopoly, 268
  profits under, 245, 245f
  public policy toward, 284–302
  and supply curve, 245
  as union in competitive market, 350–351, 351f
Monopoly equilibrium
  long-run, 246
  short-run, 244–245, 245f
Monopoly firm, 241, 245
  demand curve for, 241
Monopoly industry, 245
Monopoly power, as source of inefficiency, 389–390
Monopsony, 351–356, 354f–355f
  definition of, 351
  versus monopoly, 354–355
Moral hazard, 167, 392–393
Moral suasion, 712
MP. *See* Marginal product
MPC. *See* Marginal propensity to consume
MPP. *See* Marginal physical product
MPS. *See* Marginal propensity to save
MR. *See* Marginal revenue
MRP. *See* Marginal revenue product
MRS. *See* Marginal rate of substitution
MST. *See* Manufacturer's sales tax
Multilateral balance of payments, 853
Multilateral trading system, crisis in, 497–498
Multinational enterprise. *See* Transnational corporations
Multiple counting, 546
Multiplier, 577–583. *See also* Simple multiplier
  algebraic approach to, 582
  balanced budget, 599
  definition of, 577
  export
    under fixed exchange rates, 862, 863f
    under flexible exchange rates, 866
  greater than unity, 577–578
  less than unity, 603
  numerical example of, 580
  open-economy, and aggregate supply, 864
  and price level variations, 619–622, 621f
Multiprice monopolist, 250–255
Multivariate relationship, 59n
Municipal government
  services, relative cost of, 445
  spending and taxation, 588
Muscovy Company, 173

NAFTA. *See* North American Free Trade Agreement
NAIRU, 526, 526n, 733–734, 734t, 746n, 762–763, 770–776
Nash, John, 271
Nash equilibrium, 271f, 271–272
National Bureau of Economic Research, 772
National debt, 587n, 787–789, 788f. *See also* Government budget deficit
  combined, 789, 790f
  examples of, 793, 794f
  importance of, 796–797
National defense, 487
National Energy Policy, 506
National income, 518. *See also* Equilibrium national income; Gross domestic product
  and aggregate demand, 694–699, 698f
  and aggregate expenditure
    consumption and investment, 564–585
    in open economy with government, 586–605
  and balance of trade, 860–867
  changes in, 575–583, 576f, 806, 807f
    and price level, 617–625
  and employment, 524–528
  historical experience, 519–521
  importance of, 523–524
  long-term growth of, 524
  maximization of, and protectionism, 488–491
  measurement of, 554–555, 555t, 560
    interpretation of, 554–560
  and monetary forces, 689–699
    in long run, 700, 700f
    in short run, 700–703, 701f
  and national output, 518f, 518–524
  nominal, 519, 521n
    calculation of, 556

as policy variable, 714–715
omissions from, 557–560
potential, 521, 521*n*
and GDP gap, 521–523, 523*f*, 628–629, 629*f*
and price level, 694–699, 698*f*
in long run, 628–651
in short run, 606–627
real, 519, 521*n*
calculation of, 554–556
in short and long run, 637–639, 638*f*
short-term fluctuations in, 524
National-income accounting, 546–554
National Income and Product Account, 546
Nationalized industry, 296
National output
concepts, 545–546
and national income, 518*f*, 518–524
real, 519
National Policy, 500
National product, 516, 518
National standards, and federal provincial transfers, 443
National Training Act, 781
National Transport Agency, 415
National treatment, 312, 501–502, 504
Natural entry barriers, 246, 276
Natural monopoly, 246
direct control of, 292–295
market failure arising from, 406
Natural rate of unemployment. *See* NAIRU
Natural resources. *See* Nonrenewable resources
NDP. *See* New Democratic Party
Near money, 677–678
Necessities, definition of, 161
Nelson, Richard, 316, 819
Neoclassical growth theory, 814–818
Neomercantilism, 855
Net advantage, equalization of, 337–338
Net domestic income at factor cost, 552
Net domestic product at market price, 552
Net export(s), 550–551, 588–592
autonomous, 595–596
changes in, and price level, 608
and equilibrium national income, 595–596
and government budget deficit, 795
induced, 596
Net export function, 588–589, 590*f*
shifts in, 589–592
Net export schedule, 589, 589*t*
Net taxes, 587
Neutrality
of money, 654–655
Ricardo, 793
New Democratic Party, 358
Newly industrialised countries (NICs), 490
New Technology Employment Programme, 780
New Zealand-U.S.-Australia free trade agreement, 497
Next-generation banks, 673
NGOs. *See* Nongovernmental organizations
NIPA. *See* National Income and Product Account
Nixon, Richard, 386, 754
Nominal flows. *See* Money flows
Nominal GDP, measurement of, 554–555

Nominal interest rate, 533, 535*f*
Nominal money balances, 688–689
Nominal national income, 519, 521*n*
calculation of, 556
as policy variable, 714–715
Nominal shock, 740
Nominal values, 519
Non-accelerating inflationary rate of unemployment. *See* NAIRU
Noncooperative equilibrium, 270
Nonfactor payments, 552
Nongovernmental organizations, 827
Nonmarketed activities, and GDP, 558
Nonmarket sector, 49
Nonmaximizing theories, 315–317
importance of, 317
Nonprice competition, 264
Nonprofit organizations, as decision makers, 44*n*
Nonrenewable resources, 325
definition of, 367
economics of, 367–373
price system as conservation mechanism for, 370–373
rate of extraction, determination of, 367–369, 370*f*
rents to, 370
Nonresalability, 255
Nonstrategic behaviour, 268
Nontariff barriers, 492–494
definition of, 484
Normal goods, 63*n*, 91, 94
Normal profits, 180*n*
Normative judgements, in social policy, need for, 453–454
Normative statements
definition of, 23
in economics, 25
versus positive statements, 23–26
North, Douglas, 171
North American Free Trade Agreement, 501, 507–511
background of, 508
contents of, 507
criticisms of, 508–511
environmental aspects of, 510
fallacious arguments against, 494–495
NTBs. *See* Nontariff barriers
NX. *See* Net export(s)

OAS (old age security). *See* Elderly, benefits for
Observations, graphing of, 38–41, 40*t*, 40*f*–41*f*
Occupation(s), gender discrimination within, 362–363
Occupational segregation, 363
Official reserves, and balance of payments, 851, 856
Ohlin, Bertil, 475
Oil industry. *See* Nonrenewable resources; Organization of Petroleum Exporting Countries
Okun, Arthur, 767
Old age security. *See* Elderly, benefits for
Oligopoly, 219, 247, 249*n*, 267–280
basic dilemma of, 270–272, 271*f*
causes of, 268–270
characteristics of, 268

cooperation versus competition under, 272–275
definition of, 268
direct control of, 295–297
skepticism about, 295–296
efficiency in, 288
and functioning of economy, 279–280
long-run behaviour in, 275–279
One price, law of, 79
OPEC. *See* Organization of Petroleum Exporting Countries
Open economy
with fixed exchange rate, 861*f*, 862–863
with flexible exchange rate, 863–866, 865*f*
with government, aggregate expenditure and national income in, 586–605
macroeconomic policy in, 860–874
and social policy, 454–455
transmission mechanism in, 696
Open-economy multiplier, and aggregate supply, 864
Open-market operations, 708–710, 709*t*, 715
Opportunity cost, 4*f*, 4–5, 176, 373
applications of, beyond economics, 177
and budget line, 129
and demand for money, 686
differing
gains from trade arising from, 473–475, 474*t*
reasons for, 475
of economic growth, 810–813, 813*t*
Orderly marketing schemes, for agricultural products, 122–123
Organization
business, forms of, 170–173
of production, 170–174
Organization of Petroleum Exporting Countries, 89, 249*n*, 273–275, 488–489, 742, 753
Our Common Future (Brundtland Commission), 826–827
Output(s)
aggregated total, 519
and costs, 613–614
decisions about, and input decisions, 324–325
definition of, 176
demand for, elasticity of, 329–330
least-cost method of, determination of, 214–215, 215*f*
lost, with unemployment, 763
national
concepts, 545–546
and national income, 518*f*, 518–524
real, 519
under price discrimination, 255
and prices, 614–615
restrictions on, enforcement of, 250
short-run price and, 292–293, 294*f*
units of, discrimination among, 253–254
value added as, 545–546
Output gap
and factor prices, 629–631
inflationary, 522, 629, 631
removal of, 5ä*f*, 643, 698–699
potential income and, 521–523, 523*f*, 628–629, 629*f*

Output gap (*continued*)
  recessionary, 522, 629, 631
    removal of, 641–643, 643*f*, 699
Outside assets, 607
Overhead cost, 189
Overshooting, of exchange rate, 847–849
Ownership
  of resources, 8–9
  separation of, from control, 314–315
Ownership-coordination mix, 9
Own price elasticity of demand, 84

Panzar, John, 277
Paper money, 660–661
Paradox of thrift, 644–646
Paradox of value, 160–161
Pareto, Vilfredo, 285–287, 286*f*
Pareto optimality (efficiency), 285
Partial derivative, 59*n*
Partnership
  advantages and disadvantages of, 172
  definition of, 170
  limited, 172
Patents, 179, 246
Paternalism, 396, 419–420
Pay. *See* Wage(s)
Pay equity, 338, 363
  government policies on, 363–364
Payments accounts, 849*t*, 849–851
  balances/imbalances, meaning of, 851–856
Payoff matrix, 270, 271*f*
Peak, 522
Pegged rate. *See* Fixed exchange rate
Pensions, private-sector, 462
Per capita values, and productivity, 555–557
Perfect competition, 219
  appeal of, 237
  assumption of, 220
  demand under, 222–223
  efficiency and inefficiency in, 287–290, 290*f*
  firm in
    demand for, 220–223, 221*f*
    revenue for, 220–223, 224*t*, 224*f*
  theory of, 220–223
Perfect contestable market, 278
Perfectly competitive equilibrium, effects of cartelization on, 249, 249*f*
Perfectly competitive market structure, 219
Perfect price discrimination, 253, 254*f*
Permanent-income theory, 566
Perpetuities, 662, 683
Personal costs
  of economic growth, 813
  of unemployment, 763
Personal income, 554
  disposable, 554
  taxes on, 428–429, 429*t*
Personal services contracts, 374
Petroleum industry. *See* Nonrenewable resources; Organization of Petroleum Exporting Countries
Phillips curve, 734, 736–737
  expectations-augmented, 748–749
Physical (real) capital, 173, 662, 816
Plant, investment in, 549, 571
Plurilateral regionalism, versus hub and spoke model, 509

Point elasticity, 98
  approximation of, arc elasticity as, 98–101, 99*f*–101*f*
  precise definition, 101–102, 102*f*
Point of diminishing average productivity, 185
Point of diminishing marginal productivity, 186
Poison pills, 307
Policy constraints, of free trade agreement, 504–506
Policy issues, and factor price differentials, 338–339
Political economy, of government budget deficit, 802–803
Political sovereignty, and free trade agreement, 506
Pollution
  control of, 408*f*, 409–415, 411*f*
  and economic growth, 828–829
  economics of, 407–415
Pollution externalities, 407, 407*f*
Population
  and shifts in demand, 64
  variation in, and labour supply, 332
Porter, Michael, 316, 492, 821
Portfolio balance theory, 692
Portfolio investment, 307, 850–851
Positive statements
  definition of, 23
  in economics, 25
  versus normative statements, 23–26
Potential entry, 277–279
Potential national income, 521, 521*n*
  and GDP gap, 521–523, 523*f*, 628–629, 629*f*
Poverty, in Canada, 460–461
Power, decentralization of, 389
PPP exchange rate. *See* Purchasing power parity exchange rate
PRA. *See* Purchase and resale agreement
Precautionary balances, 687–688
Predatory pricing, 277
Predictions, 29–30
  rejection or acceptance of, 32–33
Preferences, regional differences in, 439–440
Present value, 374
  calculation of, 684–685
  definition of, 682
  of future returns, 374–377
  and interest rate, 682–683
  and market price, 683–684
Price(s). *See also* Equilibrium price; Factor price(s); Market price; Relative price
  absolute (money), 75, 129
    proportional changes in, 130–131
  administered, 263
  bargain-basement, 663
  base period, 554
  break-even, 230
  change in, household reaction to, 149–150, 151*f*
  consumer, 104
  demand and, 59–61
  determination of, by demand and supply, 70–75, 71*t*, 72*f*
  disequilibrium, 105–106, 106*f*
    definition of, 71
  entry-attracting, 228–229, 230*f*
  exit-inducing, 229

fixed (frozen). *See* Price controls
  and inflation, 74–75
  input, changes in, and SRAS curve, 615–616
  international, relative, and net export function, 590–592, 591*f*
  and output, 614–615
  protectionist policy that directly raises, 484–485
  purchase
    of capital, 373–374
    of labour, 374
  reductions in, and quantity demanded, 84, 84*t*
  relative
    classical view of, 654
    modern view of, 655
  rental
    of capital, 373
    of labour, 374
  selection of, by firms, 263–264
  seller, 104
  short-run, and output, 292–293, 294*f*
  shut-down, 224
  supply and, 67–68
  world, 79–80
    agricultural exports at, 118*f*, 118–119
Price ceilings, 107*f*, 107–109
  case study of, 109–112
  definition of, 107
Price-consumption line, 149–150, 151*f*
Price controls
  definition of, 105
  government, 105–109
  and monetary gradualism, 753
Price discrimination, 250–255
  consequences of, 254*f*, 255
  definition of, 251
  normative aspects of, 255
  perfect, 253, 254*f*
  possibility of, 254–255
  profitability of, 253–254
Price elasticity of demand, 82–90, 83*f*
  calculation of, with averages, 86
  and changes in total expenditure, 85–87, 88*f*, 88*t*–89*t*
  definition of, 84
  measurement of, 83–87
Price floors, 106–107, 107*f*
Price index
  calculation of, 542, 543*t*
  example of, 656, 656*f*
  implicit, 555
  weights for, calculation of, 542, 543*t*
  wholesale, Canadian, 655*f*, 655–656
Price level, 516, 519
  and aggregate demand, 694–699, 698*f*
  definition of, 528
  exogenous changes in, 606–613
  inflation and, 528–532, 530*f*
  money and, 655–656, 655*f*–656*f*
  and national income, 694–699, 698*f*
    changes in, 617–625
    equilibrium, 613–617
    in long run, 628–651
    in short run, 606–627
  as policy variable, 715
  variations in, and multiplier, 619–622, 621*f*

Price makers, 263
Price profiles, of nonrenewable resources, 372–373
Price rigidity, and NAIRU, 775
Price stabilization
  for agricultural goods, 119
  policy of, Bank of Canada, 722–723, 756–757, 872–873
  short-run, 264
Price system
  definition of, 50–51
  example of, 50–51
  free-market
    agricultural problems in, 112–123
    versus centrally planned economies, 11
    and resource allocation, 114–115
    and market coordination, 385–387
  multiple, 250n
  as natural resource conservation mechanism, 370–373
Price taker, 204, 336, 614–615
Price-taking firm
  in long-run equilibrium, 230
  revenue for, 221–223, 224t, 224f
  rules for, 225–226
Price theory, 75
Pricing
  average cost, 293
    example of, 294–295
  factor, 324
  full-cost, 316
  marginal cost, 293, 294f
  in natural monopoly, 292–293, 294f
  predatory, 277
Primary budget balance, 789
Primary deficit, 789, 800
Principal-agent problem, 172, 314, 393, 402
Principle
  of comparative advantage, 42
  of substitution, 199–200, 215–216, 216f
Private cost, 390, 391f
  marginal, 407–408
Private investment, and government budget deficit, 794–795
Private-ownership economy, 9
Private productive facilities, investment in, 308
Private sector, 49
  and public sector, allocation between, 445–446
Private-sector pensions, 462
Privatization, 297
Process innovation, 208, 492
Procyclical fiscal policy, 644
Producers
  and consumers, interactions between, 51–53, 52f
  resistance of, to market-based environmental policies, 416
Producers' surplus, 289, 289f
Product(s). See also Marginal product
  average, 185
    diminishing, 185t, 187
  homogeneous, 220, 265
  intermediate, 176
  national, 516, 518
  net domestic, at market price, 552
  new, 18, 208

selection of, by firms, 263
  total, 185, 185t, 186f
Product development
  costs of, 202, 491, 491n
  subsidies for, 491
Product differentiation, 263, 265–267
  gains from specialization with, 502–503
Product innovation, 208, 492
Production
  costs of, government intervention in, 399
  decisions about, for firm, 224–225
  definition of, 3
  factors of. See Factors of production
  globalisation of, 18, 260
  knowledge intensive, 824
  lean, 43, 206–208
  in long and very long run, 196–216
  marketed, 49
  nonmarketed, 49
  organization of, 170–174
  in short run, 183–195
  stages of, 545
    value added through, 547
Production costs, 202
Production function, 184–185, 212
  and long-run average cost curve, 200
Production possibilities, 5
Production possibility boundary (curve), 5, 5f, 476
  effects of economic growth on, 6f, 6–7
Productive capacity, growth of, 6–7
Productive efficiency, 285–286, 286f
  in monopoly, 288
  in perfect competition, 287
Productive facilities, private, investment in, 308
Productivity
  agricultural, growth of, 113
  definition of, 204
  diminishing average, point of, 185
  diminishing marginal, point of, 186
  growth of, significance of, 205
  increases in, and SRAS curve, 616, 616f
  labour, 524
    in modern economy, 13–14, 15f
  measurement of, 204n
  total and per capita values and, 555–557
Profit(s), 552
  calculation of, 179, 180f
  definition of, 176, 179–180
  distributed, 552
  loss of, and foreign investment, 311
  meaning and significance of, 179–180
  under monopoly, 245, 245f
  normal, 180n
  under oligopoly, 279
  and resource allocation, 180
  role of, in market coordination, 385–387
  super normal, 180n
  undistributed, 552
  definition of, 172
Profitability, of firm, in short run, 227–228, 229f
Profit maximization, 47, 175–176
  and cost minimization, 198–199
  and resource allocation, 114–115
Profit-maximizing firm, rules for, 224–226
Profit seeking, by banks, 667–668
Progressive marginal tax rate, 428

Progressive tax system, 426
Propensity to spend out of national income, 572–573
Property rights
  importance of, 391
  inadequate, and resource extraction, 371–372
Property taxes, 430
  incidence, 436, 437f
Proportional tax system, 426
Protection
  against competition, 296–297
  contingent, 493
  of individuals, 396
  of infant industries, 490
  of specific groups, 487
  against unfair trade actions, by foreign firms/governments, 490
Protectionism. See also Commercial policy; Trade policy
  attitudes toward, 497–498
  case for, 487–494
  fallacious arguments concerning, 494
  methods of, 484–485, 486f
Provincial government
  deficits, 786–787
  spending and taxation, 588
Proxy, definition of, 314
Public, resistance of, to market-based environmental policies, 416
Public assistance programs, 458
Public choices, inefficient, and government failure, 400
Public education, 396, 456
Public expenditure, 437–445, 438t
  and income distribution, 444
  and resource allocation, 444–445
  types of, 437–438, 439t, 440f
Public good(s), 406. See also Collective consumption goods
  health and safety information as, 415–420
  pure, 415
Public health care system, 463
Public-ownership economy, 9
Public policy
  evolution of, 446
  toward monopoly and competition, 284–302
Public provision, 397
  of goods and services, 437–438, 439t
  preferences for, 394–396
Public sector, 49
  and private sector, allocation between, 445–446
Public Service Alliance, 358
Purchase and resale agreement, 665
Purchased factors of production, 177
Purchase price
  of capital, 373–374
  of labour, 374
Purchasing power
  household, 131
    constant, 133, 133n
  of money, 529
Purchasing power parity exchange rate, 846–847
Pure profits. See also Profit(s)
  definition of, 179
Pure public goods, 415

Purvis, Douglas, 802
PV. *See* Present value

Quality control, in centrally planned
    economies, failure of, 10
Quality of life, 560
Quantity
    of factor demanded, 325–326
    protectionist policy that directly lowers,
        485
Quantity actually bought, 59
Quantity actually sold, 67
Quantity adjusters, 615
Quantity demanded, 58–59, 62
    change in, 65
    determinants of, 59
    increases in, and price reductions, 84, 84*t*
    and substitution effect, 135–136, 137*f*
Quantity exchanged, 59, 67
Quantity supplied, 67, 69
    change in, 70
    determinants of, 67
Quantity theory of money, 690
Quotas
    agricultural, 120–122, 121*f*
    import, 485
    on Japanese cars, 488–489

Random shocks, 733*n*
Rate of inflation, 6, 528
    measurement of, 544
    stable, 755–756
Rational expectations, 735
Rationality, consumer, assumption of,
    159–160
Rationalization, of domestic industry, 503
Rationing, 108
RBC theory. *See* Real business cycle theory
R&D. *See* Research and development
Reagan, Ronald, 456
Real business cycle theory, 768–769
Real (physical) capital, 173, 662, 816
Real costs, 114
Real flows, 51, 53, 53*n*
Real GDP. *See* Constant-dollar GDP
Real income, 131
    and relative prices, 131–132
Real interest rate, 533, 535*f*
    investment and, 570–571
Real money balances, 688–689
Real national income, 519, 521*n*
    calculation of, 554–556
Real national output, 519
Real shock, 740
Real value, 519
Real value of money, 529
Real wage, 517
Recession, 517, 522
    Canadian, 756
Recessionary gap, 522, 629, 631
    removal of, 641–643, 643*f*, 699
Reciprocity treaty, between British North
    America and United States, 499
Recovery, 522
    Canadian, 872
    and inflation, 720–723, 751*f*, 752
Redistribution, and economic growth,
    808–809
Red raspberries case, 507

Red tape, 399
Reforming Regulation (Economic Council of
    Canada), 421
Refutation, of theory, 30
Regional agreements, trade-liberalizing, 496
Regional differences, in preferences,
    439–440
Regional income equalization, 338–339
Regionalism, plurilateral, versus hub and
    spoke model, 509
Registered Retirement Savings Plan, 462
Regressive tax system, 426
Regulated industry, 296
Regulation
    economic, 292
    entry barriers created by, 246
    environmental, 406–425
        resistance to, 416–417
    government, 397
    health, 415–420
    pollution, 409–415
    safety, 415–420
    social, 292*n*, 406–425
        benefit-cost analysis of, 420–422
        definition of, 407
Regulatory reform, 421–422
Regulatory Reform Strategy (Progressive
    Conservative government), 422
Relative price, 75, 129
    and budget line, 129–132, 132*f*
    classical view of, 654
    international, and net export function,
        590–592, 591*f*
    modern view of, 655
    and relative costs, 388–389
    and resource allocation, 531*n*
Renewable resources
    definition of, 367
    and economic growth, 828
Rent(s), 551
    economic, 339–342
    definition of, 340
    to natural resources, 370
Rental accommodations, and rent controls,
    110–111
Rental price
    of capital, 373
    of labour, 374
Rent controls, 109–112
    advantages and disadvantages of, 111–112
    effects of, 107*f*, 109–112
    and housing shortage, 111, 112*f*
    in Toronto, 110
Rent-seeking, 399
Replacement investment, 549
Required reserves, 667, 670–672
Resale, prevention of, 255
Resaleable assets, 178
Research and development, 183, 259–260,
    818, 825
    expenditures, 202, 261
    by transnational corporations, 309, 313
Reserve(s)
    bank, 669–672
        need for, 669–670
        target, 670–672
    excess, 672
    falls in, 710
    official, and balance of payments, 851, 856

zero required, monetary policy with, 713
Reserve ratio, 670
    fixed, 672
    target
        changes in, and money supply, 712
        constant, 708
        variable, 675
Reserve requirements, 667, 670–672
Residential investment, 308, 549, 571
Resort hotels, and declining demand, 236
Resource(s), 3. *See also* Nonrenewable
    resources
    exhaustion, 825–828
    in government intervention, costs of,
        398–399
    ownership of, 8–9
    renewable
        definition of, 367
        and economic growth, 828
Resource allocation
    and agriculture, 116
    definition of, 6, 43
    and government intervention, 114–115
    within households, 45*n*
    profits and, 180
    and public expenditure, 444–445
    and relative price, 531*n*
Responsible Regulation (Economic Council of
    Canada), 421
Restrictive Trade Practices Commission, 298
Retained earnings. *See* Undistributed profits
Retirement income security programs,
    462–463
Revenue. *See also* Average revenue; Marginal
    revenue
    for firm in perfect competition, 220–223,
        224*t*, 224*f*
    for single-price monopolist, in short run,
        241–243
    total, 221
Revenue Canada, 459
Revenue stabilization, for agricultural goods,
    119
Ricardo, David, 322, 341, 470
Ricardo neutrality, 793
Right of establishment, 504
Risk averse, definition of, 663, 688, 688*n*
Riskiness, definition of, 663
Risk pooling, 165–166, 166*t*
Risk sharing, 166–167
Risk taking, and imputed costs, 179
Robb, Roberta, 364
Romer, Paul, 822
Roosevelt, Franklin D., 646
Rosenberg, Nathan, 173, 818
RRSP. *See* Registered Retirement Savings
    Plan
Rule of 72, 14
Rules of origin, 496

Safety information, as public good,
    415–420, 418*f*
Safety regulations, 415–420
Sales maximization, 315, 315*f*
Sales taxes, 429–430, 432, 552
    incidence, 103–105, 104*f*
Satisficing theory, 316–317
Saving
    definition of, 566

and economic growth, 809–810
Saving function, 568–569, 569f, 570t
Saving schedule, 568–569, 570t
Scale and Scope: The Dynamics of Industrial Capitalism, 269
Scarce goods, 162–163
Scarcity, 3–4
Scatter diagrams, 38–41, 40t, 40f–41f
Schelling, Thomas, 388
Schumpeter, Joseph, 247, 280, 818
Science Policy Research Unit, 818
Scientific approach, 25–27
SDRs. *See* Special drawing rights
Search unemployment, 770
Seaside Inn, 236
Seasonal adjustment, 521n
Second-generation banks, 673, 674t
Sectors, of economy, 48–49
Securities, definition of, 662
Securities markets, 726–730
Security, versus adjustment, and social policy, 455
Self-realizing expectations, 728
Seller price, 104
Sellers' preferences, 108
Semiconductor industry, Japanese, 492
Services, 588–589
    final, 17–18, 546
    government purchases of, 549–550
    intermediate, 546
    in manufacturing, growth of, 17
    public provision of, 437–438, 439t
    subsidies on, 552
Service sector, growth of, deindustrialisation and, 352–353
Set-up costs, 246
    as entry barrier, 276, 277f
Share(s), 662
Shareholders, definition of, 172
Short run
    agricultural fluctuations in, 116f–117f, 116–118
    choices for firms in, 185–187
    cost and revenue in, under monopoly, 241–243
    cost variation in, 188–193
    definition of, 184
    demand elasticity in, 89–90, 90f
    equilibrium price in, 227
    firm profitability in, 227–228, 229f
    monetary forces in, and national income, 700–703, 701f
    monetary policy variables in, 714–715
    national income in, 606–627, 637–639, 638f
    price in, and output, 292–293, 294f
    price level in, 606–627
    price stability in, 264
    production and cost in, 183–195
    rent controls in, 111, 112f
    saving and investment in, effect on economic growth, 809–810
    supply elasticity in, 95
Short-run aggregate supply curve, 613
    Keynesian, 619
    and multiplier, 619–620, 621f
    shape of, 624
        importance of, 620–622, 622f–623f
    shifts in, 615–616, 616f, 702, 736–737

slope of, 613–615, 615f, 702
    and wages, 738
Short-run average total cost curve, and long-run average cost curve, relationship between, 200–203, 203f–204f
Short-run cost curves, 189t, 191f, 191–192
    family of, 193
    and long-run costs, relationship between, 202–203
    shifts in, 192f, 192–193
Short-run equilibrium. *See also* Firm(s), equilibrium of
    of economy, 378–379
Short-run supply curve, 226–227, 227f–228f
    versus long run, 226–227
Shut-down price, 224
Simon, Herbert, 273, 316
Simple multiplier, 595
    and aggregate demand curve, 613, 614f
    definition of, 578–579, 579f
    in open economy
        with fixed exchange rate, 861, 861f
        with flexible exchange rate, 863–866, 865f
    size of, 579–583, 581f
    and tax rates, 597–598
Single-price monopolist, 241–247
Single proprietorship
    advantages and disadvantages of, 172
    definition of, 170
Size distribution of income, 322–325, 323t
    definition of, 323
Slope
    of curved lines, 37, 39f
    definition of, 36
    of demand curve, 83–84
    of straight lines, 36–37, 38f
Slumps, 522
Slutsky effect, 133n, 153
Small open economy, 834
Smith, Adam, 43, 46, 50, 200, 284, 322, 470, 855
Social advantage, versus comparative advantage, 487
Social assistance, 444, 458
Social behaviour, and nonrenewable resources, 369
Social choice mechanism, of majority rule, 401
Social choice theory, 400–402
Social cost, 390, 391f
    of economic growth, 813
    marginal, 408
    versus social benefit, 408
    of tax and transfer system, 454
Social goals, and market failure, 394–396
Social insurance, 397, 444
Social obligations, in free-market system, 396
Social policy
    Canadian, 450–468
        federal spending on, 451, 451t
        federal-provincial perspective on, 452–453
    and free trade agreement, 506
    interactions, 453
    objectives of, 453–455
    universality of, 455–456

Social programs
    assessment of, issues in, 453–455
    Canadian, outline of, 456–466
    fiscal, economic, and demographic setting of, 451
    variety of, 450–451
Social rate of discount, 372
Social regulation, 292n, 406–425
    benefit-cost analysis of, 420–422
    definition of, 407
Social science, economics as, 23–41
Social values, and resource extraction, 372
Society, economics and, 2–22
SOE. *See* Small open economy
Solow, Robert, 816
Solow residual, 816–817, 817f
Special drawing rights, 851
Special interests, and government failure, 400
Specialization
    gains from, 471
        absence of, without comparative advantage, 473, 473t
        with absolute advantage, 471
        with comparative advantage, 472–473, 473t
        with differentiated products, 502–503
        with differing opportunity costs, 473–475, 474t
        with variable costs, 477–480
    of labour, 42–43
    risks of, 487
Specific tax. *See* Excise tax
Speculative balances, 688
Speculative booms, 728–729
Spending power, of federal government, 441
SPRU. *See* Science Policy Research Unit
SRAS curve. *See* Short-run aggregate supply curve
SRATC curve. *See* Short-run average total cost curve
Stabilization policy, 596, 633–634
Stagflation, 750–752, 751f
    definition of, 517
Start-up firm, 259
Statistical analysis, 30–32
Statistics Canada, 460, 525, 542, 546, 558, 722, 872
Sticky wages, 624, 633–634, 765, 766f
Stigler, George, 297
Stiglitz, Joseph, 266
Stockholders, definition of, 172
Stockman, Alan, 768
Stock markets, 726–730
Stocks, 662
Stock variables, 60
Straight line(s), and their slopes, 36–37, 38f
Straight-line depreciation, 178
Strategic behaviour, 268–270, 272
Strategic trade advantage, creation or exploitation of, with trade restrictions, 490–491
Strategic trade policy, and competitiveness, 491–492
Structural change
    adjustment to, 780–781
    definition of, 846
    and exchange rates, 846
    increasing, and NAIRU, 776
    resistance to, and unemployment, 780

Structural unemployment, 526, 764, 770–773
  and frictional unemployment, relationship between, 772
  reduction of, 780–781
Stykholt, Stephen, 500, 502
Subsidies
  agricultural, 120
  on goods and services, 552
  for product development, 491
Substitutes, 63
  and demand elasticity, 87, 94
  money, 678
Substitution
  and elasticity of factor demand, 329
  marginal rate of
    definition of, 147
    diminishing, hypothesis of, 147–148, 148t
  principle of, 199–200, 215–216, 216f
Substitution effect, 132f, 132–136
  definition of, 133
  example of, 133, 134f, 135t
  and indifference theory, 152–154, 153f
  and quantity demanded, 135–136, 137f
  and wage rate, 334
Sumatoma, 309
Summer Canada, 780
Sunk costs, 178–179, 189
  of entry, 278
Super normal profits, 180n
Supply, 66–70. See also Aggregate supply; Factors of production, supply of; Money supply
  in action, 103–126
  of agricultural goods, 113
  change in, 70
  definition of, 68–69
  of effort, 332
  excess, 71
  of foreign exchange, 839–840
  inelastic, agricultural fluctuations with, 117f, 117–118
  of insurance, 165–167
  of labour, 332, 334
    total, 332–333
  law of, 61, 72–74, 73f
  and price, 67–68
  price determination by, 70–75, 71t, 72f
  of rental accommodations, and rent controls, 110–111
Supply curve, 68. See also Aggregate supply curve
  example of, 68, 68f
  industry, long-run, 232–233, 233f
  of labour, backward-bending, 334
  and monopoly, 245
  and sales tax, 104
  shape of, and supply elasticity, 93, 100–101, 101f
  shifts in, 69t, 69f–70f, 69–70
    and laws of supply and demand, 72–74, 73f
    versus movements along, 70
  short-run, 226–227, 227f–228f
    versus long-run, 226–227
Supply elasticity, 93–95
  definition of, 93
  determinants of, 94–95

long-run and short-run, 95
  and sales tax incidence, 104–105, 105f
  terminology, 94
Supply management, agricultural, 120, 121f, 122
Supply schedule, 68
  and equilibrium price, 70, 71t
  example of, 68, 68t
Supply shock(s), 51, 740–741
  aggregate, 622–625, 623f
    definition of, 618
  isolated, 741f, 741–742
  monetary validation of, 741f, 741–744, 743f
  repeated, 742–744, 743f
Supply-shock inflation, 740
Supply-side economics, and taxation, 435, 436f
Surplus. See also Budget surplus; Consumers' surplus
  balance-of-payments, 854
  full employment, 792n
  producers', 289, 289f
  and trade, 42–43
Sustainability, of fiscal plan, 800–801
Sustainable development, 826–827
Sustained inflation, 744–752
  reduction of, 747–752, 751f

Tacit collusion, 272
Tacit cooperation, and oligopoly, 273
Tacit knowledge, 819
Takeover(s), 303–307
  backward, 304
  conglomerate, 304
  defense against, 306–307
  definition of, 303
  effects of, 304–305
  forward, 304
  horizontal, 303–304
  hostile, 304
  types of, 303–304
  vertical, 304
Takeover bid. See Tender offer
Target ratio, 670
Target reserve, 670–672
Target reserve ratio
  changes in, and money supply, 712
  constant, 708
Tariffs
  argument for, 491–492
  Canadian, 500
  definition of, 484
  on Japanese cars, 488–489
  rates, 484, 485t
Tastes
  role of, in household choices, 137–141
  and shifts in demand, 64
Tax(es)
  business, indirect, 552, 554
  corporate, 429
  diversity and yield of, 426, 427t
  emissions, 411–413, 412f
  and equity, 431–434
  excise, 429–430
  federal sales, 432
  goods and services, 430, 430f, 432, 434, 552
  indirect, 430

manufacturer's sales, 430, 432
  net, 587
  personal income, 428–429, 429t
  property, 430
    incidence, 436, 437f
  sales, 429–430, 432, 552
    incidence, 103–105, 104f
  value added, 430
Taxation, 426–430
  supply-side effects of, 435, 436f
Tax cascading, 432–433
Tax expenditures, 427, 450
Tax functions, of government, 587–588, 588t, 588f
Tax incidence, 435–437
  definition of, 103, 436
Tax liability, postponed, and government budget deficit, 793
Tax rate
  average, 428
  changes in, effects of, 597f, 597–598, 598t
  marginal, 428
  progressive, 428
Tax-related incomes policy, 754
Tax revenues, 587
  government, and economic performance, 789
Tax shifting, 435–436
Tax system
  aspects of, 426–427
  Canadian, 428–430, 434
  distributive effects of, 397
  efficiency and social costs of, 454
  efficiency of, 434–435
  evaluation of, 430–437
  incentives provided by, 398
  progressive, 426
  proportional, 426
  regressive, 426
TC. See Total cost
Technical efficiency, 197, 285n
Techniques, new, 208
Technological change, 204–209. See also Innovation
  and capital stock, 379, 379f
  definition of, 204
  disembodied, 817–818
  and economic growth, 817–818
  embodied, 817
  endogenous, 204
  exogenous, 818
  with industrialisation, 559
  kinds of, 208
  and long-run equilibrium, 234, 235f
  and market economies, 16–18
  and monopoly, 247
  and supply, 69–70
Telecommunication industry, as natural monopoly, 295
Tenants, and property tax incidence, 436, 437f
Tender offer, 304
Term deposit, 676
Term to maturity, definition of, 662
Terms of trade, 480–481
  alteration of, with trade restrictions, 488–490
Testable statement, definition of, 23
Texaco Oil Company, 298, 304
TFC. See Total fixed cost

Theories
  importance of, 28
  representation of, on graphs, 36–38, 37f–39f
  structure of, 28–30
  testing of, 30–33, 31f
Theory of games, and oligopoly, 270–272, 271f
Theory of the Leisure Class, The, 138
Third-generation banks, 673–674
Third-party effects, 390
Thrift, paradox of, 644–646
Tight money, 756
Time horizons, for decision making, 183–184. *See also* Long run; Short run; Very long run
Time series, 41, 41f
Time-series data, 40t, 40f–41f, 41
TIP. *See* Tax-related incomes policy
TNCs. *See* Transnational corporations
Tobin, James, 688
Toronto, rent controls in, 110
Total cost, 189
  average, 189
  short-run, 192
Total cost curve, average, short-run, and long-run average cost curve, relationship between, 200–203, 203f–204f
Total demand for money, 689, 691f
Total employment, Canadian, changes in, 762–763
Total expenditure, 85
  changes in, price elasticity and, 85–87, 88f, 88t–89t
  and GDP, 551
Total fixed cost, 189
Total output, aggregated, 519
Total product, 185, 185t, 186f
Total revenue, 221
Total utility, definition of, 155
Total value
  and demand elasticity, 161–162, 162f
  versus market value, 160, 161f
  and productivity, 555–557
Total variable cost, 189
  short-run, 191f, 192
TP. *See* Total product
TR. *See* Total revenue
Trade. *See also* Free trade; Gains from trade; International trade
  balance of, 855
    and national income, 860–867
  Canadian
    composition of, 500, 501t
    outlook for, 511
  interpersonal, 470–471
  interregional, 470–471
  managed, 497–498
  purpose of, 471
  and surplus, 42–43
  terms of, 480–481
    alteration of, with trade restrictions, 488–490
  volume of, 855
Tradeable emissions permits, 413–415
Trade account, 849
Trade advantage, strategic, creation or exploitation of, with trade restrictions, 490–491

Trade liberalization, 504. *See also* Free trade
Trademarks, and opportunity cost, 179
Trade policy. *See also* Commercial policy; Protectionism
  fallacious arguments concerning, 494–495
  strategic, and competitiveness, 491–492
Trade remedy laws, 490, 492–494
Trading system, multilateral, crisis in, 497–498
Traditional economy, 7
Transactions balances, 686–687
Transactions costs, 315
Transfer earnings, 339n
Transfer payments, 53n, 438, 550, 587
  to individuals, 444
  intergovernmental, 440–443, 441f, 442t
Transfer system, efficiency and social costs of, 454
Transmission mechanism, 692–694, 693f–695f, 714
  definition of, 692
  in open economy, 696
Transnational corporations, 18, 173–175, 260, 824
  attitudes toward, 308–310
  Canadian, 310–313
  research and development by, 309, 313
Treasury bill, 307, 662
Treaty of Rome, 497, 506
Trends, 538–539
Triad set of countries, 307
Trough, 522
Turnover, of firms, 259
TVC. *See* Total variable cost
Twin deficits, 860, 867–869
Two-variable graph, 36, 37f

UAW. *See* United Automobile Workers
UI. *See* Unemployment insurance
Unavoidable cost, 189
Uncertainty, household behaviour under, 163–167
Underground economy, and GDP, 558
Undistributed profits, 552
  definition of, 172
Unemployed, definition of, 524
Unemployment, 762–784
  Canadian, 762–764
    changes in, 763
    historical experience, 526, 527f
  consequences of, 763
  cyclical, 526, 764–770, 765f–766f
    definition of, 764
    reduction of, 777
  deadweight loss of, 521
  deficient-demand, 526
  frictional, 526, 764, 770
    reduction of, 777–779
    and structural unemployment, relationship between, 772
  and industrial change, 778–779
  kinds of, 763–764
  rate of, 6
  reduction of, 457, 777–781
    and protectionism, 495
  search, 770
  significance of, 527–528
  structural, 526, 764, 770–773

  and frictional unemployment, relationship between, 772
    reduction of, 780–781
Unemployment insurance, 444, 457–458, 777–779
Unemployment rate
  accuracy of, 525
  definition of, 524–525
  estimation of, 525
  natural. *See* NAIRU
Unfair trade practises, protection against, 490
Unfavourable balance of payments, 854
Union(s), 346
  absence of, monopsonistic labour markets in, 351–354, 354f
  customs, definition of, 496
  definition of, 350
  entry of, in monopsonistic labour markets, effects of, 354–355, 355f
  modern, 357–359
  monopoly as, 350–351, 351f
  and wages, 357–359
Unit costs, 613, 629
United Automobile Workers, 359
United Kingdom, entry into EEC, 500n
United Nations
  Food and Agricultural Organization, 90
  and transnational corporations, 174–175
United States
  auto industry in, integration with Canadian auto industry, 500–501
  and British North America, reciprocity treaty between, 499
  Department of Commerce, 507
  Environmental Protection Agency, 415
  free trade agreement
    with Canada. *See* Canada-U.S. Free Trade Agreement
    and Mexico. *See* North American Free Trade Agreement
    with Israel, 497
    with New Zealand and Australia, 497
  interest rates, and Canadian monetary restraint, 871–872
  International Trade Commission, 507
  Jones Act, 487
  protectionist sentiment in, 497–498, 501
Unit elasticity, 85, 94
Unit labour costs, 629–631
Unit of account, money as, 657
Universality, of social policy, 455–456
Universities, 456–457
Unlimited liability, 172
Unreported activities, and GDP, 558
Urbanisation, with industrialisation, 559
Uruguay Round (GATT), 122, 484, 496
Used-car prices, 164
User charges, taxes as, 433
Utility
  definition of, 155
  incremental, 155n
  marginal, 155–158
    definition of, 155
    diminishing, hypothesis of, 155
  maximization of, 156–158
  total, definition of, 155
Utility graphs, 156
Utility schedules, 156, 156t

Value(s). *See also* Present value
  and cost, 176
  of currency
    external, 536
      exchange rate and, 536
    internal, 536
  liquidation, 663
  marginal, 160
  market, versus total value, 160, 161*f*
  of money. *See* Purchasing power, of
    money
  money as store of, 657, 678, 678*t*
  nominal, 519
  paradox of, 160–161
  per capita, and productivity, 555–557
  real, 519
    of money, 529
  and resource extraction, 372
  total
    and demand elasticity, 161–162, 162*f*
    and productivity, 555–557
Value added
  definition of, 546
  as output, 545–546
  through stages of production, 547
Value added taxes, 430
Value-free economics, possibility of, 33
Value judgements, 23, 33
Variable(s), 28–29
  definition of, 28
  endogenous, 28–29
  exogenous, 28–29
  flow, 60
  macroeconomic, measurement of,
    545–563
  relations among
    expression of, 30
    graphing of, 36–41, 36*f*–41*f*
  stock, 60
Variable cost
  average, 189
    short-run, 191*f*, 191–192

  total, 189
    short-run, 191*f*, 192
Variable factor, definition of, 184
Variable proportions, law of. *See*
  Diminishing returns, law of
Variable reserve ratio, 675
VAT. *See* Value added taxes
Veblen, Thorstein, 138
Velocity of circulation, 690
VER. *See* Voluntary export restriction
Vertical equity, 454
Vertical merger, 304
Very long run
  competition in, and oligopoly, 273, 279
  definition of, 184
  innovation in, and oligopoly, 274–275
  natural monopoly in, 295
  production in, 203–209
Voluntary export restriction, 485
  on Japanese cars, 488–489
von Hippel, Eric, 819

Wage(s), 551
  changes in, 733–738
  efficiency, 768–770
  versus employment, 357–359
  equilibrium, 338–339
  flexible, 633, 634*f*
  minimum, 355–357
    definition of, 355
    structural unemployment caused by,
      771–772
  one, for homogeneous labour, 348
  real, 517
  rigidity, and NAIRU, 775
  rising, in modern economy, 14, 16*f*
  sticky, 624, 633–634, 765, 766*f*
Wage controls, and monetary gradualism, 753
Wage-cost push inflation. *See* Supply-shock
  inflation
Wage differentials, in competitive markets,
  348–350

Wage pressures, upward and downward,
  630
Wage rate
  and labour market discrimination,
    359–360, 360*f*
  labour markets and, 346–355
  and labour supply, 332–334
Wartime Labour Relations Regulations Act
  of 1944, 358
Wealth
  and consumption function, 569, 570*f*
  influence on demand for money, 688
Wealth of Nations, The (Smith), 46, 50, 284,
  470
Welfare, 438, 457–458
  long-term growth in, and GDP, 559
Western Hemispheric Free Trade Agreement
  (WHFTA), 507–508
White, Bob, 359
Wholesale price index, Canadian, 655*f*,
  655–656
Williamson, Oliver, 171
Willig, Robert, 277
Winter, Sidney, 316, 819
Wolf, Charles, Jr., 24
Working conditions
  minimum standards of, 396
  wage differentials arising from, 348–350
World attitudes, toward transnational
  corporations, 308–309
World price, 79–80
  agricultural exports at, 118*f*, 118–119
World problems, economic consequences of,
  2–3

Yield, definition of, 663

Zero balance of trade, 855
Zero inflation policy, 757
Zero-profit equilibrium, 229
Zero required reserves, monetary policy
  with, 713